THE INDEX OF PSYCHOANALYTIC WRITINGS

ALEXANDER GRINSTEIN, M.D.

Preface by Ernest Jones, M.D.

INTERNATIONAL UNIVERSITIES PRESS, INC.

New York, N. Y.

THE INDEX OF PSYCHOANALYTIC WRITINGS

VOLUME X

AARONS—FYE

65001—73945

INTERNATIONAL UNIVERSITIES PRESS, INC.

New York, N. Y.

Manufactured in the United States of America

CONTENTS

INTRODUCTION

When the first five volumes of *The Index of Psychoanalytic Writings*, which list psychoanalytic literature from its inception to 1952, were originally published in 1956, we explained that the project was undertaken to present an organized listing of psychoanalytic writings and to provide a subject index of these publications in order to make this material accessible to research workers in psychoanalysis and related fields.

Our aim of usefulness to research workers seemed to be well realized, so that a further project following similar principles and organization was undertaken which resulted in the publication of four additional volumes covering the psychoanalytic literature from 1952 through 1959.

The present project was implemented to bring the *Index* up to date by providing a comprehensive listing of the psychoanalytic literature from 1960 through 1969. At the same time, we have endeavored to correct errors and omissions from the earlier volumes of the *Index*. Support for this project was provided by the National Institute of Mental Health (Grant #MH 15369), the Wayne State University School of Medicine, the Michigan Psychoanalytic Institute, and the Foundation for Research in Psychoanalysis.

In general, the procedure with respect to selection and inclusion was similar to that followed in the earlier works. As before, we have endeavored to follow the principle of inclusiveness within the general framework of psychoanalysis, avoiding consideration of the quality, point of view, or the merit of a particular formulation in any given work, leaving judgments of this kind to the individual investigator.

CRITERIA FOR SELECTION OF MATERIAL

It should be stressed that, even within the framework of inclusiveness, no topic could be exhausted from a bibliographic standpoint, since this would mean extending the references in the *Index* to include extensive bibliographies in peripheral fields. Every effort was made to be as thorough as possible as outlined below, subject to the limitations of time and financial resources.

The publications listed in these supplementary volumes to the *Index* include the following:

1. Available articles, books, monographs, and pamphlets of a psychoanalytic nature, dealing specifically with psychoanalysis or applying psychoanalytic thinking to other fields, published in any language from 1960 through 1969. This includes books classified under "psychoanalysis" by the Library of Congress and the contents of official psychoanalytic journals and major annuals of collected works.

Reprints or new editions, unless significantly revised, are not listed; neither are articles in popular magazines or newspapers—even though some of these were written by analysts whose bibliographies were otherwise included.

2. Relevant material published before 1960 which had been omitted from the *Index*. Most of the material in this category was derived from the bibliographies sent in by the respondents to our letters of inquiry, as described below under PROCEDURE.

    a. If the author is or was a psychoanalyst, the publication is included. However, if the title is clearly *non*analytic, it is omitted.

    b. Titles of questionable relevance by nonanalysts are omitted.

3. Articles, books, monographs, and pamphlets published from 1960 through 1969 by members of the International Psycho-Analytical Association, even though not obviously analytic, unless the subject matter is solely physical or organic. It is felt that the approach of these authors makes their writings pertinent since their point of view is necessarily influenced by psychoanalytic concepts. An exception to this is made in the case of reviews and abstracts published in nonanalytic journals. These are not included.

4. All abstracts and reviews appearing in "official" psychoanalytic journals in English. Abstracts and reviews in the foreign-language "official" journals are included as available. Abstracts and reviews in other journals are not included, even though written by psychoanalysts, as indicated under point 3, above.

PROCEDURE

Work on the first nine volumes of *The Index of Psychoanalytic Writings* emphasized the wide dissemination of psychoanalytic thinking and the extent to which psychoanalytic concepts influenced publications in many fields. Consequently, any attempt to provide a comprehensive listing of literature that is of interest to psychoanalysis had to find a way to search out psychoanalytic material published in other than official psychoanalytic journals. This problem lent itself to approach from two different directions. One involved contacting possible writers directly; the other, searching the literature. In some ways our approach in this project was the same as in our previous projects. There were, however, some differences.

A. *Survey of Authors*

In November 1968, a letter was prepared for distribution to members of various professional groups, outlining the purpose of the project and soliciting their bibliographies from 1960 on. The letter pointed out the difficulty in finding psychoanalytically oriented literature that appears in periodicals that are not strictly psychoanalytic, and books and monographs whose titles do not indicate their contents. The recipients of the letters were also asked to check their bibliographies as they appeared in the published volumes of the *Index* and to advise us of any errors or omissions in this material. In addition, they were requested to indicate possible subject index classifications for their publications which would not be readily obvious from the titles. This letter was sent to the following groups:

1. All members of the American Psychoanalytic Association.

2. All members and affiliate members of the Component Societies of the International Psycho-Analytical Association.

3. Members of other professional organizations of psychoanalysts: Mexico Society of Psychoanalysis; National Psychological Association for Psychoanalysis; Societé Française de Psychanalyse; Syndicat National des Psychologues Psychanalystes. We did not include members of the Academy of Psychoanalysis, the American Institute for Psychoanalysis, and the Society of Medical Psychoanalysts, as we had for Volumes VI-IX, since we were unable to obtain the rosters of these organizations.

4. A selected group of members of the American Psychiatric Association. These were chosen by checking the latest roster of the Association and examining the listing for each member to see if he had had any psychoanalytic training, connection with psychoanalysis, or had published any writings that indicated an interest in psychoanalysis.

5. Members of the American Orthopsychiatric Association under the following categories: Anthropology, Education, Guidance, Law, Marriage Counseling, Medicine, Pediatrics, Psychiatry, Psychology, Social Work, and Sociology.

The lists of names obtained from these various sources were carefully compared to prevent duplication and thus avoid the appearance of a mass, random type of query. We endeavored to facilitate replies to our inquiry by including with each letter reply sheets, indicating the specific information desired, and stamped self-addressed envelopes. For foreign respondents, we enclosed international reply coupons which prepay airmail postage to the United States.

In our survey of authors for the *Index* in Volumes VI-IX, we sent letters to a large group of psychologists, including selected members of the American Psychological Association and approximately 1000 psychologists practicing outside the United States whose names were chosen from the International Directory of Psychologists, published by the National Academy of Sciences of the National Research Council. This step was not included in the present project due to budgetary considerations. For the same reason, we were forced to omit sending any follow-up letters to the psychoanalysts in groups 1 and 2 listed above.

In this way a total of some 7,250 were queried: 2,750 analysts and 4,500 nonanalysts. About two fifths (39%) of the former group responded and, of those replying, almost two out of three listed publications of psychoanalytic interest while the remainder listed no publications.

Replies were received from approximately one third (32%) of the nonanalytic group. Of these, about two fifths (39%) sent in their bibliographies while the remainder listed no publications.

It may be noted that the replies received from the psychoanalysts in response to our query for Volumes VI-IX showed the same proportion of those sending bibliographies and those indicating no publications. However, the percentage of total replies (39% of the analysts for the present project as compared with 72% in the earlier project) indicates the value of follow-up letters for a mail query of this type.

B. *Search of Literature*

The search of literature involved primary and secondary sources.

1. Primary Sources. Complete contents of the "official" psychoanalytic journals, annuals, and collections published in English from 1960-1969 are included:

American Imago
The Annual Survey of Psychoanalysis
Bulletin of the Philadelphia Association for Psychoanalysis
International Journal of Psycho-Analysis
Journal of the American Psychoanalytic Association
Psychoanalysis and Psychoanalytic Review
The Psychoanalytic Forum
The Psychoanalytic Quarterly
The Psychoanalytic Review
The Psychoanalytic Study of the Child
Science and Psychoanalysis

The total contents (articles, abstracts, and reviews) in these publications were listed for inclusion in the *Index*.

The complete contents (articles, abstracts, and reviews) of "official" psychoanalytic journals in languages other than English are included as available. These publications include the following:

Cuadernos de Psicoanalisis
Jahrbuch der Psychoanalyse
Japanese Journal of Psycho-Analysis
Revista brasileira de Psicanálise
Revista de Psicoanálisis, Buenos Aires
Revista Uruguaya Psicoanálisis
Revue Française de Psychanalyse
Rivista di Psicoanalisi

2. Secondary Sources. Unlike the method used in the previous volumes of the Index, where many peripheral publications were searched for articles of psychoanalytic interest, the present project relies heavily on secondary sources. There are several reasons for this change in methodology.

The wide dissemination of psychoanalytic thinking into so many different fields, and the proliferation of journals into great numbers made it imperative to use a different and more efficient technique. We thus found it highly worthwhile to avail ourselves of secondary sources that had already done much of this work rather than repeat work that had already been done. Moreover, our limitations of budget made it imperative to use whatever secondary sources were available rather than time-consuming procedures that were completely beyond our means. The difficulties and sources of error in using these secondary sources are discussed below under *Difficulties and Problems*.

a. The most important secondary source available for journal articles was the *Index Medicus* from 1960 to 1964, and MEDLARS of the National Library of Medicine from 1964 to 1969. The computer printout by MEDLARS covered a large number of categories among which were such headings as: Psychoanalysis, Psychoanalytic Interpretation, Psychoanalytic Theory, Symbolism, Defense Mechanisms, Depersonalization, Guilt, Masturbation, Self, Anxiety, Castration Anxiety, Body Image, Consciousness, Hysteria, Love, Masochism, Transference (Psychology), Regression, Psychoanalytic Therapy, Narcissism, Conflict (Psychology), Parent-Child Relations, Obsessive-Compulsive Neuroses, Post-Traumatic Neuroses, War Neuroses, Dreams, Instinct.

The material thus obtained was scrutinized for relevance as to subject or author. The references that we kept were further checked against material obtained from other sources. It is important to note that the indexing service of the National Library of Medicine does not cover books, monographs, reviews or abstracts. Other methods had to be relied upon to obtain such information.

b. The Index of the Library of the Chicago Institute for Psychoanalysis. This indexing service covers a multitude of articles, books, monographs, reviews, and abstracts of psychoanalytic interest. It covers "official" journals, journals in peripheral fields, contents of books—some completely, some only in part. The coverage provides a careful subject indexing of the titles selected.

c. *Psychological Abstracts* for the years 1960 through the spring of 1971 were searched for abstracts of relevant material published from 1960 to 1969. Although this publication, in the main, lists articles, it also includes some books and monographs. Unfortunately, there is no consistency in the completeness of coverage of journals or books.

d. *Excerpta Medica,* Section VIII (Neurology and Psychiatry) for the years 1960-1966 and Section VIII B (Psychiatry) for 1967 on were also searched through the spring of 1971 for abstracts of relevant material published from 1960-1969. This publication covers primarily journal articles but also includes some books. As with *Psychological Abstracts,* there is no consistency in the completeness of coverage of particular journals.

e. Various indices to periodical literature for the period 1960-1969. These include the *Art Index, Educational Index, Essays and General Literature Index, International Index, Social Science and Humanities Index,* and *Music Index.* In addition, *the Internationale Bibliographie der Zeitschriften Literatur aus allen Gebieten des Wissens* was a valuable guide to European periodical literature. These were checked under a variety of subject headings for articles pertinent to psychoanalysis and for authors on a master list prepared from our survey of authors.

The following secondary sources were used in our search for books and monographs:

f. Catalog cards from the Library of Congress for all books under the following categories: Abnormal Psychology, Anthropology, Characterology, Clinical Psychology, Criminology, Depth Psychology, Dreams, Educational Psychology, Ego, Fantasy, Folklore, Sigmund Freud, Mental Health, Mental Hygiene, Neurosis, Phobias, Psychiatry, Psychoanalysis, Psychoneurosis, Psychotherapy, Social Psychology, Symbolism.

These Library of Congress cards were sorted into three categories: (1) those of psychoanalytic interest, which were included; (2) those definitely not of psychoanalytic interest, which were excluded; and (3) questionable ones. Then, books of possible psychoanalytic interest were chosen for inclusion from the questionable category on the basis of author, title, or subject heading indicated on these cards, or from reviews in various journals. Some books were checked by a member of our staff.

g. The journal *Contemporary Psychology* from 1960 through Spring 1971 was searched for reviews and notices of books of psychoanalytic interest for the years 1960-1969.

h. The *Mental Health Book Review Index* provided references to reviews of books in the field. These reviews were then studied to select those titles that were relevant.

i. *Books in Print.*

j. Lists of books sent to official psychoanalytic journals for reviews were studied for possible relevant titles.

k. Book notices, lists of publishers, and lists distributed by book dealers.

DIFFICULTIES AND PROBLEMS

All the difficulties confronted in the first nine volumes of *The Index of Psychoanalytic Writings* presented themselves to an even greater degree in the preparation of these volumes. This was partly because of the sheer quantity of writings resulting from the fact that psychoanalytic thinking has pervaded such a great area of literature in general. An even greater stumbling block, however, has been the fact that psychoanalytic thinking and concepts, which were formerly distinct as to content, have become accepted and integrated into so many disciplines that the lines of demarcation have at times become blurred to a point where calling a given publication psychoanalytic or not is virtually arbitrary. Examples of this are publications dealing with ego psychology, hypnosis, psychopharmacology, group therapy, and existentialism, to mention but a few areas where this has become a problem.

In facing the problem of inclusiveness we quickly reached a point where it was evident that the funds available for research would be exhausted long before we could even approach our goal of an index completed along the lines of procedure followed for Volumes VI-IX. At the same time that our costs rose considerably beyond our budgetary projections due to the inflation that plagued research in all areas, the funds allotted for pursuing this research were cut. In order to deal with this practical difficulty, the decision was made to reduce the actual search of the literature by our staff and to rely more on secondary sources.

With respect to the broad coverage thus made possible, this decision was highly advantageous. The experienced staffs of the National Library of Medicine working on MEDLARS, of the Chicago Institute Library, and of the publishers who provide the specialized indices to periodical literature, were able to list and to abstract a much wider variety of publications in much greater numbers than would have been possible for our limited staff. On the other hand, there were certain disadvantages.

1. There was no way for us to determine how completely a given journal was covered. We could not ascertain whether *every* issue had been checked for the years in which we were interested, whether the journal had been checked for only the current year, or if only occasional years and issues were checked.

2. Titles were often incomplete and subtitles were frequently missing.

3. First names of authors were sometimes indicated by initial only, creating some confusion in identification.

4. Multiple authors frequently are not listed completely; those beyond the first two or three are indicated simply by "et al."

5. MEDLARS provides only an English translation of the titles of articles appearing in foreign journals. We had, in the past, endeavored to provide the *original* title, which was then used in alphabetizing the titles, in addition to the English translation.

Some of these difficulties, although by no means all, were neutralized by the fact that we received material pertaining to the same reference from several sources. This permitted verification of titles, provided an opportunity to have the full titles, subtitles, and complete listing of all co-authors with their first names, and in the instance of foreign titles, the titles in the original language of publication. Where possible, and where the journal was readily available, we tried to obtain this information from the primary source. Understandably, however, this further verification and checking involved a great deal of extra work and hence added to the cost of the project.

In facing the problem of inclusiveness for the *Index,* a point was rapidly reached where the funds available for research were exhausted. There was the related practical point that the cost of search for psychoanalytic material in the more obscure journals and books became prohibitive. Once more, the goal of a *complete* index of psychoanalytic material that would include *all* articles by psychoanalysts or about psychoanalysis had to be modified by practical considerations. By using the method we did, our goal became approximately commensurate with our resources.

Insofar as possible, we have checked the bibliographic data for accuracy. Many of the references were derived from several sources, which thus provided verification. Some of the references, however, particularly those obtained only from the authors themselves, were incomplete, and there was no way compatible with the resources of our funds and staff, to verify them. These have, nevertheless, been included with the thought that if they come within the scope of a particular research problem, the investigator will have at least some clues by which he can find previous publications on his topic.

All titles of non-English publications have been translated into English. Although efforts were made to be consistent in the translations, this aim was not always achieved. Some variations in translation reflect nuances in meaning; others result from the fact that they represent the work of different translators, or different sources, e.g., MEDLARS, *Chicago, Psychological Abstracts, Excerpta Medica,* etc. Users of the *Index* will notice certain inconsistencies in spelling and form, for example, color/colour; psychoanalysis/psycho-analysis. These generally reflect differences between British and American usage as followed by the journals and/or book publishers, and these differences have been retained.

AUTHOR INDEX

The listing of the material in these supplementary volumes follows the general organizational schema of Volumes I-IX. The material is arranged alphabetically by author. Under the author, the references appear alphabetically according to the original title of the publication if it is available. Where it is not, the translation of the title into English is used.

Where the publication appeared in translation, the bibliographic information for each translation is given after the complete data for the original publication. In the case of foreign-language publications which did not also appear in English, a translation of the title into English, in brackets, directly follows the original title. In some instances, particularly with those publications which appeared first in languages where the original title was not available or where the original title was in a language using a non-Roman alphabet, the entry begins with the English translation of the title set off in brackets. This title is then used for the purposes of alphabetization. The known abstracts and reviews in psychoanalytic journals are listed under each title.

All material dealing with a given title bears a single number which appears in the left-hand margin. The references are numbered consecutively from the beginning to the end, starting with 65001. There are, however, exceptions to this.

First, it will be noted that occasionally a number has been omitted or is repeated followed by a letter. Omission of a number indicates that the numbered reference was deleted after the numbering had been completed. However, additions that were discovered after the numbering had been done were inserted in the appropriate place and numbered accordingly with the number followed by a letter A, B, C, etc.

Second, it will be noted that a relatively large number of references are identified by a number apparently out of sequence, preceded by an "S." These numbers identify items included in earlier volumes of the *Index* for which *additional* material has been published since 1959. This includes such items as new translations, some new editions, abstracts, and reviews. For these references only the title as it appeared in the earlier volumes is repeated. Readers interested in such a reference must check all the data in both the original volumes and the supplementary volumes. For example, at the beginning of Volume X under ABADI, MAURICIO, there is the following reference:

S-40009   Complejo de edipo—re planteo de su estructura originaria.
    Abs   Vega   Q 1961,   30:461-462

The "S" indicates that a reference with this title appeared in an earlier volume of the *Index*. In this instance, the abstract was published after 1959. For the translation of the title and complete publication data, readers must refer to the earlier volume. Since the number is over 40000, this reference appeared in the second series of *Index* volumes, in this instance, Volume VI, page 2803.

Numbers under 40000 refer to items published in the first five volumes of the *Index*. Supplementary material for some of these appeared in the second series of volumes in addition to being included in the current series. For example, in Volume X, under ABRAHAM, KARL, there is a reference:

S-36 Beiträge der Oralerotik zur Charakterbildung. Psa Stud Char 1969 205-216.

Here again, the information cited refers to publication after the reference was first published in the *Index*. Since the index reference number is under 40000, the readers know that the reference first appeared in Volumes I-V of the *Index*, in this case, Volume I. The readers, however, should further check the *Index* Volumes V and VI-IX for data that became available at the time these volumes were published. For this reference, they will indeed find in Volume VI, page 2808, data referring to the publication by Abraham, also indicated by the number S-36.

We would like to remind the users of the *Index* that, because of the way this *Index* developed over the years since the original publication of Volume I in 1956, and our endeavor to be as complete and accurate as possible, material with regard to any reference may be scattered throughout the volumes. It must be borne in mind that corrections and additions to the first four volumes were included in Volume V. Further corrections and additions, identified by "S" and the original number will be found in the next series, Volumes VI-IX. Now, additions and corrections to *all* of the previous volumes will be found in Volumes X-XIII. The last volume of this series, Volume XIV, will contain, besides the subject index, further additions and corrections to the preceding thirteen volumes as such material becomes available to us.

The "S" numbers in the second series and in the current series of the *Index* volumes serve to alert users to check *earlier* volumes for complete bibliographic information. We wish, however, to take this opportunity to urge users of the first and second series to check later volumes of the *Index* for possible additional information pertaining to a reference in which they are interested.

For example, users who check in the subject index in Volume V under "object choice, type of, in men" are referred to reference 10409. This is a paper by Sigmund Freud, the data on which are to be found in Volume I, pages 585-586. By following the suggestions made in the preceding paragraphs to check the *later* volumes of the *Index* for additional information, users will find additional material pertaining to this paper by Freud in Volume V, page 2759; in Volume VI, page 3228; and in Volume X, page 5415.

In the listing of Freud's works, a second identifying number appears in brackets below our Index number. This number refers to the year of publication and corresponds to the identifying number used by James Strachey in the *Standard Edition*. Another number in parentheses may appear below this in those instances where Mr. Strachey has indicated that the year in which a particular work was written differed from the year of publication. It will be noted that some of the English translations of the titles of Freud's works, as well as their location in the *Standard Edition*, differ from those given in Volume I. The titles which were used in Volume I were obtained from Mr. Strachey. He had very graciously supplied for use in that Volume his "working titles" together with his proposed list of contents for projected volumes of the *Standard Edition*. As he proceeded with his work, however, he changed some of the titles so that they appeared in the *Standard Edition* in their present form. The location of certain articles was also changed, and some were omitted in the final version. These changes have been incorporated in the Freud bibliography in Volume X.

In order to enable users of the *Index* to locate Freud's publications more readily, this Volume contains an appendix listing Freud's writings according to their more familiar English titles. This Appendix not only lists the titles in English but provides the *Index* reference number, the volumes of the *Index* in which material about the particular publication appears, and also the volume and pages of the *Standard Edition* where the English translation may be found.

The journals and collected works referred to are generally indicated by abbreviations. A key to these abbreviations, other than those taken from the *World List of Scientific Periodicals, 1900-1950* (3rd edition, New York: Academic Press; London: Butterworth Publications, 1952) is given in Table 1. Abstractors, reviewers, and translators whose work appears most frequently in the literature are indicated by initials. A key to these initials is given in Table 2.

SUBJECT INDEX

The entire author index is followed by an extensive subject index based upon information derived from the following sources:

1. The titles of the articles and books.

2. Material sent in by the authors as to subjects dealt with in their writings.

3. The abstracts and reviews of articles and books found in the psycho-analytic journals.

4. The abstracts of articles and books found in *Psychological Abstracts* and *Excerpta Medica.*

5. The subject listing found in *Index Medicus,* and the subjects indicated on MEDLARS print-out and Chicago Institute Library cards.

6. The actual survey of the articles and books in question whenever and wherever possible.

References which were included in Volumes I-IX, that is, those references which are identified by an "S" number, have not been indexed again in this supplement.

The resulting subject index is by no means exhaustive, covering all the ideas in a given publication. Rather, it strives to deal with the *main* topics only. For a more detailed description of the procedures used in preparation of the subject index and suggestions for its use, the reader is referred to the Introduction to Volumes V, IX, and XIV.

ACKNOWLEDGEMENTS

The preparation of this *Index* would have been impossible without the help of a great many people. In addition to thanking my friends and colleagues for their cooperation and encouragement, I wish to express my special personal thanks to

Those organizations that helped to finance the project:
The National Institute of Mental Health
Wayne State University School of Medicine
The Michigan Psychoanalytic Institute
The Foundation for Research in Psychoanalysis.

The many individuals who took the time and effort to contribute their bibliographies.

Dr. K. R. Eissler and the Sigmund Freud Archives, Inc., for help in providing additional material for the Freud bibliography.

Mrs. Lottie M. Newman for her help with the Anna Freud bibliography.

Miss Charlotte Kenton and the staff of the National Library of Medicine.

Miss Liselotte Bendix and Mrs. Phyllis Rubinton, librarians of the Abraham A. Brill Library of the New York Psychoanalytic Institute.

Mr. Glen Miller, librarian of the Chicago Institute of Psychoanalysis.

Mrs. Frances Shepherd of the Michigan Psychoanalytic Institute.

The professional staffs of various other libraries: Library of Congress, Detroit Public Library, Libraries of Wayne State University, and Libraries of the University of Michigan at Ann Arbor.

Dr. Richard Sterba, Dr. Editha Sterba, Dr. Norman Schkloven, Dr. Donald Oken, Dr. Ralph R. Greenson, and Dr. Morton Levitt for their help.

Dr. Roger Dufresne of Montreal for his listing of Freud's writings available in French translation; Mrs. Hella Bernays for her aid with foreign journals; Mrs. Bep Chompff, Miss Ida Chompff, Mrs. Adolph Deutsch, and Dr. Baqar Husaini for translating some of the titles into English.

Mrs. Heiju Oak Packard and Mrs. Deena Silverman for their conscientious and meticulous help in the search for material as well as for their assistance in the preparation of the manuscript. I am especially grateful to Mrs. Silverman for her work on the subject index.

Mrs. Edith C. Polk for her continuous help in the many labors associated with the *Index* since its inception with the first volume. Without her dedicated and conscientious assistance throughout these many years, bringing about the completion of this undertaking as well as the previous volumes of the *Index* could not have been accomplished as well.

My sons, David and Richard, for their continued interest and good-natured acceptance over the years of this very time-consuming project.

And finally, I want to express my special thanks to my wife, Adele, help-mate through the years, for her many sacrifices, her encouragement, and her devoted help with this entire undertaking.

ALEXANDER GRINSTEIN, M.D.

Detroit, Michigan

TABLE 1

LIST OF ABBREVIATIONS

Act Np Arg	Acta Neuropsiquíatrica Argentina
Acta psychother psychosom orthopaedag	Acta Psychotherapeutica, Psychosomatica et Orthopaedagogica
Acting Out	Abt, L. E. & Weissman, S. L. (Eds) *Acting Out: Theoretical and Clinical Aspects.* NY/London: Grune & Stratton 1965
Adolescents	Lorand, S. & Schneer, H. I. (Eds) *Adolescents: Psychoanalytic Approach to Problems and Therapy.* NY: Hoeber 1961
Adv ch Develop Behav	Lippsitt, L. P. & Spiker, C. C. (Eds) *Advances in Child Development and Behavior.* NY/London: Academic Pr, Vol 1, 1963; Vol 2, 1965; Vol 3, 1967
Adv PSM	Advances in Psychosomatic Medicine. Fortschritte der psychosomatischen Medizin. Progrès en Médecine Psychosomatique
AJP	American Journal of Psychology
Am Hbk Psychiat III	Arieti, S. (Ed) *American Handbook of Psychiatry.* NY: Basic Books 1966
Am Im	American Imago
Am Psych	American Psychologist
AMA ANP	A.M.A. Archives of Neurology and Psychiatry
An Surv Psa	Frosch, J. (Ed) *The Annual Survey of Psychoanalysis.* NY: IUP
Ann Np Psico-anal	Annali di Neuropsichiatria e Psicoanalisi
Ann Prog child Psychiat	Chess, S. & Thomas, A. (Eds) *Annual Progress in Child Psychiatry and Child Development.* NY: Brunner/Mazel
Arch crim Psychodyn	Archives of Criminal Psychodynamics
ASP	Journal of Abnormal and Social Psychology
Beh Sci	Behavioral Science
BMC	Bulletin of the Menninger Clinic
Bull Ass psa Fran	Bulletin de l'Association Psychanalytique de France
Bull Phila Ass Psa	Bulletin of the Philadelphia Association for Psychoanalysis
Ch Anal Wk	Geleerd, E. R. (Ed) *The Child Analyst at Work.* NY: IUP 1967
Chld Dth Pres	Wolfenstein, M. & Kliman, G. (Eds) *Children and the Death of a President: Multi-Disciplinary Studies.* Garden City, NY: Doubleday 1965
Clin Path	Journal of Clinical and Experimental Psychopathology
Clin Psych	Journal of Clinical Psychology
Compreh Txbk Psychiat	Freedman, A. M. & Kaplan, H. I. (Eds) *Comprehensive Textbook of Psychiatry.* Baltimore: Williams & Wilkins 1967

Table 1   XX

Contempo PT	Stein, M. I. (Ed) *Contemporary Psychotherapies*. Free Pr of Glencoe 1961
Crosscurrents in Ps & Psa	Gibson, R. W. (Ed) *Crosscurrents in Psychiatry & Psychoanalysis*. Phila/Toronto: J. B. Lippincott 1967
Cuad Psa	Cuadernos de Psicoanálisis. (Associatión Psicoanalítica Mexicana, México)
Curr psychiat Ther	Masserman, J. H. (Ed) *Current Psychiatric Therapies*. NY/London: Grune & Stratton 1961-69
Death & Identity	Fulton, R. (Ed) *Death and Identity*. NY/London/Sydney: John Wiley & Sons, Inc. 1965
Dev Mind	Lampl-de Groot, J. *The Development of the Mind. Psychoanalytic Papers on Clinical and Theoretical Problems*. NY: IUP 1965
Dr Af Beh 2	Schur, M. (Ed) *Drives, Affects, Behavior, Vol. 2. Essays in Memory of Marie Bonaparte*. NY: IUP 1965
Dreams Contempo Psa	Adelson, E. T. (Ed) *Dreams in Contemporary Psychoanalysis*. NY: Soc Med Psa 1963
Encéph	Encéphale (et Hygiène Mentale)
Ency Ment Hlth	Deutsch, A. & Fishman, H. (Eds) *The Encyclopedia of Mental Health*. NY: Franklin Watts 1963, 1965
Ess Ego Psych	Hartmann, H. *Essays on Ego Psychology*. NY: IUP 1964
50 Yrs Psa	Wangh, M. (Ed) *Fruition of an Idea: Fifty Years of Psychoanalysis in New York*. NY: IUP 1962
Fortschr PSM	Fortschritte der psychosomatischen Medizin. Advances in Psychosomatic Medicine. Progrès en Médecine Psychosomatique
Fortschr Psa	Fortschritte der Psychoanalyse. Internationale Jahrbuch zur Weiterentwicklung der Psychoanalyse
GAP	Group for the Advancement of Psychiatry
Group PT	Group Psychotherapy
Hbh Kinderpsychother	Biermann, G. (Ed) *Handbuch der Kinderpsychotherapie*. Munich/Basel: Reinhardt 1969
Heirs Freud	Ruitenbeek, H. M. (Ed) *Heirs to Freud. Essays in Freudian Psychology*. NY: Grove Pr 1966
HPI	The Hogarth Press and the Institute of Psycho-Analysis
IJP	Indian Journal of Psychology
Int J grp PT	International Journal of Group Psychotherapy
Int J Np	International Journal of Neuropsychiatry
Int Psa Cong	International Psycho-Analytical Congress
Int Psychiat Clin	International Psychiatry Clinics. Boston: Little, Brown
Int Rec Med	International Record of Medicine
IPC	Imago Publishing Company
IUP	International Universities Press
J	International Journal of Psycho-Analysis
J Am Psa Ass	Journal of the American Psychoanalytic Association
J anal Psych	Journal of Analytical Psychology
J genet Psych	Journal of Genetic Psychology
J ind Psych	Journal of Individual Psychology
J Pers	Journal of Personality
J proj Tech	Journal of Projective Techniques and Personality Assessment

J Psa in Groups	The Journal of Psychoanalysis in Groups
J PSM	Journal of Psychosomatic Medicine
JAbP	Journal of Abnormal Psychology
JAMA	Journal of the American Medical Association
Jap J Psa	The Japanese Journal of Psycho-Analysis
Jb Psa	Dräger, K. et al (Eds) *Jahrbuch der Psychoanalyse. Beiträge zur Theorie und Praxis.* Bern: Huber
Jb Psychol Psychother	Jahrbuch für Psychologie und Psychotherapie
JMS	Journal of Mental Science
JNMD	Journal of Nervous and Mental Diseases
Lav Np	Lavoro Neuropsichiatrico
Learn Love	Ekstein, R. & Motto, R. L. (Eds) *From Learning for Love to Love of Learning. Essays on Psychoanalysis and Education.* NY: Brunner/Mazel Publ 1969
Lit & Psych	Literature and Psychology
M	British Journal of Medical Psychology
Marriage Relat	Rosenbaum, S. & Alger, I. (Eds) *The Marriage Relationship: Psychoanalytic Perspectives.* NY/London: Basic Books 1968
Menn Q	Menninger Quarterly
Meth Res PT	Gottschalk, L. & Auerbach, A. H. (Eds) *Methods of Research in Psychotherapy.* NY: Appleton-Century-Crofts 1966
MH	Mental Hygiene
MMW	Münchner medizinische Wochenschrift
Mod Con Psa	Salzman, L. & Masserman, J. H. (Eds) *Modern Concepts of Psychoanalysis.* NY: Philos Libr 1962
Mod Psa	Marmor, J. (Ed) *Modern Psychoanalysis: New Directions and Perspectives.* NY/London: Basic Books 1968
MPN	Monatsschrift für Psychiatrie und Neurologie
NPPA J	National Probation and Parole Association Journal
NTvG	Nederlandsch Tijdschrift voor Geneeskunde
NYSJM	New York State Journal of Medicine
Ops	American Journal of Orthopsychiatry
Ops Law	Levitt, M. & Rubenstein, B. (Eds) *Orthopsychiatry and the Law. A Symposium.* Detroit: Wayne Univ Pr 1968
Out Patient Schiz	Scher, S. C. & Davis, H. R. (Eds) *The Out-Patient Treatment of Schizophrenia.* NY/London: Grune & Stratton 1960
P	American Journal of Psychiatry
PPR	Psychoanalysis and the Psychoanalytic Review
Prax PT	Praxis der Psychotherapie
Problems in Psa	Raclot, M. et al: *Problèmes de Psychanalyse.* Paris: Fayard 1957. *Problems in Psychoanalysis.* A Symposium. Baltimore: Helicon Pr 1961
Proc III World Cong Psychiat 1961	Third World Congress of Psychiatry, Proceedings Montreal, Canada, 4-10 June 1961. Univ of Toronto Pr & McGill Univ Pr
Proc IV World Cong Psychiat 1966	Proceedings of the Fourth World Congress of Psychiatry. Amsterdam/NY/London: Excerpta Medica Foundation 1967-68

Table 1   xxii

Proc RSM	Proceedings of the Royal Society of Medicine
Prog clin Psych	Riess, B. & Abt, L. E. (Eds) *Progress in Clinical Psychology.* NY: Grune & Stratton
Prog Neurol Psychiat	Spiegel, E. A. (Ed) *Progress in Neurology and Psychiatry.* NY: Grune & Stratton
Prog PT	Masserman, J. H. & Moreno, J. L. (Eds) *Progress in Psychotherapy.* NY: Grune & Stratton
Ps	Psychiatry
Psa	American Journal of Psychoanalysis
Psa Amer	Litman, R. E. (Ed) *Psychoanalysis in the Americas: Original Contributions from the First Pan-American Congress for Psychoanalysis.* NY: IUP 1966
Psa Clin Inter	Paul, L. (Ed) *Psychoanalytic Clinical Interpretation.* NY: The Free Pr of Glencoe 1963
Psa Curr Biol Thought	Greenfield, N. S. & Lewis, W. C. (Eds) *Psychoanalysis and Current Biological Thought.* Madison/Milwaukee: Univ Wisconsin Pr 1965
Psa Forum	The Psychoanalytic Forum
Psa–Gen Psychol	Loewenstein, R. M. et al (Eds) *Psychoanalysis–A General Psychology. Essays in Honor of Heinz Hartmann.* NY: IUP 1966
Psa Pioneers	Alexander, F. et al (Eds) *Psychoanalytic Pioneers.* NY/London: Basic Books 1966
Psa St C	Eissler, R. S. et al (Eds) *The Psychoanalytic Study of the Child.* NY: IUP
Psa St Soc	Muensterberger, W. & Axelrad, S. (Eds) *The Psychoanalytic Study of Society.* NY: IUP
Psa Stud Char 1969	Abraham, K. *Psychoanalytische Studien zur Charakterbildung und andere Schriften.* Frankfurt: Fisher 1969
Psa Tech	Wolman, B. B. (Ed) *Psychoanalytic Techniques: A Handbook for the Practicing Psychoanalyst.* NY: Basic Books 1967
PSM	Psychosomatic Medicine
Psych Issues	Psychological Issues
Psychiat Comm	Psychiatric Communications
Psychiat Q	Psychiatric Quarterly
Psychiat Res Rep	Psychiatric Research Reports
Psychodyn St Aging	Levin, S. & Kahana, R. J. (Eds) *Psychodynamic Studies on Aging: Creativity, Reminiscing, and Dying.* NY: IUP 1967
PT	American Journal of Psychotherapy
PT Pervers	Ruitenbeek, H. M. (Ed) *Psychotherapy of Perversions.* NY: Citadel Pr 1967
PUF	Presses Universitaires de France
Q	The Psychoanalytic Quarterly
R	The Psychoanalytic Review
R P PT	Nelson, M. C. (Ed) *Roles and Paradigms in Psychotherapy.* London/NY: Grune & Stratton 1968
Ra Pgc	Rassegna di Psicologia Generale e Clinica
Rass Np	Rassegna di Neuropsichiatria

Recent Adv biol Psychiat	Wortis, J. (Ed) *Recent Advances in Biological Psychiatry.* NY: Plenum Pr 1960-68
Rev Psicoanál	Revista de Psicoanálisis, Buenos Aires
Rev Psiquiat Psicol	Revista de Psicquiatria y Psicología Médica de Europa y America Latinas
Rev urug Psa	Revista Uruguaya Psicoanálisis
RFPsa	Revue Française de Psychanalyse
Riv Pat nerv ment	Rivista di Patologie Nervosa e Mentale
Riv Psa	Rivista di Psicoanalisi
The Roots of Crime	Glover, E. *Selected Papers on Psycho-Analysis, Volume II. The Roots of Crime.* London: Imago Publishing Co.; NY: IUP 1960
Rv Np inf	Revue de Neuropsichiatrie infantile et d'Hygiène Mentale de l'Enfance
Schweiz ANP	Schweizer Archiv für Neurologie und Psychiatrie
Schweiz Z Psychol	Schweizerische Zeitschrift für Psychologie und ihre Anwendungen. Revue Suisse de Psychologie Pure et Appliquée, Bern
Sci Psa	Masserman, J. H. (Ed) *Science and Psychoanalysis.* NY: Grune & Stratton
SE	Strachey, J. (Ed) *Standard Edition of the Complete Psychological Works of Sigmund Freud.* London: Hogarth Pr
Sel P EB	Bergler, E. *Selected Papers of Edmund Bergler, M.D. 1933-1961.* NY/London: Grune & Stratton 1969
Soc	American Journal of Sociology
Soc Casewk	Social Casework
Soc Psych	Journal of Social Psychology
Soc S R	Social Service Review
Teach Dyn Psychiat	Bibring, G. (Ed) *The Teaching of Dynamic Psychiatry.* NY: IUP 1968
Ther Nurs Schl	Furman, R. A. & Katan, A. (Eds) *The Therapeutic Nursery School: A Contribution to the Study and Treatment of Emotional Disturbances in Young Children.* NY: IUP 1969
Tokyo J Psa	Tokyo Journal of Psychoanalysis
WMW	Wiener medizinische Wochenschrift
Why Rep	Freeman, L. & Theodores, M. (Eds) *The Why Report.* NY: Arthur Bernhard 1964
Youth	Erikson, E. H. (Ed) *Youth: Change and Challenge.* NY/London: Basic Books 1963
Z Kinderpsychiat	Zeitschrift für Kinderpsychiatrie
Z PSM	Zeitschrift für psychosomatische Medizin and Psychoanalyse
Z Psychol	Zeitschrift für Psychologie

TABLE 2

ABBREVIATIONS USED
FOR NAMES OF ABSTRACTORS,
REVIEWERS, AND TRANSLATORS

AaSt	Aaron Stein		EVN	Eugene V. Nininger
AEC	Alfred E. Coodley		EW	Emory Wells
AHM	Arnold H. Modell			
AJE	Alan J. Eisnitz		FB	Frank Berchenko
AL	Alfred Lilienfeld		FTL	Frank T. Lossy
AN	Alfredo Namnum			
ARK	Arthur R. Kravitz		GD	George Devereux
AS	Austin Silber		GLG	Gerald L. Goodstone
ASt	Alix Strachey		GPK	Geraldine Pederson-Krag
			GZ	Gregory Zilboorg
BB	Bernhard Berliner			
BEM	Burness E. Moore		HA	Herbert Aldendorff
BFM	Bennett F. Markel		HD	Hartvig Dahl
BL	Barbara Low		HFM	Henry F. Marasse
			HK	Hans Kleinschmidt
CBr	Charles Brenner		HL	Herbert Lehmann
CFH	Charles F. Hesselbach		HRB	H. Robert Blank
CG	Claude Girard		HS	Harry Slochower
CK	Curtis Kendrick		HW	Herbert Weiner
CR	Charles Rycroft			
			IBa	I. Barande
DB	Clement A. Douglas Bryan		ICFH	Ivan C. F. Heisler
DJM	David J. Myerson		IK	Irving Kaufman
DRu	David L. Rubinfine		IS	Irwin Solomon
DW	Daniel Weitzner			
			JA	Joseph Afterman
EBMH	Ethilde B. M. Herford		JAA	Jacob A. Arlow
EBu	Edith Buxbaum		JAL	John Arnold Lindon
ECM	E. Colburn Mayne		JB	J. Bernays
EDJ	Edward D. Joseph		JBa	Jose Barchilon
EFA	Edwin Frederick Alston		JBi	Joseph Biernoff
EG	Edward Glover		JC	Joseph Coltrera
EJ	Ernest Jones		JCS	J. Chasseguet-Smirgel
ELG	Eugene L. Goldberg		JFr	John Frosch
EMD	Edward M. Daniels		JKl	John Klauber
EMW	Edward M. Weinshell		JLan	Joseph Lander
ESt	Erwin Stengel		JLL	Jean-Louis Langlois

JLS	Jerome L. Saperstein	RCM	R. C. McWatters
JLSt	Julian L. Stamm	RdeS	Raymond de Saussure
JMa	J. Massoubre	RDT	Robert D. Towne
JO	Joel Ordaz	RHB	Ricardo H. Bisi
JPG	Joseph P. Gutstadt	RJA	Renato J. Almansi
JRiv	Joan Riviere	RLG	Renee L. Gelman
JS	James Strachey	RRG	Ralph R. Greenson
JTM	James T. McLaughlin	RSB	Richard S. Bralove
JWS	Joseph William Slap	RTh	Ruth Thomas
		RZ	Robert Zaitlin
KHG	Kenneth H. Gordon, Jr.		
KOS	Kurt O. Schlessinger	SAS	S. A. Shentoub
KR	Kenneth Rubin	SG	Sigmund Gabe
		SGo	Stanley Goodman
LCK	Lawrence C. Kolb	SL	Sidney Levin
LDr	L. Dreyfus	SLe	S. Lebovici
LRa	Leo Rangell	SLP	Sydney L. Pomer
		SO	Shelley Orgel
MBr	Marjorie Brierley	SRS	Stewart R. Smith
MG	Martin Grotjahn	STa	Sidney Tarachow
MGr	Milton Gray		
MK	Mark Kanzer	TC	Theodore Cherbuliez
		TFr	Thomas Freeman
NR	Norman Reider	TGS	Tom G. Stauffer
NRo	Nathaniel Ross		
NZ	Norman E. Zinberg	VC	Victor Calef
		Vega	Gabriel de la Vega
OS	Oscar Sachs		
		WAF	William A. Frosch
PB	P. Blos, Jr.	WAS	Walter A. Stewart
PCR	P. C. Racamier	WCW	William C. Wermuth
PLe	Pierre Levy	WH	Willi Hoffer
PS	Philip Spielman	WPK	William P. Kapuler

A

AARONS, LOUIS

65001 (& Schulman, J.; Masserman, J. H.; Zimmar, G. P.) Behavioral adaptations after parietal cortex ablation in the neonate macaque. Recent Adv biol Psychiat 1962, 4:347-359

65002 (& Masserman, J. H.; McAvoy, T.) Brain stimulation, experience, and behavior. P 1962, 118:982-994

See Masserman, Jules H.

AARONS, Z. ALEXANDER

65003 Indications for analysis and problems of analyzability. (Read at Am Psa Ass, May 1961) Q 1962, 31:514-531

S-40002 Notes on a case of *maladie des tics.*
Abs ARK An Surv Psa 1958, 9:140-141

65004 On analytic goals and criteria for termination. (Read at Am Psa Ass, 30 April 1965) Bull Phila Ass Psa 1965, 15:97-109
Abs EFA Q 1967, 36:627

65005 On negativism and the character trait of obstinacy. (Read at San Francisco Psa Soc, 12 Nov 1962) Bull Phila Ass Psa 1963, 13:182-197
Abs EFA Q 1965, 34:134-135. PLe RFPsa 1967, 31:307

65006 On the psychogenesis of an asthmatic attack. (Read at Am Psa Ass, Dec 1958) Bull Phila Ass Psa 1962, 12:32-37
Abs PLe RFPsa 1963, 27:340

S-40003 Psychotherapy versus psychoanalysis. A case illustration.
Abs Cowitz, B. An Surv Psa 1958, 9:342

65007 Therapeutic abortion and the psychiatrist. (Read at Am Psa Ass, 8 May 1967) P 1967, 124:745-754

65008 The therapeutic function of a community psychiatric training clinic. Soc Casewk 1961, 42:128-133

REVIEW OF:
65009 Masserman, J. H. (Ed) Science and Psychoanalysis, Vol. VI: Violence and War. Q 1965, 34:286-289

AARONSON, BERNARD S.

65010 Hypnosis, responsibility, and the boundaries of self. Amer J clin Hyp 1967, 9:229-246

65011 Lilliput and Brobdignag—self and world. Amer J clin Hyp 1968, 10:160-166

ABADI, MAURICIO

65012 Las angustias arquetipicas. [Archetypical anxieties.] Act Np Arg 1960, 6:569-571

Abs Vidal, G. Rev Psicoanál 1961, 18:386

S-40009 Complejo de edipo—re planteo de su estructura originaria.

Abs Vega Q 1961, 30:461-462

S-40011 Consideraciones psicoanalíticas acerca de algunos aspectos de una psicosis con amaurosis congenita—contribucion al estudio del aparto de influencia.

Abs AN An Surv Psa 1956, 7:187-188

65013 Dante y la Divina Comedia. Introducción a su estudio psicoanalítico. [Dante and *The Divine Comedy*. Introduction to a psychoanalytic study.] Rev Psicoanál 1961, 18:96-117

Dante e la Divina Commedea. Riv Psa 1962, 8:195-213

65014 El dilema del psicoanalísta. [The dilemma of the psychoanalyst.] (Read at Latin Am Psa Cong, Jan 1960) Rev Psicoanál 1961, 18:4-8

Abs Vega Q 1962, 31:591-592

S-40015 Dioniso: estudio psicoanalítico del mito y culto dionisíacos.

Abs An Surv Psa 1955, 6:403-404

65015 Discussion of Alvarez de Toledo, L. G. et al: "Terminacion del análisis didáctico." Rev Psicoanál 1967, 24:282-283

65016 (& Bleger, J.; Pichon Rivière, E.; Rodrigué, E.) Discussion of Ekstein, R. "Termination of analysis and working through." Psa Amer 238-239

65017 Fantasía y realidad del diálogo psicoanalítico. [Fantasy and reality of the psychoanalytic dialogue.] Act Np Arg 1960, 6:39-46

65018 La hipocondría. Proposiciones acerca de su tema inconciente. [Hypochondria. Considerations of its unconscious nature.] Rev Psicoanál 1961, 18:370-373

Abs Fernández, A. A. Rev urug Psa 1963, 5:464-466

S-40021 Interpretación y verbalización: la comunicación a distancia.

Abs RHB An Surv Psa 1957, 8:254

S-40023 Nota acerca de algunos mechanismos en la psicogénesis de la obesidad.

Abs Rodrigué, E. An Surv Psa 1956, 7:200-201

65019 Notas para una semántica psicoanalítica: abreaccion. [Notes for a psychoanalytic semantics: abreaction.] Rev Psicoanál 1961, 18:374-375

65020 Protoanhelo y protoculpa del nacimiento impedido. [Oedipus complex-restatement of its original structure.] Rev Psicoanál 1960, 17:165-189

65021 Psicoanálisis del jugar. Rev Psicoanál 1964, 21:366-373

Psychoanalysis of playing. Psychother Psychosom 1967, 15:85-93. In Philippopoulos, G. S. *Dynamics in Psychiatry*, Basel/NY: Karger 1968, 1-9

65022 Psicoterapia e psicodisleptici. [Psychotherapy and psychedelics.] Riv Psa 1967, 13:277-278

65023 [Psychoanalysts in the world at large.] (Sp) (Read at Latin Am Psa Cong, Jan 1960) Rev Psicoanál 1961, 18:9-11

Abs Vega Q 1962, 31:591-592

S-40027 Renacimento de Edipo. La Vida del Hombre en la Dialéctica del Adentro y del Afuera.

Rev AN Q 1962, 31:399-401. Martinez, C. M. Rev Psicoanál 1963, 20:184

65024 El significado inconsciente de las fantasias orales. [The unconscious significance of oral fantasies.] Rev Psicoanál 1962, 19:6-13
Abs Vega Q 1964, 33:144

65025 El suicidio. [Suicide.] Act Np Arg 1960, 5:366-374

65026 El suicidio: enfoque psicoanalítico. [Suicide: a psychoanalytic approach.] Act Np Arg 1959, 5:366-374

S-40030 El torno a la muerte.
Abs Vega Q 1962, 31:298

65027 Los tres roles del ser humano y la dinamica de su explicitacion en la relacion bipersonal psicoanalítica. [The three roles in the human being and their manifestation in the psychoanalytic bipersonal relationship.] Act Np Arg 1960, 6:567-569
Abs Vidal, G. Rev Psicoanál 1961, 18:386

ABARBANEL, ALBERT

See Ellis, Albert

ABBAGNANO, N.

65028 (Ed) Storia della psicologia. [History of psychology.] Storia delle Scienze 1963, 3:623-864

ABBATE, GRACE McLEAN

65029 (Reporter) Child analysis at different developmental stages. (Panel: Am Psa Ass, May 1963) J Am Psa Ass 1964, 12:135-150

65030 Notes on the first year of the analysis of a young child with minimum participation by the mother. Ch Anal Wk 14-23

ABBOTT, JOHN A.

65031 Freud's repressed feelings about Athena on the Acropolis. Am Im 1969, 26:355-363

65032 A note on Freud's dandelion memory. Am Im 1966, 23:208-209

ABDOUCHELI

65033 [Phobia in children.] (Fr) Méd Infant 1961, 68(5):13-17

ABE, K.

65034 (& Shimakawa, M.) Genetic and developmental aspects of sleeptalking and teeth-grinding. Acta paedopsychiat 1966, 33:339-344

ABEL, THEODORA M.

65035 The dreams of a Chinese patient. Psa St Soc 1962, 2:280-309

65036 Idiosyncratic and cultural variations in the resolution of oral-oedipal motivational patterns and conflicts. J Psychol 1964, 57:377-390

65037 Shift in intermediary object-gradient during the course of psychotherapy. PT 1960, 14:691-704

ABELL, RICHARD GURLEY

65038 Etiology and treatment of the passive male. Psa 1960, 20:212-220
65039 Group psychoanalysis. Curr psychiat Ther 1964, 4:175-182
65040 A new technique for facilitating insight into dissociated material. Sci Psa 1963, 6:247-253

ABELS, E.

ABSTRACTS OF:
65041 David, M. & Appel, G. La relation mère-infant. RFPsa 1968, 32:336
65042 Diatkine, R. & Simon, J. Étude nosologique à propos de trois cas de phobies chez les adolescents. RFPsa 1968, 32:335
65043 Lebovici, S. et al: À propos de calculateurs de calendrier. RFP 1968, 32:335
65044 Mack, J. E. Cauchemars, conflit et développement du moi chez l'enfant. RFPsa 1968, 32:336

ABELS, M.-E.

ABSTRACTS OF:
65045 Godin, J. Le développement de la personne chez l'enfant paralysé. RFPsa 1967, 31:190
65046 Herren, H. Les enfants deficients de l'ouie. RFPsa 1967, 31:190
65047 Herren, H. Les enfants handicapés moteurs. RFPsa 1967, 31:190
65048 Irvine, E. Le "social casework" d'après la formulation de Florence Hollis. RFPsa 1968, 32:334
65049 Lebovici, S. Freud et Jung. RFPsa 1968, 32:334
65050 Zazzo, R. Les débiles mentaux. RFPsa 1967, 31:190

REVIEWS OF:
65051 Corboz, R. J. Les Syndromes Psycho-Organiques de l'Enfant et de l'Adolescent. RFPsa 1968, 32:333
65052 Kreisler, L. et al: Le Syndromes Psycho-Organiques de l'Enfant et d'Adolescent. RFPsa 1968, 32:333
65053 Soulé, M. & Soulé, N. L'Énurésie. RFPsa 1968, 32:329

ABELS, P.

65054 Riding with Batman, Superman, and the Green Hornet: experiences in a very special group. Ment Retard 1969, 7:37-39

ABÉLY, PAUL

65055 (& Thomas, J.) À propos de la notion d'inhibition en psychiatrie. [Apropos of the idea of inhibition in psychiatry.] Ann méd-psychol 1965, 123:355-361
65056 (& Melman, C.) Le jeu, le ludisme, la parade, en pathologie mentale. Étude clinique et approche psychanalytique. La jocothérapie. [Games, play and the parade in mental pathology. Clinical study and psycho-analytic approach. Play therapy.] Ann méd-psychol 1963, 121:353-390

ABEND, SANDER M.

65057 (& Kachalsky, H.; Greenberg, H. R.) Reactions of adolescents to short-term hospitalization. P 1968, 124:949-954

ABTRACTS OF:
65058   Chodoff, P. A critique of Freud's theory of infantile sexuality. Q 1968, 37:475
65059   Cobliner, W. G. Psychoanalysis and developmental psychology. Q 1968, 37:317
65060   Siggins, L. D. Mourning: a critique of the literature. Q 1968, 37:475

ABENHEIMER, KARL M.

S-40075 Critical observations on Fairbairn's theory of object relations. Abs An Surv Psa 1955, 6:51-53

ABERASTURY, ARMINDA

65061   Ansiedades en los padres y en los niños frente a la experiencia odontologica. [Parents' and children's anxieties during the odontological treatment.] Bol Asoc arg Odontol Niños 1962, 4(2-3):42. Cuad Psicoter 1967, 2:28-39
65062   Aspectos psicodinámicos de la epilepsia infantil. [Psychodynamic aspects in the child epilepsy.] Rev Sem med arg 1967, 130(38):1294-1303
65063   El bebé antes de la dentición. [The baby before dentition.] Bol Asoc arg Odontol Niños 1962, 4:8
65064   La dentición, su significado y sus consecuencias en el desarrollo. [Dentition, its meaning and its consequences in general development.] Bol Asoc arg Odontol Niños 1961, 3:110
65065   (& Cesio, F. R.; Liberman, D.; Mom, J. M.; Rascovsky, A.) Discussion of Arlow, J. A. & Brenner, C. "The psychoanalytic situation." Psa Amer 44-50
65066   La enseñanza del psiconanálisis. [Psychoanalytic teaching.] In author's Historia, Enseñanza y Ejercicio Legal del Psicoanálisis 51-55
65067   La existencia de la organización genital en el lactante. [The existence of genital organization in the infant.] Rev bras Psicoanál 1967, 1:18-45
65068   La fase genital previa. [The preliminary genital phase.] Rev Psicoanál 1964, 21:203-212
        Abs Vega Q 1965, 34:625-626
65069   (& Cesio, F. R.; Aberastury, M.) Historia, Enseñanza y Ejercicio Legal del Psicoanálisis. (Pref: Garma, A.) [History, Development and Legal Exercise of Psychoanalysis.] Buenos Aires: Omeba 1967, 141 p
65070   (& Knobel, M.) La masturbación y los mecanismos maniacos. [Masturbation as a manic mechanism.] Rev urug Psa 1966, 8:209-216
65071   El Niño y sus Juegos. [The Child and His Games.] Buenos Aires: Editorial Paidós 1968, 86 p
65072   La primera sesión de análisis en una niña de 5 años. [The first analytic session with a 5-year-old girl.] Rev Psicoanál 1965, 22:13-25
65073   (& Garma, E. G. de; Langer, M.; Rascovsky, A.) Psicologia de la mujer. [Psychology of women.] Rev Psicoanál 1966, 23:37-49
65074   Teoria y Técnica del Psicoánalisis de Niños. [Theory and Technique in Child Analysis.] Buenos Aires: Editorial Paidós 1962, 281 p

See Smolensky de Dellarossa, Guiliana

ABSTRACTS OF:

65075 Barnett, M. Vaginal awareness in the infancy and childhood of girls. Rev Psicoanál 1966, 23:206

65076 Lewis, W. Coital movements in the first year of life. Rev Psicoanál 1966, 23:204-205

ABERASTURY, MARCELO

See Aberastury, Arminda

ABERCROMBIE, M. J. JOHNSON

65077 The Anatomy of Judgment. An Investigation into the Processes of Perception and Reasoning. NY: Basic Books; London: Hutchinson 1960, 156 p
Rv Bellak, L. Q 1961, 30:120-122. Home, H. J. J 1961, 42:127-128

ABOULKER, P.

65078 (& Chertok, L.) Emotional factors in stress incontinence. PSM 1962, 24:507-510

65079 (& Chertok, L.; Sapir, M.) Psychologie des Accidents. [Psychology of Accidents.] Paris: L'Expansion Scientifique Française 1961, 169 p

65080 (& Chertok, L.; Sapir, M.) (Eds) Psychosomatique et Gastro-entéro-logue. [Psychosomatics and Gastroenterology.] Paris: Masson 1962

See Chertok, Léon

ABRAHAM, GEORGES

65081 A propos de quelques cas de résistance à l'induction hypnotique. [Some cases of resistance to the induction of hypnosis.] In Lassner, J. *Hypnosis and Psychosomatic Medicine*, Berlin/Heidelberg/NY: Spring-er 1967, 7-11

65082 Attività aggressiva e distruttiva nelle nevrosi cosiddette di carattere. [Aggressive and destructive activity in certain character neuroses.] Riv Psa 1965, 11:33-43

65083 Considérations cliniques et sociales sur la névrose de caractère. [Clinical and social considerations with respect to character neurosis.] Méd Hyg 1966, 24:734-735

65084 Contribution a l'étude de l'activité onirique chez les vieillards. [Contri-bution to the study of dream activity in the aged.] Ann méd-psychol 1963, 121(2):201-210

65085 [Hypnosis and psychoanalysis.] (It) Minerva Med 1969, 60:1960-1963

65086 Le problème de la catamnèse des psychothérapies et la question des critères objectifs d'appréciation des résultats thérapeutiques. [The problem of catamnesis of psychotherapies and the problem of objective criteria for the evaluation of the results of therapy.] Acta psycho-ther psychosom 1964, 12:203-236

65087 Psychodynamique Essentielle Normale et Pathologique. [Essential Psychodynamics: Normal and Pathological.] Paris: Doin 1964, 278 p
Rv Carloni, G. Riv Psa 1965, 11:67

65088 Sulla funzionalità del senso di colpa. [On the function of the sense of guilt.] Riv Psa 1963, 9:257-267
65089 Transfert et contretransfert en médecine générale. [Transference and countertransference in general medicine.] Méd Hyg 1962, 20:471-472

See Schneider, Pierre-Bernard

ABRAHAM, HILDA C.

65090 The contribution of psychoanalysis to problems of marriage guidance. London: The Marriage Guidance Council, n. d.
S-40080 A contribution to the problem of female sexuality.
       Abs SLP An Surv Psa 1956, 7:148
65091 (& Kanter, V. B.; Rosen, I.; Standen, J. L.) A controlled clinical trial of imipramine (Tofranil) with outpatients. Brit J Psychiat 1963, 109:286-293
65092 New aspects of the psycho-pathology of patients presenting for termination of pregnancy (abortion on psychiatric grounds). n.p. n.d. 23 p
65093 (& Freud, E. L.) (Eds) A Psychoanalytic Dialogue. The Letters of Sigmund Freud and Karl Abraham 1907-1926. (Tr: Marsh, B. & Abraham, H. C.) NY: Basic Books 1965, xvii + 406 p
       Correspondence 1907-1926 de Sigmund Freud et Karl Abraham. (Tr: Cambon, F. & Grossein, J.-P.) Paris: Gallimard 1969, 415 p
       Rv HS Am Im 1966, 23:279-280. Curtis, H. C. Q 1967, 36:91-93

See Marsh, Bernard

ABRAHAM, KARL

S-34   Beitrag zur "Tic Diskussion." Psa Study Char 1969, 64-68
S-36   Beiträge der Oralerotik zur Charakterbildung. Psa Stud Char 1969, 205-216
       The influence of oral erotism on character-formation. In author's On Character and Libido Development 36-60
S-38   Bemerkungen zur Psychoanalyse eines Falles von Fuss-und-Korsett-Fetischismus.
       Remarks on the psychoanalysis of a case of foot and corset fetishism. PT Pervers 192-203
65094 On Character and Libido Development: Six Essays. (Ed: Lewin, B. D.) (Tr: Bryan, D.; Strachey, A.) NY: Basic Books 1966, 206 p
       Abs J Am Psa Ass 1967, 15:219. Rv Gero, G. Q 1968, 37:283-285
S-47   Zur Charakterbildung auf der "genitalen" Entwicklungsstufe. Psa Stud Char 1969, 217-228
       Character-formation on the genital level of libido. In author's On Character and Libido Development 188-198
S-52   Über die determinierende Kraft des Namens. Psa Stud Char 1969, 39-40
S-56   Einige Belege zur Gefühlseinstellung weiblicher Kinder gegenüber den Eltern. Psa Stud Char 1969, 237-239
S-58   Einige Bemerkungen über die Rolle der Grosseltern in der Psychologie der Neurosen. Psa Stud Char 1969, 229-231

S-59   Über Einschränkungen und Umwandlungen der Schaulust bei den Psychoneurotikern nebst Bemerkungen über analoge Erscheinungen in der Völkerpsychologie. Psa Stud Char 1969, 324-382

S-60   Über Ejaculatio praecox. Psa Stud Char 1969, 43-60

S-61   Ergänzungen zur Lehre vom Analcharakter. Psyche 1961, 15:162-180. Psa Stud Char 1969, 184-204

        Contributions to the theory of the anal character. In author's *On Character and Libido Development* 165-187

S-66   Das Geldausgeben im Angstzustand. Psa Stud Char 1969, 61-63

S-67   Die Geschichte eines Hochstaplers im Lichte psychoanalytischer Erkenntnis. Psa Stud Char 1969, 69-83

S-78   Koinzidierende Phantasien bei Mutter und Sohn. Psa Stud Char 1969, 240

65094A Letters to Sigmund Freud. In Abraham, H. C. & Freud, E. L. *A Psychoanalytic Dialogue. The Letters of Sigmund Freud and Karl Abraham 1907-1926*, (Tr: Marsh, B. & Abraham, H. C.) NY: Basic Books 1965

        French: In *Correspondance 1907-1926 de Sigmund Freud et Karl Abraham*, (Tr: Cambon, F. & Grossein, J.-P.) Paris: Gallimard 1969

S-86   Zur narzisstischen Bewertung der Exkretionsvorgänge in Traum und Neurose. Psa Stud Char 1969, 241-244

S-88   Über neurotische Exogamie. Ein Beitrag zu den Übereinstimmungen im Seelenleben der Neurotiker und der Wilden. Psa Stud Char 1969, 383-387

S-97   Psychische Nachwirkungen der Beobachtung des elterlichen Geschlechtsverkehrs bei einem neunjährigen Kinde. Psa Stud Char 1969, 233-236

S-108   Psychoanalytische Studien zur Charakterbildung. Psa Stud Char 1969, 184-228

65095   Psychoanalytische Studien zur Charakterbildung und andere Schriften. [Psychoanalytic Studies on Character Formation and Other Writings.] Frankfurt: Fischer 1969, 320 p

S-109   Zur Psychogenese der Strassenangst im Kindesalter. Psa Stud Char 1969, 41-42

S-118A Sollen wir die Patienten ihre Träume aufschreiben lassen?

        Shall we have patients write down their dreams? Heirs Freud 63-67

S-121   Die Spinne als Traumsymbol. Psa Stud Char 1969, 245-251

S-128   Traum and Mythus. Eine Studie zur Völkerpsychologie. Psa Stud 1969, 261-323

S-133   Untersuchungen über die früheste prägenitale Entwicklungsstufe der Libido. Psa Stud Char 1969, 84-112

        The first pregenital stage of the libido. In author's *On Character and Libido Development* 35-66

S-138   Versuch einer Entwicklungsgeschichte der Libido auf Grund der Psychoanalyse seelischer Störungen. Psa Stud Char 1969, 113-183

        A short study of the development of the libido, viewed in the light of mental disorders. In author's *On Character and Libido Development* 67-150

S-146   Zwei Beiträge zur Symbolforschung. Psa Stud Char 1969, 252-260

ABRAHAM, NICOLAS

65096 Discussion of Barande, I. "Le vu et l'entendu dans la cure." RFPsa 1968, 32:93-96
65097 Discussion of Geahchan, D. J. "Deuil et nostalgie." RFPsa 1968, 32:63-65
65098 (& Torok, M.) Preface to Klein, M. *Essais de Psychanalyse*, Paris: Payot 1967, 7-18

ABRAHAMS, JOSEPH

65099 [Contributor to] Discussion of Arieti, S. "Etiological considerations of schizophrenia." Out-Patient Schiz 30-32
65100 [Contributor to] Discussion of Hoch, P. H. "Concepts of schizophrenia." Out-Patient Schiz 17-23
65101 [Contributor to] Discussion of Kanner, L. "Schizophrenia as a concept." Out-Patient Schiz 52-59
65102 [Contributor to] Discussion of Williams, G. E. "Crisis in the evaluation of the schizophrenic patient." Out-Patient Schiz 74-86
65103 Group methods in the treatment of schizophrenic out-patients. Out-Patient Schiz 146-154

ABRAHAMS, ROGER D.

65104 (& Dundes, A.) On elephantasy and elephanticide. R 1969, 56:225-241

ABRAHAMSEN, DAVID

65105 The Emotional Care of Your Child. NY: Trident 1969, 287 p
S-40094 The Psychology of Crime.
    Rv Shapiro, L. N. Q 1961, 30:591. Greenwald, H. PPR 1962, 49(4):139
65106 A study of Lee Harvey Oswald: psychological capacity of murder. Bull NY Acad Med 1967, 43:861-888

ABRAHAMSON, STEPHEN

65107 Letter to the editors [re Dr. Kubie's article "Reflections on training."] Psa Forum 1966, 1:141

REVIEW OF:
65108 Hendrick, I. Psychiatry Education Today. Psa Forum 1966, 1:308-309

ABRAM, HARRY S.

65109 Adaptation to open heart surgery: a psychiatric study of response to the threat of death. P 1965, 122:659-668
65110 (& McCourt, W. F.) Interaction of physicians with emergency ward alcoholic patients. Quart J Stud Alcohol 1964, 25:679-688
65111 (& Wadlington, W.) On the selection of patients for artificial and transplanted organs. Ann intern Med 1968, 69:615-620
65112 (& Gill, B. F.) Predictions of postoperative psychiatric complications. New Engl J Med 1961, 265:1123-1128

65113 Pseudocyesis followed by true pregnancy in the termination phase of an analysis. M 1969, 42:255-262

65114 The psychiatrist, the treatment of chronic renal failure, and the prolongation of life, I. P 1968, 124:1351-1358

65115 (Ed) Psychological Aspects of Surgery. (Int psychiat Clin 1967, Vol. 4, No. 2) Boston: Little, Brown 1967, xvi + 208 p

65116 Psychological problems of patients after open-heart surgery. Hosp Topics 1966, 44:111-113

65117 Psychotherapy in renal failure. Curr psychiat Ther 1969, 9:86-92

65118 Some psychological aspects of surgery. Alabama GP 1966, 16:12

65119 (& Hallman, G. L.; Franklin, M.; Leachman, R. D.; Lowrey, O. W.; Rosenberg, H. S.; McNamara, D. G.; Singleton, W. B.; Arst, D. B.) Spotting and saving patients with congenital heart disease. Patient Care 1967, 1:23-55

65120 The Van Gogh syndrome: an unusual case of polysurgical addiction. P 1966, 123:478-481

See Chafetz, Morris E.; de la Torre, Joaquín I.; Hale, M. L.

ABRAMOVITZ, A.

See Lazarus, Arnold A.

ABRAMS, ARNOLD

65121 (& Garner, H. H.; Toman, J.) (Eds) Unfinished Tasks in the Behavioral Sciences. Baltimore: Williams & Wilkins 1964, 264 p

See Rhead, Clifton

ABRAMS, SAMUEL

See Ross, Nathaniel

ABRAMS, STANLEY

65122 A refutation of Eriksen's sensitization: defense hypotheses. J proj Tech 1962, 26:259-265

65123 The relationship of repression, projection and preference in the realm of hostility. Diss Abstr 1961, 22:635-636

ABRAMSON, HAROLD A.

65124 The cronus complex and the psychodynamics of intractable asthma. In Harms, E. *Somatic and Psychiatric Aspects of Childhood Allergies*, Oxford: Pergamon; NY: Macmillan 1963, 171-201

65125 The father-son relationship in eczema and asthma. J Asthma Res 1961, 1:349-399; 1963, 1:173-206; 1964, 1:317-349; 1964, 2:65-94, 147-174; 1967, 5:29-81

65126 Intractable asthma: conflict of period of toilet training. J Psychol 1961, 52:223-229

65127 Introduction to Harms, E. *Somatic and Psychiatric Aspects of Childhood Allergies*, Oxford: Pergamon; NY: Macmillan 1963, ix-x

65128 Is psychoanalysis relevant to tomorrow's world: an editorial. J Asthma Res 1969, 6:133-134

65129 Lysergic acid diethylamide (LSD-25), XXXII: Resolution of counter-identification conflict of father during oedipal phase of son. J Psychol 1961, 51:33-87

65130 (Ed) Neuropharmocology. (Transactions of the Fifth Conference, May 1959) NY: Josiah Macy, Jr. Foundation 1960, 251 p
Rv Goolker, P. Q 1961, 30:449

65131 Psychological Problems in the Father-Son Relationship: A Case of Eczema and Asthma. NY: October House 1969, xx + 223 p

65132 (& Peshkin, M. M.) Psychosomatic group therapy with parents of children with intractable asthma, III: Sibling rivalry and sibling support. Psychosomatics 1965, 6:161-165

65134 Some aspects of the psychodynamics of intractable asthma in children. In Schneer, H. I. The Asthmatic Child, NY: Harper & Row 1963, 27-38

S-40117 (Ed) The Use of LSD in Psychotherapy.
Rv Goolker, P. Q 1961, 30:448-449

65135 The use of LSD in the therapy of children. J Asthma Res 1967, 5:139-144

ABRAMSON, J. H.

65136 The complaints of mothers and their daughters. S Afr med J 1960, 34(33):681-683

65137 Observations on the health of adolescent girls in relation to cultural change. PSM 1961, 23:156-165
Abs JPG Q 1961, 30:603

ABRAMSON, M.

65138 (& Torghele, J. R.) Weight, temperature changes and psychosomatic symptomatology in relation to the menstrual cycle. Amer J Obs Gyn 1961, 81:223-232

ABSE, DAVID WILFRED

65139 (& Dahlstrom, W. G.; Tolley, A. G.) Evaluation of tranquilizing drugs in the management of acute mental disturbance. P 1960, 116:973-980

65140 Hysteria and Related Mental Disorders. An Approach to Psychological Medicine. Baltimore: Williams & Wilkins; Bristol, England: Wright 1966, 279 p

65141 Hysteria, hypnosis and the hypnoid state. Proc 3rd World Cong Psychiat 1961, 2:856-859

65142 Investigative psychotherapy and cancer. In Kissen, D. M. & LeShan, L. L. Psychosomatic Aspects of Neoplastic Disease, Phila: Lippincott; London: Pitman Med Publ 1964, 131-137

65143 Psychiatric aspects of human male infertility. Fertility & Sterility 1966, 17:133-139

65144 Psychoanalysis and group process. Grp Anal 1968, 1(2):87-90

65145 Sexual disorder and marriage. In Nash, E. et al: Marriage Counseling in Medical Practice, Chapel Hill, N Carolina: Univ of N Carolina Pr 1964, 41-73

65146 (& Ewing, J. A.) Some problems in psychotherapy with schizophrenic patients. PT 1960, 14:505-519

65147 Some psychologic and psychoanalytic aspects of perception. In Stipe, R. E. *Perception and Environment: Foundations of Urban Design*, Chapel Hill, N Carolina: Univ of N Carolina, Inst of Govt 1966, 11-16

See Clarke, Mary G.; Cochrane, Carl M.; Curtis, Thomas E.; Dahlstrom, W. Grant; Ewing, John A.; Fortin, John N.; Jessner, Lucie; Monroe, John T., Jr.; Nash, Ethel M.

ABT, LAWRENCE EDWIN

65148 Acting out in group psychotherapy: a transactional approach. Acting Out 173-182

65149 (& Weissman, S. L.) (Eds) Acting Out: Theoretical and Clinical Aspects. (Foreword: Bellak, L.) NY/London: Grune & Stratton 1965, xiii + 336 p

Rv J Am Psa Ass 1967, 15:226-227. Kaplan, D. M. R 1964, 54:710-712. WAS Q 1967, 36:106. Deltheil, P. RFPsa 1968, 32:790

65150 Clinical psychology in Latin America. Prog clin Psych 1964, 6:235-241

* * * (& Weissman, S. L.) Preface. Acting Out xiii

65151 (& Reiss, B. F.) (Eds) Progress in Clinical Psychology. NY/London: Grune & Stratton Vol. IV 1960, x + 181 p; Vol. V 1963, 209 p; Vol. VI 1964, xi + 252 p; Vol. VII 1966, ix + 309 p; Vol. VIII: Dreams and Dreaming 1969, vi + 192 p

Rv Radomisli, M. R 1967, 54:552

65152 A transactional view of interpretation. In Hammer, E. F. *Use of Interpretation in Treatment: Technique and Art*, NY: Grune & Stratton 1968, 228-231

ABUCHAEM, JAMIL

65153 (& Ferrer, S. de; Goldstein, N.; Rovatti, J.) La interpretación según la concepción Kleiniana. [Interpretation according to the concepts of Melanie Klein.] Rev Psicoanál 1962, 19:39-41

ABURY, J.

See Guiton, Micheline

ACHAINTRE, A.

See Bergeret, J.

ACHARD ARROSA, L.

65154 Formas particulares de identificación en el actor. [Particular forms of identification in an actor.] Rev Psicoanál 1962, 19:42-47

ACHTÉ, KARL AIMO

65155 On Prognosis and Rehabilitation in Schizophrenic and Paranoid Psychoses. A Comparative Follow-up Study of Two Series of Patients First Admitted to Hospital in 1950 and 1960 Respectively. Copenhagen: Munksgaard 1967, 217 p

65156 (& Vauhkonen, M.-L.) Syöpä ja psyyke. Duodecim 1967, 83:678-685
       Cancer and the psyche. Ann Med Intern Fenn 1967, 49(Suppl):5-33
65157 Der Verlauf der Schizophrenien und der schizophreniformen Psychosen.
       Eine vergleichende Untersuchung der Veränderungen in der Krankeits-
       bildern, der Prognosen und des Verhältnisses zwischen dem Kranken
       und dem Arzt in den Jahren 1933-1935 und 1953-1955. [The course
       of schizophrenia and schizophreniform psychoses. A comparative study
       of changes in disease pictures, prognoses and the patient-physician
       relationship in the years 1933-1935 and 1953-1955.] Acta Psychiat
       Scand 1961, 36 (Suppl 15), 273 p

       See Rechardt, E.

ACK, MARVIN

65158 Julie: the treatment of a case of developmental retardation. Psa St C
       1966, 21:127-149
65159 The management of anxiety in the diagnostic evaluation. Nord Psykol
       1968, 20:49-56

ACKART, RICHARD

       See Leavy, Stanley A.

ACKER, MARY

       See McReynolds, Paul

ACKERLY, WILLIAM C.

65160 Latency-age children who threaten or attempt to kill themselves. J
       Amer Acad Child Psychiat 1967, 6:242-261
65161 (& Gibson, G.) Lighter fluid "sniffing." P 1964, 120:1056-1061

ACKERMAN, J. M.

       See Johnson, R. C.

ACKERMAN, NATHAN WARD

65162 Adolescent problems: a symptom of family disorder. Fam Proc 1962,
       1:202-213
65163 Adolescent struggle as protest. In Farber, S. M. et al: Man and Civiliza-
       tion, NY: McGraw-Hill 1965, 81-93
65164 Challenge to agree on a typology. (Panel discussion: the classification
       of family types.) In author's Expanding Theory and Practice in Family
       Therapy 78-82
65165 A challenge to traditionalism. Int J Psychiat 1967, 4:71-73
65166 Child and family psychiatry today: a new look at some old problems.
       MH 1963, 47:540-545
65167 Cultural factor in psychoanalytic therapy. Bull Am Psa Ass 1951, 7(4)
65168 Developments in family psychotherapy. Curr psychiat Ther 1968,
       8:126-136
65169 [Contributor to] Discussion of Arieti, S. "Etiological considerations of
       schizophrenia." Out-Patient Schiz 30-32

65170 [Contributor to] Discussion of Hoch, P. H. "Concepts of schizophrenia." Out-Patient Schiz 17-23

65171 [Contributor to] Discussion of Kanner, L. "Schizophrenia as a concept." Out-Patient Schiz 52-59; 194-202

65172 Discussion of Shapiro, R. L. "Identity and ego autonomy in adolescence." Sci Psa 1966, 9:24-26

65173 [Contributor to] Discussion of Williams, G. E. "Crisis in the evaluation of the schizophrenic patient." Out-Patient Schiz 74-86

65174 Divorce and alienation in modern society. In Fried, J. *Jews and Divorce*, NY: Ktav Publ House 1968

65175 A dynamic frame for the clinical approach to family conflict. In author's *Exploring the Base for Family Therapy*

65176 The emergence of family psychotherapy: a personal account. In Paterson, J. A. *Marriage and Family Counseling*, NY: Assoc Pr 1968, 154-170

65177 The emergence of family therapy and treatment, a personal view. Psychotherapy 1967, 4:125-129

65178 Emergency of family psychotherapy on the present scene. Contempo PT 228-244

65179 The emotional impact of in-laws and relatives. In Liebman, S. *Emotional Forces in the Family*, Phila: Lippincott 1959, 71-84

65180 (& Beatman, F. L.; Sherman, S. N.) (Eds) Expanding Theory and Practice in Family Therapy. NY: Fam Serv Ass Am 1967, 182 p

65181 (& Beatman, F. L.; Sherman, S. N.) (Eds) Exploring the Base for Family Therapy. NY: Fam Serv Ass Am 1961, 159 p

65182 (& Behrens, M. L.) The family approach and levels of intervention. PT 1968, 22:5-14

65183 The family approach to marital disorders. In Greene, B. L. *The Psychotherapies of Marital Disharmony*, NY: Free Pr 1965, 153-167

65184 The family as a unit in mental health. Proc III World Cong Psychiat 1961

65185 Family diagnosis and therapy. Int MH Newsletter 1961. Curr psychiat Ther 1963, 3:205-210

65186 Family diagnosis and treatment: some general principles. In Kurian, M. & Hand, M. H. *Lectures in Dynamic Psychiatry*, NY: IUP 1963, 127-137

65187 (& Franklin, P. F.) Family dynamics and the reversibility of delusional formation: a case study in family therapy. In Boszormenyi-Nagy, I. & Framo, J. L. *Intensive Family Therapy*, NY: Harper & Row 1965, 245-287

65188 The family in crisis. Bull NY Acad Med 1964, 40:171-187

65189 Family-focused therapy of schizophrenia. Out-Patient Schiz 156-173

65190 Family psychotherapy. Ency Ment Hlth 612-623

65191 Family psychotherapy and psychoanalysis: the implications of difference. Fam Proc 1962, 1:30-43

65192 Family psychotherapy—theory and practice. PT 1966, 20:405-414
Familientherapie—Theorie und Praxis. Hbh Kinderpsychother 666-677

65193 Family psychotherapy today: some areas of controversy. Comprehen Psychiat 1966, 7:375-388. In Freyhan, F. A. *Family Therapy and Marriage Counseling*, NY: Grune & Stratton 1966

65194 Family study and treatment. Children 1961, 8:130-134

65195 Family therapy. Am Hbk Psychiat III, 201-212
65196 (& Kempster, S.) Family therapy. Compreh Txbk Psychiat 1244-1248
65197 Family Therapy. Boston: Little, Brown 1967, 182 p
65198 (& Richardson, H. B.) Family therapy: an ideal for the future. In Lief,
       H. I. et al: *The Psychological Basis of Medical Practice*, NY/Evans-
       ton/London: Harper & Row 1963, 545-552
65199 Family therapy in schizophrenia: theory and practice. Int Psychiat
       Clin 1964, 1:929-943
65200 A family therapy session. In author's *Expanding Theory and Practice
       in Family Therapy* 135-177
* * * Foreword to Burrow, T. & Galt, W. E. (Eds) *The Preconscious Foun-
       dations of Human Experience.*
* * * Foreword to Grollman, E. *Judaism in Sigmund Freud's World.*
* * * Foreword to Riese, H. *Heal the Hurt Child.*
65201 The functions of a family therapist: a personal viewpoint. Dyn Psy-
       chiat 1968, 1:99-108; Abs (Ger) 108-109
65202 Further comments on family psychotherapy. Contempo PT 245-255
65203 The future of family therapy. In author's *Expanding Theory and
       Practice in Family Therapy* 3-16
S-40142 Interaction processes in a group and the role of the leader.
            Abs An Surv Psa 1955, 6:431-432
65204 Introduction. (Panel discussion: the classification of family types.) In
       author's *Expanding Theory and Practice in Family Therapy* 59-60
65205 Mental illness—1963. Psychiatry in a changing society. J Kansas Med
       Soc 1964, 65:6-11
65206 Prejudicial scapegoating and neutralizing trends in the family group.
       Int J soc Psychiat 1964 (Cong Issue)
65207 Prejudice and scapegoating in the family. In Zuk, G. H. & Boszormeny-
       Nagi, I. *Family Therapy and Disturbed Families,* Palo Alto: Sci &
       Behav Books 1967, 48-57
65208 Preventive implications of family research. In Caplan, G. *Prevention of
       Mental Disorders in Childhood,* NY: Basic Books 1961, 142-167
S-40153 Psychoanalytic principles in a mental health clinic for the preschool
       child and his family: a critical appraisal of an experiment in community
       mental health.
            Abs JA An Surv Psa 1956, 7:291-292
65209 Psychotherapy with the family group. Sci Psa 1961, 4:150-156
65210 Reflections on the program of the Council Child Development Center.
       Quart J child Behav 1950, 2:390-403
65211 The role of the family in the emergence of child disorders. In Miller,
       E. *Foundations of Child Psychiatry,* Oxford: Pergamon Pr 1968, 509-
       533
65212 The schizophrenic patient and his family relationships—a conceptual
       basis for family-focused therapy of schizophrenia. In Greenblatt, M.
       et al: *Mental Patients in Transition,* Springfield, Ill: Thomas 1961, 273-
       282
65213 Sexual delinquency among middle-class girls. In Pollak, O. & Friedman,
       A. S. *Family Dynamics and Female Sexual Delinquency,* Palo Alto,
       Calif: Sci & Behav Books 1969, 45-50

65214 The social psychology of prejudice. MH 1965, 49:27-35. In Powers, G. P. & Baskin, W. *New Outlooks in Psychology,* NY: Philos Libr 1968, 154-167

65215 Some theoretical aspects of group psychotherapy. In Moreno, J. L. *Group Psychotherapy: A Symposium,* NY: Beacon House 1945, 117-124

65216 Symptom, defense, and growth in group process. Int J grp PT 1961, 11:131-142

65217 Techniques of therapy: a case study. Ops 1940, 10:665-680

S-40159 Theory of family dynamics.

      Abs Vilar, J. Rev Psicoanál 1963, 20:188

S-40160 Transference and counter-transference

      Abs Vilar, J. Rev Psicoanál 1962, 19:270-273

65218 Treating the Troubled Family. NY: Basic Books 1966, xiii + 306 p

65219 The unity of the family. Arch Pediat 1938, 55(11):51-56

65220 (& Behrens, M. L.) The uses of family psychotherapy. Ops 1967, 37:391-392

See Friedman, Emerick; Glueck, Bernard C., Sr.; Mudd, Emily H.; Sherman, Murray H.

ACKMAN, PHYLLIS

65221 The effects of induced regression on thinking processes. Diss Abstr 1960, 21:365

ACKNER, BRIAN

65222 (& Grant, Q. A. F. R.; Maxwell, A. E.) The prognostic significance of depersonalization in depressive illnesses treated with electroconvulsive therapy. Statistical appendix. J Neurol Ns Psychiat 1960, 23:242-246

ACORD, LOREN D.

65223 Sexual symbolism as a correlate of age. J consult Psychol 1962, 26:279-281

ACTON, W. P.

See Wolff, Sula

ADAM, JOHN C.

65224 (& Rachiele, L. D.; Young, M. A.) An evaluation of parental complaints. P 1965, 121:1209-1210

ADAM, K. S.

65225 Suicide: a critical review of the literature. Canad Psychiat Ass J 1967, 12:413-420

ADAM, R.

65226 [Failure of performance from the viewpoints of education and depth psychology.] (Ger) Praxis Kinderpsychol 1964 (Suppl 6):11-21

ADAMOWSKI, T. H.

65227   The aesthetic attitude and narcissism in "Othello." Lit & Psych 1968,
18:73-81

ADAMS, ANNE

See Heath, E. Sheldon

ADAMS, DARRELL

See Little, Kenneth

ADAMS, ELSIE B.

65228   (& Sarason, I. G.) Relation between anxiety in children and their
parents. Child Develpm 1963, 34:237-246

ADAMS, GEORGE R.

65229   Sex and clergy in Chaucer's "General Prologue." Lit & Psych 1968,
18:215-222

ADAMS, HENRY B.

65230   (& Cooper, G. D.) Three measures of ego strength and prognosis for
psychotherapy. Clin Psych 1962, 18:490-494

See Cooper, G. David

ADAMS, HENRY E.

65231   (& Noblin, C. D.; Butler, J. R.; Timmons, E. O.) Differential effect
of psychoanalytically-derived interpretations and verbal conditioning
in schizophrenics. Psychol Rep 1962, 11:195-198
65232   (& Butler, J. R.; Noblin, C. D.) Effects of psychoanalytically-derived
interpretations: a verbal conditioning paradigm? Psychol Rep 1962,
10:691-694

See Berg, Irwin A.; Timmons, Edwin O.; Weingold, Harold P.

ADAMS, JAMES F.

65233   A developmental and historical analysis of psychology within the
universities of Austria and Germany over a ten-year period: 1955-1965.
Trans NY Acad Sci 1966, 28:754-760

ADAMS, JOHN E.

See Hamburg, David A.; Horowitz, Mardi J.

ADAMS, PAUL L.

65234   (& Schwab, J. J.; Aponte, J. F.) Authoritarian parents and disturbed
children. P 1965, 121:1162-1167
65235   Childhood as a world apart. Proc Conf Florida Ass on Children under
Six 1963

65236 Childhood ulcerative colitis: outlines of psychotherapy. Psychosomatics 1968, 9:75-80
65237 Children of change. Young Children 1965, 20:202-208
65238 (& McDonald, N. F.) Clinical cooling-out of poor people. Ops 1968, 38:457-463
65239 Dental symbols and dreamwork. In *Psychiatry and Pedodontics,* Florida State Dent Soc 1963
65240 Empathic parenting of the elementary school child. Southern med J 1965, 58:642-647
65241 Helping the child's heart and world. Ass Childhood Education Bull, Np. 14-A, 1967
65242 Introduction to *Psychiatry and Pedodontics,* Florida State Dent Soc 1963
65243 A pediatrician's checklist for adolescents. Clin Ped 1966, 5(1):54-58
65244 (& McDonald, N. F.; Huey, W. F.) School phobia and bisexual conflict: a report of 21 cases. P 1966, 123:541-547

ADAMS, WILLIAM R.

65245 Obituary: Dr. James F. Berwald: 1910-1965. Bull Phila Ass Psa 1965, 15:240

ABSTRACTS OF:
65246 Dratman, M. L. Affects and consciousness. Bull Phila Ass Psa 1964, 14:246-247
65247 Stein, M. H. Reality and the superego. Bull Phila Ass Psa 1964, 14:170-171

ADAMSON, J. D.

65248 (& Schmale, A. H., Jr.) Object loss, giving up, and the onset of psychiatric disease. PSM 1965, 27:557-576
65249 (& Prosen, H.; Bebchuk, W.) Training in formal psychotherapy in the psychiatric residency program. Canad Psychiat Ass J 1968, 13:445-454

ADAMSON, WILLIAM C.

65250 History of child psychiatry, I: Frederick H. Allen, M. D., child psychiatrist. Trans Coll Physicians Phila 1968, 36:96-103
65251 The needs of teachers for specialized information in the area of pediatric psychiatry. In Cruickshank, W. M. *The Teacher of Brain-Injured Children,* Syracuse, NY: Syracuse Univ Pr 1966, 271-290

ABSTRACT OF:
65253 Ritvo S. Psychoanalysis in late adolescence. Bull Phila Ass Psa 1969, 19:253-256

ADATTO, CARL P.

S-40177 Ego reintegration observed in analysis of late adolescents. Abs JLS An Surv Psa 1958, 9:288-289
65254 The impact of dynamic psychiatry. Louisian 1961, 113:204-209
65255 The inner life of the adolescent. In Usdin, G. *Adolescence,* Phila: Lippincott 1967, 130-149

65256 On play and the psychopathology of golf. (Read at New Orleans Psa
       Soc, 11 Jan 1963; at Am Psa Ass, 4 May 1963) J Am Psa Ass 1964,
       12:826-841
           Abs JLSt Q 1967, 36:470
S-40178 On pouting.
           Abs CK An Surv Psa 1957, 8:121
65257 On the metamorphosis from adolescence into adulthood. (Read at
       New Orleans Psa Soc, Feb 1964; at Am Psa Ass, Dec 1964) J Am Psa
       Ass 1966, 14:485-509
           Abs Cuad Psa 1967, 3:56. CG RFPsa 1968, 32:356. JLSt Q 1969,
       38:338
65258 (& Freedman, D.) On the precipitation of seizures in an adolescent
       boy. PSM 1968, 30:437-447

       See Freedman, David A.

       REVIEW OF:
65259 The Psychoanalytic Study of the Child, Vol. XXI. Q 1968, 37:131-132

ADCOCK, C. J.

See Adcock, Ngaire V.

ADCOCK, NGAIRE V.

65260 (& Adcock, C. J.) A factorial study of the ego reference system. J
       genet Psych 1967, 110:105-115

ADELMAN, CRUSA

See Bellak, Leopold

ADELSON, EDWARD T.

65261 Critique. Dreams Contempo Psa 262-271
65262 (Ed) Dreams in Contemporary Psychoanalysis. NY: Soc Med Psa
       1963, x + 271 p
65263 Facts and theories of the psychology of dreams. Dreams Contempo
       Psa 1-33
65264 Introduction to papers on the dream in the therapeutic process. Dreams
       Contempo Psa 133

ADELSON, JOSEPH

65265 Creativity and the dream. Merrill-Palmer Q 1960, 6:92-97
65266 The dream as a riddle. Ps 1966, 29:306-309
65267 (& Green, B.; O'Neil, R.) Growth of the idea of law in adolescence.
       Developm Psychol 1969, 1:327-332
65268 The mystique of adolescence. Ps 1964, 27:1-5
           Abs Laderman, P. Q 1965, 34:623-624
65269 Personality. Ann Rev Psychol 1969, 20:217-252
65270 The teacher as a model. In Sanford, N. The American College, NY:
       Wiley 1962, 396-417

       See Douvan, Elizabeth

ADKINS, L. JOHN

65271 The independent self: link between science and religion. Pastoral Psychol 1960, 11(103)

65272 Self-confidence: skill or value? J Ass Secretaries YMCA 1961, Jan-Feb

ADLAND, MARVIN L.

65273 Discussion of McLaughlin, F. "On the concept of health." Crosscurrents in Ps & Psa 176-178

65274 A social laboratory for freedom. Ment Hosp 1962, 13:476-478

ADLER, A.

See Lesse, Stanley

ADLER, ALEXANDER

65275 Individual psychology [interviewed by Perkins, M. E.]. In Ziskind, R. *Viewpoint on Mental Health,* NY: NYC Comm Ment Hlth Board 1967, 438-442

° ° ° Introduction to Way, L. M. *Adler's Place in Psychology.*

65276 Office treatment of the chronic schizophrenic patient. In Hoch, P. H. & Zubin, J. *Psychopathology of Schizophrenia,* NY/London: Grune & Stratton 1966, 366-371

65277 Psychotherapy, its present and future. PT 1962, 16:307-310

ADLER, ALFRED

S-437 (& Freud, S.; Friedjung, J. K.; Molitor, K.; Oppenheim, D. E.; Reitler, R.; Sadger, J.; Stekel, W.) Über den Selbstmord inbesondere den Schülerselbstmord.

On Suicide: With Particular Reference to Suicide Among Young Students. (Discussions of the Vienna Psychoanalytic Society—1910) (Ed: Friedman, P.) NY: IUP 1967, 141 p

Abs Am Im 1968, 25:194. J Am Psa Ass 1968, 16:182. Rv ESt J 1968, 49:741-742. Furer, M. Q 1969, 38:130-132

S-440 Der Sinn des Lebens.

Social Interest, a Challenge to Mankind. (Tr: Linton, J.; Vaughan, R.) NY: Capricorn Books 1964, 313 p

Le Sens de la Vie, Étude de Psychologie Individuelle Comparée. (Tr. Schaffer, H.) Paris: Payot 1968, 224 p

S-443 Studie über Minderwertigkeit von Organen. (Unveränderter reprografischer Nachdruck der Ausg. München 1927) Darmstadt: Wiss Buchgscht 1965, 92 p

65278 Superiority and Social Interest, a Collection of Later Writings. (Ed: Ansbacher, H. L.; Ansbacher, R.) Evanston, Ill: Northwestern Univ Pr 1964, xix + 432 p

ADLER, F.

See Beech, Harold R.

ADLER, GERALD

ABSTRACT OF:
65279 Pinderhughes, C. A. & Thompson, D. R. Temporal relationships between patterns of illness. Bull Phila Ass Psa 1969, 19:246-248

ADLER, GERHARD

65280 Current Trends in Analytical Psychology. London: Tavistock 1961, 15 plates + 326 p
65281 Foreword to Kirsch, J. *Shakespeare's Royal Self*, NY: Putnam 1966
65282 Methods of treatment in analytical psychology. Psa Tech 338-378
65283 (Contributor to) *Psychotherapeutische Probleme* [Psychotherapeutic Problems], Zurich: Rascher 1964
65284 Die Sinnfrage in der Psychotherapie. [The problem of meaning in psychotherapy.] Psyche 1963, 17:379-400

ADLER, H.

65285 Handbuch der tiefenpsychologischen Symbolik. [Handbook of Psychoanalytic Symbolism.] Zurich: Rhein 1969

ADLER, JOSHUA

65286 Philosophy of Judaism. NY: Philos Libr 1960, 160 p
       Rv Malev, M. Q 1961, 30:446-447

ADLER, KURT ALFRED

65287 Adler's individual psychology. Psa Tech 299-337
65288 Depression in the light of individual psychology. J ind Psych 1961, 17:56-67
65289 (& Deutsch, D.) (Eds) Essays in Individual Psychology: Contemporary Application of Alfred Adler's Theories. NY: Grove Pr 1959, xvii + 480 p
65290 Life style, gender role, and the symptom of homosexuality. J ind Psych 1967, 23:67-78
65291 The structure of a nervous breakdown. Treatment Monographs on Analytic Psychotherapy, No. 2, Fall 1968

ADLER, LETA McKINNEY

See Enelow, Allen J.

ADLER, M.

65292 Untersuchungen zur Begriffsstruktur Defektschizophrener. [Studies on the concept structure of schizophrenic defect states.] Psychiat Neurol, Basel 1967, 154:129-143

ADLER, NATHAN

65293 The antinomian personality: the Hippie character type. Ps 1968, 31:325-338

ADLERSTEIN, ARTHUR M.

See Alexander, Irving E.

ADSETT, C. ALEX

65294 (& Schottstaedt, W. W.; Wolf, S. G.) Changes in coronary blood flow and other hemodynamic indicators induced by stressful interviews. PSM 1962, 24:331
Abs Aslan, C. M. Rev Psicoanál 1963, 20:93

65295 Emotional reactions to disfigurement from cancer therapy. Canad Med Ass J 1963, 89:389-391

65296 Psychological health of medical students in relation to the medical education process. J med Educ 1968, 43:728-734

AFASIŽEV, M.

65297 Frejdizm i modernistskaja estetika. [Freudianism in modern esthetics.] Iskusstvo 1965, 28(3):70-72

AFFEMANN, RUDOLF

S-40208 Das Über-Ich bei Freud.
Abs An Surv Psa 1955, 6:37-38

AFFLERBACH, LOIS

See Bry, Ilse

AFTERMAN, JOSEPH

65298 (Participant in round table) A psychoanalytic view of the family: a study of family member interactions. Psa Forum 1969, 3:11-65

See Heinicke, Christoph M.

ABSTRACTS OF:

65299 Ackerman, N. W. Psychoanalytic principles in a mental health clinic for the preschool child and his family. An Surv Psa 1956, 7:291-292

65300 Almansi, R. J. Cloud fantasies. Q 1962, 31:585

65301 Arlow, J. A. A typical dream. Q 1962, 31:585

65302 Beckett, P. G. S. et al: Studies in schizophrenia at the Mayo Clinic, I: The significance of exogenous traumata in the genesis of schizophrenia. An Surv Psa 1956, 7:182

65303 Beres, D. Vicissitudes of superego functions and superego precursors in childhood. An Surv Psa 1958, 9:124-126

65304 Bergen, M. E. The effect of severe trauma on a four-year-old child. An Surv Psa 1958, 9:304-307

65305 Bierman, J. S. et al: A depression in a six-year-old boy with acute poliomyelitis. An Surv Psa 1958, 9:300-301

65306 Bird, H. W. & Martin, P. A. Countertransference in the psychotherapy of marriage partners. An Surv Psa 1956, 7:349

65307 Boyer, L. B. Notes on the personality structure of a North American Indian Shaman. 1962, 31:136

65308   Charatan, F. B. & Galef, H. A case of transvestitism in a six-year-old boy. Q 1967, 36:320

65309   Chassan, J. B. On probability theory and psychoanalytic research. An Surv Psa 1956, 7:46-47

65310   Devereux, G. The lifting of a refractory amnesia through a startle reaction to an unpredictable stimulus. Q 1961, 30:451

65311   Devereux, G. Weeping, urination, and grand mal. Q 1967, 36:320

65312   Eissler, K. R. Notes on problems of technique in the psychoanalytic treatment of adolescents. An Surv Psa 1958, 9:318-322

65313   Ekstein, R. & Wallerstein, J. Observations on the psychotherapy of borderline and psychotic children. An Surv Psa 1956, 7:288-289

65314   Fajrajzen, S. On a case of depersonalization. Q 1961, 30:149

65315   Fink, G. et al: The 'superobese' patient. Q 1963, 32:290

65316   Freud, A. Adolescence. An Surv Psa 1958, 9:284-286

65317   Furman, E. An ego disturbance in a young child. An Surv Psa 1956, 7:282-285

65318   Geleerd, E. R. Borderline states in childhood and adolescence. An Surv Psa 1958, 9:307-308

65319   Geleerd, E. R. Clinical contribution to the problem of the early mother-child relationship. An Surv Psa 1956, 7:142-143

65320   Gitelson, M. On the problem of character neurosis. Q 1967, 36:134

65321   Glauber, I. P. Further contributions to the concept of stuttering. Q 1963, 32:291

65322   Glover, E. The frontiers of psycho-analysis. An Surv Psa 1956, 7:67-68

65323   Glover, E. The future development of psycho-analysis. An Surv Psa 1956, 7:50

65324   Goolker, P. Affect communication in therapy. Q 1962, 31:585

65325   Gottschalk, L. A. The relationship of psychologic state and epileptic activity. An Surv Psa 1956, 7:275-279

65326   Graubert, D. N. & Levine, A. The concept of the representational world. Q 1967, 36:321

65327   Greenberg, I. M. An exploratory study of reunion fantasies. Q 1967, 36:319

65328   Grinstein, A. Some comments on breast envy in women. Q 1963, 32:291

65329   Grotjahn, M. Ego identity and the fear of death and dying. Q 1961, 30:450

65330   Grotjahn, M. Jewish jokes and their relation to masochism. Q 1962, 31:585

65331   Harris, I. D. The dream of the object endangered. An Surv Psa 1957, 8:177

65332   Hurvitz, M. The treatment of a septuagenarian. Q 1967, 36:136

65333   Jarvis, V. Clinical observations on the visual problem in reading disability. An Surv Psa 1958, 9:302-304

65334   Jessner, L. The genesis of a compulsive neurosis. Q 1967, 36:136

65335   Johnson, A. M. et al: Studies in schizophrenia at the Mayo Clinic, II: Observations on ego functions in schizophrenia. An Surv Psa 1956, 7:182

65336   Kanzer, M. Freud and the demon. Q 1962, 31:585

65337   Kaplan, E. H. Attitudes toward automobiles. Q 1962, 31:136

65338 Kaplan, E. H. Organic visual defects in a case of obsessional neurosis. Q 1963, 32:290

65339 Kardiner, A. Adaptational theory: the cross cultural point of view. An Surv Psa 1956, 7:66

65340 Kay, P. The phenomenology of schizophrenia in childhood. Q 1963, 32:291

65341 Kaywin, L. Orientation and conviction in the psychotherapist. Q 1962, 31:585-586

65342 Keiser, S. An observation concerning the somatic manifestations of anxiety. Q 1962, 31:586

65343 Khan, M. M. R. Ego ideal, excitement, and the threat of annihilation. Q 1967, 36:136-137

65344 Klein, H. R. The Columbia Psychoanalytic Clinic. An Surv Psa 1956, 7:365-366

65345 Lefer, J. Psychosis, somatic disease, and the perceived body. Q 1967, 36:319

65346 Lidz, T. et al: The intrafamiliar environment of the schizophrenic patient, I: The father. An Surv Psa 1957, 8:149-150

65347 Lorand, S. The body image and the psychiatric evaluation of patients for plastic surgery. Q 1962, 31:586

65348 Lorand, S. Regression. Technical and theoretical problems. Q 1967, 36:135

65349 Murphy, G. The prevention of mental disorder. Q 1961, 30:450

65350 Niederland, W. G. Clinical observations on the "Little Man" phenomenon. An Surv Psa 1956, 7:144-145

65351 Niederland, W. G. The problem of the survivor. Part I: Some remarks on the psychiatric evaluation of emotional disorders in survivors of Nazi persecution. Q 1962, 31:586-587

65352 Oliveira, W. I. de: The psychoanalytic approach to group psychotherapy. Q 1967, 36:136

65353 Ovesey, L. Masculine aspirations in women; an adaptational analysis. An Surv Psa 1956, 7:147-148

65354 Pavenstedt, E. The effect of extreme passivity imposed on a boy in early childhood. An Surv Psa 1956, 7:248-249

65355 Peller, L. E. The school's role in promoting sublimation. An Surv Psa 1956, 7:256-258

65356 Potter, H. W. & Klein, H. R. On nursing behavior. An Surv Psa 1957, 8:209

65357 Prall, R. C. & Dealy, M. N. Countertransference in therapy of childhood psychosis. Q 1967, 36:320

65358 Rado, S. Adaptational psychodynamics: a basic science. An Surv Psa 1956, 7:59

65359 Robbins, L. L. Character neuroses. Therapeutic problems. Q 1967, 36:135

65360 Robertson, J. A mother's observations on the tonsillectomy of her four-year-old daughter. An Surv Psa 1956, 7:265-267

65361 Roth, N. Disorders of visual perception as detected in psychoanalysis. Q 1963, 32:290

65362 Roth, N. Perception and memory. Q 1967, 36:137

65363 Savitt, R. A. Turning point in the analysis of a borderline problem. Q 1962, 31:587

65364 Schildkrout, M. S. Clinical symposium: observations on the process of identification. Q 1967, 36:321

65365 Schildkrout, M. S. & Stahl, A. S. The treatment of "provocative" behavior in the disturbed adolescent. Q 1962, 31:427

65366 Schneider, D. E. Dream flying and dream weightlessness. Q 1961, 30:450

65367 Searles, H. F. The psychodynamics of vengefulness. An Surv Psa 1956, 7:185

65368 Sperling, M. A note on some dream symbols and the significance of their changes during analysis. Q 1962, 31:587

65369 Spiegel, L. A. Comments on the psychoanalytic psychology of adolescence. An Surv Psa 1958, 9:286-287

65370 Spitz, R. A. No and Yes—on the Genesis of Human Communication. An Surv Psa 1957, 8:186-198

65371 Sterba, R. F. Therapeutic goal and present-day reality. Q 1961, 30:451

65372 Tarachow, S. Supervisors' conference: the problem of reality and the therapeutic task. Q 1963, 32:289-290

65373 Wallach, S. S. et al: Observations of involuntary eye movements in certain schizophrenics: a preliminary report. Q 1961, 30:451

65374 Walsh, M. N. A psychoanalytic interpretation of a primitive dramatic ritual. Q 1963, 32:289

65375 Weakland, J. H. Orality in Chinese conceptions of male genital sexuality. An Surv Psa 1956, 7:407-408

65376 Weigert, E. Human ego functions in the light of animal behavior. An Surv Psa 1956, 7:90

65377 Weiss, J. M. A. The gamble with death in attempted suicide. An Surv Psa 1957, 8:145

65378 Weissman, P. Antigone—a preoedipal old maid. Q 1967, 36:319

65379 Weissman, P. The primacy of mania in some forms of cyclothymic states. Q 1962, 31:136-137

65380 Weissman, P. Psychiatry and the theater. Q 1967, 36:320

65381 Windholz, E. Some technical problem in character analysis. Q 1967, 36:135

65382 Winick, C. & Holt, H. Eye and face movements as nonverbal communication in group psychotherapy. Q 1963, 32:290

65383 Wolfenstein, M. Analysis of a juvenile poem. An Surv Psa 1956, 7:414

AGLE, DAVID P.

65384 (& Ratnoff, O. D.; Wasman, M.) Conversion reactions in autoerythrocyte sensitization: their relationship to the production of ecchymosis. Arch gen Psychiat 1969, 20:438-447

65385 (& Mattsson, A.) Psychiatric and social care of patients with hereditary hemorrhagic disease. Mod Treatm 1968, 5:111-124

65386 Psychiatric studies of patients with hemophilia and related states. Arch intern Med 1964, 144:76-82

65387 (& Ratnoff, O. D.) Purpura as a psychosomatic entity—a psychiatric study of autoerythrocyte sensitization. Arch intern Med 1962, 109:685-694

65388 (& Ratnoff, O. D.; Wasman, M.) Studies in autoerythrocyte sensitiza-
       tion. The induction of purpuric lesions by hypnotic suggestion. PSM
       1967, 29:491-503

       See Tripp, L. E.

AGNER, I.

65389 [1000 bears—and we have no revolver. Course of a play therapy with
       a 5-year-old boy.] (Ger) Prax Kinderpsychol 1964 (Suppl 6):28-36

AGNEW, P. C.

65390 Culture deprivation and mental illness. Quart Bull Northw Univ Med
       Sch 1961, 35:54-60

AGORIO, RODOLFO

65391 (& Garbarino, M. F. de; Garbarino, H.; Lacava, M.; Prego, V. M. de;
       Prego, L. E. de) [Additional comments about present concepts.] (Sp)
       Rev urug Psa 1966, 8:125-138
       Abs Vega Q 1967, 36:476-477
65392 Enfoque psicoanalitica sobre algunos aspectos de la obra de Gerardo
       de Nerval. [Psychoanalytic study of some aspects of the work of
       Gerard de Nerval.] Rev urug Psa 1964, 6:357-398
65393 Identificación y personaje. [Identification and personality.] Rev urug
       Psa 1961-62, 4:253-270

       See Prego, Vida M. de

ABSTRACTS OF:
65394 Altman, L. L. On the oral nature of acting out. Rev urug Psa 1966,
       8:411
65395 Balint, M. Changing therapeutic aims and techniques in psychoanaly-
       sis. Rev urug Psa 1961-62, 4:356
65396 Balint, M. The final goal of psycho-analytic treatment. Rev urug Psa
       1961-62, 4:359
65397 Balint, M. & Balint, A. On transference and counter-transference. Rev
       urug Psa 1961-62, 4:181
65398 Kanzer, M. Acting out, sublimation and reality testing. Rev urug Psa
       1966, 8:412-413
65399 Loewenstein, R. M. Remarks on some variation in psycho-analytic
       technique. Rev urug Psa 1965, 7:380
65400 Rosenfeld, H. A. Note on the psychopathology and analytic treatment
       of schizophrenia in psychotic states. Rev urug Psa 1965, 7:385
65401 Segal, H. Fantasy and other mental processes. Rev urug Psa 1965,
       7:277
65402 Zeligs, M. A. Acting in. A contribution to the meaning of some postural
       attitudes observed during analysis. Rev urug Psa 1966, 8:413

AGOSTON, TIBOR

65403 The classical Freudian approach to psychoanalysis in groups. J Psa in
       Groups 1962, 1:6-13

65404 (& Garcia, P. F.; Tuatay, H.) Complementary delusions. Ohio Res Q 1968, 1:147-154
65405 Insight Therapy: Methodology, Psychostematics and Differential Dynamics. Ohio: Ohio Dept of Mental Hygiene and Correction 1969, 334 p
65406 (& Landman, L.; Papanek, H.) The management of anxiety in group psychoanalysis. (Round table) Psa 1961, 21:74-84
65407 (& Garcia, P. F.; Tuatay, H.) Metamorphosis, identity theme, and folie à deux. Proc IV World Cong Psychiat 1966, 1693-1696
65408 Psychotherapeutic interpretations. Ohio Res Q 1967, 1:91-96
65409 Theory and method of analytical psychotherapy. Dept Ment Hyg of Ohio, Monogr 1961, 46 p

AGRAS, STEWART

65410 Instructions and reinforcement in the modification of neurotic behavior. P 1969, 125:1435-1439

AGRESTI, ENZO

65411 (& Longhi, S.) Considerazioni sul significato dei mandela nelle opere figurative dei malati mentali. [Considerations on the significance of mandala in the drawings of mental patients.] Riv sper Freniat 1965, 89:829-848
65412 Il problema dell'io nell'ambito della fenomenologia e dell'empirismo logico. [Problem of the self in area of phenomenology and logical empiricism.] Arch Psicol Neurol Psichiat 1965, 26:370-379
65413 [Psychoanalysis and existential analysis in phenomenological prospective.] (It) Rass Np 1965, 19:813-824

AGRIN, ALFRED

65414 Who is qualified to treat the alcoholic. Comment on the Krystal-Moore discussion. Quart J Stud Alcohol 1964, 25:347-349

AGUILAR, G.

65415 (& Auersperg, A.; Varas, M.) Die neuropsychiatrisch oriente pluridimensionale Diagnostik in der vergleichenden Psychiatrie. [Neuropsychiatrically oriented pluridimensional diagnostics in comparative psychiatry.] Bibl Psychiat Neurol 1967, 133:197-206

AHBEL, G.

See Starer, Emanuel

AHMAD, FARRUKH ZAHUR

65416 Aspects of psychotherapy related to psychotherapists' responses to dependency. Diss Abstr 1961, 21:3519

See Winder, Clarence L.

AHMAD, SHAHZĀD

65417 [Religion, Culture, and Death.] (Urdu) Lahore, West Pakistan 1963

AHRENFELDT, ROBERT H.

See Soddy, Kenneth

TRANSLATION OF:
Chertok, L. [69901]

AHRENS, JOHN B.

See Foulkes, David

AICHHORN, AUGUST

65418 Delinquency and Child Guidance: Selected Papers. (Ed: Fleischmann, O.; Kramer, P.; Ross, H.) (Introd: Freud, A.) NY: IUP; London: Bailey Bros 1965, 244 p
Abs J Am Psa Ass 1966, 14:234. Rv Esman, A. H. Q 1966, 35:149-150

65419 Delinquency in a new light. In author's *Delinquency and Child Guidance* 218-235

S-517 Über die Erziehung in Besserunganstalten.
On education in training schools. In author's *Delinquency and Child Guidance* 15-48

S-518 Zur Erziehung Unsozialer.
The education of the unsocial. In author's *Delinquency and Child Guidance* 193-217

65420 Ein haufig Vorkommender, eigenartig determnierter Erziehungsnotstand und dessen Behebung. [A frequent specially determined educational problem and its therapy.] In Bolterauer, L. *Aus der Werkstatt der Erziehungsberaters,* Vienna: Verlag für Jugend und Volk 1960, 9-23

S-525 Kann der jugendlische Straffällig werden? In Bittner, G. & Rehm, W. *Psychoanalyse und Erziehung,* Bern/Stuttgart: Hans Huber 1964
The juvenile court: is it a solution? In author's *Delinquency and Child Guidance* 55-79

S-527 Lohn oder Strafe als Erziehungsmittel?
Reward or punishment as a means of education? In author's *Delinquency and Child Guidance* 80-100

S-541 Die Übertragung.
On the technique of child guidance: the process of transference. In author's *Delinquency and Child Guidance* 101-192

S-542 Verwahrloste Jugend
Rv Kaziwara, T. Jap J Psa 1965, 11(5):29

S-543 Zum Verwahrlosten-Problem.
On the problem of wayward youth. In author's *Delinquency and Child Guidance* 49-54

AIGRISSE, GILBERTE

65421 Psychanalyse de la Grèce Antique. [Psychoanalysis of Ancient Greece.] Paris: Les Belles Lettres 1960, 254 p

65422 Psychothérapies Analytiques, Huit Cas. [Eight Cases of Analytic Psychotherapy.] Paris: Éditions Universitaires 1967, 293 p

AINBINDER, MARTIN

See Deutsch, Albert L.

AINSWORTH, MARY DINSMORE (SALTER)

65423 Infancy in Uganda: Infant Care and the Growth of Love. Baltimore: Johns Hopkins Pr 1967, xvii + 471 p

See Bowlby, John

AISENSON KOGAN, AIDA

65424 El Yo y el Si Mismo. [The Ego and the Self.] Buenos Aires: Centro Editor de America Latina 1969, 107 p

AIZA, VÍCTOR MANUEL

65425 (& Cesarman, F.) Correlato sobre el tema "mania." [Round table on the subject of mania.] Rev urug Psa 1966, 8:163-172
65426 (& Cesarman, F.; Gonzalez, A.) Discussion of Rangell, L. "An overview of the ending of an analysis." Psa Amer 166-167
65427 La simbiosis madre-hijo. [The mother-infant symbiosis.] Cuad Psa 1965, 1:281-290
65428 Los valores culturales en el psicoanálisis. [Cultural values in psychoanalysis.] Cuad Psa 1966, 2:87-102

AIZENBERG, SERGIO

65429 (& Bianchedi, E. T. de; Sor, D.) Concepto de continente-contenido (identificación proyectiva) en el proceso de integración del objeto. [The concept of "container-contained" (projective identification) in the process of object integration.] Rev Psicoanál 1967, 24:131-135

See Luchina, Isaac L.

ABSTRACTS OF:
65430 Bion, W. R. Language and the schizophrenic. Rev Psicoanál 1967, 24:379-381
65431 Bion, W. R. On arrogance. Rev Psicoanál 1967, 24:386-387

AJIKI, M.

65432 [Identification.] (Jap) Jap J Nurs 1968, 32:64-65

AJMAL, MUHAMMAD

65433 Acceptance in psychoanalysis. J Psychol, Lahare 1966, 3:1-10
65434 Words and analytical therapy. J Psychol, Lahare 1964, 1:46-56

AJURIAGUERRA, JULIEN DE

65435 Le Choix Thérapeutique en Psychiatrie Infantile. [Therapeutic Choice in Child Psychiatry.] Paris: Masson 1967, 156 p
65436 (& Angelergues, R.) De la psycho-matricité au corps dans la relation avec autrui (à propos de l'oeuvre de H. Wallon). [On the psycho-

metricity of the body in relation to others (in relation to the works of H. Wallon).] Évolut psychiat 1962, 27:13
   Abs Auth Rev Psicoanál 1963, 20:79
S-40252 (& Diatkine, R.; Garcia Badaracco, J.) Psychanalyse et neurobiologie.
   Abs WAF An Surv Psa 1956, 7:97-98
65437 (& Diatkine, R.; Lebovici, S.) La Psychiatrie de l'Enfant. Paris: PUF Vol. VI 1963-64, 606 p; Vol. VIII 1965, 622 p; Vol. IX 1966, 633 p; Vol. X 1967, 575 p

AKERET, ROBERT U.

65438 (& Stockhamer, N.) Countertransference reactions to college drop-outs. Value of group supervision. PT 1965, 19:622-632

AKIMOTO, TATSUO

65439 [Study on the psycho-analytic process of a patient suffering from depressive state.] (Jap) (Read at Jap Psa Ass, 13 Oct 1963) Jap J Psa 1965, 11(6):21-24, 28-29

AKINS, K. B.

See Rossi, Ascanio M.

AKMAKJIAN, HIAG

65440 Psychoanalysis and the future of literary criticism. PPR 1962, 49:3-28
   Abs LDr RFPsa 1962, 27:352

REVIEWS OF:
65441 Benjamin, H. The Transsexual Phenomenon. R 1966, 53:684-685
65442 Levitas, G. B. (Ed) The World of Psychoanalysis. R 1966, 53:495
65443 Tedlock, E. W., Jr. (Ed) D. H. Lawrence and Sons and Lovers: Sources and Criticism. R 1966, 53:321-322

AKUTAGAWA, DONALD

65444 Basic concepts of anxiety: a synthesis. Psychology 1968, 5:29-49
65445 (& Sisko, F. J.; Keitel, N. B.) "Beartrapping"—a study in interpersonal behavior. PT 1965, 19:54-65

ALANEN, YRJö O.

65446 The family in the pathogenesis of schizophrenic and neurotic disorders. Acta psychiat Scand 1966, 42(Suppl 189):1 +
65447 (& Rekola, J.; Stewen, A.; Touvinen, M.; Takala, K.; Rutanen, E.) Mental disorders in the siblings of schizophrenic patients. Acta psychiat Scand 1963, 39(Suppl 169):167-175
65448 [Psychodynamic family studies and their influence on psychiatric concepts.] (Dan) Nord Psyk Tidsskr 1964, 18:409-419
65449 Round table conference on family studies and family therapy of schizophrenic patients. Acta psychiat Scand 1963, 39(Suppl 169):420-426
65450 Some thoughts of schizophrenia and ego development in the light of family investigations. Arch gen Psychiat 1960, 3:650-656

65451 Über die Familiensituation der Schizophrenie-Patienten. [The family situation of the schizophrenic patient.] Acta psychother psychosom 1960, 8:89-104

See Lidz, Theodore

ALARCO, F.

65452 Psicoterapia y medicación en las depresiones. [Psychotherapy and medication in depression.] Rev Psiquiat Peru 1961, 4:42-54

ALARIE, RENÉ

65453 Psychologie: le "moi." [Psychology: the "self."] Cah Nurs 1968, 41:165-166

ALBARANES, S.

See Darcourt, Guy

ALBAUGH, JUDSON K.

See Hollender, Marc H.

ALBERONI, FRANCESCO

65454 Discussion of Fornari, F. "La psychanalyse de la guerre." RFPsa 1966, 30(Suppl):269-278

ALBERT, GERALD

65455 If counseling is psychotherapy: what then? Personn Guid J 1966, 45:124-129

ALBERT, ROBERT S.

65456 (& Gallagher, E. B.) Separation phenomena as a basis for resistance to hospitalization. Int J soc Psychiat 1966, 13:59-66

See Greenblatt, Milton

ALBERTI, G.

See Balduzzi, E.

ALBINI, JOSEPH L.

See Dinitz, Simon; Pasamanick, Benjamin

ALBRECHT, A.

See Freud, Sigmund

ALBY, J. M.

65457 Identité et rôles sexuels. [Sexual identity and sexual roles.] Évolut psychiat 1962, 27:189
       Abs Auth Rev Psicoanál 1963, 20:84

65458   (& Alby, N.; Caen, J.) [The influence of psychological factors on the scholastic achievements of the hemophiliac.] (Fr) Bibl Haemat 1966, 26:179-183

65459   Les problèmes d'identification chez l'adolescent. [Identification problems in adolescents.] Gaz méd Fran 1968, 75:2451-2459

See Alby, Nicole

ALBY, NICOLE

65460   (& Alby, J. M.; Chassigneux, J.) Aspects psychologiques de l'évolution et du traitement des leucémiques, enfants et jeunes adultes, dans un centre spécialisé. [Psychological aspects of the evolution and treatment of children and young adults with leukemia in a specialized center.] Nouv Rev fran Hemat 1967, 7:577-588

See Alby, J. M.

ALCOCK, THEODORA

65461   The Rorschach in Practice. Phila: Lippincott 1964, xii + 252 p
65462   Some personality characteristics of asthmatic children. M 1960, 33:133-141

ALDAY, G.

See Soifer, Raquel

ALDENDORFF, HERBERT

ABSTRACTS OF:
65463   Berna, J. Die "réalisation symbolique" in der Kinderanalyse. An Surv Psa 1956, 7:289-291
65464   Bonnard, A. Bewusste und unbewusste Treue. An Surv Psa 1956, 7:274-275
65465   Boor, C. de: Ekzem der Hände: ein Beitrag zur psychoanalytischen Behandlung Ekzemkranker. An Surv Psa 1957, 8:156-157
65466   Cremerius, J. Diabetes mellitus: the importance of oral factors: concomitant depressive states. An Surv Psa 1957, 8:166-167
65467   Cremerius, J. Freud als Bergründer der psychosomatischen Medizin. An Surv Psa 1956, 7:197
65468   Graber, G. H. Zur Psychoanalyse eines Ekzem- und Asthmakranken. An Surv Psa 1957, 8:158
65469   Kemper, W. W. Subjekstufen- und Kategoriale Interpretation des Traumes. An Surv Psa 1957, 8:173-174
65470   Kemper, W. W. Über das Prospektive im Traum. An Surv Psa 1956, 7:236-238
65471   Kries, I. von: Zur Differentialdiagnose der Angstneurose und Angsthysterie. An Surv Psa 1957, 8:111-112
65472   Lampl-de Groot, J. Psychoanalytische Ich-Psychologie und ihre Bedeutung für die Fehlentwicklung bei Kindern. An Surv Psa 1956, 7:249-251
65473   Richter, H.-E. Über Formen der Regression. An Surv Psa 1957, 8:34-35

65474 Stokvis, B. Freud als Jude. An Surv Psa 1956, 7:35
65475 Strotzka, H. Versuch über den Humor. An Surv Psa 1957, 8:333
65476 Thomä, H. Männlicher Transvestismus und das Verlagen nach
       Geschlechtsumwandlung. An Surv Psa 1957, 8:137-138
65477 Wucherer-Huldenfeld, K. von: Freud und die Philosophie. An Surv Psa
       1956, 7:39
65478 Wulff, M. Probleme der Psychosomatik. An Surv Psa 1956, 7:197-198

ALDOUS, JOAN

65479 (& Hill, R.) International Bibliography of Research in Marriage and the
       Family, 1900-1964. Minneapolis: Univ of Minnesota Pr 1967, 508 p

ALDRICH, CLARENCE KNIGHT

65480 Another twist to The Turn of the Screw. Modern Fiction Studies 1967,
       13:167-178
65481 Brief psychotherapy: a reappraisal of some theoretical assumptions.
       P 1968, 125:585-592
65482 (& Bernardt, H. E.) Evaluation of a change in teaching psychiatry to
       medical students. Ops 1963, 33:105-114
       Abs JMa RFPsa 1964, 28:449
65483 Expectations of antisocial behavior. Acta paedopsychiat 1966, 33:6-7;
       196
65484 Impact of community psychiatry on casework and psychotherapy.
       Smith Coll Stud soc Wk 1968, 38:102-115
65485 An Introduction of Dynamic Psychiatry. (Foreword: Carstairs, G. M.)
       NY: McGraw-Hill 1966, xv + 392 p
65486 Psychiatric social work. Compreh Txbk Psychiat 1622-1624
65487 Social service information. Compreh Txbk Psychiat 541-542
65488 What price autonomy? Sci Psa 1961, 4:172-185

       See Offenkrantz, William

ALEKSANDROWICZ, DOV R.

65489 Fire and its aftermath on a geriatric ward. BMC 1961, 25:23-32
       Abs HD Q 1962, 31:294
65490 The meaning of metaphor. BMC 1962, 26:92-101
       Abs HD Q 1964, 33:141

ALEXANDER, A. A.

65491 (& Rossler, R.; Greenfield, N. S.) Ego strength and physiological re-
       sponsivity, III: The relationship of the Barron Ego Strength Scale to
       spontaneous periodic activity in skin resistance, finger blood volume,
       heart rate, and muscle potential. Arch gen Psychiat 1963, 9:142-145

       See Greenfield, Norman S.

ALEXANDER, CHARLOTTE

65492 The "stink" of reality: mothers and whores in James Baldwin's fiction.
       Lit & Psych 1968, 18:9-26

ALEXANDER, D. M.

65493 Oedipus in Victorian New York. Amer Quart 1960, 12:417-421

ALEXANDER, DUANE

See Money, John

ALEXANDER, ESTHER

See Ilan, Eliezer

ALEXANDER, FRANCES S.

65494 Obituary: John C. Gustin. R 1964, 51:673

ALEXANDER, FRANZ GABRIEL

S-40298 Adventure and security in a changing world. In author's *The Scope of Psychoanalysis* 462-472

S-579 Analyse der therapeutischen Faktoren in der psychoanalytischen Behandlung.
Analysis of the therapeutic factors in psychoanalytic treatment. In author's *The Scope of Psychoanalysis* 261-275

S-582 Der biologische Sinn psychischer Vorgänge (Über Buddhas Versenkungslehre).
Buddhistic training as an artificial catatonia: the biological meaning of psychic occurrences. In author's *The Scope of Psychoanalysis* 74-89

S-587 The castration complex in the formation of character. In author's *The Scope of Psychoanalysis* 3-30

S-40301 A contribution to the theory of play.
Abs Swartz, J. An Surv Psa 1958, 9:79-80

65495 Crime and the psychoanalyst. Mass Society 1964, 46-50

S-40302 Current problems in dynamic psychotherapy in its relationship to psychoanalysis. In author's *The Scope of Psychoanalysis* 305-309

65496 Current problems in psychosomatic medicine. Psychosomatics 1964, 5:1-2

S-40303 Current views on psychotherapy. In author's *The Scope of Psychoanalysis* 276-289

65497 The development of psychosomatic medicine. PSM 1962, 24:13-24

S-595 Development of the ego psychology. Heirs Freud 222-234

S-601 The Don Quixote of America. In author's *The Scope of Psychoanalysis* 381-383

65498 The dynamics of psychiatry in the light of learning theory. P 1964, 120:441-449
Abs Loeb, L. Q 1965, 34:140-141

65499 The dynamics of psychotherapy in the light of learning theory. (Read at South Calif Psa Soc, 21 Oct 1963) P 1963, 120:440-448. Int J Psychiat 1965, 1:189-207. With title: Psychoanalysis and learning theory. In Berenson, B. G. & Carkhuff, R. R. *Sources of Gain in Counseling and Psychotherapy*, NY: Holt, Rinehart & Winston 1967, 147-161
Abs Peck, J. S. Bull Phila Ass Psa 1964, 14:47-49

S-606 Educative influence of personality factors in the environment. In author's *The Scope of Psychoanalysis* 424-439

65500   Evaluation of psychotherapy. Proc Amer Psychopath Ass 1964, 52:176-193
65501   An experimental approach to study of physiological and psychological effects of emotional stress situations. In Tourlentes, T. T. et al: *Research Approaches to Psychiatric Problems*, NY/London: Grune & Stratton 1962, 189-203
65502   (& Flagg, G. W.; Foster, S.; Clemens, T.; Blahd, W.) Experimental studies of emotional stress, I: Hyperthyroidism. PSM 1961, 23:104-111. In author's *The Scope of Psychoanalysis* 364-377
        Abs JPG Q 1961, 30:602
65503   (& Selesnick, S. T.) Freud-Bleuler correspondence. Arch gen Psychiat 1965, 12:1-9
        Abs KR Q 1966, 35:314
S-624   Fundamentals of Psychoanalysis.
        Principes de Psychanalyse. Paris: Payot 1968, 304 p
S-626   Zur Genese des Kastrationskomplexes.
        Concerning the genesis of the castration complex. In author's *The Scope of Psychoanalysis* 112-115
65504   (& Selesnick, S. T.) The History of Psychiatry: An Evaluation of Psychiatric Thought and Practice from Prehistoric Times to the Present. NY: Harper & Row 1966, xvi + 471 p; NY: Amer Libr 1966, 584 p; London: Allen & Unwin 1967, 472 p
65505   (& Ross, H.) (Eds) The Impact of Freudian Psychiatry. Chicago: Univ of Chicago Pr 1961, 304 p
S-40314 Impressions from the Fourth International Congress of Psychotherapy. In author's *The Scope of Psychoanalysis* 548-557
65506   Introduction to *Group Psychology and the Analysis of the Ego* by Sigmund Freud. In author's *The Scope of Psychoanalysis* 473-480
S-636   Introduction to *What Man Has Made of Man* by Mortimer J. Adler. In author's *The Scope of Psychoanalysis* 511-518
S-641   The logic of emotions and its dynamic background. In author's *The Scope of Psychoanalysis* 116-128
S-646   Mental hygiene in the atomic age. In author's *The Scope of Psychoanalysis* 447-454
S-649   Metapsychologische Darstellung des Heilungsverganges.
        A metapsychological description of the process of cure. In author's *The Scope of Psychoanalysis* 205-224
65507   Neurosis and creativity. Psa 1964, 24:116-130
S-652   Der neurotische Charakter, seine Stellung in der Psychopathologie und in der Literatur.
        The neurotic character. In author's *The Scope of Psychoanalysis* 56-73
S-655   A note on Falstaff. In author's *The Scope of Psychoanalysis* 501-510
* * *   (& Eisenstein, S.; Grotjahn, M.) Preface. Psa Pioneers v-viii
* * *   Preface to author's *The Scope of Psychoanalysis* xvii-xix
S-664   The problem of psychoanalytic technique. In author's *The Scope of Psychoanalysis* 225-243
S-672   Psychiatric contributions to crime prevention. In author's *The Scope of Psychoanalysis* 412-423
* * *   Psychoanalysis and learning theory. See [65499]

S-677 Psychoanalysis and medicine. In author's *The Scope of Psychoanalysis* 483-500

S-40327 Psychoanalysis and psychotherapy. In author's *The Scope of Psychoanalysis* 310-318

S-40328 Psychoanalysis and Psychotherapy: Developments in Theory, Technique, and Training.
Abs Auth An Surv Psa 1956, 7:300; 419-425

S-678 Psychoanalysis and social disorganization. In author's *The Scope of Psychoanalysis* 384-411

65508 Psychoanalysis and the human condition. In Marmorston, J. & Stainbrook, E. *Psychoanalysis and the Human Situation*, NY: Vantage Pr 1964, 68-83

S-679 Psychoanalysis comes of age. In author's *The Scope of Psychoanalysis* 525-531

S-40330 Psychoanalysis in Western culture. In author's *The Scope of Psychoanalysis*, 170-182
Abs RZ An Surv Psa 1956, 7:392-393

S-680 Psychoanalysis revised. In author's *The Scope of Psychoanalysis* 137-164

65509 Psychoanalytic education for practice. Sci Psa 1962, 5:162-180. In author's *The Scope of Psychoanalysis* 568-586

65510 (& Eisenstein, S.; Grotjahn, M.) (Eds) Psychoanalytic Pioneers. NY/London: Basic Books 1966, xvii + 616 p
Rv J Am Psa Ass 1967, 15:225. SG Am Im 1966, 23:265-273. Balint, M. Psa Forum 1967, 2:373-374. Meyer, B. C. Q 1967, 36:595-598

S-40332 On the psychodynamics of regressive phenomena in panic states. In author's *The Scope of Psychoanalysis* 455-461
Abs An Surv Psa 1955, 6:435

S-687 Psychological aspects of medicine. In Kaufman, M. R. & Heiman, M. *Evolution of Psychosomatic Concepts*, NY: IUP 1964, 56-77

65511 (& Flagg, G. W.) The psychosomatic approach. In Wolman, B. B. *Handbook of Clinical Psychology*, NY: McGraw-Hill 1965, 855-947

S-40335 The psychosomatic approach in medical therapy. In author's *The Scope of Psychoanalysis* 345-358

S-694 Psychosomatic Medicine. Its Principles and Applications. NY: Norton 1965, 300 p
Rv J Am Psa Ass 1966, 14:227

65512 (& French, T. M.; Pollock, G. H.) (Eds) Psychosomatic Specificity, Vol. I: Experimental Study and Results. Chicago: Univ of Chicago Pr 1968, vi + 263 p

S-40334 (& Visotsky, H.) Psychosomatic study of a case of asthma. In author's *The Scope of Psychoanalysis* 359-363

S-701 The relation of structural and instinctual conflicts. In author's *The Scope of Psychoanalysis* 90-111

S-702 Remarks about the relation of inferiority feelings to guilt feelings. In author's *The Scope of Psychoanalysis* 129-136

S-40336 A review of two decades. In author's *The Scope of Psychoanalysis* 538-547

65513 Sandor Rado b. 1890. The adaptational theory. Psa Pioneers 240-248

65514   The scope of psychoanalysis. JNMD 1963, 137:402-405
65515   The Scope of Psychoanalysis, 1921-1961: Selected Papers of Franz
        Alexander. NY: Basic Books 1961, xix + 594 p
65516   Social significance of psychoanalysis and psychotherapy. Arch gen
        Psychiat 1964, 11:235-244
              Abs KR Q 1965, 34:470
S-713   Strafbedürfnis und Todestrieb.
              The need for punishment and the death instinct. In author's *The
              Scope of Psychoanalysis* 37-49
S-717   Training principles in psychosomatic medicine. In author's *The Scope
        of Psychoanalysis* 561-563
S-722   Teaching psychodynamics. In author's *The Scope of Psychoanalysis*
        564-567
S-723   A tentative analysis of the variables in personality development. In
        author's *The Scope of Psychoanalysis* 519-524
S-727   Three fundamental dynamic principles of the mental apparatus and
        of the behavior of learning organisms. In author's *The Scope of Psycho-
        analysis* 165-169
S-729   Träume mit peinlichen Inhalt.
              About dreams with unpleasant content. In author's *The Scope of
              Psychoanalysis* 50-55
S-40341 Two forms of regression and their therapeutic implications. In author's
        The Scope of Psychoanalysis 290-304
              Abs AHM An Surv Psa 1956, 7:134-135
S-730   Über Traumpaare und Traumreihen.
              Dreams in pairs and series. In author's *The Scope of Psychoanalysis*
              31-36
S-40342 Unexplored areas in psychoanalytic theory and treatment—Part I &
        Part II. In author's *The Scope of Psychoanalysis* 183-201; 319-335. In
        Daniels, G. et al: *New Perspectives in Psychoanalysis,* NY: Grune &
        Stratton 1965
              Abs Gerard, D. L. An Surv Psa 1958, 9:28-30
S-734   Values and science. In author's *The Scope of Psychoanalysis* 532-537
S-737   "The voice of the intellect is soft . . ." In author's *The Scope of Psy-
        choanalysis* 244-260
S-40344 The Western Mind in Transition: An Eyewitness Story.
              Abs J Am Psa Ass 1962, 10:455. Rv MG J 1961, 42:123-126. Wolfe,
              M. O. Q 1961, 30:108-109
S-741   A world without psychic frustration. In author's *The Scope of Psycho-
        analysis* 440-446
S-742   (& McCulloch, W. S.; Carlson, H. B.) Zest and carbohydrate metabo-
        lism. In author's *The Scope of Psychoanalysis* 339-344

        See Goldstein, Michael J.; Rado, Sandor

ALEXANDER, GEORGE J.

65517   (& Szasz, T. S.) Mental illness as an excuse for civil wrongs. Notre
        Dame Lawyer 1967, 43:24-28

        See Szasz, Thomas S.

ALEXANDER, IRVING E.

65518 (& Adlerstein, A. M.) Affective responses to the concept of death in a population of children and early adolescents. J genet Psychol 1958, 93:167-177. Death & Identity 111-123

65519 (& Colley, R. S.; Adlerstein, A. M.) Is death a matter of indifference? J Psychol 1957, 43:277-283. Death & Identity 82-89

65520 Postdoctoral training in clinical psychology. In Wolman, B. B. *Handbook of Clinical Psychology*, NY/Toronto/London: McGraw-Hill 1965, 1415-1426

ALEXANDER, JAMES M.

65521 De l'ironie. [On irony.] RFPsa 1969, 33:441-450

65522 (& Isaacs, K. S.) The function of affect. M 1964, 37:231-237
   Abs Hirsch, H. Q 1965, 34:472

65523 (& Isaacs, K. S.) Obéissance à la réalité: contribution à la théorie psychanalytique de la dépression. [Obedience to reality: a contribution to the psychoanalytic theory of depression.] RFPsa 1963, 27:223-230

65524 On courage. Bull Phila Ass Psa 1969, 19:16-27

65525 On surprise. Bull Phila Ass Psa 1968, 18:116-125
   Überraschung. Psyche 1969, 23:854-861

S-40350 The psychology of bitterness.
   Psychologie de l'amertume. PRFsa 1961, 25:945-958
   Abs JBi Q 1962, 31:123

65526 (& Isaacs, K. S.) The psychology of the fool. (Read at Int Psa Cong, July 1967) J 1968, 49:420-423
   Abs LHR Q 1969, 38:670

65527 The psychology of treason. Bull Phila Ass Psa 1969, 19:158-166

65528 (& Isaacs, K. S.) Seriousness and preconscious affective attitudes. J 1963, 44:23-30
   Abs EVN Q 1965, 34:463-464

65529 Die Zeit und der metapsychologische Begriff der Anpassung. [Time and the metapsychological concept of adaptation.] Psyche 1967, 21:693-698

   See Isaacs, Kenneth S.; Whitman, Roy M.

ALEXANDER, LEO

65530 The conditional psychogalvanic reflex: its contribution to psychiatric diagnosis. Recent Adv biol Psychiat 1962, 4:38

65531 Effects of physical treatment of mental disease upon the life instinct and the death instinct. Recent Adv biol Psychiat 1966, 8:36

65532 Hypnosis in primarily organic illness. Amer J clin Hyp 1966, 8:250-253

65533 Military psychiatry, occupation, and refugee problems in Israel. Milit Med 1968, 133:265-274

65534 Tackling the problem of enuresis. RN 1966, 29:46-50

ALEXANDER, P.

65535 Rational behaviour and psychoanalytic explanation. Mind 1962, 71 (283):326-342

ALEXANDER, RICHARD P.

65536 Contribution to the psychological understanding of pruritis ani, report of a case (in psychoanalysis). PSM 1959, 21:182-192

65537 Letter to the editors [re Berliner, B. "Depressive character."] Psa Forum 1967, 2:101-103

S-40360 (& Pope, H. L., Jr.) The negative transference: some comments on its manifestations, development and management.
Abs RZ An Surv Psa 1956, 7:340

65538 Omnipotence and the avoidance of pleasure: a contribution to the problem of separation anxiety. Psa Forum 1966, 1:278-282, 287-288
Abs Cuad Psa 1967, 3:165-166

ALFONSO, OLGA

65539 (& Fernandez, A.; Pizzolanti, G. M. D.; Prego, V. M. d.; Prego Silva, L. E.; Sopena, C.) Caracteristicas de la relación con el analista en algunos pacientes psicopáticos. [Characteristics of the relation between the analyst and some psychopathic patients.] Rev urug Psa 1966, 8:321-323

65540 La seducción en la psicopatia. [Seduction in psychopathy.] Rev urug Psa 1966, 8:317-320

ALFORD, ROBERTA (MURRAY) FANSLER

65541 Francisco Goya and the intentions of the artist. J Aesthet art Crit 1960, 18(June):482-493

ALGER, IAN

65542 The clinical handling of the analyst's responses. Psa Forum 1966, 1:290-297; 301-302
Abs Cuad Psa 1967, 3:166

65543 Freedom in analytic therapy. Curr psychiat Ther 1969, 9:73-78

65544 (& Hogan, P.) The impact of videotape recording on involvement in group. J Psa in Groups 1966-67, 2(1):50-56

65545 Joint psychotherapy of marital problems. Curr psychiat Ther 1967, 7:112-117

65546 Joint sessions: psychoanalytic variations, applications, and indications. Marriage Relat 251-265

See Rosenbaum, Salo

ALI, SAMI MAHMOUD

65547 Le corps et ses métamorphoses (contribution à l'étude de la dépersonnalisation). [The body and its metamorphoses; a contribution to the study of depersonalization.] RFPsa 1961, 25:333-378
Abs RJA Q 1962, 31:433

65548 Étude de l'image du corps dans l'urticaire. [Study of the body image in urticaria.] RFPsa 1969, 33:201-226

ALIKAKOS, LOUIS C.

65549 Analytical group treatment of the post-hospital schizophrenic. Int J grp PT 1965, 15:492-504
        Abs GPK Q 1967, 36:475

S-40369 (& Starer, E.; Winich, W.) Observations on the meaning of behavior in groups of chronic schizophrenics.
        Abs AaSt An Surv Psa 1956, 7:360-361

ALIMARAS, PETER E.

65550 Ambivalence in situations of negative interpersonal attitudes. J Psychol 1967, 65:9-13

ALKER, HENRY A.

65551 Cognitive controls and the Haan-Kroeber Model of ego functioning. JAbP 1967, 72:434-440
65552 Coping, defense and socially desirable responses. Psychol Rep 1968, 22:985-988

ALLARDICE, B. S.

65553 (& Dole, A. A.) Body image in Hansen's disease patients. J proj Tech 1966, 30:356-358

ALLEN, ARNOLD

65554 Stealing as a defense. Q 1965, 34:572-583

ALLEN, BROCK

See Allen, David W.

ALLEN, CHARLES A.

65555 Mark Twain and conscience. In Malin, I. *Psychoanalysis and American Fiction*, NY: Dutton 1965

ALLEN, D. C.

65556 Genesis of Donne's dreams. Modern Language Notes 1960, 75:293-295

ALLEN, DAVID W.

65557 (& Allen, B.) Cross porpoises [a short story]. Horizons 1961, 56(26)
65558 Exhibitionistic and voyeuristic conflicts in learning and functioning. Q 1967, 36:546-570
        Abs Cuad Psa 1968, 4:43

ALLEN, FREDERICK H.

65559 The beginning phase of therapy. In Haworth, M. R. *Child Psychotherapy*, NY/London: Basic Books 1964, 101-105
65560 Child psychotherapy. Curr psychiat Ther 1962, 2:41-47
65561 The ending phase of therapy. In Haworth, M. R. *Child Psychotherapy*, NY/London: Basic Books 1964, 292-297

65562 Positive Aspects of Child Psychiatry. NY: Norton 1963, 300 p
      Rv Stein, M. Q 1964, 33:444
65563 Therapy as a living experience. In Moustakas, C. *Existential Child Therapy*, NY: Basic Books 1966, 134-151

ALLEN, JAMES R.

65564 (& West, L. J.) Flight from violence: hippies and the green rebellion. P 1968, 125:120-126

See West, Louis Jolyon

ALLEN, M. HARRIET

65565 The Adlerian approach to counseling. J Rehab 1968, 34(Sept-Oct): 11-13

ALLEN, MARTIN G.

65566 Childhood experience and adult personality—a cross-cultural study using the concept of ego strength. Soc Psych 1967, 71:53-68
65567 Psychoanalytic theory on infant gratification and adult personality. J genet Psych 1964, 104:265-274

ALLEN, PRISCILLA

65568 Social environmental factors in the etiology of functional esotropia. Amer Orthopt J 1965, 15:72-84

ALLEN, RICHARD C.

65569 (& Ferster, E. Z.; Rubin, J. G.) Readings in Law and Psychiatry. Baltimore: Johns Hopkins Pr 1968, xvi + 519 p

ALLEN, ROBERT M.

65570 Student's Rorschach Manual. NY: IUP 1966

ALLEN, SYLVIA

S-781A Reflections on the wish of the analyst to "break" or change the basic rule.
      Abs AaSt An Surv Psa 1956, 7:327-328

ALLEN, THOMAS E.

65571 Acting out as a manifestation of a phobic equivalent. PT 1966, 20:646-654
65572 Suicidal impulse in depression and paranoia. J 1967, 48:433-438

See Rosenberger, John W.

ALLEN, WALTER R.

See White, William F.

ALLENBY, A. I.

65573   The church and the analyst. J anal Psych 1961, 6:137-155

ALLENDER, J.

See Beiser, Helen R.

ALLERS, RUDOLPH

65574   The unconscious. In *Philosophy of Science*, St. John's Univ Pr 1960, 131-158

See Pötzl, Otto

ALLIEZ, J.

65575   (& Antonelli, H.) Les rêves de bataille (battle-dreams). Aspects cliniques et pathogéniques à propos de deux observations, dont l'une très prolongée. [Battle dreams. Clinical and pathogenic aspects apropos of 2 cases, one of which was over a long period of time.] Ann méd-psychol 1968, 126(1):505-538

ALLINSMITH, BEVERLY BALCH

65576   Directiveness with which anger is expressed. In Miller, D. R. & Swanson, G. E. *Inner Conflict and Defense*, NY: Henry Holt 1960, 315-336

ALLINSMITH, WESLEY

65577   The learning of moral standards. In Miller, D. R. & Swanson, G. E. *Inner Conflict and Defense*, NY: Henry Holt 1960, 141-176
65578   (& Goethals, G. W.) The Role of Schools in Mental Health. NY: Basic Books 1962, xiv + 337 p

ALLISON, GERDA E.

65579   Primary prevention of mental disorders in children. J Amer Med Wom Ass 1964, 19:301-306
65580   Psychiatric implications of religious conversion. Canad Psychiat Ass J 1967, 12:55-61

ALLISON, JOEL

65581   Adaptive regression and intense religious experiences. JNMD 1967, 145:452-463
65582   (& Blatt, S. J.; Zimet, C. N.) The Interpretation of Psychological Tests. NY: Harper & Row 1968, x + 342 p

ALLISON, R. S.

65583   (& Hurwitz, L. J.; White, J. G.; Wilmot, T. J.) A follow-up study of a patient with Balint's syndrome. Neuropsychologia 1969, 7:319-333

ALLISON, ROGER B.

See Cole, Nyla J.

ALLISON, ROGER B., JR.
See Korner, Ija N.

ALLPORT, GORDON WILLARD

65584 Behavioral science, religion, and mental health. J Relig Hlth 1963, 2:187-197. In Belgum, D. *Religion and Medicine,* Ames, Iowa: Iowa State Univ Pr 1967, 83-95

65585 (Ed) Letters from Jerry. NY: Harcourt, Brace & World 1965, xii + 223 p

65586 Mental health: a generic attitude. J Relig Hlth 1964, 4:7-21. In Belgum, D. *Religion and Medicine,* Ames, Iowa: Iowa State Univ Pr 1967, 45-60

65587 Pattern and Growth in Personality. NY: Holt, Rinehart & Winston 1961, ix + 592 p

65588 The Person in Psychology: Selected Essays. Boston: Beacon Pr 1968, 440 p

65589 Personality and Social Encounter: Selected Essays. Boston: Beacon Pr 1960, x + 386 p

65590 Psychological models for guidance. Harv educ Rev 1962, 32:373-381. In Rosenblith, J. F. & Allinsmith, W. *The Causes of Behavior,* Boston: Allyn & Bacon 1966, 6-11. In Matson, F. W. & Montagu, A. *The Human Dialogue,* NY: Free Pr 1967, 214-223

65591 (Participant in) Symposium on Karl Bühler's contributions to psychology. J gen Psychol 1966, 75:181-219

65592 (Ed) William James Psychology. The Briefer Course. NY: Harper & Bros 1961, xxiii + 343 p

ALLSOP, KENNETH

65593 The technicolor wasteland. On drugs & literature. Encounter 1969, 32(3):64-72

ALMANSI, RENATO J.

65594 (& Kanzer, M.) Applied psychoanalysis. An Surv Psa 1955, 6:397-465

65595 Applied psychoanalysis, I: Mythology and folklore. An Surv Psa 1956, 7:376-383

65596 Applied psychoanalysis, I: Religion, mythology and folklore. An Surv Psa 1957, 8:296-310; 1958, 9:439-449

65597 Applied psychoanalysis, II: Sociological studies and anthropology. An Surv Psa 1957, 8:311-324; 1958, 9:449-474

65598 Applied psychoanalysis, II: Sociology and anthropology. An Surv Psa 1956, 7:383-408

65599 Cloud fantasies. J Hillside Hosp 1961, 10:143-153
      Abs JA Q 1962, 31:585

65600 Ego-psychological implications of a religious symbol: a cultural and experimental study. (Panel on mythology and ego psychology: Psa Ass NY, 21 May 1962) Psa St Soc 1964, 3:39-70

S-40414 The face-breast equation.
      Abs JTM Q 1961, 30:593-594

S-40416 A hypnagogic phenomenon.
Abs SL An Surv Psa 1958, 9:141-143

ABSTRACTS OF:

65601 Ali, S. M. The body and its metamorphoses: a contribution to the body of depersonalization. Q 1962, 31:433

65602 Balint, M. Examination of the patient by himself. Q 1962, 31:435

65603 Barande, R. Of silence and its time. Q 1962, 31:139

65604 Baudoin, C. Les éléments de la situation analytique. An Surv Psa 1956, 7:337-338

65605 Bolk, L. The problem of human genesis. Q 1962, 31:139-140

65606 Bouvet, M. Depersonalization and object relations. Q 1961, 30:312-313

65607 Bouvet, M. The psychoanalytic clinic. Object relations. Q 1961, 30:608

65608 Carp, E. A. D. E. Le complexe de sauvetage. An Surv Psa 1956, 7:165

65609 Chertok, L. et al: Regarding the psychological meanings of vomiting in pregnancy. Q 1962, 31:435

65610 Devereux, G. The anthropological roots of psychoanalysis. An Surv Psa 1958, 9:450-451

65611 Diatkine, R. The concept of regression. Q 1961, 30:156

65612 Diatkine, R. La notion de régression. An Surv Psa 1957, 8:33-34

65613 Dracoulides, N. N. Fétichisme du pied. An Surv Psa 1956, 7:213

65614 Erikson, E. H. Young Man Luther. An Surv Psa 1958, 9:479-487

65615 Favez-Boutonier, J. Psychanalyse et criminologie. An Surv Psa 1957, 8:318-319

65616 Gessain, R. "Vagina dentata" dans la clinique et la mythologie. An Surv Psa 1957, 8:107-108

65617 Grunberger, B. Study of the anal object relation. Q 1961, 30:155

65618 Held, R. The peculiarity of the obsessional pattern: technical requirements and necessities. Q 1962, 31:432-433

65619 Held, R. Psychopharmacology and psychotherapy in psychosomatic medicine. Q 1962, 31:436

65620 Henny, R. Some structural and psychotherapeutic aspects of adolescence. Q 1962, 31:433

65621 Klotz, H. P. et al: Presentation of a case of mental anorexia which required hospitalization in a female identical twin. Q 1962, 31:436

65622 Luquet, C. J. The obsessional structure: technical problems. Q 1962, 31:432

65623 Mayer, M. et al: Psychosomatic aspects of the infant-mother relationship. Q 1962, 31:435

65624 Nacht, S. On technique at the beginning of psychoanalytic treatment. Q 1961, 30:155

65625 Nacht, S. et al: The teaching of psychoanalysis. Q 1961, 30:310-311

65626 Nacht, S. Technical problems in the treatment of obsessional neurosis. Q 1962, 31:432

65627 Pasche, F. Freud and the Judaeo-Christian orthodoxy. Q 1962, 31:138

65628 Perrotti, N. Theoretical survey of depersonalization. Q 1961, 30:312

65629 Pichot, P. Regarding the placebo effect. Q 1962, 31:436-437

65630 Racamier, P. C. & Blanchard, M. De l'angoisse à la manie. An Surv Psa 1957, 8:152

65631 Racamier, P. C. From anxiety to mania. Clinical and psychological study of mania in its relationship to depression. Q 1961, 30:156

65632 Rappaport, E. A. L'arbre de la science. Recherce psychanalytique sur l'origine de l'humanité. An Surv Psa 1957, 8:298-299

65633 Stein, C. Castration as negation of femininity. Q 1962, 31:139

65634 Stein, C. Sado-masochistic inversion of the Oedipus complex and paranoid object relations. Q 1961, 30:311-312

65635 Teil, R. du: Clauricane ou les tribulations d'Oedipe. An Surv Psa 1957, 8:19

65636 Valabréga, J.-P. L'anthropologie psychanalytique. An Surv Psa 1957, 8:313-314

65637 Viderman, S. On the death instinct. Q 1962, 31:138

65638 Wittkower, E. Twenty years of psychosomatic medicine in North America. Q 1962, 31:436

REVIEWS OF:

65639 Cain, J. Le Problème des Névroses Expérimentales. Q 1961, 30:122-124

65640 Valabréga, J.-P. La Relation Thérapeutique. Q 1965, 34:125-126

ALMCIDA PRADO, MARIO PACHCCO DE

65641 [Regression as a defense to depression.] (Por) Rev bras Psicanal 1968, 2(2)

ALONSO FERNANDEZ, F.

65642 Die gezielten Indikationen und die psychodynamische Wirkung des Chlordiazepoxyd (Librium) als antialkoholisches Psychopharmakon. [Indications and psychodynamic effects of chlordiazepoxide (Librium) as an anti-alcoholic drug.] Schweiz ANP 1964, 93:150-164

ALPER, ARTHUR E.

65643 Negative transference and the rehab client. Rehab Rec 1965, 6:14-16

ALPER, THELMA G.

65644 (& Levin, V. S.; Klein, M. H.) Authoritarian vs. humanistic conscience. J Pers 1964, 32:313-333

ALPERT, AUGUSTA

65645 A brief communication on children's reactions to the assassination of the President. Psa St C 1964, 19:313-320

65646 Children without families: comments. J Amer Acad Child Psychiat 1965, 4:272-278

65647 Choice of defenses used by prelatency children in reaction to the assassination. Chld Dth Pres 99-106

65648 (& Bernstein, I.) Dynamic determinants in oral fixation. Psa St C 1964, 19:170-195

65649 Institute on programs for children without families: introductory remarks. J Amer Acad Child Psychiat 1965, 4:163-167

65650 Prenursery project: indications and counterindications for therapeutic intervention in the prenursery via the mother. (Read at Am Psa for Child Psa, June 1967) Psa St C 1967, 22:139-155

S-40443 Reversibility of pathological fixations associated with maternal deprivation in infancy.
Abs RTh J 1961, 42:471-472

S-40444 A special therapeutic technique for certain developmental disorders in prelatency children.
Abs AJE An Surv Psa 1957, 8:234-235

65651 A special therapeutic technique for prelatency children with a history of deficiency in maternal care. Ops 1963, 33:161-182
Abs JMa RFPsa 1964, 28:450. PS Q 1964, 33:307

65652 Treatment of an autistic child. J Amer Acad Child Psychiat 1964, 3:591-616

S-40446 The treatment of emotionally disturbed children in a therapeutic nursery.
Abs An Surv Psa 1955, 6:283-285

S-40447 (& Neubauer, P. B.; Weil, A. P.) Unusual variations in drive endowment.
Abs SGo An Surv Psa 1956, 7:246-248

ALPERT, MURRAY

65653 (& Hekimian, L. J.; Frosch, W. A.) Evaluation of treatment with recorded interviews. P 1966, 122:1258-1264

65654 (& Frosch, W. A.; Fisher, S. H.) Teaching the perception of expressive aspects of vocal communication. P 1967, 124:202-211

See Fish, Barbara

ALPERT, RICHARD

See Harfield, John S.; Sears, Robert R.

ALSEN, V.

65655 Über Struktur, Differenzierung und Substanz der Persönlichkeit. [On the structure, differentiation, and substance of the personality.] Bibl Psychiat Neurol 1968, 137:149-155

ALSHAN, LEONARD

See Davidson, Helen H.

ALSTON, EDWIN FREDERICK

65656 Bibliotherapy and psychotherapy. Libr Trends 1962, 2:159-176
Japanese: Jap-Amer Forum 1963, 7:34-47

65657 Discussion of Alexander, R. P. "Omnipotence and the avoidance of pleasure." Psa Forum 1966, 1:285-286

65658 (& Wilder, A.; Hoch, S.) Ego strengthening. Med Times 1961, 89:852-861

65659 (Participant) On regression: a workshop. (Read at West Coast Psa Soc, 14-16 Oct 1966) Psa Forum 1967, 2:293-316

65660 Psychic structure and function. Calif Med 1960, 93:13-18

S-40448 Psycho-analytic psychotherapy conducted by correspondence. Report
of therapy with patient hospitalized for tuberculosis.
Abs SLP An Surv Psa 1957, 8:285-286

ABSTRACTS OF:

65661 Aarons, Z. A. On analytic goals and criteria for termination. Q 1967,
36:627

65662 Aarons, Z. A. On negativism and the character trait of obstinacy. Q
1965, 34:134-135

65663 Badal, D. W. Transitional pre-psychotic symptoms in depression.
Q 1966, 35:155

65664 Bergler, E. The "aristocracy" among homosexuals: lovers of "trade."
Q 1963, 32:289

65665 Bettelheim, B. Early ego development in a mute autistic child. Q 1967,
36:628

65666 Bromberg, N. On polygamous women. Q 1962, 31:583

65667 Cath, S. H. & Fischberg, B. Some psychological implications of comic
strips. Q 1965, 34:135

65668 Cohen, K. D. A case of postpartum psychosis following pregnancy by
artificial insemination. Q 1968, 37:159

65669 Conrad, S. W. Phallic aspects of obesity. Q 1967, 36:629

65670 Conrad, S. W. On phantasies and their functions. Q 1968, 37:157

65671 Conrad, S. W. Physiologic determinants in fantasy formation. Q 1966,
35:155

65672 Devereux, G. Obsessive doubt: concealment or revelation? Q 1961,
30:600

65673 Dratman, M. D. Affects and consciousness. Q 1965, 34:620

65674 Eissler, K. R. On the possible proof of psychic energy. Q 1968, 37:157-
158

65675 Feldman, S. S. Luck: bad and good. Q 1965, 34:135

65676 Ferber, L. & Grey, P. Beating fantasies. Clinical and theoretical considerations. Q 1968, 37:159-160

65677 Fiedler, E. Excerpt from the analysis of a boy with congenital club
feet. Q 1967, 36:628

65678 Fink, P. J. The pacifier as a transitional object. Q 1964, 33:139

65679 Flumerfelt, J. M. On reconstruction. Q 1964, 33:139

65680 Francis, J. J. Passivity and homosexual predisposition in latency boys.
Q 1967, 36:628

65681 Frankl, L. & Hellman, I. A specific problem in adolescent boys: difficulties in loosening the infantile tie to the mother. Q 1965, 34:133

65682 Freeman, A. & Slap, J. W. A functional classification of identification.
Q 1961, 30:600

65683 Friedman, A. The role of the psychoanalyst in training psychiatric
residents. Q 1968, 37:158

65684 Galinsky, M. D. & Pressman, M. D. Intellectualization and the intellectual resistances. Q 1965, 34:134

65685 Gardiner, M. M. Introduction to Memoirs of the Wolf-Man, 1914-1919.
Q 1962, 31:295-296

65686 Gauthier, Y. Observations on ego development: the birth of a sibling. Q 1961, 30:600-601
65687 Greenson, R. R. The enigma of modern woman. Q 1968, 37:159
65688 Greenspan, J. The original persecutor—a case study. Q 1965, 34:135
65689 Holland, N. N. A literary critic's view of Heinz Hartmann's concept of adaptation. Q 1966, 35:154
65690 Huffer, V. Fee problems in supervised analysis. Q 1964, 33:300
65691 Kaplan, A. Maturity in religion. Q 1965, 34:133
65692 Kaplan, A. J. An oral transference resistance. Q 1961, 30:601
65693 Kaplan, L. S. Snow White: a study in psychosexual development. Q 1964, 33:300
65694 Kelly, W. E. Regression of the superego. Q 1967, 36:629
65695 Kleiner, H. T. Vicissitudes of the superego in the adult. Q 1968, 37:158-159
65696 Kolansky, H. Treatment of a three-year-old girl's severe infantile neurosis: stammering and insect phobia. Q 1961, 30:601
65697 Levin, S. Problems in the evaluation of patients for psychoanalysis. Q 1961, 30:601
65698 Menninger, K. The course of illness. Q 1962, 31:582
65699 Paul, L. Some ethical values of the psychoanalyst. Q 1965, 34:620
65700 Pearson, G. H. J. The importance of peer relationship in the latency period. Q 1968, 37:158
65701 Pearson, G. H. J. The psychological significance of the omen by which dreams were interpreted. Q 1965, 34:133
65702 Pearson, G. H. J. Some observations on a mild sleep disturbance in a three month old girl. Q 1965, 34:134
65703 Pearson, G. H. J. A young girl and her horse. Q 1967, 36:628-629
65704 Peller, L. E. About "telling the child" of his adoption. Q 1962, 31:582-583
65705 Peller, L. E. Biological foundations of psychology: Freud versus Darwin. Q 1967, 36:627
65706 Peller, L. E. Further comments on adoption. Q 1964, 33:300
65707 Peller, L. E. Language and its prestages. Q 1965, 34:135
65708 Pressman, M. D. On the analytic situation: the analyst is silent. Q 1962, 31:584
65709 Pressman, M. D. Silence in analysis. Q 1962, 31:582
65710 Purves, W. L. The problem of anxiety revisited. Q 1968, 37:158
65711 Silberstein, R. M. The problem of enuresis. Q 1964, 33:140
65712 Silberstein, R. M. Psychoanalysis and community psychiatry. A case report. Q 1968, 37:157
65713 Terzian, A. S. A psychoanalytic review of music. Q 1965, 34:620
65714 van den Haag, E. Psychoanalysis and utopia. Q 1967, 36:626-627
65715 Weiner, N. D. The drivers test as a modern puberty rite. Q 1965, 34:133-134
65716 Memoirs, 1905-1908 by the Wolf-Man. Q 1965, 34:136
65717 Memoirs, 1914-1919 by the Wolf Man. Q 1962, 31:296

ALT, EDITH

See Alt, Herschel

ALT, HERSCHEL

65718 (& Alt, E.) The New Soviet Man. His Upbringing and Character Development. NY: Bookman Assoc 1964, 304 p
Rv Fries, M. E. Q 1966, 35:304-305

65719 Residential Treatment of the Disturbed Child. Basic Principles in Planning and Design of Programs and Facilities. NY: IUP 1960, xiii + 437 p
Rv Geleerd, E. R. J Am Psa Ass 1964, 12:242-258. Fraiberg, S. Q 1965, 34:121-123

ALTENBERG, HENRY E.

REVIEW OF:
65720 Mendel, W. & Green, G. Therapeutic Management of Psychological Illness. R 1968-69, 55:710

ALTMAN, HENRY G.

See Mushatt, Cecil

ABSTRACT OF:
65721 Levin, S. Further comments on a common type of marital incompatibility. Bull Phila Ass Psa 1968, 18:100-102

ALTMAN, KARIN M.

TRANSLATION OF:
Reik, T. [87513]

ALTMAN, LEON L.

65722 The Dream in Psychoanalysis. NY: IUP 1969, xiii + 227 p
S-40498 On the oral nature of acting out: a case of acting out between parent and child.
Abs OS An Surv Psa 1957, 8:141. Agorio, R. Rev urug Psa 1966, 8:411

65723 (Reporter) Panel on theory of psychoanalytic theory. (Am Psa Ass, Dec 1963) J Am Psa Ass 1964, 12:620-631
S-40500 The waiting syndrome.
Abs SO An Surv Psa 1957, 8:124-125

REVIEW OF:
65724 Psychiatrists as Teachers in Schools of Social Work. Report No. 53. Q 1963, 32:382

ALTMAN, SIDNEY I.

See Dunn, John M.; Settlage, Calvin F.

ALTMANN, STUART A.

65725 (Ed) Social Communication among Primates. Chicago, Ill: Univ of Chicago Pr 1967, xiv + 392 p

ALTROCCHI, J.

See Palmer, John

ALTSCHUL, SOL

65726 Denial and ego arrest. (Read at Am Psa Ass, May 1966) J Am Psa Ass 1968, 16:301-318
65727 Parent-loss. Bull Chicago Psa Soc 1965, 1:29-33

See Fleming, Joan

ALTSCHULE, MARK DAVID

S-40510 Roots of Modern Psychiatry. Essays in the History of Psychiatry. NY/London: Grune & Stratton 1965 (2nd ed), viii + 208 p
Rv Shengold, L. Q 1967, 36:126

ALTSHULER, KENNETH Z.

65728 Comments on recent sleep research related to psychoanalytic theory. Arch gen Psychiat 1966, 15:235-239
Abs PB Q 1969, 38:512
65729 Personality traits and depressive symptoms in the deaf. (Read at Ass Psa Med, 3 Jan 1963) Recent Adv biol Psychiat 1963, 6:63-73
Abs Auth Q 1963, 32:472-475
65730 Snoring: unavoidable nuisance or psychological symptom. (Read at Ass Psa Med, 3 March 1964) Q 1964, 33:552-560
65731 (& Barad, M.; Goldfarb, A. I.) A survey of dreams in the aged, II: Noninstitutionalized subjects. Arch gen Psychiat 1963, 8:33-37
65732 Theoretical considerations in development and psychopathology of the deaf. In Rainer, J. D. & Altshuler, K. Z. Psychiatry and the Deaf, Wash DC: US GPO 1968

See Barad, Martin; Rainer, John D.

ALTUCHER, NATHAN

See Moulton, Robert W.

ALVAREZ, WALTER C.

65733 Some psychoanalysts who blame the family. J Schiz 1968, 2:1-2

ALVAREZ DE TOLEDO, LUISA G. DE

S-40513 El análisis del "asociar" del interpretar y de las "palabras."
Abs Garbarino, M. F. de Rev urug Psa 1961-62, 4:350
65734 Psicoanálisis de la comunicación verbal. [Psychoanalysis of verbal communication.] Acta psiquiat psicol Arg 1962, 8:16-24
65735 (& Grinberg, L.; Langer, M.) Terminación del análisis didáctico. Rev Psicoanál 1967, 24:259-310
Termination of training analysis. Psa Amer 174-192; 205-208

See Cesio, Fidias R.; Pichon-Rivière, Arminda A. de

ALVIM, FRANCISCO

65736 (& Santos, J. Dos; Silva, A. M. Da) Aspects fonctionnels de la vie
        onirique. [Functional aspects of the dream life.] RFPsa 1963, 27
        (Suppl):373-378

65737 (& Santos, J. Dos; Silva A. M. Da) Discussion of Bofill, P. & Folch-
        Mateau. "Problèmes cliniques et techniques de contretransfert." RFPsa
        1963, 27(Spec No):213-216

65738 [Problems of identity and identification.] (Por) J Med (Por) 1963,
        50:607-614

65739 [Psychoanalysis and treatment of depressions.] (Por) J Med (Por)
        1960, 42:600-601

65740 Troubles de l'identification et image corporelle. [Disturbances of
        identification and body image.] RFPsa 1962, 26(Suppl):5-116

AMACHER, PETER

65741 Freud's Neurological Education and Its influence on Psychoanalytic
        Theory. (Psychol Issues, Vol. 4(4). NY: IUP 1965, 93 p

AMADO, ÉLIANE (LÉVY-VALENSI)

65742 Le Dialogue Psychanalytique: les Rapports Intersubjectifs en Psy-
        chanalyse; la Vocation de Sujet. [The Psychoanalytic Dialogue: Inter-
        subjective Rapport in Psychoanalysis; The Role of the Subject.] Paris:
        PUF 1962, 222 p

AMADO, GEORGES

65743 A propos de: "L'Enuresie" de M. et N. Soule. [Discussion of Soule,
        M. & N. "L'enuresie."] Évolut psychiat 1967, 32:999-1004

65744 L'Affectivité de l'Enfant, Conceptions Psychologiques. [Affectivity of
        the Infant, Psychological Conceptions.] Paris: PUF 1969, 320 p

65745 La bonne mère: prévention et thérapeutique unique en psychiatrie
        infantile. [The good mother: the only prevention and therapy in child
        psychiatry.] Acta paedopsychiat 1963, 30:387-392

65746 Psychanalyse et assistance. La psychothérapie dans l'institution. [Psy-
        choanalysis and help. Institutional psychotherapy.] Rev Np Inf 1967,
        15:847-855

65747 La psychiatrie infantile parmi les signes de notre culture. [Child
        psychiatry among the signs of our culture.] Évolut psychiat 1964,
        29:381-410

AMADO-HAGUENAUER, G.

65748 (& Gladston, E.-R.; Picard, M.; Klapahouk, F.) Étude des preoccupa-
        tions somatiques des schizophrènes. [Study of the somatic complications
        of schizophrenics.] Ann méd-psychol 1961, 119:473-500

AMANN, A.

65749 Der Traum als diagnostischer und therapeutischer Faktor. [The dream
        as a diagnostic and therapeutic factor.] In Wheelwright, J. B. The
        Realities of the Psyche, NY: Putnam 1968, 85-97

AMAR, ANDRÉ

S-40522 Essai psychanalytique sur l'argent.
Abs Woodbury, M. A. An Surv Psa 1956, 7:394-495

AMARAL, LYGIA ALCANTARA DO

65750 Adolescência. [Adolescence.] Rev bras Psicanál 1967, 1:94-107; Abs (Eng) 107

AMARO, J. W.

65751 [Psychotherapy. Comprehension of self. Maturation.] (Por) Hosp, Rio 1965, 68:1107-1126

AMBINDER, WALTER

65752 (& Fireman, L.; Sargent, D.; Wineman, D.) Role phenomena and foster care for disturbed children. Ops 1962, 32:32-41

AMBROSE, J. ANTHONY

65753 The age of onset of ambivalence in early infancy: indications from the study of laughing. J Child Psychol Psychiat 1963, 4:167-181
65754 The comparative approach to early child development: the data of ethology. In Miller, E. Foundations of Child Psychiatry, Oxford/NY: Pergamon Pr 1968, 188-232
65755 The development of the smiling response in early infancy. In Foss, B. M. Determinants of Infant Behavior I, London: Methuen; NY: Wiley 1961, 179-201
65756 Personality development: 0-5 years. In The Seven Ages of Man, New Society Mongr 1964
65757 Ritualization in the human infant-mother bond. Phil Trans R Soc, Set B (Foy) 1966, 251:359-362
65758 The smiling and related responses in early human infancy: an experimental and theoretical study of their course and significance. Ph D Thesis. London Univ 1960
65759 The study of human social organization: a review of current concepts and approaches. Symp Zool Soc Lond 1965, 14:301-314

AMEEN, LANE

65760 (& Laffal, J.) The response of locked ward patients to the change of doctors in a residency program. Dis nerv Sys 1960, 21:695-697

AMENT, AARON

See Ammon, Günter

AMERONGEN, SUZANNE TAETS VAN

65761 Postgraduate experience for the child psychiatric clinician. J Amer Acad Child Psychiat 1967, 6:200-212

AMES, LOUISE BATES

65762 Children's stories. Genet Psychol Monogr 1966, 73:337-396

AMICI DI SAN LEO, GINO

S-40529 Reacciones transferenciales ante los honorarios; aspecto parcial de una neurosis obsesiva.
Abs An Surv Psa 1955, 6:342-343

AMINI, FARIBORZ

See Selzer, Melvin L.

AMMON, GISELA

See Ammon, Günter

AMMON, GÜNTER

65763 Abrupter Durchbruch destruktiver Aggression als psychiatrisches Problem. [Sudden eruption of destructive aggression as a psychiatric problem.] In Beiträge zur gerichtlichen Medizin, Vol. 27, Vienna 1969

65764 Beobachtungen und Erfahrungen eines Psychiaters und Psychoanalytikers bei den Lacandon-Maja Mittelamerikas. [Observations and experiences of a psychiatrist and psychoanalyst with the Lacandon-Maya of Middle America.] Mitt Berliner Gscht Anthropol Ethnol Urgeschichte 1966, 1(2):52

65765 Dynamische Psychiatrie. [Dynamic psychiatry.] Dyn Psychiat 1968, 1:6-18

65766 (& Ekstein, R.) Freuds Psychoanalyse: Perspektiven 1968 für Europa und Amerika. [Freudian psychoanalysis: perspectives 1968 for Europe and America.] Dyn Psychiat 1968, 1:46-51

65767 Herrschaft und Aggression: zur Psychoanalyse der Aggression. [Authority and aggression: on psychoanalysis of aggression.] Dyn Psychiat 1969, 2:122-133; Abs (Eng) 133

65768 (& Ammon, G.) Lehrbuch für Gruppenpsychotherapie auf psychoanalytischer Grundlage. [Textbook for Group Psychotherapy on Psychoanalytic Principles.] W Berliner Verlag 1969-70, 380 p

65769 Oralität, Identitätsdiffusion und weibliche Homosexualität: eine psychoanalytische Studie. [Orality, identity-diffusion and female homosexuality: a psychoanalytic study.] Dyn Psychiat 1969, 2:63-79; Abs (Eng) 79-82

65770 Psychoanalytic group psychotherapy. Grp Anal 1969, 2(2):9-10

65771 Psychoanalytische Gruppenpsychotherapie—Indikation und Prozess. [Psychoanalytic group psychotherapy—indication and process.] In Kleine Schriftenreihe der Pinel-Gesellschaft e.V., Berlin 1969

65772 Die "schizophrenogenic mother" in der Übertragung. [The "schizophrenogenic mother" in the transference.] Dyn Psychiat 1968, 1:34

65773 (& Ament, A.) The terminal phase of the dynamic process of a group-dynamic teaching group. Int J grp PT 1967, 17:35-43

65774 Verifikation von Psychotherapie bei schizophrener Reaktion. [Verification of psychotherapy with schizophrenic reaction.] Confin psychiat 1969, 12:65-71

65775 Zur Psychodynamik und Gruppendynamik der Aggression. [On psychodynamics and group dynamics of aggression.] Wege zum Menschen 1969, 21:166-177

65776 Zur Psychodynamik und Therapie der schizophrenen Reaktion. [On the Psychodynamics and Therapy of the Schizophrenic Reaction.] W Berliner Verlag 1969-70, 200 p

See Ekstein, Rudolf

AMOSOV, N. M.

65777 [Simulation of thinking and of the Psyche.] (Rus) Kiev, USSR: Naukova Dumka 1965, 304 p

AMRITH, M. V.

65778 Theoretical and transference analysis. Samiksa 1965, 19(3):103-106

AMSEL, ABRAHAM

65779 Judaism and Psychology. NY: Philipp Feldheim 1969, xv + 213 p

AMSTER, FANNY

65780 Differential uses of play in treatment of young children. In Haworth, M. R. Child Psychotherapy, NY/London: Basic Books 1964, 11-19

ANASTASIADIS, Y. S.

65781 A study on the psychopathological influence of parental environment on neurotic and schizoid patients. Acta psychother psychosom 1963, 11:370-390

ANASTASIOW, NICHOLAS J.

65782 Success in school and boys' sex-role patterns. Child Develpm 1965, 36:1053-1066

ANASTASOPOULOS, GEORGIOS K.

65783 Die Halluzination. Ein werdendes Nebenbewusstsein von sich selbst. [Hallucination. A progressive extra-consciousness of oneself.] Wien Z Nervenheilk 1964, 21:324-340

ANAVITARTE, JUAN PEREIRA

65784 Acerca de una interpretación del silencio. [One interpretation about silence in the analytic hour.] Rev urug Psa 1958, 3:298-318
        Abs Vega An Surv Psa 1958, 9:409-410

ANCONA, LEONARDO

65785 [Analytic-dynamic therapy and its comparison with other forms of psychotherapy.] (It) Arch Psicol Neurol Psichiat 1961, 22:391-428

65786 I dinamisi interni nell'esercizio della libertà individuale. [Internal dynamisms in the exercise of individual freedom.] Contributi Ist Psicol 1967, 29:87-101

65787 L'evoluzione delle tecniche di approccio psicoterapico alla schizofrenia. [Evolution of techniques in the psychotherapeutic approach to schizophrenia.] Arch Psicol Neurol Psichiat 1967, 28:205-219

65788 Fattori psicodinamici dell'aggressività. [Psychodynamic factors of aggressivity.] Arch Psicol Neurol Psichiat 1968, 29:507-528

65789 [Freud's pansexualism: a gross error to be corrected.] (It) Arch Psicol Neurol Psichiat 1960, 21:115-119

65790 (& Cesa-Bianchi, M.; Bocquet, F.) Identificazione al padre in assenza di modello paterno. [Identification with the father in the absence of a paternal model.] Arch Psicol Neurol Psichiat 1963, 24:119-172; 1964, 25:103-128

65791 (& Cesa-Bianchi, M.; Bocquet, F.) Identificazione al padre in assenza di modello paterno: ricerca applicata di figli degli ufficiali di marina. [Identification with the father in absence of the paternal model: research applied to children of navy officers.] Arch Psicol Neurol Psichiat 1963, 24:341-361

65792 Interpretazione clinica del comportamento religioso. [The clinical interpretation of religious behavior.] Arch Psicol Neurol Psichiat 1961, 22:7-28

65793 La motivazione. [Motivation.] Contributi Ist Psicol 1967, 29:44-73

65794 [The problem of the preparation of the psychotherapists.] (It) Arch Psicol Neurol Psichiat 1961, 22:431-435

65795 La Psicoanalisi. Brescia, Italy; La Scoula Ed 1963, 230 p
La Psychanalyse. (Tr: Hudon, E.) Sherbrooke, Québec: Éditions Paulines 1967, 237 p

65796 Il viràggio tra la dinàmica autoplàstica e la dinàmica alloplàstica. [The turning point between autoplastic dynamics and alloplastic dynamics.] Arch Psicol Neurol Psichiat 1966, 27:504-518

ANDERS, GÜNTHER

65797 Die Antiquiertheit des Menschen. [The Obsolescence of Man.] Munich: Verlag C. H. Beck 1961, 353 p
Rv HS Am Im 1966, 23:87-88

ANDERSON, A. RUSSELL

65798 Dreams and the uses of regression. JNMD 1960, 131:268-270

65799 (& McLaughlin, F.) Some observations on psychoanalytic supervision. Q 1963, 32:77-93

See Kohut, Heinz

REVIEWS OF:

65800 Gibson, R. W. (Ed) Crosscurrents in Psychiatry and Psychoanalysis. Q 1969, 38:657-660

65801 Jacobson, E. The Self and the Object World. Q 1965, 34:584-589

65802 Joseph, E. D. (Ed) Beating Fantasies and Regressive Ego Phenomena in Psychoanalysis. Q 1966, 35:599-600

ANDERSON, BEVERLY L.

65803 A sense of inferiority as a neurotic defense in women. (Read at Am Psa Ass, Dec 1960) R 1964, 51:219-230
Abs SRS Q 1965, 34:469

ABSTRACT OF:

65804 Rosenbaum, J. B. Songs of the transference. Bull Phila Ass Psa 1962, 12:177-178

ANDERSON, CAMILLA MAY

65805 Depression and suicide reassessed. J Amer Med Wom Ass 1964, 19:467-471

65806 Variations in the dynamics of the analytic relationship in the clinic and in private practice. Psa 1960, 20:73-78

ANDERSON, CHARLES C.

65807 The psychology of the metaphor. J genet Psych 1964, 105:53-73

ANDERSON, E. W.

65808 The official concept of psychopathic personality in England. In Kranz, H. *Psychopathologie Heute*, Stuttgart: Georg Thieme 1962, 243-251

ANDERSON, EILEEN G.

65809 Theories of children's play. Austral occup Ther J 1968, 15:22-34

ANDERSON, H. E., JR.

See White, William F.

ANDERSON, HAROLD H.

65810 (Ed) Creativity in Childhood and Adolescence: A Diversity of Approaches. Palo Alto, Calif: Sci & Behav Books 1965, xii + 107 p

ANDERSON, JOHN EDWARD

65811 Experience and Behavior in Early Childhood and the Adjustment of the Same Persons as Adults. Minneapolis, Univ of Minnesota, Inst of Child Development 1963

ANDERSON, LULEEN S.

65812 Fantasied and consciously perceived parent-child interactions in psychosomatic skin disorders. Diss Abstr 1965, 26:3482-3483

See Jacobs, Martin A.

ANDERSON, M. M.

See Inwood, E. R.

ANDERSON, PHILIP C.

65813 (& Cross, T. N.) Body cathexis and neurodermatitis. Comprehen Psychiat 1963, 4:40-46

ANDERSON, R. B.

See Winch, Robert F.

ANDERSON, ROBERT E.

65814 Where's dad. Paternal deprivation delinquency. Arch gen Psychiat
1968, 18:641-649

ANDESON, ROBERT P.

65815 Physiological and verbal behavior during client-centered counseling.
J counsel Psychol 1956, 3:174-184. In Goldstein, A. P. & Dean, S. J.
The Investigation of Psychotherapy, NY: Wiley 1966, 332-341

ANDERSON, WILLIAM F.

See Dorpat, Theodore L.

ANDERSSON, JENNY

See Friedman, Merton H.

ANDERSSON, OLA

65816 Studies in the Prehistory of Psychoanalysis: The Etiology of Psychoneuroses and Some Related Themes in Sigmund Freud's Scientific
Writings and Letters, 1886-1896. Stockholm: Svenska Bokförlaget
1962, 238 p
Abs J Am Psa Ass 1963, 11:662-663

ANDEWEG, JOHANNES

65817 Scientific principles and psychoanalytic theory. A dialogue between
Karen Horney and Isaac Newton. BMC 1967, 31:96-104

ANDRADE LIMA, HEITOR DE

See LIMA, HEITOR DE ANDRADE

ANDREAS-SALOMÉ, LOU

65818 The dual orientation of narcissism. (Tr: Leavy, S. A.) Q 1962, 31:1-30
65818A Letters to Sigmund Freud.
French: In Andreas-Salomé, L. *Correspondance avec Sigmund Freud
1912-1936,* (Tr: Jumel, L.) Paris: Gallimard 1970
German: In *Sigmund Freud. Lou Andreas-Salomé. Briefwechsel.*
(Ed: Pfeiffer, E.) Frankfurt: S. Fischer 1966
65819 In der Schule bei Freud. Tagebuch eines Jahres, 1912/1913. Munich:
Kindler 1965, 213 p
The Freud Journal of Lou Andreas-Salomé. (Tr: Leavy, S. A.) NY:
Basic Books 1964, v + 211 p
Rv J Am Psa Ass 1966, 14:226-227. MG Q 1965, 34:274-276.
Kaplan, D. M. R 1965, 52:488-491

ANDREWS, ERNEST E.

65820 Identity maintenance operations and group therapy process. Int J grp
PT 1964, 14:491-499

65821   The struggle for identity in mothers undergoing group therapy. Int J grp PT 1963, 13:346-353

ANDREWS, GEORGE

65822   (& Vinkenoog, S.) (Eds) The Book of Grass: An Anthology of Indian Hemp. NY: Grove Pr 1967, ix + 242 p
    Rv Gurvitz, M. S. R 1969, 56:488

ANDREWS, JOHN D. W.

65823   Psychotherapy of phobias. Psychol Bull 1966, 66:455-480

ANDREY, B.

See Fau, R. B.

ANGEL, ERNEST

65824   (Ed) Existence, Vol. IV. NY: Simon & Schuster 1967, 445 p
    Existencia, Vol. IV. Madrid: Ed Gredos 1967, 523 p
65825   Where-to, therapy and theatre? (Editorial) Council News, Council Psa Psychotherapists 1969, Jan: 1-2

See May, Rollo

ANGEL, G.

See Lizarazo, A.

ANGEL, KLAUS

65826   Loss of identity and acting out. (Read at Am Psa Ass, Dec 1964) J Am Psa Ass 1965, 13:79-84
    Abs JLSt Q 1968, 37:467
65827   On symbiosis and pseudosymbiosis. (Read at Am Psa Ass, Dec 1966) J Am Psa Ass 1967, 15:294-316

ABSTRACT OF:
65828   McDevitt, J. B. Pre-oedipal determinants of an infantile neurosis. Q 1969, 38:345

ANGEL, RONALD W.

65829   Jackson, Freud, and Sherrington on the relation of brain and mind. P 1961, 118:193-197

ANGELERGUES, R.

65830   [The body and its images: attempted dynamic comprehension of the specificity and polymorphism of the somatognosic organization.] (Fr) Évolut psychiat 1964, 29:181-216

See Ajuriaguerra, Julien de

ANGRILLI, ALBERT F.

65831   Psychosexual identification of pre-school boys. J genet Psych 1960, 97:329-340

ANGRIST, SHIRLEY
See Dinitz, Simon

ANGULO, F.
65832 Aspects fonctionnels de la vie onrique. [Functional aspects of the dream life.] RFPsa 1963, 27(Suppl):397-399

ANGYAL, ANDRAS
65833 Neurosis and Treatment: A Holistic Theory. (Ed. Hanfmann, E.; Jones, R. M.) NY: Wiley 1965, xxi + 328 p

ANNE, L.
See Couléon, H.

ANNIN, SUZETTE H.
* * * (& Fenichel, H.) Editors of Fenichel, O. "Psychoanalysis as the nucleus of a future dialectical-materialistic psychology."

ANRICH, ERNST
65834 Moderne Physik und Tiefenpsychologie: Zur Einheit der Wirklichkeit und damit der Wissenschaft, ein Versuch. [Modern Physics and Depth Psychology: On the Unity of Reality and Knowledge; an Essay.] Stuttgart: Klett 1963, xxiv + 622 p

ANSBACHER, HEINZ LUDWIG
65835 Adler and the 1910 Vienna symposium on suicide. A special review. J ind Psych 1968, 24:181-192
65836 The concept of social interest. J ind Psych 1968, 24:131-149
65837 Ego psychology and Alfred Adler. Soc Casewk 1964, 45:268-272
* * * Introduction to Adler, A. *Problems of Neurosis: A Book of Case-Histories.*
65838 (& Ansbacher, R. R.; Shiverick, D.; Shiverick, K.) Lee Harvey Oswald: an Adlerian interpretation. R 1966, 53:379-390
      Abs SRS Q 1967, 36:630-631
65839 Life style: a historical and systematic review. J ind Psych 1967, 23:191-212
65840 Sensus privatus versus sensus communis. J ind Psych 1965, 21:48-50
65841 Suicide: the Adlerian point of view. In Farberow, N. L. & Shneidman, E. S. *The Cry for Help,* NY: McGraw-Hill 1961, 204-219
65842 (& Ansbacher, R. R.) (Eds) Superiority and Social Interest: A Collection of Later Writings by Alfred Adler. London: Routledge 1965, 432 p
65843 Was Adler a disciple of Freud? A reply. J ind Psych 1962, 18:126-135

      See Rom, Paul; Van Dusen, Wilson

ANSBACHER, ROWENA R.
See Ansbacher, Heinz L.

ANSELL, CHARLES

65844   The unconscious: agency of the occult. R 1966, 53:664-672
        Abs SRS Q 1968, 37:316-317

ANSHEN, RUTH NANDA

° ° °   Editor of Fromm, E. *The Heart of Man. Its Genius for Good and Evil. Religious Perspectives.*
° ° °   Editor of Fromm, E. *The Revolution of Hope: Toward a Humanized Technology.*

ANSHIN, ROMAN

65845   Emotional problems of the chronically ill. J Amer Geriat Soc 1962, 10:447-454
65846   How the psychiatrist appears to his colleagues. JNMD 1963, 136:187-195

ANTEBI, RAYMOND N.

65847   A pitfall in the diagnosis of myasthenia gravis. Acta Psychiat Scand 1963, 39:477-480
65848   Seven principles to overcome resistances in hypnoanalysis. M 1963, 36:341-349
65849   Successes and failures in hypnosis. A study of 50 cases. Acta Psychiat Scand 1966, 42:162-170

ANTHONISEN, NIELS L.

65850   The ghost in Hamlet. Am Im 1965, 22:232-249

ANTHONY, ARISTOTLE A.

65851   The relationship between neuroticism, stress, and qualitative porteus maze performance. J consult Psychol 1963, 27:513-519

ANTHONY, ELWYN JAMES

65852   Age and syndrome in group psychotherapy—two workshops. J Long Island Consult Center 1960, 1(2)
65853   The child's discovery of his body. Phys Ther 1968, 48:1103-1114
65854   Communicating therapeutically with the child. J Amer Acad Child Psychiat 1964, 3:106-125
65855   Developments in child psychotherapy. Varieties and vicissitudes of the therapeutic situation in the treatment of children. Psychother Psychosom 1965, 13:15-28.
65856   The dynamics of child development in the Kibbutz. In Neubauer, P. B. *Children in Collectives*, Springfield, Ill: Thomas 1965
65857   Effects of training under stress in children. In Tanner, J. M. *Stress and Psychiatric Disorder*, Oxford: Blackwell Sci Publ 1960, 34-46
65858   An experimental approach to the psychopathology of childhood—micropsia. Psychiat Res Rep 1960, 13:63-107

65859 Follow-up studies in child psychiatry. Proc III World Cong Psychiat
       1961
65860 The generic elements in dyadic and in group psychotherapy. Int J grp
       PT 1967, 17:57-70
65861 Impressions of research on parental attitudes and child behavior from
       the point of view of a psychiatrist. In Glidewell, J. C. *Parental Attitudes
       and Child Behavior*, Springfield, Ill: Thomas 1961, 149-153; 162-163
65862 "It hurts me more than it hurts you"—an approach to discipline as a
       two-way process. Reiss-Davis Clin Bull 1965, 2:7-22. Learn Love 117-
       131
65863 (Reporter) Learning difficulties in childhood. (Panel: Am Psa Ass, May
       1960) J Am Psa Ass 1961, 9:124-134
65864 Low grade psychosis in childhood. Proc London Cong on Mental Re-
       tardation 1960
65865 The Madeleine and the Doughnut. A study of "screen sensations."
       (Read at Chicago Psa Soc, 24 Jan 1961) Psa St C 1961, 16:211-245
           Abs Seitz, P. F. D. Bull Phila Ass Psa 1961, 11:94-95
65866 (& Scott, P.) Manic-depressive psychosis in childhood. J child Psychol
       Psychiat 1960, 1:53-72
65867 On observing children. In Miller, E. *Foundations of Child Psychiatry*,
       Oxford/NY: Pergamon Pr 1968, 71-123
65868 One can hear the one-hand clapping. Int J Psychiat 1967, 3:117-121
65869 Piaget et le clinicien. [Piaget and the clinician.] In Inhelder, B. *"Psycho-
       logie et Epistemologie Genètique," Hommage a Jean Piaget*, Paris:
       Dunod 1966
65870 Psychoneurotic disorders. Compreh Txbk Psychiat 1387-1406
65871 The reactions of adults to adolescents and their behavior. In Caplan,
       G. & Lebovici, S. *Adolescence: Psychosocial Perspectives*, NY: Basic
       Books 1969, 54-78
65872 Reflections on twenty-five years of group psychotherapy. Int J grp PT
       1968, 18:277-301
65873 (& Schwartz, A. S.) Sleep disturbances in infancy and childhood. In
       Feelings and Their Medical Significance (Ross Laboratories) 1963, 5:10
65874 Stress in childhood. In *The Nature of Stress Disorder*, Springfield, Ill:
       Thomas 1959, 199-224
65875 Studies on bowel disorders in children. In *Report of 44th Ross Congress
       on Pediatric Research* 1963
S-40596 The system makers: Piaget and Freud.
           Abs CK An Surv Psa 1957, 8:185-186
65876 The talking doctor has begun to shoot! Bull Inst Med, Chicago 1965,
       25(10):274-289
65877 Taxonomy is not one man's business. Int J Psychiat 1967, 3:173-179
65878 Varieties and vicissitudes of the therapeutic situation in the treatment of
       children. Psychother Psychosom 1965, 13:1-14

       See Corah, Norman L.; Foulkes, Sigmund H.; Koff, Robert H.

ANTHONY, H. SYLVIA

65879 Anxiety as a function of psychomotor and social behaviour. Brit J Psy-
       chol 1960, 51:141-152

ANTHONY, NICHOLAS

65880 A longitudinal analysis of the effect of experience on the therapeutic approach. Clin Psych 1967, 23:512-516

ANTHONY, RUSSELL A.

REVIEW OF:
65881 Friedman, L. J. Psychoanalysis: Uses and Abuses. Bull Phila Ass Psa 1969, 19:96

ANTONELLI, FERRUCIO

65882 Psicoanálisis y confesión. [Psychoanalysis and confession.] Rev Psicol gen apl, Madrid 1965, 20:73-78
65883 [Indications for depth psychotherapeutic treatment in psychosomatic medicine.] (It) Arch Psicol Neurol Psichiat 1961, 22:391-428

ANTONELLI, H.

See Alliez, J.

ANTONI, NILS

65884 Erik XIV och schizofrenien. [Erik XIV and schizophrenia.] Nord Med 1964, 72:1284-1293
65885 Obituary: Poul Bjerre 24. V. 1876—15. VII. 1964. [In Memoriam; Poul Bjerre, 24 May 1876—15 July 1964.] Nord Med 1965, 73:81-85

ANTONITIS, J. J.

See Scott, John P.

ANTONOVSKY, AARON

65886 Like everyone else, only more so: identity, anxiety, and the Jew. In Stein, M. R. et al: *Identity and Anxiety*, Glencoe, Ill: Free Pr 1960, 428-434

ANTROBUS, JOHN S.

65887 (& Coleman, R.; Singer, J. L.) Signal-detection performance by subjects differing in predisposition to daydreaming. J consult Psychol 1967, 31:487-491

See Antrobus, Judith S.

ANTROBUS, JUDITH S.

65888 (& Antrobus, J. S.; Fisher, C.) Dreaming and nondreaming sleep. Arch gen Psychiat 1965, 12:395-401
65889 (& Dement, W.; Fisher, C.) Patterns of dreaming and dream recall: an EEG study. ASP 1964, 69:341-344

ANZEL, ANNE S.

65890 Whitehorn and Betz's A-B typing and patient socio-economic and personality characteristics in a quasitherapeutic situation. Diss Abstr 1968, 29(6-B):2198

ANZIEU, ANNIE

65891 Les débuts du bégaiement chez le jeune enfant. [Beginning of stuttering in young children.] Revue de Psychologie et des Sciences de l'Éducation 1967-8, 207-212

65892 Discussion de l'exposé de F.-C. Lavie, "Le souvenir dans la cure." [Discussion of the report of F.-C. Lavie, "Le souvenir dans la cure."] Bull Ass psa Fran 1967, (2)

65893 L'influence psychothérapeutique des rééducations du langage chez l'enfant. [Psychotherapeutic influence of speech re-educations in children.] Rv Np inf 1968, 16:595-601

65894 L'interprétation: son écoute et sa compréhension par le patient. [Interpretation: listening and understanding by the patient.] Bull Ass psa Fran 1969, No. 5:33-43

65895 (& Dugas, M.) Mutisme hystérique et mutisme psychotique. [Hysterical and psychotic dumbness.] J fran Oto-Rhino-Laryngol 1968, 17(3):181-182

65896 Sur quelques traits de la personnalité du bègue. [Some features of stutterer's character.] Bull Psychol, Paris 1968, 21(15-19):1022-1028

ANZIEU, DIDIER

S-40625 L'Auto-analyse. Son Rôle dans la Découverte de la Psychanalyse par Freud. Son Fonction en Psychanalyse.
   Rv Friedman, P. Q 1961, 30:431-433

65897 Comment on Dr. Brenner's paper, "Archaic features of ego functioning." (Read at Int Psa Cong, July 1967) J 1968, 49:429-430

65898 Contre Lacan: une doctrine hérétique. [Against Lacan's psychoanalytic deviance.] Quinzaino Lit 1967, 1(20):14-15

65899 De la mythologie particulière à chaque type de masochisme. [Of the particular mythology of each type of masochism.] Bull Ass psa Fran 1968, (4):84-91

65900 Difficulté d'une étude psychanalytique de l'interprétation. [Difficulty of a psychoanalytic study of interpretation.] Bull Ass psa Fran 1969, (5):12-132

65901 Le discours de l'obsessionnel dans les romans de Robbe-Grillet. [Obsessional speech in Robbe-Grillet's novels.] Temps mod 1965, 21(233):608-637

65902 Étude psychanalytique des groupes réals. [Psychoanalytic approach of natural groups.] Temps mod 1966, 22(242):56-73

65903 Le moment de l'apocalypse. [Psychoanalysis as an apocalyptic time.] La Nef 1967, 24(31):127-132

65904 Oedipe avant le complexe, ou: De l'interprétation psychanalytique des mythes. [Oedipus before his complex, or: about psychoanalytic interpretation of myths.] Temps mod 1966, 22(245):675-715

65905 Quelques problèmes posés par la formation dite en profonduer. [Some problems presented by depth analysis training.] Psychol Franc 1962, 7(2):85-93

65906 La régression dans la situation de tests projectifs. [Regression in a situation of projective tests.] Rev belg Psychol Pédag 1967, 29:33-36. Rv Np inf 1967, Suppl:5-7

APFELBAUM, BERNARD

65907 Ego psychology, psychic energy, and the hazards of quantitative explanation in psycho-analytic theory. J 1965, 46:168-182
Abs EVN Q 1967, 36:317

65908 On ego psychology: a critique of the structural approach to psychoanalytic theory. J 1966, 47:451-475
Abs EVN Q 1968, 37:463

65909 Some problems in contemporary ego psychology. J Am Psa Ass 1962, 10:526-537
Abs JBi Q 1963. 32:446-447. CG RFPsa 1964, 28:457. Guiard, F. F. Rev Psicoanál 1964, 21:76

APONTE, JOSEPH F.

See Adams, Paul L.

APPAIX, A.

65910 (& Striglioni, L.; Hénin-Robert, N.; Baurand, G.) A propos de quelques observations caractéristiques des problèmes psychiatriques rencontrés dans la dyslexie-dysorthographie. [Apropos of various typical cases with the psychiatric problems encountered in dyslexia-dysorthography.] Rev Laryng, Bordeaux 1967, 88:245-253

See Striglioni, L.

APPALARAJU, DUVVI

See Hollender, Marc H.

APPEL, GERALD

65911 Some aspects of transference and countertransference in marital counseling. Soc Casewk 1966, 47:307-312

APPEL, KENNETH E.

65912 Basic psychotherapy. J S Carolina Med Ass 1961, 57:95-101

65913 (& Zerof, H. G.; Mudd, E. H.) Community psychiatry: integration of medical and non-medical community resources. P 1966, 122:1014-1017

65914 Discussion of Aldrich, C. K. "What price autonomy?" Sci Psa 1961, 4:185-189

65915 Foreword to Resnik, H. L. P. (Ed) Suicidal Behaviors, Boston: Little, Brown 1968, xi-xii

S-40641 Freud and psychiatry.
Abs Schmale, H. T. An Surv Psa 1956, 7:28-29

° ° ° Introduction to Nemiah, J. C. Foundations of Psychopathology.

65916 (& Kety, S.; Koelle, G.; Stein, M.) Mental illness. Amer Practit 1961, 12:315-325

65917 (& Morris, H. H., Jr.) Psychiatry. Ency Ment Hlth 1567-1585

65918 Some perspectives in psychoanalysis. In Hoch, P. H. & Zubin, J. The Future of Psychiatry, NY: Grune & Stratton 1962, 127-136

65919   (& Goodwin, H. M.; Wood, H. P.; Askren, E. L.) Training in psycho-
        therapy: the use of marriage counseling in a university teaching clinic.
        P 1961, 117:709-712

See Bartemeier, Leo H.; Ewalt, Jack R.; Morris, Harold H., Jr.

APPELBAUM, ANN

65920   Transactions, Topeka Psychoanalytic Society. BMC 1968, 32:63-66;
        130-134; 199-202; 266-270; 335-338

See Sargent, Helen D.

APPELBAUM, STEPHEN A.

65921   The end of the test as a determinant of responses. BMC 1961, 25:120-
        128
            Abs HD Q 1962, 31:295
65922   (& Siegal, R. S.) Half-hidden influences on psychological testing and
        practice. J proj Tech 1965, 29:128-133
65923   Interpretation: a psychoanalytic dialogue. In Hammer, E. F. *Use of
        Interpretation in Treatment: Technique and Art,* NY/London: Grune
        & Stratton 1968, 351-363
65924   The Kennedy assassination. R 1966, 53:393-404
65925   The pleasure and reality principles in group process teaching. M 1963,
        36:49-56
65926   Psychological testing for the psychotherapist. Dyn Psychiat 1969,
        3(2):158-161; Abs (Ger) 161-163
65927   The quest for identity of adjunctive therapists. BMC 1968, 32:271-279
65928   Speaking with the second voice. Evocativeness. J Am Psa Ass 1966,
        14:462-477
            Abs Cuad Psa 1967, 3:56. JLSt Q 1969, 38:337
65929   The world in need of a "leader": an application of group psychology
        to international relations. M 1967, 40:381-392

ABSTRACTS OF:
65930   Farina, A. Patterns of role dominance and conflict in parents of schizo-
        phrenic patients. Q 1961, 30:310
65931   Goldstein, M. J. & Barthol, R. P. Fantasy responses to subliminal stim-
        uli. Q 1961, 30:149-150
65932   Holzman, P. S. & Gardner, R. W. Leveling-sharpening and memory or-
        ganization. Q 1961, 30:309
65933   O'Connell, W. E. The adaptive functions of wit and humor. Q 1961,
        30:310
65934   Pine, F. Incidental stimulation: a study of preconscious transforma-
        tions. Q 1961, 30:150
65935   Weiner, M. & Schiller, P. H. Subliminal perception or perception of
        partial cues. Q 1961, 30:310

APPELL, GENEVIÈVE

See David, Myriam

APPERSON, LOUISE BEHRENS

65936 Childhood experiences of schizophrenics and alcoholics. J genet Psych 1965, 106:301-313

65937 (& McAdoo, W. G., Jr.) Parental factors in the childhood of homo-sexuals. JAbP 1968, 73:201-206

65938 (& McAdoo, W. G., Jr.) Paternal reactions in childhood as described by schizophrenics and alcoholics. Clin Psych 1965, 21:369-373

APPLEBY, LAWRENCE

65939 (& Scher, J. M.; Cumming, J.) (Eds) Chronic Schizophrenia. Explorations in Theory and Treatment. (Foreword: Menninger, K.) Glencoe, Ill: Free Pr 1960, xv + 368 p

APPLETON, WILLIAM S.

65940 (& Chien, C.-P.) American·psychopharmacology: second class status. Brit J Psychiat 1967, 113:637-641

65941 Concentration. The phenomenon and its disruption. Arch gen Psychiat 1967, 16:373-381

APPLEY, MORTIMER H.

See Cofer, Charles N.

APTEKAR, HERBERT H.

65942 Review article on Rank, O. "Modern Education." J Otto Rank Ass 1968, 3(2):90-93

APTER, ABRAHAM

TRANSLATION OF:
Kasanin, J. S. [17935]

APTER, N. S.

65943 A brief summary of our concepts regarding transference in the transference neuroses and the narcissistic neuroses. In "Traditional Subjects Reconsidered," Proc 2nd regional conf Chicago Psa Soc 1968

ARANGO, CELSO R.

65944 Psicoterapia de grupo. [Group psychotherapy.] Folia Clín Int 1964, 14:380-387

ARASTEH, A. REZA

65945 Final integration in the adult personality. Psa 1965, 25:61-73

65946 Normative psychoanalysis: a theory and technique for the development of healthy integration. J gen Psychol 1965, 73:81-91

ARASTEH, JOSEPHINE D.

65947 Creativity and related processes in the young child: a review of the literature. J genet Psych 1968, 112:77-108. Ann Prog child Psychiat 1969, 152-184

ARAY, JULIO

65948 Aborto—Estudio Psicoanalítico. [Abortion—A Psychoanalytical Study.]
(Preface: Garma, A.) Buenos Aires: Horme 1968
65949 (& Kalina, E.) Aborto y parasitiosis. [Abortions and parasitism.] Rev
Psicoanál 1968, 25:211-217

ARCHER, LOIS

65950 (& Hosley, E.) Educational program. Ther Nurs Schl 21-63

ARCHER, RALPH HARRISON

65951 A preliminary study of hostility: the hostility ratio. Psychiat Q 1961,
35:562-574

ARCHIBALD, HERBERT C.

65952 (& Bell, D.; Miller, C.; Tuddenham, R. D.) Bereavement in childhood
and adult psychiatric disturbance. PSM 1962, 24:343-352
Abs ELG Q 1963, 32:608

ARDALI, CAHIT

See Kraft, Irvin A.

ARDEN, EUGENE

65953 Hawthorne's "Case of Arthur D." Am Im 1961, 18:45-55

ARENSBURG, BERNARDO

See Ganzaraín Cajiao, Ramón

ARGELANDER, HERMANN

65954 Die Analyse psychischer Prozesse in der Gruppe. [Analysis of psychological processes in groups.] Psyche 1963, 17:450-479; 481-515
65955 Angewandte Psychoanalyse in der ärztlichen Praxis. [Psychoanalysis
applied in medical practice.] Jb Psa 1969, 6:119-140
65956 Das Erstinterview in der Psychotherapie. [The first interview in psychotherapy.] Psyche 1967, 21:341-368; 429-467; 475-512
65957 Gruppenanalyse unter Anwendung des Strukturmodells. [Group analysis using a structural model.] Psyche 1968, 22:915-933
Abs J 1969, 50:401
65958 Der Patient in der psychotherapeutischen Situation mit seinem be-
handelnden Arzt. [The patient in the psychotherapeutic situation with
his attending physician.] Psyche 1966, 20:926-941
65959 Der psychoanalytische Befund. [The psychoanalytic diagnosis.] Psyche
1968, 22:748-753
Abs J 1969, 50:398
65960 Der psychoanalytische Dialog. [The psychoanalytical dialogue.] Psyche
1968, 22:325-339
65961 Die Übertragung als Determinante eines integrativen Prozesses. [Trans-
ference as a determinant of any integration process.] Psyche 1965,
18:701-720

65962 Zur Psychodynamik des Erstinterviews. [Psychodynamics of the initial interview.] Psyche 1966, 20:40-53

ARGEN, G. C.

65963 (& Traversa, C.) Children's Drawings and Their Bearing on the Doctor-Patient Relationship. (7 pages, 12 color plates) Basel/NY: Karger
Rv Bychowski, G. Am Im 1966, 23:275-276

ARGRETT, S.

See Blank, H. Robert; Greenberg, Harvey R.

ARGÜELLES DE MENDEZ, S.

See Rascovsky, Arnaldo

ARGYLE, MICHAEL

65964 Introjection: a form of social learning. Brit J Psychol 1964, 55:391-402
65965 Psychology and Social Problems. London: Methuen 1964, 232 p
65966 The Psychology of Interpersonal Behavior. Baltimore: Penguin Books 1967, 223 p

ARICO, JOSEPH F.

See Bandler, Bernard

ARIEFF, ALEX JOSEPH

65967 Denial of illness and the practice of medicine. Psychiat Dig 1968, 29:23-26

ARIÈS, PHILIPPE

65968 L'Enfant et la Vie Familiale Sous l'Ancien Régime. [Childhood and Family Life in Prerevolutionary France.] Paris: Librairie Plon 1960, 503 p
Rv Loewenstein, R. M. Q 1962, 31:559-560

ARIETI, SILVANO

65969 (Ed) American Handbook of Psychiatry, Vol. III. New York/London: Basic Books 1966, xiii + 778 p
Abs J Am Psa Ass 1967, 15:732. Rv Brody, M. W. Q 1969, 38:152
65970 Aspects of psychoanalytically oriented treatment of schizophrenia. Out-Patient Schiz 114-118
65971 Conceptual and cognitive psychiatry. P 1965, 122:361-366
65972 Contributions to cognition from psychoanalytic theory. Sci Psa 1965, 8:16-37
65973 [Contributor to] Discussion of Hoch, P. H. "Concepts of schizophrenia." Out-Patient Schiz 17-23
65974 [Contributor to] Discussion of Kanner, L. "Schizophrenia as a concept." Out-Patient Schiz 52-59; 174-177
65975 [Contributor to] Discussion of Rado, S. "Theory and therapy." Out-Patient Schiz 102-113

65976 Discussion of Weinstein, E. A. "Symbolic aspects of ego function."
       Sci Psa 1967, 11:144-146
65977 [Contributor to] Discussion of Williams, G. E. "Crisis in the evaluation
       of the schizophrenic patient." Out-Patient Schiz 74-86
65978 Emphasis on the healthy aspects of the patient in psychoanalysis. A
       round table discussion. Psa 1966, 26:198-200
65979 Etiological considerations of schizophrenia. Out-Patient Schiz 24-29
65980 Further training in psychotherapy. P 1968, 125:96-97
65981 Hallucinations, delusions, and ideas of reference treated with psycho-
       therapy. PT 1962, 16:52-60
65982 The interpersonal and the intrapsychic. Int J Psychiat 1967, 4:522-524
65983 The Intrapsychic Self: Feeling, Cognition, and Creativity in Health and
       Mental Illness. NY: Basic Books 1967, xvi + 487 p
65984 Introductory notes on the psychoanalytic therapy of schizophrenics. In
       Burton, A. Psychotherapy of the Psychoses, NY: Basic Books 1961,
       69-89
65985 The loss of reality. PPR 1961, 48(3):3-24
            Abs LDr RFPsa 1962, 27:348
65986 The microgeny of thought and perception. Arch gen Psychiat 1962,
       6:454-468
65987 New views on the psychodynamics of schizophrenia. P 1967, 124:453-
       458
65988 Preface to Gralnick, A. (Ed) The Psychiatric Hospital as a Thera-
       peutic Instrument, NY: Brunner/Mazel 1969, vii-viii
65989 The present status of psychiatric theory. P 1968, 124:1630-1639
65990 Il processo secondario nella psicodinamica della schizofrenia. [Sec-
       ondary process in the psychodynamics of schizophrenia.] Arch Psicol
       Neurol Psichiat 1967, 28:255-269
65991 The psychodynamics of schizophrenia: a reconsideration. PT 1968,
       22:366-381
65992 Psychopathic personality: some views on its psychopathology and psy-
       chodynamics. Comprehen Psychiat 1963, 4:301-312
65993 The psychotherapeutic approach to depression. PT 1962, 16:397-406
65994 Psychotherapy of schizophrenia. Arch gen Psychiat 1962, 6:112-122
            Abs KR Q 1963, 32:141
65995 The psychotherapy of schizophrenia in theory and practice. Psychiat
       Res Rep 1963, 17:13-29
65996 Rapida rassegna degli studi del pensiero schizofrenico da Bleuler ai
       giorni nostri. [Swift review of studies on schizophrenic thinking from
       Bleuler to the present.] Arch Psicol Neurol Psichiat 1967, 28:237-254
65997 Recent conceptions and misconceptions of schizophrenia. PT 1960,
       14:3-29
65998 A re-examination of the phobic symptom and of symbolism in psycho-
       pathology. P 1961, 118:106-110
65999 The rise of creativity: from primary to tertiary process. Contempo
       Psa 1964, 1:51-68
66000 Schizophrenic cognition. Proc Amer Psychopath Ass 1966, 54:37-48
66001 The schizophrenic patient in office treatment. In Müller, C. & Benedet-
       ti, G. Psychotherapy of Schizophrenia, Basel: Karger 1965, 7-23

66002 Sexual conflict in psychotic disorders. In Wahl, C. W. *Sexual Problems: Diagnosis and Treatment in Medical Practice,* NY: Free Pr 1967, 228-237

66003 Some elements of cognitive psychiatry. PT 1968, 21:723-736

66004 Some memories and personal views. Contempo Psa 1968, 5:85-88

66005 Studies of thought processes in contemporary psychiatry. P 1963, 120:58-64

66006 Toward a unifying theory of cognition. General Systems 1965, 10:109-115. In Gray, W. et al: *General Systems Theory and Psychiatry,* Boston: Little, Brown 1969, 193-208

66007 [Transference and counter-transference in the treatment of the schizophrenic patient.] (Por) J Bras Psiquiat 1966, 15:163-174

66008 Volition and value: a study based on catatonic schizophrenia. Comprehen Psychiat 1961, 2:74-82

See Felix, Robert H.; Lesse, Stanley

ARIZMENDI CH., FERNANDO

66009 (& Bellón, R.; Carrera, J.; Hinojosa, J. R.; Montano, G.; Ortega, R.; Ramírez, S.; Sánchez, C.; Valner, G.) El aparato psíquico. Sus estructuras. Aproximación metodológia. [The psychic apparatus. Its structures. Methodological approximation.] Cuad Psa 1967, 3:187-193

See Palacios López, Augustin

ARKIN, ARTHUR M.

66010 Post-hypnotically stimulated sleep-talking. JNMD 1966, 142:293-309

ARKIN, FRANCES S.

66011 Discussion of Silverberg, W. V. "An experimental theory of the process of psychoanalytic therapy." Sci Psa 1961, 4:166-167

66012 Preface: presidential address. Sci Psa 1962, 5:viii-x

66013 Response to presidential address. (Read at Acad Psa, 8 May 1960) Sci Psa 1961, 4:xii

ARLEN, MONROE SIGMUND

66014 Conjoint therapy and the corrective emotional experience. Fam Proc 1966, 5:91-104

ARLOW, JACOB A.

66015 Character and conflict. J Hillside Hosp 1966, 15:139-151

66016 Conflict, regression, and symptom formation. (Read at Int Psa Cong, July-Aug 1963) J 1963, 44:12-22
Conflit, régression et formation des symptômes. RFPsa 1963, 27:31-52
Konflikt, Regression und Symptombildung. Psyche 1963, 17:23-43
Conflicto, regresión y formación de síntomas. Rev Psicoanál 1963, 20:1-19
Abs Vega Q 1964, 33:331. EVN Q 1965, 34:463

66017   Depersonalization and derealization. Psa–Gen Psychol 456-478
66018   (& Brenner, C.) Discussion of Zetzel, E. R. "The analytic situation."
        Psa Amer 133-138
66019   Ego psychology and the study of mythology. (Read at Am Psa Ass,
        7 May 1961) J Am Psa Ass 1961, 9:371-393
            Abs FB Q 1962, 31:416. SAS RFPsa 1962, 26:617
66020   Fantasy, memory, and reality testing. (Read at Columbia Univ Psa
        Clin, 1 Mar 1968) Q 1969, 38:28-51
            Phantasie, Erinnerung und Realitätsprüfung. Psyche 1969, 23:881-899
S-40716 Fantasy systems in twins.
            Abs Sapochnik, L. Rev Psicoanál 1961, 18:403. LDr RFPsa 1962,
        26:332
66021   The future of an idea. 50 Yrs Psa 77-84
S-40719 The Legacy of Sigmund Freud.
            Abs WAS An Surv Psa 1956, 7:425-433
66022   The Madonna's conception through the eyes. (Panel on mythology and
        ego psychology: Psa Ass NY, 21 May 1962) Psa St Soc 1964, 3:13-25
S-40722 Notes on oral symbolism.
            Abs An Surv Psa 1955, 6:169
66023   (& Freud, A.; Lampl-de Groot, J.; Beres, D.) Panel discussion (Read at
        Int Psa Cong, July 1967) J 1968, 49:506-512
S-40723 Perversion: theoretical and therapeutic aspects. PT Pervers 56-69
66024   (& Brenner, C.) Psychoanalytic Concepts and Structural Theory. NY:
        IUP 1964, xii + 201 p
            Abs J Am Psa Ass 1966, 14:226. Rv Brandt, L. W. R 1965, 52:485-
        486. Ekstein, R. J 1966, 47:581-583. Loewald, H. W. Q 1966, 35:430-
        436
S-40726 (Reporter) The psychoanalytic theory of thinking. (Panel)
            Abs JFr An Surv Psa 1958, 9:90-100
66025   (& Brenner, C.) The psychopathology of the psychoses: a proposed
        revision. (Panel at Int Cong Psa, 1969) J 1969, 50:5-14
            Zur Psychopathologie der Psychosen. Psyche 1969, 23:402-418
66026   The reaches of intrapsychic conflict. P 1965, 122:425-431. BMC 1966,
        30:275-283
66027   Sigmund Freud. Ency Ment Hlth 632-642
66028   Silence and the theory of technique. J Am Psa Ass 1961, 9:44-55
            Abs Soifer, R. Rev Psicoanál 1961, 18:399. FB Q 1962, 31:288. SAS
        RFPsa 1962, 26:615
S-40727 On smugness.
            Abs SLP An Surv Psa 1957, 8:121-122
66029   Some reflections on memory and reality testing. Bull Ass psa Med 1968,
        8:8-11
S-40728 The structure of the déjà vu experience.
            Abs JTM Q 1961, 30:141. SAS RFPsa 1961, 25:158
S-40729 (Reporter) Sublimation. (Panel)
            Abs An Surv Psa 1955, 6:119-120
66030   The supervisory situation. J Am Psa Ass 1963, 11:576-594
            Abs Dubcovsky, S. Rev Psicoanál 1963, 20:396-397. Ennis, J. Q
        1964, 33:455-456

66031 Symptom formation and character formation. Contributions to discussion of prepublished papers [by Lampl-de Groot and Arlow]. Summary of discussion. J 1964, 45:167-170
       Resumé de la discussion. RFPsa 1966, 30:264-270
       Abs EVN Q 1966, 35:454-455
66032 A typical dream. J Hillside Hosp 1961, 10:154-158
       Abs JA Q 1962, 31:585
66033 Unconscious fantasy and disturbances of conscious experience. (Read at NY Psa Soc, 24 Nov 1963) Q 1969, 38:1-27
       Abs WAS Q 1964, 33:316-317

       See Brenner, Charles

ARLUCK, EDWARD WILTCHER

66034 Hypnoanalysis: A Case Study. NY: Random House 1964, 164 p

ARMITAGE, STEWART G.

       See King, Gerald F.

ARMON, VIRGINIA

66035 Some personality variables in overt female homosexuality. J proj Tech 1960, 24:292-308

ARMOR, DAVID J.

       See Lazare, Aaron

ARMSTRONG, EDWARD A.

66036 Shakespeare's Imagination: A Study of the Psychology of Association and Inspiration. Lincoln, Neb: Univ of Nebraska Pr 1963, 230 p

AMSTRONG, J. J.

       See Ball, J. R.

ARMSTRONG, LOUISE

66037 A Child's Guide to Freud. NY: Simon & Schuster 1963

ARMSTRONG, RENATE GERBOTH

66038 (& Hauck, P. A.) Sexual identification and the first figure drawn. J consult Psychol 1961, 25:51-54

ARNDS, H. G.

66039 (& Hillenbrand, D.; Studt, H. H.) [Stationary psychotherapeutic treatments.] (Ger) MMW 1967, 109:467-471

       See Studt, H. H.

ARNETT, BARBARA MELCHIORI

       TRANSLATION OF:
       Praz, M. [86897]

ARNFRED, A. H.

66040 [Materiopsychological comments on metapsychology and psychopathologic causality.] (Dan) Nord Psyk Tidsskr 1964, 18:627-632

ARNHEIM, RUDOLF

66041 Toward a Psychology of Art. Berkeley, Calif: Univ of Calif Pr 1966, 269 p

66042 What is art for? Teachers Coll Rec 1964, 66:46-53

ARNHOFF, FRANKLIN N.

66043 (& Damianopoulos, E. N.) Self-body recognition and schizophrenia. J gen Psychol 1964, 70:353-361

66044 Stimulus generalization and anxiety. J gen Psychol 1960, 59:131-136

ARNOLD, JACK

See Chance, Erika

ARNOLD, JOHN

66045 Poe's "Lionizing": the wound and the bawdry. Lit & Psych 1967, 1967, 17:52-54

ARNOLD, MAGDA B.

66046 Emotion and Personality. Vol. I: Psychological Aspects. Vol. II: Neurological and Physiological Aspects. NY: Columbia Univ Pr 1960, 296 p; 430 p
        Rv Niederland, W. G. Q 1961, 30:444-445

66047 Emotions. Ency Ment Hlth 547-557

66048 In defense of Arnold's theory of emotion. Psychol Bull 1968, 70:283-284

ARNOLD, O. H.

66049 Die Bedeutung der tiefenpsychologischen Anthropologie für die Psychiatrie. [The meaning of depth psychological anthropology for psychiatry.] In Edelweiss, M. L. et al: *Personalisation*, Vienna/Freiburg/Basel: Herder 1964, 3-10

66050 (& Hift, S.; Hoff, H.) Die Behandlung der Melancholie. [The therapy of melancholia.] Wien Z Nervenheil 1960, 18:16-45

66051 (& Hoff, H.) Fortschritte in der Behandlung der endogenen Psychosen. [Advances in the treatment of endogenous psychoses.] Wien klin Wschr 1961, 73:501-510

66052 (& Hoff, H.) Intensive therapy of the psychoses in a university hospital. Curr psychiat Ther 1961, 1:175-185

66053 Die körperlichen Behandlungsmethoden der Schizophrenie. [Physical therapeutic methods in schizophrenia.] In Hoff, H. *Therapeutische Fortschritte in der Neurologie und Psychiatrie*, Vienna, Innsbruck: Urban & Schwarzenberg 1960, 262-278

66054 (& Gastager, H.; Hofmann, G.) Pharmakologische Behandlungen in der Psychiatrie. [Pharmacological treatments in psychiatry.] In Hoff,

H. *Therapeutische Fortschritte in der Neurologie und Psychiatrie,* Vienna/Innsbruck: Urban & Schwarzenberg 1960, 305-329

66055 (& Hoff, H.) The role of biological treatment in comprehensive psychiatric treatment—Academic address. Recent Adv biol Psychiat 1961, 3:12-29

66056 (& Hift, S.; Hoff, H.) The role of psychotropic drugs in current psychiatric therapy. Comprehen Psychiat 1962, 3:330-342

66057 (& Hift, S.; Hofmann, G.) Die Therapie des manisch-depressiven Krankheisgeschehens. [Treatment of manic-depressive psychosis.] In Hoff, H. *Therapeutische Fortschritte in der Neurologie und Psychiatrie,* Vienna/Innsbruck: Urban & Schwarzenberg 1960, 279-289

66058 (& Tschabitscher, H.) Die Wiener Neurologisch-Psychiatrische Schule unter H. Hoff. [The Viennese Neurological Psychiatric School under H. Hoff.] Wien med Wschr 1967, 117:1128-1131

66059 (& Hoff, H.; Hofmann, G.) Zur multifaktoriellen Genese der Schizophrenie. [On the multifactorial genesis of schizophrenia.] Schweiz ANP 1963, 91:226-232

ARNOUX, H.

66060 (& Gelly, R.; Damey, E.; Hadni, J. C.) Contribution à l'investigation psychosomatique de la rétinite centrale angiospastique. Étude de 6 observations. [Psychosomatic investigation of angiospastic central retinitis. A study of 6 cases.] Rev Méd psychosom 1965, 7:365-381

ARNSØ, FOLMER

66061 Anorexia nervosa, illustrated by a psychotherapeutic casuistry. Acta Psychiat Scand 1966, 42(Suppl 191):107-123

ARNSTEIN, HELENE S.

66062 Your Growing Child and Sex. Indianapolis/Kansas City/NY: Bobbs-Merrill 1967, xiii + 188 p

ARON, WILLIAM

66063 Freud and Spinoza. Hebrew med J 1963(2):242-260; 1964(1):265-284; (2):242-260. Hebrew med J (Annual Israel edition) 1964, 282-300; 1965, 264-283
    Hebrew: Hebrew med J 1963(2):137-155; 1964(1):119-128; (2):136-146. Hebrew med J (Annual Israel edition) 1964, 109-127

66064 Hahnemann and Spinoza: a comparative study of their psychologies. The Layman Speaks 1959, 12:371-375

ARONFREED, JUSTIN

66065 (& Reber, A.) Internalized behavioral suppression and the timing of social punishment. J Pers soc Psychol 1965, 1:3-16

ARONOFF, JOEL

66066 Freud's conception of the origin of curiosity. J Psychol 1962, 54:39-45

ARONSON, ARNOLD E.

66067 (& Peterson, H. W., Jr.; Litin, E. M.) Psychiatric symptomatology in functional dysphonia and aphonia. J speech hear Disord 1966, 31:115-127

ARONSON, ELLIOT

66068 (& Mills, J.) The effect of severity of initiation on liking for a group. ASP 1959, 59:177-181. In Dulany, D. E., Jr. et al: *Contributions to Modern Psychology*, NY: Oxford Univ Pr 1964, 444-452

66069 (& Carlsmith, J. M.) Effect of the severity of threat on the devaluation of forbidden behavior. ASP 1963, 66:584-588

ARONSON, GERALD

66070 Discussion. In May, P. R. A. *Treatment of Schizophrenia,* NY: Sci House 1968, 294-297

66071 Discussion of Alger, I. "The clinical handling of the analyst's responses." Psa Forum 1966, 1:300-301

ARONSON, H.

66072 (& Weintraub, W.) Certain initial variables as predictors of change with classical psychoanalysis. JAbP 1969, 74:490-497

66073 (& Weintraub, W.) Patient changes during classical psychoanalysis as a function of initial status and duration of treatment. Ps 1968, 31:369-379

66074 (& Weintraub, W.) Sex differences in verbal behavior related to adjustive mechanisms. Psychol Rep 1967, 21:965-971

66075 (& Weintraub, W.) Social background of the patient in classical psychoanalysis. JNMD 1968, 146(2):91-97

66076 (& Weintraub, W.) Verbal productivity as a measure of change in affective status. Psychol Rep 1967, 20:483-487

See Overall, Betty; Weintraub, Walter

ARONSON, JASON

See Field, Mark G.

ARONSON, MARVIN L.

66077 Acting out in individual and group psychotherapy. J Hillside Hosp 1964, 13:43-48

66078 (& Furst, H. B.; Krasner, J. D.; Liff, Z. A.) The impact of the death of a leader on a group process. PT 1962, 16:460-468

66079 Resistance in individual and group psychotherapy. PT 1967, 21:86-94

66080 Technical problems in combined therapy. Int J grp PT 1964, 14:425-432

See Krasner, Jack D.

ARORA, SATISH K.

66081 Political communications and socialization in transitional societies. Samiksa 1964, 18(4):166-174

66082 Regression, imitation and innovation in transitional societies. Samiksa 1965, 19(4):170-175

ARRAU, CLAUDIO

66083 A performer looks at psychoanalysis. Hi Fi 1967, 17(2):50-54

ARROSA, LAURA ACHARD

66084 Aportaciones al estudio de la creación teatral. [Contributions to the study of theatrical acting.] Rev urug Psa 1961-62, 4:575-585
       Abs Vega Q 1964, 33:146-147

66085 Formas particulares de identificación en el actor. [Particular forms of identification in the actor.] Rev Psicoanál 1962, 19:42-48

66086 [Psychoanalytic study of the actor and his character.] (Sp) Rev urug Psa 1961-62, 4:389-416
       Abs Vega Q 1963, 32:458-459

ABSTRACTS OF:

66087 Berge, A. L'équation personnelles ou de l'art psychanalytique. Rev urug Psa 1961-2, 4:379

66088 Perrier, F. Phobies et hystérie d'angoisse. Rev urug Psa 1961-62, 4:563

ARSENIAN, JOHN

66089 (& Semrad, E. V.; Shapiro, D.) An analysis of integral functions in small groups. Int J grp PT 1962, 12:421-434

66090 (& Semrad, E. V.) Current conceptual depth levels in individual and group manifestations. Int J grp PT 1967, 17:82-97

66091 Life cycle factors in mental illness. A biosocial theory with implications for prevention. MH 1968, 52:19-26

66092 (& Semrad, E. V.) Schizophrenia and language. Some formulations based on experience in group therapy. Psychiat Q 1966, 40:449-458

See Refsnes, Carolyn C.

ARST, D. B.

See Abram, Harry S.

ARTH, MALCOLM J.

66093 An interdisciplinary view of the aged in Ibo culture. J geriat Psychiat 1968, 2:33-39

ARTHER, R. O.

See Kline, Milton V.

ARTHUR, ARTUR Z.

66094 Theories and explanations of delusions: a review. P 1964, 121:105-115

ARTHUR, B.

See Zrull, Joel P.

ARTHUR, BETTIE

66095 (& Kemme, M. L.) Bereavement in childhood. J child Psychol Psychiat 1964, 5:37-49
66096 (& Birnbaum, J. L.) Professional identity as a determinant of the response to emotionally disturbed children. Ps 1968, 31:138-149

ARTHUR, RANSOM J.

See Dodgen, John C.

ARTISS, KENNETH L.

66097 (& Schiff, S. B.) Education for practice in the therapeutic community. Curr psychiat Ther 1968, 8:233-247
66098 Environmental-therapy (milieu). Curr psychiat Ther 1964, 4:46-54
66099 Language and the schizophrenic quandary. Contempo Psa 1966, 3:39-54
66100 Milieu Therapy and Schizophrenia. NY/London: Grune & Stratton 1962, 169 p
       Rv Eldred, S. H. Q 1963, 32:258-260
66101 (& Bullard, D. M.) Paranoid thinking in everyday life. The function of secrets and disillusionment. Arch gen Psychiat 1966, 14:89-93
66102 Patient-therapist logic systems: their translation in the change from estrangement to membership. In Lesse, S. *An Evaluation of the Results of the Psychotherapies*, Springfield, Ill: Thomas 1968, 292-304

ARVIDSON, ROBERT M.

66103 A note on psychoanalysis in Canada. Canad Psychol 1969, 10:65-67

ARVIDSON, ROLF

ABSTRACT OF:
66104 Modell, A. H. On having the right to a life. Bull Phila Ass Psa 1964, 14:225-228

ASAI, MASAHIRO

REVIEW OF:
66105 Szondi, L. Lehrbuch der experimentellen Triebdiagnostik. Jap J Psa 1965, 11(5):26-28

ASCH, STUART S.

66106 Claustrophobia and depression. J Am Psa Ass 1966, 14:711-729
66107 Crib deaths: their possible relationship to post-partum depression and infanticide. J Mount Sinai Hosp 1968, 35:214-220
66108 Depression: three clinical variations. (Read at NY Psa Soc, 25 Feb 1964) Psa St C 1966, 21:150-171
       Abs Fine, B. D. Q 1964, 33:463-465

66109 Mental and emotional problems. In Rovinsky, J. J. & Guttmacher, A. F. *Medical, Surgical and Gynecologic Complications of Pregnancy*, Baltimore: Williams & Wilkins 1960, 1965, 461-472

ASCHER, EDUARD

66110 Motor syndromes of functional or undetermined origin: tics, cramps, Gilles de la Tourette's disease, and others. Am Hbk Psychiat III, 148-157

ASHBY, W. ROSS

66111 Design for a Brain. NY: Wiley 1960 (2nd ed), 286 p
Rv Kubie, L. S. Q 1962, 31:277-279

ASHWORTH, P. L.

See Scott, R. D.

ASKEVOLD, FINN

66112 (& Hals, H.) A comparative investigation with two personality models. Acta Psychiat Scand 1964, 40(Suppl 180):79-86

ASKEW, MELVIN W.

66113 Catharsis and modern tragedy. PPR 1961, 48(3):81-88
Abs LDr RFPsa 1962, 27:349
66114 Courtly love: neurosis as institution. R 1965, 52:19-29
Abs SRS Q 1966, 35:469
66115 Psychoanalysis and literary criticism. R 1964, 51:211-218

ASKREN, EDWARD L.

See Appel, Kenneth E.

ASLAN, CARLOS M.

66116 (& Horne, B.) La destrucción del objeto bueno ene triunfo maniaco. [The destruction of the good object in the manic triumph.] In Rascovsky, A. & Liberman, D. *Psicoanalisis de la Manía y la Psicopatia*, Buenos Aires: Editorial Paidos 1966, 171-175

ABSTRACTS OF:
66117 Adsett, C. A. et al: Changes in coronary blood flow and other hemodynamic indicators induced by stressful interviews. Rev Psicoanál 1963, 20:93
66118 Castelnuovo Tedesco, P. Emotional antecedents of perforation of ulcers of the stomach and duodenum. Rev Psicoanál 1963, 20:93
66119 Meinhardt, K. & Robinson, H. A. Stokes-Adams syndrome precipitated by emotional stress. Rev Psicoanál 1963, 20:92

ASMAR, W.

66120 [Considerations on object-relationships.] (Por) J Bras Psiquiat 1966, 15:75-77

66121 Do-it-yourself psychoanalysis by an octogenarian. J Amer Geriat Soc 1964, 12:170-179

ASSAEL, M.

66122 (& Gabbay, F.; Halpern, B.) Clinical experience in surmontil treatment. Harefuah 1965, 67/68:86-87; 1965, 69:86-87

66123 (& Avrouskine, M.) Hysterectomy: a psychosomatic case study. Acta neurol psychiat Belg 1962, 62:927-938

66124 (& Dasberg, H.; Winnik, H. Z.) Myocardial infarction in mental patients. Interrelations in the clinical course of myocardial infarction and mental disease. Israel Ann Psychiat 1965, 3:229-248

See Winnik, H. Z.

ASSAL, G.

66125 [Incest in psychotics.] (Fr) Évolut psychiat 1964, 29:75-82

See Schneider, Pierre-Bernard

ASTIGUETA, DIEGO

66126 Psicoterapia psicoanaliticamente orientada. [Psychoanalytically oriented psychotherapy.] Act Np Arg 1961, 7:279-283. Nicaragua Med 1963, 19:53-54

ASTIGUETA, FERNANDO D.

66127 Psiquiatría y sociología. [Psychiatry and sociology.] Acta psiquiat psicol Arg 1962, 8:41-45

ASTIN, ALEXANDER W.

66128 The functional autonomy of psychotherapy. Amer Psych 1961, 16:75-78. In Goldstein, A. P. & Dean, S. J. *The Investigation of Psychotherapy*, NY: Wiley 1966, 62-65

See Monroe, Jack J.

ASTLEY, M. ROYDEN C.

66129 Comment on Dr Lorand's paper "Psycho-analytic therapy of religious devotees." J 1962, 43:56-58
    Abs FTL Q 1963, 32:284

66130 Group I for study of curriculum and diadactic teaching: a sketch of their meeting and their work. (Read at Am Psa Ass, May 1961) J Am Psa Ass 1962, 10:145-152

66131 A pivotal problem revisited: a paper delivered before the Annual Pennsylvania Mental Health Conference, April 29, 1968. 19 p (Multi-lithographed)

ASTRACHAN, BORIS M.

66132 (& McKee, B.) The impact of staff conflict on patient care and behaviour. M 1965, 38:313-320

See Harrow, Martin; Redlich, Frederick C.

ASTRACHAN, JOHN A.

66133 (& Simon, B.) Study of psychosis in a pair of identical twins. Arch gen Psychiat 1963, 8:582-589

ASTRUP, CHRISTIAN

66134 De eksperimentelle dyreneuroser. [Experimental animal neuroses.] Nord Med 1960, 64:1313-1316

66135 (& Sersen, E. A.; Wortis, J.) Further psychophysiological studies of retarded, neurotic, psychotic, and normal children. Recent Adv biol Psychiat 1967, 9:301-312

66136 Suicidene og suicidalforsøkenes psykiske bekgrunn. [The psychological background of suicides and suicide attempts.] Nord Med 1965, 73:405-408

See Ugelstad, Endre

ATHANASSIADES, THOMAS J.

66137 (& McCuskey, J. M., Jr.) The role of maternal rejection in atopic eczema.

ATKIN, SAMUEL

66138 Discussion [in the 1964 symposium on "Vicissitudes of the terminal phase of life."] Psychodyn St Aging 206-211

66139 Discussion of Ekstein, R. "Termination of analysis and working through." Psa Amer 240-246

66140 The fruition of an idea. 50 Yrs Psa 23-29

66141 Psychoanalytic considerations of language and thought. A comparative study. (Read at Am Psa Ass, May 1967; at NY Psa Soc, Sept 1968) Q 1969, 38:549-582

ATKINS, FRANCES

66142 The social meaning of the Oedipus myth. J ind Psych 1966, 22:173-184

ATKINS, NORMAN B.

66143 Acting out and psychosomatic illness as related regressive trends. (Read at Int Cong Psa, July 1967) J 1968, 49:221-223
Abs LHR Q 1969, 38:668

66144 Comments on severe and psychotic regressions in analysis. (Read at Los Angeles Psa Soc, 21 Oct 1965; at Am Psa Ass, Dec 1965) J Am Psa Ass 1967, 15:584-605
Abs Shane, M. Bull Phila Ass Psa 1966, 16:160-162

66145 (Participant) On regression: a workshop. (West Coast Psa Soc, 14-16 Oct 1966) Psa Forum 1967, 2:293-316

ATKINS, ROBERT

See Salzman, Leonard F.

ATTARDO, NETTIE

66146   Psychodynamic factors in mother-child relationship in adolescent drug
        addiction. Psychiat Dig 1966, June:932. In *Proceedings of the VII
        International Congress of Anthropology and Ethnography, Vol. 1,* 1964
66147   Psychodynamic factors in the mother-child relationship in adolescent
        drug addiction: a comparison of mothers of schizophrenics and mothers
        of normal adolescent sons. Psychother Psychosom 1965, 13:249-255
66148   Symbiotic factors in adolescent addiction. J Long Island Consult Center
        1966, 4:30-46

ATWOOD, GEORGE E.

See Golding, Stephen L.

AUBRY, J.

66149   (& Dalloz, J. C.; Stern, A. L.) [Psychosomatic pediatrics: diabetes in-
        sipidus and phobic behavior, suspected cerebral tumor. Clinical and
        psychoanalytical study of diagnostic elements and their significance.]
        (Fr) Rev Méd psychosom 1966, 8:25-37
66150   (& Bargues, R.) [The foster-mothers in a family home for the cure of
        severe emotional deprivation of the early childhood.] (Fr) Évolut psy-
        chiat 1964, 29:411-436
66151   (& Klotz, H. P.; Lacan, J.) [Round table discussion: the place of psy-
        choanalysis in medicine.] (Fr) Cah Coll Med Hop Paris 1966, 7:761-
        774

See Guiton, Micheline

AUDEN, W. H.

66152   For Sigmund Freud (verse). Kenyon Rev 1940, 2:1, 30. With title: In
        Memory of Sigmund Freud. In *The Collected Poems of W. H. Auden,*
        NY: Knopf 1945

AUERBACH, ARTHUR H.

66153   (& Luborsky, L.) Accuracy of judgments of psychotherapy and the
        nature of the "good hour." In Shlien, J. et al: *Research in Psycho-
        therapy, Vol. III,* Wash DC: APA 1968, 155-168
66154   Appendix A: a survey of selected literature on the psychotherapy of
        schizophrenia. In Scheflen, A. E. *A Psychotherapy of Schizophrenia:
        Direct Analysis,* Springfield, Ill: Thomas 1961, 240-268
66155   An application of Strupp's method of content analysis to psychother-
        apy. Ps 1963, 26:137-148

See Gottschalk, Louis A.; Luborsky, Lester

AUERBACK, ALFRED

66156   The psychiatrist looks at professional courtesy. P 1962, 119:520-526
66157   (Ed) Schizophrenia: An Integrated Approach. NY: Ronald Pr 1959,
        224 p
        Rv Laing, R. D. J 1961, 42:478

AUERSPERG, A.

66158 Psychophysiologische Deutung der Schmerzhaftigkeit. [Psychophysiological meaning of pain.] In Lassner, J. *Hypnosis and Psychosomatic Medicine,* Berlin/Heidelberg/NY: Springer 1967, 12-24

See Aguilar, G.

AUERSWALD, EDGAR

See Minuchin, Salvador

AUFREITER, JOHANN

66159 The dilemma with aggression: primary need or consequence of frustration. Canad Psychiat Ass J 1969, 14:493-496
66160 Psychanalyse et état conscient. [Psychoanalysis and the conscious state.] RFPsa 1961, 25:669-680
66161 Psychoanalytic nosology and hysteria: a discussion of Dr. R. A. Cleghorn's paper, "Hysterical personality and conversion: theoretical aspects." Canad Psychiat Ass J 1969, 14:569-571

See Wittkower, Eric D.

AUGENBRAUN, BERNICE

66162 (& Reid, H. L.; Friedman, D. B.) Brief intervention as a preventive force in disorders of early childhood. Ops 1967, 37:697-702
Abs JMa RFPsa 1968, 32:801
66163 (& Tasem, M.) Differential techniques in family interviewing with both parents and preschool child. J Amer Acad Child Psychiat 1966, 5:721-730

See Garwood, Dorothy S.; Mohr, George J.; Selesnick, Sheldon T.; Tasem, Marjorie

AUGENFELD, FELIX

See Gardiner, Muriel M.

TRANSLATIONS OF:
(& Gardiner, M. M.) "The Wolf Man" [95249, 95251, 95253]

AULAGNIER-SPAIRANI, PIERA

66164 (& Clavreul, J.; Perrier, F.; Rosolato, G.; Valabrega, J.-P.) Le Désir et la Perversion. [Desire and Perversion.] Paris: Editions du Seuil 1967, 208 p
66165 [Perversion as structure.] (Fr) Inconscient 1967, (2)
Rv Urtubey, L. de Rev urug Psa 1967, 244-247
66166 Remarques sur la fémininité et ses avatars. [Remarks on femininity and its manifestations.] In author's *Le Désir et la Perversion*

AULD, FRANK, JR.

66167 (& Dollard, J.) Measurement of motivational variables in psychotherapy. Meth Res PT 85-92

66168 (& Goldenberg, G. M.; Weiss, J. V.) Measurement of primary-process thinking in dream reports. J Pers soc Psychol 1968, 8:418-426

S-40923 (& White, A. M.) Sequential dependencies in psychotherapy. In Goldstein, A. P. & Dean, S. J. *The Investigation of Psychotherapy*, NY: Wiley 1966, 342-347

66169 Vicissitudes of communication in psychotherapy. In Shlien, J. M. et al: *Research in Psychotherapy, Vol. III*, Wash DC: APA 1968, 169-178

See Goldenberg, Gary M.

AULL, GERTRUDE JOAN

66170 (& Strean, H. S.) The analyst's silence. Psa Forum 1967, 2:72-80; 86-87
66171 (& Kew, C. E.) Treatment by two therapists. Pastoral Counselor 1966, 4:23-30

AUSTARHEIM, KRISTEN

See Baltrusch, Hans-Joachim

AUSTIN, GEORGE A.

See Brunner, Jerome S.

AUSTIN, V.

See Kraft, Irvin A.

AUSUBEL, DAVID P.

66172 Ego Development and the Personality Disorders. NY: Grune & Stratton 1952, 564 p

66173 Neobehaviorism and Piaget's views on thought and symbolic functioning. Child Develpm 1965, 36:1029-1032

66174 Personality disorder is disease. Am Psych 1961, 16:69-74. In Scheff, T. J. *Mental Illness and Social Processes*, NY: Harper & Row 1967, 254-266

66175 Symbolization and symbolic thought: response to Furth. Child Develpm 1968, 39:997-1001

AVELLA, ARTHUR N.

66176 Prevention of suicide. NYSJM 1966, 66:3023-3025

AVENBURG, RICARDO

66177 Modificaciones estructurales en un paciente esquizofrénico a través del primer mes de análisis. [Structural modifications in a schizophrenic patient through the first month of analysis.] Rev Psicoanál 1962, 19: 351-365

See Liberman, David

AVRAMOVICI, J.

66178 Studiul actelor automate necoordonate (acteratate) în lumina unor date recente de psihologie, neurofiziologie si cibernetică. [The study of incoordinate automatic actions in the light of recent data of psychology, neurophysiology and cybernetics.] Neurol Psichiat Neurochir 1964, 9:401-412

AVROUSKINE, M.

See Assael, M.

AXELRAD, SIDNEY

S-40938 Comments on anthropology and the study of complex cultures. Abs An Surv Psa 1955, 6:418-420

66179 Infant care and personality reconsidered: a rejoinder to Orlansky. Psa St Soc 1962, 2:75-132

66180 Juvenile delinquency: a study of the relationship between psychoanalysis and sociology. Smith Coll Stud soc Wk 1965, 35:89-109

See Brody, Sylvia; Muensterberger, Warner

REVIEWS OF:
66181 Hsu, F. L. K. (Ed) Psychological Anthropology. Q 1963, 32:278-280
66182 Sullivan, H. S. The Fusion of Psychiatry and Social Science. Q 1968, 37:141-142

AXLINE, R. V.

See Gottheil, Edward

AXLINE, VIRGINIA M.

66183 Accepting the child completely. In Haworth, M. R. *Child Psychotherapy*, NY/London: Basic Books 1964, 239-242

66184 Dibs: In Search of Self. London: Gollancz 1966; NY: Ballantine Books 1967, 186 p

66185 The eight basic principles. In Haworth, M. R. *Child Psychotherapy*, NY/London: Basic Books 1964, 93-94

66186 Establishing rapport. In Haworth, M. R. *Child Psychotherapy*, NY/London: Basic Books 1964, 95-101

66187 Nondirective therapy. In Haworth, M. R. *Child Psychotherapy*, NY/London: Basic Books 1964, 34-39

66188 Recognition and reflection of feelings. In Haworth, M. R. *Child Psychotherapy*, NY/London: Basic Books 1964, 262-264

AXTELL, BRYAN

66189 Symbolic representation of an unresolved oedipal conflict: Gulliver in Lilliput. Psychology 1967, 4:22-23

AYRES, CONRAD M.

66190 Clinical hypnosis. Dis nerv Sys 1961, 22(4, Suppl):116-117

AZIMA, FERN J.

See Azima, Hassan

AZIMA, HASSAN

66191 (& Warnes, H.) Anaclitic therapy: discussion of theory and techniques of treatments based upon the concept of regression. Top Probl PT 1963, 4:58-69

S-40955 (& Wittkower, E. D.) Anaclitic therapy employing drugs: a case of spider phobia with Isakower phenomenon.
Abs AHM An Surv Psa 1957, 8:284-285

66192 (& Vispo, R. H.; McKenna, R.) Anaclitic therapy induced by drugs. Comprehen Psychiat 1961, 2:281-293

66193 (& Vispo, R. H.; McKenna, R.) Drug induced anaclitic situation. Recent Adv biol Psychiat 1961, 3:183

66194 Dynamic occupational therapy. Dis nerv Sys 1961, 22(4, Suppl):138-142

S-40957 (& Wittkower, E. D.) Gratifications of basic needs in treatment of schizophrenics.
Abs Shapiro, P. An Surv Psa 1956, 7:362

66195 (& Lemieux, M.; Azima, F. J.) Isolement sensoriel: étude psychopathologique et psychanalytique de la regression et du schema corporel. [Sensory isolation: a psychopathological and psychoanalytical study of regression and physique.] Évolut psychiat 1962, 27:259-280
Abs Auth Rev Psicoanál 1963, 20:85

66196 Object relations therapy of schizophrenic states: technique and theory. Psychiat Res Rep 1963, 17:30-39

66197 (& Vispo, P.; Azima, F. J.) Observations on anaclitic therapy during sensory deprivation. In Solomon, P. et al: *Sensory Deprivation,* Cambridge, Mass: Harvard Univ Pr 1961, 143-160

66198 (& Sarwer-Foner, G. J.) Psychoanalytic formulations of the effects of drugs in pharmacotherapy. Rev Canad Biol 1961, 20:603-614

66199 Psychodynamic alterations concomitant Tofranil administration. Canad Psychiat Ass J 1959, 4 (Spec Suppl):172-181

66200 Psychodynamic and psychotherapeutic problems in connection with imipramine (Tofranil) intake. JMS 1961, 107:74-82

66201 (& Glueck, B. C., Jr.) Psychotherapy of Schizophrenic and Manic-Depressive States. Contributions of Basic Sciences to Psychiatry: Definitive Statements and Future Problems. (Psychiat Res Rep #17) Wash DC: Amer Psychiat Ass 1963, 175 p

66202 Psylocybin disorganization. Recent Adv biol Psychiat 1963, 5:184-198

See Wittkower, Eric D.

AZRIN, A. H.

66203 (et al) Pain-aggression toward inanimate objects. J exp Anal Behav 1964, 7:223-228

AZRIN, NATHAN H.

66204 (& Lindsley, O. R.) The reinforcement of cooperation between children. ASP 1956, 52:100-102. In Dulany, D. E. et al: *Contributions to Modern Psychology,* NY: Oxford Univ Pr 1958, 141-146; (2nd ed) 1963, 157-162. In Ullman, L. P. & Krasner, L. *Case Studies in Be-*

havior Modification, NY: Holt, Rinehart & Winston 1965, 330-333. In Park, R. D. *Readings in Social Development,* NY: Holt, Rinehart & Winston 1968

AZULAY, JACOB DAVID

See Oliveira, Walderedo Ismael de

AZUREK, S. A.

66205 The psychoses of very early life. Int J Psychiat 1967, 3:380-382

B

BAAK, W. W.

66206 (& Clower, C. G.; Kalman, G. J.; Mittel, N. S.; Stern, S.) Therapeutic leadership in milieu treatment. Int J grp PT 1966, 16:163-173

BABA, KENICHI

66207 [The family dynamics of "Schreber case": symposium.] (Jap) Jap J Psa 1968, 14(2):26-31; Discussion 32-34

BABA, REIKO

66208 [The comparative study on the borderline cases with neurotic and schizophrenic patients—psychoanalytic study by Rorschach testing.] (Jap) (Read at Jap Psa Ass, 13 Oct 1963) Jap J Psa 1965, 11(6):2-20; Abs (Eng) 27-28

See Okonogi, Keigo

BABCOCK, CHARLOTTE G.

66209 Inner stress in illness and disability. In Parad, H. J. & Miller, R. R. *Ego-Oriented Casework, Problems and Perspectives*, NY: Fam Serv Ass Am 1963, 45-64

66210 (Reporter) The manifest content of the dream. (Panel: Am Psa Ass, April 1965) J Am Psa Ass 1966, 14:154-171

66211 On some psychodynamic factors in foster parenthood. Part I & II. Child Welfare 1965, 44:485-493, 522; 570-577, 586

66212 Reflections on dependency phenomena as seen in Nisei in the United States. In Smith, R. J. & Beardsley, R. K. *Japanese Culture, Its Development and Characteristics*, Chicago: Aldine Pr 1962, 172-185

66213 Social work as work. Soc Casewk 1953, 34:415-422

See Hunter, Doris M.

BABIGIAN, HAROUTUN M.

66214 (& Gardner, E. A.; Miles, H. C.; Romano, J.) Diagnostic consistency and change in a follow-up study of 1215 patients. P 1965, 121:895-901

See Gardner, Elmer A.; Salzman, Leonard F.

BACAL, H. A.

See Heath, E. Sheldon; Malan, David H.

BACCIAGGLUPPI, MARCO

66215 La psichiatria sociàle: rasségna critica. [Social psychiatry: a critical review.] Arch Psicol Neurol Psichiat 1966, 27:567-582

BACH, GEORGE R.

S-40982 Intensive Group Psychotherapy.
Rv Semrad, E. V. & Day, M. J Am Psa Ass 1966, 14:591-618

See Welch, E. Parl

BACH, HELMUT

S-40985 Analytische Behandlung einer Schizophrenie und einer schizoiden Psychopathie: Vergleich.
Abs Wolff, P. H. An Surv Psa 1957, 8:281

66216 Behandlungsergebnisse und besondere Schwierigkeiten bei der analytischen Psychotherapie eines psychosomatischen Krankheitsbildes (Tetanie). [Results of treatment and special difficulties in the psychoanalytic therapy of a psychosomatic disease picture (Tetany).] Z PSM 1968, 14:188-199

66217 Bemerkungen über die Indikation zur Unterbringung in der Klinik bei ambulanter psychoanalytischer Behandlung von Schizophrenen. [Remarks on the indication for allocation to clinics of schizophrenics in ambulatory psychoanalytical treatment.] Z Psychother med Psychol 1966, 16:94-104

66218 Förderung und Behinderung der natürlichen Reifungstendenzen des Menschen. [Promotion and inhibition of the natural maturation tendencies in man.] Prax Kinderpsychol 1965, 14:33-40

66219 Psychosebehandlungen in Psychiatrischen Institutionen durch niedergelassene Psychotherapeuten. [Treatment of psychoses in psychiatric institutions by practicing psychotherapists.] Z PSM 1967, 13:196-212

66220 Psychosomatische und psychotherapeutische Strömungen in der Medizin unserer Zeit. Konzepte und kritische Reflexion. 9. Zur Psychotherapie der Psychosen. [Psychosomatic and psychotherapeutic trends in current medicine. Concepts and critical reflection. 9. On psychotherapy of psychoses.] Hippokrates 1968, 39:344-349

66221 Das sogenanntepraegenitale Erleben und seine Bedeutung bei der Behandlung einer Angstkranken. [The importance of pregenital feelings in the treatment of a case of anxiety neurosis.] Z PSM 1960, 6:254-261

BACHELARD, GASTON

66222 La Formation de l'Esprit Scientifique, Contribution à une Psychanalyse de la Connaissance Objective. [The Formation of the Scientific Spirit; Contribution to a Psychoanalysis of Objective Knowledge.] (5th ed) Paris: J. Vrin 1967, 257 p

66223 La Psychanalyse de Feu. Paris: Gallimard 1967, 184 p
The Psychoanalysis of Fire. (Tr: Ross, A. C. M.) Boston: Beacon
Pr; London: Routledge 1964, viii + 119 p
Abs Am Im 1965, 22:219

BACHRACH, ARTHUR J.

66224 (Ed) Experimental Foundations of Clinical Psychology. NY: Basic
Books 1962, xii + 641 p

BACK, KURT W.

See Kerckhoff, Allan C.

BACKLAR, MARILYNN

See Call, Justin D.

BACON, CATHERINE LILLIE

S-40988 A developmental theory of female homosexuality. PT Pervers 437-462
66225 Discussion of Kross, A. M. "Woman's role." Sci Psa 1966, 10:127
66226 Discussion of Tabachnick, N. & Litman, R. E. "Character and life
circumstance in fatal accident." Psa Forum 1966, 1:71-72
S-40990 The role of aggression in the asthmatic attack.
Abs SO An Surv Psa 1956, 7:205-206

See English, O. Spurgeon; Hampe, Warren W.; Renneker, Richard E.

BACON, HELEN H.

66227 Woman's two faces: Sophocles' view of the tragedy of Oedipus and his
family. Sci Psa 1966, 10:10-24

BADAL, DANIEL W.

S-40992 Analysis of an anal character.
Abs Cowitz, B. An Surv Psa 1958, 9:170
66228 Comment on Dr. Grinberg's paper, "Two kinds of guilt—their relations
with normal and pathological aspects of mourning." J 1964, 45:371-372
Abs EVN Q 1966, 35:464
66229 Comment on Dr. Scott's paper, "Mania and mourning." J 1964, 45:377-
379
Abs EVN Q 1966, 35:464
66230 Neurocirculatory asthenia. In Conn, H. F. & Conn, R. Current Diagnosis 2, Phila: Saunders 1968
66231 The repetitive cycle in depression. (Read at Am Psa Ass, December
1960) J 1962, 43:133-141
Abs FTL Q 1963, 32:287
66232 Suicide. Bull Acad Med Cleveland 1967, Jan:8-9
66233 Transitional and pre-psychotic symptoms in depression. Bull Phila Ass
Psa 1965, 15:10-25
Abs EFA Q 1966, 35:155. PLe RFPsa 1967, 31:309
66234 Treatment of neurocirculatory asthenia. In Conn, H. F. Current Therapy, Phila: Saunders 1962, 1964

BADER, ALFRED

66235 (& Pasini, W.) [Apropos of the schizoid aspects of certain contemporary art.] (Fr) Confin psychiat 1965, 8:215-222
66236 [Psychiatry and film.] (Fr) Schweiz ANP 1967, 99:138-139

See Müller, Christian

BAER, DONALD M.

66237 An operant view of child behavior problems. Sci Psa 1969, 14:137-146

BAER, PAUL E.

66238 (& Bandura, A.) Behavior theory and identificatory learning. Ops 1963, 33:591-601

BAERWOLFF, H.

66239 One year's experience in psychosomatic group training of general practitioners. Adv Psm Med 189-194

BAEYER, WALTER VON

66240 (& Griffith, R. M.) (Eds) Conditio Humana: Erwin W. Straus on his 75th Birthday. Berlin/Heidelberg/NY: Springer 1966, 337 p
66241 Ein Fall von schizophrenem Schuldwahn (mit Bemerkungen über das Schuldproblem in der Psychopathologie). [A case of schizophrenic delusions of guilt (with remarks on the guilt problem in psychopathology).] In Kranz, H. Psychopathologie Heute, Stuttgart: Georg Thieme 1962, 108-122
66242 (& Hufner, H.) Prinzhorn's Basic Work on the Psychopathology of the "Gestaltung." (6 pages, 16 color plates)
Rv Bychowski, G. Am Im 1966, 23:275-276
66243 Psychische Folgezustände nach schweren Stress-Situationen. [Psychic conditions resulting from severe stress situations.] Proc IV World Cong Psychiat 1966, 905-906

TRANSLATION OF:
(& Selbach, O. C.) Rümke, H. C. [88834]

BAEYER-KATTE, WANDA VON

66244 Nachträgliche Gedanken zu einem Symposion über die psychologischen und sozialen Voraussetzungen des Antisemitismus. [Additional thoughts on a symposium on the psychological and social presuppositions of anti-Semitism.] Psyche 1962, 16:312-317
66245 Die Sprache bei Sigmund Freud. [Language in the work of Sigmund Freud.] Psychother U Med Anthrop 1962, 8:334-349

BAGGETT, ALLEN T., JR.

66246 The effect of early loss of father upon the personality of boys and girls in late adolescence. Diss Abstr 1967, 28:356-357

BAGH, D.

66247 A case of psychoneurosis. Samiksa 1966, 20(3):157-168

BAGRAMOV, E. A.

66248 Burzhuaznaya sotsiologiya i problema "natsional'nogo kharaktera."
[Bourgeois sociology and the problem of "national character."]
Voprosy Filosofi 1964, 18:99-109

BAHIA, ALCYON BAER

66249 Repressão, Lembrança e Amnésia. [Repression, Remembrance, and
Amnesia.] Rio de Janeiro: Ministério da Educação e Cultura 1962,
69 p

BAHN, ANITA K.

66250 (& Conwell, M.; Hurley, P.) Survey of private psychiatric practice.
Report on a field test. Arch gen Psychiat 1965, 12:295-302

See Gardner, Elmer A.; Oleinick, Martha S.

BAHNSON, CLAUS B.

66251 (& Bahnson, M. B.) Cancer as an alternative to psychosis: a theoretical
model of somatic and psychologic regression. In Kissen, D. M. &
LeShan, L. L. *Psychosomatic Aspects of Neoplastic Disease*, London:
Pitman Med Publ; Phila/Montreal: Lippincott 1964, 184-202
66252 (& Bahnson, M. B.) Denial and repression of primitive impulses and
of disturbing emotions in patients with malignant neoplasms. In Kissen,
D. M. & LeShan, L. L. *Psychosomatic Aspects of Neoplastic Disease*,
London: Pitman Med Publ; Phila/Montreal: Lippincott 1964, 42-62
66253 [Psychiatric and psychologic aspects in cancer patients.] (Ger) Verh
Dtsch Ges inn Med 1967, 73:536-550
66254 (& Bahnson, M. B.) Role of the ego defenses: denial and repression in
the etiology of malignant neoplasm. Ann NY Acad Sci 1966, 125:827-
845

See Knapp, Peter H.

BAHNSON, MARJORIE B.

See Bahnson, Claus B.

BAIER, KURT

66255 (& Rescher, N.) (Eds) Values and the Future. The Impact of Tech-
nological Change on American Values. NY: Free Pr 1969

BAIL, BERNARD W.

66256 The psychoanalysis of a bequest: a study in reparation. (Read at Los
Angeles Psa Soc, 16 Dec 1965)
Abs Shane, M. Bull Phila Ass Psa 1966, 16:230-231

See Motto, Rocco L.

BAILEY, DANIEL E.

See Sarbin, Theodore R.

BAILEY, MATTOX A.

66257 (& Berrick, M. E.; Lachmann, F. M.; Ortmeyer, D. H.) Manifest anxiety in psychiatric outpatients. Clin Psych 1960, 16:209-210
66258 (& Warshaw, L.; Eichler, R. M.) A study of factors related to length of stay in psychotherapy. Clin Psych 1959, 15:442-444

See Lachmann, Frank M.

BAILEY, PEARCE

66259 The Psychological Center, Paris—1934. (Read at Otto Rank Ass, 13 May 1967) J Otto Rank Ass 1967, 2(2):10-25
66260 Two brochures from the Psychological Center. J Otto Rank Ass 1967, 2(2):26-29

TRANSLATION OF:
Guillain, G. [75870]

BAILEY, PERCIVAL

S-41023 Janet and Freud.
Abs RZ An Surv Psa 1956, 7:49-50
66261 Pavlov or Freud. Lancet 1961, Part 1:492-493
66262 A rigged radio interview—with illustrations of various ego-ideals. Perspect Biol Med 1961, 4:199-265
66263 Sigmund the Unserene: A Tragedy in Three Acts. (Foreword: Grinker, R. R., Sr.) Springfield, Ill: Thomas 1965, xvii + 127 p

BAIRD, H. W., III

See Harley, R. D.

BAIRD, V. C.

See Knight, James A.

BAITTLE, BRAHM

66264 Current considerations of affect theory and their clinical implications. In "Traditional subjects reconsidered." Proc 2nd Regional Conf Chicago Psa Soc 1968
66265 Discussion of Spiegel, J. P. "The social and psychological dynamics of militant Negro activism: a preliminary report." Sci Psa 1968, 13:155-157
66266 On early infantile precursors in fetishism: a case study. (Read at Chi Psa Soc, 26 Sept 1967)
Abs Beigler, J. S. Bull Phila Ass Psa 1967, 17:245-247
66267 Psychiatric aspects of the development of a street corner group: an exploratory study. Ops 1961, 31:703-712

BAITTLE, MARGERY

See Schlessinger, Nathan

BAK, ROBERT C.

66268　Comments on object relations in schizophrenia and perversions. (Read at NY Psa Soc, 24 Nov 1964)
　　　Abs WAS Q 1965, 34:473-475
66269　Heinz Hartmann—a tribute to the person. Bull Phila Ass Psa 1965, 15:1-3
66270　The phallic woman: the ubiquitous fantasy in perversions. (Read at NY Psa Soc, 27 Feb 1968) Psa St C 1968, 23:15-36
　　　Abs Fine, B. D. Q 1969, 38:516
66271　Sul rapporto oggettuale nella schizofrenia e nelle perversioni. [Current report on schizophrenia and perversions.] Riv Psa 1967, 13:273-277

BAKAN, DAVID

66272　Disease, Pain & Sacrifice; Toward a Psychology of Suffering. Chicago: U of Chicago Pr 1968, x + 134 p
66273　The Duality of Human Existence: An Essay in Psychology and Religion. Chicago: Rand McNally 1966, x + 242 p
66274　Freud and the Zohar. Commentary 1960, 29:65-66
66275　The mystery-mastery complex in contemporary psychology. Am Psych 1965, 20:186-191
66276　On Method: Toward a Reconstruction of Psychological Investigation. San Francisco: Jossey-Bass 1967, xviii + 187 p
66277　Science, mysticism and psychoanalysis. Cath psychol Rec 1966, 4:1-9
66278　Sigmund Freud and the Jewish Mystical Tradition. London: Bailey Bros & Swinfen; NY: Schocken Books 1965, xxi + 326 p
　　　Rv MBr J 1967, 48:470-471
66279　Some thoughts on reading Augustine's "Confessions." J scient Stud Relig 1965, 5:149-152

BAKER, ELLIOT

See Hanfmann, Eugenia

BAKER, ELSWORTH F.

66280　Man in the Trap: The Causes of Blocked Sexual Energy. NY: Collier-Macmillan 1967, xxi + 354 p

BAKER, FRANK

See Schulberg, Herbert C.

BAKER, HOWARD J.

66281　(& Stoller, R. J.) Can a biological force contribute to gender identity? P 1968, 124:1653-1658
66282　(& Stoller, R. J.) Sexual psychopathology in the hypogonadal male. Arch gen Psychiat 1968, 18:631-634

BAKER, LAURA NELSON
See Stoutenburg, Adrien

BAKST, HYMAN
See Kennedy, Janet A.

BALAKIAN, ANNA ELIZABETH

66283 Breton and the surrealist mind—the influences of Freud and Hegel. In author's *Surrealism: The Road to the Absolute*, NY: Noonday, 1959, 91-111

BALCONI, M.

66284 (& Berrini, M. E.; Fornari, E.) Alienation of the human figure and total investment in inanimate objects. Inf Abnorm 1961, 44(Sept-Oct)
   Abs Roi, G. RFPsa 1962, 26:611

See Fornari, Franco

BALDRIDGE, BILL J.

66285 (& Kramer, M.; Whitman, R. M.; Ornstein, P. H.) Self-associations of schizophrenics. Dis nerv Sys 1968, 29(Suppl):124-128

See Kramer, Milton; Whitman, Roy M.

BALDUZZI, E.

66286 (& Alberti, G.) [Italian contributions to psychiatric humanism. 3. Time, space, body.] (It) Riv sper Freniat 1966, 90:527-565

BALDWIN, ALFRED LEE

66287 Theories of Child Development. NY: Wiley 1967

BALDWIN, INGRAM TRYON

66288 Selected interpersonal interactions for regressed schizophrenics. Clin Psych 1965, 21:73-75

BALDWIN, JOHN A.

66289 (& Millar, W. M.) (Eds) Community Psychiatry. (Int Psychiat Clin, Vol. 1, No. 3) Boston: Little, Brown 1964, xii + 501-698

BALFOUR, F. H. G.
See Malan, David H.

BALIER, C.
See Klotz, H. P.

BALINT, ALICE

S-1320 Liebe zur Mutter und Mutterliebe. [Love for the mother and mother love.] Psyche 1962, 16:481-496

See Balint, Michael

BALINT, ENID

S-41051 Drei Phasen einer Übertragungsneurose.
    Abs EW An Surv Psa 1957, 8:260-261

66290   Marital conflicts and their treatment. Comprehen Psychiat 1966, 7:403-407

66291   On being empty of oneself. (Read at Brit Psa Soc, 20 Feb 1963) J 1963, 44:470-480
    Abs Resta, G. Riv Psa 1965, 11:68. EVN Q 1966, 35:309

66292   On the feeling of being empty of oneself. (Read at So Cal Psa Soc, 2 June 1963)
    Abs Peck, J. S. Bull Phila Ass Psa 1963, 13:205-207

66293   The possibilities of patient-centered medicine. J Roy Coll Gen Pract 1969, 17:269-276

66294   Remarks on Freud's metaphors about the "mirror" and the "receiver." Comprehen Psychiat 1968, 9:344-348

66295   Training as an impetus to ego development. Psa Forum 1967, 2:56-62; 69-70

    See Balint, Michael

REVIEW OF:
66296   Barnes, E. (Ed) Psychosocial Nursing: Studies from the Cassel Hospital. J 1969, 50:412-413

BALINT, MICHAEL

66297   The Basic Fault: Therapeutic Aspects of Regression. London: Tavistock 1968, xii + 205 p

66298   The benign and malignant forms of regression. In Daniels, G. E. *New Perspectives in Psychoanalysis.* NY: Grune & Stratton 1965

S-1330 Changing therapeutic aims and techniques in psycho-analysis.
    Abs Agorio, R. Rev urug Psa 1961-62, 4:356

S-41055 The concepts of subject and object in psychoanalysis.
    Abs Frisch, A. An Surv Psa 1958, 9:109-110

S-1331 A contribution on fetishism. PT Pervers 189-191

66299   Discussion of Greenacre, P. & Winnicott, D. W. "The theory of the parent-infant relationship. Further remarks." J 1962, 43:251-252

S-41058 The Doctor, his Patient and the Illness.
    Abs An Surv Psa 1955, 6:359-360

66300   The doctor's responsibility. Med World 1960, 92:529-535

66301   The doctor's therapeutic function. Lancet 1965, (1):1177-1180
    La fonction thérapeutique du médecin. Rev Méd psychosom 1966, 8:145-154

S-41060 Die drei seelischen Bereiche.
    Abs JAL An Surv Psa 1958, 9:69-70

66302   Erfahrungen mit Ausbildungs- und Forschungs- Seminaren. [Experiences with teaching- and research-seminars.] Psyche 1968, 22:679-688

66303   (& Balint, E.; Gosling, R. H.; Hildebrand, P.) The Evaluation of a Training Scheme. London: Tavistock 1965

66304   [Examination of the patient by himself.] (Fr) Rev Méd psychosom 1961, 3:19-26
    Abs RJA Q 1962, 31:435

S-1336 The final goal in psycho-analytic treatment.
Abs Agorio, R. Rev urug Psa 1961-62, 4:359

66305 Foreword to Courtenay, M. *Sexual Discord in Marriage: A Field of Brief Psychotherapy*, London: Tavistock; Phila: Lippincott 1968

66306 Foreword to Friedman, L. J. *Virgin Wives*, London: Tavistock; Springfield, Ill: Thomas 1962

66307 Foreword to Greco, R. S. & Pittenger, R. A. *One Man's Practice*, London: Tavistock 1966

S-41064 Friendly expanses—horrid empty spaces.
Abs An Surv Psa 1955, 6:204-206; 314. Prego, Vida M. de Rev urug Psa 1961-62, 4:557

66308 [How to understand the patient?] (Fr) Rev Méd psychosom 1965, 7:197-211

66309 Letter to the editor [re Vincent Brome's book, *Freud and his Early Circle*]. J 1968, 49:99

66310 Medicine and psychosomatic medicine—new possibilities in training and practice. Comprehen Psychiat 1968, 9:267-274

S-41067 Notes on parapsychology and parapsychological healing.
Abs An Surv Psa 1955, 6:334-335

66311 Obituary: Willi Hoffer 1897-1967. (Read at Brit Psa Soc, 16 Oct 1968) J 1969, 50:262

66312 The other part of medicine. Lancet 1961, (1):40-42

66313 Pädiatrie und Psychotherapie in der ärztlichen Praxis. [Pediatrics and psychotherapy in medical practice.] Hbh Kinderpsychother 1030-1036

66314 Perversionen und Genitalität. [Perversions and genitality.] Psyche 1966, 20:520-528

66315 Der Platz der Psychotherapie in der Medizin. [The place of psychotherapy in medicine.] Psyche 1962, 16:355-373

S-1355A Primary Love, and Psycho-Analytic Technique.
Die Urformen der Liebe und die Technik der Psychoanalyse. Bern, Switzerland: Hans Huber 1965, 357 p
Rv Chazaud, J. RFPsa 1966, 30:504

S-41071 Primary narcissism and primary love.
Primärer Narzissmus und primäre Liebe. Jb Psa 1960, 1:3-34
Narcisismo primario y amor primario. Rev urug Psa 1965, 7:57-92
Abs LDr RFPsa 1961, 25:160. Sapochnik, L. Rev Psicoanál 1961, 18:185

66316 Psycho-analysis and medical practice. (Read at Chicago Inst Psa, 9 Oct 1964; at Melbourne Inst Psa) J 1966, 47:54-62
Psychanalyse et pratique médicale. Rev Méd psychosom 1967, 9:243-257
Abs Korin, S. Rev Psicoanál 1967, 24:952-954. EVN Q 1968, 37:156

66317 (& Balint, E.) Psychotherapeutic Techniques in Medicine. London: Tavistock; Phila: Lippincott 1961; Springfield, Ill: Thomas 1962, xiv + 236 p
Techniques Psychothérapeutiques en Médecine. Paris: Payot 1966
Rv Stewart, H. J 1962, 43:358-359. PLe RFPsa 1964, 28:289-290. Sapir, M. RFPsa 1968, 32:615-619

66318 (& Balint, E.) La psychothérapie par des non-psychiatres. [Psychotherapy by non-psychiatrists.] Rev Méd psychosom 1966, 8:71-79

66319 The pyramid and the psychotherapeutic relationship. Lancet 1961, (2):1051-1054

66320 The regressed patient and his analyst. Ps 1960, 23:231-243
    Der regredierte Patient und sein Analytiker. Psyche 1961, 15:253-273

S-41076 Sexualität und Gesellschaft.
    Abs Richardson, G. A. An Surv Psa 1956, 7:397-399

S-1366 On the termination of analysis.
    Sobre la terminación del análisis. (Tr: Baranger, M.) Rev urug Psa 1961-62, 4:310-317

66321 Die Struktur der "Training-cum-Research"—Gruppen und deren Auswirkungen auf die Medizin. [The structure of "training with research" —groups and their consequences for medicine.] Jb Psa 1968, 5:125-146

66322 (& Balint, E.; Gosling, R.; Hildebrand, P.) A Study of Doctors: Mutual Selection and the Evaluation of Results in a Training Programme for Family Doctors. London: Tavistock; Phila: Lippincott 1966, xii + 146 p

66323 Die technischen Experimente Sandor Ferenczis. Psyche 1966, 20:904-925
    Sandor Ferenczi's technical experiments. Psa Tech 147-167

66324 Therapeutische Regression, Urform der Liebe und die Grundstorung. [Therapeutic regression, primary love and the basic fault.] Psyche 1967, 21:713-727

S-41077 Thrills and Regressions.
    Rv Torok, M. RFPsa 1962, 26:135

S-41079 Training general practitioners in psychotherapy.
    Abs EW An Surv Psa 1958, 9:435-437

66325 Training for psychosomatic medicine. Fortschr PSM 1960, 1:167-179

66326 (& Ball, D. H.; Hare, M. L.) Training medical students in patient-centered medicine. Comprehen Psychiat 1969, 10:249-258
    Unterrichtung von Medizinstudenten in patientenzentrierter Medizin. Psyche 1969, 23:532-546

66327 Trauma and object relationship. J 1969, 50:429-435

S-1368 On transference and counter-transference.
    Abs Agorio, R. Rev urug Psa 1961-62, 4:181

66328 Two forms of regression—benign and malignant. (Read at South Calif Psa Soc, 1 June 1963)
    Abs Peck, J. S. Bull Phila Ass Psa 1963, 13:203-205

66329 Die Verantwortung des Arztes. [The responsibility of doctors.] Psyche 1959, 13:561-573

66330 The younger sister and prince charming. J 1963, 44:226-227
    La hermana menor y el príncipe azul. Rev Psicoanál 1965, 22:10-12
    Abs Gaddini, E. Riv Psa 1965, 11:184. EVN Q 1965, 34:617

66331 Zur neuauflage der "Bausteine zur Psychoanalyse" von Sandor Ferenczi. [On the new edition of "Bausteine zur Psychoanalyse" by Sandor Ferenczi.] Psyche 1967, 21:254-255

66332 Ein Zwischenfall. [An incident.] Jb Psa 1961-62, 2:161-173

REVIEW OF:
66333 Alexander, F. et al (Eds) Psychoanalytic Pioneers. Psa Forum 1968, 2:373-374

BALKANYI, CHARLOTTE

66334 Language, verbalization and superego, some thoughts on the development of the sense of rules. (Read at Psa Ass NY, Apr 1967; Brit Psa Soc, June 1967) J 1968, 49:712-718
Abs Lilleska, R. Q 1968, 37:484-485
66335 Obituary: Lajos Lévy 1875-1961. J 1962, 43:81-82
66336 On verbalization. J 1964, 45:64-74
Abs EVN Q 1966, 35:311
66337 Psychoanalysis of a stammering girl. J 1961, 42:97-109
Abs WPK Q 1962, 31:283

BALL, DOROTHEA H.

See Balint, Michael

BALL, J. R.

66338 (& Armstrong, J. J.) The use of L.S.D. 25 (D-lysergic acid diethylamide) in the treatment of the sexual perversions. Canad Psychiat Ass J 1961, 6:231-235

BALLONI, AUGUSTO

66339 Riflessioni su un caso di tentato suicido allargato. [Reflections on a case of an extended suicide attempt.] Annali di Neurologia e Psichiatria 1966, 60:243-256

See Castellani, A.

BALLY, GUSTAV

66340 Die Bedeutung der Angst für die menschliche Verfassung. [The significance of anxiety for the human state of mind.] Z Psychother med Psychol 1964, 14:123-139
66341 Die Bedeutung des Spiels für Reifen der menschlichen Persönlichkeit. [The meaning of play for the maturing of the human personality.] Hbh Kinderpsychother 40-45
66342 Einführung in die Psychoanalyse Sigmund Freuds. [Introduction to the Psychoanalysis of Sigmund Freud.] Reinbek bei Hamburg: Rowohlt 1961, 297 p
De Psychoanalyse van Sigmund Freud. (Foreword: Uchtenhagen, A.) (Tr: Houwink, R. H.) Utrecht/Antwerp: Het Spectrum 1966, 336 p
66343 Erfahrung und Theorie in der Tiefenpsychologie. [Experience and theory in depth psychology.] Schweiz ANP 1963, 91:103-115
[Spanish] Archivos Panameños de Psicologia 1965, 1:199-215
66344 Ludwig Binswangers Weg zu Freud. [Ludwig Binswanger's way to Freud.] Schweiz Z Psychol 1966, 25:293-308
66345 Die notwendige Interpretation der Anschauungen Freuds. [The necessary interpretation of Freud's observations.] Fortschr Med 1963, 81:914-915
S-41097 Ordnung und Ursprünglichkeit, Zuwendung und Ziel.
Abs An Surv Psa 1955, 6:357-359

66346 Psychoanalysis and social change. Psa 1964, 24:145-152
66347 Sociological aspects of psychoanalysis. Psa 1966, 26:5-19 Bull NY Acad Med 1966, 42:343-355
66348 The sociology of psychoanalysis. (Read at South Calif Psa Soc, 1 Oct 1963)
Abs Peck, J. S. Bull Phila Ass Psa 1964, 14:44-47
66349 Soziologische Aspekte der Tiefenpsychologie. [Sociological aspects of depth psychology.] Nervenarzt 1965, 36:66-70

BALOGH, PENELOPE

66350 Psychoanalysis and psychotherapy: parallels and deviations. Association of Psychotherapists Bulletin 1965, 6:35-42
66351 The psychological aspects of aggression. MAPW Bulletin 1965, 29:10-19

BALSER, BENJAMIN HARRIS

66352 (& Mumford, E.; Chaplan, A.; Gratwick, M.; Mumford, R. S.; Clinton, W.) A mental health study in preparatory schools: proposed plan. Psychol in Schools 1966, 3:6-16
66353 (& Wacker, E.; Gratwick, M.; Mumford, R. S.; Clinton, W.; Balser, P. B.) Predicting mental disturbance in early adolescence. P 1965, 121 (Suppl 12):xi-xix
S-41103 (Ed) Psychotherapy of the Adolescent. NY: IUP 1957, 270 p

BALSER, PAUL B.

See Balser, Benjamin H.

BALTER, LEON

66354 The mother as source of power. A psychoanalytic study of three Greek myths. Q 1969, 38:217-274

BALTRUSCH, EVA

See Baltrusch, Hans-Joachim

BALTRUSCH, HANS-JOACHIM

66355 (& Austarheim, K.; Baltrusch, E.) Psyche—Nervensystem—Neoplastischer Prozess: ein altes Problem mit neuer Aktualität. Teil II: Neutrale Relationen. Teil III: Klinische Beobachtungen und Untersuchungen zur Psychosomatik der Krebskrankheit mit vorzugsweise psychoanalytischer Methodik. [Psyche—nervous system—neoplastic process: an old problem with new timeliness. Part II: Neutral relations. Part III: Clinical observations and studies on the psychosomatic aspects of cancer with prevalent psychoanalytic and psychosomatic methodology.] Z PSM 1963, 9:229-245; 1964, 10:1-10; 157-169

BAN, THOMAS

See Cameron, D. Ewen; Lehmann, Heinz Edgar

BAND, RAYMOND ISAAC

66356 (& Brody, E. B.) Human elements of the therapeutic community: a study of the conflicting values and attitudes of people upon whom patients must be dependent. Arch gen Psychiat 1962, 6:307-314

BANDINI, TULLIO

See Canepa, Giacomo

BANDLER, BERNARD

66357 The American Psychoanalytic Association and community psychiatry. P 1968, 124:1037-1042
66358 Development of an inpatient service. Int Psychiat Clin 1966, 3(3):3-10
66359 Discussant of "Medical Education." Teach Dyn Psychiat 56-62
66360 Evolution of a community mental health center. Int Psychiat Clin 1966, 3(3):249-266
* * * Foreword to Pavenstedt, E. (Ed) *The Drifters.*
66361 Introduction to Summary Report of the Preparatory Commission on Content. In Early, L. W. et al: *Teaching Psychiatry in Medical School,* Wash DC: Am Psychiat Ass 1969, 306-309
66362 Opening remarks. [Symposium on a developmental approach to problems of acting out.] J Amer Acad Child Psychiat 1963, 2:4-5
66363 (Ed) Psychiatry in the General Hospital. (Int Psychiat Clin, Vol. 3, No. 3) Boston: Little, Brown 1966, xii + 275 p
       Rv Brody, M. W. Q 1969, 38:151-152
S-41115 (& Kaufman, I. C.; Dykens, J. W.; Schleifer, M. M.; Shapiro, L. N.; Arico, J. F.) Role of sexuality in epilepsy: hypnosis; analysis of two seizures.
       Abs RSB An Surv Psa 1958, 9:209-210
S-41118 Some conceptual tendencies in the psychosomatic movement.
       Abs SO An Surv Psa 1958, 9:55-57

BANDLER, LOUISE S.

66364 Casework—a process of socialization: gains, limitations, conclusions. Int Psychiat Clin 1967, 4(4):255-296
66365 Family functioning: a psychosocial perspective. Int Psychiat Clin 1967, 4(4):225-253

BANDURA, ALBERT

66366 (& Walters, R. H.) Aggression. Nat Soc Study of Educ Yrbk 1962, Part I, 1963:364-415
66367 (& Ross, D.; Ross, S. A.) A comparative test of the status envy, social power, and secondary reinforcement theories of identificatory learning. ASP 1963, 67:527-534. In Rosenblith, J. F. & Allinsmith, W. *The Causes of Behavior,* Boston: Allyn & Bacon 1966, 159-166
66368 (& Menlove, F. L.) Factors determining vicarious extinction of avoidance behavior through symbolic modeling. J Pers soc Psychol 1968, 8:99-108
66369 (& Huston, A. C.) Identification as a process of incidental learning. ASP 1961, 63:311-318

66370 (& Whalen, C. K.) The influence of antecedent reinforcement and divergent modeling cues on patterns of self-reward. J Pers soc Psychol 1966, 3:373-382

66371 (& Mischel, W.) Modification of self-imposed delay of reward through exposure to live and symbolic models. J Pers soc Psychol 1965, 2:698-705. In Rosenblith, J. F. & Allinsmith, W. *The Causes of Behavior*, Boston: Allyn & Bacon 1966, 437-444

66372 (& Grusec, J. E.; Menlove, F. L.) Observational learning as a function of symbolization and incentive set. Child Develpm 1966, 37:499-506

66373 On empirical disconfirmations of equivocal deductions with insufficient data. J consult clin Psychol 1968, 32:247-249

S-41123 (& Lipsher, D. H.; Miller, P. E.) Psychotherapists' approach-avoidance reactions to patients' expressions of hostility. J consult Psychol 1960, 24:1-8. In Goldstein, A. P. & Dean, S. J. *The Investigation of Psychotherapy*, NY: Wiley 1966, 271-278

66374 Psychotherapy as a learning process. Psychol Bull 1961, 58:143-159

66375 (& Perloff, B.) Relative efficacy of self-monitored and externally imposed reinforcement systems. J Pers soc Psychol 1967, 7:111-116

66376 (& Grusec, J. E.; Menlove, F. L.) Some social determinants of self-monitoring reinforcement systems. J Pers soc Psychol 1967, 5:449-455

66377 (& Ross, D.; Ross, S. A.) Transmission of aggression through imitation of aggressive models. ASP 1961, 63:575-582

66378 (& Grusec, J. E.; Menlove, F. L.) Vicarious extinction of avoidance behavior. J Pers soc Psychol 1967, 5:16-23

See Baer, Paul E.; Winder, Clarence L.

BANERJEE, SARADINDU

66379 Concept of ego in Freud and Hartmann. Samiksa 1966, 20(4):226

66380 Observations on psychoanalysis and existentialism. Samiksa 1968, 22(2):50-72

BANG, RUTH

66381 (Ed) Sexuelle Fehlhaltungen. [Sexual Deviations.] Munich/Basel: Ernst Reinhardt Verlag 1966

BANG, VINH

See Piaget, Jean

BANKIER, ROBERT GORDON

66382 Capgras' syndrome: the illusion of doubles. Canad Psychiat Ass J 1966, 11:426-429

BANKS, ALBERT LAWRENCE

See Rutherford, Robert N.

BANKS, HUGH CHRISTOPHER

66383 The relationship of the flexibility of ego defenses to the rate of recovery in tuberculosis patients. Diss Abstr 1963, 24(2):830

BANKS, ROBIN

See Cappon, Daniel

BANKS, SAMUEL A.

66384 Psychotherapy: values in action. Int Psychiat Clin 1965, 2:497-514

BANKS, SAMUEL H.

See Barnard, George W.

BANNISTER, DONALD

66385 (& Salmon, P.) Schizophrenic thought disorder: specific or diffuse?
M 1966, 39:215-219

See Willis, J. H.

BANNISTER, K.

66386 (& Pincus, L.) Shared Phantasy in Marital Problems: Therapy in a
Four-Person Relationship. London: Tavistock 1965, 77 p

BARACCHINI, G.

See Carlo Giannini, G. del

BARACH, A. L.

66387 The impulse to yield—a contemporary evaluation of an instinctive
drive. J Amer Geriat Soc 1963, 11:228-234
66388 In defense of Promethean anxieties. The Promethean hazard of creativity compared to nonfruitful endemic anxiety. J Amer Geriat Soc
1967, 15:1096-1113

BARAD, MARTIN

66389 (& Altshuler, K. E.; Goldfarb, A. I.) A survey of dreams in the aged.
Arch gen Psychiat 1961, 4:419-424

See Altshuler, Kenneth Z.

BARAG, D.

66390 [The snake and the scorpion in the ancient east.] (Heb) Dapim
Refuiim 1962, 21:730-732

BARAG, GERDA

66391 Psychiatric disturbances of holocaust ("Shoa") survivors. (Read at
Israel Psa Soc, 9 July 1966) Israel Ann Psychiat 1967, 5(1)

BARAHAL, HYMAN S.

66392 Auto-interpretation of dreams and art productions. Hypnoanalysis of a
case of amnesia. Psychiat Q 1967, 41:607-630
66393 Psychodynamic approach to psychoneurosis. NYSJM 1967, 67:1737-
1744

BARAHONA FERNANDES, H. J. DE

66394   Nicolai Hartmann und die Psychopathologie. [Nicolai Hartmann and psychopathology.] In Kranz, H. *Psychopathologie Heute*, Stuttgart: Thieme 1962, 6-10

66395   Le test psychosomatique de l'ischémie. [The psychosomatic test for ischemia.] In Lassner, J. *Hypnosis and Psychosomatic Medicine*, Berlin/Heidelberg/NY: Springer 1967, 25-28

BARAJAS CASTRO, RAFAEL

S-41137 Analyse d'un rêve apporté au début d'un traitement.
        Abs TC An Surv Psa 1957, 8:175-176

66396   El padre, la filiación, la identidad. [The father, the filial relationship, and identity.] Cuad Psa 1965, 1:179-188

66397   Reflexiones sobre el tratamento clásico. [Thoughts on classical treatment.] Cuad Psa 1966, 2:39-44

BARANDE, ILSE

66398   Commentaire (sur la régression). [Commentary (on regression).] RFPsa 1966, 30:485-489

66399   Intégration et régression. [Integration and regression.] RFPsa 1966, 30:470-472

66400   Lecture des "Mémoires" de Schreber. [On reading the Schreber memoirs.] RFPsa 1966, 30:27-39

66401   Le vu et l'entendu dans la cure. [Sight and insight in healing.] RFPsa 1968, 32:67-96

See Barande, Robert

ABSTRACTS OF:

66402   Berna, J. Die Indikations zur Kinderanalyse. RFPsa 1964, 28:464

66403   Bruckner, P. Sigmund Freud Privatlektüre. RFPsa 1964, 28:462

66404   Cajiano, R. G. Die Forschungsarbeit in der Gruppentherapie, ihre Probleme, Methoden und Aufgaben. RFPsa 1962, 26:622

66405   Ezriel, H. Übertragung und psychoanalytische Deutung in der Einzel- und Gruppen-Therapie. RFPsa 1962, 26:622

66406   Furman, E. Some features of the dream function of a severely disturbed young child. RFPsa 1964, 28:455

66407   Greenson, R. R. On enthusiasm. RFPsa 1964, 28:453

66408   Harley, M. The role of the dream in the analysis of a latency child. RFPsa 1964, 28:455

66409   Herbert, E. L. Die Anwendung von Gruppen-Verfahren in der Lehrerbildung. RFPsa 1962, 26:620

66410   Hochheimer, W. Probleme einer politischen Psychologie. RFPsa 1964, 28:462

66411   Keiser, S. Disturbance of ego functions of specific and abstract thinking. RFPsa 1964, 28:454

66412   Kuiper, P. C. Betrachtungen über die psychoanalytische Technik bei der Behandlung neurotischer Patientinnen. RFPsa 1964, 28:461

66413   Lampl de Groot, J. Die Behandlungstechnik bei neurotischen Patientinnen. RFPsa 1964, 28:462

66414 Loch, W. Zur Problematik des Seelenbegriffes in der Psychoanalyse. RFPsa 1962, 26:624

66415 Loch, W. Schulpsychiatrie. Psychoanalyse in Konvergenz? RFPsa 1962, 26:620

66416 Meyer, A. E. & Staewen, R. Beobachtungen über Analysenverläufe bei nicht-indizierten Therapeutenwechsel. RFPsa 1962, 26:626

66417 Merian, D. Phantasiegeschichten in der Kindertherapie. RFPsa 1964, 28:464

66418 Mitscherlich, A. Anmerkungen über die Chronifizierung psychosomatischen Geschehens. RFPsa 1962, 26:621

66419 Mitscherlich-Nielsen, M. Besonderheiten der Behandlungstechnik bei neurotischen Patientinnen. RFPsa 1964, 28:462

66420 Moser, U. Übertragungsproblem in der Psychoanalyse eines chronisch schwergenden Charakterneurotikers. RFPsa 1964, 28:460

66421 Norman, E. "Unglück steckt an": ein besonderer Aspekt in der Lehrerbildung. RFPsa 1962, 26:620

66422 Root, N. N. Some remarks on anxiety dreams in latency and adolescence. RFPsa 1964, 28:456

66423 Rosenfeld, E. M. Analyse einer Angsthysterie, nach 21 Jahren kritisch betrachtet. RFPsa 1964, 28:463

66424 Rosenfeld, H. A. Über Rauschgiftsucht. RFPsa 1962, 26:621

66425 Scheunert, G. Die Abstinenzregel in der Psychoanalyse. RFPsa 1962, 26:626

66426 Searles, H. F. The differentiation between concrete and metaphorical thinking in the recovering schizophrenic patient. RFPsa 1964, 28:454

66427 Winnik, H. Z. Bemerkungen zu einem tanatophilen Aspekt des Masochismus. RFPsa 1964, 28:461

66428 Zulliger, H. Heilende Kräfte im kindlichen Spiel. RFPsa 1962, 26:144

BARANDE, ROBERT

66429 À la recherche du processus psychanalytique. [On research into the psychoanalytic process.] Interprétation 1969

66430 À propos d'une prédiction de Freud et de ses avatars. [On a prediction of Freud and his worshippers.] RFPsa 1966, 30:807-811

66431 L'angoisse névrotique. [Neurotic anxiety.] Certificat de Neuro-Psychiatrie, 1960-61.

66432 Aperçu clinique de la dépression névrotique. [Clinical survey of neurotic depression.] Perspectives psychiat 1963, (3)

66433 Discussion of Fornari, F. "La psychanalyse de la guerre." RFPsa 1966, 30(Suppl):285-288

66434 Discussion of Rouart, J. "Investment and counterinvestment." RFPsa 1967, 31:241-242

66435 Discussion of Viderman, S. "Régression et situation analytique." RFPsa 1966, 30:483-484

66436 Du temps d'un silence. Approche technique, contre-transférentielle et psychodynamique. [Of silence and its time. A technical approach. Countertransference and psychodynamics.] RFPsa 1961, 25:177-220 Abs RFA Q 1962, 31:139

66437 La Dynamique du Couple. [The dynamics of the couple.] Ecole d'Assistantes Sociales, Vitry, Nov 1961

66438   Essai métapsychologique sur le silence: de l'objet total phallique dans
        la clinique du silence. [Metapsychological essay on silence: on the
        total phallic object in the clinic of silence.] RFPsa 1963, 27:53-115
           Abs Donadeo, J. Q 1964, 33:613
66439   L'inachièvement de l'analyse: loi biologique ou contre-transfert. [Non-
        achievement of analysis: biologic law or countertransference?] RFPsa
        1968, 32:263-272
66440   L'inachièvement de l'homme comme structure de son temps. [Man's
        lack of achievement as the measure of his times.] RFPsa 1965, 29:281-
        303
           Abs Nascimbene, T. Riv Psa 1966, 12:329-331
66441   Mélanie Klein parmi nous? [Melanie Klein among us?] Inconscient
        1969
66442   Pathologie de la vie amoureuse. [Pathology of love life.] Traité Psa
        1965, 1
66443   Le problème de la regression. Essai critique sur l'histoire et les vicis-
        situdes de l'hypothèse freudienne. [The problem of regression. Critical
        essay on the history and the vicissitudes of the Freudian hypothesis.]
        RFPsa 1966, 30:349-420
66444   Problèmes cliniques et techniques du contre-transfert. [Clinical and
        technical problems of countertransference.] RFPsa 1963, 27(Suppl):
        229-232
66445   Psychothérapies de la pratique courante. [Psychotherapies in current
        practice.] In L'Encyclopedie Medico-Chirurgicale 1966, Nov, 37 810
        C10
66446   La "pulsion de mort" comme nontransgression: survie et transfiguration
        du tabou de l'inceste. [The "death-drive" as nontransgression: survival
        and transfiguration of the incest taboo.] RFPsa 1968, 32:465-502
66447   Remarques sur la relation analytique concue comme "passage à l'acte
        incestueux" et ses effets sur le personnage de l'analyste dans son champ
        professionnel. [Remarks on the analytic relation conceived as "passage
        to the incestuous act" ("passage to the first act") and its effects
        ("passages to the second acts") notably on the personage of the analyst
        in his professional field.] RFPsa 1968, 32:1077-1084
66448   (& Barande, I.; Dalibard, Y.) Remarques sur le narcissisme dans le
        mouvement de la cure. [Remarks on narcissism in the movement of
        therapy.] RFPsa 1965, 29:601-611
66449   Revue critique sur les troubles du sommeil chez l'enfant. [Critical sur-
        vey on the problems of sleep of the infant.] Psychiat Enfant 1959, 1(2)
66450   Structure et mécanisme de défense névrotique. [Structure and mechan-
        ism of neurotic defense.] Traité Psa 1965, 1
66451   Le suicide en psychiatrie. [Suicide in psychiatry.] Problèmes 1959, May

REVIEW OF:
66452   Grinberg, L. et al: Psicoterapia del Grupo su Enfoque Psicoanalitica.
        RFPsa 1962, 26:138

BARANGER, MADELEINE

66453   El "insight" en la situación analitica. ["Insight" in the psychoanalytic
        situaton.] Rev urug Psa 1964, 6:19-38

66454 (& Baranger, W.) Insight in the analytic situation. Psa Amer 56-72
66455 (& Baranger, W.; Fernandez, A.; Garbarino, M. F. de; Mendilaharsu, S. A. de; Nieto, M.) Mecanismos hipocondriacos "normales" en el desarrollo femenino. ["Normal" hypochondriac mechanisms in feminine development.] Rev urug Psa 1961-62, 4:3-54
66456 (& Baranger, W.) La situación como campo dinámico. [The analytic situation.] Rev urug Psa 1964, 6:19-38
      Abs Vega 1962, 31:593-594

TRANSLATIONS OF:
Balint, M. [1366]. Klein, M. [18472]. Rosenfeld, H. [57498]

ABSTRACTS OF:
66457 Bridger, H. Criteria for the termination of analysis. Rev urug Psa 1961-62, 4:366
66458 Britzer, J. R. & Murray, J. M. On the transformation of early narcissism during pregnancy. Rev urug Psa 1965, 7:104
66459 Buxbaum, E. Technique of terminating analysis. Rev urug Psa 1961-62, 4:367
66460 Greenacre, P. Certain technical problems in the transference relationship. Rev urug Psa 1961-62, 4:198
66461 Grunberger, B. Préliminaires à une étude topique du narcissisme. Rev urug Psa 1965, 7:105
66462 Hoffer, W. Three psychological criteria for the termination of treatment. Rev urug Psa 1961-62, 4:363
66463 Little, M. Counter-transference and the patient's response to it. Rev urug Psa 1961-62, 4:194
66464 Little, M. On delusional transference (transference psychosis). Rev urug Psa 1961-62, 4:191
66465 Milner, M. A note on the ending of an analysis. Rev urug Psa 1961-62, 4:361
66466 Payne, S. Short communication on criteria for terminating analysis. Rev urug Psa 1961-62, 4:363
66467 Reich, A. On counter-transference. Rev urug Psa 1961-62, 4:188
66468 Reich, A. On the termination of analysis. Rev urug Psa 1961-62, 4:364

REVIEWS OF:
66469 Kemper, W. W. New Phylogenetic Contributions to the Psychology of Women. Rev urug Psa 1964, 6:509-514
66470 Luquet-Parat, C. J. Le Changement d'Objet. Rev urug Psa 1964, 6:514-517

BARANGER, WILLY

66471 Aspectos problemáticos de la teoría de los objetos en la obra de Melanie Klein. [Problematic aspects of the theory of objects according to the works of Melanie Klein.] Rev Psicoanál 1962, 19:14-19
66472 Discussion of Liberman, D. "Entropy and information in the therapeutic process." Rev Psicoanál 1967, 24:63-65
S-41147 The ego and the function of ideology.
      Abs GLG An Surv Psa 1958, 9:126-127

66473   (& Garbaríno, H.) La enfermedad infantil del psicoanálisis. [The "infantile illness" of psychoanalysis.] Rev Psicoanál 1961, 18:12-17
        Abs Vega Q 1962, 31:591-592
66474   El enfoque economico de Freud a Melanie Klein. [An economic clarification of Freud and Melanie Klein.] Rev Psicoanál 1968, 25:297-344
S-41149 Interpretación e ideología (sobre la regla de abstención ideológica).
        Abs RHB An Surv Psa 1957, 8:255
66475   El muerto-vivo. Estructura de los objetos en el duelo y los estados depresivos. [The dehumanization of body ego (dead-living partial objects).] Rev urug Psa 1961-62, 4:586-603
        Abs Vega Q 1964, 33:147
66476   La noción de "material" y el aspecto temporal prospectivo de la interpretación. [The notion of "material" and the prospective temporal aspect of the interpretation.] Rev urug Psa 1961-62, 4:215-251
S-41151 Notas acerca del concepto de fantasía inconsciente.
        Abs Vega An Surv Psa 1956, 7:83
66477   (& Mom, J.) Sintesis final de los relatos y discusiones sobre material clinico en el VI Congreso Psicanalitico Latinamericano. [Synthesis of clinical material presented and discussed at the Sixth Psychoanalytic Congress of Latin America.] Rev urug Psa 1968, 8:347-362
        Abs Vega Q 1968, 37:633

        See Baranger, Madeleine; Koolhaas, Gilberto; Muñoz, Jorge G.

ABSTRACTS OF:
66478   Lagache, D. Sur le polyglottisme dans l'analyse. Rev urug Psa 1961-62, 4:369
66479   Lewin, B. The analytic situation: topographic considerations. Rev urug Psa 1961-62, 4:369
66480   Loewenstein, R. Some remarks on the role of speech in psychoanalytic technique. Rev urug Psa 1961-62, 4:370
66481   Renard, M. The Freudian conception of narcissistic neurosis. Rev urug Psa 1963, 5:467
66482   Rodrigué, E. Notes on menstruation. Rev urug Psa 1964, 6:522
66483   Weissman, P. Psychosexual development in a case of neurotic virginity and old maidenhood. Rev urug Psa 1964, 6:523-525

REVIEW OF:
66484   Racker, H. Estudios sobre Técnica Psicoanalítica. Rev urug Psa 1961-62, 4:164

BARATGIN, A.

REVIEW OF:
66485   Bowlby, J. Maternal Care and Mental Health. RFPsa 1962, 26:136

BARBARA, DOMINICK A.

66486   Emotional factors in communicating. Psa 1962, 22:93-98
66487   (& Goldart, N.; Oram, C.) Group psychoanalysis with adult stutterers. Psa 1961, 21:40-57

66488 (Ed) New Directions in Stuttering: Theory and Practice. Springfield,
       Ill.: Thomas 1965, ix + 188 p
66489 (Ed) Psychological and Psychiatric Aspects of Speech and Hearing.
       Springfield, Ill.: Thomas 1960, xii + 776 p
66490 (Ed) The Psychotherapy of Stuttering. Springfield, Ill.: Thomas 1962,
       x + 269 p
66491 The psychotherapy of stuttering. Curr psychiat Ther 1963, 3:114-123
66492 Questions and Answers on Stuttering. Springfield, Ill.: Thomas 1965,
       vii + 102 p

BARBER, C. L.

66493 The death of Zenocrate: "conceiving and subduing both" in Marlowe's
       Tamburlaine. Lit & Psych 1966, 16:15-24

BARBER, THEODORE XENOPHON

66494 Death by suggestion: a critical note. PSM 1961, 23:153-155
       Abs JPG Q 1961, 30:603
66495 (& Calverley, D. S.) Effects on recall of hypnotic induction, motivation-
       al suggestions, and suggested regression: a methodological and experi-
       mental analysis. JAbP 1966, 71:169-180
66496 Hypnotic age regression: a critical review. PSM 1962, 24:286-299
       Abs RDT Q 1963, 32:291
66497 Toward a theory of hypnosis: posthypnotic behavior. Arch gen Psychiat
       1962, 7:321-342
       Abs KR Q 1964, 33:140
66498 Toward a theory of "hypnotic" behavior: the "hypnotically induced
       dream." JNMD 1962, 135:206-221. In Moss, C. S. *The Hypnotic In-
       vestigation of Dreams*, NY/London/Sydney: Wiley 1967, 214-235

BARBU, ZEVEDEI

66499 Problems of Historical Psychology. NY: Grove 1960, vii + 222 p

BARCAI, AVNER

66500 "But who listens"—therapeutic values of replayed tape recorded inter-
       views. PT 1967, 21:286-294
66501 The therapeutic utilization of defense mechanisms: rapid improvement
       in in-patients. Psychotherapy 1967, 4:155-158

       See Minuchin, Salvador

BARCHILON, JOSE

66502 Analysis of a woman with incipient rheumatoid arthritis. A contribu-
       tion to the understanding of somatic equivalents of withdrawal into
       sleep. (Read at Am Psa Ass, 5 May 1962) J 1963, 44:163-177
       Abs Gaddini, E. Riv Psa 1965, 11:75. EVN Q 1965, 34:615
66503 Development of artistic stylization: a two-year evolution in the draw-
       ings of a normal child. (Read at Am Psa Ass, May 1964) Psa St C
       1964, 19:256-274
66504 Emotions and respiration. Conference on regulation and respiration.
       Ann NY Acad Sci 1963, 109:619-630

66505 The Fall. (Read at Chicago Psa Soc, 25 Oct 1966)
       Abs Beigler, J. S. Bull Phila Ass Psa 1967, 17:106-111
66506 *The Fall* by Albert Camus: a psychoanalytic study. (Read at Int Psa
       Cong, July 1967) J 1968, 49:386-389
66507 (& Kovel, J. S.) Huckleberry Finn: a psychoanalytic study. (Read at
       Am Psa Ass, May 1965; Phila Ass Psa, 11 Feb 1966) J Am Psa Ass
       1966, 14:775-814
       Abs Magran, L. & Resnick, A. B. Bull Phila Ass Psa 1966, 16:163-167
66508 Introduction to Foucault, M. *Madness and Civilization: A History of
       Insanity in the Age of Reason,* NY: Pantheon Books 1965
S-41165 On countertransference "cures."
       Abs AL An Surv Psa 1958, 9:400-401
66509 Psychiatric teaching models, old and new. In Early, L. W. et al:
       Teaching Psychiatry in Medical School, Wash DC: Am Psychiat Ass
       1969, 333-347
66510 Some unconscious aspects of the different teaching methods. NY:
       Proc 3rd Onchiota Conf, Albert Einstein College 1963, 3:27-43

       See Rosenbaum, Milton

ABSTRACTS OF:
66511 Baudoin, C. Freud et la dialectique de l'exogène et de l'endogène. An
       Surv Psa 1956, 7:13-14
66512 Kouretas, D. Psychanalyse et mythologie: la névrose sexuelle des
       Dandaïdes. An Surv Psa 1957, 8:310
66513 Lacombe, P. Réactions inconscientes au conflit international du Canal
       de Suez. An Surv Psa 1957, 8:319-320
66514 Lechat, F. Autour du principe du plaisir. An Surv Psa 1957, 8:30-31
66515 Loewenstein, R. M. Réflexions sur le traitement d'un cas de névrose
       compulsionelle. An Surv Psa 1956, 7:322-324
66516 Nacht, S. Instinct de mort ou instinct de vie? An Surv Psa 1956,
       7:52-53
66517 Pasche, F. Autour de quelques propositions freudiennes contestées. An
       Surv Psa 1956, 7:53-55
66518 Racker, H. Considérations psychanalytique sur le Cocu Magnifique de
       F. Crommelynck. An Surv Psa 1957, 8:344-345
66519 Shentoub, S. A. De quelques problèmes dans l'homosexualité mascu-
       line active: fragment d'analyse. An Surv Psa 1957, 8:134-135

REVIEW OF:
66520 Racker, H. Estudios sobre Técnica Psicoanalitica. Q 1963, 32:427-431

BARCLAY, ALLAN GENE

66521 (& Cusumano, D. R.) Father absence, cross-sex identity, and field-
       dependent behavior in male adolescents. Child Develpm 1967, 38:243-
       250

       See Thaman, Audrey M.

BARCLAY, ANDREW M.

66522 (& Haber, R. N.) The relation of aggressive to sexual motivation. J
       Pers 1965, 33:462-475

BARCLAY, JAMES R.

66523 Franz Brentano and Sigmund Freud. J existent Psychiat 1964-65, 5:1-36

BARD, J. A.

See Wittenbrook, John M.

BARDON, E. J.

66524 Transference reactions to the relationship between male and female co-therapists in group psychotherapy. J Amer Coll Health Ass 1966, 14:287-289

BARDON, JACK I.

66525 (& Bennett, V. D. C.) Preparation for professional psychology: an example from a school psychology training program. Am Psych 1967, 22:652-656

BARDWICK, JUDITH M.

66526 (& Behrman, S. J.) Investigation into the effects of anxiety, sexual arousal, and menstrual cycle phase on uterine contractions. PSM 1967, 29:468-482

66527 Need for individual assessment of SS in psychosomatic research. Psychol Rep 1967, 21:80-86

66528 Uterine contractions as a function of anxiety, sexual arousal and menstrual cycle phase. Diss Abstr 1964, 25:3683

See Ivey, M. E.

BAREIKIS, ROBERT

66529 Arthur Schnitzler's "Fräulein Else": a Freudian novella? Lit & Psych 1969, 19:19-32

BARENDREGT, J. T.

66530 (et al) Research in Psychodiagnostics. The Hague: Mouton 1961, viii + 221 p
Rv Wisdom, J. O. J 1966, 47:585-588

BARENHOLTZ, BENJAMIN

66531 (& Edelson, R. B.) The evaluation of emotional health in the selection and education of students. Nurs Outlook 1967, 15:40-43

BARGER, PATRICIA M.

See Schulman, Jerome L.

BARGLOW, PETER

66532 (& Gunther, M. S.; Johnson, A.) Hysterectomy and tubal ligation: a psychiatric comparison. Obstet Gynec 1965, 25:520-527

66533 (Reporter) Panel: Identity crisis in adolescence. Bull Chicago Soc Adol Psychiat 1966, 1(1):17-19

66534 Pseudocyesis and psychiatric sequelae of sterilization. Arch gen Psychiat 1964, 11:571-580
       Abs KR Q 1966, 35:164
66535 (& Bornstein, M.; Exum, D. B.) Some psychiatric aspects of illegitimate pregnancy in early adolescence. Ops 1968, 38:672-687

See Offer, Daniel; Patt, Stephen L.

BARGUES, R.

See Aubry, J.

BARISH, J. A.

66536 Veritable Saint Genet. Wis Stud Contemp Lit 1965, 6:267-285

BARISH, JULIAN I.

66537 The adolescent within an adolescent treatment program. In Nichtern, S. *Mental Health Services for Adolescents*, Frederick A. Praeger Publ 1968, 131-142
66538 Discussion of Gelb, L. A. "Psychotherapy in a corrupt society." Sci Psa 1969, 14:227-228
66539 Discussion of Gralnick, A. "Psychoanalysis and the treatment of adolescents in a private hospital." Sci Psa 1966, 9:108-110
66540 A multidimensional view of sexual acting out in the residential treatment of adolescents. Newsletter, National Ass Private Psychiat Hosp 1966, 15(2):2-4
66541 (& Buchenholz, B.) A teaching technique for inferring psychodynamics. Psychiat Q 1960, 34:103-116

BARKER, CURTIS H.

See Schein, Edgar H.

BARKER, MICHAEL J.

See Wolowitz, Howard M.

BARKER, WARNER J.

66542 (Reporter) Female sexuality. (Panel: Am Psa Ass, 6 May 1967) J Am Psa Ass 1968, 16:123-145
66543 The nonsense of Edward Lear. (Read at Pittsburgh Psa Soc, Mar 1966) Q 1966, 35:568-586
S-41184 The stereotyped Western story: its latent meaning and psycho-economic function.
       Abs An Surv Psa 1955, 6:463-464
66544 The Western story, sports and games. In Slovenko, R. & Knight, J. A. *Motivations in Play, Games, and Sports*, Springfield, Ill.: Thomas 1967, 573-581

BARKIN, LEONARD

ABSTRACT OF:
66545 Blum, H. Transference and structure. Q 1969, 38:170-171

BARMACK, J. E.

See Kahn, Edwin

BARMAN, ALICEROSE

66546 Mental Health in Classroom and Corridor. NY: Western Publ Co 1968, 158 p

BARNARD, GEORGE W.

66547 (& Banks, S. H.) Motor psychotherapy: a method for ego enhancement. MH 1967, 51:604-611

BARNARD, JAN

66548 Dreams, a "royal road to the unconscious." RN 1967, 30(2):49-53; 86-88
66549 Psychiatry today. Freud's legacy, and how his heirs have used it. RN 1967, 30(1):50-56; 96-97

BARNARD, MARGARET W.

See Kolb, Lawrence C.

BARNERT, MILDRED

See Dreger, Ralph M.

BARNES, EDWARD J.

66550 Psychotherapists' conflicts, defense preferences, and verbal reactions to certain classes of client expressions. Diss Abstr 1964, 25:618-619

BARNES, ELIZABETH

66551 (Ed) Psychosocial Nursing: Studies from the Cassel Hospital. London: Tavistock Publ 1968, 316 p
Rv Balint, E. J 1969, 50:412-413

BARNES, HAZEL E.

66552 Adler and Sartre: comment. J ind Psych 1965, 21:201

BARNES, J. A.

66553 Anthropology after Freud. Austral J Philos 1959, 37:14-27

BARNES, JAMES

66554 Coitus interruptus as a cause of anxiety neurosis. J Irish Med Ass 1960, 47:153-155

BARNES, K.

See Lefcourt, Herbert M.

BARNES, L. B.

See Dalton, Gene W.

BARNES, MARION J.

66555   Reactions to the death of a mother. Psa St C 1964, 19:334-357

BARNES, ROBERT H.

66556   Psychodynamic psychiatry: perspectives USA 1968. Dyn Psychiat 1968, 1(2):82-90; Abs (Ger) 90-91

See Ebaugh, Franklin G.

BARNETT, JOSEPH

66557   Cognition, thought and affect in the organization of experience. Sci Psa 1968, 12:237-247
66558   Cognitive repair in the treatment of obsessional neuroses. Proc IV World Cong Psychiat 1966, 752-757
66559   On aggression in the obsessional neuroses. Contempo Psa 1969, 6:48-57
66560   On cognitive disorders in the obsessional. (Read at Int Forum Psa, July 1965) Contempo Psa 1966, 2(2):122-134
66561   A structural analysis of theories in psychoanalysis. (Read at William Alanson White Psa Soc, 8 Jan 1965) R 1966, 53:85-98

BARNETT, MARJORIE C.

66562   "I can't" versus "he won't." Further considerations of the psychical consequences of the anatomic and physiological differences between the sexes. (Read at Am Psa Ass, 6 May 1967) J Am Psa Ass 1968, 16:588-600
66563   Vaginal awareness in the infancy and childhood of girls. (Read at Am Psa Ass, May 1962) J Am Psa Ass 1966, 14:129-151
        Abs Aberastury, A. Rev Psicoanál 1966, 23:206. CG RFPsa 1968, 32:350. JLSt Q 1969, 38:334

BARNETT, SAMUEL ANTHONY

66564   Attack and defense in animal societies. UCLA Forum Med Sci 1967, 7:35-56
66565   The biology of aggression. Lancet 1964,(2):803-807
66566   (& Burn, J.) Early stimulation and maternal behaviour. Nature 1967, 213:150-152
66567   Instinct and Intelligence: Behavior of Animals and Man. Englewood Cliffs, N.J.: Prentice-Hall 1967
66568   The Rat: A Study in Behavior. Chicago: Aldine Publ Co 1963, xvi + 288 p

BAROFF, GEORGE S.

66569   (& Tate, B. G.) The use of aversive stimulation in the treatment of chronic self-injurious behavior. J Amer Acad Child Psychiat 1968, 7:454-470

BAROLIN, G. S.

66570   Principes de la psychotherapie sous agents psycholytiques. [Principles of psychotherapy using psycholytic agents.] Evolut psychiat 1962, 27:283
        Abs Auth Rev Psicoanál 1963, 20:86

BARON, P.

See Schneider, Pierre-Bernard

BARON, SAMUEL

66571   Levels of insight and ego functioning in relation to hypnoanalysis. Int J clin exp Hypnos 1960, 8:141-146
S-41203 Transference and counter-transference in the classroom.
        Abs Ekboir, J. G. Rev Psicoanál 1961, 18:182

BARPAL, HEDDY

66572   Aspectos transferenciales e inferencias teóricas en un caso con fobia a la desfloración y al embarazo. [Aspects of transference and theoretical inferences in a case of defloration and pregnancy.] Rev Psicoanál 1962, 19:49-54

BARR, ALAN P.

66573   Cervantes' probing of reality and psychological realism in "Don Quixote." Lit & Psych 1968, 18:111-122

BARR, HARRIET LINTON

See Klein, George S.

BARR, RICHARD H.

66574   (& Hill, G.) Acquired spasmodic torticollis in a male homosexual. JNMD 1960, 130:325-330

BARRAL, MARY ROSE

66575   Merleau-Ponty: The Role of the Body-Subject in Interpersonal Relations. Pittsburgh: Duquesne Univ Pr 1965, xi + 297 p
        Rv Gorman, W. R 1968, 55:152-153

BARRAU, B.

66576   La capacité de changement. [The capacity to change.] Bull Ass Psa Fran 1966, 3

BARRE, ALAN

66577   Psychoanalysis for psychiatrists is now tax-deductible. NYSDB Bull 1968, 10(5):4

ABSTRACT OF:
66578   Freud, A. Difficulties in the path of psychoanalysis. Q 1969, 38:676-679

BARRES, P.

66579 [Apropos of indications for psychoanalysis and analytic psychotherapy.] (Fr) Toulouse Med 1964, 65:1263-1264

BARRETT, BEATRICE H.

66580 Acquisition of operant differentiation and discrimination in institutionalized retarded children. Ops 1965, 35:862-885
Abs JMa RFPsa 1967, 31:328

66581 (& Lindsley, O. R.) Deficits in acquisition of operant discrimination and differentiation shown by institutionalized retarded children. Amer J ment Defic 1962, 67:424-436

BARRETT, JAMES E., JR.

See Grunebaum, Henry U.

BARRETT, JEAN

66582 The conflict of generations in college counseling. MH 1966, 50(1)

BARRETT, WILLIAM G.

66583 Irrational Man. NY: Doubleday 1958
Rv Coltrera, J. T. J Am Psa Ass 1962, 10:166-215
S-41209 On the meaning of Tom Sawyer.
Abs An Surv Psa 1955, 6:454-456

BARRET-LENNARD, GODFREY T.

66584 Dimensions of Therapist Response as Causal Factors in Therapeutic Change. Wash DC: APA 1962, 36 p

BARRIGUETE C., ARMANDO

ABSTRACTS OF:
66585 Boyer, L. B. Desarrollo histórical de la terapia psicoanalítica de la esquizofrenia: contribuciones de los discípulos de Freud. Cuad Psa 1967, 3:245
66586 Cesio, F. Sobre técnico psicoanalítica. Cuad Psa 1967, 3:245-246
66587 Grinberg, R. Interpretación psicoanalítica de "Las Cabezad Trocadas." Cuad Psa 1967, 3:246
66588 Leeuw, P. J. van der: Simposio: criterios de selección para la formación de estudiantes de psicoanálisis. Cuad Psa 1967, 3:61-62

BARRON, ARTHUR T.

See Burlingham, Dorothy T.

BARRON, BRUCE A.

See Glucksman, Myron L.

BARRON, DAVID B.

66589 *Coriolanus:* portrait of the artist as infant. Am Im 1962, 19:171-193
66590 *Endymion:* the quest for beauty. Am Im 1963, 20:27-47

BARRON, DAVID WILLIAM

66591 Fundamental aspects of Kaiserian-oriented process therapy. J existent
Psychiat 1967, 6:58-73

BARRON, FRANK X.

66592 Creative Person and Creative Process. NY: Holt, Rinehart, & Winston
1969, x + 212 p
66593 Creativity and Psychological Health: Origins of Personal Vitality and
Creative Freedom. London: Van Nostrand 1963, x + 292 p
    Rv Hammer, E. F. R 1967, 54:382-384

BARRON, JULES

REVIEW OF:
66594 Knight, J. A. For the Love of Money. R 1968-69, 55:713-714

BARRON, S. H.

See Mohr, George J.

BARRUCAND, D.

66595 (& Barrucand, M.) Psychopathologie de l'expression chez A. Kubin.
[Psychopathology of the expression in A. Kubin.] Ann méd-psychol
1967, 125(2):389-405

See Kissel, P.

BARRUCAND, M.

See Barrucand, D.

BARRY, HERBERT, JR.

66596 (& Lindemann, E.) Critical ages for maternal bereavement in psychoneuroses. PSM 1960, 22:166-181
    Abs EMW Q 1961, 30:305
66597 (& Barry, H., III; Lindemann, E.) Dependency in adult patients following early maternal bereavement. JNMD 1965, 140:196-206
    Abs BFM Q 1967, 36:142
S-1544 Significance of maternal bereavement before age of eight in psychiatric patients. Death & Identity 206-216

BARRY, HERBERT, III

See Barry, Herbert, Jr.

BARRY, MAURICE J.

66598 Depression, shame, loneliness and the psychiatrist's position. PT 1962,
16:580-590

BARRY, MAURICE J., JR.

66599 Incest. In Slovenko, R. Sexual Behavior and the Law, Springfield, Ill:
Thomas 1965, 521-538

S-41227 (& Johnson, A. M.) The incest barrier.
Abs NZ An Surv Psa 1958, 9:132-133
66600 Psychologic aspects of smoking. Proc Mayo Clin 1960, 35:386-389

See Rome, Howard P.

BARSA, JOSEPH ALBERT

66601 The fallacy of the "double blind." P 1963, 119:1174-1175

BARSIS, OLGA

TRANSLATION OF:
Fenichel, O. [72710]

BARTA, JAMES

66602 A study of the concurrence of anxiety and hostility. Diss Abstr 1963, 23(9):3471-3472

BARTEMEIER, LEO H.

66603 Address. In Kenworthy, M. E. *William C. Menninger Memorial Volume,* NY: Clarke & Way 1967
66604 Character formation. BMC 1969, 33:346-351
66605 The church's role in combating prejudice. J pastoral Counsel 1967, 2(2)
66606 Clinical brief. Newsletter, Mich Soc Neurol Psychiat, 1963, 5(8):123
66607 Comments on Lemercier, G. "A benedictine monastery in psycho-analysis." Bull Guild Cath Psychiatrists 1966, 13:11-12
66608 A contribution of psychiatry to medical practice. Q Newsletter, National Ass Private psychiat Hosp 1966, 15(1)
66609 Death and dying: attitudes of patient and doctor: discussion. GAP Symp #11 1965, 5:650-651
66610 Discussion of Aarons, Z. A. "Therapeutic abortion and the psychiatrist." P 1967, 124:753-754
66611 Discussion of Hendrick, I. "Our generation of psychiatrists: changes in our words and changes in our thinking." Cross-currents in Ps & Psa 36-38
66612 Discussion of Seguin, C. A. "Human values in psychotherapy." Proc IV World Cong Psychiat 1966, 1006-1007
66613 (& Braceland, F. J.) Emotional aspects of aging. In Farnsworth, D. L. & Braceland, F. J. *Psychiatry, the Clergy, and Pastoral Counseling,* Collegeville, Minn: Inst for Mental Health, St. John's Univ Pr 1969, 163-179
66614 Emotional development in adolescence. Teenage Problems in Amer Culture 1963, 7:82-91
66615 Emotional reactions to illness. Maryland State med J 1961, 10(May)
66616 Exposition: Proc First Int Cong Direct Psa 1964. Doylestown Foundation Paper 1965
66617 (& Appel, K. E.; Ewalt, J. R.; Barton, B. E.) The future of psychiatry. The report of the joint commission on mental illness and health. P 1962, 118:973-981

66618   Healthy and unhealthy patterns of religious behavior. J Relig Hlth
        1965, 4:309-314
66619   In appreciation. JNMD 1969, 149:19-20
66620   An introspective account of Meniere's syndrome. BMC 1967, 31:193-
        196
66621   Man and his molecules. Georgetown med Bull 1965, 19(1)
66622   Married women after fifty. Bull Women's Aux, AMA 1960, 22:56-57
66623   The meaning of discipline. Teenage Problems in Amer Culture 1964,
        6:67-72
66624   Meniere's syndrome. Proc IV World Cong Psychiat 1966, 2738-2739
66625   Obligations of the medical profession. State Govt 1962, 35(1):12
66626   Occupational therapy and psychiatry. Ment Hosp 1964, 15:138-139
66627   Preface to *Psychiatry and Public Affairs*, GAP Rep & Sump 1966
66628   Psychiatric aspects of medical practice. Emotional reactions to illness.
        Maryland State med J 1961, 10:240-242
66629   (& Greenwald, A. F.) Psychiatric discharges against medical advice.
        Arch gen Psychiat 1963, 8:117-119
66630   Psychiatric problems of the aging. Ment Hosp 1960, 11:8
66631   The psychiatrist in the hospital setting. Hosp Prog 1962, 43:69-70
66632   (& Rosen, H.) The psychiatry resident as participant therapist. P 1967,
        123:1371-1378
66633   Psychoanalysis and religion. BMC 1965, 29:237-244
        Psychanalyse et religion. La Vie Spirituelle 1967, Suppl No. 80:176-
        184
66634   Psychological factors in doctor-patient relations. Med Ann DC 1961,
        30:553-555
66635   The psychological factors in illness. J Arkansas Med Soc 1960, 56:298
66636   The psychological significance of excessive fatigue. Dallas med J
        1960, 46:135-138
66637   Relationship of the psychiatric unit to private hospitals. In Kaufman,
        M. R. *The Psychiatric Unit in a General Hospital—Its Current and
        Future Role*, NY: IUP 1965, 438-441; 461-482
66638   The secret of medical practice. MH 1961, 45:323-326
66639   (& Farnsworth, D. L.) Sexual deviation. In Farnsworth, D. L. & Brace-
        land, F. J. *Psychiatry, the Clergy, and Pastoral Counseling*, College-
        ville, Minn: Inst for Mental Health, St. John's Univ Pr 1969, 267-279
66640   Structure and function of the predominating symptom in some border-
        line cases. P 1960, 116:825-827
        Abs Leavitt, M. Q 1961, 30:144
66641   Testimony: hearings before the Subcommittee on Labor and Public
        Welfare, U. S. Senate, S. 755 and 756. Wash DC: US GPO, March
        85-89
66642   Treatment of the spouse of the alcoholic. Mod Treatment 1966, 3:542-
        547
        Trattamento del conjuge dell'alcoolista. Terapia dell'alcoolismo a
        cura di Marvin A. Block. Terapia Moderna 1967, 111:114-119
66643   Working with the community. Q Newsletter, National Ass Private
        Psychiat Hosp 1959-60, 9(4)

        See Carmichael, Hugh T.; Ewalt, Jack R.; Rosen, Harold

REVIEW OF:
66644 Pruyser, P. W. A Dynamic Psychology of Religion. BMC 1968, 32:258

BARTEN, HARVEY H.

See Bellak, Leopold

BARTER, JAMES T.

66645 (& Langsley, D. G.) The advantages of a separate unit for adolescents.
Hosp Comm Psychiat 1968, 19(8):25-27

BARTH, L.

66646 Freud und die Psychotherapie in der Sicht des praktischen Arztes.
[Freud and psychotherapy as seen by the practicing physician.]
Fortschr Med 1963, 81:919-920

BARTHEL, ARNFRIED

See Tausch, Anne-Marie

BARTHOL, RICHARD P.

See Goldstein, Michael J.

BARTHOLOMAY, ANTHONY F.

See Fox, Henry M.

BARTLETT, F. H.

66647 Pavlov and Freud. Sci & Soc 1961, 25:129-138

BARTOLESCHI, BENEDETTO

66648 (& Ferreti, E.) Contributo alla psicoterapia delle psicosi in età evolutiva.
[Contribution to the psychotherapy of psychoses in a state of evolution.] Riv Psa 1961, 7:111-123
66649 The crisis of acute anxiety at an evolutionary age. Inf Anorm 1961,
44:Sept-Oct
Abs Roi, G. RFPsa 1962, 26:611
66650 (& Novelletto, A.) L'influenza di gravi malattie fisiche nella prima infanzia sulla sviluppo mentale. Riv Psa 1967, 13:149-162
The influence of severe bodily illnesses in early childhood on mental
development. Symposium: child analysis and pediatrics. (Read at Int
Psa Cong, July 1967) J 1968, 49:294-297
Abs LHR Q 1969, 38:669

BARTOLINI, JORGE P.

S-41264 Incorporación visual e incorporación anal.
Abs Vega An Surv Psa 1956, 7:95
S-41265 Sucesivos desplazamientos de la incorporación preoral.
Abs RHB An Surv Psa 1957, 8:134

See Rascovsky, Arnaldo; Weil, Jorge M.

BARTON, B. E.
See Bartemeier, Leo H.

BARTON, HELEN B
66651 Nervous Tension, Behavior and Body Function. NY: Philos Libr 1965, 336 p

BARTON, R.
66652 Science and psychiatry. Lancet 1963, (2):566-568

BARTON, R. T.
66653 The whispering syndrome of hysterical dysphonia. Ann Otol 1960, 69:156-164

BARTON, WALTER E.
66654 (et al) Impressions of European Psychiatry. Washington: Am Psychiat Ass 1961, 128 p
66655 Introduction to Glasscote, R. M. (et al): *The Community Mental Health Center. An Analysis of Existing Models.* Washington, D.C.: Joint Information Service 1964
66656 (& Brosin, H. W.; Farrell, M. J.) Obituary: William Claire Menninger 1899-1966. P 1966, 123:614-617

See Katz, Martin M.

BARTSCH, WOLFGANG
66657 Psychoanalyse in der Bundesrepublik. [Psychoanalysis in the Bund Republic.] Tribüne 1964, 3:1191-1199

BARUA, M.
S-41268 Freud and Horney on anxiety and neurosis.
Abs An Surv Psa 1955, 6:22-23

BARUCH, DOROTHY W.
66658 Little mocking bird. In Moustakas, C. *Existential Child Therapy,* NY: Basic Books 1966, 30-34
66659 Transference and counter-transference in the classroom. MH 1960, 44:86-90

See Miller, Henry

BARUCH, GRACE K.
66660 Anne Frank on adolescence. Adolescence 1968-69, 3:425-434

BARUCH, J. Z.
66661 [Motion sickness is often caused by anxiety over the trip.] (Dut) T Ziekenverpl 1966, 19:521

BARUK, HENRI

66662 Freud et l'occultisme. [Freud and occultism.] Ann méd-psychol 1969, 127(2):179

66663 Nouvelles recherches sur Freud et la psychanalyse. [New research on Freud and psychoanalysis.] Ann méd-psychol 1968, 126(1):595-601

66664 Observation sur les suites d'une psychothérapie d'inspiration psychanalytique. [Observation on the after-effects of a psychoanalytically inspired psychotherapy.] Ann méd-psychol 1967, 125(2):141-143

66665 [The problem of hysteric accidents and mental images in the hysteric personality.] (Sp) Prensa Med Argent 1965, 52:2441-2445

66666 Psychanalyse et homosexualité. [Psychoanalysis and homosexuality.] Ann méd-psychol 1967, 125(1):136-138

66667 La Psychiatrie Française de Pinel à nos Jours. [French Psychiatry from Pinel to Our Day.] Paris: PUF 1967, 153 p

66668 Psychoses et Névroses. [Psychoses and Neuroses.] (9th ed) Paris: PUF 1968, 128 p

66669 La signification de la psychanalyse et le judaisme. [The significance of psychoanalysis and Judaism.] Rev Hist med hebr 1966, 19:15-29; 53-65; 131-132

BARZA, S.

See Malmo, Robert B.

BARZILAY, SHOSHANA

66670 (& Winnik, H. Z.; Davies, M.) Postpartum mental disturbances. Harefuah 1969, 76:104-106

See Moses, Rafael

BARZUN, JACQUES

66671 Romanticism today. Encounter 1961, 17(3):50-56

BASAGLIA, F.

66672 [Anxiety and insincerity: the human condition of the neurotic.] (It) Riv sper Freniat 1964, 88:392-404

66673 [Body, look and silence. The enigma of subjectivity in psychiatry.] (Fr) Evolut psychiat 1965, 30:11-26

66674 Silence in the dialogue with the psychotic. J existent Psychiat 1965, 6:99-102

BASAMANIA, BETTY W.

66675 The family as the unit of study and treatment: IV. The emotional life of the family: inferences for social casework. Workshop, 1959. Ops 1961, 31:74-86

BASCH, MICHAEL FRANZ

66676 Perception, subliminal perception and Freud's "project." (Read at Chicago Psa Soc, 26 Nov 1968) 17 p (litho)
       Abs Handler, J. S. Bull Phila Ass Psa 1969, 19:238-242

66677 (& Gamm, S. R.) (Reporters) A reconsideration of the clinical and theoretical aspects of narcissism. In "Traditional subjects reconsidered." Proc reg Conf Chicago Psa Soc 1968

BASCHET, C.

66678 Discussion of Luquet, P. "Ouvertures sur l'artiste et le psychanalyste: la fonction esthetique du moi." RFPsa 1963, 27:606

BASH, NICHOLAS

See Graff, Harold

BASKIN, WADE

See Roback, Abraham A.

TRANSLATION OF:
Kolle, K. [79251]

BASQUIN, M.

66679 [Anxiety and anxiety neurosis.] (Fr) Concours Méd 1965, 87:4967-4974

BASS, BERNARD M.

See Petrullo, Luigi

BASSAN, MARVIN

See Chessick, Richard D.

BASSANETTI, F.

See Landucci-Rubini, L.

BASSESCU, SABERT

66680 Creativity and the dimensions of consciousness. Humanitas 1968, 4:133-144

BASSIN, ELLEN G.

See Strickler, Martin

BASSIN, F. V.

66681 A critical analysis of Freudianism [Soviet view]. Soviet Rev 1960, 1(5):3-14. In Zawdony, J. K. Man and International Relations, Vol. II, San Francisco, Calif: Chandler Publ 1966, 119-125
66682 K probleme "bessoznatel'-nogo." [On the problem of the "unconscious."] Voprosy Filosofi 1962, 16:112-124
66683 A neofreudizmus kritikája. [Criticism of neofreudism.] Magyar pszichol Szle 1961, 18:3-25

BASTIAANS, JAN

66684 [Non-directive counseling and psychoanalysis.] (Dut) Ned Tijdschr Psychol 1959, 14:519-532

Psychiatric training problems in psychosomatic medicine. Fortschr PSM 1960, 1:179-189
66686 Psychiatrische Bemerkungen zu Problemen der Fettsucht und Magersucht. [Psychiatric notes on problems connected with obesity and pathological leanness.] Psyche 1963, 16:615-630
66687 Psychoanalytic investigations on the psychic aspects of acute myocardial infarction. Psychother Psychosom 1968, 16:202-209
S-41302 Some problems of the transference in the treatment of psychosomatic patients.
Abs An Surv Psa 1955, 6:362-363

See Musaph, Herman; Reichsman, F.

BASTIDE, ROGER

66688 (Ed) Sens et Usages du Terme de Structure dans les Sciences Humaines et Sociales. [The Meaning and Usage of the Term Structure in Human and Social Sciences.] Le Haye: Mouton 1962, 165 p
66689 Sociologie et psychanalyse. Sociology and psychoanalysis. Sociología y psicoanálisis. Hum Context 1968, 1:23-36; 37-49; 50-52
66690 The sociology of the dream. In Grunebaum, G. E. von & Caillois, R. *The Dream and Human Societies*, Berkeley/Los Angeles: Univ Calif Pr 1966, 199-211
66691 (& Raveau, F.) (Eds) Table Ronde sur l'Adaptation des Africains en France. [Round table on the Adaptation of Africans in France.] Paris: (Mimeo) 1965

BASTIE, J.

66692 (& Bastie, Y.; Lacassih, A.) [A psychosis of interpretation and the interpretations of this psychosis.] (Fr) Encéph 1961, 50:190-202

BASTIE, Y.

66693 (& Bleandonu, G.; Chabrand, P.) L'erotomanie passionnelle. [Passional erotomania.] Ann méd-psychol 1965, 123(2):317-332

See Bastie, J.

BASTOS, OTHON

66694 L'activité onirique dans les états dépressifs. [Dream activity in depressive states.] Evolut psychiat 1963, 28:99-127
66695 (& Suerinck, E.) Les rêves de maniaques. [Dreams of manics.] Evolut psychiat 1963, 28:129-137

BATCHELOR, IVOR R. C.

See Henderson, David

BATESON, GREGORY

66696 Communication theories in the etiology of the neuroses. In Merin, J. H. & Nagler, S. H. *The Etiology of the Neuroses*, Palo Alto, Calif: Sci & Behav Books 1966, 28-35

66697 (Ed) Perceval's Narrative: A Patient's Account of His Psychosis, 1830-
       1832. Stanford, Calif.: Stanford Univ Pr 1961; London: Hogarth 1962,
       xxii + 331 p

       See Ruesch, Jurgen

BATLIWALA, BAPAI M.

66698 Mental Health Service in a Nursery School. Bombay, India: Dept Psy-
       chological Services, Parsi Punchayet Trust 1960, xiv + 55 p

BATTAGGIA, PIER G.

       See Rovera, Gian G.

BATTEGAY, RAYMOND

66699 Geschwisterrelationen als Funktionsmuster der (therapeutischen)
       Gruppen. [Sibling relations as a functional model of (therapeutic)
       groups.] Psychother Psychosom 1966, 14:251-263
66700 Die Gruppe als therapeutisches Milieu. [The group as a therapeutic
       medium.] Z Psychother med Psychol 1964, 14:29-35
66701 Gruppenpsychotherapie und modernes psychiatrisches Spital. [Group
       psychotherapy and the modern psychiatric hospital.] Nervenarzt 1965,
       36:250-253
66702 Medikamentensucht als psychiatrisches Problem. [Drug addiction as a
       psychiatric problem.] Schweiz med Wschr 1965, 95:1247-1250
66703 Professor Dr. med. Heinrich Meng: Zum 80. Geburtstag. [Professor Dr.
       med. Heinrich Meng: on his 80th birthday.] Prax Kinderpsychol 1968,
       17:33-34. Z PSM 1968, 14:1-2
66704 Psychodynamische Verhältnisse bei der Gruppenpsychotherapie. [Psy-
       chodynamic aspects of group psychotherapy.] Psychiat Neurol Neuro-
       chir 1960, 63:333-342
66705 Psychotherapy of schizophrenics in small groups. Int J grp PT 1965,
       15:316-320
66706 Das therapeutische Gruppengespräch. [Therapeutic communication in
       the group.] Prax PT 1967, 12:32-41
66707 Zur Ausbildung von Gruppentherapeuten. Arbeit mit analytischen
       Selbsterfahrungsgruppen. [On the training of group psychotherapists.
       Work with groups practicing psychoanalytic self-experience.] Schweiz
       ANP 1964, 93:346-361

BATTEN, C.

       TRANSLATION OF:
       Raclot, M. et al [87126]

BATTIE, WILLIAM

66708 A Treatise on Madness. (Introd & Annot: Hunter, R. & Macalpine, I.)
       London: Dawson 1962, 60 p

BATTISTA, O. A.

66709 Mental Drugs: Chemistry's Challenge to Psychotherapy. Phila: Chilton
       1960, xx + 155 p

BATTLE, ALLEN OVERTON

66710 Culture conflict and psychotherapy of adolescent patients. GP 1966, 34:140-144

BATTLE CAROLYN C.

See Hoehn-Saric, Rudolf; Nash, Earl H.; Truax, Charles D.

BAUDOUIN, CHARLES

S-41315 Les éléments de la situation analytique.
    Abs RJA An Surv Psa 1956, 7:337-338
S-41316 Freud et la dialectique de l'exogène et de l'endogène.
    Abs JBa An Surv Psa 1956, 7:13-14
S-41317 Métamorphoses de l'instinct et conduites symboliques.
    Symbolic behaviour and the metamorphoses of instinct. Problems in Psa 10-23
S-41322 Transfert et projection en situation analytique.
    Abs An Surv Psa 1955, 6:319-322

    See Raclot, Marcel

BAUDRY, FRANCIS (FRANK)

66711 (& Wiener, A.) The family of the surgical patient. Surgery 1968, 63:416-422
66712 (& Wiener, A.; Hurwitt, E. S.) Indications for psychiatric consultation on a surgical service. Surgery 1966, 60:993-1000
66713 (& Wiener, A.) Preoperative preparation of the surgical patient. Surgery 1968, 63:885-889

BAUER, J.-P.

66714 (& Wetta, J.-M.; Bucher-Andlauer; Philonenko, L.; Durand de Bousingen, R.) Le rôle du père dans la désadaptation universitaire. [The role of the father in maladjustment to the university.] Rv Np inf 1965, 13:783-794

BAUER, WILLIAM WALDO

66715 All You Need to Know About Insomnia, Sleep, and Dreams. NY: Essandess Special Editions 1967, 95 p
66716 (Ed) Today's Health Guide. Chicago: AMA 1965

BAUGH, ANNIE P.

See West, J. V.

BAUGH, JAMES R.

66717 The relationship between reported memories of childhood experience and present behavior. Diss Abstr 1968, 29(1-A):141-142

BAUGH, V. S.

66718 (& Stanford, G. A.) Psychological factors in ulcer patients. Dis nerv Sys 1964, 25:553-557

    See West, J. V.

BAUM, O. EUGENE

66719 (& Felzer, S. B.) Activity in initial interviews with lower class patients. Arch gen Psychiat 1964, 10:345-353

66720 Countertransference. (Read at Phila Psa Inst, 28 Jan 1967) R 1969-70, 56:621-637

66721 The "difficult" patient. Unless a patient's hidden anxieties and needs are recognized, the difficult situation is the end result of the physician-patient interaction. Penn Med 1967, 70:82-83

66722 (& Ross, M.) How psychiatric training methods might be improved. Resident Physician 1968, 14(12):52-59

66723 (& Felzer, S. B.; D'Zmura, T. L.; Shumaker, E.) Psychotherapy, dropouts and lower socioeconomic patients. Ops 1966, 36:629-635
Abs JMa RFPsa 1968, 32:379

66724 (& Felzer, S. B.) Psychotherapy of lower socioeconomic patient. Int Psychiat Clin 1964, 1:461-474

REVIEW OF:
66725 Racker, H. Transference and Countertransference. Bull Phila Ass Psa 1969, 19:45-50

BAUMAN, GERALD

See Dorsey, Joseph; Rosenbaum, Milton

BAUMEYER, FRANZ

66726 Arbeitsstörungen bei Studenten. [Learning disorders in students.] Z PSM 1968, 14:79-90

66727 Erfahrungen über die Behandlung psychogener Erkrankungen in Berlin. [Practical experiences in the treatment of the psychogenically ill in Berlin.] Z PSM 1962, 8:167-183

S-41333 Der Fall Schreber.
Abs An Surv Psa 1955, 6:10-12. JAL An Surv Psa 1956, 7:29; 178-179

66728 Der psychogene akute Herzanfall. [The psychogenic acute heart attack.] Z PSM 1966, 12:12-26

66729 Zur Symptomatologie und Genese der Agoraphobie. [On the symptomatology and the origin of agoraphobia.] Z PSM 1959-60, 6:231-245

BAUMGARTEN, FRANZISKA

66730 Seelische Not und Vorurteil: Einglick in verworrene menschliche Beziehungen. [Psychic Need and Prejudice.] Munich: Karl Albert 1961, 218 p

BAUMRIND, DIANA

66731 Effects of authoritative parental control on child behavior. Child Develpm 1966, 37:887-907

66732 Parental control and parental love. Children 1965, 12:230-234

66733 (& Black, A. E.) Socialization practices associated with dimensions of competence in preschool boys and girls. Child Develpm 1967, 38:291-327

BAURAND, G.

See Appaix, A.; Striglioni, L.

BAXTER, JAMES C.

66734   (& Becker, J.) Anxiety and avoidance behavior in schizophrenics in response to parental figures. ASP 1962, 64:432-437

66735   (& Williams, J.; Zerof, S.) Child-rearing attitudes and disciplinary fantasies of parents of schizophrenics and controls. JNMD 1965, 141:567-
579

66736   Family relations and variables in schizophrenia. Psychiat Res Rep 1966,
20:43-53

66737   Family relationship variables in schizophrenia. Acta Psychiat Scand
1966, 42:362-391

66738   (& Horton, D. L.; Wiley, R. E.) Father identification as a function of
mother-father relationship. J ind Psych 1964, 20:167-171

66739   (& Lerner, M. J.; Miller, J. S.) Identification as a function of the rein-
forcing quality of the model and the socialization background of the
subject. J Pers Soc Psychol 1965, 2:692-697

66740   Parental complementarity and parental conflict. J ind Psych 1965,
21:149-153

BAXTER, SEYMOUR

66741   (& Chodorkoff, B.; Underhill, R.) Psychiatric emergencies: disposi-
tional determinants and the validity of the decision to admit. P 1968,
125:1542-1548

BAYER, SANFORD

66742   Each Man Kills. (Introd: Greenwald, H.) NY: Ballantine Books 1962,
342 p
Rv Sherman, M. H. PPR 1962, 49(4):127-128

BAYET, ROLAND

S-41347 Étude d'un cas de constipation. Recherche de ses facteurs psychodynamiques.
Abs An Surv Psa 1955, 6:218-220

BAYLEY, HELEN C.

See Cummings, S. Thomas

BAYLEY, N.

See Schaefer, Earl S.

BAYNE, HELEN

66743   (& Bry, I.) Problems and projects in the bibliography of psychiatry and
psychology. In Proc I Int Cong Med Librarianship, 20-25 July 1953.
Libri, Copenhagen 1954, 3:363-387

BAYNES, HELTON GODWIN

66744   Mythology of the Soul: A Research into the Unconscious from Schizo-
        phrenic Dreams and Drawings. London: Rider 1969, xxii + 980 p.

BAZA, B.

See Soifer, Raquel

BAZELON, DAVID L.

66745   The interface of law and the behavioral sciences. New Engl J Med
        1964, 271:1141-1145
66746   Justice for juveniles. New Repub 1967, Apr 22:13-16
66747   Justice stumbles over science. Trans-action 1967, 4(8):8
66748   Mental disorders: the need for a unified approach. Ops 1964, 34:39-44
66749   Mental retardation: legal and moral considerations. Ops 1965, 35:838-
        844
            Abs JMa RFPsa 1967, 31:328
66750   (& Boggs, E.) President's panel on mental retardation. Report of the
        Task Force on Law, Jan 1963
66751   The responsibility of the accused and the psychiatrist. Bull NY State
        District Branches, Am Psychiat Ass 1962, 4(1)

BAZIN, P.

See Danon-Boileau, Henri

BAZIT, ZEEV

66752   [Erich Fromm's socio-psychological theory.] (Heb) Urim 1963-64,
        55-59:112-115

BEACH, F. A.

See Scott, John P.

BEACH, KENNETH H.

See Stehlin, John S., Jr.

BEACHER, A. I.

66753   Psychoanalytic treatment of a sociopath in a group situation. PT 1962,
        16:278-288

BEALL, LYNNETTE

66754   Character and neurosis revisited—the case of Miss K. J consult clin
        Psychol 1968, 32:348-354
66755   Vocational choice: the impossible fantasy and the improbable choice.
        J counsel Psychol 1967, 14:86-92

BEAN, LEE L.

See Myers, Jerome K.

BEAN, WILLIAM B.

66756 Of doctors and priests: foreword to Belgum, D. *Religion and Medicine*, Ames, Iowa: Iowa State Univ Pr 1967, v-ix

66757 Some notes on parodies, with an example. Arch intern Med 1962, 10:819-822

BEAR, ROBERTA MEYER

See Hess, Robert D.

BEARDSLEE, DAVID C.

See Dulany, Donelson E., Jr.

BEARDSLEY, K.

66758 Analysis of psychological tests of persons diagnosed sociopathic personality disturbances. Arch crim Psychodyn 1961, Suppl:389-411

BEATMAN, FRANCES LEVINSON

66759 Family interaction: its significance for diagnosis and treatment. Soc Casewk 1957, 38:111-118. In Kasius, C. *Social Casework in the Fifties*, NY: Fam Serv Ass Amer 1962, 212-225

66760 Intergenerational aspects of family therapy. In Ackerman, N. W. et al: *Expanding Theory and Practice in Family Therapy*, NY: Fam Serv Ass Amer 1967, 29-38

See Ackerman, Nathan W.

BEBCHUK, W.

See Adamson, J. D.

BECK, AARON T.

66761 Depression: Clinical, Experimental, and Theoretical Aspects. NY: Harper & Row 1967, xiv + 370 p

66762 (& Ward, C. H.) Dreams of depressed patients: characteristic themes in manifest content. Arch gen Psychiat 1961, 5:462-467

66763 A systematic investigation of depression. Comprehen Psychiat 1961, 2:163-170

66764 Thinking and depression: I. Idiosyncratic content and cognitive distortions. II. Theory and therapy. Arch gen Psychiat 1963, 9:324-333; 1964, 10:561-571

See Saul, Leon J.; Ward, Clyde H.

BECK, ANNE G.

See Beck, Samuel J.

BECK, DIETER

66765 Die auslösende Situation beim Reizmagen. Ein Beitrag zur Psychodynamik der funktionellen Magenbeschwerden. [The causative situation in irritated stomach. A contribution on the psychodynamics of functional stomach disorders.] Schweiz med Wschr 1967, 97:739-745

66766 Die Indikation zur psychoanalytischen Kurztherapie. [Indication for psychoanalytic short time therapy.] Z PSM 1967, 13:257-265

66767 Die Kurzpsychotherapie. [Short-term psychotherapy.] Schweiz med Wschr 1968, 98:1859-1864

66768 Psychosomatische Aspekte der funktionellen Herzbeschwerden. [Psychosomatic aspects of functional heart diseases.] Schweiz med Wschr 1965, 95:395-399

66769 Schwangerschaftsunterbrechung und Schuldgefühl. [The interruption of pregnancy and guilt feelings.] Schweiz med Wschr 1964, 94:357-362

66770 Zur Behandlungstechnik der psychoanalytischen Kurztherapie. [On the management technic of intensive psychoanalytic therapy.] Z PSM 1968, 14:125-136

See Kielholz, Paul

BECK, HELEN L.

66771 Casework with parents of mentally retarded children. Ops 1962, 32:870-877

Abs JMa RFPsa 1964, 28:445

BECK, MARIA

66772 Rehabilitation eines chronischen Trinkers mit der Methode des katathymen Bilderlebens. [Rehabilitation of a chronic alcoholic with the catathymic imagery experience method.] Psychother Psychosom 1967, 15:7. Prax PT 1968, 13:97-103

BECK, SAMUEL J.

66773 Abraham's ordeal: creation of a new reality. R 1963, 50:335-349

66774 Biographical sketch of Hermann Rorschach. Encyclopedia Britannica 1960

66775 Emotions and understanding. Int Psychiat Clin 1966, 3:93-114

66776 Emotions, knowing, and Rorschach. In Muller, J. J. The Clinical Interpretation of Psychological Tests, Boston: Little, Brown 1966

66777 Families of schizophrenic and of well children: method, concepts, and some results. Ops 1960, 30:247-275

66778 Hermann Rorschach. International Encyclopedia of the Social Sciences 1967

66779 (& Nunnally, J. C.) Parental attitudes in families. A semantic differential study of parental attitudes in families of children resident in a therapeutic school and in families with well children. Arch gen Psychiat 1965, 13:208-213

66780 Psychological Processes in the Schizophrenic Adaptation. NY: Grune & Stratton 1965, viii + 421 p

66781 Research in childhood schizophrenia. Ops 1962, 32:336

66782 The Rorschach Experiment. Ventures in Blind Diagnosis. NY: Grune & Stratton 1960, 256 p

Rv Kurth, G. M. Q 1962, 31:411-413

66783 The Rorschach test, communication, and psychotherapy. Meth Res PT
       551-572
66784 Rorschach's *Erlebnistypus:* an empiric datum. Beih Schweiz Z Psychol
       Anwend No. 45. Rorschachiana 1963, 8:8-25
66785 (& Beck, A. G.; Levitt, E. E.; Molish, H. B.) Rorschach's Test: I.
       Basic Processes. 3d rev ed NY/London: Grune & Stratton 1961, x +
       237 p
66786 (& Molish, G. B.) Rorschach's Test: II. A Variety of Personality Pic-
       tures. 2nd ed NY: Grune & Stratton 1967, viii + 440 p
66787 Schizophrenia: interadaptation of person, family and culture. In Ro-
       mano, J. *The Origins of Schizophrenia,* Amsterdam/NY: Excerpta Med-
       ica Found 1967, 249-269
66788 SR-2. Affect autonomy in schizophrenia. Arch gen Psychiat 1960,
       2:408-420
66789 Symptom and trait in schizophrenia. Ops 1964, 34:517-526

BECK-DVORŽAK, M.

See Betlheim, Stjepan; Persic, N.

BECKER, ALOIS M.

66790 "Fortschritt" und "Orthodoxie" in der Psychoanalyse. ["Progress" and
       "orthodoxy" in psychoanalysis.] Psyche 1965, 18:881-887
66791 Jahrbuch der Psychoanalyse. [Yearbook of Psychoanalysis.] Psyche
       1964, 18:829-833
66792 Suggestion als sozialer Vorgang und als ärztliches Mittel, mit beson-
       derer Berücksichtigung der Irreführungs- und Placebofrage. [Sugges-
       tion as social process and medication with special consideration of mis-
       leading and placebo questions.] Psyche 1963, 17:357-378
S-41384 Zur Gliederung des Über-Ichs.
       Abs BB An Surv Psa 1956, 7:138-139

BECKER, ALVIN

66793 (& Sheldon, D., Greenblatt, M.) Prevention of hospitalization for the
       geriatric mentally ill. Curr psychiat Ther 1968, 8:187-194

BECKER, BENJAMIN J.

66794 Alienation and the group anaytic process. Psa 1961, 21:273-279
66795 A concept of total psychiatric theory. Penn psychiat Q 1969, 9(2):5-14
66796 Dreams in group psychoanalysis. J Psa in Groups 1964, 1(2):28-35
66797 The obese patient in group psychoanalysis. PT 1960, 14:322-337
66798 Sexual rivalry in group psychoanalysis. Psa 1960, 20:201-204

BECKER, ERNEST

66799 Angel in Armor; a Post-Freudian Perspective on the Nature of Man.
       NY: G. Braziller 1969, xi + 195 p
66800 Anthropological notes on the concept of aggression. Ps 1962, 25:328-
       338
66801 The Birth and Death of Meaning. NY: Free Pr of Glencoe 1962, 210 p

66802 A note on Freud's primal horde theory. Q 1961, 30:413-419

66803 The psychotherapeutic meeting of East and West. Am Im 1961, 18:3-20

66804 Psychotherapeutic observations on the Zen discipline: one point of view. Psychologia 1960, 3:100-112

66805 The relevance to psychiatry of recent research in anthropology. PT 1962, 16:600-617

66806 The Revolution in Psychiatry; The New Understanding of Man. Glencoe, Ill.: Free Pr 1964, 276 p

66807 Social science and psychiatry: the coming challenge. Antioch Rev 1963, 23:353-366

66808 Socialization, command performance, and mental illness. Soc 1962, 67:494-501. In Bergen, B. J. & Thomas, C. S. *Issues and Problems in Social Psychiatry*, Springfield, Ill: Thomas 1966, 198-211

66809 The Structure of Evil. An Essay on the Unification of the Science of Man. NY: Braziller 1968, xviii + 430 p
  Rv Slochower, H. Am Im 1969, 26:94

66810 Toward a comprehensive theory of depression: a cross-disciplinary appraisal of objects, games and meaning. JNMD 1962, 135:26-35

66811 Zen: A Rational Critique. NY: Norton 1961, 192 p

BECKER, EUGENE

See Deutsch, Albert L.

BECKER, GEORGE S.

66812 (& Israel, P.) Integrated drug and psychotherapy in the treatment of alcoholism. Quart J Stud Alcohol 1961, 22:610-633

BECKER, GILBERT

66813 Ego-defense patterns in extroverts and introverts. Psychol Rep 1967, 20:387-392

BECKER, HORTENSE KOLLER

66814 Carl Koller and cocaine. Q 1963, 32:309-373

BECKER, HOWARD

66815 The sorrow of bereavement. In Ruietenbeek, H. M. *Death: Interpretations*, NY; Dell 1969, 195-216

BECKER, JOSEPH

See Baxter, James C.; Spielberger, Charles D.

BECKER, PHILIP L.

66816 Edward Hitschmann 1871-1957. Psychoanalysis of great men. Psa Pioneers 160-168

See Grotjahn, Martin

BECKER, R. E.

See Harrow, Martin

BECKER, RAYMOND DE

66817 Rêve et sexualité. [Dream and Sexuality.] Paris: La Table Ronde 1965, 216 p
66818 La Vie Tragique de Sigmund Freud. [The Tragic Life of Sigmund Freud.] Paris: Éditions Planète 1967, 312 p
Rv Delattre, J. RFPsa 1968, 32:794-795

BECKER, TED E.

66819 (Reporter) Latency. (Panel: Am Psa Ass, Dec 1964) J Am Psa Ass 1965, 13:584-590
Abs Kalina, E. Rev Psicoanál 1966, 23:199-204

See Esman, Aaron

BECKER, W.

66820 Selbstmorde im Jugendalter. [Suicide in youth.] Med Klin 1965, 60:226-231

BECKETT, PETER GORDON STEWART

66821 Adolescents Out of Step. Their Treatment in a Psychiatric Hospital. Detroit: Wayne State Univ Pr 1965, 190 p
Rv Evans, F. M. Q 1967, 36:451-452
66822 (& Lennox, K.; Grisell, J. L.) Responsibility and reward in treatment. A comparative follow-up study of adolescents. JNMD 1968, 146:257-263
S-41396 (& Robinson, D. B.; Frazier, S. H.; Steinhilber, R. M.; Duncan, G. M.; Estes, H. R.; Litin, E. M.; Grattan, R. T.; Lorton, W. L.; Williams, G. E.; Johnson, A. M.) Studies in schizophrenia at the Mayo Clinic, I: The significance of exogenous traumata in the genesis of schizophrenia.
Abs JA An Surv Psa 1956, 7:182
66823 (& Bleakley, T. H.) A Teaching Program in Psychiatry. Vol. I. Schizophrenia, Paranoid Conditions, Depression. Detroit: Wayne State Univ Pr 1968

See Johnson, Adelaide M.

BECKETT, THOMAS

66824 A candidate's reflections on the supervisory process. Contempo Psa 1969, 5(2):169-179

BECKH-WIDMANSTETTER, H. A.

66825 Two letters to a patient. J ind Psych 1966, 22:112-115

BECKMAN, A. C.

66826 Hidden themes in the frontier thesis: an application of psychoanalysis to historiography. Comp Stud Soc & Hist 1966, 8:361-382

BECKMANN, D.

66827 (& Richter, H.-E.; Scheer, J. W.) Kontrolle von Psychotherapieresultaten. [Controls of psychotherapeutic results.] Psyche 1969, 23:805-823

66828 (& Richter, H.-E.) Selbstkontrolle einer klinischen Psychoanalytikergruppe durch ein Forschungsprogram. [Self control of a clinical psychoanalytical group using a research program.] Z Psychother med Psychol 1968, 18:201-218

See Richter, Horst-Eberhard

BECKWITT, MORRIS

66829 On the vicissitudes of sibling penis envy in a girl twin. Israel Ann Psychiat 1968, 6:13-29

BECQ, M.

66830 (& Gleizes, L.) A propos de quelques conduites suicidaires chez des mélancoliques. [The suicidal behavior of some melancholic patients.] Toulouse Méd 1960, 61:649-653

BEDAT, M.

66831 [Psychotherapeutic technics.] (Fr) Infirm Franc 1968, Feb:31-34

BEDEE, C.

66832 [Activities as a therapeutic aid.] (Dut) NTvG 1968, 112:725-727

BEDFORD, ZENOBIA

See Kraft, Irvin A.

BEEBE, JOHN, III

See Gendlin, Eugene T.

BEECH, HAROLD REGINALD

66833 (& Nace, E. P.) Asthma and aggression: the investigation of a hypothetical relationship employing a new procedure. Brit J soc clin Psychol 1965, 4:124-130

66834 (& Fransella, F.) Research and Experiment in Stuttering. NY: Pergamon Pr 1968, xi + 224 p

66835 (& Adler, F.) Some aspects of verbal conditioning in psychiatric patients. Behav Res Ther 1963, 1:273-282

66836 The symptomatic treatment of writer's cramp. In Eysenck, H. J. Behaviour Therapy and the Neuroses, Oxford, NY: Pergamon Pr 1960, 349-372

BEECKMANS-BALLE, M.

See Morthier-Nizet, O.

BEER, COLIN G.

66837 Ethology on the couch. Sci Psa 1968, 12:198-213

BEERE, D. B.

See Kidd, Aline H.

BEETS, NICHOLAS

66838 Ego psychology and the meeting face-to-face in psychotherapy. Rev existent Psychol Psychiat 1967, 7:72-93
66839 [Freud and Erikson. Notes for a chapter on ego psycholoy and adolescent psychotherapy.] (Dut) Nederl Tijdschr Psychol 1967, 22:360-378

BEGELMAN, DAVID ARTHUR

66840 (& Tolor, A.) A taste of honey: Dr. Guttmacher on Dr. Szasz. Psychol Rep 1966, 18:531-534
66841 Two criticisms of the mental illness concept. JNMD 1966, 141:598-604

BEGLEY, CARL

66842 (& Lebo, D.) Dylan Thomas' "If I Were Tickled by the Rub of Love": a psychoanalytic interpretation. Psychology 1968, 5:68-75

BÉGOIN, J.

66843 Tuberculose pulmonaire et problèmes psychosomatiques. [Pulmonary tuberculosis and psychosomatic problems.] Rev Méd psychosom 1965, 7:159-195

BEHARRIELL, FREDERICK J.

66844 Freud's "double": Arthur Schnitzler. J Am Psa Ass 1962, 10:722-730
          Abs JBi Q 1963, 32:449
66845 Psychology in the early works of Thomas Mann. PMLA 1962, 77 (March):149-155

BEHRENS, MARJORIE L.

66846 (& Meyers, D. I.; Goldfarb, W.; Goldfarb, N.; Fieldsteel, N. D.) The Henry Ittelson Center Family Interaction Scales. Genet Psychol Monogr 1969, 80:203-295
66847 (& Goldfarb, W.) A study of patterns of interaction of families of schizophrenic children in residential treatment. Ops 1958, 28:300-312

See Ackerman, Nathan W.

BEHRMAN, S. J.

See Bardwick, Judith M.

BEHYMER, ALICE F.

66848 (& Canida, J.; Cooper, S.; Faden, P. D.; Kahne, M. J.) Mental health films in group psychotherapy. Ps 1957, 20:27-38

BEIDELMAN, T. O.

66849 The ox and Nuer sacrifice: some Freudian hypotheses about Nuer symbolism. Man, London 1966, 1:453-467

BEIER, E.

See Korner, Ija N.

BEIER, ERNST G.

66850 Preventive measures in the mental health area: some theoretical considerations on justification and a fantasy about the future. Int Psychiat Clin 1969, 6(3):193-211
66851 The Silent Language of Psychotherapy; Social Reinforcement of Unconscious Processes. Chicago: Aldine 1966, xiii + 338 p

REVIEW OF:
66852 Goldstein, A. P. & Dean, S. J. (Eds) The Investigation of Psychotherapy. R 1967, 54:547-548

BEIGEL, HUGO G.

66853 Three transvestites under hypnosis. Int J clin exp Hyp 1965, 13:71-82

BEIGLER, JEROME S.

66854 (Reporter) The assessment of change resulting from psychoanalytic treatment. (Panel: Chicago Psa Soc, 28 Feb 1967) Bull Phila Ass Psa 1968, 18:95-100
66855 Discussion of Weisman, A. D. "The dying patient." Forest Hosp Publ 1962, 1:20-21
66856 Liaison psychiatry. Chicago Med 1961, 64:12-16. Ill med J 1962, 122:247-248

ABSTRACTS OF:
66857 Baittle, B. On early infantile precursors in fetishism: a case study. Bull Phila Ass Psa 1967, 17:245-247
66858 Barchilon, J. The Fall. Bull Phila Ass Psa 1967, 17:106-111
66859 Bettelheim, B. Child rearing in the Israel Kibbutzim. Bull Phila Ass Psa 1968, 18:139-143
66860 Freud, A. Some aspects of the relation between neurotic pathology in childhood and in adult life. Bull Phila Ass Psa 1967, 17:111-114
66861 Kavka, J. The fractionated dream narrative as transference communication. Bull Phila Ass Psa 1968, 18:205-209
66862 Kernberg, O. F. Prognostic factors in the psychoanalytic treatment of narcissistic personalities. Bull Phila Ass Psa 1968, 18:143-148
66863 Lipton, S. D. Observations on rapid manifestations of drives and defenses. Bull Phila Ass Psa 1967, 17:176-177
66864 Loewenstein, R. M. An historical review of the theory of psychoanalytic technique. Bull Phila Ass Psa 1969, 19:58-60
66865 Seitz, P. F. D. Cycles and subcycles in the analytic process. Bull Phila Ass Psa 1969, 19:97-100
66866 Seitz, P. F. D. Representations of adaptive and defense mechanisms in the concrete imagery of dreams. Bull Phila Ass Psa 1968, 18:91-95

66867 Steele, B. F. Parental abuse of infants and small children. A study of the effect of early experience on adult parenting behavior. Bull Phila Ass Psa 1968, 18:209-213

BEIN, K.

66868 School phobia. J Med Soc New Jersey 1967, 64:67-70

BEIRNAERT, LOUIS

66869 Un monitum du Saint-Office. [On psychoanalysis.] Etudes 1961, 311:116-119

BEISER, HELEN R.

66870 Discrepancies in the symptomatology of parents and children. J Amer Acad child Psychiat 1964, 3:457-468

66871 Fifty-seven years of child guidance: the experience of the institute for juvenile research. Proc IV World Cong Psychiat 1966, 1640-1642

66872 (& Allender, J.) Personality factors influencing medical school achievement. J med Educ 1964, 39:175-182

66873 Personality factors influencing medical school achievement: a follow-up study. J med Educ 1967, 42:1087-1095

66874 Psychiatric diagnostic interviews with children. J Amer Acad Child Psychiat 1962, 1:656-670

66875 (Reporter) A reappraisal of Waelder's "The principle of multiple function." In Traditional Subjects Reconsidered," Proc 2nd Regional Conf Chicago Psa Soc 1968

66876 Self-listening during supervision of psychotherapy. Arch gen Psychiat 1966, 15:135-139
Abs PB Q 1969, 38:511

See Mathews, W. Mason

BEISSER, ARNOLD R.

66877 The Madness in Sports; Psychosocial Observation on Sports. NY: Appleton-Century-Crofts 1967, 241 p

66878 Psychodynamic observations of a sport. PPR 1961, 48:69-76

66879 (& Harris, H.) Psychological aspects of the civil rights movement and the Negro professional man. P 1966, 123:733-737

66880 Transference and countertransference in the psychiatric joke. PT 1963, 17:78-82

BEITNER, MARVIN S.

66881 Word meaning and sexual identification in paranoid schizophrenics and anxiety neurotics. ASP 1961, 63:289-293

BEKEI, MARTA

66882 [The influence of constitutional and environmental factors on child development.] (Sp) Acta psiquiat psicol Arg 1963, 9:53

66883 Medicina Psicosomática en Pediatria. [Psychosomatic Medicine in Childhood.] Buenos Aires: Ed. Medica Panam 1965
Rv Salas, E. J. Rev Psicoanál 1967, 24:937-938

66884 [Psychologic aspects of hospital care of children.] (Sp) El día Médico 1961, (75):2330
66885 [The rehabilitation of Indoamericans through psychosomatic medicine.] (Sp) Médico Moderno 1966, 4(9)
66886 [Spontaneous manifestations of the newborn.] (Sp) Rev Arch Arg Pediat 1963, 59(5):6

BÉLAIR, CLAUDETTE

See Bigras, Julien; Mackay, Jacques

BÉLANGER, DAVID

66887 (& Saunier, M.) Étude analytique des processus psychophysiologiques dans la maladie de Parkinson. [Analytical study of the psychophysiological processes in Parkinson's disease.] Rev Canad Biol 1961, 20:539-544

BELCHIOR, CORNELIO DA SILVA

66888 A instrucão sexual e a psicanálise. [On sexual instruction and psychoanalysis.] Rev ecclesiástica bras 1962, 22:174-181

BELINKOFF, JULIUS

66889 (& Bross, R.; Stein, A.) The effect of group psychotherapy on anaclitic transference. Int J grp PT 1964, 14:474-481

BELKÁNYI, CHARLOTTE

REVIEW OF:
66890 Pichon, E. & Borel-Maisonny, S. Le Bégaiement. Sa Nature et son Traitement. J 1965, 46:397-398

BELL, ANITA I.

66891 Additional aspects of passivity and feminine identification in the male. (Read at Washington Psa Inst, Jan 1968; Am Psa Ass, May 1968) J 1968, 49:640-647
66892 Bowel training difficulties in boys: prephallic and phallic considerations. J Amer Acad child Psychiat 1964, 3:577-590
66893 (& Levine, M. I.) The psychologic aspects of pediatric practice. II. Masturbation. J Pediat 1956, 18(5)
66894 The role of parents. Adolescents 273-281
66895 The significance of scrotal sac and testicles for the prepuberty male. (Read at Amer Psa Ass, Dec 1963; Western New England Psa Soc, Oct 1964) Q 1965, 34:182-206
        Abs LDr RFPsa 1966, 30(Suppl):326
66896 Some observations on the role of the scrotal sac and testicles. (Read at Amer Psa Ass 1959, 1960; NY Psa Soc, 29 Nov 1960) J Am Psa Ass 1961, 9:261-286
        Abs Brauer, P. H. Q 1961, 30:318-319. FB Q 1962, 26:617. SAS RFPsa 1962, 26:617. Auth Rev Psicoanál 1963, 20:89

S-41438 Some thoughts on postpartum respiratory experiences and their relationship to pregenital mastery, particularly in asthmatics.
Abs GLG An Surv Psa 1958, 9:205-206

REVIEW OF:
66897 Winokur, G. (Ed) Determinants of Human Sexual Behavior. Q 1965, 34:127

BELL, CLIVE

66898 Dr. Freud on art. In Strom, W. *A Dial Miscellany,* Syracuse, NY: Syracuse Univ Pr 1963, 227-230

BELL, D. S.

66899 (& Trethowan, W. H.) Amphetamine addiction. JNMD 1961, 133:489-496

BELL, DANIEL

REVIEW OF:
66900 Rokeach, M. The Open and Closed Mind. Investigations into the Nature of Belief Systems and Personality Systems. Q 1961, 30:435-438

BELL, DOROTHY

See Archibald, Herbert C.

BELL, NORMAN W.

66901 (& Vogel, E. F.) (Eds) A Modern Introduction to the Family. Glencoe, Ill.: Free Press 1960. x + 691 p
66902 (& Spiegel, J. P.) Social psychiatry. Arch gen Psychiat 1966, 14:337-345
Abs PB Q 1969, 38:167
66903 (& Thieschman, A.; Vogel, E.) A sociocultural analysis of the resistances of working-class fathers treated in a child psychiatric clinic. Ops 1961, 31:388-405
Abs JMa RFPsa 1962, 26:327
66904 Terms of a comprehensive theory of family psychopathology relationships. In Zuk, G. H. & Boszormenyi-Nagy, I. *Family Therapy and Disturbed Families,* Palo Alto, Calif: Sci & Behav Books 1967, 2-10

See Eldred, Stanley H.; Vogel, Ezra F.

BELL, RICHARD Q.

66905 Developmental psychology. Ann Rev Psychol 1965, 16:1-38
66906 A reinterpretation of the direction of effects in studies of socialization. Psychol Rev 1968, 75:81-95
66907 Retrospective and prospective views of early personality development. Merrill-Palmer Q 1960, 6:131-144
66908 Structuring parent-child interaction situations for direct observation. Child Devlpm 1964, 35:1009-1020

See Gordon, Norma S.; Waldrop, Mary F.

BELLAGAMBA, HUGO F.

66909 (& Horne, B. C.; Salvarezza, L.; Salvarezzo, R. R. de; Simoes, G.; Winocur, J.) Ampliación del concepto de idealición. [Amplification of the concept of idealization.] Rev Psicoanál 1962, 19:55-56

BELLAH, ROBERT N.

66910 Father and son in Christianity and Confucianism. R 1965, 52:92-114
Abs SRS Q 1966, 35:472-473

BELLAK, LEOPOLD

66911 Acting out: some conceptual and therapeutic considerations. PT 1963, 17:375-389
66912 (& Chassan, J. B.) An approach to the evaluation of drug effect during psychotherapy: a double-blind study of a single case. JNMD 1964, 139:20-30
66913 The Broad Scope of Psychoanalysis: Selected Papers of Leopold Bellak. (Ed: Spence, D. P.) NY: Grune & Stratton 1968, 392 p
66914 CAT-H (An adaptation of the C. A. T. with human figures.) Larchmont, NY: C. P. S. Inc 1964
66915 (& Adelman, C.) The Children's Apperception Test (CAT). In Rabin, A. I. & Haworth, M. R. *Projective Techniques with Children,* NY/London: Grune & Stratton 1960, 62-94
66916 A community mental health centre in a hospital. M 1960, 33:287-290
66917 The concept of acting out: theoretical considerations. Acting Out 3-19
66918 Contemporary European psychiatry. JNMD 1962, 135:82-87
66919 (Ed) Contemporary European Psychiatry. NY: Grove Pr 1962, 372 p
Rv AN Q 1963, 32:420-423. ESt J 1963, 44:382
S-41444 Creativity: some random notes to a systematic consideration.
Abs ARK An Surv Psa 1958, 9:489-490
66920 Depersonalization as a variant of self-awareness. In Abrams, A. *Unfinished Tasks in the Behavioral Sciences,* Baltimore: Williams & Wilkins 1964
66921 Discussion: the children's apperception test: its use in developmental assessments of normal children. J proj Tech 1968, 32:425-427
66922 (& Rosenberg, S.) Effects of anti-depressant drugs on psychodynamics. Psychosomatics 1966, 7:106-114
S-41449 An ego-psychological theory of hypnosis. Abs An Surv Psa 1955, 6:136-137
66923 (& Small, L.) Emergency Psychotherapy and Brief Psychotherapy. NY/London: Grune & Stratton 1965, ix + 254 p
Rv HRB Q 1967, 36:124-125
S-41450 (& Smith, M. B.) An experimental exploration of the psychoanalytic process.
Abs SO An Surv Psa 1956, 7:60-62
66924 (& Meyer, E. J.; Rosenberg, S.; Zuckerman, M.) An experimental study of brief psychotherapy. In Lesse, S. *An Evaluation of the Results of the Psychotherapies,* Springfield, Ill.: Thomas 1968, 101-152
° ° ° Foreword. Acting Out x-xii

* * * Foreword to Chassan, J. B. *Research Design in Clinical Psychology and Psychiatry*
* * * Foreword to Haworth, M. R. *The CAT: Facts about Fantasy*
* * * Foreword to Klopfer, W. G. *The Psychological Report. Use and Communication of Psychological Findings*
66925 Free association: conceptual and clinical aspects. J 1961, 42:9-20
       Über theoretische und klinische Aspekte der freien Assoziation. Psyche 1961, 15:382-404
       Abs WPK Q 1962, 31:281. PCR RFPsa 1964, 28:297
66926 A general hospital as a focus of community psychiatry. A trouble shooting clinic combines important functions as a part of hospital's emergency service. JAMA 1960, 174:2214-2217
66927 (Ed) Handbook of Community Psychiatry and Community Mental Health. NY: Grune & Stratton 1963, 530 p; 1964, viii + 465 p
       Rv WAF Q 1966, 35:617
66928 (& Hurvich, M. S.) A human modification of the Children's Apperception Test (CAT-H). J proj Tech 1966, 30:228-242
66929 Intensive design drug therapy and the psychotherapeutic process. Psychosomatics 1965, 6:287-289
66930 Introduction to Hunt, M. M. et al: *The Talking Cure*, NY: Harper & Row 1963
66931 (& Chassan, J. B.) An introduction to intensive design in the evaluation of drug efficacy during psychotherapy. Meth Res PT 478-499
66932 Methodology and research in the psychotherapy of psychoses. Psychiat Res Rep 1963, 17:30-39
66933 Personality structure in a changing world. Arch gen Psychiat 1961, 5:183-185
66934 (& Salk, L.; Rosenhan, D.) A process study of the effects of Deprol on depression. Exemplification of a method of a psychodynamic process study of psychotropic drugs. JNMD 1961, 132:531-538
66935 (& Barten, H. H.) (Eds) Progress in Community Mental Health, Vol. I. NY: Grune & Stratton 1969, viii + 272 p
66936 The psychiatric unit in the general hospital [interviewed by Perkins, M. E.]. In Ziskind, R. *Viewpoint on Mental Health*, NY: NYC Comm Ment Hlth Board 1967, 22-28
66937 (& Prola, M.; Meyer, E. J.; Zuckerman, M.) Psychiatry in the medical-surgical emergency clinic. Arch gen Psychiat 1964, 10:267-269
S-41460 Psychoanalytic principles discernible in projective testing.
       Abs Frisch, A. An Surv Psa 1958, 9:120
66938 Psychological test reporting; a problem in communication between psychologists and psychiatrists. Introduction: the scope of the problem. Ops 1959, 29:528-546
66939 Psychoses. In *International Encyclopedia of the Social Sciences*, NY: Crowell Collier & Macmillan 1968
66940 (& Hurvich, M.; Crawford, P.) Psychotic egos. Symposium: The emergence of ego psychology. R 1969-70, 56:526-542
66941 (& Black, B.) The rehabilitation of psychotics in the community. Ops 1960, 30:346-355
66942 Research in psychoanalysis. (Read at the Phila Psa Soc, 20 Jan 1960) Q 1961, 30:519-548

66943   The role and nature of emergency psychotherapy. Amer J publ Hlth
        1968, 58(2)
S-41465 (& Benedict, P. K.) (Eds) Schizophrenia: A Review of the Syndrome.
        NY: Grune & Stratton 1966, xx + 1010 p
            Abs SLP An Surv Psa 1958, 9:181. Rv Rosenfeld, H. J 1961, 42:126
66944   (& Loeb, L.) (Eds) The Schizophrenic Syndrome. NY: Grune & Strat-
        ton 1969, 864 p
66945   Somerset Maugham: a thematic analysis of ten stories. In White, R. W.
        The Study of Lives, NY: Atherton Pr 1966, 142-159
66946   Soviet psychiatric lag. P 1969, 125:1267
S-41468 Studying the psychoanalytic process by the method of short-range
        prediction and judgment.
            Abs Frisch, A. An Surv Psa 1958, 9:342-343
66947   The systematic diagnosis of the schizophrenic syndrome. Dyn Psychiat
        1969, 3:148-156; Abs (Ger) 156-157
66948   (& Hurvich, M.) A systematic study of ego functions. JNMD 1969,
        148:569-585
66949   (& Hurvich, M.; Silvan, M.; Jacobs, D.) Towards an ego psychological
        appraisal of drug effects. P 1968, 12:593-604
66950   The treatment of schizophrenia and psychoanalytic theory. JNMD
        1960, 131:39-46
66951   Les urgences psychiatriques pour les médecins practiciens. [Psychiatric
        emergencies for practicing physicians.] Méd Hyg 1964, (649)

        See Chassan, Jacob B.; Hurvich, Marvin S.; Rosenberg, Sidney

        REVIEWS OF:
66952   Abercrombie, M. J. J. The Anatomy of Judgment. An Investigation into
        the Processes of Perception and Reasoning. Q 1961, 30:120-122
66953   Masserman, J. H. (Ed) Current Psychiatric Therapies, Vol. I & Vol. II.
        Q 1963, 32:278
66954   Peatman, J. G. & Hartley, E. L. (Eds) Festschrift for Gardner Murphy.
        Q 1961, 30:135
66955   Rosen, J. N. Direct Psychoanalytic Psychiatry. Q 1964, 33:281-283

BELLANOVA, PIERO

66956   Discussion of Fajrajzen, S. "Alcune considerazione sull' aggressività
        controtransferenziale nel trattamento di pazienti psicotici." Riv Psa
        1966, 12:107
66957   Rapporti fra terapia ed espressione pittorica nel'analisi di un omosessu-
        ale. [Reports on therapy and pictorial expression from the analysis of
        a homosexual.] Riv Psa 1966, 12:93-98

BELLÓN, RAÚL

        See Arizmendi Ch., Fernando

BELLS, E. K.

66958   (& Neubauer, P. B.) Sex differences and symptom patterns in early
        childhood. J child Psychiat 1963, 2:417-433

BELMONT, HERMAN S.

66959 Community mental health and dynamic child psychiatry. Penn Med 1968, 71:53-56

* * * Contributor to Pearson, G. H. J. *A Handbook of Child Psychoanalysis*

66960 In Memoriam. Gerald H. J. Pearson, M. D. 1893-1969. Bull Phila Ass Psa 1969, 19:109-113

S-41479 Remarks on the etiology and management of ego disturbances in children.
Abs An Surv Psa 1955, 6:287-288

REVIEW OF:

66961 Blos, P. On Adolescence. A Psychoanalytic Interpretation. Bull Phila Ass Psa 1962, 12:116-117

BELO, JANE

66962 Trance in Bali. (Pref: Mead, M.) NY: Columbia Univ Pr 1960, 283 p
Rv Muensterberger, W. Q 1961, 30:290-292

BELSASSO, GUIDO

See Palacios López, Agustin

BEMELMANS, FELIX

66963 Le test de dessin d'A. Rey. [The drawing test of A. Rey.] Bull Orient scol profess 1958, 7:11-30

BEMPORAD, JULES R.

66964 (& Sours, J. A.; Spalter, H. F.) Cataracts following chronic headbanging: a report of two cases. P 1968, 125:245-249

66965 Perceptual disorders in schizophrenia. P 1967, 123:971-976

BÉNASSY, MAURICE

66966 Discussion of Held, R. "Contribution à l'étude psychanalytique du phénomène religieux." RFPsa 1962, 26:261

66967 Discussion of Lebovici, S. "Colloque sur les interprétations en thérapeutique psychanalytique." RFPsa 1962, 26:32

66968 Discussion of Luquet, P. "Ouvertures sur l'artiste et le psychanalyste." RFPsa 1963, 27:609

66969 En relisant "Analyse terminable et analyse interminable." [On rereading "Terminable analysis and interminable analysis."] RFPsa 1968, 32:246-262

S-41495 Evolution de la psychanalyse.
Abs JLL An Surv Psa 1956, 7:39-40

66970 (& Diatkine, R.) Ontogenèse du fantasme. RFPsa 1964, 28:539-565
Symposium on fantasy: On the ontogenesis of fantasy. (Read at Int Psa Cong, July-Aug 1963) J 1964, 45:171-179
Abs EVN Q 1966, 35:455-456

66971 Psychanalyses didactiques et expériences réligieuses. [Training psychoanalyses and religious experiences.] RFPsa 1965, 29:31-41

S-41500 Psychanalyse et psychologie.
Abs HFM An Surv Psa 1957, 8:18

66972 Psychanalyse générale et problème du narcissisme. [General psychoanalysis and the problem of narcissism.] Bull Psychol, Paris 1966, 19:816-828; 1173-1183

66973 Psychanalyse théorique. [Theoretical psychoanalysis.] Bull Psychol, Paris 1967, 20:563-567; 1043-1046

66974 Théorie du narcissisme de Federn (psychologie du Moi). [Federn's theory of narcissism (ego psychology).] RFPsa 1965, 29:533-559

66975 Les théories du "moi" en psychanalyse. [Psychoanalytic theories of the ego.] Bull Psychol, Paris 1963, 16:568-573

REVIEWS OF:

66976 Foissin, H. Mecanismes Perceptifs et Structure de la Personnalité. RFPsa 1966, 30:324

66977 Koch, S. Psychology: A Study of a Science, I. RFPsa 1962, 26:769

66978 Nacht, S. The Presence of the Analyst. RFPsa 1967, 31:293-298

BENATTI, C.

See Cavazzuti, G. B.

BENDA, CLEMENS E.

66979 Discussion of Bender, L. "Childhood schizophrenia: a review." J Hillside Hosp 1967, 16:1

66980 The existential approach in psychiatry. J existent Psychiat 1960, 1:24-40

66981 The existential approach to religion. Int Psychiat Clin 1969, 5(4):37-48

66982 Existentialism in philosophy and science. J existent Psychiat 1960, 1:284-314

66983 Die geistigen Entwicklungsstörungen in Kindesalter. Grundlegende Ausführungen. [Disorders of mental development in childhood. Basic remarks.] Nervenarzt 1964, 35:97-101

66984 The Image of Love. Modern Trends in Psychiatric Thinking. NY: Free Pr of Glencoe 1961, viii + 206 p
Rv Eidelberg, L. Q 1963, 32:125-126

66985 Language, consciousness, and problems of existential analysis. (Daseinsanalyse). PT 1960, 14:259-276

66986 Language, intelligence, and creativity. J existent Psychiat 1962-63, 3:27-44

66987 Motivation and conscience. Humanitas 1968, 3:241-258

66988 "Narcissism" in psychoanalysis and the "love of oneself" in existential psychotherapy. Dis nerv Sys 1961, 22(4,Suppl):69-77

66989 Neuroses of conscience. J existent Psychiat 1967, 28:425-442

66990 (& Squires, N. D.; Ogonik, J.) The relationship between intellectual inadequacy and emotional and sociocultural privation. Comprehen Psychiat 1964, 5:294-313

66991 What is existential psychiatry? P 1966, 123:288-296

BENDER, H.

66992 The Gotenhafen case of correspondence between dreams and future events: a study of motivation. Int J Neuropsychiat 1966, 2:398-407

BENDER, LAURETTA

66993 (& Faretra, G.) Body image problems in children. In Lief, H. I. et al: *The Psychological Basis of Medical Practice*. NY: Harper & Row 1963, 431-439

66994 The brain and child behavior. Arch gen Psychiat 1961, 4:531-547

66995 Childhood schizophrenia: a review. J Hillside Hosp 1967, 16:10-22. Int J Psychiat 1968, 5:211-220; 234-236
Schizophrenie de l'enfance. Méd Hyg 1961, 19:499-500

66996 Clinical research from in-patient services for children, 1920-1957. Psychiat Q 1961, 15:88-120

66997 The concept of plasticity in childhood schizophrenia. In Hoch, P. & Zubin, J. *Psychopathology of Schizophrenia*, NY: Grune & Stratton 1966, 354-365

66998 Current techniques in the management of the anxious child. PT 1961, 15:341-347

66999 Developmental neuropsychiatry: the child psychiatry of the future. In Hoch, P. H. & Zubin, J. *The Future of Psychiatry*, NY/London: Grune & Stratton 1962, 200-215

° ° ° Editor of Schilder, P. *Contributions to Developmental Neuropsychiatry*.

67000 Emotional deprivation in infancy and its implications in child psychiatry. Criança Port 1960, 19:83-107

S-1910 Genesis of hostility in children. R 1963, 50:625-632. In Zawodny, J. K. *Man and International Relations, Vol. 1,* San Francisco, Calif: Chandler Publ 1966, 76-82

67001 Offended and offender children. In Slovenko, R. *Sexual Behavior and the Law,* Springfield, Ill: Thomas 1965, 687-703

67002 The origin and evolution of the Gestalt function, the body image and delusional thoughts in schizophrenia. Recent Adv biol Psychiat 1963, 5:38-62

67003 Prognosis of infantile psychosis and neurosis. Proc IV World Cong Psychiat 1966, 124-126

67004 A psychiatrist looks at deviancy as a factor in juvenile delinquency. Fed Probation 1968, 2:35-41

67005 Some art work of emotionally disturbed boys at puberty. J Hillside Hosp 1968, 17:349-361

67006 Theory and treatment of childhood schizophrenia. Acta paedopsychiat 1967, 34:298-307

67007 Treatment in early schizophrenia. Prog PT 1960, 5:177-184

See Siva Sankar, D. V.

BENDIX, LISELOTTE

REVIEWS OF:
67008 Grinstein, A. The Index of Psychoanalytic Writings. Q 1967, 36:295-297

67009 Sigmund Freud in Übersetzungen. Q 1967, 36:130

BENE, EVA

67010 Anxiety and emotional impoverishment in men under stress. M 1961, 34:281-289

67011 On the genesis of female homosexuality. Brit J Psychiat 1965, 111:815-821

67012 On the genesis of male homosexuality: an attempt at clarifying the role of the parents. Brit J Psychiat 1965, 111:803-813

BENEDEK, E.

See Harrison, Saul I.

BENEDEK, THERESE

S-41542 A contribution to the problem of termination of training analysis.
Abs An Surv Psa 1955, 6:393-395

67013 Discussion of Sherfey, M. J. "The evolution and nature of female sexuality in relation to psychoanalytic theory." J Am Psa Ass 1968, 16:424-448

67014 The functions of the sexual apparatus and their disturbances. In Alexander, F. *Psychosomatic Medicine. Its Principles and Applications.* NY: Norton 1965

67015 An investigation of the sexual cycle in women: methodologic considerations. Arch gen Psychiat 1963, 8:311-322
Abs KR Q 1964, 33:302

67016 Obituary: Franz Alexander 1891-1964. J Am Psa Ass 1964, 12:877-881

67017 On the psychic economy of developmental process. Arch gen Psychiat 1967, 17:271-276

S-41550 The organization of the reproductive drive.
Abs JBi Q 1961, 30:296. PCR RFPsa 1964, 28:290

S-41551 Parenthood as a developmental phase. A contribution to the libido theory.
Elternschaft als Phase der Entwicklung. Jb Psa 1960, 1:35-61
Abs JTM Q 1961, 30:137

67018 (& Fleming, J.) Psychoanalytic Supervision. NY: Grune & Stratton 1966, 252 p

S-41558 Toward the biology of the depressive constellation.
Abs OS An Surv Psa 1956, 7:182-184

67019 Training analysis—past, present and future. (Read at Conf on Training Analysis 1965) J 1969, 50:437-445

67020 Über Orgasmus und Frigidität. [On orgasm and frigidity.] Jb Psa 1963, 3:11-29

See Fleming, Joan

REVIEW OF:

67021 Stone, L. The Psychoanalytic Situation. Q 1962, 31:549-551

BENEDETTI, GAETANO

67022 Alcuni aspetti dello sviluppo del carattere nella nostra cultura occidentale. [Some aspects of character development in our western culture.] Psichiatria Generale e dell'età Evolutiva 1965, 2(1)

67023 Analogien zwischen Kinderpsychotherapie und Psychotherapie mit regredierten schizophrenen Erwachsenen. [Comparison between psychotherapy in children and in regressed schizophrenic adults.] Acta paedopsychiat 1962, 29:320-330

67024 La Angustia. [Anxiety.] Tribuna de la Revista de Occidente, Madrid 1960

67025 Aspetti neurofisiologici dell'ansia, fatti e problemi. [Neurophysiological problems of anxiety, facts and problems.] Milano: Incontri Ciba 1966, April

67026 Aspetti odierni dello sviluppo psicosessuale. [Present-day aspects of psychosexual development.] Psichiatria Generale e dell'età Evolutiva 1965, 3(3)

67027 Begüssung. [Welcoming remarks.] In Müller, C. & Benedetti, G. *Psychotherapy of Schizophrenia (3rd Int Symp 1964)*, Basel/NY: Karger 1965, vi-x

67028 Ch. Blumhardt, seine Seelsorge im Lichte heutiger psychotherapeutischer Kenntnisse. [Ch. Blumhardt, his ministerial work in the light of today's therapeutic knowledge.] Reformatio 1960, 9(9):10

67029 La comunicazione in psichiatria. [Communication in psychiatry.] Arch Psicol Neurol Psichiat 1967, 28(3-4)

67030 La concezione moderna della psichiatria. [The conception of modern psychiatry.] In *Biblioteca de Psichiatria e Psicologia Clinica*, Milan: Feltrinelli 1962

67031 (& Miller, C.) Contemporary Swiss psychiatry. In Bellak, L. *Contemporary European Psychiatry*, NY: Grove Pr 1962

67032 Die Daseinsanalyse in der Sicht eines Psychiaters. ["Das—einanalysis" as seen by a psychiatrist.] Jb Psychol Psychother med Anthropol, 11(3-4)

67033 Dialektische Gegensatzpaare in der Psychiatrie. [Dialectic antithesis in psychiatry.] Jb Psychol Psychother med Anthropol, 9

67034 Dialettica della situazione in psicoterapia. [Dialectics of the situation in psychotherapy.] In *La Psicoterapia delle Psicosi Schizofreniche*, Milan: Centro di Studii de Psicoterapia Clinica 1964

67035 Entwicklung der Psychotherapie Schizophrener. [Development of psychotherapy for schizophrenics.] Z Psychother med Psychol 1962, 12:59-62

67036 Il fattore personale nella psichiatria odierna. [The personal factor in present day psychiatry.] Arch Psicol Neurol Psichiat 1960, 21:335-355

67037 Forschungen zur Schizophrenielehre 1956-1961. [Survey of theory of schizophrenia 1956-1961.] Fortschr Neurol Psychiat 1962, 30(7-8)

67038 (& Kind, H.; Wenger, V.) Forschungen zur Schizophrenielehre 1961-1965. [Investigations on schizophrenia theory 1961-1965.] Fortschr Neurol Psychiat 1967, 35:1-34; 41-121

67039 Die Fürsorge um den psychisch Kranken. [Care of the mentally ill.] Der Fürsorger 1960, 28:41

67040 Grundprobleme der Psychotherapie bei Schizophrenen. [Basic problems of psychotherapy with schizophrenics.] In Hoff, H. *Therapeutische Fortschritte in der Neurologie und Psychiatrie*, Vienna/Innsbruck: Urban & Schwarzenberg 1960, 364-378

67041 Grundzüge der psychotherapie bei Schizophrenen. [Characteristics of psychotherapy with schizophrenics.] In author's *Psychotherapy of Schizophrenia (1st Int Symp 1956)* 1-6

67042 Die Handhabung der Regression in der individuellen Psychotherapie schizophrener Psychosen. [The operation of regression in the individual psychotherapy of schizophrenic psychoses.] Psychother Psychosom 1965, 13:87-100

67043 Die Heilungstat eines Seelsorgers. [The sanctification of a minister.] Kirchenbote 1960, 3(70)

67044 Homosexualität Homophilie in medizinisch-psychologischer Sicht. [Homophile homosexuality from a medico-psychological viewpoint.] In *Probleme der Homophilie*, Bern und Tübingen 1965

67045 L'immigration italienne en Suisse. [Italian immigration in Switzerland.] In *Industrialisation and Mental Health*, Geneva: World Federation for Mental Health 1965

67047 Klinische Psychotherapie. [Clinical Psychotherapy.] Bern: Huber Verlag 1964

67048 Menschliche Umwelt und Schizophrenie. [The human environment and schizophrenia.] Seele 1965, 6

67049 Neuropsychologie Heute: eine Standortbestimmung. [Neuropsychology today.] Schweiz Ärztezeitung 1968, 49:1201-1208

67050 Neurose und Gesellschaft im Lichte der neueren Kriegspsychiatrie. [Neurosis and society in the light of the new war psychiatry.] Schweiz ANP 1965, 95(2)

67051 Nevrosi e psicoterapia. [Neuroses and psychotherapy.] Enciclopedia medica Italiana 1960

67052 El Paciente Psiquico y su Mundo. [The Psychiatric Patient and His World.] Madrid: Ediciones Morata 1966

67053 Das Problem der Schuld in Medizinisch-Anthropologischer Sicht. [The Problem of Guilt from the Medical-Anthropological Point of View.] Stuttgart: Universitas, Wissenschaftliche Verlagsgesellschaft 1960

67054 Il problema della produttività individuale nell'educazione e nella personalità odierna. [The problem of individual productivity in education and in present day personality.] Psichiatria dell'età Evolutiva 1964, 2(4)

67055 Le problème de la régression psychotique dans la psychothérapie individuelle. [The problem of psychotic regression in individual psychotherapy.] In Müller, C. & Benedetti, G. *Psychotherapy of Schizophrenia (3rd Int Symp 1964)*, Basel/NY: Karger 1965, 168-176

67056 Prognostische Gesichtspunkte zur Psychotherapie schizophrener Psychosen. [Prognostic criteria for psychotherapy of schizophrenic psychoses.] Z Psychother med Psychol 1966, 16:61-69

67057 Psichiatria e psicoterapia. [Psychiatry and psychotherapy.] In *Problemi di Psicoterapie*, Milan: Centro Studii di Psicoterapia Clinica 1962

67058 La psichiatria nelle varie civiltà e culture. [Psychiatry in various civilizations and cultures.] In *Psicoterapia e Science Umane*, Milan: Centro Studii di Psicoterapia Clinica 1967, 1(2-3)

67059 La psichiatria oggi. [Psychiatry today.] In *L'Uomo, L'Universo, La Scienza*, Rome: Edilindustria Editoriale 1964

67060   Psicoterapia e Psicodinamica della schizofrenia paranoide. [Psychother-
         apy and psychodynamics of paranoid schizophrenia.] In *La Psicoter-
         apia delle Psicosi Schizofreniche*, Milan: Centro di Studii di Psicoter-
         apia Clinica 1964
67061   Psychiatrie und Psychotherapie in Widerspruch und Übereinstimmung.
         [Psychiatry and psychotherapy: contradictions and agreements.] Acta
         psychother psychosom 1962, 10:206-218
67062   Psychiatrische Prophylaxe. [Psychiatric prophylaxis.] Int J prophylak-
         tische Medizin & Sozialhygiene 1962, 6(3)
67063   Der Psychisch Leidende und seine Welt. [The Psychiatrically Ill and
         His World.] Stuttgart: Hippokrates Verlag 1964
67064   Psychopharmakotherapie neuro-vegetativer Funktionsstörungen und
         psychosomatischer Krankheiten. [Psycho-pharmacotherapy of disturb-
         ances in neuro-vegetative function and psychosomatic illness.] In
         Monnier, M. von: *Pathophysiologie*, II, Stuttgart: Hippokrates 1963
67065   (& Müller, C.) (Eds) Psychothérapie de la Schizophrénie. Psychother-
         apie der Schizophrenie. Psychotherapy of Schizophrenia. (1st Int Symp,
         Oct 1956) Basel/NY: Karger 1957, 264 p
67066   (& Müller, C.) (Eds) Psychothérapie de la Schizophrénie. Psycho-
         therapie der Schizophrenie. Psychotherapy of Schizophrenia. (2nd Int
         Symp, 1959) Basel/NY: Karger 1960, viii + 300 p
67067   Psychotherapie und Seelsorge. [Psychotherapy and pastoral care.] In
         Wort und Gemeinde, EVZ Verlag 1968
67068   Psychotherapie und Seelsorge in Widerspruch und Übereinstimmung.
         [Psychotherapy and pastoral care: agreements and contradictions.]
         Beiträge zu Psychiatrie und Seelsorge 1964, (6), Oct
67069   The psychotherapy of a schizophrenic patient. In Burton, A. *Modern
         Psychotherapeutic Practice*, Palo Alto, Calif: Sci & Behav Books 1965,
         37-57
67070   Die Quellen des sozialen Kontaktes. [The sources of social contact.]
         Acta paedopsychiat 1964, 31:145-162
67071   Die Schuld in psychotherapeutischer und seelsorgerischer Sicht. [Guilt
         in the light of psychotherapy and of pastoral care.] Universität und
         Christ. Evangelischer Verlag Zollikon 1960
67072   Die Schule im Spiegel des später seelisch Erkrankten. [School as a
         mirror of later mental illness.] Schriften des Schweiz, Lehrervereins,
         Zurich 1961, 34
67073   Übertragungen und Schizophrenietherapie. [Transference and the ther-
         apy of schizophrenia.] Schweiz ANP 1963, 91:122-128
67074   Wahnsinn als lebensgeschichtliches Phänomen. (Über die Verstand-
         lichkeit der chronisch schizophrenen Psychose.) [Delusion as a phe-
         nomenon in one's life-history. (An attempt to understand chronic
         schizophrenic psychosis.] Z Psychother med Psychol 1964, 14:186-195
67075   Das Werden des Paranoid Kranken in unserem Psychotherapeutischen
         Handeln. [Development of fate of the paranoic in our psychothera-
         peutic dealings.] In *Werden und Handeln*, Stuttgart: Hippokrates Ver-
         lag 1963
67076   Wie sieht der Therapeut seine Aufgabe? [How does the therapist see
         his problem?] Kirchenbote 1961, 47(7)

67077 Zum Begriff der Begegnungen in der Psychotherapie. [On the concept of treatment in psychotherapy.] Prax PT 1966, 11:201-207

See Müller, Christian

BENEDICT, PAUL K.

67078 Psychotherapy of alcoholism. Prog PT 1960, 5:148-155

See Bellak, Leopold

BENEDICT FOX, E. G.

67079 Was General Lee a victim of group psychology? R 1961, 48(3):62-68

BENFARI, ROBERT C.

67080 Defense and control: further indications. Percept mot Skills 1966, 22:736-738

67081 (& Calogeras, Roy C.) Levels of cognition and conscience typologies. J proj Tech 1968, 32:466-474

67082 The scanning control principle and its relationship to affect manipulation. Percept mot Skills 1966, 22:203-216

BEN-HORIN, PESSAH

See Vogel, Gerald W.

BENJAMIN, ANNE

S-41592 (Reporter) Childhood phobias. (Panel)
Abs An Surv Psa 1955, 6:263-266

BENJAMIN, HARRY

67083 (& Masters, R. F. L.) Prostitution and Morality. NY: Julian Pr 1964, 494 p
Rv Woltmann, A. G. R 1966, 53:303-308

67084 The Transsexual Phenomenon. NY: Julian Pr 1966, 286 p
Rv Akmakjian, H. R 1966, 53:684-685

BENJAMIN, JOHN D.

67085 Developmental biology and psychoanalysis. Psa Curr Biol Thought 57-80

67086 Discussion of Hartmann's ego psychology and the problem of adaptation. (Read at Chicago Psa Soc, 28 Jan 1964) Psa—Gen Psychol 28-42

67087 Further comments on some developmental aspects of anxiety. In Gaskill, H. S. Counterpoint: Libidinal Object and Subject, NY: IUP 1963, 121-153

67088 Some developmental observations relating to the theory of anxiety. (Read at Am Psa Ass, Dec 1958) J Am Psa Ass 1961, 9:652-668
Abs FB Q 1962, 31:423-424

BENJAMIN, LORNA S.

67089 The beginning of thumbsucking. Child Develpm 1967, 38:1065-1078

BENKENDORF, J.

See Furman, Robert A.

BENNET, EDWARD ARMSTRONG

67090 What Jung Really Said. London: Macdonald; NY: Schocken 1966, 185 p
Rv Hood, J. J 1967, 48:472

BENNETT, ABRAM ELTING

67091 (& Engle, B.) Psychiatric nursing and occupational therapy. Prog Neurol Psychiat 1960, 15:577-588; 1961, 16:575-584; 1962, 17:572-582; 1963, 18:659-669; 1964, 19:638-647

BENNETT, EDWARD

67092 Personality Assessment and Diagnosis. A Clinical and Experimental Technique. NY: Ronald Pr 1961, xii + 287 p
Rv Siegel, M. G. Q 1963, 32:124

BENNETT, EDWARD L.

See Dennis, Wayne

BENNETT, IVAN F.

See Southworth, John W.

BENNETT, IVY

S-41603 Delinquent and Neurotic Children. London: Tavistock; NY: Basic Books 1961, xii + 532 p
Rv Fountain, G. Q 1961, 30:580-582. EG Q 1961, 42:291-292. Geleerd, E. R. J Am Psa Ass 1964, 12:242-258

BENNETT, STEPHEN L.

67093 (& Klein, H. R.) Childhood schizophrenia: 30 years later. P 1966, 122:1121-1124

BENNETT, VIRGINIA D. C.

See Bardon, Jack I.

BENNEY, CELIA

See Black, Bertram J.

BENNIS, WARREN G.

67094 A critique of group therapy research. Int J grp PT 1960, 10:63-76
Abs GPK Q 1961, 30:604-605
67095 (& Schein, E. H.; Steele, F. I.; Berlew, D. E.) (Eds) Interpersonal Dynamics. Essays and Readings on Human Interaction. Homewood, Ill: Dorsey Pr 1968
67096 A psychoanalytic inquiry into the "two cultures" dilemma. Psa Forum 1969, 3:161-174; 182-183

67097 (& Slater, P. E.) The Temporary Society. NY: Harper & Row 1968, x + 147 p

67098 Toward a genetic theory of group development. J grp Psa Proc 1968, 1(2):23-25

BENOISTON, JEAN E.

67099 (& Mouzet, C.; Tanguy, M.) La symbolique prélogique d'un délirant. [Pre-logical symbolism of a delirious patient.] Evolut psychiat 1963, 28:283-304

BENOÎT, G.

See Lebovici, Serge

BENOIT, J. C.

67100 [The dream function. Psychiatric and psychologic interest in contemporary studies devoted to nocturnal dreams.] (Fr) Sem Hop Paris 1964, 40:2782-2786

67101 [Psychotherapy and use of medications in the practice of psychiatry. 3. Individual and collective aspects of the care.] (Fr) Pr méd 1968, 830-832

See Bergeron, Marcel

BENSMAN, JOSEPH

67102 (& Vidich, A.) Business cycles, class and personality. PPR 1962, 49(2): 30-52

BENTAL, VICKY

67103 Psychiatric disturbances of holocaust ("Shoa") survivors. Remarks and case-representation in a symposium of the Israel Psa Soc. Israel Ann Psychiat 1967, 5(1)

67104 Psychic mechanisms of the adoptive mother in connection with adoption. Israel Ann Psychiat 1965, 3:24-34
    Die Psychischen Mechanismen der Adoptivmutter in Verbindung mit der Adoption. Psyche 1966, 20:282-293

See Winnik, Heinrich Z.

BENTE, D.

67105 (& Bradley, T. B.) (Eds) Neuro-psychopharmacology. Vol. IV. Proceedings of the Collegium Internationale Neuro-Psychopharmacologicum, Birmingham 1964. London: Elsevier Publ Co. 1965; NY: Amer Elsevier Publ Co. 1966, xix + 518 p
    Rv Ostow, M. R 1967, 54:553-554

BENTZ, HANS W.

67106 Sigmund Freud in Übersetzungen. [Sigmund Freud in Translation.] Eine Bibliographie seiner in Buchform und Anthologien erschienen übersetzungen 1945-1960/1961. Frankfurt/Mainz: Bentz 1961, 60 p
    Abs J Am Psa Ass 1966, 14:233-234. Rv Kalmanovitch, J. RFPsa 1967, 31:298-299, Bendix, L. Q 1967, 36:129-130

BERADT, CHARLOTTE

67107 The Third Reich of Dreams. (Tr: Gottwald, A.) (With an essay by B. Bettelheim.) Chicago: Quadrangle Books 1968, 176 p
Abs J Am Psa Ass 1969, 17:279. Rv Katz, J. R 1969, 56(2):351-353

BERBLINGER, KLAUS W.

67108 Brief psychotherapy and the psychiatric consultation. Psychosomatics 1967, 8:6-10

See Simon, Alexander

BERCHENKO, FRANK

ABSTRACTS OF:
67109 Arlow, J. A. Ego psychology and the study of mythology. Q 1962, 31:416
67110 Arlow, J. A. Silence and the theory of technique. Q 1962, 31:288
67111 Bell, A. I. Some observations on the role of the scrotal sac and testicles. Q 1962, 31:292
67112 Benjamin, J. D. Some developmental observations relating to the theory of anxiety. Q 1962, 31:423-424
67113 Brandt, L. W. Some notes on English Freudian terminology. Q 1962, 31:294
67114 Eisnitz, A. J. Mirror dreams. Q 1962, 31:418-419
67115 Ekstein, R. & Rangell, L. Reconstruction and theory formation. Q 1962, 31:424-425
67116 Ferreira, A. J. Empathy and the bridge function of the ego. Q 1962, 31:290
67117 Fleming, J. What analytic work requires of an analyst: a job analysis. Q 1962, 31:425
67118 Fountain, G. Adolescent into adult: an inquiry. Q 1962, 31:417-418
67119 Fries, M. E. Some factors in the development and significance of early object relationships. Q 1962, 31:424
67120 Geleerd, E. R. Some aspects of ego vicissitudes in adolescence. Q 1962, 31:416-417
67121 Greenson, R. R. On the silence and sounds of the analytic hour. Q 1962, 31:289
67122 Grinstein, A. Freud's dream of the botanical monograph. Q 1962, 31:419
67123 Hammerman, S. Masturbation and character. Q 1962, 31:292-293
67124 Harley, M. Some observations on the relationship between genitality and structural development at adolescence. Q 1962, 31:418
67125 Lichtenstein, H. Identity and sexuality: a study of their interrelationship in man. Q 1962, 31:291-292
67126 Lipton, S. D. The last hour. Q 1962, 31:293
67127 Loewenstein, R. M. Introduction to panel "the silent patient." Q 1962, 31:286-287
67128 Loomie, L. S. Some ego considerations in the silent patient. Q 1962, 31:288-289
67129 McLaughlin, J. T. The analyst and the hippocratic oath. Q 1962, 31:290-291

67130 Modell, A. H. Denial and the sense of separateness. Q 1962, 31:420
67131 Murphy, W. F. A note on trauma and loss. Q 1962, 31:419-420
67132 Pfeffer, A. Z. Follow-up study of a satisfactory analysis. Q 1962, 31:425
67133 Rangell, L. The role of early psychic functioning in psychoanalysis. Q 1962, 31:420-421
67134 Rosenbaum, J. B. The significance of the sense of smell in the transference. Q 1962, 31:293
67135 Rubinfine, D. L. A survey of Freud's writings on early psychic functionings. Q 1962, 31:421-422
67136 Spiegel, L. A. Disorder and consolidation in adolescence. Q 1962, 31:417
67137 Spitz, R. A. Some early prototypes of ego defenses. Q 1962, 31:422-423
67138 Van der Heide, C. Blank silence and the dream screen. Q 1962, 31:290
67139 Warren, M. The significance of visual images during the analytic session. Q 1962, 31:419
67140 Zeligs, M. A. The psychology of silence: its role in transference, countertransference and the psychoanalytic process. Q 1962, 31:287

REVIEW OF:
67141 Menaker, W. & Menaker, E. Ego in Evolution. Q 1967, 36:283-284

BERCZELLER, EVA

67142 The "aesthetic feeling" and Aristotle's catharsis theory. J Psychol 1967, 65:261-271

BERDICHEVSKY, M.

See Zimmermann, D.

BERECZ, JOHN M.

67143 Phobias of childhood: etiology and treatment. Psychol Bull 1968, 70:694-720. Ann Prog child Psychiat 1969, 558-601

BERENSON, BERNARD G.

67144 (& Carkhuff, R. R.) Introduction: a personalized approach to counseling and psychotherapy. In authors' Sources of Gain in Counseling and Psychotherapy 1-7
67145 (& Carkhuff, R. R.) (Eds) Sources of Gain in Counseling and Psychotherapy: Readings and Commentary. NY/Chicago/San Francisco: Holt, Rinehart & Winston 1967, xii + 449 p
67146 (& Carkhuff, R. R.) Summary: emerging directions: a synthesis. In authors' Sources of Gain in Counseling and Psychotherapy 439-449

See Carkhuff, Robert R.

BERENSON, MARVIN H.

67147 Introjection in the countertransference. (Read at Los Angeles Psa Soc, 19 May 1966)
        Abs Shane, M. Bull Phila Ass Psa 1967, 17:118-121

BERENSTEIN, ISIDORO

67148   La pareja conjugal: vinculos, roles y niveles de comunicación. [The married couple: bondage, roles, levels of communication.] Acta psiqui-at psicol Arg 1962, 8:105-110

BERENT, IRVING

67149   A ritualistic aspect of smoking. Am Im 1961, 18:305-309

See Finkelstein, Lionel

BERES, DAVID

67150   Character formation. Adolescents 1-9

S-41649 Communication in psychoanalysis and in the creative process: a parallel. In Ruitenbeek, H. M. *The Creative Imagination,* Chicago: Quadrangle Books 1965, 207-222
     Abs EDJ An Surv Psa 1957, 8:78-80

S-41650 The contribution of psycho-analysis to the biography of the artist.
     Abs PCR RFPsa 1961, 25:284

67151   Discussion of Engel, G. L. "Some obstacles to the development of research in psychoanalysis." J Am Psa Ass 1968, 16:205-210

67152   (& Gale, C.; Oppenheimer, L.) Disturbances of identity function in childhood: psychiatric and psychological observations. Ops 1960, 30:369-381

S-41652 Ego deviation and the concept of schizophrenia.
     Abs SGo An Surv Psa 1956, 7:279-282

67153   Ego disturbances associated with early deprivation. J Amer Acad child Psychiat 1965, 4:188-205

67154   The functions of the superego. Psa Amer 275-288

67155   The humanness of human beings: psychoanalytic considerations. (Read at NY Psa Soc, 28 Nov 1967) Q 1968, 37:487-522

67156   Obituary: John F. Kennedy. (Read at Am Psa Ass, 8 Dec 1963) J Am Psa Ass 1964, 12:401-403

S-41653 Perception, imagination, and reality. (Read at NY Psa Soc, 31 May 1960)
     Perception, imagination et réalité. RFPsa 1961, 25:651-667
     Abs Jackel, M. M. Q 1961, 30:160-162. JBi Q 1962, 31:117-118.
     Urtubey, L. D. Rev urug Psa 1965, 7:280

67157   Psychoanalysis, science and romanticism. Dr Af Beh 2:397-417

67158   Psychoanalytic notes on the history of morality. (Read at Am Psa Ass, 6 Dec 1964) J Am Psa Ass 1965, 13:3-37
     Abs JLSt Q 1968, 37:465-466

S-41655 The psychoanalytic psychology of imagination.
     Abs JTM Q 1961, 30:597. SAS RFPsa 1962, 26:613

67159   The role of empathy in psychotherapy and psychoanalysis. J Hillside Hosp 1968, 17:362-369

67160   Structure and function in psycho-analysis. (Read at NY Psa Soc, 12 Jan 1965; Los Angeles Psa Soc, 21 Jan 1965)
     Abs HW Q 1965, 34:629-631. RZ Bull Phila Ass Psa 1966, 16:47-50.
     EVN Q 1967, 36:313

67161   Superego and depression. (Read at NY Psa Soc, 27 Sept 1966) Psa—
        Gen Psychol 479-498
            Abs Harrison, I. B. Q 1967, 36:635-636
67162   Symbol and object. BMC 1965, 29:3-23
67163   The unconscious fantasy. (Read at Western NY Psa Soc, 8 Apr 1961;
        Chicago Psa Soc, 26 Sept 1961) Q 1962, 31:309-328
            Abs Seitz, P.F.D. Bull Phila Ass Psa 1961, 11:194-195. LDr RFPsa
        1963, 27:357
S-41656 Vicissitudes of superego functions and superego precursors in child-
        hood.
            Abs JA An Surv Psa 1958, 9:124-126

        See Arlow, Jacob A.

        REVIEWS OF:
67164   Church, J. Language and the Discovery of Reality. A Developmental
        Psychology of Cognition. Q 1962, 31:267-269
67165   Eissler, K. R. Goethe. A Psychoanalytic Study 1775-1786. Q 1965,
        34:447-450
67166   Furst, S. S. (Ed) Psychic Trauma. Q 1969, 38:132-135
67167   Russel, G. W. The Candle of Vision. Q 1967, 36:120-121
67168   Veith, I. Hysteria. The Theory of a Disease. Q 1967, 36:284-287
67169   Von Leyden, W. Remembering. A Philosophical Problem. Q 1963, 32:
        103-105

BEREZIN, MARTIN A.

67170   Applied psychoanalysis. III. Literature, arts and aesthetics. An Surv
        Psa 1958, 9:474-500
67171   Comment on Miss Bicudo's paper: "Persecutory guilt and ego restric-
        tions." J 1964, 45:363-365
            Abs EVN Q 1966, 35:463-464
67172   Comment on Dr. Luquet's paper: "Early identifications and structura-
        tion of the ego." J 1964, 45:269-271
            Abs EVN Q 1966, 35:459-460
67173   Discussion [in the 1964 symposium on "Vicissitudes of the terminal
        phase of life."] Psychodyn St Aging 211-213
67174   Discussion of Giovacchini, P. L. "Characterological aspects of marital
        interaction." Psa Forum 1967, 2:18-19
* * *   Foreword to Zinberg, N. E. & Kaufman, I. Normal Psychology of the
        Aging Process
67175   (& Cath, S. H.) (Eds) Geriatric Psychiatry: Grief, Loss and Emotional
        Disorders in the Aging Process. NY: IUP; London: Bailey Bros 1966,
        380 p
            Abs J Am Psa Ass 1967, 15:224
S-41673 Note-taking during the psychoanalytic session.
            Abs DJM An Surv Psa 1957, 8:286
67176   (& Fern, D. J.) Persistence of early emotional problems in a seventy-
        year-old woman. J geriat Psychiat 1967, 1
67177   Some intrapsychic aspects of aging. In Zinberg, N. E. & Kaufman, I.
        Normal Psychology of the Aging Process, NY: IUP 1963, 93-117

S-41676 Some observations on art (music) and its relationship to ego mastery. Abs Cowitz, B. An Surv Psa 1958, 9:488-489

67178 (Reporter) The theory of genital primacy in the light of ego psychology. (Panel: Am Psa Ass, NY, 21 Dec 1968) J Am Psa Ass 1969, 17:968-987

See Blau, David

ABSTRACTS OF:

67179 Colby, K. M. Energy and Structure in Psychoanalysis. An Surv Psa 1955, 6:58, 466-475

67180 Fiedler, L. A. The failure of love in American fiction. An Surv Psa 1956, 7:417-418

67181 Munden, K. J. A contribution to the psychological understanding of the origin of the cowboy and his myth. An Surv Psa 1958, 9:447-448

REVIEWS OF:

67182 Grotjahn, M. Psychoanalysis and the Family Neurosis. Q 1961, 30:283-285

67183 Kaplan, B. & Wapner, S. (Eds) Perspectives in Psychological Theory. Essays in Honor of Heinz Werner. Q 1964, 33:278-279

BERG, CHARLES

67184 Madkind: The Origin and Development of the Mind. London: Allen & Unwin 1962, 277 p

S-41685 The problem of homosexuality. Abs RZ An Surv Psa 1956, 7:214-215; 1957, 8:133-134

BERG, IRWIN AUGUST

67185 (& Adams, H. E.) The experimental bases of personality assessment. In Bachrach, A. J. *Experimental Foundations of Clinical Psychology,* NY: Basic Books 1962, 52-93

BERG, JAN HENDRIK VAN DEN

67186 Kleine Psychiatric voor Studenten en Degenen die de Psychiater Vervangen of Bijstaan. [A Little Bit of Psychiatry for Students and Those in Need of Psychiatric Help.] Nijkerk: G. F. Callenbach 1967, 240 p

67187 The Psychology of the Sickbed. Pittsburgh: Duquesne Univ Pr 1966, 136 p

BERGAN, JOHN R.

67188 Pitch perception, imagery, and regression in the service of the ego. J Res mus Educ 1965, 13:15-32

BERGE, ANDRÉ

67189 L'art et la psychanalyse. [Art and psychoanalysis.] (Introduction) In *Entretiens sur l'Art et la Psychanalyse,* Editions Mouton 1968

67190 L'attitude du médecin devant la masturbation chez l'enfant et l'adolescent. [The doctor's attitude toward masturbation in child and adolescent.] J Méd Lyon 1962, 20 Sept

67191 Attitudes parentales et rendement scolaire. [Parental attitudes and scholastic performance.] (Texte imprimé pour les journées du Centre Xème anniversaire) 1966

67192 Le Centre psychopédagogique Claude Bernard. [The psychopedagogic center of Claude Bernard.] Réadaptation 1966, Spec no 130 (May)

67193 Coéducation des enfants dans la famille. [Coeducation of children in the family.] Échanges 1966, Spec no 76

67194 Conjoints et parents. [Husband and wife, and parents.] L'École des Parents 1967, Sept/Oct

67195 Contre la peur de vivre et l'angoisse de mourir. [Against the fear of living and the pangs of death.] Paris: Éditions Bernard Grasset 1963

67196 Culpabilité et responsabilité: article radiodiffusé. [Guilt and responsibility.] École des Parents 1961, (4)

S-41696 Les Défauts des Parents. Éditions Sudel 1960

67197 Les difficultés scolaires en tant que symptômes. [School difficulties as symptoms.] Revue Réadaptation 1964, (110)

67198 L'échec scolaire chez les surdoués. [School failure in gifted children.] Revue Réadaptation 1964, (110)

67199 L'écolier difficile. [The problem student.] 1962

67200 L'éducation de l'adulte et la préparation au vieillissement. [Adult education and preparation for old age.] École des Parents 1963, (8)

67201 Éducation et sexualité—quel rôle le médecin peut-il jouer? [Education and sexuality. What part should the doctor play?] École des Parents 1967, June (6)

67202 L'éducation sexuelle. [Sexual education.] École des Parents 1963, (9)

67203 L'Éducation Sexuelle Chez l'Enfant. [Sexual Education for the Child.] Paris: PUF 1961

S-41705 Educazione sessuale et affettica.
L'éducation sexuelle et affective. Éditions du Scarabée 1960

67204 L'émergence du problème éthique (collection Documents—Santé mentale). [The emergence of the ethical problem.] Éditions Prévot 1966

67205 L'enfant désiré et l'enfant non désiré. [The wanted and the unwanted child.] Planning Familial 1964 (I)

67206 L'enfant et ses différents milieux de Vie, I. [The child and the different spheres of his life.] Ecole des Parents 1965, (3) (5)

S-41706 L'équation personnelle ou de l'art psychanalytique.
Abs Arrosa, L. A. Rev urug Psa 1961-62, 4:379

67207 L'évolution psychanalytique de l'enfant. [Psychoanalytic evolution of the child.] In Le Guide de la Seconde Enfance, Editions Sociales françaises 1960, Chap 1

67208 La femme et son image corporelle. [The woman and her body image.] In "Aspects de la Femme," Le Groupe Familial 1965, April (27) (Spec no)

67209 Fonction de l'adolescence de la vie actuelle. [The function of adolescence in present day life.] Rv Np inf 1964, 12(10&11)

67210 L'hygiène mentale à l'école [Mental hygiene in the school.] 8éme année 1960, (3-4)

67211 L'inadaptation scolaire. [Scholastic maladjustment.] Vie sociale—cahiers du CEDIAS 1965

67212 Libéralisme éducatif et délinquance juvénile. [Educational liberalism and juvenile delinquency.] Rv Np inf 1968, 16:315-322

67213 La Liberté dans l'Éducation. [Freedom in Education.] Éditions du Scarabée 1961

67214 Les Maladies de la Vertu. [The Maladies of Virtue.] Paris: Grasset 1961
       Rv SLe RFPsa 1962, 26:311

67215 Les Maladies de la Vertu, la Morale Pour ou Contre l'Homme? [The Maladies of Virtue: Morality for or against Mankind?] Paris: Payot 1969, 224 p

67216 La mère célibataire et son enfant. [The unmarried mother and her child.] Reproduction d'articles pour le Planning 1966

67217 Le Métier de Parent, du Mariage, des Parents, au Mariage des Enfants. [The Craft of Parenthood: from Marriage to Parenthood to the Marriage of the Children.] Paris: Édition Montaigne 1961

67218 Les milieux familiaux. [The family environment.] In Psychologie de l'Enfant, Éditions Bourrelier 1961

67219 Mixité et coéducation. [Coeducation.] Cahiers Pédagogiques 1966, No 59

67220 Morale et hygiène mentale. [Morality and mental hygiene.] In La Table Ronde, 1961, (161)

67221 La notion de virilité s'est-elle modifiée. [The idea of virility is being modified.] Le Groupe Familial 1966, April (31)

67222 Participation à la morale devant la biologie et la psychanalyse. [Contribution to morality of biology and psychoanalysis.] (Collection Recherches et Débats) 1966

67223 Perspective d'un médecine psychologique scientifique. [Prospect for scientific psychological medicine.] Rv Np inf 1968, 16:463-471

67224 Pourquoi je suis contre les idées du Professeur Baruk. [Why I oppose the ideas of Professor Baruk.] Les Nouvelles Littéraires 1965, Nov

* * *   Preface to Mauco, G. Psychanalyse et Éducation

67225 Préface et notes. [Preface and notes.] In L'Éducation Sexuelle de Havelock Ellis, 1965

67226 Propos aux Parents et aux Éducateurs. [Remarks for Parents and Teachers.] Paris: Éditions Montaigne 1961

67227 La psychanalyse dans la psychologie de l'enfant. [Psychoanalysis in child psychology.] In Psychologie de l'Enfant, Éditions Armand Colin 1967

S-41724 Psychanalyse et prophylaxie mentale.
       Abs JLL An Surv Psa 1956, 7:292-293

67228 Psychothérapie du groupe familial. [Psychotherapy of the family group.] Rv Np inf 1965, 13:Sept

67229 Les Psychothérapies. [Psychotherapies.] Paris: PUF 1968, 214 p

67230 Reflexions sur l'article du Docteur Jan. C. Booman. [Remarks on the article by Dr. Jan. C. Booman.] Association Montessori Internationale 1964, (3 & 4)

67231 Relations intérieures du groupe familial. [Internal relations of the family group.] École des Parents 1962, (3) Jan

67232 Le rôle du père dans la société actuelle. [The role of the father in present-day society.] Revue des Travaux de l'Académie des Sciences Morales et Politiques 1964

67233 Sexualité chez l'adolescent. [Sexuality in the adolescent.] Bulletin official de la Société Française de Psycho-Prophylaxie Obstétricale 1967

67234 Signification actuelle de la sexualité et sens de la vie. [Present day significance of sexuality and consciousness of life.] Le Groupe Familial 1968, April (39)

67235 Le surmoi, son origine, sa nature et sa relation avec la conscience morale. [The superego, its origin, its nature, and its relation to the moral conscience.] RFPsa 1967, 31:1079-1080

67236 Troubles caractériels chez l'enfant. [Characterological difficulties in the infant.] Bull Psychol, Paris 1962, (205, 207, 208)

67237 The understanding adult. (Report of the World Assembly of the World Organization for Early Childhood Education.) 1963

BERGEN, BERNARD J.

67238 Discussion of Symonds, M. "Growing up poor." Sci Psa 1969, 14:213-214

BERGEN, M.

See Spock, Benjamin

BERGEN, MARY E.

S-41733 The effect of severe trauma on a four-year-old child.
Abs JA An Surv Psa 1958, 9:304-307

67239 Some observations of maturational factors in young children and adolescents. Psa St C 1964, 19:275-286

See Kennell, John H.

BERGER, A.

See Holzman, Philip S.

BERGER, D.

TRANSLATIONS OF:
Freud, S. [10438, 10453, 10505, 10525, 10599, 10622]

BERGER, ELLEN TESSMAN

67240 (& Prentice, N. M.; Hollenberg, C. K.; Korstvedt, A. J.; Sperry, B. M.) The development of causal thinking in children with severe psychogenic learning inhibitions. Child Develpm 1969, 40:503-515

BERGER, IRVING L.

67241 Group psychotherapy training institutes: group process, therapy or resistance to learning? Int J grp PT 1967, 17:505-512

67242 Modifications of the transference as observed in combined individual and group psychotherapy. Int J grp PT 1960, 10:456-469
Abs GPK Q 1961, 30:605-606

67243 (& Markey, O. B.) Psychiatry and medical practice; discussion of an approach to teaching psychiatry to practicing physicians. Ohio State med J 1964, 60:754-757

BERGER, LOUIS

67244 Conformity as a function of the ability to express hostility. J Pers 1963, 31:247-257

BERGER, MARK

67245 (Reporter) Current considerations of the topographic theory. In "Traditional subjects reconsidered." Proc 2nd Regional Conf Chicago Psa Soc 1968

BERGER, MILTON MILES

67246 (& Rosenbaum, M.) Notes on help-rejecting complainers. Int J grp PT 1967, 17:357-370
       Abs GPK Q 1968, 37:632
67247 The place of psychoanalysis in contemporary group psychotherapy. Top Probl PT 1960, 2:155-163
67248 Poetry as therapy—and therapy as poetry. In Leedy, J. J. *Poetry Therapy*, Phila/Toronto: Lippincott 1969, 75-87

       See Beukenkamp, Cornelius, Jr.; Rosenbaum, Max

BERGER, PETER L.

67249 Towards a sociological understanding of psychoanalysis. Soc Res 1965, 32:26-41

BERGER, PHYLLIS LENORE DODD

67250 Investigation of two theories of neurotic anxiety: Freud vs Mowrer. Diss Abstr 1963, 24(2):830-831

BERGER, RALPH J.

67251 Experimental modification of dream content by meaningful verbal stimuli. Brit J Psychiat 1963, 109:722-740
67252 (& Oswald, I.) Eye movements during active and passive dreams. Science 1962, 137:601
67253 When is a dream is a dream is a dream? Exp Neurol Suppl 1967 (4):15-28

BERGER, STANLEY

67254 Some psycho-economic aspects of analytic interpretation in the light of intrasystemic conflict. In Hammer, E. F. *Use of Interpretation in Treatment: Technique and Art*, NY: Grune & Stratton 1968, 81-90

BERGERET, J.

67255 (& Callier, J.) A propos de deux cas d'agoraphobie chez l'homme: hystérie d'angoisse et d'autres possibilités économiques. [About two cases of masculine agoraphobia: anxiety hysteria and other economic possibilities.] RFPsa 1969, 33:577-588
67256 A propos de l'acting out dit "d'adolescence" et du contretransfert. [About the acting out "of adolescence" and the countertransference.] RFPsa 1968, 32:1001-1004

67257 A propos de la pathologie du caractère. [About the pathology of the character.] Publ Soc Neuro-Psych reg Lyon 1963, 12 p

67258 A propos du comportement de passivité. [About the demeanour of passivity.] J Méd Lyon 1966, Suppl:92-99

67259 Un cas particulier de psychopathologie de la senescence. [With regard to a rather special case of psycho-pathological senescence.] Rev Hyg et Med Soc 1968, E16(6):617

67260 (& Achaintre, A.) Essai sur la fonction structurante du plaisir. [Essay on the structuring function of pleasure.] Coll psych sex, Lyon 1963, 11 p

67261 Les états limites. [The border-lines.] Confin psychiat 1969, (3)

67262 Le masochisme. [Masochism.] In Psychanalyse et Psychologie, Paris: Int H. P. 1967

BERGERON, A.

ABSTRACT OF:

67263 Bergeron, M. Les conceptions psycho-biologiques de H. Wallon. Rev Psicoanál 1963, 20:79

BERGERON, MARCEL

67264 Les conceptions psycho-biologiques de H. Wallon. [The psycho-biological conceptions of H. Wallon.] Evolut psychiat 1962, 27:27
Abs Bergeron, A. Rev Psicoanál 1963, 20:79

67265 (& Benoit, J.-C.; Jamet, F.; Sejournet, B.; Zagdoun, R.) Les fugues de l'adulte recherches etiopathogeniques. [Fugues in adults. Etiopathogenic investigations.] Ann méd-psychol 1966, 124(1):17-43

67266 Psychologie du Premier Âge. De la Naissance à 3 Ans. [Early Psychology. From Birth to 3 Years.] Paris: PUF (n.d.)
Rv Clancier, A. RFPsa 1967, 31:302

BERGHOLZ, HARRY

67267 Comment on Evert Sprinchorn's "Strindberg and the Psychiatrists." Lit & Psych 1965, 15:45

BERGIN, ALLEN E.

67268 The effects of psychotherapy; negative results revisited. J counsel Psychol 1963, 10:244-250. In Goldstein, A. P. & Dean, S. J. *The Investigation of Psychotherapy*, NY: Wiley 1966, 160-165. With title: Negative results revisited. In Berenson, B. G. & Carkhuff, R. R. *Sources of Gain in Counseling and Psychotherapy*, NY: Holt, Rinehart & Winston 1967, 47-55

67269 An empirical analysis of therapeutic issues. In Arbuckle, D. S. *Counseling and Psychotherapy*, NY: McGraw-Hill 1967, 175-212

° ° ° Negative results revisited. See [67268]

67270 A self-regulation technique for impulse control disorders. Psychotherapy 1969, 6:113-118

67271 Some implications of psychotherapy research for therapeutic practice. JAbP 1966, 71:235-246. Int J Psychiat 1967, 3:136-150. In Berenson, B. G. & Carkhuff, R. R. *Sources of Gain in Counseling and Psychotherapy*, NY: Holt, Rinehart & Winston 1967, 401-421

BERGLER, EDMUND

S-2077 On acting and stage fright. Sel P EB 786-791

67272 The "aristocracy" among homosexuals: lovers of "trade." Bull Phila Ass Psa 1962, 12:1-9
     Abs EFA Q 1963, 32:289. PLe RFPsa 1963, 27:340

67273 A basic oversight in the discussion of violence on TV. Dis nerv Sys 1962, 23:255-259

S-2089 A clinical contribution to the psychogenesis of humor. Sel P EB 38-54

67274 The clinical importance of "Rumpelstiltskin" as anti-male manifesto. Am Im 1961, 18:65-70
     Abs Hojman, R. K. de Rev Psicoanál 1961, 18:390

S-41743 The confusionist—a neglected neurotic type. Sel P EB 907-913

S-41745 A contribution to the multiple meaning of psychogenic phenomena.
     Abs An Surv Psa 1955, 6:151

S-41746 A contribution to the psychology of the snob. Sel P EB 941-944

S-2095 "Crime and punishment;" why punishment fails to prevent crime. Sel P EB 754-785

67275 Curable and Incurable Neurotics: Problems of "Neurotic" versus "Malignant" Masochism. NY: Liveright 1961, 471 p

S-2096 The danger neurotics dread most: loss of the "basic fallacy." Sel P EB 274-279

S-41750 Depression as after-effect of missed masochistic opportunities. Sel P EB 945-949

S-2099 Did Freud really advocate a "hands-off" policy toward artistic creativity? Sel P EB 412-416

67276 Differential diagnosis between a calculated risk and a masochistic action. Dis nerv Sys 1960, 21:30-31

S-2100 Differential diagnosis between "normal" and "neurotic" aggression. Sel P EB 197-202

S-2101 Differential diagnosis between spurious homosexuality and perversion homosexuality. Sel P EB 614-622

S-2102 On the disease-entity boredom ("alysosis") and its psychopathology. Sel P EB 742-753

S-2108 Eight prerequisites for the psychoanalytic treatment of homosexuality. Sel P EB 537-567

S-41754 On exaggeration. Sel P EB 928-937

S-41756 Fear of heights. Sel P EB 813-817
     Abs CK An Surv Psa 1957, 8:100-101

S-41758 A few examples of superego's cruelty.
     Abs An Surv Psa 1955, 6:138-139

S-2115 Five aims of the psychoanalytic patient. Sel P EB 287-300

S-2116 On a five-layer structure in sublimation. Sel P EB 94-109

S-2119 Four types of dreams indicating progress during psychoanalytic treatment. Sel P EB 223-230

S-41760 Further contributions to the problem of blushing. Sel P EB 807-812
     Abs CK An Surv Psa 1957, 8:158-159

S-2125 Further observations on the clinical picture of "psychogenic oral aspermia." Sel P EB 466-496

S-2126 Further studies on beating fantasies. Sel P EB 209-214

S-2127 Further studies on depersonalization. Sel P EB 215-222

S-41761 G. Bose's psychology of smell and a case of "stink-neurosis."
Abs An Surv Psa 1955, 6:151-152

S-2128 The gambler: a misunderstood neurotic. Sel P EB 687-699

S-41762 The habit of not returning books; a contribution to half-accepted "social stealing." Sel P EB 925-927

67277 L'homosexualité masculine. [Male homosexuality.] Méd Hyg 1960, 18

S-41765 Homosexuality: Disease or Way of Life?
Abs Harrison, I. An Surv Psa 1956, 7:212-213, 433-436

67278 "I want the job done and refuse to accept a memorandum why it cannot be done." Dis nerv Sys 1960, 21:281-282

S-41767 The "I'm damned if I do, and damned if I don't" technique.
Abs BEM An Surv Psa 1956, 7:219-220

67279 On the irrational anger of some wives when witnessing their husbands' "weak and silly" behavior. Dis nerv Sys 1962, 23:48-49

67280 (& Meerloo, J. A. M.) Justice and Injustice: The Origin of the Sense of Justice and its Relation to Everyday Life, the Law, and the Problems of Juvenile Delinquency and Crime. NY: Grune & Stratton 1963, 170 p

S-41775 Laughter and the Sense of Humor.
Abs IS An Surv Psa 1956, 7:436-442

S-2139 The "leading" and the "misleading" basic identifications. Sel P EB 140-168

S-41776 "Little Dorrit" and Dickens' intuitive knowledge of psychic masochism. Sel P EB 796-806
Abs JC An Surv Psa 1957, 8:328

S-2142 Logorrhoea. Sel P EB 700-712

S-41778 "Making a case" type of depression—a predictable test-mechanism in psychotherapy. Sel P EB 349-354

67281 (& Eidelberg, L.) Der Mammakomplex des Mannes. [The mammary complex of the male.] Psyche 1966, 20:670-699

S-2150 Morning erections. Sel P EB 896-900

S-2151 Mystery fans and the problem of "potential murderers." Sel P EB 851-861

S-2153 The myth of a new national disease. Homosexuality and the Kinsey Report. Sel P EB 633-651

S-2154 Neurosis—a progressive or self-limiting disease? Sel P EB 280-286

67282 A new approach to the psychology of crime. JNMD 1961, 133:254-258

S-2158 A new approach to the therapy of erythrophobia. Sel P EB 713-724

S-2160 Newer genetic investigations on impotence and frigidity. Sel P EB 623-632

S-41786 The "old-man act" of the middle-aged man. Sel P EB 938-940

S-2165 Paradoxical tears—tears of happiness. Sel P EB 904-906

67283 Parents Not Guilty! Of Their Children's Neuroses. NY: Liveright Publ Corp 1964, 283 p
Rv M. M. RFPsa 1968, 32:332

S-2167 Personality traits of alcohol addicts. Sel P EB 885-888

S-41790 Post-analytic misuse of pre-analytic symptoms. A contribution to the "self-allotted fraction" of psychic masochism. Sel P EB 355-359

S-41791 Practical and technical problems presented by the patient's lies about the analyst during psychoanalytic treatment.
Abs An Surv Psa 1955, 6:347-348

S-2172 On a predictable mechanism: enabling the patient even at the beginning of analysis to check the veracity of interpretations. Sel P EB 261-273

S-2174 Preliminary phases of the masculine beating fantasy. Sel P EB 55-72

S-2175 Premature ejaculation. Sel P EB 652-658

° ° ° A preventive technique for avoidance of postpartum depression. See [S-41799]

S-2177 The problem of frigidity. Sel P EB 568-581

S-2178 The problem of "magic gestures." Sel P EB 110-122

67284 Psychic "pointers" for the general practitioner and internist treating psychosomatic diseases. Dis nerv Sys 1959, 20(9)

S-2191 Psychoanlysis of a case of agoraphobia. Sel P EB 672-686

S-2194 Psychoanalysis of writers and of literary productivity. Sel P EB 368-402

S-41797 Psychoanalytic aspects of the personality of the obese. Sel P EB 792-795

67285 Psychological factors in the decline of an industry. Dis nerv Sys 1960, 21:461-463

S-2199 Psychology of "daily routine." Sel P EB 901-903

S-2200 Psychology of friendship and acquaintanceship. Sel P EB 867-875

S-41798 The Psychology of Gambling.
Abs Gilder, R. An Surv Psa 1957, 8:142-144

67286 Psychopathic personalities are unconsciously propelled by a defense against a specific type of psychic masochism—"malignant masochism." Arch crim Psychodyn 1961, (Suppl):416-434. Sel P EB 818-831

S-2210 Psychopathology of impostors. Sel P EB 725-741

S-2211 Psychopathology of ingratitude. Sel P EB 862-866

S-2213 Psychopathology of the "first impulse" and "first thought" in neurotics. Sel P EB 889-895

S-41799 Psychoprophylaxis of postpartum depression. Sel P EB 360-366. With title: A preventive technique for avoidance of postpartum depression. In Kroger, W. S. *Psychosomatic Obstetrics, Gynecology and Endocrinology*, Springfield, Ill: Thomas 1962, 50-57

67287 The published works of Edmund Bergler. Sel P EB 953-966

S-2216 The relation of the artist to society. Sel P EB 403-411

S-41800 The relation of writers to literary criticism.
Abs An Surv Psa 1955, 6:453

S-2217 On the resistance situation: the patient is silent. Sel P EB 246-260

S-2218 The respective importance of reality and phantasy in the genesis of female homosexuality. Sel P EB 512-536

S-41803 "Salome," the turning point in the life of Oscar Wilde. Sel P EB 433-441

S-41804 The second book and the second play. Sel P EB 426-432
Abs An Surv Psa 1955, 6:164

67288 Selected Papers of Edmund Bergler, M.D. 1933-1961. NY/London: Grune & Stratton 1969, x + 981 p

S-41805 The seven paradoxes in Shakespeare's "Hamlet." Sel P EB 445-464

S-2220 A short genetic survey of psychic impotence (II). Sel P EB 582-597

67289 The six herculean labors of the psychic masochist. Dis nerv Sys 1961, 22:218-222

S-2221 Six types of neurotic reaction to a husband's request for a divorce. Sel P EB 876-884

S-41808 Smoking and its infantile precursors. Sel P EB 914-924

S-2224 Some recurrent misconceptions concerning impotence. Sel P EB 497-511

S-2226 On a specific source of resistance in psychotherapy hitherto underestimated: the quasi-moral connotation of neurotic symptoms. Sel P EB 323-339

67290 On a specific type: "the approval-hungry neurotic." Dis nerv Sys 1961, 22:441-442. Sel P EB 950-952

S-2227 Specific types of resistance in orally regressed neurotics. Sel P EB 598-613

S-41813 Technical problems with couples simultaneously analyzed by the same analyst. Sel P EB 340-348

67291 Tensions Can Be Reduced to Nuisances. NY: Collier Books 1960

S-2236 On the theory of therapeutic results in psychoanalysis. Sel P EB 232-245

S-2237 A third function of the "day residue" in dreams. Sel P EB 81-93

S-2238 Thirty some years after Ferenczi's "Stages in the Development of the Sense of Reality." Sel P EB 123-139

S-2241 Three tributaries to the development of ambivalence. Sel P EB 203-208

S-2243 Two forms of aggression in obsessional neurosis. Sel P EB 73-80

S-41819 Unconscious mechanisms in "writer's block." Sel P EB 417-425
        Abs An Surv Psa 1955, 6:163-164

S-41820 Unconscious reasons for husbands' "confessions" to their jealous wives.
        Abs AaSt An Surv Psa 1956, 7:157

S-2248 Use and misuse of analytic interpretations by the patient. Sel P EB 301-322

S-41882 Victor Hugo's identifications. Sel P EB 442-444
        Abs DJM An Surv Psa 1958, 9:476

S-2249 Vorläufige Mitteilung: über obszöne Worte.
        Obscene words. Sel P EB 834-850

S-41823 Voyeurism. Sel P EB 659-669

67292 To what length the neurotic's distortions can go. . . . Am Im 1961, 18:391-398

67293 What would you say to a man who complains, "Lately, I've had the strangest thoughts about other men . . . I think I'm homosexual"? Why Rep 253-263

67294 Why must men and women punish themselves? Why Rep 129-140

S-2252 "Working through" in psychoanalysis. Sel P EB 169-196

S-41825 Writers of half-talent.
        Abs JC An Surv Psa 1957, 8:328

See Branfman, Theodore G.; Jekels, Ludwig

BERGLER, MARIANNE

* * * Preface. Sel P EB ix-x

BERGMAN, MARIA V.

67295   A psychoanalytic approach to the genesis of promiscuity. In Goldman,
        G. D. & Milman, D. S. *Modern Woman*, Springfield, Ill: Thomas 1969,
        211-228

BERGMAN, PAUL

67296   An experiment in filmed psychotherapy. Meth Res PT 35-49
67297   (& Malasky, C.; Zahn, T. P.) Oral functions in schizophrenia. JNMD
        146:351-359
S-41829 The role of faith in psychotherapy.
        Abs SO An Surv Psa 1958, 9:332-333

BERGMAN, ROBERT

67298   A case of stuttering. J Amer Acad child Psychiat 1968, 7:13-30

BERGMANN, MARTIN S.

67299   Free association and interpretation of dreams: historical and methodo-
        logical considerations. In Hammer, E. F. *Use of Interpretation in
        Treatment: Technique and Art*, NY: Grune & Stratton 1968, 270-279
67300   The impact of ego psychology on the study of the myth. (Read at
        Psa Ass NY, 21 May 1962) Am Im 1966, 23:257-264
67301   The intrapsychic and communicative aspects of the dream. Their role
        in psycho-analysis and psychotherapy. (Read at Int Psa Cong, July
        1965) J 1966, 47:356-363
        Abs EVN Q 1968, 37:314
67302   Obituary: John L. Herma: in memoriam. (Read at National Psychol
        Ass for Psa, 25 Sept 1966) R 1966, 53:676-677
67303   The place of Paul Federn's ego psychology in psychoanalytic meta-
        psychology. J Am Psa Ass 1963, 11:97-116
        Abs JBi Q 1964, 33:135. Guiard, F. Rev Psicoanál 1966, 23:233

BERGMANN, THESI

67304   Application of analytic knowledge to children with organic illness. In
        Weinreb, J. *Recent Developments in Psychoanalytic Child Therapy*,
        NY: IUP 1960, 139-148
67305   (& Freud, A.) Children in the Hospital. NY: IUP 1955, 162 p; Teachers
        College Pr 1966, xii + 153 p
        Abs J Am Psa Ass 1967, 15:223-224. Rv Bussel, L. R. Q 1968,
        37:137-138. J. S. RFPsa 1968, 32:330
67306   Personality development of two chronically ill children. Bull Phila Ass
        Psa 1967, 17:158-168
67307   (& Freud, A.) Typical reactions to specific illness. In authors' *Children
        in the Hospitals* 59-71
        Das Verhalten kranker Kinder im Verlauf orthopädischer Behand-
        lungen. Hbh Kinderpsychother 859-865

BERGREEN, STANLEY W.

67308   (& Hacker, F. J.; Illing, H.) Regression: a psychological process related
to aging. Acta Geront Belg 1964, 2:102-104. J Amer Geriat Soc 1966,
14:62-66

See Hacker, Frederick J.

BERGSTROM, L.

67309   (& Bergstrom, R. M.) [An analysis of concept formation in psychiatry
in the light of the theory of sensory physiology.] (Ger) Ann Acad Sci
Fenn (Med) 1964, 106(Suppl 21):1-16

BERGSTROM, R. M.

See Bergstrom, L.

BERK, G.

See Masterson, James F., Jr.

BERK, ROBERT

67310   (& Cuker, R.; Goldart, N.; Wolf, L.; Swerdloff, B.) A profile study of
the applicant not accepted for treatment at analytic clinics. Psychiat Q
1964, 38:64-80

BERKELEY, RUTH P.

REVIEW OF:
67311   Reik, T. Voices from the Inaudible: The Patients Speak. R 1965,
52:486-487

BERKEY, BARRY R.

67312   (& Roberts, L. M.) Sandor Ferenczi. (The man, his work, and evolving
forms of active psychotherapy.) Dis nerv Sys 1968, 457-461

BERKOVITZ, IRVING H.

67313   Discussion of Heilbrunn, G. "How 'cool' is the beatnik?" Psa Forum
1967, 2:45-47
67314   (& Chikahisa, P.; Lee, M. L.; Murasaki, E. M.) Psychosexual development of latency-age children and adolescents in group therapy in a
residential setting. Int J grp PT 1966, 16:344-356

BERKOWER, LARY

67315   The enduring effect of the Jewish tradition upon Freud. P 125:1067-
1075

BERKOWITS, G. A.

See Rosenthal, Maurice J.

BERKOWITZ, BERNARD

See Bowers, Margaretta K.

BERKOWITZ, LEONARD

67316 Aggressive cues in aggressive behavior and hostility catharsis. Psychol Rev 1964, 71:104-122

67317 Aggressive stimuli, aggressive responses and hostility catharsis. Sci Psa 1963, 6:18-29

67318 Anti-semitism, judgmental processes, and displacement of hostility. ASP 1961, 62:210-215

67319 Experiments on automatism and intent in human aggression. UCLA Forum Med Sci 1967, 7:243-266

67320 (& Green, J. A.; Macaulay, J. R.) Hostility catharsis as the reduction of emotional tension. Ps 1962, 25:23-31

67321 (Ed) Roots of Aggression; A Re-examination of the Frustration-Aggression Hypothesis. NY: Atherton Pr 1969, 136 p

67322 Some factors affecting the reduction of overt hostility. ASP 1960, 60:14-21

BERKOWITZ, LOUIS

67323 (& Chwast, J.) A community center program for the prevention of school dropouts. Fed Probation 1967, 31:36-40

67324 (& Lurie, A.; Chwast, J.; Seigle, N.; Wachspress, M.) Community center resocialization of former psychiatric patients. MH 1965, 49:266-273

67325 The devil within. R 1968, 55:28-36
    Abs SRS Q 1969, 38:340

67326 (& Lurie, A.) Socialization as a rehabilitative process. Comm ment Hlth J 1966, 2:55-60

BERKOWITZ, PEARL H.

67327 (& Rothman, E. P.) The Disturbed Child: Recognition and Psycho-educational Therapy in the Classroom. NY: NY Univ Pr 1960, x + 204 p
    Rv Rexford, E.N. Q 1960, 29:417-419. Raylesberg, D. PPR 1961, 48(2):126-127

67328 (& Rothman, E. P.) (Eds) Public Education for Disturbed Children in New York City: Application and Theory. Springfield, Ill: Thomas 1966, x + 376 p

BERKWITS, GLORIA A.

See Rosenthal, Maurice J.

BERL, SOLL

See Kaye, Harvey E.

BERLE, BEATRICE BISHOP

67329 (& Nyswander, M.) Ambulatory withdrawal treatment of heroin addicts. NYSJM 1964, 64:1846-1848

BERLEW, DAVID E.

See Bennis, Warren G.

BERLIEN, IVAN C.

67330 Toward the theory of schizoaffective states. Behav Np 1969, 1(2):7-11

BERLIN, IRVING N.

67331 The atomic age, the non-learning child, the parent. Educ Ldrshp 1964, 21:444-447

67332 Bibliography of Child Psychiatry, No. 1. Wash DC: Am Psychiat Ass 1963, iv + 94 p

67333 The child's "inalienable right" to psychological disorder. Ops 1965, 35:638-639

67334 Consultation and special education. In Philips, I. *Prevention and Treatment of Mental Retardation*, NY: Basic Books 1966, 270-293

67335 Contribution to Career Training in Child Psychiatry. (Report of Conference on Training in Child Psychiatry, 10-15 Jan 1963) Wash DC: Am Psychiat Ass 1964

67336 (& Yeager, C. L.) Correlation of epileptic seizures, electroencephalograms and emotional state: some preliminary observations in several children. Amer J Dis Childr 1951, 81:664-670

67337 Crises and action potentials for citizens. Canad Ment Hlth 1968, 16(5):18-22

67338 Desegregation creates problems too. Sat Rev 1963, 46(June 15):66-67. In Humphrey, H. *School Desegregation*, NY: Crowell 1964, 230-234

67339 Education for community psychiatry. Ops 1968, 38:569-571

67340 The emotional and learning problems of the psychosocially deprived child. In *The Adults Around the Child*, Telecourse Viewer's Guide, Univ of Washington 1966

67341 The emotional and learning problems of the socially and culturally deprived child. MH 1966, 50:340-347

67342 From teachers' problems to problem teachers. MH 1960, 44:80-83

67343 Guilt as an etiological factor in war neuroses. JNMD 1950, 111:239-245

67344 A history of challenges in child psychiatry training. MH 1964, 48:557-565

67345 Infancy and childhood. In Feldman, R. & Buck, D. *Proceedings of Seventh Annual Training Sessions for Psychiatrist-Teachers of Practicing Physicians, 1966,* Boulder, Colorado: Western Interstate Commission for Higher Education 1967

67346 (& Szurek, S. A.) (Eds) Learning and Its Disorders. (Clinical Approaches to Problems of Childhood, Vol. I.) Palo Alto, Calif: Sci & Behav Books 1965, xviii + 295 p

67347 Learning as therapy. Sat Rev 1966, 49(Oct 15):78-79

67348 Learning mental health consultation. History and problems. MH 1964, 48:257-266

67349 Love and mastery in the educational process. Educ Forum 1966, 31:43-49

67350 Mental health consultation in schools as a means of communicating health principles. J Amer Acad Child Psychiat 1962, 1:671-679

67351 Mental health consultation in schools: who does it and why. Comm ment Hlth J 1965, 1:19-22. In Lindgren, H. C. *Readings in Educational Psychology*, NY: Wiley 1968, 391-396

67352 Mental health consultation with a juvenile probation department. Crime Delinq 1964, 10:67-73

67353 New directions in AOA: one view. Ops 1964, 34:801-804

67354 Preventive aspects of mental health consultation to schools. MH 1967, 51:34-40. In Szurek, S. A. & Berlin, I. N. *The Antisocial Child: His Family and His Community,* Palo Alto, Calif: Sci & Behav Books 1969, 207-215

67355 Psychiatric consultation on the anti-delinquency project. Calif J sec Educ 1960, 35:198-202

67356 Psychiatric social work teaching of medical students through collaboration. Some aspects of psychiatric social work teaching of medical students. Amer Assoc Soc Wk 1957, Jan:27-31

67357 Psychosomatic disorders of childhood: an overview. In Szurek, S. A. & Berlin, I. N. *Psychosomatic Disorders and Mental Retardation in Children,* Palo Alto, Calif: Sci & Behav Books 1968, 37-53

67358 (& Szurek, S. A.) The question of therapy for the trainee in the psychiatric training program. J Amer Acad Child Psychiat 1966, 5:155-165

67359 A review of some elements of neurology. Soc Casewk 1956, 37:427-433; 493-500

67360 School child guidance services, retrospect and prospect. Psychol Sch 1966, 3:229-236

67361 The school counselor: his unique mental health function. Person Guid J 1963, 41:409-414. In Bently, J. C. *The Counselor's Role: Commentary and Readings,* Boston: Houghton Mifflin 1968, 144-150

67362 Secondary prevention. Compreh Txbk Psychiat 1541-1548

67363 Some implications of ego psychology for the supervisory process. PT 1960, 14:536-544

67364 Some observations in child psychology. West Med 1963, 4:240-244

67365 Special learning problems of deprived children. NEA J 1966, 55(3): 23-24

67366 (& Szurek, S. A. Teaching administration in the training of child psychiatrists. J Amer Acad Child Psychiat 1964, 3:551-560

67367 The theme in mental health consultation sessions. Ops 1960, 30:827-828

67368 Training in child psychiatry: challenges historical and current. In Levy, J. & McNickle, R. K. *Meeting the Treatment Needs of Children,* Boulder, Colorado: Western Interstate Commission for Higher Education, 1963, 84-96

67369 Training in community psychiatry: its relation to clinical psychiatry. Comm ment Hlth J 1965, 1:357-360

67370 Transference and countertransference in community psychiatry. Arch gen Psychiat 1966, 15:165-172
           Abs PB Q 1969, 38:512

67371 (& Christ, A. E.) The unique role of the child psychiatry trainee on an inpatient or day care unit. J Amer Acad Child Psychiat 1969, 8:247-252

67372 Unrealities in teacher education. Sat Rev 1964, 47(65):56-58

67373 What help can the educator expect from the mental health specialist? Calif J elem Educ 1962, 31:7-15

67374 Working with children who won't go to school. Children 1965, 12:109-112. Children's Champion 1965-66, 3:8-12. Careers, No. R650 (Soc

Wrker 195, p. 27), Largo, Florida, May 1966. In Saltzman, G. A. & Peters, H. J. *Pupil Personnel Services*, Itasca, Ill: Peacock Publ 1967, 134-140

See Boatman, Maleta J.; Szurek, Stanislaus A.

BERLINER, BERNHARD

67375 Psychodynamics of the depressive character. Psa Forum 1966, 1:244-251; 262-264; 420; 1967, 2:103
   Abs Cuad Psa 1967, 3:165
S-41855 The role of object relations in moral masochism.
   Abs Swartz, J. An Surv Psa 1958, 9:167-169

ABSTRACTS OF:
67376 Becker, A. M. Zur Gliederung des Über-Ichs. An Surv Psa 1956, 7:138-139
67377 Görres, A. Die Technik der Psychoanalyse. Zu Edward Glover: the Technique of Psycho-Analysis. An Surv Psa 1956, 7:62
67378 Lampl-de Groot, J. Anmerkungen zur psychoanalytischen Triebtheorie. An Surv Psa 1956, 7:91-92
67379 Laqueuey, W. Psychoanalyse in sowjetischer Perspektive. An Surv Psa 1956, 7:77-79
67380 Lebovici, S. Die Aspekte der Frühen objekt—Beziehungen: Die analitische Beziehung. An Surv Psa 1956, 7:99-100
67381 Meng, H. Sigmund Freud in Brief, Gespräch, Begegung und Werk. An Surv Psa 1956, 7:17-18
67382 Mitscherlich, A. Aggression und Anpassung. An Surv Psa 1956, 7:92-93
67383 Scheunert, G. Einige Entwicklungstendenzen der neueren psychoanalytischen Ich-Psychologie. An Surv Psa 1956, 7:57-58
67384 Schottländer, F. Blendung durch Bilder. An Surv Psa 1956, 7:254-255
67385 Victorius, K. Der "Moses des Michelangelo" von Sigmund Freud. An Surv Psa 1956, 7:18, 412
67386 Zulliger, H. Zur Psychoanalyse einer "Blitz"-Heilung. An Surv Psa 1956, 7:354-356

BERLYNE, DANIEL E.

67387 Conflict and arousal. Sci Am 1966, 215:820-827
67388 Conflict, Arousal, and Curiosity. NY: McGraw-Hill 1960, xiv + 350 p
67389 A decade of motivation theory. Amer Sci 1964, 52:447-451
67390 Motivational problems raised by exploratory and epistemic behavior. In Koch, S. *Psychology: A Study of a Science, Vol. 5*, NY/Toronto/London: McGraw-Hill 1963, 284-364
67391 Structure and Direction in Thinking. NY: John Wiley 1965, xi + 378 p
   Rv Fine, B. D. Q 1967, 36:439-442

BERMAN, ANNE

TRANSLATION OF:
(& Grossein, J.-P.) Freud, S. [46284, 73578]

BERMAN, LEO H.

67392 (& Freedman, L. Z.) Clinical perception of sexual deviates. J Psychol 1961, 52:157-160

S-2390 Countertransferences and attitudes of the analyst in the therapeutic process. In Zinberg, N. E. *Psychiatry and Medical Practice in a General Hospital*, NY: IUP 1964, 17-27

67393 Discussion of Aldrich, C. K. "What price autonomy?" Sci Psa 1961, 4:185

S-41869 Mental hygiene for educators: report on an experiment using a combined seminar and group psychotherapy approach. In Zinberg, N. E. *Psychiatry and Medical Practice in a General Hospital*, NY: IUP 1964, 253-263

67394 Panel on the humanistic approach to sexuality: freedom and sexuality. Dis nerv Sys 1969, 30:784-786

S-2394 Psychoanalysis and group psychotherapy. In Zinberg, N. E. *Psychiatry and Medical Practice in a General Hospital*, NY: IUP 1964, 264-270

S-41872 Some problems in the evaluation of psychoanalysis as a therapeutic procedure.
Abs An Surv Psa 1955, 6:315-316

S-41866 Some recent trends in psychoanalysis.
Abs AJE An Surv Psa 1957, 8:14-15

See Daniels, Edward M.; Snyder, Benson R.

BERMAN, LILA
See Weiland, I. Hyman

BERMAN, M.
See Lewis, William C.

BERMAN, RAQUEL
See Ramírez, Santiago

BERMAN, SIDNEY

67395 The psychological implications of intractable asthma in childhood. Clin Proc Child Hosp DC 1967, 23:210-218

67396 The role of children in the family. In Liebman, S. *Emotional Forces in the Family*, Phila/Montreal: Lippincott 1959, 51-69

67397 Techniques of treatment of a form of juvenile delinquency, the antisocial character disorder. J Amer Acad Child Psychiat 1964, 3:24-52

BERMONT, HUBERT INGRAM

67398 Psychoanalysis is a Great Big Help! NY: Stein & Day 1963

BERMÚDEZ ROJAS, JAIME G.

67399 ¿Qué es el Psicodrama? [What is Psychodrama?] Buenos Aires: Genitor 1966
Rv Pavlovsky, E. Rev Psicoanál 1967, 24:209

BERNA, JACQUES M.

67400 Aspekte der Objektbeziehung und Ich-Entwichlung. [Some aspects of object-relation and ego-development.] Almanach (Stutt) 1965, 171-208

67401 Ich-Psychologie und psychoanalytische Technik. [Ego-psychology and psychoanalytic technique.] Psyche 1968, 22:161

67402 Ich-psychologische Deutungstechnik und Kinderanalyse. [The technique of the interpretation of ego psychology and analysis of children.] Psyche 1967, 21:31-43. Hbh Kinderpsychother 321-332

67403 Die Indikation zur Kinderanalyse. [Indications for child analysis.] Psyche 1962, 16:81-99. Hbh Kinderpsychother 247-264
    Abs IBa RFPsa 1964, 28:464

67404 Kinder und Erwachsenen-Analyse. [Analysis for Children and Adults.] Jb Psa 1969, 6:157-170

S-41881 Kinderanalyse eines Aggressiven.
    Abs An Surv Psa 1955, 6:290-292

67405 Kinderanalyse und Erziehung. [Analysis of children and education.] Schweiz Z Psychol 1964, 23:329-338

67406 Obituary: Hans Zulliger. Cuad Psa 1967, 3:66-67

67407 Die Pubertätsrevolte in Robinson Crusoe. [The revolution of adolescence in Robinson Crusoe.] Almanach (Stutt) 1966, 144-150

S-41883 Die "Réalisation symbolique" in der Kinderanalyse.
    Abs HA An Surv Psa 1956, 7:289-291

BERNABEU, EDNITA P.

S-41885 The effects of severe crippling on the development of a group of children.
    Abs WCW An Surv Psa 1958, 9:299

S-41887 Science fiction: a new mythos.
    Abs SO An Surv Psa 1957, 8:334-335

S-41888 Underlying ego mechanisms in delinquency.
    Abs DJM An Surv Psa 1958, 9:311-312

REVIEW OF:
67408 Bloch, H. A. & Niederhoffer, A. The Gang. A Study in Adolescent Behavior. Q 1961, 30:129-133

BERNAL DEL RIESGO, ALFONSO

TRANSLATION OF:
Salter, A. [89020]

BERNAL Y DEL RIO, V.

67409 The sexual syndromes. Bol Asoc med P Rico 1964, 56:203-212

BERNARD, F.

67410 (& Flavigny, H.) [The role of the father in obsessions of children.] (Fr) Rv Np inf 1965, 13:730-739

BERNARD, J. L.

See Eisenman, Russell

BERNARD, P.

See Ey, Henri

BERNARD, VIOLA W.

67411 Adoption. Ency Ment Hlth 70-108

67412 Child and adolescent services. In Ziskind, R. *Viewpoint on Mental Health*, NY: NYC Comm Ment Hlth Board 1967, 69-73

67413 Community administrative training program. Ment Hosp 1961, 12(2): 66-67

67414 Community mental health programming. J Amer Acad Child Psychiat 1965, 4:226-242

67415 Community psychiatry. In Neubauer, P. B. *Children in Collectives*, Springfield, Ill: Thomas 1965, 1-7

67416 (& Ottenberg, P.; Redl, F.) Dehumanization: a composite psychological defense in relation to modern war. In Schwebel, M. *Behavioral Science and Human Survival*, Palo Alto, Calif: Sci & Behav Books 1965, 64-82

67417 Discussion of Geiger, H. J. "Of the poor, by the poor, or for the poor: the mental health implications of social control of poverty programs." Psychiat Res Rep 1967, 21:68-71

67418 The division of community psychiatry and the Washington Heights program. In Kolb, L. C. et al: *Urban Challenges to Psychiatry*, Boston: Little, Brown 1969, 119-152

67419 Education for community psychiatry. In Kolb, L. C. et al: *Urban Challenges to Psychiatry*, Boston: Little, Brown 1969, 319-360

67420 Education for community psychiatry in a university medical center (with emphasis on the rationale and objectives of training). In Bellak, L. *Handbook of Community Psychiatry*, NY: Grune & Stratton 1963, 82-122

67421 (& Crandell, D. L.) Evidence for various hypotheses of social psychiatry. In Zubin, J. & Freyhan, F. A. *Social Psychiatry*, NY: Grune & Stratton 1968, 172-219

67422 Obituary: Sol Wiener Ginsburg, M.D. 1899-1960. Ops 1960, 30:829-831

67423 Other mental health-related services and groups in the community. In Kolb, L. C. et al: *Urban Challenges to Psychiatry*, Boston: Little, Brown 1969, 193-233

67424 Roles and functions of child psychiatrists in social and community psychiatry: implications for training. J Amer Acad Child Psychiat 1964, 3:165-176

S-41895 School desegregation—some psychiatric implications.
          Abs WCW An Surv Psa 1958, 9:460-461

67425 Some aspects of training for community psychiatry in a university medical center. In Goldston, S. E. *Concepts of Community Psychiatry: A Framework for Training*, NIMH 1965, 57-67

67426 Some interrelationships of training for community psychiatry, community mental health programmes, and research in social psychiatry. Proc III World Cong Psychiat 1961, 3:67-71

67427 Some principles of dynamic psychiatry in relation to poverty. P 1965, 122:254-267

67428 The training of mental health specialists in schools of public health. In author's *Mental Health Teaching in Schools of Public Health* (Arden-House Conference 1959), Columbia University, School of Public Health and Administrative Medicine 1961, 291-338

67429 A training program in community psychiatry. Ment Hosp 1960, 11(5): 6-10

67430 Why people become the victims of medical quackery. Amer J Pub Hlth 1965, 55:1142-1147

See Dohrenwend, Bruce P.; Kolb, Lawrence C.; Marmor, Judd; Redl, Fritz

BERNARDEZ, TERESA

67431 The feminine role: case report. BMC 1965, 29:198-205

BERNARDI, SERGIO

67432 Problemi relativi al condizionamento emotivo nei fenomeni parapsicologici. [Problems relative to emotional conditioning by parapsychological phenomena.] Rass ital Ricerca psichica 1966, 1:41-52

BERNARDT, H. E.

See Aldrich, C. Knight

BERNASCONI, MARION

See Gartley, Wayne

BERNAYS, HELLA FREUD

TRANSLATION OF:
Bühler, C. [69067]

BERNDT, HEIDE

67433 (& Lorenzer, A.; Horn, K.) Architektur als Ideologie. [Architecture as Ideology.] Frankfurt: Suhrkamp 1968, 243 p

BERNE, ERIC

67434 The cultural problem psychopathology in Tahiti. P 1960, 116:1076-1081

67435 Difficulties of comparative psychiatry: the Fiji islands. P 1959, 116: 104-109

67436 Discussion of Giovacchini, P. L. "Characterological aspects of marital interaction." Psa Forum 1967, 2:16-18

67437 Ego. Ency Ment Hlth 515-520

67438 Games People Play: The Psychology of Human Relationships. NY: Grove Pr 1964; London: Deutsch 1966, 192 p
       Hvad er det vi Leger? Gyldendalske Boghandel. Copenhagen: Nordisk Forlag A. S. 1967
       Mens Erger je Niet. The Hague: Stichting Uitgeverij 1967

Kanssakäymisen Kuviot. Jyvaskyla, Finland: K. J. Gummerus 1967
Des Jeux et des Hommes. Paris: Editions Stock 1964
Spiele der Erwachsenen. Hamburg: Rowohlt Verlag 1967
A Che Gioco Giochiamo. Milan: Il Saggiatore 1967
Japanese: Tokyo: Kawade Shobo 1967
Mennesker og Masker. Oslo: J. W. Cappelens Forlag 1967
Los Jeugos en que Participamos. Mexico: Editorial Diana 1966
Sa Bär vi oss åt. Stockholm: Almquist & Wiksell 1967
Rv Haley, J. R 1965, 52:489-492

67439 Intuition: VI. The psychodynamics of intuition. Psychiat Q 1962, 36: 294-300

67440 Notes on games and theatre; interview by A. Wagner. Tulane Drama Rev 1967, 11:89-91

67441 Principles of Group Treatment. NY: Oxford Univ Pr 1966, xviii + 379 p

67442 Principles of transactional analysis. Curr psychiat Ther 1964, 4:35-45

S-41903 The psychological structure of space with some remarks on Robinson Crusoe.
Abs So An Surv Psa 1956, 7:128-130

67443 Recent advances in transactional analysis. Curr psychiat Ther 1966, 6:114-124

67444 Reply to Dr. Shapiro's critique. Psychol Rep 1969, 25:478

67445 Staff-patient staff conferences. P 1968, 125:286-293

67446 The Structure and Dynamics of Organizations and Groups. Phila/Montreal: J. B. Lippincott 1964, NY: Grove Pr 1966, xi + 260 p
German: Hamburg: Rowohlt Verlag 1968
Rv Semrad, E. V. & Day, M. J Am Psa Ass 1966, 14:591-618

67447 Transactional Analysis in Psychotherapy; A Systematic Individual and Social Psychiatry. NY: Grove Pr 1961, 270 p

BERNER, P.

67448 Beeinträchtigung durch Lärm und Lärmbekämpfung—aus psychiatrischer Sicht. [Damage from, and overcoming noise from the psychiatric viewpoint.] Mitt Öst Sanit—Verwalt 1965, 66:313-316

67449 (& Kryspin-Exner, K.) Zum Problem der Identitätskrisen bei Primitivpersönlichkeiten. [On the problem of identification in primitive personalities.] Wien Z Nervenheilk 1966, 24:198-203

BERNFELD, SIEGFRIED

S-2440 Über die einfache männliche Pubertät.
On simple male adolescence. Sem Psychiat 1969, 1:113-126

67450 On psychoanalytic training. Q 1962, 31:453-482
Abs Dubcovsky, S. Rev Psicoanál 1964, 21:87-89

S-2483 Über Sexuelle Aufklärung. In Bittner, G. & Rehm, W. *Psychoanalyse und Erziehung*, Bern/Stuttgart: Hans Huber 1964

BERNHARD, ROBERT

67451 Chemical homologue of the model presented in Freud's "Project." Q 1964, 33:357-374
Abs Rosarios, H. Rev Psicoanál 1964, 21:264

BERNHEIM, H.

67452 De la Suggestion et de Ses Applications à la Thérapeutique.
Hypnosis and Suggestion in Psychotherapy. (Tr: Herter, C. A.)
New Hyde Park, NY: Univ Books 1963, 1964, xvi + 428 p
Rv Stewart, H. J 1965, 46:277-278. Niederland, W. G. Q 1966,
35:138-141

BERNICK, NILES

See Cartwright, Rosalind D.

BERNS, ROBERT S.

67453 Discussion of Heilbrunn, G. "How 'cool' is the beatnik?" Psa Forum
1967, 2:47-49
67454 Regressive emotional behavior in college students. P 1966, 122:1378-
1384

BERNSTEIN, ANNE E.

67455 (& Blacher, R. S.) The recovery of a memory from three months of age.
(Read at Am Psa Ass, 16 Dec 1966) Psa St C 1967, 22:156-161

BERNSTEIN, ARNOLD

67456 The psychoanalytic technique. In Wolman, B. B. *Handbook of Clinical
Psychology*, NY: McGraw-Hill 1965, 1168-1199

See Lennard, Henry L.

BERNSTEIN, ARTHUR

67457 (& Simon, F.) Anxiety and angina pectoris. Angiology 1962, 13:17-22

BERNSTEIN, BENEDICT

67458 On the history of the New Jersey Psychoanalytic Society. Bull New
Jersey Psa Soc 1968, 1:3-6

BERNSTEIN, BENJAMIN L.

See Linn, Louis

BERNSTEIN, HASKELL

67459 Identity and sense of identity. (Read at Chicago Psa Soc, 26 Feb 1963)
Abs Kavka, J. Bull Phila Ass Psa 1964, 14:157-162

See Miller, Arthur A.; Sklansky, Morris

BERNSTEIN, ISIDOR

67460 Dreams and masturbation in an adolescent boy. (Read at Am Psa Ass,
4 Dec 1959) J Am Psa Ass 1962, 10:289-302
Abs JBi Q 1963, 32:132

S-41911 The importance of characteristics of parents in deciding on child analysis.
Abs IS An Surv Psa 1958, 9:313

67461 (& Fine, B. D.) The manifest content of the dream. Monograph Series of the Kris Study Group of the NY Psychoanalytic Institute 1969, No. 3:58-113

S-41912 (Reporter) Panel: indications and goals of child analysis as compared with child psychotherapy.
Abs CK An Surv Psa 1957, 8:227-228

S-41913 The role of narcissism in moral masochism.
Abs SO An Surv Psa 1957, 8:118-120

See Alpert, Augusta

REVIEW OF:
67462 Pearson, G. H. J. (Ed) A Handbook of Child Psychoanalysis. Bull Phila Ass Psa 1968, 18:132-135

BERNSTEIN, LEWIS

67463 (& Turrell, E. S.; Dana, R. H.) Motivation for nursing. Nurs Res 1965, 14:222-226

67464 (& Purcell, K.; Rosenbaum, S.; Wasserman, H.; Stewart, A.; Metz, J. R.) Organization and functions of the psychological services at the Jewish National Home for Asthmatic Children. In Harms, E. *Somatic and Psychiatric Aspects of Childhood Allergies,* Oxford: Pergamon; NY: Macmillan 1963, 203-249

BERNSTEIN, M. H.

See Linn, Louis

BERNSTEIN, STANLEY

67465 (& Kaufman, M. R.) The psychiatrist in a general hospital: his functional relationship to the nonpsychiatric services. J Mount Sinai Hosp 1962, 29:385-394

67466 (& Kaufman, M. R.) A psychological analysis of apparent depression following Rauwolfia therapy. J Mount Sinai Hosp 1960, 27:525

67467 (& Kaufman, M. R.; Brown, F.; Laski, L.; Graydon, C.; Mendlowitz, M.; Kantor, I.) Psychological implications of apparent depression following Rauwolfia therapy. Proc Ist Int Cong of Neuro-Pharmacology (1958), Amsterdam: Elsevier Publ 1960

BERNSTEIN, STEPHEN

67468 (& Wacks, J.; Christ, J.) The effect of group psychotherapy on the psychotherapist. PT 1969, 23:271-282

BERRICK, M. E.

See Bailey, Mattox A.; Lachmann, Frank M.

BERRINI, M. E.

See Balconi, M.; Fornari, Franco

BERRYMAN-SIMPSON, EILEEN

67469 Psychoanalysis in Paris today. PT 1967, 21:18-31; 256-274

67470 The simultaneous treatment of a mother and child: the mother's side. PT 1963, 17:266-274

67471 The treatment of adolescents—effecting the transference. Management problems in private practice. PT 1960, 14:338-345

BERSANI, LEO

67472 Anxious imagination. Partisan Rev 1968, 35(Winter):49-66

BERTALANFFY, LUDWIG VON

S-41926 Comments on aggression.
Abs SO An Surv Psa 1958, 9:76-77

67473 Robots, Men, and Minds; Psychology in the Modern World. NY: G. Braziller 1967, x + 150 p

BERTRAND, MARIE-ANDRÉE

67474 Prophylaxie et traitement. [Prevention and treatment.] Ann Intern Crim 1965, (2)
Abs Delteil, P. RFPsa 1968, 32:178

BERTHELSDORF, SIEGFRIED

67475 (Participant) On regression: a workshop. (Held at West Coast Psa Soc, 14-16 Oct 1966) Psa Forum 1967, 2:293-316

BERTINI, M.

67476 (& Lewis, H. B.; Witkin, H. A.) Some preliminary observations with an experimental procedure for the study of hypnagogic and related phenomena. Arch Psicol Neurol Psichiat 1964, 25:493-534. In Tart, C. T. *Altered States of Consciousness: A Book of Readings,* NY: John Wiley & Sons 1969, 93-111

BERTINI, MARIO

67477 Il tratto difensivo dell'isolamento nella sua determinazione dinamica e strutturale. [The defensive trait of isolation in its dynamic and structural determination.] Contributi Ist Psicol 1962, 24:307-326

BERTINO, JOSEPH R.

See Klee, Gerald D.

BERTOCCI, PETER ANTHONY

67479 Existential phenomenology and psychoanalysis. Rev Metaphysics 1965, 18:690-710

67480 Mind. Ency Ment Hlth 1231-1234

67481 (& Millard, R. M.) Personality and the Good, Psychological and Ethical Perspectives. NY: David McKay 1963, xxi + 711 p

BERTRAM, P.

See Karen, Edward S.

BERTRAND, SHARON

67482 (& Masling, J.) Oral imagery and alcoholism. JAbP 1969, 74:50-53

BERWALD, CATHARINE DONOVAN

See Matsushima, John

BESANÇON, ALAIN

67483 Histoire et psychanalyse. [History and psychoanalysis.] Annales, Paris 1964, 19:237-249

67483A Psychoanalysis: auxiliary science or historical problem? In Laqueur, W. et al: *Reappraisals: A New Look at History; the Social Sciences and History*, London: Weidenfeld & Nicholson 1968

BESDINE, MATTHEW

67484 Jocasta and Oedipus: another look. In *Pathways in Child Guidance*, Bureau of Child Guidance, Board of Ed of the City of NY 1968, 1-4

67485 The Jocasta complex, mothering and genius. R 1968, 55:259-277; 574-600

67486 Mrs. Oedipus. Psychol Today 1969, 2(8):40-47, 67

BETH, E. W.

67487 (& Piaget, J.) Épistémologie Mathématique et Psychologie. [Mathematical Epistemology and Psychology.] Paris: PUF 1961, 352 p

BETLHEIM, STJEPAN

67488 [Brief psychotherapy.] (Cro) Neuropsihijatrija 1967, 15:7-18

67489 (& Blažević, D.; Beck-Dvoržak, M.) [Effect of physical injuries on the etiology and structure of neuroses.] (Ser) Neuropsihijatrija 1963, 11: 143-149

67490 (& Blažević, D.; Beck-Dvoržak, M.; Bućan, N.; Cividini, E.; Radošević, Z.) The general practitioner as psychotherapist. Med J 1966, 88:1419-1423

67491 (& Bućan, N.; Koporcic, P.) [On psychotherapy of psychical impotence.] (Ser) Lijecn Vjesn 1959, 81:493-502

67492 Das Problem der Einzelbesprechung innerhalb der Gruppenpsychotherapie. [The problem of the individual interview in the course of group therapy.] Z Psychother med Psychol 1963, 13:21-27

67493 [The relationship between group and individual psychotherapy.] (Ser) Neuropsihijatrija 1963, 11:253-260

67494 (& Blažević, D.; Beck-Dvoržak, M.; Bućan, N.; Cividini, E.; Katicic, N.; & Radošević, Z.) [Role of psychological tests during psychotherapy of neurotic patients.] (Ser) Neuropsihijatrija 1960, 8:254-260

67495 Soziale Grenzen der Behandlungsfähigkeit von Neurosen mit Psychotherapie. [Social limits on the ability to treat neuroses with psychotherapy.] (Abs) Psychother Psychosom 1967, 15:8

67496 Zur Frage der Gruppenpsychotherapie Homosexueller. [On the question of group psychotherapy of homosexuals.] Top Probl PT 1963, 4:154-162

See Persic, N.

BETTELHEIM, BRUNO

67497 Art: a personal vision. In *Art*, NY Museum of Modern Art 1964
67498 Aspects of appreciation. In Smith, E. R. & Tyler, R. W. *Appraising and Recording Student Progress*, NY: Harper 1942, 276-306
67499 Child Guidance: A Community Responsibility. Institute for Community Development and Services, Continuing Education Service, Michigan State Univ 1962, 18 p
67500 Child rearing in the Israel Kibbutzim. (Read at Chicago Psa Soc, 24 Mar 1967)
    Abs Beigler, J. S. Bull Phila Ass Psa 1968, 18:139-143
67501 The Children of the Dream. NY/London: Macmillan-Collier 1969, xiii + 345 p
67502 Class, color and prejudice. Nation 1963, 197:231-234
67503 The courage to be: fragments of the case history of an autistic girl. (Read at Chicago Psa Soc, 27 Feb 1962)
    Abs Miller, A. A. Bull Phila Ass Psa 1962, 12:87-89
67504 The decision to fail. Schl Rev 1961, 69:377-412
67505 Dialogues with Mothers. NY: The Free Pr of Glencoe 1962, 216 p
    Rv Roiphe, H. Q 1963, 32:268-269. Levine, M. D. R 1967, 54:714
67506 Does communal education work? Commentary 1962, 33:117-125
67507 Early ego development in a mute autistic child. (Read at Phila Ass Psa, 28 May 1965) Bull Phila Ass Psa 1965, 15:127-136
    Abs EFA Q 1967, 36:628. PLe RFPsa 1967, 31:310
67508 The education of emotionally and culturally deprived children. Learn Love 235-244
67509 Eichmann; the system; the victims. New Repub 1963, 148(24): 23-33
67510 The Empty Fortress. Infantile Autism and the Birth of the Self. NY: Free Pr; London: Collier-Macmillan 1967, xiv + 484 p
    Rv Ekstein, R. Q 1968, 37:296-297
S-2576 (& Janowitz, M.) Ethnic tolerance: a function of social and personal control. In Berelson, B. & Janowitz, M. *Reader in Public Opinion and Communication*, Glencoe, Ill.: Free Pr 1950, 94-105
67511 Growing up female. Harper's Mag 1962, 225(1349):120-128
67512 Harry—a study in rehabilitation. ASP 1949, 44:231-265
S-41954 The Informed Heart; Autonomy in a Mass Age.
    Rv Rubin, I. A. Q 1962, 31:108-111
67513 Interpersonal relationships in behavior control. In *20th Annual Conference on Youth and Community Service*, State of Illinois: Dept of Public Welfare 1951, 100-111
S-2580 Love is Not Enough. NY: Macmillan 1965, 350 p
    L'Amore Non Basta. Milan: Ferro 1967
    Rv Momigliano, L. N. Riv Psa 1967, 13:86-88
67514 News and comment: toward a new school. Elem Sch J 1958, 59(2): 61-67

67515 A non-contribution to educational research. Harv educ Rev 1963, 33:326-335

67516 Notes on the future of education. Univ Chicago Mag 1966, 58(5): 12-14

S-2583 (& Sylvester, E.) Notes on the impact of parental occupations: some cultural determinants of symptom choice in emotionally disturbed children. With title: Parental occupations and children's symptoms. In Bell, N. W. & Vogel, E. F. *A Modern Introduction to the Family,* Glencoe, Ill: Free Pr 1960, 499-509

67517 Obsolete youth. Towards a psychograph of adolescent rebellion. Encounter 1969, 33(3):29-42

* * * (& Sylvester, E.) Parental occupations and children's symptoms. See [S-2583]

67518 Personality formation in the kibbutz. Psa 1969, 29:3-9

67519 Portnoy psychoanalyzed. Midstream 1969, 15(6):3-10

67520 (& Janowitz, M.) Prejudice. Sci Am 1950, 183(4):11-13

67521 The problem of generations. Daedalus 1962, 91:68-96. Youth 64-92

67522 Psychiatric consultation in residential treatment. (Workshop 1957, I. The Director's View.) Ops 1958, 28:256-265

67523 Reading the signs of mental health. PTA Mag 1959, 53(7):16-19

67524 Segregation: new style. Schl Rev 1958, 66:251-272

67525 (& Janowitz, M.) Social Change and Prejudice: Including Dynamics of Prejudice. NY: Free Pr of Glencoe 1964, xi + 337 p

67526 The study of man—the victim's image of the anti-Semite. Commentary 1948, 5:173-179

67527 Teaching the disadvantaged. NEA J 1965, 54(6):8-12

67528 To nurse and to nurture. Nurs Forum 1962, 1(3):60-76

67529 Training the child-care worker in a residential center. Ops 1966, 36:694-705

Abs JMa RFPsa 1968, 32:380

67530 The ultimate limit. Midway 1968, 9(2):3-25

67531 Violence: a neglected mode of behavior. Ann Am Acad Pol Soc Sci 1966, 364:50-59. Reflections 1966, 1(4):26-41

67532 What students think about art. In Dunkel, H. B. *General Education in the Humanities,* Wash DC: Amer Council on Education 1947, 177-227

67533 Women: emancipation is still to come. New Repub 1964, 151(19):48-58

REVIEW OF:

67534 Neubauer, P. D. (Ed) Children in Collectives. Child-rearing Aims and Practices in the Kibbutz. Q 1967, 36:300-304

BETTSCHART, W.

See Crot, M.

BETWEE, MARCUS C.

See Rubin, Eli Z.

BETZ, BARBARA J.

67535 Bases of therapeutic leadership in psychotherapy with the schizophrenic patient. PT 1963, 17:196-212
67536 Freud's personality at 40. Am Im 1965, 22:180-185

BEUCHER, MAX

67537 À propos de certaines guérisons magiques au cours de psychothérapies d'adolescents. [Apropos of certain magical cures during psychotherapy of adolescents.] Ann méd-psychol 1966, 2:534
67538 La Psychanalyse est-elle nuisible? [Is Psychoananlysis Harmful?] Paris: Hachette 1968, 274 p

BEUCLER, A.

TRANSLATION OF:
Freud, S. [10431]

BEUGEN, M. VAN

See Boeke, Pieter E.

BEUKENKAMP, CORNELIUS, JR.

67539 The existence of the individual in his group. Voices 1965, 1(1):79-82
67540 A few leisure hours. Voices 1966, 2(2):47
67541 Health for what? Psychologia 1965, 8:151-152
67542 Hostility in female sexual identification. Voices 1966, 2(1):90-92
67543 The importance of despair. Bibl Psychiat Neurol 1963, 118:69-75
67544 Is health enough? Int ment Hlth Res N L 1961, 3(1 & 2)
67545 Meaning as structure in psychotherapy. J existent Psychiat 1967, 7:473-479
67546 Parental suicide as a source of resistance to marriage. Int J grp PT 1961, 11:204-208
67547 Phantom patricide. Arch gen Psychiat 1960, 3:282-288
67548 The similarity and differences between therapy groups and educational groups. Proc 7th Int Cong Ment Hlth 1968
67549 (& Berger, M. M.) Training in group psychotherapy: a symposium. PT 1958, 12(3):3-13. In Rosenbaum, M. & Berger, M. M., *Group Psychotherapy and Group Function*, NY/London: Basic Books 1963, 553-557
67550 When the Troubled Meet (Fortunate Strangers). NY: Rinehart; Dover, Delaware: Pickett Enterprises 1966, 269 p

BEVAN, WILLIAM

67551 The concept of adaptation in modern psychology. J Psychol 1965, 59:73-93

BEYER, ROBERT CARLYLE

67552 Search for identity: two very different approaches. J Inter-Amer Stud 1968, 10:345-349

BEYME, F.

67553 Archetypal dreams and frigidity. J anal Psych 1967, 12:3-22

67554 Archetypischer Traum (Todeshochzeit) und psychosomatisches Symptom (weibliche Impotenz) im Lichte der Forschungen von J. J. Bachofen, C. G. Jung und E. Neumann. [Archetype dream (death marriage) and psychosomatic symptoms (female impotence) in the light of studies by J. J. Bachofen, C. G. Jung and E. Neumann.] Schweiz ANP 1963, 92:140-173; 1964, 93:100-136; 94:125-153

67555 Das neue Schlafmittel Mogadon und das Traumgeschehen. [The new soporific Mogadon and the occurrence of dreams.] Psychiat Neurol, Basel 1965, 149:136-141

67556 Obituary: [In memoriam: C. G. Jung (1875-1961).] (Ger) Schweiz ANP 1962, 90:357-361

BHADRA, M. K.

67557 Existential psycho-analysis—its various aspects. Samiksa 1967, 21(4): 139-157

BHANDARI, LALIT C.

67558 Some aspects of psychoanalytic therapy in India. Prog PT 1960, 5:218-220

BHASKARAN, KRISHNASWAMY

67559 Genital self-mutilation: psychodynamic study of a case. Ind J Psychiat 1959, 1(3):112-117

BIANCHEDI, ELIZABETH T. DE

67560 (& Sor, D.) Revertir la perspectiva, su problemática en el proceso analítico. [Problems of perspective reversal in the analytic process.] Rev Psicoanál 1967, 24:143-150

See Aizenberg, Sergio

ABSTRACTS OF:

67561 Bion, W. R. Experiences in groups. Rev Psicoanál 1967, 24:391-393

67562 Boyer, L. B. A hypothesis regarding the time of appearance of the dream screen. Rev Psicoanál 1961, 18:90

67563 Devereux, G. Retaliatory homosexual triumph over the father. Rev Psicoanál 1961, 18:178

67564 Harris, I. D. Unconscious factors common to parents and analysts. Rev Psicoanál 1961, 18:177

67565 Jacques, E. Disturbances in the capacity to work. Rev Psicoanál 1961, 18:391

67566 James, M. Premature ego development. Some observations on disturbances in the first three months of life. Rev Psicoanál 1961, 18:395-396

67567 Khan, M. M. R. Regression and integration in the analytic setting. Rev Psicoanál 1961, 18:178

67568   Reich, A. Further remarks on counter-transference. Rev Psicoanál 1961, 18:394
67569   Rosenfeld, H. A. On drug addiction. Rec Psicoanál 1961, 18:393
67570   Tidd, C. W. The use of psychoanalytic concepts in medical education. Rev Psicoanál 1961, 18:392

67571   Williams, A. H. A psychoanalytic approach to the treatment of the murderer. Rev Psicoanál 1961, 18:395

REVIEW OF:
67572   Bowlby, J. Separation Anxiety. Rev Psicoanál 1961, 18:89

BIANCHI, Z.

See Brughera, F.

BIBACE, ROGER

See Denner, Bruce; Sonstroem, Anhe M.

BIBRING, EDWARD

S-42004 Psychoanalysis and the dynamic psychotherapies. In Zinberg, N. E. *Psychiatry and Medical Practice in a General Hospital*, NY: IUP 1964, 51-71
S-2629 Zur Entwicklung und Problematik der Triebtheorie.
        The development and problems of the theory of the instincts. J 1969, 50:293-308

BIBRING, GRETE L.

67573   Can psychiatry be taught? Teach Dyn Psychiat 5-20
67574   (& Kahana, R. J.) Lectures in Medical Psychology: An Introduction to the Care of Patients. NY: IUP 1969, xiv + 289 p
67575   Old age: its liabilities and its assets; a psychological discourse. (Read at Boston Psa Soc, 23 Feb 1966) Psa—Gen Psychol 253-271
        Das hohe Alter: Passiva und Aktiva. Eine psychobiologische Studie. Psyche 1969, 23:262-279
        Abs Kravitz, A. R. Bull Phila Ass Psa 1967, 17:43-47
* * *   Preface. Teach Dyn Psychiat 1-4
* * *   Preface to Zinberg, N. E. *Psychiatry and Medical Practice in a General Hospital* NY: IUP 1964, xi-xii
S-2642 Psychiatric principles in casework. In Zinberg, N. E. *Psychiatry and Medical Practice in a General Hospital*, NY: IUP 1964, 41-50
S-42011 Psychiatry and medical practice in a general hospital. In Zinberg, N. E. *Psychiatry and Medical Practice in a General Hospital*, NY: IUP 1964, 75-87
S-2643 Psychiatry and social work. In Zinberg, N. E. *Psychiatry and Medical Practice in a General Hospital*, NY: IUP 1964, 28-40
S-42013 Some considerations of the psychological processes in pregnancy.
        Abs RTh J 1961, 42:469
67576   Some considerations regarding the ego ideal in the psychoanalytic process. J Am Psa Ass 1964, 12:517-521
        Abs JLSt Q 1967, 36:132. CG RFPsa 1968, 32:175

67577 (& Dwyer, T. F.; Huntington, D. S.; Valenstein, A. F.) A study of the psychological processes in pregnancy and of the earliest mother-child relationship. Psa St C 1961, 16:9-72

67578 (Ed) The Teaching of Dynamic Psychiatry: A Reappraisal of the Goals and Techniques in the Teaching of Psychoanalytic Psychiatry. NY: IUP 1968, x + 277 p

67579 Work with physicians. In Weinreb, J. *Recent Developments in Psychoanalytic Child Therapy,* NY: IUP 1960, 39-52

See Hamburg, David A.; Kahana, Ralph J.

BICK, ESTHER

67580 The experience of the skin in early object-relations. (Read at 25th Int Psa Cong, July 1967) J 1968, 49:484-486

67581 Notes on infant observation in psycho-analytic training. (Read at Brit Psa Soc, July 1963) J 1964, 45:558-566
  Notas sobre la observación de lactantes en la ensenanza del psico-análisis. Rev Psicoanál 1967, 24:97-115
  Abs Q 1966, 35:622

67582 Symposium on child analysis. I. Child analysis today. (Read at Int Psa Cong, July-Aug 1961) J 1962, 43:328-332; 342
  La psychanalyse infantile aujourd'hui. RFPsa 1964, 28:139-148; 165-168
  Abs RLG Q 1963, 32:605-606

BICKFORD, R. G.

See Schwarz, Berthold E.

BICUDA, VIRGINIA LEONE

67583 Consecuencias del fracoso de la defensa maniaca. [Consequences of the breakdown of manic defences.] Rev urug Psa 1966, 8:303-315

67584 Correlato sobre el tema "Mania." El alcance de la regresión en la mania. [Round table on mental illness. Regression in mental illness.] Rev urug Psa 1966, 8:139-147

67585 Discussion of Sandford, B. "Cinderella." Psa Forum 1967, 2:133-135

67586 Persecutory guilt and ego restrictions. Characterization of a pre-depressive position. (Read at Int Psa Cong, July-Aug 1963) J 1964, 45:358-363
  Culpabilité pérsecutoire et restrictions du Moi. Caractérisation d'une position prédépressive. RFPsa 1965, 29:219-232
  Abs EVN Q 1966, 35:463-464

67587 Relação economica entre "splitting," sublimação e sintomas obsessivos. [Economic relationship between "splitting," sublimation, and obsessive symptoms.] Rev bras Psicanál 1967, 1:67-76; Abs (Engl) 77-78

BIDDLE, W. EARL

67588 Crime and delinquency. Abstracts Vol. 4, No. 3. Chevy Chase, Maryland: U. S. Dept of Health, Education and Welfare Public Health Service, 393-588

67589   Hypnosis in the Psychoses. Springfield, Ill: Thomas 1967, xi + 139 p
67590   Images: the objects psychiatrists treat. Arch gen Psychiat 1963, 9:464-
        470

BIDERMAN, ALBERT D.

67591   (& Zimmer, H. M.) (Eds) The Manipulation of Human Behavior. NY:
        Wiley 1961, xx + 323 p

BIDNEY, DAVID

67592   Myth, symbolism, and truth. In Vickery, J. B. *Myth and Literature;*
        Contemporary Theory and Practice, Lincoln, Neb: Univ of Neb Pr
        1966, 3-13
67593   So-called primitive medicine and religion. In Galdston, I. *Man's Image*
        in Medicine and Anthropology, NY: IUP 1963, 141-156

BIEBER, IRVING

67594   Advising the homosexual. Med Asp hum Sexual 1968, 2(3):34-39
67595   Anxiety and phobias. In Kurian, M. & Hand, M. H. *Lectures in Dy-*
        namic Psychiatry, NY: IUP 1963, 78-89
67596   Biosocial determinants of neurosis. In Merin, J. & Nagler, S. *Etiology*
        of Neurosis, Palo Alto, Calif: Sci & Behav Books 1966, 16-27
67597   Clinical aspects of male homosexuality. In Marmor, J. *Sexual Inversion,*
        NY: Basic Books 1965, 248-267
67598   Discussion of Bridger, W. H. & Birns, B. M. "An analysis of the role
        of sucking in early infancy." Sci Psa 1968, 12:161-165
67599   Discussion of Dement, W. C. "Experimental dream studies." Sci Psa
        1964, 7:177-178
67600   Discussion of Gershman, H. "Homosexuality and some aspects of crea-
        tivity." Psa 1964, 24:35-38
67601   Discussion of psycho-physiological papers [by N. Kleitman & E. A.
        Weinstein]. Dreams Contempo Psa 102-115
67602   Discussion of White, R. W. "Competence and the growth of person-
        ality." Sci Psa 1967, 11:49-54
67603   (& Dain, H. J.; Dince, P. R.; Drellich, M. G.; Grand, H. G.; Gundlach,
        R. H.; Kremer, M. W.; Rifkin, A. H.; Wilbur, C. B.; Bieber, T. B.)
        Homosexuality: A Psychoanalytic Study of Male Homosexuals. NY:
        Basic Books 1962; Vintage Books 1965, viii + 358 p
            Homosexualidad. Estudio Psicoanalítico. Mexico, DF: Editorial Pax
        Mexico
            Rv JCS RFPsa 1962, 26:490. Socarides, C. W. Q 1963, 32:111-114.
        Guarner, E. Cuad Psa 1965, 1:210
67605   Introduction to papers on the psycho-physiology of dreams. Dreams
        Contempo Psa 34-36
67606   (& Gershman, H.; Ovesey, L.; Weiss, F. A.) The meanings of homo-
        sexual trends in therapy. A round table discussion. Psa 1964, 24:60-76
67607   (& Drellich, M. G.) Psychological adaptation to serious illness and or-

gan ablation. In Lief, H. I. et al: *The Psychological Basis of Medical Practice*, NY: Harper & Row 1963, 318-327

67608 Sadism and masochism. Am Hbk Psychiat III 256-270

67609 Sex in psychoanalysis. In Allison, A. *The Biology of Sex*, London: Penguin Science Survey 1967, 242-256

67610 Sexual deviations. I. Introduction. Compreh Txbk Psychiat 959-962

67611 Sexual deviations. II: Homosexuality. Compreh Txbk Psychiat 963-976

See Bieber, Toby B.; Drellich, Marvin G.; Martin, Alexander R.

BIEBER, TOBY B.

67612 Acting out in homosexuality. Acting Out 142-151

S-42029 The emphasis on the individual in psychoanalytic group therapy. Abs MK An Surv Psa 1957, 8:279

67613 Group psychotherapy today. Case discussion. Top Probl PT 1965; 5:189-193

67614 The lesbian patient. Med Asp hum Sexual 1969, 3(1):6; 9-10; 12

67615 On treating male homosexuals. Arch gen Psychiat 1967, 16:60-63

67616 (& Bieber, I.) Psychotherapeutic focus in social psychiatry. Arch gen Psychiat 1965, 13:62-66
Abs PB Q 1967, 36:144

67617 The psychotherapy of homosexuality, 3: female therapist's view. Psychiat Opin 1967, 4(2):12-13

67618 (& Bieber, I.) Resistance to marriage. Marriage Relat 47-58

67619 (& Cappon, D.; Durkin, H. E.) A symposium on combined individual and group psychotherapy discussion. Int J grp PT 1964, 14:433-454

See Bieber, Irving

BIELICKA, IZABELA

67620 (& Olechnowicz, H.) A note on the rehabilitation of the family in the treatment of the orphan syndrome in infants. J child Psychol Psychiat 1967, 8:139-142

67621 (& Olechnowicz, H.) Technika psychoterapii najmlodszego dziecka. [Technique of psychotherapy in the very young child.] Pediat Pol 1966, 41:779-788

67622 (& Olechnowicz, H.) [Theoretical assumptions of psychotherapy at the pre-verbal level.] (Pol) Pediat Pol 1966, 41:771-777

BIERENFELD, F. R.

S-42031 Justice, aggression, and Eros.
Giustizia, aggressione ed Eros. Riv Psa 1963, 9:241-255
Abs AEC An Surv Psa 1957, 8:317

BIERI, JAMES

67623 (& Lobeck, R.) Self-concept differences in relation to identification, religion and social class. ASP 1961, 62:94-98

BIERMAN, JOSEPH S.

S-42034 (& Silverstein, A. B.; Finesinger, J. E.) A depression in a six-year-old boy with acute poliomyelitis.
Abs JA An Surv Psa 1958, 9:300-301

67624 Necrophilia in a thirteen-year-old boy. Q 1962, 31:329-340

BIERMANN, GERD

67625 Analytische Müttergruppentherapie bei verhaltensgestörten Kindern und Jugendlichen. [Analytic group therapy of mothers of children and adolescents with behavior disturbances.] Therapiewoche 1966, 16:792. Hbh Kinderpsychother 760-771

67626 Aufgaben des Kinderpsychotherapeuten in der Kinderklinik. [Lessons for child psychotherapy from a children's clinic.] Hbh Kinderpsychother 981-989

67627 Behandlung einer psychogenen Depression. [Treatment of psychogenic depression.] Acta psychother psychosom 1960, 8:307-318

67628 Berufs- und Ausbildungsweg des Kinderpsychotherapeuten. [Education for and the profession of child therapist.] Hbh Kinderpsychother 619-630

67629 Die Familien-Neurose in ihrer Projektion im Familien-Zeichentest. [The family neurosis in its projection in the family drawing test.] Psyche 1962, 16:127-141

67630 Gruppentherapie bei verhaltensgestörten Kindern und Jugendlichen und deren Eltern. [Group therapy in children and adolescents with behavior disorders and their parents.] Prax Kinderpsychol 1964, 13:40-47

67631 (Ed) Handbuch der Kinderpsychotherapie. [Handbook of Child Psychotherapy.] Munich/Basel: Reinhardt 1969, xvi + 617 p; xii + 619-1190 p

67632 Identitätsprobleme judischer Kinder and Jugendlicher in Deutschland. [Identity problems of Jewish children and adolescents in Germany.] Prax Kinderpsychol 1964, 13:213-221

67633 Katamnesenprobleme in der Kinderpsychotherapie. [The problem of catamnesis in child psychotherapy.] Pädiatr Pädol 1968, 4:233. Hbh Kinderpsychother 1157-1169

67634 Kinderpsychotherapie in der ärztlichen Praxis. [Child psychotherapy in the practice of medicine.] Pädiatr Prax 1967, 6:445. Hbh Kinderpsychother 1018-1030

67635 Psychotherapeutische Probleme bei psychosomatischen Erkrankungen im Kindes- und jugendalter. [Psychotherapeutic problems in psychosomatic illnesses of children and adolescents.] Pädiatr Prax 1968, 7:337, 503. Hbh Kinderpsychother 865-886

67636 Die Rolle der Mutter in der Erziehungsberatung und Psychotherapie des Kindes, Teil II. [The role of the mother in educational counseling and psychotherapy of children.] Prax Kinderpsychol 1967, 16:295-298

67637 Die Rolle des Vaters in der Erziehungsberatung. [The role of the father in educational counseling.] Prax Kinderpsychol 1963, 12:298-308

67638 Die seelische Entwicklung des Kindes im Familienmilieu schizophrener.

[The psychic development of children in the family environment of schizophrenics.] Schweiz ANP 1966, 97:87-132; 329-360

67639   Symbiotische Mutter-Kind-Beziehungen. [Symbiotic mother-child relations.] Psyche 1968, 22:875-895
        Abs J 1969, 50:400

67640   Vom Umgang mit Eltern verhaltensgestörten Kinder. [On a visit with parents of children with behavior disorders.] Mschr Kinderheilk 1964, 112:214-216

67641   Zur Geschichte der analytischen Kinderpsychotherapie. [The history of analytical child psychotherapy.] Mschr Kinderheilk 1968, 116(2):41-49. Hbh Kinderpsychother 1-18

See Kos-Robes, Marta

BIERNAERT, LOUIS

67461A [Freud, religion and civilization.] (Fr) In Problèmes de Psychanalyse, Paris: Fayard 1957, 173-183
        English: Problems in Psa 194-206

See Raclot, Marcel

BIERNOFF, JOSEPH

ABSTRACTS OF:

67642   Alexander, J. The psychology of bitterness. Q 1962, 31:123

67643   Apfelbaum, B. Some problems in contemporary ego psychology. Q 1963, 32:446-447

67644   Beharriell, F. J. Freud's "double": Arthur Schnitzler. Q 1963, 32:449

67645   Benedek, T. The organization of the reproductive drive. Q 1961, 30:296

67646   Beres, D. Perception, imagination, and reality. Q 1962, 31:117-118

67647   Bergmann, M. S. The place of Paul Federn's ego psychology in psychoanalytic metapsychology. Q 1964, 33:135

67648   Bernstein, I. Dreams and masturbation in an adolescent boy. Q 1963, 32:132

67649   Bonnard, A. The primal significance of the tongue. Q 1962, 31:117

67650   Bowlby, J. Separation anxiety. Q 1961, 30:297

67651   Boyer, L. B. The time of appearance of the dream screen. Q 1961, 30:297-298

67652   Brenner, A. B. Onan, the levirate marriage and the genealogy of the Messiah. Q 1963, 32:448-449

67653   Bronson, G. A neurological perspective on ego development in infancy. Q 1964, 33:134

67654   Devereux, G. Retaliatory homosexual triumph over the father. A further contribution to the counter-Oedipal sources of the Oedipus complex. Q 1961, 30:299

67655   Dickes, R. Fetishistic behavior: a contribution to its complex development and significance. Q 1964, 33:137

67656   Erikson, E. H. Reality and actuality: an address. Q 1963, 32:446

67657   Feldman, S. R. Blushing, fear of blushing, and shame. Q 1963, 32:133

67658   Fraiberg, S. Technical aspects of the analysis of a child with a severe behavior disorder. Q 1963, 32:132-133

67659 Furman, E. Some features of the dream function of a severely disturbed young child. Q 1963, 32:131

67660 Garma, A. et al: Symposium on disturbances of the digestive tract. Q 1962, 31:120-121

67661 Glauber, I. P. Federn's annotation of Freud's theory of anxiety. Q 1964, 33:135

67662 Greenacre, P. Considerations regarding the parent-infant relationship. Q 1962, 31:123-124

67663 Greenson, R. Empathy and its vicissitudes. Q 1962, 31:119

67664 Greenson, R. R. On enthusiasm. Q 1963, 32:130

67665 Harley, M. The role of the dream in the analysis of a latency child. Q 1963, 32:131-132

67666 Harris, I. D. Typical anxiety dreams and object relations. Q 1962, 31:124

67667 Harris, I. D. Unconscious factors common to parents and analysis. Q 1961, 30:298

67668 Heiman, M. Sexual response in women: a correlation of physiological findings with psychoanalytic concepts. Q 1964, 33:138-139

67669 Holt, R. R. A critical examination of Freud's concept of bound vs. free cathexis. Q 1963, 32:446

67670 James, M. Premature ego development. Some observations upon disturbances in the first three months of life. Q 1962, 31:116

67671 Jarvis, W. Some effects of pregnancy and childbirth on men. Q 1963, 32:448

67672 Kahn, M. M. R. Clinical aspects of the schizoid personality: affects and techniques. Q 1962, 31:119-120

67673 Katan, M. Dream and psychosis: their relationship to hallucinatory processes. Q 1962, 31:118

67674 Keiser, S. Disturbance of ego functions of speech and abstract thinking. Q 1963, 32:130-131

67675 Kligerman, C. A psychoanalytic study of Pirandello's "Six Characters in Search of an Author." Q 1963, 32:449

67676 Knapp, P. H. Short-term psychoanalytic and psychosomatic predictions. Q 1964, 33:136-137

67677 Lebovici, S. et al: Symposium on psychotic object relationships. Q 1962, 31:123

67678 Lidz, T. et al: Ego differentiation and schizophrenic symptom formation in identical twins. Q 1963, 32:131

67679 Little, M. On basic unity. Q 1962, 31:118-119

67680 Loewald, H. W. On the therapeutic action of psychoanalysis. Q 1961, 30:296

67681 Miller, I. Confrontation, conflict, and the body image. Q 1964, 33:134-135

67682 Myerson, P. G. Awareness and stress: post-psycho-analytic utilization of insight. Q 1961, 30:298

67683 Novey, S. The principle of "working through" in psychoanalysis. Q 1963, 32:448

67684 Ostow, M. The metapsychology of autoscopic phenomena. Q 1962, 31:125

67685   Pfeffer, A. Z. The meaning of the analyst after analysis: a contribution to the theory of therapeutic results. Q 1964, 33:136

67686   Rangell, L. On friendship. Q 1964, 33:134

67687   Reich, A. Further remarks on counter-transference. Q 1962, 31:119

67688   Richardson, G. A. & Moore, R. A. On the manifest dream in schizophrenia. Q 1964, 33:137

67689   Ritvo, S. & Solnit, A. J. The relationship of early ego identification to superego formation. Q 1962, 31:116-117

67690   Root, N. N. Some remarks on anxiety dreams in latency and adolescence. Q 1963, 32:132

67691   Rose, G. J. Unconscious birth fantasies in the ninth month of treatment. Q 1963, 32:448

67692   Rosenfeld, H. A. On drug addiction. Q 1962, 31:121

67693   Rosner, A. A. Mourning before the fact. Q 1963, 32:447

67694   Ross, D. W. & Kapp, F. T. A technique for self-analysis of counter-transference: use of the psychoanalyst's visual images in response to patient's dreams. Q 1963, 32:447-448

67695   Rycroft, C. The analysis of a paranoid personality. Q 1961, 30:296-297

67696   Sandler, J. The background of safety. Q 1962, 31:118

67697   Sarlin, C. N. Depersonalization and derealization. Q 1963, 32:450

67698   Schur, M. Phylogenesis and ontogenesis of affect- and structure-formation and the phenomenon of repetition compulsion. Q 1962, 31:116

67699   Searles, H. F. The differentiation between concrete and metaphorical thinking in the recovering schizophrenic patient. Q 1963, 32:130

67700   Shevin, F. F. Countertransference and identity phenomena manifested in the analysis of a case of "phallus girl" identity. Q 1964, 33:137-138

67701   Siegman, A. J. A type of transference elation. Q 1964, 33:136

67702   Silverman, S. Ego function and bodily reactions. Q 1962, 32:447

67703   Socarides, C. W. The historical development of theoretical and clinical concepts of overt female homosexuality. Q 1964, 33:139

67704   Sperling, M. The psychoanalytic treatment of a case of chronic regional ileitis. Q 1962, 31:124-125

67705   Stamm, J. L. Altered ego states allied to depersonalization. Q 1963, 32:449-450

67706   Stokes, A. D. A game that must be lost. Q 1961, 30:297

67707   Suslick, A. The phallic representation of the voice. Q 1964, 33:138

67708   Tidd, C. W. et al: Symposium on psychoanalysis and ethology. Q 1962, 31:117

67709   Weissman, P. The psychology of the critic and psychological criticism. Q 1963, 32:449

67710   Winnicott, D. W. The theory of the parent-infant relationship. Q 1962, 31:124

67711   Zeligs, M. A. The role of silence in transference, countertransference, and the psychoanalytic process. Q 1962, 31:119

67712   Zetzel, E. R. et al: Symposium on "depressive illness." Q 1962, 31:121-122

BIGGAR, JEAN

67713   Psychotherapy and Child Development; An Introduction for Students. London: Tavistock 1966, 142 p

BIGHAM, THOMAS JAMES

67714 (et al) (Eds) Moral Values in Psychoanalysis. NY: Academy of Religion and Mental Health 1965, ix + 131 p
Psychanalyse et Valeurs Morales. (Tr: Desvignes, F.) Paris: Éditions du Cerf 1967, 199 p

See Bowers, Margaretta K.

BIGNOLD, B. C.

67715 Agoraphobia: a review of ten cases. Med J Aust 1960, 47(2):332-333

BIGRAS, JULIEN

67716 La conception doctrinale de Béla Grunberger sur la structure névrotique. [The theoretical concepts of Béla Grunberger on the neurotic structure.] Cah Psychol 1965, April

67717 (& Mackay, J.; Melvyn, C.; Bélair, C.; Trétrault, L.) Les diagnostics pedo-psychiatriques selon l'age et le sexe dans un centre canadien français de Montreal. [Pedopsychiatric diagnosis according to age and sex in a French Canadian center in Montreal.] Rev Np inf 1968, 16:739-750

67718 En decà et au-delà de l'enceste chez l'adolescente. [On this side and that of incest in adolescents.] Canad Psychiat Ass J 1966, 11:189-204

67719 Esquisse d'une théorie de l'adolescence centrée sur le point de vue économique freudien. [The outline of an adolescence theory centered on the Freudian economic point of view.] Inconscient 1968, (6):89-104

67720 Étude de la fonction du père au cours d'une psychanalyse d'enfant. [A study of the function of the father during the psychoanalysis of a child.] Evolut psychiat 1966, 31:547-579

67721 Étude du fantasme de viol chez l'adolescente. [Study of the rape-fantasy in adolescent girls.] Canad Psychiat Ass J 1964, 9:131-139

67722 Le fantasme, avoir un enfant du père, comme organisateur de désir féminin. [The fantasy, having a child from the father, as the organizing principle of feminine desire.] Interprétation 1967, 1(3):71-110

67723 L'identification des objets et l'identification au père-idéal. [The identification of objects and the identification with the idéal-father.] Interprétation 1968, 2(3):5-20

67724 L'identification féminine chez l'adolescente. [Feminine identification in the adolescent girl.] Psychiat Enfant 1965, 6:163-274

67725 La scène du récit du rêve. [The scene of the dream narration.] Inconscient 1967, 3:107-110

67726 Le sens moral et le masochisme dans l'inceste père-fille. [Moral sense and masochism in father-daughter incest.] Interprétation 1967, 1(1): 35-63

67727 (& Gauthier, Y.; Bouchard, C.; Tassé, Y.) Suicidal attempts in adolescent girls. A preliminary study. Canad Psychiat Ass J 1966, 11(Suppl): S275-S282

See Mackay, Jacques

BILIKIEWICZ, T.

67728 Zur Frage der Umkehrbarkeit des homosexuellen Triebes. [Reversibility of the homosexual instinct.] Psychiat Neurol med Psychol 1968, 20:7-9

BILLAUD, R.

67729 La bouderie. Essai psychoclinique et psychopathologique. [Sulking. A clinical and psychopathological study.] Encéph 1960, 49:243-273

BILLER, HENRY B.

67730 Father absence, maternal encouragement and sex role development in kindergarten-age boys. Child Develpm 1969, 40:539-546

67731 A multiaspect investigation of masculine development in kindergarten age boys. Genet Psychol Monogr 1968, 78:89-138

67732 A note on father absence and masculine development in lower-class negro and white boys. Child Develpm 1968, 39:1003-1006

BILLINSKY, JOHN M.

67733 Jung and Freud (The end of a romance). Andover Newton Quart 1969, 10:39-43

BILMES, MURRAY

67734 The delinquent's escape from conscience. PT 1965, 19:633-640

67735 Shame and delinquency. Contempo Psa 1967, 3(2):113-133

BILZ, RUDOLF

67736 Menschliche Aggressivität. Versuch einer verhaltensphysiologischen Differenzierung. [Human aggression, attempt at a behavior-physiological differentiation.] Z Psychother med Psychol 1967, 17:157-177

67737 Die Übermütungs-Panik (II): Eine psychosomatische Erörterung über die neurasthenische Leistungsschwäche. [The over-fatigue panic. II. A psychosomatic discussion on neurasthenic incapacity.] Med Welt 1964, 39:2099-2102

BINDEGLAS, PAUL MELVIN

67738 Therapeutic approaches to projection, some limitations of the classical view. Psychiat Q 1965, 39:293-302

BINDER, S.

67739 Die unzurechnungsfähige Sexualerbrecher im Rorschachtest. [The irresponsible sexual offender in the Rorschach test.] Nervenarzt 1968, 39:62-67

BINDRA, DALBIR

67740 An interpretation of the "displacement" phenomenon. Brit J Psychol 1959, 50:263-268

Abs Schlesinger, H. J. Q 1961, 30:154-155

BING, JAMES F.

S-42110 (& McLaughlin, F.; Marburg, R. O.) The metapsychology of narcissism.
Abs RTh J 1961, 42:467

67741 (& Marburg, R. O.) (Reporters) Panel on narcissism. (Amer Psa Assoc, Dec 1961) J Am Ass 1962, 10:593-605

BING, R.

See Offenkrantz, William

BINGER, CARL A. L.

67742 Conflicts in the life of Thomas Jefferson. P 1969, 125:1098-1107
67743 Discussion of Kubie, L. S. "Reflections on training." Psa Forum 1966, 1:100-101
67744 The doctor's job twenty years later. PSM 1964, 26:381-386
67745 The dreams of Benjamin Rush. P 1969, 125:1653-1659
67746 Emotional disturbances among college women. In Blain, G. B., Jr.; & McArthur, C. C. *Emotional Problems of the Student*, NY: Appleton-Century-Crofts 1961, 192-206
67747 Emotional maturity. Ency Ment Hlth 533-546
67748 The psychiatrist in the looking glass. Harper's Mag 1964, June
67749 Psychological conflicts of adolescents. Workshop Proceedings, Albuquerque, N. M., 11-13 April 1960
67750 Revolutionary Doctor. Benjamin Rush 1746-1813. NY: Norton 1966, 326 p
Rv Bookhammer, R. S. Q 1967, 36:608-609
67751 The two faces of medicine. New Engl J Med 1966, 275:193-195
67752 The Two Faces of Medicine. NY: Norton 1967, 208 p
Rv Cooper, A. M. Q 1969, 38:143-144

BINION, RUDOLPH

67753 Frau Lou: Nietsche's Wayward Disciple. Princeton, N. J.: Princeton Univ Pr 1968, xi + 587 p

BINOIS, R.

67754 La fatigue en milieu professional. [Fatigue in the professional environment.] Rev Med psychosom 1966, 8:243-273

BINSTOCK, WILLIAM A.

67755 (& Semrad, E. V.; Bloom, J. D.) The role of brief psychotherapy. Proc IV World Cong Psychiat 1966, 424-432

See Semrad, Elvin V.

BINSWANGER, HERBERT

S-42124 Freuds Psychosentherapie.
Abs HK An Surv Psa 1956, 7:35-36

67756 Grundpositionen der Psychoanalyse und die Konzeption von Ludwig
       Klages. [Basic positions in psycho-analysis and the concept of Ludwig
       Klages.] Z PSM 1963, 9:124-133
67757 Psychotherapeutische und graphologische Aspekte zur Genese und
       Struktur der Zwangsneurosen. [Psychotherapeutic and graphologic as-
       pects of the genesis and structure of obsessive-compulsive neuroses.]
       Z PSM 1966, 12:178-185
67758 Qualitatives Erleben und quantitativer Aspekt. [Qualitative experience
       and its quantitative aspects. A contribution to the methodological
       problem in psychiatry.] Schweiz ANP 1963, 91:78-84

BINSWANGER, LUDWIG A.

67759 Being-in-the-World: Selected Papers. (Tr: Needleman, J.) NY/Lon-
       don: Basic Books 1963, ix + 364 p
           Rv Slochower, H. Am Im 1964, 21(1-2):183. Levine, J. M. J Am
       Psa Ass 1967, 15:166-212
S-42131 Daseinanalyse und Psychotherapie. Acta psychother psychosom 1960,
       8:251-260
S-42133 Erinnerungen an Sigmund Freud.
           Abs SLP An Surv Psa 1956, 7:29; 443-447
67760 Existential analysis, psychiatry, schizophrenia. J existent Psychiat 1960,
       1:157-165
67761 Foreword to Häfner, H. *Psychopathen,* Berlin: Springer 1961
67762 Jakob Wyrsch. Zum 70. Geburtstag am 12. Juni 1962. [Jakob Wyrsch
       on his 70th birthday, 12 June 1962.] Psychiat Neurol, Basel 1962,
       143:369-378
67763 Melancholie und Manie. Phänomenologische Studien. [Melancholia
       and Mania. Phenomenological Studies.] Pfullingen, Germany: Verlag
       Gunther Neske 1960, 149 p
           Rv Fessler, L. Q 1961, 30:433-435
67764 Symptom and time: a casuistic contribution. Existent Inqu 1960,
       1(2):14-18
67765 Weisen der sprachlichen Kommunikation und ihre Einschränkung auf
       die "symbolische Ausdrucksweise." [Modes of communication in speech
       and its limitation to the "symbolic expressive mode."] Psyche 1960,
       13:686-709
           Modalitá della communicazione verbale e sua limitazione all' espres-
       sione simbolica presentate in un ossessivo dicisettene. Arch Psicol
       Neurol Psichiat 1960, 21:357-369

BION, D.

See Castets, Bruno

BION, WILFRED RUPRECHT

S-42146 On arrogance. In author's *Second Thoughts* 86-92
           Abs GLG An Surv Psa 1958, 9:163-164. Aizenberg, S. Rev Psicoanál
       1967, 24:386-387
S-42147 Attacks on linking. In author's *Second Thoughts* 93-109
           Ataques al vinculo. Rev urug Psa 1965, 7:355-371

Abs PRC RFPsa 1961, 25:291. Grimaldi, P. Rev Psicoanál 1967, 24:388-390

67766 Commentary. In author's *Second Thoughts* 120-166

S-42148 Development of schizophrenic thought. In author's *Second Thoughts* 36-42
Abs SLP An Surv Psa 1956, 7:175. Grimaldi, P. Rev Psicoanál 1967, 24:382-383

S-42149 Differentiation of the psychotic from the non-psychotic personalities. In author's *Second Thoughts* 43-64
Abs SLP An Surv Psa 1957, 8:153-154. Schlossberg, N. Rev Psicoanál 1967, 24:385-386

67767 Elements of Psycho-Analysis. London: Heinemann; NY: Basic Books 1963, v + 110 p
Elementos del Psicoanálisis. (Foreword: Grinberg, L.) Buenos Aires: Ed Paidós 1966
Rv Money-Kyrle, R. E. J. 1965, 46:385-388. Silverman, D. Q 1965, 34:281-282

67768 Experiences in Groups and Other Papers. London: Tavistock; NY: Basic Books 1961, 198 p
Abs J Am Psa Ass 1962, 10:639. Rv J 1964, 45:609. AaSt Q 1964, 33:441-442. Semrad, E. V. & Day, M. J Am Psa Ass 1966, 14:591-618. Bianchedi, E. T. de Rev Psicoanál 1967, 24:391-393

67769 The grid. (Unpublished work, 1964)
Abs Sor, D. Rev Psicoanál 1967, 24:395-399

S-2875A Group dynamics. A re-view.
Abs Sor, D. Rev Psicoanál 1967, 24:375-377

S-42150 On hallucination. In author's *Second Thoughts* 65-85
Abs GLG An Surv Psa 1958, 9:184-185. Grimaldi, P. Rev Psicoanál 1967, 24:387-388

67770 The imaginary twin. (Read at Brit Psa Soc, 1 Nov 1950) In author's *Second Thoughts* 3-22

* * * Introduction. In author's *Second Thoughts* 1-2

S-42151 Language and the schizophrenic.
Abs Aizenberg, S. Rev Psicoanál 1967, 24:379-381

67771 Learning from Experience. London: Heinemann; NY: Basic Books 1962, xii + 111 p
Aprendiendo de la Experiencia. (Foreword: Grinberg, L.) Buenos Aires: Ed Paidos 1965
Rv Guntrip, H. J 1965, 46:381-385

67772 Notes on memory and desires. Psa Forum 1967, 2:272-273; 279-280

S-42152 Notes on the theory of schizophrenia. In author's *Second Thoughts* 23-25
Abs Grimaldi, P. Rev Psicoanál 1967, 24:377-379

67773 (& Rosenfeld, H.; Segal, H.) Obituary: Melanie Klein. J 1961, 42:4-7

S-2877 Psychiatry at a time of crisis.
Abs Rolla, E. H. Rev Psicoanál 1967, 24:371-375

67774 Research on Small Groups. Paris: PUF n.d.
Rv Chazaud, J. RFPsa 1966, 30:499

67775 Second Thoughts: Selected Papers on Psycho-Analysis. London: William Heinemann Medical Books 1967, iii + 173 p; NY: Basic Books 1968

67776 Symposium: the psycho-analytic study of thinking. II. A theory of thinking. (Read at Int Psa Cong, July-Aug 1961) J 1962, 43:306-310.
    In author's *Second Thoughts* 110-119
        Théorie de la pensée. RFPsa 1964, 28:75-84
        Abs RLG Q 1963, 32:602-604. Granel, J. A. Rev Psicoanál 1967, 24:393

67777 Transformations. Change from Learning to Growth. NY: Basic Books; London: Heinemann Medical Books 1965, 183 p

REVIEW OF:

67778 Eissler, K. R. Medical Orthodoxy and the Future of Psychoanalysis. J 1966, 47:575-579

67779 Slovenko, R. (Ed) Sexual Behavior and the Law. J 1966, 47:579-581

BIRAN, SIGMUND

67780 Die Ausserpsychologischen Voraussetzungen der Tiefenpsychologie. [Metaphysical Assumptions of Depth Psychology.] Munich/Basel: Ernst Reinhardt Verlag 1966, 180 p

67781 Dynamische Psychologie der männerlichen Sexualneurosen: I. Aufbau und Inhalt der Symptome. II. Die sexualkonflikte als Basis der Sexualneurose. [Dynamic psychology of the male sexual neuroses: I. Pattern and content of the symptoms. II. Sexual conflict as the basis of sexual neurosis.] Z PSM 1960, 7:10-20; 1961, 7:92-106; 175-190; 267-279

67782 Der Freitod und die Lust-Unlust Bilanz des Lebens. [Suicide and the pleasure-pain principle of life.] Z Psychother med Psychol 1969, 19: 51-58

67783 Die Hypochondrie und der Sammelbegriff des eingebildeten Krankseins. [Hypochondria and the general concept of imaginary sickness.] Acta psychother psychosom 1963, 11:343-369

67784 Die Psychopathie im Lichte der seelischen Grundgegebenheiten. [Psychopathy in the light of basic psychic data.] Z PSM 1965, 11:36-45; 128-137; 180-193

67785 Über den Bildungsweg der psychosomatischen Erkrankungen. [On the manner of development of psychosomatic diseases.] Psychiat Neurol Neurochir 1967, 70:39-57

67786 Über Möglichkeiten und Wege, die Dauer der psychoanalytischen Behandlung zu verkürzen. [Possibilities and ways to shorten duration of psychoanalytic therapy.] Z PSM 1969, 15:153-181

S-42160 Der Unterschied zwischen Phobie und Angsthysterie.
        Abs An Surv Psa 1955, 6:145

67787 Versuch einer Psychologie der Todesfurcht. [Attempt at the psychological analysis of the fear of death.] Confin psychiat 1968, 11:154-176

67788 Versuch zur Psychopathogenese der Schizophrenie. [The psychopathogenesis of schizophrenia.] Psychiat Neurol Neurochir 1960, 63:252-281

67789 Zum Problem der Homosexualität. [The problem of homosexuality.] Acta psychother psychosom 1964, 12:402-453

BIRCH, HERBERT G.

67790 (& Thomas, A.; Chess, S.) Behavioral development in brain-damaged children, three case studies. Arch gen Psychiat 1964, 11:596-603

See Chess, Stella; Thomas, Alexander

BIRD, BRIAN

67791 On candidate selection and its relation to analysis. (Read at Pre-Cong Conf on Training, July 1967) J 1968, 49:513-526

S-42163 A consideration of the etiology of prejudice.
Abs AL An Surv Psa 1957, 8:127-129

S-42164 The curse of insight.
Abs DJM An Surv Psa 1957, 8:272

S-42167 Feelings of unreality.
Abs SLP An Surv Psa 1957, 8:103-104

67792 Mother-daughter vexation: a study of the phallic phase of female development. (Read at Los Angeles Psa Soc, 26 March 1964)
Abs RZ Bull Phila Ass Psa 1964, 14:238-240

67793 A mother's paradoxical response to advice. Amer J Dis Childr 1964, 107:383-385

S-42170 A specific peculiarity of acting out.
Abs OS An Surv Psa 1957, 8:140-141. Fernández, A. Rev urug Psa 1966, 8:414

S-42171 A study of the bisexual meaning of the foreskin.
Abs Margolis, N. M. An Surv Psa 1958, 9:294-297

BIRD, DUDLEY

See Woodward, Katharine F.

BIRD, H. WALDO

S-42174 (& Martin, P. A.) Countertransference in the psychotherapy of marriage partners.
Abs JA An Surv Psa 1956, 7:349

See Martin, Peter A.

BIRLEY, J. L. T.

See Brown, George W.

BIRMINGHAM, WILLIAM

67794 (& Cuneen, J. E.) (Eds) Cross Currents of Psychiatry and Catholic Morality. NY: Pantheon Books 1964, 396 p

BIRNBACH, MARTIN

67795 Neo-Freudian Social Philosophy. Palo Alto, Calif: Stanford Univ Pr 1961; London: Oxford Univ Pr 1962, vi + 283 p

BIRNBAUM, J.

See Witkin, Herman A.

BIRNBAUM, JUDITH L.

See Arthur, Bettie

BIRNER, LOUIS

67796   The James Bond phenomenon. J Contempo PT 1968, 1:13-18

BIRNEY, ROBERT CHARLES

67797   (& Teevan, R. C.) (Eds) Measuring Human Motivation. London: Van
Nostrand 1962, 181 p
67798   (& Teevan, R. C.) Reinforcement, an Enduring Problem in Psychology:
Selected Readings. London: Van Nostrand 1961, 230 p

See Teevan, Richard C.

BIRNS, BEVERLY H.

67799   (& Blank, M.; Bridger, W. H.; Escalona, S. K.) Behavioral inhibition
in neonates produced by auditory stimuli. Child Develpm 1965, 36:
639-645

See Bridger, Wagner H.

BIRREN, JAMES E.

67800   (Ed) Handbook of Aging and the Individual. Chicago, Ill.: Univ Chicago Pr 1959, xii + 939 p
67801   (& Butler, R. N.; Greenhouse, E. W.; Skoloff, L.; Yarrow, M. R.)
(Editorial collaboration: Perlin, S.) Human Aging: A Biological and
Behavioral Study. Bethesda, Md.; PH Serv Publ No. 986, 1963, xi +
328 p

BIRTCHNELL, JOHN

67802   The possible consequences of early parent death. M 1969, 42:1-12

BISCHOF, LEDFORD J.

67803   Interpreting Personality Theories. NY/Evanston/London: Harper &
Row 1964, ix + 694 p

BISHOP, FRANCES V.

67804   The anal character: a rebel in the dissonance family. J Pers soc Psychol
1967, 6:23-36

BISHOP, MELVIN P.

See Lief, Harold I.

BISI, NORA RASCOVSKY DE

67805   Discussion of Liberman, D. "Entropia e information en el proceso
terápeutico." Rev Psicoanál 1967, 24:65-67
67806   Rilke y el problema de la muerte. [Rilke and the problem of death.]
Rev Psicoanál 1963, 20:237-252

BISI, RICARDO H.

S-42178 Dermatosis in a case of postpartum psychosis.
Abs SO An Surv Psa 1956, 7:185-186

ABSTRACTS OF:

67807   Abadi, M. Interpretación y verbalización: la comunicación a distancia.
An Surv Psa 1957, 8:254

67808   Baranger, W. Interpretación e ideología (sobre la regla de abstención
ideológica). An Surv Psa 1957, 8:255

67809   Bartolini, J. P. Sucesivos desplazamientos de la incorporación preoral.
An Surv Psa 1957, 8:134

67810   Campo, A. J. La interpretación y la acción en el análisis de los niños.
An Surv Psa 1957, 8:233-234

67811   Campo, V. La interpretación de la entrevista con los padres en el
análisis de niños. An Surv Psa 1957, 8:228

67812   Cesio, F. R. El lenguaje no-verbal: su interpretación. An Surv Psa
1957, 8:254

67813   Cesio, F. R. Psicoanálisis del hábito de fumar. An Surv Psa 1957,
8:125-126

67814   Garcia Reinoso, D. La interpretación en pacientes con trastornos de
conversión. An Surv Psa 1957, 8:253-254

67815   Garma, A. Interpretaciones en sueños del psiquismo fetal. An Surv Psa
1957, 8:174-175

67816   Gonzalez, A. Relaciones de objeto y oscilaciones en el ciclo depresión
hipomanía. An Surv Psa 1957, 8:150-151

67817   Grinberg, L. Perturbaciones en la interpretación por la contraidentifi-
catión proyectiva. An Surv Psa 1957, 8:253

67818   Grinberg, L. Si yo fuera usted: contribución al estudio de la identificación proyectiva. An Surv Psa 1957, 8:129

67819   Langer, M. La interpretación basada en la vivencia contratransferencial
de conexión o desconexión con el analizado. An Surv Psa 1957, 8:255-
256

67820   Liberman, D. Interpretación correlativa entre relato y repetición: su
aplicación en una paciente con personalidad esquizoide. An Surv Psa
1957, 8:254-255

67821   Mom, J. M. Algunas consideraciones sobre interpretación en las fobias
An Surv Psa 1957, 8:255

67822   Pichon-Rivière, A. A. de La inclusión de los padres en el cuadro de la
situación analítica y el manejo de esta situación a través de la interpretación. An Surv Psa 1957, 8:229

67823   Racker, G. T. de Consideraciones sobre la formulación de la interpretación. An Surv Psa 1957, 8:252

67824   Rascovsky, A. (et al): La integración de la interpretación con los
niveles preorales. An Surv Psa 1957, 8:201-202

67825   Rascovsky, A. Sobre la génesis y evolución de las tendencias escopto-
fílicas a partir de la percepción interna. An Surv Psa 8:76-78

67826   Rolla, E. H. Análisis de una esquizofrenia. An Surv Psa 1957, 8:283-
284

67827   Weil, J. N. Psicoanálisis de una obesa con perversiones sexuales. An
Surv Psa 1957, 8:167

BISTER, WOLFGANG

67828 Bemerkungen zur psychoanalitisch orientierten Therapie bei Schizophrenen. [Remarks on the psychoanalytically oriented therapy of schizophrenics.] Psyche 1960, 14:360-381

67829 Gesichtspunkte bei der Indikation zur Psychotherapie von Schizophrenen. [Viewpoints in the indication for the psychotherapy of schizophrenics.] Nervenarzt 1962, 33:511-513

67830 Psychodynamische und soziale Aspekte der Schizophreniebehandlung. [Psychodynamic and social aspects of the treatment of schizoprenia.] Schwiez Z Psychol 1968, 27:18-29

67831 Über das Schulderleben bei Schizophrenen in psychotherapeutischer Sicht. [On the school life of schizophrenics from the psychotherapeutic viewpoint.] In Benedetti, G. & Müller, C. *Psychotherapy of Schizophrenia (2nd Int Symp 1959)*, Basel/NY: Karger 1960, 258-275

67832 Über kommunikative Einflüsse bei der klinischen und ambulanten Psychotherapie von Schizophrenen. [Concerning the influence of communication in hospital and ambulatory therapy of schizophrenics.] In Müller, C. & Benedetti, G. *Psychotherapy of Schizophrenia*, Basel/NY: Karger 1965, 82-89

67833 Zur Anwendung des psychoanalytischen Modells auf Psychopathologiesche Phanomene bei Psychosen. [Use of the psychoanalytical model for psychopathologic phenomena in psychoses.] Z Psychother med Psychol 1969, 19:153-162

BITTLE, ROBERT M.

See Shagass, Charles

BITTNER, EGON

See Ostwald, Peter

BITTNER, GÜNTHER

67834 Dynamische Psychologie in der Schule. [Dynamic psychology in school.] Prax Kinderpsychol 1966, 15:105-109

67835 Erraten als psychoanalytische Technik. [Guessing as a psychoanalytic technique.] Psyche 1968, 22:384-397

67836 Für und Wider die Leitbilder; Idealische Lebensformen in Pädagogisch-Psychologischer Kritik. [For and against leading images. Idealistic pedagogic-psychological criticism.] Heidelberg: Quelle & Meyer 1964, 154 p

67837 Pädagogische Überlegungen zum Realitätsprinzip. [Pedagogical considerations on the reality principle.] Psyche 1966, 20:128-142

67838 (& Rehm, W.) Psychoanalyse und Erziehung. [Psychoanalysis and education.] In authors' *Psychoanalyse und Erziehung*

67839 (& Rehm, W.) (Eds) Psychoanalyse und Erziehung. [Psychoanalysis and Education.] Munich: Goldmann 1966, 186 p

67840 Sublimierungstheorie und paedagogische Psychoanalyse. [Sublimation theory and pedagogic psychoanalysis.] Psyche 1964, 18:292-304

67841   Über die Symbolik weiblicher Reifung in Volksmärchen. [On the symbolism of female maturation in fairy tales.] Prax Kinderpsychol 1963, 12:210-213

BIXLER, RAY H.

67842   Limits are therapy. In Haworth, M. R. *Child Psychotherapy*, NY/London: Basic Books 1964, 134-137

BJERRE, POUL

67843   Die Lehrbarkeit der Seelenheilkunst. [The teaching of psychotherapy.] Prax PT 1964, 9:193-201

BJÖRK, STIG

67844   Aggressiivisuus ja psykoanalyysi. [Aggression and psychoanalysis.] Medisiinari 1967, (3) 7 p
67845   Hypnoosi lääkärin apuna. [Hypnosis as an aid to medical therapy.] Terveydenhoitolehti 1965, (10) 4 p
67846   Neuroosidiagnoosin rajat. [The boundaries of neurosis.] Duodecim 1965, (6) 10 p
67847   Psykoanalyyttinen käsitys sielunelämän kehityksestä. Lyhyt katsaus. [The Psychoanalytic View of Mental Development. A Short Survey.] Finland, Helsinki: Otava 1962, 66 p

BJORKSTEN, CHRISTEL

67848   Variability in normal ego-structure during school-age. Nord Psykol 1965, 17:371-424

BJÖRNSSON, SIGURJÓN

67849   Freud og Jung. [Freud and Jung.] Andvari 1961, 86:142-147
67850   Hjátrú og hugsýki. [Superstition and neurosis.] Almanak hins Ísl. Pjóvinafél 1963, 89:25-41
67851   Úr Hugarheimi. [An Outline of Clinical and Psychotherapeutic Psychology.] Heimskringla, Reykjavík 1964, 218 p
67852   Klinisk sálarfrøoi. [Clinical Psychology.] In *Vísindin Efla alla Daø*, Hlabuø, Reykjavík 1961, 69-90
67853   Leiøin til Skáldskapar. [The Road to Poetry.] Menningarspour, Reykjavík 1964, 109 p
67854   Salfrøilegar bókmenntaskýringar. [Psychological theories on literature.] Lesbók Morgunblaøsins 41(4):5-6, 12-15; (5):5-7, 12-13

BJORUM, N.

67855   [The phenomenological method in psychiatry.] (Dan) Nord Psyk Tidsskr 1968, 22:3-9

BLACHER, RICHARD S.

67856   Discussion of Flarsheim, A. "The psychological meaning of the use of marijuana and LSD in one case." Psa Forum 1969, 3:124-126

67857 (& Winkelstein, C.) The initial contact with the cancer patient—some psychiatric considerations. J Mount Sinai Hosp 1968, 35:423-428

See Bernstein, Anne E.; Meyer, Bernard C.; Winkelstein, Charles

BLACK, A. E.
See Baumrind, Diana

BLACK, BERTRAM J.

67858 Psychiatric rehabilitation in the community. In Bellak, L. *Handbook of Community Psychiatry and Community Mental Health,* NY: Grune & Stratton 1964, 248-264

67859 (& Benney, C.) Rehabilitation. In Bellak, L. & Loeb, L. *The Schizophrenic Syndrome,* NY/London: Grune & Stratton 1969, 735-756

67860 Rehabilitation and aftercare. In Ziskind, R. *Viewpoint on Mental Health,* NY: NYC Comm Ment Hlth Board 1967, 291-297; 305-310

See Bellak, Leopold

BLACK, ISABELLA

67861 Was it Arnold's doing? A psychological study of Arthur Hugh Clough. PPR 1961, 48:104-110

BLACK, MICHAEL S.

67862 (& London, P.) The dimensions of guilt, religion, and personal ethics. Soc Psych 1966, 69:39-54

See London, Perry

BLACKER, KAY HILL

67863 Obsessive-compulsive phenomena and catatonic states—a continuum. A five-year case study of a chronic catatonic patient. Ps 1966, 29:185-194

BLACKMAN, NATHAN
See Hellman, Daniel S.

BLACKMAN, SHELDON

67864 (& Mandell, W.; Goldstein, K. M.; Silberstein, R. M.) An approach to a community mental health theory. Proc APA 1964

67865 (& Silberstein, R. M.; Goldstein, K. M.) Status problems in the mental health team. MH 1965, 49:577-580

See Silberstein, Richard M.

BLACKWELL, AMELIA
See Blitzer, John R.; Rollins, Nancy

BLACKWOOD, WILLIAM
See Hunter, Richard A.

BLAHD, WILLIAM
See Alexander, Franz G.

BLAIN, DANIEL

67866 (& Potter, H.; Solomon, H.) Manpower studies with special reference to psychiatrists. P 1960, 116:791-797

67867 Mental health and hospital care in California. Calif Med 1963, 99:70-73

67868 A program for mental hygiene in California. Calif Med 1960, 93:263-268

BLAINE, GRAHAM B., JR.

67869 (& McArthur, C. C.) Basic character disorders and homosexuality. In authors' *Emotional Problems of the Student* 110-127

67870 Divided loyalties: the college therapist's responsibility to the student, the university and the parents. Ops 1964, 34:481-485
Abs JMa RFPsa 1966, 30:519

67871 (& McArthur, C. C.) (Eds) Emotional Problems of the Student. (Introd: Erikson, E. H.) NY: Appleton-Century-Crofts 1961, 254 p; NY: Anchor Books, Doubleday; Cambridge, Mass: Harvard Univ Pr 1966, xx + 283 p

67872 Patience and Fortitude. The Parents' Guide to Adolescence. Boston: Little, Brown 1962, 206 p

67873 (& McArthur, C. C.) Problems connected with studying. In authors' *Emotional Problems of the Student* 83-109

67874 Some emotional problems of adolescents. Med Clin N Amer 1965, 49:387-404

67875 Therapy. In author's *Emotional Problems of the Student* 257-276

67876 Youth and the Hazards of Affluence. NY: Harper & Row 1967, xi + 144 p

BLAIR, MARIE
See Hart, Juanita T.

BLAISE, EDUARDO

S-42209 Inhibición de la expresión proyectiva de la agresión. Regresión. Obsidad. Análisis de la fantasía básica.
Abs AN An Surv Psa 1956, 7:202

BLAKE-PALMER, G.

67877 Jung's influence on psychiatry and anthropology. New Zeal med J 1962, 61:450-453

BLAKESLEE, CLEMENT
See Gunther, Meyer S.

BLANC, CLAUDE

67878 Les modèles ontologiques de l'esprit en psychiatrie. [Ontologic models of the mind in psychiatry.] Évolut psychiat 1968, 33:421-428

67879 La psychopharmacologie: les mots, les drogues et l'esprit. [Psychopharmocology: words, drugs, and mind.] Évolut psychiat 1966, 31:707-740

BLANC, MARC

67880 Des idées et des mots en psychiatrie contemporaine. [Some ideas and words in contemporary psychiatry.] Ann méd-psychol 1967, 125(2): 501-517

67881 Syndrome de Turner et troubles neuropsychiatriques. [Turner's syndrome and neuropsychiatric disorders.] Ann méd-psychol 1966, 124(2): 346-353

BLANCHARD, M.

See Racamier, Paul C.

BLANCHARD, WILLIAM H.

67882 Psychodynamic aspects of the peak experience. R 1969, 56:87-112

67883 Rousseau and the Spirit of Revolt: A Psychological Study. Ann Arbor: Univ of Mich Pr 1967, xiv + 300 p
Rv Daly, R. W. R 1969, 56:158-160

BLANCK, GERTRUDE

67884 Crossroads in the technique of psychotherapy. Symposium: The emergence of ego psychology. R 1969-70, 56:498-510; 552-555

67885 Education for Psychotherapy: A Guide to the Major Training Facilities in the Field of Psychotherapy in the United States. NY: The Institute for Psychoanalytic Training and Research, Inc. 1962, 89 p

67886 Some technical implications of ego psychology. J 1966, 47:6-13
Einige technische Folgerungen aus der Ich-Psychologie. Psyche 1968, 22:199-214
Abs EVN Q 1968, 37:155

See Blanck, Rubin

BLANCK, RUBIN

67887 (& Blanck, G.) Marriage and Personal Development. NY/London: Columbia Univ Pr 1968, xiv + 191 p

BLANE, HOWARD T.

67888 (Hill, M. J.; Brown, E.) Alienation, self-esteem and attitudes toward drinking in high-school students. Quart J Stud Alcohol 1968, 29:350-354

67889 Characterological patterns of defense. Int Psychiat Clin 1966, 3:139-162

See Chafetz, Morris E.

BLANK, H. ROBERT

67890 (& Greenberg, H. R.; Argrett, S.) The anatomy of elopement from an acute adolescent service: escape from engagement. Psychiat Q 1968, 42:17-27

67891 Birth control and poverty. Bull NY State District Branches, Am Psychiat Ass 1965, 8:2 & 9

67892 The challenge of rehabilitation. Israel med J 1961, 20(5-6):127-142. New Outlook Blind 1962, 56:203-209
　　　Swedish: Social med Tidskr 1964, 41:345-354
　　　Abs Auth Q 1962, 31:141

67893 Community psychiatry and the psychiatrist in private practice. In Bellak, L. *Handbook of Community Psychiatry and Community Mental Health,* NY: Grune & Stratton 1964, 300-318

67894 Contributions of Freudian psychoanalysis. Prog clin Psych 1960, 4:100-115

67895 Dream analysis in the treatment of the blind. Dreams Contempo Psa 188-211

S-42232 Dreams of the blind. In Levitas, G. B. *The World of Psychology,* NY: Braziller 1963
　　　Abs SL An Surv Psa 1958, 9:224-226

67896 Drugs and accidents (maternal drug intoxication as a cause of injury to children). Children 1963, 10(5):204

67897 Helping the client accept his disability. In Jacobs, A. et al: *Counseling in the Rehabilitation Process,* NY: Teachers Coll, Columbia Univ 1961

67898 Humane abortion law or more criminal abortions. Westchester med Bull 1966, 34

67899 (& Greenberg, H. R.; Greenson, D. P.) The jelly baby. Psychiat Q 1968, 42:211-216

67900 Mourning. In Kutscher, A. H. *Death and Bereavement,* Springfield, Ill: Thomas 1969, 204-206

67901 The multidisciplinary treatment and research team. New Outlook Blind 1960, 54:115-118

67902 Must a handicap be a disability to a child? Why Rep 377-393

67903 Obituary: I. Peter Glauber, M.D. 1899-1966. Q 1967, 36:588

67904 Poverty, public health and mental health. Westchester med Bull 1965, 33(3):10-24

67905 Preventable murder. Bull NY State District Branches, Am Psychiat Ass 1966, 8:2 & 8

67906 The psychiatrist in improved services for the blind: a view from a twenty-one-year perspective. Blindness 1968:41-53

S-42237 Psychoanalysis and blindness.
　　　Abs AHM An Surv Psa 1957, 8:161-163

67907 The psychoanalyst in community work. Westchester med Bull 1964, 32

67908 Reactions to loss of body parts—some research priorities in rehabilitation. New Outlook Blind 1968, 62:137-143

67909 Recent advances in management of alcoholics. Westchester med Bull 1962, Oct

67910 Rehabilitation in Israel. New Outlook Blind 1962, 56(3):92-195

See Greenberg, Harvey R.; Klein, Donald F.

ABSTRACTS OF:
67911 Brody, E. B. Color and identity conflict in young boys. Observations of
       Negro mothers and sons in urban Baltimore. Q 1964, 33:457
67912 De Vos, G. The relation of guilt toward parents to achievement and
       arranged marriage among the Japanese. Q 1961, 30:300-301
67913 Dreikur, R. The interpersonal relationship in hypnosis. Q 1963, 32:140
67914 Enelow, A. J. The silent patient. Q 1961, 30:299-300
67915 Gladstone, H. P. A study of techniques of psychotherapy with youthful
       offenders. Q 1963, 32:139
67916 Glauber, I. P. Dysautomatization: a disorder of preconscious ego
       functioning. Q 1968, 37:327-330
67917 Goldfarb, W. Childhood Schizophrenia. Q 1963, 32:589-591
67918 Grunebaum, H. U. et al: The baby on the ward. A mother-child
       admission to an adult psychiatric hospital. Q 1964, 33:143-144
67919 Heine, R. W. & Trosman, H. Initial expectations of the doctor-patient
       interaction as a factor in continuance in psychotherapy. Q 1961,
       30:300
67920 Kars, P. C. The existential moment in psychotherapy. Q 1962, 31:428-
       429
67921 Kleiner, R. J.; Tuckman, J. & Lavell, M. Mental disorder and status
       based on race. Q 1961, 30:300
67922 LeShan, L. & LeShan, E. Psychotherapy and the patient with a limited
       life span. Q 1962, 31:429
67923 Lidz, T. (et al): Schizophrenic patients and their siblings. Q 1964,
       33:143
67924 Lu, Y. Mother-child role relations in schizophrenia. A comparison of
       schizophrenic patients with nonschizophrenic siblings. Q 1962, 31:428
67925 McCord, W. et al: The familial genesis of psychoses. Q 1963, 32:139
67926 Monroe, J. T., Jr. & Abse, D. W. The psychopathology of trichotillo-
       mania and trichophagy. Q 1964, 33:144
67927 Newman, R. et al: The experimental situation as a determinant of
       hypnotic dreams. Q 1961, 30:299
67928 Sarvis, M. A. & Garcia, B. Etiological variables in autism. Q 1962,
       31:429
67929 Schaffer, L. et al: On the nature and sources of the psychiatrist's
       experience with the family of the schizophrenic. Q 1963, 32:138-139
67930 Shapiro, D. Aspects of obsessive compulsive style. Q 1963, 32:139
67931 Silber, E. The analyst's participation in the treatment of an adolescent.
       Q 1963, 32:140
67932 Vogel, E. F. The marital relationship of parents of emotionally dis-
       turbed children: polarization and isolation. Q 1961, 30:299
67933 Ward, C. H. Some further thoughts on the examination dream. Q
       1962, 31:429-430

REVIEWS OF:
67934 Bellak, L. & Small, L. Emergency Psychotherapy and Brief Psycho-
       therapy. Q 1967, 36:124-125
67935 Brain, L. Diseases of the Nervous System. Sixth Edition. Q 1964,
       33:298-299
67936 Caplan, G. Principles of Preventive Psychiatry. Q 1964, 33:588-589

67937 Cappon, C. Toward an Understanding of Homosexuality. Q 1966, 35:137-138

67938 Carroll, T. J., Rev. Blindness, What It Is, What It Does, and How to Live with It. Q 1962, 31:563-565

67939 Dellis, N. P. & Stone, H. K. (Eds) The Training of Psychotherapists. Q 1962, 31:408-409

67940 Erikson, E. Childhood and Society. Q 1964, 33:581

67941 Faergeman, P. M. Psychogenic Psychoses. A Description and Follow-up of Psychoses following Psychological Stress. Q 1964, 33:436-437

67942 Forbes, T. R. The Midwife and the Witch. Q 1969, 38:660-661

67943 Fraser, J. T. (Ed) The Voices of Time. A Cooperative Survey of Man's Views of Time as Understood and Described by the Sciences and by the Humanities. Q 1967, 36:297-300

67944 Furth, H. G. Thinking Without Language. Psychological Implications of Deafness. Q 1967, 36:617-619

67945 Hastings, D. W. Impotence and Frigidity. Q 1964, 33:448

67946 Henderson, D. & Batchelor, I. R. C. Henderson and Gillespie's Text-book of Psychiatry. 9th Ed., Rev. Q 1964, 33:288-289

67947 Levine, E. S. The Psychology of Deafness, Techniques of Appraisal for Rehabilitation. Q 1961, 30:115-116

67948 Marmor, J. (Ed) Sexual Inversion. The Multiple Roots of Homosexuality. Q 1966, 35:137-138

67949 Lloyd, C. W. (Ed) Human Reproduction and Sexual Behavior. Q 1965, 34:461-462

67950 Noyes, A. P. & Kolb, L. C. Modern Clinical Psychiatry. 6th Ed. Q 1964, 33:447-448

67951 Redlich, F. C. & Freedman, D. X. The Theory and Practice of Psychotherapy. Q 1967, 36:436-439

67952 White, R. W. (Ed) The Study of Lives. Essays on Personality in Honor of Henry A. Murray. Q 1966, 35:150-151

BLANK, LEONARD

67953 (Ed) Nudity and Nudism: Studies in Voyeurism and Exhibitionism. Chicago, Ill: Aldine Publ 1966, 310 p

67954 Psychological Evaluation in Psychotherapy. Ten Case Histories. A Guide to the Use of Psychological Test Results in Understanding Behavior in Psychotherapy. Chicago, Ill: Aldine Publ 1965; London: Allen & Unwin 1966, xii + 364 p

67955 (& David, H. P.) (Eds) Sourcebook for Training in Clinical Psychology. NY: Springer Publ Co 1964, ix + 337 p

67956 Training problems in clinical psychology. Prog clin Psych 1964, 6:184-199

67957 (& Roth, R. H.) Voyeurism and exhibitionism. Percept mot Skills 1967, 24:391-400

BLANK, MARION

67958 (& Bridger, W. G.) Deficiencies in verbal labeling in retarded readers. Ops 1966, 36:840-847

Abs JMa RFPsa 1968, 32:383

67959 The mother's role in infant development: a review. J Amer Acad Child Psychiat 1964, 3:89-105

67960 Some maternal influences on infants' rates of sensorimotor development. J Amer Acad Child Psychiat 1964, 3:668-687

See Birns, Beverly H.

BLANKENBURG, WOLFGANG

67961 Lebensgeschichtliche Faktoren bei manischen Psychosen. [Biographic factors in manic psychoses.] Nervenarzt 1964, 35:536-539

67962 Psychosomatische und psychotherapeutische Strömungen in der Medizin unser Zeit. Konzepte und kritische Reflexion, 10: Die daseinanalytische Auffassung. [Psychosomatic and psychotherapeutic trends in current medicine. Concepts and critical reflections. 10. Existential analytic interpretation.] Hippokrates 1968, 39:379-384

BLANTON, R. L.

See Kodman, Frank, Jr.

BLANTON, SMILEY

67963 Freud and theology. Pastoral Counselor 1963, 1:3-8

67964 Pastoral counseling in industry. Pastoral Counselor 1964, 2:3-12

67965 The use of poetry in individual psychotherapy. In Leedy, J. J. *Poetry Therapy*, Phila/Toronto: Lippincott 1969, 171-179

67966 What are the causes of promiscuity? Why Rep 195-204

BLARER, ARNO V.

67967 Über die Ich-Struktur bei Primärinfantilen. [On the ego structure of people with primary infantilism.] Schweiz Z Psychol 1962, 21:222-246

BLASER, PETER

67968 (& Poeldinger, W.) Angst als Geistesgeschichtliches Phänomen und naturwissenschaftliches Problem. [Anxiety as a spiritual, historical phenomenon and as a scientific problem.] In Kielholz, P. *Angst: Psychische und Somatische Aspekte*, 11-36

67969 (& Gehring, A.; Poeldinger, W. J.) Toward a measurement of depressive symptoms. Int Psychiat Clin 1969, 6(2):27-52

BLATT, EVA FISHELL

67970 The relationship between severity of disease and extent of psychopathology in psychosomatic illness. A test of regression theory. Psychosomatics 1963, 4:207-214

BLATT, S.

See Marcus, David

BLATT, SIDNEY J.

67971 The Wechsler Scales and acting out. Acting Out 242-251

See Allison, Joel; Roth, David

BLAU, ABRAM

67972 (& Lenzner, A. S.) Attitudes and prognosis of naval psychiatric discharges. Ops 1946, 16:455-480
67973 Discussion of Greenacre, P. & Winnicott, D. W. "The theory of the parent-infant relationship. Further remarks." J 1962, 43:249-250
67974 (& Slaff, B.; Easton, K.; Welkowitz, J.; Springarn, J.; Cohen, J.) The psychogenic etiology of premature births. PSM 1963, 25:201-211
     Abs ELG Q 1964, 33:304
S-42299 A unitary hypothesis of emotion: 1. anxiety, emotions of displeasure, and affective disorders.
     Abs An Surv Psa 1955, 6:310-311

See Easton, Karl; La Vietes, Ruth L.; Mohacsy, Ildiko

BLAU, DAVID

67975 (& Berezin, M. A.) Introduction: some ethnic and cultural considerations in aging. J geriat Psychiat 1968, 2:3-5

ABSTRACT OF:
67976 Myerson, P. G. The hysteric's experience in psychoanalysis. Bull Phila Ass Psa 1969, 19:173-176

BLAUFARB, HERBERT

67977 Introduction. Reiss-Davis Clin Bull 1967, 4:66-67

BLAUNER, ROBERT

REVIEW OF:
67978 Gorer, G. Death, Grief, and Mourning. R 1968, 55:521-522

BLAYA, MARCELO

67979 [Concept of dynamic psychiatry.] (Por) Rev Ass Med Bras 1963, 9:41-45
67980 Mecanismos de defesa e formação de sintomas. [Defense mechanisms and symptom formation.] Arch Gastroent, S. Paulo 1966, 3(2):71-80
67981 [Psychoanalytic psychotherapy.] (Por) Med Cir Farm 1959, 284:550-561
67982 O Tratamento de psicóticos pela psicoterapia psicanalítica de grupo. [The treatment of psychotics with group psychoanalytic psychotherapy.] J Bras Psiquiat 1966, 15:33-52
67983 El uso de defensas maniacas in una obra teatral: "O Pagador de Promeasas." [The use of manic defenses in a drama: "O Pagador of Prometheus."] Rev urug Psa 1966, 8:281-287

TRANSLATIONS OF:
Menninger, K. [53996, 83574]

BLAYLOCK, BARBARA

See Byrne, Donn E.

BLAY NETO, BERNARDO

67984 [Some aspects of countertransference in the group.] (Por) J Bras Psiquiat 1965, 14:235-243

Zur Gegenübertragung in der Gruppentherapie. Z PSM 1966, 12: 138-143

Algunos aspectos de contratransferencia en grupo. Rev Psicol norm patol 1966, 12:436-440

67985 Das Verschleiern von Gruppenphantasievorstellungen. [Disguising of group fantasy ideas.] Z PSM 1969, 15:277-282

BLAZER, JOHN A.

67986 Fantasy and its effects. J gen Psychol 1964, 70:163-182

67087 The Fliess Biorhythm Theory: a preliminary report. Psychology 1964, 1:13-17

BLAŽEVIĆ, D.

See Betlheim, Stjepan; Persic, N.

BLEAKLEY, THOMAS H.

See Beckett, Peter G. S.

BLEANDONU, G.

See Bastie, Y.

BLEGER, JOSÉ

67988 Estudio sobre la simbiosis en "El reposo del guerrero." [Study of symbiosis in "El reposo del guerrero."] Rev Psicoanál 1962, 19:173-200

Abs Vega Q 1963, 32:612

67989 Meta final ficticia y fantasía inconsciente: estudio comparativo. [Unreal goal and unconscious fantasy: a comparative study.] Acta psiquiát psicol Amér Latina 1967, 13:127-140

67990 Modalidades de la relación objetal. [Modalities of object relationships.] Rev Psicoanál 1962, 19:58-62

67991 Notas para una semántica psicoanalítica. [Notes on psychoanalytical semantics.] Rev Psicoanál 1961, 18:375-376; 1962, 371-373; 19:1963, 20:76-78; 180-183; 283-284

67992 Psicoanálisis del encuadre psicoanalítico. Rev Psicoanál 1967, 24:241-258

Psycho-analysis of the psycho-analytic frame. J 1967, 48:511-519

67993 La simbiosis. [Symbiosis.] Rev Psicoanál 1961, 18:360-369

Abs Vega Q 1962, 31:593

67994 Simbiosis. Estudio de la parte psicótica de la personalidad. [Symbiosis. Study of the psychotic part of personality.] Rev urug Psa 1964, 6:159-279

Abs Vega Q 1965, 34:627

67995 [Study of dependence-independence in relation to the process of projection-introjection.] (Sp) Rev Psicoanál 1961, 17:456-479

See Abadi, Mauricio; Bleger, Lily S.; Grinberg, León

ABSTRACTS OF:
67996 Heuyer, G. Influence médicale et psychiatrique dans l'oeuvre de H. Wallon. Rev Psicoanál 1963, 20:80-82
67997 Lagache, D. Pouvoir et personne. Rev Psicoanál 1963, 20:82
67998 Spitz, R. À propos de la genèse des composantes de surmoi. Rev Psicoanál 1963, 20:76-78
67999 Tarachow, S. Ambiguity and human imperfection. Rev Psicoanál 1966, 23:501
68000 Zazzo, R. La dialectique de l'intelligence chez H. Wallon. Rev Psicoanál 1963, 20:84

BLEGER, LILY S.

68001 (& Bleger, J.) Algunas correlaciones entre Freud, M. Klein y Fairbairn. [Some correlations between Freud, M. Klein and Fairbairn.] Rev Psicoanál 1962, 19:63-65

BLEICH, DAVID

68002 The determination of literary value. Lit & Psych 1967, 17:19-30

BLESS, EVELYN

See Freedman, Jonathan L.

BLEULER, EUGEN

S-3154 (& Hess, R. et al) Lehrbuch der Psychiatrie. Berlin/New York 1966, 1969, xvi + 659 p

BLEULER, MANFRED

68003 Biologie und Entwicklungslehre der Persönlichkeit. [Biology and theory on the development of the personality.] Verh Schweiz Naturforsch Ges Bern 1952, 26-43
68004 Conception of schizophrenia within the last fifty years and today. Proc RSM 1963, 56:945-952. Int J Psychiat 1965, 1:501-514
68005 Early Swiss sources of Adolf Meyer's concepts. P 1962, 119:193-196
68006 Endocrinological psychiatry and psychology. Henry Ford Hosp med J 1967, 15:309-317
68007 Endokrinologische Behandlungsverfahren bei psychischen Störungen. [Endocrinological methods of treatment for mental disturbances.] In Hoff, H. Therapeutische Fortschritte in der Neurologie und Psychiatrie, Vienna/Innsbruck 1960, 294-305
68008 Die Entwicklung der wissenschaftlichen Psychiatrie und medizinischen Psychologie in Zürich im vorigen halben Jahrhundert (1895-1945). [The development of scientific psychiatry and medical psychology in Zurich during the last half century (1895-1945).] Festschrift zur 200 Jahrfeier der Naturforsch. Ges. Zürich 1946
68009 Entwicklungslinien psychiatrischer Praxis und Forschung in jüngster Zeit. [Lines of development of recent psychiatric practice and research.] Schweiz med Wschr 1961, 91:1549-1555

* * * Foreword to Ernst, K. et al: *Ergebnisse der Verlaufsforschung bei Neurosen*

68010 Forschungen zur Schizophreniefrage. [Research concerning schizophrenia.] Wien Z Nerveneilk 1948, 1:129-148

68011 The genesis and nature of schizophrenia. Psychiat Dig 1969, 30:17-26

68012 Geschichte des Burghölzlis und der psychiatrischen Universitätsklinik. [History of "Burghölzli" and the psychiatric university clinic.] In *Zürcher Spitalgeschichte,* herausgg. vom Regierungsrat des Kantons Zürich, Buchdruckerei Berichthaus, Zürich 1951, 377

68013 Iatrogene Geistesstörungen. [Iatrogenic mental disorders.] Praxis 1961, 50:249-254

68014 [List of publications by M. Bleuler.] (Ger) Schweiz ANP 1963, 91:5-10

68015 [Mental hygiene.] (Ger) Praxis 1965, 54:131-133

68016 Neurose und Unfallbehandlung. [Neurosis and treatment of accidents.] Schweiz med Wschr 1943, 73:113

68017 Die psychiatrische Krankengeschichte: Spiegel, Bremsklotz und Bahnbrecher des Fortschrittes. [The psychiatric case history: mirror, brake shoe and pioneer of advance.] Wien Z Nervenheilk 1967, 25:125-130

68018 Psychopathologic reactions in acute somatic distress. Acta psychother psychosom 1967, 15:94-104. In Philippopoulos, G. S. *Dynamics in Psychiatry,* Basel/NY: Karger 1968, 10-20

68019 Schizophreniartige Psychosen und ätiologie der Schizophrenie. [Schizophrenia-like psychoses and etiology of schizophrenia.] Schweiz med Wschr 1962, 92:1641-1647

68020 The teaching of psychiatry: a Swiss viewpoint. WHO PH Pap 1961, 9:177-186

68021 Der Werdegang einer Kinderneurose. [The development of an infantile neurosis.] Schweiz med Wschr 1947, 77:494

68022 Zur Psychotherapie der Schizophrenie. [On the psychotherapy of schizophrenia.] Dtsch med Wschr 1954, 79:841-842

BLEWETT, LAURA

68023 Object loss and its implications to nursing. Arizona Nurse 1968, 21(3):8-12

BLINDER, B.

See Luborsky, Lester

BLINDER, MARTIN GEORGE

68024 Classification and treatment of depression. Int Psychiat Clin 1969, 6(2):3-26

68025 (& Kirschenbaum, M.) Married couple group therapy. Curr psychiat Ther 1968, 8:137-142

BLISS, C. M.

See Knapp, Peter H.

BLISS, EUGENE L.

68026 (& Branch, C. H. H.) Anorexia Nervosa. Its History, Psychology, and
       Biology. NY: Paul B. Hoeber 1960, 210 p
          Rv Bond, D. D. Q 1961, 30:447-448
68027 (Ed) Roots of Behavior. NY: Paul B. Hoeber 1962

       See Branch, C. H. Hardin

BLITZER, JOHN R.

68028 (& Rollins, N.; Blackwell, A.) Children who starve themselves: ano-
       rexia nervosa. PSM 1961, 23:369-383
          Abs RDT Q 1962, 31:427
68029 (& Murray, J. M.) On the transformation of early narcissism during
       pregnancy. (Read at Am Psa Ass, Dec 1961; Boston Psa Soc & Inst,
       Apr 1962) J 1964, 45:89-97
          Abs Baranger, M. Rev urug Psa 1965, 7:104. EVN Q 1966, 35:312

       ABSTRACT OF:
68030 Sandler, J. Research with the Hampstead Psychoanalytic Index. Bull
       Phila Ass Psa 1961, 11:92-94

BLOCH, ADELE

68031 Kazantsakis and the image of Christ. Lit & Psych 1965, 15:2-11

BLOCH, CLAUDE

68032 (& Rapoport, L.) Problèmes particuliers de la psychothérapie individ-
       uelle d'étudiants en période d'examens. [Special problems in individual
       psychotherapy of students taking examinations.] Confin psychiat 1968,
       11:51-57
68033 La psychothérapie en practique médicale. [Psychotherapy in medical
       practice.] Bruxelles méd 1960, 40:1743-1758

BLOCH, DONALD A.

68034 Ecology of mental health models. Sci Psa 1965, 8:150-158

BLOCH, DOROTHY

68035 Feelings that kill: the effect of the wish for infanticide in neurotic
       depression. R 1965, 52:51-66
          Abs SRS Q 1966, 35:470. CG RFPsa 1968, 32:170
68036 Some dynamics of suffering: effect of the wish for infanticide in a
       case of schizophrenia. R 1966, 53:531-554
          Abs SRS Q 1968, 37:316
68037 The use of interpretation in the psychoanalytic treatment of children.
       In Hammer, E. F. Use of Interpretation in Treatment: Technique and
       Art, NY: Grune & Stratton 1968, 300-320

BLOCH, HERBERT AARON

68038 (Ed) Crime in America. NY: Philos Libr 1961, 355 p
68039 (& Niederhoffer, A.) The Gang. A Study in Adolescent Behavior. NY: Philos Libr 1958, 231 p
         Rv Bernabeu, E. P. Q 1961, 30:129-133

BLOCH, IWAN

68040 Das Sexualleben unserer Zeit in seinen Beziehungen zur modernen Kultur. Berlin: Marcus Verlagbuchhandlung 1919, xvi + 816 p
         The Sexual Life of Our Time in Its Relation to Modern Civilization. (Tr: Eden, P. M.) NY: Allied Books 1928, xvi, + 790 p

BLOCH, JULIA B.

68041 The white worker and the Negro client in psychotherapy. Soc Wk 1968, 13:36-42

BLOCH, RENÉ

68042 Über die Bedeutung der Todessehnsucht für psychogene Störungen des Ernährungstriebes. [The importance of a longing for death for the psychogenous disturbance of appetite for food.] Z PSM 1967, 13:63-69

BLOCH, SAUL K.

See Seward, Georgene H.

BLOCK, J.

See Haan, Norma

BLOCK, JACK

68043 (& Turula, E.) Identification, ego control, and adjustment. Child Develpm 1963, 34:945-953

See Block, Jeanne; Chang, Judy

BLOCK, JEANNE

68044 (& Patterson, V.; Block, J.; Jackson, D.) A study of the parents of schizophrenic and neurotic children. Ps 1958, 27:387-397
         Abs WCW An Surv Psa 1958, 9:294

BLOCK, STANLEY L.

68045 Anxiety and the rabbi. Amer Rabbi 1966, 2:23-31
68046 Correspondence. P 1962, 119:589-590
68047 Definition of transference in group psychotherapy. Psychiat Dig 1966, 27:18
68048 The effect of mephenesin upon anxiety. AMA ANP 1953, 69:727-731
68049 The first 146 years: a chronicle of the Department of Psychiatry, University of Cincinnati. Comprehen Psychiat 1968, 9:453

68050   Hippocrates on psychotherapy by the general practitioner. New Engl
        J Med 1957, 256:559-561
68051   (& Powles, W. E.) Integrating training in group psychotherapy with
        psychiatric residency training: a program note. Psychiat Spectator
        1965, 2:May
68052   Multi-leadership as a teaching and therapeutic tool in group psycho-
        therapy. Comprehen Psychiat 1961, 2:211-218
68053   Notes on regression in groups. Comprehen Psychiat 1969, 10:128-135
68054   St. Augustine: on grief and other psychological matters. P 1966, 122:
        943-946
68055   Some notes on transference in group psychotherapy. Comprehen Psy-
        chiat 1966, 7:31-38

        See Ross, William D.

BLOCK, WILLIAM E.

68056   (& Ventur, P. A.) A study of the psychoanalytic concept of castration
        anxiety in symbolically castrated amputees. Psychiat Q 1963, 37:518-
        526
        Abs Engle, B. Q 1964, 33:456

BLOM, GASTON E.

68057   (& Waite, R. R.) Brief statement of research ideas: motivational con-
        tent analysis of primers. Proj Literacy Rep 1964, No. 3:51-56
68058   The community confronts psychoanalysis. n.p.n.d. 24 p (multilitho-
        graphed)
68059   The concept of stewardship—burnt offerings or redefining our values.
        Children's Relig 1960, Nov
68060   The concept "perceptually handicapped": its assets and limitations.
        Sem Psychiat 1969, 1:253-261
68061   (& Waite, R. R.; Zimet, S.) A content analysis of first grade reading
        textbooks. Reading Teacher 1968, 21:317-323
68062   (& Finzer, W. F.) The development of specific treatment approaches
        to the emotionally disturbed child: psychiatric inpatient and day care
        treatment. Amer J med Sci 1962, 243:112-123
68063   (& Waite, R. R.; Zimet, S.) Ethnic integration and urbanization of a
        first grade reading textbook: a research study. Psychol Sch 1967,
        4:176-181
68064   (& Waite, R. R.; Zimet, S.) Motivational content analysis of primers.
        Proj Literacy Rep 1966, No. 7:1-12
68065   The psychoeducational approach to learning disabilities. Sem Psychiat
        1969, 1:318-329
68066   Psychoeducational aspects of classroom management. Except Children
        1966, 32:377-383
68067   (& Rudnick, M.; Weiman, E.) A psychoeducational treatment program:
        implications for the development of potentialities in children. In Otto,
        H. A. Human Potentialities, NY: Grune & Stratton 1968
68068   Relatos de mesas redondas de la Asociación Psicoanalítica Americana:
        el papel de los sueños en el analisis de niños. [Reports on a conference

of the American Psychoanalytic Association: the role of dreams in the analysis of children.] Rev Psicoanál 1969, 26:217-226

68069   (& Rudnick, M.; Searles, J.) Some principles and practices in the psychoeducational treatment of emotionally disturbed children. Psychol Sch 1966, 3:30-38

See Waite, Richard R.; Zimet, S.

BLOMART, JEANNINE

68070   Attitudes maternelles et réactions a l'entrée au jardin d'enfants. [Maternal attitudes and reactions of the child on commencing kindergarten.] Acta Psychol 1963, 21(2):75-99

BLONDHEIM, S. H.

See Masling, Joseph

BLOOM, JOSEPH D.

See Binstock, William A.

BLOOM, LEON

68071   Further thoughts on tipping. PPR 1962, 49:135-137

BLOOM, LEONARD

68072   Some comments upon recent trends in social psychology. Soc Psych 1961, 53:211-224

BLOOM, MARTIN

68073   Toward a developmental concept of love. J hum Relat 1967, 15:246-263

BLOOM, RICHARD D.

See Deutsch, Martin

BLOOM, VICTOR

68074   An analysis of suicide at a training center. P 1967, 123:918-925
68075   (& Dobie, S. I.) The effect of observers on the process of group therapy. Int J grp PT 1969, 19:79-87

BLOOMBERG, CLAIRE M.

* * *   Editor of Colm, H. *The Existential Approach to Psychotherapy with Adults and Children.*

BLOOMER, RICHARD H.

68076   Characteristics of portrayal and conflict and children's attraction to books. Psychol Rep 1968, 23:99-106

BLOS, PETER

68077 Character formation in adolescence. (Read at Am Psa Ass, 16 Dec 1967) Psa St C 1968, 23:245-263

68078 The concept of acting out in relation to the adolescent process. (Read at NY Psa Soc, 25 Sept 1962) J Amer Acad Child Psychiat 1963, 2(1):118-143

Die Funktion des Agierens im Adoleszenzprozess. Psyche 1964-65, 18:120-138

Abs Weissman, P. Q 1963, 32:146-148

68079 Delinquency. Adolescents 132-151. J Tokyo Inst Psa 1965; 132-151

68080 The initial stage of male adolescence. Psa St C 1965, 20:145-164

68081 Intensive psychotherapy in relation to the various phases of the adolescent period. Ops 1962, 32:901-910

Abs PS Q 1963, 32:453. JMa RFPsa 1964, 28:446

68082 On adolescence. JNMD 1962, 135:268-270

68083 On Adolescence. A Psychoanalytic Interpretation. NY: Free Pr of Glencoe 1962 & 1965, xii + 269 p

Les Adolescents, Essai de Psychanalyse. Paris: Éditions Stock 1967, 282 p

Rv Belmont, H. S. Bull Phila Ass Psa 1962, 12:116-117. Strean, H. S. PPR 1962, 49(4):128-129. Fraiberg, S. Q 1963, 32:432-436

68084 (& Kanzer, M.; Karush, A.; Keiser, S.; Schur, M.) Panel on working through. (Read at Psa Ass NY, 15 Nov 1965)

Abs Blum, H. P. Q 1966, 35:633-635

S-42361 Preadolescent drive organization.

Abs EDJ An Surv Psa 1958, 9:273-274

S-42362 Preoedipal factors in the etiology of female delinquency.

Abs Skolnick, A. An Surv Psa 1957, 8:221-223

68085 The second individuation process of adolescence. (Read at Cleveland Psa Ass 17 Feb 1967; Mich Ass Psa, 18 Feb 1967) Psa St C 1967, 22:162-186

68086 Three typical constellations in female delinquency. In Pollak, O. & Friedman, A. S. Family Dynamics and Female Sexual Delinquency, Palo Alto: Sci & Behav Books 1969, 99-110

Drei typische Konstellationen in der Delinquenz des Madchens. Psyche 1964, 17:649-663

La criminalita minorile femminile: tre gruppi tipici. Quad Criminol clin 1965, 1:193-212

68087 Youth unrest: a symposium. P 1969, 125:1155-1159

See Solnit, Albert J.

BLOS, PETER, JR.

ABSTRACTS OF:

68088 Altshuler, K. Z. Comments on recent sleep research related to psychoanalytic theory. Q 1969, 38:512

68089 Beiser, H. R. Self-listening during supervision of psychotherapy. Q 1969, 38:511

68090 Bell, N. & Spiegel, J. P. Social psychiatry. Q 1969, 38:167

68091 Berlin, I. N. Transference and countertransference in community psychiatry. Q 1969, 38:512

68092 Bieber, T. B. & Bieber, I. Psychotherapeutic focus in social psychiatry. Q 1967, 36:144

68093 Bowers, M. B., Jr. & Freedman, D. X. "Psychedelic" experiences in acute psychosis. Q 1969, 38:512

68094 Bruch, H. Psychotherapy with schizophrenics. Q 1969, 38:167

68095 Bursten, B. Munchausen's syndrome. Q 1968, 37:318

68096 Davis, J. M. Efficacy of tranquilizing and anti-depressant drugs. Q 1968, 37:320

68097 Donnelly, J. Aspects of the treatment of character disorders. Q 1969, 38:343-344

68098 Easson, W. M. The ego-ideal in the treatment of children and adolescents. Q 1969, 38:513

68099 Elson, A. et al: Follow-up study of childhood elective mutism. Q 1967, 36:145

68100 Fine, P. & Offer, D. Periodic outbursts of antisocial behavior. Q 1968, 37:317-318

68101 Fiss, H. et al: Waking fantasies following interruption of two types of sleep. Q 1969, 38:342

68102 Goldfarb, W. et al: Treatment of childhood schizophrenia. Q 1969, 38:166

68103 Gregory, I. Anterospective data following childhood loss of a parent. I. Delinquency and high school dropout. II. Pathology, performance, and potential among college students. Q 1967, 36:144

68104 Harrison, S. I. et al: Social class and mental illness in children. Q 1968, 37:319-320

68105 Hirsch, S. J. Left, right, and identity. Q 1968, 37:630

68106 Horowitz, M. J. Body image. Q 1969, 38:341

68107 Jackson, D. D. & Yalom, I. Family research on the problem of ulcerative colitis. Q 1969, 38:514

68108 Kales, A. et al: Somnambulism: psychophysiological correlates. I. All night EEG studies. II. Psychiatric interviews, psychological testing and discussion. Q 1969, 38:342

68109 Kanfer, F. H. & Phillips, J. S. Behavior therapy. Q 1969, 38:511

68110 Keith, C. Multiple transfer of psychotherapy patients. Q 1969, 38:166-167

68111 Kiersch, T. A. & Nikelly, A. J. The schizophrenic in college. Q 1969, 38:344

68112 Langs, R. J. Manifest dreams from three clinical groups. Q 1969, 38:343

68113 Lustig, N. et al: Incest: a family group survival pattern. Q 1968, 37:629-630

68114 Meyerson, A. T. Amnesia for momicide ("pedicide"). Q 1969, 38:341-342

68115 Nemetz, P. & Weiner, H. Some factors in the choice of psychiatry as a career. Q 1968, 37:318

68116 Oleinick, M. S. et al: Early socialization experiences and intra-familial environment. Q 1969, 38:513

68117 Pauly, I. B. Male psychosexual inversion: transsexualism. Q 1967, 36:144

68118 Rubin, B. Psychological aspects of human artificial insemination. Q 1967, 36:144

68119 Schlessinger, N. Supervision of psychotherapy. Q 1969, 38:511

68120 Schonfeld, W. A. Body image disturbances in adolescence. Q 1969, 38:343

68121 Schopler, E. Early infantile autism and receptive processes. Q 1968, 37:319

68122 Schwab, J. J. & Clemmons, R. S. Psychiatric consultations. Q 1969, 38:341

68123 Simon, N. M. & Senturia, A. G. Psychiatric sequelae of abortion. Q 1969, 38:513-514

68124 Smith, S. The adolescent murderer. Q 1968, 37:318-319

68125 Tabachnick, N. et al: Comparative psychiatric study of accidental and suicidal death. Q 1968, 37:630

68126 Trunnell, T. L. Thought disturbance in schizophrenia. Q 1967, 36:143-144

68127 Ullman, M. An experimental approach to dream and telepathy. Q 1969, 38:343

68128 Wittkower, E. D. & Rin, H. Transcultural psychiatry. Q 1968, 37:319

REVIEW OF:

68129 Kiell, N. The Universal Experience of Adolescence. Q 1965, 34:296-298

BLUESTONE, HARVEY

68130 Correctional psychiatry. In Ziskind, R. *Viewpoint on Mental Health,* NY: NYC Comm Ment Hlth Board 1967, 402-408

68131 (& McGahee, C. L.) Reaction to extreme stress: impending death by execution. P 1962, 119:393-396

See Snow, Emasue

BLUM, ARTHUR

See Polansky, Norman A.

BLUM, ERNST

68132 Antropologia y psicoanálisis. [Anthropology and psychoanalysis.] Arch Estud psicoan Psicol med 1967, 4:45-47

68133 Betrachtungen über das Problem der "Wiederholung." [The problem of "repetition."] Confin psychiat 1964, 7:197-215

68134 Psychoanalytische und anthropologische Betrachtungen über Zeit, Wort und Gestalt. [Psychoanalytical and anthropological considerations on time, word and gestalt.] Schweiz Z Psychol 1965, 24:321-335

68135 Psychoanalyse und Ethik. Herr Professor Dr. med. Heinrich Meng zu seinem 80. Geburtstag. [Psychoanalysis and ethics. On the occassion of the 80th birthday of Prof. Heinrich Meng.] Schweiz Z Psychol 1967, 26:213-216

S-42371 Über Sigmund Freud: Der Mann Moses und die monotheistische Religion.
Abs EW An Surv Psa 1956, 7:23-24

BLUM, EVA MARIA

68136 (& Blum, R. H.) Alcoholism: Modern Psychological Approaches to Treatment. (Foreword: Chafetz, M. E.) San Francisco: Jossey-Bass 1967, xvi + 373 p

68137 Psychoanalytic views of alcoholism. A review. Quart J Stud Alcohol 1966, 27:259-299

68138 Who is qualified to treat the alcoholic? Comment on the Krystal-Moore discussion. Quart J Stud Alcohol 1964, 25:350

BLUM, FRED H.

68139 Dynamic psychology and the social sciences. Clin Path 1961, 22:41-50

BLUM, GERALD S.

68140 Defense preferences among university students in Denmark, France, Germany, and Israel. J proj Tech 1964, 28:13-19

68141 A guide for research use of the Blacky Pictures. J proj Tech 1962, 26: 3-29

68142 A Model of the Mind: Explored by Hypnotically Controlled Experiments and Examined for Its Psychodynamic Implications. London/NY: Wiley 1961, xi + 229 p

68143 Psychoanalytic behavior theory: a conceptual framework for research. In David, H. P. & Brengelmann, J. C. *Perspectives in Personality Research*, NY: Springer 1960, 107-138

68144 Psychodynamics: the Science of Unconscious Mental Forces. Belmont, Calif.: Wadsworth Publ Co 1966, x + 82 p

See Minkowich, Abram

BLUM, HAROLD P.

68145 Childhood physical illness and invalid adult personality. (Read at Int Psa Cong, July 1967) J 1968, 49:502-505

68146 Color in dreams. (Read at Psa Ass NY, 16 Mar 1964) J 1964, 45:519-529
    Abs Auth Q 1964, 33:621. Yazmajian, R. V. Q 1964, 33:621-623. EVN Q 1966, 35:621

68147 Notes on the written dream. J Hillside Hosp 1968, 17(2 & 3):67-78

68148 A psychoanalytic view of *Who's Afraid of Virginia Woolf?* J Am Psa Ass 1969, 17:888-903

68149 Transference and structure. (Read at Psa Ass NY, 16 Oct 1967)
    Abs Barkin, L. Q 1969, 38:170-171

S-42380 Van Gogh's chairs.
    Abs AS An Surv Psa 1956, 7:413

See Eidelberg, Ludwig; Kanzer, Mark

ABSTRACTS OF:

68150 Blos, P. et al: Panel on working through. Q 1966, 35:633-635

68151 Dicks, R. On alteration in the state of consciousness and its defensive function: a hypnoid state. Q 1965, 34:480-482

68152 Ross, N. Beyond the future of an illusion. Q 1965, 34:322-323

REVIEWS OF:

68153 Lorenz, K. On Aggression. Q 1967, 36:609-612
68154 The Psychoanalytic Study of the Child, Vol. XXII. Q 1969, 38:483-488

BLUM, LUCILLE HOLLANDER

68155 (& Geller, M.) Toward a closer alliance between psychoanalytic and genetic schools of psychology. J genet Psych 1961, 99:289-300

BLUM, MILTON L.

See Hutt, Max L.

BLUM, RICHARD H.

68156 (et al) Utopiates. The Use and Users of LSD 25. NY: Atherton Pr 1964; London: Tavistock 1965, 303 p
       Rv Winick, C. Am Im 1966, 23:82-83

See Blum, Eva Maria

BLUMBERG, STANLEY

68157 (& Giller, D. W.) Some verbal aspects of primary-process thought: a partial replication. Pers soc Psychol 1965, 1:517-520
68158 (& Maher, B. A.) Trait attribution as a study of Freudian projection. Soc Psych 1965, 65:311-316

See Hunt, William A.

BLUMEN, G.

68159 Une expérience d'un an comme résident en psychiatrie infantile aux États-Unis (Boston). [One year's experience as a resident in child psychiatry in the United States (Boston).] Ann méd-psychol 1968, 126(1):135

BLUMEN, H. L.

See Deutsch, J. A.

BLUMENFELD, DAVID C.

68160 The psychoanalytic concept of freedom. Diss Abstr 1967, 27:2173

BLUMENFIELD, MICHAEL

See Deutsch, Albert L.

BLUMENTHAL, MORTIMER J.

REVIEW OF:

68161 Slavson, S. R. Reclaiming the Delinquent by Para-Analytic Group Psychotherapy and the Inversion Technique. Q 1969, 38:147-148

BOARD, RICHARD

S-42390 Intuition in the methodology of psychoanalysis.
        Abs WCW An Surv Psa 1958, 9:329-330

BOATMAN, MALETA J.

68162 (& Paynter, J.; Parsons, C.) Nursing in hospital psychiatric therapy for psychotic children. Ops 1962, 32:808-817
    Abs JMa RFPsa 1964, 28:445

68163 (& Berlin, I. N.) Some implications of incidental experiences with psychopharmacologic drugs in a children's psychotherapeutic program. J. Amer Acad Child Psychiat 1962, 1:431-442

BOAZ, WILLARD D.

68164 Man's psychological development in the mind. In Schroeder, O. A *Law-Medicine Problem,* Cincinnati: W. H. Anderson Co. 1962

S-42396 A technical problem expressed in the first interview.
    Abs AS An Surv Psa 1956, 7:324-325

See Kennell, John H.

BOBBITT, RUTH A.

See Jensen, Gordon D.

BOBON, J.

68165 (& Dongier, M.; Dongier, S.; Demaret, A.) Les composantes paranoïaques dans les névroses caractérielles. Illustrations littéraires et picturales. [Paranoiac components in character neuroses. Literary and pictorial illustrations.] Acta neurol psychiat Belg 1965, 65:99-107

68166 (& Gomez, J.; Gernay, J. M.; Goffioul, F.) Gynecomastie provoquée chez un ambisexuel. [Gynecomasty induced in a bisexual.] Acta neurol psychiat Belg 1965, 65:108-115

BOCKHOVEN, J. S.

See Goodrich, D. Wells

BOCQUET, C.

See Ancona, Leonardo

BOCQUET, F.

See Ancona, Leonardo

BODENHEIMER, J.

68167 Der Fall Hanna. Eine psychoanalytische Heilung bei beginnender Schizophrenie. [The case of Hanna. A psychoanalytic cure of a beginning schizophrenia.] Acta psychother psychosom 1964, 12:188-202

BODIAN, C.

See Miles, Harold C.

BODIN, ARTHUR M.

68168 (& Geer, J. H.) Association responses of depressed and non-depressed patients to words of three hostility levels. J Pers 1965, 33:392-408

See Jackson, Don D.

BODKIN, MAUD

68169 Literature and the individual reader. Lit & Psych 1960, 10:39-44

BOEGNER-PLICHET, M. J.

REVIEW OF:
68170 Lewin, K. Field Theory in Social Science. RFPsa 1962, 26:140

BOEHM, FELIX

(See also Böhm, Felix)

S-42402 Freud als Forscher und Mensch.
Abs Spiegel, N. An Surv Psa 1956, 7:14

BOEHM, LEONORE

68171 (& Nass, M. L.) Social class differences in conscience development. Child Develpm 1962, 33:565-574

BOEKE, PIETER E.

68172 (& Ostermann) De invloed van psychische faktoren op de lactatie. [The influence of psychological factors on lactation.] Ned Tijdschr Verlosk Gyn 1962, 62:1-16
68173 (& Hart de Ruyter, T.; Beugen, M. Van) Het Moeilijk Opvoedbare Kind in het Pleeggezin. [The Problem Child in the Foster Home.] Assen, Netherlands: Van Gorcum 1968
68174 Psychoanalytische therapie in de puberteit. [Psychoanalytic therapy in adolescence.] In *Capita Selecta uit de Kinderpsychiatrie onder Redactie von Prof. Dr. Th. Hart De Ruyter,* Zeist: W. de Haan 1963
68175 Psychologie in de medische situatie. [Psychology in the medical situation.] Openbare Les. Groningen 1965
68176 Psychologische faktoren in de tandheelkunde. [Psychological factors in dentistry.] De behandeling van het kauwstelsel. Amsterdam 1962

BOENHEIM, CURT

68177 A group training method in transference and other problems. Sci Psa 1964, 7:262-264
68178 The importance of creativity in contemporary psychotherapy. Psychiat Opin 1967, 4(2):21; 24-27

See Pine, Irving

BOER, JOSEPHINE DE

68179 Four Mallorcan satirists. Symposium 1960, 14:188-198

BOER, JULIUS DE

68180 A System of Characterology. Assen, Netherlands: Royal Vangorcum 1966, xvi + 454 p

BOESKY, DALE

68181   (& Katz, L.) Factors associated with the psychiatric referral techniques of a group of physicians. Mich Med 1960, 50:1356-1360

68182   (& Cross, T. N.; Morley, G. W.) Postpartum psychoses. Amer J Obs Gyn 1960, 80:1209-1217

68183   The reversal of *déjà raconté*. (Read at Mich Psa Soc, 28 Oct 1967; Am Psa Ass, May 1968) J Am Psa Ass 1969, 17:1114-1141

BOETTCHER, D.

68184   (& Stoerger, R.) Wiederholungen in spontanen Bildnereien im Verlauf schizophrener Psychosen. [Repetitions in spontaneous drawings in the course of schizophrenic psychoses.] Nervenarzt 1966, 37:223-224

BOFILL, P.

68185   Discours inaugural. [Inaugural address.] RFPsa 1966, 30:5-6

68186   (& Folch-Mateu, P.) Problèmes cliniques et techniques du contre-transfert. [Clinical and technical problems of countertransference.] RFPsa 1963, 27(Suppl):31-129
       Abs Auth Rev Psicoanál 1963, 20:398

BOFILL TAULER, P.

68187   [Psychoanalytical study on anorexia nervosa.] (Sp) Med Clin, Barc 1964, 42:57-67

BOGACHENKO, V. P.

68188   [Neuro-psychotic disorders in burn sickness.] (Rus) Voennomed Zh 1965, 1:26-30

BOGAN, LOREY G.

See Coe, Henry W.

BOGDONOFF, M. D.

68189   (& Nichols, C. R.; Klein, R. F.; Eisdorfer, C.) The doctor-patient relationship. A suggested practical and purposeful approach. JAMA 1965, 192:45-48

BOGGS, ELIZABETH

See Bazelon, David L.

BOGIĆEVIĆ, DJORDJE

68190   [Countertransference.] (Cro) Neuropsihijatrija 1968, 16:39-47

See Klajn, V.

BOHM, EWALD

68191   (& Moser, U.) Eine phobische Neurose mit sehr früh Fixierung im Rorschach- und Szondi-Test. [Phobic neurosis with very early fixation in Rorschach and Szondi test.] In *Beiträge zur Diagnostik, Prognostik und Therapie des Schicksals,* Bern/Stuttgart: Huber 1962, 117-125

TRANSLATION OF:
Nyman, A. [85567]

BÖHM, FELIX

(See also Boehm, Felix)

S-3428 Über den Weiblichkeitskomplex des Mannes. [On the femininity complex in men.] Psyche 1960, 14:38-59

BOIGON, HELEN W.

68192 Discussion on irrational complications of the cancer problem. Psa 1965, 25:58-61
68193 Discussion on the philosophical aspect of the changing image of human nature. Psa 1966, 26:145-148
68194 Horney's concept of basic anxiety. Its relationship to the phenomenon of violence. Psa 1965, 142-157
68195 Problems in learning: "Why do they tell me I can when I can't." Psa 1968, 28:25-34
68196 The psychoanalyst and the welfare state. Psa 1968, 28:122-123

BOIGON, MELVIN

68197 Discussion of Chodoff, P. "Feminine psychology and infantile sexuality." Sci Psa 1966, 10:42-44
68198 Emphasis on the healthy aspects of the patient in psychoanalysis. A round table discussion. Psa 1966, 26:193
68199 What leads to basic change in psychoanalytic therapy. A round table discussion. Psa 1965, 25:129-130

BOISEN, ANTON T.

68200 The Exploration of the Inner World: A Study of Mental Disorder and Religious Experience. NY: Harper 1962, viii + 322 p

BOKERT, EDWIN

See Fiss, Harry

BOLAFFIO, M. T.

TRANSLATION OF:
(& Tolentino, I.) Grunberger, B. [75812]

BOLEN, DARRELL W.

68201 (& Boyd, W. H.) Gambling and the gambler. A review and preliminary findings. Arch gen Psychiat 1968, 18:617-630

BOLEWSKI, MARLENE

68202 Zur Frage der therapeutischen Indikation bei psycho-somatischen Krankheiten. [On the problem of therapeutic indication in psychosomatic diseases.] Z PSM 1964, 10:219-220

BOLGAR, HEDDA

68203 The case study method. In Wolman, B. *Handbook of Clinical Psychology*, NY: McGraw-Hill 1965, 28-39

68204 Contributions toward a general theory of mental development: Jean Piaget and Heinz Hartmann. Sci Psa 1964, 7:39-53

BOLIN, RICHARD R.

See Chessick, Richard D.

BOLK, L.

68205 Le problème de la genèse humaine. [The problem of human genesis.] RFPsa 1961, 25:243-279
Abs Auth Rev Psicoanál 1961, 18:195. RJA Q 1962, 31:139-140

BOLLAND, JOHN

68206 (& Sandler, J.) The Hampstead Psychoanalytic Index: A Study of the Psychoanalytic Case Material of a Two-Year-Old Child. (Pref: Freud, A.) NY: IUP 1965; London: Hogarth 1967, xiii + 203 p
Abs J Am Psa Ass 1967, 15:223. Rv Furer, M. Q 1968, 37:439-440

See Nagera (Perez), Humberto

BOLLES, ROBERT C.

68207 Theories of Motivation. NY: Harper & Row 1966, 546 p

BOLMAN, WILLIAM M.

68208 Cross-cultural psychotherapy. P 1968, 124:1237-1244

68209 (& Katz, A. S.) Hamburger hoarding: a case of symbolic cannibalism resembling Whitico psychosis. JNMD 1966, 142:424-428

68210 (& Westman, J. C.) Prevention of mental disorder: an overview of current programs. P 1967, 123:1058-1068

BOLSI, D.

68211 (& Torre, M.) Coscienza individuale e coscienza social: aspetti psicopatologici. [Individual and social conscience: psychopathological aspects.] Riv Psicol soc 1961, 28:223-233

BOLTE-CORNELISSEN, H. M.

68212 [Problems on the theory regarding indications for psychotherapy in children in the latency period.] (Dut) NTvG 1965, 20:194-218

BOLTEN, MART P.

See Stokvis, Berthold

BOLTERAUER, LAMBERT

68213 (Ed) Aus der Werkstatt des Erziehungsberaters. Gedenkschrift zur 10. Wiederkehr des Todestages August Aichhorns. [From the Workshop of the Educational Counselor. Commemorative Volume on the 10th Anniversary of the Death of August Aichhorn.] Vienna: Verlag Jugend Volk 1960

68214 Lust und Unlust als Motivationfaktoren im Entscheidungsgeschehen. [Pleasure and unpleasure as motivation factors in decision making.] Psyche 1969, 23:641-665

BOLTON, A.

68215 The indications for separating children from their parents. Med Pr 1960, 243:388-391

BONACCORSI, MARIE-THÉRÈSE

68216 L'anxieté au cours de la formation psychiatrique. [Anxiety in the course of psychiatric education.] Canad Psychiat Ass J 1965, 10:188-193

68217 (& Destrooper, J.) Rêves et revision secondaire. [Dreams and secondary elaboration.] Arch Psicol Neurol Psichiat 1967, 28:485-498

68218 (& Caplan, H.) Psychotherapy with a blind child. Canad Psychiat Ass J 1965, 10:393-398

BONAN, A. FERDINAND

68219 Psychoanalytic implications in treating unmarried mothers with narcissistic character structures. Soc Casewk 1963, 44:323-329

BONAPARTE, MARIE

68220 Discussion of Pasche, F. "Freud et l'orthodoxie judéo-chrétienne." RFPsa 1961, 25:81

68221 L'epilepsie et le sado-masochisme dans la vie et l'oeuvre de Dostoïevski. [Epilepsy and sadomasochism in the life and works of Dostoyevski.] RFPsa 1962, 26:715-730
        Abs Auth Rev Psicoanál 1963, 20:193. Soavi, G. C. Riv Psa 1965, 11:83

S-42442 Eros, Saul de Tarse et Freud.
        Abs TC An Surv Psa 1957, 8:305

S-42458 Psychanalyse et sexologie.
        Abs HFM An Surv Psa 1956, 7:91

S-3509 Réflexions biophysiques sur le sado-masochisme.
        Some biopsychical aspects of sado-masochism. Heirs Freud 164-193

68222 [Three Discussions on Psychoanalysis.] (Greek) Athens 1950, 96 p

S-42460 Vitalisme et psychosomatique.
        [Vitalism and psychosomatics.] (Ger) Psyche 1961, 14:561-588

BOND, ALMA H.

68223 Sadomasochistic patterns in an 18-month-old child. J 1967, 48:596-603

BOND, DOUGLAS D.

68224 Discussant: "Psychiatric residents." Teach Dyn Psychiat 131-133

68225 Discussant: "Medical education." Teach Dyn Psychiat 62-68

68226 Some perspectives in psychoanalysis. P 1965, 122:481-484
68227 Teaching ethical concepts to medical students and psychiatric residents. P 1969, 126:241-243

See Earley, LeRoy W.

REVIEWS OF:
68228 Bliss, E. L. & Branch, C. H. H. Anorexia Nervosa. Its History, Psychology, and Biology. Q 1961, 30:447-448
68229 Lifton, R. J. Thought Reform and the Psychology of Totalism. Q 1962, 31:279-280

BONDURANT, J. V.

See Hume, Portia B.

BONE, HARRY

68230 Two proposed alternatives to psychoanalytic interpreting. In Hammer, E. F. *Use of Interpretation in Treatment: Technique and Art*, NY: Grune & Stratton 1968, 169-196

BONE, RONALD N.

68231 (& Coriett, F.) Brief report: frequency of dream recall, creativity and a control for anxiety. Psychol Rep 1968, 22:1355-1356
68232 Extraversion, neuroticism and dream recall. Psychol Rep 1968, 23:922

BONFILS, S.

See M'Uzan, Michel de

BONHAM, MARILYN

68233 The Laughter and Tears of Children. NY: Macmillan 1968

BONIER, RICHARD J.

68234 Research design and clinical practice: the interface: reciprocal influences. Proc 77th Ann Convention Am Psychol Assoc 1969, 4(2):533-534

BONILLA, EDUARDO SEDA

68235 Spiritualism, psychoanalysis, and psychodrama. Amer Anthropologist 1969, 71:493-497

BONIME, WALTER

68236 A case of depression in a homosexual young man. (Read at Acad Psa, 2 May 1965) Contempo Psa 1966, 3:1-20
68237 The Clinical Use of Dreams. A Practical Handbook for Analyst and Patient. (Foreword: Ullman, M.) NY: Basic Books 1962, xxiii + 343 p
    Rv Spotnitz, H. R 1963, 50(1):152-155. Noble, D. Q 1964, 33:432-433. Levine, J. M. J Am Psa Ass 1967, 15:166-212

68238 Competitiveness and cynicism as factors in personality distortion. In Merin, J. H. *The Etiology of Neuroses*, Palo Alto, Calif: Sci & Behav Books 1966, 152-158

68239 Depression as a practice; dynamic and psychotherapeutic considerations. Comprehen Psychiat 1960, 1(3):194-198

68240 Discussion of Kelman, H. "Techniques in dream interpretation." Psa 1965, 25:20-23

68241 Discussion of Kramer, M. et al: "Depression: dreams and defenses." P 1965, 122:417-419

68242 Discussion of Lower, R. B. "Psychotherapy of neurotic dependency." P 1967, 124:104-105

68243 Discussion of Robbins, B. S. "The dream as an instrument of rational psychotherapy." Dreams Contempo Psa 180-187

68244 Discussion of Ulman, M. "The social roots of the dream." Psa 1960, 20:189-192

68245 Discussion of Weiss, F. A. "The significance of the emotional experiencing of dreams in psychoanalytic therapy." Sci Psa 1963, 6:231-233

68246 Disregard of dream data in psychotherapy. Sci Psa 1966, 9:170-173

68247 The dream as human experience. In Kramer, M. *Dream Psychology and the New Biology of Dreaming*, Springfield, Ill: Thomas 1969

68248 Dynamics and psychotherapy of depression. Current psychiat Ther 1962, 2:137-146

68249 Intellectual insight, changing consciousness, and the progression of processes during psychoanalysis. Comprehen Psychiat 1961, 2:106-112
        Abs Saucier, J. L. RFPsa 1962, 26:608

68250 Marital conflict, analytic resistance, and therapeutic progress. Marriage Relat 209-224

68251 Masturbatory fantasies and personality functioning. Sci Psa 1969, 15:32-47

68252 New emphases and revisions in the role of dreams in psychoanalysis. Fortschr Ps 1966, 2:141-151

68253 The psychodynamics of neurotic depression. Am Hbk Psychiat III 239-255

68254 A psychotherapeutic approach to depression. Contempo Psa 1965, 2:48-53

68255 The pursuit of anxiety-laden areas in therapy of schizoid patient. Ps 1959, 22:239-244

68256 Role of dreams in psychoanalysis. Sci Psa 1964, 7:185-192

S-42479 The use of dream evidence of evolving health—a therapeutic tool.
        Abs WCW An Surv Psa 1958, 9:215-216

68257 The use of dreams in the therapeutic engagement of patients. Contempo Psa 1969, 6:13-30

BONN, ETHEL M.

68258 (& Boorstein, S.) Regressive electroshock therapy and anaclitic psychotherapy. A case report. BMC 1959, 23:190-201

BONNAFE, L.

68259 [The personage of the psychiatrist or metamorphoses. 3.] (Fr) Évolut psychiat 1967, 32:1-36

BONNARD, AUGUSTA

S-42481 Conscious and unconscious loyalties in children.
   Abs HA An Surv Psa 1956, 7:274-275
68260 Impediments of speech: a special psychosomatic instance. (Read at
   Brit Soc Psa, 21 Mar 1962; Chicago Psa Soc, 25 Sept 1962) J 1963,
   44:151-162
      Abs Kavka, J. Bull Phila Ass Psa 1962, 12:174-176. Gaddini, E. Riv
   Psa 1965, 11:74. EVN Q 1965, 34:614-615
S-42484 Pre-body ego types of (pathological) mental functioning.
      Über pathologische Funktionsweisen auf der Vorstufe des Körper-
   Ichs. Psyche 1961, 15:274-297
      Abs CFH An Surv Psa 1958, 9:246-249
S-42485 The primal significance of the tongue.
      La signification fondamentale de la langue. (Dans les conditions
   normales et anormales.) RFPsa 1961, 25:601-614
      Die primäre Bedeutung der Zunge in normalen und abnormen
   Zuständen. Psyche 1961, 14:690-700
      Abs JBi Q 1962, 31:117
68261 Primary process phenomena in the case of a borderline psychotic child.
   J 1967, 48:221-236
      Abs EVN Q 1969, 38:158-159
68262 Die Schulphobie eines Dissozialen Jungen. [School phobia of an unsocial youth.] In Bolterauer, L. *Aus der Werdstatt des Erziehungsberaters,* Vienna: Verlag Jugend Volk 1960, 24-46
68263 Tongue swallowing. Proc RSM 1960, 53: 784-785
68264 Truancy and pilfering associated with bereavement. Adolescents 152-
   179

BONNAUD, M.

See Chertok, Léon

BONNET, ANDRÉ

68265 Comment stabiliser votre équilibre psychique mis en péril par la vie
   moderne. [How to Stabilize Your Psychic Equilibrium Endangered by
   Modern Life.] Paris: Dangles 1961, 186 p

BONNETT, SARA A.

68266 Development of the educational program. (Read at Am Psa Ass, May
   1961) J Am Psa Ass 1962, 10:127-138

BONSTEDT, THEODOR

68267 (& Worpell, D. F.; Lauriat, K.) Difficulties in treatment of school
   phobia, with report of a case. Dis nerv Sys 1961, 22:75-83

BONZI, A.

68268 (& Ploeger, A.) Psychodynamik und Therapie Trichotillomanie in der
   Adoleszenz. [Psychodynamics and treatment of trichotillomania in adolescence.] Psychother Psychosom 1965, 13:380-386

BOOKBINDER, LAWRENCE J.

68269 The application of psychodynamic thinking to hypnotic behavior. Psychiat Q 1961, 35:488-496

BOOKHAMMER, ROBERT S.

68270 (& Meyers, R. W.; Schober, C. C.; Piotrowski, Z. A.) A five year clinical follow-up study of schizophrenics treated by Rosen's "direct analysis" compared with controls. P 1966, 123:602-604

REVIEWS OF:
68271 Binger, C. Revolutionary Doctor. Benjamin Rush 1746-1813. Q 1967, 36:608-609
68272 Hendrick, I. (Ed) The Birth of an Institute. Q 1962, 31:560-562
68273 Kubie, L. S. The Riggs Story. The Development of the Austin Riggs Center for the Study and Treatment of the Neuroses. Q 1961, 30:286-288

BOOMER, DONALD STUART

68274 (& Goodrich, D. W.) Speech disturbances and judged anxiety. J consult Psychol 1961, 25:160-164

See Goodrich, D. Wells

BOONS, M. C.

68275 [Act and word in psychoanalysis.] (Fr) RFPsa 1968, 32:1001-1004; 1095-1098

BOONS-GRAFÉ, M. C.

68276 Discussion of Rouart, J. "Investment and counter-investment." RFPsa 1967, 31:243

REVIEW OF:
68277 Laplanche, J. Hölderlin and the question of the father. RFPsa 1964, 28:283

BOOR, CLEMENS DE

68278 Die Colitis ulcerosa als psychosomatisches Syndrom. [Ulcerative colitis as a psychosomatic syndrome.] Psyche 1964, 18:107-119
68279 Comment on Dr. Musaph's paper, "Psychodynamics in itching states." (Read at Int Psa Cong, July 1967) J 1968, 49:339-340
68280 Der Einfluss der Entwicklung der psychoanalytischen Theorie auf die Behandlungstechnik. [The development of psychoanalytic theory and its influence on analytic technique.] Psyche 1968, 22:738-746
    Abs J 1969, 50:398
S-42494 Ekzem der Hände: ein Beitrag zur psychoanalytischen Behandlung Ekzemkranzer.
    Abs HA An Surv Psa 1957, 8:156-157
68281 Hysterie: Konversionsneurotisches Symptom oder Charakterstruktur? [Hysteria: conversion neurotic syndrome or character structure?] Psyche 1966, 20:588-599

68282 (& Hügel, K.) (Eds) Psychoanalyse und Soziale Verantwortung. [Psychoanalysis and Social Responsibility.] Stuttgart: Klett 1968, 271 p

68283 (& Künzler, E.) Die psychosomatische Klinik und ihre Patienten: Erfahrungsbericht der psychosomatischen Universitäts-Klinik Heidelberg. [The Psychosomatic Clinic and Its Patients: Progress Report of the Psychosomatic Clinic of the University of Heidelberg.] (Foreword: Mitscherlich, A.) Bern: Hans Huber; Stuttgart: Ernst Klett 1963, 274 p
Rv Thorner, H. A. J 1965, 46:277

68284 Strukturunterschiede unbewusster Phantasien bei Neurosen und psychosomatischer Krankheiten. [Structural differences between unconscious phantasies in neuroses and in psychosomatic illnesses.] Psyche 1965, 18:664-673

68285 Über psychosomatische Aspekte der Allergie (dargestellt an einem Fall von chronischer Urticaria). [On psychosomatic aspects of allergy (described by a case of chronic urticaria).] Psyche 1965, 19:365-378

68286 Zur Frage der psychosomatischen Spezifität unter besonderer Berücksichtigung des Asthma bronchiale. [The question of psychosomatic specificity, with special reference to bronchial asthma.] Psyche 1961, 15:801-814

See Künzler, Erhard; Rosenkötter, Lutz; Weisker, Angela

BOOR, M.

See Schill, Thomas R.

BOOR, W. DE

68287 Über medikamentöse Interferenzphänomene. [Drug interference phenomena.] In Kranz, H. *Psychopathologie Heute,* Stuttgart: Georg Thieme 1962, 162-166

BOORSTEIN, SEYMOUR

68288 A psychoanalytic overview of the offender: implications for therapy. Psa Forum 1967, 2:246-256; 267-269

See Bonn, Ethel M.

BOOTH, GOTTHARD

68289 The auspicious moment in somatic medicine. Psa 1969, 29:84-88

68290 Cancer and humanism (psychosomatic aspects of evolution.) In Kissen, D. M. & LeShan, L. L. *Psychosomatic Aspects of Neoplastic Disease,* London: Pitman Med Publ; Phila/Montreal: Lippincott 1964, 159-169

68291 Disease as a message. J Relig Hlth 1962, 1:309-318

68292 Irrational complications of the cancer problem. Psa 1965, 25:41-60

68293 Krebs und Tuberkulose im Rorschachschen Formdeuteversuch. [Cancer and tuberculosis in Rorschach's psychodiagnostic experiment.] Z PSM 1964, 10:176-188

68294 Values in nature and in psychotherapy. Arch gen Psychiat 1963, 8:22-33

68295   The voice of the body. Introduction to Siirala, A. *The Voice of Illness*, Phila: Fortress Pr 1964, 1-25. In Belgum, D. *Religion and Medicine*, Ames, Iowa: Iowa State Univ Pr 1967, 96-118

BORDELEAU, J.-M.

See Hillel, J.-M.

BORDI, SERGIO

68296   Discussion of Bak, R. C. "Sul rapporto oggettuale nella schizofrenia e nelle perversioni." Riv Psa 1967, 13:276-277
68297   Introduzione (e traduzione) di M. Klein: Contributions to Psychoanalysis, 1921-1945. [Introduction and notes (with Italian translation) to M. Klein's Contributions to Psychoanalysis, 1921-1945.] Florence: Martinelli 1961
68298   Su "la fugacita" (una nota sul processo creativo). [On "transience" (a note on the creative process).] Psiche 1967, 4:20
68299   Valutazione dell'Io all'inizio del trattamento psicoterapeutico. (An ego valuation in beginning a psychotherapeutic treatment.] Psiche 1964, 1:159

See Tolentino, Isidoro

BORDIN, EDWARD S.

69300   Commentary: patient-therapist interaction. In Shlien, J. M. et al: *Research in Psychotherapy, Vol. III*, Wash DC: APA 1968, 416-421
68301   Free association: an experimental analogue of the psychoanalytic situation. Meth Res PT 189-208
68302   Personality and free association. J consult Psychol 1966, 30:30-38

See Harway, Norman I.

BOREHAM, JOHN L.

68303   The psycho-dynamic diagnosis and treatment of vocational problems. Brit J soc clin Psychol 1967, 6:150-158

BOREL, JACK C.

68304   Security as a motivation of human behavior. Arch gen Psychiat 1964, 10:105-108
        Abs KR Q 1965, 34:141

BOREL-MAISONNY, S.

See Pichon, Edouard

BORELLI, M.

See Chertok, Léon

BORELLI, NELSON

See Masserman, Jules H.

BORGATTA, EDGAR F.

68305 New principle of psychotherapy. Clin Psych 1959, 15:330-334

BORGHI, JOHN HENRY

68306 Premature termination of psychotherapy and patient-therapist expectations. PT 1968, 22:460-473

BORGNA, EUGENIO

68307 [Considerations on the existential motivations which are at the foundation of some forms of neurotic experience.] (It) Sist Nerv 1964, 16:104-127

68308 [Experience of guilt in endogenous depression.] (It) Sist Nerv 1965, 17:95-109

68309 Sul problema della spersonalizzazione nella depressione endogena. [On the problem of depersonalization in endogenous depression.] Riv sper Freniat 1965, 89:568-593

BORING, EDWIN GARRIGUES

68310 (Ed) Harvard List of Books in Psychology. Cambridge, Mass: Harvard Univ Pr 1964, viii + 111 p

68311 (& Lindzey, G.) (Eds) A History of Psychology in Autobiography, Vol. V. NY: Appleton-Century-Crofts 1967, xiii + 449 p

68312 The nature of psychology; excerpt from "Psychology." In Sourcebook in Psychology, NY: Philos Libr 1960, 3-12

68313 The Physical Dimensions of Consciousness. NY: Dover 1963, xviii + 251 p

68314 Psychologist at Large. An Autobiography and Selected Essays. NY: Basic Books 1961, 371 p
         Rv VC Q 1963, 32:436-441

68315 The psychologist's concept of mind. J psychol Res, Madras 1960, 4:95-101

BORKENAU, FRANZ

68316 The concept of death. Twentieth Century 1955, 157:313-329. Death & Identity 42-56

BORKOWSKI, JOHN GREGG

68317 (& Mann, T.) Effects of anxiety and interference on short-term memory. J exp Psychol 1968, 78:352-354

BORNE, ÉTIENNE

S-42514 Une pensée dangereuse.
         A dangerous doctrine. Problems in Psa 207-219

         See Raclot, Marcel

BORNHEIM, CURT

68318 The importance of creativity in contemporary psychotherapy. J music Ther 1967, 4:3-6

BORNSTEIN, BERTA

S-3595 The analysis of a phobic child. Some problems of theory and technique in child analysis.
L'analyse d'un enfant phobique. Quelque problèmes de théorie et de technique dans l'analyse d'enfant. (Tr: Lagache, D.) Paris: Sorbonne, Laboratoire de Psychopathologie. Document de travail. Dactylogramme 1965, 84 p

68319 Disorders of language. Harefuah 1965, 69:280-282

BORNSTEIN, M.

See Barglow, Peter

BORNSTEIN-WINDHOLZ, S.

68320 Missverständnisse in der psychoanalytischen Pedagogik. [Misconceptions in the psychoanalytic pedagogy.] In Bittner, G. & Rehm, W. *Psychoanalyse und Erziehung*, Bern/Stuttgart: Hans Huber 1964

68321 Unbewusstes der Eltern in der Erziehung der Kinder. [Unconsciousness of the parents in the education of children.] In Bittner, G. & Rehm, W. *Psychoanalyse und Erziehung*, Bern/Stuttgart: Hans Huber 1964

BOROWITZ, GENE H.

68322 Some ego aspects of alcoholism. M 1964, 37:257-263
Abs JCS RFPsa 1967, 31:320

68323 The utilization of evoked attitudes in the diagnostic evaluation of children. Proc IV World Cong Psychiat 1966, 1577-1580

BOROWITZ, GENE

See Cartwright, Rosalind D.

BORRERO, HERNANDO PASTRANA

68324 Circuncisión—factor disociativo—antisemitismo. El proceso melancólico par la perdida del prepucio. [Circumcision—dissociative factor—antisemitism. The melancholy process over the loss of the foreskin.] Rev Psicoanál 1962, 19:331-343

BORTNER, RAYMAN W.

68325 The relationship between age and measures of id, ego, and super-ego functioning. J Gerontol 1963, 18:286-289

68326 Super-ego functioning and institutional adjustment. Percept mot Skills 1962, 14:375-379

BORTZ, EDWARD L.

68327 Who is qualified to treat alcoholics. Comment on the Krystal-Moore discussion. Quart J Stud Alcohol 1964, 25:351

BOSE, BEJOYKETU

68328 Concept of defense. Samiksa 1960, 14:28-32
68329 Observations on body mind parallelism. Samiksa 1965, 19:147-162

S-42523 The phenomenon of compulsion to repeat and its metapsychological significance.
Abs Gerard, D. L. An Surv Psa 1958, 9:71-72

BOSE, GIRINDRASEKHAR

68330 A new theory of mental life. Samiksa 1966, 20:1

BOSHIER, ROGER

68331 (& Hamid, P. N.) Academic success and self concept. Psychol Rep 1968, 22:1191-1192
68332 Attitudes toward self and one's proper names. J ind Psych 1968, 24:63-66
68333 Self esteem and first names in children. Psychol Rep 1968, 22:762

BOSINELLI, M.

See Carloni, Glauco

BOSS, MEDARD

68334 Die Bedeutung der Daseinanalyse für die psychoanalytische Praxis. [Significance of Daseinanalysis for psychoanalytic practice.] In Hoff, H. *Therapeutische Fortschritte in der Neurologie und Psychiatrie,* Vienna/Innsbruck: Verlag Urban & Schwarzenberg 1960, 162-172
68335 Begegnung in der Psychotherapie. [Encounter in psychotherapy.] Psychother Psychosom 1965, 13:332-341
68336 The conception of man in natural science and Daseinanalysis. Comprehen Psychiat 1962, 3:193-214
68337 Daseinanalytische Bemerkungen zu Freuds Vorstellung des "Unterbewussten." [Daseinanalytic observations on Freud's conception of "subconsciousness."] Z PSM 1960, 7:130-141
68338 Ego? Motivation? J existent Psychiat 1960-61, 1:275-283
68339 Entmythologisierung der psychosomatischen Medizin. [De-mystification of psychosomatic medicine.] In Lassner, J. *Hypnosis and Psychosomatic Medicine,* Berlin/NY: Springer 1967, 35-53
68340 (& Condrau, G.) Existential psychoanalysis. Psa Tech 443-467
68341 Grosse Psychotherapie der psychosomatischen Krankheiten. [Major psychotherapy of psychosomatic diseases.] Schweiz med Wschr 1960, 90:173-177
68342 Models and antimodels in psychosomatic medicine. Ther Umsch 1967, 24:536-545
68343 Le problème du moi dans la motivation. [The problem of the ego in motivation.] Évolut psychiat 1960, 25:481-489
68344 Psychanalyse et analyse du "Dasein." [Psychoanalysis and "Dasein" (existential) analysis.] Acta psychother psychosom 1960, 8:161-171
Abs SLe RFPsa 1961, 25:156
68345 Psychoanalysis and Daseinanalysis. (Tr: Lefebre, L.) NY: Basic Books 1963, viii + 295 p
Rv Curry, A. E. R 1964, 51(2):159-160. Levine, J. M. J Am Psa Ass 1967, 15:166-212

68346 Psychosomatische Störungen und Organneurosen—Erkenntnisse heutiger Psychotherapie. [Psychosomatic disorders and organ-neuroses—insights by modern psychotherapy.] Universitas 1967, 22:1163-1172

68347 Sinn und Gehalt der Sexuellen Perversionen: Ein Daseinsanalytischer Beitrag zur Psychopathologie des Phänomens der Liebe. [The Nature and Function of Sexual Perversity: An Existential Analytic Contribution to the Psychopathology of the Phenomenon of Love.] Bern: Hans Huber 1966, 142 p
        Rv Veszy-Wagner, L. J 1967, 48:609

BOSSÉ, J.

See Monod, Mireille

BOSSELMAN, BEULAH CHAMBERLAIN

68348 Castration anxiety and phallus envy: a reformulation. Psychiat Q 1960, 34:252-259
        Abs Engle, B. Q 1961, 30:301

68349 (& Rosenthal, I. M.; Schwarz, M.) Introduction to Developmental Psychiatry. Springfield, Ill: Thomas 1965, v + 139 p
        Rv Kestenberg, J. Q 1966, 35:292-294

S-3733 Neurosis and Psychosis.
        Spanish: (Tr: LaFarga Corona, J.) La Prensa Medica Mexicana 1967

BOSSIO, V.

See Pringle, M. L. K.

BOSTON, M.

See Bowlby, John

BOSWELL, JOHN I., JR.

See Schopler, Eric

BOSWELL, JOHN J., JR.

68350 (& Lewis, C. P.; Freeman, D. F.; Clark, K. M.) Hyperthyroid children: individual and family dynamics: a study of twelve cases. J Amer Acad Child Psychiat 1967, 6:64-85

BOSWELL, JOHN W.

See Dorpat, Theodore L.

BÖSZÖRMÉNYI, Z.

68351 Creative urge as an after effect of model psychoses. Confin psychiat 1960, 3:117-126

BOSZORMENYI-NAGY, IVAN

68352 Communication versus internal programing of relational attitudes. (Panel discussion: communication within the family.) In Ackerman,

N. W. et al: *Expanding Theory and Practice in Family Therapy*, NY: Fam Serv Ass Amer 1967, 89-92

68353 (& Framo, J. L.) Family concept of hospital treatment of schizophrenia. Curr psychiat Ther 1962, 2:159-166

68354 (& Framo, J. L.) (Eds) Family Treatment of Schizophrenia. NY: Harper & Row 1963

68355 (& Framo, J. L.) (Eds) Intensive Family Therapy: Theoretical and Practical Aspects. NY: Harper & Row 1965, xix + 507 p
Rv Freedman, A. J 1968, 49:103-107; Q 1968, 37:140-141. Panken, S. R 1968-69, 55:709

68356 Intensive family therapy as process. In author's *Intensive Family Therapy* 87-142

68357 Relational modes and meaning. In Zuk, G. H. & Boszormenyi-Nagy, I. *Family Therapy and Disturbed Families*, Palo Alto, Calif: Sci & Behav Books 1967, 58-73

68358 A theory of relationships: experience and transaction. In author's *Intensive Family Therapy* 33-86

68359 Types of pseudo-individuation. (Panel discussion: the classification of family types.) In Ackerman, N. W. et al: *Expanding Theory and Practice in Family Therapy*, NY: Fam Serv Ass Amer 1967, 66-69

See Framo, James L.; Friedman, Alfred S.; Zuk, Gerald H.

BOTT, ELIZABETH

68360 Psychoanalysis and ceremony. In Sutherland, J. D. *The Psychoanalytic Approach*, London: Baillière & Cassell 1968, 52-77

BOTT-BODENHAUSEN, MANFRED

68361 Der Zugang zum Verbrecher. Die Bedeutung der Tiefenpsychologie für Strafrechtswesen und Kriminologie. [The Approach to the Criminal. The Significance of Depth Psychology for Criminal Law and Criminology.] Hamburg, Kriminalistik Verlag 1965, 112 p

BÖTTCHER, H. R.

68362 Zur Analyse des Elternbilds neurotischer und gesunder Person. [On the analysis of the parental image in neurotic and healthy persons.] Z Psychother med Psychol 1968, 18:15-20

BOTVIN, CONSTANCE S.

See Messier, Michel

BOUCHARD, COLETTE

See Bigras, Julien

BOUCHARD, F.

68363 [The pediatrician and psychoanalysis.] (Fr) Méd Infant 1959, 66: 23-28

BOUDIER, C. E.

68364   Een wijsgerige interpretatie van Freud. [A philosophical interpretation of Freud.] Gawein 1967, 15:394-410

BOULANGER, JEAN BAPTISTE

68365   Depression in childhood. Canad Psychiat Ass 1966, 11(Suppl):S309-S312
68366   Discours inaugural. [Inaugural address.] RFPsa 1966, 30(Suppl):7-8
68367   Group analytic psychodrama in child psychiatry. Canad Psychiat Ass J 1965, 10:427-432
68368   Group psychoanalytic therapy in child psychiatry. Canad Psychiat Ass J 1961, 6:272-275
68369   The metapsychology of depression. Psychiat Res Rep 1963, (17):103-105
68370   Les options thérapeutiques en psychiatrie infantile. [The therapeutic options in child psychiatry.] Canad Psychiat Ass J 1965, 10:125-128
68371   Psychologue et psychiatre ou "Le Mariage Forcé." [Psychologist and psychiatrist or "The Enforced Marriage." Canad Psychiat Ass J 1962, 7:170-173
68372   Les psychothérapies collectives chez l'enfant et l'adolescent. [Collective psychotherapy in the child and adolescent.] Canad Psychiat Ass J 1968, 13:323-326
68373   Psychothérapies et psychanalyse. [Psychotherapy and psychoanalysis.] Canad Psychiat Ass J 1961, 6:123-126
68374   Psychotherapy of adolescents. Canad Psychiat Ass J 1968, 13:103-104

BOULDING, KENNETH EWART

68375   Conflict and Defense: A General History. NY: Harper 1962, ix + 349 p
68376   The Impact of the Social Sciences. NY/Brunswick, N. J.: Rutgers Univ Pr 1966, iv + 117 p

BOUR, PIERRE

68377   [Alternate psychotherapy of a neurotic couple.] (Fr) Évolut psychiat 1960, 25:255-269
68378   Découverte et maniement de l'agressivité inconsciente en psycho-thérapie de groupe. [The discovery and management of unconscious aggressiveness in group psychotherapy.] Évolut psychiat 1967, 32:961-983
68379   Elements catalyseurs dans la psychotherapie de groupe des schizo-phrènes. [Catalytic elements in group psychotherapy of schizophrenics.] Ann méd-psychol 1964, 122(2):491-514
68380   Entraves psychologiques du premier développement de l'enfant: comment les prévenir. [Psychological hindrances to the early development of the child: how to prevent them.] Pr méd 1966, 74:1699-1701
68381   Hommage à René Laforgue. [Homage to René Laforgue.] Psyché, Paris 1963, 18(Suppl):61 p
68382   Hommage à René Laforgue. Pionnier de la psychanalyse en France.

[Homage to Rene Laforgue, pioneer of psychoanalysis in France.] Pr méd 1962, 70:2717-2719

68383 Psychothérapie croisée d'un couple névrotique. [Overlapping therapy with a neurotic couple.] Evolut psychiat 1960, 25:255-269

BOURDIER, PIERRE

68384 [Acting out of the transference and important decisions during psycho-analytic therapy.] RFPsa 1968, 32:1035-1040

68385 La céphalée de l'enfant ou contribution à l'étude des états pré-morbides de l'enfance. [The child's brain or contribution to the study of pre-morbid states of infancy.] RFPsa 1962, 26:633-654
Abs Auth Rev Psicoanál 1963, 20:191

68386 Début de psychanalyse d'un scoptophile. [Commencement of the psy-choanalysis of a scoptophiliac.] RFPsa 1968, 32:531-554

68387 Réflexions sur le bonheur et l'amour le possible, l'impossible et l'in-terdit. [Reflections on happiness and love, possible, impossible and for-bidden.] RFPsa 1967, 31:883-889

BOURGEOIS, M.

68388 (& Henry, P.) Le parricide et son père. [The parricide and his father.] Ann méd-psychol 1967, 125(1):595-600

See Blanc, Marc

BOURGUIGNON, ANDRÉ

68389 La discussion entre Freud et Laforgue sur la "scotomisation." [The discussion between Freud and Laforgue on "scotomization.] Bull Ass psa Fran 1967, 2:243-249

68390 Un grand médecin, René Laforgue. [A great doctor. René Laforgue.] Sem Hôp (Informations) 1962, 38(17):4-5

68391 Neurophysiologie du rêve et théorie psychanalytique. [Neurophysiology of the dream and psychoanalytic theory.] Psychiat Enfant 1968, 11:1-69

68392 Phase paradoxale et métapsychologie freudienne. [Paradoxal phase and freudian metapsychology.] In Wertheimer, P. Rêve et Conscience, Paris: PUF 1968

* * * Preface to Laforgue, R. Réflexions Psychanalytiques

68393 Le premier modèle freudien de l'appareil psychique et la neurophysio-logie du rêve. [The first Freudian model of the mental apparatus and the neurophysiology of the dream.] Ann Thér psychiat 1967, 3:49-55. Ann méd-psychol 1967, 125(1):139

68394 Recherches récentes sur le rêve. Métapsychologie freudienne et neuro-physiologie. [Recent research on the dream. Freudian metapsychology and neurophysiology.] Temps mod 1966, 22(238):1, 603-1, 628

68395 Les relations épistolaires de Freud et Laforgue. [The epistolary rela-tions between Freud and Laforgue.] Ann méd-psychol 1968, 126(1): 169-176

68396 Le rêve et le corps: contribution à la théorie psychosomatique. [The dream and the body: contribution to psychosomatic theory.] Rev Méd psychosom 1967, 9:175-185

BOURNE, HAROLD

68397   Main's syndrome and a nurse's reaction to it. Arch gen Psychiat 1960, 2:576-581
        Abs KR Q 1961, 30:309

BOUSINGEN, D. DE

68398   (& Chercheve, R.) [Psychosomatic articulation in implantology.] (Fr) Chir Dent France 1967, 37:29-37

BOUTHREUIL, O.

See Chertok, Léòn

BOUTOURLINE YOUNG, H.

68399   Deprivation of maternal care. Developm child Neurol 1963, 5:520-521

See Mussen, Paul Henry

BOUVET, MAURICE

S-42573 La clinique psychanalytique: la rélation d'objet.
        Abs WAF An Surv Psa 1956, 7:170-172. RJA Q 1961, 30:608
S-42577 Dépersonnalisation et rélations d'objet.
        Abs Rev Psicoanál 1961, 18:76. RJA Q 1961, 30:312-313
68400   La Rélation d'Objet: Névrose Obsessionelle, Dépersonnalisation. [Object Relations: Obsessional Neurosis, Depersonalization.] Paris: Payot 1967, 435 p
68401   Resistances Transfert: Écrits Didactiques. [Transference Resistances: Didactic Writings.] Paris: Payot 1968, 310 p
S-42585 (& Marty, P.; Sauguet, H.) Transfert, contre-transfert et réalité.
        Abs HFM An Surv Psa 1956, 7:348
S-42587 Les variations de la technique. Distance et variation.
        Abs Fernández, A. A. Rev urug Psa 1965, 7:378. GLG An Surv Psa 1958, 9:345-347

See Nacht, Sacha

BOUVIER, EUGENE A.

See Farberow, Norman L.

BOWEN, WILLIAM T.

See Reinert, Raymond E.

BOWEN, ZACK

68402   Goldenhair: Joyce's archetypal female. Lit & Psych 1967, 17:219-228

BOWER, ELI MICHAEL

68403   (& Hollister, W. G.) (Eds) Behavioral Science Frontiers in Education. NY: Wiley 1967, 539 p
68404   Primary prevention of mental and emotional disorders: a frame of reference. Ment Hlth Monogr No. 5, 1964:1-9

BOWER, GORDON H.

See Hilgard, Ernest R.

BOWERS, MALCOLM BAKER, JR.

68405 (& Chipman, A.; Schwartz, A.; Dann, O. T.) Dynamics of psychedelic drug abuse. A clinical study. Arch gen Psychiat 1967, 16:560-566

68406 The onset of psychosis—a diary account. Ps 1965, 28:346-358

68407 (& Freedman, D. X.) "Psychedelic" experiences in acute psychoses. Arch gen Psychiat 1966, 15:240-248
Abs PB Q 1967, 38:512

BOWERS, MARGARETTA K.

68408 Address to the ministry studies board conference. In DeWire, H. *Guidance of Ministerial Candidates,* Dayton, Ohio: Ministry Studies Board 1966

68409 (& Berkowitz, B.) Clinical observations of the effects of electroconvulsive therapy in the hypnotic state. JNMD 1953, 118:355-364

68410 Conflicts of the Clergy; A Psychodynamic Study with Case Histories. Edinburgh/NY: T. Nelson 1963, xvi + 252 p
Rv Clinton, J. K. Am Im 1965, 22:203-204

68411 (& Jackson, E. N.; Knight, J. A.; LeShan, L.) Counseling the Dying. NY: Thomas Nelson & Sons 1964, v + 183 p
Rv Levin, R. R 1965, 52(1):136-137

68412 (& Bigham, T. J.) The cross as a command to suffer. Int Rec Med 1958, 171:753-760

68413 Discussion of Christensen, C. W. "Standing in the need of prayer." Voices 1966, 2(4):34-36

68414 Discussion of Guze, H. "The female body-image in personality and culture." In Goldman, G. D. & Milman, D. S. *Modern Woman: Her Psychology and Sexuality.* Springfield, Ill: Thomas 1969, 117-120

68415 Experimental study of the creative process by means of hypnoanalytic association to a painting done in occupational therapy. The magic ring of Walter Positive. Int J clin exp Hyp 1966, 14:1-21

68416 (& Perrone, H.; Brecher, S.; Berkowitz, B.; Krinsky, A.) Frenquel as an adjunct to psychotherapy. Trans Acad Psychosom Med 1958

68417 Friend or traitor? Hypnosis in the service of religion. Int J clin exp Hyp 1959, 7:205-215

68418 (& Brecher-Marer, S.; Polatan, A. H.) Hypnosis in the study and treatment of schizophrenia, a case report. Int J clin exp Hyp 1961, 9:119-138

68419 Hypnosis in the treatment of offenders. Focus 1953, 32:33-38

68420 Hypnotic aspects of Haitian Voodoo. Int J clin exp Hyp 1961, 9:269-282

68421 (Ed) Introductory Lectures in Medical Hypnosis. NY: Inst Res Hyp 1958, 90 p

68422 Passive submission to the will of God. Pastoral Psychol 1965, 16(158):11-17

68423 Protestantism in its therapeutic implications. (Ann Psychother Monogr #2) NY: Am Acad Psychother 1959

68424 (& Magill, L.) Psychotherapy of homosexuality; a preliminary (annotated) bibliography. Published by author 1966

68425 Psychotherapy of religious conflict. Int Psychiat Clin 1969, 5(4):233-242

68426 Psychotherapy of religious personnel; some observations and recommendations. In Cook, S. W. *Research Plans in the Fields of Religion, Values and Morality*, NY: Relig Educ Assoc 1962. J pastoral Care 1963, 17(1):11-16

68427 Report of investigation of the development of multiple personalities. In Landis, C. & Bolles, M. M. *Textbook of Abnormal Psychology*, NY: Macmillan 1950, 91-96

68428 (& Warkenten, J.; Leland, T.) Respect for phobias (phone dialogue). Voices 1967, 3(3):53-61

68429 Symbolism in worship. Transactions (J Dept Psychiat, Marquette School of Med) 1969, 1(2):1-6

68430 (& Murphy, R., Jr.; Guze, H.) Tenderness in psychotherapy. Voices 1966, 2(1):5-19

68431 Theoretical considerations in the use of hypnosis in the treatment of schizophrenia. Int J clin exp Hyp 1961, 9:39-46

S-42600 (& Berkowitz, B.; Brecher, S.) Therapeutic implications of analytic group psychotherapy of religious personnel.
Abs RSB An Surv Psa 1958, 9:428

68432 A triangle of treatment. Focus 1951, 30:161-167; 186-187

68433 The use of hypnosis in the treatment of schizophrenia. R 1964, 51: 451-460

See Howard, W. Marcus; Zacharis, James L.

BOWLBY, JOHN

68434 Attachment and Loss. NY: Basic Books; London: HIP 1969, xx + 428 p
Rv JWS Bull Phila Ass Psa 1969, 19:226-228

68435 Childhood bereavement and psychiatric illness. In Richter, D. et al: *Aspects of Psychiatric Research*, London/NY/Toronto: Oxford Univ Pr 1962, 262-293

68436 Childhood mourning and its implications for psychiatry. P 1961, 118: 481-498. With title: Childhood mourning and psychiatric illness. In Lomas, P. *The Predicament of the Family*, London: HIP 1967, 140-168
Abs Leob, L. Q 1963, 32:292

* * * Childhood mourning and psychiatric illness. See [68436]

68437 Comment on Gewirtz, J. L. "A leaning analysis of the effects of normal stimulation and deprivation on the acquisition of social motivation and attachment." In Foss, B. M. *Determinants of Infant Behaviour*, London: Methuen; NY: Wiley 1961, 301-303

68438 Deprivation of Maternal Care. Together with author's *Maternal Care and Mental Health*, NY: Schocken Books 1966

68439 Disruption of affectional bonds and its effects on behavior. Canad ment Hlth Suppl 1969, No. 59, 12 p

S-42612 (& Ainsworth, M.; Boston, M.; Rosenbluth, D. M.) The effects of mother-child separation: a follow-up study.
Abs AJE An Surv Psa 1956, 7:261-262

° ° ° Foreword to Foss, B. M. (Ed) *Determinants of Infant Behaviour,* London: Methuen; NY: Wiley 1961, xiii-xv

° ° ° Foreword to Foss, B. M. (Ed) *Determinants of Infant Behaviour IV,* London: Methuen 1969, xiii-xiv

° ° ° Foreword to Heinicke, C. M. & Westheimer, I. J. *Brief Separations,* NY: IUP 1966, ix-xi

S-42615 Grief and mourning in infancy and early childhood. In Daniels, G. E. *New Perspectives in Psychoanalysis,* NY: Grune & Stratton 1965

S-3832 (et al) I. Maternal Care and Mental Health. II. Deprivation of Maternal Care. [Two books in one] NY: Schocken Books 1966, 360 p
Soins Maternels et Santé Mentale. Geneva: WHO 1954
Rv Baratgin, A. RFPsa 1962, 26:136

S-42623 The nature of the child's tie to his mother.
Abs JAL An Surv Psa 1958, 9:240-241

68440 Note on Dr. Lois Murphy's paper, "Some aspects of the first relationship." J 1964, 45:44-46
Abs EVN Q 1966, 35:310

68441 Note on Dr. Max Schur's comments on grief and mourning in infancy and early childhood. Psa St C 1961, 16:206-208

68442 Pathological mourning and childhood mourning. (Read at Chicago Inst Psa, 4 May 1961) J Am Psa Ass 1963, 11:500-541
Abs Ennis, J. Q 1964, 33:454-455

68443 Processes of mourning. (Read at Sandor Rado Lectures, NY, April 1960; at Brit Psa Soc, Oct 1960) J 1961, 42:317-340. In Daniels, G. E. *New Perspectives in Psychoanalysis,* NY: Grune & Stratton 1965
Abs WPK Q 1962, 31:576. PCR RFPsa 1964, 28:298-299

68444 (& Carstairs, M.) Psychiatric research: new mental million. Brit med J 1963, 1:1342-1343

S-42634 Separation anxiety.
Die Trennungsangst. Psyche 1961, 15:411-464
Abs Rev Psicoanál 1961, 18:89. JBi Q 1961, 30:297

68445 Separation anxiety: a critical review of the literature. J child Psychol Psychiat 1961, 1:251-269

S-42639 Symposium on "Psychoanalysis and Ethology." II. Ethology and the development of object relations.
L'ethologie et l'évolution des relations objectales. RFPsa 1961, 25:623-631
Ethologisches zur Entwicklung der Objektbeziehungen. Psyche 1961, 15:508-516
Abs JBi Q 1962, 31:117

68446 A Two-Year-Old Goes to Hospital. NY: NY Univ Film Libr, 50 Minutes.

See Durbin, Evan Frank Mottram; Melges, Frederick T.

BOWMAN, KARL M.

68447 (& Crook, G. H.) Emotional changes following castration. (In explorations in the physiology of emotions.) Psychiat Res Rep 1960, (12):81-96

68448 Review of psychiatric progress 1959: Alcoholism. P 1960, 116: 626-628

68449   (& Engle, B.) Review of psychiatric progress 1959: Geriatrics. P 1960, 116:629-630
68450   (& Engle, B.) Sexual psychopath laws. In Slovenko, R. *Sexual Behavior and the Law,* Springfield, Ill: Thomas 1965, 757-778

BOYAR, JEROME I.

68451   Suicide in adolescence. Straub Clin Proc 1968, 34(1):19-23

BOYD, HARRY

68452   Love versus omnipotence: the narcissistic dilemma. Psychotherapy 1968, 5:272-277

BOYD, ROBERT D.

68453   Analysis of the ego-stage development of school-age children. J exp Educ 1964, 32:249-257

BOYD, STUART

See Macdonald, John M.

BOYD, WILLIAM H.

See Bolen, Darrell W.

BOYER, FRED L.

See Gantt, W. Horsley

BOYER, L. BRYCE

68454   (& Boyer, R. M.) Algunos efectos de la aculturación sobre las vicisitudes del impulso agresivo. [Some effects of acculturation on changes in the aggressive impulse.] Psiquiat soc 1967, 1:36-59
68455   (& Boyer, R. M.; Brawer, F. B.; Kawai, H.; Klopfer, B.) Apache age groups. J proj Tech 1964, 28:397-402
68456   (& Boyer, R. M.; Kawai, H.; Klopfer, B.) Apache "learners" and "non-learners." II. Quantitative Rorschach signs of influential adults. J proj Tech pers Assess 1967, 31:22-29; 1968, 32:146-159
68457   (& Boyer, R. M.) Aportes psicoanalíticos y antropológicos a la tarea con minorias étnicas. [Contributions of psychoanalysis and anthropology to the care of ethnic minorities.] Acta psiquiát psicol Amer Latina 1969, 15:25-33
68458   (& Boyer, R. M.; Klopfer, B.; Scheiner, S. B.) Características que influyen individualmente en las vidas de los niños de la Tribu apache, tanto los analfabetos como los medianamente instruidos: sus signos diferenciales cuantitativos. [Characteristics which individually influence the lives of Apache tribe children, illiterates as well as the fairly well-educated: their quantitative differential signs.] Rev Psicol mex 1968, 1968, 3:73-96   ◈
S-42670 Christmas "neurosis."
        Abs An Surv Psa 1955, 6:167-168
68459   (& Boyer, R. M.) A combined anthropological and psychoanalytical contribution to folklore. Psychopath afr 1967, 3:333-372

68460   (& Klopfer, B.; Brawer, F. B.: Kawai, H.) Comparisons of the Shamans and pseudoshamans of the Apaches of the Mescalero Indian Reservation: a rorschach study. J proj Tech 1964, 28:173-180

68461   Desarrollo histórico de la terapia psicoanalítica de la esquizofrenia: contribuciones de los discípulos de Freud. Rev Psicoanál 1966, 23(2): 91-148
   Historical development of psychoanalytic therapy of the schizophrenias: contributions of the followers of Freud. In author's *Psychoanalytic Treatment of Schizophrenic and Characterological Disorders* 80-142
   Abs Barriguete C. A. Cuad Psa 1967, 3:245

68462   Desarrollo histórico en la psicoterapia psicoanalítica de las esquizofrenias: contribuciones de Freud. Cuad Psa 1965, 1:355-381
   Historical development of psychoanalytic psychotherapy of the schizophrenias: Freud's contributions. Background infromation. In author's *Psychoanalytic Treatment of Schizophrenic and Characterological Disorders* 40-79
   Freuds Beitrag zur Psychotherapie der Schizophrenie. Psyche 1967, 21:870-894

68463   (& Klopfer, B.; Boyer, R. M.; Brawer, F. B.; Kawai, H.) Effects of acculturation on the personality traits of the old people of the Mescalero and Chiricahua Apaches. Int J soc Psychiat 1965, 11:264-271

68464   Example of legend distortion from the Apaches of the Mescalero Indian reservation. J Amer Folklore 1964, 77:118-142

68465   Folk psychiatry of the Apaches of the Mescalero Indian Reservation. In Kiev, A. *Magic, Faith and Healing: Studies in Primitive Psychiatry Today*, Glencoe, Ill: Free Pr 1964, 384-419

68466   Further remarks concerning Shamans and shamanism. (Read at West Coast Psa Soc, Aug 1962; Am Psa Ass, Dec 1962) Israel Ann Psychiat 1964, 2:235-257

* * *   Introduction to author's *Psychoanalytic Treatment of Schizophrenic and Characterological Disorders* 17-39

S-42672 A hypothesis regarding the time of appearance of the dream screen. Abs JBi Q 1961, 30:297-298. Bianchedi, E. T. de Rev Psicoanál 1961, 18:90

68467   Notes on the personality structure of a North American Indian Shaman. J Hillside Hosp 1961, 10:14-33
   Abs JA Q 1962, 31:136

68468   Obituary: Donald Andrews Macfarlane, 1897-1964. SF Psa Soc Inst N L 1965, Jan:1-3

68469   Office treatment of schizophrenic patients by psychoanalysis. Psa Forum 1966, 1:337-356; 1967, 2:100-101; 190-195
   Abs Cuad Psa 1967, 3:247

S-42673 On maternal overstimulation and ego defects. Abs SGo An Surv Psa 1956, 7:251-252

68470   (Participant) On regression: a workshop. (Held at West Coast Psa Soc, 14-16 Oct 1966) Psa Forum 1967, 2:293-316

68471   Pioneers in the psychoanalysis of schizophrenia. Psa Forum 1967, 3:215-227; 233-235

* * *   Preface to author's *Psychoanalytic Treatment of Schizophrenic and Characterological Disorders* 7-10

68472 Provisional evaluation of psycho-analysis with few parameters employed in the treatment of schizophrenia. (Read at Asociacíon Psicoanalítica Mexicana, July 1958) J 1961, 42:389-403
        Tratamiento ambulatorio de pacientes esquizofrénicos: terapía psi-
coanalítica con un mínimo de parametros. Acta psiquiát psicol Amér
Latina 1965, 11:147-154
        Abs WPK Q 1962, 31:557. PCR RFPsa 1964, 28:299

68473 Psychoanalytic insights in working with ethnic minorities. Soc Casewk
1964, 45:519-526

68474 (& Giovacchini, P. L.) Psychoanalytic Treatment of Characterological
and Schizophrenic Disorders. NY: Science House 1967, 379 p
        Rv Linden, J. A. Psa Forum 1967, 2:375-377. Richter, P. Q 1967,
36:598-601. Holt, H. R 1969, 56:150-154

68475 Psychological problems of a group of Apaches: alcoholic hallucinosis
and latent homosexuality among typical men. Psa St Soc 1964, 3:203-
277

68476 Remarks on the personality of Shamans: with special reference to the
Apache of the Mescalero Indian reservation. (Read at Asoc Psa Mexicana, July 1958; San Francisco Psa Soc, Feb 1959) Psa St Soc 1962,
2:233-254

68477 Remarks to an experiment in the treatment of schizophrenic patients:
the use of psychoanalysis with minimal parameters. (Read at Los
Angeles Psa Soc, 16 Jan 1964)
        Abs RZ Bull Phila Ass Psa 1964, 14:174-177

68478 (& Klopfer, B.; Boyer, R. M.; Brawer, F. B.; Kawai, H.) El Rorschach
en el estudio de los grupos apaches. [The Rorschach in the study of
Apache groups.] Rev mex Psicol 1965, 1:565-574

68479 Shamans: to set the record straight. Amer Anthropologist 1969, 71:
307-309

68480 (& Boyer, R. M.) Some influences of acculturation on the personality
traits of the old people of the Mescalero and Chiricahua Apaches.
(Read at V Cong Psa Latinamer, 28 Feb 1964; Am Psa Ass, 1 May
1964) Psa St Soc 1967, 4:170-182
        Algunos efectos de la aculturación sobre los caracteres de la personal-
idad en los actuales Apaches viejos de la reservación Mescalero (Mes-
caleros y Chiricahuas). Cuad Psa 1968, 4:1-8

68481 Stone as a symbol in Apache mythology. Am Im 1965, 22:14-39
        La piedra como un simbolo: datos ulteriores. (Temas preedipicos y
edipicos en la mitologie Apache). Cuad Psa 1965, 1:123-145
        Abs Cuad Psa 1966, 2:126-127. JWS Q 1966, 35:163

68482 La terapia psicoanalitica della schizofrenia. [Psychoanalytic therapy in
schizophrenia.] Riv Psa 1966, 12:3-30

68483 Tratamiento de pacientes esquizofrénicos en consultorio. El uso de la
terapia psicoanalítica con escasos parámetros. Rev Psicoanál 1966,
23:287-317
        Office treatment of schizophrenic patients: the use of psychoanalytic
therapy with few parameters. Introduction. In author's *Psychoanalytic
Treatment of Schizophrenic and Characterological Disorders* 143-188

See Klopfer, Bruno

REVIEWS OF:
68484 Kiev, A. Curanderismo. Mexican-American Folk Psychiatry. Q 1969, 38:329-332
68485 Kiev, A. (Ed): Magic, Faith and Healing. Studies in Primitive Psychiatry Today. Q 1965, 34:606-610

BOYER, RUTH M.

See Boyer, L. Bryce

BRABANT, G.-P.

68486 Masochism et principe de réalité. [Masochism and the reality principle.] Bull Ass psa Fran 1968, (4):54-57

TRANSLATIONS OF:
Rosenfeld, H. A. [88354]. Rycroft, C. [58135]. (& Moscovici, M.) Winnicott, D. W. [95042]

BRACELAND, FRANCIS JAMES

68487 The art of psychotherapy. Curr psychiat Ther 1963, 3:1-7
68488 Books. America 1959, 101(Apr 4):47-49
68489 Emotional problems of everyday life. MH 1968, 52:7-18
* * * Foreword to Harms, E. Origins of Modern Psychiatry, Springfield, Ill: Thomas 1967, v-viii
68490 Insight. Ency Ment Hlth 850-858
68491 (& Stock, M.) Modern Psychiatry: A Handbook for Believers. Garden City, NY: Doubleday and Co. 1963, xix + 346 p
          Abs Am Im 1964, 21(1-2):189. Rv Hiltner, S. Am In 1965, 22:202-203. Sta Q 1965, 34:126-127
68492 Pervasive anxiety and the need for wisdom. P 1968, 125:241-242
68493 Usage and abusage of a standard diagnostic nomenclature. Int J Psychiat 1969, 7:407-411

See Bartemeier, Leo H.; Farnsworth, Dana, L.

BRACHFELD, OLIVER

68494 (& Stokvis, B.) Aus der Praxis der gelenkten Tagträume (anhand eines Beispieles). [From the practice of directed daydreams (with an example).] Z Psychother med Psychol 1963, 13:73-81

BRACK, ESTHER

68495 Bifokale Gruppentherapie von Schizophrenen: Einige Erfahrungen nach zweijährigem Versuch. [Bifocal group therapy of schizophrenics: some experiences after two years of trial.] Z PSM 1962, 8:133-141

BRACKBILL, YVONNE

68496 (Ed) Infancy and Early Childhood. A Handbook and Guide to Human Development. NY: Free Pr 1967, x + 523 p
          Rv Kestenberg, J. S. Q 1969, 38:647-650

See Hetherington, Eileen M.

BRADLEY, G.

See Renneker, Richard E.

BRADLEY, JOHN B.

See Miller, Peter M.

BRADLEY, MARIAN

See Heinicke, Christoph M.

BRADLEY, NOEL

68497 The doll: some clinical, biological and linguistic notes on the toy-baby and its mother. (Read at West Coast Psa Soc, 8 Oct 1960) J 1961, 42:550-555

Abs WPK Q 1962, 31:581

68498 Phantasy and theory: notes on a seventeenth-century scholar. Am Im 1963, 20:331-343

68499 Primal scene experience in human evolution and its phantasy derivatives in art, proto-science and philosophy. Psa St Soc 1967, 4:34-79

68500 The vulture as mother symbol: a note on Freud's *Leonardo*. Am Im 1965, 22:47-56

Abs Cuad Psa 1966, 2:127. JWS Q 1966, 35:315

BRADLEY, T. B.

See Bente, D.

BRADLOW, PAUL A.

See Loftus, Thomas A.

BRADY, JOHN PAUL

68501 (& Lind, D. L.) Experimental analysis of hysterical blindness. Operant conditioning techniques. Arch gen Psychiat 1961, 4:331-339

68502 Hysteria versus malingering: a response to Grosz and Zimmerman. Behav Res Ther 1966, 4:321-322

68503 Psychotherapy, learning theory, and insight. Arch gen Psychiat 1967, 16:304-311

68504 Publication trends in American psychiatry: 1844-1960. II. Treatment and geographical distribution of authors. JNMD 1962, 135:252-257

See Levitt, Eugene E.

BRADY, JOSEPH V.

68505 Behavioral stress and physiological change: a comparative approach to the experimental analysis of some psychosomatic problems. Trans NY Acad Sci 1964, 26:483-496. In Palmer, J. O. & Goldstein, M. J. *Perspectives in Psychopathology*, NY: Oxford Univ Pr 1966, 196-208

BRAGG, ROBERT L.

68506 Risk of admission to mental hospital following hysterectomy or cholecystectomy. Amer J Pub Hlth 1965, 55:1403-1410

BRAGIER, M. A.

68507   Brain Function, Vol. 5: Aggression and Defense. Los Angeles: Univ of Calif Pr 1967

BRAIN, D. J.

68508   (& Maclay, I.) Controlled study of mothers and children in hospital. Brit med J 198, (1):278-280

BRAIN, WALTER RUSSELL

68509   The concept of hysteria in the time of William Harvey. Proc RSM 1963, 56:317-324

BRAJOVIĆ, C.

68510   (& Milatović, B.; Maŕjanović, A.) Psychische Einflüsse auf die Milchproduktion bei der stillenden Mutter. [Psychic influences on milk production in breast-feeding mothers.] MMW 1966, 108:2116-2119

BRAKELMANN, E.

See Opitz, Erich

BRALOVE, RICHARD S.

ABSTRACTS OF:

68511   Bandler, B. et al: Role of sexuality in epilepsy: hypnosis; analysis of two seizures. An Surv Psa 1958, 9:209-210
68512   Bowers, M. K. et al: Therapeutic implications of analytic group psychotherapy of religious personnel. An Surv Psa 1958, 9:428
68513   Eidelberg, L. Technical problems in the analysis of masochists. An Surv Psa 1958, 9:358-360
68514   Greenberg, N. H. & Rosenwald, A. K. Transvestism and pruritus perinei. An Surv Psa 1958, 9:179-180
68515   Hamburger, W. W. The occurrence and meaning of dream of food and eating: I. Typical food and eating dreams of four patients in analysis. An Surv Psa 1958, 9:221
68516   Jackson, J. & Grotjahn, M. The treatment of oral defenses by combined individual and group psychotherapy. An Surv Psa 1958, 9:428-429
68517   Marmor, J. Some comments on ego psychology. An Surv Psa 1958, 9:58-59
68518   Orens, M. H. The genesis of environment. An Surv Psa 1958, 9:51
68519   Orgel, S. Z. Effect of psychoanalysis on the course of peptic ulcer. An Surv Psa 1958, 9:410-411
68520   Tarachow, S. et al: Studies in ambivalence. An Surv Psa 1958, 9:73-75

BRAM, FREDERICK M.

68521   The gift of Anna O. M 1965, 38:53-58
        Abs Hirsh, H. Q 1966, 35:317. JCS RFPsa 1967, 31:322

BRAMEL, DANA

68522   Selection of a target for defensive projection. ASP 1963, 66:318-324

BRAMMER, LAWRENCE M.

68523 (& Shostrom, E. L.) Threapeutic Psychology: Fundamentals of Counseling and Psychotherapy. Englewood Cliffs, N. J.: Prentice-Hall 1960, xx + 447 p; 1968, ix + 486 p

BRAMS, JEROME

68524 From Freud to Fromm. Psychol Today 1968, 1:32-35, 64-65

BRAMS, J. M.

See Rychlak, J. F.

BRANCH, C. H. HARDIN

68525 (& Bliss, E. L.) Anorexia nervosa. Compreh Txbk Psychiat 1062-1063
68526 Discussion of Kubie, L. S. "Reflections on training." Psa Forum 1966, 1:102-103
68527 Henry Walter Brosin, M.D. builder of bridges. P 1968, 125:18-24
68528 Therapy *sine* psychiatry. Curr psychiat Ther 1962, 2:1-7

See Bliss, Eugene L.; Cole, Nyla J.

BRANCH, J. B.

See Kellam, Sheppard G.

BRANDÃO LOPES, MIRTES

TRANSLATION OF:
Segal, H. [90262]

BRANDCHAFT, BERNARD S.

REVIEW OF:
68529 Rosenfeld, H. A. Psychotic States: A Psycho-Analytical Approach. J 1966, 47:569-575

BRANDT, ELISABETH PASZTOR

TRANSLATION OF:
(& Brandt, L. W.) Décarie, T. G. [70856]

BRANDT, L.

See Riess, Bernard F.

BRANDT, LEWIS WOLFGANG

68530 Castration: fantasy and reality. Psychotherapy 1966, 3:85-87
68531 Process or structure. R 1966, 53:50-54
68532 Some notes on English Freudian terminology. J Am Psa Ass 1961, 9:331-339
   Abs FB Q 1962, 31:294
68533 Some notes on penis loss anxiety. PT 1961, 15:246-250

68534   The unobserving participant. R P PT 120-149

See Brandt, Elisabeth Pasztor

TRANSLATIONS OF:
Hartmann, H. [13644, 13688]

REVIEWS OF:
68535   Action for Mental Health. The Final Report of the Joint Commission on Mental Illness and Health, 1961. PPR 1961, 48(4):139-141
68536   Arlow, J. A. & Brenner, C. Psychoanalytic Concepts and the Structural Theory. R. 1965, 52:485-486
68537   Fierman, L. B. (Ed) Effective Psychotherapy: The Contribution of Hellmuth Kaiser. R 1967, 54:182-184
68538   Goldman, G. S. & Shapiro, D. (Eds): Developments in Psychoanalysis at Columbia University. R 1969, 56:357-358
68539   Gurin, G. et al: Americans View Their Mental Health. A Nationwide Interview Survey. PPR 1962, 49(1):139-140
68540   Mahrer, A. L. (Ed): The Goals of Psychotherapy. R 1967, 54:549-550
68541   Schur, M. The Id and the Regulatory Principles of Mental Functioning. R 1968, 55:151-152

BRANDT, RICHARD M.

68542   Self: missing link for understanding behavior. MH 1957, 41:24-33. In Crow, L. D. & Crow, A. *Readings in Child and Adolescent Psychology*, NY/London/Toronto: Longmans 1961, 320-332

BRANDT, RUDOLPH J.

S-42738 Aus der Analyse einer Mörders.
Abs EW An Surv Psa 1958, 9:175-177

BRANDZEL, ESTHER

68543   Working through the Oedipal struggle in family-unit sessions. Soc Casewk 1965, 46:414-422

BRANFMAN, THEODORE G.

S-42742 Modesty as a quasi-moral resistance.
Abs An Surv Psa 1955, 6:209
S-42743 Psychology of music and musicians: two clinical examples.
Abs An Surv Psa 1955, 6:164
S-42744 (& Bergler, E.) Psychology of "perfectionism."
Abs An Surv Psa 1955, 6:208-209

BRANHAM, EYA FECHIN

68544   Sound and movement in psychotherapy. Prog PT 1960, 5:112-115

BRANN, BEATE M.

68545   Unconscious motivation in medication errors. Ment Hosp 1965, 16:348-351

BRANN, HENRY WALTER

68546 C. G. Jung und Schopenhauer. [C. G. Jung and Schopenhauer.] Schopenhauer Jahrbuch 1965, 36:76-87

68547 The role of parapsychology in Schopenhauer's philosophy. Int J Parapsychol 1966, 8:397-415

BRANTLEY, H. T.

See Wallach, Michael A.

BRASK, B. H.

68548 [Chronic childhood psychoses. A review.] (Dan) Ugeskr Laeg 1964, 126:959-968

BRAST, ROSMARIE

68549 Beitrag zur Zwangsneurose in Kindesalter und Pubertät. [Contribution to obsessive-compulsive neurosis in infancy and puberty.] Schweiz ANP 1967, 313-347

68550 Psychiatrische Probleme in der Erziehungsberatung. [Psychiatric problems in counseling for children.] Heilpadag Werkbl 1960, 29:6-16

BRATFOS, OLE

68551 Parental deprivation in childhood and type of future mental disease. Acta Psychiat Scand 1967, 43:453-461

BRAUER, PAUL H.

ABSTRACTS OF:

68552 Bell, A. I. Some observations on the role of the scrotal sac and testicles. Q 1961, 30:318-319

68553 Holt, R. R. Beyond vitalism and mechanism: Freud's concept of psychic energy. Q 1966, 35:476-477

68554 Rosenbaum, M. Dreams in which the analyst appears undisguised: a statistical study. Q 1965, 34:475-477

68555 Rubinfine, D. L. Maternal stimulation, psychic structure, and early object relations (with special reference to aggression and denial). Q 1962, 31:147-148

68556 Weissman, P. The effect of preoedipal paternal attitudes on development and character. Q 1963, 32:462-464

REVIEWS OF:

68557 Kelman, H. (Ed) New Perspectives in Psychoanalysis; Contributions to Karen Horney's Holistic Approach. Q 1968, 37:291-293

68558 Zinberg, N. (Ed) Psychiatry and Medical Practice in a General Hospital. Q 1966, 35:448-451

BRAUN, JOHN RICHARD

68559 (Ed) Clinical Psychology in Transition: A Selection of Articles from the American Psychologist. Cleveland: Howard Allen Inc 1961, 211 p; World Pub Co 1966, 426 p

Rv Levine, M. D. PPR 1962, 49(1):141-142

BRAUNSCHWEIG, DENISE

68560 De certaines mécanismes antidépressifs tels qu'ils apparaissent au cours du traitement psychanalytique des névroses. [Certain antidepressive mechanisms as they appear in the course of psychoanalytic treatment of neuroses.] RFPsa 1968, 32:599-603

68561 Discussion of Kestemberg, E. & Kestemberg, J. "Contributions à la perspective génétique en psychanalyse." RFPsa 1966, 30:715-719

68562 Discussion of Luquet-Parat, C.-J. "L'organisation oedipienne." RFPsa 1967, 31:853-857

68563 Le narcissisme. [Narcissism.] RFPsa 1965, 29:471-474; 589-600; 613-615

68564 (& Diatkine, R.; Kestemberg, E.; Lebovici, S.) À propos des méthodes de formation en groupe. [About training-methods in different training-groups—the part of the psychoanalyst.] Psychiat Enfant 1968, 11(1): 71-180

See Lebovici, Serge

BRAUNSTEIN, PATRICIA

See Goldfarb, William

BRÄUTIGAM, WALTER

68565 Begriff, Erlebnisweise und Genese der Neurose. [Concept, mode of experience and genesis of neurosis.] Nervenarzt 1965, 36:56-65

68566 Die Beziehungen zwischen Psychiatrie und Psychoanalyse in Deutschland. [The connection between psychiatry and psychoanalysis in Germany.] Nervenarzt 1967, 38:394-397
French: Évolut psychiat 1967, 32:287-297

68567 L'importance des concepts neurologiques de Freud pour la théorie psychanalytique. [The importance of Freud's neurological concepts in psychoanalytic theory.] Évolut psychiat 1960, 25:62-76

68568 Indikation und Prognose bei analytisch nicht behandelbaren Krankheitsbildern (Kontaktpsychotherapie bei 12 Sexualdelinquenten). [Indication and prognosis in analytically unmanageable clinical cases. (Contact psychotherapy of 12 sexual delinquents.) Z Psychother med Psychol 1966, 16:105-113

68569 Körperliche Faktoren bei der sexuellen Partnerwahl und ihre Bedeutung für die Homosexualität. [Physical factors in the choice of a sexual partner and their importance for homosexuality.] Stud Gen 1966, 19:303-315

68570 Krankheitsbewusstsein und Krankheitseinsicht im Verlauf der Psychose. [Awareness of and insight into illness during psychoses.] In Kranz, H. *Psychopathologie Heute*, Stuttgart: Georg Thieme 1962, 53-60

68571 Reaktionen, Neurosen, Psychopathien. Ein Grundiss der kleinen Psychiatrie. [Reactions, Neuroses, Psychopathies.] Stuttgart: Georg Thieme 1968

68572 Typus, Psychodynamic und Psychotherapie herzphobischer Zustände. [Type, psychodynamics, and psychotherapy of cardiophobic conditions.] Z PSM 1964, 10:276-285

68573 Zur Erkrankungssituation und psychotherapeutischen Indikation bei Schizophrenen. [On schizophrenics' experience of being sick and indications for psychotherapy.] In Müller, C. & Benedetti, G. *Psychotherapy of Schizophrenia*, Basel/NY: Karger 1965, 177-188

68574 (& Müller, C.) Zur Kritik der Schizophreniediagnose bei psychotherapeutisch behandelten Kranken. (Aus den Krankengeschichten der Fälle von Sechehaye, Benedetti, Elrod und Chr. Müller.) [Contribution to the critical appraisal of the diagnosis of schizophrenia in patients treated with psychotherapy. (From the case histories of the cases of Sechehaye, Benedetti, Elrod and Chr. Müller.)] Nervenarzt 1962, 33:342-349

BRAVERMAN, MALVIN

68575 (& Hacker, F. J.) Posttraumatic hyperirritability. R 1968, 55:601-614

68576 (& Hacker, F. J.) Psychotraumatic reactions. Indust Med Surg 1966, 35:957-966. J forens Med 1966, 13:101-114

BRAWER, FLORENCE B.

See Boyer, L. Bryce

BRAYBOY, T.

See Sager, Clifford J.

BRAYBOY, THOMAS LEE

68577 (& Marks, M. J.) Transference variations evoked by racial differences in co-therapists. PT 1968, 22:474-480

BRAZELTON, T. BERRY

68578 The early mother-infant adjustment. Pediatrics 1963, 32:931-937

See Gifford, Sanford

BRECHER, EDWARD

See Brecher, Ruth

BRECHER, RUTH

68579 (& Brecher, E.) (Eds) An Analysis of Human Sexual Response. Boston: Little, Brown; NY: New Amer Libr 1966, 318 p

BRECHER-MARER, SYLVIA

See Bowers, Margaretta K.

BREEIJEN, ARIE DEN

See Levitt, Eugene E.

BREGER, ELI

68580 Etiologic factors in enuresis: a psychobiologic approach. J Amer Acad Child Psychiat 1963, 2:667-676

BREGER, LOUIS

* * * (& McGaugh, J. L.) Another view of behavior therapy. See [68583]
68581 (Ed) Clinical-Cognitive Psychology; Models and Integrations. Englewood Cliffs, N. J.: Prentice-Hall 1969, vii + 299 p
68582 Conformity as a function of the ability to express hostility. J Pers 1963, 31:247-257
68583 (& McGaugh, J. L.) Critique and reformulation of "learning theory" approaches to psychotherapy and neuroses. Psychol Bull 1965, 63:338-358. With title: Another view of behavior therapy. In Berenson, B. G. & Carkhuff, R. R. Sources of Gain in Counseling and Psychotherapy, NY/Chicago/San Francisco: Holt, Rinehart & Winston 1967, 323-357
68584 Function of dreams. JAbP 1967, 72(Suppl):1-28
68585 Motivation, energy, and cognitive structure in psychoanalytic theory. Mod Psa 44-65
68586 (& Ruiz, C.) The role of ego-defense in conformity. Soc Psych 1966, 69:73-85

BREGGIN, PETER R.

See Malev, Jonathan S.

BREMER, JOHAN

68587 Asexualization. A Follow-Up Study of 244 Cases. Oslo, Norway: Oslo Univ Pr 1958, 366 p
Rv Gero, G. Q 1961, 30:587-589. CG RFPsa 1962, 26:136

BRENDER, MYRON

68588 Discussion: Hospers on psychoanalysis: a critique. Philos Sci 1965, 32:73-83

BRENER, ELLIOT M.

68589 Castration anxiety, sexual fantasy, and sexual adjustment. Diss Abstr Int 1969, 30(5-B):2412

BRENGELMANN, J. C.

See David, Henry P.

BRENMAN, MARGARET

S-3930 Dreams and hypnosis. In Moss, C. S. The Hypnotic Investigation of Dreams, NY/London: Wiley 1967, 127-136
68590 (& Gill, M.) Hypnotherapy. A Survey of the Literature. NY: IUP 1947, 276 p
68591 Obituary: Robert Palmer Knight, 1902-1966. (Read at West New England Soc & Inst, 4 June 1966) Q 1966, 35:594-596

BRENNAN, JAMES F.

68592 Self-understanding and social feeling. J ind Psych 1967, 23:53-57
68593 Upright posture as the foundation of individual psychology: a comparative analysis of Adler and Straus. J ind Psych 1968, 24:25-32

BRENNEIS, CHARLES B.

68594 Differences in male and female ego styles in manifest dream content. Diss Abstr 1968, 28:3056

BRENNER, ARTHUR B.

68595 Onan, the levirate marriage and the genealogy of the Messiah. J Am Psa Ass 1962, 10:701-721
Abs JBi Q 1963, 32:448-449. Salmovici, E. Rev Psicoanál 1964, 21:381-383

See Rothenberg, Simon

BRENNER, CHARLES

68596 Archaic features of ego functioning. (Read at 25th Int Psa Cong, July 1967) J 1968, 49:426-429
Abs LHR Q 1969, 38:671
68597 Contributions to *The World Book Encyclopedia*, Chicago: Field Educ Enterprises 1958-1967
68598 Discussion of Boyer, L. B. "Office treatment of schizophrenic patients by psychoanalysis." Psa Forum 1966, 1:347
68599 Discussion of Gardner, R. W. "Organismic equilibration and the energy-structure duality in psychoanalytic theory: an attempt at theoretical refinement." J Am Psa Ass 1969, 17:41-53
68600 (& Arlow, J. A.) Dreams and the structural theory. (Read at Westchester Psa Soc, 4 Apr 1961)
Abs HFM Q 1961, 30:324-325
68601 Dreams in clinical psychoanalytic practice. JNMD 1969, 149:122-132
S-42766 An Elementary Textbook of Psychoanalysis. NY: Doubleday 1957; IUP 1966, 224 p
Psykoanalysens Grundbegreber. (Tr: Boisen, M.) Copenhagen: Trajan Pr 1967, 196 p
Grundzüge der Psychoanalyse. (Tr: Müller, H. G.) Frankfurt a.M.: S. Fischer Verlag 1967, 236 p
Breve Corso de Psicoanalisi. (Tr: Mori, F.) Florence: G. Martinelli 1967, 239 p
Japanese: (Tr: Yomone, T.; Motomura, H.) Tokyo: Seishin Shobo Co 1965, 273 p
Persian: (Tr: Djavaher-Kalam, F.) Teheran: B.T.N.K. 1968, 298 p
Psykoanalysens Grunder. (Tr: Kihlbom, M.) Stockholm: Bokförlaget Prisma 1968, 187 p
Rv Ravasini, C. Riv Psa 1967, 13:85
S-42767 Facts, coincidence and the psi hypothesis.
Abs SLP An Surv Psa 1957, 8:20
68602 The mechanism of repression. Psa—Gen Psychol 390-399
S-42769 The nature and development of the concept of repression in Freud's writings
Abs EMW An Surv Psa 1957, 8:93-96
68603 Obituary: Charles Davison: 1891-1965. Q 1966, 35:275-276
68604 Obituary: Albert A. Rosner 1910-1962. Q 1962, 31:382-384

S-42772 (Reporter) Panel: Re-evaluation of the libido theory.
Abs IS An Surv Psa 1956, 7:51-52
68605 Psychoanalysis and science. (Read at Am Psa Ass, 12 May 1968) J
Am Psa Ass 1968, 16:675-696
68606 Psychoanalysis, classical theory. In *Encyclopedia of the Social Sciences*,
Macmillan & Free Pr 1968
68607 The psychopathology of the psychoses. (Read at NY Psa Soc, 13 Nov
1962)
Abs WAS Q 1963, 32:301-305
S-42773 A reformulation of the psychoanalytic theory of parapraxes.
Abs An Surv Psa 1955, 6:137-138
68608 Some comments on technical precepts in psychoanalysis. (Read at NY
Psa Soc, Nov 1966) J Am Psa Ass 1969, 17:333-352

See Arlow, Jacob A.

ABSTRACT OF:
68609 Madison, P. Freud's Concept of Repression and Defense, Its Theoretical and Observational Language. Q 1962, 31:562-563

REVIEW OF:
68610 Schur, M. The Id and the Regulatory Principles of Mental Functioning.
Q 1968, 37:597-602

BRENNER, DONALD R.

See Caprio, Frank S.

BRÈS, Y.

68611 Le biologisme freudien. [Freudian biology.] Rev philos Fran 1965,
155:303-325

BRESSER, P. H.

68612 Kinder- und jugendpsychiatrie aus der Sicht des Psychopathologen.
[Infant and adolescent psychiatry from a psychopathological point of
view.] In Kranz, H. *Psychopathologie Heute*, Stuttgart: Georg Thieme
1962, 363-370

BRESSLER, BERNARD

68613 The concept of identity: a review. M 1965, 38:191-210
Abs JCS RFPsa 1967, 31:324
68614 The concept of the self: its significance in the etiology and therapy of
psychic disorders. R 1965, 52(3):95-115
Abs SRS Q 1966, 35:627
68615 First dreams in analysis: their relationship to early memories and the
pre-oedipal mother. PPR 1961, 48(4):60-82
Abs LDr RFPsa 1962, 27:352. Vilar, J. Rev Psicoanál 1963, 20:288
68616 A note on the bisexual significance of the testes. M 1961, 34:277-280
68617 The psychotherapeutic nurse. Amer J Nurs 1962, 62:87-90

See Silverman, Albert J.

BRESSLER, J.
See Spence, Donald P.

BREWSTER, HENRY H.
S-3975A Separation reaction in psychosomatic disease and neurosis. Death & Identity 216-226

BRICEÑO, ANTONIO
68618 Correlato sobre el tema "mania." [Round table on the subject of mental illness.] Rev urug Psa 1966, 8:173-180

BRICKMAN, HARRY R.
68619 The psychedelic "hip scene": return of the death instinct. P 1968, 125:766-772
68620 (& Schwartz, D. A.; Doran, S. M.) The psychoanalyst as community psychiatrist. P 1966, 122:1081-1087
    Abs Loeb, L. Q 1968, 37:629
68621 Some social psychiatric considerations. Arch gen Psychiat 1960, 2:470-476

BRIDGE, CARL JAMES
68622 Schizophrenia and the Oedipus complex. Psychiat Q Suppl 1965, 39:324-333

BRIDGER, H.
S-3982 Criteria for the termination of analysis.
    Abs Baranger, M. Rev urug Psa 1961-62, 4:366

BRIDGER, WAGNER H.
68623 Adolescent idealism in the civil rights movement. Sci Psa 1966, 9:61-67
68624 (& Birns, B. H.) An analysis of the role of sucking in early infancy. Sci Psa 1968, 12:156-161
68625 (& Mandel, I. J.) Cognitive expectancy and automatic conditioning: extension of schizokinesis. Recent Adv biol Psychiat 1965, 7:79-83
68626 Ethological concepts and human development. Recent Adv biol Psychiat 1962, 4:95-107
68627 (& Birns, B.) Neonates' behavioral and autonomic responses to stress during soothing. Recent Adv biol Psychiat 1963, 5:1-6
68628 The neurophysiological accompaniments of sensory and sleep deprivation and their role in the production of psychological disturbances. Recent Adv biol Psychiat 1964, 6:105-110

See Birns, Beverly H.; Blank, Marion

BRIEHL, MARIE H.
68629 Helene Deutsch b. 1884. The maturation of woman. Psa Pioneers 282-298

BRIEHL, WALTER

68630   Wilhelm Reich 1897-1957. Character analysis. Psa Pioneers 430-438

BRIEN, A.

68631   Old Freudian bull. New Statesm 1966, 72(Aug 12):227-228

BRIERLEY, MARJORIE

68632   Discussion of Bion, W. R. "Notes on memory and desire." Psa Forum
        1967, 2:277-278
68633   "Hardy perennials" and psychoanalysis. J 1969, 50:447-452

REVIEWS OF:
68634   Bakan, D. Sigmund Freud and the Jewish Mystical Tradition. J 1967,
        48:470-471
68635   Freud, S. The Standard Edition of the Complete Psychological Works
        of Sigmund Freud. Vol. I: J 1967, 48:323-326. Vol. III: J 1962, 43:
        468-471. Vol. VI: J 1961, 42:288. Vol. VIII: J 1961, 42:123. Vol. XV:
        J 1964, 45:584-586. Vol. XVI: J 1964, 45:584-586. Vol. XIX: J 1965,
        46:251-254. Vol. XXI: J 1965, 46:521-525. Vol. XXII: J 1965, 46:
        251-254. Vol. XXIII: J 1965, 46:521-525
68636   Hartmann, H. Psychoanalysis and Moral Values. J 1962, 43:351-352
68637   Laing, R. D. The Divided Self. A Study of Sanity and Madness. J
        1961, 42:288-291

BRIEWIG, EVA-MARIA

See Leonhard, Karl

BRIGG, ELVIRA HUGHES

68638   The application problem: a study of why people fail to keep first
        appointments. Soc Wk 1965, 10(2):71-78
68639   (& Mudd, E. H.) An exploration of methods to reduce broken first
        appointments. Fam Coordinator 1968, 17(1):41-46

BRIGGS, D. L.

See Molish, H. G.

BRIGGS, R. F.

68640   The hospitalized child faces emotional hazards. Hosp Manag 1967,
        103(5):90-92

BRIGHT, FLORENCE

68641   Deprivation: barriers to nurse-patient communication. Parental anxiety
        —a barrier to communication. ANA Clin Sess 1968, 13-20
68642   (& France, M. L.) The nurse and the terminally ill child. Ment Retard
        1966, 4(Dec):39-42
68643   The pediatric nurse and parental anxiety. Nurs Forum 1965, 4:30-47

BRILL, F.

68644 [Mental problems in adolescence.] (Heb) Dap refuiim 1961, 20:475-480

BRILL, ABRAHAM ARDEN

S-4198 The psychology of Sigmund Freud. In Shapley, H. et al: *A Treasury of Science*, Harper 1963, 635-652
S-4222 Sexuality and its role in the neuroses. Heirs Freud 68-86

BRILL, HENRY

68645 (& Patton, R. E.) The evaluation of patients following treatment in a state hospital. Proc Amer Psychopath Ass 1964, 52:254-270
68646 Nosology. Compreh Txbk Psychiat 581-589

BRIL, NORMAN Q.

68647 (Contributor) Anderson, R. S. *Neuropsychiatry in World War II*. Wash DC: Office of the Surgeon General, Dept of the Army 1966
68648 General biological studies. In Bellak, L. & Loeb, L. *The Schizophrenic Syndrome*, NY/London: Grune & Stratton 1969, 114-154
68649 Gross stress reaction, II: Traumatic war neurosis. Compreh Txbk Psychiat 1031-1035
68650 (& Glass, J. F.) Hebephrenic schizophrenic reactions. Arch gen psychiat 1965, 12:545-551
68651 Milieu of the medical school and undergraduate psychiatric education. In Early, L. W. et al: *Teaching Psychiatry in Medical School*, Wash DC: Am Psychiat Ass 1969, 133-135
68652 The need for psychiatric assistants. Psychiat Dig 1967, 28:13-23
68653 (& Liston, E. H., Jr.) Parental loss in adults with emotional disorders. Arch gen Psychiat 1966, 14:307-314
68654 (& Weinstein, R.; Garratt, J.) Poverty and mental illness: patients; perception of poverty as an etiological factor in their illness. P 1969, 125:1172-1179
* * * Preface to author's *Psychiatry and Medicine* v-xii
68655 (& Storrow, H. A.) Prognostic factors in psychotherapy. JAMA 1963, 183:913-916
68656 (Ed) Psychiatry in Medicine. Berkeley/Los Angeles: Univ Calif Pr 1962, xvi + 195 p
68657 The psychotherapeutic process. In author's *Psychiatry in Medicine* 1-25
68658 Results of psychotherapy. Calif Med 1966, 104:249-253
68659 (& Storrow, H. A.) Social class and psychiatric treatment. Arch gen Psychiat 1960, 3:340-344
68660 (Ed) Symposium on Psychiatry in Medicine. Berkely/Los Angeles: Univ Calif Pr 1962, 195 p

See Koegler, Ronald R.

REVIEW OF:
68661 Hendrick, I. Psychiatry Education Today. Psa Forum 1966, 1:306-308

BRIM, ORVILLE G., JR.

68662 Education for Child Rearing. NY: Russell Sage Found 1959, 362 p

BRIND, ANNA

See Bühler, Charlotte

BRINKER-FRANKE, M.

68663 Symbolismus I & II. [Symbolism I & II.] Agnes Karll-Schwest 1966, 20:291-292; 331-332

BRION, SERGE

See Delay, Jean Paul Louis

BRIONES, L.

See Gauthier, Yvon

BRISAC, DREYFUS

See Doumic-Girard, Alice

BRISAC, IERIQUE

See Doumic-Girard, Alice

BRISSENDEN, A.

See Kapp, Frederic T.; Ross, William D.

BRISSET, CHARLES

68664 À propos de: "Névroses et Troubles Psychosomatiques" de M. Dongier. [Concerning M. Dongier's "Neuroses and Psychosomatic Troubles."] Évolut psychiat 1967, 32:987-989
68665 Conversion et psychosomatique. [Conversion and psychosomatic medicine.] Ann méd-psychol 1969, 127(1):482
68666 Le culturalisme en psychiatrie. [Culturalism in psychiatry.] Évolut psychiat 1963, 28:369-405
68667 Hystérie et pathologie psychosomatique. [Hysteria and psychosomatic pathology.] Rev Prat 1964, 14:1459-1470
68668 [Psychoanalysis in the contemporary French psychiatric movement. A letter to Dr. Koupernik.] (Fr) Concours Méd 1963, 85:1933-1940

See Ey, Henri.

REVIEW OF:
68669 Osborn, R. Marxisme et psychanalyse. RFPsa 1968, 32:627-629

BROADHURST, BETTY P.

See Greene, Bernard L.

BROCHER

68670 [The future of the families.] (Ger) Prax Kinderpsychol 1964, (Suppl 6):5-7

BROCHER, TOBIAS

68671 Aggressionsabwehr und Anpassung in Gruppen. [On defense mechanism and adaptation in groups.] In Mitscherlich, A. *Bis Hierher und Nicht Weiter,* Munich: Piper 1969

68672 Aggressionstrieb und Politik. [Aggressive drives and politics.] In Schultz, H. J. *Politik und Wissenschaft,* Stuttgart: Kreuz 1969

68673 Autorität. [Authority.] In Schmidt, W. *Kollegs für Junge Leute,* Bunse: Mainz 1969, 33-45

68674 Begleitende Verfahren bei der Überprüfung des medizinischen Unterrichts. [Methods employed in connection with evaluation of medical training.] In Uexkuell, T. von: *Probleme des Medizinunterrichts,* Munich/Berlin: Urban & Schwarzenberg 1968

68675 Comment on paper by Drs. Joffe and Sandler, "Comments on the psychoanalytic psychology of adaptation, with special reference to the role of affects and the representational world." (Read at Int Psa Cong, July 1967) J 1968, 49:454-456

68676 Dein Kind—Partner oder Gefolge? [Your child—partner or follower?] In *Konflikte der Generationen,* Stuttgart: Klett 1966, 53-69

68677 Die Elternschule. [School for parents.] Hbh Kinderpsychother 684-692

68678 Erkennen und Handeln. [Perception and acting.] In *Nürnberger Gespräche,* Freiburg: Rombach 1967, 13-36

68679 Die Erziehung zur Geschlechtlichkeit. [Sexual education.] In *Krise der Ehe?* Munich: Piper 1966, 187-206

68680 Fachärztliches Gutachten. [A specialist's opinion.] In Giese, H. "Aufklärung in Illustrierten?" B Sexfschg 1968, (44):41-73

68681 Die Funktion der Erziehungsberatung in der modernen Gesellschaft. [The function of child guidance in modern society.] Schleswholst Ärzteblatt 1966, 19(5)

68682 Gefährdete Demokratie. [Democracy in danger.] In *Kontexte II,* Stuttgart: Kreuz 1966, 41-50

68683 Das gemeinsame Leben. [Life in togetherness.] In *Christliche Erziehung Heute,* Munich: Ehrenwirth 1963, 35-60

68684 Gruppendynamik und Erwachsenenbildung. [Group Dynamics and Adult Education.] Braunschweig: Westermann 1968, 173 p

68685 Herausforderung der Zukunft. [Provocations of the future.] In Schulz, H. J. *Was Weiss Man von der Seele,* Stuttgart: Kreuz 1967, 203-213

68686 Homosexuelles Verhalten als Entwicklungsstörung. [Homosexual behavior as developmental disturbance.] In *Plädoyer für die Abschaffung des ¶ 175,* Frankfurt: Suhrkamp 1966 (175) 12 p

68687 Das Ich und die Anderen in Familie und Gesellschaft. [The Ego and the Others in Family and Society.] Stuttgart: Bonz 1967, 104 p
El Yo et los Otros. Salamanca: Sigueme 1968, 162 p

68688 Ideologie, Legende und Wirklichkeit in der Erziehung. [Ideology, legend, and reality in education.] In *Gesellschaft und Neurose,* Stuttgart: Klett 1965, 43-80

68689 Jugend- Tor zur Welt. [Youth- gate to the world.] Almanach (Stutt) 1962. With title: Prägende Kindeheitserinnerungen, Tor zur Welt. [Imprinting memories of childhood, gate to the world.] Göttingen: Hogrefe 1963, 25-43

68690 Das Kind und seine Eltern. [The child and his parents.] In *Christliche Erziehung Heute*, Munich: Ahrnenwirth 1963

68691 Eine Kleine Elternschule. [Short School for Parents.] Stuttgart: Klett 1964, 78 p

68692 Kritische Überlegungen zur Sexualerziehung in der Schule. [Critical thoughts on sexual education in schools.] In *Kritische Beiträge zur Bildungstheorie*, Frankfurt: Diesterweg 1968

68693 Misslungene Werbung in der Neurose. [Unsuccessful wooing in neurosis.] In *Neurose, ein Psychosoziales Problem*, Stuttgart: Klett 1960, 7-38

* * * Prägende Kindeheitserinnerungen, Tor zur Welt. See [68689]

68694 Prävention in den sozialmedizinischen Berufen. [Prevention in sociomedical professions.] Kongressbericht IPA, Wiesbaden/Basel: Karger 1969, 10 p

68695 Prävention in der Erziehung, Symposionbericht. [Symposium report on prevention of psychic disturbances in the area of education.]. Kongressbericht IAP, Part I, Basel: Karger 1969, 8 p

68696 Psychoanalytische Aspekte der Depression. [Psychoanalytic aspects of depression.] Wegezum Menschen 1966, 18:267-284

68697 Psychologische Aspekte des Friedens. [Psychological aspects of peace.] Briefe zur Völksverständigung 1967, 40:1-26 (Ger, Eng, Fr)

68698 Psychosoziales Feld und Pubertät. [Psychosocial field and puberty.] In *Jugend Zwischen Gestern und Morgen- in Psychotherapeutischer Sicht*, Stuttgart: Klett 1961, 7-24

68699 Revolution oder Innovation. [Revolution or innovation.] Zum Jugendprotest in der Monat, Ztschr 1968, (8), 18 p

68700 Die Rezeption Freuds in Deutschland. [Recognition of Freud in Germany.] In *Aufklärung Heute, Probleme der Deutschen Gesellschaft*, Freiburg: Rombach 1967, 205-217

68701 Die Rolle des Kindes in der Gesellschaft der Zukunft. [The role of the child in future society.] In *Die Zukunft unserer Kinder*, Freiburg: Walter/Olten 1967, 22-42

68702 Schule ohne Sozialerziehung. [School without social education.] Neue Sammlung 1967, 7:429-435

68703 Die Situation des Erziehers. [The situation of the teacher.] In Hörl, R. *Konzepte f. e. Neue Schule*, Cologne: Luchterhand 1968, 33-45

68704 Sprache; uber die Weise mit Kindern zu sprechen. [On language; the way to communicate with children.] In *Die Zukunft unserer Kinder*, Freiburg: Walter/Olten 1967, 68-74

68705 Die Unterhaltungssendung als Instrument gesellschaftspolitischer Bewusstseinsbildung. [Television and broadcasting as an element of developing social awareness.] In *Fernesehen in Deutschland*, Mainz: Hase & Koehler 1967, 283-295

68706 Untersuchungen zum Lehr- und Lehrsystem des Medizinischen Unterrichts. [Research Study on the Teaching and Learning System in Medical Education.] Giessen: med Fakultät (Inst Sozialmedizin) 1968, 20 p

68707 Über averbale Kommunikation. [On non-verbal communication.] Psyche 1967, 21:634-653

68708 Verleugnung oder Einsicht? [Denial or insight?] Z Verständnis Judentums 1968, 7(28)
68709 Vorurteile- Erforschung und Bekämpfung. [Prejudices- research and prevention.] Hess Blätter Volksbildung 1965, (5):352-359
68710 Zukunft gruppenpsychologischer Forschung. [Future of group psychology research.] Gruppendyn 1969, 1
68711 Zum Vorurteil des Antisemitismus. [On the prejudice of antisemitism.] Tribüne 1966, 5:2121-2135

See Mitscherlich, Alexander

BROCK, HELENE

68712 Untersuchungen über die Entwicklung der Kinder nervenkranker Mütter. [Investigations on the development of children whose mothers have nervous diseases.] Acta paedopsychiat 1962, 29:116-123

BROCK, TIMOTHY C.
See Buss, Arnold H.

BROCKBANK, REED

68713 Analytic group psychotherapy. Curr psychiat Ther 1966, 6:145-156
68714 Aspects of mental health consultation. Arch gen Psychiat 1968, 18:267-275
68715 Letter to the editors [re Gull, G. & Strean, H. S. "Analyst's silence."] Psa Forum 1967, 2:288
68716 (& Westby-Gibson, D.) (Eds) Mental Health in a Changing Community. A Symposium. NY: Grune & Stratton 1966, ix + 163 p
68717 (Participant) On regression: a workshop. (Held at West Coast Psa Soc, 14-16 Oct 1966) Psa Forum 1967, 2:293-316
68718 Problems of self-identity in mental illness and mental health. In author's Mental Health in a Changing Community 26-33
68719 The psychology of humanism. Humanist 1963, 23(2)

BRÖCKER, F. J.

68720 Oorspronkelijke stukken. Oedipus complex of Oedipus-fictie? [On the hypothesis of the incestuous young child conflict.] NTvG 1965, 109:1376-1381

BRODERICK, CARLFRED B.

68721 Sexual behavior among pre-adolescents. J soc Issues 1966, 22:6-21

BRODEUR, CLAUDE

68722 Du Problème de l'inconscient à une Philosophie de l'Homme: 1. Les Théories Freudiennes sur la Structure de l'Organisme Psychique. 2. La Structure de la Pensée Humaine. [From the Problem of the Unconscious to a Philosophy of Man: 1. Freudian Theories on the Structure of the Psychic Organism. 2. The Structure of Human Thought.] Montreal: Inst Rech Psychol 1969, 118 p; 156 p

68723   La négation comme facteur essentiel de formation du sujet humain. [Denial as an essential factor in the formation of the human being.] Interprétation 1968, 2(3)

BRODEY, WARREN M.

68724   The family as the unit of study and treatment: III. Images, object and narcissistic relationships. Workshop, 1959. Ops 1961, 31:69-73
68725   The need for a system approach. In Ackerman, N. W. et al: *Expanding Theory and Practice in Family Therapy*, NY: Fam Serv Ass Amer 1967, 17-19
68726   On the dynamics of narcissism: I. Externalization and early ego development. Psa St C 1965, 20:165-193
68727   Processes of family change. (Panel discussion: the classification of family types.) In Ackerman, N. W. et al: *Expanding Theory and Practice in Family Therapy*, NY: Fam Serv Ass Amer 1967, 60-66

BRODIE, RICHARD D.

68728   Some aspects of psychotherapy in a residential treatment center. Ops 1966, 36:712-719

BRODRICK, ALAN HOUGHTON

TRANSLATION OF:
Tucci, G. [93421]

BRODSKY, BERNARD

68729   (Reporter) The application of psychoanalytic method and theory to social problems. (Panel: Am Psa Ass, NY, Dec 1966) J Am Psa Ass 1967, 15:686-694
68730   Two contributions to the theory of working through. (Read at NY Psa Soc, 13 Oct 1964)
        Abs IS Q 1965, 34:319-321
68731   Working through: its widening scope and some aspects of its metapsychology. (Read at Am Psa Ass, May 1964) Q 1967, 36:485-496
        Abs Cuad Psa 1968, 4:41

ABSTRACT OF:
68732   Rosen, V. H. The relevance of "style" to problems of defense and the organizing function of the ego. Q 1961, 30:466-469

REVIEWS OF:
68733   Fulton, R. (Ed) Death and Identity. Q 1967, 36:106-108
68734   Meerloo, J. A. M. Illness and Cure. Studies on the Philosophy of Medicine and Mental Health. Q 1965, 34:301-302
68735   Rado, S. Psychoanalysis and Behavior; Collected Papers. Vol. II: 1956-1961. Q 1964, 33:272-274
68736   Rochlin, G. Griefs and Discontents. The Forces of Change. Q 1967, 36:606-607

BRODSKY, C.

See Ruesch, Jurgen

BRODY, BENJAMIN

68736A Is the unconscious necessary. The denial of the unconscious: a great leap backward. Int J Psychiat 1969, 8:590-595
68736B The present status of psychoanalysis: an addendum to Dr. Arieti. Int J Psychiat 1969, 9:630-639

See Shatan, Chaim F.

BRODY, CHARLES

See Nichtern, Sol

BRODY, EUGENE B.

68737 Adolescents as a United States minority group in an era of social change. In author's *Minority Group Adolescents in the United States*, Baltimore: Williams & Wilkins 1968, 1-16
68738 Algunos problemas conceituais e metodogicos relacionados com pesquisa em sociedade, cultura e doenca mental. J Bras Psiquiat 1963, 12:117-142
   Conceptual and methodological problems in research in society, culture and mental illness. JNMD 1964, 139:62-74
68739 The ambulatory schizophrenic as a medical patient. Psychosomatics 1961, 2:435-437
68740 An appreciation for Lawrence S. Kubie. JNMD 1969, 149:3-4
68741 Borderline state, character disorder, and psychotic manifestations— some conceptual formulations. Psa 1960, 23:75-80
68742 Color and identity conflict in young boys. Observations of Negro mothers and sons in urban Baltimore. Ps 1963, 26:188-201. In Palmer, J. O. & Goldstein, M. J. *Perspectives in Psychopathology*, NY: Oxford Univ Pr 1966, 338-353
   Abs HRB Q 1964, 33:457
68743 Color and identity conflict in young boys. II: Observations of white mothers and sons in urban Baltimore. Arch gen Psychiat 1964, 10:354-360
68744 A contemporary history of the Journal of Nervous and Mental Disease, an editorial. JNMD 1967, 145:1-5
68745 Continuing problems in the relationship between training in psychiatry and psychoanalysis in the U.S.A. JNMD 1963, 136:58-67
68746 Cultura, communicación y emoción en el proceso educativo. [Culture, communication and emotion in the educational process.] Reimpreso Educ med Salud 1968, 2(1)
68747 Cultural exclusion, character and illness. P 1966, 122:852-858
68748 Culture, symbol and value in the social etiology of behavioral deviance. Proc Amer Psychopath Ass 1968, 57:8-41. In Zubin, J. & Freyhan, F. A. *Social Psychiatry*, NY: Grune & Stratton 1968, 8-13
68749 The development of the psychiatric resident as a therapist. In Dellis, N. P. & Stone, H. K. *The Training of Psychotherapists*, Baton Rouge: Louisiana State Univ Pr 1960, 86-89
68750 Discussion of Eisenberg, L. "Social class and individual development." Crosscurrents in Ps & Psa 81-84

68751 Endocrine factors in growth and development. In *The Cyclopedia of Medicine, Surgery and Specialities*, F. A. Davis Co. 1952

68752 Existence, action and context in psychotherapy with schizophrenic patients. A commentary on Mullahy's presentation of Sullivan's theory of schizophrenia. Int J Psychiat 1967, 4:525-529

68753 Factors in the recognition and management of the non-hospitalized schizophrenic as a medical patient. Modern Treatment 1969, 6(4): 695-703

68754 Foreword to Pope, B. & Scott, W. H. *Psychological Diagnosis in Clinical Practice*, NY: Oxford Univ Pr 1967, xiii

68755 Foreword to Robinson, L. *Psychological Aspects of the Care of Hospitalized Patients*, Phila: F. A. Davis 1968, vii-x

68756 Freud's theory of psychosis and the role of psychotherapist. JNMD 1961, 133:36-45

68757 From schizophrenic to homosexual: a crisis in role and relating. PT 1963, 17:579-595

68758 (& Derbyshire, R.; Schliefer, C. B.) How the young adult Baltimore Negro male becomes a mental hospital statistic. Psychiat Res Rep 1967, (22):206-219

68759 Mental health planning and directed social change. Psychiat Res Rep 1967, (22):368-374

68760 (& Derbyshire, R. L.) Mental status, anti-semitic and anti-foreign prejudice in Negro college students. Arch gen Psychiat 1963, 619-628

68761 (Ed) Minority Group Adolescents in the United States. Baltimore, Md.: Williams & Wilkins; Edinburgh: Livingstone 1968, 243 p
      Rv Taylor, C. N. Contempo Psa 1969, 5(2):190-192

68762 Minority group status and behavioral disorganization. In author's *Minority Group Adolescents in the United States* 227-243

68763 The new urban America: implications for medical education. In Early, L. W. et al: *Teaching Psychiatry in Medical School*, Wash DC: Am Psychiat Ass 1969, 69-78

68764 Obituary: Jacob E. Finesinger, M.D. P 1959, 116:383

68765 (& Sata, L. S.) Personality disorders. In Freedman, A. M. & Kaplan, H. I. *Comprehensive Textbook of Psychiatry*, Baltimore: Williams & Wilkins 1967, 937-950

68766 Planeamiento de la Salud Mental de la comunidad, epidemiologia psiquiatrica y cambio social dirigido. [Community mental health planning, psychiatric epidemiology and directed social change.] Rev lat-amer Salud ment 1967, No. 11:353-363

68767 Psychiatric implications of space flight. P 1959, 115:1112

68768 Psychiatric problems of the German occupation. P 1948, 286:105

68769 The psychiatrist's decision to refer a patient for psychological testing. [Symposium on psychology and psychiatry.] JNMD 1959, 129:88-91

68770 Psychiatry and prejudice. Am Hbk Psychiat III 629-642

68771 Psychiatry and the social order. P 1965, 122:81-87

68772 Psychiatry in Portuguese America (Brazil). P 1964, 120:959-961

68773 The psychiatry of Latin America. Editorial. P 1966, 123:475-477

68774 Psychiatry's continuing identity crisis: confusion or growth? Psychiat Dig 1969, 30(June):12-17

68775   Psychoanalysis and social research. Discussion. In Goldman, G. S. & Shapiro, D. *Developments in Psychoanalysis at Columbia University*, NY: Hafner Publ 1966, 295-300

68776   Psychologic tension and serum iodine levels in psychiatric patients without evidence of thyroid disease. PSM 1949, 11:70

68777   The public mental hospital as a symptom of social conflict. Maryland State med J 1960, 9:330-334

68778   Recording cross-culturally useful interview data: experience from Brazil. P 1966, 123:446-456

68779   The role of the clinical-nurse specialist in nursing administration. J psychiat Nurs 1964, 2:254-262

68780   The role of the psychiatrist: staffing patterns. In Kaufman, M. R. *The Psychiatric Unit in a General Hospital*, NY: IUP 1965, 26-35; 88-109

68781   Social conflict and schizophrenic behavior in young adult Negro males. Ps 1961, 24:337-346

68782   Sociocultural influences on vulnerability to schizophrenic behavior. In Romano, J. *Origins of Schizophrenia*, Excerpta Medica Int Cong Series No. 151, 1968, 228-238

68783   Some conceptual and methodological issues involved in research on society, culture, and mental illness. JNMD 1964, 139:62-74
        Abs BFM Q 1966, 35:157

68784   (& Newman, R.; Redlich, F. C.) Sound recording and the problem of evidence in psychiatry. Science 1951, 113:379

68785   Status and role determinants of initial interview behavior. PT 1968, 22:1-11

68786   Status and role influence on initial interview behavior in psychiatric patients. In Lesse, S. *An Evaluation of the Results of the Psychotherapies*, Springfield, Ill: Thomas 1968, 269-279

S-42908 Superego, introjected mother, and energy discharge in schizophrenia: contribution from the study of anterior lobotomy.
        Abs CK An Surv Psa 1958, 9:189-190

68787   (& Fishman, M.) Therapeutic response and length of hospitalization of psychiatrically ill veterans: social determinants. Arch gen Psychiat 1960, 2:174-181

68788   Thumb-sucking in adults. Questions and answers. JAMA 1964, 189:971

68789   Toward a psychiatry of international decision-makers. Int J Psychiat 1968, 5:338-340

68790   (& Sata, L. S.) Trait and pattern disturbances. Compreh Txbk Psychiat 937-950

68791   Transcultural psychiatry, human similarities, and socioeconomic evolution. Proc IV World Cong Psychiat 1966, 239-244. P 1967, 124:616-622

68792   Urban disintegration and the psychiatrist's dilemna. P 1969, 125:1719-1721

68793   What do schizophrenics learn during psychotherapy and how do they learn it? JNMD 1958, 127:66

        See Band, Raymond I.; Derbyshire, Robert L.; Gallahorn, George; Monroe, Russell R.

REVIEW OF:
68794 Searles, H. F. The Nonhuman Environment in Normal Development and in Schizophrenia. Q 1962, 31:104-106

BRODY, LEON

See Dunbar, Flanders

BRODY, MATTHEW

68795 Depression and somatic illness (the neuro-patho-neuroses). Psychosomatics 1968, 9:245-247
68796 (& Golden, M. M.; Lichtman, H. S.) Experience with small group seminars for practicing physicians. P 1965, 122:497-500
68797 (& Golden, M. M.) Mental health research and training. In Ziskind, R. *Viewpoint on Mental Health*, NY: NYC Comm Ment Hlth Board 1967, 368-374
68798 Phylogenesis of sexual morality; psychiatric exegesis on Onan and Samson. NYSJM 1968, 68(19):2510

BRODY, MORRIS WOLF

S-42912 Clinical manifestations of ambivalence.
          Abs SO An Surv Psa 1956, 7:164-165
68799 (& Mahoney, V. P. Introjection, identification and incorporation. J 1964, 45:57-63
          Abs EVN Q 1966, 35:311
68800 The psychiatric case conference. Ps 1961, 24:361-366. With title: The use of the conference. Int Psychiat Clin 1964, 1:357-366
68801 (& Harrison, S. I.) Stutterers. In Slavson, S. R. *The Fields of Group Psychotherapy*, NY: IUP 1956, 96-107
S-42920 Transference and countertransference in psychotherapy.
          Abs An Surv Psa 1955, 6:360-361
* * * The use of the conference. See [68800]

See Hoffman, Francis H.

REVIEWS OF:
68802 Arieti, S. (Ed) American Handbook of Psychiatry, Vol. III. Q 1969, 38:152
68803 Bandler, B. (Ed) Psychiatry in the General Hospital. Q 1969, 38: 151-152
68804 Kelman, H. (Ed) Advances in Psychoanalysis. Contributions to Karen Horney's Holistic Approach. Q 1964, 33:586
68805 Knapp, P. H. (Ed) Expression of the Emotions in Man. Q 1964, 33: 435-436
68806 Scher, S. C. & Davis, H. R. (Eds) The Out-Patient Treatment of Schizophrenia. Q 1961, 30:285-286
68807 Solomon, P. & Glueck, B. C. (Eds) Recent Research on Schizophrenia. Q 1965, 34:604-605
68808 Stein, M. R. et al: (Eds) Identity and Anxiety. Survival of the Person in Mass Society. Q 1961, 30:116-117

BRODY, PAULA

68809   Shylock's omophagia: a ritual approach to "The Merchant of Venice."
Lit & Psych 1967, 17:229-234

BRODY, SELWYN

68810   Community therapy of child delinquents. Curr psychiat Ther 1963,
3:197-204

68811   Psychiatric observations on juvenile delinquents in residential treatment.
Dis nerv Sys 1961, 22:632-635

68812   Simultaneous psychotherapy of married couples: preliminary observations. PPR 1961, 48(4):94-107. Curr psychiat Ther 1961, 1:139-144

68813   Syndrome of the treatment rejecting patient. R 1964, 51:243-252
Abs SRS Q 1965, 34:469

68814   Value of group psychotherapy in patients with "polysurgery addiction."
Psychiat Q 1959, 33:260-283

REVIEWS OF:

68815   Rubinstein, R. & Lasswell, H. D. The Sharing of Power in a Psychiatric
Hospital. R 1969, 56:161-162

68816   Wahl, C. W. (Ed) New Dimensions in Psychosomatic Medicine. R
1964, 51:691-693

BRODY, STUART A.

68817   (& Savino, M. T.) A case of *folie à deux* in early California. Psychiat
Q Suppl 1964, 38:111-118

BRODY, SYLVIA

68818   Aims and methods in child psychotherapy. J Amer Acad Child Psychiat
1964, 3:385-412

68819   (& Axelrad, S.) Anxiety, socialization, and ego formation in infancy.
(Read at 24th Int Psa Cong, July 1965; NY Psa Soc, 31 May 1966) J
1966, 47:218-229
Abs Harrison, I. B. Q 1967, 36:480-481. EVN Q 1968, 37-311

68820   (& Axelrad, S.) Mother-infant interaction: forms of feeding. (Read at
NY Psa Soc, 13 Feb 1968)
Abs Donadeo, J. Q 1969, 38:346-347

68821   Passivity: A Study of Its Development and Expression in Boys. NY:
IUP; London: Bailey Bros 1964, viii + 184 p
Abs J Am Psa Ass 1966, 14:231-232. Rv Esman, A. H. Q 1965,
34:290-293. Lomas, P. J 1965, 46:394

S-42925 Patterns of Mothering: Maternal Influence during Infancy.
Abs Auth An Surv Psa 1956, 7:245-246; 447-462

68822   Preventive intervention in current problems of early childhood. In
Caplan, G. *Prevention of Mental Disorders in Children*, NY: Basic
Books 1961, 168-191

S-42926 Self-rocking in infancy.
Abs LDr RFPsa 1962, 26:331. JTM Q 1962, 31:127-128

68823   Some aspects of transference resistance in prepuberty. (Read at Am
Psa Ass, Dec 1960; NY Psa Soc, June 1961) Psa St C 1961, 16:251-274
Abs EVN 1961, 30:620-622

68824 Some infantile sources of childhood disturbance. J Amer Acad Child Psychiat 1967, 6:615-643

REVIEW OF:

68825 Foss, B. M. (Ed) Determinants of Infant Behavior. Q 1963, 32:269-271

BROEDEL, JOHN W.

See Fast, Irene

BROEKMAN, J. M.

68826 Phänomenologisches Denken in Philosophie und Psychiatrie. [Phenomenological thinking in philosophy and psychiatry.] Confin psychiat 1965, 8:165-187

BROEN, WILLIAM ERNEST, JR.

68827 Schizophrenia; Research and Theory. NY: Academic Press 1968, x + 240 p

BROMBERG, NORBERT

S-42930 Maternal influences in the development of moral masochism.
Abs An Surv Psa 1955, 6:199-201

68828 On polygamous women. (Read at Am Psa Ass, May 1960) Bull Phila Ass Psa 1961, 11:155-167. With title: Polygamous women. In Slovenko, R. *Sexual Behavior and the Law*, Springfield, Ill: Thomas 1964, 341-355
        Japanese: (Tr: Ohtsuki, K.) Tokyo J Psa 1967, 25:24-31
        Abs EFA Q 1962, 31:583. PLe RFPsa 1963, 27:335
* * * Polygamous women. See [68828]

BROMBERG, WALTER

68829 Advances in group therapy. Curr psychiat Ther 1961, 1:152-158
68830 An analysis of therapeutic artfulness. P 1958, 114:719-725
S-4409 Crime and the Mind, A Psychiatric Analysis of Crime and Punishment. NY: Macmillan 1965, xiv + 431 p
68831 Developments in group and action methods. Prog PT 1960, 5:59-66
68832 Discussion of Boorstein, S. "A psychoanalytic overview of the offender: implications for therapy." Psa Forum 1967, 2:262-267
68833 History of treatment of mental disorders. Ency Ment Hlth 737-746
68834 Homosexuality. Ency Ment Hlth 747-764
68835 The Mold of Murder. A Psychiatric Study of Homicide. NY/London: Grune & Stratton 1961, viii + 230 p
        Rv Sta Q 1963, 32:442-444
68836 The nature of psychology. JNMD 1963, 137:609-610
68837 The Nature of Psychotherapy: A Critique of the Psychotherapeutic Transaction. NY: Grune & Stratton 1962, vii + 108 p
68838 (& Simon, F.) The "protest" psychosis. A special type of reactive psychosis. Arch gen Psychiat 1968, 19:155-160
68839 Psychiatrists in court: the psychiatrist's view. P 1969, 125:1343-1347
68840 Psychopathic personality concept evaluated and re-evaluated. Arch gen Psychiat 1967, 17:641-645

68841 The psychopathic personality concept re-evaluated. Arch crim Psychodyn 1961, (Spec No.):435-442
68842 Sex offense as a disguise. Corrective Psychiat 1965, 11:293-298
68843 Sexual deviation. Ency Ment Hlth 1848-1857

See Halleck, Seymour L.

BROME, VINCENT

68844 Freud and His Early Circle. NY: Morrow, [1967] 1968, xii + 275 p

BRONFENBRENNER, URIE

68845 Freudian theories of identification and their derivatives. Child Develpm 1960, 31:15-40
68846 Parenthood and child rearing. Ency Ment Hlth 1437-1448
68847 The psychological costs of quality and equality in education. Child Develpm 1967, 38:909-925
68848 Toward a theoretical model for the analysis of parent-child relationships in a social context. In Glidewell, J. C. *Parental Attitudes and Child Behavior*, Springfield, Ill: Thomas 1961, 90-109

BRONISCH, F. W.

68849 Klinische und psychopathologische Anmerkungen zur gegenwärtigen Stellung der Elektro-Krampfbehandlung im therapeutischen Gesamtplan. [Clinical and psychopathological observations on the modern position of ECT within the overall planning of therapeutics.] In Kranz, H. *Psychopathologie Heute*, Stuttgart: Georg Thieme 1962, 155-161

BRONNER, ALFRED

68850 Psychotherapy with religious patients. Review of the literature. PT 1964, 18:475-487

BRONSON, F. H.

See Scott, John P.

BRONSON, GORDON

68851 A neurological perspective on ego development in infancy. J Am Psa Ass 1963, 11:55-65
        Abs JBi Q 1964, 33:134

BRONSON, WANDA C.

68852 Dimensions of ego and infantile identification. J Pers 1959, 27:532-545. In Crow, L. F. & Crow, A. *Readings in Child and Adolescent Psychology*, NY: Longmans 1961, 167-178
68853 Early antecedents of emotional expressiveness and reactivity control. Child Develpm 1966, 37:794-810

BROOKS, GEORGE W.

See DiMascio, Alberto; Greenblatt, Milton

BROOKS, SAMUEL H.

See Eiduson, Bernice T.

BROPHY, BRIGID

68854   Black Ship to Hell. London: Secker & Warburg 1962, 490 p
68855   Mozart the Dramatist; A Psychological and Historical Study of Genius.
NY: Harcourt, Brace & World 1964, 328 p
Rv Coltrera, J. T. J Am Psa Ass 1965, 13:634-703. Deri, O. Am Im
1965, 22:212-215
68856   Sex-'n'-violence. New Statesman 1965, 69:677-678

BROSIN, HENRY W.

68857   Acute and chronic brain syndromes. Compreh Txbk Psychiat 708-711
68858   The adolescent's crisis today. Adolescent crises. NYSJM 1967, 67:2003-2011
68859   Biographical sketch. In Menninger, W. C. A Psychiatrist for a Troubled World, NY: Viking 1967, xv-xix
68860   Brain syndromes associated with trauma. Compreh Txbk Psychiat 748-759
68861   The changing curriculum. In Stokes, A. B. Psychiatry in Transition, 1966-1967, Toronto: Univ Toronto Pr 1967, 39-55
68862   The clinicians search for values. Bull Guild Cath Psychiat 1967, 14: 207-209
68863   Combat fatigue. Encyclopedia Britannica 1967, 6:119-120
68864   Communication and mental health. Ency Ment Hlth 321-336
68865   Communication systems in the newer clinical settings. Hosp Comm Psychiat 1967, 18:321-326
68866   Communication systems of the consultation process. In Mendel, W. M. & Solomon, P. Psychiatric Consultation, NY: Grune & Stratton 1968, 1-12
68867   Computers in psychiatry. Introduction. P 1969, 125(Suppl):1-2
68868   (& Menninger, W. C.; et al) The consultant system. In Anderson, R. S. et al: Neuropsychiatry in World War II, Vol. 1, Washington: US GPO 1967, 67-96
68869   Current psychiatric therapies; transition without precedent. Curr psychiat Ther 1967, 7:1-6
68870   Dedication speech. P 1968, 124:1012-1014
68871   Discussion of Pollack, I. "Language as behavior." In Darley, F. L. Brain Mechanisms Underlying Speech and Language, NY: Grune & Stratton 1967, 97-100
68872   Evolution and understanding diseases of the mind. In Tax, S. Evolution After Darwin, Vol. 2: Evolution of Man, Chicago: Univ Chicago Pr 1960, 373-400
68873   Federal legislation, local psychiatric societies and changing patterns of practice. MH 1967, 51:479-485
° ° °   Foreword. Meth Res PT ix-xi
° ° °   Foreword to Schwab, J. T. Handbook of Psychiatric Consultation.
68874   Franz Alexander, M. D.: scientist and teacher; twenty-three years after

Freud. In Marmorston, J. & Stainbrook, E. *Psychoanalysis and the Human Situation,* NY: Vantage Pr 1964, 42-65

68875 General hospitals. In Anderson, R. S. et al: *Neuropsychiatry in World War II, Vol. 1,* Washington: US GPO 1967, 297-323

68876 Human aggression in psychiatric perspective. UCLA Forum med Sci 1967, 7:267-296

68877 Information explosion—information retrieval. P 1965, 122:453-454

68878 Introduction. P 1969, 125, 7(Suppl):1-2

68879 (Ed) Lectures on Experimental Psychiatry. Pittsburgh Bicentennial Conference. Western Psychiatric Institute and Clinic, March 5-7, 1959. Pittsburgh: Univ Pitt Pr 1961, x + 361 p
Rv Schur, M. Q 1963, 32:260-266

68880 Linguistic-kinesic analysis using film and tape in a clinical setting. P 1966, 122(Suppl):33-37

68881 The management of the neurotic and emotionally disturbed patient. Chicago Med 1962, 65:13-17

68882 Obsessive-compulsive disorders. In Sills, D. L. *International Encyclopedia of the Social Sciences,* Vol. 11, NY: Macmillan & Free Pr 1968, 241-245

68883 Preface to Western Psychiatric Institute *Lectures on Experimental Psychiatry,* Pittsburgh: Univ of Pitt Pr 1961, v-vi

68884 Presidential address: Adaptation to the unknown. P 1968, 125:1-16

S-42974 The primary processes and psychoses.
Abs JLan An Surv Psa 1957, 8:31-32

68885 The problem and obligations of psychiatric research. In U.S. Veterans Administration *Cooperative Chemotherapy Studies in Psychiatry and Research Approaches to Mental Illness; Transactions, Vol. 5,* Washington, 1960, 236-241

68886 The psychology of appetite. In Wohl, M. G. & Goodhart, R. S. *Modern Nutrition in Health and Disease,* Phila: Lea & Febiger 1960, 82-95; (4th ed) 1968, 83-75

68887 Remarks. In *Memorial for William C. Menninger,* NY: Privately printed 1967, 36-39

68888 Response to the presidential address. P 1967, 124:7-8

68889 Shell shock. Encyclopedia Britannica 1967, 20:374

68890 Stress and adaptation; some unanswered questions. In *Stress and Adaptation, Part II: The Age of Anxiety; Guest Lecture Series, 1965-1966,* Des Plaines, Ill: Forest Hospital Foundation 1966, 32-40

68891 Studies in human communication in clinical settings using sound film and tape. Wisc med J 1964, 63:503-506

68892 Toward a more scientific study of human behavior and communication. Folia psychiat neurol Jap 1964, (Suppl 7):460-463

68893 Transition without precedent. Curr psychiat Ther 1967, 7:1-6

68894 Tribute to Franz Alexander. In *Franz Alexander, M.D., 1891-1964,* Chicago: Inst for Psa 1964, 14-20

S-42984 (Reporter) Validation of psychoanalytic theory.
Abs An Surv Psa 1955, 6:16-20, 66-67

68895 Vistas in psychotherapy. In Koskoff, Y. D. & Shoemaker, R. J. *Vistas in Neuropsychiatry,* Pittsburgh Neuropsychiatric Society: Univ Pitt Pr 1964, 95-122

68896 Ways in which state mental health agencies and colleges and univ-
ersities can collaborate in in-service training programs. In *Planning for
Comprehensive Inservice Training in a State Mental Health Program,*
Albany 1964, 50-59

See Barton Walter E.; Simmons, Leo W.

BROSS, RACHEL B.

68897 Termination of analytically oriented psychotherapy in groups. Int J
PT 1959, 9:326-337

BROSS, ROBERT

See Belinkoff, Julius

BROTMAN, RICHARD E.

See Freedman, Alfred M.

BROTMAN, SANFORD

See Mendel, Werner M.

BROTTO, M.

68898 Contributo allo studio dell'omosessualità nevrotica. Genesi e psicoterapia
di tre casi di omosessualità maschile. [Contribution to the study of
neurotic homosexuality. Genesis and psychotherapy of 3 cases of male
homosexuality.] Riv sper Freniat 1962, 86:277-341

BROUILLIOT, MAURICE

68899 (& Riggenbach, O.) L'utilisation de l'échelle de "Wittenborn" à l'hôpital psychiatrique. [The use of the "Wittenborn" scale in the psychiatric
hospital.] Schweiz ANP 1965, 95:205-207

BROUSSELLE, A.

See Danon-Boileau, Henri; Douady, D.

BROWER, BROCK

68900 Psychotherapy in America—the contemporary scene. In Rolo, C. J.
Psychiatry in American Life, Boston: Little, Brown 1963, 31-51
68901 Who's in among the analysts. Or how to tell one from the other *before*
you settle for the couch. Esquire 1961, 56(July):79-84

BROWN, A.

TRANSLATION OF:
Lély, G. [80419]

BROWN, B.

See Ravich, Robert A.

BROWN, BERT R.

See Deutsch, Martin

BROWN, CONSTANCE M.

68902 (& Ferguson, L. W.) Self-concept and religious belief. Psychol Rep 1968, 22:266

BROWN, DANIEL G.

68903 (& Young, A. J.) Body image and susceptibility to contact dermatitis. M 1965, 38:261-267
68904 Emotional disturbance in eczema: a study of symptom-reporting behaviour. J psychosom Res 1967, 11:27-40
68905 Psychosexual disturbances: transvestism and sex-role inversion. Marriage fam Liv 1960, 22:218-227

BROWN, DOROTHY

See Woodward, Katharine F.

BROWN, ELLIOT

See Blane, Howard T.

BROWN, F.

See Bernstein, Stanley; Zucker, Howard D.

BROWN, FELIX

68906 Bereavement and lack of a parent in childhood. In Miller, E. *Foundations of Child Psychiatry*, Oxford/NY: Pergamon Pr 1968, 435-455
68907 (& Epps, P.) Childhood bereavement and subsequent crime. Brit J Psychiat 1966, 112:1043-1048
68908 Childhood bereavement and subsequent psychiatric disorder. Brit J Psychiat 1966, 112:1035-1041
68909 Depression and childhood bereavement. JMS 1961, 107:754-777

BROWN, FRED

68910 The Bender Gestalt and acting out. Acting Out 320-332
68911 Clinical psychology. Compreh Txbk Psychiat 1618-1621
68912 How the clinical psychologist can help the nonpsychiatric physician. Med Clin N Amer 1967, 51:1477-1483
68913 (& Katz, H.; Kaufman, R.) The patient under study for cancer: a personality evaluation. PSM 1961, 23:166-171
    Abs JPG Q 1961, 30:603-604

See Meyer, Bernard C.

REVIEWS OF:
68914 Schafer, R. Projective Testing and Psychoanalysis. Selected Papers. Q 1968, 37:617
68915 Weiner, I. B. Psychodiagnosis in Schizophrenia. Q 1968, 37:144

BROWN, GEORGE W.

68916 (& Birley, J. L. T.) Crises and life changes and the onset of schizophrenia. J Health soc Behav 1968, 9:203-214

BROWN, HARRISON

* * * Foreword to Eiduson, B. T. *Scientists: Their Psychological World*, NY:
Basic Books 1962, v-vi

BROWN, JAMES ALEXANDER CAMPBELL

68917 Freud and the Post-Freudians. Baltimore, Md.: Penguin 1961; London:
Cassell 1963, viii + 227 p
68918 In defence of Freud. Discovery 1961, 22:495-499

BROWN, JAMES HENRY

68919 Homosexuality as an adaptation in handling aggression. J Louisiana
med Soc 1963, 115:304-311
68920 An uncommon type of transient loss of memory. Canad Med Ass J
1968, 98:878

BROWN, JANET L.

68921 Differential hand usage in three-year-old children. J genet Psych 1962,
100:167-175
68922 Follow-up of children with atypical development (infantile psychosis).
Ops 1963, 33:855-861
       Abs PS Q 1964, 33:610-611
68923 Prognosis from presenting symptoms of preschool children with atypical
development. Ops 1960, 30:382-390. In Palmer, J. O. & Goldstein,
M. J. *Perspectives in Psychopathology*, NY: Oxford Univ Pr 1966, 398-
405
       Abs JMa RFPsa 1962, 26:315
68924 States in newborn infants. Merrill-Palmer Q 1964, 10:313-327

       See Reiser, David E.

BROWN, JUDITH M.

       See Schwab, John J.

BROWN, L. B.

68925 (& Thouless, R. H.) Animistic thought in civilized adults. J genet Psych
1965, 107:33-42

BROWN, MARTHA MONTGOMERY

68926 (& Brown, P. R.; Glidewell, J. C.; Hunt, R. G.) Nurses, Patients and
Society Systems. (Ed: Weiss, J. M. A.) (Foreword: Redlich, F. C.)
Columbia, Mo: Univ Missouri Pr 1968, xx + 203 p
68927 (& Fowler, G. R.) Psychodynamic Nursing; A Biosocial Orientation.
2nd ed. Phila: Saunders 1961, 315 p

BROWN, NORMAN OLIVER

68928 Love's Body. NY: Random House 1966, 276 p
Rv HS Am Im 1966, 23:273-275

BROWN, O. H.

See Richek, H. G.

BROWN, PATRICIA R.

See Brown, Martha M.

BROWN, PAUL

See Schmidt, Elsa

BROWN, ROBERT G.

See Busse, Ewald W.

BROWN, SARA G.

See Polansky, Norman A.

BROWN, SAUL L.

68929 Clinical impressions of the impact of family group interviewing on child and adolescent psychiatric practice. J Amer Acad Child Psychiat 1964, 3:688-696
68930 Diagnosis, clinical management and family interviewing. Sci Psa 1969, 14:188-194
68931 Discussion of Selesnick, S. T. "Historical perspectives in the development of child psychiatry." Int J Psychiat 1967, 3:368-382

See Rogawski, Alexander S.; Tasem, Marjorie

BROWN, STUART L.

See Freedman, David A.

BROWN, SYDNEY

68932 (& Nyswander, M.) The treatment of masochistic adults. Ops 1956, 26:351-364

BROWN, THELMA E.

68933 An index for assessing levels of ego functioning based on homeostatic principles. Psychiat Dig 1966, 27:35-36 passim

BROWN, W. T.

See Cleghorn, Robert A.

BROWN, WILFRED

See Jaques, Elliott

BROWN, WILLIAM

68934 Psychology of personality. In *Source Book in Psychology*, NY: Philos Libr 1960, 150-164

See Ekstein, Rudolf

BROWN, WILLIAM PATERSON

68935 Further comments on perceptual defence. Brit J Psychol 1965, 56: 312-313

68936 The homosexual male: treatment in an out-patient clinic. In Rosen, I. *The Pathology and Treatment of Sexual Deviation,* London: Oxford Univ Pr 1964, 196-220

BROWNE, I.

See McCourt, William F.

BROWNE, IVOR W.

68937 American psychiatry and the cult of psychoanalysis. J Irish Med Ass 1964, 54:11-17

BROWNE, WILLIAM F.

68938 (& May, M. A.; Kane, R. P.) Psychosocial aspects of hemophilia: a study of twenty-eight hemophilic children and their families. Ops 1960, 30:730-740

Abs JMa RFPsa 1962, 26:320

BROWNE, WILLIAM J.

68939 The alcoholic bout as an acting out. Q 1965, 34:420-437

BROWNE-MAYERS, ALBERT NORDEMAN

68940 Push-pull psychotherapy. Dis nerv Sys 1966, 27(Suppl):66-67

See McKinley, Robert A.

BROWNFIELD, BERNARD

See Illing, Hans A.

BROWNFIELD, CHARLES ALLEN

68941 Hypnosis in sensory deprivation: a brief case report. Psychologia 1966, 9:215-216

BROWNING, THOMAS B.

See Kazan, Avraam T.

BROZOVSKY, M.

See Schneer, Henry I.

BRUCE, PAUL

68942   Three forces in psychology and their ethical and educational implications: classical psychoanalysis. Educ Forum 1966, 30:277-285

BRUCH, HILDE

68943   Activity in the psychotherapeutic process. Curr psychiat Ther 1962, 2:69-74

68944   Anorexia nervosa and its differential diagnosis. JNMD 1965, 141:555-566

68945   Changing approaches to the study of the family. Psychiat Res Rep 1966, 20:1-7

68946   Changing concepts on anorexia nervosa. Med Rec Rep 1966, 59:140-144; 181-186

68947   Conceptual confusion in eating disorders. JNMD 1961, 133:46-54

68948   (& Palombo, S. R.) Conceptual problems in schizophrenia. JNMD 1961, 132:114-117

   Abs Powelson, H. Q 1961, 30:606

68949   Cooperation between medical services in primary prevention. Acta paedopsychiat 1962, 29:356-358

S-43017 Developmental obesity and schizophrenia.

   Abs WCW An Surv Psa 1958, 9:203-204

68950   Disturbed communication in eating disorders. Ops 1963, 33:99-104. In Irving, F. & Powell, M. *Psychosomatic Ailments in Childhood and Adolescence*, Springfield, Ill: Thomas 1967, 90-99

   Abs PS Q 1964, 33:306. JMa RFPsa 1964, 28:449

68951   Disturbed hunger awareness. In *The Regulation of Food and Water Intake*, 1962

S-43018 Don't Be Afraid of Your Child.

   No le Tenga Miedo A Su Hijo. Buenos Aires: Guia de Padres Perplejos 1966, 293 p

68952   Eating disorders. Forest Hosp Publ 1962, 1:9-15

68953   Eating disorders and schizophrenic development. In Usdin, G. L. *Psychoneurosis and Schizophrenia*, Phila: J. B. Lippincott 1966, 113-124

68954   Effectiveness in psychotherapy or the constructive use of ignorance. Psychiat Q 1963, 37:332-339

   Abs Engle, B. Q 1964, 33:456

68955   The effects of modern psychiatric theories on our society—a psychiatrist's view. J existent Psychiat 1961, 2:213-232. Med Rec Ann 1965, 58:329-332; 367-370; 413-415

68956   (& Coddington, R. D.; Sours, J. A.) Electrogastrographic findings associated with affective changes. P 1964, 121:41-44

68957   The experience of reality in childhood schizophrenia. JNMD 1964, 138:196-197

68958   (& Palombo, S. R.) Falling apart: the verbalization of ego failure. Ps 1964, 27:248-258

68959   Falsification of bodily needs and body concept in schizophrenia. Arch gen Psychiat 1962, 6:18-24. Proc 3rd World Cong Psychiat 1962, 2:1117-1119

   Abs KR Q 1963, 32:140

68960   How psychology can help the overweight patient. Physician's Pano-
        rama 1966, 4:4-10
68961   Hunger and instinct. JNMD 1969, 149:91-114
68962   The insignificant difference: discordant incidence of anorexia nervosa
        in monozygotic twins. P 1969, 126:85-90
68963   (& Thum, L. C.) Maladie des tics and maternal psychosis. JNMD
        1968, 146:446-456
68964   Mass murder: the Wagner case. P 1967, 124:693-698
68965   Obesity. In Irving, F. & Powell, M. *Psychosomatic Ailments in Child-
        hood and Adolescence,* Springfield, Ill: Thomas 1967, 103-123. In
        Sills, D. L. *International Encyclopedia of the Social Sciences,* NY:
        Macmillan & Free Pr 1968, 227-232
68966   Obesity and orality. Contempo Psa 1969, 5(2):129-144
68967   Obesity and overnutrition. In Gellis, S. S. & Kagan, B. M. *Current
        Pediatric Therapy,* Phila: Saunders 1964, 2-3
68968   Obesity in adolescence. In Caplan, G. & Lebovici, S. *Adolescence,* NY:
        Basic Books 1969, 213-225
68969   100 years of psychiatry (Kraepelin)—50 years later. Arch gen Psychiat
        1969, 21:257-261
68970   Overnutrition and obesity. In Holt, M. & Barnett, P. *Pediatrics* 1962,
        255-258
68971   The overprivileged delinquent. Folia psychiat neurol Jap 1964, (Suppl
        7):226
68972   Perceptual and conceptual distrubances in anorexia nervosa. PSM
        1962, 24:187-194
            Abs RDT Q 1962, 31:588-589
68973   Perturbations neuropsychiques et obésité. In *Extrait de L'Obésité,*
        Paris: Expansion Scientifique 1963, 176-179
            Neuro-psychological disturbances in obesity. Psychiat Dig 1966, 27:
            37-41
68974   Present concepts of schizophrenia, formal discussion. Folia psychiat
        neurol Jap 1964, (Suppl 7):294
68975   Prognosis and treatment of obesity from a psychiatrist's point of view.
        J Amer Wom Med Ass 1964, 19:745-749
            French: Probl Actuel Endocr Nutr 1963, 7:319-326
68976   The psychiatric differential diagnosis of anorexia nervosa. In *Anorexia
        Nervosa* (Symposium, Gottingen 24-25 April 1965), Stuttgart: Thieme
        70-87
68977   Psychological aspects of overeating and obesity. Psychosomatics 1964,
        5:269-274
68978   (& Rosenkotter, L.) Psychotherapeutic aspects of teaching emotion-
        ally disturbed children. Psychiat Q 1960, 34:648-657
68979   Psychotherapeutic problems in eating disorders. R 1963, 50:573-587
            Abs SRS Q 1964, 33:608
68980   Psychotherapy in obesity. Curr psychiat Ther 1968, 8:63-69
68981   Psychotherapy with schizophrenics. Int Psychiat Clin 1964, 1:863-890.
        Arch gen Psychiat 1966, 14:346-351
            Abs PB Q 1969, 38:167
68982   Social and emotional factors in diet changes. J Amer Dent Assoc 1961,
        63:461-465. Nutrition News 1963, 26:13-14

68983 Some comments on talking and listening in psychotherapy. Ps 1961, 24:269-272

68984 Symposium on obesity. Feelings 1960, 2(8)

68985 Transformation of oral impulses in eating disorders: a conceptual approach. Psychiat Q 1961, 35:458-481
Abs Engle, B. Q 1962, 31:587-588

68986 Treatment of obesity (overnutrition). In Shirkey, H. C. *Pediatric Therapy*, St. Louis: C. V. Mosby Co 1964, 235-240
Psychotherapie der kindlichen Fettsucht. Hbh Kinderpsychother 935-942

68987 Über die psychologischen Aspekte der Fettleibigkeit. Med Klin 1960, 55:295-300
Psychological aspects of obesity. In *From Occurrence, Causes and Prevention of Overnutrition*, Stockholm, Sweden: Almquist & Wiksell 1964, 37-46. Med Rec Ann 1965, 58:187-192

See Palombo, Stanley R.

BRÜCKNER, PETER

68988 Die grosse Freud-Biographie. [The major Freud biography.] Psyche 1961, 14:881-894

68989 (Ed) Psychoanalyst. [Psychoanalysis.] Frankfurt: Europ Verlagsanstalt 1968, 112 p

68990 Sigmund Freuds Privatlekture. [Sigmund Freud's private reading list.] Psyche 1962, 15:881-902; 16:721-743; 1963, 16:881-895
Abs IBa RFPsa 1964, 28:462

68991 Zur gesellschaftlichen Biographie Sigmund Freuds: die Genese seiner sozialen Ideen. [On the societal biography of Sigmund Freud: the genesis of his social ideas.] Psyche 1963, 17:801-814

BRÜEL, OLUF

68992 Integritätskomplex und zwangsneurose. Über die psychischen Zusammenhänge bei einigen sogennanten zwangsneurotischen Charaktereigenschaften, dargestellt anhand von Bruckstücken einer 3 jährigen analytischen Psychotherapie. [Integrity complex and compulsive neurosis. On the psychological correlates of various so-called compulsive neurotic character traits, described with the aid of fragments of a 3-year analytic psychotherapy.] Z Psychother med Psychol 1963, 13:127-133

BRUGGER, THOMAS CARL

68993 (& Caesar, G. R.; Frank, A.; Marty, S. C.) Peer supervisor as a method of learning psychotherapy. Comprehen Psychiat 1962, 3:47-53

BRUGHERA, F.

68994 (& Bianchi, Z.) [Comparison of the psychomotor development of children deprived of maternal care with that of children raised by mothers and by mother substitutes.] (It) Lattante 1965, 36:85-89

BRUGMANN, ANNE M.

See Fernandez Cerdeño, A.

BRUGMANS, HENRI F.

TRANSLATION OF:
Ellenberger, H. F. [72100]

BRÜLL, F.

68995 The trauma—theoretical considerations. Israel Ann Psychiat 1969, 7:96-108

BRULL, H. FRANK

68996 Beatnik. Psa Forum 1967, 2:379

BRUN, RUDOLF

S-43048 Die biologischen Grundlagen der Übertragung.
     Abs An Surv Psa 1955, 6:318
68997 Die Freud'sche Psychoanalyse als Verhaltensforschung beim Menschen. [Freudian psychoanalysis as human behavior research.] Psyche 1961, 15:306-321
68998 Psychoanalytische Behandlung und Heilung eines Schreibkrampfes verbunden mit Steifigkeit und Paraesthesien in den Armen. [Psychoanalytic treatment and cure of writer's cramp associated with stiffness and paresthesia in the arms.] Acta psychother psychosom 1964, 12:382-390
68999 Die Schädel- und Hirnverletzung. [Skull and Brain Damage.] Bern/Stuttgart: Huber 1963

See Zimmermann, David

BRUNER, E. M.

See Ross, Alan O.

BRUNER, JEROME SEYMOUR

S-43064 (et al) Contemporary Approaches to Cognition.
     Rv Holt, R. R. J Am Psa Ass 1964, 12:650-665
S-43065 Freud and the image of man. In author's On Knowing, 149-158
     Abs AEC An Surv Psa 1956, 7:19
69000 On Knowing; Essays for the Left Hand. Cambridge, Mass: Harvard Univ Pr 1962; NY: Atheneum 1965, 165 p
69001 (& Kenney, H. J.) Representation and mathematical learning. Monogr Soc Res child Develop 1965, 30:50-59
69002 (& Olver, R. R.; Greenfield, P. M., et al) Studies in Cognitive Growth; a Collaboration at the Center for Cognitive Studies. NY: Wiley 1966, xviii + 343 p
69003 (& Goodnow, J. J.; Austin, G. A.) A Study of Thinking. NY: Wiley 1956, xii + 330 p; NY: Sci Ed 1962, 321 p
     Rv Holt, R. R. J Am Psa Ass 1964, 12:650-665

BRUNNER, CORNELIA

69004 Die Anima als Schicksalsproblem des Mannes. [Anima as Man's Problem of Fate.] Zürich: Rascher 1963, 331 p

BRUNO, ANTONIO

69005 Note sulla teoria psicoanalitica dei deliri. [A note on the psychoanalytic theory of mental illness.] Riv Psa 1961, 7:53-62
69006 La psicodinamica sperimentale nei suoi aspetti metodologici. [Experimental psychodynamics in its methodological aspects.] Riv Psa 1961, 7:133-142

BRUNO, NELSON

69007 (& Tanco Duque, R.) ¿Puede sustituir la terapia analitica de grupo al psicoanálisis individual? [Can analytic group therapy be substituted for individual psychoanalysis?] Arch Estud psicoanal Psicol med 1967, 4:115-124

BRUNSWICK, DAVID

S-43070 A comment on E. Servadio's "A presumptive telepathic-precognitive dream during analysis."
    Abs SLP An Surv Psa 1957, 8:178
69008 The drives and affects. (Read at Los Angeles Psa Soc, 18 Mar 1965)
    Abs RZ Bull Phila Ass Psa 1965, 15:244-246
* * * (& Lachenbruch, R.) Introduction to *Freud's Letters to Ernst Simmel.*
69009 Le point de vue physiologique. [The physiological point of view.] RFPsa 1961, 25:741-746

    See Deri, Frances

BRUNSWICK, RUTH MACK

S-4700F The preoedipal phase of the libido development.
    La phase préoedipienne du développement de la libido. RFPsa 1967, 31:267-291

BRUNT, M. Y.

    See Pulver, Sydney E.

BRUSSEL, JAMES ARNOLD

69010 (& Cantzlaar, G. L.) The Layman's Dictionary of Psychiatry. NY: Barnes & Noble 1967, xiv + 269 p
    Rv Woltmann, A. G. R 1969-70, 56:648-649
69011 The Layman's Guide to Psychiatry. What You Should Know About Nervous Tension, Emotional Problems and Mental Illness. (Preface: Hoch, P. H.) NY: Barnes & Noble 1961, xi + 235 p
    Rv Woltmann, A. G. R 1969-70, 56:648-649

BRY ILSE

69012 (& Afflerbach, L.) Bibliographical challenges in the age of the computer; excerpts from editorial. Libr J 1965, 90:813-818

69013 (& Rifkin, A. H.) Freud and the history of ideas: primary sources, 1886-1910. Sci Psa 1962, 5:6-36

69014 (& Afflerbach, L.) In search of an organizing principle for the behavioral science literature. Comm ment Hlth J 1968, 4:75-84

See Bayne, Helen

BRY, THEA

See Leser, Louis S.; Loesch, John G.; Loesser, Lewis H.

BRYAN, DOUGLAS

TRANSLATION OF:
(& Strachey, A.) Abraham, K. [65094]

BRYAN, L. L.

See Lipton, H. R.

BRYANT, CHARLES MARTEL

69015 (& Grunebaum, H. U.) The theory and practice of the family diagnostic. I. Practical aspects and patient evaluation. Psychiat Res Rep 1966, No. 20:140-149

See Grunebaum, Henry U.

BRYANT, K.

See Ramzy, Ishak

BRYANT, KEITH N.

69016 (& Hirschberg, J. C.) Helping the parents of a retarded child. The role of the physician. Amer J Dis Childr 1961, 102:52-66

69017 Some clinical notes on reading disability. A case report. BMC 1964, 28:323-338

    Abs McGowan, L. Q 1966, 35:468-469

See Ekstein, Rudolf

BRYDONE, GILLIAN

TRANSLATION OF:
Thomä, H. [93140]

BRYER, JACKSON R.

69018 A psychiatrist reviews *Tender is the Night*. Lit & Psych 1966, 16:198-199

BRYGOO, F.

See Shentoub, S. A.

BRYT, ALBERT

69019 Discussion of Cohen, S. B. "Rebel and reactionary, siblings under the skin?" Sci Psa 1968, 13:52-55

69020 Discussion of Wolberg, A. & Lawson, E. P. "The goals of community mental health consultation." Sci Psa 1965, 8:259-261

69021 Dropout of adolescents from psychotherapy: failure in communication. In Caplan, G. & Lebovici, S. *Adolescence,* NY/London: Basic Books 1969, 293-303

69022 Modifications of psychoanalysis in the treatment of adolescents. Sci Psa 1966, 9:80-90

BUĆAN, N.

See Betlheim, Stjepan; Persic, N.

BUCHANAN, R. F.

69023 (& Ripley, H. S.) Religiosity and paranoid schizophrenia. Amer Psychiat Ass Summ 1964:169-170

BUCHENHOLZ, BRUCE

S-43081 Models for pleasure.
Abs ARK An Surv Psa 1958, 9:83-84

69024 Program therapy with adolescents. Curr psychiat Ther 1964, 4:79-82

See Barish, Julian I.

BUCHER-ANDLAUER

See Bauer, J.-P.

BUCHSBAUM, M.

See Henkin, R.

BÜCHSENSCHÜTZ, BERNHARD

69025 Traum und Traumdeutung im Alterthume. [Dream and Dream Interpretation in Antiquity.] Wiesbaden: Sändig 1967, 94 p

BUCHWALT, N. A.

See Lesse, Henry

BUCKEY, C.

See Offenkrantz, William

BUCKLE, DONALD F.

69026 (& Lebovici, S.) Les Centres de Guidance Infantile. Geneva, Switzerland: O. M. S. 1958, 133 p
Child Guidance Centers. Geneva: WHO 1960, 133 p

69027 (& Lebovici, S.) The child in the family. WHO PH Pap 1965, 28:34-40

69028 Child psychiatry and the World Health Organization. In Miller, E. *Foundations for Child Psychiatry,* Oxford/NY: Pergamon Pr 1968, 3-8

69029   Mental health services for adolescents—an introduction. In Caplan, G.
        & Lebovici, S. *Adolescence,* NY/London: Basic Books 1969, 363-371
69030   (& Lebovici, S.; Tizard, J.) Le traitement des enfants placés en insti-
        tution en Europe. [Treatment of institutionalized children in Europe.]
        Psychiat Enfant 1964, 7:497-546
           Stationäre Kinderpsychiatrische Behandlung in Europa. Prax Kinder-
        psychol 1965, 14:17-25; 69-77

BUCKLE, R. C.

See McConaghy, N.

BUCKLEW, JOHN

69031   Paradigms for Psychopathology: A Contribution to Case History Analy-
        sis. Phila: Lippincott 1960, xii + 236 p

BUCKMAN, JOHN

69032   LSD in the psychotherapy of psychosomatic disorders. The nature of
        unconscious material produced. In Shlien, J. M. et al: *Research in
        Psychotherapy, Vol. III,* Wash DC: APA 1968, 425-448
69033   Theoretical aspects of L.S.D. therapy. Int J soc Psychiat 1967, 13:126-
        138

BUCOVE, ARNOLD DAVID

69034   Postpartum psychoses in the male. Bull NY Acad Med 1964, 40:961-
        971

BUDA, B.

69034A [Homosexuality.] (Hun) Orv Hetil 1969, 110:2137-2145

BUDDEN, JULIAN

69035   Music on the couch: a study in analysis. Music & Musicians 1963,
        11(March):14-16

BUELL, FRANK ANDREW

69036   School phobia. Dis nerv Sys 1962, 23(2):79-64

BUGENTAL, JAMES F. T.

69037   The challenge that is man. In author's *Challenges of Humanistic Psy-
        chology* 5-11
69038   (Ed) Challenges of Humanistic Psychology. NY/Toronto/London: Mc-
        Graw-Hill 1967, xiv + 362 p
69039   (et al) Contribuciones de Karl Bühler a la psicología. [Contributions of
        Karl Bühler to psychology.] Rev de Psicología General y Aplicada
        1969, 24:240-287
69040   A critique of Peter Koestenbaum's "The Vitality of Death." J existent
        Psychiat 1964-65, 5:433-436
69041   The Existential Orientation in Intensive Psychotherapy: Workshop in
        Clinical Psychology, Arizona State Univ, April 1963. Los Angeles,
        Calif: Psychol Service Ass 1963, 63 p

69042 Humanistic psychology and the clinician. Prog clin Psych 1966, 7:223-239

69043 The nature of the therapeutic task in intensive psychotherapy. J existent Psychiat 1964-65, 5:199-204

69044 The person who is the psychotherapist. J consult Psychol 1964, 28:272-277

69045 Psychodiagnostics and the quest for certainty. Ps 1964, 27:73-77

69046 The Search for Authenticity: An Existential Analytic Approach to Psychotherapy. NY: Holt, Rinehart & Winston 1965, xix + 437 p

69047 (Participant) Symposium on Karl Bühler's contributions to psychology. J gen Psychol 1966, 75:181-219

69048 The third force in psychology. J humanist Psychol 1964, 4:19-25

69049 Values and existential unity. In Bühler, C. & Massarik, F. *The Course of Human Life*, NY: Springer 1968, 383-392

BUGGLE, FRANZ

69050 (& Wirtgen, P.) Gustav Theodor Fechner und die psychoanalytischen Modellvorstellungen Sigmund Freuds: Einflüsse und Parallelen. [Gustav Theodor Fechner and Sigmund Freud's psychoanalytic conceptual models: influences and parallels.] Archiv für die gesamte Psychologie 1969, 121(2-4):148-201

BÜHLER, CHARLOTTE

69051 Aiding the patient to find his identity and the values consonant with it. Psychotherapy 1965, 2:89-91

69052 (& Marschak, M.) Basic tendencies of human life. In author's *The Course of Human Life*, 92-102

69053 Considerations about the role of values and beliefs in human life. J existent Psychiat 1961-62, 2:147-174

69054 (& Massarik, F.) (Eds) The Course of Human Life—A Study of Goals in the Humanistic Perspective. NY: Springer 1968, ix + 422 p

69055 The course of human life as a psychological problem. Hum Develpm 1968, 11(3):184-200

69056 The developmental structure of goal setting in group and individual studies. In author's *The Course of Human Life* 27-54

69057 Early environmental influences on goal setting. In author's *The Course of Human Life* 173-188

69058 (& Horner, A. J.) Existential and humanistic psychology: a hope for the future in philosophy, psychotherapy, and research. Int Psychiat Clin 1969, 6(3):55-73

69059 Fulfillment and failure of life. In author's *The Course of Human Life* 400-403

69060 The general structure of the human life cycle. In author's *The Course of Human Life* 12-26

69061 Genetic aspects of the self. Ann NY Acad Sci 1962, 96:730-764

69062 Goals of life and therapy. Psa 1962, 22:153-175

69063 Human life as a whole as a central subject of humanist psychology. In Bugental, J. F. T. *Challenges of Humanistic Psychology*, NY/Toronto/London: McGraw-Hill 1967, 83-91

69064 The integrating self. In author's *The Course of Human Life* 330-350
* * * Introduction to author's *The Course of Human Life* 1-10
69065 (& Brind, A.; Horner, A. J.) Old age as a phase of human life: questionnaire study. Hum Develpm 1968, 11:53-63
69066 (& Spitz, R.) Probleme der Interaktion von Anlage und Umwelt. Ein Diskussion zwischen Charlotte Bühler und René Spitz. [Problems of the interaction between hereditary factors and environment. A discussion between Charlotte Bühler and René Spitz.] Psyche 1968, 22: 143-152
69067 Psychologie im Leben unserer Zeit.
       Psychology for Contemporary Living (Tr: Bernays, H. F.) NY: Hawthorn Books 1969, xvi + 334 p
69068 Rélation de la psychothérapie et de la psychologie sous le rapport du concept de normalité et de santé. [Relation of psychotherapy and psychology in respect to the concept of normality and health.] Rev Psychol appl 1961, 11:103-104
69069 (& Horner, A. J.) The role of education in the goal-setting process. In author's *The Course of Human Life* 231-245
69070 (& Goldenberg, H.) Structural aspects of the individual's history. In author's *The Course of Human Life* 54-63
69071 Therapy in an existential crisis. In Moustakas, C. *Existential Child Therapy*, NY: Basic Books 1966, 102-118
69072 Values in Psychotherapy. (Pref: Stainbrook, E. J.) NY: Free Pr of Glencoe 1962, v + 251 p
       Japanese: Tokyo: Charles E. Tuttle 1962
       Swedish: Stockholm: Natur Och Kultur 1968
       Rv Linn, L. Q 1964, 33:119-120. Wohl, J. R 1964, 51(1):164-165
69073 Die Wiener Psychologische Schule in der Emigration. [The Vienna School of psychology in exile.] Psychol Rdsch 1965, 16:187-196

BUICK, DAVID

See Stroh, George

BUIS, C.

69074 A child's spectacles as fetish. Psychiat Neurol Neurochir 1966, 69:359-362
69075 Oedipus, Dionysus and Eros. Psychiat Neurol Neurochir 1964, 67: 427-438

BULL, JAMES

See Hunter, Richard A.

BULLARD, DEXTER M.

69076 Discussion of Frank, J. D. "Relief of distress and attitudinal change." Sci Psa 1961, 4:121-124
69077 Psychotherapy of paranoid patients. Arch gen Psychiat 1960, 2:137-141

See Artiss, Kenneth L.

BULLARD, DEXTER M., JR.

69078 (& Glaser, H. H.; Geagarty, M. C.; Pivchik, E. C.) Failure to thrive in the "neglected" child. Ops 1967, 37:680-690

69079 (& Hoffman, B. R.; Havens, L. L.) The relative value of tranquilizing drugs and social and psychological therapies in chronic schizophrenia. Psychiat Q 1960, 34:293-306

ABSTRACT OF:

69080 Fraiberg, S. Repression and repetition in child analysis. Bull Phila Ass Psa 1967, 17:99-106

BULLITT, WILLIAM CHRISTIAN

See Freud, Sigmund

BULLOCK, MICHAEL

TRANSLATION OF:
Worringer, W. [95445]

BUMMER, BARRY

69081 (& Rosenthal, R.) Anxiety level and the retention of neutral and affectively toned verbal material. J proj Tech 1963, 27:47-50

BUNNERY, W. E.

See Schiff, Sheldon K.

BUNNEY, WILLIAM EDWARD

69082 (& Hamburg, D. A.) Methods for reliable longitudinal observation of behavior. Development of a method for systematic observation of emotional behavior on psychiatric wards. Arch gen Psychiat 1963, 9:280-294

BUNTING, MARY

69083 Discussion of Kross, A. M. "Woman's role." Sci Psa 1966, 10:127-129

BUNZEL, RUTH LEAH

See Mead, Margaret

BURACK, JOSEPH

See Kanter, Stanley S.

BURBANK, JAN

See Straus, Jessie H.

BURCH, JOHN E.

69084 Hostility and interpersonal relationships. Winnipeg clin Quart 1964, 17:93-102

BURCHARD, EDWARD M. L.

S-43120 The evolution of psychoanalytic tasks and goals.
Abs WCW An Surv Psa 1958, 9:14-15

69085 Mystical and scientific aspects of the psychoanalytic theories of Freud, Adler, and Jung. PT 1960, 14:289-307

69086 Obituary: Dr. Lawrence W. Kaufman. Contemp Psa 1969, 5(2):180-181

S-43121 Psychoanalysis, cultural history and art.
Abs JLan An Surv Psa 1958, 9:467-468

BURCHARD, JOHANN M.

69087 Struktur und Soziologie des Transvestitismus und Transsexualismus. [Structure of sociology of transvestism and transsexualism.] B Sexfschg 1961, (21):1-69

69088 Vergleichende Psychopathologie. [Comparative psychopathology.] Nervenarzt 1966, 37:388-394

BURDON, ARTHUR PEMBERTON

69089 (& Neely, J. H.) Chronic school failure in boys: a short-term group therapy and educational approach. P 1966, 122:1211-1219

69090 (& Neely, J. H.; Thorpe, A. L.) Emotionally disturbed boys failing in school: treatment in an outpatient clinic school. Southern med J 1964, 57:829-835

69091 (& Ryan, W.) Group therapy as primary treatment in an outpatient setting. Curr psychiat Ther 1963, 3:229-233

BURGER, MARTHE

69092 L'organisation orale chez une hystérique cleptomane. [Oral makeup in an hysterical kleptomaniac.] RFPsa 1962, 26:423-446

BÜRGER-PRINZ, H.

69093 Über Antriebe. [On impulses.] In Kranz, H. *Psychopathologie Heute,* Stuttgart: Georg Thieme 1962, 49-52

BURGESS, ANN C.

69094 Depressive and aggressive behavior: intervention techniques used in resolving adolescent conflicts: a descriptive clinical case study in nursing therapy. Diss Abstr 1967, 28(3-B):960

BURGESS, C. F.

69095 The seeds of art: Henry James' *Donnée.* Lit & Psych 1963, 13:67-73

BURGUM, EDWIN BERRY

69096 Freud and fantasy in contemporary fiction. Sci & Soc 1965, 29:224-231

REVIEWS OF:
69097 Crews, F. C. The Sins of the Fathers: Hawthorne's Psychological Themes. Am Im 1966, 23:367-374

69098 Holland, N. N. The Dynamics of Literary Response. Am Im 1969, 26:79-82
69099 Weiss, D. A. Oedipus in Nottingham: D. H. Lawrence. Am Im 1966, 23:180-183

BURK, E. D.

See Powles, William E.

BURKE, JOAN L.

69100 (& Lee, H.) An acting-out patient in a psychotic group. Int J grp PT 1964, 14:194-201

BURKE, KENNETH

69101 Caldwell: maker of grotesques. In Malin, I. *Psychoanalysis and American Fiction*, NY: Dutton 1965
69102 Freud—and the analysis of poetry. In author's *The Philosophy of Literary Form* 258-292. In Ruitenbeek, H. M. *Psychoanalysis and Literature*, NY: Dutton 1964, 114-141
69103 Language as Symbolic Action: Essays on Life, Literature, and Method. Berkeley: Univ of Calif Pr 1966, xiv + 514 p
69104 Mind, body, and the unconscious. In author's *Language as Symbolic Action* 63-80
69105 On the first three chapters of genesis. In May, R. *Symbolism in Religion and Literature*, NY: Braziller 1960, 118-151
69106 Permanence and Change; an Anatomy of Purpose. Indianapolis: Bobbs-Merrill 1965 (2nd rev ed)
69107 The Philosophy of Literary Form; Studies in Symbolic Action (2nd ed). Baton Rouge: Louisiana State Univ Pr 1967, xxvi + 455 p
69108 The Rhetoric of Religion: Studies in Logology. Boston: Beacon Pr 1961, vi + 327 p
69109 The thinking of the body. Comments on the imagery of catharsis in literature. R 1963, 50:375-413. In author's *Language as Symbolic Action* 308-343
        Abs SRS Q 1964, 33:605

BURKHARDT, H.

69110 Das erotische Verhältnis zur Wirklichkeit. [The erotic relationship to reality.] Nervenarzt 1968, 39:56-62
69111 Die Inkorporation als Urphänomen des Sichfühlens und der Partnerschaft. [The incorporation of self-sentiment and partnership as primordial phenomenon.] Nervenarzt 1966, 37:246-252
69112 Die schizophrene Wehrlosigkeit. [Schizophrenic defenselessness.] Nervenarzt 1962, 33:306-312

BURKS, HENRY L.

69113 (& Harrison, S. I.) Aggressive behavior as a means of avoiding depression. Ops 1962, 32:416-422
        Abs RLG Q 1963, 32:137

69114 (& Hoekstra, M.) Psychiatric emergencies in children. Ops 1964, 34:
134-137
69115 (& Good, J. A.; Higginbotham, E. S.; Hoffman, C. A.) Treatment of
language lags in a psychotherapeutic nursery school. J Educ 1967,
1(2):197-206

See Finch, Stuart M.; Harrison, Saul I.

BURLINGAME, ROGER

69116 The analyst's couch and the creative mind. In Rudman, H. W. &
Rosenthal, I. A *Contemporary Reader*, NY: Ronald 1961, 313-319

BURLINGHAM, DOROTHY T.

69117 Developmental considerations in the occupations of the blind. Psa St
C 1967, 22:187-198
69118 Discussion of Greenacre, P. & Winnicott, D. L. "The theory of the
parent-infant relationship. Further remarks." J 1962, 43:254
S-4886 Die Einfühlung des Kleinkindes in die Mutter.
Empathy between infant and mother. J Am Psa Ass 1967, 15:764-
780
69119 Hearing and its role in the development of the blind. Psa St C 1964,
19:95-112
S-4889 Kinderanalyse und Mutter. In Bittner, G. & Rehm, W. *Psychoanalyse
und Erziehung*, Bern/Stuttgart: Hans Huber 1964. Hbh Kinderpsychother 631-637.
Child analysis and the mother. In Haworth, M. R. *Child Psychotherapy*, NY/London: Basic Books 1964, 70-76
69120 Occupations and toys for blind children. (Read at Int Psa Cong, July
1967) J 1968, 49:477-480
S-4894 Probleme des psychoanalytischen Erziehers. In Bittner, G. & Rehm, W.
Psychoanalyse und Erziehung, Bern/Stuttgart: Hans Huber 1964
69121 (& Goldberger, A.) The re-education of a retarded blind child. (Read
at Am Psa Ass for Ch Analysis, 20 Apr 1968) Psa St C 1968, 23:369-
385
S-43135 (& Goldberger, A.; Lussier, A.) Simultaneous analysis of mother and
child.
Abs An Surv Psa 1955, 6:279-283
69122 Some notes on the development of the blind. Psa St C 1961, 16:121-145
69123 Some problems of ego development in blind children. Psa St C 1965,
20:194-208
69124 (& Barron, A. T.) A study of identical twins, their analytic material
compared with existing observation data of their early childhood. Psa
St C 1963, 18:367-423
S-4897 Twins—a gang in miniature.
Zwillinge—eine Bande im Kleinen. In Bolterauer, L. *Aus der Werkstatt des Erziehungsberaters*, Vienna: Verlag Jugend & Volk 1960,
47-51

BURN, J.

See Barnett, Samuel A.

BURNELL, GEORGE M.

69125 (& Solomon, G. F.) Early memories and ego function. Arch gen Psychiat 1964, 11:556-567

BURNER, MARCEL

See Schneider, Pierre-Bernard; Weinstein, Glorice

BURNHAM, DONALD L.

69126 Autonomy and activity-passivity in the psychotherapy of a schizophrenic man. In Burton, A. *Psychotherapy of the Psychoses*, NY: Basic Books 1961, 208-236

69127 Identity definition and role demand in the hospital careers of schizophrenic patients. Ps 1961, 24(Suppl 2):96-122

69128 (& Gladstone, A. I.) Method of studying the relationship between pathological excitement and hidden staff disagreement. Ps 1966, 29: 339-343

69129 The need-fear dilemma in August Strindberg's object relations. (Abs) Bull Los Angeles Psa Soc Inst 1969, 6(1)

69130 Schizophrenia. In Conn, H. F. *Current Therapy*, Phila: W. B. Saunders 1967, 632-635

69131 (& Gladstone, A. I.; Gibson, R. W.) Schizophrenia and the Need-Fear Dilemma. NY: IUP 1969, 488 p

69132 Separation anxiety. A factor in the object relations of schizophrenic patients. Arch gen Psychiat 1965, 13:346-358

S-43150 Some problems in communication with schizophrenic parents.
         Abs An Surv Psa 1955, 6:189-190

69133 The special-problem patient: victim or agent of splitting. Ps 1966, 29:105-122

BURNHAM, JOHN CHYNOWETH

S-43151 The beginnings of psychoanalysis in the United States.
         Abs AS An Surv Psa 1956, 7:40-41

69134 Psychoanalysis and American Medicine, 1894-1918: Medicine, Science and Culture. (Psychol Issues 5 (4) Monogr 20) NY: IUP 1968, vi + 250 p
         Abs J Am Psa Ass 1969, 17:274-275. Rv Padel, J. H. J 1969, 50:254-256

BURNS, EDWARD M.

69135 Psychological foundations of political theory. In author's *Ideas in Conflict*. NY: Norton 1960, 387-425

BURNS, MARY E.

69136 (& Glasser, P. H.) Similarities and differences in casework and group work practice. Social S R 1963, 37:416-428

BURNS, PAUL

TRANSLATION OF:
Meseguer, P. [83650]

BURNYEAT, J. P.

69137 Mental health insights in literature. I. MH 1966, 50:184-185

BURRILL, DONALD R.

69138 The notion of reality in Freud's analysis of religion. Med Arts Sci 1965, 19:8-19

BURROW, TRIGANT

69139 Preconscious Foundations of Human Experience. (Ed: Galt, W. E.) (Foreword: Ackerman, N. W.) NY: Basic Books 1964, xxvi + 164 p

BURSTEIN, ALVIN G.

69140 Some verbal aspects of primary process thought in schizophrenia. ASP 1961, 62:155-157

See Chapman, Loren J.; Miller, Arthur A.; Muslin, Hyman L.

BURSTEN, BEN

69141 Family dynamics and illness behavior. GP 1964, 29:142-145
69142 (& D'Esopo, R.) The obligation to remain sick. Arch gen Psychiat 1965, 12:402-407
69143 On Munchausen's syndrome. Arch gen Psychiat 1965, 13:261-268
69144 (& Russ, J. J.) Preoperative psychological state and corticosteroid levels of surgical patients. PSM 1965, 27:309-316
69145 The psychiatric consultant and the nurse. Nurs Forum 1963, 2:7-23

BURSTIN, JACQUES

69146 Désagrégation, régression et reconstruction dans la schizophrénie. [Aggression, Regression and Reconstruction in schizophrenia.] Toulouse: Editions Privat, n. d.
        Abs Auth RFPsa 1964, 28:625

BURT, CYRIL

69147 Baudoin on Jung. Brit J Psychol 1964, 55:477-484
69148 Brain and consciousness. Brit J Psychol 1968, 59:55-69
69149 The concept of consciousness. Brit J Psychol 1962, 53:229-242
69150 The concept of mind. J psychol Res, Madras 1960, 4:54-64
69151 Logical positivism and the concept of consciousness. Brit J statis Psychol 1960, 13(1):55-77

BURSTEIN, EUGENE

See Moulton, Robert W.

BURT, V.

See Stunkard, Albert J.

BURTON, ARTHUR

69152 Beyond the transference. Psychotherapy 1964, 1:49-53
69153 (& Harris, R. E.) (Eds) Clinical Studies of Personality, Vol. II. NY: Harper & Row 1966, v + 469 p
69154 The clinician as moralist. J existent Psychiat 1960, 1:207-218
69155 A commentary on the problem of human identity. J existent Psychiat 1965, 5:257-263
69156 Death as a countertransference. PPR 1962, 49(4):3-20
       Abs HL Q 1963, 32:610-611. Ekboir, J. G. de Rev Psicoanál 1964, 21:80
69157 Existential conceptions in John Hersey's novel: *The Child Buyer*. J existent Psychiat 1961-62, 2:243-258
69158 The meaning of psychotherapy. J existent Psychiat 1967, 7:49-64
69159 Modern Humanistic Psychotherapy. San Francisco: Jossey-Bass 1967, xvi + 171 p
69160 (Ed) Modern Psychotherapeutic Practice: Innovations in Technique. Palo Alto: Sci & Behav Books 1965, xi + 399 p
69161 The moment in psychotherapy. Psa 1960, 20:41-48
69162 On the nature of loneliness. Psa 1961, 21:34-39
69163 The psychotherapy of a non-diseased person. In author's *Modern Psychotherapeutic Practice* 381-399
69164 (Ed) Psychotherapy of the Psychoses. NY: Basic Books 1961, viii + 386 p
       Rv Rosenfeld, H. J 1962, 43:184-188
69165 The quest for the golden mean: a study in schizophrenia. In author's *Psychotherapy of the Psychoses* 172-207
69166 Schizophrenia and existence. Ps 1960, 23:385-394
69167 Therapeutic interruption: planned and unplanned. Psa 1966, 26:81-87
69168 Time, space, and ascensionism. J existent Psychiat 1963-64, 4:289-300
69169 (& Heller, L. G.) The touching of the body. R 1964, 51:122-134
       Abs SRS Q 1965, 34:311
69170 The transference and countertransference of acting-out behavior. Psa 1965, 25:79-84

BURTON, GENEVIEVE

69171 An alcoholic in the family. Nurs Outlook 1964, 12(5):30-33
69172 (& Kaplan, H. M.) Group counseling in conflicted marriages where alcoholism is present: clients' evaluation of effectiveness. J Marriage Fam 1968, 30(1):74-79
69173 (& Kaplan, H. M.) Marriage counseling with alcoholics and their spouses, I: a critique of the methodology of a follow-up study. Brit J Addiction 1968, 63:151-160
69174 (& Kaplan, H. M.) Marriage counseling with alcoholics and their spouses, II: the correlation of excessive drinking behavior with family pathology and social deterioration. Brit J Addiction 1968, 63:161-170
69175 Nurse and Patient. The Influence of Human Relationships. London: Tavistock 1965, 212 p
69176 (& Kaplan, H. M.) Sexual behavior and adjustment of married alcoholics. Quart J Stud Alcohol 1968, 29(A):603-609; (B):(Abs)737-738

BURTON, ROGER V.

See Yarrow, Marian J.

BUSCAINO, VITO MARIA

69177 "Dementia Praecox: 1965." Évolut psychiat 1966, 31:185-195

BUSCH, FRED

69178 Transference in psychological testing. J proj Tech pers Assess 1968, 32:509-512

See Ekstein, Rudolf

BUSER, M.

69179 Psychotherapeutische Probleme des Internisten. [Psychotherapeutic problems of the internist.] Helv Med Acta 1965, 32:526-531

BUSH, GEORGE

69180 Transference, countertransference, and identification in supervision. Contempo Psa 1969, 5:158-162

BUSH, MARSHALL

69181 The problem of form in the psychoanalytic theory of art. R 1967, 54:5-35
     Abs SRS Q 1968, 37:471
69182 Psychoanalysis and scientific creativity: with special reference to regression in the service of the ego. J Am Psa Ass 1969, 17:136-190

BUSHNELL, DONNA D.

69183 Level of arousal and the primary process properties of associative responses. Diss Abstr 1968, 29(1-B):363-364

BUSKIRK, MARTHA

69184 (& Cunningham, J.; Kent, C. A.) Disturbed children: therapeutic approaches to separation and individuation. Amer J occup Ther 1968, 22:289-293

BUSS, ARNOLD HERBERT

69185 (& Murray, E. N.) Activity level and words connoting mood. Percept mot Skills 1965, 21:684-686
69186 (& Fischer, H.; Simmons, A. J.) Aggression and hostility in psychiatric patients. J consult Psychol 1962, 26:84-89
69187 (& Portnoy, N. W.) Pain tolerance and group identification. J Pers soc Psychol 1967, 6:106-108
69188 The Psychology of Aggression. NY: Wiley 1961, x + 307 p
     Rv Rosen, V. H. Q 1963, 32:106-108
69189 The psychology of aggression. JNMD 1962, 135:180-182

69190 Psychopathology. NY: John Wiley & Sons 1966, xi + 483 p
       Rv Weiss, S. S. Q 1968, 37:457-459. Siller, J. R 1969, 56:485-486
69191 (& Brock, T. C.) Repression and guilt in relation to aggression. ASP
       1963, 66:345-350
69192 (& Murray, E. N.; Buss, E.) Stimulus generalization and fear of snakes.
       J Pers soc Psychol 1968, 10:134-141
69193 (& Daniell, E. F.) Stimulus generalization and schizophrenia. JAbP
       1967, 72:50-53
69194 (& Buss, E. H.) Stimulus generalization with words connoting anxiety.
       J Pers soc Psychol 1966, 4:707-710
69195 (& Buss, E. H.) (Eds) Theories of Schizophrenia. NY: Atherton Pr
       1969, 175 p

       See Zuckerman, Marvin

BUSS, EDITH H.

       See Buss, Arnold H.

BUSSCHER, J. DE

69196 Le thème de l'inceste dans les psychoses paranoïdes. [The theme of
       incest in paranoid psychoses.] Acta neurol psychiat Belg 1963, 68:862-
       891

BUSSE, EWALD WILLIAM

69197 (& Dovenmuehle, R. H.; Brown, R. G.) Psychoneurotic reactions of the
       aged. Geriatrics 1960, 15:97-105
69198 The senile psychoses. Ency Ment Hlth 1829-1836

       See Earley, Leroy W.

BUSSEL, LILI R.

       REVIEWS OF:
69199 Bergmann, T. & Freud, A. Children in the Hospital. Q 1968, 37:137-
       138
69200 Haworth, M. R. (Ed) Child Psychotherapy. Practice and Theory. Q
       1965, 34:453-456

BUSTAMANTE, JOSÉ ANGEL

69201 Cultural factors in hysterics with schizophrenic clinical picture. Int J
       soc Psychiat 1968, 14:113-118
69202 [Folklore and psychiatry.] (Sp) Rev Psiquiat Peru 1960, 3:110-124
       Abs Vega Q 1961, 30:463
69203 [Folklore in psychiatry.] (Sp) Rev Arch Neurol Psiquiat (Cuba) 1960,
       10:197-212
       Abs Vega Q 1961, 30:611
S-43208 El sacrificio totémico nel Baroko ñañigo.
       Abs Vega An Surv Psa 1958, 9:469-470

BUSTAMANTE, M.

69204 Die Funktion der Träume: psychoanalytische und neurophysiologische Zusammenhänge. [The function of dreams: psychoanalytic and neurophysiologic connections.] Z PSM 1969, 15:51-56

69205 Psicoanálisis y medicina psicosomática. [Psychoanalysis and psychosomatic medicine.] Folia Clín Int 1964, 14:289-303

BUTLER, ALFRED J.

See Culbertson, Ellen

BUTLER, JOEL ROBERT

69206 Behavioral analysis of psychoanalytically derived interpretations presented on operant schedules of reinforcement. Diss Abstr 1962, 23: 1069-1070

See Adams, Henry E.; Timmons, Edwin O.

BUTLER, ROBERT N.

69207 Aspects of survival and adaptation in human aging. P 1967, 123:1233-1243

69208 The destiny of creativity in later life: studies of creative people and the creative process. Psychodyn St Aging 20-63

69209 Discussion in the 1964 symposium on "Vicissitudes of the terminal phase of life." Psychodyn St Aging 198-201

69210 The facade of chronological age: an interpretative summary of the multidisciplinary studies of the aged conducted at the National Institutes of Mental Health. P 1963, 119:721-728

69211 Intensive psychotherapy for the hospitalized aged. Geriatrics 1960, 15:644-653

69212 The life review: an interpretation of reminiscence in the aged. Ps 1963, 26:65-76. In Kastenbaum, R. *New Thoughts on Old Age*, NY: Springer 1964, 265-280

69213 Planning an intensive psychotherapeutic inpatient program for the aged. Maryland State med J 1961, 10:138-144

69214 Privileged communication and confidentiality in research. Arch gen Psychiat 1963, 8:139-141

69215 (& Sulliman, L. G.) Psychiatric contact with the community-resident, emotionally disturbed elderly. JNMD 1963, 137:180-186

69216 Psychiatric evaluation of the aged. Geriatrics 1963, 18:220-232

69217 Research and clinical observations on the psychologic reactions to physical changes with age. Mayo Clin Proc 1967, 42:596-619

69218 Some observations on culture and personality in aging. Soc Wk 1963, 6:79-84

69219 Toward a psychiatry of the life-cycle: implications of sociopsychologic studies of the aging process for the psychotherapeutic situation. Psychiat Res Rep 1968, 23:233-248

See Birren, James E.; Werner, Martha M.

BUTTERS, NELSON

See Kellner, Harold

BUTTS, HUGH F.

69220 (& Lindo, T.) Continuity of care on an intensive psychiatric treatment unit. A two year evaluation. J Nat Med Ass 1968, 60:408-414

69221 The Harlem Hospital Center Psychiatric Day Hospital—a three year evaluation. J Nat Med Ass 1967, 59:273-277

69222 The organization of a psychiatric day hospital. J Nat Med Ass 1964, 56:381-389

69223 Post-partum psychiatric problems—a review of the literature dealing with etiological theories. J Nat Med Ass 1969, 61:136-139; 204

69224 (& Wachtel, A. A.) The psychiatric sequelae of heart surgery. J Nat Med Ass 1961, 53:268-270

69225 Psychodynamic and endocrine factors in post-partum psychoses. J Nat Med Ass 1968, 60:224-227

69226 Skin color perception and self-esteem. J Negro Educ 1963, 32:122-128

See Schachter, Judith S.

BUTZ, JOHN L.

See Hollender, Marc H.

BUXBAUM, EDITH

69227 Aggression und die Bedeutung der Gruppe für die Adoleszenz. [Aggression and the role of the group for adolescence.] In *Aggression und Aupassung*, Munich: R. Piper & Co. Verlag

69228 Discussion of Segal, H. "Melanie Klein's technique." Psa Forum 1967, 2:217-219

69229 The parents' role in the etiology of learning disabilities. Psa St C 1964, 19:421-447
Die Rolle der Eltern in der Ätiologie der Lernstörungen. Psyche 1966, 20:161-188. Hbh Kinderpsychother 700-714.

S-43222 (Reporter) Panel: the psychology of adolescence.
Abs JFr An Surv Psa 1958, 9:274-284

69230 (Participant) On regression: a workshop. (West Coast Psa Soc, 14-16 Oct 1966) Psa Forum 1967, 2:293-316

S-5031 Technique of terminating analysis.
Abs Baranger, M. Rev urug Psa 1961-62, 4:367

69231 Three great psychoanalytic educators. Reiss-Davis Clin Bull 1966, 3:5-13. Learn Love 28-35

69232 Understanding Your Child: A Guidebook for Parents. NY: Grove 1962, xv + 204 p
Conosco Mio Figlio. Oscar Mondadori 1968

BUYTENDORP, ALBERT

See Nichtern, Sol

BYCHOWSKI, GUSTAV

69233 An approach to psychotic anxiety. PT 1961, 15:409-418
69234 The archaic object and alienation. (Read at Psa Soc, Rome, 2 Nov 1966) J 1967, 48:384-393
S-43255 Art, magic and the creative ego.
       Abs JLan An Surv Psa 1957, 8:332
69235 A brief visit to India: observations and psychoanalytic implications. Am Im 1968, 25:59-76
       Abs JWS Q 1969, 38:339
69236 Continuum and antimony: two principles of psychoanalytic dialectics. J Hillside Hosp 1968, 17(2 & 3):79-93
69237 Contributor to Krystal, H. *Massive Psychic Trauma*, NY: IUP 1968
S-43257 Dictatorship and paranoia.
       Abs An Surv Psa 1955, 6:432-433
69238 Diktatoren: Beiträge zu einer psychoanalytischen Persönlichkeits und Geschichts Deutung. [Dictators: Contributions to a Psychoanalytical Interpretation of Their Personalities and History.] Munich: Szczesny Verlag 1965
69239 Discussion of Baranger, M. & Baranger, W. "Insight in the analytic situation." Psa Amer 73-78
69240 Discussion of Bennis, W. G. "A psychoanalytic inquiry into the 'two cultures' dilemma." Psa Forum 1969, 3:179-182
69241 Discussion of Boyer, L. B. "Office treatment of schizophrenic patients by psychoanalysis." Psa Forum 1966, 1:349-350
S-43259 The ego and the introjects: origins of religious experience.
       Abs AHM An Surv Psa 1956, 7:173-175. Swartz, J. An Surv Psa 1958, 9:439-442
69242 The ego and the object of the homosexual. (Read at Am Psa Ass, Dec 1959) J 1961, 42:255-259
       Das Ich und das Objekt des Homosexuellen. Psyche 1961, 15:465-474
       Abs WPK Q 1962, 31:285
S-5064 The ego of homosexuals. PT pervers 372-408
69243 Escapades: a form of dissociation. (Read at NY Psa Soc, March 1961) Q 1962, 31:155-174
       Abs EDJ Q 1961, 30:613-614. LDr RFPsa 1963, 27:356
69244 Evil in Man: The Anatomy of Hate and Violence. NY: Grune & Stratton 1968, vi + 98 p
       Rv Frank, J. D. Am Im 1968, 25:384-386
69245 Freud and Jung: an encounter. (Read at Israel Psa Soc, 1963) Israel Ann Psychiat 1964, 2:129-143
69246 Frigidity and object relationship. (Read at Am Psa Ass, Dec 1960) J 1963, 44:57-62
       Abs EVN Q 1965, 34:464
S-43260 General aspects and implications of introjection.
       Abs SO An Surv Psa 1956, 7:388-390
S-43263 Interaction between psychotic partners, II: schizophrenic partners.
       Abs Shevin, F. F. An Surv Psa 1956, 7:179-181
69247 Obituary: Bela Mittelmann 1899-1959. J Am Psa Ass 1961, 9:362-364
69248 Obituary: Sidney Tarachow 1908-1965. Am Im 1966, 23:89-90

69249 Obsessive compulsive facade in schizophrenia. (Read at Int Psa Cong, July 1965) J 1966, 47:189-197

Façade compulsive-obsessionnelle dans la schizophrénie. RFPsa 1967, 31:669-692

La fachada obsesivo-compulsiva en la esquizofrenia. Rev Psicoanál 1967, 24:341-367

Abs EVN Q 1968, 37:310

69250 Patterns of anger. Psa St C 1966, 21:172-192

69251 Platonic love and the quest for beauty. The drama of J. J. Winckelmann. (Read at Am Psa Ass, May 1961; at NY Psa Soc, Feb 1963) Am Im 1964, 21(3-4):80-94

Platonische Liebe und die Suche nach der Schonheit. Das Drama Winckelmanns. Psyche 1966, 20:700-714

Abs Slap, J. W. Q 1965, 34:621

69252 The potential of psychoanalytic biography: Zeligs on Chambers and Hiss. Am Im 1969, 26:233-241

69253 The psychoanalysis of the psychotic core. Psychiat Res Rep 1963, (17):1-12

69254 Psychopathology of aggression and violence. Bull NY Acad Med 1967, 43:300-309

69255 Psychosis precipitated by psychoanalysis. (Read at Am Psa Ass, May 1965) Q 1966, 35:327-339

Abs Cuad Psa 1966, 2:123-124. Rosarios, H. Rev Psicoanál 1967, 24:440. LDr RFPsa 1968, 32:183

69256 The quest for beauty and the pitfalls of sublimation. (Read at NY Psa Soc, 12 Feb 1963)

Abs Furer, M. Q 1963, 32:466-468

S-43267 The release of internal images.

Abs SLP An Surv Psa 1956, 7:125-126

69257 Social climate and resistance in psychoanalysis. J 1969, 50:453-459

69258 Structure des dépressions chroniques et latentes. [The structure of chronic and latent depressions.] RFPsa 1961, 25:927-935

S-43270 Struggle against the introjects.

Abs JAL An Surv Psa 1958, 9:123-124

S-43271 Symposium on "depressive illness."

Abs JBi Q 1962, 31:121-122

69259 Thought and language. Int J Psychiat 1967, 4:530

REVIEWS OF:

69260 Argen, G. C. & Traversa, C. Children's Drawings and Their Bearing on the Doctor-Patient Relationship. Am Im 1966, 23:275-276

69261 de Groot, A. Saint Nicholas. A Psychoanalytic Study of his History and Myth. Am Im 1966, 23:277-278

69262 Lebovici, S. & McDougall, J. Un Cas de Psychose Infantile: Étude Psychanalytique. Q 1962, 31:262-264

69263 Milner, M. On Not Being Able to Paint. Am Im 1968, 25:192-193

69264 Nagera, H. Vincent Van Gogh: A Psychological Study. Am Im 1968, 25:191-192

69265 Richter, H.-E. Eltern, Kind und Neurose. Psychoanalyse der kinderlichen Rolle. Q 1964, 33:579-580

69266 Roazen, P. Freud: Political and Social Thought. J 1968, 49:739-741
69267 Spoerri, T. Adolf Wölfli's Picture World. Am Im 1966, 23:275-276
69268 v. Baeyer, W. & Hufner, H. Prinzhorn's Basic Work on the Psycho-pathology of the "Gestaltung." Am Im 1966, 23:275-276

BYRNE, DONN ERWIN

69269 Childrearing antecedents of repression-sensitization. Child Develpm 1964, 35:1033-1039
69270 (& Blayblock, B.; Goldberg, J.) Dogmatism and defense mechanisms. Psychol Rep 1966, 18:739-742
69271 Parental antecedents of authoritarianism. J Pers soc Psychol 1965, 1:369-373
69272 (& Hamilton, M. L.) (Eds) Personality Research: A Book of Readings. Englewood Cliffs, N. J.: Prentice-Hall 1966, xiii + 411 p
69273 (& Sheffield, J.) Response to sexually arousing stimuli as a function of repressing and sensitizing defenses. JAbP 1965, 70:114-118

See Worchel, Philip

BYRUM, MILDRED

See Ruebush, Britton K.

BZHALAVA, YOSIF T.

69274 K probleme bessoznatel'nogo v teorii ustanovki D. N. Uznadze. [The problem of the unconscious in D. N. Uznadze's theory of set.] Voprosy Psikhologii 1967, 13:155-159

C

CABBABÉ, GILBERT

See Luzes, Pedro

CABELLO, V. P.

69275 [A new form of scientific quackery: the psychological.] (Sp) Sem Med, B Air 1963, 123:1658-1661

CABERINTE, LEÃO

69276 Ideas sobre una concepción formal, del instincto en su teoría monistica. [Thoughts on a formal conception of instinct in its monistic theory.] Rev Psicoanál 1961, 18:18-25

CACHELOUS, R.

See Danon-Boileau, Henri

CADER, GORDON

See Lichtenberg, Joseph D.

CAEN, J.

See Alby, J. M.

CAESAR, GEORGE R.

See Brugger, Thomas C.

CAFFARATTO, TIRSI MARIO

69277 Due poco comuni metodi di cura psichica: l'ipnotisme e la narco-analisi. Loro applicazione nel campo ostetrico-ginecologico. [Two un-usual methods of psychotherapy: hypnotism and narcoanalysis. Their application in the obstetrico-gynecological field.] Minerva Ginec 1959, 11:820-824

CAGNO, L. DI

69278 (& Ravetto, F.) L'anoressia del primo anno di vita quale espressione dell'alterato rapporto madre-figlio. Indagine catamnestica e rilievi psicopatologici. Minerva Pediat 1968, 20:416-423

Anorexia in the first year of life as an expression of changes in the mother-child relationship. A catamnestic study and psychopathological findings in 30 cases. Panminerva Med 1968, 10:465-471

69279 [Effects of maternal deprivation on a pair of pygopagic twins hospitalized from birth.] (It) Lattante 1965, 36:204-207

69280 (& Castello, D.) [Partial deprivation of maternal care: consequences on psychomotor development of the hospitalized child and its prophylaxis in the clinica pediatrica of University of Turin.] (It) Lattante 1965, 36:202-204

See Castello, D.

CAHEN, M.

See Nacht, Sacha

CAHEN, ROLAND

69281 L'être et l'analyse.' [Being and analysis.] Évolut psychiat 1967, 32:547-572

69281A [The law of specific blindness.] (Fr) Évolut psychiat 1969, 34:681-689

69282 The psychology of the dream: its instructive and therapeutic uses. In Grunebaum, G. E. von & Caillois, R. *The Dream and Human Society*, Berkeley/Los Angeles: Univ Calif Pr 1966, 119-143

69283 Thème et symbolisme de l'eau en psychanalyse à travers l'évolution d'un cas. [Theme and symbolism of water in psychoanalysis during development of a case.] Évolut psychiat 1969, 34:27-46

See Raclot, Marcel

CAHN, P.

69284 Psychologie des relations entre le nourrisson et sa mère au cours des 30 premiers mois. [Psychology of the relations between mother and child during the first thirty months.] Strasbourg Méd 1966, 17:310-313

CAHN, RAYMOND

69285 (& Mouton, T.) Affectivité et Troubles du Langage Écrit chez l'Enfant et l'Adolescent. [Affectivity and Disturbances of the Written Language of the Child and of the Adolescent.] Privat Editeur 1967, 134 p

69286 Discussion of Mendel, G. "La sublimation artistique." RFPsa 1964, 28:805

69287 Perspectives psychanalytiques sur la place des thérapeutiques de relaxation dans la cadre des psychothérapies de l'adolescent. [Psychoanalytic perspectives on the place of relaxation therapy within the framework of adolescent psychotherapy.] Rv Np inf 1968, 16:525-530

69288 Problématique psychosomatique. À propos d'un cas à troubles digestifs fonctionnels prévalents. [Psychosomatic problems. Functional digestive disorders.] Rev Méd psychosom 1965, 7:31-43

69288A [Psychoanalysis and heredity.] (Fr) Évolut psychiat 1969, 34:691-717

69289 Psychopathologique de la fatigue chez l'adolescent. [Psychopathology of the fatigue of the adolescent.] In *La Fatigue* (III Congrès International de Médecine Psychosomatique), Edouard Privat Editeur 1967, 468-475

69290 Le tonus. Approche génétique, différentielle et psychanalytique. [Muscular tonus. Genetic, differential and psychoanalytical approach.] Cah Psychiat 1962, No. 16/17:25-39

CAHOON, DELWIN DUANE

69291 Symptom substitution and the behavior therapies: a reappraisal. Psychol Bull 1968, 69:149-156

CAILLOIS, ROGER

See Grunebaum, G. E. von

CAIN, ALBERT C.

69292 (& Fast, I.) Children's disturbed reactions to parent suicide. Ops 1966, 36:873-880
       Abs JMa RFPsa 1968, 32:383
69293 (& Fast, I.; Erickson, M. E.) Children's disturbed reactions to the death of a sibling. Ops 1964, 34:741-752
69294 (& Erickson, M. E.; Fast, I.; Vaughn, R. A.) Children's disturbed reactions to their mother's miscarriage. PSM 1964, 26:58-66
69295 Discussion of Malmquist, C. "A critique of the education of the child psychiatrist." Int J Psychiat 1968, 6:296-316
69296 (& Maupin, B. M.) Interpretation within the metaphor. BMC 1961, 25:307-311
       Abs HD Q 1962, 31:584
69297 (& Fast, I.) The legacy of suicide. Observations on the pathogenic impact of suicide upon marital partners. Ps 1966, 29:406-411
69298 (& Cain, B. S.) On replacing a child. J Amer Acad Child Psychiat 1964, 3:443-456
       Remplacer un enfant. Méd Hyg 1963, 21(603)
69299 On the meaning of "playing crazy" in borderline children. Ps 1964, 27:278-289
69300 The perils of prevention (editorial). Ops 1967, 37:640-642
69301 The presuperego "turning-inward" of aggression. Q 1961, 30:171-208
69302 Special "isolated" abilities in severely psychotic young children. Ps 1969, 32:137-149
69303 A supplementary dream technique with the Children's Apperception Test. Clin Psych 1961, 17:181-183
69304 Too long, too little. Int J Psychiat 1968, 6:307-313

       See Fast, Irene; Finch, Stuart M.; Harrison, Saul I.; Kemph, John P.

CAIN, ARTHUR J.

ABSTRACT OF:
69305 Murray, J. M. On the transformation of narcissism into ego ideal. Bull Phila Ass Psa 1963, 13:143-145

CAIN, BARBARA S.

See Cain, Albert C.; Weiss, Morris

CAIN, JACQUES

69306 Essai de comprehension psycho-somatique de l'état allergique. [The psychosomatic concept of allergy.] Evolut psychiat 1962, 27:339-363

69307 Le masochisme chez Masoch. [The masochism of Masoch.] Bull Ass psa Fran 1968, No. 4:64-75

69308 Le Problème des Névroses Expérimentales. [The Problem of Experimental Neuroses.] Bruges: Desclée de Brouwer 1959, 168 p
    Rv RJA Q 1961, 30:122-124

69309 Le symptôme psychosomatique. [The psychosomatic symptom.] Rev Méd psychosom 1967, 9:77-101. Ann méd-psychol 1967, 1:287

CAINE, THOMAS MCKENZIE

69310 (& Smail, D. J.) Attitudes of psychiatric nurses to their role in treatment. M 1968, 41:193-197

69311 (& Smail, D. J.) Attitudes of psychiatric patients to staff roles and treatment methods in mental hospitals. M 1968, 41:291-294

69312 (& Smail, D. J.) Attitudes of psychiatrists to staff roles and treatment methods. M 1967, 40:179-182

69313 Response consistency and testing levels. Brit J soc clin Psychol 1967, 6:38-42

69314 (& Smail, D. J.) The Treatment of Mental Illness. Science, Faith and the Therapeutic Personality. NY: IUP 1969, 192 p

69315 (& Hope, K.) Validation of the Maudsley Personality Inventory E Scale. Brit J Psychol 1964, 55:447-452

See Martin, Denis V.

CAJIAO, RAMON GAUZARAIN

69316 Die Forschungsarbeit in der Gruppen Therapie, ihre Probleme, Methoden und Aufgaben. [Research in group therapy, its problems, methods and purposes.] Psyché, Paris 1962, 26(8)
    Abs IBa RFPsa 1962, 26:622

CALDARINI, G.

See Generali, I.

CALDEN, GEORGE

69317 (& Dupertuis, C. W.; Hokanson, J. E.; Lewis, W. C.) Psychosomatic factors in the rate of recovery from tuberculosis. PSM 1960, 22:345-355
    Abs JPG Q 1961, 30:453

CALDER, KENNETH T.

69318 How psychoanalytic institutes evaluate applicants: replies to a questionnaire. (Read at Pre-Cong Conf on Training, July 1967) J 1968, 49:540-547

S-43294 (Reporter) Technical aspects of regression during psychoanalysis.
    Abs JFr An Surv Psa 1958, 9:350-357

ABSTRACT OF:
69319 Wangh, M. A psychoanalytic study of anti-semitism: the psychodynamics and psychogenesis of prejudice, anti-semitism, and Nazi
anti-semitism. Q 1963, 32:299-301

CALDER-MARSHALL, ARTHUR

69320 The Sage of Sex: A Life of Havelock Ellis. NY: G. P. Putnam 1960,
292 p

CALDERONE, MARY STEICHEN

69321 Conception control and sexual problems. In Wahl, C. W. *Sexual Problems*, NY: Free Pr; London: Collier-Macmillan 1967, 71-78
69322 (Ed) Manual of Contraceptive Practice. Baltimore: Williams & Wilkins
1964, xxi + 295 p
Tecnicas Anticoncepcionales. S. A.: Ed Interamericana 1966
69323 Sexual health and family planning. Amer J Pub Hlth 1968, 58:223-231

CALDWELL, BETTYE M.

69324 Assessment of infant personality. Merrill-Palmer Q 1962, 8:71-81
69325 (& Watson, R. I.) An evaluation of sex hormone replacement in aged
women. In McGuigan, F. J. & Calvin, A. *Current Studies in Psychology*,
NY: Appleton-Century-Crofts 1958, 91-95
69326 (& Richmond, J. B.) The impact of theories of child development.
Children 1962, 9:73-78
69327 (& Hersher, L.) Mother-infant interaction during the first year of life.
Merrill-Palmer Q 1963, 10:119-128
69328 (& Hersher, L.; Lipton, E. L.; Richmond, J. B.; Stern, G. A.; Eddy,
E.; Drachman, R.; Rothman, A.) Mother-infant interaction in mono-
matric and polymatric families. Ops 1963, 33:653-664
69329 On reformulating the concept of early childhood education—some whys
needing wherefores. Young Children 1967, 22:348-356
69330 On the effects of infant care. In Hoffman, M. L. & Hoffman, L. W.
Review of Child Development Research, Vol. 1, NY: Russell Sage
Foundation 1964, 9-87
69331 The usefulness of the critical period hypothesis in the study of filiative
behavior. Merrill-Palmer Q 1962, 8:229-242. In Rosenblith, J. F. &
Allinsmith, W. *The Causes of Behavior*, Boston: Allyn & Bacon 1966,
310-317
69332 What is the optimal learning environment for the young child? Ops
1967, 37:8-21. Ann Prog child Psychiat 1968, 149-165

See Richmond, Julius B.

CALEF, VICTOR

69333 Alcoholism and ornithophobia in women. Q 1967, 36:584-587
69334 Discussion of Friedman, L. J. "From Gradiva to the death instinct."
Psa Forum 1966, 1:59-62
69335 Lady Macbeth and infanticide or "how many children had Lady Macbeth murdered?" J Am Psa Ass 1969, 17:528-548

69336   (Reporter) Report of discussion of acting out—English language section
        II. J 1968, 49:225-227
            Abs LHR Q 1969, 38:668
69337   The unconscious fantasy of infanticide manifested in resistance. (Read
        at Los Angeles Psa Res Group, Feb 1964; at Topeka Psa Soc, March
        1964; at San Francisco Psa Soc, Feb 1965) J Am Psa Ass 1968, 16:
        697-710

        REVIEWS OF:
69338   Boring, E. G. Psychologist at Large. An Autobiography and Selected
        Essays. Q 1963, 32:436-441
69339   Hoch, P. H. & Zubin, J. (Eds) The Future of Psychiatry. Q 1964,
        115-119
69340   Kaufman, M. R. & Heiman, M. (Eds) Evolution of Psychosomatic Con-
        cepts. Anorexia Nervosa: A Paradigm. Q 1965, 34:451-453
69341   Schaar, J. H. Escape from Authority: the Perspectives of Erich Fromm.
        Q 1964, 33:291-293

CALHOUN, D. W.

See Nelson, Benjamin N.

CALIGOR, LEOPOLD

69342   (& May, R.) Dreams and Symbols: Man's Unconscious Language.
        NY: Basic Books 1968-69, vii + 307 p

See Witenberg, Earl G.

CALJE, J. F.

69343   Quelques considérations sur le concept de la psychasthénie. [Some
        considerations on the concept of psychasthenia.] Acta neurol psychiat
        Belg 1961, 61:22-33

CALL, JUSTIN D.

69344   From anaclitic depression to "toughness" in an infant male twin. Acta
        Genet Med, Rome 1963, 12:134-143
69345   Lap and finger play in infancy, implications for ego development.
        (Read at Int Psa Cong, July 1967) J 1968, 49:375-378
69346   Newborn approach behaviour and early ego development. (Read at
        Int Psa Cong, 30 July 1963) J 1964, 45:286-294
            Les comportements d'approche du nouveau-né et le developpement
        du moi primitif. RFPsa 1967, 31:464-483
            Sobre el desarrollo psíquico del recién nacido. Cuad Psa 1965, 1:
        237-256
            Abs EVN Q 1966, 35:460-461
69347   (& Christianson, M.; Penrose, F. R.; Backlar, M.) Psychogenic mega-
        colon in three preschool boys: a study of etiology through collaborative
        treatment of child and parents. Ops 1963, 33:923-928
69348   (& Marschak, M.) Styles and games in infancy. J Amer Acad Child
        Psychiat 1966, 5:193-210

See Marschak, Marianne; Work, Henry H.

CALLAHAN, DANIEL M.

69349 Freud saw it coming. Commonweal 1966, 84(June 3):312-313; Discussion. 1966, 84(July 1):405 + ; (July 22):483-484

See McNair, Douglas M.

CALLAHAN, ROBERT

See Eron, Leonard D.

CALLAHAN, ROGER J.

69350 Overcoming religious faith: a case history. Rational Living 1967, 2:16-21

CALLAWAY, ENOCH

69351 Discussion of Savage, C. "The analysis of an 'outsider.'" Psa Forum 1969, 3:298-299

See Klee, Gerald D.

CALLENBACH, ERNEST

69352 Freud (film). Film Quart 1963, 16(Summer):50-51

CALLIER, J.

See Bergeret, J.

CALLIERI, BRUNO

69353 (& D'Agostino, N.) Antropologia esistenziale e psicoanalisi di fronte al sentimento di colpa. [Existential anthropology and psychoanalysis dealing with guilt feelings.] Arch Psicol Neurol Psychiat 1962, 23:7-18
69354 Aspetti psicopatologico-clinici della "Wahnstimmung." [Psychopathological-clinical aspects of "Wahnstimmung."] In Kranz, H. *Psychopathologie Heute*, Stuttgart: Georg Thieme 1962, 72-80
69355 (& Frighi, L.) Il concetto di angoscia nell'esistenzialismo e nella psicoanalisi. [The concept of anxiety in existentialism and psychoanalysis.] Riv sper Freniat 1961, 85:374-385

CALMAS, WILFRED E.

69356 Fantasies of the mother-son relationship of the rapist and the pedophile. Diss Abstr 1965, 26:2875-2876

CALOGERAS, ROY C.

69357 Silence as a technical parameter in psycho-analysis. J 1967, 48:536-558
Abs LHR Q 1969, 38:507

See Benfari, Robert C.

CALVERLEY, DAVID SMITH

See Barber, Theodore X.

CAMBON, FERNAND

TRANSLATION OF:
(& Grossein, J.-P.) Abraham, H. C. & Freud, E. L. [65093]

CAMBOR, C. GLENN

69358 Preoedipal factors in superego development: the influence of multiple mothers. Q 1969, 38:81-96

See Carroll, Edward J.

CAMERON, DALE C.

69359 (Contributor) Concluding statement. Out-Patient Schiz 234-239

CAMERON, DONALD EWEN

69360 The day hospital. In Proc IV World Cong Psychiat 1966, 377-379
69361 Evolving concepts of memory. Recent Adv biol Psychiat 1967, 9:1-12
69362 (Ed) Forensic Psychiatry and Child Psychiatry. (International Psychiatry Clinics 1965, Vol. 2, No. 1) Boston: Little, Brown 1965, x + 3-217
69363 Psychotherapy in Action. NY: Grune & Stratton 1968, ix + 228 p
69364 (& Greenblatt, M.) (Eds) Recent Advances in Neuro-Physiological Research. Wash DC: Amer Psychiat Assoc 1959, 136 p
        Rv Pappenheim, E. Q 1961, 30:591-592
69365 (& Levy, L.; Ban, T.; Rubenstein, L.) Repetition of verbal signals in therapy. Curr psychiat Ther 1961, 1:100-111
69366 Uncovering in psychotherapy. Psychiat et Neurol 1965, 150:334-344

CAMERON, JOHN LEWIS

S-43350 (& Freeman, T.; McGhie, A.) Clinical observations on chronic schizophrenia.
        Abs Shapiro, P. An Surv Psa 1956, 7:181-182
S-43351 (& Freeman, T.) Group psychotherapy in affective disorders.
        Abs AaSt An Surv Psa 1956, 7:359-360

See Freeman, Thomas

CAMERON, NORMAN ALEXANDER

69367 Introjection, reprojection, and hallucination in the interaction between schizophrenic patient and therapist. J 1961, 42:86-96
        Abs WPK Q 1962, 31:283. PCR RFPsa 1964, 28:299-300
69368 Paranoid reactions. Compreh Txbk Psychiat 665-675
69369 Personality Development and Psychopathology. A Dynamic Approach. Boston: Houghton, Mifflin Co 1963, xxi + 793 p
        Rv J Am Psa Ass 1964, 12:261
69370 The Psychology of Behavior Disorders, A Biosocial Interpretation. Boston: Houghton Mifflin 1947, 662 p

CAMERON, PAUL

69371 Confirmation of the Freudian psychosexual stages utilizing sexual symbolism. Psychol Rep 1967, 21:33-39

69372 Ego strength and happiness of the aged. J Gerontol 1967, 22:199-202
69373 Introversion and egocentricity among the aged. J Gerontol 1967, 22:465-468

CAMINHA, MIRIAM E.

See Leme, Wanda P.

CAMPAIGNE, HOWARD M.

See Scher, Jordan M.

CAMPANA, M.

69373A [Possibility of an esthetic interpretation.] (It) Riv Sper Freniat 1968, 92(Suppl 1): 255-259

CAMPBELL, JOHN D.

See Raush, Harold L.; Yarrow, Marian J.

CAMPBELL, JOSEPH

69374 (Ed) Man and Transformation. (Tr: Manheim, R.) NY: Pantheon Books 1964, xviii + 413 p
Rv Am Im 1965, 22:220

CAMPBELL, MAGDA

See Fish, Barbara

CAMPBELL, MIRIAM C.

69375 Some observations concerning the choice of time in applying to a child study center. Reiss-Davis Clin Bull 1967, 4:77-81

CAMPBELL, RUTH

69376 Violence in adolescence. J anal Psych 1967, 12:161-173

CAMPO, ALBERTO J.

69377 La hipocresia como trastorno del carácter. [Feigning as a character disorder.] Rev Psicoanál 1967, 24:623-643
S-43372 La interpretación y la acción en el análisis de los niños.
Abs RHB An Surv Psa 1957, 8:233-234
69378 Introducción al estudio genético y evolutivo de la omnipotencia. [Introduction to the study of genesis and the evolution of omnipotency.] Rev Psicoanál 1963, 20:359-376
Abs Vega Q 1965, 34:143
69379 (& Carpelan, H.) La manifestation de la défense maniaque dans un groupe de psychodrame psychanalytique. [The manifestation of manic defence in a group of psychoanalytic psychodrama.] Acta psychother psychosom 1962, 10:439-453

See Grinberg, Léon

CAMPO, VERA

69380 Aportación al estudio de la mania en el niño. [Contribution to the study of mania in children.] Rev Psicoanál 1962, 19:66-70
Abs Vega Q 1964, 33:144

S-43377 La interpretación de la entrevista con los padres en el análisis de niños.
Abs RHB An Surv Psa 1957, 8:228

S-43378 La introducción del elemento traumático.
Abs JO An Surv Psa 1958, 9:316

CAMPOS, LEONARD P.

69381 Relationship between time estimation and retentive personality traits. Percept mot Skills 1966, 23:59-62

CANAVAN, DONNAH

See Glass, David C.

CANCRO, ROBERT

69382 (& Voth, H. M.; Voth, A. C.) Character organization and the style of hospital treatment. Arch gen Psychiat 1968, 19:161-164

69383 Elopements from the C. F. Menninger Memorial Hospital. BMC 1968, 32:228-238

See Voth, Harold M.

CANEPA, GIACOMO

69384 La contribution des théories de personnalité à la recherche criminologique: aspects cliniques. [The contribution of theories of personality in criminological research: clinical aspects.] Arch Psicol Neurol Psichiat 1966, 27:336-352

69385 (& Bandini, T.) The personality of victims of incest (criminological study). Int Crim Police Rev 1967, 22(208):140-145

CANESTRARI, ROBERT E., JR.

69386 Spatial stimulus generalization gradients and id, ego, and superego strength. Percept mot Skills 1964, 19:51-55

CANIDA, JACK

See Behymer, Alice F.

CANNING, JERRY W.

69387 A logical analysis of criticisms directed at Freudian psychoanalytic theory. Diss Abstr 1966, 27:1078-1079

CANNON, ANN

69388 Transference as creative illusion. J anal Psych 1968, 13(2):95-108

CANNON, J. ALFRED

See Koegler, Ronald R.

CANSEVER, GÖKÇE

69389 Language structure of primary-process thinking. Diss Abstr 1960, 21:954
69390 Psychological effects of circumcision. M 1965, 38:321-331

CANTER, ARTHUR

See Meyer, Eugene

CANTOR, DAVID

See Feldman, Fred

CANTOR, MORTON B.

69391 The initial interview. In Kelman, H. *New Perspectives in Psychoanalysis,* NY: Morton 1965, 191-215
69392 Karen Horney on psychoanalytic technique: mobilizing constructive forces. Psa 1967, 27:188-199
69393 Problems in diagnosing and prognosing with occult schizophrenic patients. Psa 1969, 29:36-49
69394 The quality of the analyst's attention. In Kelman, H. *Advances in Psychoanalysis,* NY: Norton 1964, 220-229

CANTOR, ROBERT

See Curtis, Thomas A.

CANTRELL, WILLIAM A.

69395 Discussion of Balint, E. "Training as an impetus to ego development." Psa Forum 1967, 2:68-69

CANTRIL, HADLEY

* * * A fresh look at the human design. See [69396]
69396 The human design. J ind Psych 1964, 20:129-136. With title: A fresh look at the human design. In Bugental, J. F. T. *Challenges of Humanistic Psychology,* NY/Toronto/London: McGraw-Hill 1967, 13-18
69397 Obituary: Gordon W. Allport (1897-1967). J ind Psych 1968, 24:97-98

CANTZLAAR, GEORGE LA FOND

See Brussel, James A.

CAPDEVILLE, C.

See Darcourt, Guy

CAPELL, MARTIN D.

69398 The ethical basis of psychoanalysis. R 1967, 54:688-696
       Abs SRS Q 1969, 38:164
69399 Passive mastery of helplessness in games. Am Im 1968, 25:309-332

CAPLAN, GERALD

69400 (& Cadden, V.) Adjusting Overseas—A Message to Each Peace Corps Trainee. Wash DC: The Peace Corps 1962

69401 (& Lebovici, S.) (Eds) Adolescence: Psychosocial Perspectives. NY: Basic Books 1969, xx + 412 p

69402 An Approach to Community Mental Health. NY: Grune & Stratton; London: Tavistock 1961, 262 p

69403 An approach to the study of family mental health. In Galdston, I. *The Family: A Focal Point in Health Education*, NY: IUP 1961, 52-73

69404 Common Problems of Early Childhood. Atlanta, Georgia: Georgia Department of Public Health 1961 (Pamphlet)

69405 Community psychiatry—introduction and overview. In Goldston, S. E. *Concepts of Community Psychiatry—A Framework for Training*, Public Health Service Publication No. 1319, U.S. Dept of Health, Education and Welfare 1965, 3-18

69406 Conception, pregnancy, and childbirth. Ency Ment Hlth 337-354

69407 A conceptual model for primary prevention. In van Krevelen, A. *Child Psychiatry and Prevention*, Bern: Huber 1964

69408 Concluding discussion. In author's *Prevention of Mental Disorders in Children* 398-416

69409 Crisis in the family. Med Opin Rev 1966, 1(8):21-23

69410 Current issues relating to the education of psychiatric residents in community psychiatry. In *Proc 3rd Annual Conf Mental Health Career Development Program, May 26-28, NIMH*, Bethesda, Maryland: Public Health Service Publication No. 1245 1964. In Goldston, S. E. *Concepts of Community Psychiatry—A Framework for Training*, Public Health Service Publication No. 1319, U.S. Dept of Health, Education, and Welfare 1965, 167-182

69411 (Ed) Curriculum content. In *Mental Health Teaching in Schools of Public Health*, NY: Columbia Univ Pr 1961, 195-234

69412 (& Caplan, R. B.) Development of community psychiatry concepts. Compreh Txbk Psychiat 1499-1516

69413 Elements of a comprehensive community mental health program for adolescents. In author's *Psychiatric Approaches to Adolescence* 81-91. In author's *Adolescence* 372-386

69414 Emotional crisis. Ency Ment Hlth 521-532

69415 Emotional implications of pregnancy and influences on family relationships. In Stuart, H. C. & Prugh, D. G. *The Healthy Child*, Harvard Univ Pr 1960, 72-82

69416 (Ed) Emotional Problems of Early Childhood. NY: Basic Books 1955, xiv + 544 p

69417 Foreword to Huessy, H. R. (Ed) *Mental Health with Limited Resources*, NY: Grune & Stratton 1966

69418 (& Mason, E. A.; Kaplan, D. M.) Four studies of crisis in parents of prematures. Comm ment Hlth J 1965, 1:149-161

69419 General introduction and overview. In author's *Prevention of Mental Disorders in Children* 3-30

69420 Growing up and society. In *Proceedings of the White House Confer-*

ence on Health, No. 3-4, 1965, Wash DC: Department of Health, Education, and Welfare 1967, 530-532

69421 (& Lebovici, S.) Introduction. In authors' *Psychiatric Approaches to Adolescence* 9-11

69422 Introduction to Roberts, L. *Comprehensive Mental Health: The Challenge of Evaluation,* Madison: Univ of Wisc 1968

69423 Manual for Psychiatrists Participating in the Peace Corps Program. Wash DC: Medical Program Division, Peace Corps 1962

69424 Opportunities for school psychologists in the primary prevention of mental disorders in children. MH 1963, 47:525-539. Ment Hlth Monogr 1964, No. 5:9-22. In Miller, E. *The Foundations of Child Psychiatry,* Oxford/NY: Pergamon Pr 1968, 671-687

69425 Patterns of parental response to the crisis of premature birth. Ps 1960, 23:365-374

69426 (& Grunebaum, H. U.) Perspectives on primary prevention: a review. Arch gen Psychiat 1967, 17:331-346

69427 Prevention of mental disorders. Ency Ment Hlth 1556-1566

69428 (Ed) Prevention of Mental Disorders in Children. Initial Explorations. (Foreword: Felix, R. H.) NY: Basic Books 1961, xxii + 425 p
Rv Roiphe, H. Q 1962, 31:264-266

69429 Primaire preventie van geestelijke stoornissen bij kinderen door hulpverlening tijdens crisisperioden. [Primary prevention for mental disorders of children through preventive intervention during periods of crisis.] Geneesk Gids 1962, No. 14

69430 Principles of Preventive Psychiatry. (Foreword: Felix, R. H.) NY/London: Basic Books; London: Tavistock 1964, xii + 304 p
Principios de Psiquiatria Preventiva. Buenos Aires: Paidos 1968
Rv HRB Q 1964, 33:588-589

69431 Problems of training in mental health consultation. In Goldston, S. E. *Concepts of Community Psychiatry—A Framework for Training,* Public Health Service Publication No. 1319, U.S. Dept of Health, Education, and Welfare 1965, 91-108

69432 (& Lebovici, S.) (Eds) Psychiatric Approaches to Adolescence. Amsterdam: Excerpta Medica Foundation 1966, 182 p

69433 Psychological aspects of pregnancy. In Lief, H. et al: *The Psychological Basis of Medical Practice,* NY/Evanston/London: Harper & Row 1963, 441-448

69434 The role of pediatricians in community mental health (with particular reference to the primary prevention of mental disorders in children). In Bellak, L. *Handbook of Community Psychiatry and Community Mental Health,* NY: Grune & Stratton 1964, 287-299

69435 The roots of human relationships: mother and infant. In Stuart, H. C. & Pugh, D. G. *The Healthy Child,* Cambridge, Mass: Harvard Univ Pr 1960, 209-220

69436 Some comments on "community psychiatry and social power." Soc Probl 1966-67. 14:23-25

69437 Types of mental health consultation. Ops 1963, 33:470-481
Abs JMa RFPsa 1964, 28:452

See Mason, Edward A.; Parad, Howard J.; Schulberg, Herbert C.

CAPLAN, HYMAN

69438 Some aspects of parent guidance in child psychiatry. Canad Psychiat Ass J 1968, 13:311-315

See Bonaccorsi, Marie T.

CAPLAN, LLOYD M.

69439 Identification, a complicating factor in the inpatient treatment of adolescent girls. Ops 1966, 36:720-724
Abs JMa RFPsa 1968, 32:380

CAPLAN, RUTH B.

69440 (& Caplan, G.) Psychiatry and the Community in Nineteenth Century America: the Recurring Concern with the Environment in the Prevention and Treatment of Mental Illness. NY: Basic Books 1969, xx + 360 p

See Caplan, Gerald

CAPONE, G.

69441 Dinamioa dell'inconscio nell-arte. [Dynamics of the unconscious in art.] Arch Pat Clin med 1961, 38:79-130

CAPPADONIA, ANTHONY C.

69442 (& Herrick, G. W.) Some psychological aspects of intonation. Sch Musician 1963, 34(Jan):44-45; (Feb):44-45; (March):34-35

CAPPON, DANIEL

69443 (& Banks, R.) Distorted body perception in obesity. JNMD 1968, 146:465-467
69444 Experiments in time perception. Canad Psychiat Ass J 1964, 9:396-410
69445 The fear of dying. Pastoral Psychol 1961, 12:35-44
69446 Myths in psychotherapy. Curr psychiat Ther 1968, 8:47-55
69447 (& Banks, R.) Orientational perception. II. Body perception in depersonalization. Arch gen Psychiat 1965, 13:375-379
69448 Orientational perception: IV. Time and length perception in depersonalization and derealized patients and controls under positive feedback conditions. P 1969, 125:1214-1217
69449 The psychology of dying. Pastoral Psychology 1961, Feb. In Ruitenbeek, H. M. Death: Interpretations, NY: Dell Publ 1969, 61-72
69450 Results of psychotherapy. Brit J Psychiat 1964, 110:35-45
69451 The results of psychotherapy. An evaluation of analytical type psychotherapy in private practice. Top Probl PT 1963, 4:259-274
69452 Toward an Understanding of Homosexuality. Englewood Cliffs, N.J.: Prentice-Hall 1965, xi + 302 p
Rv HRB Q 1966, 35:137-138

See Bieber, Toby B.

CAPRINI, G.

69452A (& Rebecchi, G.; Perbellini, G.) [A new method of pharmacoanalysis: diazanalysis.] (It) Riv Sper Freniat 1969, 93:822-824

CAPRIO, FRANK S.

69453 Female Homosexuality: A Modern Study of Lesbianism. NY: Grove Pr 1962; 1964, xvii + 334 p

69454 The Modern Woman's Guide to Sexual Maturity. NY: Grove Pr 1965, 256 p

69455 Only in Psychiatry. NY: Citadel Pr 1962, 188 p

69456 A Psychiatrist Talks about Sex. NY: Belmont 1968, 125 p

69457 (& Brenner, D. R.) Sexual Behavior: Psycho-Legal Aspects. NY: Citadel Pr 1961, 384 p

69458 Variations in Sexual Behavior. (Foreword: Henry, G. W.) NY: Grove Pr 1962, x + 344 p

CAQUANT-DIDIER, E.

See Haim, A.

CAQUOT, A.

69459 (& Leibovici, M.) (Eds) La Divination, Vol. II. [Divination.] Paris: PUF 1968

CARAPANOS, FROSSO

69460 (& Potamianou, A.) Genèse et évolution de deux fantasmes au cours de la thérapie d'un enfant psychotique. [Genesis and development of 2 fantasies during therapy of a psychotic child.] Rv Np inf 1967, 15:115-133

CARBALLO, JUAN ROF

69461 Constitution, transference, and co-existence. Acta psychother psychosom 1960, 8:400-414

69462 Thanatos. Ciba Symp 1964, 12:79-86

69463 Corrélations entre médecine interne et psychanalyse. [Correlations between internal medicine and psychoanalysis.] RFPsa 1963, 27(Spec. No.):9-28

CARDEN, NORMAN L.

69464 (& Schamel, D. J.) Observations of conversion reactions seen in troops involved in the Viet Nam conflict. P 1966, 123:21-31

CARDEÑA, JAIME

69465 (& Féder, L.; Díaz Infante, F.; Moreno Corzo, L.; Parres, R.; Ramirez, S.; Valner, G.) Algunos conceptos acerca de feminidad. [Some concepts concerning femininity.] (Round Table) Cuad Psa 1965, 1:205-206

CARDON, S. Z.

See Iberall, A. S.

CAREK, DONALD J.

69466 Group therapy as a study in behavioral expression. Int Psychiat Clin 1964, 1:123-135

69467 (& Watson, A. S.) Treatment of a family involved in fratricide. Arch gen Psychiat 1964, 11:533-542

See Harrison, Saul I.; Waggoner, Raymond W., Sr.

CAREK, MILDRED

69468 Psychosis in childhood. In Miller, E. *Foundations of Child Psychiatry,* Oxford/NY: Pergamon Pr 1968, 323-338

CARENZO, M.-F.

See Guasch, G.-P.

CARGNELLO, DANILO

69469 From psychoanalytic naturalism to phenomenological anthropology (Daseinanalyse): from Freud to Binswanger. Hum Context 1968, 1:70-92; 213-230; 421-435

CARINI, LOUIS

69470 Note on the theory of symbolic transformations. Percept mot Skills 1966, 22:750

CARKHUFF, ROBERT R.

69471 (& Berenson, B. G.) Beyond Counseling and Therapy. NY: Holt, Rinehart & Winston 1967, x + 310 p

69472 (& Pierce, R.) Differential effects of therapist race and social class upon patient depth of self-exploration in the initial clinical interview. J consult Psychol 1967, 31:632-634

* * * An integration of practice and training. See [69473]

* * * Requiem or reveille? See [69474]

69473 Toward failure or fulfillment: training and practice in counseling and psychotherapy. In *The Counselor's Contribution to Facilitative Processes,* Urbana, Ill: Parkinson 1966, 1-18. With title: An integration of practice and training. In Berenson, B. G. & Carkhuff, R. R. *Sources of Gain in Counseling and Psychotherapy,* NY/Chicago/San Francisco: Holt, Rinehart & Winston 1967, 423-436

69474 Training in counseling and psychotherapy: requiem or reveille? J of Counseling Psychol 1966, 13:360-367. With title: Requiem or reveille? In Berenson, B. G. & Carkhuff, R. R. *Sources of Gain in Counseling and Psychotherapy,* NY/Chicago/San Francisco: Holt, Rinehart & Winston 1967, 8-20

See Berenson, Bernard G.; Truax, Charles B.

CARLET, HELEN A.

69475 A study of the fantasy behavior of children at three age levels. Diss Abstr 1965, 26:1167-1168

CARLISKY, MARIO

69476 Oedipus. Beyond complex. R 1967, 54:296-302
Abs SRS Q 1968, 37:473
S-43425 The Oedipus legend and "Oedipus Rex."
Abs ARK An Surv Psa 1958, 9:446
69477 Primal scene, procreation and the number 13. Am Im 1962, 19:19-20

CARLO GIANNINI, G. DEL

69478 (& Baracchini, G.) [Psychopathologic aspects of school phobia.] (It)
Riv Neurobiol 1967, 13:328-335

CARLONI, GLAUCO

69479 (& Giorgio, A. Di; Gozzi, M. T.; Vanzelli, U.) Bonifica dell' ambiente
familiare in situazioni di disadattamento: la psicoterapia di gruppo alle
madri di preadolescenti nevrotici. [Improvement of familial environment in situations of maladjustment: group-psychotherapy for mothers
of neurotic preadolescents.] Riv ital Sicurezza soc 1965, 3:282-286
69480 (& Bosinelli, M.) I Concetti di Ansia e di Angoscia. [The Conceptions
of Anxiety and Anguish.] Riv sper Freniat 1960, 84(Monogr), 250 p
69481 La fiaba al lume della psicoanalisi. [The fairy tale in the light of psychoanalysis.] Riv Psa 1963, 9:169-186
69482 I mostri delle fiabe. [The demons of fairy tales.] Atlante 1967, (29):
70-77
69483 (& Spadoni, A.; Zucchini, G.) Psicoterapia di gruppo con psicotici
all'interno dell'ospedale psichiatrico. [Group psychotherapy for psychotics in a psychiatric hospital.] Riv ital Sicurezza soc 1965, 3:282-286
Psychothérapie de groupe de psychotiques à l'intérieur d'un hôpital
psychiatrique. Inform psychiat 1966, 42:235-240
69484 (& Spadoni, M. G.) Puo l'assistente sociale svolgere un lavoro psicoterapico in ospedale psichiatrico? [Can the social worker carry out
psychotherapeutic work in a mental hospital?] In Atti della Tavola
Rotonda Sul Servizio Sociale Ospedaliero, Rome: Instituto Italiano di
Medicina Sociale 1965, 172-175

REVIEW OF:
69485 Abraham, G. Psychodynamique essentielle, normale et pathologique.
Riv Psa 1965, 11:67

CARLSMITH, JAMES MERRILL

See Aronson, Elliot

CARLSON, ERIC T.

See Dain, Norman

CARLSON, HELEN B.

69486 Identity and character formation. P 1966, 122:821-823
69487 Identity-confusion. Sci Psa 1964, 7:230-236

69488 Identity-confusion (acute confusional state): research design for identification of the syndrome and analysis of preliminary results. Int J Np 1965, 1:452-465

69489 The relationship of the acute confusional state to ego development. J 1961, 42:517-536
       Abs WPK Q 1962, 31:581. PCR RFPsa 1964, 28:306

       See Alexander, Franz G.

CARLSON, P. V.
See Schechter, M. D.

CARLSON, R.

69490 Identification and personality structure in preadolescents. ASP 1963, 67:566-573

CARLUCCIO, CHARLES

69491 (& Sours, J. A.; Kolb, L. C.) Psychodynamics of echo-reactions. Arch gen Psychiat 1964, 10:623-629. JAMA 1964, 188:1148-1149
       Abs KR Q 1965, 34:313

CARMACK, WILLIAM R.

69492 Communication and community readiness for social change. Ops 1965, 35:539-543
       Abs JMa RFPsa 1966, 30:527

CARMEN, LAWRENCE M.
See Hollender, Marc H.

CARMICHAEL, HUGH T.

69493 (& Gerty, F. J.; Bartemeier, L. H.) Better relationships between psychiatrists and other physicians: a new concept in psychiatry. Round table on private practice. In Scientific Papers and Discussions, Divisional Meeting, Amer Psychiat Assoc, Detroit, Oct 1959

69494 The case seminar in psychotherapy. In Report of the 12th Annual Institute in Psychiatry and Neurology, Little Rock, Ark: Consolidated V.A. Hospital 1960, 22-23

69495 Continuing education for psychiatrists. P 1968, 125:135-136

69496 Continuing education in medicine. Alaska Med 1968, 10(4):157-159

69497 (& Noonan, W. J.; Kenyon, A. T.) The effects of testosterone proprionate in impotence. P 1941, 97:919-943

69498 The initial psychiatric interview. In Report of the 12th Annual Institute in Psychiatry and Neurology, Little Rock, Ark: Consolidated V.A. Hospital 1960, 17-18

69499 (& Muslin, H. L.; Fisher, L. A.) A learning project for psychiatry instructors. In Scientific Proceedings, 124th Annual Meeting, Amer Psychiat Ass 1967, 76-77

69500 Perspectives on the American Board of Psychiatry and Neurology. Arch gen Psychiat 1963, 8:405-417

69501 Psychiatry in Chicago 1935-1957 as I saw it. Ill med J 1958, 114:1-10
69502 The psychosomatic approach. ROK Armed Forces med J 1961, 1(2): 5-12. Texas State J Med 1963, 59:80-85
69503 (& Masserman, J. H.) Results of treatment in a psychiatric outpatient department: a follow-up study of 166 cases. JAMA 1939, 113:2292-2298
69504 Sound-film recording of psychoanalytic therapy: a therapist's experiences and reactions. J Iowa State Med Soc 1956, 46:590-595. Meth Res PT 50-59

See Muslin, Hyman L.

CARMICHAEL, ROBERT

See Eiduson, Bernice T.

CARP, EUGÈNE ANTOINE DÉSIRÉ ÉMILE

69505 Angst en Vrees. [Anxiety and Fear.] Utrecht/Antwerp: Het Spectrum 1966, 160 p
69506 Le besoin d'un optimisme thérapique. [The need for a therapeutic optimism.] Acta psychother psychosom 1964, 12:111-118
S-43436 Le complexe de sauvetage.
        Abs RJA An Surv Psa 1956, 7:165
69507 The world conception of the mentally deficient human being. J existent Psychiat 1960-61, 1:121-126

CARP, FRANCES M.

69508 Differences among older workers, volunteers, and persons who are neither. J Gerontol 1968, 23:497-501
69509 Psychosexual development of stutterers. J proj Tech 1962, 26:388-391

CARPELAN, HENRIK

69510 Fredsforskning och psykoanalys. [Peace research and psychoanalysis.] Psykisk Hälsa 1969, 10:22-40
69511 Några psykoanalytiska synpunkter på psykiatrisk nosologi. [Some psychoanalytic viewpoints concerning psychiatric nosology.] Nord Psyk Tidsskr 1964, 18:604-617
69512 Psykoanalyyttinen ryhmähoito—käytännön näkökohtia. [Practical views on psychoanalytic group therapy.] Sosiaali-lääketieteellinen Aikakauslehti 1968, 6:223-232

See Campo, Alberto

CARPENTER, BOB L.

See Raphling, David L.

CARPENTER, SUSANNE I.

69513 Psychosexual conflict, defense, and abstraction. Diss Abstr 1966, 26: 7445

CARPENTER, THOMAS P.

69514 Abnormal psychology in twentieth-century novels. Lit & Psych 1966,
16:43-47

CARPENTIER, RENÉ

69515 S. Congrégation du Saint-Office: Monitum du 15 Juillet 1961, relatif
à l'enseignement de la théologie morale en metière d'imputabilité des
actes humaines, et à l'usage de la psychanalyse par les clercs et les
religieux. [Concerning the teaching of moral theology with respect to
the imputability of human behavior and the use of psychoanalysis by
clerics and religious.] Nouv Rev théolog 1961, 93(83):856-861

CARPILOVSKY, JOSÉ C.

69516 Frustração, inveja e ódio em um grupo terapêutico. [Frustration, envy
and hate in a therapeutic group.] J Bras Psiquiat 1964, 13:365-371

69517 [Oral phase of the primary scene in group therapy.] (Por) J Bras
Psiquiat 1966, 15:211-218

69518 [Fantasies of a therapeutic group concerning the admission of the
"observer."] (Por) J Bras Psiquiat 1965, 14:277-284

CARPINACCI, JORGE A.

69519 (& Liberman, D.; Schlossberg, N.) Perturbaciones de la communicación y neurosis de contratransferencia. [Disturbances in communication
and countertransference neurosis.] Rev Psicoanál 1963, 20:63-69

See Liberman, David; Zac, Joel

REVIEW OF:
69520 Freud, M. Sigmund Freud. Mi Padre. Rev Psicoanál 1967, 24: 210-213

CARR, ARTHUR C.

69521 (& Forer, B. R.; Henry, W. E.; Hooker, E.; Hutt, M. L.; Piotrowski,
Z. A.) The Prediction of Overt Behavior through the Use of Projective
Techniques. Springfield, Ill: Thomas 1960; Oxford: Blackwell 1961,
vii + 177 p

69522 Psychological defect and psychological testing. Int Psychiat Clin 1964,
1:773-798

69523 Psychological testing and reporting. J proj Tech 1968, 32:513-521

69524 Symposium on "reinterpretations of the Schreber case: Freud's theory
of paranoia." II. Observations on paranoia and their relationship to the
Schreber case. J 1963, 44:195-200
Abs EVN Q 1965, 34:615

See Frazier, Shervert H.; Hendin, Herbert; Kolb, Lawrence C.; Mesnikoff, Alvin M.; Rainer, John D.; Schoenberg, Bernard

CARR, H. E., JR.

See Knapp, Peter H.

CARR, JOHN E.

See Rabkin, Leslie Y.

CARRERA, JOSÉ

See Arizmendi Ch., Fernando

ABSTRACT OF:

69525 Ekstein, R. On the acquisition of speech in the autistic child. Cuad Psa 1965, 1:298

CARRETIER, L.

See Racamier, Paul C.

CARRIERO, F.

69526 [Comprehensive anthropological analysis of a case of homicide. Criminogenetic considerations.] (It) Zacchia 1967, 42(3):288-297

CARRINGTON, PATRICIA

See Ephron, Harmon S.

CARROLL, EDWARD J.

69527 Family therapy—some observations and comparisons. Fam Proc 1964, 3:178-185
69528 General systems theory and psychotherapy. Curr psychiat Ther 1966, 6:8-12
69529 Instinct and the basis of behavior. Penn psychiat Q 1962, 2:3-12
69530 (& Cambor, C. G.; Leopold, J. V.; Miller, M. D.; Reis, W. J.) Psychotherapy of marital couples. Fam Proc 1963, 2:25-53.
69531 Steady state and change in family interviews In Gray, W. et al: *General Systems Theory and Psychiatry*, Boston: Little, Brown 1969, 457-467
69532 A Study of Interpersonal Relations Within Families. Pitt: Craig House for Children 1966, 108 p
69533 Treatment of the family as a unit. Penn med J 1960, 63:57-62

See Charny, E. Joseph; Loeb, Felix F., Jr.

REVIEW OF:

69534 Mazlish, B. (Ed) Psychoanalysis and History. Q 1964, 33:585

CARSON, ROBERT C.

See Daniels, Robert S.

CARSON, R. L.

See Cummings, S. Thomas

CARSTAIRS, GEORGE MORRIS

69535 Cross-cultural interviewing. In Kaplan, B. *Studying Personality Cross-Culturally*, NY/Evanston/London: Harper & Row 1961, 533-548

69536 Foreword to Aldrich, C. K. *An Introduction to Dynamic Psychiatry*, NY: McGraw-Hill 1966, v-vi

See Bowlby, John; Giel, R.

REVIEW OF:
69537 Kardiner, A. & Preble, E. They Studied Man. J 1964, 45:588-590

CARSTENS, ERIK

69538 Had. Antivirkelighed. Løgnagtigt sjaeleliv. Virkelighed og kontakt. Personlighed og omverden. [Hate. Anti-Reality. False Spiritual Life. Reality and Contact. Personality and the World Around.] Copenhagen: Dansk Psykoterapeutforening 1967, 135 p

CARTER, GEORGE H.

69539 Admission and diagnostic procedures. In Boulder, B. *Psychiatry in the General Hospital*, Boston: Little, Brown 1966, 11-25
S-43470 History making and interviewing technique.
        Preparación de historial clínico y técnica de intervistas. Bol Oficina Sanetoria Panamer 1965, 59(3):236-246

ABSTRACT OF:
69540 Lamont, J. H. Hawthorne's last novels: a study in creative failure. Bull Phila Ass Psa 1962, 12:38-39

CARTER, PAULINE

69541 (& Lockey, A.) Teaching the hyperactive child. Provo Pap 1967, Summer:124-131

CARTHY, JOHN D.

69542 (& Ebling, F. J.) (Eds) The Natural History of Aggression. London/NY: Academic Pr 1964

CARTWRIGHT, DESMOND S.

69543 Effectiveness of psychotherapy: a critique of the spontaneous remission argument. J counsel Psychol 1955, 2:290-296. In Goldstein, A. P. & Dean, S. J. *The Investigation of Psychotherapy*, NY: Wiley 1966, 222-227

See Sweney, Arthur B.

CARTWRIGHT, DORWIN

69544 (& Zander, A.) Group Dynamics. Research and Theory. Evanston, Ill/Elmsford, NY: Row, Peterson & Co 1960, xii + 826 p
        Rv Woltmann, A. G. PPR 1962, 49(4):125

See Dennis, Wayne

CARTWRIGHT, ROSALIND DYMOND

69545 (& Vogel, J. L.) A comparison of changes in psychoneurotic patients during matched periods of therapy and no therapy. J consult Psychol 1960, 24:121-127

69546 A comparison of the response to psychoanalytic and client-centered psychotherapy. Meth Res PT 517-529

69547 Dream and drug-induced fantasy behavior. A comparative study. Arch gen Psychiat 1966, 15:7-15

69548 (& Bernick, N.; Borowitz, G.) Effect of an erotic movie on the sleep and dreams of young men. Arch gen Psychiat 1969, 20:262-271

69549 (& Monroe, L. J.; Palmer, C.) Individual differences in response to REM deprivation. Arch gen Psychiat 1967, 16:297-303

69550 (& Monroe, L. J.) Relation of dreaming and REM sleep: the effects of REM dperivation under two conditions. J pers soc Psychol 1968, 10:69-74

CARUSO, IGOR A.

69551 (& Frühmann, E.) Activation and symbolization of delusions in schizophrenia. In Burton, A. *Psychotherapy of the Psychoses*, NY: Basic Books 1961, 237-255

69552 Aggressivität oder "Todestrieb?" Der Wiederholungszwang und primäre Leugnung. [Aggression or death instinct? Repetition compulsion and early disavowal.] Fortschr Psa 1968, 3:105-121

69553 Die "Akzeptierung" Freuds und die Grundeinstellung zum psychotherapeutischen Heilungsverlauf. [The acceptance of Freud and the fundamental attitude to the outcome of psychotherapeutic treatment and its limits.] In Graber, G. H. *Der psychotherapeutische Heilungsverlauf und seine Grenzen*, Bern/Ratingen-Düsseldorf: Ardschuna 1965, 6-11

69554 O alibi do Bem-Estar. [Ambivalence in the affluent society.] Circulo bras Psicol profunda 1960, 1
El Bienestar como coartada de la Reificación. Rev jav 1961, 56:248-260
L'ambivalence dans la Société du Bien-Être. Bull Psychol, Paris 1963, 16:613-618

69555 An Dr. Gustav Hans Graber (zum 70. Geburtstag). [To Dr. Gustav Hans Graber (on his 70th birthday).] Psychol, Bern 1963, 15 (5/6): 169-171

69556 O aspeto social da Higiene Mental. [The social aspect of mental hygiene.] Criança Port 1960, 19:117-124

69557 Beantwortung der Enquête über "Le Risque." [Reply to the investigation on "Le Risque."] Esprit 1965, 33(1):167-172

69558 Beantwortung der Enquête "Zum Stressbegriff in der psychosomatischen Medizin." [Reply to the investigation, "On the concept of stress in psychosomatic medicine."] Z PSM 1965, 11:262-263

S-43475 (& Frühmann, E.; Schindler, S.; Wegeler, A.; Wucherer-Huldenfeld, K. v.) Bios, Psyche, Person.
Bios, Psique, Persona. Madrid: Credos 1965, 335 p

69559   Contribución al estudio de los conceptos de pulsion de muerte y de agresividad en Freud. [Contribution to the study of Freud's concepts of the instincts for death and for aggression.] Arch Estud psicoanal Psicol med 1965, 2:5-70
        Contribution à l'étude des concepts de pulsion de mort et d'aggressivité chez Freud. Bull Psychol, Paris 1965, 19:1-36

69560   Crise du monde technique et psychologie. [Technical and psychological world crisis.] In *La Technique et l'Homme, "Recherches et Débats,"* Paris: Libr Artheme Fayard 1960, 54-65
        Psychologia a kryzys wieku techniki. In *Nauka i Technika a Wiara,* Warsaw: Pax 1964, 189-202

69561   El devenir del hombre y la utopia. [The evolution of man and utopia.] Rev Univ México 1966, 20(11):8-10

69562   Einheit and Vielheit in der Psychoanalyse. [Unity and diversity in psychoanalysis.] Prax Kinderpsychol 1966, 15:152-154

69563   Foreword to Gabel, J. Ideologie und Schizophrenie. *Foremen der Entfremdung,* Frankfurt a.M.: Fischer 1967, 27-40

69564   Freud, un muerto venerado y traicionado. [Freud, after his death, worshipped and betrayed.] Eco 1964, 9:414-428

69565   Geschichtliches und Kritisches über Mutterliebs- und Geburtsphantasien [Historical and critical comments on fantasies of mother love and birth.] Psychol, Bern 1961, 13(8/9):308-313

69566   Hacia un Conocimiento Simbólico de la Persona Humana. [Toward a symbolic understanding of the human personage.] México: Guadalajara 1961

° ° °   How social is psychoanalysis? See [69579]

69567   Das Ich und die Kultur. [Ego and culture.] De Facto, Salzburg 1968, 5:i-xi. Jb Psychol Psychother med Anthropol 1968, 16:18-29
        Le moi et la civilisation. Bull Psychol, Paris 1968, 22(3-4):129-136

69568   Interkollektive Dialektik in der psychoanalytischen Situation. Psychoanalytische Situation als mikrosoziales Modell. [Intercollective dialectics in the psychoanalytic situation. The psychoanalytic situation as a microsocial model.] Z PSM 1963, 9:197-208. Fortschr Psa 1966, 2:37-52
        A situáçao psicanalitica, modelo microsocial. Circulo bras Psicol Profunda 1962, 2(2):3-22
        Dialectica intercolectiva en la situación psicoanalítica, la situación psicoanalítica como modelo micro-social. Rev mex psicol 1963, 1(2):149-174

69569   Mit der Trennung leben. [Living with separation.] In Graber, G. H. *Probleme moderner Psychotherapie,* Bern/Ratingen-Düsseldorf: Arschuna 1966, 12-21

69570   (& Edelweiss, M. L.) Moral, super-ego e complexo de bode expiatório. [Morality, superego and complex of expiatory wedding.] Circulo bras Psicol profunda 1963, 3(1-2):67-80

69571   Note sur la nécessité et l'ambivalence de l'aliénation. [Note on necessity for and ambivalence of alienation.] Bull Psychol, Paris 1960, 14(1-4):29-32

69572   Notiz über den Traum als Intelligenzleistung. [Note on the dream as the result of intelligence.] Psychol, Bern 1960, 12 (7-8):284-286

69573 La Personalizacion. Biologia y Sociedad. [Personalization. Biological and Sociological Aspects.] Bogota: Circulo Vienes de Psicologia Profunda Grupo Bogota 1964, 75 p
Rv Vega Q 1965, 34:450-451. Vega R 1966, 53:308-310

69574 La perspectiva social falsifica el psicoanalisis? [Is there a false social perspective in psychoanalysis?] Arch Estud psicoanal Psicol med 1965, 2:109-113

69575 Die prekäre Hoffnung: Wiederholungszwang, Todestrieb und Kultur. [The precarious expectation: repetition compulsion, the death urge, and culture.] Jb Psychol Psychother med Anthropol 1966, 14:186-229

69576 El psicoanálisis como método y como técnica. [Psychoanalysis as method and as technique.] Rev Psicol, Bogota 1963, 8(2):131-147

69577 El Psicoanálisis, Lenguaje Ambiguo. [Psychoanalysis: Ambiguous Language.] México: Fondo de Cultura Economica 1966, 218 p

69578 Psicoanálisis y civilisación. [Psychoanalysis and civilization.] Eco 1963, 8:188-205

69579 La psychanalyse est-elle sociale? Esprit 1961, 29:420-437
Is the psychoanalysis social? Cross Currents 1963, Winter. With title: How social is psychoanalysis? In Birmingham, W. & Cunneen, J. E. *Cross Currents of Psychiatry and Catholic Morality,* NY: Pantheon Books 1964, 357-372
Es Social el Psicoanalisis? Universidad de Antioquia (Colombia) 1961, 144(Jan-Mar.):30-46

69580 Psychanalyse et souveraieneté de l'homme. [Psychoanalysis and the supremacy of man.] Esprit 1966, 34:3-20. Epoches 1966

69581 Psychanalyse pour la Personne. [Psychoanalysis for the Individual.] Paris: Seuil 1962
Psicanalisis per la Persona. Milan: Comunitá 1965, 196 p
Psicanálisis e Dialética. Rio de Janeiro: Bloch 1967
Psicoanálisis para la persona. Barcelona: Seix Barral 1965, 246 p

S-43488 Psychoanalyse und Synthese der Existenz.
Existential Psychology: From Analysis to Synthesis. (Tr: Krapf, E.) NY: Herder & Herder; London: Darton, Longman & Todd 1964, xx + 227 p
Rv Donadeo, J. Q 1961, 30:117-118

69582 Die Psychoanalyse zwischen Ideologie und Ideologiekritik. [Psychoanalysis between ideology and criticism of ideology.] Z PSM 1968, 14:204-211

69583 Psychological systems and the psychology of symbolism. Criança Port 1956-57, 15-16(1)

69584 Schuld und Schuldgefühl. [Guilt and feelings of guilt.] Prax PT 1968, 13(5):202-207

69585 El simbolo, criterio de conocimiento e instrumento del psicoanalisis. [The symbol, criterion of knowledge and tool of psychoanalysis.] Eco 1962, 5:73-87. With title: Hacia un conocimiento simbolico de la persona humana. Actas luso-esp Neurol Psiquiat 18

S-43491 Soll es eine tiefenpsychologische "orthodoxie" geben?
Debe haber una "Ortodoxia" psicoanalitica? Rev Psicol norm patol 1960, 6(1-2):210-216

Debe haber una "Ortodoxia" psicoanalitica? Vervielfältigtes Skriptum des Wiener Arbeitskreises für Tiefenpsychologie, s. d. 1960

69586　Soziale Aspekte der Psychoanalyse. [Social Aspects of Psychoanalysis.] Stuttgart: Ernst Klett Verlag 1962, 89 p
De sociale aspecten van de Psychoanalyse. Utrecht/Antwerp: Spectrum 1967
Psicoanálisis Dialéctico. Buenos Aires: Paidós 1964, 143 p

69587　(& Schindler, R.) Das Team in der Behandlung neurotischer Kinder und die spezifische Funktion des Psychiaters. [The team in the treatment of neurotic children and the specific function of the psychiatrist.] Criança Port 1962-63, 21:211-221

69588　La technique analytique en tant que technique "existentielle." [The analytic technique as an "existential" technique.] Acta psychother psychosom 1960, 8:17-22
La técnica analitica como técnica existencial. Rev Psiquiat Psicol med, Barcelona 1959, 7:171-174. Rev Psicol, Bogota 1960, 5(2). IV Congrese Internacional de Psicoterapia, Barcelona, Editorial Scientia 1963

69589　Die Trennung der Liebenden: Eine Phänomenologie des Todes. [The Separation of Lovers: A Phenomenology of Death.] Bern: Hans Huber 1968, 316 p

69590　Über einige Aspekte der Forschung und Praxis in der Tiefenpsychologie. [Some aspects of research and practice in depth psychology.] Jb Psychol Psychother med Anthropol 1967, 15(3/4):199-207
Algunas concideraciones sobre nuestro trabajo. Arch Estud psicoanal Psicol med 1967, 4:17-25

69591　Über Selbstverwirklichung und Kultur. [On self realization and culture.] Psychol, Bern 1968, 20:6-11

S-43496　Übertragung und Symbol.
Abs An Surv Psa 1955, 6:319

69592　(& Tanco-Duque, R.) Valores espirituales y psicoanálisis. [Psychoanalysis and spiritual values.] Rev Espir 1960, 19:51-55

69593　Die Verdinglichung. Gedanken zu "La fausse Conscience: Essai sur la Réification" von Joseph Gabel. [Substantiation. Ideas about "The False Conscience" by Joseph Gabel.] Jb Psychol Psychother med Anthropol 1962, 9:319-326

69594　Veröffentlichungen. [Publications.] In Edelweiss, M. L. et al: *Personalisation,* Vienna/Freiburg/Basel: Herder 1964, 163-168

69595　Vida y separación. [Life and separation.] Rev Psicoanal Psiquiat Psicol 1967, 5:26-33

69596　Vie pulsionelle et religion. [Life instinct and religion.] Revue de Psychologie et des Sciences de l'Education 1966-67, 2(1):12-20

69597　Der Vorstoss ins Weltall als psychologisches Problem. [All the world pushing forward as a psychological problem.] Psychol, Bern 1960, 12(11):424-429; (12):463-467
Las conquistas espaciales como problomo psicológico. Indice, Barcelona 1961, 12. With title: La angustia del Otto Mundo. In *El Espectador, Dominical,* 8 de Enero, 1961, p VII

69598　Werden und "Entwerden" im Handeln. [Becoming and "unbecoming" in action.] In Wiesenhütter, E. *Werden und Handeln,* Stuttgart: Hippokrates 1963, 218-234

69599 Zur Doppelsinnigkeit der Gegenübertragung. [The ambiguity of countertransference.] In Graber, G. H. *Probleme moderner Psychotherapie,* Bern/Ratingen-Düsseldorf: Ardschuna 1966, 26-29

69600 Zum Problem der Psychoanalyse in fremder Sprache. [On the problem of psychoanalytic treatment in a foreign language.] Z PSM 1964, 10(1):36-49; (2):126-140; (3):209-219; (4):285-295

El problema de psicoanálisis en lengua extranjera. Arch Estud psicoanal Psicol med 1966, 78 p

See Raclot, Marcel; Walcher, W. von

CARUTH, ELAINE

69601 (& Ekstein, R.) Certain phenomenological aspects of the countertransference in the treatment of schizophrenic children. Reiss-Davis Clin Bull 1964, 1:80-88

69602 Comics—neither condemned nor condoned. Reiss-Davis Reporter 1968, 7(1):2

69603 Hercules and Superman: the modern-day mythology of the comic book. Some clinical applications. J Amer Acad Child Psychiat 1968, 7:1-12

69604 (& Ekstein, R.) Interpretation within the metaphor: further considerations. J Amer Acad Child Psychiat 1966, 5:35-45. In Ekstein, R. *Children of Time and Space, of Action and Impulse,* NY: Appleton-Century-Crofts 1966, 158-165

69605 The onion and the Moebius strip. R 1968, 55:415-425

See Ekstein, Rudolf; Meyer, Mortimer M.

CARY, ARA C.

69606 (& Reveal, M. T.) Prevention and detection of emotional disturbances in preschool children. Ops 1967, 37:719-724

CASADY, RICHARD R.

69607 Sexual problems of children—their detection and management. In Wahl, C. W. *Sexual Problems. Diagnosis and Treatment in Medical Practice,* NY: Free Pr; London: Collier-Macmillan 1967, 115-132

CASCELLA, G.

69608 [Delire and deliriant interpretations of jealousy.] (It) Rass Np 1966, 19:685-705

CASEY, ROBERT PIERCE

69609 Psychoanalytic study of religion. In Strunk, O. *Readings in the Psychology of Religion,* NY: Abingdon Pr 1959, 62-74

CASLER, LAWRENCE

69610 Maternal deprivation: a critical review of the literature. Monogr Soc Res child Develop 1961, 26(2):1-64

CASRIEL, DANIEL

69611   So Fair a House: The Story of Synanon. Englewood Cliffs, N.J.: Prentice-Hall 1963, xiv + 224 p

CASS, LORETTA K.

69612   (& Wessen, A. E.) Determinants of parental attitudes. In Glidewell, J. C. *Parental Attitudes and Child Behavior*, Springfield, Ill: Thomas 1961, 207-214

CASSEE, A. P.

69613   Het Begrip Ik-Sterkte in de Psychoanalyse (with summary in English). [The Concept of Ego-Strength in Psychoanalysis.] Amsterdam: Swets en Zeitlinger 1967, 150 p

CASSELL, WILFRED A.

69614   (& Fisher, S.) Body image boundaries and histamine flare reaction. PSM 1963, 25:344-351
          Abs ELG Q 1964, 33:305-306
69615   Body perception and symptom localization. PSM 1965, 27:171-176
69616   (& Duboczy, J. B.) Cardiac symptoms and tachistoscopic recognition of the heart image. Canad Psychiat Ass J 1967, 12:73-76
69617   (& Richman, J. L.) Negatively correlated external and internal symptom clusters. PSM 1968, 30:121-124
69618   A projective index of body-interior awareness. PSM 1964, 26:172-177
69619   A tachistoscopic index of body perception. I. Body boundary and body interior awareness. J proj Tech 1966, 30:31-36

CASSEM, N. H.

See Hackett, Thomas P.

CASSENS, JAMES

See Gendlin, Eugene T.

CASTAGNOLA, ROBERT L.

See Kanter, Stanley S.

CASTALDO, VINCENZO

69620   (& Holzman, P. S.) The effects of hearing one's own voice on sleep mentation. JNMD 1967, 144:2-13

CASTANOS, J. N.

See Koller, K. M.

CASTELLANI, A.

69621   [Anthropo-analytical contribution to the study of obsessive disease.] (It) G Psichiat Neuropat 1962, 90:79-111
69622   (& Balloni, A.) [Clinical classification and psychopathological study of pyromania.] (It) G Psichiat Neuropat 1966, 94:571-623

69623 [On the psychopathological and clinical problem of depressions with obsessions. Obsessive dysthymia.] (It) Arch Psicol Neurol Psichiat 1964, 25:325-350

69624 [Phenomenological and anthropological analysis of some constitutive aspects of the "phobic" world.] G Psichiat Neuropat 1964, 92:347-354

69625 [Recent contribution to the study of phobic psychoneuroses by means of analysis of the "phobic space."] (It) G Psichiat Neuropat 1963, 91:21-37

CASTELLANI, LEONARD

69626 Freud en Cifra. [Freud in Code.] Buenos Aires: Cruz y Fierro 1966, 70 p

CASTELLO, D.

69627 (& Cagno, L. Di.) [Importance of the mother-child relationship on rhythm of psychomotor development of twins.] (It) Minerva Nipiol 1965, 15:253-255

69628 Importanza del rapporto madre-figlio nell'immaturo ospedalizzato. [Importance of the mother-child relationship in hospitalized premature infants.] Minerva Pediat 1966, 18:331-336

69629 [On a case of kleptomania traceable to affective maternal deprivation.] (It) Lattante 1965, 36:207-209

See Cagno, L. di

CASTELNUOVO-TEDESCO, PIETRO

69630 Brief psychotherapeutic treatment of the depressive reactions. Int Psychiat Clin 1966, 3(4):197-210

69631 The doctor's attitude and his management of patients with sexual problems. In Wahl, C. W. *Sexual Problems*, NY: Free Pr; London: Collier-Macmillan 1967, 238-246

69632 Emotional antecedents of perforation of ulcers of the stomach and duodenum. PSM 1962, 24:398
Abs Rev Psicoanál 1963, 20:93

69633 Psychiatric observations on attacks of gout in a patient with ulcerative colitis. Report of a case. PSM 1966, 28:781-788

69634 The Twenty-Minute Hour: A Guide to Brief Psychotherapy for the Physician. Boston: Little, Brown 1965, xii + 184 p

69635 Ulcerative colitis in an adolescent boy subjected to a homosexual assault. PSM 1962, 24:148-155

CASTETS, BRUNO

69636 (& Czesnowicka, M. N.; Bion, D.; Gibello, B.) A propos de la place du père dans la structure psychotique: réflexions sur la psycho-genèse des psychoses à partir de quatre observations. [Apropos of the position of the father in the psychotic structure: reflections on the psychogenesis of psychoses from four observations.] Ann méd-psychol 1966, 124:447-462

69636A [On sadism and masochism. Apropos of the contemporary novel, *The Story of O* by Pauline Reage.] (Fr) Évolut psychiat 1969, 34:47-63

69637 Un père et sa pulsion de mort. [A father and his death wish.] Ann méd-psychol 1968, 126(1):217-230

69638 Réflexion critique sur la notion de "moi." [Critical reflection on the notion of "ego."] Evolut psychiat 1967, 32:603-616

CASTIGAN, GIOVANNI

69639 Sigmund Freud: A Short Biography. NY: Macmillan 1965, xiv + 306 p

CASTILLA DEL PINO, CARLOS

69640 La angustia, las ideas sobrevaloradas y el sentimiento de culpabilidad en los enfermos depresivos. [Anguish, fixed ideas and guilt feelings in depressives.] Rev Psiquiat Psicol 1966, 7:371-393

69641 Los dinamismos de la tristeza y de la inhibición en los enfermos depresivos. [The dynamics of sadness and inhibition in depressive patients.] Arch Neurobiol 1966, 29:205-231

69642 Foundations of a dialectic anthropology. Hum Context 1969, 1:398-420

CASTRO DE LA MATA, G.

69643 (& Gingras, G.; Wittkower, E. D.) Impact of sudden, severe disablement of the father upon the family. Canad Med Ass J 1960, 82:1015-1020

CASUSO, GABRIEL

S-43501 Anxiety related to the "discovery" of the penis. An observation.
Abs EMW An Surv Psa 1957, 8:205-206

69644 A psychoanalyst's observation during a totalitarian take-over. (Read at Phila Ass Psa, 16 March, 1962)
Abs Cowitz, B. Bull Phila Ass Psa 1962, 12:178-181

69645 (Reporter) The relationship between child analysis and the theory and practice of adult psychoanalysis. (Panel: Am Psa Ass, Los Angeles, May 1964) J Am Psa Ass 1965, 13:159-171
Abs Kalina, E. Rev Psicoanál 1966, 23:348

CATEMARIO, ARMANDO

69646 La Società Malata; Saggio Sulla Filosofia di Fromm. [The Sick Society: Samples of the Philosophy of Fromm.] Naples: Giannini 1962, viii + 620 p

CATH, STANLEY H.

69647 (& Fischberg, B.) An Al Capp strip on psychiatry. Tufts Folia Med 1963, 9:96-98

69648 Beyond depression—the depleted state. A study in ego psychology in the aged. Canad Psychiat Ass J 1966, 11(Suppl):S329-S339

69649 Discussion in the 1964 symposium on "Vicissitudes of the terminal phase of life." Psychodyn St Aging 213-218

69650 (& Cohen, H.) Elbow rubbing and the wish to be beaten. A study of a case and the possible genesis of perversion. Israel Ann Psychiat 1967, 5:185-197

69651 (& Fischberg, B.) How to beat your friends at bridge. A psychiatrist looks at comic strips. Tufts Folia Med 1963, 9:88-96

69652 Psychodynamics of the three generation home. Tufts Folia Med 1962, 8(2):43-53

69653 Some dynamics of middle years—a study in depletion and restitution. Smith Coll Stud soc Wk 1963, 33(2):97-126. In Berezin, M. A. & Cath, S. L. *Geriatric Psychiatry; Grief, Loss and Emotional Disorder in the Aging Process,* NY: IUP 1965, 21-72

69654 (& Fischberg, B.) Some psychological implications of comic strips. Bull Phila Ass Psa 1964, 14:29-36
Abs EFA Q 1965, 34:135. PLe RFPsa 1967, 31:307

69655 The student-teacher alliance and the formation of the professional ego: an experiment in small-group seminars in the second year of medical school. Int J grp PT 1965, 15:303-315

See Berezin, Martin A.

ABSTRACT OF:
69656 Gitelson, M. The curative importance of the first phase in psychoanalysis. Bull Phila Ass Psa 1961, 11:132-135

CATLIN, GEORGE E.

69657 Library of dreams. Int J soc Psychiat 1965, 11:306-308

CATTELL, JAMES P.

69658 The adolescents' crises today: discussion. NYSJM 1967, 67:1998

69659 Avoiding the mistakes of bereavement. In Kutscher, A. H. *But Not to Lose,* NY: Frederick Fell 1969

69660 Behavioral disorders. In Kutscher, A. H. et al: *Pharmacotherapeutics of Oral Disease,* NY: McGraw-Hill 1964, 483-488

69661 Depersonalization phenomena. Am Hbk Psychiat III 88-102

69662 Deprivation and fantasy: early experiences, later developments and therapeutic connotations. Comprehen Psychiat 1961, 2:304-307

69663 (& Forster, E.) Evaluation of patients following treatment in general hospital out-patient clinics. Proc Amer Psychopath Ass 1964, 52:247-253

S-43507 The holiday syndrome.
Abs An Surv Psa 1955, 6:166-167

69664 (& MacKinnon, R. A.; Forster, E.) Limited goal therapy in a psychiatric clinic. P 1963, 120:255-260

69665 Personality and behavior changes following trauma. In *Traumatic Medicine and Surgery for the Attorney, Vol. 6,* London: Butterworth 1962

69666 Pseudoneurotic schizophrenia: clinical course and social outcome. Int Psychiat Clin 1964, 1:753-772

69667 Psychiatric implications of bereavement. In Kutscher, A. H. *Death and Bereavement,* Springfield, Ill: Thomas 1969, 153-162

69668 Psychodynamic and clinical aspects of depersonalization. Bull Ass psa Med 1965, Oct

69669 A psychodynamic view of pseudoneurotic schizophrenia. In Hoch, P. H.

& Zubin, J. *Psychopathology of Schizophrenia*, NY: Grune & Stratton 1966, 19-36

69670 (& Malitz, S.) Revised survey of selected psychopharmacological agents. P 1960, 117:449-453

69671 Some observations on "the case of Ellen West." Ann PT 1961, 2:6

See Daniels, George E.; Hoch, Paul H.

CATTELL, RAYMOND BERNARD

69672 Anxiety and motivation: theory and crucial experiments. In Spielberger, C. D. *Anxiety and Behavior*, NY/London: Academic Pr 1966, 23-62

69673 (& Warburton, F. W.) A cross-cultural comparison of patterns of extraversion and anxiety. Brit J Psychol 1961, 52:3-15

69674 (& Rickels, K.) Diagnostic power of IPAT objective anxiety neuroticism tests with private patients. Arch gen Psychiat 1964, 11:459-465

69675 (& Rickels, K.; Weise, C.; Gray, B.; Yel, R.) The effects of psychotherapy upon measured anxiety and regression. PT 1966, 20:261-269

69676 Evaluating therapy as total personality change: theory and available instruments. PT 1966, 20:69-88

69677 (& Scheier, I. H.) Extension of meaning of objective test personality factors: especially into anxiety, neuroticism, questionnaire and physical factors. J gen Psychol 1959, 61:287-315

69678 (& Howarth, E.) Hypotheses on the principal personality dimensions in children and tests constructed for them. J genet Psych 1962, 101:145-163

69679 (& Scheier, I. H.) The Meaning and Measurement of Neuroticism and Anxiety. NY: Ronald Pr 1961, 535 p
Rv Karush, A. Q 1964, 33:124-127

69680 Objective personality tests: a reply to Dr. Eysenck. Occupational Psychol 1964, 38:69-86. In Megargee, E. I. *Research in Clinical Assessment*, NY/London: Harper & Row 1966, 174-188

69681 (& Meredith, G. M.) Other psychological personality theories. Compreh txbk Psychiat 410-417

69682 The parental early repressiveness l.ypothesis for the "authoritarian" personality factor, U.I. 28. J genet Psych 1964, 105:333-349

69683 (& Peterson, D. R.) Personality structure in four and five year olds in terms of objective tests. Clin Psych 1959, 15:355-369

69684 Personality theory derived from quantitative experiment. Compreh Txbk Psychiat 388-410

69685 Personality theory growing from multivariate quantitative research. In Koch, S. *Psychology: A Study of a Science*, Vol. 3, NY/Toronto/London: McGraw-Hill 1959, 257-327

69686 Psychological definition and measurement of anxiety. J Neuropsychiat 1964, 5:396-402

69687 Psychological measurement of anxiety and depression: a quantitative approach. Canad Psychiat Ass J 1962, 7(Suppl):11-28

69688 (& Rickels, K.) The relationship of clinical symptoms and IPAT-factored tests of anxiety, regression and asthenia: a factor analytic study. JNMD 1968, 146:147-160

69689 The Scientific Analysis of Personality. Baltimore: Penguin Books 1965, 399 p

69690 Trait-view theory of perturbations in ratings and self ratings (L(BR) and Q-data): its application to obtaining pure trait score estimates in questionnaires. Psychol Rev 1968, 75:96-113

69691 (& Howarth, E.) Verification of objective test personality factor patterns in middle childhood. J genet Psych 1964, 104:331-349

See Damarin, Fred Louis, Jr.; Hundleby, John D.; Scheier, Ivan H.

CAUDILL, WILLIAM

69692 Discussion of "Some ethnic and cultural considerations in aging: a symposium." J geriat Psychiat 1968, 2:40-43

69693 (& Doi, L. T.) Interrelations of psychiatry, culture, and emotion in Japan. In Galdston, I. *Man's Image in Medicine and Anthropology*, NY: IUP 1963, 374-421

CAUTELA, JOSEPH R.

69694 A behavior therapy approach to pervasive anxiety. Behav Res Ther 1966, 4:99-109

69695 Desensitization factors in the hypnotic treatment of phobias. J Psychol 1966, 64:277-288

CAVALCANTI, O.

See Zimmerman, David

CAVALIN, HECTOR

69696 Incestuous fathers: a clinical report. P 1966, 122:1132-1138

CAVANAH, JOHN R.

69697 The psychotherapy of homosexuality, 1: Some thoughts on individual therapy. Psychiat Opin 1967, 4(2):5-8

CAVANNA, ROBERTO

69698 (& Servadio, E.) ESP experiments with LSD 25 and psiococybin. (Parapsychol Monogr No. 5) NY: Parapsychol Found 1964, 123 p

CAVAZZUTI, G. B.

69699 (& Bennatti, C.; Foschi, F.) Gli spasmi respiratori affettivi dell'età infantile: aspetti psicologici, II. [Affective respiratory spasms in the infantile age: psychological aspects. II.] Riv sper Freniat 1966, 90: 1543-1562

CAVIOR, NORMAN

See Kurtzberg, Richard L.

CAZAVELAN, JANE

69700 (& Epstein, S.) Daydreams of female paranoid schizophrenics. Clin Psych 1966, 22:27-32

CAZZULLO, A. GUARESCHI

69701 (& Cocchi, A.; Generali, I.) Obésité de l'enfance: contribution a l'étude psychodynamique. [Obesity in childhood: contribution to a psychodynamic study.] Acta paedopsychiat 1968, 35:324-326

CAZZULO, CARLO L.

69702 Biological and clinical studies on schizophrenia related to pharmacological treatment—academic address. Recent Adv biol Psychiat 1963, 5:114-143

69703 Della coscienza: funzione analitica e sintetica. [On consciousness: analytic and collective function.] Riv sper Freniat 1965, 89:1580-1582

69704 [Juvenile delinquency. Psychopathologic and psychodynamic aspects of juvenile maladjustment.] (It) Minerva Med 1965, 56:4032-4036

69705 (& Mancia, M.) Psychopathological aspects of the relation between vigilance and consciousness. Acta Neurochir 1964, 12:366-378

69706 (& Martis, D. De; Leonardi, P.) Psychotherapy and pharmacotherapy of neuroses. Top Probl PT 1963, 4:169-176

69707 (& Ermentini, A.; Montanini, R.) [Therapeutic prospects in psychogeriatrics.] (It) G Geront 1963, 11:789-805

CEDERCREUTZ, C.

69708 [Migraine in women.] (Sw) Finsk Lakaresallsk Handl 1964, 108:226-229

CÉNAC-THALY, H.

69709 (& Mérienne, C.; Charbaut, J.) Un cas de pénis fantôme chez une délirante paranoïde. [A case of phantom penis in a paranoid deliriant.] Ann méd-psychol 1968, 126(2):372-376

CENTERS, LOUISE

69710 (& Centers, R.) Body cathexes of parents of normal and malformed children for progeny and self. J consult Psychol 1963, 27:319-323

CENTERS, RICHARD

69711 The anal character and social severity in attitudes. J proj Tech pers Assess 1969, 33:501-506

See Centers, Louise

CERDA, ENRIQUE

69712 Algunas contribuciones de la psicología científica al psicoanálisis. [Some contributions of scientific psychology to psychoanalysis.] Rev Psicol gen apl, Madrid 1965, 20:79-94

CERF, F.

See Mayer, M.

CERQUEIRA, LUIZ

See Oliveira, Walderedo Ismael de

CESA-BIANCHI, MARCELLO

See Ancona, Leonardo

CESARMAN, FERNANDO C.

69713 Complejo de edipo y recuerdó encubridor. [The Oedipus complex and uncovering memories.] Cuad Psa 1965, 1:189-193

69714 Discussion of Namnum, A. "Consideraciones psicoanalíticas sobre el secreto." Cuad Psa 1967, 3:125-127

69715 Querer y deber. [To wish and to owe.] Cuad Psa 1967, 3:141-149

69716 Sublimación y pseudosublimación. [Sublimation and pseudo sublimation.] Cuad Psa 1967, 3:37-42

See Aiza, Victor M.

REVIEW OF:

69717 Ramirez, S. El Mexicano Psicologia de Suis Motivaciones. Cuad Psa 1966, 2:49

CESIO, FIDIAS R.

S-43553 Un caso de úlcera duodenal.
Abs An Surv Psa 1955, 6:217-218

69718 La comunicación extraverbal en psicoanálisis. Transferencia, contratransferencia e interpretación. [Extraverbal communication in psychoanalysis. Transference, countertransference and interpretation.] Rev Psicoanál 1963, 20:124-127
Abs Vega Q 1964, 33:458

S-43555 Contribución al estudio de la reacción terapeutica negativa.
Abs Vega Q 1962, 31:140

69719 Discussion of Toledo, L. G. et al: "Terminación del análisis didáctico." Rev Psicoanál 1967, 24:283-288

69720 La disociación y el letargo en la reacción terapéutica negativa. [Dissociation and lethargy in negative therapeutic reactions.] Rev Psicoanál 1962, 19:20-25

69721 (& Álverez de Toledo, L.; Mom, J.; Schlossberg, T.; Storni, L.; Morera, M.; Evelson, E.) Duelo, melancolía y depresión. [Mourning, melancholia and depression.] Rev Psicoanál 1963, 20:128-132
Abs Vega Q 1964, 33:458

S-5413 Estudio psicoanalítico de un caso de depresión hipocondríaca a través de su tratamiento por electro-schock y psicoterapia.
Abs Meharu, M. L. Rev urug Psa 1963, 5:486

S-43556 El individuo y la sociedad: un estudio psicoanalítico.
Abs AN An Surv Psa 1956, 7:388

S-43557 El lenguaje no-verbal: su interpretación.
Abs RHB An Surv Psa 1957, 8:254

69722 El letargo, la melancolía y el duelo en la reacción terapéutica negativa. [Lethargy, melancholia and mourning in the negative therapeutic reaction.] Rev Psicoanál 1962, 19:317-322

S-43558 El letargo, contribución al estudio de la reacción terapéutica negativa.
Abs Vega Q 1961, 30:460-461

69723   El letargo. Una reacción a la pérdida de objeto. Contribución al estudio
        de la reacción terapéutica negativa. [Lethargy: a reaction to the loss
        of an object. A contribution to the study of the negative therapeutic
        reaction.] Rev Psicoanál 1964, 21:19-27
            Abs Vega Q 1965, 34:314
69724   El letargo. Una representación de lo latente. Sa relacion con la re-
        presión. [Lethargy, a manifestation of latency. Its relation to repres-
        sion.] Rev urug Psa 1966, 8:217-222
            Abs Vega Q 1968, 37:162
69725   Obituary: Heinrich Racker. Rev Psicoanál 1961, 18:282-285
69726   Palabras de apertura (Symposium on the works of Melanie Klein).
        [Opening remarks.] Rev Psicoanál 1962, 19:1-5
S-43560 Psicoanálisis de hábito de fumar.
            Abs RHB An Surv Psa 1957, 8:125-126
69727   Sobre técnica psicoanalítica. La interpretación en al aqui y ahora.
        Valoración de esta formulatión conceptual fundada en las ideas de
        Freud sobre la atemporalidad de lo inconsciente. [On psychoanalytic
        technique. The interpretation here and now. Evaluation of this special
        formulation of concepts based on Freud's ideas about nontemporality
        of the unconscious.] Rev Psicoanál 1966, 23:149-160
            Abs Barriguete C., A. Cuad Psa 1967, 3:245-246. Vega Q 1967,
        36:475-476
69728   La transferencia en el sueño y en el tratamiento psicoanalítico. [Trans-
        ference in sleep and in psychoanalytic treatment.] Rev Psicoanál 1967,
        24:809-816

        See Aberastury, Arminda; Smolensky de Dellarossa, Guiliana

        REVIEW OF:
69729   Racker, H. Estudios Sobre Técnica Psicoanalítica. Rev Psicoanál 1961,
        18:384

CHABB, ALBERTO

See Rolla, Edgardo H.

CHABRAND, P.

See Bastie, Y.

CHADWICK, MARY

S-5421 Education of the educationist.
            Die Erziehung des Erziehers. In Bittner, G. & Rehm, W. *Psycho-
        analyse und Erziehung,* Bern/Stuttgart: Hans Huber 1964
S-5433 Notes upon the fear of death. In Ruitenbeek, H. M. *Death: Interpreta-
        tions,* NY: Dell 1969, 73-86

CHAFETZ, MORRIS E.

69730   (& Blane, H. T.; Abram, H. S.; Golner, J.; Lacy, E.; McCourt, W. F.;
        Clark, E.; Meyers, W.) Establishing treatment relations with alcoholics.
        JNMD 1962, 134:395-409

69731 (& Blane, H. T.; Abram, H. S.; Clark, E.; Golner, J. E.; Hastie, E. L.; McCourt, W. F.) Establishing treatment relations with alcoholics: a supplementary report. JNMD 1964, 138:390-393

69732 Foreword. In Blum, E. M. & Blum, R. H. *Alcoholism: Modern Psychological Approaches to Treatment,* San Francisco: Jossey-Bass 1967, ix-x

69733 Who is qualified to treat the alcoholic. Comment on the Krystal-Moore discussion. Quart J Stud Alcohol 1964, 25:358-360

CHAIEB, M. C.

See Luquet, Pierre

CHAIKEN, NINA

See Steisel, Ira M.

CHAIO, JOSÉ

S-43575 Algunos aspectos de la actuación de las interpretaciones en el desarrollo del "insight" y en la reestructuración mental del niño.
Abs JO An Surv Psa 1958, 9:314-315

CHALFEN, LEO

69734 The use of dreams in psychoanalytic group psychotherapy. R 1964, 57:461-468

REVIEW OF:
69735 Kuiper, P. C. On Being Genuine and Other Essays. R 1969, 56:350-351

CHALIFF, CYNTHIA

69736 The psychology of economics in Emily Dickinson. Lit & Psych 1968, 18:93-100

CHALLMAN, ALAN

69737 Hostility and disease. Minn Med 1966, 49:523-528

CHALPIN, GEORGE

69738 The fathers' group. An effective therapy medium for involving fathers in a child psychiatric clinic treatment program. J Amer Acad Child Psychiat 1966, 5:125-133

CHAMBERLAIN, PAMELA

See Minuchin, Salvador

CHAMBERLIN, CECIL R., JR.

69739 Running away during psychotherapy. BMC 1960, 24:288-294

CHAMBERLIN, ROBERT W., JR.

69740 Approaches to child rearing: early recognition and modification of vicious-circle parent-child relationships. Clin Ped 1967, 6:469-479

69741   Approaches to child rearing: their effects on child behavior. An analysis
        of reported surveys. Clin Ped 1966, 5:688-698
69742   Approaches to child rearing—their identification and classification. Clin
        Ped 1965, 4:150-159

CHAMBERS, A. B.

69743   Three notes on Eve's dream in Paradise lost. Philol Q 1967, 46:186-193

CHAMBERS, CHARLES H.

69744   Leo Kanner's concept of early infantile autism. M 1969, 42:51-54

CHAMBERS, HELEN H.

69745   Oral erotism revealed by hypnosis. Int J clin exp Hyp 1968, 16:151-157

CHAMBERS, JACK A.

69745A Beginning a multidimensional theory of creativity. Psychol Rep 1969,
        25:779-799

CHAMBERS, JUDITH

69746   Maternal deprivation and the concept of time in children. Ops 1961,
        31:406-419
        Abs JMa RFPsa 1962, 26:327

        TRANSLATION OF:
        Piaget, Jean et al: [00000]

CHAMPAGNE, EMILY

        See Jacobs, Martin A.

CHAMPERNOWNE, H. IRENE

69747   (& Lewis, E.) Psychodynamics of therapy in a residential group. J anal
        Psych 1966, 11:163-180

CHANCE, ERIKA

69748   (& Arnold, J.; Tyrrell, S.) Communality and stability of meaning in
        clinical case description. ASP 1962, 64:389-406
69749   Content analysis of verbalizations about interpersonal experience. Meth
        Res PT 127-145
69750   (& Arnold, J.) The effect of professional training, experience, and pref-
        erence for a theoretical system upon clinical case description. Hum
        Relat 1960, 13:195-213
69751   The father's perception of his first child. In Stolz, L. M. *Father-Child
        Relationships of Warborn Children,* Palo Alto, Calif: Stanford Univ Pr
        1954, 75-105
69752   Group psychotherapy and community psychiatry. Ops 1967, 37:920-
        925
69753   Group psychotherapy and the psychiatric social worker. J ment Hlth
        1948, 8(1)

69754   Group psychotherapy in community mental health programs. Ops 1967, 37:921-925

69755   Implications of interdisciplinary differences in case description. Ops 1963, 33:672-677
        Abs JMa RFPsa 1964, 28:465

69756   (& Arnold, J.; Tyrrell, S.) Professional background and themes used in clinical case description. Hum Relat 1962, 15:53-61

69757   Training in analytic group psychotherapy: observations on some learning problems in the dimension of power. Int J grp PT 1965, 15:291-302
        Abs GPK Q 1967, 36:475

CHANCE, N. A.

See Murphy, H. B. M.

CHANDLER, CAROLINE A.

69758   (& Lourie, R. S.; Peters, A. D.) Early Child Care: The New Perspectives. (Ed & Int: Dittmann, L. L.) NY: Atherton 1968, x + 385 p

See Kern, Howard M., Jr.; Lourie, Reginald S.

CHANDLER, E.

69758A (& Holden, H. M.; Robinson, M.) Treatment of a psychotic family in a family psychiatry setting. Psychother Psychosom 1968, 16:339-347

CHANDLER, TERTIUS

69759   Ikhnaton and Moses. Am Im 1962, 19:127-139

CHANG, JUDY

69760   (& Block, J.) Study of identification in male homosexuals. J consult Psychol 1960, 24:307-310

CHANG, SUK CHOO

69761   The cultural context of Japanese psychiatry and psychotherapy. PT 1965, 19:593-606

69762   Depression: an aspect of phenomenology and semantics. Canad Psychiat Ass J 1966, 11(Suppl):S7-S10

69763   Dream-recall and themes of hospitalized schizophrenics. Arch gen Psychiat 1964, 10:119-122

CHANOVER, E. PIERRE

69764   Marcel Proust: a medical and psychoanalytic bibliography. R 1969-70, 56:638-641

CHAO, D. H.

See Knight, James A.

CHAPIN, FRANCIS B.

69765   A paradigm of dream interpretation. Diss Abstr Int 1969, 30(6-B):2889

CHAPIRO, MARC

69766   La Revolution Originelle. [The Original Revolution.] Paris: Vrin 1958
        Rv RdeS RFPsa 1961, 25:149

CHAPLAN, ABRAHAM

See Balser, Benjamin H.

CHAPLIK, M.

See Linn, Louis

CHAPLIN, J. P.

69767   Commentary on three Oswald interpretations. J ind Psych 1967, 23:
        48-52

CHAPLIN, WILLIAM H.

69768   Form and psychology in *King Lear*. Lit & Psych 1969, 19(3-4):31-45

CHAPMAN, ARTHUR HARRY

69769   Further observations on the nemesis concept. Psychiat Q 1962, 36:720-
        726
        Abs Engle, Bernice S. Q 1963, 32:450
69770   Iatrogenic problems in psychotherapy. Psychiat Dig 1964, 25:23-29
69771   Management of Emotional Disorders: A Manual for Physicians. Phila:
        Lippincott 1962, 259 p
69772   (& Gibbons, M. J.; Loeb, D. G.) Psychiatric aspects of hospitalizing
        children. Arch Pediat 1956, 73:77-88
69773   Psychiatrogenic illness. P 1960, 116:873-877
        Abs Leavitt, M. Q 1961, 30:145
69774   (& Loeb, D. G.) Psychosomatic gastrointestinal problems in children.
        Amer J Dis Childr 1955, 89:717-724
69775   (& Loeb, D. G.; Young, J. E.) A psychosomatic study of five children
        with duodenal ulcer. J Pediat 1956, 48:248-261
69776   Textbook of Clinical Psychiatry: An Interpersonal Approach. Phila:
        J. B. Lippincott 1967, xiii + 480 p
        Rv Whitaker, C. A. R 1969, 56:490

CHAPMAN, J. DUDLEY

69777   The Feminine Mind and Body: the Psychosexual and Psychosomatic
        Reactions of Women. NY: Philos Libr 1967, 325 p

CHAPMAN, JAMES

69778   (& McGhie, A.) An approach to the psychotherapy of cognitive dys-
        function in schizophrenia. M 1963, 36:253-260
S-43602 (& Freeman, T.; McGhie, A.) Clinical research in schizophrenia—
        the psychotherapeutic approach. With title: Disorders of attention and
        perception in schizophrenia. In Dulany, D. E., Jr. et al: *Contributions
        to Modern Psychology*, NY: Oxford Univ Pr 1964, 389-405

* * *   (& Freeman, T.; McGhie, A.) Disorders of attention and perception in schizophrenia. See [S-43602]

See McGhie, Andrew

CHAPMAN, JEAN
See Hernberg, Rae Shifrin

CHAPMAN, LOREN J.
69779   (& Burstein, A. G.; Day, D.; Verdone, P.) Regression and disorders of thought. ASP 1961, 63:540-545

See Klarman, Rafael

CHAPMAN, RICHARD F.
69780   Group mental health consultation. Milit Med 1966, 131:30-35
69781   Suicide during psychiatric hospitalization. BMC 1965, 29(2):35-44

CHARATAN, FRED B.
69782   (& Galef, H.) A case of transvestitism in a six-year-old boy. J Hillside Hosp 1965, 14:160-177
        Abs JA Q 1967, 36:320

CHARBAUT, J.
See Cénac-Thaly, H.

CHARBONNIER, GABRIELLE
69783   Importance de la phase cannibale dans l'évolution sexuelle et affective de la femme. [Importance of the cannibal phase in the sexual and emotional development of the woman.] Ann méd-psychol 1968, 1(3):460
69784   Les incidences de la phase cannibale sur l'évolution sexuelle et affective de la femme. [Effects of the cannibal phase on sexual and affective development of women.] Évolut psychiat 1968, 33:731-741
69785   (& Granier, J.) La technique des images du Docteur Guillerey: méthode psychothérapie. [Technique of images of Dr. Guillerey: psychotherapeutic method.] Évolut psychiat 1966, 31:849-866

CHARLES, LOIS
See Reding, Georges R.

CHARNY, E. JOSEPH
69786   (& Carroll, E. J.) General systems theory and psychoanalysis. I. Theoretical considerations. (Read at Am Psa Ass, Nov 1964) Q 1966, 35:377-398
        Abs Cuad Psa 1966, 2:124-125
69787   Psychosomatic manifestations of rapport in psychotherapy. PSM 1966, 28:305-315. In Gray, W. et al: General Systems Theory and Psychiatry, Boston: Little, Brown 1969; 267-284

See Scheflen, Albert E.

REVIEW OF:
69788 Ostwald, P. F. Soundmaking. The Acoustic Communication of Emotion. Q 1965, 34:128-130
69789 Scheflen, A. E. Stream and Structure of Communicational Behavior. Context Analysis of a Psychotherapy Session. Q 1967, 36:113-116

CHARNY, ISRAEL W.

69790 Integrated individual and family psychotherapy. Fam Proc 1966, 5: 179-198
69791 Marital love and hate. Fam Proc 1969, 8:1-24
69792 The psychotherapist as teacher of an ethic of nonviolence. Voices 1967, 3:57-66
69793 Regression and reorganization in the "isolation treatment" of children: a clinical contribution to sensory deprivation research. J child Psychol Psychiat 1963, 4:47-60
69794 Teaching the violence of the holocaust: a challenge to educating potential future oppressors and victims for nonviolence. Jewish Educ 1968, 38:15-24

See Cohen, Richard L.

CHARRIER, JEAN-PAUL

69795 L'Inconscient et la Psychanalyse. [The Unconscious and Psychoanalysis.] Paris: PUF 1968, 126 p

CHASE, C. THURSTON

69796 The psychotherapy of the adolescent from a schoolmaster's point of view. In Balser, B. H. *Psychotherapy of the Adolescent,* NY: IUP 1957, 182-246

CHASE, LOUIS S.

69797 The concept of ambivalence. Philippine J Psychiat Neurol 1967, 7:7-13
69798 (& Hire, A. W.) Countertransference in the analysis of borderlines. (Read at Boston Psa Soc, 23 Mar 1966)
       Abs Reichard, J. F. Bull Phila Ass Psa 1967, 17:48-51

CHASE, RICHARD VOLNEY

69799 An approach to Melville. In Malin, I. *Psychoanalysis and American Fiction,* NY: Dutton 1965, 111-120

CHASIN, RICHARD M.

69800 (& Semrad, E. V.) Interviewing a depressed patient. Hosp Comm Psychiat 1966, 17:283-286

CHASSAN, JACOB B.

69801 (& Bellak, L.) An introduction to intensive design in the evaluation of drug efficacy during psychotherapy. Meth Res PT 478-499

S-43614 On probability theory and psychoanalytic research.
Abs JA An Surv Psa 1956, 7:46-47
69802 Research Design in Clinical Psychology and Psychiatry. (Foreword: Bellak, L.) NY: Appleton-Century-Crofts 1967, xviii + 280 p
Rv Esman, A. H. Q 1969, 38:503-504

See Bellak, Leopold; Strupp, Hans H.

CHASSEGUET-SMIRGEL, JANINE

69803 L'analité et les composantes anales du vécu corporel. [Anality and the anal components of the body ego.] Canad Psychiat Ass J 1962, 7:16-24
69804 Apropos de "L'Année Dernière à Marienbad." [On "Last Year at Marienbad."] RFPsa 1969, 33:415-440
69805 [Considerations on penis envy.] (Fr) RFPsa 1968, 32:273-278
69806 Corps vécu et corps imaginaire dans les premiers travaux psychanalytiques. [The actual and the imaginary body in early psychoanalytic work.] RFPsa 1963, 27:255-270
69807 Diskussionsbemerkung zu dem Beitrag von L. Veszy-Wagner: Zwangsneurose und latente Homosexualität. [Remarks on the contribution of L. Veszy-Wagner: compulsion neurosis and latent homosexuality.] Psyche 1967, 21:616-623
69808 En relisant "Analyse terminée et analyse interminable." [On rereading "Analysis terminable and interminable."] RFPsa 1968, 32:301-304
69809 Note clinique sur les rêves d'examen. [Clinical note on examination dreams.] RFPsa 1967, 31:173-177
69810 Notes cliniques sur un fantasme commun à la phobie et à la paranoïa. [Clinical notes on a fantasy common to phobia and paranoia.] RFPsa 1966, 30:121-144
69811 Notes de lecture en marge de la révision du cas Schreber. [Marginal notes on revision of the Schreber case.] RFPsa 1966, 30:41-61
69812 Oedipe et religion. [Oedipus and religion.] RFPsa 1967, 31:875-882
69813 Psychanalyses et psychothérapies des tuberculeux pulmonaires récents. [Psychoanalyses and psychotherapies of patients with pulmonary tuberculosis.] RFPsa 1969, 33:463-504
69814 (& David, C.; et al) Recherches Psychanalytiques Nouvelles sur la Sexualité Féminine. [New Psychoanalytical Inquiries Concerning Female Sexuality.] Paris: Payot 1964, 275 p
Rv Mendilaharsu, S. A. de Rev urug Psa 1964, 6:517-522
69815 Réflexions sur le concept de "réparation" et la hiérarchie des actes créateurs. [Reflections on the concept of "reparation" on the hierarchy of creative actions.] RFPsa 1965, 29:17-29
69816 Le rossignol de l'empereur de Chine: essai psychanalytique sur le "Faux." [The emperor of China's nightingale: psychoanalytic essay on the "Fake."] RFPsa 1969, 33:115-142

See Racamier, P.-C.

ABSTRACTS OF:
69817 Borowitz, G. H. Some ego aspects of alcoholism. RFPsa 1967, 31:320
69818 Bram, F. M. The gift of Anna O. RFPsa 1967, 31:322

69819 Bressler, B. The concept of identity. RFPsa 1967, 31:324
69820 Davie, J. & Freeman, T. Disturbances of perception and consciousness in schizophrenic states. RFPsa 1963, 27:331
69821 Fairbairn, W. R. D. A note on the origin of male homosexuality. RFPsa 1967, 31:319
69822 Frankl, L. Susceptibility to accidents. RFPsa 1967, 31:325
69823 Guntrip, H. Psychodynamic theory and the problem of psychotherapy. RFPsa 1967, 31:314
69824 Guntrip, H. The schizoid problem, regression and the struggle to preserve an ego. RFPsa 1963, 27:332
69825 Hawkins, D. R. A review of psychoanalytic dream theory in the light of recent psychological-physiological studies of sleep and dreaming. RFPsa 1967, 31:326
69826 Hayman, A. Some aspects of regression in non-psychotic puerperal breakdown. RFPsa 1964, 28:309
69827 Heyat, V. v. Der: The role of the father in early mental development. RFPsa 1967, 31:320
69828 Honig, A. M. Pathological identifications. RFPsa 1967, 31:318
69829 Jackson, M. Jung's later work. RFPsa 1964, 28:310-311
69830 Khan, M. M. The role of polymorph-perverse body experience and object-relations in ego integration. RFPsa 1964, 28:312-313
69831 Noy, P. et al: Clinical observations on the psychogenesis of impotence. RFPsa 1967, 31:326
69832 Sachs, L. J. & Stern, B. H. Bernard Shaw and women. RFPsa 1967, 31:321
69833 Schmidt, E. & Brown, P. Experimental testing of two psychoanalytic hypotheses. RFPsa 1967, 31:323
69834 Searles, H. F. The sources of the anxiety in paranoid schizophrenia. RFPsa 1963, 27:332
69835 Thomas, H. Some psychoanalytic observations on anorexia nervosa. RFPsa 1967, 31:317
69836 Winnicott, D. W. Regression as therapy. RFPsa 1967, 31:313

REVIEWS OF:
69837 Bauchau, H. Heartbreak. RFPsa 1967, 31:298
69838 Bieber, I. et al: Homosexuality: A Psychoanalytic Study. RFPsa 1962, 26:490
69839 Kiell, N. (Ed) Psychoanalysis, Psychology and Literature. RFPsa 1964, 28:310

CHASSELL, JOSEPH O.

69840 Old wine in new bottles: superego as a structuring of roles. Crosscurrents in Ps & Psa 203-218
S-43616 (Reporter) Psychoanalysis and psychotherapy. (Panel) Abs An Surv Psa 1955, 6:353-357

REVIEW OF:
69841 Sullivan, H. S. Schizophrenia as a Human Process. Q 1962, 31:556-559

CHASSIGNEUX, J.

See Alby, Nicole

CHATEAU, J.-F.

69842 Esquisse d'une methodologie pour l'abord des nevroses de groupe (choix du lieu de l'analyste). [Outline of a methodology for an approach to group neuroses (choice of the analyst's place).] Rv Np inf 1968, 16:499-502

CHATFIELD, E. HALE

69843 Levels of meaning in Melville's "I and my chimney." Am Im 1962, 19:163-169

CHATTERJEE, G. P.

69844 The effect of maternal deprivation on the development of child's personality. Psychol Ann 1966-67, 1:44-46

CHATTERJEE, T. K.

69845 A case of obsessional neurosis. Samiksa 1966, 20:169-176
69846 Study of personality of an epileptic homicide. Samiksa 1963, 17:207-223

CHATTERJI, N. N.

69847 The agoraphobic's companion. Samiksa 1967, 21:81-92
69848 A case of compulsion neurosis resembling drug addiction. Samiksa 1963, 17:108-111
69849 A case of hysteria. Samiksa 1965, 19:135-142
69850 Delusion formation in paranoia. Samiksa 1964, 18(Spec.No.2):9-67
69851 Delusional ideas in a case of borderland psychosis. Samiksa 1960, 14:9-23
69852 Drug addiction and psychoses. Samiksa 1963, 17:130-149
69853 Ego psychology. Samiksa 1965, 19:163-169
S-43624 A new theory of paranoia.
Abs An Surv Psa 1955, 6:41-43, 190
69854 Onset of schizophrenia in a case of obsessional neurosis. Samiksa 1963, 17:5-11
69855 Psychoanalysis of a case of manic depressive psychosis. Samiksa 1963, 17:1-26
69856 Psychoanalysis of a case of obsessional and compulsion psychoneurosis. Samiksa 1964, 18:62-82
69857 Psychoanalysis of an artist with obsessional symptoms. Samiksa 1963, 17:173-197
69858 A psychoanalytical study of a case of peptic ulcer. Samiksa 1964, 18: 125-141
69859 Psychoanalytical study of a case of schizophrenia. Samiksa 1960, 14:51-65
69860 Psychodynamics of paranoia. Psychother Psychosom 1967, 15:105-113. In Philippopoulos, G. S. Dynamics in Psychiatry, Basel/NY: Karger 1968, 21-113
69861 Theories of paranoia. Samiksa 1964, 18:105-120
69862 Treatment of paranoia. Samiksa 1965, 19:94-100

CHAUDHURI, ARUN KUMAR RAY

S-43631 A psycho-analytic study of the Hindu Mother Goddess (Kali) concept. Abs AS An Surv Psa 1956, 7:377-379

CHAUDHURY, PRAVAS JIVAN

69863 Catharsis in the light of Indian aesthetics. J Aesthet art Crit 1965, 24(1,Suppl):151-163

CHAYES, CHARLES M.

See Schwartz, Laszlo

CHAYES, I. H.

69864 Kubla Khan and the creative process. Stud Romanticism 1966, 6:1-21; 1967, 6:128

CHAZAUD, JACQUES

69865 La conception de la maladie mentale dans l'oeuvre de Harry Stack Sullivan. [The concept of mental illness in the work of Harry Stack Sullivan.] Évolut psychiat 1961, 26:161-176

69866 Contribution à la théorie psychanalytique de la paranoïa. Autour de la relation d'objet et de la problematique homosexuelle-anale. [Contribution to the psychoanalytic theory of paranoia. On object-relation and the homosexual-anal problem.] RFPsa 1966, 30:93-119

69867 Regard sur la psychothérapie des schizophrènes à tendances catatoniques. [Concerning the psychotherapy of schizophrenics with catatonic tendencies.] Évolut psychiat 1965, 30:246-298

REVIEWS OF:

69868 Balint, M. Primary Love and Psycho-Analytic Technique. RFPsa 1966, 30:504

69869 Bion, W. R. Research on Small Groups. RFPsa 1966, 30:499

69870 Ortigues, M. C. & Ortigues, E. Oedipe African. RFPsa 1967, 31:503-507

69871 Ricoeur, P. On interpretation: an essay on Freud. RFPsa 1967, 31:499-503

CHEBABI, WILSON DE LYRA

69872 (& Lima, H. de A.) Fantasias de "acasalamento" no grupo terapeutico. [The pairing fantasy in a therapeutic group.] J Bras Psiquiat 1963, 12:327-342

See Oliveira, Walderedo Ismael de

CHEEK, DAVID B.

69873 (& LeCron, L. M.) Clinical Hypnotherapy. NY: Grune & Stratton 1968, viii + 245 p

69874 Some newer understandings of dreams in relation to threatened abortion and premature labor. Pacif Med Surg 1965, 73:379-384

CHEEK, FRANCIS E.

69875 (& Rosenhaupt, M.) Are sociologists incomprehensible? An objective study. Soc 1968, 73:617-627
69876 Family interaction patterns and convalescent adjustment of the schizophrenic. Arch gen Psychiat 1965, 13:138-147
69877 The father of the schizophrenic. The function of a peripheral role. Arch gen Psychiat 1965, 13:336-345
69878 Parental role distortions in relation to schizophrenic deviancy. Psychiat Res Rep 1966, 20:54-64

See Lewis, Nolan D. C.

CHEIN, ISIDOR

69879 (& Gerard, D. L.; Lee, R. S.; Rosenfeld, E.) The Road to H: Narcotics, Delinquency and Social Policy. NY/London: Basic Books 1964, xii + 482 p
      Rv Winick, C. Am Im 1965, 22:205-206

CHEN, EDITH

69880 (& Cobb, S.) Family structure in relation to health and disease. A review of the literature. J chron Dis 1960, 12:544-567

CHEN, RONALD M.

69881 The emotional problems of retirement. J Amer Geriat Soc 1968, 16: 290-295
69882 (& Tirard, N.) The Menninger Foundation. World ment Hlth 1963, 15:16-22

See Thompson, Prescott W.

CHENEY, WARREN D.

69883 The neurosis-specific psychoanalytic techniques and personality theory of Fritz Riemann. Psa 1966, 26:20-28

CHERBULIEZ, THEODORE

ABSTRACTS OF:
69884 Barajas Castro, R. Analyse d'un rêve apporté au début d'un traitement. An Surv Psa 1957, 8:175-176
69885 Bonaparte, M. Eros, Saul de Tarse et Freud. An Surv Psa 1957, 8:305
69886 Dalibard, Y. Autour de l'analyse d'un cas de fantasme sadique. An Surv Psa 1957, 8:102-103
69887 Fain, M. À propos d'un cas d'hypertension artérielle. An Surv Psa 1957, 8:163-164
69888 Favreau, J.-A. & Doumic, A. Psychanalyse et éducation. An Surv Psa 1956, 7:242-245
69889 Lang, J.-L. L'abord psychanalytique des psychoses chez l'enfant. An Surv Psa 1958, 9:309-310
69890 Leclaire, S. À propos de l'épisode psychotique que présenta "l'homme aux loups." An Surv Psa 1958, 9:190-191

69891 Male, P. Étude psychanalytique de l'adolescence. An Surv Psa 1956, 7:258-261

69892 Mallet, J. Psychanalyse et troubles de la sexualité: II. Les troubles névrotiques de la sexualité. An Surv Psa 1956, 7:209-211

69893 Marty, P. & Fain, M. Psychanalyse et médecine psychosomatique. Le mouvement psychosomatic dans la médecine. An Surv Psa 1956, 7: 198-200

69894 Nodet, C.-H. Psychanalyse et sens du péché. An Surv Psa 1957, 8:132-133

69895 Pasche, F. & Renard, M. Psychanalyse et troubles de la sexualité: des problèmes essentiels de la perversion. An Surv Psa 1956, 7:209-211

69896 Reding, G. R. Les états de dépendance en clinique psychanalytique. An Surv Psa 1957, 8:244-246

69897 Rosolato, G. & Widlocher, D. Karl Abraham: lecture de son oeuvre. An Surv Psa 1958, 9:9-10

69898 Schweich, M. Principles d'action thérapeutique de la psychothérapie des schizophrènes hospitalisés. An Surv Psa 1958, 9:419-420

CHERCHEVE, R.

See Bousingen, D. de

CHERKAS, MARSHALL S.

69899 Discussion of Sandford, B. "A patient and her cats." Psa Forum 1966, 1:181-182

CHERTOK, LÉON

69900 (& Mondzain, M. L.; Bonnaud, M.) À propos de la signification psychologique des vomissements gravidiques. [The psychological meaning of the vomiting in pregnancy.] Rev Méd psychosom 1961, 3:57-67
   Abs RJA Q 1962, 31:435

69901 La découverte du transfert. Essai d'interprétation épistémologique. RFPsa 1968, 32:503-530
   The discovery of the transference: towards an epistemological interpretation. (Tr: Ahrenfeldt, R. H. & Chertok, L.) (Read at Swiss Psa Soc, 28 Jan 1967; at Am Psa Ass, May 1968) J 1968, 49:560-576

69902 (& Masserman, J. H.; Snezhnevsky, R. V.) Differences and agreements between East and West as to the etiology and treatment of behavior disorders. Proc IV World Cong Psychiat 1966, 1121-1131

69903 (& Michel-Wolfromm, H.) Les étudiants, les médecins et l'approche psychosomatique de la médecine. [Students, doctors, and the psychosomatic approach to medicine.] In Deutsch, F. et al: Advances in Psychosomatic Medicine, IV: Training in Psychosomatic Medicine. Basel: Karger 1964

69904 Évolution des recherches sur l'hypnose. [Evolution of research on hypnosis.] Pr méd 1968, 76:39-41

69905 (& Bonnaud, M.; Borelli, M.; Donnet, J.-L.; Revault d'Allonnes, C.) Féminité et Maternité: Étude Clinique et Expérimentale sur l'Accouchement sans Douleur. Paris: Desclée de Brouwer 1966, 279 p

Motherhood and Personality; Psychosomatic Aspects of Childbirth. (Tr: Graham, D.) (Foreword: Morris, N.) London: Tavistock; Phila: J. B. Lippincott 1969, vi + 303 p

69905A [Freud in Paris: decisive stage. Psychobiographic essay.] (Fr) Évolut psychiat 1969, 34:733-750

69906 From Liébeault to Freud. PT 1968, 22:96-101

69907 From suggestion to metapsychology. M 1968, 41:95-116

69908 Hope of reconciliation. Int J Psychiat 1968, 5:237-242

69909 L'hypnose depuis le premier Congrès International tenu à Paris en 1889. [Hypnosis since the 1st International Congress held in Paris in 1889.] Pr méd 1965, 73:1495-1500. In Lassner, J., *Hypnosis and Psychosomatic Medicine*, Berlin/Heidelberg/NY: Springer 1967, 67-82

69910 An introduction to the study of tensions among psychotherapists. M 1966, 39:237-243

69911 La médecine psychosomatique à l'est et à l'ouest. [Psychosomatic medicine in the West and in Eastern European countries.] PSM 1969, 31:510-521

69912 [Obstetrical psychoprophylaxis and psychotherapy.] (Cz) Ceskoslov Psychiat 1962, 58:73-82

69913 On the discovery of the cathartic method. (Tr: Graham, D.) J 1961, 42:284-287
   Abs WPK Q 1962, 31:286

69914 (& Bouthreuil, O.; Aboulker, P.) La préparation de l'étudiant en médecine à la relation médicale. [Preparation of the medical student for the physician-patient relation.] Pr méd 1968, 76:1371-1374

69915 Psychiatric dialogue between East and West. M 1968, 41:295-298

69916 Psychoprophylaxe oder Psychotherapie in der Geburtshilfe? Über die Theorien der psychoprophylaktischen Entbindung. [Psychoprophylaxis or psychotherapy in obstetrics? On the theories of psychoprophylactic delivery.] Zbl Gynäk 1962, 84:657-667
   Psychoprophylaxie ou psychothérapie obstétricale. Adv PSM 1963, 3:134-138

69917 Psychosomatic methods of preparation for childbirth. Spread of the methods, theory, and research. Amer J Obs Gyn 1967, 98:698-707

69918 (& Fontaine, M.) Psychosomatics in veterinary medicine. J psychosom Res 1963, 7:229-235

69919 Relaxation and psychosomatic methods of preparation for childbirth. Amer J Obs Gyn 1961, 82:262-267

69920 ["Sleep and related states" by A. A. Liebeault. From suggestion to metapsychology.] (Fr) Évolut psychiat 1966, 31:779-901

69921 Tensions among psychotherapists. P 1965, 121:1106-1108

69922 Theory of hypnosis since 1889. Int J Psychiat 1967, 3:188-199

69923 (& Mondzain, M. L.; Bonnaud, M.) Der Wunsch nach dem Kind und das Schwangerschaftserbrechen. Z Psychother med Psychol 1962, 12:181-186
   Vomiting and the wish to have a child. PSM 1963, 25:13-18
   Abs ELG Q 1964, 33:302-303

See Aboulker, P.; Montausset, M.

CHESHIRE, NEIL

69924 On the rationale of psychodynamic argumentation. M 1964, 37:217-230

CHESNI, Y.

69925 [Various remarks on dreams and their relation with the theory of knowledge.] (Fr) Rev Otoneuroophtal 1968, 40:361-366
69925A [Inner words, dream thought, phantom members.] Confin Neurol 1969, 31:374-382]

CHESS, STELLA

69926 (& Thomas, A.) (Eds) Annual Progress in Child Psychiatry and Child Development, 1968, 1969. NY: Brunner/Mazel 1968, x + 565 p; 1969, x + 700 p
69927 (& Thomas, A.; Birch, G. H.) Behavior problems revisited: findings of an anterospective study. J Amer Acad Child Psychiat 1967, 6:321-331. Ann Prog child Psychiat 1968, 335-344
69928 Diagnosis and treatment of the hyperactive child. NYSJM 1960, 60: 2379-2385
69929 (& Thomas, A.; Birch, H. G.) Distortions in developmental reporting made by parents of behaviorally disturbed children. J Amer Acad Child Psychiat 1966, 5:226-234
69930 Family climate in relation to character structure. Psa 1964, 24:198-201
69931 Healthy responses, developmental disturbances, and stress or reactive disorders. I. Infancy and childhood. Compreh Txbk Psychiat 1358-1366
69932 (& Thomas, A.; Birch, H. G.; Hertzig, M.) Implications of a longitudinal study of child development for child psychiatry. P 1960, 117:434-441
69933 Individuality in children, its importance to the pediatrician. J Pediat 1966, 69:676-684
69934 (& Thomas, A.; Rutter, M.; Birch, H. G.) Interaction of temperament and environment in the production of behavioral disturbances in children. P 1963, 120:142-148. In Palmer, J. O. & Goldstein, M. J. *Perspectives in Psychopathology,* NY: Oxford Univ Pr 1966, 390-397
69935 An interactive concept of childhood schizophrenia. Int J Psychiat 1968, 5:222-223
69936 Interactive implications of childhood schizophrenia. J Hillside Hosp 1967, 16:75-84
69937 A longitudinal study of children with resulting anterospective data. In Merin, J. H. & Nagler, S. H. *The Etiology of the Neuroses,* Palo Alto, Calif: Sci & Behav Books 1966, 80-93
69938 Mal de mère. Ops 1964, 34:613-614
69939 Psychiatric treatment of the mentally retarded child with behavior problems. Ops 1962, 32:863-869
         Abs JMa RFPsa 1964, 28:445
69940 (& Lyman, M. S.) A psychiatric unity in a general hospital pediatric clinic. Ops 1969, 39:77-85
69941 Psychiatry of the first three years of life. Am Hbk Psychiat III 18-29
69942 The role of temperament in the child's development. Acta paedopsychiat 1967, 34(4-5):91-103

69943 (& Thomas, A.; Birch, H. G.) Your Child Is a Person: A Psychological Approach to Parenthood Without Guilt. NY: Viking Pr 1965, ix + 213 p

See Birch, Herbert G.; Marcus, Joseph; Thomas, Alexander; Wolff, Sula

CHESSICK, RICHARD D.

69944 *Acus Malefactorum* (Needle of the evil persons.) Bulletin of the North Shore Branch of the Chicago Medical Society 1965, Feb

69945 The alcoholic-narcotic addict. Quart J Stud Alcohol 1961, 22:261-268

69946 The asthmatic narcotic addict. Psychosomatics 1960, 1:346-350

69947 (& Clark, R. K.; McFarland, R. L.) Automatic data processing: compromises and considerations. Psychophysiol NL 1962, 8:15-20

69948 Critique: anxiety and maternal love. PT 1967, 21:325-327

69949 Critique: Bertrand Russell. PT 1968, 22:304-307

69950 Critique: Books to begin the study of man. PT 1968, 22:102-105

69951 Critique: literature as a necessity of life. PT 1968, 22:502-504

69952 Critique: man's evolutionary inheritance. PT 1967, 21:685-688

69953 Critique: on being unbearably alone. PT 1967, 21:860-862

69954 The "crucial dilemma" of the therapist in the psychotherapy of borderland patients. PT 1968, 22:655-666

69955 Differential diagnosis of abdominal pain: neuropsychiatric aspects. J Ky State Med Ass 1960, 58:1167-1169

69956 (& Kronholm, J.; Beck, M.; Maier, G.) Effect of pretreatment with tryptamine, tryptophen and DOPA on LSD reaction in tropical fish. Psychopharmacologia 1964, 5:390-392

69957 Empathy and love in psychotherapy. PT 1965, 19:205-219

69958 Ethical and psychodynamic aspects of payment for psychotherapy. Voices 1968, 3:26-30

69959 (& Bassan, M.) Experimental approaches to the concept of empathy in psychotherapy. In Lesse, S. *An Evaluation of the Results of Psychotherapies*, Springfield, Ill: Thomas 1968, 49-69

69960 Greed and vanity in the life of the psychotherapist. Psychiat Dig 1967, 28:40-43

69961 How Psychotherapy Heals; The Process of Intensive Psychotherapy. NY: Science House 1969, 227 p

69962 The identification of "pseudoneurotic" or "borderline" schizophrenic patients in general medical practice. J Med Ass Georgia 1963, 52: 217-218

69963 Meditations from the library of a psychotherapist, I: America. II: Secret phantasies. III: Secret perversions. IV: Time. Voices 1967, 3:58-61, 81-84; 92-94; 1968, 4:63-65

69964 *Orgia* and *omophagia*. JAMA 1965, 192:310-312

69965 Periodic hyperingestion. J Obesity 1964, 1:17-18

69966 Periodic hyperingestion as a problem for the general practitioner. Clin Med 1966, 73:31

69967 The "pharmacogenic orgasm" in the drug addict. Arch gen Psychiat 1960, 3:545-556
　　　Abs KR Q 1962, 31:134-135

69968 The problem of addiction. Med Times 1962, 90:247-252

69969 The problem of tobacco habituation. JAMA 1964, 188:932-933

69970 (& Bolin, R. R.) Psychiatric study of patients with psychomotor seizures. JNMD 1962, 134:72-79
69971 (& Wasserman, E. M.; Huels, M. A.; Gerty, F. J.) The psychiatric
ward administrator. Ment Hosp 1959, 10(3):7-10
69972 A psychiatrist is beaten. J Amer Acad PT 1966, 2:20-25
69973 The psychotherapy of borderline patients. PT 1966, 20:600-614
69974 A resident looks at psychiatry. Resident Physician 1957, 3(7):94-103
S-43650 The sense of reality, time and creative inspiration.
Abs JC An Surv Psa 1957, 8:332
69975 Some problems and pseudo-problems in psychiatry. Psychiat Q 1961,
35:711-719
69975A Was Machiavelli right. Am J PT 1969, 23:633-644

See Kaplan, Gerson H.; Lal, Harbans; Milton, Leroy M.

CHETHIK, MORTON

69976 (& Fleming, E.; Mayer, M. F.; McCoy, J. N.) A quest for identity:
treatment of disturbed Negro children in a predominantly white treatment center. Ops 1967, 37:71-77
69977 The therapy of an obsessive-compulsive boy: some treatment considerations. J Amer Acad Child Psychiat 1969, 8:465-484

See Harrison, Saul.

CHEZ, RONALD

69978 The female patient's sexual history. In Wahl, C. W. *Sexual Problems,*
NY: Free Pr; London: Collier-Macmillan 1967, 1-12

CHIBA, TANENARI

69979 On the proper consciousness. Psychologia 1960, 3:65-72

CHICAGO PSYCHOANALYTIC SOCIETY

69980 Traditional Subjects Reconsidered. Proc 2nd Regional Conference held
at the Center for Continuing Education of the University of Chicago,
23-24 March 1968, 89 p

CHICKERING, HOWELL D., JR.

69981 Robert Frost, romantic humorist. Lit & Psych 1966, 16:139-150

CHIEN, CHING-PIAO

See Appleton, William S.

CHIKAHISA, PAUL

See Berkovitz, Irving H.

CHILD, CHARLES MANNING

69982 (et al) The Unconscious, a Symposium. Freeport, NY: Books for
Libraries Press 1966, 260 p

CHILD, IRVIN L.

69983 (& Cooperman, M.; Wolowitz, H. M.) Esthetic preference and other correlates of active versus passive food preference. J Pers soc Psychol 1969, 11:75-84

69984 Problems of personality and some relations to anthropology and sociology. In Koch, S. *Psychology: A Study of a Science, Vol. 5*, NY/Toronto/London: McGraw-Hill 1963, 593-638

CHINAGLIA, LINO

69985 Sulle sindromi depressive. [About depressive syndromes.] Riv Psicol soc 1965, 32:159-176

CHIOZZA, L.

69986 (& Laborde, V.; Obstfeld, E.; Pantolini, S.) El uso del pensamiento logico en la interpretación puesto al servicio de la contrarésistencia. [The use of logical thinking in interpretation, in the service of the counter-resistance.] Rev urug Psa 1966, 8:223-229
    Abs Vega Q 1968, 37:162

CHIPMAN, ABRAM

See Bowers, Malcolm B., Jr.

CHISTONI, G.

See Schneider, Pierre-Bernard

CHIVERS, NORMAN CAMPBELL

69987 (& Dorpat, T. L.) Emotional reactions to surgical procedures. GP 1958, 17:108-111

See Dorpat, Theodore L.

CHKARTISHVILI, SH. N.

69988 Problema Bessoznatel'nogo v Sovetskoĭ psikhologii. [Problem of the Unconscious in Soviet Psychology.] Tbilisi, USSR: Metsniereba 1966, 64 p

CHODOFF, PAUL

69989 Chronic or persisting identity diffusion. P 1964, 121:282-283

69990 A critique of Freud's theory of infantile sexuality. P 1966, 123:507-518. Int J Psychiat 1967, 4:35-48
    Abs Abend, S. M. Q 1968, 37:475

69991 Discussion of Fernandez, J. W. "Filial piety and power: psychosocial dynamics in the legends of Shaka and Sundiata." Sci Psa 1969, 14:60-63

69992 Discussion of Hoppe, K. D. "The emotional reactions of psychiatrists when confronting survivors of persecution." Psa Forum 1969, 3:203-204

69993 Discussion of Hoppe, K. D. "The psychodynamics of concentration camp victims." Psa Forum 1966, 1:81-83

69994 Discussion of Niederland, W. G. "A contribution to the psychology of gambling." Psa Forum 1967, 2:184

69995 Effects of extreme coercive and oppressive forces: brainwashing and concentration camps. Am Hbk Psychiat III 384-405

69996 Feminine psychology and infantile sexuality. Sci Psa 1966, 10:28-42

69997 Hysteria, the mimicry of disease. Med Ann DC 1965, 34:536-539

69998 Identity. Sci Psa 1962, 5:249-259

69999 Late effects of the concentration camp syndrome. Arch gen Psychiat 1963, 8:323-333

70000 Neurophysiology, psychiatry and psychiatrists. Med Ann DC 1964, 33:280-282

70001 The problem of psychiatric diagnosis: can biochemistry and neuro-physiology help? Ps 1960, 23:185-191

70002 Psychoanalysis and fees. Comprehen Psychiat 1964, 5:137-145

70003 (& Friedman, S. B.; Hamburg, D. A.) Stress, defenses and coping behavior: observations in parents of children with malignant disease. P 1964, 120:743-749

See Friedman, Stanford B.

CHODORKOFF, BERNARD

70004 About alcoholism. Contact—MPPPA J 1963, March

70005 Alcoholism and ego function. Quart J Stud Alcohol 1964, 25:292-299

70006 Alcoholism education in a psychiatric institute: I. Medical students: attitudes toward alcoholism and achievement. Quart J Stud Alcohol 1967, 28:723-230

70007 (& Krystal, H.; Nunn, J.; Wittenberg, R.) Employment character-istics of hospitalized alcoholics. Quart J Stud Alcohol 1961, 22:106-110

70008 The medical-psychiatric emergency. New Physician 1965, 14:6-8

70009 Self-perception, perceptual defense and adjustment. In Byrne, D. & Hamilton, M. L. Personality Research: A Book of Readings, NY Pren-tice-Hall 1966

See Baxter, Seymour; Chodorkoff, Joan R.

CHODORKOFF, JOAN R.

70010 (& Chodorkoff, B.) Psychiatric referral of a pediatric patient. Mich Med 1969, 68:215-216

CHODURA, V.

70011 [Family situation and sexual anamnesis in the paraphrenic syndrome.] (Cz) Ceskoslov Psychiat 1968, 64:349-352

CHODUROVÁ, A.

See Haas, Ladislav

CHOISY, MARYSE

70012 L'homme et l'oeuvre. [The man and his work.] Psyché (Paris) 1963, 18(Sp Issue)

70013 Psychoanalysis and Catholicism. In Birmingham, W. & Cuneen, J. E. *Cross Currents of Psychiatry and Catholic Morality*, NY: Pantheon 1964, 62-83

70014 Psychoanalysis of the Prostitute. NY: Philos Libr 1961, 138 p

70015 Sigmund Freud: A New Appraisal. NY: Philos Libr; Citadel 1963, 141 p
   Rv EDJ Q 1964, 33:439-440

CHOMBART DE LAUWE, P.

70016 Hypothèses pour une psychosociologie de la fatigue. [Hypotheses for a psychosociology of fatigue.] Rev Méd Psychosom 1966, 8:275-286

CHOPRA, SUKHENDRA LAL

70017 A comparative study of achieving and underachieving students of high intellectual ability. Except Children 1967, 33:631-634

CHORNY, HAROLD H.

70018 Fantasy aggression and the injuriousness of induced aggression. Diss Abstr 1964, 25:622

CHORON, JACQUES

70019 Discussion of Friedman, L. J. "From Gradiva to the death instinct." Psa Forum 1966, 1:59

70020 Modern Man and Mortality: The Ultimate Problems of Interest To Every Man: Human Destiny and the Meaning of Life. NY: Macmillan 1964, vii + 276 p

CHOROST, S.

See Levine, Murray; Silberstein, Richard M.

CHOTLOS, JOHN W.

See Miller, Milton H.

CHRIST, ADOLPH E.

70021 Attitudes toward death among group of acute geriatric psychiatric patients. J Gerontol 1961, 16:56-59. In Death & Identity 146-152

70022 (& Wagner, N. N.) Iatrogenic factors in residential treatment: a problem in staff training. Ops 1966, 36:725-729
   Abs JMa RFPsa 1968, 32:381

70023 Juvenile delinquency—always a hopeless prognosis. Postgrad Med 1964, 36:551-554

70024 (& Griffiths, R.) Parent-nurse therapeutic contact on a child psychiatry unit. Ops 1965, 35:589-593

70025 Sexual countertransference problems with a psychotic child. J Amer Acad Child Psychiat 1964, 3:298-316

See Berlin, Irving N.; Townes, Brenda

CHRIST, JACOB

70026 Psychoanalytical treatment of a dissociative state with hallucinations. Int Psychiat Clin 1968, 5(1):47-59

See Bernstein, Stephen; Grunebaum, Henry U.

CHRISTAKOS, A. C.

See McDonald, Robert L.

CHRISTENSEN, CARL W.

70027 The mental health of clergymen. Int Psychiat Clin 1969, 5(4):191-200
70028 The occurrence of mental illness in the ministry: introduction; family background; psychotic disorders; psychoneurotic disorders; personality disorders. J pastoral Care 1959, 13:79-87; 1960, 14:13-20; 1961, 15:153-159; 1963, 17:1-10; 125-135
70029 Religious conversion. Arch gen Psychiat 1963, 9:207-216
70030 Standing in the need of prayer. Voices 1966, 2(4):33-34

CHRISTENSEN, DARREL E.

70031 Hegel's phenomenological analysis and Freud's psychoanalysis. Int Philos Q 1968, 8:356-378

CHRISTIANSEN, KENNETH

See Dana, Richard H.

CHRISTIANSON, MARY

See Call, Justin D.

CHRISTIE, GEORGE L.

70032 Psychiatrists and psychoanalysis. Med J Aust 1964, (1):964-965
70033 Therapeutic community and psychotherapy: The Austen Riggs Centre. Med J Aust 1964, (1):458-460

CHRISTOFFEL, HANS

S-5665 Exhibitionism and exhibitionists. PT Pervers 255-284

CHRISTOZOV, CHRISTO

70034 Phénomènes obsessionnels dans les psychoses (investigations cliniques et physiopathologiques). [Obsessional phenomena in psychoses (clinical and physiopathologic investigations).] Ann méd-psychol 1965, 123(1):43-72
70035 Réflexions sur le rôle névrosogène de l'angoisse. [The role of anxiety in inducing neuroses.] Maroc Med 1968, 48(510):94-109
70036 Sur quelques aspects du probleme névrotique sous l'optique de l'analyse comparative. [On some aspects of the problem of neuroses in the light of comparative analysis.] Ann méd-psychol 1966, 124(2):155-173

CHRZANOWSKI, GERARD

70037   Community mental health. Sci Psa 1965, 8:238-242

70038   Dinamica e genetica dei distrubi del pensiero negli stati schizopatici. [Dynamics and genetics of disturbances in the process of thinking in schizophrenia.] Arch Psicol Neurol Psichiat 1967, 28:295-305

70039   Discussion of Drellich, M. G. & Waxenberg, S. E. "Erotic and affectional components of female sexuality." Sci Psa 1966, 10:54-55

70040   Einige Grundpositionen der interpersonellen Theorie. [Some basic tenets of the interpersonal theory.] Z PSM 1968, 14:291-297

70041   The independent roots of ego psychology and their therapeutic implications. Sci Psa 1967, 11:150-158

70042   An interpersonal view of phobias. Voices 1967, 3:10-15

70043   Neurasthenia and hypochondriasis. Compreh Txbk Psychiat 1163-1168

70044   (Participant) Panel discussion: the management of depression in children and adults. Contempo Psa 1965, 2:26-29; 54-61

70045   The psychotherapeutic management of sociopathy. PT 1965, 19:372-381
        Abs Auth Rev Psicoanál 1966, 23:70

70046   Symptom choice in schizophrenic manifestations. Contempo Psa 1967, 4:41-52

70047   Termination in psychoanalysis, goals and technical principles evolving from Sullivanian conceptions. Ops 1960, 14:48-62

CHURCH, JOSEPH

70048   Language and the Discovery of Reality. A Developmental Psychology of Cognition. NY: Random House 1961, 245 p
        Rv Beres, D. Q 1962, 31:267-269

70049   (Ed) Three Babies: Biographies of Cognitive Development. NY: Random House 1966, ix + 323 p

See Stone, Lawrence Joseph

CHURCH, MARGARET

70050   Dostoevsky's "Crime and Punishment" and Kafka's "The Trial." Lit & Psych 1969, 19(3-4):47-55

CHURCHILL, S. R.

70051   Travail social en groupe: outil de diagnostic en guidance infantile. [Group social work, a diagnostic tool in child guidance.] RFPsa 1966, 30:527

CHURCHILL, WAINWRIGHT

70052   Homosexual Behavior Among Males: A Cross Cultural and Cross-Species Investigation. NY: Hawthorn Books 1967, ix + 349 p
        Rv Woltmann, A. G. R 1969, 56:489. WAS Q 1969, 38:141-143

CHWAST, JACOB

70053   Alienation as a factor in delinquency. Fed Probation 1964, 28:25-30

70054   Control—the key to offender treatment. Journal of Offender Therapy 1963, 7(1). PT 1965, 19:116-125

70055 Delinquency and criminology: an acting out phenomenon. Acting Out 100-108

70056 Depressive reactions as manifested among adolescent delinquents. PT 1967, 21:575-584

70057 (Harari, C.; Delany, L.) Experimental techniques in group psychotherapy with delinquents. J Crim Law Criminol Police Sci 1961, 52: 156-165

70058 Group process in leadership training for older adults. Adult Leadership 1963, 11:301-302; 310

70059 Groupwork with gangs: its possibilities and limitations. J psychiat Treatm Offenders 1960, Dec, 4(3)

70060 Jewish delinquency. Workmen's Circle CALL 1962, March

70061 The malevolent transformation. J crim Law Criminol Police Sci 1963, 53:42-47

70062 Mental health consultation with street gang workers. Canad J Corr 1965. In *Interdisciplinary Problems in Criminology: Papers of American Society of Criminology 1964*, Columbus, Ohio: Publication Services, The College of Commerce and Administration, Ohio State Univ 1965

70063 The parameters of delinquency treatment. Int ment Hlth N L 1961, June, 3:1 & 2

70064 Principles and techniques of offender therapy. Cur psychiat Ther 1966, 6:136-144

70065 Reading, spelling and delinquency. Spelling Prog Bull 1962

70066 (& Lurie, A.) The resocialization of the discharged depressed patient. Canad Psychiat Ass J 1966, 11(Suppl):131-140

70067 Reversibility-irreversibility. Problems in the treatment of offenders. PT 1961, 15:221-232

70068 The role of the community center in the socialization of the ex-patient. *Proceedings of a Professional Institute. The Social Rehabilitation of the Mentally Ill: Impact on the Community*, NY: Hillside Hospital 1964, 44-46

70069 The selection of personnel for a police juvenile service. J crim Law Criminol Police Sci 1960, 51:357-362

70070 A small goal is big enough—minimal objective in treating the delinquent. Crime Delinq 1963, 9:159-162

70071 The social function of guilt. Soc Wk 1964, 9(2):58-63. In Proceedings of the Third World Congress of Psychiatry, Cameron 1963

70072 Therapeutic intervention in reversing gang pathogenicity. J Offender Ther 1961, June, 5:1

70073 Value conflicts in law enforcement. Crime Delinq 1965, 11:151-161

70074 (& Seller, S.) The violent gang: etiology and treatment. In Endleman, S. *Violence in the Streets*, Chicago: Quadrangle Books 1968, 237-252

See Berkowitz, Louis; Harari, Carmi; Weisman, Irving

CIARLO, DOROTHY D.

70075 (& Lidz, T.; Ricci, J.) Word meaning in parents of schizophrenics. Arch gen Psychiat 1967, 17:470-477

CIBELLI, LOUIS ALFRED

70076 The analytically-oriented psychotherapeutic process. J Med Ass Georgia 1962, 51:360-361

CITRIN, E.

See Kitchener, Howard

CITTERIO, C.

70077 [Presuppositions for an interpretation of the phenomenology of anxiety in endogenous depression.] (It) Rass Stud Psichiat 1962, 51:199-208

CIVIDALLI, N.

See Moses, Rafael

CIVIDINI, E.

70078 (& Klain, E.) [Countertransference and interactions in group psychotherapy.] (Cro) Neuropsihijatrija 1966, 14:109-117

70079 (et al) [Transference and countransference in group psychotherapy.] (Cro) Neuropsihijatrija 1967, 15:191-199

See Betlheim, Stjepan; Persic, N.

CLAESSENS, DIETER

70080 Angst, Furcht und gesellschaftlicher Druck und andere Aufsätze. [Anxiety, Fear and Social Pressure, and Other Essays.] Dortmund: Ruhfus 1966, 167 p

70081 Instinkt Psyche Geltung: Bestimmungsfaktoren Menschlichen Verhaltens. [Instinct, Psyche and Values: Determining Factors of Human Behavior.] Cologne, W. Germany: Westdeutscher 1967, 218 p

70082 Ein Theorem zur Struktur der Psyche. [A theorem for the structure of the psyche.] Jb Psychol Psychother med Anthropol 1966, 14:736-759

CLAEYS, W.

70083 Ontstaan en statuut van het geweten volgens S. Freuds cerste oqvattingen. [The creation and dictates of the conscience according to S. Freud's conceptions.] Tijdschr Philos 1963, 25:500-529

CLAMAN, LAWRENCE

70084 (& Trieschman, A.) Adjustment to surgery of children with ulcerative colitis. Amer J Dis Childr 1964, 107:131-137

70085 (& Johnstone, R. E.) Effect of emotions on use of medication in myasthenia gravis. Texas State J Med 1965, 61:49-51

70086 The psychosis of general paresis. JNMD 1957, 125:57-63

70087 Short-term analytic group psychotherapy with undergraduate college students. St. Med 1958, 6:80-93

CLANCIER-GRAVELAT, ANNE

70088 Discussion of Fornari, F. "La psychanalyse de la guerre." RFPsa 1966, 30:279-280

70089 Discussion of Grunberger, B. "Study on depression." RFPsa 1965, 29:183-184
70090 Discussion of Kestemberg, E. & Kestemberg, J. "Contributions à la perspective génétique en psychanalyse." RFPsa 1966, 30:760-761
70091 Discussion: Remarques sur le narcissisme dans le mouvement de la cure. [Remarks about narcissism in the analytic process.] RFPsa 1965, 29:609-611
70092 Oedipe et création littéraire. [Oedipus and literary creation.] RFPsa 1967, 31:891-895

REVIEWS OF:
70093 Bergeron, M. Early Psychology. RFPsa 1967, 31:302
70094 David, M. La Psicoanalisi nella Cultura Italiana. RFPsa 1968, 32:329
70095 Grenial, P. Dictionnaire de la Mythologie Grecque et Romaine. RFPsa 1968, 32:152
70096 Sandreau, T. La Main Sur la Bouche. RFPsa 1966, 30:510

CLARE, JACK

See Kaye, Harvey E.

CLARIDGE, G.

See Eysenck, Sybil B. G.

CLARK, ELEANOR

See Chafetz, Morris E.

CLARK, J. H.

70097 Adaptive machines in psychiatry. Prog brain Res 1963, 2:224-235

CLARK, KENNETH M.

See Boswell, John J., Jr.

CLARK, LINCOLN D.

70098 A comparative view of aggressive behavior. P 1962, 119:336-341

CLARK, MARY G.

See Hawkins, D. R.

CLARK, R. K.

See Chessick, Richard D.; Scharfman, Melvin Allen

CLARK, ROBERT A.

70099 Analytic psychology today. PT 1961, 15:193-204
70100 Discussion of Forbush, B. "Moses Sheppard's interest in mental illness." Crosscurrents in Ps & Psa 18-20
S-43718 Jung and Freud: a chapter in psychoanalytic history. Abs An Surv Psa 1955, 6:7-8

70101 Jungian and Freudian approach to dreams. PT 1961, 15:89-100
70102 Psychiatrists and psychoanalysts on war. PT 1965, 19:540-558

CLARKE, ALAN DOUGLAS BENSON

70103 Problems in assessing the later effects of early experience. In Miller, E.
       Foundations of Child Psychiatry, Oxford/NY: Pergamon Pr 1968, 339-
       368
70104 (& Clarke, A. M.) Some recent advances in the study of early depriva-
       tion. J child Psychol Psychiat 1960, 1(1):26-36

CLARKE, ANN MARGARET

See Clarke, Alan Douglas Benson

CLARKE, MARY G.

70105 (& Curtis, T. E.; Abse, D. W.) Etiological factors in peptic ulcer as
       revealed in group-analytic psychotherapy. Int Rec Med 1960, 173(2):
       92-96

See Curtis, Thomas E.; Hawkins, David R.

CLARKE, O. NORA J.

See Goforth, Eugene G.

CLARKE, PETER ROBIN FRANKLIN

70106 (& Stengel, E.) The teaching of psychology to medical students. Proc
       IV World Cong Psychiat 1966, 966-969

CLARKSON, A. R.

See Cramond, W. A.

CLAUSER, GÜNTER

70107 Psychotherapie-Fibel; Einführung in die Psychotherapie innerer Krank-
       heiten. [Psychotherapy Primer: Introduction to Psychotherapy of Inner
       Illnesses.] (Foreword: Heilmeyer, L.) Stuttgart: G. Thieme 1963, xii
       + 213 p
70108 Verhaltensanalyse und aktiv-analytische Psychotherapie pubertäts-
       magersüchtiger Mädchen. [Analysis of the behavior and active-analyti-
       cal psychotherapy of emaciated girls during puberty.] Prax Kinder-
       psychol 1961, 10:278-287

See Hiltmann, Hildegard

CLAVREUL, JEAN

70109 Le couple pervers. [The perverted couple.] In Aulagnier-Spairani, P.
       et al: *Le Désire et la Perversion*, Paris: Seuil 1967

See Aulagnier-Spairani, Piera

CLAY, DENNIS D.

70110 Interpretation, reward, and freedom of communication in psychotherapy. Proc 77th Ann Convention Am Psychol Assoc 1969, 4(2):499-500

CLAYTON, PAULA J.

See Reich, Theodore; Winokur, George

CLEGHORN, JOHN MARNOCH

See Cleghorn, Robert A.; Gottschalk, Louis A.

CLEGHORN, ROBERT ALLEN

70111 Foreword to Lesse, S. *An Evaluation of the Results of the Psychotherapies,* Springfield, Ill: Thomas 1968, 51-52
70112 Hysterical personality and conversion: theoretical aspects. Canad Psychiat Ass J 1969, 14:553-567
70113 Pitfalls in thinking big. Psychiat Q 1964, 38:607-617
70114 The place of theory, observation and scientific method in psychosomatic
medicine. Proc IV World Cong Psychiat 1966, 580-585
70115 (Ed) Proceedings of the 3rd World Congress of Psychiatry. Toronto,
Canada: Univ of Toronto Pr 1951-53, 3 Volumes
70116 (& Pivnicki, D.) Psychodynamic aspects of altered proprioception and
motility in Parkinson's disease. Rev Canad Biol 1961, 20:643-648
10117 (& Brown, W. T.) Psychogenesis of emesis. Canad Psychiat Ass J 1964,
9:299-312
70118 (& Cleghorn, J. M.) Training in psychosomatic research. Adv PSM
1967, 5:166-179
70119 The two cultures in psychiatry. Canad Med Ass J 1965, 93:49-57

CLEMENS, THEODORE

See Alexander, Franz; Goldstein, Michael J.

CLEMENTS, M.

70120 Mythology and psychological presupposition. Educ Theory 1964, 14:
224-228

CLEMES, STANLEY R.

70121 (& Dement, W. C.) Effect of REM sleep deprivation on psychological
functioning. JNMD 1967, 144:485-491

CLEMMONS, ROY S.

See Schwab, John J.

CLARK, GABRIELLE

70122 Reflection on the role of the mother in the development of language in
the schizophrenic child. Canad Psychiat Ass J 1961, 6:252-256

CLIFFORD, W.

70123 (& Scott, M.) The mutually defensive roles of depression and mania. Canad Psychiat Ass J 1966, 11(Suppl):S267-S274

CLINCO, ARTHUR A.

70124 Discussion of Lubin, A. J. "The influence of the Russian Orthodox Church on Freud's Wolf-Man: a hypothesis." Psa Forum 1967, 2:166-168

See Wayne, G. J.

CLINTON, J. KEW

REVIEW OF:
70125 Bowers, M. K. Conflicts of the Clergy. A Psychodynamic Study with Case Histories. Am Im 1965, 22:203-204

CLINTON, WILLIAM

See Balser, Benjamin H.

CLOSSON, W. G., JR.

See Hall, Robert A.

CLOTHIER, FLORENCE

S-43739 The unmarried mother of school age as seen by a psychiatrist. In Crow, L. D. & Crow, A. *Readings in Child and Adolescent Psychology*, NY/London/Toronto: Longmans 1961, 502-515

CLOUGH, WILSON O.

70126 Psychology and the art of literature. Educ Forum 1967, 31:173-179

CLOUZET, MARYSE

See under CHOISY, MARYSE

CLOWER, COURTNEY G.

See Baak, W. W.

CLUNE, FRANCIS J., JR.

See Robinson, Ira E.

CLYNE, M. B.

70127 Der Anruf bei Nacht. Eine psychologische Untersuchung aus der ärztlichen Praxis. [The Night Call. A Psychological Study from General Practice.] Bern/Stuttgart: Huber/Klett 1964, 303 p

COAN, RICHARD W.

70128 (& Zagona, S. V.) Contemporary ratings of psychological theorists. Psychol Rec 1962, 12:315-322

COBB, SIDNEY

See Chen, Edith

COBB, STANLEY

70129 Brain and personality. P 1960, 116:938-939
70130 Mind-body relationships. In Lief, H. E. et al: *The Psychological Basis of Medical Practice*, NY/Evanston/London: Harper & Row 1963, 36-43
70131 Some clinical changes in behavior accompanying endocrine disorders. JNMD 1960, 130:97-106

COBBS, PRICE M.

See Grier, William H.

COBLINER, W. GODFREY

70132 Psychoanalysis and the Geneva school of genetic psychology: parallels and counterparts. Int J Psychiat 1967, 3(2):82-116; 128
    Abs Abend, S. M. Q 1968, 37:317

See Spitz, René A.

COBRINIK, LEONARD

70133 (& Faretra, G.) Verbal stereotypy in childhood emotional disorder. Recent Adv biol Psychiat 1966, 8:1-8

See Bender, Lauretta

COBURN, WALLACE A.

See Rutherford, Robert N.

COCCHI, A.

See Cazzullo, A. Guareschi; Generali, I.

COCHRANE, CARL M.

70134 (& Prange, A. J., Jr.; Abse, D. W.) Reserpine-produced changes in the direction of aggressive drives. Proceedings of 3rd World Cong of Psychiat 1961, 1:370-373

See Schopler, Eric

COCHRANE, HORTENCE S.

See Seidenberg, Robert

CODDINGTON, R. DEAN

70135 (& Offord, D. R.) Psychiatrists' reliability in judging ego function. Arch gen Psychiat 1967, 16:48-55

See Bruch, Hilde

CODERCH, JUAN

70136 La enseñanza de la psicología al estudiante de medicina. [The teaching of psychology to the medical student.] Rev Psiquiat Psicol Méd 1968, 8:430-451

CODLING, LAURA

See Lewis, Melvin

CODY, JOHN J.

70137 Emily Dickinson's Vesuvian face. Am Im 1967, 24:161-180
Abs JWS Q 1969, 38:165
70138 Mourner among the children. The psychological crisis of Emily Dick- · inson. I & II. Psychiat Q 1967, 41:12-37; 233-263

See Pancrazio, James J.

COE, HENRY W.

70139 (& Bogan, L. G.) The Freud Center. Ment Hosp 1965, 16:238-240

COELHO, GEORGE V.

70140 (& Silber, E.; Hamburg, D. A.) Use of the Student-TAT to assess coping behavior in hospitalized, normal, and exceptionally competent college freshmen. Percept mot Skills 1962, 14:355-365

See Murphey, Elizabeth B.; Silber, Earle

COFER, CHARLES N.

70141 (& Appley, M. H.) Motivation: Theory and Research. NY: John Wiley 1964, 958 p
Rv Linn, L. Q 1965, 34:610-611

COGHI, ISABELLA

See Landelli, Carlo L.

COHEN, ARNOLD D.

See Kazan, Avraam T.

COHEN, F. M.

See Horowitz, Mardi J.

COHEN, HASKEL

See Cath, Stanley H.

COHEN, IRVIN H.

70142 (& Lichtenberg, J. D.) Alopecia areata. Arch gen Psychiat 1967, 17: 608-614

70143   (Ed) Family Structure, Dynamics, and Therapy. (Psychiat Res Report
        #20.) Wash: Amer Psychiat Assoc 1966, 234 p

See Knight, James A.

COHEN, J.

See Blau, Abram

COHEN, JACOB

See Ortmeyer, Dale

COHEN, JOHN

70144   (Ed) Readings in Psychology. London: George Allen & Unwin 1964,
        414 p

COHEN, KENNETH D.

70145   A case of postpartum psychosis following pregnancy by artificial in-
        semination. Bull Phila Ass Psa 1966, 16:136-146
            Abs EFA Q 1968, 37:159
70146   Significance of illness to the patient. J Einstein Med Cent 1960, 8:5-6

REVIEW OF:
70147   Deutsch, H. Selected Problems of Adolescence. Bull Phila Ass Psa 1969,
        19:167-168

COHEN, L. H.

See Sears, R. R.

COHEN, MABEL BLAKE

70148   Manic-depressive psychosis. Ency Ment Hlth 958-964
70149   Personal identity and sexual identity. Ps 1966, 29:1-14

See Cohen, Robert A.

COHEN, MAURICE

70150   Chaucer's Prioress and her tale. A study of anal character and anti-
        semitism. Q 1962, 31:232-249

COHEN, MIMI

See Norbeck, Edward

COHEN, N. J.

See Kaffman, Mordecai

COHEN, RAQUEL E.

70151   (& Grinspoon, L.) Limit setting as a corrective ego experience. Arch
        gen Psychiat 1963, 8:74-79

COHEN, RICHARD L.

70152 Developments in the isolation therapy of behavior disorders of children. Curr psychiat Ther 1963, 3:180-187

70153 (& Charny, I. W.; Lembke, P.) Parental expectations as a force in treatment: the identification of unconscious parental projections onto the children's psychiatric hospital. Arch gen Psychiat 1961, 4:471-478

COHEN, ROBERT A.

70154 Discussion of Novey, S. "Behavior and inner experience: parallels and contradictions in the appraisal of treatment." Crosscurrents in Ps & Psa 163-167

70155 Foreword to Rothwell, N. D. & Doniger, J. M. *The Psychiatric Halfway House: A Case Study,* Springfield: Ill: Thomas 1966, vii-ix

70156 Manic-depressive reactions. Compreh Txbk Psychiat 676-688

70157 (& Cohen, M. B.) Research in psychotherapy: a preliminary report. Ps 1961, 24(2, Suppl):46-61

COHEN, ROSALYN S.

70158 (& La Vietes, R.) Clinical principles of curriculum selection. In Hellmuth, J. *Educational Therapy, Vol. I.,* Seattle: Special Child Publ 1966, 137-154

70159 (& La Vietes, R.; Reens, R.; Rindsberg, B.) An inquiry into variations of teacher-child communication: implications for the treatment of emotionally ill children. In Knoblock, P. *Proceedings of First Annual Conference on Education of Emotionally Disturbed Children,* Syracuse Univ Pr 1966

70160 Some childhood identity disturbances: educational implementation of a psychiatric treatment plan. J Amer Acad Child Psychiat 1964, 3:488-499

70161 Therapeutic education and day treatment: a new professional liaison. Except Children 1965, 32:23-28

See La Vietes, Ruth L.

COHEN, RUDOLF

70162 Die testpsychologische Begutachtung im Dienste der Indikationsstellung zur Analyse. [Psychological test expert testimony in the determination of the indication for analysis.] Psyche 1960, 14:77-80

COHEN, S.

See Haim, A.; Sapir, M.

COHEN, SANFORD

70163 (& Silverman, A. J.; Shmavonian, B. M.) Influence of psychodynamic factors on central nervous system functioning in young and aged subjects. PSM 1961, 23:123-137

See Silverman, Albert J.

COHEN, SHELDON B.

70164   The ontogenesis of prophetic behavior: a study in creative conscience formation. PPR 1962, 49:100-122
        Abs RLG Q 1963, 32:135
70165   Rebel and reactionary, siblings under the skin? Sci Psa 1968, 13:39-52

COHEN, SIDNEY

70166   The Beyond Within. (Foreword: Murphy, G.) NY: Atheneum 1964, 268 p
70167   Contact deprivation in infants. Psychosomatics 1966, 7:85-88
70168   Discussion of Savage, C. "The analysis of an 'outsider'." Psa Forum 1969, 3:290

        See McGlothlin, William H.

COHEN, STANLEY

        See Linn, Louis

COHEN, STEPHEN H.

70169   Neurotic ambiguity and the neurotic hiatus between knowledge and action. J existent Psychiat 1963, 3:75-96

COHEN, STEWART

70170   The development of aggression. Diss Abstr 1968, 28:4705-4706

COHEN, SYDNEY

70171   The origin and function of sadistic behavior. J contempo PT 1969, 2:3-7

COHEN, YEHUDI A.

70172   The Transition from Childhood to Adolescence: Cross-Cultural Studies of Initiation Ceremonies, Legal Systems, and Incest Taboos. Chicago: Aldine 1966, 254 p
        Rv J Am Psa Ass 1969, 17:276. Glenn, J. Q 1965, 34:605-606

COHLER, BERTRAM JOSEPH

70173   (& Woolsey, S. H.; Weiss, J. L.; Grunebaum, H. U.) Childrearing attitudes among mothers volunteering and revolunteering for a psychological study. Psychol Rep 1968, 23:603-612

COHN, ALFRED EINSTEIN

70174   No Retreat from Reason, and Other Essays. Port Washington, NY: Kennikat Pr 1969, xi + 279 p

COHN, FAYE

        See Gordon, Jesse E.

COHN, FRANZ S.

70175 Fantasy aggression in children as studied by the doll play technique. Child Develpm 1962, 33:235-250

S-43776 Time and the ego.
Abs AHM An Surv Psa 1957, 8:80-81

COHN, ISADORE H.

70176 (& Hulse, W. C.) The use of a group psychotherapy program for adolescents as a training unit in child psychiatry. Ops 1961, 31:521-535
Abs JMa RFPsa 1962, 26:329

70177 Intra-psychic changes in an adolescent girl during group psychotherapy. Top Probl PT 1965, 5:176-188

COHN, JAY B.

70178 Man and his dentist. Anesthesia Prog 1968, 15:34-36

See Tabachnick, Norman

COHN, NORMAN

70179 The cult of the free spirit: a medieval heresy reconstructed. PPR 1961, 48:51-68

70180 The myth of the Jewish world-conspiracy: a case study in collective psychopathology. Commentary 1966, 41(5):35-42

COHN, RUTH C.

70181 A child with a stomach ache. In Fagan, J. & Shephard, I. Gestalt Therapy Now, NY: Social and Behavioral Sciences 1969

70182 From couch to circle to community. In Ruitenbeck, H. Group Therapy Today: Styles, Methods and Theories, NY: Atherton Pr 1969

70183 Group therapeutic techniques as educational means in the training of psychoanalysts. Top Probl PT 1965, 5:48-58

70184 A group therapeutic workshop in countertransference. Int J grp PT 1961, 11:284-296

70185 "I must do what I want to." Voices 1968, 4(2):29-33

70186 Psychoanalytic, experiential and Gestalt therapy in groups. In Fagan, J. & Shephard, I. Gestalt Therapy Now, NY: Social and Behavioral Sciences 1969

70187 Psychoanalytic or experiential group psychotherapy: a false dichotomy. R 1969, 56:333-345

70188 The sexual fantasies of the psychotherapist and their use in psychotherapy. J Sex Res 1966, 2:219-226

70189 Das Thema als Mittelpunkt der Gruppe. [Theme-centered interactional groups.] In Gruppen Psychotherapie und Gruppen Dynamik, Band 3, Verlag für Medizinische Psychologie (Vandenhoek und Ruprecht), Göttingen 1969

70190 Training group therapists in interactional seminars. In Proc Int Cong of Group Psychotherapy. Vienna: Wiener med Akad 1968

70191 Training intuition. In Otto, H. & Mann, J. Ways of Growth, NY: Grossman Publ 1968, 167-177

COHRSSEN, J.

See Werry, John S.

COIMBRA DE MATOS, A.

70191A [Apropos of ideologies.] (Fr) RFPsa 1969, 33:894-897

COL, C.

See Launay, C.

COLARUSSO, CALVIN A.

See Kolansky, Harold

COLBY, KENNETH MARK

70192 Causal correlations in clinical interpretation. Psa Clin Inter 189-199. From author's *A Skeptical Psychoanalyst*, NY: Ronald pr Co 1958

70193 Commentary: report to plenary session on psychopharmacology in relation to psychotherapy. In Shlien, J. M. et al: *Research in Psychotherapy, Vol. III*, Wash DC: APA 1968, 536-540

70194 (& Watt, J. B.; Gilbert, J. P.) A computer method of psychotherapy: preliminary communication. JNMD 1966, 142:148-152

70195 Computer simulation of change in personal belief systems. Beh Sci 1967, 12:248-253

S-43783 Energy and Structure in Psychoanalysis.
Abs Berezin, M. A. An Surv Psa 1955, 6:58, 466-475

70196 Experiment on the effects of an observer's presence on the imago system during psychoanalytic free-association. Beh Sci 1960, 5:216-232

70197 Experimental treatment of neurotic computer programs. Arch gen Psychiat 1964, 10:220-227

S-43786 An Introduction to Psychoanalytic Research.
Abs J Am Psa Ass 1962, 10:444. Rv Pfeffer, A. Z. Q 1962, 31:260-261

70198 On the greater amplifying power of causal-correlative over interrogative inputs on free association in an experimental psychoanalytic situation. JNMD 1961, 133:233-239
Abs Powelson, H. Q 1963, 32:293-294

70199 (& Gilbert, J. P.) Programming a computer model of neurosis. J math Psychol 1964, 1:405-417

70200 Psychotherapeutic processes. Ann Rev Psychol 1964, 15:347-370

70201 Research in psychoanalytic information theory. Amer Sci 1961, 49:358-369

70202 Sex differences in dreams of primitive tribes. Amer Anthropologist 1963, 65:1116-1122

S-43788 A Skeptical Psychoanalyst.
Abs HK An Surv Psa 1958, 9:26-28

70203 Therapeutic person-computer conversation. In Stollak, G. E. et al: *Psychotherapy Research; Selected Readings*, Chicago: Rand McNally 1966

COLE, A. A.

See Wilson, Charles P.

COLE, EDWIN M.

70204 Discussion of Defries, Z. et al: "Treatment of secondary reading disability in young boys: a pilot study." Sci Psa 1969, 14:107-109

COLE, JONATHAN O.

70205 (& Klerman, G. L.; Jones, R. T.) Drug therapy. Prog Neurol Psychiat 1960, 15:540-576; 1961, 16:539-574
70206 (& Cole, K. G.) Psychopharmacology. Ency Ment Hlth 1654-1663

See Jenkins, Richard L.; Katz, Martin M.

COLE, KATHLEEN G.

See Cole, Jonathan O.

COLE, M.

See Lourie, Reginald S.

COLE, NYLA J.

70207 (& Branch, C. H. H.; Allison, R. B.) Some relationships between social class and the practice of dynamic psychotherapy. P 1962, 118:1004-1012

COLE, SPURGEON

See Steward, Horace

COLE, WILLIAM GRAHAM

70208 Sex in Christianity and Psychoanalysis. NY/London: Oxford Univ Pr 1966, xvi + 329 p

COLEMAN, JAMES S.

70209 (& Johnstone, J. W. C.; Jonassohn, K.) The Adolescent Society. The Social Life of the Teenager and its Impact on Education. NY: The Free Pr of Glencoe 1961, xvi + 368 p
      Rv Wolfenstein, M. Q 1963, 32:126-128

COLEMAN, JOHN

70210 Shot at Freud. New Statesman 1963, 66(6 Sept):297

COLEMAN, JOSEPH C.

70211 The levels hypothesis: a re-examination and reorientation. J proj Tech 1969, 33:118-122

COLEMAN, JULES VICTOR

70212 Aims and conduct of psychotherapy. Arch gen Psychiat 1968, 18:1-6
70213 Banter as psychotherapeutic intervention. Psa 1962, 22:69-74
70214 Social factors influencing the development and containment of psychi-

atric symptoms. In Scheff, T. J. *Mental Illness and Social Processes,*
NY: Harper & Row 1967, 158-168

See Errera, Paul; Hirschberg, J. Cotter

COLEMAN, MARSHALL DONALD

70215 Emergency psychotherapy. Prog PT 1960, 5:78-85
70216 (& Rosenbaum, M.) The walk-in psychiatric clinic. Israel Ann Psychiat
       1963, 1:99-106

COLEMAN, ROLAND

See Antrobus, John S.

COLES, ROBERT

70217 Achievement of Anna Freud. Massachusetts Rev 1966, 7:203-220
70218 Bullitt to Wilson. New Repub 1967, 156(28 Jan):27-30
70219 Children of Crisis; A Study of Courage and Fear. Boston: Little, Brown
       1967, xiv + 401 p
70220 Discussion of Bridger, W. H. "Adolescent idealism in the civil rights
       movement." Sci Psa 1966, 9:68
70221 Erikson's search for Gandhi. Int J Psychiat 1969, 7:477-483
70222 The Jamesian psychoanalyst. Contempo Psa 1967, 3:167-172
70223 On courage. Contempo Psa 1965, 1:85-98

COLIN, BOURJADE

70224 (& Colin, R.) Aperçu sur l'inceste. [A survey of incest.] Acta Med Leg
       Soc (Liège) 1966, 19:213-219

COLIN, ROSIER

See Colin, Bourjade

COLLETTE, ALBERT

70225 Introduction à la Psychologie Dynamique; des Théories Psychanali-
       tiques à la Psychologie Moderne. [Introduction to Dynamic Psychol-
       ogy; from Psychoanalytic Theories to Modern Psychology.] Brussels:
       Univ Libre de Bruxelles, Institut de Sociologie 1963, 267 p

COLLEY, RUDOLPH S.

See Alexander, Irving E.

COLLIER, MARY JEFFREY

70226 (& Gaier, E. L.) The childhood story preferences of adolescent Finnish
       girls. Am Im 1961, 18:187-204
S-43824 (& Gaier, E. L.) Preferred childhood stories of college women.
       Abs Swartz, J. An Surv Psa 1958, 9:272-273
70227 The psychological appeal in the Cinderella theme. Am Im 1961, 18:
       399-411

See Gaier, Eugene L.

COLLIER, REX M.

70228 A figure-ground model replacing the conscious-unconscious dichotomy. J ind Psych 1964, 20:3-16
70229 Selected implications from a dynamic theory of consciousness. Am Psych 1964, 19:265-269

COLLINS, CARVEL EMERSON

70230 The interior monologues of the sound and the fury. In Malin, I. *Psychoanalysis and American Fiction*, NY: Dutton 1965, 223-243

COLLINS, D. J.

See Sadoff, Robert L.

COLLINS, GAROLD W.

70231 Dreaming and adaptation to stress. Diss Abstr 1967, 27:4119

COLLINS, W.

See Petrie, Asenath

COLLINSON, J. B.

70232 Brain model for clinicians. Arch gen Psychiat 1964, 11:495-502
70233 The concept. Arch gen Psychiat 1962, 6:168-181

COLM, HANNA N.

70234 The affirmation of distance and closeness in psychotherapy. Rev existent Psychol Psychiat 1961, 1:33-43
70235 The Existentialist Approach to Psychotherapy with Adults and Children. (Ed: Bloomberg, C. M.) (Introd: Weigert, E.) NY: Grune & Stratton 1966, vii + 229 p
S-43837 A field-theory approach to transference and its particular application to children. In Haworth, M. R. *Child Psychotherapy*, NY/London: Basic Books 1964, 242-256
    Abs An Surv Psa 1955, 6:324-326
S-43839 Phobias in children.
    Abs Vilar, J. Rev Psicoanál 1962, 19:275-277
70236 The role of affirmation in analysis. Ps 1960, 23:279-285

COLODNY, DOROTHY

See Kurlander, LeRoy Frank

COLODNY, ROBERT GARLAND

70237 (Ed) Frontiers of Science and Philosophy. Pittsburgh, Pa.: Univ Pitt Pr 1962, 288 p

COLOMBO, EDUARDO R.

70238 (& Moccio, F.) El vampiro: estudio de un rumor. [The vampire: study of a rumor.] Act Np Arg 1961, 7:12-19

COLONNA, ALICE B.

70239 A blind child goes to the hospital. Psa St C 1968, 23:391-422
70240 Discussion of Burlingham, D. "The re-education of a retarded blind child." Psa St C 1968, 23:386-390

See Nagera (Perez), Humberto

COLONNA, MARIA T.

See Iandelli, Carlo L.

COLPE, C.

70241 [A physician in a dialogue. Reminiscences of Ludwig Binswanger, died on 5 February 1966.] (Ger) Landarzt 1967, 43:277-283

COLTART, NINA E. C.

REVIEW OF:
70242 Laing, R. D. & Cooper, D. G. Reason and Violence. A Decade of Sartre's Philosophy 1950-1960. J 1965, 46:394-395

COLTON, S.

See Ship, A. G.

COLTRERA, JOSEPH T.

70243 On the creation of beauty and thought: the unique as vicissitude. J Am Psa Ass 1965, 13:634-703
70244 (& Ross, N.) Freud's psychoanalytic technique—from the beginning to 1923. Psa Tech 13-50
70245 The gifts of Daedalus: an adaptive aspect of the superego in the maintenance of psychic structure. (Read at Boston Psa Soc, 24 Apr 1963) Abs Kahn, E. Bull Phila Ass Psa 1963, 13:145-147
70246 Psychoanalysis and existentialism. J Am Psa Ass 1962, 10:166-215

ABSTRACTS OF:
70247 Bergler, E. "Little Dorrit" and Dickens' intuitive knowledge of psychic masochism. An Surv Psa 1957, 8:328
70248 Bergler, E. Writers of half-talent. An Surv Psa 1957, 8:328
70249 Chessick, R. D. The sense of reality, time and creative inspiration. An Surv Psa 1957, 8:332
70250 Ehrenzweig, A. The creative surrender. A comment on "Joanna Field's" book An Experiment in Leisure. An Surv Psa 1957, 8:331-332
70251 Grotjahn, M. The defense against creative anxiety in the life and work of James Barrie. Commentary to John Skinner's research of "The Boy Who Wouldn't Grow Up." An Surv Psa 1957, 8:327-328
70252 Ostow, M. Virtue and necessity. An Surv Psa 1957, 8:24-25
70253 Posinsky, S. H. The problem of Yurok anality. An Surv Psa 1957, 8:320-323
70254 Racker, H. Character and destiny. An Surv Psa 1957, 8:87-88

70255 Schnier, J. Restitution aspects of the creative process. An Surv Psa 1957, 8:87
70256 Zierer, E. & Zierer, E. Leonardo da Vinci's artistic productivity and creative sterility. An Surv Psa 1957, 8:345-347

COMESS, LEONARD J.

70257 Discussion of Krystal, H. "A psychoanalytic contribution to the theory of cyclicity of the financial economy." Psa Forum 1966, 1:371-372

COMFORT, ALEX

70258 Anxiety in adults. Publ Hlth Rep 1968, 82:279-290
70259 Darwin and Freud. Lancet 1960, (2):107-111
70260 Darwin and the Naked Lady. Discursive Essays on Biology and Art. NY: George Braziller 1962, xi + 174 p
70261 On ecstasy and originality. Extase et originalité. Hum Context 1969, 1:253-258; 259-264
70262 The Rape of Andromeda. Lit & Psych 1960, 10:14-28
70263 Summing up. J psychosom Res 1968, 12:117-120
70264 A technology of the emotions? Une technologie des émotions? Hum Context 1968, 1:53-61; 62-70

CONDON, WILLIAM S.

70265 Discussion of Boyer, L. B. "Pioneers in the psychoanalysis of schizophrenia." Psa Forum 1969, 3:230-232
70266 Psychoanalysis and civilization. Psychiat Comm 1960, 3:5-20
70267 A segmentation of behavior. J psychiat Res 1967, 5:221-235

CONDRAU, GION

70268 [The psychotherapeutic encounter with guilt and guilt feelings.] (Ger) Praxis 1960, 49:534-538
70269 Psychotherapie eines Schreibkrampfes. [Psychotherapy of writer's cramp.] Z PSM 1961, 7:255-267

See Boss, Medard

CONDRY, JOHN C., JR.

See Dana, Richard H.

CONE, FAIRFAX MASTICK

70270 Symbology in advertising. In Whitney, E. *Symbology: The Use of Symbols in Visual Communication,* Hastings House 1960, 69-86

CONGER, JOHN JANEWAY

70271 (& Gaskill, H. S.) Accident proneness. Compreh Txbk Psychiat 1107-1110
70272 Accidents. Ency Ment Hlth 29-36

See Mussen, Paul Henry

CONGER, KYRIL B.

70273 (& Fischer, K.; Winn, H.) Castration anxiety. Penn Med 1967, 70(7): 71-73

CONKLING, MARK

70274 Sartre's refutation of the Freudian unconscious. Rev existent Psychol Psychiat 1968, 8:86-101

CONLON, M. F.

See Trethowan, William H.

CONN, JACOB H.

70275 Meanings and motivations associated with spontaneous regression. J clin exp Hyp 1958, 6:21-44
70276 The psychodynamics of recovery under hypnosis. Int J clin exp Hyp 1960, 8:3-16

See Lawrey, Lawson G.

CONNELL, PHILIP

70277 The early years: preparation for parenthood. J Roy Inst PH Hyg 1963, 26:275-280

CONNER, JACK

70278 Is it true? Or is it so? Psychiat Res Rep 1961, 14:49-61

CONNOR, THOMAS B.

See Huffer, Virginia

CONOLLY, JOHN

70279 The Construction and Government of Lunatic Asylums. (Introd: Hunter, R. & Macalpine, I.) London: Dawson 1968, 183 p
70280 An Inquiry Concerning the Indications of Insanity (1830). (Introd: Hunter, R. & Macalpine, I.) London: Dawson 1964, 496 p

CONRAD, K.

70281 Die Gestaltanalyse in der psychiatrischen Forschung. [Gestalt analysis in psychiatric research.] Nervenarzt 1960, 31:267-273

CONRAD, STANLEY W.

70282 Management of obesity. In Nodine, J. *The First Hahnemann Symposium of Psychosomatic Medicine,* Phila: Lea & Febiger 1962, 890-896
70283 Phallic aspects of obesity. (Read at Am Psa Ass, 5 Dec 1964) Bull Phila Ass Psa 1965, 15:207-223
    Abs EFA Q 1967, 36:629. PLe RFPsa 1967, 31:311

70284 On phantasies and their functions. (Read at Am Psa Ass, 4 Dec 1965)
Bull Phila Ass Psa 1966, 16:4-19
Abs EFA Q 1968, 37:157. PLe RFPsa 1967, 31:311
70285 Physiologic determinants in phantasy-formation. (Read at Am Psa Ass,
1 May 1964) Bull Phila Ass Psa 1965, 15:26-42
Abs EFA Q 1966, 35:155. PLe RFPsa 1967, 31:310

REVIEW OF:
70286 Pearson, G. H. J. (Ed) A Handbook of Child Psychoanalysis. Bull
Phila Ass Psa 1968, 18:136-138

CONSOLE, WILLIAM A.

See Keiser, Sylvan; Lorand, Sandor

CONSTANTINE, H.

See Heim, Edgar

CONSTANTINOPLE, ANNE

70287 An Eriksonian measure of personality development in college students.
Developm Psychol 1969, 1:357-372

CONTICELLI, MARIO

70288 Psicologia e cibernetica. [Psychology and cybernetics.] Cultura e Scu-
ola 1966, No. 17. Studi e Ricerche de Psicologia 1967, 10: 8 p

CONWELL, MARGARET

See Bahn, Anita K.

COODLEY, ALFRED E.

70289 A comprehensive book review of Beyond Laughter. Dyn Psychiat 1968,
1(Suppl):1-8
70290 Discussion of Devereux, G. "The cannibalistic impulses of parents."
Psa Forum 1966, 1:125
70291 Psychiatric considerations in surgery. J Int Coll Surg 1961, 35:745-751

ABSTRACTS OF:
70292 Bierenfeld, F. R. Justice, aggression, and Eros. An Surv Psa 1957,
8:317
70293 Bruner, J. S. Freud and the image of man. An Surv Psa 1956, 7:19
70294 Erikson, E. H. The first psychoanalyst: crisis and discovery. An Surv
Psa 1956, 7:8-9
70295 Garma, A. Oral-digestive superego aggressions and actual conflicts in
peptic ulcer patients. An Surv Psa 1957, 8:159-160
70296 Grotjahn, M. Beyond Laughter. An Surv Psa 1957, 8:332-333
70297 Hacker, F. J. Freud, Marx, and Kierkegaard. An Surv Psa 1956, 7:19-20
70298 Herberg, W. Freud, the revisionists, and the social reality. An Surv
Psa 1956, 7:20
70299 Hyman, S. E. Psychoanalysis and the climate of tragedy. An Surv Psa
1956, 7:25

70300 Jones, E. The nature of genius. An Surv Psa 1956, 7:4-5
70301 Jones, E. Psychiatry before and after Freud. An Surv Psa 1956, 7:6
70302 Jones, E. Sigmund Freud: the man and his achievements. An Surv Psa 1956, 7:3-4
70303 Kaplan, A. Freud and modern philosophy. An Surv Psa 1956, 7:21
70304 Kardiner, A. Freud: the man I knew, the scientist, and his influence. An Surv Psa 1956, 7:33
70305 Kazin, A. The Freudian revolution analyzed. An Surv Psa 1956, 7:18
70306 Levin, A. J. Oedipus and Samson: the rejected hero-child. An Surv Psa 1957, 8:308-309
70307 Maritain, J. Freudianism and psychoanalysis: a thomist view. An Surv Psa 1956, 7:21-22
70308 Moloney, J. C. The precognitive cultural ingredients of schizophrenia. An Surv Psa 1957, 8:150
70309 Murphy, G. The current impact of Freud upon American psychology. An Surv Psa 1956, 7:20
70310 Niebuhr, R. Human creativity and self-concern in Freud's thought. An Surv Psa 1956, 7:22-23
70311 Novey, S. Utilization of social institutions as a defense technique in the neuroses. An Surv Psa 1957, 8:249-250
70312 Ostow, M. The erotic instincts—a contribution to the study of instincts. An Surv Psa 1957, 8:64-66
70313 Schnier, J. The Tibetan Lamaist Ritual: Chöd. An Surv Psa 1957, 8:303-304
70314 Stokes, A. D. Listening to clichés and individual words. An Surv Psa 1957, 8:126
70315 Weizsäcker, V. von: Reminiscences of Freud and Jung. An Surv Psa 1956, 7:33-34
70316 Zilboorg, G. The changing concept of man in present-day psychiatry. An Surv Psa 1956, 7:19

REVIEW OF:
70317 Grotjahn, M. Psycho-analysis and the Family Neurosis. J 1961, 42: 475-477

COOK, JOHN A.

ABSTRACTS OF:
70318 Nininger, E. V. Unconscious hallucinations in normal thinking. Q 1965, 34:633-636
70319 Ostow, M. Pathogenesis, symptom formation, and energetics. Q 1963, 32:614-616
70320 Peterfreund, E. Psychoanalysis: an evolutionary biological approach. Part I. Some fundamental difficulties in current psychoanalytic theory. (& Schwartz, J. T.) Part II. Psychological phenomena and the nature of biological order. Q 1966, 35:631-633
70321 Peto, A. Variations of archaic thinking in neurotics, in borderlines and in schizophrenics. Q 1964, 33:461-463

REVIEW OF:
70322 Davidson, H. A. Forensic Psychiatry. Q 1966, 35:297-298

COOKE, ROBERT E.

70323 (& Levin, S.) (Eds) The Biologic Basis of Pediatric Practice. (2 volumes) NY/Toronto/Sydney/London: McGraw-Hill 1968, xxi-890; 891-1739

See Kolb, Lawrence C.

COOLIDGE, JOHN C.

70324 (& Grunebaum, M. G.) Individual and group therapy of a latency age child. Int J grp PT 1964, 14:84-96

70325 (& Tessman, E.; Waldfogel, S.; Willer, M. L.) Patterns of aggression in school phobia. Psa St C 1962, 17:319-333
Abs SLe RFPsa 1964, 28:814

70326 (& Willer, M. L.; Tessman, E.; Waldfogel, S.) School phobia in adolescence: a manifestation of severe character disturbance. Ops 1960, 30:599-607

70327 Unexpected death in a patient who wished to die. J Am Psa Ass 1969, 17:413-420

COON, GAYLORD P.

70328 Acute psychosis, depression, and elation. In Blaine, G. B., Jr. & McArthur, C. C. *Emotional Problems of the Student*, Garden City/NY: Anchor Books 1966, 128-146

COONS, WESLEY H.

70329 The dynamics of change in psychotherapy. Canad Psychiat Ass J 1967, 12:239-245

COOPER, A.

See Mandell, W.

COOPER, ALAN J.

70330 Hostility and male potency disorders. Comprehen Psychiat 1968, 9: 621-626

COOPER, ALLAN

70331 Problems in therapy of a patient with masked depression. A White Institute clinical services conference. (27 Feb 1968) Contempo Psa 1968, 5(1):45-56

COOPER, ALLEN

See Silberstein, Richard M.

COOPER, ARNOLD MICHAEL

70332 (& Karush, A.; Easser, B. R.; Swerdloff, B.) The adaptive balance profile and prediction of early treatment behavior. In Goldman, G. S.

& Shapiro, D. *Developments in Psychoanalysis at Columbia University*, NY: Hafner Publ Co 1966, 183-215

See Karush, Aaron

REVIEW OF:
70333   Binger, C. The Two Faces of Medicine. Q 1969, 38:143-144

COOPER, BEATRICE

70334   The parallel process as it emerges in casework. Reiss-Davis Clin Bull 1964, 1:89-99

COOPER, D. G.

See Laing, R. D.

COOPER, G. DAVID

70335   (& Adams, H. B.; Gibby, R. G.) Ego strength changes following perceptual deprivation. Report on a pilot study. Arch gen Psychiat 1962, 7:213-217

See Adams, Henry B.

COOPER, JOSEPH B.

70336   Parent evaluation and social ideology. Psychol Rep 1960, 7:414

COOPER, LESLIE M.

See Hilgard, Ernest R.

COOPER, MAX

70337   Interpretation in the early phase of therapy. In Hammer, E. *Use of Interpretation in Treatment. Technique and Art*, NY: Grune & Stratton 1968, 27-30

COOPER, RUTH

See Peck, Robert F.

COOPER, SAUL

See Behymer, Alice F.

COOPER, SHAWN

70338   An exploration of ego defense mechanisms and related processes in clinic and non-clinic families. Diss Abstr 1969, 29(9-B):3478-3479

COOPER, SHIRLEY

70339   Emergencies in a psychiatric clinic. Soc Casewk 1960, 41:134-139
70340   (& Krantzler, B.) A polemic in response to a tribute. Soc Wk 1968, 13:3-4; 117-119

70341 (Participant in round table) A psychoanalytic view of the family: a study of family member interactions. (Ed: Lindon, J. A.) Psa Forum 1969, 3:11-65
70342 The swing to community mental health. Soc Casewk 1968, 49:275-280
70343 Work with parents—change or progress? Soc Casewk 1961, 42:342-347

See Heiman, Nanette; Sylvester, Emmy

COOPERMAN, MARC

See Child, Irvin L.

COOPERMAN, STANLEY

70344 Willa Cather and the bright face of death. Lit & Psych 1963, 13:81-87

COOPERSMITH, STANLEY

70345 The Antecedents of Self-Esteem. San Francisco: W. H. Freeman 1967, ix + 283 p
70346 Studies in self-esteem. Sci Am 1968, 218 (Feb):96-106

COPEL, SIDNEY L.

70347 Psychodiagnostic Study of Children and Adolescents. Springfield, Ill: Thomas 1967, xii + 200 p

COPELAND, A.

70348 Basic factors in interview technique. GP 1962, 25:97-100

COPELMAN, LOUIS S.

70349 Souvenirs sur l'application du psycho-diagnostic Rorschach, en remontant trente ans d'histoire de la médecine. [Remembrances concerning the application of the Rorschach psychodiagnostic test, going back 30 years into the history of medicine.] Paris: Comptes Rendus du VIe Congres Int Rorschach Meth proj 1968, 1:57-60

COPPEN, ALEC J.

70350 Biochemical aspects of depression. Int Psychiat Clin 1969, 6(2):53-81
70351 The Marke-Nyman temperament scale: an English translation. M 1966, 39:55-59
70352 (& Walk, A.) (Eds) Recent Developments in Affective Disorders: A Symposium. London: Headley 1967, 158 p

COPPOLILLO, HENRY P.

70353 Conversion, hypochondriasis and somatization: a diagnostic problem for internists. J Arkansas Med Soc 1965, 62:67-71
70354 (& Harrison, S. I.) The emotionally disturbed child. In Conn, H. F. & Conn, W. B. Current Diagnosis, Phila: Saunders 1968, 898-903
70355 Maturational aspects of the transitional phenomenon. J 1967, 48:237-246
Abs EVN Q 1969, 38:159

70356 The questioning and doubting parent. J Pediat 1965, 67:371-380
70357 A technical consideration in child analysis and child therapy. J Amer Acad Child Psychiat 1969, 8:411-435

COR, J.
See Danon-Boileau, Henri

CORAH, NORMAN L.
70358 (& Anthony, E. J.; Painter, P.; Stern, J. A.; Thurston, D. L.) Effects of perinatal anoxia after seven years. Psychol Monogr 1965, 79(3):1-34

CORBIN, EDWIN I.
70359 Muscle action as nonverbal and preverbal communication. (Read at Psa Ass NY, 20 Nov 1961) Q 1962, 31:351-363
    Abs SO Q 1962, 31:305-306

REVIEWS OF:
70360 Greenfield, N. S. & Lewis, W. L. (Eds) Psychoanalysis and Current Biological Thought. Q 1966, 35:441-443
70361 Grossman, C. M. & Grossman, S. The Wild Analyst. The Life and Work of Georg Groddeck. Q 1966, 35:290-292
70362 The Psychoanalytic Study of the Child, Vol. XIX. Q 1966, 35:280-284

CORDAY, ROBERT J.
70363 Limitations of therapy in adolescence. J Amer Acad Child Psychiat 1967, 6:526-538
70364 Toilet training and "the terrible two's," comments on the prevention and management of behavior problems at this age. Clin Ped 1967, 6(1):41-46

CORDECH, JUAN
70365 Consideraciones sobre el concepto de neurosis de renta. [Psychologic aspects of compensation cases.] Rev Psiquiat Psicol 1958, 3:467-474
    Abs Vega An Surv Psa 1958, 9:209

COREN, HARRY Z.
70366 (& Saldinger, J. S.) Visual hallucinosis in children; a report of two cases. Psa St C 1967, 22:331-356

COREY, DOUGLAS Q.
70367 The use of a reverse format in now psychotherapy. R 1966, 53:431-450
    Abs SRS Q 1967, 36:631-632

CORI, FERRUCCIO A. DI
70368 Unconscious motivation as a source of creative expression. Dis nerv Sys 1960, 21(Suppl No. 2):119-123

CORIETT, FAITH

See Bone, Ronald N.

CORMACK, PETER H.

70369 A study of the relationship between body image and the perception of physical ability. Diss Abstr 1966, 27:961-962

CORMAN, GERTRUDE

See Corman, Louis

CORMAN, HARVEY H.

70370 (& Escalona, S. K.; Reiser, M. F.) Visual imagery and preconscious thought processes. Arch gen Psychiat 1964, 10:160-172
   Abs KR Q 1965, 34:141

See Wilson, Charles P.

CORMAN, LOUIS

70371 Agressivité masculine par surcompensation à une identification féminine. [Masculine aggressiveness as an overcompensation of feminine identification, its relationship to delinquency.] Rv Np inf 1964, 12:647-653

79372 Le diagnostic du dépassement de l'Oedipe par le test du gribouillis. [Diagnosis of post-Oedipal development by the scribble test.] Ann méd-psychol 1966, 124(2):530-531

70373 [The double in the family-drawing test: its psychopathological significance.] (Fr) Évolut psychiat 1967, 32:117-147

70374 [The family drawing test. Significance of added persons.] (Fr) Rv Np inf 1965, 13:67-81

70375 L'interprétation dynamique du test du dessin de famille. Signification des personnages barrés. [The dynamic interpretation of the "draw-the-family" test. The significance of the figures crossed out.] J Méd Nantes 1968, 8:33-45

70376 (& Defever, A.) Interprétation projective par le test P.N. d'un cas de mélancolie chez l'enfant. [Interpretation of the PN projective test in the case of a melancholy child.] Rev Psychol appl 1965, 15:271-282

70377 La rivalité fraternelle et l'identification régressive au rival. [Sibling rivalry and the regressive identification with the rival.] Canad Psychiat Ass J 1963, 8:167-181

70378 (& Corman, G.; Foulard, F.) Une technique nouvelle des tests de projection: la méthode des préférences-identifications. [A new technique for projective tests: the identification-preference method.] Rev Psychol appl 1960, 10:25-37

70379 Le test du dessin de famille (symbolisation par un animal des tendances interdites). [Family drawing test (animal symbolization of forbidden tendencies).] Canad Psychiat Ass J 1964, 9:417-430

CORMAN, RENA

See Hunt, Morton M.

CORMIER, BRUNO M.

70380 Depression and persistent criminality. Canad Psychiat Ass J 1966, 11 (Suppl):208-220
70381 (& Kennedy, M.; Sangowicz, J.) Psychodynamics of father-daughter incest. Canad Psychiat Ass J 1962, 7:203-217
70382 (& Kennedy, M.; Sangowicz, J. M.) Sexual offenses, episodic recidivism and the psychopathological state. In Slovenko, R. *Sexual Behavior and the Law,* Springfield, Ill: Thomas 1965, 707-741

CORN, HARRY Z.

70383 (& Saldinger, J. S.) Visual hallucinosis in children: a report of two cases. Psa St C 1967, 22:331-356

CORNELISON, A.

See Fleck, Stephen

CORNELISON, ALICE R.

See Lidz, Theodore

CORNELISON, FLOYD SHOVINGTON, JR.

70384 Anna Freud doctoral award address. J Am Psa Ass 1967, 15:828-831
70385 Behavioral reactions to surgical procedures. Trans Coll Physicians Phila 1966, 33:194-196
70386 Learning about behavior. A new technique: self-image experience. MH 1966, 50:584-587
70387 (& Tausig, T. N.) A study of self-image experience using video-tapes at Delaware State Hospital. Delaware med J 1964, 36:229-231

See West, Louis J.

CORNEY, ROBERT T.

See Volkan, Vamik D.

CORNIER, A.

70388 [Indications and contraindications for psychoanalysis.] (Fr) Clinique 1962, 57:465-468

CORNUBERT, C.

70389 Freud et Romain Rolland. Essai sur la Découverte de la Pensée Psychanalytique par Quelques Écrivains Français. [Freud and Romain Rolland. Essay on the Discovery of Psychoanalytic Thought by Some French Writers.] Paris: Thèse de Médecine 1966, 74 p

CORNYETZ, PAUL

70390 Classical psychoanalysis: the future of an idea. R 1966, 53:576-594
70391 Psychoanalysis and social reality. (Panel: Nat Psychol Ass Psa, 29 Oct 1965) R 1967, 54:453-457
       Abs SRS Q 1969, 38:162

70392   Remarks on insight and interpretation. In Hammer, E. F. *Use of Interpretation in Treatment: Technique and Art,* NY: Grune & Stratton 1968, 253-259

CORRAO, FRANCESCO

70393   Metapsicologia del contro-transfert. [The metapsychology of countertransference.] Riv Psa 1962, 8:85-96
70394   Discussion of Muratori, A. M. "Sogni di progresso e sogni di regresso nella pratica psicoanalitica." Riv Psa 1963, 9:123

CORRAZE, J.

70395   La trichotillomanie: étude psychopathologique. [Trichotillomania. A psychopathological study.] Rev Méd Toulouse 1966, 2(2,I):97-110. Bull Soc Franc Derm Syph 1966, 73:100-102

CORRÊA, PAULO DIAS

70396   A amizade. [On friendship.] Rev bras Med 1950, 7:798
70397   Atirar objetos e . . . Goethe. [On the throwing of objects and . . . Goethe.] Rev bras Med 1950, 7:114
70398   Os caminhos do amor. [On the paths of love.] Rev bras Med 1951, 8:572
70399   O casamento, êsse desconhecido. [Marriage, this unknown.] Rev bras Med 1951, 8:264
70400   O ciúme. [On jealousy.] Rev bras Med 1949, 6:550
70401   Condições para o matrimônio feliz. [On the conditions for a happy marriage.] Rev bras Med 1949, 6:812
70402   Condutas terapêuticas na psicopatia e na neurose. [On therapeutic handling in psychopathy and neurosis.] J bras Psiquiat 1969, 12:69
70403   O drama das perturbações emocionais. [On the drama of emotional disturbances.] Rev bras Med 1951, 8:43
70404   A escolha amorosa. [On love choice.] Rev bras Med 1949, 6:687
70405   Os estados de depressão. [On depressive states.] Bras-Med 1949, 63
70406   Etiologia e tratamento do fogacho. [On the etiology and treatment of flushing.] Rev bras Med 1950, 7:347
70407   Os fatôres emocionais na hipertensão arterial. [On the emotional factor of high blood pressure.] Rev bras Med 1951, 8:724
70408   "Freud Desmascarado" e o Simbolismo dos Sonhos. ["Der Entzauberte Freud" (Emil Ludwig's) and Dream's Symbolism.] Belo Horizonte: Edições Acaiaca 1948, 15 p
70409   Honorário de colega para colega. [Fees from colleague to colleague.] Rev Ass Med M.G. 1954, 5:91
70410   A incapacidade para amar. [On the incapacity for love.] Rev bras Med 1950, 7:48
70411   O inconsciente e a responsabilidade—aparente antinomia. [The unconscious and responsibility—apparent antinomy.] Bras-Med 1948, 62:56
70412   O inconsciente e a responsabilidade perante a Legislação penal. [The unconscious and responsibility concerning criminal legislation.] Rev bras Med 1949, 6:168. Rev Ass Med M.G. 1949, 1:39. Vigília 1949, 1:151

70413 Máscaras. [On masks.] Hosp, Rio 1949, 36:97

70414 O mêdo aos mortos. [On fear of the dead.] Rev bras Med 1950, 7:188

70415 O mistério da criação literária. [On the mystery of literary creation.] Acaiaca 1948, 1:11

70416 Notas sôbre a compreensão do doente mental. [Some notes on the understanding of the mental patient.] J Bras Psiquiat 1962, 11:113

70417 Podem prevenir-se os acidentes? [Can accidents be prevented?] Seguridade soc 1950, 1:24

70418 Porque os homens amam. [Why men love.] Rev bras Med 1949, 6:457

70419 A psicogênese das doenças somáticas. [On the psychogenesis of somatic diseases.] Rev bras Med 1951, 8:193

70420 A psicografia (escrita automática) à luz da psicologia médica. [The psychography (automatic writing) in the light of medical psychology.] Hosp, Rio 1947, 32:121

70421 Psicologismo? . . . [Psychologism? . . .] Rev bras Med 1950, 7:332

70422 Rubor, sinal de vergonha. [Blushing, sign of shame.] Rev bras Med 1949, 6:306

70423 Sôbre a psicologia do casamento. [On the psychology of marriage.] Rev bras Med 1949, 6:629

70424 O suicídio orgânico. [On organic suicide.] Rev Ass Med M.G. 1951, 2:187

70425 Transferência, fenômeno neurótico. [Transference, a neurotic phenomenon.] Rev bras Med 1950, 7:465

See Oliveira, Walderedo Ismael de

CORREAL, JOSÉ

See Rascovsky, Arnaldo

CORRENTI, SAMUEL

70426 A comparison of behaviorism and psychoanalysis with existentialism. J existent Psychiat 1965, 5:379-388

CORRIGAN, ROBERT W.

70427 (Ed & Int) Comedy: Meaning and Form. San Francisco: Chandler Publ 1966

70428 (Ed) Theatre in the Twentieth Century. NY: Grove Pr 1965, 320 p Rv Seidenberg, R. Q 1967, 36:121-122

CORROTHERS, MARIE LAWRENCE

70429 Sexual themes in an adolescent girls' group. Int J grp PT 1963, 13:43-51

CORSA, HELEN STORM

70430 A fair but frozen maid: a study of Jane Austen's *Emma*. Lit & Psych 1969, 19:101-123

70431 Is this a Mannes Herte? Lit & Psych 1966, 16:184-191

CORSINI, RAYMOND J.

70432 (& Daniels, R. S.; McFarland, R. L.) Group psychotherapy. Prog Neurol Psychiat 1960, 15:526-534

70433 (& Rosenberg, B.) Mechanisms of group psychotherapy: processes and dynamics. JAbP 1955, 15:406-411. In Rosenbaum, M. & Berger, M. *Group Psychotherapy and Group Function,* NY/London: Basic Books 1963, 340-351

CORSON, SAMUEL A.

70434 Cerebrovisceral theory—a physiologic basis for psychosomatic medicine. Int J Psychiat 1967, 4:234-241

CORTES, CARLOS F.

70435 (& Fleming, E. S.) The effects of father absence on the adjustment of culturally disadvantaged boys. J spec Educ 1968, 2:413-420

CORTES, W. A.

70435A [Psychological development of personality.] (Por) Rev bras Med 1969, 26:334-335

CORTESÃO, E. L.

70436 [Depressions. The psychodynamic aspect.] (Por) J Med, Porto 1965, 56:356-362

70437 [Psychodynamics of depressive neuroses and syndromes in group analytical psychotherapy.] (Por) J Med, Porto 1960, 42:730-734

70438 [Psychodynamics of human relations.] (Por) J Med, Porto 1964, 54: 580-587

70439 [Psychotherapy and psychotherapists.] (Por) J Med, Porto 1963, 51: 791-799

CORTEZ, FERNAND

70440 L'identification au rôle social. Le métier du père. [Identification with social role. The father's occupation.] Rv Np inf 1965, 13:819-828

CORVAL, PHILLIPE

70441 Thèmes de la psychologie Adlerienne. [Themes of Adlerian psychology.] Bull Psychol, Paris 1965, 19:30-39

CORWIN, HOWARD A.

ABSTRACT OF:

70442 Mack, J. E. Children's nightmares: a developmental study. Bull Phila Ass Psa 1964, 14:228-231

COSER, LEWIS A.

70443 The functions of dissent. Sci Psa 1968, 13:158-168

70444 Violence and the social structure. Sci Psa 1963, 6:30-42. In Endleman, S. *Violence in the Streets,* Chicago: Quadrangle Books 1968, 71-84

COSNIER, JACQUES

70445 Les Névroses Expérimentales, de la Psychologie Animale à la Pathologie Humaine. [Experimental Neuroses, from Animal to Human Psychology.] Paris: Éditions du Seuil 1966, 175 p
   Rv PLe RFPsa 1967, 31:491
70445a [A thought disorder.] (Fr) RFPsa 1969, 33:845-855

COSSA, PAUL

70446 Pourquoi devient-on psychanalyste? [Why does one become a psychoanalyst?] Pr méd 1967, 75:2137-2138

See Raclot, Marcel

COSTELLO, CHARLES GERARD

70447 Psychology for Psychiatrists. Oxford/NY: Pergamon 1966, xi + 328 p

See Rachman, Stanley

COSTELLO, TIMOTHY W.

See Coville, Walter J.

COSTIGAN, GIOVANNI

70448 Sigmund Freud: A Short Biography. NY: Macmillan 1965, xiv + 306 p; Collier Bks 1968, xiv + 392 p
   Rv GPK Q 1966, 35:142-143

COTTINGHAM, ALICE

See Schwartz, Emanuel K.

COTTLE, B.

See Knights, L. C.

COTTLE, J. T.

70449 The location of experience: a manifest time orientation. Acta Psychol 1968, 28:129-149

COUADAU, A.

See Israël, L.; Porot, Maurice

COUCHMAN, M.

See Rotkin, I. D.

COULÉON, H.

70450 (& Couléon, M.; Anne, L.; Desplanches, J.) La place de la narcoanalyse dans la thérapeutique psychiatrique. [The place of narcoanalysis in psychiatric therapy.] Ann méd-psychol 1963, 121(2):367-376

COULÉON, M.

See Couléon, H.

COULT, ALLAN D.

70451 Unconscious inference and cultural origins. Amer Anthropologist 1963, 65:32-35

COUNTS, ROBERT M.

70452 Family crises and the impulsive adolescent. Arch gen Psychiat 1967, 17:64-71

See Shore, Milton F.

COURCHET, J.-L.

70453 Le vide social et la révolte. [The social void and revolt.] RFPsa 1966, 30:114-116

COURT, J. H.

See Cramond, W. A.

COURTECUISSE-MIRAL, J.

See Smirnoff, Victor N.

COURTENAY, MICHAEL

70454 Sexual Discord in Marriage: A Field for Brief Psychotherapy. (Foreword: Balint, M.) Mind & Medicine Monogr No. 16. London: Tavistock; Phila: Lippincott 1968, xiv + 137 p

COURTLESS, T. F.

See Silber, David E.

COURTNEY, BARBARA M.

70455 Other voices, other rooms. Voice changes as manifestations of ego changes. Ps 1965, 28:375-379

COURTNEY, JON

70456 (& Davis, J. M.; Solomon, P.) Sensory deprivation: the role of movement. Percept mot Skills 1961, 13:191-199

See Davis, John M.

COVI, L.

See Meyer, Eugene

COVILLE, WALTER J.

70457 (& Costello, T. W.; Rouke, F. L.) Abnormal Psychology. NY: Barnes & Noble Publ 1960, xv + 298 p

COWAN, LAURENCE H.

70458   Psychotherapy—terminable and interminable. (Abs) Psychother Psychosom 1967, 15:13

COWEN, EMORY L.

70459   The experimental analogue: an approach to research in psychotherapy. Psychol Rep 1961, 8:9-10. In Goldstein, A. P. & Dean, S. J. *The Investigation of Psychotherapy,* NY: Wiley 1966, 42-44

COWEN, JOHN

70460   The art of medicine. Psa 1962, 22:208-212
70461   A commentary on ontic perspectives. Psa 1961, 21:92-97

COWEN, JOSEPH ROBERT

70462   A note on the meaning of television to a psychotic woman. BMC 1959, 23:202-203

COWITZ, BERNARD

ABSTRACTS OF:
70463   Aarons, Z. A. Psychotherapy versus psychoanalysis. A case illustration. An Surv Psa 1958, 9:432
70464   Badal, D. W. Analysis of an anal character. An Surv Psa 1958, 9:170
70465   Berezin, M. A. Some observations on art (music) and its relationship to ego mastery. An Surv Psa 1958, 9:488-489
70466   Casuso, G. A psychoanalyst's observation during a totalitarian take-over. Bull Phila Ass Psa 1962, 12:178-181
70467   Frankl, L. & Hellman, I. The effect of an early fixation on adolescent detachment from infantile ties. Bull Phila Ass Psa 1963, 13:147-148
70468   Frosch, J. Delusional fixity, sense of conviction and the psychotic conflict. Bull Phila Ass Psa 1965, 15:183-186
70469   Galinsky, M. & Pressman, M. D. Intellectualization and the intellectual resistance. Bull Phila Ass Psa 1963, 13:202-203
70470   Geleerd, E. R. Review of Melanie Klein's last book *Narrative of a Child Analysis.* Bull Phila Ass Psa 1963, 13:39-41
70471   Kaplan, L. S. Snow White: a study in psychosexual development. Bull Phila Ass Psa 1963, 13:94-95
70472   Katan, M. Fetishism, splitting of the ego and denial. Bull Phila Ass Psa 1964, 14:40-42
70473   Klein, G. S. On hearing one's own voice: an aspect of cognitive control in spoken thought. Bull Phila Ass Psa 1964, 14:241-244
70474   Levin, S. A study of fees for control analysis. An Surv Psa 1958, 9:435
70475   Markovitz, E. Auto-identification in the development of the self-image. Bull Phila Ass Psa 1965, 15:53-56
70476   Moore, W. T. Concern about a bee-sting in the analysis of an eleven-year-old boy. An Surv Psa 1958, 9:310-311
70477   Niederland, W. G. The psychoanalysis of a severe obsessive-compulsive neurosis. An Surv Psa 1958, 9:148-149

70478 Pressman, M. D. An unusual technical problem in the analysis of an agoraphobia. An Surv Psa 1958, 9:360-361

70479 Rapaport, D. An historical survey of psychoanalytic ego psychology. An Surv Psa 1958, 9:57-58

70480 Rubinfine, D. L. On beating fantasies. Bull Phila Ass Psa 1964, 14: 38-40

70481 Stein, M. Trauma and dream-like states. Bull Phila Ass Psa 1962, 12: 93-95

70482 Sterba, R. & Sterba, E. Remarks concerning the personality of Michelangelo Buonarroti. Bull Phila Ass Psa 1961, 11:195-197

70483 Terzian, A. A psychoanalytic review of music. Bull Phila Ass Psa 1964, 14:244-246

COX, JAMES L. D.

70484 Impasse in adolescence. J Med Ass Georgia 1963, 52:145-146

70485 A patient's view of psychotherapy. Lancet 1965, 1:103-104

COX, RACHEL DUNAWAY

70486 Stress and mastery. J Otto Rank Ass 1969, 4(1):37-48

COYNE, LOLAFAYE

See Sargent, Helen D.; Voth, Harold M.

CRABTREE, LOREN H., JR.

70487 A psychotherapeutic encounter with a self-mutilating patient. Ps 1967, 30:91-100

CRADDICK, RAY A.

70488 Identification with the aggressor through figure drawings. Percept mot Skills 1969, 28:547-550

CRAFT, MICHAEL

70489 (& Stephenson, G.; Granger, C.) A controlled trial of authoritarian and self-governing regimes with adolescent psychopaths. Ops 1964, 34: 543-554
  Abs JMa RFPsa 1966, 30:519

CRAIN, IRVING J.

70490 Panel on the humanistic approach to sexuality: sex and love. Dis nerv Sys 1969, 30:774-776

CRAMER, PHEBE

70491 A restandardization of the Menninger Word Association Test. J gen Psychol 1968, 78:119-125

CRAMER, ROBERT L.

See Dowd, Patrick J.

CRAMOND, W. A.

70492 Medical, moral and legal aspects of organ transplantation and long-term resuscitative measures: psychological, social and community aspects. Med J. Aust 1968, 2:622-627

70493 (& Knight, P. R.; Lawrence, J. R.; Higgins, B. A.; Court, J. H.; Mac-Namara, F. M.; Clarkson, A. R.; Miller, C. D. J.) Psychological aspects of the management of chronic renal failure. Brit med J 1968, (1): 539-543

CRANDALL, DEWILL L.

See Bernard, Viola W.

CRANDALL, V. J.

See Rafferty, Janet E.

CRANEFIELD, PAUL F.

70494 Freud and the "School of Helmholtz." Gesnerus 1966, 23:35-39
S-43921 Joseph Breuer's evaluation of his contribution to psychoanalysis.
Abs SLP An Surv Psa 1958, 9:9

CRANK, H. HARLAN

REVIEW OF:
70495 Jaco, E. G. The Social Epidemiology of Mental Disorders—A Psychiatric Survey of Texas. Q 1962, 31:565-567

CRAVIOTO, JAQUIN

70496 (& Robles, B.) Evolution of adaptive and motor behavior during rehabilitation from Kwashiorkor. Ops 1965, 35:449-464
Abs JMa RFPsa 1966, 30:525

CRAWFORD, ELIZABETH

S-43922 The wolf as condensation.
Abs An Surv Psa 1955, 6:414-415

CRAWFORD, PATRICIA

See Bellak, Leopold

CREEGAN, ROBERT F.

70497 A symbolic action during bereavement. ASP 1942, 37. In Ruitenbeek, H. M. Death: Interpretations, NY: Dell 1969, 217-221

CREMERIUS, JOHANNES

70498 Abriss der psychoanalytischen Abwehrtheorie (unter besonderer Berücksichtigung der Klinik). [Outline of psychoanalytic defense theory (with special consideration to the clinic).] Z Psychother med Psychol 1968, 18:1-15

S-43927 Die Bedeutung der Oralität für den altersdiatetes und die mit ihm verbundenen depressiven Phasen.
Abs HA An Surv Psa 1957, 8:166-167

70499 Beobachtung dynamischer Prozesse beim Pflegepersonal, insbesondere von Wiederstand und Übertragung, während der psychoanalytischen Behandlung einer Schizophrenen. [Observation of dynamic processes among treatment personnel, particularly resistance and transference, during the psychoanalytic treatment of a schizophrenic.] Psyche 1963, 16:686-704

S-43930 Freud als Bergründer der psychosomatischen Medizin.
Abs HA 1956, 7:197

S-43931 Freuds Bedeutung für die psychosomatische Medizin.
Abs HK An Surv Psa 1956, 7:17

70500 Problems and difficulties in teaching psychosomatic medicine to medical students in Germany. Adv PSM 1960, 1:201-205

70501 Die Reaktionsbildung im Lebel Phillipps II. und ihre Bedeutung für das Schicksal Spaniens. [Reaction formation in the life of Philip II and its importance for the fate of Spain.] Psyche 1968, 22:118-142

70502 Schweigen als Probleme der psychoanalytischen Technik. [Keeping silent as a problem in psychoanalytic technique.] Jb Psa 1969, 6:69-103

70503 (& Elhardt, S.; Klüwer, R.) Wurzeln und Entwicklung des neurotischen Charackters. Kasuistischer Beitrag mit einer Diskussion über Diagnostik und ärztliche Einstellung. [Roots and development of the neurotic character. Case report with a discussion on diagnosis and the physician's attitude.] Z PSM 1963, 9:16-26; 94-108

70504 Zur prognose unbehandelter neurosen. [On the prognosis of untreated neuroses.] Z PSM 1966, 12:106-111

CRÉPIN, D.

70505 (& Crépin, J.) Promenades et transferts en institutions. [Walks and transference in institutions.] Ann méd-psychol 1968, 126(2):587

CRÉPIN, J.

See Crépin, D.

CREWS, FREDERICK C.

70506 Love in the western world. Partisan Rev 1967, 34:272-287

70507 Ruined wall: unconscious motivation in The Scarlet Letter. New Engl Q 1965, 38:312-320

70508 The Sins of the Fathers: Hawthorne's Psychological Themes. NY: Oxford Univ Pr 1966, viii + 279 p
Rv Burgum, E. B. Am Im 1966, 23:367-374

CRICK, JOYCE

70509 Psycho-analytical elements in Thomas Mann's novel Lotte in Weimar. Lit & Psych 1960, 10:69-75

70510 Thomas Mann and psycho-analysis: the turning-point. Lit & Psych 1960, 10:45-55. In Manheim, L. & Manheim, E. Hidden Patterns, NY: Macmillan 1966, 171-191

CRIE, ROBERT D.

70511 "The Minister's Black Veil": Mr. Hooper's symbolic fig leaf. Lit & Psych 1967, 17:211-218

CRISP, A. H.

70512 An attempt to measure an aspect of "transference." M 1964, 37:17-30

70513 Development and application of a measure of "transference." J psychosom Res 1964, 8:327-335

70514 Psychological aspects of breast-feeding with particular reference to anorexia nervosa. M 1969, 42:119-132

70515 (& Moldofsky, H.) A psychosomatic study of writer's cramp. Brit J Psychiat 1965, 111:841-858

70516 Some approaches to psychosomatic clinical research. M 1968, 41:323-341

70517 (& Moldofsky, H.) Therapy of writer's cramp. Curr psychiat Ther 1967, 7:69-72

70518 "Transference," "symptom emergence" and "social repercussion" in behaviour therapy. A study of fifty-four treated patients. M 1966, 39:179-196

CROCKER, DAVID

70519 Discussion of Bergmann, T. "Application of analytic knowledge to children with organic illness." In Weinreb, J. *Recent Developments in Psychoanalytic Child Therapy*, NY: IUP 1960, 149-153

70520 (Reporter) Panel on psychoanalytic considerations concerning the development of language in early childhood. J Am Psa Ass 1963, 11:143-150

S-43947 The study of a problem of aggression.
Abs An Surv Psa 1955, 6:268-270

CROCKER, DOROTHY BRIN

See Dreikurs, Rudolf

CROCKET, RICHARD

70521 Acting-out as a mode of communication in the psychotherapeutic community. Brit J Psychiat 1966, 112:383-388

CROCKETT, DAVID

70522 (& Suinn, R. M.) Identification and authoritarianism. M 1966, 39:65-66

CROCKETT, NORMA D.

70523 An elaboration of the Hockett-Ascher-Endleman interpretation of "The Human Revolution." R 1967, 54:706-707

CROCKETT, RICHARD

70524 (& Sandison, R. A.; Walk, A.) (Eds) Hallucinogenic Drugs and Their Psychotherapeutic Use. Springfield, Ill: Thomas; London: Lewis 1963, xiii + 191 p

CROCQ, LOUIS

70525 (& Lefebvre, P.; Girard, V.) [Considerations on the development of concepts in war psychopathology. Apropos of 3 typical cases.] (Fr) Rev Méd psychosom 1965, 7:253-262

CROFTS, I.
See Walters, Richard H.

CROMER, MARJORIE
See Gershon, Elliot S.

CROMWELL, RUE L.
See Orr, William F.; Shakow, David

CRONBACH, LEE J.
See Edwards, Allen J.

CRONHOLM, B.

70526 L'application des méthodes psychologiques dans l'analyse des troubles de la mémoire. [Application of psychological methods to the analysis of disturbances of memory.] Rev Psychol appl 1963, 13:171-188

CROOK, GUY HAMILTON
See Bowman, Karl M.

CROSBY, DONALD H.

70527 Psychological realism in the works of Kleist: "Penthesilea" and "Die Marquise von O . . ." Lit & Psych 1969, 19:3-16

CROSS, THOMAS N.
See Anderson, Philip C.; Boesky, Dale

CROSSON, FREDERICK J.

70528 The concept of mind and the concept of consciousness. J existent Psychiat 1965-66, 6:449-457

CROT, M.

70529 (& Bettschart, W.) Traitement psychothérapeutique par le psychodrame analytique. [Psychotherapeutic treatment by means of analytic psychodrama.] Acta Paedopsychiatrica 1960, 36:130-141

CROTHERS, ROBERT R.

70530 The Word and the World. (Foreword: Menninger, K.) Topeka, Kansas: Robert R. Crothers 1963

CROUSE, FARRELL R.

See Loftus, Thomas A.

CROW, ALICE (VON BAUER)

See Crow, Lester D.

CROW, LESTER DONALD

70531 (& Crow, A.) Adolescent Development and Adjustment. NY/Toronto/ London: McGraw-Hill 1965 (2nd Ed), ix + 523 p
70532 (& Crow, A.) (Eds) Readings in Child and Adolescent Psychology. NY/London/Toronto: Longman, Green & Co 1961, xii + 592 p

CROWE, A. S.

70533 Psychopathology: manifestation of a disturbed self-system. ANA Reg Clin Conf 1967, 268-273

CROWLEY, PATRICK J.

70534 School phobia. Brit med J 1960, (2):1312

CROWLEY, RALPH M.

70535 Foreword to Chartam, R. *Husband and Lover: The Art of Sex for Men.* NY: New Amer Libr 1967
70536 (Participant) Panel discussion: the psychoanalyst's motivation to help. Contempo Psa 1964, 1(1):30-37; 49-50
70537 Presidential address: the medical model in psychoanalysis. (Read at Am Acad Psa, 7 May 1967) Sci Psa 1968, 12:1-11
70538 (& Laidlaw, R. W.) Psychiatric opinion regarding abortion, preliminary report of a survey. P 1967, 124:559-562
70539 What are the causes of premature ejaculation? Why Rep 225-233; 590-591

CROWN, SIDNEY

70540 Criteria for the measurement of outcome in psychotherapy. M 1968, 41:31-38
70541 Psychoanalysis and science. In Sutherland, J. D. *The Psychoanalytic Approach,* London: Baillière & Cassell 1968, 44-51
70542 (& Crisp, A. H.) A short clinical diagnostic self-rating scale for psychoneurotic patients. The Middlesex Hospital Questionnaire (M.H.Q.). Brit J Psychiat 1966, 112:917-923

CRUMBAUGH, JAMES C.

70543 The application of logotherapy. J existent Psychiat 1965, 5:403-412
70543A The automobile as part of the body-image in America. MH 1968, 52: 349-350

CRUTCHER, ROBERT A.

70544 The usefulness of group therapy with character disorders. Int J grp PT 1961, 11:431-439

CRUVANT, BERNARD
See Karpman, Benjamin

CRYDER, H.
See White, William F.

CUELI, JOSÉ
70545   Algunos aspectos téchnicos en el manejo del huérfano temprano. [Some technical aspects in the management of separation anxiety.] Cuad Psa 1966, 2:109-113

ABSTRACTS OF:
70546   Kaplan, S. M. The negative ego ideal. Cuad Psa 1965, 1:313
70547   Segal, M. M. Transvestism as an impulse and a defense. Cuad Psa 1965, 1:383

CUKER, RUTH
See Berk, Robert

CULBERTSON, ELLEN
70548   (& Guthrie, G. M.; Butler, A. J.; Gorlow, L.) Patterns of hostility among the retarded. Amer J ment Defic 1961, 66:421-427

CULPIN, MILLAIS
70549   The conception of nervous disorder. M 1962, 35:73-80
        Abs ICFH Q 1963, 32:141-142

CUMES, JEFFREY
70550   Contrasting systems of explanation in psychology. Psychological Scene 1967, 1:30-33

CUMMING, ELAINE
70551   (& Henry, W. E.) Growing Old. The Process of Disengagement. (Foreword: Parsons, T.) NY: Basic Books 1961, xiii + 293 p
        Rv MG Q 1963, 32:125

See Cumming, John

CUMMING, JOHN
70552   (& Cumming, E.) Ego & Milieu; Theory and Practice of Environmental Theory. (Foreword: Stanton, A. H.) NY: Atherton Pr 1962; London: Tavistock 1964, 292 p
        Rv Am Im 1965, 22:218
70553   (& Turner, R. J.) Social structure and psychiatric disorder: a theoretical note. Proc Amer Psychopath Ass 1967, 55:52-62

See Appleby, Lawrence

CUMMINGS, S. THOMAS

70554 (& Stock, D.) Brief group therapy of mothers of retarded children outside the specialty clinic setting. Amer J ment Defic 1962, 66:739-748

70555 (& Bayley, H. C.; Rie, H. E.) Effects of the child's deficiency on the mother: a study of mothers of mentally retarded, chronically ill and neurotic children. Ops 1966, 36:595-608
Abs JMa RFPsa 1968, 32:379

70556 (& Carson, R. L.) Maternal personality and the externalizing-internalizing symptom dimension in neurotic children. Proceedings of the 75th Annual Convention of the American Psychological Assoc 1967, 2:181-182

CUNEEN, JOSEPH E.

See Birmingham, William

CUNLIFFE, MARCUS

70557 Where Freud-Bullitt went wrong. Encounter 1967, 29(1):86-88; 90

CUNNINGHAM, JULIE

See Buskirk, Martha

CURLEE, JOAN

70558 Alcoholism and the "empty nest." BMC 1969, 33:165-171

CURPHEY, T.

See Litman, Robert E.

CURRAN, FRANK JOSEPH

70559 To help the child, we must also help the parent. P 1968, 124:1448-1449

CURRIER, CAROL BEVERLY

70560 Patient-therapist relationships and the process of psychotherapy. Diss Abstr 1964, 24:5539-5540

CURRIER, LAURENCE M.

70561 The psychological impact of cancer on the cancer patient and his family. Rocky Mtn med J 1966, 63(2):43-48; 68

CURRY, ANDREW E.

70562 Myth, transference and the black psychotherapist. R 1964-65, 51:547-554
Abs SRS Q 1966, 35:160-161

70563 Some comments on transference when the group therapist is negro. Int J grp PT 1963, 13:363-365

70564 Toward the phenomenological study of the family. J existent Psychiat 1967, 6:35-44

70565 The world of a schizophrenic woman. PPR 1962, 49(1):129-135

REVIEWS OF:

70566　Boss, M. Psychoanalysis and Daseinanalysis. R 1964, 51:327-328

70567　Lederer, W. Dragons, Delinquents, and Destiny. An Essay on Positive Superego Functions. R 1966, 53:143-144

70568　Watts, A. Psychotherapy East and West. PPR 1962, 49(3):128

CURTI, MERLE

70569　The American exploration of dreams and dreamers. J Hist Ideas 1966, 27:391-416

CURTIS, GEORGE C.

70570　Discussion of Savage, C. "The analysis of an 'outsider.'" Psa Forum 1969, 3:300-301

See Saul, Leon J.

CURTIS, HOMER C.

REVIEW OF:

70571　Abraham, H. C. & Freud, E. L. (Eds) A Psychoanalytic Dialogue. The Letters of Sigmund Freud and Karl Abraham, 1907-1926. Q 1967, 36: 91-93

CURTIS, JACK H.

70572　Social Psychology. NY: McGraw-Hill 1960, x + 435 p

CURTIS, JAMES L.

REVIEW OF:

70573　Rohrer, J. H. & Edmonson, M. S. (Eds) The Eighth Generation Grows Up. Cultures and Personalities of New Orleans Negroes. Q 1965, 34: 303-305

CURTIS, MARGARET

See Nichtern, Sol

CURTIS, THOMAS A.

70574　(& Cantor, R.) The maxillofacial rehabilitation of President Grover Cleveland and Dr. Sigmund Freud. J Amer Dent Ass 1968, 76:359-361

CURTIS, THOMAS E.

70575　(& Clarke, M. G.; Abse, D. W.) Etiological factors in peptic ulcer as revealed in group-analytic psychotherapy. Int Rec Med 1960, 173(2): 92-96

See Clarke, Mary G.

CUSHING, JANE

See Gallahorn, George

CUSHNA, B.

See Greene, Marshall A.

CUSTANCE, JOHN

70576   Wisdom, Madness, and Folly: The Philosophy of a Lunatic. (Pref: Jung, C. G.) NY: Pellegrini & Cudahy 1952

CUSUMANO, D. R.

See Barclay, Allan G.

CUTLER, M.

See Renneker, Richard E.

CUTLER, R.

See Renneker, Richard E.

CUTLER, RICHARD E.

See Mushatt, Cecil

CUTLER, RICHARD LOYD

S-43973 Countertransference effects in psychotherapy. In Goldstein, A. P. & Dean, S. J. *The Investigation of Psychotherapy*, NY: Wiley 1966, 263-270

CUTNER, MARGOT

70577   Analytical work with LSD 25. Psychiat Q 1959, 33:715-757

CVIK, NATALIO

ABSTRACTS OF:
70578   Nunberg, H. Téoria general de las neurosis. Rev Psicoanál 1966, 23:280
70579   Freud, S. The ego and the id. Rev Psicoanál 1966, 23:257

CYPHER, JAMES R.

70580   The tangled sexuality of Temple Drake. Am Im 1962, 19:243-252

CYTRYN, LEON

70581   (& Lourie, R. S.) Mental retardation. Compreh Txbk Psychiat 817-856
70582   (& Uihlein, A.) Training of volunteers in the field of mental retardation and experiment. Ops 1965, 35:493-499
      Abs JMa RFPsa 1966, 30:526

CZERNIK, A.

See Klages, W.

CZERWENKA-WENKSTETTEN, HERIBERT

70583 Klinisch-psychiatrische und tiefenpsychologische Gesichtspunkte der Beurteilung des Schweredgrades von Neurosen. [Clinical-psychiatric and depth psychology points of view in the evaluation of degrees of severity of neuroses.] Wien Z Nervenheilk 1966, 24:236-246

CZESNOWICKA, M. N.

See Castets, Bruno

D

DABRITZ, LINDA

70584 (& Gillis, S.; Van Epps, J.) Rescue fantasy in the nurse therapist relationship with a psychotic child. J psychiat Nurs 1968, 6:71-85

DABROWSKI, KAZIMIERZ

70585 Le milieu psychique interne. [The internal psychic environment.] (Fr) Ann Méd-Psychol 1968, 2:457-485

70586 Positive Disintegration. Boston: Little, Brown, & Co. 1964, xviii + 132 p

70587 Psychothérapie des Névroses et des Psychonévroses. L'Instinct de la Mort d'après la Theorie de la Désintégration Positive. [Psychotherapy of Neuroses and Psychoneuroses. The Death Instinct According to the Theory of Positive Disintegration.] Warsaw: Państwowe Wydawn. Naukowe 1965, 22 p

DACO, PIERRE

70588 Guide de la Psychologie Moderne. [Guide to Modern Psychology.] Paris: Centre National du Livre Familial 1968, 516 p

70589 Les Prodigieuses Victoires de la Psychologie Moderne. [The Prodigious Victories of Modern Psychology.] Verviers: Gérard & Co. 1968, 511 p

70590 Les Triomphes de la Psychanalyse. [The Triumphs of Psychoanalysis.] (Pref: Jamont, C.) Verviers: Gérard; Paris: l'Inter 1966, 445 p

D'AGOSTINO, ANGELO

70591 (Ed) Family, Church and Community. NY: P. J. Kenedy & Sons 1965

D'AGOSTINO, N.

See Callieri, Bruno

DAHL, HARTVIG

70592 Observations on a "natural experiment": Helen Keller. (Read at Seattle Psa Soc, 10 Feb 1964; Am Psa Ass, 1 May 1964) J Am Psa Ass 1965, 13:533-550

Abs Rosarios, H. Rev Psicoanál 1966, 23:76. JLST Q 1968, 37:625-626

70593   (Reporter) Psychoanalytic theory of the instinctual drives in relation to recent developments. (Panel: Am Psa Ass, NY, Dec 1967) J Am Psa Ass 1968, 16:613-637

ABSTRACTS OF:

70594   Aleksandrowicz, D. R. Fire and its aftermath on a geriatric ward. Q 1962, 31:294

70595   Aleksandrowicz, D. R. The meaning of metaphor. Q 1964, 33:141

70596   Appelbaum, S. A. The end of the test as a determinant of responses. Q 1962, 31:295

70597   Cain, A. & Maupin, B. M. Interpretation within the metaphor. Q 1962, 31:584

70598   Dement, W. The effect of dream deprivation. Q 1961, 30:150-151

70599   Felix, R. H. The psychiatric training of the medical student and psychiatrist. Q 1962, 31:584

70600   Freud, A. Regression as a principle in mental development. Q 1964, 33:604-605

70601   Gardner, R. W. & Lohrenz, L. J. Leveling–sharpening and serial reproduction of a story. Q 1961, 30:451-452

70602   Gitelson, M. The place of psychoanalysis in psychiatric training. Q 1963, 32:134

70603   Hall, B. H. & Wallerstein, R. S. Termination studies. Q 1961, 30:147-148

70604   Harlow, H. F. & Harlow, M. K. The effect of rearing conditions on behavior. Q 1964, 33:142-143

70605   Holzman, P. S. Repression and cognitive style. Q 1964, 33:602

70606   Kaufman, I. The defensive aspects of impulsivity. Q 1964, 33:603-604

70607   Keith, C. R. Some aspects of transference in dream search. Q 1964, 33:602

70608   Klein, G. S. Credo for a "clinical psychologist": a personal reflection. Q 1964, 33:604

70609   Levin, L. A. A sexual preoccupation in a little girl. Q 1962, 31:295.

70610   Levy, E. Z. The subject's approach: important factor in experimental isolation? Q 1963, 32:133-134

70611   Piaget, J. Three lectures. Q 1964, 33:141-142

70612   Ramzy, I. Freud's understanding of anxiety. Q 1962, 31:294

70613   Roosenburg, A. M. The treatment of criminals in institutions. Q 1962, 31:295

70614   Santos, J. F. et al: How attention influences what is perceived: some experimental evidence. Q 1964, 33:603

70615   Siegal, R. S. & Ehrenreich, G. A. Inferring repression from psychological tests. Q 1964, 33:141

70616   Solley, C. M. & Munden, K. Toward a description of mental health. Q 1964, 33:142

70617   Stengel, E. Self-destructiveness and self-preservation. Q 1963, 32:133

70618   Stross, L. & Shevrin, H. Differences in thought organization between hypnosis and the waking state: an experimental approach. Q 1964, 33:143

70619   Voth, H. A note on the function of dreaming. Q 1962, 31:294

70620 Voth, H. M. et al: Situational variables in the assessment of psycho-therapeutic results. Q 1963, 32:134
70621 Wallerstein, R. S. & Robbins, L. L. Initial studies. Q 1961, 30:147

DAHLBERG, CHARLES CLAY

70622 Abortion. In Slovenko, R. *Sexual Behavior and the Law*, Springfield, Ill: Thomas 1965, 379-393
70623 Discussion of Kuhns, R. F. "Modernity and death: *The Leopard* by Giuseppe di Lampedusa." Contempo Psa 1969, 5(2):124-126
70624 Discussion of Schimel, J. L. "The grammar of psychoanalysis: Sullivan revisited." Contempo Psa 1968, 5(1):41-43
70625 LSD as an aid to psychoanalytic treatment. Sci Psa 1963, 6:255-266
70626 LSD facilitation of psychoanalytic treatment. A case study of depth. In Abramson, H. A. *The Use of LSD in Psychotherapy and Alcoholism*, NY: Merrill 1967, 237-257
70627 Obituary: Mrs. Lloyd Merrill. Contempo Psa 1969, 5(2):183-194
70628 The 100 minute hour. Contempo Psa 1967, 4(1):1-18
70629 Pharmacologic facilitation of psychoanalytic therapy. Curr psychiat Ther 1963, 3:91-99
70630 A survey of the LSD question: a review of four books. Contempo Psa 1965, 2(1):62-82

See Jaffe, Joseph

DAHLHEIM, L. G.

70631 Training in psychosomatic research. Advances Psychosom Med 1967, 5:119-125

DAHLSTROM, W. G.

70632 (& Tolley, A. G.; Abse, D. W.) Evaluation of tranquilizing drugs in the management of acute mental disturbance. P 1960, 116:973-980
70633 (& Abse, D. W.) The value of chemotherapy in senile mental disturbances. JAMA 1960, 174:2036-2042

See Abse, D. Wilfred

DAILEY, CHARLES A.

70634 Natural history and phenomenology. J ind Psych 1960, 16:36-44

DAIM, WILFRED

70635 Depth Psychology and Salvation. (Tr, Ed, Intro: Reinhardt, Kurt, F.) NY: Frederick Ungar Publ Co. 1963, 315 p

DAIN, H.

See Riess, Bernard F.

DAIN, HARVEY J.

See Bieber, Irving

DAIN, N.

70636 (& Carlson, E. T.) Moral insanity in the United States 1835-1866. P 1962, 118:795-801

DALACK, JOHN D.

See Silberstein, Richard M.

DALE, LAURA A.

See Murphy, Gardner

DALEY, JAMES W.

70637 Freud and moral philosophy. Dissertation Abstr 1967, 27:3487

DALIBARD, YVES

S-43996 Autour de l'analyse d'un cas de fantasme sadique.
Abs TC An Surv Psa 1957, 8:102-103

70638 Discussion of Barande, R. Essai métapsychologique sur le silence: de l'objet total phallique dans la clinique du silence. RFPsa 1963, 27: 98-99

70639 Discussion of Diatkine, R. Agressivité et fantasmes d'aggression. RFPsa 1966, 30:119-120

70640 Discussion of Fornari, F. La psychanalyse de la guerre. RFPsa 1966, 30:281-283

70641 Discussion of Geahchan, D. J. Deuil et nostalgie. RFPsa 1968, 32:60-61

70642 Discussion of Kestemberg, E. & Kestemberg, J. Contributions à la perspective génétique en psychanalyse. RFPsa 1966, 30:753-754

70643 Discussion of Lebovici, S. Colloque sur les interprétations en thérapeutique psychanalytique. RFPsa 1962, 26:28

70644 Discussion of Luquet, P. Ouvertures sur l'artiste et le psychanalyste. RFPsa 1963, 27:606-608

70645 Discussion of Mendel, G. La sublimation artistique. RFPsa 1964, 28: 794-795

70646 Discussion of Schmitz, B. Les états limites. RFPsa 1967, 31:264

70647 Discussion of Viderman, S. Régression et situation analytique. RFPsa 1966, 30:482-483

DALLOZ, J. C.

See Aubrey, J.

DALMA, GIOVANNI

70648 Tendenze tanatiche in Leonardo: saggio so di un aspetto della sua personalita. [Thanatic tendencies in Leonardo: the study of one aspect of his personality.] Nevrasse 1959, 9:669-718

DALMA, JUAN

70649 Patogenia por situación conflictual y mecanismos de regresión: des coincidencias en varias doctrinas sobre neurosis. [Pathogenesis in conflictual situations and the mechanisms of regression: two coincidences in various doctrines on neurosis.] Acta psiquíat psicol Amér Latina 1965, 11:267-277

70650 Reflexiones sobre el instinto tanático. [Reflections on the thanatic instinct.] Act Np Arg 1960, 6:63-67

70651 Tension entre madre e hija como causa morbigena en las neurosis juveniles. [Tension between mother and daughter as a morbigenic cause of juvenile neurosis.] Act Np Arg 1961, 7(3):208-214

DALMAU, CARLOS J.

70652 Anthropocentric aspects of religion. R 1967, 54:679-687
Abs SRS Q 1969, 38:164

70653 Problems of transference analysis. Arch crim Psychodyn 1960, 4:13-31

70654 Psychopathy and psychopathic behaviors: a psychoanalytic approach. Arch crim Psychodyn 1961, 4:443-455

DALRYMPLE, WILLARD

See Pervin, Lawrence A.

DALSIMER, JAMES S.

See Khantzian, Edward J.

DALSIMER, WALTER

ABSTRACT OF:

70655 Karasic, J. Symptoms, transference, and the past. Bull Phila Ass Psa 1966, 16:104-106

DALTON, GENE W.

70656 (& Zaleznik, A.; Barnes, L. B.) The Distribution of Authority in Formal Organization. Boston: Harvard U, Div of Research, Graduate School of Bus Ad 1968

DALTON, K.

70657 The influence of the mother's health on her child. Proc RSM 1966, 59:1014-1016

70658 Menstruation and crime. M 1961, 5269:1752-1753

DALY, ROBERT W.

70659 Schizoid rule-following. R 1968, 55:400-414
Abs SRS Q 1969, 38:673-674

70660 Social reality and the concept of defense. (Symposium: The psychoanalyst as mediator and double agent.) R 1965, 52:391-399

70661 Values: a view from the clinic. J Relig & Health 1967, 6(2):126-136

REVIEWS OF:

70662 Blanchard, W. H. Rousseau and the Spirit of Revolt: A Psychological Study. R 1969, 56:158-160

70663 Dunham, H. W. Community and Schizophrenia. R 1967, 54(1):184-188

70664 Geiger, T. The Conflicted Relationship: The West and the Transformation of Asia, Africa and Latin America. R 1969, 56:481-482
70665 Klausner, S. Z. (Ed) The Quest for Self-Control. R 1966, 53:680-683
70666 Menaker, W. & Menaker, E. Ego in Evolution. R 1967, 54(1):184-188

DAMARIN, FRED LOUIS, JR.

70667 (& Cattell, R. B.) Personality factors in early childhood and their relation to intelligence. Monogr Soc Res child Developm 1968, 33:1-95

DAMBACHER, BEATRICE M.

70668 Hostility and counter-transference: nursing therapy of a schizophrenic woman. Dissertation Abstr 1967, 28(3-B):962

DAME, NENABELLE, G.

70669 (& Finck, G. H.; Mayos, R. G.) Conflict in marriage following premarital pregnancy. Ops 1966, 36:468-475

See Reiner, Beatrice S.

DAMEY, E.

See Arnoux, H.

DAMIANOPOULOS, ERNEST N.

See Arnhoff, Franklin N.

DANA, RICHARD H.

70670 Anxiety and humanization. Psychol Rep 1967, 21:1017-1024
70671 (& Condry, J. C., Jr.) A criterion for analyses of interpersonal perception. J gen Psychol 1965, 72:233-238
70672 Foundations of Clinical Psychology: Problems of Personality and Adjustment. Princeton/London: Van Nostrand 1966, viii + 322 p
70673 From therapists anonymous to therapeutic community. J ind Psych 1963, 19(2):185-190
70674 The impact of fantasy on a treatment program. Corrective Psychiat & J soc Ther 1964, 10(4):202-212
70675 Psychopathology: a developmental interpretation. J ind Psych 1965, 21:58-65
70676 (& Christiansen, K.) Repression and psychopathology. J proj Tech 1959, 23:412-416
70677 (& Smith, B.) Repression-sensitization and clinical judgment. Psychol Rep 1968, 22:252
70678 Six constructs to define Rorschach M. J proj Tech 1968, 32:138-145
70679 Thematic techniques and clinical practice. J proj Tech 1968, 32:204-214

See Bernstein, Lewis; Hirsch, C. L.

DANDURAIN, CARLOS WHITING

70680 Psicopatalogia de una denomination: analisis didactic. [Psychopathology of a so-called training analysis.] Rev Psicoanál 1961, 18:138-144
       Abs Vega Q 1962, 31:591-592

DANEHY, JOHN J.

See Hollender, Marc H.; Malev, Jonathan S.; Pittenger, Robert E.

DANIEL, JAMES P.

70681 Child of Fury. The Story of the Psychological Development of a Psychotic Child. (Foreword: Geist, H.) NY: Exposition Pr 1961, 78 p
Rv Roiphe, H. Q 1963, 32:123-124

DANIELL, E. F.

See Buss, Arnold H.

DANIELS, D. N.

70682 (& Rubin, R. S.) The community meeting. An analytical study and a
theoretical statement. Arch gen Psychiat 1968, 18:60-75

DANIELS, DAVID N.

70683 Task groups in the therapy of mental patients. Curr psychiat Ther 1969,
9:186-194

DANIELS, EDWARD M.

70684 Discussion of Winnicott, D. W. "Clinical regression compared with
defense organization." Int Psychiat Clin 1968, 5:12-15
70685 (& Snyder, B. R.; Wool, M. L.; Berman, L.) A group approach to predelinquent boys, their teachers and parents, in a junior high school.
Int J grp PT 1960, 10:346-352. In Zinberg, N. E. *Psychiatry and Medical Practice in a General Hospital*, NY: IUP 1964, 301-307

See Fox, Henry M.

ASTRACTS OF:
70686 Fox, H. M. Narcissistic defenses during pregnancy. An Surv Psa 1958,
9:144-145
70687 Friedman, L. J. Toward an integration of psychoanalytic and philosophic esthetics. An Surv Psa 1958, 9:497-499
70688 Jensen, V. W. & Petty, T. A. The fantasy of being rescued in suicide.
An Surv Psa 1958, 9:174-175
70689 Kanzer, M. Image formation during free association. An Surv Psa 1958,
9:104-106
70690 Kubie, L. S. Neurotic Distortion of the Creative Process. An Surv Psa
1958, 9:490-496
70691 Kubie, L. S. Research into the process of supervision in psychoanalysis.
An Surv Psa 1958, 9:433-435
70692 Lax, R. F. Infantile deprivation and arrested ego development. An
Surv Psa 1958, 9:317-318
70693 Marmor, J. The psychodynamics of realistic worry. An Surv Psa 1958,
9:166-167
70694 Miller, A. A. An interpretation of the symbolism of Medusa. An Surv
Psa 1958, 9:448-449

70695 Palm R. On the symbolic significance of the Star of David. An Surv Psa 1958, 9:445

70696 Rappaport, E. A. The grandparent syndrome. An Surv Psa 1958, 9:291-293

70697 Rosenzweig, S. The idiocultural dimension of psychotherapy: pre- and post-history of the relations between Sigmund Freud and Josef Popper-Lynkeus. An Surv Psa 1958, 9:10-12

DANIELS, GEORGE E.

70698 The Columbia University Psychoanalytic Clinic: an experiment in university teaching in psychoanalysis. J med Educ 1960, 35:164-171

70699 (& Catell, J. P.; Rogers, T. C.; Gaylin, W. M.; Shapiro, D.) History of the Sandor Rado Lectureship. In author's *New Perspectives in Psychoanalysis*, NY: Grune & Stratton 1965

70700 (& Catell, J. P.; Rogers, T. C.; Gaylin, W. M.; Shapiro, D.) (Eds) New Perspectives in Psychoanalysis, Sandor Rado Lectures 1957-1963. (The Psychoanalytic Clinic for Training and Research, Columbia University and the Alumni Assoc of the Columbia Univ Psychoanalytic Clinic, NY) NY: Grune & Stratton 1965, viii + 328 p

70701 (& O'Connor, J. F.; Karush, A.; Moses, L.; Flood, C. A.; Leopore, M.) Three decades in the observation and treatment of ulcerative colitis. PSM 1962, 24(1)

Tre decenni di osservazioni di terapia della colite ulcerosa. Med Psicosomática 1963, 8(3)

Abs Musacchio, A. E. Rev Psicoanál 1964, 21:190

See Karush, Aaron; Kolb, Lawrence C.; O'Connor, John F.; Rado, Sandor

DANIELS, MARVIN

70702 The dynamics of morbid envy in the etiology and treatment of chronic learning disability. R 1964-65, 51:585-596

Abs CG RFPsa 1968, 32:167, SRS Q 1966, 35:161-162

70703 Pathological vindictiveness and the vindictive character. R 1969, 56: 169-196

DANIELS, ROBERT SANFORD

70704 (& Prosen, H.) The contribution of visual observation to an interview. Int J grp PT 1962, 12:230

70705 (& McFarland, R. L.; Solon, E.) Group psychotherapy. Prog Neurol Psychiat 1962, 17:526-535

70706 (& Lieberman, M.) Group psychotherapy. Prog Neurol Psychiat 1965, 20:717-722

70707 (& Margolis, P. M.; Carson, R. C.) Hospital discharges against medical advice. I. Origin and prevention. Arch gen Psychiat 1963, 8:120-130

70708 Psychotherapy of depression—a rational approach by the family physician. Postgraduate Med 1962, 32:436

70709 (& Lessow, H.) Severe postpartum reactions. An interpersonal view. Psychosomatics 1964, 5:21-26

70710 Some early manifestations of transference: their implications for the first phase of psychoanalysis. J Am Psa Ass 1969, 17:995-1014

70711 (& Draper, E.; Rada, R.) Training in the adaptive psychotherapies. Comprehen Psychiat 1968, 9:383-391.

See Corsini, Raymond J.; Draper, Edgar; Lieberman, Morton A.; McFarland, Robert L.; Reding, Georges R.

DANN, O. T.

See Bowers, Malcolm B., Jr.

DANN, SOPHIE

See Freud, Anna

DANNEBERG, ERIKA

70712 Dynamische und ökonomische Aspekte der Entwicklung des Über-Ichs. [Dynamic and economic aspects of the development of the superego.] Psyche 1968, 22:365-383

DANNENBERG, HANNS-JOACHIM

70713 Jugendliches Stottern und Homosexualität. [Adolescent stuttering and homosexuality.] Jb Psa 1960, 1:253-274

DANON-BOILEAU, HENRI

70714 (& Delesalle, S.; Lab, P.; Levy, E.; et al) L'abord médico-pédagogique des étudiants schizophrènes. [The medical-pedagogical approach to schizophrenic students.] Rev Np inf 1967, 15(7-8):589-617

70715 (& Lab, P.; Cachelou, R.) L'amitryptilline dans les états dépressifs atypiques. [Amitryptilline in atypical depressive states.] Ann médpsychol 1962, 5:741-745

70716 L'angoisse des examens et des concours. [Examination anxiety.] Rev Np inf 1957, 5(3-4):3-7

70717 (& Lab, P.; Peraud, C.; Tuset, A.) A propos d'un cas de bouffée délirante accompagnée de signes d'hyperthyrodidie. [Concerning a case of delirious flushing accompanied by signs of hyperthyroidism.] Rev Méd psychosom 1966, 4

70718 (& Lab, P.; Levy, E.; Peraud, C.) À propos d'un type particulier de pères de schizophrènes: les pères-mères de schizophrènes. [Apropos of a particular type of fathers of schizophrenics: the "mothers of schizophrenics"—type fathers.] Rev Np inf 1965, 13:805-812

70719 Aspects psychothérapiques de la reprise du travail en milieu intellectuel. [Psychotherapeutic aspects of resumption of work in an intellectual atmosphere.] Rev Np inf 1957, 5(11-12):635-642

70720 La colère et l'angoisse. [Anger and anxiety.] Évolut Psychiat 1964, 29:463-495

70721 (& Dupré, J.; Lab, P.; Levy, E.) Conséquences lointaines du délabrement familial lié à la guerre chez les étudiants juifs. [Long range consequences in Jewish students from families shattered by the war.] Rev Np inf 1965, 13:563-575

70722 (& Levy, E.) Diverses modalités de prise en charge des étudiants malades mentaux a la Clinique Dupré et au Centre Pierre Janet à Sceaux. [Different methods of handling mentally ill students at the Dupré Clinic and at the Pierre Janet Center at Sceaux.] Inform psychiat 1968, 44(3)

70723 (& Lab, P.; Levy, E.) Les échecs universitaires. [University failures.] Revue d'Hygiène et de Médecine Sociales 1965, 13:177-188

70724 (& Lavitry, S.; Levy, E.; Rousseau, A.; Laborit, H.) Essais thérapeutiques de la semi-aldéhide succinique chez les malades mentaux. [Therapeutic experiments with succinic semi-aldehyde for the mentally ill.] Rev Agressologie 1964, 2:189-195

70725 Fonctionnement de la Maison Universitaire Médico-Psychologique de Sceaux. [Operation of the University Medico-Psychological House at Sceaux.] Perspectives Psychiat 1965, 10

70726 (& Lab, P.) L'inhibition intellectuelle. [Intellectual inhibition.] Psychiat Enfant 1962, 5(1):43-173. Presse Méd 1963, 5:2543-2544

70727 (& Lab, P.) Le médecin en face de la maladie mortelle. [The doctor confronted with terminal illness.] Abbottempo Livre 2–1966:8-11

70728 (& Delesalle, S.; Lab, P.; Bazin, P.; Frontisi, F.; Goldberg, J.; Guibout, D.) Orthopedagogie de l'étudiant: essai clinique sur certaines disciplines littéraires: aspects symptomatiques, relationnels et techniques. [Orthopedagogy of the student. Clinical essay on certain literary disciplines.] Psychiat Enfant 1967, 10:381-463

70729 (& Lab, P.) Participants: 2ème congrès international de Morale Médicale. Table ronde: Psychiatrie moderne et responsabilités médicales. [2nd International Congress on Medical Ethics. Round Table: Modern psychiatry and medical responsibilities.] Paris, May 1966. Report published by l'Ordre National des Médecins, II:420-428

70730 (& Lab, P.; Cachelous, R.) Le problème des échecs universitaires. [The problem of university failures.] Presse Méd 1962, 70(34):1665-1666

70731 Problèmes posés par l'hygiène mentale des étudiants. [Problems presented by the mental hygiene of students.] Évolut Psychiat 1956, 4:809-842

70732 Les psychothérapies brèves dans une institution médicopédagogique. [Brief psychotherapies in a medicopedagogical institution.] In IV Congres mondial de psychiatrie, Madrid 5-11 Sept 1966. Excerpta Medica, 117, 157

70733 Quelques aspects de problèmes psycho-pathologiques chez les étudiants. [Some aspects of psychopathological problems in students.] Bull Psychol, Paris 1960

70734 (& Lab, P.) Quelques aspects psychologiques des difficultés scolaires de l'enfant normal à la puberté. [Some psychological aspects of scholastic difficulties at puberty of the normal child.] Congrès International d'Hygiène Scolaire et Universitaire—Unesco 1959

70735 Réadaptation au travail chez les étudiants. [Readjustment to work in students.] Rev Np inf 1958

70736 (& Brousselle, A.; Lab, P.; Levy, E.) La réadaptation des étudiants atteints de troubles mentaux. [The readjustment of students affected by mental problems.] Revue Santé de l'Homme 1965, 140

70737   (& Lab, P.; Levy, E.) La réadaptation des étudiants malades mentaux. [The readjustment of mentally ill students.] Revue Réadaptation B.U.S., Paris 1963, 105:21-30

70738   (& Delesalle, S.; Gaugue, D.; Lab, P.; Levy, E.; Plumyene, J.; Ruffiot, A.) Le rôle d'une orthopédagogie dans le traitement des maladies mentales de l'adolescent scolaire et universitaire. [The role of orthopedagogy in the treatment of mental illness in adolescent and university students.] Ann méd-psychol 1963, 1:13-28

70739   (& Cor, J.) Tuberculose et troubles mentaux. [Tuberculosis and mental problems.] L'Encyclopédie Médico-Chirurgicale 1964, 37610 A 10

70740   (& Lab, P.; Levy, E.; Lavitry, S.; Ruffiot, S.; Laborit, H.) Utilisation en psychiatrie du Gamma OH. [The utilization in psychiatry of Gamma OH.] Presse Méd 1962, 47:2205-2207

See Douady, D.

DANSEREAU, M.

70741   L'emotion. Essai d'introduction phénoménologique à une ontogonese psychosomatique de la personne. [Emotion. Attempt at a phenomenologic introduction to a psychosomatic ontogenesis of the personality.] (Fr) Psychother Psychosom 1965, 13:449-465

DANTO, BRUCE

70742   Contributor to Krystal, H. *Massive Psychic Trauma*, NY: IUP 1969

DANTZIG, A. VAN

70743   Neurotic mechanisms of grandeur and omnipotence. Psychiat Neurol Neurochir 1967, 70:197-211

70744   Das Verhältnis zwischen existentialistischen und psychoanalytischen Theorien über die Angst. [The relation between the existential and psychoanalytic theory of anxiety.] Psychiat Neurol Neurochir 1964, 67:24-38

DANTZIG-VAN AMSTEL, B. VAN

70745   Obituary: Nel Tibout: 1899-1968. J 1969, 50:132-133

DARBES, ALEX

70746   A single psychotherapy session: an analysis of its content and form with implications for a theory of the therapy process. Proc W Va Acad Sci 1959, 31:75-78

DARCOURT, GUY

70747   Définition clinique de masochisme moral. [Clinical definition of moral masochism.] Bull Ass Psa Fran 1968, (4):3-34; 63

70748   (& Capdeville, C.; Albaranes, S.) Masochisme, narcissisme et masochisme narcissique: étude clinique. [Masochism, narcissism, and narcissistic masochism: a clinical study.] Ann méd-psychol 1968, 1(4):621

DARE, CHRISTOPHER

70749 An aspect of the ego psychology of religion: a comment on Dr. Guntrip's paper. M 1969, 42:335-340

DARROW, CHARLOTTE

70750 (& Lowinger, P.) The Detroit uprising: a psychosocial study. Sci Psa 1968, 13:120-133

DA SILVA, GUY

70751 Considérations psychodynamiques sur le viellissement. [Psychodynamic considerations concerning ageing.] Laval Méd 1967, 38:567-576. Un Méd Canada 1967, 96:570-577

70752 The loneliness and death of an old man: three years' psychotherapy of an eighty-one-year-old depressed patient. J geriat Psychiat 1967, 1:5-27

DATTA, L.-E.

See Parloff, Morris B.

DAUMEZON, G.

70753 (& Huguet, P.) Apparence da procédés surréalistes comme moyen de défense d'un malade. [Appearance of surrealistic procedures as a defense mechanism in a patient.] (Fr) Ann méd-psychol 1960, 118(1): 291-299

DAUNTON, ELIZABETH

70754 Description, evaluation and follow-up of case treated via the mother. Ther Nurs Schl 215-230
70755 Diagnosis. Ther Nurs Schl 204-214
70756 Some aspects of ego and superego resistance in the case of an asthmatic child. (Read at Am Psa Ass 1960) Ch Anal Wk 206-228

See Sandler, Anne-Marie

DAUVEN, J.

70757 Les Pouvoirs de l'Hypnose. [The Powers of Hypnosis.] (Preface: Servadio, E.) Paris: Planète 1965

DAVAL, R.

70758 Psycho-sociologie de la décision: décision collective et identification au groupe. [Psycho-sociology of decision making: group decision and identification with the group.] Bull Psychol, Paris 1967, 20:559-562

DAVANZO, HERNAN

70759 Contribuiçao psicanalítica ao ensino da psicologia médica. [Psychoanalytic contribution to the teaching of medical psychology.] Rev Medicina 1962, 1:123-126

70760   A contribution to the analysis of resistances in neurotic dependence. J 1962, 43:441-447
          Abs EVN Q 1965, 34:308
70761   The family group in dynamic psychiatric diagnosis. Int J grp PT 1962, 12:496-502
70762   A method of teaching reparative psychotherapy to medical students. J med Educ 1965, 785-791
70763   [Teaching psychiatry and medical psychology in the medical school of Ribeiro Preto (1956-1963).] (Por) Psiquiatria 1963, 3:5-17
          Abs Vega Q 1966, 35:630

   See Neto, David Azoubel

DAVENPORT, C. W.

   See Harrison, Saul I.

DAVENPORT, H. T.

   See Werry, John S.

DAVID, CHARLES BROWN

70764   Toward a definition of psychotherapy. Dis nerv Syst 1961, 22:106-108

DAVID, CHRISTIAN

70765   L'Attitude Conceptuelle en Médecine Psychosomatique. [The Conceptual Attitude in Psychosomatic Medicine.] Paris: Foulon 1961
          Rv SLe RFPsa 1961, 25:405
70766   De la valeur mutative des remaniements post-oedipiens. [On the changing value of post-oedipal dealings.] RFPsa 1967, 31:813-817
70767   Discussion of Fornari, F. "La psychanalyse de la guerre." RFPsa 1966, 30:284
70768   Discussion of Geahchan, D. J. "Deuil et nostalgie." RFPsa 1968, 32:61-62
70769   Discussion of Marty, P. "Régression et instinct de mort." RFPsa 1967, 31:27-28
70770   Discussion of Mynard, J. "À propos d'un facteur d'interminabilité encore peu degagé en 1937." RFPsa 1968, 32:279-283
70771   Discussion of Rouart, J. "Investment and counter-investment." RFPsa 1967, 31:223-230
70772   État amoureux et travail du deuil. [Being in love and the work of mourning.] Interpretation 1967, 1(4):45-71
70773   L'heterogénéité de l'inconscient et les continuités psychiques. [Unconscious heterogeneity and the psychic continuity.] Inconscient 1967, 4:1-35
70774   [Heterogeneity of acting out and ambiguity of transference.] RFPsa 1968, 32:1005-1010
70775   Psychosomatique et théorie du stress. [Psychosomatic and the stress theory.] Temps mod 1962, 18(199):1108-1120
70776   Quelqu'un manque. [Somebody's missing.] Études Freudiennes (Tchou) 1969

70777   Réflexions métapsychologiques concernant l'état amoureux. [Metapsychological reflections concerning the state of being in love.] RFPsa 1966, 30:195-225

See Chasseguet-Smirgel, Janine; Fain, Michel; Marty, Pierre

DAVID, HENRY

70778   Discussion of Wedge, B. Psychiatry and international affairs. Int J Psychiat 1968, 5:330-344

DAVID, HENRY P.

70779   Discussion of Goldman, G. D. "The clinical psychologist as a therapist: training and practice." Prog clin Psych 1963, 5:189-192

70780   (& Brengelmann, J. C.) (Eds) Perspectives in Personality Research. NY: Springer 1960, ix + 370 p

See Blank, Leonard

DAVID, KENNETH

70781   Ego-strength, sex differences, and description of self, ideal, and parents. J gen Psychol 1968, 79:79-81

DAVID, MICHELE

70782   L'idealismo italiano e la psicoanalisi. [Italian idealism and psychoanalysis.] Riv Psa 1963, 9:189-234

70783   (& Appel, G.) La relation mère-enfant. Étude de cinq "patterns" d'interaction entre mère et enfant à l'âge d'un an. [The mother-child relationship. Study of five patterns of interaction between mother and a one year old child.] Psychiat de l'Enfant 1966, 9:445-531
Abs Abels, E. RFPsa 1968, 32:336

DAVIDMAN, HOWARD

70784   Contributions of Sandor Rado to psychodynamic science. Sci Psa 1964, 7:17-34

70785   Evaluation of psychoanalysis: a clinician's view. Proc Am Psychopath Ass 1964, 52:32-44

70786   Psychiatrie correctionnelle de comportement criminel et délinquant; développement d'un cours spécial pour psychiatres diplômés. [Correctional psychiatry of criminal and delinquent behaviour; development of a special course for certifying psychiatrists.] Méd et Hyg 1965, 23:680

70787   Psychological problems of deafness, blindness and muteness in children. In Lief, H. I. (et al): Psychological Basis of Medical Practice, NY: Harper & Row 1963

70788   Sandor Rado. Compreh Txbk Psychiat 355-362

70789   (& Preble, E.) Schizophrenia among adolescent street gang leaders. In Hoch, P. H. & Zubin, J. Psychopathology of Schizophrenia, NY: Grune & Stratton 1966, 372-383. In Lefton, M. (et al): Approaches to

Deviance; Theories, Concepts, and Research Findings, Meredith Corp 1968, 189-199

70790 What you should know about homosexuality. State of Mind, Ciba 1958, 2(4)

DAVIDS, ANTHONY

70791 (& DeVault, S.; Talmadge, M.) Anxiety and childbirth abnormalities. J consult Psychol 1961, 25:74-77

70792 Ego functions in disturbed and normal children: aspiration, inhibition, time estimation, and delayed gratification. J consult Psychol 1969, 33:61-70

70793 (& Oliver, G. R.) Fantasy aggression and learning in emotionally disturbed and normal children. J proj Tech 1960, 24:124-128

70794 Psychodynamic and sociocultural factors related to intolerance of ambiguity. In White, R. W. *The Study of Lives,* NY: Atherton Pr 1966, 160-177

70795 (& Silverman, M.) A psychological case study of death during pregnancy. ASP 1960, 11:287-291

70796 The relation of cognitive-dissonance theory to an aspect of psychotherapeutic practice. Am Psych 1964, 19:329-332

70797 (& Lawton, M. J.) Self-concept, mother-concept, and food aversions in emotionally disturbed and normal children. ASP 1961, 62:309-314
    Abs Rosen, I. C. Q 1962, 31:590-591

DAVIDSON, AUDREY

70798 (& Fay, J.) Fantasy in middle childhood. In Haworth, M. R. *Child Psychotherapy,* NY/London: Basic Books 1964, 401-406

DAVIDSON, D.

70799 A problem of identity in relation to an image of a damaged mother. J anal Psych 1965, 10:67-76

70800 Transference as a form of active imagination. J anal Psych 1966, 11: 135-146

DAVIDSON, G. M.

70801 The anxiety in reference to existential-analytics. Dis nerv Sys 1960, 21:267-274

70802 Dostoevsky and the perennial drama of man. Psychiat Q Suppl 1963, 37:88-105

DAVIDSON, GERSON N.

S-44071 Concerning the biological aspects of the Oedipus complex.
    Abs An Surv 1955, 6:67-68

DAVIDSON, H. H.

70803 (& Greenberg, J. W.; Alshan, L.) The identification of caution, a correlate of achievement functioning. J proj Tech 1966, 30:381-384

DAVIDSON, HENRY A.

70804 The doctor as a parent. J Med Soc NJ 1967, 64:560-562
70805 Medical-legal aspects of traumatic psychoneurosis. Industr Med Surg 1966, 35:936-938
70806 The new war on psychiatry. P 1964, 121:528-534
70807 Rationalizations for continued smoking. NYSJM 1964, 64:2993-3001
70808 The reversible superego. P 1963, 120:192-193

DAVIDSON, JOAN

70809 Infantile depression in a "normal" child. J Amer Acad child Psychiat 1968, 7:522-535

See Widroe, H.

DAVIDSON, KENNETH S.

See Sarason, Seymour B.

DAVIDSON, P. WAVERLY, III

See Slawson, Paul F.

DAVIDSON, S. I.

70810 Auto-enucleation of the eye: a study of self-mutilation. Acta psychother psychosom 1962, 10(4):286-300

DAVIDSON, SONNY

70811 Discussion of Greenacre, P. & Winnicott, D. W. "The theory of the parent-infant relationship. Further remarks." Contributions to discussion (xiv) J 1962, 43:254-255

DAVIDSON, SUSANNAH

70812 Bereavement in children. Nurs Times 1966, 62:1650-1652
70813 School phobia as a manifestation of family disturbance: its structure and treatment. J child Psychol Psychiat 1961, 1:270-287

DAVIE, JAMES McKELLAR

70814 (& Freeman, T.) Disturbances of perception and consciousness in schizophrenic states. M 1961, 34:33-41
         Abs RDT Q 1961, 30:610. JCS RFPsa 1963, 27:331
70815 (& Freeman, T.) The nonpsychotic residue in schizophrenia. M 1961, 34:117-127
         Abs RDT Q 1962, 31:137
70816 Observations on some defensive aspects of delusion formation. M 1963, 36:67-74

DAVIES, I. J.

70817 (& Ellenson, G.; Young, R.) Therapy with a group of families in a psychiatric day center. Ops 1966, 36:134-146
         Abs JMa RFPsa 1968, 32:181

DAVIES, M.
See Barzilai, Shoshana

DAVIN, MICHEL
70818　La psicoanalisi nella cultura italiana. [Psychoanalysis in Italian culture.] Turin: Boringhieri 1966
　　　　Rv Clancier, A. RFPsa 1968, 32:329

DAVIS, ALLEN
See Raphling, David L.

DAVIS, ALLISON
70819　(& Dollard, J.) Children of Bondage. The Personality Development of Negro Youth in the Urban South. (Orig publ by Amer Council of Ed 1940) NY/Evanston/London: Harper & Row 1964, xxiv + 299 p
　　　　Rv Davis, E. B. Q 1965, 34:302-303

DAVIS, ANNETTE
See Sher, Elizabeth

DAVIS, CARROLL
70820　Room to Grow: A Study of Parent-Child Relationships. Toronto: Univ Toronto Pr 1966, xxvi + 214 p

DAVIS, CHARLES A.
See Klaf, Franklin, S.

DAVIS, D. RUSSELL
70821　The family triangle in schizophrenia. M 1961, 34:53-63
70822　Interventions into family affairs. M 1968, 41:73-79
70823　A re-appraisal of Ibsen's Ghosts. Fam Proc 1963, 2:81-94

DAVIS, ELIZABETH B.
70824　The clinical practice of community psychiatry at Harlem Hospital. J Hillside Hosp 1968, 17:3-12

See Lerner, Burton

REVIEW OF:
70825　Davis, A. & Dollard, J. Children of Bondage. The Personality Development of Negro Youth in the Urban South. Q 1965, 34:302-303

DAVIS, ETHEL H.
See Miller, Donald S.

DAVIS, HAROLD L.
70826　Short-term psychoanalytic therapy with hospitalized schizophrenics. R 1965-66, 52(Winter):81-108
　　　　Abs CG RFPsa 1968, 32:365. SRS Q 1966, 35:628-629

DAVIS, HARRY K.

70827 Management of the hostile patient. Southern Med J 1964, 57:563-566
70828 (& Farley, A. J.) Psychodynamics of depressive illness. (Fantasy love-object loss as an etiologic factor.) Dis nerv Sys 1967, 28:105-110

DAVIS, HOWARD R.

See Scher, Sam C.

DAVIS, J. A.

70829 The attitude of parents to the approaching death of their child. Developm Med child Neurol 1964, 6:286-288

DAVIS, J. E.

70830 Corrective therapy, its changing roles. J Ass Phys Ment Rehab 1964, 18:98-100 Passim

DAVIS, J. F.

See Malmo, Robert B.

DAVIS, JOHN M.

70831 (& McCourt, W. F.; Solomon, P.) The effect of visual stimulation on hallucinations and other mental experiences during sensory deprivation. P 1960, 116:889-892
  Abs Leavitt, M. Q 1961, 30:146
70832 Efficacy of tranquilizing and anti-depressant drugs. Arch gen Psychiat 1965, 13:552-572
  Abs PB Q 1968, 37:320
70833 (& McCourt, W. F.; Courtney, J.; Solomon, P.) Sensory deprivation: the role of social isolation. Arch gen Psychiat 1961, 5:84-90

See Courtney, Jon

DAVIS, MARTIN D.

ABSTRACT OF:
70834 Sperling, O. E. Recompenses for learning. Q 1963, 32:149-150

DAVIS, WINBORN E.

See Knight, James A.

DAVISON, G. C

See Lazarus, Arnold A.

DAWES, CAROL J.

70835 Experiments on selected aspects of "primary process" thinking. Dissertation Abstr 1966, 27:607

DAWES, LYDIA G.

70836 Discussion of Furman, E. "Treatment of under-fives by way of their parents." In Weinreb, J. *Recent Developments in Psychoanalytic Child Therapy*, NY: IUP 1960, 135-138

DAWS, PETER P.

70837 The aetiology of mental disorder. Bull Brit Psychol Soc 1967, 20:45-47

DAWSON, JOSEPH G.

70838 (& Noblin, C. D.; Timmons, E. O.) Dynamic and behavioral predictors of hypnotizability. J consult Psychol 1965, 29:76-78
70839 (& Stone, H. K.; Dellis, N. P.) (Eds) Psychotherapy with Schizophrenics. Baton Rouge, La.: Louisiana St Univ Pr 1961, vi + 156 p
          Rv Rey, J. H. J 1962, 43:471-476. First, H. G. Q 1963, 32:416-419

DAY, DOROTHY

See Chapman, L. J.

DAY, JULIANA

See Schaffer, Leslie

DAY, MAX

70840 The natural history of training groups. Int J grp PT 1967, 7:436-447
70841 (& Samrad, E. V.) Psychoanalytically oriented group psychotherapy. Psa Tech 511-532

See Schniewind, H. E.

ABSTRACT OF:
70842 Winnicott, D. W. Dependence in infant care, in child care, and in the psychoanalytic setting. Bull Phila Ass Psa 1963, 13:32-34

DAY, ROBERT A.

70843 The rebirth of Leggatt. Lit & Psych 1963, 13:74-81

DAYMAS, S.

See Launay, C.

DE, NAGENDRANATH

S-44091 Bose's theory of the opposite wish. Abs An Surv Psa 1955, 6:68

DE AJURIAGUERRA, J.

See AJURIAGUERRA, J. DE

DEALY, MARGARET N.

See Prall, Robert C.

DEAN, ARCHIE L.

See Green, Maurice R.

DEAN, EDWARD S.

S-44092 Drowsiness as a symptom of countertransference.
Abs AHM An Surv Psa 1957, 8:271-272

70844 Process, schizophrenic and therapeutic: some misconceptions resulting from language and philosophy. P 1961, 118:61-65

70845 A psychotherapeutic investigation of nagging. R 1964-65, 51(Winter): 555-561

DEAN, SANFORD J.

See Goldstein, Arnold P.

DEAN, STANLEY ROCHELLE

70846 Beyond the unconscious: the ultraconscious. P 1965, 122:471. Bol Asoc Med P Rico 1968, 60:349-354

DE ANDRADE LIMA, HEITOR

See LIMA, HEITOR DE ANDRADE

DEANE, WILLIAM N.

70847 The culture of the patient: an underestimated dimension in psycho-therapy. Int J soc Psychiat 1961, 7:181-186

DEARMAN, HENRY BURKETT

70848 (& Smith, B. M.) Unconscious motivation and the polygraph test. P 1963, 119:1017-1020

DEB, AJIT KUMAR

70849 History of development of psychiatry. Calcutta Med J 1960, 57(9): 313-315

DEB, MAYA

70850 Personality pattern of post-polio paralytics. Samiksa 1967, 21(3):131-138

DE BARAHONA FERNANDES, H. J.

See BARAHONA FERNANDES, H. J. DE

DE BECKER, RAYMOND

70851 The Understanding of Dreams and Their Influence on the History of Man. (Tr: Heron, M.) NY: Hawthorne; London: Allen & Unwin 1968, 432 p
Abs J Am Psa Ass 1969, 17:275

DEBELL, DARYL E.

70852 A critical digest of the literature on psychoanalytic supervision. J Am
Psa Ass 1963, 11:546-575
Abs Dubcovsky, S. Rev Psicoanál 1963, 20:395. Ennis, J. Q 1964,
33:455

DE BELL, GRACE

REVIEW OF:
70853 Fleming, J. & Benedek, T. Psychoanalytic Supervision. A Method of
Clinical Teaching. Q 1968, 37:128-131

DE BERKER, P. U.

70854 What is psychotherapy? Ass PT Bull 1967, 7:12-23

DE BOER, JULIUS

See BOER, JULIUS DE

DE BONO, EDWARD

70855 New Think. NY: Basic Books 1967, 156 p
Rv Sachs, D. M. Bull Phila Ass Psa 1969, 19:229-233

DE BOOR, CLEMENS

See BOOR, CLEMENS DE

DEBRAY, R.

See Lebovici, Serge

DE BUCK, R.

See BUCK, R. DE

DE BUSSCHER, J.

See BUSSCHER, J. DE

DÉCARIE, THÉRÈSE GOUIN

70856 Intelligence and Affectivity in Early Childhood: An Experimental
Study of Jean Piaget's Object Concept and Object Relations. (Fore-
word: Piaget, J.) (Tr: Brandt, E. P. & Brandt, L. W.) NY: IUP 1965;
London: Bailey Bros 1966, xvi + 230 p
Rv Shapiro, T. Q 1968, 37:135-137
70857 A study of the mental and emotional development of the thalidomide
child. In Foss, B. M. *Determinants of Infant Behaviour, IV*, London:
Methuen 1969, 167-187

DE CAROLIS, U.

See CAROLIS, U. DE

DE CENCIO, D.

See Ziller, Robert C.

DECHARMS, RICHARD

70858 (& Wilkins, E. J.) Some effects of verbal expression of hostility. ASP 1963, 66:462-470

DECOBERT, SIMONE

70859 Discussion of Barande, I. Le vu et l'entendu dans la cure. RFPsa 1968, 32:85-86

70860 Discussion of Barande, R. La pulsion de mort. RFPsa 1968, 32:493

70861 Discussion of Geahchan, D. J. Deuil et nostalgie. RFPsa 1968, 32:59-60

70862 Discussion of Gillibert, J. La réminiscence et la cure. RFPsa 1968, 32:418

70863 Discussion of Grunberger, B. En marge de "l'homme aux rats." RFPsa 1967, 31:608

70864 Discussion of Neyraut, M. À propos de l'inhibition intellectuelle. RFPsa 1968, 32:785-786

70865 Discussion of Rouart, J. Les notions d'investissement et de contre-investissement à travers l'évolution des idées freudiennes. RFPsa 1967, 31:237

70866 Discussion of Schmitz, B. Les états limites. RFPsa 1967, 31:261

70867 Discussion of Viderman, S. Narcissisme et rélation d'objet dans la situation analytique. RFPsa 1968, 32:119

70868 Discussion of Viderman, S. Le rapport sujet-objet et la problématique du désir. RFPsa 1968, 32:757-759

70869 Étude clinque d'un cas d'agoraphobie. [Clinical study of a case of agoraphia.] RFPsa 1969, 33:531-546

See Kestemberg, Jean

DECURTINS, F.

70870 Das Erlebnis eines beginnenden schizophrenen Schubes auf Grund einer selbstschilderung. [The experience of a beginning schizophrenic relapse on the basis of a self description.] Schweiz Arch Neurol Neurochir Psychiat 1966, 98:100-105

DE DEMARIA, LAURA ACHARD

See DEMARIA, LAURA ACHARD DE

DEESE, JAMES

70871 The Structure of Association in Language and Thought. Johns Hopkins/London: Oxford Univ Pr 1966, 216 p

DEETZ, JAMES J. F.

See Owen, Roger C.

DE FAILLA, MARIA I.

See FAILLA, MARIA I. DE

DE FERRER, SUSANA L.

See FERRER, SUSANA L. DE

DEFEVER, A.

See Corman, L.

DE FIASCHE, DORA N.

See FIASCHE, DORA N. DE

DE FOKS, GILDA S.

See FOKS, GILDA S. DE

DEFRIES, ZIRA

70872 (& Natchez, G.; Verdiani, F.) Treatment of secondary reading disability in young boys: a pilot study. Sci Psa 1969, 14:89-107

DE GARMA, ELISABETH G.

See GARMA, ELISABETH G. DE

DE GEORGE, RICHARD T.

70873 (Ed) Ethics and Society: Original Essays on Contemporary Moral
Problems. Garden City, NY: Doubleday-Anchor 1966
70874 Psychoanalysis, metaphysics and self-knowledge. Proc Amer Cath Phil
Ass 1961, 35:197-204

DEGKWITZ, RICHARD

70875 Über die Bedeutung von Erwartungen für Übertragung und Wiederholungszwang. [The significance of anticipation for transference and
repetition compulsion.] Nervenarzt 1966, 37(6):263-266

DE GRINBERG, REBECCA V.

See GRINBERG, REBECCA V. DE

DE GROOT, ADRIAAN D.

See GROOT, ADRIAAN D. DE

DEGROOT, JOANNE C.

70876 (& Gleser, G. C.; Gottschalk, L. A.) The relationship between field
dependence-independence, a psychometric measure of response-tend-
ency and certain affect dimensions. Clin Psych 1969

DEHAUDT, H.

See Fau, R. B.

DE HIRSCH, K.

70877 Two categories of learning difficulties in adolescents. Ops 1963, 33:
87-91
Abs JMa RFPsa 1964, 28:448

DE HOYOS, A.

70878 (& De Hoyos, G.) The future direction of social work. 2. The professional mobility of social work and its middle-class orientation. Ops 1968, 38:18-24

DE HOYOS, G.

See De Hoyos, Arturo

DEIKMAN, ARTHUR J.

70879 De-automatization and the mystic experience. Ps 1966, 29:324-338
70880 Discussion of Jenkins, H. "Semantic restraints and the psychedelics." ETC 1966, 142(2):101-116
70881 Experimental meditation. JNMD 1963, 136:329-343
70882 Implication of experimentally induced contemplative meditation. JNMD 1966, 142:101-116

DEIN, ERLING

70883 On the concept of autism. Acta Psychiat Scand 1966, 42:124-135

DEITZ, G. E.

70883A A comparison of delinquents with nondelinquents on self-concept, self-acceptance, and parental identification. J genet Psych 1969, 115: 285-295

DE JARAST, SARA

See JARAST, SARA DE

DEJUNG, BEAT

70884 Regressionen im Verhalten des Menschen. Eine Untersuchung über Probleme der Psychischen Entwicklung und der Psychogenen Regressionen. [Regression in Human Behavior. An Examination of the Problem of Psychic Development and of Psychogenic Regression.] Zürich: Juris-Verlag 1967, 164 p

DE LA FUENTE, RAMÓN

See FUENTE, RAMÓN DE LA

DELALOYE, R.

See Genevard, G.; Schneider, Pierre-Bernard

DE LA MATA, R. G.

70885 (& Gingras, G.; Wittkower, E. D.) Impact of sudden, severe disablement of the father upon the family. Canad Med Ass J 1960, 82:1015-1020

DELANDE, CATHERINE

TRANSLATION OF:
Freud, A. [10307]

DELANO, JAMES GREASON

70886 Psychiatric implications of the teen-ager's problems. JAMA 1963, 184: 539-543
70887 Separation anxiety as a cause of early emotional problems in children. Mayo Clin Proc 1964, 39:743-749

See Saul, Leon J.

DELANY, LLOYD

See Chwast, Jacob

DE LA TORRE, JOAQUÍN

See TORRE, JOAQUÍN DE LA

DELATTRE, JACQUES

REVIEW OF:
70888 de Becker, R. La Vie Tragique de Freud. RFPsa 1968, 32:794-795

DE LA VEGA, GABRIEL

See VEGA, GABRIEL DE LA

DELAY, JEAN PAUL LOUIS

70889 (& Pichot, P.; Lempérière, T.; Ochonisky, A.; Lechevalier, B.; Lefrançois, J.-J.) Etats confusionnels et manifestations d'allure hystérique au cours d'une porphyrie mixte. [States of confusion and manifestations of hysteric character in the course of a mixed porphyria.] Ann med-psychol 1965, 123(1):109-117
70890 (& Volmat, R.) Painting and Chemotherapy in Psychopathology and Pictorial Expression. Basel/NY: Karger 1964, Series I
70891 (& Pichot, P.; Perse, J.) Personnalité obsessionelle, et caractère dit obsessionel: étude clinique et psychométrique. [Obsessive personality and so-called obsessive character: a clinical and psychometric study.] Rev Psychol appl 1962, 12(4):233-262
70892 (& Brion, S.) Le Syndrome de Korsakoff. [Korsakoff's Syndrome.] Paris: Masson & Cie 1969
70893 The Youth of André Gide. (Tr & Abr: Guicharnaud, J.) Chicago/London: Univ Chicago Pr 1963, x + 498 p

DEL CARLO GIANNINI, G.

See CARLO GIANNINI, G. DEL

DELESALLE, S.

70894 (& Plumyene, J.) Avatars de la relation pédagogique à la clinique Dupré. [Avatars of the pedagogical relationship to the Dupré clinic.] Perspectives Psychiat 1965, 10

See Danon-Boileau, Henri

DE LEVITA, DAVID J.

70895 The Concept of Identity. Paris: Mouton 1965, NY: Basic Books 1966, 209 p
Rv Lomas, P. J 1967, 48:124. Miller, A. A. Q 1968, 37:142-143

70896 On the psycho-analytic concept of identity. J 1966, 47:299-305
Abs EVN Q 1968, 37:312

DELGADO, HONORIO

70897 Acerca del tratamiento de las depresiones. [Treatment of depressions.] Rev Neuro-Psiquiat 1960, 23:157-164

70898 [The ego ideal and the identification with the ego.] (Sp) Folia Clin Int 1964, 14:21-24

DELGADO, RAFAEL A.

70899 (& Mannino, F. V.) Some observations of trichotillomania in children. J Amer Acad Child Psychiat 1969, 8:229-246

See Mannino, Fortune V.

D'ELIA, FRANK G.

See Gralnick, Alexander; Silverberg, J. William

DELISLE, FRANÇOISE

70900 Friendship's Odyssey: In Love with Life. London: Delisle 1964, xix + 323 p

DELIUS, L.

70901 Psychologische und psychotherapeutische Aspekte der Rehabilitation von Herzkranken. [Psychological and psychotherapeutic aspects in the rehabilitation of heart patients.] (Ger) Z Kreislaufforsch 1968, 57:84-87

70902 (& Fahrenberg, J.) Psychovegetative Syndrome (Psychosomatic Syn-.dromes). Stuttgart: Georg Thieme Verlag 1966, xi + 290 p

DELLAERT, RENÉ

70903 L'expression libre en psychothérapie. [Free drawing in psychotherapy.] Acta neurol psychiat Belg 1964, 64:9-22

70904 Psychotherapie des schizophrènes par la méthode de la participation engagée. [Psychotherapy of schizophrenia by the method of committed participation.] Psychother Psychosom 1966, 14:118-132

DELLAROSSA, ALIJO

70905 Coexistencia de dos mecanismos defensivos: maníacos y depresivos. [Coexistence of two defensive mechanisms: manic and depressive.] Rev Psicoanál 1962, 19:71-74

See Grinberg, Léon

DELLIS, NICHOLAS P.

70906 (& Stone, H. K.) (Eds) The Training of Psychotherapists—A Multidisciplinary Approach. Baton Rouge: Louisiana St Univ Pr 1961, xii + 195 p
Rv HRB Q 1962, 31:408-409. Payne, S. J 1963, 44:378-380

See Dawson, Joseph G.

DELOR, C. J.

70907 The irritable bowel syndrome. Amer J Gastroent 1967, 47:427-434

DELPIERRE, GUY

70908 Apports de Jung à la psychologie. [Jung and psychology.] Évolut Psychiat 1963, 28(4):589-607
70909 Les Psychothérapies, Finalités, Méthodes, Caracteristiques Relationnelles. [Psychotherapies, Finalities, Methods, Related Characteristics.] Toulouse: E. Privat 1969, 143 p
70910 Les sept instances de la personnalité selon Charles Baudouin. [The seven foundations of personality according to Charles Baudouin.] Cahiers Psychol 1964, 7:31-43

DELTEIL, PIERRE

70911 [Psychotic object relations.] (Fr) Évolut Psychiat 1961, 26:365-397
70911A [Depersonalization, depression acting out and refusal of reality.] (Fr) Ann méd psychol 1969, 1:543-579

ABSTRACTS OF:
70912 Abt, L. E. & Weissman, S. L. Acting out: theoretical and clinical aspects. RFPsa 1968, 32:790
70913 Bertaud, M.-A. Prophylaxie et traitement. RFPsa 1968, 32:178
70914 Fully, G. Médicine pénitentiare et criminologie. RFPsa 1968, 32:633
70915 Gigeroff, A. K. Methods of treatment. RFPsa 1968, 32:178-179
70916 Milutinovic, M. Les tendances récentes de la recherche criminologique et de la pénologie en Yougoslavia. RFPsa 1968, 32:177
70917 Moutin, P. Étude comparative des militaires délinquants avec et sans antécédents judiciares. RFPsa 1968, 32:177
70918 Mucchielli, R. Comment ils deviennent délinquants. RFPsa 1967, 31:497-499
70919 Pinatel, J. Science de l'homme et droit pénal. RFPsa 1968, 32:633
70920 Pinatel, J. Les travaux du Congrès. RFPsa 1968, 32:178
70921 Trotter, M. Scientific research: presentation of conclusions. RFPsa 1968, 32:179

DELUCA, J.

70922 Psychosexual conflict in adolescent enuretics. J Psychol 1968, 68:145-149

DELUCA, JOSEPH NICHOLAS

70923 The structure of homosexuality. J proj Tech 1966, 30:187-191

DE LUCA, P. L.

See LUCA, P. L. DE

DELUCIA, LENORE A.

70924 The toy preference test: a measure of sex-role identification. Child Developm 1963, 34:107-117

DE LYRA CHEBABI, WILSON

See CHEBABI, WILSON DE LYRA

DEMAREST, ELINOR W.

S-44141 (& Winesteine, M. C.) The initial phase of concomitant treatment of twins.
Abs An Surv Psa 1955, 6:292-295

DEMARET, A.

See Bobon, J.

DEMARIA, LAURA ACHARD DE

70925 Homosexual acting out. [Symposium: Acting out.] (Read at Int Psa Cong, July 1967) J 1968, 49:219-220
Abs LHR Q 1969, 38:668

See Alfonso, Olga

DE MARTINO, MANFRED F.

S-44143 (Ed) Dreams and Personality Dynamics.
Abs J Am Psa Ass 1961, 9:168. Rv Pollock, G. H. Q 1961, 30:586-587
70926 (Ed) Sexual Behavior and Personality Characteristics. NY: Citadel Pr 1963, Grove Pr 1966, 412 p

DE MARTINO, RICHARD

See Fromm, Erich

DE MARTIS, DARIO

See MARTIS, DARIO DE

DEMBER, CYNTHIA FOX

See Krug, Othilda

DEMBERG, C. F.

See Schafer, Roy

DEMENT, WILLIAM C.

70927 Discussion of Snyder, F. "Toward an evolutionary theory of dreaming." P 1966, 123:136-142

70928 The effect of dream deprivation. Science 1960, 131:1705-1707
         Abs HD Q 1961, 30:150-151
70929 Experimental dream studies. Sci Psa 1964, 7:129-162, 176-177
70930 (& Fisher, C.) Experimental interference with the sleep cycle. Canad
         Psychiat Ass J 1963, 8:400-405
70931 (& Kahn, E.; Roffwarg, H. P.) The influence of the laboratory situation
         on the dreams of the experimental subject. JNMD 1964, 139:119-131
         Abs BFM Q 1967, 36:141
70932 Possible physiological determinants of a possible dream-intensity cycle.
         Exp Neurol Suppl 1967, 4:38-55
70933 The psychophysiology of dreaming. In Grunebaum, G. E. von & Cail-
         lois, R. *The Dream and Human Societies,* Berkeley/Los Angeles: Univ
         of Calif Pr 1966, 77-107
70934 Recent studies of the biological role of rapid eye movement sleep.
         P 1965, 122:404-408
         Abs Loeb, L. Q 1967, 36:473
70935 (& Wolpert, E. A.) The relation of eye movement, body motility, and
         external stimuli to dream content. J exper Psychol 1958, 55:543-553
70936 Sleep and dreams. Compreh Txbk Psychiat 77-87

         See Antrobus, Judith S.; Clemes, Stanley R.; Fisher, Charles; Gulevich,
         George D.; Kahn, Edwin; Rechtschaffen, Allan; Roffwarg, Howard P.

DEMERITT, S.
See Guerney, Bernard G., Jr.

DE MIJOLLA, A.
See Soulairac, André

DE MONCHAUX, CECILY
See MONCHAUX, CECILY DE

DE MONCHY, RENÉ
See MONCHY, RENÉ DE

DE MONCHY, S. J. R.
70937 Adam—Cain—Oedipus. Am Im 1962, 19:3-17

DEMOULIN, P.
70938 Névrose et Psychose: Essai de Psychopathologie Phénoménologique.
         [Neurosis and Psychosis: Essay on Phenomenological Psychopathology.]
         Louvain, Belgium: Nauwelaerts 1967, 196 p

DE M'UZAN, MARTY
See M'UZAN, MARTY DE

DE M'UZAN, MICHEL
See M'UZAN, MICHEL DE

DE MYER, MARIAM

See Tilton, James R.

DENBER, HERMAN C. B.

70939 Note on the treatment of depression. Canad Psychiat Ass J 1966, 11(Suppl):S141-S145

70940 A study of the therapeutic community. Prog PT 1960, 5:116-121

DEN BREEIJEN, ARIE

See BREEIJEN, ARIE DEN

DENFORD, J. D.

70941 Combined use of drugs and psychotherapy. In *Symposium: Drugs and the Mind*, New Zealand: Univ Otago Med School 1967, 129-135

70942 Depressive reactions of short duration. M 1967, 40:45-53

70943 Emotional problems of doctors starting general practice. New Zeal med J 1969, 69:136-139

70944 The psychodynamics of homosexuality. New Zeal med J 1967, 66(Ps Sp. No.):743-744

DENGROVE, EDWARD

70945 Behavior therapy. [Symposium: The Clinical Relevance of Affect Theory.] (Read at Scient Conf, Council Psa PT, 14 Feb 1965) R 1966, 53:293-298

Abs SRS Q 1967, 36:472

DEN HARTOG, GLORIA

See Kanter, Stanley S.

DENIKER, P.

70946 (& Sempe, J. C.) Les personnalités psychopathique. Essai de définition structurale. [The psychopathic personalities. Attempt at a structural definition.] (Fr) Encéph 1967, 56:5-32

See Green, André

DENIS PEGGE, C.

70947 The mode of the dream. JMS 1962, 108:26-36

DENKER, HENRY

70948 A Far Country, a Drama in Three Acts. NY: French 1961, 98 p

70949 Preliminary journey to far country. Theatre Arts 1962, 46(Dec):26-27

DENKER, ROLF

70950 Aufklärung über Aggression; Kant, Darwin, Freud, Lorenz, u. a. [Clarification of Aggression: Kant, Darwin, Freud, Lorenz, etc.] Stuttgart: Kohlhammer 1966, 144 p

DENN, R.

70951 Psychoanalysis and psychiatric nursing. Nurs Res 1963, 12:93-98

DENNEHY, C. M.

70952 Childhood bereavement and psychiatric illness. Brit J Psychiat 1966, 112:1049-1069

DENNER, BRUCE

70953 (& Bibace, R.) A developmental analysis of the amnesic syndrome. M 1967, 40:163-168

DENNIS, WAYNE

70954 (& Cartwright, D.; Kelly, E. L.; Skinner, B. F.; Fisher, A. E.; Rosenzweig, M. R.; Krech, D.; Bennett, E. L.; Milner, P. M.; Estes, W. K.; Newell, A.; Simon, H. A.; Kendler, H. H.; Mowrer, O. H.) Current Trends in Psychological Theory: A Bicentennial Program. Pittsburgh, Pa.: Univ of Pittsburgh Pr 1961, x + 229 p

DENNY, JOSEPH V.

See Steisel, Ira M.

DENNY, REUEL

See Riesman, David

DE-NOUR, A. KAPLAN

See Noy, Pinchas

DENT, ALAN

70955 Birds and words [Freud; film]. Illustrated London News 1963, 243 (14 Sept):396

DE OLIVEIRA, WALDEREDO ISMAEL

See OLIVEIRA, WALDEREDO ISMAEL DE

DE OTAOLA, JR.

See OTAOLA, JR., DE

DE PAIVA, LUIZ MILLER

See PAIVA, LUIZ MILLER DE

DEPREZ, HUGUETTE

70956 [A psychological understanding of the corrida.] (Fr) In Ey, H. *Entretiens Psychiatriques, #10*, Toulouse, France: Edouard Privat 1964

DE PERROT, E.

See PERROT, E. DE

DE RACKER, GENEVIÈVE T.

See RACKER, GENEVIÈVE T. DE

DERBOLOWSKY, UDO

70956A [Guided position changes as a technic in psychoanalyzed groups.] (Ger) Z Psychother med Psychol 1969, 19:204-207

70957 [Multilateral resistance in patient groups.] (Ger) Z Psychother med Psychol 1964, 14:74-79

70958 Psycholytische Intervalltherapie mit LSD 25 oder ambulante analytische Psychotherapie? [Psycholytic interval therapy with LSD 25 or ambulant analytical psychotherapy?] Z Psychother med Psychol 1966, 16:33-38

70959 Über den Abstinenzbegriff bei Sigmund Freud mit seinen Konsequenzen für die Gruppenpsychotherapie. [On Sigmund Freud's concept of abstinence with its consequences for group psychotherapy.] (Ger) Z Psychother med Psychol 1968, 18:177-184

70960 Über eine Dreistufentechnik der Traumbearbeitung. [A three stage technique of dream elaboration.] Prax PT 1968, 13:145-156

DERBYSHIRE, ROBERT L.

70961 Adolescent identity crisis in urban Mexican Americans in East Los Angeles. In Brody, E. B. *Minority Group Adolescents in the United States*, Baltimore: Williams & Wilkins 1968, 73-110

70962 (& Brody, E. B.; Schleifer, C.) Family structure of young adult Negro male mental patients: preliminary observations from urban Baltimore. JNMD 1963, 136:245-251

70963 (& Brody, E. B.) Identity and ethnocentrism in American Negro college students. MH 1964, 48:202-208

70964 (& Brody, E. B.) Marginality, identity and behaviour in the American Negro: a functional analysis. Int J soc Psychiat 1964, 10:7-13

70965 (& Brody, E. B.) Personal identity and ethnocentrism in American Negro college students. MH 1964, 48:65-69

70966 (& Brody, E. B.) Social distance and identity conflict in Negro college students. Sociol & soc Res 1964, 48:301-314

See Brody, Eugene B.

DERCKSEN, S. J.

70967 [Man in his future environment.] (Dut) T soc Geneesk 1964, 42:716-719

DE REUCK, A. V. S.

70968 (& Knight, J.) (Eds) Conflict in Society. London: Churchill 1966, 467 p

70969 (& Porter, R.) (Eds) The Mentally Abnormal Offender: A Ciba Foundation Symposium. Int Psychiat Clin, 5(3), Boston: Little, Brown 1968, xii + 260 p

70970 (& Porter, R.) (Eds) Transcultural Psychiatry. London: Churchill 1965, 396 p

DERI, FRANCES

TRANSLATION OF:
(& Brunswick, D.) Freud, S. [73588]

DERI, OTTO

REVIEW OF:
70971 Brophy, B. Mozart the Dramatist: A Psychological and Historical Study
       of Genius. Am Im 1965, 22:212-215

DERI, SUSAN K.

70972 Changing concepts of transference in depth-psychology. Schweiz Z
       Psychol 1967, 51(Suppl):114-125
70973 Freedom in psychotherapy. (Read at Ass Applied Psa, 21 Oct 1960)
       PPR 1961, 48(3):97-115
70974 Interpretation and language. In Hammer, E. F. *Use of Interpretation
       in Treatment: Technique and Art*. NY: Grune & Stratton 1968, 141-147
70975 The role of genotropism in borderline states. In *Beiträge zur Diagnostik,
       Prognostik and Therapie des Schicksals*. Bern: Hans Huber

DE RISIO, C.

See RISIO, C. DE

DERKSEN, H. E.

See Musaph, Herman

DE RODRIGUÉ, EMILIO

See RODRIGUÉ, EMILIO DE

DE ROSA, R.

See ROSA, R. DE

DE ROSIS, HELEN

70976 A homogeneous group. J Psa in Groups 1966-67, 2(1):1-8
70977 A preventive community psychiatry project and its relationship to
       psychoanalytic principles. Psa 1968, 28:129-138
70978 Preventive psychiatry: a homecoming for psychoanalysis? J Psa in
       Groups 1968, 2(2):1-3

DE ROSIS, LOUIS EDWARD

70979 Alienation and group analysis. Psa 1961, 21:263-272
70980 (& Becker, B. J.; Wassell, B. B.; Kraft, I. A.; Abell, R. G.) Sexuality in
       group psychoanalysis: a round table discussion. Emotional distortion
       of sexuality in group psychoanalysis. Psa 1960, 20:197-220
70981 Suicide: the Horney point of view. In Farberow, N. L. & Schneidman,
       E. S. *The Cry for Help*, NY/Toronto/London: McGraw-Hill 1961,
       236-254

D'ERRICO, A.

See ERRICO, A. D'

DERSHOWITZ, ALAN M.

See Katz, Jay

DE SAIX, CHRISTINE

See Polansky, Norman A.

DE SALAZAR, M. P.

See SALAZAR, M. P. DE

DE SAUSSURE, JANICE

See SAUSSURE, JANICE DE

DE SAUSSURE, RAYMOND

See SAUSSURE, RAYMOND DE

DE SAUVAGE NOLTING, W. J. J.

See SAUVAGE NOLTING, W. J. J. DE

DE SAVITSCH, EUGENE

70982 Homosexuality. Transvestism and Change of Sex. Springfield, Ill.: Thomas 1958

DESCHIN, C. S.

70983 The future direction of social work. I. From concern with problems to emphasis on prevention. Ops 1968, 38:9-17

DE SCHUTT, FANNY ELMAN

See SCHUTT, FANNY ELMAN DE

DESCOMBES, GASTON

70984 Le symbolisme du feu et de l'urine dans un cas de névrose. [The symbolism of fire and urine in a case of neurosis.] Schweiz Z Psychol 1963, 22:304-337

DESHAIES, M.

70985 Les significations de la psychotherapie. [The meaning of psychotherapy.] Bull Psychol, Paris 1965, 18:934-941

DE SILVA, MANIKKU W.

70986 A study of motivational theory in early Buddhism with references to the psychology of Freud. Dissertation Abstr 1968, 28:4209

DE SIMONE GABURRI, G.

See SIMONE GABURRI, G. DE

DES LAURIERS, AUSTIN M.

70987 The Experience of Reality in Childhood Schizophrenia. Monograph
Series on Schizophrenia No. 6. NY:IUP; London: Tavistock 1962, 215 p
Rv Geleerd, E. R. Q 1964, 33:110-113
70988 The schizophrenic child. Arch gen Psychiat 1967, 16:194-201

DESMEDT, D.

70989 Psychodrame analytique en externat médico-pédagogique pour enfants
débiles. [Analytical psychodrama in special education for defective
children.] Rev Np inf 1967, 15:869-882

DESMONDE, WILLIAM H.

70990 Magic Myth and Money: The Origin of Money in Religious Ritual.
NY: Free Pr of Glencoe 1962, 208 p
Abs Am Im 1964, 21:190. Rv Hartogs, R. PPR 1962, 49(4):124.
MK Q 1963, 32:122-123
S-44177 The ritual origins of Shakespeare's *Titus Andronicus.*
Abs An Surv Psa 1955, 6:461

DESOILLE, ROBERT

70991 The directed daydream. (Tr: Haronian, F.) Psychosynthesis Res
Foundation 1966, (18), iii + 33 p
70992 Psychanalyse et rêve éveillé dirigé. [Psychoanalysis and directed daydream.] Inform Psychol 1962, 8:13-23
70993 [Outline of the technic of the directed daydream in psychotherapy.]
(Fr) Évolut Psychiat 1959, (4):575-583

D'ESOPO, ROSE

See Bursten, Ben

DESPERT, JULIETTE LOUISE

70994 The Emotionally Disturbed Child—Then and Now. NY: Vantage Pr
1965
Rv J.S. RFPsa 1968, 32:330
70995 Introducing the child to the therapeutic situation. In Haworth, M. R.
Child Psychotherapy, NY/London: Basic Books 1964, 87-90
70996 Using the first interview as a basis for therapeutic planning. In Haworth, M. R. *Child Psychotherapy,* NY/London: Basic Books 1964,
110-114

DESPLANCHES, J.

See Couléon, H.

DESROCHES, HARRY FRANCIS

70997 (& Kaiman, B. D.) The relationship between dream recall and symptoms of emotional instability. Clin Psych 1964, 20:350-352

DESTROOPER, J.

See Bonaccorse, Marie T.

DESVIGNES, FRANÇOIS

TRANSLATION OF:
Bigham, T. J. (Ed): [67714]

DE SZILVAY, G.

See SZILVAY, G. DE

DETENGOF, F. F.

70998 [Critique of psychosomatic medicine and its basis—freudianism and neofreudianism.] (Rus) Med Zh Uzbek 1961, 9:6-12

DE TONI, G.

See TONI, G. DE

DE TRAUBENBERG, N. R.

See TRAUBENBERG, N. R. DE

DETRE, T.

70999 Sleep disorder and psychosis. Canad Psychiat Ass J 1966, 11(Suppl): S169-S177

DETTMERING, PETER

71000 Dichtung und Psychoanalyse. Thomas Mann, Rainer Maria Rilke, Richard Wagner. [Poetry and Psychoanalysis. Thomas Mann, Rainer Maria Rilke, Richard Wagner.] Munich: Nymphenburger Verlag 1969, 200 p
71001 Die Inzestsproblematik im späteren Werk Thomas Mann's. [The problem of incest in Thomas Mann's later works.] Psyche 1966, 20:440-465
71002 [Suicide problems in Thomas Mann's work.] Psyche 1965, 19:547-569

DEUTSCH, ALBERT

71003 Challenges for orthopsychiatry: community perspectives. Ops 1956, 26:675-682
71004 Current trends in psychiatric research. In Brill, N.Q. *Psychiatry in Medicine*, Berkeley/Los Angeles: Univ of Calif Pr 1962, 120-135
71005 (& Fishman, H.) (Eds) The Encyclopedia of Mental Health. Vols. I & V. NY: Franklin Watts 1963, xxiv + 2,228 p
        Rv McDevitt, J. B. Q 1965, 34:299-300
71006 (Ed) Sex Habits of American Men. NY: Prentice-Hall, 194 p

DEUTSCH, ALBERT L.

71007 (& Ainbinder, M.; Becker, E.; Blumenfield, M.) Group therapy schizophrenics in an outpatient clinic. J Psa in Groups 1966-67, 2(1):30-38

See Edwards, John W.

DEUTSCH, ALICE R.

71008 Malingering and conversion reactions in opthalmology. J Tenn Med
Ass 1968, 61:694-698

DEUTSCH, CYNTHIA P.

See Deutsch, Martin; Freedman, Alfred M.

DEUTSCH, DANICA

71009 Alfred Adler and Margaret Mead: a juxtaposition. J ind Psych 1966,
22:228-233

See Adler, Kurt

DEUTSCH, FELIX

71010 (& Jones, A.; Stokvis, B.; Freyberger, H.; Stunkard, A.) (Eds) Advances in Psychosomatic Medicine, Vol 4. Training in Psychosomatic
Medicine. Basel: Karger; London: Bailey Bros; NY: Hafner Publ Co
1964, 221 p
Abs J Am Psa Ass 1966, 14:228
71011 Analytic posturology and synesthesiology: some important theoretical
and clinical aspects. R 1963, 50:40-67
S-44186 The associative anamnesis and sector therapy as a psychoanalytically
oriented approach to patients.
Abs DW An Surv Psa 1958, 9:361-363
71012 Body, mind, and art. In Kepes, G. The Visual Arts Today, Wesleyan
Univ Pr 1960, 34-45
71013 (& Thompson, D.; Pinderhughes, C.; Goodglass, H.) Body, Mind, and
the Sensory Gateways. NY: Basic Books 1963, 106 p
Abs J Am Psa Ass 1964, 12:259-260. Rv Kaplan, D. M. R 1963,
50:686-687. Engel, G. L. Q 1964, 33:433-435
S-44190 Correlations of verbal and nonverbal communication in interviews
elicited by the associative anamnesis.
Abs Lebovici, S. RFPsa 1961, 25:156
S-44191 The creative passion of the artist and its synthetic aspects.
Abs Racamier, P. C. RFPsa 1961, 25:284
71014 Entering the mind through the sensory gateways in associative anamnesis. PSM 1960, 22:466-479
Abs JPG Q 1961, 30:454
S-44193 A footnote to Freud's "Fragment of an Analysis of a Case of Hysteria."
Abs SO An Surv Psa 1957, 8:9-10
71015 Mind, body, and art. II. Studies of the pictographic reflections of the
body image on the drawings of children. Acta psychother psychosom
1963, 11:181-192

71016 Principios de "terapia de sector." Medicina Clinica 1959, 33(6):413
    Principles of sector therapy. Acta psychother psychosom 1960, 8: 209-219
    Abs SLe RFPsa 1961, 25:156

S-6717 Psychoanalyse und innere Medizin. In Kaufman, M. R. & Heiman, M. *Evolution of Psychosomatic Concepts,* NY: IUP 1964, 47-55

71017 Psychodynamics. In Brill, N. Q. *Psychiatry in Medicine,* Berkeley/Los Angeles: Univ of Calif Pr 1962, 79-99

S-44204 Reflections on Freud's one hundredth birthday.
    Abs RZ An Surv Psa 1956, 7:9-10

71018 Some principles of correlating verbal and non-verbal communication. Meth Res PT 166-184

71018A Training in psychosomatic medicine. Adv PSM 1964, 4

See Waller, John V.

DEUTSCH, HELENE

S-6759 Absence of grief. In author's *Neuroses and Character Types* 226-236

71019 Acting out in the transference relationship. J Amer Acad Child Psychiat 1963, 2:160-175. In author's *Neuroses and Character Types* 363-373

S-6761 Über bestimmte Widerstandsformen.
    A discussion of certain forms of resistance. In author's *Neuroses and Character Types* 248-261. Heirs Freud 235-252

71020 Bisexuality and immortality in the Dionysus myth. (Read at NY Psa Soc, 11 Apr 1967)
    Abs Donadeo, J. Q 1968, 37:321-322

71021 The contemporary adolescent girl. Sem in psychiat 1969, 1:99-112

71022 Discussant: "House Officers." Teach Dyn Psychiat 268-270

S-6763 Don Quijote und Don Quijotismus.
    Don Quixote and Don Quixotisms. In author's *Neuroses and Character Types* 218-225

S-6764 Der erste Liebeskummer eines 2 jährigen Knaben.
    A two-year-old boy's first love comes to grief. In author's *Neuroses and Character Types* 159-164

S-6765 Ein Fall von Hühnerphobie.
    A case of hen phobia. In author's *Neuroses and Character Types* 84-96

S-6766 Ein Fall Von hysterischer Schicksalneurose.
    Hysterical fate neurosis. In author's *Neuroses and Character Types* 14-28

S-6767 Ein Fall von Katzen phobie.
    Anxiety states: diffused anxiety—a case of cat phobia. In author's *Neuroses and Character Types* 74-83

71023 Frigidity in women. In author's *Neuroses and Character Types* 358-362

S-6772 Zur Genese der Platzangst.
    Agoraphobia. In author's *Neuroses and Character Types* 97-116

S-6773A Hysterische Konversionssymptome—Anfälle. Dämmerzustände.
    Hysterical conversion symptoms: fits, trance states. In author's *Neuroses and Character Types* 57-73

S-6773B Hysterische Konversionssymptome: Lähmung, Sprachstörungen, Fresslust.
>Hysterical conversion symptoms: paralysis, speech defects, gluttony. In author's *Neuroses and Character Types* 43-56

S-6773c Hysterische Konversionssymptome: Nachtangst, Bettnässen, Potenzstörungen.
>Hysterical conversion symptoms: pavor nocturnus, bedwetting, impotence. In author's *Neuroses and Character Types* 29-42

S-44209 The impostor: contribution to ego psychology of a type of psychopath. In author's *Neuroses and Character Types* 319-338. In Levitt, M. *Readings in Psychoanalytic Psychology* 124-139
>Abs An Surv Psa 1955, 6:196-199

S-6774 Über das induzierte Irresein (folie à deux).
>Folie à deux. In author's *Neuroses and Character Types* 237-247

71024 *Lord Jim* and depression. In author's *Neuroses and Character Types* 353-357

S-6777 Melancholische und depressive Zustände.
>Melancholic and depressive states. In author's *Neuroses and Character Types* 145-158
>Stati melanconici e depressivi. Riv Psa 1962, 8:15-24

S-6778 Mütterlichkeit und Sexualität.
>Motherhood and sexuality. In author's *Neuroses and Character Types* 190-192

71025 Neuroses and Character Types. NY: IUP; London: HIP 1965, xii + 388 p
>Abs J Am Psa Ass 1966, 14:234. Rv Gulotta, G. Riv Psa 1966, 12:220-221

71026 Posttraumatic amnesias and their adaptive function. Psa—Gen Psychol 437-455

71027 The psychiatric component in gynecology. Prog Gyn 1950, 2:207-217. In author's *Neuroses and Character Types* 305-318

71028 A Psychoanalytic Study of the Myth of Dionysus and Apollo: Two Variants of the Son-Mother Relationship. NY: IUP 1969, 101 p

S-44212 Psychoanalytic therapy in the light of follow-up. In author's *Neuroses and Character Types* 339-352
>Abs JTM Q 1961, 30:138

S-6786 Psychologie der manisch-depressiven Zustände insbesondere der chronischen Hypomanie.
>The psychology of manic-depressive states, with particular reference to chronic hypomania. In author's *Neuroses and Character Types* 203-217

S-6789A Die Rolle des aktuellen Konfliktes in der Neurosenbildung.
>The part of the actual conflict in the formation of neurosis. In author's *Neuroses and Character Types* 3-13

71029 Selected Problems of Adolescence. NY: IUP 1967; London: Hogarth 1968, 134 p
>Rv Cohen, K. D. Bull Phila Ass Psa 1969, 19:167-168

71030 Some clinical considerations of the ego ideal. J Am Psa Ass 1964, 12:512-516
>Abs JLSt Q 1967, 36:131-132. CG RFPsa 1968, 32:174

S-6791 Some forms of emotional disturbance and their relationship to schizo-phrenia. In author's *Neuroses and Character Types* 262-281
S-6792 Some psychoanalytic observations in surgery. In author's *Neuroses and Character Types* 282-304
S-6796 Über die weibliche Homosexualität.
Homosexuality in women. In author's *Neuroses and Character Types* 165-189
S-6798A Zwangsvorstellungen.
Obsessional ideas. In author's *Neuroses and Character Types* 134-144
S-6798B Zwangszeremoniell und Zwangshandlungen.
Obsessional ceremonial and obsessional acts. In author's *Neuroses and Character Types* 117-133

DEUTSCH, J. A.

71031 (& Blumen, H. L.) Counter-injection: a new technique for the analysis of drinking. Nature, London 1962, 196(4850):196-197

DEUTSCH, LAWRENCE

ABSTRACTS OF:
71032 Ekstein, R. & Wallerstein, J. Choice of interpretation in the treatment of borderline and psychotic children. An Surv Psa 1957, 8:237-239
71033 Hirschberg, J. C. Parental anxieties accompanying sleep disturbance in young children. An Surv Psa 1957, 8:210-212
71034 Rubenstein, B. O. & Levitt, M. Some observations regarding the role of fathers in child analysis. An Surv Psa 1957, 8:229-231
71035 Shengold, L. L. The parent as Sphinx. Q 1962, 31:304-305

DEUTSCH, MARTIN

71036 Cognition. Compreh Txbk Psychiat 158-166
71037 (& Bloom, R. D.; Brown, B. R.; Deutsch, C. P.; Goldstein, L. S.; John, V. P.; Katz, P. A.; Levinson, A.; Peisach, E. C.; Whiteman, M.) The Disadvantaged Child. NY: Basic Books 1967, xii + 400 p
71038 The role of social class in language development and cognition. Ops 1965, 35:78-88
Abs JMa RFPsa 1966, 30:522
71039 (& Jensen, A.; Katz, I.) (Eds) Social Class, Race and Psychological Development. NY: Holt, Rinehart & Winston 1968, 423 p

See Freedman, Alfred M.; Ravich, Robert A.

DEUTSCH, MORTON

° ° ° Foreword to Sanford, N. *The American College. A Psychological and Social Interpretation of the Higher Learning*, NY/London/Sydney: Wiley 1962
71040 (& Krauss, R. M.) Theories in Social Psychology. NY/London: Basic Books, x + 244 p

DEUTSCHER, MAX

71041 Adult work and developmental models. Ops 1968, 38:882-892
71042 (& Green, M. R.) Mental health is a *social* problem. Ops 1967, 37:832-834

DE VALOIS, RUSSELL L.

See Dulaney, Donelson E., Jr.

DEVAULT, SPENCER

See Davids, A.; Mora, George

DEVEREUX, GEORGE

71043 The abduction of Hippodameia as "Aition" of a Greek animal husbandry rite. Studi e Materiali di Storia delle Religioni 1965, 36:3-25
71044 (Adultery). Sexology 1959, 26:84-85
S-44220 The anthropological roots of psychoanalysis.
         Abs RJA An Surv Psa 1958, 9:450-451
71045 (& La Barre, W.) Art and mythology: a general theory. In Kaplan, B. *Studying Personality Cross-Culturally*, NY/Evanston/London: Harper & Row 1961, 361-403
S-44223 The awarding of a penis as compensation for rape.
         Abs JAL An Surv Psa 1957, 8:309-310
71046 Der Begriff der Vaterschaft bei den Mohave Indianern. [The concept of fatherhood among the Mohave Indians.] Z Ethnologie 1937, 69:27-78
71047 The cannibalistic impulses of parents. Psa Forum 1966, 1:114-124; 129-130
S-44226 Charismatic leadership and crisis.
         Abs An Surv Psa 1955, 6:437-440
71048 Comment on Lessa's review. Amer social Rev 1956, 21:88-89
71049 Compte rendu d'enseignement. [Report on education.] In *Annuaire 1963/4, École Pratique des Hautes Études (6e Section)* 1964; 1965, 251-252; 1966, 206-208; 1967, 183-184; 1968, 183-184
71050 Considérations psychanalytiques sur la divination, particulièrement en Grèce. [Psychoanalytic notes on divination, particularly in Greece.] In Caquot, A. & Leibovici, M. *La Divination, Vol. II,* Paris: PUF 1968, 449-471
71051 Considérations ethnopsychanalytiques sur la notion de parenté. [Ethno-psychoanalytic considerations on the idea of kinship.] Homme 1965, 5:224-247
S-44229 A counteroedipal episode in Homer's *Iliad.*
         Abs An Surv Psa 1955, 6:404-405
71052 Cultural factors in hypnosis and suggestion: an examination of primitive data. Int J clin exp Hyp 1966, 14:273-291
71053 La délinquence sexuelle des jeunes filles dans société "puritaine." [Sexual delinquency of young girls in "puritanical" society.] Temps mod 1964, 29:621-659
71054 Discussion of Lipton, E. L. et al: "Autonomic function in the neonate." PSM 1960, 22:65-67

71055 Discussion of Viderman, S. "Narcissisme et relation d'objet dans la situation analytique." RFPsa 1968, 32:119-120
71056 The displacement of modesty from pubis to face. R 1965-66, 52:391-399
S-44234 Dream learning and individual ritual differences in Mohave shamanism. Abs JLan An Surv Psa 1957, 8:323
71057 Education and discipline in Mohave society. Primitive Man 1950, 23:85-102
71058 The Enetian Horse of Alkman's Partheneion. Hermes 1966, 94:129-134
71059 The Enetian horses of Hippolytos. Antiquité Classique 1964, 33:375-383
71060 Essais d'Ethnopsychiatrie Générale. [Essays on General Ethno-Psychiatry.] Paris: Gallimard 1969
71061 An ethnopsychiatric note on property destruction in Cargo-Cults. Man 1964, 64:184-185
71062 Ethnopsychological aspects of the terms "deaf" and "dumb." Anthropol Q 1964, 37:68-71
71063 The exploitation of ambiguity in Pindaros O. Rheinisches Museum für Philologie 1966, 109:298
71064 Fausse non-reconnaissance. Clinical sidelights on the role of possibility in science. BMC 1967, 31:69-78
S-44239 Finger nails.
        Japanese: Tokyo J Psa 1960, 18(6):1-3
71065 From Anxiety to Method in the Behavioral Sciences. Paris/The Hague: Mouton 1967, xx + 376 p
71066 Funcion complementaria de la psicoterapia y de la educacion. [The complementary function of psychotherapy and education.] Criminalia 1956, 22(2):90-94
71067 Functioning units in Há(rhn)de:an(ng) Society. Primitive Man 1937, 10:1-7
71068 Greek pseudo-homosexuality. Symbolae Osloenses 1967, 42:69-92
71069 A heuristic measure of cultural affinity. Anthropol Q 1961, 35:24-28
71070 Homer's wild she-mules. J Hellenic Studies 1965, 85:29-32
71071 Homosexuality among the Mohave Indians. In Owen, R. C. et al: The North American Indians, NY: Macmillan 1967, 410-416
71072 The human animal: a rejoinder. Man 1955, 55(124):111-112
71073 L'image de l'enfant dans deux tribus, Mohave et Sedang, et son importance pour la psychiatrie infantile. [The image of the child in 2 tribes: Mohave and Sedang. Its importance in child Psychology.] Rv Np inf 1968, 16:375-390
71074 [Intervention.] (Fr) Évolut psychiat 1966, 31:507-512
71075 The Kolaxaian Horse of Alkman's Partheneion. Classical Q 1965, 15:176-184
71076 Laws to live by—not under. Comm Educ 1965, 1:299-312
71077 The lifting of a refractory amnesia through a startle reaction to an unpredictable stimulus. J Hillside Hosp 1960, 9:218-223
        Abs JA Q 1961, 30:451
71078 Loss of identity, impairment of relationships, reading disability. Q 1966, 35:18-39
        Abs LDr RFPsa 1967, 31:330

71079 Maladie mentale et société. [Mental illness and society.] Adventure Humaine 1967, 4:115-118

71080 Mohave Ethnopsychiatry and Suicide: The Psychiatric Knowledge and the Psychic Disturbances of an Indian Tribe. Washington, D.C.: Smithsonian Inst, Bureau of American Ethnology, Bulletin 175, 1961, 586 p
Rv Gorer, G. J 1963, 44:245-248

71081 Mohave Indian personality. Bull Amer Psa Ass 1950, 6:33-35

71082 Mumbling. The relationship between a resistance and frustrated auditory curiosity in childhood. J Am Psa Ass 1966, 14:478-484
Abs Cuad Psa 1967, 3:56. CG RFPsa 1968, 32:356. JLSt Q 1969, 38:337

71083 La naissance d'Aphrodite. [The birth of Aphrodite.] In *Mélanges Claude Lévi-Strauss*, Paris/The Hague: Mouton 1969

71084 La nature du stress. [The nature of stress.] Rev Méd psychosom 1966, 8:103-113

71085 Neurotic downward identification. Am Im 1965, 22:77-95
Abs Cuad Psa 1966, 2:127. JWS Q 1966, 35:315

71086 (& Hoffman, F. H.) Non-recognition of the patient by the therapist. An analysis of a countertransference distortion related to the therapist's professional stance. PPR 1961, 48(3):41-61
Abs LDr RFPsa 1962, 27:348

S-44249 Normal and abnormal: the key problem of psychiatric anthropology.
Abs WAF An Surv Psa 1956, 7:383-385

S-44250 A note on the feminine significance of the eyes.
Abs AS An Surv Psa 1956, 7:161

71087 Notes sur une "introduction à l'ethnologie." [Notes on "introduction to ethnology."] Ethnologia Europaea 1967, 1:232-237

71088 Obituary: Geza Roheim 1891-1953. Amer Anthropologist 1953, 55:420

71089 Observation and belief in Aischylos' accounts of dreams. Psychother Psychosom 1967, 15:114-134. In Philippopoulos, G. S. *Dynamics in Psychiatry*, Basel/NY: Karger 1968, 30-50

S-44254 Obsessive doubt: concealment or revelation?
Abs EFA Q 1961, 30:600

71090 Les origines sociales de la schizophrénie. [Social origins of schizophrenia.] Inform psychiat 1965, 41:783-799

71091 Orthopraxis: the cancelling of one parapraxis by another. Psychiat Q 1968, 42:726-737

71092 Pathogenic dreams in non-Western societies. In Grunebaum, G. E. von & Caillois, R. *The Dream and Human Society*, Berkley, Calif: Univ Calif Pr 1966, 213-228

S-44256 Penelope's character.
Abs SO An Surv Psa 1957, 8:343-344

71093 The perception of motion in infancy related to development of physical theory of motion. BMC 1965, 29:143-147

71094 The posthumous voices. Contempo Psychol 1959, 4:253-254

71095 Preface to special issue in honor of Prof. D. Kouretas. Psychother Psychosom 1967, 15:vi-vii

71096 Primitive psychiatric diagnosis: a general theory of the diagnostic process. In Galdston, I. *Man's Image in Medicine and Anthropology*, NY: IUP 1963, 337-373

S-44260 A primitive slip of the tongue.
Abs JLan An Surv Psa 1957, 8:111

71097 La psychanalyse et l'histoire: une application à l'histoire de Sparte. [Psychoanalysis and history: an application to the history of Sparta.] Annales, Paris 1965, 20:18-44

S-44262 Psychoanalysis as anthropological field work: data and theoretical implications.
Abs Schmale, H. T. An Surv Psa 1957, 8:315-316

S-44263 (Ed) Psychoanalysis and the Occult.
Rv Löfgren, L. B. J Am Psa Ass 1968, 16:146-178

71098 Psychoanalytic reflections on experiences of "levitation." Int J Parapsychol 1960, 2(2):39-60

S-44264 A psychoanalytic scrutiny of certain techniques of direct analysis.
Abs Sapochnik, L. Rev psicoanál 1961, 18:180

71099 A psychoanalytic study of contraception. (Mimeograph) NY: Planned Parenthood Federation of America 1960. J Sex Res 1965, 1:105-134

71100 Rapports cliniques et phylogénétiques entre les odeurs et les emotions dans la névrose caracterielle d'un hottentot griqua. [Clinical and phylogenetic relationships between odors and emotions in the character neurosis of a Hottentot.] Psychopathol afr 1966, 2(1):65-76

71101 The realistic basis of fantasy. Its relation to testicular castration anxiety and the unconscious equation: testicles = breasts. J Hillside Hosp 1968, 17:13-20

S-6853 Reality and Dream: The Psychotherapy of a Plains Indian. (Pref: Mead, M.) NY: Anchor Books 1969 (rev. ed), xlviii + 615 p

71102 Réflexions ethno-psychanalytiques sur la fatique névrotique. [Ethnopsychoanalytic observations concerning nervous fatigue.] Rev Méd Psychosom 1966, 8:235-241. In Travaux du Troisième Congrès International de Médecine Psychosomatique 1967, 159-165

S-44267 A regressively determined parapraxis.
Japanese: Tokyo J Psa 1960, 18(7):1-5

71103 Rejoinder to Parsons and Wintrob. Transcultural psychiat Res 1964, 1:167-169

71104 La rénonciation à l'identité: défense contre l'aneantissement. [Renunciation of identity: defense against destruction.] RFPsa 1967, 31:104-142

S-44269 Retaliatory homosexual triumph over the father. A further contribution to the counter-Oedipal sources of the Oedipus complex.
Abs Bianchedi, E. T. de Rev Psicoanál 1961, 18:178. JB Q 1961, 30:299

71105 Schizophrenia vs. neurosis and the use of "premature" deep interpretations as confrontations in classical and in direct analysis. Psychiat Q 1960, 34:710-721

71106 Une science de la sexualité: pourquoi? [A science of sexuality: why?] Preface to Henriquez, F. La Sexualité Sauvage, Paris 1965

71106A [Separation: subject and observer.] (Fr) Rev med Psychosom 1969, 11:335-351

71107 Shamans as neurotics. Amer Anthropologist 1961, 63:1088-1090

S-44270 The significance of the external female genitalia and of female orgasm for the male.
Abs AL An Surv Psa 1958, 9:469

71108 Sociopolitical functions of the Oedipus myth in early Greece. Q 1963, 32:205-214
Greek: Epoches 1964, 17:18-22

S-6862 Some criteria for the timing of confrontations and interpretations. Psa Clin Inter 79-92

71109 Los sueños patogenos en las sociedades no occidentales. In Grunebaum, G. E. von & Caillois, R. *Los Suenos y las Sociedades Humanas,* Buenos Aires: Editorial Sudamericana 1964
Pathogenic dreams in non-western societies. In Grunebaum, G. E. von & Caillois, R. *The Dream and Human Societies,* Berkeley, Calif: Univ Calif Pr 1966, 213-228
Rêves pathogènes dans les sociétés non-occidentales. In Caillois, R. & Grunebaum, G. E. von: *Le Rêve et les Sociétés Humaines,* Paris: Gallimard 1967

71110 Une théorie ethnopsychiatrique de l'adaptation. [An ethnopsychiatric theory of adaptation.] In Bastide, R. & Raveau, F. *Table Ronde sur l'Adaptation des Africains en France,* Paris: (Mimeograph) 1965

71111 Transference, screen memory and the temporal ego. JNMD 1966, 143:318-323

71112 Two types of modal personality models. In Kaplan, B. *Studying Personality Cross-Culturally,* NY/Evanston/London: Harper & Row 1961, 227-241

71113 An unusual audio-motor synesthesia in an adolescent. Significance of this phenomenon in psychoanalytic therapy. Psychiat Q 1966, 40:459-471

71114 The validity of psychoanalysis. Bull Amer Psa Ass 1950, 6:30-31

71115 The voices of children: psychocultural obstacles to therapeutic communication. PT 1965, 19:4-19

71116 Weeping, urination, and grand mal. J Hillside Hosp 1965, 14:97-107
Abs JA Q 1967, 36:320

71117 What would you say to a married man or woman who complains, "There's no fun, no excitement, or discovery any more—we come at each other like machines turning over for the thousandth time?" Why Rep 51-63

DE VERTEUIL, ROGER L.

71118 A psychiatric approach to the study of nightmare. Canad Psychiat Ass J 1962, 7:151-158

DE VON FLINDT, ROBERT

71119 An investigation of the relationship between defense effectiveness and ego strength under simulated stress conditions. Diss Abstr 1967, 28(3-B):1187

DE VOS, GEORGE A.

71120 (Ed) Culture Change and Psychological Adjustment. Berkeley, Calif: Univ of Calif Pr 1969

71121 (& Wagatsuma, H.) (Eds) Japan's Invisible Race: Caste in Culture and Personality. Berkeley/Los Angeles: Univ Calif Pr 1966, xvii + 415 p

71122 (& Murakami, E.; Murase, T.) Recent research, psychodiagnosis, and therapy in Japan. Prog clin Psych 1964, 6:226-234

71123 The relation of guilt toward parents to achievement and arranged marriage among the Japanese. Ps 1960, 23:287-301
       Abs HRB Q 1961, 30:300-301

71124 Symbolic analysis in the cross-cultural study of personality. In Kaplan, B. *Studying Personality Cross-Culturally*, NY/Evanston/London: Harper & Row 1961, 599-634

DE VRIES, R.

71124A Constancy of generic identity in the years three to six. Monogr Soc Res Child Develop 1969, 34:1-67

DEWALD, PAUL A.

71125 Forced termination of psychoanalysis. Transference, countertransference and reality responses in five patients. BMC 1966, 30:98-110

71126 Learning problems in psychoanalytic supervision: diagnosis and management. Comprehen Psychiat 1969, 10:107-121

71127 Psychotherapy, a Dynamic Approach. NY: Basic Books 1964, xvii + 307 p
       Rv Wallerstein, R. S. J Am Psa Ass 1966, 14:183-225. Wolberg, A. R. R 1966, 53:139-142. Rachlin, H. L. Q 1967, 36:307-308

71128 Reactions to the forced termination of analysis. (Read at Chicago Psa Soc, 28 May 1963)
       Abs Kavka, J. Bull Phila Ass Psa 1964, 14:231-234

71129 Reactions to the forced termination of therapy. Psychiat Q 1965, 39: 102-126

71130 The termination of psychotherapy. Psychiat Dig 1967, 28:33-43

71131 Therapeutic evaluation and potential: the psychodynamic point of view. Comprehen Psychiat 1967, 8:284-298

71132 Transference, countertransference and reality responses in five patients. BMC 1966, 30:98-100

       See Eidelberg, Ludwig

REVIEWS OF:

71133 Harrison, S. I. & Carek, D. J. A Guide to Psychotherapy. Q 1968, 37:306-307

71134 Hollender, M. H. The Practice of Psychoanalytic Psychotherapy. Q 1967, 36:455-456

71135 Wolberg, L. R. (Ed) Short-term Psychotherapy. Q 1967, 36:455-456

DEWEESE, POLLY

71136 Focusing the intake process to aid determination of treatability. In Weinreb, J. *Recent Developments in Psychoanalytic Child Therapy*, NY: IUP 1960, 84-92

       See Shore, Milton F.

DEWHURST, KENNETH

71137 A seventeenth-century dream interpreted. JNMD 1963, 136:594-596
71138 A seventeenth-century symposium on manic-depressive psychosis. M
1962, 35:113-125

See Todd, John

DE WILMARS, M.

See WILMARS, M. DE

DE WIND, A.

See WIND, A. DE

DE WIND, E.

See WIND, E. DE

DE WIT, GERARD A.

71139 Symbolism of masculinity and femininity; An Empirical Phenomen-
ological Approach to Developmental Aspects of Symbolic Thought in
Word Associations and Symbolic Meanings of Words. NY: Springer
Pub Co 1963, 107 p

DE WIT, J.

71140 Some critical remarks on "maternal deprivation." Acta paedopsychiat
1964, 31:240-253

DE YOUNG, CAROL D.

See Langsley, Donald G.; Pittman, Frank S.

DE ZUBIRÍA, R.

See ZUBIRÍA, R. DE

DIAMOND, BERNARD L.

71141 The children of Leviathan: psychoanalytic speculations concerning
welfare law and punitive sanctions. Calif Law Rev 1966, 54:357-369
71142 Clues to spotting mental illness in misdemeanants, No. 2. Municipal
Court Rev 1965, 5:50-57
71143 (Contributor to) Confidentiality and privileged communication in the
practice of psychiatry. NY, GAP, June 1960
71144 The criminal responsibility of the mentally ill. Stanford Law Rev 1961,
14:59-86
71145 The fallacy of the impartial expert. Arch crim Psychodyn 1959, 3:221-
236
71146 From M'Naughten to Currens, and beyond. Calif Law Rev 1962, 50:
189-205
71147 Identification and the sociopathic personality. [Symposium on psychopathy.] Arch crim Psychodyn 1961, 4:456-465

71148 Law and psychiatry. Ency Ment Hlth 908-929
71149 (& Louisell, D.) Law and psychiatry: detente, entente, or concomitance? Cornell Law Q 1965, 50:217-234
71150 Legal psychiatry. (Film) San Francisco, Science in Action, Calif Acad of Sci 1965
71151 (Contributor to) The mentally ill offender, London, J. & A. Churchill Ltd., 1968
71152 (& Platt, A. M.) The origins and development of the "wild beast" concept of mental illness and its relation to theories of criminal responsibility. J Hist behav Sci 1965, 1:355-367
71153 (& Platt, A. M.) The origins of the "right and wrong" test of criminal responsibility and its subsequent development in the United States: an historical survey. Calif Law Rev 1966, 54:1227-1260
71154 Preparing psychiatric testimony. In California Criminal Law Practice, Berkeley: Univ Calif, Continuing Education of the Bar 1964, 611-627
71155 Psychiatric testimony from the psychiatrist's standpoint. In Cohen, N. Criminal Law Seminar, Brooklyn 1961
71156 The psychiatrist as a medical witness. In Proceedings, National Medicolegal Symposium, AMA & ABA, March 1965, 135:141
71157 (& Louisell, D.) The psychiatrist as an expert witness: some ruminations and speculations. Mich Law Rev 1965, 63:1335-1354
71158 Psychiatry and the criminal. Part I: Rules of criminal responsibility of the mentally ill. Postgrad Med 1964, 36(2):A-46; A-48; A-50; A-52; A-54
71159 The psychodynamics of the offender. In The Mentally Ill Offender, A Symposium, Atascadero State Hospital 1960, 35-39
71160 The scientific method and the law. Hastings Law J 1967, 19:179-199
71161 Some observations about the genesis of the Gorshen case. In Donnelly, R. C. et al: Criminal Law, NY: Free Pr of Glencoe 1962, 688-691
71162 (Participant) Special commissions on insanity and criminal offenders. First report, July 7, 1962, Sacramento, Calif. Second report, Nov 15, 1962, Oakland, Calif
71163 On the spelling of Daniel M'Naughten's name. Ohio State Law J 1964, 25:84-88
71164 (Participant) Survey of California state mental facilities. San Francisco, CMA, Jan 18, 1965
71165 (Participant) Survey of mental health needs and resources of British Columbia. Washington, D.C., APA 1961
71166 (Editor of) Symposium: What is insanity? Arch crim Psychodyn 1961, 4:285-316
71167 Ten great books in the history of psychiatry. Ment Hosp 1961, 12(9): 32-33

       See Karpman, Benjamin

DIAMOND, EDWIN

71168 The Science of Dreams: An Analysis of What You Dream and Why. NY: Doubleday 1962, 264 p
       Rv Spotnitz, H. R 1963, 50(1):152-155

DIAMOND, LEON SIDNEY

71169 (& Marks, J. B.) Discontinuance of tranquilizers among chronic schizophrenic patients receiving maintenance dosage. JNMD 1960, 131:247-
251

DIAMOND, M. DAVID

71170 (& Weiss, A. J.; Grynbaum, B.) The unmotivated patient. Arch phys
Med Rehabil 1968, 49:281-284

DIAMOND, STANLEY

71171 The search for the primitive. In Galdston, I. *Man's Image in Medicine
and Anthropology*, NY: IUP 1963, 62-115

See Hollender, Marc H.

DIASIO, KAREN

71172 Psychiatric occupational therapy: search for a conceptual framework in
light of psychoanalytic ego psychology and learning theory. Amer J
occup Ther 1968, 22:400-414

DIATKINE, RENÉ

71173 L'abord psychanalytique de l'hystérie. [Psychoanalytic approach to
hysteria.] Confrontations psychiat 1968, No. 1:85-99
71174 Agressivité et fantasmes d'agression. [Aggression and hallucinations of
aggression.] RFPsa 1966, 30(Spec No):15-90; 133-134
S-44338 (& Favreau, J. A.) Le caractère névrotique.
Abs Noble, D.; Woodbury, M. A. An Surv Psa 1956, 7:190-196
71175 Difficultés de l'approche épidémiologique en psychiatre infantile. [Dif-
ficulties of the epidemiological approach in child psychiatry.] Évolut
psychiat 1968, 33:217-237
71176 Discussion of Bofill, P. & Folch-Mateau, P. "Problémes cliniques et
techniques du contre-transfert." RFPsa 1963, 27(Spec No):227-228
71177 Discussion of Geahchan, D. J. "Deuil et nostalgie." RFPsa 1968, 32:65
71178 Discussion of Held, R. "Contribution a l'étude psychanalytique du
phénomène religieux." RFPsa 1962, 26:259
71179 Discussion of Lebovici, S. "Colloque sur les interprétations en thérapeutique psychanalytique." RFPsa 1962, 26:30
71180 Du normal et du pathologique dans l'évolution mentale de l'enfant.
[About the normal and the pathological in the mental evolution of the
infant.] Psychiat Enfant 1967, 10:1-42
71181 En relisant en 1966 "Analyse terminable et interminable." [On rereading in 1966 "Analysis, terminable and interminable."] RFPsa 1968,
32:226-230
71182 (& Simon, J.) Étude nosologique à propos de trois cas de phobies chez
des adolescentes. [A nosological study of three cases of phobia in adolescents.] Psychiat Enfant 1966, 9:289-339
Abs Abels, E. RFPsa 1968, 32:335
71183 Facteurs psychiques dans la genèse, l'évolution le traitement du
bégaiement. [Psychic factors in the origin and the evolution of treatment of stammering.] Rev J.F.O.R. L. No. IX, 1960

71184 Indications and contraindications for psychoanalytic treatment. [Symposium: Indications and counterindications.] (Read at 25th Int Psa Cong, July 1967) J 1968, 49:266-270
    Abs LHR Q 1969, 38:669
71185 Névrose et caractère. (Discussion) RFPsa 1966, 30:318-323
S-44341 La notion de régression.
    Abs RJA An Surv Psa 1957, 8:33-34. RFA Q 1961, 30:156
71186 (& Simon, J.) Le point de vue de la régression en psychanalyse d'enfants. [The point of view of regression in the psychoanalysis of children.] RFPsa 1966, 30:457-466
71187 Le psychanalyse et la femme de 50 ans. [Psychoanalysis and the 50-year-old woman.] Rev Méd 1966, No. 15:755-763
71188 (& Favreau, J. A.) Le psychiatrie et les parents. [Psychiatry and relatives.] Psychiat Enfant 1960, 3:227-259
71189 Remarques à propos de la conférence de Mme Frijling-Schreuder. [Comments on the lecture by Mrs. Frijling-Schreuder.] RFPsa 1968, 32:139-144
71190 Remarques sur les particularités de la structure hystérique: hystérie de conversion et hystérie d'angoisse. [Remarks on the peculiarities of the hysteric structure: conversion hysteria and anxiety hysteria.] Ann mèd-psychol 1969, 1:481
S-44346 Symposium on psychotic object relationships.
    Abs JBi Q 1962, 31:123

See Ajuriaguerra, Julien De; Benassy, Maurice; Braunschweig, Denise; Chasseguet-Smirgel, Janine; Lebovici, Serge; Nacht, Sacha

REVIEW OF:
71191 Lebovici, S. & MacDougall, J. Un cas de psychose infantile (étude psychanalytique.) RFPsa 1963, 27:320

DIATKINE-KALMANSON, D.
See Lebovici, Serge

DÍAZ INFANTE, FERNANDO
71192 Estudio psicoanalitico de la cultural Nahuatl en relation con el complijo de edipo. [Psychoanalytic study of the Nahuatl in relation to the Oedipus complex.] Cuad Psa 1965, 1:147-169

See Cardeña, Jaime

DIAZ PORTILLO, ISABEL
TRANSLATION OF:
Freud, A. [73550]

ABSTRACT OF:
71193 Yarrow, L. J. & Goodwin, M. S. Some conceptual issues in the study of mother-infant interaction. Cuad Psa 1965, 1:384

DIBNER, ANDREW S.
See Rhudick, Paul J.

DIBON, PIERRE

See Jacob, Maurice

DI CAGNO, L.

See CAGNO, L. DI

DICKES, ROBERT

71194 The defensive function of an altered state of consciousness: a hypnoid state. J Am Psa Ass 1965, 13:356-403
71195 Fetishistic behavior: a contribution to its complex development and significance. (Read at Psa Ass NY, 19 Feb 1962) J Am Psa Ass 1963, 11:303-330
       Abs Auth Q 1962, 31:446-467. Rumore, T. R. Q 1962, 31:447-448. JBi Q 1964, 33:137
71196 On alteration in the state of consciousness and its defensive function: a hypnoid state. (Read at Psa Ass NY, 14 Dec 1964)
       Abs Blum, H. P. Q 1965, 34:480-482
71197 Psychoanalytic therapy. An Surv Psa 1958, 9:323-430
71198 Psychotherapy and the practitioner. Psychosomatics 1962, 3:438-446
71199 Severe regressive disruptions of the therapeutic alliance. (Read at Am Psa Ass, Dec 1965) J Am Psa Ass 1967, 15:508-533
71200 Some observations on lying, a derivative of secrecy. J Hillside Hosp 1968, 17:94-109

See Waxenberg, Sheldon E.; Weisfogel, Jerry

DICKEY, BRENDA A.

71201 Attitudes toward sex roles and feelings of adequacy in homosexual males. J consult Psychol 1961, 25:116-122

DICKIE, GEORGE

71202 Francis Hutcheson and the theory of motives. AJP 1961, 74:625-629

DICKINSON, JOHN M.

71203 Aggression and the status of evil in man: a critical analysis of Sigmund Freud's assumptions from the theological perspective of Reinhold Niebuhr. Diss Abstr 1964, 25:3097-3098

DICKOFF, JAMES

71204 (& James, P.; Wiedenbach, E.) Theory in a practice discipline. I. Practice oriented discipline. Nurs Res 1968, 17:415-435

DICKS, HENRY V.

71205 Concepts of marital diagnosis and therapy as developed at the Tavistock Family Psychiatric Units, London, England. In Nash, E. M. et al: *Marriage Counseling in Medical Practice*, Chapel Hill: Univ North Carolina Pr 1964, 255-275

* * * Foreword to Guntrip, H. J. S. *Healing the Sick Mind*, NY: Appleton-Century-Crofts 1964, 1965
71206 Marital Tensions: Clinical Studies Towards a Psychological Theory of Interaction. NY: Basic Books; London: Routledge 1967, xiv + 354 p
Rv Gorer, G. J 1968, 49:107-109
71207 Object relations theory and marital studies. M 1963, 36:125-129
71208 The state of psychotherapy in British psychiatry: special section. P 1969, 125:1238-1239

DICKS, RUSSELL L.

See Hiltner, Seward

DICKSON, RONALD J.

71209 Archetypal symbolism in Lorca's *Bodas de Sangre*. Lit & Psych 1960, 10:76-79

DI CORI, FERRUCCIO A.

See CORI, FERRUCCIO A. DI

DICYON, I.

See Riess, Bernard F.

DIECKMANN, HANS

71210 Die Differenz zwischen dem anschaulichen und dem abstrahierenden Denken in den Psychologien von C. G. Jung and Freud. [The difference between intuitive and abstract thought in the psychology of Jung and Freud.] Z PSM 1959-60, 6:287-292; 1960, 7:58-65
71211 Herzneurose. Dargestellt an einem Fall von paroxysmaler Tachykardie. [Cardiac neurosis and dependence upon the mother, discussed on the basis of a case of paroxysmal tachycardia.] Z PSM 1966, 12:26-39
71212 Integration process of the ego-complex in dreams. J anal Psych 1965, 10:49-66
71213 Das Lieblingsmärchen der Kindheit als therapeutischer Faktor in der Analyse. [The favored fairy tale of childhood as a therapeutic factor in analysis.] Prax Kinderpsychol 1968, 17:288-292
71214 Märchen und Träume als Helfer des Menschen. [Fairy Tales and Dreams as Helpers of Mankind.] Stuttgart: Bonz 1966, 99 p
71215 Über einige Beziehungen zwischen Traumserie und Verhaltensänderungen in einer Neurosenbehandlung. [On various relations between dream series and behavioral changes in the treatment of a neurosis.] Z PSM 1962, 8:273-281
71216 Zum Aspekt des Grausamen in Märchen. [On the cruelty aspect in fairy tales.] Prax Kinderpsychol 1967, 16:298-306

DIEL, PAUL

71217 Journal d'un Psychanalysé. [Diary of a Psychoanalysand.] Paris: Plon 1964, 273 p

71218 Les Principes de l'Éducation et de la Rééducation. [Principles of Education and Re-education.] Neuchâtel, Switzerland: Delachaux & Niestlé 1961, 250 p

DIENELT, KARL

71219 Von Freud zu Frankl. Die Entwicklung der Tiefenpsychologie und deren Anwendung in der Pädagogik. [From Freud to Frankl. The Development of Depth Psychology and Its Application to Pedagogy.] Vienna/Munich: Österreichischer Bundesverlag 1967, 143 p

DIENER, HARRY

See Kleinschmidt, Hans J.

DIERKENS, JEAN

71220 Freud. Anthologie Commentée. [Freud. Annotated Anthology.] Brussels: Éditions "Labor" 1965, 231 p

DIESING, ULRICH

71221 Die pragmatischen Psychotherapieverfahren—Suggestion, Hypnose und autogenes Training—in der Kinderpsychotherapie. [Pragmatic management in psychotherapy—suggestion, hypnosis and autogenous training in psychotherapy of children.] Hbh Kinderpsychother 525-541

DIETHER, JACK

S-44381 Mahler and psychoanalysis.

Abs JLan An Surv Psa 1958, 9:476

DIETRICH, HEINZ

71222 Anakastische Eifersucht. [Anankastic jealousy.] Int J Np 1966, 2:98-110
71223 Capgras' Syndrom und Déjà vu. [Capgras' syndrome and déjà vu.] Fortschr Neurol Psychiat 1962, 30:617-625
71224 Wahrträume und Wahn. [Truth dreams and delusions.] Nervenarzt 1965, 36:114-118

DIGGORY, JAMES C.

71225 Self-Evaluation: Concepts and Studies. NY: Wiley 1966, xiii + 477 p
71226 (& Rothman, D. Z.) Values destroyed by death. ASP 1961, 63:205-210. Death & Identity 152-161

DI GIORGIO, A.

See GIORGIO, A. DI

DIGNAN, MARY HOWARD

71227 Ego identity and maternal identification. J Pers soc Psychol 1965, 1:476-483

DI GRASSO, P. G.
See GRASSO, P. G. DI

DIJK, W. K. VAN

71228 Diagnostiek, klinische psychiatrie en psycho-analyse. [Diagnostics, clinical psychiatry and psychoanalysis.] In van der Leeuw, P. J. et al: *Hoofdstukken uit de Hedendaagse Psychoanalyse,* Arnhem: van Loghum Slaterus 1967, 129-142
71229 Iets over diagnostiek en diagnostiseren in de psychiatrie. [Some remarks on diagnostics in psychiatry.] Groningen: Wolter 1964, 19 p
71230 Psychopathologische en Klinische Aspecten van de Psychogene Psychose. [Psychopathologic and Clinical Aspects of the Psychogenic Psychosis.] Groningen: van Denderen 1963, 286 p

DIJKHUIS, J. H.

71231 Over duiden en interpreteren in de psychoanalytische situatie. [On clarification and interpretation in the psychoanalytical situation.] Ned Tijdschr Psychol 1965, 20:348-363

DILLING, C. A.
See Mueller, William J.

DILLON, FREDERICK
See Inman, W. S.

DILLON, HAROLD
See Leopold, Robert L.

DILNOT, ALAN F.
See Faber, Mel D.

DIMANT, F.

71232 (& Raimbault, G.) Preparation à la maternité: observations psychanalytiques. [Preparation for maternity: psychoanalytic observations.] Rev Méd psychosm 1965, 7:383-400
71233 (& Raimbault, G.) Preparation a la maternité? Le vécu de l'accouchement. [Preparation for maternity? Regarding the experience of childbirth.] Rev Méd psychosom 1966, 8:137-144

DI MASCIO, ALBERTO

71234 (& Brooks, G. W.) Free association to a fantasied psychotherapist: a case report. Arch gen Psychiat 1961, 4:513-516

See Kanter, Stanley S.; Shader, Richard I.

DIMITROV, CHRISTO T.

71235 E.v. Hartmanns "Philosophie des Unbewussten" und Freuds "Tiefenpsychologie." [E.v. Hartmann's "Philosophy of the unconscious" and Freud's "depth psychology."] Z PSM 1969, 15:131-146

71236 (& Jablenski, A.) Nietzsche und Freud. [Nietzsche and Freud.] Z PSM 1967, 13:282-298

       Nietzsche y Freud. Rev Psicoanal Psiquiat Psicol 1968, (9):46-65

71237 (& Krestnikov, A. N.) Posibilidades de expansión y enriquecimiento del método de reproducción de N. Krestnikov. [Possibilities of expansion and enrichment of the reproduction method of N. Krestnikov.] Arch Estud psicoanal Psicol med 1967, 4:144-152

71238 (& Kolev, N.) Réflexions et notes critiques sur quelques notions psychanalytiques classiques en psychopathologie. [Reflections and critical notes on some classical psychoanalytic ideas in psychopathology.] Ann méd-psychol 1965, 123(2):303-316

DIMOCK, GEORGE E.

71239 Oedipus: the religious issue. Hudson Rev 1968, 21:430-456

DINARD, CÉCILE

71239A [Adolescence, paternal neglect.] (Fr) Acta Paedopsychiat 1969, 36: 210-215

71240 A propos du masochisme chez l'enfant. [Concerning masochism in children.] Bull Ass psa Fran 1968, No. 4:103-108

71241 [Apropos of theft by children before puberty.] (Fr) Pediatrie 1962, 194-200

71242 Contribution à l'étude des phobies de l'école. Le rôle du père. [Contribution to the study of school phobias. The role of the father.] Rev Np inf 1965, 13:797-804. Pediatrie 1965, 20:983-989

71243 [Early nutritional difficulties in a girl.] (Fr) Pediatrie 1964, 19:853-857

DINCE, PAUL R.

71244 General considerations of major sexual disturbances in marriage. Marriage Relat 145-156

71245 Maternal depression and failures of individuation during adolescence. Sci Psa 1966, 9:27-37

See Bieber, Irving

DINGMAN, HARVEY F.

See Frisbie, Louise V.; Silverstein, Arthur B.

DINGMAN, JOSEPH F.

See Lief, Harold I.

DINITZ, SIMON

71246 (& Scarpitti, F. R.; Albini, J. L.; Lefton, M.; Pasamanick, B.) An experimental study in the prevention of hospitalization of schizophrenics. Ops 1965, 35:1-9

       Abs JMa RFPsa 1966, 30:521

71247 (& Lefton, M.; Angrist, S.; Pasamanick, B.) Psychiatric and social attributes as predictors of case outcome in mental hospitalization. Soc Probl 1961, 8:322-328. In Scheff, T. J. *Mental Illness and Social Processes*, NY: Harper & Row 1967, 119-130

See Pasamanick, Benjamin

DINKELKAMP, THEODORE

71248 Verzeichnis der Publikationen von M. Bleuler. [An index to M. Bleuler's publications.] Schweiz ANP 1963, 91:5010

DINKMEYER, DON C.

71249 Child Development: The Emerging Self. Englewood Cliffs, N. J.: Prentice-Hall 1965, xi + 434 p

71250 (& Dreikurs, R.) Encouraging Children to Learn: The Encouragement Process. Englewood Cliffs, N. J.: Prentice-Hall 1963, 162 p

DINNERSTEIN, DOROTHY

71251 "The little mermaid" and the situation of the girl. Contempo Psa 1967, 3:104-112

DINSMOOR, JAMES A.

71252 Studies in abnormal behavior in animals. In Waters, R. H. et al: *Principles of Comparative Psychology*, NY: McGraw-Hill 1960, 289-324

DIO, E.

See Soifer, Raquel

DI PIAZZA, P.

See PIAZZA, P. DI

DI SCIPIO, WILLIAM J.

See Fox, Beatrice

DISERTORI, BEPPINO

71253 Psicologia, parapsicologia e atemporalita del sogno (a proposito del trattato di castelli e del saggio di Maria Zambrano.) [Psychology, parapsychology and timelessness of dreams (apropos of the Castelli's treatise and Maria Zambrano's essay).] Riv sper Freniat 1961, 85:40-51

DISTLER, LUTHER S.

71254 (& May, P. R. A.; Tuma, A. H.) Anxiety and ego strength as predictors of response to treatment in schizophrenic patients. J consult Psychol 1964, 28:170-177

71255 Patterns of parental identification: an examination of three theories. Diss Abstr 1965, 26:1168-1169

DITMAN, KEITH S.

71256 Initial treatment of the skid row alcoholic. Int Psychiat Clin 1966, 3(4):177-181

71257 (& Hayman, M.; Whittlesey, J. R. B.) Nature and frequency of claims following L.S.D. JNMD 1962, 134:346-352

See Hayman, Max

DITTES, JAMES E.

S-44392 Galvanic skin response as a measure of patient's reaction to therapist's permissiveness. In Goldstein, A. P. & Dean, S. J. *The Investigation of Psychotherapy*, NY: Wiley 1966, 294-303

See Gollob, Harry F.

DITTMANN, ALLEN T.

71258 (& Goodrich, D. W.) A comparison of social behavior in normal and hyperaggressive preadolescent boys. Child Develpm 1961, 32:315-327

71259 (& Wynne, L. C.) Linguistic techniques and the analysis of emotionality in interviews. ASP 1961, 63:201-204. In Meth Res PT 146-152

See Goodrich, D. Wells; Harway, Norman I.; Klein, Marjorie H.; Mathews, W. Mason; Shakow, David

DITTMANN, LAURA L.

* * * (Editor of) Chandler, C. et al: *Early Child Care: The New Perspectives.*

DIXON, JAMES CANNON

71260 The relation between perceived change in self and in others. J gen Psychol 1965, 73:137-142

DIXON, NORMAN FRANK

S-44397 Symbolic associations following subliminal stimulation. Abs SLP An Surv Psa 1956, 7:114-116

DIZMANG, LARRY H.

71261 Loss, bereavement, and depression in childhood. Int Psychiat Clin 1969, 6(2):175-195

DLIN, BARNEY M.

71262 The doctor, his emotions and his heart. Minn Med 1969, 52:369-374

71263 Emotional factors in coronary occlusion. Minn Med 1961, 44:124-125; 170-173; 212-213

71264 Emotional reactions in myocardial infarctions: covert primal anxiety in a medical ward setting. Psychiat Spectator 1964, 2(3):15-16

71265 Myocardial infarction—factors in delayed recovery. Trans Coll Physicians Phila 1961, 28:211-213

71266 Post-coronary emotional problems. Psychiat Prog 1965, Nov
71267 Primal anxiety and psychiatric emergencies. Postgrad Med 1961, 30:
       200-206
71268 Psychologic adaptation to pacemaker and open heart surgery. Arch gen
       Psychiat 1968, 19:599-610
71269 Psychological adaptation to pacemaker following cardiac arrest. Psy-
       chosomatics 1966, 7:73-80
71270 (& Perlman, A.; Ringold, E.) Psychosexual response to ileostomy and
       colostomy. P 1969, 126:374-381

       See Fischer, H. Keith

DOBIE, SHIRLEY I.

       See Bloom, Victor; Lowinger, Paul

DOBROTKA, G.

71271 [Paranoid defense as motivation for a criminal act.] (Slovak) Ceskoslov
       Psychiat 1967, 63:318-324

DOBRY, J.

71271A [Theoretical and philosophical foundations of psychosomatic directions
       and schools.] (Cz) Cesk Psychiat 1969, 65:52-61

DOBZHANSKY, THEODOSIUS GRIGORIEVICH

71272 The Biology of Ultimate Concern. The New Amer Libr 1967, xvii +
       152 p
71273 (Ed) Evolutionary Biology, Vol. II. NY: Appleton-Century-Crofts
       1968
71274 Mankind Evolving; The Evolution of the Human Species. New Haven:
       Yale Univ Pr 1962, 381 p

DOCKAR-DRYSDALE, BARBARA E.

71275 Problems of communication in the treatment of adolescents. Ass Psy-
       chotherapists Bull 1967, No. 7:24-31
71276 Therapy in Child Care: Collected Papers. (Foreword: Winnicott,
       D. W.) Harlow, England: Longmans 1968, xviii + 163 p

DODDS, ERIC ROBERTSON

71277 Pagan and Christian in an Age of Anxiety. Some Aspects of Religious
       Experience from Marcus Aurelius to Constantine. NY: Cambridge Univ
       Pr 1965, xii + 144 p
       Rv Posinsky, S. H. Q 1966, 35:606-608

DODGEN, JOHN C.

71278 (& Arthur, R. J.) Psychotherapy of a sexagenarian. Dis nerv Sys 1967,
       28:680-683

DODS, LORIMER

71279 Oedipus: myth or history? Med J Aust 1968, (1):367-368

DOHRENWEND, BRUCE PHILIP

71280 (& Bernard, V. W.; Kolb, L. C.) The orientation of leaders in an urban area toward problems of mental illness. P 1962, 118:683-691

See Kolb, Lawrence C.

DOI, L. TAKEO

71281 Discussion of Flarsheim, A. "The psychological meaning of the use of marijuana and LSD in one case." Psa Forum 1969, 3:126-129
71282 Discussion of Havens, L. "Main current of psychiatric development." Int J Psychiat 1968, 5:288-327
71283 ["Hitomishiri" as a Japanese concept of stranger anxiety: Symposium on "Hitomishiri."] (Jap) Jap J Psa 1969, 15(2):12
71284 Is psychiatry not scientific? Int J Psychiat 1968, 5:310-312
71285 Methodology and mythology. Int J Psychiat 1966, 2:567-568
71286 [On the "Amae" theory: Symposium on the Amae theory.] (Jap) Jap J Psa 1968, 14(3):14-19
71287 [The psychodynamics of schizophrenia: Symposium.] (Jap) Auth Abstr (Eng) Jap J Psa 1966, 12(4):14; 32-33

See Caudill, William

DOLANOVÁ, HELGA

See Žižkovà, Alena

DOLE, ARTHUR A.

See Allardice, B. S.

DOLGAN, J.

See Mosher, Donald L.

DOLGIN, J.

See Silberstein, Richard M.

DOLLARD, JOHN

71288 (& Miller, N. E.) Personality and Psychotherapy: An Analysis in Terms of Learning, Thinking, and Culture. NY: McGraw-Hill 1963, xv + 488 p

See Auld, Frank, Jr.; Davis, Allison; White, Alice M.

DOLTO-MARETTE, FRANÇOISE

S-6965 Cure psychanalytique a l'aide de la poupée-fleur.
        Psychoanalytische Kinderhandlung mit Hilfe der "Blumenpuppe." Hbh Kinderpsychother 379-392
* * *   Preface to Mannoni, M. Le Premier Rendez-vous avec le Psychanalyste, Paris: Gonthier 1965

71289 Psychanalyse et Pédiatrie; Les Grandes Notions de la Psychanalyse, Seize Observations d'Enfants. [Psychoanalysis and Pediatrics; the Great Ideas of Psychoanalysis, 16 Studies of Children.] Paris: Éditions de la Parole 1961, 284 p

DOMHOFF, BILL

71290 (& Calvin, S.) Aggression in dreams. Int J soc Psychiat 1963, 9:259-267
71291 But just what sort of a thing is a coping mechanism? Psychol Rep 1965, 16:234
71292 Night dreams and hypnotic dreams: is there evidence that they are different? Int J clin exp Hyp 1964, 12:159-168. In Moss, C. S. *The Hypnotic Investigation of Dreams*, NY/London/Sydney: Wiley 1967, 206-213

See Hall, Calvin S.

DOMHOFF, G. WILLIAM

71293 But why did they sit on the king's right in the first place? R 1969-70, 56:586-596
71294 Historical materialism, cultural determinism, and the origin of the ruling classes. R 1969, 56:271-287
71295 A paper-and-pencil study of Fromm's humanistic psychoanalysis. J humanist Psychol 1964, 4:149-153

DOMINGUES DE MORAES, OSWALD

See Lobo, Fabio Leite

DOMINIAN, J.

71296 Psychiatry and the Christian. NY: Hawthorn 1962, 135 p

DOMKE, H. R.

See Tapia, Fernando

DONADEO, JOHN

71297 (Reporter) Psychoanalysis and learning theory. (Meeting NY Psa Soc, 18 June 1963) Q 1964, 33:152-154

ABSTRACTS OF:
71298 Barande, R. Essai métapsychologique sur le silence. Q 1964, 33:613
71299 Brody, S. & Axelrad, S. Mother-infant interaction: forms of feeding. Q 1969, 38:346-347
71300 Deutsch, H. Bisexuality and immortality in the Dionysos myth. Q 1968, 37:321-322
71301 Fain, M. & Marty, P. Perspective psychosomatique sur le fonction des fantasmes. Q 1966, 35:319
71302 Fine, B. D. et al: Psychoanalysis and learning theory. (Dr. Charles Brenner's section of the Kris Study Group.) Q 1964, 33:152-154
71303 Gombrich, E. H. The dream of reason: propaganda symbolism in the French Revolution. Q 1963, 32:460-462

71304 Green, A. Une variante de la position phallique-narcissique. Q 1964,
       33:613
71305 Grunberger, B. De l'image phallique. Q 1966, 35:318-319
71306 Lebovici, S. et al: Symposium on interpretations in psychoanalytic
       therapy. Q 1964, 33:612-613
71307 Lorand, S. Psychoanalytic therapy of religious devotees: a theoretical
       contribution. Q 1961, 30:316-318
71308 Mises, R. L'intégration du père dans les conflits précoces. Q 1966,
       35:319
71309 Pasche, F. Régression, perversion, névrose. Q 1964, 33:613
71310 Remus, J. Some aspects in early-orphan adults' analysis. Q 1965, 34:
       316-318
71311 Stein, M. H. Self-observation, reality and the superego. Q 1967, 36:
       148-150
71312 Wangh, M. On evocation of a proxy. A defensive maneuver, its pur-
       poses, and genesis. Q 1962, 31:144-146

       REVIEWS OF:
71313 Caruso, I. A. Psychanalyse et Synthèse Personnelle: Rapports Entre
       l'Analyse Psychologique et les Valeurs Existentielles. Q 1961, 30:117-
       118
71314 Nacht, S. Le Masochism. (3rd ed) Q 1966, 35:602-603

DONAHUE, GEORGE T.

71315 (& Nichtern, S.) Teaching the Troubled Child. NY: Free Pr 1965,
       x + 202 p; 1968, xvi + 206 p
          Rv Lorand, R. L. Q 1967, 36:304. Ross, J. H. R 1969, 56:486-487

       See Nichtern, Sol

DONELLI, A.

71316 (& Faienza, C.; Moretti, M.) [Study of effects of lack of maternal care:
       investigations followed on 123 boys of prepubertal and pubertal age at
       the Institute Marchiondi Spagliardi of Milan-Baggio.] (It) Lattante
       1965, 36:291-296

DONGIER, MAURICE

71317 (& Dongier, S.) L'attrait de la prostitution et de la prostituée. [The
       attraction of prostitution and the prostitute.] Acta neurol psychiat Belg
       1964, 64:719-724
* * * Foreword and notes to Ellis, H. La Sélection Sexuelle Chez l'Homme,
       Paris: Tcou 1965
* * * Foreword and notes to Ellis, H. Les Caractères Sexuels Secondaires,
       Paris: Tcou 1965
71318 Névroses et Troubles Psychosomatiques. [Neuroses and Psychosomatic
       Disorders.] Brussels: C. Dessart 1966, 1967, 296 p
71319 Observations neurobiologiques en relation avec les structures de
       l'inconscient. [Neurobiological observations in relation to unconscious
       structures.] Évolut psychiat 1964, 29:247-266

71320 Psychologie du couple et controle des naissances. [Sexual psychology and birth control.] Marseille Méd 1966, 10:695-701

71321 Recherches psychosomatiques en cardiologie. I. Les tachycardies paroxystiques. II. Etude comparée de 100 coronariens et de 100 subjets temoins. [Psychosomatic researches in cardiology. I. Paroxysmal tachycardias. II. A comparison between 100 coronary patients and 100 controls.] Pr méd 1961, 61:839-841

71322 Le syndrome subjectif des traumatismes craniens envisage sous l'angle psychopathologique. [The subjective syndrome of cranial injuries seen from the psychopathologic angle.] Acta Orthop Belg 1965, 31:954-959

See Bobon, J.

DONGIER, SUZANNE

71323 (& Duchesne, A.) Anorexie mentale et place dans la fatrie. [Anorexia nervosa and sibling ranking.] Acta neurol psychiat Belg 1966, 66:812-819

See Bobon, J.; Dongier, Maurice

DONIGER, JOAN

71324 (& Goodrich, D. W.) An occupational therapy program in an all-research center. Amer J occup Ther 1954, 8:218-219

See Rothwell, Naomi

DONINI, G.

See Leppo, Luciano V.

DONNELLY, CHARLES

See Dyrud, Jarl E.

DONNELLY, ELLEN M.

71325 ·The quantitative analysis of parent behavior toward psychotic children and their siblings. Genet Psychol Monogr 1960, 62:331-376

DONNELLY, JOHN

71326 Aspects of the treatment of character disorders. Arch gen psychiat 1966, 15:22-28
       Abs PB Q 1969, 38:343-344

DONNET, J.-L.

See Chertok, Léon

DONOGHUE, A. K.

* * * (& Hillman, J.) Editors of Freud, S. *The Cocaine Papers.*
* * * (& Hillman, J.) Foreword to Freud, S. *The Cocaine Papers,* Vienna/Zurich: Dunquin Pr 1963, iii-viii

DOOLITTLE, HILDA

S-44449 Tribute to Freud.
Rv Niederland, W. G. J Am Psa Ass 1964, 12:223-241

DORAN, S. MARK

See Brickman, Harry R.

DOREY, R.

71327 Discussion: Changement individuel et processus analytique. [Individuel change and analytic process.] Bull Ass psa Fran 1967, (3)

DORFMAN, ELAINE

See Goodwin, Hilda M.; Hepps, Robert

DORFMAN, WILFRED

71328 Hypochondriasis as a defense against depression. Psychosomatics 1968, 9:248-251
71329 Masked depression. Bibl Psychiat Neurol 1963, 118:50-58

DORIS, JOHN

71330 (& Solnit, A. J.) Treatment of children with brain damage and associated school problems. J Amer Acad Child Psychiat 1963, 2:618-635

See Sarason, Seymour B.

DORN, ROBERT M.

71331 Crying at weddings (and) "When I grow up." J 1967, 48:298-307
71332 The pleasures and changes of educating and being educated—supervision. Riess-Davis Clin Bull 1966, 3:105-112
71333 Psychoanalysis and psychoanalytic education: what kind of "journey?" Psa Forum 1969, 3:239-254; 270-274
71334 The role of the psychoanalyst in community mental health. Comm ment Hlth J 1966, 2:5-12

REVIEW OF:
71335 Seed, P. The Psychological Problem of Disarmament. Q 1968, 37: 144-145

DORNBUSCH, A.

See Weil, Jorge N.

DÖRNER, KLAUS

71336 Interview und Exploration. [Interview and exploration.] Nervenarzt 1966, 37:18-25

DORON, M.

71337 Psychodrame et groupe de base: thérapie de formation. [Psychodrama and basic group: development therapy.] Ann méd-psychol 1968, 126 (2):759

DORON, ROLAND

71338   Résistance au changement et compulsion de répétition. [Resistance to change and repetition compulsion.] Bull Ass psa Fran 1967, (3)

DORPAT, THEODORE LORENZ

71339   (& Holmes, T. H.) Backache of muscle tension origin. N West Med 1958, 57:602-607. In Kroger, W. S. *Psychosomatic Obstetrics, Gynecology and Endocrinology,* Springfield, Ill: Thomas 1962, 425-436. With title: Psychophysiologic aspects of backache. Postgrad Med 1959, 25:713-719

71340   Before the legislature. Bull King County Med Soc 1959, 38:60

71341   (& Jackson, J. K.; Ripley, H. S.) Broken homes and attempted and completed suicide. Arch gen Psychiat 1965, 12:213-216. In Gibbs, J. P. *Suicide,* NY: Harper & Row 1968, 170-178

71342   Clinical problems with the tranquilizing durgs. In *Proceedings of the Teachers' Seminar on Pharmacology,* Seattle: Univ of Washington Pr 1957, 176-183

71343   (& Chivers, N. C.) Emotional reactions to surgery. Yale sci Mag 1957, 32:53-60

71344   Evaluation and management of suicide reactions. Med Times 1963, 91:1212-1219

71345   (& Boswell, J. W.) An evaluation of suicidal intent in suicide attempts. Comprehen Psychiat 1963, 4:117-125

71346   Loss of controls over suicidal impulses. Bull Suicidology 1968, Dec: 26-30

71347   (& Holmes, T. H.) Mechanisms of skeletal muscle pain and fatigue. AMA ANP 1955, 74:628-640

71348   Psychiatric observations on assassinations. N West Med 1968, 67:976-979

° ° °   Psychophysiologic aspects of backache. See [71339]

71349   Regulatory mechanisms of the perceptual apparatus on involuntary physiological actions. (Read at Seattle Psa Soc, 14 Feb 1966) J Am Psa Ass 1968, 319-334
        Abs Goforth, E. Psa Forum 1966, 1:321-322

71350   (& Ripley, H. S.) The relationship between attempted suicide and committed suicide. Comprehen Psychiat 1967, 8:74-79

71351   (& Anderson, W. F.; Ripley, H. S.) The relationship of physical illness to suicide. In Resnik, H. L. P. *Suicidal Behavior: Diagnosis and Management,* Boston: Little, Brown & Co 1968, 209-219

71352   (& Ripley, H. S.) A study of suicide in King County, Washington. N West Med 1962, 61:655-661

71353   (& Ripley, H. S.) A study of suicide in the Seattle area. Comprehen Psychiat 1960, 1:349-359

71354   Suicide in murderers. Psychiat Digest 1966, 27:51-55

71355   (& Holems, T. H.) Tic, torticollis, coccydynis, and muscle spasms. In Ros, A. R. *Manual de Terapeutica Clinica,* Cuba 1952

        See Chivers, Norman C.; Johnson, M. H.; Kogan, W. S.; Palola, E. G.

DORR, THOMAS O.

71356 The psychoanalysis of a female fraternal twin. Riv Neurobiol 1964, 10(Suppl):1265-1289

DORSEY, JOHN M.

71357 American Government: Conscious Self Sovereignty. Detroit, Mich: Center for Health Education 1969, xvii + 137 p
71358 Contributor to Krystal, H. *Massive Psychic Trauma.*
71359 Discovering My World of My Mind. Detroit, Mich: Center for Health Education 1968
71360 The doctor of medicine and Michigan's community mental health programs. Mich Med 1965, 64:195-197
71361 The excellence of man. In *The World of Teilhard de Chardin*, Baltimore, Md.: Helicon Pr 1961, 64-76
71362 (Ed) The Growth of Self Insight. Detroit: Wayne State Univ Pr 1962
71363 Hypnosis. Detroit, Mich: Center for Health Education 1968
71364 Illness or Allness: Conversations of a Psychiatrist. Detroit: Wayne State Univ Pr 1965, 636 p
     Rv Goldman, B. Am Im 1965, 22:206-208
71365 Living education. Mich Educ J 1956-57, 34:353-357
71366 Man's medicines. Michigan State Medical Society for College of Pharmacy, Stephen Wilson Conference publication 1968, 81-96
71367 Narcotic addiction in our community primarily an education problem. Mich Med 1961, 60:621-629
71368 The nature of man. Detroit, Mich: Center for Health Education 1968
71369 A psychoanalytic appreciation of American government. Am Im 1961, 18:207-233
71370 The psychology of language. In Travis, L. E. *Handbook of Speech Pathology*, NY: Appleton-Century-Crofts 1957
71371 Religion and medical psychology. Pastoral Psychol 1968, 19(183): 27-34
71372 Seven Annual Medical Reports. Detroit: McGregor Health Foundations
71373 The Spirit of Health. Liverpool, England: Margaret Laird Fonndation
71374 The spirit of medicine. Mich Med 1963, 62:1215-1216
71375 The university professor. Newsletter, Michigan Society of Neurology and Psychiatry 1964, 7(2), Sept
71376 Vis medicatrix naturae. Memorial Research Monographs Naka, Osaka, Japan: Committee on the Celebration of 60th Birthday of Professor S. Naka 1960, 63-74. Mich Med 1961, 60:43-48, 50

See Krystal, Henry

DORSEY, JOSEPH

71377 (& Matsunaga, G.; Bauman, G.) Training public health nurses in mental health. Arch gen Psychiat 1964, 11:214-222

DOSHI, R.

See Marshall, Helen R.

DOS SANTOS, J.

See SANTOS, J. DOS

DOSUZHKOV, F. N.

71378 [Neurosis of pathological timidity-scoptophobia.] (Rus) Zh Nevropat Psikhiat 1963, 63:130-136

DOSUŽKOV, THEODORE (BOHODAR)

71379 Considerazioni sul sonno nel corso della seduta analitica. [Considerations of sound in the course of the analytic session.] Riv Psa 1965, 11:153-165

71380 Fear of failure, the pivotal symptom of a special psychoneurosis. Psychother Psychosom 1967, 15:16

71381 [Neurologic concept of neurosis.] (Cz) Acta Univ Carol [Med] Prague 1966, 12:521-532

71382 [On Janet's psychasthenia.] (Cz) Ceskoslov Psychiat 1964, 60:37-44

71383 I princípi anatomici e fisiologici nella psicoanalisi. [Anatomic and physiologic principles in psychoanalysis.] Riv Psa 1962, 8:3-14

71384 Das Psychodrama aus der Sicht der Psychoanalyse. [Psychodrama from the psychoanalytical viewpoint.] Z Psychother med Psychol 1969, 19: 163-164

71385 Psychoneurosy a puberta. [Psychoneuroses and puberty.] Psychológia a patopsychológia diet'at'a 1969, 4:251-253; Abs (Rus) (Eng) 254
Psychoneurosen und Pubertät. Wiss Z Univ Rostock 1968, 17:563-564

71386 Quelques problèmes posés par l'éreutophobie. [Some problems posed by ereuthophobia.] Évolut psychiat 1969, 34:877-896

71387 [Scotophobia.] (Cz) Ceskoslov Psychiat 1962, 58:102-107

71388 Skoptophobie—die vierte Übertragungsneurose. [Scoptophobia—the 4th transference neurosis.] Psyche 1965, 19:537-546

71389 Some problems of pathogenesis of idiopathic stuttering. Proceedings of II European Congress of Pedopsychiatry, Rome 1963, 2(1):324-332

71390 [Two cases of erythrophobia (analysis of their differences).] (Fr) Evolut psychiat 1967, 32:427-448
Due casi di ereutofobia. Riv Psa 1967, 13:175-195

71391 Wortlose Kommunikation bei der Hysterie. [Wordless communication in hysteria.] Dyn Psychiat 1968, 1(2):74-81; Abs (Eng), 81

71392 Zur Frage der Dysmorphobie. [On the question of dysmorphobia.] Psyche 1969, 23:683-699

DOTEN, DAVID R.

71393 (& Rosenthal, M. J.) Therapeutic management of a pubescent boy's prolonged episode of hostile acting out. Child Welfare 1967, 46:326-334

DOUADY, D.

71394 (& Jeanguyot, M.; Danon-Boileau, H.) Bilan médical de trois ans de fonctionnement de la Clinique Dupré. [Medical balance sheet of three years of operation of the Dupré Clinic.] Revue Réadaptation B.U.S. Paris 1962(?), 73:17-26

71395 (& Jeanguyot, M.; Danon-Boileau, H.; Neel, D.; Lab, P.; Brousselle, A.; Levy, E.) L'organisation des cliniques médico-psychologiques de la fondation santé des étudiants de France. [The organization of medical-psychological clinics as the basis of health for French students.] Rv Np inf 1967, 15:505-535

71396 (& Danon-Boileau, H.) Le service de santé mentale universitaire. [Mental health service at the universities.] Revue Réadaptation 34, 1956

71397 (& Danon-Boileau, H.) Service de santé mentale universitaire en France—la santé mentale à l'université. [Mental health service in the university in France.] Cah Ass int Univ 1958, 3:51-61

DOUD, ROBERT M.

71398 The will and the right to believe: a study in the philosophy of William James. Penna psychiat Q 1968, 7:14-41

DOUGLAS, GWENTH

71399 Puerperal depression and excessive compliance with the mother. M 1963, 36:271-278

71400 Some emotional disorders of the puerperium. J psychosom Res 1968, 12:101-106

DOUGLAS, VIRGINIA ISABEL

71401 Children's responses to frustration: a developmental study. Canad J Psychol 1965, 19:161-171

See Werry, John S.

DOUGLAS, WILLIAM

71402 Obituary: Carl Gustav Jung: 1875-1961. AJP 1961, 74:639-641

DOUGLASS, JOSEPH H.

71403 The child, the father of the man.. Fam Coordinator 1969, 18:3-8

DOUMIC, A.

See Favreau, J.-A.

DOUMIC-GIRARD, ALICE

71404 (& Brisac, I.; Brisac, D.) Le Sommeil de l'Enfant. [Children's Sleep.] Paris: PUF 1959, 1969, 195 p
Spanish: 1963

DOUVAN, ELIZABETH

71405 (& Adelson, J.) The Adolescent Experience. NY: Wiley 1966, xii + 471 p

DOVENMUEHLE, ROBERT H.

See Busse, Ewald W.

DOWD, PATRICK J.

71406 (& Cramer, R. L.) Habituation transference in coriolis acceleration.
Aerospace Med 1967, 38:1103-1107

DOWNING, M. H.

See Rickels, K.

DOWNING, R. W.

See Rickels, K.

DOWNS, ROBERT BINGHAM

71407 Eros and death. In author's *Molders of the Modern Mind*, NY: Barnes
& Noble 1961, 368-371

DOXAS, ANGELO

71408 [Palamas (Psychoanalysis of the Life and Work of Palamus).] (Gr)
Athens: Ed. Hestia 1960
Rv Salomon, F. RFPsa 1961, 25:150

DOZIER, J. EMMETT

See Orr, William F.

DRACHMAN, ROBERT

See Caldwell, Bettye M.

DRACOULIDES, NICHOLAS N.

71409 ADIT: Test d'interpretation de dibujos abstractos. [ADIT: Abstract
Drawings Interpretation Test.] Rev Psiquiat Psicol 1960, June:527-538
71410 ADIT (with new observations). Top Probl PT 1960, 3:286-292
71411 [The aggressive feeling of atonal music.] (Gr) El. Kosmos, Athens
1967, Apr 19
71412 [Antipsychological counterfeit of the childish designs by teachers intervention.] (Gr) Athinaïki, Athens 1966, Mar 30
71413 Aristophanes: *The Clouds* and *The Wasps:* foreshadowing of psychoanalysis and psychodrama. Am Im 1966, 23:48-62
Abs JWS Q 1967, 36:138
71414 L'art psychopathologique et les déformismes de Picasso. [Psycho-
pathological art and the distortions of Picasso.] Ann Esthétique
(Athens) 1967-68, 72-77
71415 [An author of solitude and violence.] (Gr) Semaine, Athens 1966,
June 29
71416 [Cathartic tendencies of "Happenings."] (Gr) El. Kosmos, Athens
1967, Apr 20

71417 Le contact affectif interhumain: fonction, perturbations, conséquences, mesures. [Interhuman contact: function, disturbances, consequences, measures.] Ann méd-psychol 1969, (2):15-64

71418 Contact socio-affectif et solitude anxiogène. [Socio-affective contact and anxiogenic solitude.] Psychother Psychosom 1967, 15:73

71419 Créativité de l'artiste psychanalysé. [Creativity of the psychoanalyzed artist.] Acta psychother psychosom 1964, 12:391-401

71420 Déféminsation de la femme survalorisée et infantilisme d'adultes et de jeunes. [Defeminization of the overvalued woman and resulting infantilism in adult and young men.] Acta psychother psychosom 1962, 10:53-61

71421 Desegregation évolutionnelle de l'image dans l'art psychopathologique et dans le cubisme picassien. [Evolutional disaggregation of image in psychopathological art and in Picassien cubism.] Art and Psychopathology, Amsterdam 1969, 249-254

71422 L'éducation psychopédagogique des futurs parents et des maîtres et l'éducation préscolaire des enfants: doivent-elles devenir obligatoires? [The psychopedagogical education of future parents and teachers and the pre-school education of children: should they be made obligatory?] Hyg ment 1963, 52:203-220

S-44500 Essai d'interprétation des réactions de désobéissance.
        Abs An Surv Psa 1955, 6:195-196

S-44501 Fétichisme du pied.
        Abs RJA An Surv Psa 1956, 7:213

71423 [Geopsychical connections with the folkloric art.] (Gr) New Forms, Athens 1962, June

71424 [Infantile graphism in exological pictures.] (Gr) Athinaïki, Athens 1966, Sept 29

71425 Interprétation psychanalitique des "Bacchantes" d'Euripide. [Psychoanalytic interpretation of Euripides' "Bacchantes."] Acta psychother psychosom 1963, 11:14-27

71426 Interprétation psychanalytique d'un néographisme integré a un néomorphisme. [Psychoanalytical interpretation of a neographic word in a neomorphic drawing.] Acta neurol psychiat Belg 1962, 62:250-263

71427 [Killed Israeli children, drawing their life.] (Gr) Athinaïki, Athens 1965, Jan 14

71428 Manifestations de l'agressivité latente et de l'agressivité défensive de nos jours. [Manifestations of latent aggressiveness and of defensive aggressiveness in our time.] (Read at Int Psa Forum, July 1965) Ann méd-psychol 1965, 123(2):617-629

71429 [Mental preventive hygiene.] (Gr) Athens: Hygionomic Tribune 1964, 20 p

71430 Objectifs et processus psychobiologiques de la femme. [Psychobiological objectives and processes in women.] Ann méd-psychol 1962, 120 (2):667-695

71431 [Oedipus complex (and its variations).] (Gr) Athens: Hygionomic Tribune 1962, 8 p

71432 [On the life and the work of Sigmund Freud (with some personal impressions).] (Gr) Theater of Athens 1963 (Play-bill)

71433 Origine de la psychanalyse et du psychodrame. [Origin of psychoanalysis and psychodrama.] Histoire des Sciences Médicales, Paris 1967, June:101-112

71434 Les "orphelins du sein" et leur retentissement social. [The "breast orphans" and the social effects of the lack of breast-feeding.] Ann méd-psychol 1967, 125(2):375-388

71435 [Picasso.] (Gr) Athinaïki, Athens 1967, Jan 2

71436 Picasso et l'art psychopathologique. [Picasso and psychopathological art.] Action et Pensée 1967, (3) Sept.:5-8

71437 Le principe de la "Besace d'Esope" en psychodiagnostic et psychothérapie. [The principle of "The Beggar's Purse" in psychodiagnosis and psychotherapy.] Top Probl PT 1963, 4:219-232

71438 Processus identificatoires et identification chiasmatique. [The processes of identification and "chiasmatic identification."] Psychother Psychosom 1965, 13(5):342-363

71439 Projection du "Moi" de l'auteur sur son oeuvre. [The author's projection of "ego" in his work.] Action et Pensée 1962, Dec

71440 Psychanalyse d'Aristophane (de sa Vie et de ses Oeuvres). [Psychoanalysis of Aristophanes (of his Life and Works).] Paris: Ed Univ 1967, 255 p
Rv Garma, A. Rev Psicoanál 1967, 24:939-940. Gillibert, J. RFPsa 1968, 32:625-627

71441 Psychanalyse de l'Artiste et de son Oeuvre. [Psychoanalysis of the Artist and his Work.] Geneva: Mont-Blanc 1962, 240 p

71442 [Psychic complexes.](Gr) Athens: Medical Encyclopedia 1960, 20 p

71443 [Psychic factors in child drawings.] (Gr) Anexartitos 1961, Jan 3

71444 [Psychocritique and psychobiography of Edward Albee.] (Gr) Images, Athens 1965

71445 [Psychocritique and psychobiography of Tennessee Williams.] (Gr) Nea Estia, Athens 1964

71446 Psychocritique de Hedda Gabler. [Psychocritique of Hedda Gabler.] Action et Pensée 1962, Sept

71447 Psychocritique de Dionysisme. [Psychocritique of Dionysism.] In Actes du 87th Congrès National des Sociétés Savantes, Paris: Ministère de l'Education Nationale 1963, 75-120

71448 [Psychocritique of 11 comedies of Aristophanes.] (Gr) Embros, Athens 1966

71449 [Psychocritique of Jean Genet.] (Gr) Semaine, Athens 1966, June 22

71450 [Psychocritique of Palamas.] (Gr) Athens: Estia 1960, 540 p

71451 [Psychocritique of the theater of cruelty and of anti-theater.] (Gr) Semaine, Athens 1966, May 25

71452 [Psychocritique of the work of Goya.] (Gr) Embros 1963, Dec 21

71453 [Psychological analysis of the life and work of Aristophanes.] (Gr) Kathimerini, Athens 1963, June 16

71454 [Psychological analysis of the theater of Tennessee Williams.] (Gr) Semaine, Athens 1966, July 6

71455 [Psychological analysis of Vendekint's theater of sexual cruelty.] (Gr) Alpha 1966, July 21

71456 [Psychopathological Art and Picassian Cubism.] (Gr) Oss: Organon 1969 (Appeared simultaneously in English, Dutch, French, German, Italian & Spanish.)

71457 [The psychopedagogical education for parents and teachers.] (Gr)
Athens: School and Life 1961, 20 p

71458 Psychoportrait de Bernard Shaw. [Psychoportrait of Bernard Shaw.]
Action et Pensée 1964, Sept

71459 Reconversion de la situation oedipienne dans l'affectivité conjugale et
parentale. [Reconversion of the oedipal situation in conjugal and
parental affection.] Acta psychother psychosom 1961, 9:132-146

71460 [Sexual delinquency and criminality of adolescents.] (Gr) Athens:
Hygionomic Tribune 1963, 8 p

71461 [Similarities between drawings of children and the drawings of primi-
tives.] (Gr) Formes Nouvelles, Athens 1962, Nov

71462 Souvenirs personnels sur René Laforgue. [Personal memories of René
Laforgue.] Psyché, Paris 1963, 18(Sp Issue)

71463 Sur la téchnique psychanalytique et les étapes de la cure. [On psychoanalytic technic and stages of the treatment.] (Read at Int Psa
Forum, 12-14 July 1965) Ann méd-psychol 1966, 124(1):625-638

71464 Utilisation du magnétophone en psychothérapie. [Use of the tape
recorder in psychotherapy.] Psychother Psychosom 1965, 13:466-476

DRÄGER, KATHE

71465 (& Mitscherlich, A.; Richter, H. E.; Scheunert, G.; Seeger-Meistermann,
E.) Jahrbuch der Psychoanalyse. Beiträge zur Theorie und Praxis.
[Annual of Psychoanalysis. Contributions to its Theory and Practice.]
Bern: Hans Huber, Vol. I 1960; Vol. II 1961-62; Vol. III 1964, 263
p; Vol. IV 1967, 267 p; Vol. V 1968, 148 p; Vol. VI 1969, 189 p
    Rv Veszy-Wagner, L. J 1967, 48:606-607. Woltmann, A. G. R
1968-69, 55:708-709

71466 Probleme der Verwahrlosung. [Problems of neglect.] Jb Psa 1961-62,
2:124-142

71467 Übersicht über psychoanalytische Auffassungen von der Entwicklung
der wieblichen Sexualität. [Review of psychoanalytical concepts on the
development of female sexuality.] Psyche 1968, 22:410-422

See Scheunert, Glessen

DRAKE, DAVID

S-44529 A psychoanalytic interpretation of social ideology.
Abs An Surv Psa 1955, 6:440-441

DRAPEAU, P.

See Gauthier, Yvon

DRAPER, EDGAR

71468 (& Daniels, R. S.; Rada, R.) Adaptive psychotherapy: an approach
toward greater precision in the treatment of chronically disturbed.
Comprehen Psychiat 1968, 9:372-382

71469 (& Meyer, G. G.; Parzen, Z.; Samuelson, G.) On the diagnostic value
of religious ideation. Arch gen Psychiat 1965, 13:202-207

71470 Psychiatric consultation to clergymen. Int Psychiat Clin 1969, 5(4): 269-278

71471 Psychiatry and Pastoral Care. Englewood Cliffs, N.J.: Prentice-Hall 1965, 138 p
       Rv Piers, G. Q 1967, 36:126-127

71472 Psychological dynamics of religion. Int Psychiat Clin 1969, 5(4):19-36

See Daniels, Robert S.; Westberg, Granger E.

DRAPKIN, ARNOLD

See Stamm, Julian L.

DRATMAN, MITCHELL, L.

71473 Affects and consciousness. (Read at Philadelphia-Cleveland Cong, 8 June 1963) Bull Phila Ass Psa 1964, 14:183-192
       Abs Adams, W. R. Bull Phila Ass Psa 1964, 14:246-247. EFA Q 1965, 34:620. PLe RFPsa 1967, 31:309

71474 Contributor to Pearson, G. H. J. A Handbook of Child Psychoanalysis, NY/London: Basic Books 1968

See Wenar, Charles

DRAVITZ, JOEL R.

See Schonbar, Rosalea A.

DRECHSLER, ROBERT J.

71475 (& Shapiro, M. I.) A procedure for direct observation of family inter-action in a child guidance clinic. Ps 1961, 24:163-170

71476 (& Shapiro, M. I.) Two methods of analysis of family diagnostic data in a child guidance clinic. Fam Proc 1963, 2:367-379

DREGER, RALPH MASON

71477 (& Barnert, M.) Measurement of the custom and conscience functions of the superego. Soc Psych 1969, 77:269-280

71478 Perception in the context of social and personality theory. J gen Psychol 1961, 64:3-30

DREIFUSS, GUSTAV

71479 A psychological study of circumcision in Judaism. J anal Psych 1965, 10:23-32

DREIKURS, RUDOLF

71480 The Adlerian approach to psychodynamics. Contempo PT 60-79
71481 The Adlerian approach to therapy. Contempo PT 80-94
71482 Adlerian psychotherapy. In Fromm-Reichmann, F. & Moreno, J. L. Progress in Psychotherapy, NY: Grune & Stratton 1956, 111-118
71483 The current dilemma in psychotherapy. J existent Psychiat 1960-61, 1:187-206
71484 Discussion of Reich, W. J. & Nechtow, M. J. "Differential diagnosis and psychic factors in pelvic pain." In Kroger, W. S. Psychosomatic Ob-

stetrics, Gynecology and Endocrinology, Springfield, Ill: Thomas 1962, 455-459

71485 Discussion of Rutherford, R. N. et al: "Frigidity in the female partner with special reference to postpartum frigidity: some clinical observations and study programs. In Kroger, W. S. *Psychosomatic Obstetrics, Gynecology and Endocrinology,* Springfield, Ill: Thomas 1962, 415-417

71486 The dynamics of music therapy. Music Ther 1953, 3:15-23

71487 Early experiments in social psychiatry. Int J soc Psychiat 1961, 7:141-147

71488 Early experiments with group psychotherapy. PT 1959, 13:882-891

71489 Educating for self-government: a survey of four experimental schools. Humanist 1965, 25:8-12

71490 Die Ehe—eine Herausforderung. [Marriage—a Provocation.] Stuttgart: Klett 1968, 273 p

71491 Goals in psychotherapy. Psa 1956, 16:18-23. In Mahrer, A. R. *Goals in Psychotherapy,* NY: Appleton-Century-Crofts 1967, 221-237

S-44534 Group psychotherapy from the point of view of Adlerian psychology. In Rosenbaum, M. & Berger, M. *Group Psychotherapy and Group Function,* NY/London: Basic Books 1963, 168-179

71492 A humanistic view of sex. Humanist 1959, 19:84-92

71493 The impact of equality. Humanist 1964, 24:143-146

71494 The impact of the group for music therapy and music education. Music Ther 1959, 9:93-106

71495 Individual psychology: the Adlerian point of view. In Wepman, J. M. & Heine, R. W. *Concepts of Personality,* Chicago: Aldine Publ 1963, 234-256

71496 The interpersonal relationship in hypnosis; some fallacies in current thinking about hypnosis. Ps 1962, 25:219-226
         Abs HRB Q 1963, 32:140

* * * Kinderpsychotherapie durch Erziehungsberatung. See [71499]

71497 The meaning of dreams. Chicago med Sch Q 1944, 5(3):4-6; 25-26

71498 (& Crocker, D. B.) Music therapy with psychotic children. Music Ther 1955, 5:62-73

71499 Musiktherapie mit psychotischen Kindern. In Teirich, H. R. *Musik in der Medizin,* Stuttgart: Gustav Fischer 1958, 68-76. With title: Kinderpsychotherapie durch Erziehungsberatung. Hbh Kinderpsychother 95-107
         Music therapy with psychotic children. Psychiat Q 1960, 34:722-734

71500 (& Shulman, B. H.; Mosak, H. H.) Patient-therapist relationship in multiple psychotherapy. I. Its advantages to the therapist. II. Its advantages to the patient. Psychiat Q 1952, 26:219-227; 590-596

71501 Psychiatric considerations of music therapy. Music Ther 1957, 7:31-36

71502 Psychodynamic diagnosis in psychiatry. P 1963, 119:1045-1048

71503 The psychodynamics of disability—a group therapy approach. Amer Arch Rehab Ther 1954, 2(2):4-8

71504 Psychodynamics, Psychotherapy and Counseling: Collected Papers. (Mimeographed) Jamaica, W. I.: Knox Educ Serv 1958. Eugene: Univ of Oregon Pr 1963

71505 The psychological and philosophical significance of rhythm. Nat Ass mus Ther Bull 1957, 6(1):7-8, 10-11; 1961, 10(4):8-17

71506 The psychological uncertainty principle. Top Probl PT 1963, 4:23-31
71507 The religion of democracy. Humanist 1955, 15:210-215; 266-273
71508 The religion of the future. In Kuenzli, A. E. *Reconstruction in Religion: A Humanist Symposium,* Boston: Beacon Pr 1961, 3-20
71509 Die Rolle der Gruppe in der Erziehung. [The role of the group in education.] In Meyer, E. *Sozialerziehung und Gruppenunterricht, international gesehen,* Stuttgart: Ernst Klett 1963
71510 The scientific revolution. Humanist 1966, 26:8-13
71511 (& Sonstegard, M.) A specific approach to practicum supervision. Counselor Educ Supervis 1966, 6:18-25
71512 (& Mosak, H. H.) The tasks of life. I. Adler's three tasks. Indiv Psychologist 1966, 4:18-22
71513 (& Mosak, H. H.) The tasks of life. II. The fourth life task. Indiv Psychologist 1967, 4:51-56
71514 Techniques and dynamics of multiple psychotherapy. Psychiat Q 1950, 24:788-799
71515 Tele and inter-personal therapy: appraisal of Moreno's concept from the Adlerian point of view. Group PT 1955, 8:185-191
71516 The war between the generations: juvenile delinquency stumps the experts. Humanist 1961, 21:15-24
71517 The White House Conference on Children and Youth, 1960; a crittique: triumph of institutionalism. Humanist 1960, 20:281-287
71518 (& Soltz, V.) Your Child and Discipline. (Pamphlet) Washington, D.C.: Nat Educ Ass 1964
71519 Zur Frage der Selbstmordprophylaxe. [On the question of suicide prevention.] Allg Z Psychiat 1930, 93:98-114

See Dinkmeyer, Don C.; Shlien, John M.

DRELLICH, MARVIN G.

71520 (& Waxenberg, S. E.) Erotic and affectional components of female sexuality. Sci Psa 1966, 10:45-53
71521 Psychoanalysis of marital partners by separate analysts. Marriage Relat 237-250
S-44541 (& Bieber, I.) The psychologic importance of the uterus and its functions. Some psychoanalytic implications of hysterectomy.
Abs DW An Surv Psa 1958, 9:206-208

See Bieber, Irving

DRESSER, JOHN W.

See Lustig, Noel

DREYFUS, ALBERT E.

71522 Group psychoanalysis. JNMD 1960, 131:271

DREYFUS, HUBERT L.

TRANSLATION OF:
(& Dreyfus, P. A.) Merleau-Ponty, M. [83641]

DREYFUS, LAURETTE

ABSTRACTS OF:

71523 Akmakjian, H. Psychoanalysis and the future of literary criticism. RFPsa 1962, 27:352

71524 Arieti, S. The loss of reality. RFPsa 1962, 27:348

71525 Arlow, J. A. Fantasy systems in twins. RFPsa 1962, 26:332

71526 Askew, M. W. Catharsis and modern tragedy. RFPsa 1962, 27:349

71527 Balint, M. Primary narcissism and primary love. RFPsa 1961, 25:160

71528 Bell, A. I. The significance of the scrotal sac and testicles for the prepuberty male. RFPsa 1966, 30(Suppl):326

71529 Beres, D. The unconscious fantasy. RFPsa 1963, 27:357

71530 Bressler, B. First dreams in analysis: their relation to early memories and the preoedipal mother. RFPsa 1962, 27:352

71531 Brody, S. Self-rocking in infancy. RFPsa 1962, 26:331

71532 Bychowski, G. Escapades: a form of dissociation. RFPsa 1963, 27:356

71533 Bychowski, G. Psychosis precipitated by psychoanalysis. RFPsa 1968, 32:183

71534 Devereux, G. Loss of identity, impairment of relationship, reading disability. RFPsa 1967, 31:330

71535 Devereux, G. & Hoffman, F. H. Non-recognition of the patient by the analyst. RFPsa 1962, 27:348

71536 Friedman, D. B. Death anxiety and the primal scene. RFPsa 1962, 27:352

71537 Gero, G. Sadism, masochism and aggression: their role in symptom-formation. RFPsa 1963, 27:358

71538 Giovacchini, P. L. The ego and the psychosomatic state: report of two cases. RFPsa 1962, 26:331

71539 Greenacre, P. Woman as artist. RFPsa 1962, 26:332

71540 Greenberg, H. R. Pyromania in a woman. RFPsa 1967, 31:332

71541 Greenson, R. M. The working alliance and the transference neurosis. RFPsa 1966, 30(Suppl):325

71542 Hesselbach, C. F. Superego regression in paranoia. RFPsa 1963, 27:358

71543 Kanzer, M. The motor sphere of the transference. RFPsa 1968, 32:360

71544 Kanzer, M. Verbal and nonverbal aspects of free association. RFPsa 1962, 26:627

71545 Kaplan, D. M. The emergence of projection in a series of dreams. RFPsa 1962, 27:354

71546 Kestenberg, J. S. The role of movement patterns in development. Rhythms of movement. RFPsa 1966, 30:325

71547 Kleeman, J. A. Dreaming for a dream course. RFPsa 1963, 27:357

71548 Knapp, P. H. et al: Suitability for psychoanalysis: a review of 100 supervised analytic cases. RFPsa 1962, 26:334

71549 Kubie, L. S. The fallacious misuse of the concept of sublimation. RFPsa 1963, 27:355

71550 Mahler, M. S. & Furer, M. Observations on research regarding the "symbiotic syndrome" of infantile psychosis. RFPsa 1962, 26:333

71551 Meismer, W. W. The operational principle and meaning in psychoanalysis. RFPsa 1967, 31:332

71552 Menaker, E. The self-image as defense and resistance. RFPsa 1961, 25:161
71553 Monsour, K. J. Asthma and the fear of death. RFPsa 1961, 25:160
71554 Moriarty, D. M. Early loss and the fear of mothering. RFPsa 1962, 27:354
71555 Nydes, J. Creativity and psychotherapy. RFPsa 1962, 27:353
71556 Ostow, M. The psychic function of depression. RFPsa 1962, 26:334
71557 Peters, R. J. Immortality and the artist. RFPsa 1962, 27:352
71558 Roth, N. The face-genital equation. RFPsa 1961, 25:411
71559 St. John, R. Regression as a defence in chronic schizophrenia. RFPsa 1968, 32:183
71560 Schuster, D. B. Notes on "A child is being beaten." RFPsa 1968, 32:183
71561 Sherman, M. H. Siding with the resistance in paradigmatic psychotherapy. RFPsa 1962, 27:351
71562 Slap, J. W. On sarcasm. RFPsa 1967, 31:330
71563 Sperling, M. Analytic first aid in school phobias. RFPsa 1962, 26:627
71564 Spotnitz, H. The narcissistic defence in schizophrenia. RFPsa 1962, 27:350
71565 Strean, H. S. Difficulties met in the treatment of adolescents. RFPsa 1962, 27:349
71566 Waelder, R. Inhibitions, symptoms and anxiety: 40 years later. RFPsa 1968, 32:361
71567 Waldhorn, H. F. Assessment of analyzability: technical and theoretical observations. RFPsa 1962, 26:335
71568 Weiner, N. D. On bibliomania. RFPsa 1967, 31:332
71569 Weissman, P. Theoretical considerations of ego regression and ego functions in creativity. RFPsa 1968, 32:361
71570 Winick, C. & Holt, H. Differential recall of the dream as a function of audience perception. RFPsa 1962, 27:354
71571 Yazmajian, R. V. Pathological urination and weeping. RFPsa 1967, 31:330

DREYFUS, MADELEINE

TRANSLATION OF:
Orgler, H. [85785]

DREYFUS, PATRICIA ALLEN

See Dreyfus, Hubert L.

DREYFUS-MOREAU, JANINE

71572 A propos de quelques facteurs favorisant l'impuissance. [Some factors favoring sexual impotence.] Évolut psychiat 1964, 29:437-458
S-44603 Bilan d'une expérience de psychanalyse collective.
Abs An Surv Psa 1955, 6:375-378
71573 Traitement des impuissance psychogènes. [Management of psychogenic impotencies.] Pr méd 1963, 71:1654-1655

REVIEW OF:
71574 Ellis, H. Étude de Psychologie Sexuelle. RFPsa 1966, 30:321

DRINNON, RICHARD

71575 In the American heartland: Hemingway and death. R 1965, 52(2): 6-31
       Abs SRS Q 1966, 35:471

DRISCOLL, P. M. DE

TRANSLATIONS OF:
Lagache, D. [79849]. Zetzel, E. R. [95691]

DROSE VERA

See Vandenbergh, Richard L.

DRUCKER, MAUREEN N.

71576 (& Greenson, J.) The meaning of waiting for help. Reiss-Davis Clin Bull 1965, 2:97-103

DRUMHELLER, SIDNEY J.

71577 A Jung oriented rationale for a program for moral education. Relig Relig Educ 1968, 63:131-136

DRUSS, RICHARD G.

71578 Cases of suspected homosexuality seen at an army mental hygiene consultation service. Psychiat Q 1967, 41:62
71579 Foreign marriages in the military. Psychiat Q 1965, 39:330
71580 Group intake conferences at a mental hygiene consultation service. Milit Med 1964, 129:777
71581 Problems associated with retirement from military service. Milit Med 1965, 130:382
71582 (& O'Connor, J. F.; Prudden, J. F.; Stern, L. O.) Psychologic response to colectomy. Arch gen Psychiat 1968, 18:53-59
71583 (& Kornfield, D. S.) The survivors of cardiac arrest. A psychiatric study. JAMA 1967, 201:291-296
71584 Teaching psychiatry to medical students assigned to clinical medicine. Psychosomatics 1967, 8:331-333

DRY, AVIS M.

71585 Obituary: Carl Gustav Jung, 1875-1961. Brit J Psychol 1961, 52:311-315
71586 The Psychology of Jung (a Critical Interpretation). London: Methuen; NY: Wiley 1962, xiv + 329 p
       Rv Hartogs, R. R 1963, 50:693

DRYE, ROBERT C.

See Grinker, Roy R., Sr.

DUBCOVSKY, SANTIAGO

71587 (& Schutt, F. E. de; Teper, E.) Anti-Semitism: the magic reality conflict. Am Im 1966, 23:132-141
   Abs JWS Q 1967, 36:472

ABSTRACTS OF:
71588 Arlow, J. A. The supervisory situation. Rev Psicoanál 1963, 20:396-397
71589 Bernfeld, S. On psychoanalytic training. Rev Psicoanál 1964, 21:87-89
71590 DeBell, D. E. A critical digest of the literature on psychoanalytic supervision. Rev Psicoanál 1963, 20:395
71591 Eissler, K. R. Freud and the psychoanalysis of history. Rev Psicoanál 1964, 21:261
71592 Fleming, J. & Benedek, T. Supervision, a method of teaching psychoanalysis. Rev Psicoanál 1964, 21:383-385
71593 Glover, E. Freudian or neofreudian? Rev psicoanál 1964, 21:385
71594 Loewenstein, R. M. Some considerations on free association. Rev Psicoanál 1963, 20:393
71595 Needles, W. Eros and the repetition compulsion. Rev Psicoanál 1964, 21:89

REVIEW OF:
71596 Schur, M. The problem of death in Freud's writings and life. Rev Psicoanál 1967, 24:693-697

DUBLIN, CHRISTINE

See Lourie, Reginald S.

DUBLINEAU, J.

71597 L'émotion dans l'oeuvre de Wallon et le problème type évolutif. [Emotion in the work of Wallon and the typical evolutionary type.] Évolut psychiat 1962, 27:67
   Abs Auth Rev Psicoanál 1963, 20:80

DUBO, SARA

71598 (& Rabinovitch, R. D.) Child psychiatry. Prog Neurol Psychiat 1960, 15:429-441; 1961, 16:436-450; 1962, 17:436-449

DUBOCZY, JOHN B.

See Cassell, Wilfred A.

DUBOS, RENE J.

71599 Biological remembrance of things past: environmental determinants of human life. (Freud Memorial lecture, 28 Apr 1967) Bull Phila Ass Psa 1967, 17:133-148
71600 Mirage of Health. Garden City, NY: Doubleday 1961, 235 p

DUBOUCHET, JEANNE

71601 Essai de Formalisation de la Psychologie. [An Attempt at a Formulation of Psychology.] Paris: Le Francois 1965
Rv PLe RFPsa 1967, 31:299-301

DUBOWY, MILDRED W.

See Lawrence, Margaret M.

DUBREIL, G.

See Wittkower, Eric D.

DUBROVSKY, DUSYA T.

TRANSLATION OF:
Zulliger, H. [95868]

DUCHE, D. J.

71602 [The approach and therapeutic perspectives of psychoanalysis in children suffering from character disturbances.] (Fr) Clinique 1962, 57:611-615

DUCHE, J.-D.

See Lang, Jean-Louis

DUCHESNE, A.

See Dongier, Suzanne

DUCKWORTH, ELEANOR

TRANSLATION OF:
Piaget, J. [86528]

DUDEK, STEPHANIE Z.

71603 (& Lester, E. P.) The good child facade in chronic underachievers. Ops 1968, 38:153-160
71604 Regression and creativity. A comparison of the Rorschach records of successful vs. unsuccessful painters and writers. JNMD 1968, 147: 535-546

See Wittkower, Eric D.

DUDLEY, DONALD L.

71605 (& Holmes, T. H.; Martin, C. J.; Ripley, H. S.) Changes in respiration associated with hypnotically induced emotion, pain and exercise. PSM 1964, 24:46-57. Amer Psychiat Assoc Summaries 1963, 150-151
71606 (& Holmes, T. H.; Martin, C. J.; Ripley, H. S.) Hypnotically induced facsimile of pain. Arch gen Psychiat 1966, 15:198-204. JNMD 1967, 144:258-265

DUFF, D. F.

See Horowitz, Mardi J.

DUFFY, E. L.

See Wood, Howard P.

DUFFY, JAMES H.

71607 (& Kraft, I. A.) Beginning and middle phase characteristics of group psychotherapy of early adolescent boys and girls. J Psa in Groups 1966-67, 2(1):23-29
71608 Childhood schizophrenia. Med Rec Ann 1964, 57:344-345
71609 (& Kraft, I. A.) Group therapy of early adolescents: an evaluation of one year of group therapy with a mixed group of early adolescents. Ops 1965, 35:372

DUFFY, PHILIP E.

See Hollender, Marc H.

DUFFY, VERNON

71610 From Beside the Couch. NY: Vantage 1962, 44 p

DUGAS, M.

See Anzieu, Annie

DUHL, LEONARD J.

71611 (& Leopold, R. L.) Contributions of psychoanalysis to social psychiatry. Sci Psa 1965, 8:171-184
71612 Planning and predicting: or what to do when you don't know the names of the variables. Daedalus 1967, 96:779-788. In Gray, W. et al: General Systems Theory and Psychiatry, Boston: Little, Brown 1969, 337-346
71613 (& Leopold, R. L.) Relationship of psychoanalysis with social agencies: community implications. Mod Psa 577-597
71614 (Ed) Urban America and the Planning of Mental Health Services, Symposium No. 10. GAP 1964, 5:385-516
71615 (Ed) The Urban Condition: People and Policy in the Metropolis. NY: Basic Books 1963, 410 p

See Leopold, Robert L.

DÜHRSSEN, ANNEMARIE

71616 (& Jorswieck, E.) Eine empirisch-statistische Untersuchung zur Leistungsfähigkeit psychoanalytischer Behandlung. [An empirical-statistical investigation into the efficacy of psychoanalytic therapy.] Nervenarzt 1965, 36:166-169
71617 Katamnestische Ergebnisse bei 1004 Patienten nach analytischer Psychotherapie. [Catamnestic results with 1004 patients following analytic psychotherapy.] Z PSM 1962, 8:94-113

71618 Katamnestische Untersuchungen bei 150 Kindern und Jugendlichen nach analytischer Psychotherapie. [Catamnestic studies of 150 children and adolescents following analytic psychotherapy.] Prax Kinderpsychol 1964, 13:241-255

71618A [Possibilities and problems of short-term therapy.] (Ger) Z Psychosom Med Psychoanal 1969, 15:229-238

71618B [Preventive measures in the family.] (Ger) Psychother Psychosom 1968, 16:319-332

71619 Das Problem der Intelligenz in der Psychotherapie. [The problem of intelligence in psychotherapy.] Nervenarzt 1964, 35:22-28

71620 Die Prognose in der Psychoanalyse. [Prognosis in psychoanalysis.] Z PSM 1966, 12:97-105
       El pronóstico en el psicoanálisis. Rev Psicoanál Psiquiat Psicol 1967, 6:56-66

71621 Wissenschaftliche und medizinalpolitische Aspekte in der Kinderpsychiatrie. [Scientific and medico-political aspects in child psychiatry.] Psychother Psychosom 1965, 13:47-57

71622 (& Jorswieck, E.) Zur Korrektur von Eysencks Berichterstattung über psychoanalytische Behandlungsergebnisse. [On the correction of Eysenck's report on the results of psychoanalytic therapy.] Acta psychother psychosom 1962, 10:329-342

DUIJKER, H. C. J.

71623 Enkele opmerkingen over driften. [Some comments concerning drives.] Ned Tijdschr Psychol 1967, 22:549-567

DUKE, ROBERT BRADFORD

71624 (& Wrightsman, L. S.) Relation of repression-sensitization to philosophies of human nature. Psychol Rep 1968, 22:235-238

DULANY, DONELSON EDWIN, JR.

71625 (& De Valois, R. L.; Beardslee, D. C.; Winterbottom, M. R.) (Eds) Contributions to Modern Psychology: Selected Readings in General Psychology. NY: Oxford Univ Pr 1958, 1963, 1964(2nd ed, rev), xii + 484 p

DUNBAR, FLANDERS

71626 Accidents and life experience. In Dunbar, F. & Brody, L. *Basic Aspects and Applications of the Psychology of Safety*, NY: NY Univ, Center Safety Education 1959, 1-5

71627 (& Brody, L.) Basic Aspects and Applications of the Psychology of Safety. NY: NY Univ, Center Safety Education 1959, 24 p

71628 Comprehensive treatment by the non-psychiatrist. In Kroger, W. S. *Psychosomatic Obstetrics, Gynecology and Endocrinology*, Springfield, Ill: Thomas 1962, 705-718

71629 Emotional factors in spontaneous abortion. In Kroger, W. S. *Psychosomatic Obstetrics, Gynecology and Endocrinology*, Springfield, Ill: Thomas 1962, 135-143

DUNCAN, GLEN M.

See Beckett, Peter G. S.

DUNCAN, ROBERT H.

See Greenhill, Maurice H.

DUNDES, ALAN

71630 Discussion of Sandford, B. "Cinderella." Psa Forum 1967, 2:139-141
71631 Earth-diver: creation of the mythopoeic male. Amer Anthropologist 1962, 64:1032-1051
71632 The father, the son, and the holy grail. Lit & Psych 1962, 12:101-112
71633 The folklore of wishing wells. Am Im 1962, 19:27-34
71634 Summoning deity through ritual fasting. Am Im 1963, 20:213-220

See Abrahams, Roger D.

DUNKELL, SAMUEL V.

71635 Acting out, obesity and existence. Acting Out 135-141

DUNLOP, HOPE E.

See Kramer, Charles H.

DUNN, JOHN M.

71636 (& Altman, S. I.) Child psychiatry. Prog Neurol Psychiat 1967, 22:422-434

See Settlage, Calvin F.

DUNN, R. E.

See Stotland, Ezra

DUNTEMAN, G.

See Bass, Bernard M.

DUNTON, H. DONALD

See Ravich, Robert A.

DUPERTUIS, C. WESLEY

See Calden, George

DUPONT, HENRY J.

71637 Social learning theory and the treatment of transvestite behavior in an eight year old boy. Psychotherapy 1968, 5:44-45

DUPONT, ROBERT LOUIS, JR.

71638 (& Grunebaum, H. U.) The willing victims: husbands of paranoid women. P 1968, 125:151-159

DUPONT MUÑOZ, MARCO ANTONIO

ABSTRACTS OF:

71639 Garma, A. Investigaciones recientes sobre el soñar y el dormir (actualizaciones). Cuad Psa 1967, 3:246-247

71640 Rosenbaum, M. Dreams in which the analyst appears undisguised. A clinical and statistical study. Cuad Psa 1965, 1:384

DUPRE, J.

See Danon-Boileau, Henri

DURAND, CHARLES

S-44678 (& Folch, P.) Le transfert dans la cure pré-analytique. Abs An Surv Psa 1955, 6:330-331

DURAND DE BOUSINGEN, R.

See Bauer, J.-P.; Kammerer, T.

DURBAN, PIERRE

71641 A propos d'une observation selon la psychanalyse de Jung et des conceptions qui peuvent en decouler. [Apropos of a case treated by Jung's psychoanalytic method and of concepts which may arise from it.] Ann méd-psychol 1964, 122(1):747-774

71642 Psychanalyse d'un gnostique: "Psychanalyse diabolique." [Psychoanalysis of a gnostic: "Diabolical psychoanalysis."] Ann méd-psychol 1967, 125(1):657-686

71643 La psychologie des prostituées. [Psychology of prostitutes.] Ann méd-psychol 1966, 124(1):169-192

DURBIN, EVAN FRANK MOTTRAM

71644 (& Bowlby, J.) Personal aggressiveness and war. In Bramson, L. & Goethals, G. W. *War: Studies from Psychology, Sociology, Anthropology*, NY: Basic Books 1964, 81-103

DURELL, JACK

See Steinberg, Harry R.

DURHAM, JOHN

71645 The influence of John Stuart Mill's mental crisis on his thoughts. Am Im 1963, 20:369-384

DURKHEIM, EMILE

71646 (& Ellis, A.) Incest: The Nature and Origin of the Taboo. The Origins and the Development of the Incest Taboo. NY: Lyle Stuart 1963, 186 p

71647 Suicide. A Study in Sociology. (Tr: Spaulding, J. A. & Simpson, G.) (Ed: Simpson, G.) NY: Free Pr 1966, 405 p

DURKIN, HARRY, JR.

See Kaufman, Irving

DURKIN, HELEN E.

71648 (& Glatzer, H. T.; Kadis, A. L.; Wolf, A.; Hulse, W. C.) Acting out in group psychotherapy: a panel discussion. PT 1957, 12:87-105

71649 (& Glatzer, H. T.) Combined individual and group psychoanalysis. Symposium, 1959. 3. Discussion. Ops 1960, 30:242-246

71650 The Group in Depth. NY: IUP 1964; London: Bailey Bros 1965, xii + 378 p
Rv GPK Q 1966, 35:301-303

71651 Limitations of the parent's role in producing neurosis. In Merin, J. H. & Nagler, S. H. *The Etiology of the Neuroses,* Palo Alto, Calif: Sci & Behav Books 1966, 64-68; 90-93

71652 Vicissitudes of the concept of transference in the clinical practice of group psychotherapy. Ops 1962, 32:313-314

See Bieber, Toby B.; Shaskan, Donald A.

DURKIN, RODERICK

71653 Social functions of psychological interpretations. Ops 1967, 37:956-962

DUROCHER, M. A.

See Green, Morris

DURST, W.

71654 Epileptoide Psychopathie—epilepsiekorrelierte Enzephalopathie. [Epileptoid psychopathy—encephalopathy correlated with epilepsy.] In Kranz, H. *Psychopathologie Heute,* Stuttgart: Georg Thieme 1962, 185-192

DU SOLD, DONALD D.

See Masserman, Jules H.

DUVE, ANNE M.

71655 Psychodynamics and learning. Nord Psykol 1966, 18:201-209

DUYCKAERTS, FRANÇOIS

71656 La Formation du Lien Sexuel. [The Formation of the Sexual Bond.] Brussels: Dessart 1964, 326 p

71657 Les impasses dans les theories de la personnalité. [The deadlocks in the theories on personality.] Acta neurol psychiat Belg 1961, 61:658-665

71657A [Normal sexuality and genital love.] (Fr) Bruxelles méd 1969, 49:711-716

DWORSCHAK, ROSA

71658 Tiefenpsychologie als Hilfswissenschaft der Sozialarbeit. [Depth psychology as an auxiliary science in social work.] In Bolterauer, L. *Aus der Werkstatt des Erziehungsberaters,* Vienna: Verlag f. Jugend und Volk 1960, 175-183

DWYER, JOHN HARRINGTON

71659 (& Dwyer, M. L.) Vincent van Gogh: a study of the relationship between some childhood disturbances and his drive to paint. Psychiat
Comm 1963, 6:1-8

DWYER, MARYELLEN LEE

See Dwyer, John H.

DWYER, THOMAS F.

S-44701 (& Zinberg, N. E.) Psychiatry for medical school instructors. In Zinberg, N. E. *Psychiatry and Medical Practice in a General Hospital,*
NY: IUP 1964, 88-97

71660 Psychoanalytic teaching in the medical school. Teach Dyn Psychiat
23-37; 77-78

See Bibring, Grete L.

DYCK, G.

71660A "Talking the dozens." A game of insults played in a group of adolescent
boys. BMC 1969, 33:108-116

DYK, R. B.

71660B An exploratory study of mother-child interaction in infancy as related
to the development of differentiation. J Amer Acad Child Psychiat
1969, 8:657-691

DYKENS, JAMES W.

See Bandler, Bernard

DYKMAN, ROSCOE A.

See Reese, William G.

DYMOND, ROSALIND F.

71661 Adjustment changes in the absence of psychotherapy. In Goldstein,
A. P. & Dean, S. J. *The Investigation of Psychotherapy,* NY: Wiley
1966, 217-221

DYRUD, JARL E.

71662 (& Donnelly, C.) Executive function of the ego. Clinical and pro-
cedural relevance. Arch gen Psychiat 1969, 20:257-261

DYSINGER, ROBERT H.

71663 The family as the unit of study and treatment. Workshop 1959. 2. A
family perspective on the diagnosis of individual members. Ops 1961,
31:61-68

DYTRYCH, Z.

See Haas, Ladislav

D'ZMURA, THOMAS L.

71664 The function of individual supervision. Int Psychiat Clin 1964, 1:377-387

See Baum, O. Eugene; Gottschalk, Louis A.

E

EAGLE, CAROL J.

71665 An investigation of individual consistencies in the manifestations of primary process. Diss Abstr 1964, 25:2045

See Shaw, R.

EARLE, A. M.

71666 (& Earle, B. V.) Early material deprivation and later psychiatric illness. Ops 1961, 31:181-186
Abs JMa RFPsa 1962, 26:324

EARLE, BRIAN VIGORS

71667 Periodic hypersomnia and megaphagia (the Kleine-Levin syndrome). Psychiat Q 1965, 39:79-83

See Earle, A. M.

EARLEY, LEROY WILLIAM

71668 (& Gregg, L. A.) A long-term experience with joint medical-psychiatric teaching. J med Educ 1959, 34:927-930
71669 (& Bond, D. W.; Sprague, C. C.; Gaskill, H.; Holland, B.; Busse, E. W.) (Eds) Teaching Psychiatry in Medical School, Wash DC: Am Psychiat Ass 1969, ix + 587 p

EASSER, BARBARA RUTH

71670 (& Lesser, S. R.) Hysterical personality: a re-evaluation. Q 1965, 34:390-412
71671 (& Lesser, S. R.) Transference resistance in hysterical character neurosis: technical considerations. In Goldman, G. S. & Shapiro, D. *Developments in Psychoanalysis at Columbia University*, NY: Hafner Publ 1966, 69-80

See Cooper, Arnold M.; Karush, Aaron

EASSON, WILLIAM MCALPINE

71672 Adolescent inpatients in love. A therapeutic contradiction. Arch gen Psychiat 1967, 16:758-763

71673 Adolescents' environments reveal diagnostic clues. Hosp Comm Psychiat 1967, 18:119-121

71674 The anaclitic ego deficiency syndrome of adolescence. Adolescence 1967, 2(5):97-106

71675 The appearance of the adolescent as a diagnostic indicator. Pediatrics 1966, 38:842-844

71676 Body image and self-image in children. Phantom phenomenon in a 3-year-old child. Arch gen Psychiat 1961, 4:619-621

71677 Care of the young patient who is dying. JAMA 1968, 205:203-207

71678 The continued nonpatient. An adolescent dilemma. Arch gen Psychiat 1967, 16:359-363

71679 Ego defects in nonpsychotic adolescents. Psychiat Q 1968, 42:156-168

71680 The ego-ideal in the treatment of children and adolescents. Arch gen Psychiat 1966, 15:288-292
           Abs PB Q 1969, 38:513

71681 Encopresis, psychogenic soiling. Canad Med Ass J 1960, 82:624-628

71682 Gasoline addiction in children. Pediatrics 1962, 29:250-254

71683 The management of depression in children and adolescents. Ohio State med J 1968, 64:1024-1027

71684 (& Steinhilber, R. M.) Murderous aggression by children and adolescents. Arch gen Psychiat 1961, 4:1-9

71685 Myxedema with psychosis. Arch gen Psychiat 1966, 14:277-283

71686 Projection as an etiological factor in "motiveless" delinquency. Psychiat Q 1967, 41:228-232

71687 Psychopathological environmental reaction to congenital defect. JNMD 1966, 142:453-459

71688 The Severely Disturbed Adolescent; Inpatient, Residential, and Hospital Treatment. NY: IUP 1969, viii + 249 p

EASTMAN, DONALD F.

71689 An exploratory investigation of the psychoanalytic theory of stuttering by means of the Blacky Pictures Test. Diss Abstr 1960, 21:1629

EASTMAN, MAX

71689A A significant memory of Freud. New Republic 1941, 104(20):19 May

EASTON, KARL

71690 Clinical studies of the pathogenesis and personality structure of made narcotic addicts. J Hillside Hosp 1965, 14:36-53

71691 Considerations on autism in infancy and childhood. NYSJM 1962, 62:3628-3633

71692 Hysterical paralysis associated with intrapsychic conflict and unrepressed memories of a rape experience in childhood (a case report). J Hillside Hosp 1966, 15:26-35

71693 (& Blau, A.) Neonatal and mother-infant observations in child psychiatry training. J Amer Acad Child Psychiat 1963, 2:176-186

71694 Neonatal behavior, mother-baby interactions, and personality development. NYSJM 1966, 66:1874-1882

71695 Types of clinical psychiatric pictures observed in heart disease. NYSJM 1961, 61:2103-2109

71696 Welfare services. (Interviewer: Perkins, M. E.) In Ziskind, R. *Viewpoint on Mental Health*, NY: NYC Comm Ment Hlth Board 1967, 421-426

See Blau, Abram

EATON, ARTHUR

71697 Some implications and effects of intragroup acting out of pregenital conflicts. Int J grp PT 1962, 12:435-447

EATON, LOUIS

See Menolascino, Frank J.

EATON, MERRILL THOMAS

71698 (& Peterson, M. H.) Psychiatry. Flushing, NY: Medical Examination Publ Co 1967, 564 p

EBAUGH, FRANKLIN G.

71699 The case of the confused parent. P 1962, 118:1136-1138

71700 The evolution of psychiatric education: editor's notebook. P 1969, 126:97-100

71701 Mental health: goals and paths to achieving them. Rocky Mtn med J 1962, 59:33-35

71702 (& Barnes, R. H.) Psychiatric education. P 1962, 118:646-650

71703 Summary report of the Preparatory Commission on Social Climate. In Earley, L. W. et al: *Teaching Psychiatry in Medical School*, Wash DC: Am Psychiat Ass 1969, 94-100

EBENSTEIN, WILLIAM

71704 Freud. In author's *Great Political Thinkers* 844-848

71705 (Ed) Great Political Thinkers: Plato to the Present. NY: Rinehart 1951, 903 p; 1956, 940 p; 1960, 978 p

71706 (Ed) Modern Political Thought; the Great Issues. 2d ed. NY: Rinehart 1954, 806 p; 1960, 875 p

EBERHARD, GÖRAN

71707 Peptic ulcer in twins. A study in personality, heredity, and environment. Acta Psychiat Scand Suppl 1968, 205:118 p

71708 The personality at peptic ulcer. Preliminary report of a twin study. Acta Psychiat Scand Suppl 1968, 203:131-133

EBLING, F. J.

See Carthy, John D.

EBON, MARTIN

71709 Parapsychological dream studies. In Grunebaum, G. E. von & Caillois, R. *The Dream and Human Societies*, Berkeley/Los Angeles: Univ Calif Pr 1966, 163-175

REVIEWS OF:

71710 Edmunds, S. Miracles of the Mind. R 1969, 56:145-147
71711 Pratt, J. G. Parapsychology: an Insider's View of ESP. R 1969, 56: 145-147
71712 Rao, K. R. Experimental Parapsychology. R 1969, 56:145-147
71713 Schwarz, B. E. Psycho-Dynamics. R 1969, 56:145-147

EBTINGER, RENÉ

71714 L'adolescent et son corps (à propos de l'hypocondrie et du suicide). [The adolescent and his body (on hypochondria and suicide).] Strasbourg Méd 1967, (9):844-855
71715 (& Renoux, M.) Aspects psychopathologiques de la paternité. [Psychopathological aspects of fatherhood.] Proc IV World Cong Psychiat 1966, 1680-1682
71716 [Pathological reactions to paternity.] (Fr) Strasbourg Méd 1963, 14: 971-982
71717 La réalité dans l'expérience psychanalytique. [Reality in the psychoanalytic experience.] Riv sper Freniat 1965, 89:31-67

See Kammerer, T.

ECK, MARCEL

71718 Approche psychanalytique de Marcel Proust (1). A propos de deux livres récents. [The psychoanalytical approach to Marcel Proust (I). Apropos of 2 recent books.] Pr méd 1968, 76:135-138

ECKARDT, MARIANNE H.

71719 Changes in the self and identity during psychoanalysis. Self and identity: a magic deception? Psa 1963, 23:9-13
71720 The detached person: a discussion with a phenomenological bias. Psa 1960, 20:139-163
71721 Discussion of Chrzanowski, G. "The independent roots of ego psychology and their therapeutic implications." Sci Psa 1967, 11:158-160
71722 Discussion of Enelow, A. J. & Adler, L. M. "The 'here and now' as the focus of psychotherapy." Sci Psa 1965, 8:222-224
71723 Discussion of Pumpian-Mindlin, E. "Anna Freud and Erik H. Erikson." Sci Psa 1964, 7:13-16
71724 Discussion of Shainess, N. "Feminine identity and mothering." Sci Psa 1964, 7:249-252
71725 Discussion of Speigel, R. "The role of father-daughter relationships in depressive women." Sci Psa 1966, 10:119-120
71726 Overevaluation of anxiety in the treatment process. Sci Psa 1963, 6:192-200
71727 Process or programming: new emphases in psychotherapy. Proc IV World Cong Psychiat 1966, 765-769
71728 Psychotherapy of anxiety states. P 1966, 122:940-943. Curr psychiat Ther 1966, 6:62-63
71729 [Responsibility systems and psychoanalytic reflections.] (Sp) Folia Clín Int 1966, 16:34-40
71730 Therapeutic perspectives. Contempo Psa 1969, 6:1-12

71731   Values, identity and the psychoanalytic process. Sci Psa 1962, 5:265-271

See Rubins, Jack L.; Weiss, Frederick A.; Wolstein, Benjamin

ECKARDT, U. VON

See Fernández-Marina, Ramón

ECKHARDT, WILLIAM

71732   Psychoneurotic values. J Amer Osteopath Ass 1967, 66:982-983

ECKMAN, K. M.

See Zuckerman, Marcia

EDDY, EVELYN

See Caldwell, Bettye M.

EDDY, W. B.

See Glad, Donald D.

EDEL, ABRAHAM

71733   Concept of the unconscious: some analytic preliminaries. Philos Sci 1964, 31:18-33
71734   The psychopathic personality in the light of the philosophy of ethics. Arch Crim Psychodyn 1961, 4 (Spec. No.):466-471

EDEL, LEON

71735   The biographer and psycho-analysis. (Read at Boston Soc Inst, 23 March 1961) J 1961, 42:458-466
          Abs WPK Q 1962, 31:579
71736   Hawthorne's symbolism and psychoanalysis. In Manheim, L. & Manheim, E. *Hidden Patterns,* NY: Macmillan 1966, 93-111
71737   Literary criticism and psychoanalysis. Contempo Psa 1965, 1(2):151-163
71738   Psychoanalysis and the "creative" arts. Mod Psa 626-641
71739   Willa Cather and the professor's house. In Malin, I. *Psychoanalysis and American Fiction,* NY: Dutton 1965, 199-221

EDEL, ROBERTA R.

71740   What Little Hans learned: review of a learning theory approach. Contempo Psa 1968, 4(2):189-204

EDELHEIT, HENRY

71741   Binswanger and Freud. Q 1967, 36:85-90
71742   Discussion of Lubin, A. J. "The influence of the Russian Orthodox Church on Freud's Wolf-Man: a hypothesis." Psa Forum 1967, 2:165-166
71743   Jung's memories, dreams, reflections. Q 1964, 33:561-566

71744 (Reporter) Language and the development of the ego. (Panel: Am Psa Ass, 6 May 1967) J Am Psa Ass 1968, 16:113-122

71745 Speech and psychic structure. The vocal-auditory organization of the ego. (Read at Am Psa Ass, 5 May 1967) J Am Psa Ass 1969, 17:381-412

REVIEWS OF:

71746 Gutheil, E. A. The Handbook of Dream Analysis. Q 1961, 30:118-119

71747 Prelinger, E. et al: An Ego-Psychological Approach to Character Assessment. Q 1965, 34:289-290

71748 Sebeok, T. A. et al (Eds) Approaches to Semiotics: Transactions of the Indiana University Conference on Paralinguistics and Kinesics. Q 1968, 37:299-304

71749 Watzlawick, P. et al: Pragmatics of Human Communication. A Study of International Patterns, Pathologies, and Paradoxes. Q 1968, 37:299-304

EDELSON, MARSHALL

71750 Ego Psychology, Group Dynamics, and the Therapeutic Community. NY: Grune & Stratton 1964, xii + 242 p

Rv Semrad, E. V. & Day, M. J Am Psa Ass 1966, 14:591-618

71751 (& Marcus, M.) Priorities in community mental health programs: a theoretical formulation. Soc Psychiat 1967, 2(2):66-71

71752 Schizophrenia. In Conn, H. Current Therapy 1966, Phila: W. B. Saunders 1966, 621-626

71753 The sociotherapeutic function in a psychiatric hospital. J Fort Logan Ment Hlth Center 1967, 4:1-45

71754 Sociotherapy and psychotherapy in the psychiatric hospital. In Redlich, F. C. Social Psychiatry, Baltimore: Williams & Wilkins 1969, 196-211

71755 The Termination of Intensive Psychotherapy. Springfield, Ill: Thomas 1963, 84 p

Rv J Am Psa Ass 1964, 12:260. Wallerstein, R. S. J Am Psa Ass 1966, 14:183-225

EDELSON, RUTH B.

See Barenholtz, Benjamin

EDELSON, STUART ROY

71756 (& Warren, P. H.) Catatonic schizophrenia as a mourning process. Dis nerv Sys 1963, 24:527-534

71757 A dynamic formulation of childhood schizophrenia. Dis nerv Sys 1966, 27:610-615

EDELSTEIN, E. L.

71758 Psychodynamics of a transvestite. PT 1960, 14:121-131

EDELWEISS, MALOMAR LUND

71759 Las malas relaciones entre los psicoanalistas, un problema terapéutico? [Poor relations between psychoanalysts: a therapeutic problem?] Arch Estud psicoan Psicol med 1967, 4:125-134

71760 (& Tanco Duque, R.; Schindler, S.) (Eds) Personalisation. Studien zur
       Tiefenpsychologie und Psychotherapie. [Personalisation. Studies on
       Depth Psychology and Psychotherapy.] Vienna/Freiburg/Basel: Her-
       der 1964, 171 p
71761 Symbolik und Echtheit des Symbols. [Symbolism and authenticity of
       symbols.] In author's *Personalisation* 40-49

       See Caruso, Igor A.

EDEN, PAUL M.

TRANSLATION OF:
Bloch I. [68040]

EDENBAUM, ROBERT I.

71762 "Babylon Revisited": a psychological note on F. Scott Fitzgerald. Lit
       & Psych 1968, 18:27-29

EDER, MONTAGU DAVID

S-7398 The myth of progress. M 1962, 35:81-89
        Abs ICFH 1963, 32:141-142
S-7402 Psychoanalysis and politics. In Ebenstein, W. *Modern Political
        Thought,* NY: Holt 1960, 71-82

EDGAR, IRVING I.

71763 The psychoanalytic approach to Shakespeare's *Hamlet.* Canad Psychiat
       Ass J 1961, 6:353-355
71764 Shakespeare's *Hamlet:* the great modern Oedipus tragedy. Psychiat Q
       Suppl 1963, 37:1-22

EDGCUMBE, ROSE

See Thomas, Ruth

EDGE, S.

See Waite, Richard R.

EDGERTON, MILTON T.

See Meyer, Eugene

EDIE, JAMES M.

* * * Editor of Merleau-Ponty, M. *The Primary of Perception and Other
       Essays*

EDINBURG, G.

See Zinberg, Norman E.

EDINGER, DORA

71765 Bertha Pappenheim: Freud's Anna O. Highland Park, Ill: Congregation
       Solel 1968, 102 p

71766 Bertha Pappenheim: Leben und Schriften. [Life and Works.] Frankfurt: Ner-Tamid Publ 1963, 156 p
Rv MG Q 1964, 33:439

EDMINSTER, STEVEN A.

TRANSLATION OF:
Freud, S. [10351, 10362]

EDMISTON, FRANK GERALD

71767 (& Williams, R. C.) A study of object relations in a case of ulcerative colitis. Comprehen Psychiat 1963, 4:96-104

EDMONSON, MUNRO S.

See Rohrer, John H.

EDMONSTON, WILLIAM EDWARD, JR.

71768 An experimental investigation of hypnotic age-regression. Amer J clin Hyp 1961, 3:127-138

EDMUNDS, SIMEON

71769 Miracles of the Mind. Springfield, Ill: Thomas 1966 xi + 204 p
Rv Löfgren, L. B. J Am Psa Ass 1968, 16:146-178. Ebon, M. R 1969, 56:145-147

EDSON, W. DOYLE

71770 An analysis of identity from the standpoint of Erikson, Freud, Kroeber and Tillich. Diss Abstr 1969, 29(7-B):2631-2632

EDWARDS, ALLEN L.

71771 (& Cronbach, L. J.) Experimental design for research in psychotherapy. Clin Psych 1952, 8:51-59. In Goldstein, A. P. & Dean, S. J. *The Investigation of Psychotherapy*, NY: Wiley 1966, 71-79

EDWARDS, FREDERICK HATELY

71772 Aetiological patterns in delinquent adolescents. A survey of 66 cases seen at the Portman Clinic 1961-1964. Psychother Psychosom 1965, 13:256-264
71773 Psychotherapy of adolescents. In *Proceedings of the 3rd International Congress of Psychotherapy, London 1964, Part II*, Basel/NY: Karger 1965, 9 p

EDWARDS, GRIFFITH

71774 Role-playing theory vs. clinical psychiatry. Int J Psychiat 1967, 3:203-205

EDWARDS, JOHN W.

71775 (& Deutsch, A. L.) Group counseling for parents of adolescent problem children in a general hospital. J Psa in Groups 1968, 2(2):15-22

EDWARDS, MARIE

71776 Libidinal phases in the analytic treatment of a preschool child. Psa St C 1967, 22:199-215

EEG-OLOFSSON, RICHARD

71777 On dreams and personal conflicts. J existent Psychiat 1965, 6:213-214

EFRON, HERMAN Y.

See Piotrowski, Zygmunt A.

EGAN, MERRITT H.

71778 (& Robison, O. L.) Home treatment of severely disturbed children and families. Ops 1966, 36:730-735
    Abs JMa RFPsa 1968, 32:381

EGER, WILLIAM HENRY

ABSTRACT OF:
71779 Fraiberg, S. & Freedman, D. Observations on a congenitally blind child with severe ego deviations. Bull Phila Ass Psa 1963, 13:199-202

EGGAN, DOROTHY

71780 Dream analysis. In Kaplan, B. *Studying Personality Cross-Culturally,* NY/Evanston/London: Harper & Row 1961, 551-577
71781 Hopi dreams in cultural perspective. In Grunebaum, G. E. von & Caillois, R. *The Dream and Human Societies,* Berkeley/Los Angeles: Univ Calif Pr 1966, 237-265
71782 The manifest content of dreams: a challenge to social science. Amer anthropologist 1952, 54:469-485

EGGERT, DELMER C.

See Shagass, Charles

EGGERTSEN, PAUL FRED

71783 Caprice: the "cool" rebellion. Canad Psychiat Ass J 1965, 10:165-169
71784 The dilemma of power: nuclear weapons and human reliability. Ps 1964, 27:211-218
71785 Psychodynamic relationships: suicide and flying phobia. Int Psychiat Clin 1967, 4:155-175

EHEBALD, ULRICH

71786 Aufgaben einer psychoanalytischen Klinik heute. [Problems of a modern psychoanalytic clinic.] MMW 1963, 105:2196-2200
71787 (& Walser, H.) Drei Jahre Psychoanalyse in einem Krankenhaus. [3 years of psychoanalysis in a hospital.] Schweiz ANP 1960, 85:265-284

EHRENREICH, GERALD A.

71788 Headache, necrophilia, and murder. A brief hypnotherapeutic investigation of a single case. BMC 1960, 24:273-287

See Siegal, Richard S.

EHRENTHEIL, OTTO FELIX

71789 A critique of psychiatric training programs: historical perspective and
future trends. Int J Neuropsychiat 1967, 3:152-158

EHRENWALD, JAN

71790 Brief psychotherapy and the existential shift. Proc IV World Cong
Psychiat 1966, 2850-2851. Bull NY Acad Med 1967, 43:798-810
71791 Can one person catch a neurosis from another? Why Rep 271-279
71792 A childhood memory of Pablo Picasso. Am Im 1967, 24:129-139
71793 Discussion of Khan, M. M. R. "On symbiotic omnipotence." Psa Forum
1969, 3:148-150
71794 Doctrinal compliance: a history of error in psychotherapy. J Hist behav
Sci 1966, 2:51-57
71795 Family dynamics and communication theory. J Commun 1963, 13:
191-198
71796 Four years of progress in psychotherapy. Prog PT 1960, 5:25-40
71797 Freud versus Jung—the mythophobic versus the mythophilic temper in
psychotherapy. Israel Ann Psychiat 1968, 6:115-125
71798 Hippocrates' *kairos* and the existential shift. Psa 1969, 29:89-93
71799 Neurosis in the family. Arch gen Psychiat 1960, 3:232-241
71800 Neurosis in the Family and Patterns of Psychosocial Defense. A Study
of Psychiatric Epidemiology. NY: Harper & Row 1963, 203 p
Rv Spotnitz, H. R 1964, 51:676-677. Lomas, P. J 1965, 46:268-270
71801 Neurotic contagion within the family. In Merin, J. H. & Nagler, S. H.
The Etiology of the Neuroses, Palo Alto, Calif: Sci & Behav Books
1966, 45-49; 90-93
71802 Psychotherapy: Myth and Method; An Integrative Approach. NY/
London: Grune & Stratton 1966, x + 212 p
Abs J Am Psa Ass 1967, 15:730. Rv Ekstein, R. Q 1968, 37:304-305.
Servadio, E. R 1968, 55:323-324
71803 The return of Quetzalcoatl and doctrinal compliance. A case study of
Cortes and Montezuma. PT 1960, 14:308-321
S-44754 Schizophrenia, neurotic compliance, and the psi hypothesis.
Abs EMW Q 1961, 30:307
71804 The symbiotic matrix of paranoid delusions and the homosexual alter-
native. Psa 1960, 20:49-65
71805 The therapeutic process and the rival schools. PT 1967, 21:44-53
71806 The visual distortion test. A study in experimental psychiatry. Psychiat
Q 1966, 40:429-448

REVIEWS OF:
71807 Eissler, K. R. Leonardo da Vinci: Psycho-Analytic Notes on the
Enigma. R 1964, 51:329-330

71808 Kiev, A. Curanderismo: Mexican American Folk Psychiatry. Am Im 1969, 26:84-85
71809 Sherman, M. H. (Ed) Psychoanalysis in America: Historical Perspectives. Am Im 1967, 24:151-152

EHRENZWEIG, ANTON

S-44760 The creative surrender. A comment on "Joanna Field's" book *An Experiment in Leisure*.
   Abs JC An Surv Psa 1957, 8:331-332
71810 The Hidden Order in Art. A Study in the Psychology of Artistic Imagination. Berkeley: Univ Calif Pr; London: Weidenfeld & Nicolson 1967, 306 p
   Rv MG Q 1968, 37:608-612
S-44762 The Psychoanalysis of Artistic Vision and Hearing. An Introduction to a Theory of Unconscious Perception.
   Abs J Am Psa Ass 1967, 15:219-220. Rv Weissmann, P. Q 1967, 36:122-124
71811 Unconscious mental imagery in art and science. Nature 1962, 194: 1008-1012
71812 The undifferentiated matrix of artistic imagination. Psa St Soc 1964, 3:373-398

EHRLICH, DANUTA

71813 (& Sabshin, M.) A study of sociotherapeutically oriented psychiatrists. Ops 1964, 34:469-480
   Abs JMa RFPsa 1966, 30:519

EHRLICH, R. E.

See Sours, John A.

EHRMANN, JACQUES

71814 Introduction to Gaston Bachelard. Modern Language Notes 1966, 81: 572-578
71815 Rameau's Nephew: an existential psychoanalysis of Diderot by himself. J existent Psychiat 1963-64, 4:59-68

EHRMANN, JOHN C.

See Pacht, Asher R.

EIBL-EIBESFELDT, IRENÄUS

71816 Aggressive behavior and ritualized fighting in animals. Sci Psa 1963, 6:8-17
71817 Ontogenetic and maturational studies of aggressive behavior. UCLA Forum med Sci 1967, 7:57-94

EICHERT, H.

71818 Bemerkungen zur Arbeit: psychosomatische Einflüsse für die Entstehung des Lichen ruber planus von G. Veltman und R. Weitz in

Heft 1 (1966) dieser Zeitschrift. [Remarks on the article: psychosomatic influences in the development of lichen ruber planus by G. Veltman and R. Weitz in Number 1 (1966) of this journal.] Hautarzt 1967, 18:133-135

EICHLER, ROBERT M.

See Bailey, Mattox A.

EICKE, DIETER

71819 Depersonalisationsphänomene als kommunikatives Mittel. [Depersonalization as a way of communication.] In Müller, C. & Benedetti, G. *Psychotherapy of Schizophrenia (3rd Int Sym 1964)*, Basel/NY: Karger 1965, 77-81

71820 Diagnosen bei Vegetativer Dystonie. [Psychological diagnosis in vegetative dystonia.] Med Klin 1960, 55:1586-1592

71821 Die Erforschung psychosomatischer Zusammenhänge auf dem Wege der wortlosen Kommunikation. [Nonverbal communication as research field in psychosomatic conditions.] Verh Dtsch Ges inn Med 1967, 73:683-688

71822 Funktionelle Störungen und Untersuchungstechnik in psychosomatischer Sicht. [Technic of interview with nonorganic disease, a psychosomatic view. Or: How to make a psychosocial diagnosis.] Dtsch Ärzteblatt 1966, 63:2249-2252

71823 Das Gewissen und das Über-Ich. [Conscience and superego.] Wege zum Menschen 1964, 16:109-126. In Petrilowitsch, N. *Das Gewissen als Problem*, Darmstadt: Wissenschaftliche Buchgesellschaft 1966, 65-91

71824 Methoden der Milieutherapie (psychoanalytisch orientierte Soziotherapie) dargestellt an einer Schizophreniebehandlung. [Methods of milieu therapy (psychoanalytically oriented sociotherapy) exhibited in the treatment of schizophrenia.] Psychother Psychosom 1967, 15:17

71825 Probleme der Indikationsstellung zur Psychotherapie Schizophrener. [Indication of psychotherapy of schizophrenics.] Z Psychother med Psychol 1966, 16:70-78

71826 Psychotherapie einer depersonalisierten Patientin als Beitrag zur Psychopathologie der Depersonalisation. [Psychotherapy of a depersonalized patient, a contribution to the psychopathology of depersonalization.] Z PSM 1966, 12:149-163

71827 Therapeutische Gruppenarbeit mit Schizophrenen. [Group therapy (or group treatment) with schizophrenics.] Z Psychother med Psychol 1967, 17:100-111

71828 Über den Zusammenhang von Müdigkeit und Aggressionstrieb. [The relation between fatigue and the aggressive drive.] In Privat, E. *Travaux du troisième Congrès international de Medicine Psychosomatique*. Editeur Toulouse 1967, 424-428

71829 Zielsetzungen und Ergebnisse einer sozialpsychiatrischen Fachausbildung für Schwestern. [Aims and results of a postgraduate training in social psychiatry for nurses.] Moderne Krankenpflege 1967, 5:1-5

EICKHOFF, LOUISE F. W.

71830   The second childhood: observations on treatment. M 1964, 37:319-323

EIDELBERG, E.

See Lesse, Henry

EIDELBERG, LUDWIG

71831   Ein Beitrag zum Studium der ästhetischen Lust. [A contribution to the study of esthetic pleasure.] Psyche 1962, 15:588-591

S-44770 The concept of narcissistic mortification.
        Abs Fernández, A. A. Rev urug Psa 1965, 7:95

S-7550 A contribution to the study of masochism. PT Pervers 124-136

71832   A contribution to the study of the unpleasure-pleasure principle. Psychiat Q 1962, 36:312-316
        Abs Engle, B. S. Q 1963, 32:293

71833   The Dark Urge. NY: Pyramid Books 1961, 159 p
        Les Violences de l'Inconscient. Paris: Editions de la Pensée Moderne 1962

71834   (& Blum, H.; Dewald, P.; Eisnitz, A. J.; Glover, E.; Lewin, B.; Niederland, W. G.; Schneer, H.; Shengold, L.; Sperling, O. E.; Yazmajian, R.) (Eds) Encyclopedia of Psychoanalysis. NY: Free Pr; London: Collier-Macmillan 1968, xxix + 571 p
        Rv Am Im 1968, 25:194

S-44774 An introduction to the study of the narcissistic mortification.
        Abs AaSt An Surv Psa 1957, 8:38-40

S-44776 Neurotic choice of mate.
        Abs SO An Surv Psa 1956, 7:154-155

71835   Obsessional neurosis. In Kurian, M. & Hand, M. H. *Lectures in Dynamic Psychiatry*, NY: IUP 1963, 102-126

71836   (& Palmer, J. N.) Primary and secondary narcissism. Psychiat Q 1960, 34:480-487
        Abs Engle, B. Q 1961, 30:301-302

71837   Psicologia de la Violacion. [The Psychology of Violation.] Argentina: Editorial Paidos 1965

S-44779 Psychoanalyse einer Psychopathin.
        Abs HFM An Surv Psa 1958, 9:180-181

71838   Psychoanalysis: science, art, or bureaucracy?: "avec peur et reproche." Am Im 1964, 21(1-2):175-179

71839   Rescue fantasy. Dyn Psychiat 1968, 1(Suppl):9-11

71840   A second contribution to the study of the narcissistic mortification. Psychiat Q 1959, 33:636-646

71841   A suggestion for a psychoanalytic dictionary. (Read at Psa Ass NY, 21 Oct 1963)
        Abs Ralske, N. N. Q 1964, 33:320-322

S-7570 Take Off Your Mask.
        Doe Dat Masker Af. Holland: Het Erste Nederlandse Pocketboek 1962

S-44784 Technical problems in the analysis of masochists.
        Abs RSB An Surv Psa 1958, 9:358-360

71842   The theory of psychoanalytic therapy. (Panel discussion: Psa Ass NY, 15 May 1961)
Abs Shengold, L. Q 1961, 30:626-629
71843   What are the causes of frigidity? Why Rep 215-224
71844   Why do some people want something for nothing? Why Rep 455-469

See Bergler, Edmund; Kanzer, Mark

REVIEW OF:
71845   Benda, C. E. The Image of Love. Modern Trends in Psychiatric Thinking. Q 1963, 32:125-126

EIDUSON, BERNICE T.

71846   (& Eiduson, S.; Geller, E.) Biochemistry, genetics, and the nature-nurture problem. P 1962, 119:342-350. In Millon, T. *Theories of Psychopathology,* Phila: Saunders 1967, 10-19
71847   A brief overview of research at Reiss-Davis. Reiss-Davis Clin Bull 1965, 2:52-58
71848   Career patterns of scientists. In Taylor, C. W. *Aging and Achievement,* Univ Park, Pa.: Penn State Univ Pr 1968
71849   (& Lubitz, I. A.) Certain aspects of infant behavior monitored for the first 96 hours of life. Ops 1966, 36:222-223
71850   (& Johnson, T. C. M.; Rottenberg, D.) Comparative studies of learning problems seen in five child clinics. Ops 1966, 36:829-839
Abs JMa RFPsa 1968, 32:383
71851   (& Meyer, M. M.; Lucas, W. B.) Contribution of psychological testing of parents to the understanding of the child. J proj Tech 1963, 27:387-417
71852   Discussion of Lindon, J. A. "On Freud's concept of dream-action." Psa Forum 1966, 1:41-42
71853   (& Brooks, S. H.; Motto, R. L.) A generalized psychiatric information-processing system. Beh Sci 1966, 11:133-142
71854   Infancy and goal-setting behavior. In Bühler, C. & Massarik, F. *The Course of Human Life,* NY: Springer 1968, 102-123
71855   Intellectual inbreeding in the clinic. Ops 1964, 34:714-721
71856   (& Brooks, S. H.; Motto, R. L.; Platz, A.; Carmichael, R.;) New strategy for psychiatric research, utilizing the psychiatric case history event system. In Kline, N. S. & Laska, E. *Computers and Electronic Devices in Psychiatry,* NY: Grune & Stratton 1968, 45-58
71857   (& Ramsey, D. M.) Pilot studies on decision-making in psychiatry. Reiss-Davis Clin Bull 1967, 4:115-129
71858   Productivity rate in research scientists. Amer Sci 1966, 54:57-63
71859   (et al) Psychiatric Case History Event System: Transcription Procedures with Lexicons. Los Angeles: Reiss-Davis Child Study Center 1966
71860   (& Rosow, L. W.; Switzer, J.) Reactions of disturbed children to natural crisis. Reiss-Davis Clin Bull 1965, 2:69-79
71861   (& Brooks, S. H.; Motto, R. L.; Platz, A.; Carmichael, R.) Recent developments in the psychiatric case history event system. Beh Sci 1967, 12:254-267

71862 Recognition of creativity. In *When Children Live Creatively*, Santa Monica, Calif: Calif Assoc for Childhood Education 1966. Assembly I, 8 p

71863 Replacing traditional records by event reports. Hosp Comm Psychiat 1966, 17(3):28-31

71864 Retreat from help. Ops 1968, 38:910-921

71865 The scientist's image of himself. Science 1960, 132(3426):552-554

71866 Scientists and their psychological world. Calif Inst Tech Q 1963, 4(3):14-19. Engineering & Science 1963, 16(5):22-30

71867 Scientists as advisors and consultants in Washington. Bull atom Sci 1966, 22(8):26-31

71868 Scientists: Their Psychological World. (Foreword: Brown, H.) NY: Basic Books 1962, xvi + 299 p

71869 (et al) Studies in Decision Making in Psychiatry—Phase I. Los Angeles: Reiss-Davis Child Study Center 1967

71870 A study of children's attitudes toward the Cuban crisis. MH 1965, 49:113-125

71871 Summary of a study on scientists as advisors to government. In Krauch, T. *Wissenschaft und Politik*, Heidelberg: Studiengruppe für Systemforschung 1966, 140-159

71872 Two classes of information in psychiatry. Arch gen Psychiat 1968, 18: 405-419

71873 (& Johnson, T. C. M.; Rottenberg, D.) Use of psychiatric case records as information vehicles. Reiss-Davis Clin Bull 1965, 2:59-68

See Eiduson, Samuel; Meyer, Mortimer M.; Morris, Clarence; Ramsey, Diane M.; Ramsey-Klee, Diane M.

EIDUSON, SAMUEL

71874 (& Geller, E.; Yuwiler, A.; Eiduson, B. T.) Biochemistry and Behavior. (Introd: Murphy, G.) Princeton, NJ: Van Nostrand 1964, xii + 554 p

See Eiduson, Bernice T.

EINHORN, E. H.

71875 Signal exchange patterns in the genesis of extra-marital affairs. Newsletter, Soc of Med Psa 1967, 8

EINSTEIN, GERTRUDE

71876 (& Moss, M. S.) Some thoughts on sibling relationships. Soc Casewk 1967, 48:549-555

EISDORFER, CARL

See Bogdonoff, M. D.; Jeffers, Frances C.

EISELEY, LOREN

71877 Darwin, Coleridge, and the theory of unconscious creation. Library Chronicle 1965, 31(1):7-22. Daedalus 1965, 94:588-602

EISEN, ARNOLD

71878 (& Lurie, A.; Robbins, L. L.) Group processes in a voluntary psychiatric hospital. Ops 1963, 33:750-754

EISEN, NATHANIEL HERMAN

71879 Some effects of early sensory deprivation on later behavior: the quondam hard-of-hearing child. ASP 1962, 65:338-342
       Abs Rosen, I. C. Q 1963, 32:296

EISENBERG, LEON

71880 Adolescence. Ency Ment Hlth 37-69
71881 (& Gruenberg, E. M.) The current status of secondary prevention in child psychiatry. Ops 1961, 31:355-367
       Abs JMa RFPsa 1962, 26:326
71882 Deprivation and foster care.· J Amer Acad Child Psychiat 1965, 4:243-248
71883 (Ed) Digest of papers and the program of the forty-third annual meeting of the American Orthopsychiatric Association, San Francisco, California. 13-16 April 1966. Ops 1966, 36(2): 396 p
71884 Discussion of Greenblatt, M. "The nature of psychiatry: biologic aspects." In Hoch, P. H. & Zubin, J. The Future of Psychiatry, NY/London: Grune & Stratton 1962, 251-255
71885 Discussion of Dr. Solnit's paper "Who deserves child psychiatry? A study in priorities." J Amer Acad Child Psychiat 1966, 5:17-23
71886 If not now, when? Ops 1962, 31:793
       Abs JMa RFPsa 1964, 28:444
71887 (& Neubauer, P. B.) Mental health issues in Israeli collectives: Kibbutzim. J Amer Acad Child Psychiat 1965, 4:426-442
71888 The pediatric management of school phobia. J Pediat 1959, 55:758-766
71889 Psychopharmacology in childhood: a critique. In Miller, E. Foundations of Child Psychiatry, Oxford/NY: Pergamon Pr 1968, 625-641
71890 Psychotic disorders in childhood. In Cooke, R. E. & Levin, S. The Biologic Basis of Pediatric Practice, NY/Toronto/London: McGraw-Hill 1968, 1583-1591
71891 The psychiatric history. In Cooke, R. E. & Levin, S. The Biologic Basis of Pediatric Practice, NY/Toronto/London: McGraw-Hill 1968, 1359-1365
71892 Racism, the family and society: a crisis in values. MH 1968, 52:512-520. Ann Prog child Psychiat 1969, 252-264
71893 The relationship between psychiatry and pediatrics: a disputatious view. Pediatrics 1967, 39:645-647. Ann Prog child Psychiat 1968, 145-148
71894 The sins of the fathers: urban decay and social pathology. Ops 1962, 32:5-17
71895 Social class and individual development. Crosscurrents in Ps & Psa 65-80; 85-88

       See Oleinick, Marta S.

EISENBERG, MORTON S.

71896 Discussion of Heilbrunn, G. "How 'cool' is the beatnik?" Psa Forum 1967, 2:42-44

See Scheidlinger, Saul

EISENBERG, S.

71897 The relationship of depression to authoritarianism and ethnocentrism in three Israeli ethnic sub-groups. Confin psychiat 1966, 9:159-176

EISENBUD, JULE

71898 Chronologically extraordinary psi correspondences in the psychoanalytic setting. R 1969, 56:9-27

S-44803 Comments on Dr. Brenner's "Facts, coincidence and the psi hypothesis."
        Abs SLP An Surv Psa 1957, 8:20

71899 Comments on Edward Girden's review of psychokinesis. Int J Parapsychol 1964, 6:99-101

71900 Compound theories of precognition. J Soc Psychical Res 1962, 41:353-355

71901 Discussion of Bion, W. R. "Notes on memory and desire." Psa Forum 1967, 2:268

71902 Discussion of Strean & Nelson: "A further clinical illustration of the paranormal triangle hypothesis." PPR 1962, 49(3):74-76
        Abs HL Q 1963, 32:452

71903 (& Hassel, L.; Keely, H.; Sawrey, W.) A further study of teacher-pupil attitudes and results on clairvoyance tests in the fifth and sixth grades. J Amer Soc psychical Res 1960, 54(2):72-79

71904 The hand and the breast with special reference to obsessional neurosis. (Read at Topeka Psa Soc, Nov 1960; at San Francisco Psa Soc, Nov 1961) Q 1965, 34:219-248

71905 The oral side of humor. (Read at West Coast Psa, 17-19 Aug 1962) R 1964, 51:57-73
        Abs SRS Q 1965, 34:309-310

71906 Perception of subliminal visual stimuli in relation to ESP. Int J Parapsychol 1965, 7:161-181

71907 Psi and the nature of things. Int J Parapsychol 1963, 5:245-268

71908 Recently found carving as a breast symbol. Amer Anthropologist 1964, 66:141-147

71909 Reply to W. H. Rushton. J Soc Psychical Res 1968, Oct

71910 Sein oder Nichtsein—oder ist Psi notwendig? Z Parapsychol 1964, 7:25-45
        Why Psi? R 1966, 53:647-663

71911 (& Frey, H.; Lehrburger, H.; Marx, J. R.; Paley, A.; Starrett, D.; Wheeler, B. W.) Some unusual data from a session with Ted Serios. J Amer Soc psychic Res 1967, 61:241-253

71912 Suggestion at a distance. Int J Parapsychol 1962-63, 4(3):99-106

71913 A test to determine the relationship of subliminal visual stimuli and ESP in a laboratory setting. Int J Parapsychol 1965, 7(2):161-181

S-44814 Time and the Oedipus.
Abs SO An Surv Psa 1956, 7:235-236

71914 Two approaches to spontaneous case material. J Amer Soc psychical
Res 1963, 57:118-135

71915 (& Eller, J. J.; Liddon, S. C.; Merrill, F. B.) Two experiments with
Ted Serios. J Amer Soc psychical Res 1968, 62:309-319

71916 The U-phenomenon, parapsychology and psychoanalysis. J Amer Soc
psychical Res 1961, 55(4):135-141

S-44815 On the use of the psihypothesis in psycho-analysis.
Abs An Surv Psa 1955, 6:314-315

71917 The World of Ted Serios. "Thoughtgraphic Studies of an Extra-
ordinary Mind. NY: William Morrow & Co. 1967, 367 p; Simon &
Schuster 1968; Pocket Books 1968
Rv Löfgren, L. B. J Am Psa Ass 1968, 16:146-178. Ullman, M.
R 1968, 55:655-661

EISENBUD, RUTH-JEAN

71918 Female homosexuality: a sweet enfranchisement. In Goldman, G. D. &
Milman, D. S. *Modern Woman,* Springfield, Ill: Thomas 1969, 247-264

71919 Masochism revisited. R 1967, 54:561-582
Abs SRS Q 1969, 38:163

EISENMAN, RUSSELL

71920 (& Bernard, J. L.; Hannon, J. E.) Benevolence, potency, and God: a
sematic differential study of the Rorschach. Percept mot Skills 1966,
22:75-78

71921 Birth order, anxiety, and verbalizations in group psychotherapy. J
consult Psychol 1966, 30:521-526

71922 The patient who fears success. Psychology 1968, 5(4):62-68

EISENSTEIN, SAMUEL

71923 Otto Rank 1884-1939. The myth of the birth of the hero. Psa Pioneers
36-50

See Alexander, Franz

EISENTHAL, SHERMAN

71924 Suicide and aggression. Psychol Rep 1967, 21:745-751

EISLER, H. E.

S-44826 The development of the individual.
Abs An Surv Psa 1955, 6:92-94

EISMAN, H. D.

See Jacobs, Martin A.

EISNER, HENRY

ABSTRACTS OF:

71925 Guttman, S. A. The concepts of structure. Bull Phila Ass Psa 1967, 17:125-127

71926 Rosen, V. H. Sign phenomena and their relationship to unconscious meaning. Bull Phila Ass Psa 1969, 19:242-246

EISNITZ, ALAN J.

71927 Mirror dreams. (Read at NY Psa Ass, May 1959; Am Psa Ass, Dec 1959) J Am Psa Ass 1961, 9:461-479
Abs FB Q 1962, 31:418-419

71928 Narcissistic object choice, self representation. (Read at Int Cong Psa 1969) J 1969, 50:15-25
Narzisstische Objektwahl, Selbstrepräsentanz. Psyche 1969, 23:419-437

71929 The relation between adult and child analysis. Bull NY Acad Med 1968, 44:571-575

See Eidelberg, Ludwig

ABSTRACTS OF:

71930 Alpert, A. A special therapeutic technique for certain developmental disorders in prelatency children. An Surv Psa 1957, 8:234-235

71931 Berman, L. Some recent trends in psychoanalysis. An Surv Psa 1957, 8:14-15

71932 Bowlby, J. et al: The effects of mother-child separation: a follow-up study. An Surv Psa 1956, 7:261-262

71933 Fairbairn, W. R. D. Considerations arising out of the Schreber case. An Surv Psa 1956, 7:75-76

71934 Guntrip, H. J. S. Recent developments in psycho-analytical theory. An Surv Psa 1956, 7:73-75

71935 Kardos, E. & Peto, A. Contributions to the theory of play. An Surv Psa 1956, 7:127-128

71936 Marmor, J. Some observations on superstitions in contemporary life. An Surv Psa 1956, 7:382, 387-388

EISSLER, KURT ROBERT

71937 Crusaders. Psa St Soc 1964, 3:329-355

71938 Death and the pleasure principle. In author's The Psychiatrist and the Dying Patient 71-80. In Ruitenbeek, H. M. Death: Interpretations, NY: Dell 1969, 11-18

71939 Die Ermordung von wievielen seiner Kinder muss ein mensch symptomfrei ertragen können, um eine normale Konstitution zu haben? [The murder of how many of his children can a human being endure without symptoms, and still be normal?] Psyche 1963, 17:241-291

71940 Fortinbras and Hamlet. Am Im 1968, 25:199-223
Abs JWS Q 1969, 38:672

71941 Freud and the psychoanalysis of history. (Read at Am Psa Ass, 5 May 1963) J Am Psa Ass 1963, 11:675-703
Abs Dubcovsky, S. Rev Psicoanál 1964, 21:261. Ennis, J. Q 1965, 34:465-466

71942 Goethe. A Psychoanalytic Study. 1775-1786. Detroit: Wayne State Univ Pr 1963, 2 Vols., xxxv + 1538 p
Rv Illing, H. A. J 1964, 45:126-128. Slochower, H. Am Im 1964, 21:182-183. Beres, D. Q 1965, 34:447-450. Coltrera, J. T. J Am Psa Ass 1965, 13:634-703

S-44834 Goethe and science: a contribution to the psychology of Goethe's psychosis.
Abs NZ An Surv Psa 1958, 9:477-479

71943 A hitherto unnoticed letter by Sigmund Freud. J 1961, 42:197-204
Abs WPK Q 1962, 31:283

71944 Home movies and possible psychic damage? (Letter to the editor.) P 1967, 123:1307

71945 Incidental observations on a case of child murder. Dr Af Beh 2:325-368

71946 Irreverent remarks about the present and the future of psychoanalysis. J 1969, 50:461-471

S-44836 On isolation.
Abs RTh J 1961, 42:467-468

S-44837 Julius Wagner-Jaurregs Gutachten über Sigmund Freud und seine Studien zur Psychoanalyse.
Abs HK An Surv Psa 1958, 9:33-34

S-44838 Kritische Bemerkungen zu Renée Gicklhorns Beitrag "Eine mysteriöse Bildaffäre."
Abs HK An Surv Psa 1958, 9:34

71947 Leonardo da Vinci. Psycho-Analytic Notes on the Enigma. NY: IUP 1961; London: Int. Psycho-Anal. Lib. & Hogarth 1962, plates + 375 p
Abs J Am Psa Ass 1962, 10:446-447. Rv MK Q 1962, 31:269-271. Rosenfeld, E. M. J 1963, 44:113-115. Ehrenwald, J. R 1964, 51:329-330. Coltrera, J. T. J Am Psa Ass 1965, 13:634-703

71948 Mankind at its best. J Am Psa Ass 1964, 12:187-222

71949 Medical Orthodoxy and the Future of Psychoanalysis. NY: IUP; London: Bailey Bros 1965, x + 592 p
Rv Sherman, M. H. R 1965, 52:487-489. Bion, W. R. J 1966, 47:575-579. Kaplan, A. J. Q 1966, 35:597-599. Keiser, S. J Am Psa Ass 1969, 17:238-267

71950 On the metapsychology of the preconscious: a tentative contribution to psychoanalytic morphology. Psa St C 1962, 17:9-41
Abs SLe RFPsa 1964, 28:810

71951 A note on trauma, dream, anxiety, and schizophrenia. Psa St C 1966, 21:17-50

S-44841 Notes on the environment of a genius.
Abs RTh J 1961, 42:473

S-44842 Notes on problems of technique in the psychoanalytic treatment of adolescents. With some remarks on perversions.
Abs JA An Surv Psa 1958, 9:318-322

71952 Notes on the psychoanalytic concept of cure. Psa St C 1963, 18:424-463

71953 On the possible proof of psychic energy. Bull Phila Ass Psa 1966, 16:61-70
Abs EFA Q 1968, 37:157-158

71954   Perverted psychiatry? P 1967, 123:1352-1358
        Pervertierte Psychiatrie? Psyche 1967, 21:553-575
        Abs Loeb, L. Q 1969, 38:511
S-44844 The Psychiatrist and the Dying Patient.
        Abs AaSt An Surv Psa 1955, 6:221, 475-491
71955   Psychopathology and creativity. (Read at Chicago Inst for Psa, 21
        Oct 1966) Am Im 1967, 24:35-81
        Abs JWS Q 1968, 37:474
71956   The relation of explaining and understanding in psychoanalysis: dem-
        onstrated by one aspect of Freud's approach to literature. Psa St C
        1968, 23:141-177
S-44845 Remarks on some variations in psychoanalytic technique.
        Variationen in der psychoanalytischen Technik. Psyche 1960, 13:
        609-624
        Abs JAL An Surv Psa 1958, 9:327. Urtubey, L. de Rev urug Psa
        1965, 7:382-385
71957   Sigmund Freud und die Wiener Universität. Über die Pseudo-Wissen-
        schaftlichkeit der jüngsten Wiener Freud-Biographik. [Sigmund Freud
        and the University of Vienna. On the pseudo-scientific method of
        biography of the young Freud in Vienna.] Bern/Stuttgart: Huber 1966,
        191 p
S-44846 Some comments on psychoanalysis and dynamic psychiatry.
        Abs AL An Surv Psa 1956, 7:56-57
S-44847 An unusual function of an amnesia.
        Abs An Surv Psa 1955, 6:137, 155-156
71958   Weitere Bemerkungen zum Problem der KZ-Psychologie. [Additional
        comments on the problem of concentration camp psychology.] Psyche
        1968, 22:452-463
71959   Zur Notlage unserer Zeit. [On the crisis of our time.] Psyche 1968,
        22:641-657
71960   Zwei bisher übersehene Dokumente zur akademischen Laufbahn Sig-
        mund Freuds. [Two documents previously overlooked pertaining to
        Sigmund Freud's academic career.] Wien klin Wschr 1966, 78:16-19

        See Eissler, Ruth S.

        REVIEW OF:
71961   Lesky, E. Die Wiener medizinische Schule im 19 Jahrhundert. Q 1966,
        35:127-130

EISSLER, RUTH S.

71962   (& Eissler, K. R.) Heinz Hartmann: a biographical sketch. BMC 1964,
        28:298-301. Psa—Gen Psychol 3-15
        Abs McGowan, L. Q 1966, 35:467

        TRANSLATION OF:
        Freud, S. [73587]

EITINGER, G. L.

        See Winnik, Heinrich Z.

EITINGON, MAX

S-7755 Remarks on lay analysis. Heirs Freud 96-100

EKBOIR, JULIA GRINBERG DE

ABSTRACTS OF:

71963 Baron, S. Transference and counter-transference in the classroom. Rev Psicoanál 1961, 18:182

71964 Burton, A. Death as countertransference. Rev Psicoanál 1964, 21:80

71965 Feldman, H. From self-analysis to transference character traits. Rev Psicoanál 1961, 18:181

71966 Feldman, H. The id: present, past—and future. Rev Psicoanál 1961, 18:183

71967 Fry, W. F. The schizophrenic "who." Rev Psicoanál 1964, 21:86

71968 Greene, M. A. The stormy personality. Rev Psicoanál 1964, 21:85

71969 Joseph, F. Transference and countertransference in a dying patient. Rev Psicoanál 1964, 21:83

71970 Hall, C. S. Out of a dream came the faucet. Rev Psicoanál 1964, 21:86

71971 Kaufman, F. Myopia seen psychoanalytically. Rev Psicoanál 1964, 21:187

71972 Lewis, H. B. A case of watching as defense against an oral incorporation fantasy. Rev Psicoanál 1964, 21:187

71973 Meerloo, J. A. The dual meaning of human regression. Rev Psicoanál 1964, 21:185

71974 Rosenbaum, J. B. Holiday, symptom and dream. Rev Psicoanál 1964, 21:186

71975 Schneck, J. M. The psychodynamics of "déjà vu." Rev Psicoanál 1964, 21:84

71976 Schoenfeld, C. G. Three fallacious attacks upon psychoanalysis as science. Rev Psicoanál 1964, 21:84

71977 Searles, H. F. Scorn, disillusionment and adoration in the psychotherapy of schizophrenia. Rev Psicoanál 1964, 21:183-185

71978 Spotnitz, H. The need for isolation in the schizophrenic personality. Rev Psicoanál 1964, 21:81

71979 Strean, H. S. & Coleman, M. Further clinical illustration of the paranormal triangle hypothesis. Rev Psicoanál 1964, 21:187

71980 Vogel, E. & Bell, N. W. The emotionally disturbed child as a family scapegoat. Rev Psicoanál 1961, 18:184

EKSTEIN, RUDOLF

71981 The acquisition of learning readiness: task or conflict? Learn Love 172-196

71982 An den Herausgeber. [To the editor.] Dyn Psychiat 1968, 1(1):4-5

71983 (& Motto, R. L.) The borderline child in the school situation. In Gottesgen, M. G. & Gottesgen, G. B. *Professional School Psychology.* NY: Grune & Stratton 1960, 249-262. Learn Love 197-211

Das Grenzfall-Kind in der Schulsituation. Prax Kinderpsychol 1961, 10(4):113-119

71984 The boundary line between education and psychotherapy. Reiss-Davis

Clin ann Rep 1960-61, 14-15. Reiss-Davis Clin Bull 1964, 1(1):26-28.
Learn Love 157-163

71985 A bridge not a chasm: the relationship between psychoanalysis and
education. Mental Health Progress 1965

71986 (& Friedman, S. W.) Cause of the illness or cause of the cure. Int J
Psychiat 1968, 5:224-229

71987 The child, the teacher and learning. Young Children 1967, 22:195-209.
Learn Love 65-78

S-44851 (& Bryant, K.; Friedman, S. W.) Childhood schizophrenia and allied
conditions.
Esquizofrenia y estados analogos en el niño. In Bellak, L. *Esquizofrenia: Revision del Sindrome,* Barcelona: Editorial Herder 1962, 627-
766

71988 Children of Time and Space, of Action and Impulse: Clinical Studies
on the Psychoanalytic Treatment of Severely Disturbed Children. NY:
Appleton-Century-Crofts 1966, x + 466 p
Rv Leonard, M. R. Q 1968, 37:132-135. Kaplan, L. J. R 1969, 56:
344-345

S-44852 (& Wallerstein, J.) Choice of interpretation in the treatment of
borderline and psychotic children. In author's *Children of Time and
Space, of Action and Impulse* 148-157
Abs Deutsch, L. An Surv Psa 1957, 8:237-239

S-44853 A clinical note on the therapeutic use of a quasi-religious experience.
With title: The therapeutic use of a quasi-religious experience. In
author's *Children of Time and Space, of Action and Impulse* 365-372
Abs OS An Surv Psa 1956, 7:160-170

S-44854 (& Wright, D. G.) Comments on a psychotherapeutic session with the
space child. With title: A psychotherapeutic session with the space
child. In author's *Children of Time and Space, of Action and Impulse*
339-347

71989 Concerning the teaching and learning of psychoanalysis. (Read at
Committee on Psa Educ, NY, March 1966) J Am Psa Ass 1969, 17:
312-332

S-44855 (& Wallerstein, J.; Mandelbaum, A.) Countertransference in the
residential treatment of children. Treatment failure in a child with a
symbiotic psychosis. In author's *Children of Time and Space, of Action
and Impulse* 428-455
Abs RTh J 1961, 42:472

71990 Cross-sectional views of the psychotherapeutic process with an adolescent recovering from a schizophrenic episode. Ops 1961, 31:757-
775. In author's *Children of Time and Space, of Action and Impulse*
381-402. In Clark, D. H. & Lesser, G. S. *Emotional Disturbance and
School Learning,* Chicago: Sci Res Ass 1965, 102-120

71991 Discussion of Devereux, G. "The cannibalistic impulses of parents."
Psa Forum 1966, 1:127-128

71992 Discussion of Livermore, J. B. "A schizophrenic child reviews her own
treatment." Ops 1956, 26:373-375

71993 Discussion of Rosenbaum, M. "Psychological effects on the child
raised by an older sibling." Ops 1963, 33:518-520

71994 (& Caruth, E.) Distancing and distance devices in childhood schizophrenia and borderline states: revised concepts and new directions in research. Psychol Rep 1967, 20:109-110

71995 (& Meyer, M. M.) Distancing devices in childhood schizophrenia and allied conditions: quantitative and qualitative aspects of "distancing" in the psychotherapeutic process. Psychol Rep 1961, 9:145-146

71996 The dying and living of Teresa Esperanza. Psychol Today 1968, 1(8):44-48

71997 (& Motto, R. L.) Editors' introduction. Learn Love xvii-xxi

S-44860 Faith and reason in psychotherapy.
   Japanese: Tokyo J Psa 1962, 20(5):2-6
   Abs SO An Surv Psa 1958, 9:333-334

71998 (& Ammon, G.) Freuds Psychoanalyse: Perspektiven 1968 für Europa und Amerika. [Freud's psychoanalysis: perspectives for Europe and USA, 1968.] Dyn Psychiat 1968, 1:46-51

71999 (& Caruth, E.) From Eden to Utopia. (Communications.) Am Im 1965, 22:128-141
   Abs JWS Q 1966, 35:315

72000 (& Motto, R. L.) (Eds) From Learning for Love to Love of Learning. Essays on Psychoanalysis and Education. (Foreword: Redl, F.) NY: Brunner/Mazel Publ 1969, xxii + 282 p

72001 From prevention of emotional disorders to creative learning and teaching. Learn Love 107-113

S-44861 (& Friedman, S.) The function of acting out, play action and play acting in the psychotherapeutic process. In author's *Children of Time and Space, of Action and Impulse* 169-206
   Abs OS An Surv Psa 1957, 8:232-233

72002 A general treatment philosophy concerning acting out. Acting Out 162-172

72003 Group work—teaching a way of life. Boy's Work Exchange 1941, 10:2

72004 Historical notes concerning psychoanalysis and early language development. (Read at Am Psa Ass, 4 May 1962) J Am Psa Ass 1965, 13:707-731
   Abs JLSt Q 1968, 37:626-627

S-44863 A historical survey on the teaching of psychoanalytic techniques.
   Un levantomento historico sobre o ensino da tecnica psicoanalitica. Arqu Clin Pinel 1961, 1(1):69-82
   Abs JTM Q 1962, 31:128-129

72005 Impulse—acting out—purpose: psychotic adolescents and their quest for goals. (Read at Int Psa Cong, July 1967) J 1968, 49:347-352

72006 (& Motto, R. L.) Introduction: a new look at psychoanalytic understanding of discipline in education. Reiss-Davis Clin Bull 1965, 2:5-6

72007 (& Motto, R. L.) Introduction. Education and psychoanalysis: new tasks in a changing society. Reiss-Davis Clin Bull 1967, 4:2-5

72008 (& Motto, R. L.) Introduction. Psychoanalytic education: a bridge not a chasm. Reiss-Davis Clin Bull 1966, 3:2-4

72009 J. C. Hill's psychoanalytic contributions to teaching. Reiss-Davis Clin Bull 1966, 3(1):14-17. London Head Teacher J 1966, 305:245-246

72010 Karl Bühler and psychoanalysis. J gen Psychol 1966, 75:204-212

72011 The learning process: from learning for love to love of learning. Learn Love 95-98

72012　The learning process: from the phase of learning for love to the phase of the love of learning. Reiss-Davis Clin ann Rep 1961-62. Reiss-Davis Clin Bull 1964, 1(1):29-32

72013　(& Caruth, E.) Levels of verbal communication in the schizophrenic child's struggle against, for, and with the world of objects. Psa St C 1969, 24:115-137

72014　Lili E. Peller's psychoanalytic contributions to teaching. Reiss-Davis Clin Bull 1967, 4(1):6-9.

72015　(& Brown, W.; Greenbaum, N.; Hollingsworth, I.; Kobler, A.; Sargent, H.) A method of supervision for psychotherapy. Trans Kansas Acad Sci 1950, 53:254-267

* * *　The nature of the interpretive process. See [44880]

72016　(& Busch, F.; Liebowitz, J.; Perna, D.; Tuma, J.) Notes on the teaching and learning of child psychotherapy within a child guidance setting. Reiss-Davis Clin Bull 1966, 3:68-97

72017　(& Friedman, S. W.) Object constancy and psychotic reconstruction. Psa St C 1967, 22:357-374

S-44867 (& Wallerstein, J.) Observations on the psychology of borderline and psychotic children. In author's *Children of Time and Space, of Action and Impulse* 91-113

S-44868 (& Wallerstein, J.) Observations on the psychotherapy of borderline and psychotic children. In author's *Children of Time and Space, of Action and Impulse* 114-122

　　　　Abs JA An Surv Psa 1956, 7:288-289

72018　Omnipotence and omni-impotence. Int J Psychiat 1967, 4:443-447

72019　On the acquisition of speech in the autistic child. Reiss-Davis Clin Bull 1964, 1(2):63-79. In author's *Children of Time and Space, of Action and Impulse* 231-248

S-44866 (& Friedman, S. W.) On the meaning of play in childhood psychosis. In author's *Children of Time and Space, of Action and Impulse* 207-230

72020　On the nature of the psychotherapeutic process. Bull Veterans Admin 1951, Oct:3-12

72021　The opening gambit in psychotherapeutic work with a severely disturbed adolescent girl. Ops 1963, 33:862-871. In author's *Children of Time and Space, of Action and Impulse* 75-88

　　　　Abs PS Q 1964, 33:611. Kalina, E. & Rascovsky, A. Rev Psicoanál 1967, 24:441-444

72022　Origins of values in children. Educ Leadership 1964, 21:523-526

72023　The Orpheus and Eurydice theme in psychotherapy. BMC 1966, 30:207-224

　　　　El tema de Orfeo y Euridice en la psicoterapia. Cuad Psa 1966, 2(3-4):71-86

　　　　Abs Kalina, E. & Rascovsky, A. Rev Psicoanál 1967, 24:446-448

72024　Perspective: roaming the behavioral sciences. Psychiat News 1966, 1(8):7

72025　The philosophical refutation. J Philos 1941, Jan:57-67

S-44869 Philosophy of science and psychoanalysis.

　　　　Japanese: Tokyo J Psa 1963, 21(4):2-6

72026 Pleasure and reality, play and work, thought and action—variations of and on a theme. J humanist Psychol 1963, 3:20-31. In author's *Children of Time and Space, of Action and Impulse* 285-297

72027 (& Sargent, H.) Preliminary report on an experimental project in supervision in clinical psychology. Trans Kansas Acad Sci 1949, 52: 232-243

72028 The project on childhood psychosis: an introduction. Reiss-Davis Clin Bull 1964, 1:57-62

72029 (& Friedman, S. W.) Prolegomenon to a psychoanalytic technique in the treatment of childhood schizophrenia. Reiss-Davis Clin Bull 1968, 5:107-115

72030 (& Motto, R. L.) Psychoanalysis and education: a reappraisal. R 1964-65, 51:569-584

72031 (& Motto, R. L.) Psychoanalysis and education—an historical account. (Read at Am Psa Ass, 9 Dec 1961) Reiss-Davis Clin Bull 1964, 1:7-25. Learn Love 3-27

Psychoanalyse und Erziehung—Vergangenheit und Zukunft. Prax Kinderpsychol 1963, 12:213-233

Abs SRS Q 1966, 35:161

72032 Psychoanalysis and education: from prevention of emotional disorders to creative learning and teaching. Reiss-Davis Clin Bull 1968, 5:51-58

72033 Psychoanalysis and social crises. BMC 1969, 33:333-345

72034 Psychoanalysis looks at the origins of values in children. Educ Leadership 1964, 21:523-526

72035 The psychoanalyst and his relationship to the philosophy of science. In Feyerabend, P. K. & Maxwell, G. *Mind, Matter, and Method: Essays in Philosophy and Science in Honor of Herbert Feigl*, Minn: Univ Min Pr 1966, 59-69

El psicoanalisis y su relacion con la filosofia de la ciencias. Cuad Psa 1967, 3:27-36

72036 Psychoanalytic notes on the function of the curriculum. Reiss-Davis Clin Bull 1966, 3:36-46. Learn Love 47-57

72037 Psychoanalytic thoughts on learning and teaching readiness. Ops 1967, 37:356-357

* * * (& Wright, D. G.) A psychotherapeutic session with the space child. See [44854]

72038 (& Caruth, E.) Psychotic acting out: royal road or primrose path. In author's *Children of Time and Space, of Action and Impulse* 298-308

72039 Psychotic adolescents and their quest for goals. In Bühler, C. & Massarik, F. *The Course of Human Life*, NY: Springer 1968, 202-212

72040 Puppet play of a psychotic adolescent girl in the psychotherapeutic process. (Read at San Francisco Psa Soc, 8 Jan 1962) Psa St C 1965, 20:441-480. In author's *Children of Time and Space, of Action and Impulse* 249-284

Abs Kalina, E. & Rascovsky, A. Rev Psicoanál 1967, 24:445-446

72041 (& Rangell, L.) Reconstruction and theory formation. (Read at Am Psa Ass, 6 Dec 1958) J Am Psa Ass 1961, 9:684-697

Rekonstruktion und Theoriebildung. Psyche 1963, 17:414-425

Abs FB Q 1962, 31:424-425

72042 (& Motto, R. L.) The referral of the emotionally disturbed child. Calif Educational Research and Guidance Assoc., Conference Report 1960. Learn Love 164-171

72043 Reflections on parallels in the therapeutic and the social process. In Bühler, C. *Values in Psychotherapy*, NY: Free Pr 1962, 181-194. Samiksa 1963, 17(Sp. Issue):51-61

　　　　Japanese: In Bühler, C. [Values in Psychotherapy.] (Jap) Tokyo: Charles E. Tuttle 1965, 164-174

　　　　Swedish: In Bühler, C. [Values in Psychotherapy.] (Sw) Stockholm: Natur Och Kultur 1968, 194-206

72044 (Caruth, E.) The relation of ego autonomy to activity and passivity in the psychotherapy of childhood schizophrenia. Reiss-Davis Clin Bull 1968, 5:89-95

72045 The school psychologist's quest for identity. Learn Love 227-234. In *Toward a Professional Identity in School Psychology*, Calif Assoc of School Psychologists and Psychometrists, 14th ann conf publ 1963, 19-28

72046 (& King, P. E.) The search for ego controls: progression of play activity in psychotherapy with a schizophrenic child. R 1968, 54(4):83-92

72047 (& Motto, R. L.) The second education of teachers: an experiment in postgraduate training of teachers. Learn Love 218-226

72048 Siegfried Bernfeld 1892-1953. Sisyphus or the boundaries of education. Psa Pioneers 415-429

S-7783 (& Wright, D. G.) The space child. In author's *Children of Time and Space, of Action and Impulse* 311-323. In *Bobbs-Merrill Reprint Series in the Social Sciences,* 1966:211-224

72049 (& Wright, D. G.) The space child: ten years later. Forest Hosp Publ 1964, 2:36-47. In author's *Children of Time and Space, of Action and Impulse* 348-361

S-44874 The space child's time machine: on "reconstruction" in the psychotherapeutic treatment of a schizophrenoid child. In author's *Children of Time and Space, of Action and Impulse* 324-338

72050 Special training problems in psychotherapeutic work with psychotic and borderline children. Ops 1962, 32:569-583. In author's *Children of Time and Space, of Action and Impulse* 413-427

　　　　Abs RLG Q 1963, 32:137

72051 Supervision of psychotherapy: is it teaching? Is it administration? Or is it therapy? Psychotherapy 1964, 1:138-139

72052 (Participant) Symposium on Karl Bühler's contributions to psychology. J gen Psychol 1966, 75:181-219

72053 Task and conflict. Reiss-Davis Clin Bull 1967, 4:29-33

S-44878 (& Friedman, S. W.) A technical problem in the beginning phase of psychotherapy with a borderline psychotic child. In author's *Children of Time and Space, of Action and Impulse* 63-74

* * * Termination of analysis and working through. See: [72064]

S-44879 Termination of the training analysis within the framework of present-day institutes.

　　　　Abs An Surv Psa 1955, 6:391-392

* * * The therapeutic use of a quasi-religious experience. See [44853]

72054 (& Wallerstein, R. S.) Therapist and patient—learning problems. From author's *The Teaching and Learning of Psychotherapy*, NY: Basic Books 1958. In Haworth, M. R. *Child Psychotherapy*, NY: Basic Books 1964, 437-445

Terapeuta e paziente: problemi di apprendimento. In Haworth, M. R. *Psicoterapia Infantile*, Rome: Armando Editore 1967, 559-571

72055 Thoughts concerning appointment and election procedures for training analysts and other faculty members. JNMD 1969, 149:208-212

S-44880 Thoughts concerning the nature of the interpretive process. With title: The nature of the interpretive process. In author's *Children of Time and Space, of Action and Impulse* 125-147

72056 (& Caruth, E.) To sleep but not to dream: on the use of electrical tape recording in clinical research. Reiss-Davis Clin Bull 1965, 2:87-92

Abs Kalina, E. & Rascovsky, A. Rev Psicoanál 1967, 24:448-449

72057 A translation of and comments on Bernfeld's "On sexual enlightenment." Learn Love 36-44

72058 A tribute to Anne Sullivan Macy: a great teacher of discipline. Reiss-Davis Clin Bull 1965, 2:23-28. Learn Love 132-137

72059 Turmoil during puberty and adolescence: growth crises or pathology? Reiss-Davis Reporter 1966, 5:2

72060 (& Friedman, S. W.) Über einige gebräuchliche Modelle in der psychoanalytischen Behandlung kindlicher Psychosen. [On some customary models in the psychoanalytic treatment of child psychoses.] Hbh Kinderpsychother 1094-1107

S-44882 Vicissitudes of the "internal image" in the recovery of a borderline schizophrenic adolescent. In author's *Children of Time and Space, of Action and Impulse* 373-380

Abs An Surv Psa 1955, 6:300-301

72061 Willi Hoffer's contribution to teaching and education. Reiss-Davis Clin Bull 1968, 5:4-10

72062 Work with new Americans. Boy's Work Exchange 1943, 11(2):1-5

72063 (& Caruth, E.) The working alliance with the monster. BMC 1965, 29:189-197. In author's *Children of Time and Space, of Action and Impulse* 403-410

Der Arbeitspakt mit dem Ungeheuer. Therapie einer kindlichen Psychose. Hbh Kinderpsychother 1107-1115

72064 Working through and termination of analysis. (Read at Am Psa Ass, May 1964) J Am Psa Ass 1965, 13:57-78. With title: Termination of analysis and working through. Psa Amer 217-237

Abs CG RFPsa 1968, 32:338. JLSt Q 1968, 37:467

72065 Your own psychology. J Educ 1940, 123:301-302

See Ammon, Günter; Caruth, Elaine; Kass, Walter; King, Peter D.; Meyer, Mortimer M.; Motto, Rocco L.

REVIEWS OF:

72066 Arlow, J. A. & Brenner, C. Psychoanalytic Concepts and the Structural Theory. J 1966, 47:581-583

72067 Bettelheim, B. The Empty Fortress. Infantile Autism and the Birth of the Self. Q 1968, 37:296-297

72068 Ehrenwald, J. Psychotherapy: Myth and Method; An Integrative Approach. Q 1968, 37:304-305
72069 Masserman, J. H. (Ed) Science and Psychoanalysis, Vol. VII. Development and Research. Q 1966, 35:289-290

EKSTERMAN, A. J.

72070 Indicações psiquiátricas em gastroenterologia. [Indications for psychiatric treatment in gastroenterology.] Arch Gastroent, S. Paulo 1966, 3(3):111-115

ELBERT, SHIRLEY

72071 (& Rosman, B.; Minuchin, S.; Guerney, B.) A method for the clinical study of family interaction. Ops 1964, 34:885-894

ELBLINGER, SHULAMIT

See Kreitler, Hans

ELDRED, STANLEY H.

72072 Discussion of Washburn, S. L. "Milieu interventions in the treatment of psychosis." Int Psychiat Clin 1968, 5(1):29-31
72073 (& Bell, N. W.; Longabauch, R.; Sherman, L. J.) Interactional correlates of chronicity in schizophrenia. Psychiat Res Rep 1964, (19): 1-12
72074 (& Vanderpol, M.) (Eds) Psychotherapy in the Designed Therapeutic Milieu. (International Psychiatry Clinics, Vol. 5, No. 1) Boston: Little, Brown 1968, xx + 150 p
72075 Sullivan in cultural perspective. Int J Psychiat 1967, 4(6):531-533

ABSTRACT OF:
72076 Fisher, C. & Dement, W. C. Dreaming and psychosis; observations on the dream-sleep cycle during the course of an acute paranoid psychosis. Bull Phila Ass Psa 1961, 11:130-132

REVIEW OF:
72077 Artiss, K. L. Milieu Therapy and Schizophrenia. Q 1963, 32:258-260

ELDRIDGE, HERBERT G.

72078 The "mind distrest": literary allusions in Benjamin Rush's *Diseases of the Mind.* Lit & Psych 1966, 16:93-102

ELESTON, MARY R.

See Kaye, Harvey E.

ELHARDT, SIEGFRIED

72079 Angst und psycho-somatisches Geschehen. [Anxiety and psychosomatic effects.] Z PSM 1959-60, 6:16-22
S-44887 Freuds Bedeutung für Beziehung zwischen Arzt und Patient. Abs HK An Surv Psa 1956, 7:16

72080 Trauminterpretation in der psychoanalytischen Behandlung. [Dream interpretation in psychoanalytic treatment.] Z PSM 1959-60, 6:275-284
72081 Über gesunde und neurotische "aggression." [On healthy and neurotic "aggression."] Z PSM 1968, 14:175-187

See Cremerius, J.

ELIADE, MIRCEA

72082 Images and Symbols; Studies in Religious Symbolism. (Tr: Mairet, P.) NY: Sheed & Ward 1961, 189 p
72083 Initiation dreams and visions among the Siberian shamans. In Grunebaum, G. E. von & Caillois, R. *The Dream and Human Societies,* Berkeley/Los Angeles: Univ Calif Pr 1966, 331-340
72084 Myths, Dreams and Mysteries. (Tr: Mairet, P.) NY: Harper & Row 1967, 254 p

ELIASOPH, EUGENE

72085 Existence, spontaneity and anxiety, as related to the process of "merging." Prog PT 1960, 5:195-200

ELINSON, JACK

See Weber, John J.

EL-ISLAM, M. F.

72086 The psychotherapeutic basis of some Arab rituals. Int J soc Psychiat 1967, 13:265-268

ELKES, ALEXANDER

72087 (& Thorpe, J. G.) A Summary of Psychiatry. London: Faber 1967, 3-143 p

ELKES, CHARMIAN

See Rioch, Margaret J.

ELKES, JOEL

72088 Discussion of Wagner, P. S. "Psychiatry for everyman." Crosscurrents in Ps & Psa 60-64
72089 Introduction. Sci Psa 1965, 8:145-146
72090 The place of ethology in the undergraduate teaching of the behavioral sciences. In Earley, L. W. et al: *Teaching Psychiatry in Medical School,* Wash DC: Am Psychiat Ass 1969, 313-314

ELKIN, HENRY

72091 The emergence of human being in infancy. Rev existent Psychol Psychiat 1961, 1:17-26
72092 The unconscious and the integration of personality. Rev existent Psychol Psychiat 1965, 5:176-189

ELKIND, DAVID

* * * Editor of Piaget, J. *Six Psychological Studies,* NY: Random House
       1967, 192 p

       See Tenzer, Anita

ELKINS, ALAN M.

72093 (& Papanek, G. O.) Consultation with the police: an example of com-
       munity psychiatry practice. P 1966, 123:531-535
72094 The patient in community psychiatry. Current psychiat Ther 1968,
       8:182-186

ELKISCH, PAULA

72095 Free art expression. In Rabin, A. I. & Haworth, M. R. *Projective Tech-
       niques with Children,* NY: Grune & Stratton 1960, 273-288
72096 Nonverbal, extraverbal, and autistic verbal communication in the
       treatment of a child tiqueur. (Read at Am Psa for Ch Psa, 4 June
       1967) Psa St C 1968, 23:423-437
S-44911 (& Mahler, M. S.) On infantile precursors of the "influencing machine"
       (Tausk).
              Abs RTh J 1961, 42:472
S-44913 The psychological significance of the mirror.
              Abs CK An Surv Psa 1957, 8:106-107

ELKS, CHARMIAN

       See Rioch, Margaret J.

ELL, ERNST

72097 Die Jugendlichen in der seelischen Pubertät. [The Young Person in
       Emotional Puberty.] Lambertus-Verlag 1966, 186 p

ELLARD, J.

72097A The problems of the migrant. Med J Aust 1969, 2:1039-1043

ELLENBERGER, HENRI F.

72098 Alfred Adler: two letters to a patient. J ind Psych 1966, 22:112-115
S-44919 The ancestry of dynamic psychotherapy.
              Abs AaSt An Surv Psa 1956, 7:297-298
72099 Charcot and the Salpetrière school. PT 1965, 19:253-267
72100 The concept of creative illness. (Tr: Brugmans, H. F.) R 1968, 55:
       442-456
              Abs SRS Q 1969, 38:674
72101 Effects d'une maladie physique grave et prolongée d'un enfant sur sa
       famille. [Effects of a serious prolonged physical sickness of a child
       on its family.] Schweiz ANP 1967, 99:348-390
72102 The evolution of depth psychology. In Galdston, I. *Historic Deriva-
       tions of Modern Psychiatry,* NY: McGraw-Hill 1967, 159-184
S-44924 Fechner and Freud.
              Abs AaSt An Surv Psa 1956, 7:36-38

72103 Intéret et domaines d'application de l'ethno-psychiatrie. [The interest and fields of application of ethnopsychiatry.] Proc IV World Cong Psychiat 1966, 264-268

S-44925 The life and work of Hermann Rorschach.
La vida y la obra de Hermann Rorschach (1884-1922). Rev Psicol gen apl, Madrid 1958, 13:561-613

72104 Mesmer and Puysegur: from magnetism to hypnotism. R 1965, 52(2):137-153
Abs SRS Q 1966, 35:473

72105 La psychologie de Carl Gustav Jung. A propos de son autobiographie. [The psychology of Carl Gustav Jung. A propos of his autobiography.] Un méd Canad 1964, 93:993-1006

S-44928 The unconscious before Freud.
Abs AaSt An Surv Psa 1957, 8:8-9

See May, Rollo; Menninger, Karl; Wittkower, Eric D.

REVIEW OF:
72106 Sherman, M. H. et al (Eds): Psychoanalysis in America: Historical Perspectives. R 1966, 53(4):178-180

ELLENSON, GERALD

See Davies, Ida J.

ELLER, J. J.

See Eisenbud, Jule

ELLES, G. W.

72107 Family treatment from a therapeutic community. Confin psychiat 1965, 8:9-14

ELLES, GILLIAN

72108 A family pattern of distress. In Lomas, P. *The Predicament of the family,* London: HIP 1967, 57-89

72109 The mute sad-eyed child: collateral analysis in a disturbed family. (Read at Brit Psa Soc, 3 May 1961) J 1962, 43:40-49
Abs FTL Q 1963, 32:284

ELLIOTT, DELBERT S.

72110 (& Vosa, H. L.; Wendling, A.) Dropout and the social milieu of the high school: a preliminary analysis. Ops 1966, 36:808-817
Abs RFPsa 1968, 32:382

ELLIOTT, GEORGE P.

72111 Country full of blondes. Nation 1960, 190: April 23. Abstr Engl St 1960, 3:360

ELLIOT, ORVILLE

72112 (& Scott, J. P.) The development of emotional distress reactions to separation in puppies. J genet Psychol 1961, 99:3-22

ELLIOTT, ROBERT C.

72113 The Power of Satire: Magic, Ritual, Art. Princeton: Princeton Univ
Pr 1960, 300 p
Rv Posinsky, S. H. Q 1961, 30:445-446

ELLIOTT, ROBERT E.

See Hiltner, Seward

ELLIS, ALBERT

72114 An answer to some objections to rational-emotive psychotherapy.
Psychotherapy 1965, 2:108-111
72115 The Art and Science of Love. NY: Lyle Stuart, Inc. 1960, 400 p
72116 Art and sex. In author's *The Encyclopedia of Sexual Behavior* 161-179
72117 The Art of Erotic Seduction. NY: Lyle Stuart, Inc. 1968, 216 p
72118 The case against religion: a psychotherapist's view. Independent 1962,
126:4-5
72119 The Case for Sexual Liberty. Vol. I. Tucson, Arizona: Seymour Pr
1965, vi + 141 p
Rv Woltmann, A. G. R 1966, 53:303-308
72120 Constitutional factors in homosexuality: a reexamination of the evidence. In Beigel, H. *Advances in Sex Research*, NY: Paul Hober, Inc.
1963, 161-186
72121 Continuing personal growth of the psychotherapist. J humanist Psychol
1966, 7:156-169
72122 (& Harper, R. A.) Creative Marriage. NY: Lyle Stuart, Inc. 1961,
288 p
72123 (& Abarbanel, A.) The Encylopedia of Sexual Behavior. NY: Hawthorn Books 1961, 1059 p (2 Vols. Revised ed.); 1968, 1059 p (1 Vol.)
72124 The essence of sexual morality. Issue: Sex Ethics 1964, 2:20-24
72125 The Folklore of Sex. NY: Grove Pr 1961, (Revised ed.) 320 p
72126 Goals of psychotherapy. In Mahrer, A. R. *The Goals of Psychotherapy*,
NY: Appleton-Century-Crofts 1967, 206-220
72127 (& Harper, R. A.) A Guide to Rational Living. Englewood Cliffs, New
Jersey: Prentice-Hall 1961, 195 p
72128 Homosexuality: Its Causes and Cure. NY: Lyle Stuart, Inc. 1965, 288 p
72129 Homosexuality: the right to be wrong. J Sex Res 1968, 4:96-107
72130 (& Wolfe, J. L.; Moseley, S.) How to Prevent Your Child from Becoming a Neurotic Adult. NY: Crown Publishers 1966, 247 p
72131 If This Be Sexual Heresy . . . NY: Lyle Stuart, Inc. 1963, 253 p
72132 Is psychoanalysis harmful? Psychiat Opin 1968, 5(1):16-24
72133 Marriage counseling with demasculinizing wives and demasculinized
husbands. Marriage fam Liv 1960, 22:13-20
72134 Masturbation by sexually isolated individuals. In Masters, R. E. L.
Sexual Self-Stimulation, Los Angeles: Sherbourne Pr 1967, 221-231
72135 (& Sagarin, E.) Nymphomania: A Study of the Oversexed Woman.
NY: Gilbert Pr 1964, 255 p; Macfadden Books 1965, 178 p
S-44948 An operational reformulation of some of the basic principles of psychoanalysis.
Abs AHM An Surv Psa 1956, 7:45-46

72136   The Origins and the Development of the Incest Taboo. NY: Lyle Stuart, Inc. 1963, 186 p
72137   Psychotherapy and moral laxity. Psychiat Opin 1967, 4(5):18-21
72138   A rational approach to interpretation. In Hammer, E. *The Use of Interpretation in Treatment*, NY: Grune & Stratton 1968, 232-239
72139   Rational-emotive psychotherapy. In Arbuckle, D. S. *Counseling and Psychotherapy*, NY: McGraw-Hill 1967, 78-99
72140   Reason and Emotion in Psychotherapy. NY: Lyle Stuart 1962, 442 p
72141   Sexual manifestations of emotionally disturbed behavior. Ann Am Acad Pol Soc Sci 1968, 376:96-105
72142   Sexual promiscuity in America. Ann Am Acad Pol Soc Sci 1968, 378:58-67
72143   There is no place for the concept of sin in psychotherapy. J counsel Psychol 1960, 7:188-192
72144   Thoughts on theory versus outcome in psychotherapy. Psychotherapy 1964, 1:83-87

See Durkheim, Émile

ELLIS, BARBARA GRAY

72145   Unconscious collusion in marital interaction. Soc Casewk 1964, 45:79-85

ELLIS, HAVELOCK

S-7867   Studies in the Psychology of Sex.
        Étude de Psychologie Sexuelle. Paris: Ed. Hesnard, Vol. 3, (n.d.)
        Rv Dreyfus-Moreau, J. RFPsa 1966, 30(Sp. No.):321

ELLMAN, RICHARD

* * *   Foreword to Weiss, D. A. Oedipus in Nottingham: D. H. Lawrence. Seattle: Univ of Wash Pr 1962

ELMER, ELIZABETH

72146   Children in Jeopardy: A Study of Abused Minors and Their Families. Pittsburgh: Univ of Pittsburgh Pr 1967, xi + 125 p
72147   (& Gregg, G. S.) Developmental characteristics of abused children. Pediatrics 1967, 40:596-602. Ann Prog child Psychiat 1968, 555-565
72148   Failure to thrive: role of the mother. Pediatrics 1960, 25:717-725
72149   Identification of abused children. Children 1963, 10:180-184

See Reinhart, John B.

ELMS, ALAN C.

72150   Role playing, incentive, and dissonance. Psychol Bull 1967, 68:132-148

ELROD, NORMAN F.

72151   Beitrag zur Entwicklungspsychologie im Rahmen der Schizophrenen-Situation. [Contribution to developmental psychology within the framework of the situation of schizophrenics.] In Benedetti, G. & Müller, C. *Psychotherapy of Schizophrenia* (2nd Int Symp 1959), Basel/NY: Karger 1960, 17-29

ELSÄSSER, ERIKA

72152 (& Zeise, W. J.) Beitrag zur Rolle der Kotherapeutin in der analytischen Gruppentherapie von Jugendlichen, unter Berück—sichtigung grundlegender Unterschiede zwischen psychoanalytischer Einzel- und Gruppen-Therapie. [Contribution to the role of the co-therapist in analytic group therapy of adolescents with special reference to fundamental differences between psychoanalytic individual and group therapy.] Prax Kinderpsychol 1964, 13:47-51

72153 Über die Bedeutung der Vorurteilsforschung für die Erziehungsberatung. [On the significance of the study of prejudice in educational counseling.] Prax Kinderpsychol 1964, 13:134-143

72154 Über die Wiederbelebung der Einzelkindsituation in der psychoanalytischen Gruppentherapie im Anschluss an Einzeltherapie. [On the revival of the single child situation in psychoanalytic group therapy following individual psychotherapy.] Prax Kinderpsychol 1963, 12:208-210

See Zeise, Werner, J.

ELSÄSSER, GÜNTER

72155 Analytisch-psychotherapeutische Grundeinsichten und -haltungen im Umgang mit psychiatrischen Patienten. [Basic analytical—psychotherapeutic attitudes and insight in dealing with psychiatric patients.] Nervenarzt 1963, 34:488-491

72156 Analytische Psychotherapie in psychiatrischen Krankenabteilungen. [Analytic psychotherapy in psychiatric hospital department.] Z Psychother med Psychol 1960, 10:192-199

S-44983 Objektives Verschulden und Neurose.
Objective guilt and neurosis. In Belgum, D. *Religion and Medicine,* Ames, Iowa: Iowa State Univ Pr 1967, 245-255

72157 Therapieschritte und Wirkungsfaktoren in der analytischen Psychotherapie. [Steps in therapy and factors of efficacy in analytic psychotherapy.] Z PSM 1965, 11:55-64

72158 Über die Protokollierung psychoanalytischer Behandlungsverläufe. [On recording the course of psychoanalytical treatment.] Z PSM 1967, 13:138-141

ELSON, ABRAHAM

72159 (& Pearson, C.; Jones, C. D.; Schumacher, E.) Follow-up study of childhood elective mutism. Arch gen Psychiat 1965, 13:182-187
Abs PB Q 1967, 36:145

ELSON, MIRIAM A.

72160 The reactive impact of adolescent and family upon each other in separation. Ch Psychiat 1964, 3:697-708

EMCH, MINNA

S-7894A The social context of supervision.
Abs An Surv Psa 1955, 6:386-387

EMDE, ROBERT N.

72161 (& Polak, P. R.; Spitz, R. A.) Anaclitic depression in an infant raised in an institution. J Amer Acad Child Psychiat 1965, 4:545-553
72162 Limiting regression in the therapeutic community. Amer J Nurs 1967, 67:1010-1015

See Polak, Paul R.

EMDE BOAS, CONRAD VAN

72163 Las consecuencias emocionales de diferencias de situación en la terapia colectiva analíticamente orientada y el análisis individual. [Emotional consequences of situational differences in analytically oriented collective therapy and in individual analysis.] Rev Psiquiat Psicol 1967, 8:167-173
72164 Intensive group psychotherapy with married couples. Int J grp PT 1962, 12:142-153
Thérapie intensive de groupe avec des couples mariés. RFPsa 1962, 26:447-465
Abs Auth Rev Psicoanál 1963, 20:94
72165 Die Lage der Homosexuellen in den Niederlanden. [The position of homosexuals in the Netherlands.] Z PSM 1967, 13:55-63
72166 Verniging sverslagen nederlandse verniging voor psychotherapie. [Determination of the indications for analytical group psychotherapy.] Ned Tijdschr Geneesk 1966, 110:2186-2190

EMERSON, P. E.

See Schaffer, H. R.

EMERSON, RICHARD

See Titchener, James L.

EMERY, PAUL E.

See Greenblatt, Milton

EMICH, I.

72167 Zum Angsttraum des nervösen Kindes. [Nightmares of nervous children.] Mat Med Nordmark 1964, 2:3-15

EMMERICH, WALTER

72168 Parental identification in young children. Genet Psychol Monogr 1959, 60:257-308
72169 Personality development and concepts of structure. Child Develpm 1968, 39:671-690

See Weiss, Peter

EMMETT, J. L.

See Love, J. G.

ENACHESCU, CONSTANTIN

72170 Analyse psychopathologique du contenu symbolique des dessins des malades schizophrènes. [Psychopathological analysis of the symbolic content of drawings by schizophrenic patients.] Ann méd-psychol 1967, 125(2):37-65

72171 [On the symbolic representation of mental disturbances in alcoholics.] (Fr) Confin psychiat 1966, 9:236-248

72172 Recherche psychopathologique sur le phénomène de la "régression" dans les dessins des schizophrènes. [A psychopathologic study of the phenomenon of "regression" in the drawings of schizophrenic patients.] Encéph 1967, 56:166-189

See Nicolau, A.

ENDICOTT, JEAN

See Endicott, Noble A.; Mesnikoff, Alvin M.

ENDICOTT, NOBLE A.

72173 (& Endicott, J.) "Improvement" in untreated psychiatric patients. Arch gen Psychiat 1963, 9:575-585. In Goldstein, A. P. & Dean, S. J. The Investigation of Psychotherapy, NY: Wiley 1966, 207-217

See Gill, Merton M.; Simon, Justin

ENDLEMAN, ROBERT

72174 Personality and Social Life. Text and Readings. NY: Random House 1967, 624 p
Rv Nichols, C. Q 1969, 38:501-502

72175 Reflections on the human revolution. R 1966, 53:169-188
Abs SRS Q 1967, 36:470

ENDLER, NORMAN S.

72176 A behavioristic interpretation of the psychotherapy system of Karen Horney. Canad Psychol 1965, 6a:188-200

ENELOW, ALLEN J.

72177 The compensable injury. Calif Med 1967, 106:179-182

72178 Drug treatment of psychotic patients in general medical practice. Calif Med 1965, 102:1-4

* * * (& Adler, L. M.) Foreword to Fierman, L. B. (Ed) Effective Psychotherapy: The Contribution of Hellmuth Kaiser. NY: Free Pr; London: Collier-Macmillan 1965

72179 (& Adler, L. M.) The "here and now" as the focus of psychotherapy. Sci Psa 1965, 8:208-222

72180 Identity and communication. PT 1964, 18:649-659

72181 (& Adler, L. M.) An instrument for studying role-perception in physicians (its application to communication problems in medicine). Dis nerv Sys 1965, 26:209-220

72182 (& Wexler, M.) The medical interview. Med Times 1965, 93:1192-1200

72183 (& Adler, L. M.) Natural history of a postgraduate course in psychiatry. Psychosomatics 1967, 8:185-192

72184 Phenomenological principles in psychiatric diagnosis. Arizona Med 1963, 20:59-62

72185 Prevention of mental disorder. The role of the general practitioner. Calif Med 1966, 104:16-21

72186 (& Wexler, M.) Psychiatry in the Practice of Medicine. NY: Oxford Univ Pr 1966, viii + 355 p

72187 Psychotherapy in the practice of medicine. Med Arts Sci 1967, 21: 79-88

72188 The silent patient. Ps 1960, 23:153-158
Abs HRB Q 1961, 30:299-300

72189 (& Myers, V. H.) The value of psychiatric courses for practicing physicians. Hosp Comm Psychiat 1968, 19:146-149

REVIEW OF:
72190 Hendrick, I. Psychiatry Education Today. Psa Forum 1966, 1:304-305

ENELOW, MORTON L.

72191 Discussion of Snow, E. & Bluestone, H. "Fetishism and murder." Sci Psa 1969, 15:99-100

72192 Public nuisance offenses: exhibitionism, voyeurism and transvestism. In Slovenko, R. *Sexual Behavior and the Law,* Springfield, Ill: Thomas 1965, 478-486

See Monroe, Russell R.

ENG, ERLING

S-45004 Cellini's two childhood memories.
Abs AS An Surv Psa 1956, 7:416-417

TRANSLATION OF:
(& Kennedy, S. C.) Straus, E. W. M. et al: [92607]

ENGEL, GEORGE L.

72193 Anxiety and depression-withdrawal: the primary affects of unpleasure. (Read at Boston Psa Soc, 9 Nov 1961) J 1962, 43:89-97
Abs AHM Bull Phila Ass Psa 1961, 11:39-41. FTL Q 1963, 32: 285-286

72194 Biologic and psychologic features of the ulcerative colitis patient. Gastroenterology 1961, 40:313

72195 The concept of psychosomatic disorder. J psychosom Res 1967, 11:3-10

72196 Delirium. Compreh Txbk Psychiat 711-716

72197 Discussion of Gorney, R. "Of divers things: preliminary note on the dynamics of scuba diving." Psa Forum 1966, 1:271-272

72198 Ego development following severe trauma in infancy. (Read at Chicago Psa Soc, 22 Oct 1968)
    Abs Handler, J. S. Bull Phila Ass Psa 1969, 19:234-236

72199 Ego development following severe trauma in infancy: a 14 year study of a girl with gastric fistula and depression in infancy. Bull Ass psa Med 1967, 6:57.

72200 Guilt, pain, and success. PSM 1962, 24:37-48
    Abs RDT Q 1962, 31:588

72201 Humanism and science in medicine. In Brill, N. Q. *Psychiatry in Medicine*, Berkeley/Los Angeles: Univ Calif Pr 1962, 42-63

72202 Intestinal disorders. Compreh Txbk Psychiat 1054-1059

72203 Introduction to brain disorders. Compreh Txbk Psychiat 706-707

72204 Is grief a disease? A challenge for medical research. PSM 1961, 23: 18-22
    Abs JPG Q 1961, 30:601-602

72205 Letter to editor re: Percival Bailey's views on psychoanalysis. Persp Biol Med 1961, 4:386

72206 (& Schmale, A. H.) Letter to the editors re: Dr. Saul's "Sudden death at impasse." Psa Forum 1966, 1:234-236

72207 A life setting conducive to illness: the giving-up—given-up complex. BMC 1968, 32:355-365. Ann intern Med 1968, 69:293-300

72208 Medical education and the psychosomatic approach. A report on the Rochester experience 1946-1966. J psychosom Res 1967, 11:77-85

72209 Mental illness: vital balance or myth? BMC 1964, 28:145-153

72210 The psychoanalytic approach to psychosomatic medicine. Mod Psa 251-273

72211 (& Schmale, A. H., Jr.) Psychoanalytic theory of somatic disorder: conversion, specificity, and the disease onset situation. (Read at Am Psa Ass, 4 Dec 1965; at Brit Psa Soc, 16 Nov 1966) J Am Psa Ass 1967, 15:344-365
    French: Rev Méd psychosom 1968, 10:197-216
    Eine psychoanalytische Theorie der somatischen Störung. Psyche 1969, 23:241-261
    Teoria psicoanalitica de los trastornos somaticos. Conversion, especificidad y la situacion de comienzo de la enfermedad. Rev Psicoanál 1968, 25:68-118

72212 Psychogenic pain. J occup Med 1961, 3:249

72213 Psychological Development in Health and Disease. Phila/London: Saunders 1962, 435 p
    Rv Linn, L. Q 1964, 33:120-122

72214 A psychological setting of somatic disease: the giving-up—given-up complex. Proc RSM 1967, 60:553

72215 A reconsideration of the role of conversion in somatic disease. Comprehen Psychiat 1968, 9:316-326

72216 Some obstacles to the development of research in psychoanalysis. Closing comments. (Read at Am Psa Ass, 2 Dec 1965) J Am Psa Ass 1968, 16:195-204; 228-229

S-45022 (& Reichsman, F.) Spontaneous and experimentally induced depression in an infant with a gastric fistula: a contribution to the problem of depression.

Abs AL An Surv Psa 1956, 7:267-271

72217 Toward a classification of affects. In Knapp, P. *Expression of the Emotions in Man*, NY: IUP 1963, 266-294

72218 Training in psychosomatic research. Adv PSM 1967, 5:16-24

72219 A unified concept of health and disease. Persp Biol Med 1960, 3:459-485

See Schmale, Arthur H.

REVIEWS OF:

72220 Deutsch, F. Body, Mind and the Sensory Gateways. Q 1964, 33:433-435

72221 Groen, J. J. et al: Psychosomatic Research. A Collection of Papers. Q 1966, 35:611-615

72222 Levitt, E. E. The Psychology of Anxiety. Q 1969, 38:667

72223 Wahl, C. W. (Ed): New Dimensions in Psychosomatic Medicine. Q 1966, 35:300-301

72224 Wisdom, J. W. & Wolff, H. H. (Eds): The Role of Psychosomatic Disorder in Adult Life. Q 1966, 35:615-616

ENGEL, MARY

72225 (& Marsden, G.; Woodaman, S.) Children who work and the concept of work style. Ps 1967, 30:392-404

72226 Psychological testing of borderline psychotic children. Arch gen Psychiat 1963, 8:426-434
Abs KR Q 1964, 33:302

72227 Shifting levels of communication in treatment of adolescent character disorders. Arch gen Psychiat 1960, 2:94-99
Abs KR Q 1961, 30:308

ENGEL, S. W.

72228 Zur Psychopathologie des Rechtsbrechers. [Psychopathology of the offender.] In Kranz, H. *Psychopathologie Heute,* Stuttgart: Georg Thieme 1962, 328-344

ENGELHARDT, DAVID M.

See Hankoff, Leon D.

ENGELHARDT, K.

72229 Über anthropologische Gesichtspunkte in der Medizin. [On anthropological viewpoints in medicine.] Med Welt 1963, (43):2167-2173

ENGELL, R.

72230 (et al) [Neopsychoanalysis.] (Ger) Landarzt 1968, 44:6-11

ENGELMEIER, MAX P.

72231 Hauptaufgaben der Psychiatrie heute und morgen. [Principal tasks of psychiatry today and tomorrow.] Hippokrates 1967, 38:895-899

ENGELS, W. DENNIS

72232 (& Wittkower, E.) Allergic and skin disorders. Compreh Txbk Psychiat 1093-1099

ENGLE, BERNICE S.

See Bennett, Abram E.; Bowman, Karl M.

ABSTRACTS OF:

72233 Block, W. E. & Ventur, P. A. A study of the psychoanalytic concept of castration anxiety in symbolically castrated amputees. Q 1964, 33:456

72234 Bosselman, B. C. Castration anxiety and phallus envy: a reformulation. Q 1961, 30:301

72235 Bruch, H. Effectiveness in psychotherapy. Q 1964, 33:456

72236 Bruch, H. Transformation of oral impulses in eating disorders: a conceptual approach. Q 1962, 31:587-588

72237 Chapman, A. H. Further observations on the Nemesis concept. Q 1963, 32:450

72238 Eidelberg, L. A contribution to the study of the unpleasure-pleasure principle. Q 1963, 32:293

72239 Eidelberg, L. & Palmer, J. N. Primary and secondary narcissism. Q 1961, 30:301-302

72240 Federn, E. Some clinical remarks on the psychopathology of genocide. Q 1961, 30:302

72241 Federn, E. The therapeutic personality, as illustrated by Paul Federn and August Aichhorn. Q 1963, 32:292

72242 Greenberg, N. H. et al: A study in transsexualism. Q 1961, 30:301

72243 Hart, H. H. A review of the psychoanalytic literature on passivity. Q 1962, 31:587

72244 Hendin, H. Suicide in Sweden. Q 1963, 32:292

72245 Hollander, R. Compulsive cursing. Q 1961, 30:302

72246 Kaufman, M. R. The problems of the psychoanalyst as a teacher in general psychiatry. Q 1964, 33:456

72247 Levy, N. J. Notes on the creative process and the creative person. Q 1962, 31:135

72248 Lipshutz, D. M. Some dynamic factors in the problem of aggression. Q 1962, 31:136

72249 Nussbaum, K. & Michaux, W. W. Response to humor in depression; a predictor and evaluator of patient changes. Q 1964, 33:456

72250 Peyser, H. S. The fear of traveling: a discussion and report of a case. Q 1962, 31:587

72251 Scheflen, A. E. Regressive one-to-one relationships. Q 1961, 30:302

72252 Searles, H. F. Schizophrenia and the inevitability of death. Q 1962, 31:588

72253 Shoor, M. & Speed, M. H. Delinquency as a manifestation of the mourning process. Q 1964, 33:456

72254 Stevenson, I. The role of wishes in the origin of dreams and psychoses. Q 1962, 31:135

72255 Taylor, W. S. Hypnoanalysis of a fetishism. Q 1963, 32:293

72256 Weiner, I. B. Father-daughter incest. Q 1963, 32:450

72257 Whittington, H. G. Transference in brief psychotherapy: experience in a college psychiatric clinic. Q 1963, 32:293

ENGLEHARDT, DAVID M.

72258 Foreword. Adolescents ix-xi

ENGLER, BARBARA O.

72259 The concept of knowledge in the thought of Sigmund Freud. Diss Abstr 1967, 28:1845-1846

ENGLISH, AVA CHAMPNEY

See English, Horace B.

ENGLISH, HORACE BIDWELL

72260 (& English, A. C.) A Comprehensive Dictionary of Psychological and Psychoanalytical Terms, a Guide to Usage. NY: McKay 1964, xiv + 594 p
   Rv Gulotta, G. Riv Psa 1965, 11:180

ENGLISH, J. T.

See Menninger, W. Walter

ENGLISH, O. SPURGEON

72261 Anxiety and the normal heart. GP 1960, 21:82-85
72262 Clinical observations on direct analysis. Comprehen Psychiat 1960, 1:156-163
72263 The contribution of psychoanalysis to psychiatry and psychopathology. In Page, J. D. *Approaches to Psychopathology*, NY/London: Columbia Univ Pr 1966, 139-153
72264 Contributions to the development of a psychotherapist. PT 1968, 22:431-442
72265 (& Hampe, W. W., Jr.; Bacon, C. L.; Settlage, C. F.) Direct Analysis and Schizophrenia: Clinical Observations and Evaluations. NY: Grune & Stratton 1961, 128 p
   Abs J Am Psa Ass 1962, 10:445. Rv First, H. G. Q 1961, 30:571-575. Sullivan, C. T. R 1963, 50:156-157
72266 Education in mental health combined with treatment of psychosomatic illness. Psychother Psychosom 1967, 15:135-141. In Philippopoulos, G. S. *Dynamics in Psychiatry*, Basel/NY: Karger 1968, 51-58
° ° °   Foreword to Scheflen, A. E. *A Psychotherapy of Schizophrenia: Direct Analysis*, Springfield, Ill: Thomas 1961, vii
72267 Nota sobre la orientación psicoterapéutica en el tratamiento de las enfermedades psicosomáticos. [A note on the psychotherapeutic orientation in the treatment of psychosomatic illness.] Act Np Arg 1960, 6:527-529
72268 Some dynamic concepts of human emotions in relation to hypnosis. Amer J clin Hyp 1962, 4:135-140
72269 Subjective reactions to being filmed. Meth Res PT 60

72270 Values in psychotherapy: the affair. Voices 1967, 3(4):9-14
72271 Who should be trained for psychotherapy? Int Psychiat Clin 1964,
       1:271-281

ENKE, HELMUT

72272 Bipolare Gruppenpsychotherapie als Möglichkeit psychoanalytischer
       Arbeit in der stationären Psychotherapie. [Bipolar group psycho-
       therapy as a possibility of psychoanalytic procedure in hospital psycho-
       therapy.] Z Psychother med Psychol 1965, 15:116-121
72273 Eine formale Affekt- und Beziehungsanalyse in Traumserien von Pa-
       tienten mit psychosomatischen Krankheitsbildern. [A formal affect and
       social relation analysis in series of dreams in patients with psycho-
       physiologic disorders.] Z PSM 1968, 14:15-33
72274 Patientengespräche. [Conversations of patients.] Prax PT 1967, 12:
       79-88
72275 Somatisierung und gruppenpsychotherapie. [Somatization and group
       psychotherapy.] Psychiat Neurol med Psychol 1968, 20:41-45
72276 (& Ohlmeier, D.) Über die Bedeutung spontaner Bildnereien in der
       Psychotherapie. [On the significance of spontaneous creativities during
       psychotherapy.] Z PSM 1962, 8:45-48
72277 (& Michler, S.) Über einige Kriterien der Mutter-Kind-Beziehung bei
       männlichen Patienten mit den Symptomen: Asthma bronchiale, Colitis
       gravis, Herzbeschwerden und Magenbeschwerden. [On some criteria
       of the mother-child relation in male patients with the symptoms:
       bronchial asthma, colitis gravis, cardiac and stomach disorders.]
       Z PSM 1967, 13:108-115

ENNIS, BARBARA

See Reding, Georges R.

ENNIS, JEROME

ABSTRACTS OF:
72278 Arlow, J. A. The supervisory situation. Q 1964, 33:455-456
72279 Bowlby, J. Pathological mourning and childhood mourning. Q 1964,
       33:454-455
72280 DeBell, D. E. A critical digest of the literature on psychoanalytic super-
       vision. Q 1964, 33:455
72281 Eissler, K. R. Freud and the psychoanalysis of history. Q 1965, 34:
       465-466
72282 Fisher, C. & Friedman, S. On the presence of a rhythmic, diurnal, oral
       instinctual drive cycle in man: a preliminary report. Q 1967, 36:478-
       480
72283 Heiman, M. et al: A pre-examination of the significance of clitoral
       versus vaginal orgasm. Q 1969, 38:517
72284 Loewenstein, R. M. Some considerations on free association. Q 1964,
       33:454
72285 Rose, G. J. Body ego and creative imagination. Q 1965, 34:467
72286 Rosen, V. H. Variants of comic caricature and their relationship to
       obsessive-compulsive phenomena. Q 1965, 34:466

72287   Rosenbaum, J. B. & Subrin, M. The psychology of gossip. Q 1965, 34:467-468
72288   Scott, W. C. M. A finger-licking finger-flicking habit. Q 1965, 34:468
72289   Seidenberg, R. The hidden "we." Q 1964, 33:455
72290   Shengold, L. The parent as Sphinx. Q 1965, 34:466-467
72291   Stewart, W. A. An inquiry into the concept of working through. Q 1964, 33:454
72292   Whitman, R. M. Remembering and forgetting dreams in psychoanalysis. Q 1965, 34:467

ENNS, M. P.

See Klingsporn, M. J.

EPHRON, HARMON S.

72293   (& Carrington, P.) Discussion of Dement, W. C. "Experimental dream studies." Sci Psa 1964, 7:171-176
72294   (& Carrington, P.) Ego functioning in rapid eye movement sleep: implications for dream theory. Sci Psa 1967, 11:75-94; 99-102
72295   (& Carrington, P.) Rapid eye movement sleep and cortical homeostasis. Psychol Rev 1966, 73:500-526

EPHRON, LAWRENCE R.

72296   Narcissism and the sense of self. R 1967, 54:107-117
        Abs SRS Q 1969, 38:162

EPPEL, HEDDA

72297   Über Identifizierung. [On identification.] Psyche 1965, 19:516-536. With title: Die Identifizierung in der Kinderpsychotherapie. Hbh Kinderpsychother 277-287
* * *   Die Identifizierung in der Kinderpsychotherapie. See: [72297]

EPPS, PHYLLIS

See Brown, Felix

EPSTEIN, ARTHUR W.

72298   Fetishism. In Slovenko, R. Sexual Behavior and the Law, Springfield, Ill: Thomas 1965, 515-520
72299   Fetishism: a comprehensive view. Sci Psa 1969, 15:81-87

EPSTEIN, L. J.

See Koegler, R. R.

EPSTEIN, LEON J.

See Mendel, Werner M.; Simon, Alexander

EPSTEIN, N. B.

See Rakoff, V.

EPSTEIN, SEYMOUR

72300 Toward a unified theory of anxiety. Prog exp Pers Res 1967, 4:1-89

See Cazavelan, Jane; Saltz, George

ERBAUGH, J. K.

See Ward, Clyde H.

ERDBRINK, W. L.

See Sours, John A.

ERDÉLY, ZOLTAN

See Rosenkötter, Lutz

ERICKSON, M. T.

See Lesser, Ken

ERICKSON, MARY E.

See Cain, Albert C.

ERICKSON, MILTON H.

72301 The experience of interviewing in the presence of observers. Meth Res PT 61-63
72302 Hypnosis and examination panics. Amer J clin Hyp 1965, 7:356-358
72303 An introduction to the study and application of hypnosis for pain control. Psychiat Res Rep 1961, (14):83-90
72304 Selected Papers of Milton H. Erickson, M.D. Volume I. Advanced Techniques of Hypnosis and Therapy. (Ed: Haley, J.) (Foreword: Kubie, L. S.) NY/London: Grune & Stratton 1967, xviii + 557 p
72305 A special inquiry with Aldous Huxley into the nature and character of various states of consciousness. Amer J clin Hyp 1965, 8:14-33
S-8042 (& Kubie, L. S.) The translation of the cryptic automatic writing of one hypnotic subject by another in a trancelike dissociated state. In Moss, C. S. The Hypnotic Investigation of Dreams, NY/London/Sydney: Wiley 1967, 101-114

ERICKSON, RALPH W.

72306 Some historical connections between existentialism, daseinsanalysis, phenomenology and the Wurzburg school. J gen Psychol 1967, 76:3-24

ERIKSEN, CHARLES WALTER

72307 Cognitive responses to internally cued anxiety. In Spielberger, C. D. Anxiety and Behavior, NY/London: Academic Pr 1966, 327-360
72308 Perceptual defense. Proc Amer Psychopath Ass 1965, 53:222-246

See Johnson, Harold

ERIKSON, ERIK HOMBURGER

72309   (Ed) The Challenge of Youth. NY: Doubleday 1965, xxvi + 340 p
S-8055 Childhood and Society. (rev enl ed.) NY: Norton 1963, 445 p
        Danish: Copenhagen: Hans Reitzels Forlag 1967
        Het Kind en de Samenleving. Aula-Bocken 1964
        Lapsuus ja Yhteiskunta. K. J. Gummerus 1962
        Hebrew: Tel Aviv: Sifriath Poalim Pub. 1960
        Infanzia e Societa. Rome: Armando Armando Editore 1966
        Bardommen og Samfunnet. Oslo: Gyldendal Norsh Forlag 1968
        Infancia y Sociodad. Buenos Aires: Editiones Horme, Editorial
        Paidos 1959, 1966
        Rv HRB Q 1964, 33:581
72310   Childhood and society. In *Children of the Caribbean,* The Common-
        wealth of Puerto Rico, Printing Division, San Juan 1961, 18-29
72311   (et al) Children of the Caribbean: Their Mental Health Needs. (Pro-
        ceedings of the 2nd Caribbean Conference for Mental Health, 10-16
        Apr 1959, St. Thomas, Virgin Islands.) San Juan, P. R.: Dept of the
        Treasury 1961, 179 p
72312   The concept of identity in race relations: notes and queries. Daedalus
        1966, 95:145-170. In author's *Identity: Youth and Crisis,* 295-320
72313   Concluding remarks. In *Women and the Scientific Professions,* (MIT
        Symposium on American Women in Science and Engineering), Cam-
        bridge, Mass/London: MIT Pr 1965, 232-245
72314   Concluding remarks on ritualization of behavior in animals and man.
        Phil Trans R Soc 1966, 251:513-524
S-45087 The confirmation of the delinquent.
        Die Bestatigung des Rechtsbechers. Ein Richter verurteilt wegen
        Wiederrede zur Strassenarbeit. In Bolterauer, L. *Aus der Werkstatt
        des Erziehungsberaters,* Vienna: Verlag f. Jugend und Volk 1960, 184-
        194
72315   Discussant: "House officers." Teach Dyn Psychiat 247-251
S-45089 The dream specimen of psychoanalysis. In author's *Identity: Youth
        and Crisis* 142-207
S-8058 Ego development and historical change. In author's *Identity: Youth
        and Crisis* 44-90
S-45090 Ego identity and the psychosocial moratorium. In author's *Identity:
        Youth and Crisis* 142-207
° ° °   Eight ages of man. See [45091]
S-45091 Eight stages of man. With title: Eight ages of man. Int J Psychiat
        1966, 2:281-300
S-45092 The first psychoanalyst: crisis and discovery. In author's *Insight and
        Responsibility* 17-46
        Abs AEC An Surv Psa 1956, 7:8-9
S-45093 Freud's *The Origins of Psychoanalysis.*
        Abs An Surv Psa 1955, 6:4-6
72316   Gandhi's autobiography: the leader as a child. The American Scholar
        1965-66, 35:632-646
72317   Gandhi's Truth: On the Origins of Militant Nonviolence. NY: Norton
        1969, 474 p
72318   The golden rule and the cycle of life. (George W. Gay Lecture on

Medical Ethics 1963) Harv med Alumni Bull 1963, 37(2). In White, R. W. *The Study of Lives,* NY: Atherton Pr 1966, 412-428. With title: The golden rule in the light of new insight. In author's *Insight and Responsibility* 217-243

S-8060 Growth and crises of the "healthy personality." In author's *Identity: Youth and Crisis* 91-141

   Wachstum und Krisen der gesunden Persönlichkeit. Darmsstadt: Wissenschaftliche Buchgesellschaft 1967

72319 The human life cycle. In *International Encyclopedia of the Social Sciences,* NY: Crowell-Collier Publ 1968

° ° ° Human strength and the cycle of generations. See: [72339]

S-45094 Identität und Entwurzelung in unserer Zeit.

   Identity and uprootedness in our time. In author's *Insight and Responsibility* 81-107

S-45095 Identity and the Life Cycle: Selected Papers.

   Rv Lichtenstein, H. J Am Psa Ass 1963, 11:173-223

72320 Identity and the psychosocial development of the child. In *Discussions on Child Development,* Proc 3rd Meeting of the Child Study Group, WHO Vol. 3, NY: IUP 1958

72321 Identity: Youth and Crisis. NY: Norton; London: Faber & Faber 1968, 336 p

   Dutch: Vitgrverij Het Spectrum 1969
   German: Stuttgart: Klett 1969
   Italian: Mondadori Editore 1969
   Swedish: Stockholm: Natur och Kultur 1969

72322 The initial session and its alternatives. Genet Psychol Monogr 1940, 22:557. With title: The initial situation and its alternatives. In Haworth, M. R. *Child Psychotherapy,* NY/London: Basic Books 1964, 106-110

   Die Anfangssituation der Kinderanalyse und ihre Alternativen. Hbh Kinderpsychother 264-268

° ° ° The initial situation and its alternatives. See: [72322]

72323 Inner and outer space: reflections on womanhood. Daedalus 1964, 93:582-606. In author's *Identity: Youth and Crisis* 261-294. In Lifton, R. J. *The Woman in America,* NY: Houghton 1965, 1-26

72324 Insight and Responsibility. Lectures on the Ethical Implications of Psychoanalytic Insight. NY: Norton 1964; London: Faber & Faber 1966, 256 p

   French: Paris: Librairie Ernst Flammarion 1969
   German: Stuttgart: Ernst Klett Verlag 1966
   Italian: Rome: Armando Armando Editore 1967
   Spanish: Buenos Aires: Ediciones Horme 1969
   Swedish: Stockholm: Natur och Kultur 1969

   Rv Esman, A. H. Q 1965, 34:117-119. Kaplan, D. M. R 1965, 52:133-136. NRo J 1966, 47:562-568

° ° ° Introduction. In Blaine, G. B., Jr. & McArthur, C. C. *Emotional Problems of the Student,* NY: Appleton-Century Crofts 1961; Garden City/NY: Anchor Books 1966, xvii-xxx. In author's *Identity: Youth and Crisis* 142-207

72325 Late adolescence. In Funkenstein, D. H. *The Student and Mental*

Health, The World Federation for Mental Health and the International Association of Universities 1959

72326 Memorandum for the conference on the draft. In Tax, S. *The Draft: A Handbook of Facts and Alternatives,* Chicago: Univ of Chicago Pr 1967, 280-283

72327 Memorandum on identity and Negro youth. J soc Issues 1964, 20(4): 29-42

72328 Memorandum on youth for the committee on the year 2000, American Academy of Arts and Sciences. Daedalus 1967, 96:860-870. In author's *Identity: Youth and Crisis* 15-43

72329 Die menschliche Stärke und der Zyklus der Generationen. [Human strength and the cycle of generations.] Psyche 1966, 20:241-281

S-45098 The nature of clinical evidence. In author's *Insight and Responsibility* 47-80

72330 A neurological crisis in a small boy: Sam. In author's *Childhood and Society* 25-38. In Dulany, D. E., Jr. et al: *Contributions to Modern Psychology,* NY: Oxford Univ Pr 1964, 356-366

72331 On the nature of psycho-historical evidence: in search of Gandhi. Daedalus 1968, 97(3):695-730. Int J Psychiat 1969, 7:451-476

° ° ° Ontogeny of ritualization. See: [72332]

72332 The ontogeny of ritualization in man. Phil Trans R Soc 1966, 251: 147-526. With title: Ontogeny of ritualization. Psa—Gen Psychol 601-621

Ontogenese der Ritualisierung. Psyche 1968, 22:481-502

72333 Postscripts to the conference. In *Children of the Caribbean,* The Commonwealth of Puerto Rico, Printing Division, San Juan 1961, 151-154

S-45101 The problem of ego identity. In author's *Identity: Youth and Crisis* 142-207; 208-231. In Stein, M. R. et al: *Identity and Anxiety,* Glencoe, Ill: Free Pr 1960, 37-87

Abs BEM An Surv Psa 1956, 7:105-110. Guiard, F. Rev Psicoanál 1966, 23:244

72334 Psychoanalysis and ongoing history: problems of identity, hatred and nonviolence. P 1965, 122:241-253

Abs Loeb, L. Q 1967, 36:473

° ° ° Psychological reality and historical acutality. See: [72338]

72335 The psychosexual and psychosocial dimension in the interpretation of dreams. (Read at Boston Psa Soc, 22 June 1960)

Abs Long, R. T. Bull Phila Ass Psa 1961, 11:38-39

72336 Psychosexual stages in child development. In *Discussions on Child Development,* World Health Organization Study Group, IV, 1959

72337 Psychosocial identity. In *International Encyclopedia of the Social Sciences,* NY: Crowell-Collier Publ 1968

72338 Reality and actuality: an address. (Read at Am Psa Ass 1961) J Am Psa Ass 1962, 10:451-474. With title: Psychological reality and historical actuality. In author's *Insight and Responsibility* 159-215

Abs JBi Q 1963, 32:446. Rv R 1967, 54:453-468

72339 The roots of virtue. In Huxley, J. The Humanist Frame, London: George Allen & Unwin; NY: Harper & Bros 1961, 145-165. With title: Human strength and the cycle of generations. In author's *Insight and Responsibility* 109-157

S-45104 On the sense of inner identity. In author's *Identity: Youth and Crisis* 44-90

S-45106 Sigmund Freuds psychoanalytische Krise.
Abs An Surv Psa 1956, 7:14

72340 The strange case of Freud, Bullitt, and Woodrow Wilson. NY Rev Books 1967, 8(2):3-8. J 1967, 48:462-468

S-8068 Studies in the interpretation of play: clinical observation of play disruption in young 'children. In Haworth, M. R. *Child Psychotherapy*, NY/London: Basic Books 1964, 264-276

72341 Toys and reasons. In Haworth, M. R. *Child Psychotherapy*, NY/London: Basic Books 1964, 3-11

72342 Wholeness and totality. In Bramson, L. & Goethals, G. W. *War: Studies from Psychology, Sociology, Anthropology*, NY: Basic Books 1964, 119-131

S-45110 Wholeness and totality—a psychiatric contribution. In author's *Identity: Youth and Crisis* 44-90

S-45111 Young Man Luther: A Study in Psychoanalysis and History.
De Jonge Luther. Holland 1968
Nuori Luther. Helsinki: Weiliin & Goeoes 1966
Luther Avant Luther. Paris: Librairie Ernst Flammarion 1969
Der Junge Mann Luther. Munich: Szczesny Verlag 1963
Il Giovane Lutero. Rome: Armando Armando Editore 1966
Kulturkris och Religion. Stockholm: Diakonistyrelsens Bookfoerlag 1966
Abs RJA An Surv Psa 1958, 9:479-487. Rv Lichtenstein, H. J Am Psa Ass 1963, 11:173-223

72343 Youth and the life cycle, an interview. Children 1960, 7:43-49

72344 (Ed) Youth: Change and Challenge. NY/London: Basic Books 1963, xiv + 284 p

72345 Youth: fidelity and diversity. Daedalus 1962, 91:5-27. In author's *Identity: Youth and Crisis* 232-260

ERIKSON, KAI T.

72346 Notes on the sociology of deviance. Soc Probl 1962, 9:307-314. In Scheff, T. J. *Mental Illness and Social Processes*, NY: Harper & Row 1967, 294-304

72347 The role of sociology in medical and psychiatric education; the definition of areas of sociology especially relevant to medical and psychiatric education; its relevance to clinical content. In Earley, L. W. et al: *Teaching Psychiatry in Medical School*, Wash DC: Am Psychiat Ass 1969, 314-318

ERLE, JOAN B.

ABSTRACT OF:

72348 Arlow, J. A. Some aspects of the nature of evidence. Q 1968, 37:636-638

REVIEW OF:

72349 Turner, M. B. Philosophy and the Science of Behavior. Q 1968, 37:461-462

ERLENMEYER-KIMLING, L.

See Kallmann, Franz J.

ERMENTINI, A.

See Cazzullo, Carlo L.

ERNST, KLAUS

72350 (& Kind, H.; Rotach-Fuchs, M.) Ergebnisse der Verlaufsforschung bei Neurosen. [Results of Research in Neuroses] (Foreword: Bleuler, M.) Berlin/Heidelberg/NY: Springer 1968, xii + 164 p

S-45116 Praktische Probleme der individuellen Psychotherapie in der Anstalt am Beispiel einer Schizophreniebehandlung.
In Benedetti, G. & Müller, C. *Psychotherapy of Schizophrenia (1st Int Symp 1956),* Basel/NY: Karger 1957, 201-208

72351 Verlaufsforschung bei Neurosen und Indikation zur Psychotherapie. [Research in neuroses and indication for psychotherapy.] Z PSM 1962, 12:89-97

ERNST, MORRIS LEOPOLD

72352 (& Schwartz, A. U.) Censorship: The Search for the Obscene. NY: Macmillan 1964, xvi + 288 p
Rv Kaplan, D. M. R 1964, 51:683-685

72353 Communication: anniversary greetings. R 1963, 50(1):145-148

72354 (& Schwartz, A. U.) Privacy: The Right to be Let Alone. NY: Macmillan 1962

ERON, LEONARD D.

72355 (Ed) Current Concerns in Clinical Psychology. I. The Classification of Behavior Disorders. Chicago: Aldine Publ 1966, xii + 180 p

72356 (& Callahan, R.) (Eds) The Relation of Theory to Practice in Psychotherapy. Chicago: Aldine Publ 1969, vii + 176 p

72357 (& Walder, L. O.; Toigo, R.; Lefkowitz, M. M.) Social class, parental punishment for aggression, and child aggression. Child Develpm 1963, 34:849-867

See Zubin, Joseph

ERRERA, PAUL

72358 Confidentiality and the psychiatric patient. Hosp Comm Psychiat 1968, 19:347

72359 (& Coleman, J. V.) A long-term follow-up study of neurotic phobic patients in a psychiatric clinic. JNMD 1963, 136:267-271

72360 Some historical aspects of the concept: phobia. Psychiat Q 1962, 36:325-336

ERVIN, F. R.

See Mendelson, Jack H.

ESCALONA, SIBYLLE K.

72361 Children's responses to the nuclear war threat. Children 1963, 10(4): 137-142

72362 Developmental needs of children under two-and-a-half years old. Children's Bureau Research Reports 1967, (1):7

S-45123 The impact of psychoanalysis upon child psychology.
Abs DW An Surv Psa 1958, 9:227-230

72363 Mental health, the educational process and the school. Ops 1967, 37:1-4

72364 Normal development: personality and behavior. In Barnett, H. L. *Pediatrics*, NY: Appleton-Century-Crofts 1968

72365 Patterns of infantile experience and the developmental process. Psa St C 1963, 18:197-244

S-45125 (& Heider, G. M.) Prediction and Outcome.
Rv Raylesberg, D. D. PPR 1961, 48(4):138-139

72366 (& Moriarty, A.) Prediction of school age intelligence from infant tests. Child Developm 1961, 32:597-605

72367 Problems and opportunities in the application of psychoanalytic knowledge of normal development. n.p., 1961, 20 p multilithographed

72368 The Roots of Individuality: Normal Patterns of Development in Infancy. Chicago: Aldine Publ 1968-69; London: Tavistock 1968, ix + 547 p

72369 Some considerations regarding psychotherapy with psychotic children. In Haworth, M. R. *Child Psychotherapy*, NY/London: Basic Books 1964, 50-58

72370 Some determinants of individual differences in early ego development. Trans NY Acad Sci 1965, 27:802-816

72371 The study of individual differences and the problem of state. J Amer Acad Child Psychiat 1962, 1:11-37

See Birns, Beverly; Corman, Harvey H.

ESCARDO, F.

72372 [The lack of paternal figure and the transformation of the feminine role.] (Sp) Rev Hosp Psiquiat Habana 1967, 8:313-320
Abs Vega Q 1968, 37:634

ESCHENBACH, H. W.

72373 [Study on the psychology of C. G. Jung. A comprehensive model.] (Ger) Landarzt 1967, 43:1353-1361

ESCOLIER, J. C.

See Quidu, M.

ESCOLL, PHILIP J.

72374 Perception in residency training: methods and problems. P 1967, 124:187-193

ESMAN, AARON H.

72375 Childhood psychosis and "childhood schizophrenia." Ops 1960, 30: 391-396
      Abs JMa RFPsa 1962, 26:315
72376 Discussion of Flarsheim, A. "The psychological meaning of the use of marijuana and LSD in one case." Psa Forum 1969, 3:121-122
72377 The dream screen in an adolescent. Q 1962, 31:250-251
72378 Drug use by adolescents: some valuative and technical implications. Psa Forum 1967, 2:340-345; 352-353
72379 Marital psychopathology: its effects on children and their management. Marriage Relat 133-143
72380 (& Hartmann, D.; Becker, T. E.; Kaplan, E. H.) Panel on "drug use by adolescents." (Read at NY Psa Soc, 26 March 1968)
      Abs Firestein, S. K. Q 1969, 38:518
72381 Treatment of personality disorders in children. In Wolman, B. B. *Handbook of Clinical Psychology*, NY: McGraw Hill 1965, 1323-1342
72382 Visual hallucinoses in young children. Psa St C 1962, 17:334-343
      Abs SLe RFPsa 1964, 28:814

See Rosenfeld, Eva

REVIEWS OF:
72383 Bijou, S. W. & Baer, D. M. (Eds): Child Development: Readings in Experimental Analysis. Q 1969, 38:148-149
72384 Brody, S. Passivity. A Study of its Development and Expression in Boys. Q 1965, 34:290-293
72385 Chassan, J. B. Research Design in Clinical Psychology and Psychiatry. Q 1969, 38:503-504
72386 Erikson, E. H. Insight and Responsibility. Lectures on the Ethical Implications of Psychoanalytic Insight. Q 1965, 34:117-119
72387 Fleischmann, O. et al (Eds): Delinquency and Child Guidance. Selected Papers of August Aichhorn. Q 1966, 35:149-150
72388 Naumburg, M. Dynamically Oriented Art Therapy. Its Principles and Practice. Q 1968, 37:141
72389 Rosenberg, B. & Fliegel, N. The Vanguard Artist: Portrait and Self-Portrait. Q 1967, 36:116-120

ESMIOL, PATTISON

See Feinstein, Howard M.

ESPINOSA, NORBERTO

See Herrera, Julio J.

ESSEN-MÖLLER, E.

72390 Über die Schizophrenie-häufigkeit bei Müttern von Schizophrenen. [The incidence of schizophrenia among mothers of schizophrenics.] Schweiz ANP 1963, 91:260-266

ESSER, M. A.

See Simon, Alexander

ESSER, PIETER HENDRIK

72391 [Alcohol and responsibility.] (Dut) T Soc Geneesk 1964, 42:294-299
72392 [Dreams.] (Dut) T Ziekenverpl 1966, 19:119-123
72393 De menselijke beleving van zijn lichaam. [The body image in humans.] Nederl T Psychol 1963, 18:430-445
72394 De Wereld der Dromen. [The World of Dreams.] Kampen: J. H. Kok 1962, 259 p

ESSLINGER, H.

72395 [How does anxiety disappear by playing. Excerpts from the play therapy of a 7-year-old child suffering from anxiety.] (Ger) Prax Kinderpsychol 1964, (Suppl 6):22-27

ESTERSON, A.

See Laing, Ronald David

ESTES, HUBERT R.

S-45136 (& Haylett, C. H.; Johnson, A. M.) Separation anxiety.
       Abs RZ An Surv Psa 1956, 7:262-263

See Beckett, Peter G. S.

ESTES, WILLIAM K.

See Dennis, Wayne

ETCHEGOYEN, RICARDO H.

72396 Estado actual de la psicoterapia en la Argentina. [The present state of psychotherapy in Argentina.] Acta psiquiat psicol Arg 1963, 9(2): 93-113
72397 (& Gabay, J.; Quiroga, N.) Imagen del padre en un grupo de alcohólicos. [The father image in a group of alcoholics.] Acta psiquiát psicol Amér Latina 1965, 11:277-280
72398 (& Zogbi, S.; Villanueva, J. A.) La posicion dépresiva y el proceso del aprendizaje. [The depressive position and the learning process.] Acta psiquiát psicol Amér Latina 1965, 11:19-23

ETIGSON, ELIZABETH

See Tobin, Sheldon S.

ETTEDGUI, ARMAND SAMUEL

72399 Kafka ou le sens d'un échec. [Kafka, or the sense of failure.] RFPsa 1963, 27:675-682

EVAN, SARAH

72400 The compensatory work of transference. PPR 1961, 48(2):19-29
72401 The creative work of free association. PPR 1961, 48(3):89-96

REVIEW OF:
72402 Mendelson, M. Psychoanalytic Concepts of Depression. PPR 1962, 49(4):132-135

EVANS, ANNE S.

See Greenblatt, Milton

EVANS, D. R.

72403 Masturbatory fantasy and sexual deviation. Beh Res Ther 1968, 6:17-19

EVANS, FREDERIC M.

REVIEW OF:
72404 Beskett, P. G. S. Adolescents Out of Step. Their Treatment in a Psychiatric Hospital. Q 1967, 36:451-452

EVANS, JOHN

72405 Analytic group therapy on delinquents. Adolescence 1966, 1:180-196
72406 In-patient analytic group therapy of neurotic and delinquent adolescents. Some specific problems associated with these groups. Psychother Psychosom 1965, 13:265-270
72407 Rocking at night. J Child Psychol Psychiat 1961, 2:71-85

EVANS, PATRICK

TRANSLATION OF:
Lauzon, G. [80142]

EVANS, R. B.

72407A Childhood parental relationships of homosexual men. J Consult Clin Psychol 1969, 33:129-135

EVANS, RICHARD ISADORE

72408 Conversations with Carl Jung and Reactions from Ernest Jones. Princeton, N.J./London: Van Nostrand 1964, viii + 173 p
72409 Dialogue with B. F. Skinner. Psychiat soc Sci Rev 1969, 3:11-21
72410 Dialogue with Erich Fromm. NY: Harper & Row 1966, xix + 136 p
72411 Dialogue with Erik Erikson. NY: Harper & Row 1967, xvi + 142 p
72412 Psychology and Arthur Miller. NY: Dutton 1969, xvii + 136 p
72413 (& Leppmann, P. K.) Resistance to Innovation in Higher Education: A Social Psychological Exploration Focussed on Television and the Establishment. (Foreword: Sanford, N.) San Francisco: Jossey-Bass 1968, xxii + 198 p

EVANS, RICHARD K.

72414 Casework treatment of parents during child analysis. BMC 1967, 31:32-41

72414A Casework with the father of an adolescent boy. BMC 1968, 32:366-376

EVANS, WILLIAM N.

72415 The fear of being smothered. Q 1964, 33:53-70

72416 Serendipity. Q 1963, 32:165-180; 627-630

EVARTS, EDWARD V.

See Kety, Seymour S.

EVDOKAS, TAKIS

72417 [The Difficult Problems and the First Questions of Your Child.] (Gr) Athens: Athan. Karavias Publ Co 1968, 127 p

72418 [The psychogenic element in epilepsy.] (Gr) Cyprus med J 1962, 12(1-2)

EVELSON, ELENA

S-45153 Una experiencia analítica análisis simultaneo de hermanos mellizos. Abs JO An Surv Psa 1958, 9:316-317

72419 (& Grinberg, R. V. de) El niño frente a la muerte. [The child's notion of death.] Rev Psicoanál 1962, 19:344-350
        Abs Vega Q 1964, 33:146

See Cesio, Fidias R.; Grinberg, León; Grinberg, Rebeca Vaisman de

EVERETT, HENRY C.

72420 The "adversary" system in married couples' group therapy. Curr psychiat Ther 1969, 9:168-172

EVERS, NATHANIEL H.

See Switzer, Robert E.

EWALT, JACK R.

72421 Clinic and institutional therapy. Israel Ann Psychiat 1964, 2:5-10

72422 Discussant: "Physicians in the Community." Teach Dyn Psychiat 175-179

* * * Foreword to Greenblatt, M. et al: *Mental Patients in Transition*, Springfield, Ill: Thomas 1961, ix-xi

72423 History of the community psychiatry movement. P 1969, 126:43-52

72424 (& Zaslow, S.; Stevenson, P.) How nonpsychiatric physicians can deal with psychiatric emergencies. Ment Hosp 1964, 15:194-196

72425 (& Schwartz, M. S.; Appel, K. E.; Bartemeier, L. H.; Schlaifer, C.) Joint Commission on Mental Illness and Health. P 1960, 116:782-790

72426 (& Maltsberger, J. T.) Prevention. In Bellak, L. & Loeb, L. *The Schizophrenic Syndrome*, NY/London: Grune & Stratton 1969, 757-775

72427 Programs for residents in psychiatry. In Kaufman, M. R. *The Psychiatric Unit in a General Hospital,* NY: IUP 1965, 307-314; 384-401
72428 Psychotherapy and public health. Prog PT 1967, 5:67-77
72429 Psychotherapy of schizophrenic reactions. Curr psychiat Ther 1963, 3:150-170
72430 (& Farnsworth, D. L.) Textbook of Psychiatry. NY: McGraw-Hill 1963, 381 p

See Bartemeier, Leo H.; Grinspoon, Lester; Vaillant, George Eman

EWING, JOHN A.

72431 Counselling help for the alcoholic marriage. In Nash, E. M. et al: *Marriage Counseling in Medical Practice,* Chapel Hill: Univ of North Carolina Pr 1964, 92-116
72432 (& Fox, R. E.) Family therapy of alcoholism. Curr psychiat Ther 1968, 8:86-91
72433 (& Abse, D. W.) Some problems in psychotherapy with schizophrenic patients. PT 1960, 14:505-519

See Abse, D. Wilfred; Strupp, Hans H.

EXNER, JOHN E., JR.

72434 Rorschach responses as an index of narcissism. J proj Tech pers Assess 1969, 33:324-330

EXUM, D. B.

See Barglow, Peter

EY, G.

72435 (Ed) L'Inconscient. [The Unconscious.] Bruges: Descles de Brouwer 1966, 424 p

EY, HENRI

72436 Der Abbau des Bewusstseinsfeldes beim Phänomen Schlaf-Traum und seine Beziehungen zur Psychopathologie. Entwurfeiner allgemeinen Relativitätstheorie der Desorganisation des bewussten Seins für die Gesamtheit der Geisteskrankheiten. [The disorganization of the field of consciousness in the sleep-dream phenomenon and relationship to psychopathology. Outline of a theory of generalized relativity of disorganization of the conscious being to the whole of mental disorders.] Nervenarzt 1967, 38:237-242

La dissolution de la conscience dans le sommeil et le rêve et ses rapports avec la psychopathologie. Esquisse d'une théorie de la relativité généralisée de la désorganisation de l'être conscient et de diverses maladies mentales. Presse Méd 1967, 75:575-578. Proc IV World Cong Psychiat 1966, 139-157
72437 La asistencia psiquiátrica en Francia. [Psychiatric assistance in France.] Rev Psioanal Psiquiat Psicol 1967, 6:67-75
72438 [The concept of "scope of consciousness."] (Fr) Évolut psychiat 1963, 28:209-220

72439 La Conscience. [Consciousness.] Paris: PUF 1963, 439 p
72440 Le déchiffrement de l'inconscient. [Deciphering the unconscious.] Riv
       sper Freniat 1965, 89:68-77
72441 Le devenir conscient et le langage. [The development of consciousness
       and language.] Évolut psychiat 1968, 33:1-18
72442 (Ed) Entretiens psychiatriques, #10. [Psychiatric Conference No. 10.]
       Toulouse: Edouard Privat 1964, 262 p
72443 Folie et monde moderne. [Madness and the modern world.] Évolut
       psychiat 1968, 33:309-346
72444 [Introduction to the present-day study of hysteria. (History and an-
       alysis of the concept.)] (Fr) Rev Prat 1964, 14:1417-1431
72445 Kurt Schneider ou le primat de la clinique. [Kurt Schneider or the head
       of the clinic.] In Kranz, H. *Psychopathologie Heute*, Stuttgart: Georg
       Thieme 1962, 1-5
72446 (& Bernard, P.; Brisset, C.) Manuel de Psychiatrie. [Manual of Psy-
       chiatry.] Paris, France: Masson & Cie 1960, 1013 p; 1963, 1015 p;
       1967, 1212 p
72447 Naturaleza y clasificación de las enfermedades mentales. [Nature and
       classification of mental illnesses.] Rev Psicoanal Psiquiat Psicol 1967,
       5:68-82
72448 Neurobiologia del sueño y del ensueño: bosquejo de una patologia del
       campo de la consciencia. [Neurobiology of sleep and the dream: out-
       line of a pathology of the field of consciousness.] Rev Psicoanal Psi-
       quiat Psicolo 1966, 3:54-68
72449 Plan d'Organisation du Champ de la Psychiatrie. [Plan of Organization
       of the Field of Psychiatry.] Toulouse: E. Privat 1966, 103 p
72450 [The problem of consciousness in Paul Guiraud's work.] (Fr) Évolut
       psychiat 1966, 31:265-271
72451 Psychiatric therapy in France. Curr psychiat Ther 1962, 2:266-269
72452 El ser consciente y la alucinación. [The conscious being and the hal-
       lucination.] Actas Luso-esp Neurol Psiquiat 1967, 26:201-208
72453 Das Unbewusste und die Struktur des Bewussten. [The unconscious
       and the structure of the conscious.] Wien Z Nervenheilk 1961, 18:
       285-301
S-45186 Valor terapeutico del análisis existencial.
       Valeur thérapeutique de l'analyse existentielle. Acta psychother
       psychosom 1960, 8:241-251

See Straus, Erwin W. M.

EYCK, M. VAN

72454 (& Hernalsteen, L.) Les facteurs psychiques dans les maladies des
       fosses nasales et des sinus. Notion generales. [The psychological factors
       in the maladies of nose and accessory sinuses. General notions.] Acta
       Oto-Rhino-Laryng Belg 1962, 16(3):189-198

EYSENCK, HANS JURGEN

72455 (& Rachman, S. J.) The application of learning theory to child psychi-
       atry. In Howells, J. G. *Modern Perspectives in Child Psychiatry*, Spring-
       field, Ill: Thomas 1965, 104-169

72456 (Ed) Behaviour Therapy and the Neuroses; Readings in Modern Methods of Treatment Derived from Learning Theory. Oxford/NY: Symposium Publ Div, Pergamon Pr 1960, 479 p

72457 Behaviour therapy, spontaneous remission and transference in neurotics. P 1963, 119:867-871

72458 (& Rachman, S.) The Causes and Cures of Neurosis; An Introduction to Modern Behaviour Therapy Based on Learning Theory and the Principles of Conditioning. London: Routledge & K. Paul 1965, xii + 318 p

72459 Crime and Personality. Boston: Houghton Mifflin 1964; London: Routledge 1965, xv + 204 p
     Rv Williams, A. H. J 1965, 46:392-393

72460 The effects of psychotherapy. Int J Psychiat 1965, 1:97-143

72461 The effects of psychotherapy: an evaluation. J consult Psychol 1952, 16:319-324. With title: The inefficacy of therapeutic process with adults. In Berenson, B. G. & Carkhuff, R. R. *Sources of Gain in Counseling and Psychotherapy*, NY/Chicago/San Francisco: Holt, Rhinehart & Winston 1967, 22-31

72462 The effects of psychotherapy reconsidered. Acta psychother psychosom 1964, 12:38-44

72463 Fact and Fiction in Psychology. Baltimore: Penguin Books 1965, 300 p

72464 (Ed) Handbook of Abnormal Psychology. An Experimental Approach. NY: Basic Books 1961, xvi + 816 p
     Rv Siller, J. PPR 1962, 49(4):137-138

° ° ° The inefficacy of therapeutic process with adults. See: [72461]

S-45190 Learning theory and behaviour therapy. In author's *Behaviour Therapy and the Neuroses* 4-21. In Lindzey, G. & Hall, C. S. *Theories of Personality*, NY/London/Sydney: Wiley 1965, 1966, 1968, 398-410

72465 Modern learning theory. In author's *Behaviour Therapy and the Neuroses* 79-83

72466 Neurose, Konstitution und Persönlichkeit. [Neurosis, constitution and personality.] Z Psychol 1966, 172:145-181

72467 New ways of curing the neurotic. Psychol Scene 1967, 1:2-8

72468 The outcome problem in psychotherapy: a reply. Psychotherapy 1964, 1:97-100. In Goldstein, A. P. & Dean, S. J. *The Investigation of Psychotherapy*, NY: Wiley 1966, 157-160

72469 Personality and behaviour therapy. Proc RSM 1960, 53:504-508

72470 Psychoanalysis. Twentieth Century 1966, 174(Spring):15-17

72471 Psychotherapy or behaviour therapy. Ind psychol Rev 1964, 1:33-41

72472 A rational system of diagnosis and therapy in mental illness. Prog clin Psych 1960, 4:46-64

See Eysenck, Sybil B. G.; Oerton, J. R.

EYSENCK, SYBIL B. G.

72473 (& Eysenck, H. J.; Claridge, G.) Dimensions of personality, psychiatric syndromes, and mathematical models. JMS 1960, 106:581-589

EZRIEL, HENRY

S-45196 Experimentation within the psycho-analytic session. Psa Clin Inter 112-142

72474 The first session in psycho-analytic group treatment. Ned Tijdschr Geneesk 1967, 111:711-716

72475 The role of transference in psycho-analytic and other approaches to group treatment. Acta psychother psychosom 1959, 7(Suppl):101-116

S-8150 The scientific testing of psychoanalytic findings and theory: the psychoanalytic session as an experimental situation.

La sesión psicoanalítica como situación experimental. Rev urug Psa 1961-62, 4:271-279

72476 Übertragung und psychoanalitische Deutung in der Einzelund Gruppen-Psychotherapie. [Transference and psychoanalytic interpretation in individual and group psychotherapy.] Psyche 1960, 14:496-523

Abs IBa RFPsa 1962, 26:622

F

FAATZ, ANITA J.

72477 Individuals in association. An account of how the Otto Rank Association came to be formed. J Otto Rank Ass 1966, 1(1):81-88
72478 The search and the goal. J Otto Rank Ass 1967, 2(1):136-146
72479 Two realms of the will: separate or phases in a process? J Otto Rank Ass 1968, 3(1):107-117

See Robinson, Virginia P.

FABER, MEL D.

72480 Freud and Shakespeare's mobs. Lit & Psych 1965, 15:238-255
72481 Hamlet, sarcasm and psychoanalysis. R 1968, 55:79-90
72482 Lord Brutus' wife: a modern view. R 1965, 52:449-455
72483 Oedipal patterns in Henry IV. Q 1967, 36:426-434
72484 (& Dilnot, A. F.) On a line of Iago's. Am Im 1968, 25:86-90
72485 Ophelia's doubtful death. Lit & Psych 1966, 16:103-109
72486 Psychoanalytic remarks on a poem by Emily Dickinson. R 1969, 56: 247-264
72487 Shakespeare's suicides. In Shneidman, E. S. *Essays in Self-Destruction,* NY: Sci House 1968, 30-58
72488 Some remarks on the suicide of King Lear's eldest daughter. Univ Rev 1967, 23:313-317
72489 Suicide and the "Ajax" of Sophocles. R 1967, 54:441-452
      Abs SRS Q 1969, 38:162
72490 Two studies in self-aggression in Shakespearean tragedy. I. The conscience of the king: a preliminary investigation of Claudius' self-destructive urges. II. Suicidal patterns in *Othello.* Lit & Psych 1964, 14:80-85; 85-96

FABIAN, ABRAHAM A.

S-45201 Reading disability: an index of pathology.
        Abs An Surv Psa 1955, 6:266-267

FABREGA, HORACIO, JR.

72491 (& Wallace, C. A.) How physicians judge symptom statements: a cross-cultural study. JNMD 1967, 145:486-491

FABRICIUS, JOHANNES

72492   Livet før Livet. En Dybdepsykologisk Analyse af Fødslen, dens Aftryk
        i det Ubevidste og dens Symbolske Genoplevelse Som en Gen-Fødsel
        i Drømmen, Alkymien og Kunsten. [Life before Life. A Depth Psy-
        chological Analysis of Delivery, the Impression of the Unconscious and
        Symbolism in Dreams.] Copenhagen: Hermes 1966, 119 p

FACHINELLI, ELVIO

72493   Il desiderio dissidente. [The dissenting wish.] Quad piacentini 1968,
        33:74-79
* * *   Foreword to Glover, E. *Freud o Jung,* Milan: Sugar 1967
72494   Gruppo chiuso o aperto? [Closed or open group?] Quad piacentini
        1968, 36:107-124
72495   [New meaning of drawing and magic recovery of the past in the work
        of a psychotic artist.] (It) Arch Psicol Neurol Psichiat 1964, 25:27-50
72496   Nota a "Materialismo dialettico e psicanalisi" di Wilhelm Reich. [Note
        about "Dialectic materialism and psychoanalysis" by Wilhelm Reich.]
        Corpo 1966, 3:278-280
* * *   Preface to Léautaud, P. *Settor Privato,* Milan: Feterinelli 1968
72497   Su un accesso vertiginoso comparso con un sogno in una particolare
        fase del trattamento psicanalitico. [On a fit of dizziness appeared with
        a dream during a particular phase of psychoanalytic treatment.] *Atti*
        della Settimana Psicosomatica Internazionale, Rome, 11-16 Sept 1967
72498   Sul significato della negazione nell'ultimo Freud. [On the meaning of
        negation in the last Freud.] Riv Psa 1965, 11:167-176. Corpo 1965,
        1:5-12
72499   Sul tempodenaro anale. [On anal time-money.] Corpo 1965, 2:92-107

        See Molinari, Egon

        TRANSLATIONS OF:
        Freud, S. [10486]. (& Molinari, E.) Freud, S. [10495]. (& Fachinelli,
        H. T.) Freud, S. [10614]. Kris, E. [18934]. Reich, W. [26818]

FACHINELLI, H. TRETTL

        See Fachinelli, Elvio

FACKLER, WILLIAM

        See Graff, Harold

FADEN, PAUL D.

        See Behymer, Alice F.

FAERGEMAN, POUL M.

72500   [The depressive personality and manic-depressive psychosis in psy-
        choanalytic interpretation.] (Dan) Nord Psykiat Tidsskr 1964, 18:
        617-626
72501   [The development of the psychoanalytic theory on metapsychology.]
        (Dan) Nord Psykiat Tidsskr 1964, 18:291-301

72502 Discussion of Boyer, L. B. "Pioneers in the psychoanalysis of schizophrenia." Psa Forum 1969, 3:228-229

S-45205 Fantasies of menstruation in men.
Abs An Surv Psa 1955, 6:176

72503 Psychogenic Psychoses. A Description and Follow-up of Psychoses Following Psychological Stress. Wash DC/London: Butterworth 1963, x + 268 p
Rv HRB Q 1964, 33:436-437. ESt J 1964, 45:608-609

72504 Reactive psychoses: psychodynamic aspects of psychopathological conditions. A clinical illustration using a case. Acta Psychiat Scand 1968, (Suppl No. 203):9-12

FAGAN, JOEN

72505 The evaluation of sexual behavior during psychotherapy. Voices 1967, 3:50-51

FAGER, ROBERT E.

See Hollender, Marc H.

FAHRENBERG, JOCHEN

See Delius, Ludwig

FAI, LESLIE L.

See Masserman, Jules H.

FAIENZA, C.

See Donelli, A.; Landucci-Rubini, L.

FAIGEN, DELIA

See Grinberg, Rebeca V. de

FAIGENBAUM, DAVID

See Fischhoff, Joseph

FAILLA, ISABEL DE

See Rolla, Edgardo H.

FAILLA, MARIA I. DE

72506 [Transference and counter-transference in the process of psychoanalysis.] (Sp) Rev Psicoanál 1966, 23:450-467

FAIN, MICHEL

72507 A propos des troubles allergiques. [On allergic difficulties.] RFPsa 1967, 31:717-718

S-45236 A propos d'un cas d'hypertension artérielle.
Abs TC An Surv Psa 1957, 8:163-164

72508 (& Marty, P.) A propos du narcissisme et de sa genèse. [Apropos of narcissism and of its origin.] RFPsa 1965, 29:561-572

72509 Analyse du masochisme inadapté. [Analysis of maladaptive masochism.] RFPsa 1968, 32:145-149

72510 (& David, C.) Aspects fonctionnels de la vie onirique. [Functional aspects of the dream life.] RFPsa 1963, 27(Suppl):241-343
       Abs Auth Rev Psicoanál 1964, 21:398

72511 Contribution à l'étude des variations de la symptomatologie. [Contribution to the study of variations in symptomatology.] RFPsa 1962, 26(Suppl):351-378
       Abs Auth Rev Psicoanál 1963, 20:94. Retacchi, G. Riv Psa 1966, 12:216-217

72512 Le dialogue de sourds. [Dialogue of the deaf.] RFPsa 1965, 29:105-108

72513 Discussion of Alvim, F. "Troubles de l'identification et image corporelle." RFPsa 1962, 26(Suppl):267-277

72514 Discussion of Barande, I. "Le vu et l'entendu dans la cure." RFPsa 1968, 32:86-88

72515 Discussion of Grunberger, B. "Considérations sur le clivage entre le narcissisme et la maturation pulsionelle." RFPsa 1962, 26:202

72516 Discussion of Grunberger, B. "De l'image phallique." RFPsa 1964, 28: 232-233

72517 Discussion of Kestemberg, E. & Kestemberg, J. "Contributions à la perspective génétique en psychanalyse." RFPsa 1966, 30:720-728

72518 Discussion of Kestemberg, J. "A propos de la relation érotomanique." RFPsa 1962, 26:600

72519 Discussion of Lebovici, S. "Colloque sur les interprétations en thérapeutique psychanalytique." RFPsa 1962, 26:23

72520 Discussion of Luquet, P. "Les identifications précoces dans la structuration et la restructuration du moi." RFPsa 1962, 26(Suppl):267-277

72521 Discussion of Luquet-Parat, C.-J. "L'organisation oedipienne." RFPsa 1967, 31:818-824

72522 Discussion of Marty, P. "Régression et instinct de mort." RFPsa 1967, 31:1129-1133

72523 Discussion of Mendel, G. "La sublimation artistique." RFPsa 1964, 28:801-804

72524 Discussion of Mynard, J. "A propos d'un facteur d'interminabilité encore peu degagé en 1937." RFPsa 1968, 32:284-286

72525 Discussion of Pasche, F. "De la dépression." RFPsa 1963, 27:212-213

72526 Discussion of Rouart, J. "La temporisation comme maîtrise et comme défense." RFPsa 1962, 26:417

72527 Discussion of Schnitz, B. "Les états limites." RFPsa 1967, 31:262-264

72528 Discussion of Viderman, S. "De l'instinct de mort." RFPsa 1961, 25: 117-121

72529 Discussion of Viderman, S. "Narcissisme et relation d'objet dans la situation analytique." RFPsa 1968, 32:120-123

72529A [Intervention in thought disorders.] (Fr) RFPsa 1969, 33:898-904

72530 Introduction à la discussion sur "Téchnique de la cure des déprimés malades présentant une tendance dépressive." [Introduction to the discussion of "Technique of the cure of patients presenting a depressive trend."] RFPsa 1968, 32:605-609

72531 Laurence ou le labeur statufié. [Laurence on the work of erecting a statue.] RFPsa 1969, 33:273-284

72531A [Outline of a study concerning the existence of mental activities considered as prototypic of the psychoanalytic process.] (Fr) RFPsa 1969, 33:929-962

72532 (& Marty, P.) Perspective psychosomatique sur la fonction des fantasmes. [Psychosomatic perspective on the function of fantasy.] RFPsa 1964, 28:609-622
Abs Donadeo, J. Q 1966, 35:319

S-45235 Principes de clinique psychosomatique a l'occasion de l'investigation d'un cas de glaucome.
Abs HFM An Surv Psa 1957, 8:163

72533 [Reflections on acting out after reading J. Rouart's report.] (Fr) RFPsa 1968, 32:1025-1034

72534 Réflexions sur la structure allergique. [Reflections on the allergic structure.] RFPsa 1969, 33:227-242

72535 Régression et psychosomatique. [Regression and psychosomatic medicine.] RFPsa 1966, 30:451-456

See Kreisler, Léon; Marty, Pierre; Schneider, Jean

FAIRBAIRN, ROBERT H.

72536 Vincent Van Gogh—his psychopathology as reflected in his oil paintings. Canad Psychiat Ass J 1966, 11:443-444

See Langsley, Donald G.

FAIRBAIRN, W. RONALD D.

S-45276 Considerations arising out of the Schreber case.
Abs AJE An Surv Psa 1956, 7:75-76

S-45282 On the nature and aims of psycho-analytical treatment.
Abs SLP An Surv Psa 1958, 9:334-335

72537 A note on the origin of male homosexuality. M 1964, 37:31-32
Abs Hirsh, H. Q 1965, 34:142. JCS RFPsa 1967, 31:319

S-45285 Observations in defence of the object-relations theory of the personality.
Abs An Surv Psa 1955, 6:53-54

* * * Preface to Sullivan, C. T. *Freud and Fairbairn: Two Theories of Ego-Psychology*, Doylestown, Pa: Doylestown Foundation 1963

72538 Synopsis of an object-relations theory of the personality. J 1963, 44:224-225
Abs Gaddini, E. Riv Psa 1965, 11:184. EVN Q 1965, 34:617

FAIRWEATHER, GEORGE WILLIAM

72539 (et al) Relative Effectiveness of Psychotherapeutic Programs: A Multicriteria Comparison of Four Programs for Three Different Patient Groups. Washington: APA 1960, 26 p

FAJRAJZEN, STEFANO

72540 Alcune considerazioni sull'aggressività controtransferenziale nel trattamento di pazienti psicotici. [Some considerations on aggression in the countertransference, in the treatment of psychotic patients.] Riv Psa 1966, 12(1):23-48; 104-107

72541 Considerazioni su alcune difficoltà nello studio della schizofrenia. [Considerations on some difficulties in the study of schizophrenia.] Ann Np Psicoanal 1965, 12(1-2):124-133

72542 Discussion of Forti, L. "Utilizzazione della tecnica psicoanalitica in situazioni diverse durante l'infanzia." Riv Psa 1966, 12:103

72543 Discussion of Gaddini, E. "Contributo allo studio dell'effetto P.E.S. nella situazione analitica." Riv Psa 1966, 12:91

72544 Discussion of Limentani, A. "Problemi di ambivelenza, riparazione e le situazioni edipiche." Riv Psa 1967, 13:301

72545 Discussion of Matte Blanco, I. "Relazione tra i concetti di introlezione e proiezione e i concetti die spazio e tempo." Riv Psa 1967, 13:313-314

72546 Discussion of Muratori, A. M. T. "Rapporti oggettuali e struttura del l'io." Riv Psa 1966, 12:86-87

72547 Discussion of Muratori, A. M. T. Vicissitudini della relazione simbiotica e angosce d'identità." Riv Psa 1967, 13:320

72548 Discussion of Servadio, E. "Considerazioni sulla yoga." Riv Psa 1967, 13:290, 291-92, 293, 294

72549 Discussion of Turillazzi, M. S. M. "Evoluzione di alcuni condotte sessuali nel corso di un trattamento psicoanalitico." Riv Psa 1967, 13: 308-309, 310

72550 On a case of depersonalization. J Hillside Hosp 1960, 9:106-127
Abs JA Q 1961, 30:149

72551 Reazioni depressive del paziente e dell'analista nella situazione analitica, e natura del processo terapeutico. [Depressive reactions in the patient and in the analyst in the psychoanalytic situation, and nature of the therapeutic process.] Riv Psa 1967, 13(2):119-147; 315-318

TRANSLATION OF:
Boyer, L. B. [68482]

FÁLEK, ARTHUR

See Kallmann, Franz J.

FALICK, MORDECAI L.

See Levitt, Morton; Meyer, Ruben; Rubenstein, Ben O.

ABSTRACT OF:
72552 Galdston, I. Freud's influence on contemporary culture. An Surv Psa 1956, 7:25-26

FALRET, J.

See Lasègue, C.

FALSTEIN, EUGENE I.

72553 (& Offer, D.) Adolescent therapy. Prog clin Psych 1963, 5:60-73

72554 (& Feinstein, S. C.; Offer, D.; Fine, P.) Group dynamics: inpatient adolescents engage in an outbreak of vandalism. Arch gen Psychiat 1963, 9:32-45

72555 Present concepts in the management of the adolescent. Ill med J 1961, 120:334-335

72556 The uncontrollable child: some general sociopsychological observations. Southern med J 1966, 59:228-229

FANAI, F.

72556A [Course and prognosis of child neglect. Follow-up studies of juveniles with disturbed social behavior.] (Ger) Psychiat Clin (Basel) 1969, 2:1-13

FANON, FRANTZ

72557 Studies in a Dying Colonialism. NY: Monthly Review Pr 1965, 181 p
Rv Posinsky, S. H. Q 1966, 35:600-602

72558 The Wretched of the Earth. (Tr: Farrington, C.) (Pref: Sartre, J.-P) NY: Grove Pr 1965, 255 p
Rv Posinsky, S. H. Q 1966, 35:600-602

FANTEL, HANS

See Hartogs, Renatus

FARAU, ALFRED

72559 Die Entwicklung der Individualpsychologie und ihre Stellung im heutigen Amerika. [The development of individual psychology and its position in America today.] Psyche 1960, 13:881-891

72560 Fifty years of individual psychology. Comprehen Psychiat 1962, 3:242-254

FARBER, BERNARD

72561 Marital integration as a factor in parent-child relations. Child Develpm 1962, 33:1-14

FARBER, I. E.

See West, Louis J.

FARBER, IRVING J.

72562 Psychological aspects of mass disasters. J Nat Med Ass 1967, 59:340-345

72563 Psychotherapy of a patient with narcolepsy. J Hillside Hosp 1962, 11:29-56

FARBER, LESLIE H.

S-8203 (& Fisher, C.) An experimental approach to dream psychology through the use of hypnosis. In Moss, C. S. *The Hypnotic Investigation of Dreams*, NY/London/Sydney: Wiley 1967, 115-126

72564 "I'm sorry, dear." Commentary 1964, 38(5):47-54. The Commentary Reader 1966, 528-542

72565 Perfectibility and the psychoanalytic candidate. J existent Psychiat 1962-63, 3:285-292

72566 The phenomenology of suicide. In Shneidman, E. S. *On the Nature of Suicide*, San Francisco: Jossey-Bass 1969, 103-110
72567 Psychoanalysis and morality. Commentary 1965, 40(5):69-74
72568 The Ways of the Will: Essays Toward a Psychology and Psychopathology of Will. NY/London: Basic Books 1966, ix + 266 p
72569 Will and willfulness in hysteria. Rev existent Psychol Psychiat 1961, 1:229-241
72570 The will to will. J Otto Rank Ass 1969, 4(1):13-23

See Rioch, Margaret J.

FARBER, MAURICE L.

72571 Anality, political aggression, acquiescence, and questionnaire construction. ASP 1958, 56:278-279
72572 Theory of Suicide. NY: Funk & Wagnalls 1968, x + 115 p

FARBER, SEYMOUR M.

72573 (& Mustacchi, P.; Wilson, H. L.) (Eds) Man and Civilization: The Family's Search for Survival; a Symposium. NY: McGraw-Hill 1965, xii + 210 p

FARBEROW, NORMAN L.

72574 Bibliography on Suicide and Suicide Prevention. 1897-1957, 1958-1967. Wash DC: Natl Institute of Mental Health 1969, vii + 203 p
72575 (& Shneidman, E. S.; Bouvier, E. A.) Bibliography on suicide, 1897-1957. In author's *The Cry for Help* 325-388
72576 (& Shneidman, E. S.; Neuringer, C.) Case history and hospitalization factors in suicides of neuropsychiatric hospital patients. JNMD 1966, 142:32-44
72577 (& Shneidman, E. S.) (Eds) The Cry for Help. NY/London/Sydney: McGraw-Hill 1961, 1965, xvi + 398 p
       Rv Mann, J. Q 1964, 33:296-298
72578 Introduction and case history of Mr. A. S. In author's *The Cry for Help* 153-166
72579 (& McEvoy, T. L.) Suicide among patients with diagnoses of anxiety reaction or depressive reaction in general medical and surgical hospitals. JAbP 1966, 71:287-299
72580 (& Shneidman, E. S.; Leonard, C. V.) Suicide among schizophrenic mental hospital patients. In author's *The Cry for Help* 78-109
72581 (& Shneidman, E. S.; Litman, R. E.; Wold, C. I.; Heilig, S. M.; Kramer, J.) Suicide prevention around the clock. Ops 1966, 36:551-558
72582 (& Shneidman, E. S.) A survey of agencies for the prevention of suicide. In authors' *The Cry for Help* 136-149

See Litman, Robert E.; Meyer, Mortimer M.; Shneidman, Edwin S.; Tabachnick, Norman

FARETRA, GLORIA

See Bender, Lauretta; Cobrinik, Leonard

FARINA, AMERIGO

72583 (& Holzberg, J. D.) Attitudes and behaviors of fathers and mothers of male schizophrenic patients. JAbP 1967, 72:381-387

72584 (& Holzberg, J. D.) Interaction patterns of parents and hospitalized sons diagnosed as schizophrenic or nonschizophrenic. JAbP 1968, 73:114-118

72585 Patterns of role dominance and conflict in parents of schizophrenic patients. ASP 1960, 61:31-38
   Abs Appelbaum, S. A. Q 1961, 30:310

FARIS, MILDRED T.

See Mayman, Martin; Sargent, Helen D.

FARKAS, MARY E.

See Masserman, Jules H.

FARLEY, ARTHUR J.

See Davis, Harry K.

FARNHAM, LOUISE J.

See Ruebush, Britton K.

FARNSWORTH, DANA L.

72586 Concepts for educational psychiatry. JAMA 1962, 181:815-821

72587 Mental health in college. Ency Ment Hlth 1080-1090

72588 Psychiatry, Education and the Young Adult. Springfield, Ill: Thomas 1966, xv + 268 p

72589 (& Braceland, F. J.) (Eds) Psychiatry, the Clergy, and Pastoral Counseling: The St. John's Study. Collegeville, Minn: Inst for Mental Health, St. John's Univ Pr 1969, xviii + 356 p

72590 The psychotherapy of the college student. Curr psychiat Ther 1963, 3:124-130

72591 (& Munter, P. K.) The role of the college psychiatrist. In Blaine, G. B., Jr. & McArthur, C. C. Emotional Problems of the Student, Garden City/NY: Anchor Books 1966, 1-18

See Bartemeier, Leo H.; Ewalt, Jack R.

FARQUHARSON, R. F.

72592 (& Hyland, H. H.) Anorexia nervosa. A metabolic disorder of psychologic origin. JAMA 1938, 111:1085-1092. In Kaufman, R. M. & Heiman, M. Evolution of Psychosomatic Concepts, NY: IUP 1964, 202-226

FARRELL, BRIAN A.

72593 Can psychoanalysis be refuted? Inquiry 1961, 4:16-36

S-45348 Psychological theory and the belief in God.
   Abs An Surv Psa 1955, 6:48-49, 428-429

72594 The status of psychoanalytic theory. Inquiry 1964, 7:104-122
72595 Symposium on psychoanalysis and validation. II. On the character of psychodynamic discourse. M 1961, 34:7-13
    Abs RDT Q 1961, 30:609
72596 (& Wisdom, J. O.; Turquet, P. M.) Symposium: the criteria for a psychoanalytic interpretation. In Aristotelian Society for the Systematic Study of Philosophy, *Proceedings: Suppl Vol. 36,* London: Harrison 1962, 77-144

FARRELL, MALCOLM J.

See Barton, Walter E.

FARRELL, MARK P., JR.

72597 Transference dynamics of group psychotherapy. Arch gen Psychiat 1962, 6:66-76
    Abs KR Q 1963, 32:140

FARRELLY, F.

See Ludwig, Arnold M.

FARRINGTON, CONSTANCE

TRANSLATION OF:
Fanon, F. [72558]

FARROW, BOBBY J.

See Santos, John F.

FARSON, RICHARD E.

72598 Introjection in the psychotherapeutic relationship. J counsel Psychol 1961, 8:337-342. In Goldstein, A. P. & Dean, S. J. *The Investigation of Psychotherapy,* NY: Wiley 1966, 360-365

FAST, IRENE

72599 (& Broedel, J. W.) Intimacy and distance in the interpersonal relationships of persons prone to depression. J proj Tech 1967, 31(6):7-12
72600 Some relationships of infantile self-boundary development to depression. J 1967, 48:259-266
    Abs EVN Q 1969, 38:159-160
72601 (& Cain, A. C.) The step-parent role: potential for disturbances in family functioning. Ops 1966, 36:485-491
    Abs JMa RFPsa 1968, 32:377

See Cain, Albert C.; Hoffberg, Caroline

FATHĪ, MUHAMMAD

72602 [The Study of Psychoanalysis in Egypt, Related to Science, Sociology and Law.] (Arab) Cairo 1946, 228 p

FAU, R. B.

72603 (& Andrey, B.; LeMen, J.; Dehaudt, H.) Psychothérapie des Débile Mentaux. [Psychotherapy of the Mentally Deficient.] Paris: PUF 1966, 262 p

FAUCHEUX, CLAUDE

72604 La représentation sociale de la psychanalyse. [Social representation of psychoanalysis.] Temps mod 1961, 17(188):981-989

FAURE, HENRI

72605 Hallucinations et Realité Perceptive. [Hallucinations and Perceptive Reality.] Paris: PUF 1965, 255 p
72606 Les Objets dans la Folie: Les Appartenances du Délirant. [Object Investment of Insanity: The Belongings and Characteristics of Delirious Patients.] Paris: PUF 1966, 278 p
72607 Sleep-induced group psychotherapy. Int J grp PT 1960, 10:22-37

FAURE, R.

See Ridjanovic, S.

FAVEZ, GEORGES

72608 Ce qui est interprété. [That which is interpreted.] Bull Ass psa Fran 1969, (5):82-86
72609 Le complexe d'oedipe et l'ironie. [The Oedipus complex and irony.] RFPsa 1967, 31:1069-1075
72610 Présentation. [Introduction.] Bull Ass psa Fran 1965, (1)

FAVEZ-BOUTONIER, JULIETTE

72611 L'activité volontaire. [Voluntary activity.] Bull Psychol, Paris 1965, 18:913-916
72612 Les dessins de l'enfant schizophrène. [The drawings of schizophrenic children.] Rv Np inf 1960, 8:107-110
72613 L'objet. [The object.] Bull Psychol, Paris 1966, 19:894-899
S-45365 Psychanalyse et criminologie.
Abs RJA An Surv Psa 1957, 8:318-319

FAVREAU, J.-A.

72614 Discussion of Lebovici, S. "Colloque sur les interpretations en thérapeutique psychanalytique." RFPsa 1962, 26:33-43
72615 Discussion of Misès, R. "L'intégration du père dans les conflits précoces." RFPsa 1964, 28:390-391
72616 Intégration et régression. [Integration and regression.] RFPsa 1966, 30:472
S-45376 (& Doumic, A.) Psychanalyse et éducation.
Abs TC An Surv Psa 1956, 7:242-245
72617 [Technical problems raised by the psychoanalytic therapy of homosexuals.] (Fr) RFPsa 1964, 28:327-331

See Diatkine, René; Lebovici, Serge; Nacht, Sacha

FAY, JUDITH

See Davidson, Audrey

FAZEKAS, JOSEPH F.

72618 The multiple genesis and therapy of psychiatric disorders. Med Ann
DC 1960, 29:439-440

FAZIO, F. DE

72618A [Convention for the study of the use of narcoanalysis, in Reggio Emilia,
18 December 1966.] (It) Riv sper Freniat 1968, 92:1558-1591

FAZZONE, ROGER A.

See Tolor, Alexander

FEASTER, JOHN

72619 Faulkner's *Old Man:* a psychoanalytic approach. Modern Fiction
Studies 1967, 13:89-93

FEATHER, B. W.

See Hine, Frederick R.

FÉDER, LUIS

72620 (& Gonzalez Pineda, F.) Discussion of Parres, R. & Ramirez, S. "Termination of analysis." Psa Amer 267-272
72621 Editorial. Cuad Psa 1965, 1:117-118; 307-308
72622 Editorial: Nace "Cuadernos de Psicoanalisis." [Editorial: The birth of
"Cuadernos de Psicoanalisis."] Cuad Psa 1965, 1:1-2
72623 Introducción a la serie.-El eterno Edipo. [Introduction to the series:
The eternal Oedipus.] Cuad Psa 1965, 1:119-122
72624 Madre-hijo, su encuentro y rencuentro en torno a la hipogalctia sín-
drome de tres traumas básicos. Un estudio de la constelación oral.
[Mother-son, their encounter and collision with the three basic traumas
of the hypogalactia syndrome. A study of the oral constellation.] Cuad
Psa 1967, 3:195-225
72625 Un "screen acting" incestuoso. Masoquismo e ingenuidad femeninos.
[Incestuous "screen acting." Feminine masochism and sensitivity.]
Cuad Psa 1965, 1:195-203
72626 (& Gonzalez Pineda, F.) "Terminación de análisis" correlato oficial al
trabajo. [Official statement on "termination of analysis."] Cuad Psa
1965, 1:69-73

See Cardeña, Jaime

ABSTRACTS OF:
72627 Greenson, R. R. That "impossible" profession. Cuad Psa 1965, 1:387
72628 Randell, L. On friendship. Cuad Psa 1965, 1:212
72629 Shakow, D. Ethics for a scientific age. Some moral aspects of psychoanalysis. Cuad Psa 1965, 1:385

REVIEW OF:
72630 Socarides, C. Female Sexuality. Cuad Psa 1965, 1:211

FEDER, SAMUEL L.

72631 Psychological considerations in the care of patients with cancer. Ann NY Acad Sci 1966, 125:1020-1027
72632 The use of psychotherapeutic drugs in obstetrics. In Rovinsky, J. J. & Guttmacher, A. F. *Medical, Surgical, and Gynecologic Complications of Pregnancy,* Baltimore: Williams & Wilkins 1960, 1965, 511-519

FEDERN, ERNST

72633 How Freudian are the Freudians? Some remarks to an unpublished letter. J Hist behav Sci 1967, 3:269-281
72634 Some clinical remarks on the psychopathology of genocide. Psychiat Q 1960, 34:538-549
       Einige klinische Bemerkungen zur Psychopathologie des Völkermords. Psyche 1969, 23:629-639
       Abs Engle, Bernice Q 1961, 30:302
72635 The therapeutic personality; as illustrated by Paul Federn and August Aichhorn. Psychiat Q 1962, 36:39-43
       Abs Engle, B. S. Q 1963, 32:292
72636 Was Adler a disciple of Freud? A Freudian view. J ind Psych 1963, 19:80-82

       See Nunberg, Herman

FEDERN, PAUL

S-8279 Ego psychology and the psychosis.
        Abs Szpilka, J. Rev Psicoanál 1966, 23:245
S-8318 Der neurotische Stil.
        Abs AaSt An Surv Psa 1957, 8:126-127
72637   (& Meng, H.) (Eds) Psychoanalyse und Alltag. [Psychoanalysis and Everyday.] Bern/Stuttgart: Huber 1964 (5th rev), 298 p
S-8329 (& Meng, H.) Psychoanalytische Vorbeungung oder psychoanalytische Behandlung? In Bolterauer, L. *Aus der Werkstatt des Erziehungsberaters,* Vienna: Verlag f. Jugend und Volk 1960, 230-239
S-8360 Über zwei typische Traumsensationen.
        On dreams of flying. Heirs Freud 121-128

FÉDIDA, PIERRE

72638 Le corps et sa mise en scène dans le fantasme masochiste. [The body and its setting in masochistic fantasy.] Bull Ass psa Fran 1968, (4):92-102
72639 Le discours a double entente: interprétation, délire et vérité. [The words have a double meaning: interpretation, frenzy and truth.] Bull Ass psa Fran 1969, (5):51-58
72640 [Structuralism in psychopathology (history, language and relation).] (Fr) Évolut psychiat 1964, 29:85-129

FEDORENKO, E. G.

72641 (Ed) [Philosophical Problems of Medicine and Biology.] (Rus) Kiev, USSR: Zdorov'ya 1965, 255 p

FEDOTOV, D.

S-45384 A Soviet view of psychoanalysis.
Abs Leach, D. An Surv Psa 1957, 8:17

FEHR, J. J.

72642 [On some drawings of a delirious schizophrenic.] (Fr) Confin psychiat 1967, 10:36-45

FEIBEL, CHARLOTTE

72643 The archaic personality structure of alcoholics and its implications for group therapy. Int J grp PT 1960, 10:39-45

FEIBLEMAN, JAMES K.

72644 The ambivalence of aggression and the moralization of man. Persp Biol Med 1966, 9:537-548
72645 Behavior as response. Psychiat Res Rep 1961, (14):15-33
72646 The cultural circuit in psychology and psychiatry. JNMD 1959, 132: 127-145. In Bergen, B. J. & Thomas, C. S. *Issues and Problems in Social Psychiatry*, Springfield, Ill: Thomas 1966, 212-243
72647 Sexual behavior, morality and the law. In Slovenko, R. *Sexual Behavior and the Law*, Springfield, Ill: Thomas 1965, 171-190
72648 Transfer matching: a new method in psychotherapy. J Psychol 1961, 51:411-420

FEIFEL, HERMAN

S-45387 Attitudes of mentally ill patients toward death. Death & Identity 131-142
72649 Death. Ency Ment Hlth 427-450
72650 The function of attitudes toward death. J Long Island Consult Center 1967, 5:26-32
72651 (Ed) The Meaning of Death. NY: McGraw-Hill 1965, xvi + 351 p
72651A Perception of death. Ann NY Acad Sci 1969, 164:669-677
72652 (& Jones, R. B.) Perception of death as related to nearness to death. Proc 76th Annual Convention of APA 1968, 3:545-546
72653 The problem of death. Catholic Psychological Record 1965, 3(Spring). In Ruitenbeek, H. M. *Death: Interpretations*, NY: Dell 1969, 125-129

See Meyer, Mortimer M.

FEIGENBAUM, ARYEH

72654 Notes on affirmation and negation in human speech. Their linguistic expression and biological and psychological background. (Read at Israel Psa Soc, Feb 1960) Q 1961, 30:243-258
72655 Notes on negation, affirmation, and magical thinking. (Read at Israel Psa Soc, Dec 1961) Q 1963, 32:215-245

FEINBERG, C.

See Spence, Donald P.

FEINBERG, IRWIN

ABSTRACT OF:

72656 Szurek, S. A. The Roots of Psychoanalysis and Psychotherapy; A Search for Principles of General Psychotherapeutics. An Surv Psa 1958, 9:385-387

FEINER, ARTHUR H.

72657 (& Levenson, E. A.) The compassionate sacrifice: an explanation of a metaphor. R 1968, 55:552-573

72658 A note on Ravich's "Shakespeare and psychiatry." Lit & Psych 1965, 15:125-128

See Levenson, Edgar A.

FEINGOLD, BEN F.

See Freeman, Edith H.

FEINSTEIN, HOWARD MARVIN

72659 Chronicles of Reuben: a psychological test of authenticity. Amer Quart 1966, 18:637-654

72660 (& Paul, N.; Esmiol, P.) Group therapy for mothers with infanticidal impulses. P 1964, 120:882-886

72661 Hamlet's Horatio and the therapeutic mode. P 1967, 123:803-809

FEINSTEIN, SHERMAN C.

See Falstein, Eugene I.

FEIRSTEIN, ALAN

72662 Personality correlates of tolerance for unrealistic experiences. J consult Psychol 1967, 31:387-395

See Blatt, S. J.

FEJOS, PAUL

* * * Foreword to Galdston, I. Man's Image in Medicine and Anthropology, NY: IUP 1963, xi-xiii

72663 Magic, witchcraft and medical theory in primitive cultures. In Galdston, I. Man's Image in Medicine and Anthropology, NY: IUP 1963, 43-61

FELD, SHEILA C.

72664 Longitudinal study of the origins of achievement strivings. J Pers soc Psychol 1967, 7:408-414

See Gurin, Gerald

FELDER, RICHARD E.

72665 Hospitalization of the mentally ill in Georgia. (Booklet) Med. Assoc of Ga. 1957

72666 Iatrogenic heart disease. J Med Ass Georgia 1960, 49:327-328

72667 (& Malone, T. P.; Warkentin, J.; Whitaker, C. A.) Organic psychosis as picked up in psychiatric examination. J Med Ass Georgia 1960, 49: 56-60
72668 Referral to a psychiatrist. Georgia gen Practit 1955
72669 The use of the self in psychotherapy. In Arbuckle, D. S. *Counseling and Psychotherapy*, NY: McGraw-Hill 1967, 100-111

See Warkentin, John; Whitaker, Carl A.

FELDMAN, A. BRONSON

72670 Animal magnetism and the mother of Christian Science. R 1963, 50:313-320
72671 Betwixt art, revolution and religion, a chronicle of the psychoanalytic movement. Am Im 1964, 22:134-152
S-45409 Dostoevsky and father-love. Exemplified by *Crime and Punishment*.
       Abs JLan An Surv Psa 1958, 9:475
72672 Folklore light on free association. PPR 1962, 49(1):34-36
72673 The imperial dreams of Disraeli. R 1966, 53:609-641
S-45416 A moral reformer damaged in the making. From the fiction case-histories of Anton Chekhov.
       Abs JLan An Surv Psa 1957, 8:336
S-45419 The pattern of promiscuity seen in Schnitzler's "Round Dance."
       Abs EMW Q 1961, 30:306
S-45423 Shakespeare's early errors.
       Abs An Surv Psa 1955, 6:449-450
72674 Stages in the development of love. Am Im 1964, 21(3-4):64-79
72675 The word in the beginning. R 1964, 51:79-98
       Abs SRS Q 1965, 34:310

REVIEWS OF:
72676 Greenacre, P. The Quest for the Father: A Study of the Darwin-Butler Controversy, as a Contribution to the Understanding of the Creative Individual. R 1968, 55:154-156
72677 Holland, N. N. Psychoanalysis and Shakespeare. R 1966, 53:312-317

FELDMAN, ARTHUR A.

S-45430 The Davidic dynasty and the Davidic messiah.
       Abs Hojman, R. K. Rev Psicoanál 1961, 18:388

FELDMAN, BETTY

See Krasner, Jack

FELDMAN, DAVID

72678 Psychoanalysis and crime. Mass Society 1964:50-58

FELDMAN, FRED

72679 Discussion of Miller, M. L. "Manic depressive cycles of the poet Shelley." Psa Forum 1966, 1:199-201
72680 (& Cantor, D.; Soll, S.) Psychiatric study of a consecutive series of 34 patients with ulcerative colitis. Brit med J 1967, (3):14-17

72681 Results of psychoanalysis in clinic case assignments. J Am Psa Ass 1968, 16:274-300
72682 The tripartite session: a new approach in psychiatric social work consultation. Psychiat Q 1968, 42:48-61

FELDMAN, HAROLD

S-45434 How we create "fathers" and make them "sons."
         Abs An Surv Psa 1955, 6:412-414
S-45435 The id: present, past—and future?
         Abs Ekboir, J. G. de Rev Psicoanál 1961, 18:183. EMW Q 1961, 30:306-307
S-45439 From self-analysis to transference character traits.
         Abs Ekboir, J. G. de Rev Psicoanál 1961, 18:181

See Meyerowitz, Joseph H.

FELDMAN, HARRY

72683 In a Forest Dark. NY: T. Nelson 1960, 191 p

See Hollender, Marc H.

FELDMAN, M. P.

72684 Aversion therapy for sexual deviations: a critical review. Psychol Bull 1966, 65:65-79

FELDMAN, MARVIN J.

72685 (& Hersen, M.) Attitudes toward death in nightmare subjects. JAbP 1967, 72:421-425

FELDMAN, PHILIP M.

See Nesbitt, Robert E. L., Jr.

FELDMAN, RONALD B.

72686 (& Werry, J. S.) An unsuccessful attempt to treat a tiqueur by massed practice. Behav Res Ther 1966, 4:111-117

See Kravitz, Henry

FELDMAN, SANDOR S.

S-45446 Alarm-dreams.
         Abs IK An Surv Psa 1957, 8:176-177
72687 The attraction of "the other woman." J Hillside Hosp 1964, 13:3-17
S-45447 Blanket interpretations.
         Abs ARK An Surv Psa 1958, 9:357-358
72688 Blushing, fear of blushing, and shame. (Read at Psa Ass NY, 19 Oct 1959; at Western NY Psa Group, 14 Nov 1959, at Am Psa Ass, 5 Dec 1959) J Am Psa Ass 1962, 10:368-385
         Abs JBi Q 1963, 32:133

72689 Brief communications from psychoanalytical practice. Bull Phila Ass Psa 1968, 18:126-131

S-45448 Crying at the happy ending.
        Abs BEM An Surv Psa 1956, 7:161-162

72690 Discussion of Lehmann, H. "The lion in Freud's dreams." Psa Forum 1967, 2:239

72691 Luck: bad and good. (Read at Am Psa Ass, 7 Dec 1962) Bull Phila Ass Psa 1964, 14:1-12
        Abs EFA Q 1965, 34:135

72692 On romance. (Read at Am Psa Ass, 1968) Bull Phila Ass Psa 1969, 19:153-157

72693 Patterns in obedience and disobedience. Am Im 1969, 26:21-36

72694 The role of "as if" in neurosis. (Read at Mich Ass Psa, 30 April 1960; at Western NY Psa Soc, 19 Nov 1960; at Am Psa Ass, 10 Dec 1960) Q 1962, 31:43-53

S-45454 The sin of Reuben, firstborn son of Jacob.
        Abs An Surv Psa 1955, 6:405

72695 The use of adopted language in dreams. J Hillside Hosp 1968, 17:-110-115

See Lorand, Sandor

FELDMAN, THALIA

72696 Gorgo and the origins of fear. Arion 1965, 4:484-494

FELDMAN, YONATA

72697 Integration of psychoanalytic concepts into case work. Smith Coll Stud soc Wk 1960, 31:144-156

72698 Understanding ego involvement in casework training. In Parad, H. J. & Miller, R. R. *Ego-Oriented Casework,* NY: Fam Serv Ass Amer 1963, 292-306

See Love, Sidney

FELDMANN, H.

See Meyer, Joachim-Ernst

FELDMAN-TOLEDANO, Z.

See Groen, J. J.

FELDSTEIN, STANLEY

72699 (& Jaffe, J.) Language predictability as a function of psychotherapeutic interaction. J consult Psychol 1963, 27:123-126

72700 Vocal patterning of emotional expression. Sci Psa 1964, 7:193-208

See Jaffe, Joseph

FELICI, F.

72700A (& Laurenzi, G. B.) [Psychopathological study of the art of Chagall and comparisons with psychopathological art.] (It) Riv sper Freniat 1968, 92:1442-1489

FELIX, ROBERT H.

72701 Comparative study of drawings of the human hand by normal children and chronic schizophrenics. Israel Ann Psychiat 1963, 1:11-22

* * * Foreword to Caplan, G. *Prevention of Mental Disorders in Children,* NY: Basic Books 1961

* * * Foreword to Caplan, G. *Principles of Preventive Psychiatry,* NY/London: Basic Books 1964

* * * Foreword to Farberow, N. L. & Shneidman, E. S. *The Cry for Help,* NY/Toronto/London: McGraw-Hill 1961, ix

* * * Foreword to Langsley, D. G. & Kaplan, D. M. *The Treatment of Families in Crisis,* NY: Grune & Stratton 1968

72702 The National Institute of Mental Health. Ency Ment Hlth 1292-1305

72703 (& Arieti, S.) The pattern of the human hand. Israel Ann Psychiat 1966, 4:30-42

72704 The psychiatric training of the medical student and psychiatrist. BMC 1961, 25:213-224
Abs HD Q 1962, 31:584

FELL, JOSEPH P., III

72705 A critique of Jean-Paul Sartre's theory of emotion. Diss Abstr 1968, 28:4663-4664

72706 Emotion in the Thought of Sartre. NY/London: Columbia Univ Pr 1965, x + 254 p

72707 Sartre's *Words:* an existential self-analysis. R 1968, 55:426-441
Abs SRS Q 1969, 38:674

FELLMAN, GORDON A.

See Zinberg, Norman E.

FELLNER, CARL H.

72708 Provocation of suicidal attempts. JNMD 1961, 133:55-58

See Miller, Milton H.

FELTON, JEAN SENCER

See Katz, Alfred H.

FELZER, STANTON B.

See Baum, O. Eugene

FENICHEL, CARL

72709 Psycho-educational approaches for seriously disturbed children in the classroom. In Hellmuth, J. *Education Therapy, Vol. I,* Seattle: Special Child Publ 1966, 207-221

FENICHEL, HANNA

See Annin, Suzette H.

FENICHEL, OTTO

S-8553 Problems of psychoanalytic technique.
Problemas de técnica psicoanalítica. (Mex Psa Assoc publ Psa Monogr) Editorial Pax México
72710 Psychoanalysis as the nucleus of a future dialectical-materialistic psychology. (Tr: Barsis, O.) (Eds: Annin, S. H.; Fenichel, H.) Am Im 1967, 24:290-311
Abs JWS Q 1969, 38:165
S-8582 Zum Theorie der psychoanalytischer Technik.
Concerning the theory of psychoanalytic technique. Psa Clin Inter 42-64

FENSTERHEIM, H.

See Normand, William C.

FERARD, MARGARET L.

72711 (& Hunnybun, N. K.) The Caseworker's Use of Relationships. London: Tavistock 1962, 133 p

FERBER, LEON

72712 (& Gray, P.) Beating fantasies—clinical and theoretical considerations. (Read at Baltimore-Cleveland-Phila Psa Cong, 11 June 1966) Bull Phila Ass Psa 1966, 16:186-206
Abs Lichtenberg, J. D. Bull Phila Ass Psa 1966, 16:216-222. EFA Q 1968, 37:159-160
72713 Discussion of Lubin, A. J. "The influence of the Russian Orthodox Church on Freud's Wolf-Man: a hypothesis." Psa Forum 1967, 2: 168-170

FERDIÈRE, G.

72714 (& Lwoff, S.) Compréhension par l'enfant du symbolisme préhistorique. [The child's comprehension of prehistoric symbolism.] Ann méd-psychol 1965, 123(1):328-332

FERDINAND, WILLI

72715 Eine konfliktauflösende negative Übertragung ausserhalb der therapeutischen Situation. [A conflict-solving negative transference outside the therapeutic situation.] Prax Kinderpsychol 1965, 14:161-164
72716 Verhaltensprimivierung als wiederholte Reaktion auf Überforderungsituationen. [Primitivization of behavior as a repeated reaction to situations of exaggerated requirements.] Prax Kinderpsychol 1966, 15:193-196

FERENCZI, SÁNDOR

S-9078 Bausteine zur Psychoanalyse. (2nd ed) Bern: Hans Huber Verlag 1964, 567 p
Rv Illing, H. A. Q 1966, 35:136-137

S-9108 Entwicklungsstufen des Wirklichkeitssinnes.
         Stages in the development of the sense of reality. In Rosenblith, J. F.
         & Allinsmith, W. *The Causes of Behavior*, Boston: Allyn & Bacon 1966,
         476
S-9123 Freud's Einfluss auf die Medizin.
         Freud's influence on medicine. Heirs Freud 16-32
72717   Les raisons qu'ont les psychanalystes de se grouper en Association.
         [The reasons why psychoanalysts form an Association.] Bull Ass psa
         Fran 1966, (2)
S-9264 Spiritismus.
         Spiritism. (Tr: Fodor, N.) R 1963, 50(1):139-144
S-9266 Sprachverwirrung zwischen den Erwachsenen und dem Kind. Psyche
         1967, 21:256-265
S-9307 Versuch einer Genitaltheorie.
         Thalassa: Psychanalyse des Origines de la Vie Sexuelle. Paris:
         Petite Bibliothèque Payot 1962, 186 p
         Rv Veszy-Wagner, L. J 1963, 44:382

FERGUSON, EVA D.

72718   Ego involvement: a critical examination of some methodological issues.
         ASP 1962, 64:407-417

FERGUSON, JULIA

See Goodrich, D. Wells

FERGUSON, L. R.

See Hatfield, John S.

FERGUSON, LEONARD W.

See Brown, Constance M.

FERGUSON, ROBERT E.

See Glad, Donald D.

FERMI, LAURA

72719   Illustrious Immigrants; the Intellectual Migration from Europe, 1930-
         1941. Chicago: Univ Chicago Pr 1968, xi + 440 p

FERN, DONALD J.

See Berezin, Martin A.

FERNANDES, H. J.

72720   Système hormothymique de P. Guiraud et modèles théoriques de la
         personnalité. [The hormothymic system of Paul Guiraud and theor-
         etical models of personality.] Évolut psychiat 1966, 31:167-174

FERNANDES, M. A.

72721   [The contradictions in "Jungian" psychotherapy in an informative re-
         view for dynamic psychiatry.] (Por) J Med (Por) 1965, 57:741-746

72722 [Psychotherapy of schizophrenia based on an analysis of delusions.]
(Por) J Med (Por) 1964, 53:629-654; 697-709

FERNANDEZ, AIDA AURORA

72723 Confusión y acting out. Algunos aspectos del análisis de un paciente
homosexual. [Confusion and acting out. Some aspects of the analysis
of a homosexual patient.] Rev urug Psa 1967, 9:149
72724 (& Pizzolanti, C. P. de; Prego, V. M. de) Fantasia de escena primaria
en los padres que esperan. [Fantasy of the primal scene in fathers-to-
be.] Rev urug Psa 1967, 9:237-241

See Alfonso, Olga; Baranger, Madeleine

ABSTRACTS OF:
72725 Bird, B. A specific peculiarity of acting out. Rev urug Psa 1966, 8:414
72726 Bouvet, M. Les variations de la téchnique. Distance et variation. Rev
urug Psa 1965, 7:378
72727 Eidelberg, L. The concept of narcissistic modification. Rev urug Psa
1965, 7:95

REVIEWS OF:
72728 Abadi, M. Hypochondria. Rev urug Psa 1963, 5:464-466
72729 Hornstra, W. L. Homosexualidad. Rev urug Psa 1967, 9:248-254

FERNANDEZ, C.

See Reding, Georges R.

FERNANDEZ, JAMES W.

72730 Filial piety and power: psychosocial dynamics in the legends of Shaka
and Sundiata. Sci Psa 1969, 14:47-60

FERNANDEZ, M. A.

See Rato, M. M.

FERNANDEZ-CERDEÑO, A.

72731 (& Leuner, H.) Das Erleben der oralen Regression unter Einfluss von
Halluzinogenen (LSD-25 und Psylocybin). [Experience of regression
to the oral phase under the influence of hallucinogenic drugs (LSD-25
and Psilocybin).] Z PSM 1965, 11(1):45-54
72732 (& Brugmann, A. M.; Roldan, E.) Estudio comparativo entre el sueño
y el ensueño y el fenómeno onirico bajo las drogas alucinógenas.
[Comparative study between sleep, dreams and oneiric phenomena
under hallucinogenic drugs.] Arch Estud psicoan Psicol med 1967,
4:137-143

FERNÁNDEZ-MARINA, RAMÓN

72733 Cultural stresses and the schizophrenogenesis in the mothering one.
Ann NY Acad Sci 1960, 84:864-877

72734 (& Eckardt, U. von) The Horizons of the Mind. NY: Philos Libr 1964, xviii + 535 p

72735 The psychological functions of the Puerto Rican families. Inst of Caribbean Studies, Univ of P. R. 1968, November

72736 The Puerto Rican syndrome: its dynamics and cultural determinants. Ps 1961, 24:79-82

FERNANDEZ-ZOILA, ADOLFO

72737 Introduction à une étude des nevroses "existentielles": approche psychopathologique de la thematique du film de Marcel Carné, "Les Tricheurs." [Introduction to a study of "existential" neurosis: a psychopathological approach to the theme of the movie by Marcel Carné, "The Cheaters."] Évolut psychiat 1960, 25:433-459

FERNEAU, ERNEST W., JR.

72738 (& Klein, D. C.) Mental health consultation and sector psychotherapy. R 1969, 56:327-339

FERRACUTI, FRANCO

See Wolfgang, Marvin E.

FERRADINI, FRANCO G.

72739 Alcuni problemi circa la psicodiagnosi delle malattie mentali. [Some problems about psychodiagnosis of mental illness.] Ra Pgc 1961-63, 6:1-17

72740 (& Zapparoli, G. C.) Note sui fondamenti della psicoterapia analitica dell'isteria. [Notes about psychoanalytic treatment of hysteria.] Ra Pgc 1961-63, 6:18-28

72741 Il problema dell'aggressivitá nella concezione di H. Hartmann. [The problem of aggressivity in the concepts of H. Hartmann.] Riv Psa 1962, 8:57-66

See Zapparoli, Giovanni G.

FERRÃO, LAERTES MOURA

72742 Homossexualidada e defesas manícas. [Homosexuality and manic defenses.] Rev bras Psicanál 1967, 1:85-91. Abs (Engl) 91

FERRARI, ARMANDO BIANCO

72743 [The death instinct. (A contribution towards a systematic study.)] (Por) Rev bras Psicanál 1967, 1(3):324-350; (4):487-526

FERRARI, M.

72744 [Contribution to the interpretation of the psychodynamics of suicide and attempted suicide in depressed persons.] (It) Osped Psichiat 1967, 35:217-234

72745 [Contribution to the knowledge of the psychodynamics of incest.] (It) Osped Psichiat 1967, 35:253-264

FERRAUD, PAULETTE MICHON

TRANSLATION OF:
Torok, M. [93327]

FERREIRA, ANTONIO J.

72746 Emotional factors in prenatal environment. JNMD 1965, 141:108-118
       Abs BFM Q 1967, 36:143
72747 Empathy and the bridge function of the ego. J Am Psa Ass 1961,
       9:91-105
       Abs FB Q 1962, 31:290
72748 The etiology of schizophrenia. Calif Med 1961, 94:369-377
72749 Family myth and homeostasis. Arch gen Psychiat 1963, 9:457-463
       Abs KR Q 1964, 33:610
72750 Family myths. Psychiat Res Rep 1966, (20):85-90
72751 Family myths: the covert rules of the relationship. Confin psychiat
       1965, 8:15-20. In Proc 6th Int Cong PT, III. Basel: Karger 1965,
       15-20
72752 Interpersonal perceptivity among family members. Ops 1964, 34:64-70
72753 The intimacy need in psychotherapy. Psa 1964, 24:190-194
72754 Loneliness and psychopathology. Psa 1962, 22:201-207
72755 On repetition compulsion. R 1965, 52:84-93
       Abs SRS Q 1966, 35:471. CG RFPsa 1968, 32:171
72756 On silence. PT 1964, 18:109-114
72757 The pregnant woman's emotional attitude and its reflection on the new-
       born. Ops 1960, 30:553-561
       Abs JMa RFPsa 1962, 26:318
72758 Psychosis and family myth. PT 1967, 21:186-197

See Winter, William D.

FERRER, SUSANA L. DE

See Abuchaem, Jamil; Rascovsky, Arnaldo

FERRETTI, EFREM

72759 Considerazioni su un caso di ereutofobia. [Considerations on a case of
       ereuthophobia.] Riv Psa 1967, 13:71-84
72760 Discussion of Muratori, A. M. "Sogni di progresso et sogni di regressi
       nella pratica psicoanalitica." Riv Psa 1963, 9:132

See Bartoleschi, Benedetto

TRANSLATION OF:
Freud, S. [10434]

ABSTRACTS OF:
72761 Grunberger, B. Étude sur la dépression. Riv Psa 1966, 12:328
72762 Lacombe, P. Un mécanisme de pleurer pathologique. Riv Psa 1966,
       12:328
72763 Racamier, P. C. Propos sur la réalité dans la théorie psychanalytique.
       Riv Psa 1965, 11:85

72764 Spitz, R. A. A propos de la genèse des composants du surmoi. Riv Psa 1965, 11:83

FERRIER, M.-J.

72765 Emploi des méthodes projectives en psychothérapie analytique. [Use of projective methods in analytic psychotherapy.] Ann méd-psychol 1968, 126(2):109

FERRO, PHILIP L.

See Nesbitt, Robert E. L., Jr.

FERSCHTUT, GUILLERMO

72766 (& Sor, D.) Communicación y teoria Kleiniana. [Communication and the theory of Melanie Klein.] Rev Psicoanál 1962, 19:75-79
72767 Obituary: Heinrich Racker. Rev Psicoanál 1961, 18:288-292

See Liberman, David

FERSTER, CHARLES B.

72768 Operant reinforcement of infantile autism. In Lesse, S. *An Evaluation of the Results of the Psychotherapies*, Springfield, Ill: Thomas 1968, 221-236

FERSTER, ELYSE ZENOFF

See Allen, Richard C.

FESHBACH, SEYMOUR

72769 The stimulating versus cathartic effects of a vicarious aggressive activity. ASP 1961, 63:381-385. In Rosenblith, J. F. & Allinsmith, W. *The Causes of Behavior,* Boston: Allyn & Bacon 1966, 481-485

See Jessor, Richard

FESSLER, LACI

72770 The biological character of psychoanalysis. Exp Med Surg 1962, 20: 36-40

REVIEW OF:
72771 Binswanger, L. Melancholie und Manie. Phänomenologische Studien. Q 1961, 30:433-435

FEUER, LEWIS SAMUEL

72772 Anxiety and philosophy: the case of Descartes. Am Im 1963, 20:411-449
72773 The Conflict of Generations: The Character and Significance of Student Movements. NY: Basic Books 1969, ix + 543 p
72774 The dreams of Descartes. Am Im 1963, 20:3-26
72775 Karl Marx and the Promethean complex. Encounter 1968, 31(6):15-32

S-45493 Psychoanalysis and Ethics.
    Abs Auth An Surv Psa 1955, 6:424, 492-503
72776 Rejoinder on "the role of sexuality in the formation of ideas." J ind
    Psych 1961, 17:110-111
72777 The Scientific Intellectual: The Psychological and Sociological Origins
    of Modern Science. NY: Basic Books 1963, 441 p
72778 The standpoints of Dewey and Freud: a contrast and analysis. J ind
    Psych 1960, 16:119-136

FEUERSTEIN, C.
See Riess, Bernard F.

FEYS, JEAN
ABSTRACTS OF:
72779 Mallet, J. Contribution a l'étude des phobies. An Surv Psa 1956, 7:150-
    153
72780 Pasche, F. Réactions pathologiques à la réalité. An Surv Psa 1958,
    9:147-148
72781 Slavson, S. R. Émergence des facteurs dynamiques psychanalytiques
    dans une psychothérapie de groupes d'entretiens avec adultes. An
    Surv Psa 1958, 9:427-428

FIALA, S.
72782 Psychoenergetika a sjednocení vědy. [Psychoenergetics and the unifi-
    cation of science.] Activ Nerv Sup, Prague 1966, 8:265-274

FIASCHÉ, DORA N. DE
72783 Esquema corporal y concepción del mundo. Notas sobre el análisis de
    un psicótico con un sistema delirante. [Body image and conception of
    the world. Notes on the psychoanalysis of a psychotic with a delusional
    system.] Rev Psicoanál 1963, 20:268-282
    Abs Vega Q 1964, 33:459
72784 Notas sobre el conflicto edípico. Un caso clínico. [Notes on the Oedipus
    complex: a clinical case.] Rev Psicoanál 1964, 21:163-178

See Weil, Jorge N.

FICHTENBAUM, LEONARD
See White, Alice M.

FIDERER, GERALD
72785 D. H. Lawrence's *The Man Who Died:* the phallic Christ. Am Im
    1968, 25:91-96

FIEANDT, KAI VON
72786 Zur wissenschaftlichen Psychologie der sogenannten Selbsterfassung.
    [A contribution to the psychology of self-appraisal.] Psychol Beit 1960,
    5:41-52

FIEBRAND, H.

72787 (& Reimer, F.) "Masseter-Krampf." Ein Beitrag zur Differentialdiagnose der Tic-Krankheit. ["Masseteric cramp." A contribution to the differential diagnosis of tics.] Z Psychother med Psychol 1965, 15: 38-41

FIEDLER, ELEANOR

72788 Excerpts from the analysis of a boy with congenital club feet. (Read at Phila-Baltimore-Cleveland Psa Cong, 12 June 1965) Bull Phila Ass Psa 1965, 15:137-159
      Abs EFA Q 1967, 36:628

FIEDLER, LESLIE A.

72789 Come back to the raft af'in Huck honey! In Malin, I. *Psychoanalysis and American Fiction*, NY: Dutton 1965
S-45510 The failure of love in American fiction.
      Abs Berezin, M. A. An Surv Psa 1956, 7:417-418
72790 Love and death in the American novel. Commentary 1960, 29:439-447
72791 Master of dreams. Partisan Rev 1967, 34:339-356

FIELD, KAY

72792 (& Schour, E.) The application of psychoanalytic concepts of personality developments in the educative process. Ops 1967, 37:415-416

FIELD, LEWIS W.

72793 An ego-programmed group treatment approach with emotionally disturbed boys. Psychol Rep 1966, 18:47-50

FIELD, MARK G.

72794 (& Aronson, J.) The institutional framework of Soviet psychiatry. JNMD 1964, 138:305-322
      Abs BFM Q 1965, 34:311
72795 Psychiatry and ideology: the official Soviet view of western theories and practices. PT 1968, 22:602-615

REVIEWS OF:
72796 Myasishchev, N. N. Personality and the Neuroses. R 1968, 55:142-147
72797 Telberg, I. & Dmitrieff, A. Russian-English Glossary of Psychiatric Terms. R 1968, 55:142-147

FIELDING, BENJAMIN B.

72798 The dream and the session. Psychother Psychosom 1966, 14:298-312
72799 Dreams in group psychotherapy. Psychotherapy 1967, 4:74-77
72800 Intense transference reactions and the group therapist. Psychother Psychosom 1966, 14:161-170
72801 The utilization of dreams in the treatment of couples. Psychother Psychosom 1966, 14:81-89

FIELDS, JULIE E.

72802 Experiences of efficacy within the family, and adaptive ego functioning in the child. Diss Abstr 1969, 29(7-B):2632

FIELDSTEEL, NINA D.

See Behrens, Marjorie L.

FIER, MORTON

72803 Contact lens phobia. P 1964-65, 121:502-503
Abs Loeb, L. Q 1966, 35:313

FIERMAN, LOUIS B.

72804 (Ed) Effective Psychotherapy: The Contributions of Hellmuth Kaiser. (Foreword: Enelow, A. J. & Adler, L. M.) NY: Free Pr 1965, xxvi + 217 p
Abs J Am Psa Ass 1967, 15:217. Rv Brandt, L. W. R 1967, 54:182-184

FIERZ, HEINRICH KARL

72805 Die analytische Psychotherapie (C. G. Jung) in der psychiatrischen Klinik. [Analytic psychotherapy (C. G. Jung) in the psychiatric clinic.] Acta psychother psychosom 1962, 10:219-232
72806 Klinik und Analytische Psychologie. [Clinic and Analytical Psychology.] Zürich: Rascher Verlag 1963, 316 p
72807 Prof. Dr. Carl Gustav Jung, Küsnacht ZH (1875-1961). [Prof. Dr. Carl Gustav Jung, Kuesnacht near Zurich (1875-1961).] Schweiz ANP 1963, 92:223-226

FIERZ-MONNIER, H. K.

72808 Obituary: Carl Gustav Jung (1875-1961). Med Klin 1961, 56:2085-2087

FIGETAKIS, NICK

72809 Process-reactive schizophrenia: ego-strength and selected psychosexual dimensions. Diss Abstr 1964, 25:625

FIGGE, KLAUS

TRANSLATION OF:
(& Stein, W.) Laing, R. D. [79907]

FIGUEROA, JUAN ADOLFO

72810 Notas para un semantico psicoanalítica: couvade. [Notes for a psychoanalytic semantics: couvade.] Rev Psicoanál 1961, 18:170-171

FILIPPI, RONALD

72811 (& Rousey, C. L.) Delay in onset of talking; a symptom of interpersonal disturbance. J Am Acad Child Psychiat 1968, 7:316-328

FILIPPOV, L. I.

72812 Ekzistential'nyi psikhoanaliz Zh. P. Sartra: Zamysel i resultat. [The existential psychoanalysis of J. P. Sartre: conception and consequence.] Voprosy Filosofii 1968, 22(7):77-88

FILLER, WILLIAM

See Lief, Harold I.

FINCH, ROY

* * * Foreword to King, C. D. *The States of Human Consciousness,* New Hyde Park, NY: Univ Books 1963

FINCH, STUART M.

72813 (& Burks, H. L.) Early psychotherapeutic management of the school phobia. Postgrad Med 1960, 27:140-147

72814 Fundamentals of Child Psychiatry. NY: W. W. Norton 1960, 334 p
Rv Motto, R. L. Q 1961, 30:288-290

72815 Nomenclature for children's mental disorders need improvement. Int J Psychiat 1969, 7:414

72816 Personality development in the physically handicapped child. Clin Ped 1967, 6:171-172

72817 (& Cain, A. C.) Psychoanalysis of children: problems of etiology and treatment. Mod Psa 424-453

72818 Psychophysiological disorders. Compreh Txbk Psychiat 1406-1414

72819 (& Hess, J. H.) Ulcerative colitis in children. P 1962, 118:819-825
Abs Loeb, L. Q 1963, 32:607

See Kemph, John P.

FINCK, GEORGE H.

72820 Conflict in marriage following premarital pregnancy. Ops 1966, 36: 468-475

72821 The effect on the marital relationship of the wife's search for identity. Fam Life Coordinator 1965, 14:133-136

72822 Group counseling with unmarried mothers. J Marriage Fam 1965, 27: 224-229

72823 Marriage counseling—a service in behalf of children. Fam Life Coordinator 1962, 11:39-42
Familieradgivning i borneforsorgen. Bornesagens Tidende 1963, 58:148-154

See Dame, Nenabelle G.; Reiner, Beatrice S.

FINE, BERNARD D.

72824 (& Joseph, E. D.; Waldhorn, H. F.) (Eds) The Mechanism of Denial and the Manifest Content of the Dream. (The Kris Study Group of the NY Psa Inst, Monograph III.) NY: IUP 1969, 113 p

72825 (Reporter) Panel on some aspects of psychoanalytic methodology. Read at Am Psa Ass, Dec 1963) J Am Psa Ass 1964, 12:610-619

72826 (& Landau, F. L.; Lipton, E. L.; McDevitt, J. B.; Stump, J. E.) Psychoanalysis and learning theory. (Read at NY Psa Soc, 18 June 1963)
Abs Donadeo, J. Q 1964, 33:152-154

See Bernstein, Isidor; Moore, Burness E.

ABSTRACTS OF:
72827 Asch, S. S. Depression: three clinical variations. Q 1964, 33:463-465
72828 Bak, R. C. The phallic woman: the ubiquitous fantasy in perversions.
Q 1969, 38:516
72829 Greenacre, P. Overidealization of the analyst and of analysis: manifestations in the transference and countertransference relationships. Q
1967, 36:636-637
72830 Guttman, S. A. Some aspects of scientific theory construction and psychoanalysis. Q 1965, 34:631-633
72831 Harley, M. A secret in prepuberty (its bisexual aspects). Q 1963, 32:
616-617
72832 Holt, R. R. Ego autonomy re-evaluated. Q 1966, 35:479-481
72833 Loewenstein, R. M. (Chm) Reconstruction in psychoanalysis. Q 1962,
31:142-144
72834 Niederland, W. G. An analytic inquiry into the life and work of
Heinrich Schliemann (1822-1890). Q 1962, 31:595-597

REVIEWS OF:
72835 Berlyne, D. E. Structure and Direction in Thinking. Q 1967, 36:439-
442
72836 Masserman, J. H. (Ed) Current Psychiatric Therapies. Vol. VII. Q
1969, 38:149-151
72837 Scher, J. M. (Ed) Theories of the Mind. Q 1965, 34:130-132
72838 Thyne, J. M. The Psychology of Learning and Techniques of Teaching. Q 1965, 34:295-296
72839 Zaigarnik, B. V. The Pathology of Thinking. Q 1967, 36:439-442

FINE, EDWARD

72840 The psychology of stuttering. (Read at Detroit Psa Soc, 27 Apr 1964)
Abs Rosenbaum, J. B. Bull Phila Ass Psa 1964, 14:237-238

FINE, HAROLD J.

See Zimet, Carl N.

FINE, LEON

See Osworio, Abel G.

FINE, PAUL

72841 (& Offer, D.) Periodic outbursts of antisocial behavior. Arch gen
Psychiat 1965, 13:240-254
Abs PB Q 1968, 37:317-318

See Falstein, Eugene I.

FINE, REUBEN

72842 The analytic treatment of a psychotic. Psychotherapy 1964, 1:166-177

S-45533 Chess and chess masters. With title: Psychoanalytic observations on chess and chess masters. R 1956, 4:7-77. With title: The Psychology of the Chess Player. NY: Dover 1967, 74 p
Abs An Surv Psa 1956, 7:401

72843 Erotic feelings in the psychotherapeutic relationship. R 1965, 52:30-37
Abs SRS Q 1966, 35:469. CG RFPsa 1968, 32:169

72844 Freud: A Critical Re-evaluation of His Theories. NY: David McKay Co., Inc. 1962, 307 p; London: Allen & Unwin 1963, 271 p
Rv NR Q 1963, 32:581-583. Nelson, M. C. R 1964, 51:326

72845 Interpretation: the patient's response. In Hammer, E. F. *Use of Interpretation in Treatment: Technique and Art,* NY: Grune & Stratton 1968, 110-120

72846 On the nature of scientific method in psychology. Psychol Rep 1969, 24:519-540

72847 The personality of the asthmatic child. In Schneer, H. I. *The Asthmatic Child,* NY/Evanston/London: Harper & Row 1963, 39-57

° ° °   Psychoanalytic observations on chess and chess masters. See [45533]

72848 Psychoanalytic theory of sexuality. In Slovenko, R. *Sexual Behavior and the Law,* Springfield, Ill: Thomas 1965, 147-167

72849 The psychology of blindfold chess. Acta Psychol 1965, 24:352-370

° ° °   The Psychology of the Chess Player. See [45533]

72850 A transference manifestation of male homosexuals. PPR 1961, 48(2): 116-120

FINE, ROSWELL H.

72851 Apparent homosexuality in the adolescent girl. Dis nerv Sys 1960, 21:634-637

72852 Growth and development in the school age child. Institute on Growth and Development (Kentucky) 1962, 33

72853 Psychotherapy with the mildly retarded adolescent. Curr psychiat Ther 1965, 5:58-66

72854 A treatment program for the mildly retarded adolescent. J ment Deficiency 1964, 70:23-30

FINEBERG, HENRY H.

72855 Psychiatry—office problems. 2. Management of behavior problems in the office. Amer Practit 1960, 11:909-914

See Weiss, Samuel

FINEMAN, ABRAHAM D.

ABSTRACT OF:

72856 Myerson, P. G. The assimilation of unconscious material. Bull Phila Ass Psa 1963, 13:34-36

FINEMAN, JOANN B.

ABSTRACTS OF:

72857 Knapp, P. H. Short term psychoanalytic and psychosomatic predictions. Bull Phila Ass Psa 1961, 11:192-194

72858 Rochlin, G. The thought of dying: some origins of religious belief. Bull Phila Ass Psa 1963, 13:84-86

FINESINGER, JACOB E.

See Bierman, Joseph S.

FINGARETTE, HERBERT

72859 Discussion of Veszy-Wagner, L. "Little Red Riding Hood on the couch." Psa Forum 1966, 1:408-409

S-45557 The ego and mystic selflessness. In Stein, M. R. et al: *Identity and Anxiety*, Glencoe, Ill: Free Pr 1960, 552-583

72860 On Responsibility. NY: Basic Books 1967, 181 p

72861 Orestes: paradigm hero and central motif of contemporary ego psychology. R 1963, 50:437-461
         Abs SRS Q 1964, 33:606

72862 Real guilt and neurotic guilt. J existent Psychiat 1962, 145-158

72863 Self-Deception. NY: Humanities 1968, 171 p

72864 The Self in Transformation: Psychoanalysis, Philosophy and the Life of the Spirit. NY/London: Basic Books 1963, xiii + 356 p. NY: Harper & Row 1965, viii + 362 p

72865 The unprivate self. (Read at So Calif Psa Soc, 15 Feb 1963)
         Abs Peck, J. S. Bull Phila Ass Psa 1963, 13:97-99

FINK, GERALDINE

72866 Analysis of the Isakower phenomenon. (Read at Psa Ass NY, 20 Mar 1967) J Am Psa Ass 1967, 15:281-293
         Abs Urbach, H. Q 1968, 37:326-327

72867 (& Schneer, H. I.) Psychiatric evaluation of adolescent asthmatics. In Schneer, H. I. *The Asthmatic Child*, NY/Evanston/London: Harper & Row 1963, 205-223

72868 (& Gottesfeld, H.; Glickman, L.) The "superobese" patient. J Hillside Hosp 1962, 11:97-119
         Abs JA Q 1963, 32:290

See Gill, Merton M.; Simon, Justin

ABSTRACTS OF:

72869 Frank, J. Nosological and differential diagnostic considerations in the group of schizophrenias, regressophrenias. Q 1967, 36:638-639

72870 Orgel, S. & Shengold, L. The fatal gifts of Medea. Q 1969, 38:520

FINK, HANS F.

72871 Development arrest as a result of Nazi persecution during adolescence. (Read at 25th Int Psa Cong, July 1967) J 1968, 49:327-329
         Abs LHR Q 1969, 38:669

FINK, HAROLD KENNETH

72872 Guilt and the obsessive-compulsive neurotic personality. Samiksa 1963, 17(2):82-96

FINK, MAX

72873 Discussion of Dahlberg, C. C. "LSD as an aid to psychoanalytic treatment." Sci Psa 1963, 6:266-268

FINK, PAUL JAY

72874 Art as a language. J Albert Einstein Med Center 1967, 15:143-150
72875 (& Goldman, M. J.; Levick, M.) Art therapy—a new discipline. Penn Med 1967, 70(1):61-66
72876 Can normal sexual response be studied artificially? Psychiat Opin 1968, 5(4):20-26
72877 (& Goldman, M. J.; Lyons, I.) Morning glory seed psychosis. Arch gen Psychiat 1966, 15:209-213
72878 The pacifier as a transitional object. Bull Phila Ass Psa 1962, 12:69-83
Abs EFA Q 1964, 33:139

See Levick, Myra

FINKELSTEIN, HARRY

72879 Containment of acting-out adolescents in an open institution. Soc Casewk 1961, 42:134-138

FINKELSTEIN, JACQUES

72880 A propos de quelques conduits masochiques. [Concerning certain masochistic behavior.] RFPsa 1962, 6:67-86
Abs Tagliacozzo, R. Riv Psa 1965, 11:70
S-45580 Remarques à propos d'un cas de névrose obsessionelle.
Abs HFM An Surv Psa 1957, 8:102

FINKELSTEIN, LIONEL

72881 (& Berent, I.) Group therapy in a receiving hospital. Ment Hosp 1960, 11(3):43-44

FINKELSTEIN, MELVILLE

See Rosenthal, Maurice J.

FINN, MICHAEL HERBERT PAUL

S-45582 A note on a waking "blank stage" analogous to Isakower's phenomena, the dream screen and blank dreams.
Abs An Surv Psa 1955, 6:156-157

FINNERTY, RICHARD

See Messier, Michel

FINNEY, JOSEPH C.

72882 (Ed) Culture Change, Mental Health, and Poverty. Lexington: Univ Kentucky Pr 1969, xxiii + 344 p
72883 Judgments of ethnic groups. J Psychol 1968, 68:321-328
72884 Material influences on anal or compulsive character in children. J genet Psychol 1963, 103:351-367
72885 Some maternal influences on children's personality and character. Genet Psychol Monogr 1961, 63:199-278

FINZER, WILLIAM F.

72886 (& Kisley, A. J.) Localized neurotic interaction. J Amer Acad Child Psychiat 1964, 3:265-272
72887 (& Waite, R. R.) The relationship between accumulated knowledge and therapeutic techniques. J Amer Acad Child Psychiat 1964, 3:709-720
72888 Symptom contagion in children's emotional disorders. Clin Ped 1965, 4:18-22

See Blom, Gaston E.

FINZI, H.

See Rosenberg, L. M.

FIREMAN, LAURA

See Ambinder, Walter

FIRESTEIN, STEPHEN K.

72889 (Reporter) Problems of termination in the analysis of adults. (Panel: Am Psa Ass, 11 May 1968) J Am Psa Ass 1969, 17:222-237
72890 Review of literature for project to study terminations in psychoanalysis. (Multilithographed) 1967, 39 p

ABSTRACTS OF:
72891 Esman, A. et al: Panel on drug use by adolescents. Q 1969
72892 Kris Study Group: Reactions to separation. Q 1966, 35:323-325
72893 Spiegel, L. A. A psychoanalytic study of pain of mental origin in relation to self and object; its differentiation from anxiety. Q 1964, 33:314-316
72894 Stern, M. M. Fear of death and analytical technique. Q 1967, 36:324-325

FIRESTONE, MELVIN P.

72895 The physical examination as a psychotherapeutic tool. PT 1962, 16:61-63

FIRST, HELEN G.

REVIEWS OF:
72896 Dawson, J. G. et al: Psychotherapy with Schizophrenics. A Reappraisal. Q 1963, 32:416-419

72897 English, O. S. et al: Direct Analysis and Schizophrenia: Clinical Observations and Evaluations. Q 1961, 30:571-575

72898 Scheflen, A. E. A Psychotherapy of Schizophrenia: A Study of Direct Analysis. Q 1961, 30:571-575

FISCH, RICHARD

72899 Resistance to change in the psychiatric community. Alternatives. Arch gen Psychiat 1965, 13:359-366

FISCHBERG, BRUCE

See Cath, Stanley H.

FISCHEL, ANNE

72900 Learning in a lonely place. MH 1968, 52:42-44

FISCHER, A.

See Ruesch, Jurgen

FISCHER, HENRY G.

72901 The Abu symbol. Q 1966, 35:591-593

FISCHER, H. KEITH

72902 (& Dlin, B. M.; Winters, W., Jr.; Hagner, S. B.; Russell, G. W.; Weiss, E.) Emotional factors in coronary occlusions; II: Time patterns and factors related to onset. Psychosomatics 1964, 5:280-291
    Die emotionale Bedeutung von Zeitfaktoren für den Beginn des Coronarverschlusses. Psyche 1964-65, 18:161-176

72903 The problem of pain from the psychiatrist's viewpoint. Psychosomatics 1968, 9:319-325

72904 Psychosomatic medicine. Prog Neurol Psychiat 1960, 15:462-473

72905 (& Dlin, B. M.; Philippopoulos, G. S.) Psychosomatic medicine. Prog Neurol Psychiat 1961, 16:473-485; 1962, 17:473-484; 1963, 18:567-578; 1965, 20:671-681

72906 (& Dlin, B. M.) Psychosomatic medicine. Prog Neurol Psychiat 1964, 19:562-574; 1966, 21:546-552; 1967, 22:469-475; 1968, 23:504-513

72907 (& Dlin, B. M.; Rees, W. L. L.) Psychosomatic medicine. Prog Neurol Psychiat 1969, 24:452-462

72908 Some observations on psychoanalysis of psychiatric research. Psychosomatics 1962, 3:447-449

See Conger, Kyril B.

FISCHER, HERBERT

See Buss, Arnold H.

FISCHER, J.

72909 Anamnestische Verfolgung von Angaben aus dem ersten Lebensjahr bei Kindern mit psychogenen Erbrechen. [Anamnestic follow-up of

data from the first year of life in children with psychogenic vomiting.]
Acta paedopsychiat 1961, 28:249-254

FISCHER, RUTH

See Singer, Melvin

FISCHER, WILLIAM

72910   The problem of unconscious motivation. Humanitas 1968, 3:259-272

FISCHER-HOMBERGER, E.

72910A [Hysteria and misogyny—an aspect of the history of hysteria.] (Ger)
Gesnerus 1969, 26:117-127

FISCHETTI, N. M.

72910B (& Romita, F.; Gregorio, M. de) [Children, families and hospitals today.] (It) Riv Clin Pediat 1968, 81:1364-1373

FISCHHOFF, JOSEPH

72911   Family disturbances and children's non-verbal behavior. Med Times
1966, 94:151-156
72912   (& Wooley, P. V.; Faigenbaum, D.) Pediatric psychiatric supervision
in teaching of residents. Amer J Dis Childr 1965, 109:477-482
72913   Preoedipal influences in a boy's determination to be "feminine" during
the oedipal period. J Amer Acad Child Psychiat 1964, 3:273-286

FISCHMAN, HILDA S.

See Sands, Rosalind M.

FISH, BARBARA

72914   (& Shapiro, T.; Campbell, M.; Wile, R.) Classification of schizophrenia
in children under five years. P 1968, 124:1415-1423
72915   (& Shapiro, T.) A descriptive typology of children's psychiatric disorders: II: A behavioral classification. Psychiat Res Rep 1964, (18):
75-86
72916   Drug therapy in child psychiatry: psychological aspects. Comprehen
Psychiat 1960, 1:55-61. In Clark, D. H. & Lesser, G. S. *Emotional
Disturbance and School Learning*, Chicago: Sci Res Ass 1965, 163-171
72917   Drug use in psychiatric disorders of children. P 1968, 124:31-36. Ann
Prog child Psychiat 1969, 641-650
72918   Evaluation of psychiatric therapies in children. Proc Amer Psychopath
Ass 1964, 52:202-220
72919   Limitations of the new nomenclature for children's disorders. Int J
Psychiat 1969, 7:393-398
72920   (& Shapiro, T.) A method to study language deviation as an aspect of
ego organization in young schizophrenic children. J Amer Acad Child
Psychiat 1969, 8:36-56
72921   Organic therapies. Compreh Txbk Psychiat 1468-1472
72922   (& Alpert, M.) Patterns of neurological development in infants born
to schizophrenic mothers. Recent Adv biol Psychiat 1963, 5:24-37

72923   (& Wile, R.; Shapiro, T.; Halpern, F.) The prediction of schizophrenia in infancy: II. A ten-year follow-up report of predictions made at one month of age. Proc Amer Psychopath Ass 1966, 54:335-353

72924   (& Shapiro, T.; Halpern, F.; Wile, R.) The prediction of schizophrenia in infancy. III. A ten-year follow-up report of neurological and psychological development. P 1965, 121:768-775
   Abs Loeb, L. Q 1966, 35:313-314

72925   (& Campbell, M.; Shapiro, T.; Weinstein, J.) Preliminary findings on thiothixene compared to other drugs in psychotic children under five years. In Lehmann, H. E. *The Thioxanthenes*, Basel/NY: Karger 1969, 90-99

72926   Treatment of children. Int Psychiat Clin 1966, 2(4, Suppl):1-17

FISH, FRANK JAMES

72927   Clinical Psychopathology: Signs and Symptoms in Psychiatry. Bristol: J. Wright 1967, vii + 120 p

72928   The concept of schizophrenia. M 1966, 39:269-273

72929   Existentialism and psychiatry. JMS 1961, 107:978-985

72930   Experimentelle Untersuchung der formalen Denkstörung bei der Schizophrenie. Ein Überblick über die englische Literatur. [Experimental study of the formal thinking disorders in schizophrenia. A survey of the English literature.] Fortschr Neurol Psychiat 1966, 34:427-445

72931   The psychiatric aspects of paroxysmal tachycardia. Brit J Psychiat 1964, 110:205-210

FISHER, ALAN E.

See Dennis, Wayne; Scott, John P.

FISHER, ALDEN L.

72932   Freud and the image of man. Proc Amer Cath Phil Ass 1961, 35:45-77

FISHER, CHARLES

72933   A cycle of penile erecton synchronous with dreaming sleep. (Read at NY Psa Soc, 17 Mar 1964)
   Abs Furer, M. Q 1964, 33:614-617

72934   Discussion of Hartmann, E. L. "The D-state: a review and discussion of studies on the physiologic state concomitant with dreaming." Int J Psychiat 1966, 2:36-40

72935   (& Dement, W. C.) Dreaming and psychosis; observations on the dream-sleep cycle during the course of an acute paranoid psychosis. (Read at Boston Psa Soc, 26 April 1961)
   Abs Eldred, S. H. Bull Phila Ass Psa 1961, 11:130-132

72936   Dreaming and sexuality. (Read at NY Psa Soc, 23 Nov 1965) Psa— Gen Psychol 537-569

72937   Dreams. Ency Ment Hlth 498-512

S-45610 Dreams, images, and perceptions. A study of unconscious-preconscious relationships.
   Abs IS An Surv Psa 1956, 7:222-224

72938 Fluctuations in the dream-sleep cycle in relation to psychopathological states. (Read at Westchester Psa Soc, 2 April 1962)
       Abs HFM Q 1962, 31:449-450
72939 (& Dement, W.) Manipulation expérimentale du cycle rêve-sommeil par rapport aux états psychopathologiques. [Experimental manipulation of the dream-sleep cycle in relation to psychopathological states.] Rev Méd psychosom 1962, 4:5-12
72940 Obituary: Sidney Tarachow: 1908-1965. Q 1966, 35:277-279
72941 (& Friedman, S. M.) On the presence of a rhythmic diurnal, oral instinctual drive cycle in man: a preliminary report. (Read at NY Psa Soc, 17 May 1966)
       Abs Ennis, J. Q 1967, 36:478-480
72942 Psychoanalytic implications of recent research on sleep and dreaming. I: Empirical findings. II: Implications for psychoanalytic theory. J Am Psa Ass 1965, 13:197-270; 271-303
       Abs CG RFPsa 1968, 32:339-343. JLSt Q 1968, 37:468-469
72943 Psychological significance of the dream-sleep cycle. In Witkin, H. A. & Lewis, H. B. Experimental Studies of Dreaming, NY: Random House 1967, 76-127
72944 Recent trends in dream-sleep research in the United States. Proc IV World Cong Psychiat 1966, 168-177
72945 (& Dement, W. C.) Studies on the psychopathology of sleep and dreams. P 1963, 119:1160-1168
       Abs Loeb, L. Q 1964, 33:609-610
S-45616 A study of the preliminary stages of the construction of dreams and images.
       Abs Solomon, R. G. An Surv Psa 1957, 8:171-173
72946 Subliminal and supraliminal influences on dreams. P 1960, 116:1009-1017
       Abs Leavitt, M. Q 1961, 30:455-456. Loeb, L. Q 1961, 30:146

       See Antrobus, Judith S.; Dement, William C.; Friedman, Stanley M.; Hamburg, David A.; Kahn, Edwin; Rechtschaffen, Allan; Roffwarg, Howard P.; Shevrin, Howard

REVIEW OF:
72947 Hartmann, E. The Biology of Dreaming. Q 1969, 38:135-138

FISHER, GARY M.

72948 Sexual identification in mentally retarded male children and adults. Amer J ment Defic 1960-61, 65:42-45

FISHER, H. R.

See Wittenbrook, John M.

FISHER, KENNETH A.

72949 The assumptions in scientific therapy. R 1964, 51:253-273
       Abs SRS Q 1965, 34:469
72950 Crisis in the therapist. R 1967, 54:81-98
       Abs SRS Q 1968, 37:472
72951 Psychological bias. J existent Psychiat 1963-64, 4:325-342

FISHER, LAWRENCE A.

See Carmichael, Hugh T.

FISHER, RHODA LEE

72952 Body boundary and achievement behavior. J proj Tech 1966, 30:435-438

72953 Classroom behavior and the body image boundary. J proj Tech 1968, 32:450-452

72954 Mother's hostility and changes in child's classroom behavior. Percept mot Skills 1966, 23:153-154

72955 Social schema of normal and disturbed school children. J educ Psychol 1967, 58:88-92

See Fisher, Seymour

FISHER, SAUL H.

72956 Discussion of Bacon, H. H. "Woman's two faces: Sophocles' view of the tragedy of Oedipus and his family." Sci Psa 1966, 10:24-27

72957 (& Merin, J. H.; Weiss, F.) Discussion of "Clinical Psychoanalytic Concepts." In Merin, J. H. & Nagler, S. H. The Etiology of the Neuroses, Palo Alto, Calif: Sci & Behav Books 1966, 159-162

72958 Discussion of Silverberg, W. A. "On dream interpretation in psychoanalytic therapy." Dreams Contempo Psa 154-158

72959 The individual psychotherapist looks at group psychotherapy. Top Probl PT 1960, 2:57-63

72960 Psychological aspects of rehabilitation. In Lief, H. I. et al: The Psychological Basis of Medical Practice, NY/Evanston/London: Harper & Row 1963, 521-530

See Alpert, Murray

FISHER, SEYMOUR

72961 The body boundary and judged behavioral patterns in an interview situation. J proj Tech 1964, 28:181-184

72962 Body boundary and perceptual vividness. JAbP 1968, 73:392-396

72963 Body-boundary sensations and acquiescence. J Pers soc Psychol 1965, 1:381-383

72964 (& Seidner, R.) Body experiences of schizophrenic, neurotic and normal women. JNMD 1963, 137:252-257
    Abs BFM Q 1965, 34:137

72965 Body image and hypnotic response. Int J clin exp Hyp 1963, 11:152-162

72966 Body image and psychopathology. Arch gen Psychiat 1964, 10:519-529

72967 Body image boundaries and hallucinations. In West, L. J. Hallucinations, NY: Grune & Stratton 1962, 249-260

72968 (& Fisher, R. L.) Body image boundaries and patterns of body perception. ASP 1964, 68:255-262

72969 Body image in neurotic and schizophrenic patients. Further studies. Arch gen Psychiat 1966, 15:90-101

72970   (& Fisher, R. L.) The complexity of spouse similarity and difference. In Zuk, G. H. & Boszormeni-Nagy, I. *Family Therapy and Disturbed Families,* Palo Alto, Calif: Sci & Behav Books 1967, 118-132

72971   A further appraisal of the body boundary concept. J consult Psychol 1963, 27:62-74. In Megargee, E. I. *Research in Clinical Assessment,* NY/London: Harper & Row 1966, 519-534

72972   (& Mirin, S.) Further validation of the special favorable response occurring during unconscious self-evaluation. Percept mot Skills 1966, 23:1097-1098

72973   (& Renik, O. D.) Induction of body image boundary changes. J proj Tech 1966, 30:429-434

72974   Organ awareness and organ activation. PSM 1967, 29:643-647

72975   Sex designations of right and left body sides and assumptions about male-female superioriay. J Pers soc Psychol 1965, 2:576-580

72976   (& Osofsky, H.) Sexual responsiveness in women. Psychological correlates. Arch gen Psychiat 1967, 17:214-216

72977   (& Mendell, D.) The spread of psychotherapeutic effects from the patient to his family group. Ps 1958, 21:133-140
         Abs WCW An Surv Psa 1958, 9:429

See Cassell, Wilfred A.; Nesbitt, Robert E. L., Jr.

FISHMAN, CLAIRE G.

72978   Need for approval and the expression of aggression under varying conditions of frustration. J Pers soc Psychol 1965, 2:809-816

FISHMAN, HELEN

See Deutsch, Albert

FISHMAN, MICHAEL

See Brody, Eugene B.; Lourie, Reginald S.

FISK, B.

72979   The maturation of arousal and attention in the first months of life: a study of variations in ego development. J child Psychiat 1963, 2:253-270

FISK, FERN

See Hilgard, Josephine R.; Newman, Martha F.

FISS, HARRY

72980   (& Klein, G. S.; Bokert, E.) Waking fantasies following interruption of two types of sleep. Arch gen Psychiat 1966, 14:543-551
         Abs PB Q 1969, 38:342

REVIEW OF:

72981   Menninger, K. et al: The Vital Balance. The Life Process in Mental Health and Illness. Am Im 1965, 22:281-283

FITTKAU, BERND

See Tausch, Anne-Marie

FITTS, WILLIAM HOWARD

72982 The Experience of Psychotherapy; What It's Like for Client and Therapist. Princeton, N. J.; Van Nostrand 1965, iv + 188 p

FITZGERALD, DONALD

72983 (& Roberts, K.) Semantic profiles and psychosexual interests as indicators of identification. Personn Guid J 1966, 44:802-806

FITZGERALD, EDWARD T.

72984 Measurement of openness to experience: a study of regression in the service of the ego. J Pers soc Psychol 1966, 4:655-663

FITZGERALD, JOSEPH

See Levitt, Eugene

FITZGERALD, R. VANCE

72985 Letter to the editors re: Giovacchini, P. L. "Marital interaction." Psa Forum 1967, 2:287

FITZGERALD, ROGER

See Wall, Richard J.

FITZHERBERT, JOAN

72986 Healing of neurosis. For Health & Healing 1966, Nov-Dec 170-173
S-45638 Increase in I. Q. at the onset of schizophrenia. J psychophysic Res 1967
72987 The perception of apparitions. Int J Parapsychol 1963, 5:74-94
72988 The role of extra-sensory perception in early childhood. Int J Parapsychol 1961, 3:81-95
72989 Some suggestions concerning homosexuality. Brit J Psychiat 1967, 113:446
72990 The source of man's "intimations of immortatlity." Brit J Psychiat 1964, 110:859-862

FITZPATRICK, JOSEPH P.

See Martin, John M.

FITZSIMONS, RUTH M.

See Murphy, Albert T.

FIUME, S.

72990A (& Vecchia, S. de; Monaco, F. del; et al) [Parallel linguistic and psychopathological study of some disorders of verbal meaning in a case of initial schizophrenia.] (It) G Psichiat Neuropat 1969, 97:627-654

See Fiume Garelli, F.

FIUME GARELLI, F.

72990B (& Monaco, F. del; Fiume S.) [From autism to schizophrenia. Considerations on the mechanisms of psychodynamic development.] (It) G Psichiat Neuropat 1969, 97:155-183

FIZER, JOHN

72991 Problem of the unconscious in the creative process as treated by Soviet aesthetics. J Aesthet art Crit 1963, 12:399-406
S-45642 Projection and identification in the artistic perception.
        Abs An Surv Psa 1955, 6:452-453

FLAGG, GLENN W.

72992 Felix Deutsch 1884-1964. Psychoanalysis and internal medicine. Psa Pioneers 299-307

See Alexander, Franz; Goldstein, Michael J.

FLAMM, H.

72992A [Necessary new ways of psychotherapy. Psychoanalysis, a fundamental mistake of a prominent atheist.] (Ger) Praxis 1969, 58:972-973

FLANNERY, EDWARD H.

72993 Anti-Semitism: a spiritual disease. Thought 1966, 41:33-44

FLARSHEIM, ALFRED

72994 Comment on conjoint therapy. Psa Forum 1966, 1:325-326
72995 Comment on methodological problems in clinical research in psychosomatic medicine. PSM 1960, 22:409-410
72996 Delinquency in the suburbs. Ill Schools J 1967, 47:33-39
72997 The psychological meaning of the use of marijuana and LSD in one case. Psa Forum 1969, 3:103-115; 129-134
72998 Resolution of the mother-child symbiosis in a psychotic adolescent. Bull Chicago Soc Adol Psychiat 1967, 2(1):6-16
72999 The role of the psychotherapist in the university health service. J Amer Coll Hlth Ass 1967, 15(3):270-278
73000 The separation of management from the therapeutic setting in a paranoid patient. J 1967, 48:559-572
        Abs LHR Q 1969, 38:507

FLATTER, RICHARD

73001 "Solid" or "sullied," and another query. Shakespeare Q 1960, 11:490-493

FLAVELL, JOHN H.

73002 Psychoanalysis and developmental psychology. Introduction (Jean Piaget). Int J Psychiat 1967, 3:75-81

FLAVIGNY, H.

73003 [The role of the father in the psychopathological disorders of children. Conclusions.] (Fr) Rev Np inf 1965, 13:769-770

See Bernard, F.; Jardin, F.

FLECK, LILI

73004 Die Beurteilung der orgastischen Kapazität der Frau und ihrer Störungen aus psychoanalytischer Sicht. [The psychoanalytic assessment of female orgastic capacity and its disturbances.] Psyche 1969, 23:58-74
   Abs J 1969, 50:402

73005 Die Pubertätsmagersucht des jungen Mädchens und ihre Behandlung. [Underweight in an adolescent girl and its treatment.] Hbh Kinderpsychother 921-935

73006 (& Lange, J.; Thomä, H.) Verschiedene Typen von Anorexia nervosa und ihre psychoanalytische Behandlung. [Various types of anorexia nervosa and their psychoanalytic therapy.] In Meyer, J. E. & Feldmann, H. *Anorexia Nervosa*, Stuttgart: Georg Thieme 1965, 87-95

FLECK, STEPHEN

73007 (& Lidz, T.; Cornelison, A.) Comparison of parent-child relationships of male and female schizophrenic patients. Arch gen Psychiat 1963, 8:1-7

73008 Family dynamics and origin of schizophrenia. PSM 1960, 22:333-344
   Abs JPG Q 1961, 30:452-453

73009 Hysteria through the ages. Conn Med 1966, 30:615-616

° ° ° Introduction. In Rubenstein, R. & Lasswell, H. D. *The Sharing of Power in a Psychiatric Hospital*, New Haven/London: Yale Univ Pr 1966

73010 Psychotherapy of families of hospitalized patients. Curr psychiat Ther 1963, 3:211-218

73011 The role of the family in psychiatry. Compreh Txbk Psychiat 213-224

See Lidz, Theodore

FLEGEL, HORST

73012 Umgruppierung in einer psychiatrischen Abteilung als Soziotherapie. Beitrag zu einer Soziologie der Krankenhauspsychiatrie. [Regrouping in a psychiatric unit as a form of social therapy. A contribution to the sociology of institutional psychiatry.] Nervenarzt 1963, 34:384-391

73013 Vom Wachsaal zur therapeutischen Gemeinschaft. Das psychiatrische Krankenhaus auf dem Wege zum psychotherapeutischen Institut. [From the custodial room to therapeutic community. The psychiatric hospital on the way to psychotherapeutic institute.] Z Psychother med Psychol 1968, 18:41-49

See Petrilowitsch, N.

FLEGENHEIMER, FEDERICO A.

REVIEW OF:
73014 Wisdom, J. O. A Methodological Approach to the Problem of Hysteria. Rev Psicoanál 1963, 20:87

FLEISCHL, MARIA F.

73015 Comments on growth-inducing forces. Proceedings of a professional institute, co-sponsored by Hillside Hospital and the Educational Alliance 1964, 33-34
73016 A man's fantasy of a crippled girl. PT 1960, 14:741-748
73017 Poetry therapy. Int MH Res Newsletter 1968, 10(2)
73018 The role of the therapist in social club therapy. Brit J soc Psychiat 1967, 1:203-209
73019 Specific problems encountered in social rehabilitation. Theoretical formulations. PT 1964, 18:660-669
73020 (& Wolf, A.) Techniques of social rehabilitation. Curr psychiat Ther 1967, 7:202-208
73021 (& Waxenberg, S. E.) The therapeutic social club, a step toward social rehabilitation. Int MH Res Newsletter 1964, 6(1)
73022 The understanding and utilization of social and adjunctive therapies. PT 1962, 26:255-265

See Waxenberg, Sheldon E.

FLEISCHMANN, OTTO

* * *   (& Kramer, P.; Ross, H.) (Editors of) *Delinquency and Child Guidance. Selected Papers of August Aichhorn.*

FLEISS, ARTHUR N.

73023 Abstraction in art and psychiatry. NYSJM 1962, 62:2864-2866
73024 Psychotic symptoms: a disturbance in the sleep mechanism. Psychiat Q 1962, 36:727-733

See Hollender, Marc H.; Malev, Jonathan S.

FLEMING, ELIZABETH

See Chethik, Morton

FLEMING, ELYSE S.

See Cortes, Carlos F.

FLEMING, JOAN

S-45661 (& Altschul, S.) Activation of mourning and growth by psycho-analysis. J 1963, 44:419-431
        Abs Smolensky, G. Rev Psicoanál 1964, 21:259. Resta, G. Riv Psa 1965, 11:186. EVN Q 1966, 35:308
73025 The evolution of a research project in psychoanalysis. In Gaskill, H. S. *Counterpoint: Libidinal Object and Subject,* NY: IUP 1963, 75-105
73026 Philosophy, criteria and procedures for appointment of training analysts; a memorandum. 23 Nov 1968, 8 p (multilithographed)
73027 (& Benedek, T.) Psychoanalytic Supervision. A Method of Clinical Teaching. NY: Grune & Stratton 1966, x + 252 p
        Rv De Bell, G. Q 1968, 37:128-131. Keiser, S. J Am Psa Ass 1969, 17:238-267

73028 (& Benedek, T.) Supervision; a method of teaching psychoanalysis: preliminary report. Q 1964, 33:71-96
Abs Dubcovsky, S. Rev Psicoanál 1964, 21:383-385
73029 Teaching the basic skills of psychotherapy. Arch gen Psychiat 1967, 16:416-426
73030 The training analyst as an educator. In Proc of the Topeka Conf on Training Analysis, 10-13 April 1969
73031 What analytic work requires of an analyst; a job analysis. J Am Psa Ass 1961, 9:719-729
Abs FB Q 1962, 31:425

See Benedek, Therese F.

REVIEW OF:
73032 Klein, H. R. Psychoanalysts in Training. Selection and Evaluation. Q 1967, 36:435-436

FLESCH, REGINA

73033 Counseling parents of chronically ill children. The problem and suggested techniques. Pediat Clin N Amer 1963, 10:765-780

FLESCHER, JOACHIM

73034 Dual analysis. Curr psychiat Ther 1968, 8:38-46
S-45665 The "dual method" in analytic psychotherapy.
Abs Auth An Surv Psa 1958, 9:365-366
73035 Dual Therapy: Triadic Principle of Genetic Psychoanalysis. NY: D.T.R.B. Editions 1966, 560 p
Rv Kaplan, D. M. R 1969, 56:483-485
S-45666 A dualistic viewpoint on anxiety.
Abs An Surv Psa 1955, 6:38, 76-78
73036 Letter to the editors re: "Conjoint therapy." Psa Forum 1966, 1:421-426

FLETCHER, RONALD

S-45671 Instinct in Man. In the Light of Recent Work in Comparative Psychology.
Abs DJM An Surv Psa 1957, 8:40-46

FLEW, ANTONY

73037 Motives and the unconscious. In Feigl, H. & Scriven, M. *Minnesota Studies in the Philosophy of Science, I. The Foundations of Science and the Concepts of Psychology and Psychoanalysis,* Minneapolis: Univ Minnesota Pr 1956, 155-173
Abs AHM An Surv Psa 1956, 7:48

FLIEGEL, NORRIS

See Rosenberg, Bernard

FLIESS, ROBERT

S-45675 The *déjà raconté:* a transference-delusion concerning the castration complex.
  Abs AHM An Surv Psa 1956, 7:148-149

73038 Ego and the Body Ego: Contributions to Their Psychoanalytic Psychology. NY: Schulte 1961, xv + 390 p
  Rv Sloane, P. Bull Phila Ass Psa 1962, 12:118-119. EG J 1963, 44:238-242. Keiser, S. J 1963, 44:242-245

S-45676 Erogeneity and Libido, Some Addenda to the Theory of the Psychosexual Development of the Human.
  Abs WAS An Surv Psa 1957, 8:46-63

S-45679 Phylogenetic versus ontogenetic experience. Notes on a passage of dialogue between "little Hans" and his father.
  Abs SLP An Surv Psa 1956, 7:83-84

FLINT, ARDEN A., JR.

73039 Crisis in marriage—reification or reality. Ops 1968, 38:560-564

See Rioch, Margaret J.

FLINT, MAURICE S.

73040 Development of Freud's theory of causation. Diss Abstr 1964, 25:3099

FLOOD, CHARLES A.

See Daniels, George E.; O'Connor, John F.

FLORES, J.

73040A [Dynamic and economic factors in the analytic process and especially in the role of interpretation.] (Fr) RFPsa 1969, 33:981-986

FLOURNOY, OLIVER L.

73041 Colite ulcereuse et relations interpersonnelles. [Ulcerous colitis and interpersonal relationships.] Évolut psychiat 1961, 26:419-444

73042 Discussion of Diatkine, R. "Agressivité et fantasmes d'agression." RFPsa 1966, 30(Spec No):117-118

73043 Discussion of Sandler, J. & Joffe, W. G. "A propos de la sublimation." RFPsa 1967, 31:19-21

73044 Du symptôme du discours. [From the symptom to speaking about it.] RFPsa 1968, 32:807-889

73045 La notion de changement en psychanalyse. [The notion of change in psychoanalysis.] Schweiz Z Rev Suisse Psychol 1963, 22:289-303

73046 La sublimation. [Sublimation.] (Discussants: Spitz, R. A.; Gressot, M.; Roch, M.) RFPsa 1967, 31:59-99

REVIEW OF:
73047 Musatti, C. L. Gradiva. RFPsa 1962, 26:141

FLOWER, BARDWELL H.

* * * Foreword to Moriarty, D. M. *The Loss of Loved Ones: The Effects of a Death in the Family on Personality Development*, Springfield, Ill: Thomas 1967

FLUGEL, JOHN CARL

S-45692 On bringing bad news.
Abs An Surv Psa 1955, 6:211-212

FLUMERFELT, JOHN M.

73048 On reconstruction. (Read at Phila-Cleveland Psa Cong, June 1959; at Am Psa Ass, May 1960) Bull Phila Ass Psa 1962, 12:53-68
Abs EFA Q 1964, 33:139
S-45702 A problem of technique in the analysis of a transference.
Abs IK An Surv Psa 1957, 8:261-262

FLYNN, GERTRUDE E.

73049 The development of the psychoanalytic concept of depression. J psychiat Nurs 1968, 6:138-149

FLYNN, JOHN T.

73050 Identification and Individuality. Instincts Fundamental to Human Behavior. NY: Beekman Pr 1968, 82 p

FODOR, NANDOR

73051 Aberrations and traumata of olfactory function. Res J Philos soc Sci 1965, 2:73-95
73052 At-oneness. A new phenomenon for parapsychology. Res J Philos soc Sci 1964, 1:57-64
73053 Between Two Worlds. Englewood Cliffs, N.J.: Prentice-Hall; West Nyack, NY: Parker Publ 1964, xii + 268 p
S-45709 Dream recall and dream construction in the light of linguistic interchange.
Abs DJM An Surv Psa 1957, 8:173
73054 Encyclopaedia of Psychic Science. New Hyde Park, NY: Univ Books 1966
73055 Hang it all. Am Im 1961, 18:311-314
S-45713 The Haunted Mind: A Psychoanalyst Looks at the Supernatural.
Rv Löfgren, L. B. J Am Psa Ass 1968, 16:146-178
73056 Hindu on the couch. Res J Philos soc Sci 1964, 1:204-210
73057 Jung, Freud, and a newly-discovered letter of 1909 on the Poltergeist theme. R 1963, 50:279-288
73058 Jung's sermons to the dead. R 1964, 51:74-78
Abs SRS Q 1965, 34:310
S-9856 New Approaches to Dream Interpretation.
Rv Spotnitz, H. R 1963, 50(1):152-155
73059 Sandor Ferenczi's psychic adventures. Int J Parapsychol 1961, 3(3): 49-59

TRANSLATION OF:
Ferenczi, S. [9264]

REVIEWS OF:
73060 Podmore, F. Mediums of the 19th Century. R 1964, 51:693-694
73061 Sudre, R. Parapsychology. PPR 1961, 48:125-126

FOGELSON, RAYMOND D.

See Wallace, Anthony F. C.

FOISSIN, HENRI

73062 Mécanismes perceptifs et structure de la personnalité. [Perceptual mechanisms and structure of the personality.] Ann méd-psychol 1965, 123(1):713-724

FOKS, GILDA S. DE

73063 Actualización sobre autismo. [On autism.] Rev Psicoanál 1967, 24: 645-663
73064 Algunos aspectos de la importancia de la voz en relacion con la transferencia-contratransferencia. [Some aspects of the importance of the voice in relation to transference-countertransference.] Rev urug Psa 1966, 8:231-237
       Abs Vega Q 1968, 37:162

FOLCH, P.

See Durand, Charles

FOLCH-MATEU, P.

See Bofill, P.

FOLEY, J. M.

See Schulman, Jerome L.

FOLEY, LEO A.

73065 (Ed) Philosophy and Psychiatry. Proc Amer Cath Phil Ass 1961, 35, 254 p

FOLIN, W.

See Werner, Matha M.

FOLK, J. J.

See Werner, A.

FOLKART, LYDIA

See Thomas, Ruth

FOLLENS, BERTRAM

73066   The analyst's role: to interpret or to react? In Hammer, E. F. *Use of Interpretation in Treatment: Technique and Art,* NY: Grune & Stratton 1968, 101-106

FOLLETT, BARBARA NEWHALL

73067   Barbara; The Unconscious Autobiography of a Child Genius. Chapel Hill: Univ of North Carolina Pr 1966, 146 p

FOLLETT, HELEN

See McCurdy, Harold G.

FONG, STANLEY L. M.

73068   Identity conflicts of Chinese adolescents in San Francisco. In Brody, E. B. *Minority Group Adolescents in the United States,* Baltimore: Williams & Wilkins 1968, 111-132

FONSECA, P.

See Zimmermann, David

FONTAINE, M.

See Chertok, Léon

FONTAN, M.

73068A (& Ascher, J.; Lange, G.) [Some remarks on acting out.] (Fr) Ann méd-psychol 1969, 127:784-793

FONTANA, ALAN

See Rosenwald, George C.

FONTANA-LAHITTE, ALBERTO E.

S-45747 Colitis ulcerosa, presentación de un caso.
            Abs JO An Surv Psa 1958, 9:201-202
73069   (Ed) Psicoterapia con Alucinogenos. [Psychotherapy with Hallucinogens.] Buenos Aires: Losada 1965, 221 p
            Rv Vega R 1968-69, 55:709-710
73070   Psychotherapy and community—clinical observations. Proc IV World Cong Psychiat 1966, 2489-2491

FONTANARI, D.

73071   (et al) [Oneiric confusion syndrome following withdrawal of analgesics.] (It) Riv sper Freniat 1968, 92:963-977

FONTANAROSSA, H. O.

73072   [Sequences in the historical discussion of the ego.] (Sp) Sem Med, B Aires 1963, 123:1334-1336

FONTANGE, X.

See Blanc, Marc

FONTES, VICTOR

73073 Childhood mental hygiene in Portugal. Crianca Port 1956-57, 15-16(1)
73074 Childhood schizophrenia. Crianca Port 1956-57, 15-16(1)
73075 Evolution of personality during childhood. Crianca Port 1956-57, 15-16(1)
73076 Freud and child psychopathology. Crianca Port 1956-57, 15-16(1)
73077 Intelligence development at the pre-school age. Crianca Port 1956-57, 15-16(1)
73078 Psychotechnique and sports. Crianca Port 1956-57, 15-16(1)

FORBUSH, BLISS

73079 Moses Sheppard's interest in mental illness. Crosscurrents in Ps & Psa 11-17

FORD, DONALD H.

73080 (& Urban, H. B.) Psychotherapy. Ann Rev Psychol 1967, 18:333-372
73081 (& Urban, H. B.) Systems of Psychotherapy: A Comparative Study. NY: Wiley 1963, xii + 712
       Rv Moldawsky, S. R 1965, 52:492-493

FORD, E. S. C.

73082 Being and becoming a psychotherapist: the search for identity. PT 1963, 17:472-482
73083 (& Robles, C.; Harlow, R. G.) Psychotherapy with child psychotics: report of two cases. PT 1960, 14:705-718

ABSTRACTS OF:
73084 Greenacre, P. The relation of the impostor to the artist. An Surv Psa 1958, 9:161-162
73085 Niederland, W. G. Early auditory experiences, beating fantasies, and primal scene. An Surv Psa 1958, 9:130-132
73086 Olden, C. Notes on the development of empathy. An Surv Psa 1958, 9:241-242
73087 Weissman, P. Shaw's childhood and *Pygmalion*. An Surv Psa 1958, 9:473

FORD, LE ROY H., JR.

73088 (& Sempert, E. L.) Relations among some objective measures of hostility, need aggression, and anxiety. J consult Psychol 1962, 26:486

See Markowitz, Arnold

FORDHAM, FRIEDA

73089 Some views on individuation. J anal Psych 1969, 14:1-12

FORDHAM, MICHAEL

73090 Active imagination—deintegration or disintegration. J anal Psych 1967, 12:51-66

73091 (Ed) Contact with Jung: Essays on the Influence of his Work and Personality. London: Tavistock 1963; Phila/Montreal: Lippincott 1965, x + 245 p
Rv Am Im 1965, 22:219

73092 Countertransference. I. M 1960, 33:1-8
Abs IH Q 1961, 30:151

73093 Ego and the self in analytic practice. J Psychol, Lahore 1964, 1:32-45

73094 Ego, self, and mental health. M 1960, 33:249-253

73095 The empirical foundation and theories of self in Jung's works. J anal Psych 1963, 8:1-23

73096 An Evaluation of Jung's Work. London: Guild of Pastoral Psychology Lecture No. 119, 1962

73097 Memorial meeting to C. G. Jung. An interpretation of Jung's thesis about synchronicity. M 1962, 35:205-210

73098 Notes on the psychotherapy of infantile autism. M 1966, 39:299-312

73099 Obituary: C. G. Jung: 26 July 1875 to 6 June 1961. M 1961, 34:167-168

73100 The relation of the ego to the self. M 1964, 37:89-102

73101 The relevance of analytical theory to alchemy, mysticism, and theology. J anal Psych 1960, 5:113-128

73102 The self in childhood. Psychother Psychosom 1965, 13:29-35

73103 Suggestions towards a theory of supervision. J anal Psych 1961, 6:107-115

73104 Technique and counter-transference. J anal Psych 1969, 14:95-118

73105 Theorie und Praxis der Kinderanalyse aus der Sicht der analytischen Psychologie C. G. Jungs. [The theory and practice of child analysis in the light of Jung's psychology.] Hbh Kinderpsychother 168-185

REVIEW OF:

73106 Jacobson, E. The Self and the Object World. J 1965, 46:525-529

FORDYCE, W. E.

See Johnson, M. H.

FOREGGER, RICHARD

73107 The love triangle in marriage and divorce. MH 1966, 50:199-204

FORER, BERTRAM R.

73108 The taboo against touching in psychotherapy. Psychotherapy 1969, 6:229-231

See Carr, Arthur C.; Meyer, Mortimer M.

FORIZS, LORANT

73109 Some common denominators in psychotherapeutic modalities. Dis nerv Sys 1966, 27:783-788

FORMAN, ROBERT

See Switzer, Robert E.

FORNARI, E.

See Balconi, M.

FORNARI, FRANCO

73110 L'adolescenza dal punto di vista psicoanalitico. [Adolescence from the psychoanalytic point of view.] Gaz Sanitaria 1967, 38(6). In author's *Nuovi Orientamenti nelle Psicoanalisi*

S-45766 Analisi di un caso di etilismo. Rapporti tra tossicomania e istinto di morte. In author's *Nuovi Orientamenti nelle Psicoanalisi*

73111 (& Malcovati, P.; Miraglia, F.) Angoisses primaires chez la femme lors de l'accouchement. [Primary anxieties of woman during delivery.] In *I Congrès International de Médicine psychosomatique et Maternité*, Paris: Gauthier-Villars 1965

73112 Aspetti cognitivi del controtransfert nella psicoanalisi degli schizofrenici. [Cognitive aspects of countertransference in psychoanalysis of schizophrenics.] AUT AUT 1967, (98):52-61

73113 Comment on Dr. Meltzer's paper, "Terror, persecution, dread—a dissection of paranoid anxieties." (Read at 25th Int Psa Cong, July 1967) J 1968, 49:400-401

73114 Condition dépressive et condition paranoide dans la crise de la guerre. [Depressive and paranoid conditions in crises of war.] RFPsa 1964, 28:251-277

73115 La contestazione globale. [Global contestation.] AUT AUT 1968, #108:15-29

S-45767 Contributi alla teoria psicoanalitica della depressione. In author's *Nuovi Orientamenti nelle Psicoanalisi*

73116 Depersonnalisation et angoisses primaires. [Depersonalization and primary anxieties.] RFPsa 1966, 30. In author's *Nuovi Orientamenti nelle Psicoanalisi*

73117 La depressione e l'universo della colpa. [Depression and the universe of guilt.] Edited by Gruppo Milanese per lo Sviluppo della Milano 1965. In author's *Nuovi Orientamenti nelle Psicoanalisi*

S-45769 La dottrina psicoanalitica degli istinti. In author's *Nuovi Orientamenti nelle Psicoanalisi*

73118 (& Berrini, M. E.; Balconi, M.) Estraneazione della figura umana e investimento esclusivo di oggetti inanimati. [Estrangement of human figure and exclusive cathexis in animated objects.] Inf Anorm 1961, 44. In author's *Nuovi Orientamenti nelle Psicoanalisi*

S-45770 I fondamenti psicologici della psicoterapia analitica delle forme schizofreniche. In author's *Nuovi Orientamenti nelle Psicoanalisi*

73119 L'Io nelle psicosi schizofreniche. [The ego in the schizophrenic psychosis.] Edited by Gruppo Milanese per lo Sviluppo della Psicoterapia, Maggio 1963, Milan. In author's *Nuovi Orientamenti nelle Psicoanalisi*

73120 I meccanismi di difesa dalla colpa. [The mechanisms of defense from guilt.] Atti del XV Congresso degli psicologi Italiani, Turin, giungo 1965. In author's *Nuovi Orientamenti nelle Psicoanalisi*

73121 Nota psicoanalitica sul suicidio. [Psychoanalytic note on suicide.] In
       Suicidio e Tentato Suicidio in Italia, Milan: Giuffré 1966
73122 Nuovi Orientamenti nelle Psicoanalisi. [New Trends in Psychoanalysis.]
       Milan: Feltrinelli 1966, 354 p
73123 Osservazioni psicoanalitiche sul suicidio. [Psychoanalytic observations
       on suicide.] Riv Psa 1967, 13:21-36
73124 Osservazioni sulle nuove vedute sul contro-transfert. [Observations on
       new findings in countertransference.] Riv Psa 1962, 8:119-142
73125 (& Berrini, M. E.; Balconi, M.) Perturbazione nei primi rapporti og-
       gettuali e superinbestimento di oggetti inanimati. [Alterations in orig-
       inal object-relation and overcathexis of inanimated objects.] Inf Anorm
       1960, 38(May-June). In author's *Nuovi Orientamenti nelle Psicoanalisi*
73126 Principio del piacere e principio di realtà nel fenomeno "beat." [Pleas-
       ure principle and reality principle in "beat" phenomenon.] Milan:
       Centro Studi Lombardo 1968
73127 Psicanalisi della Guerra. [Psychoanalysis of War.] Milan: Feltrinelli
       Editore 1966, 354 p
73128 Psicanalisi della Guerra Atomica. [Psychoanalysis of the Atomic War.]
       Milan: Edizioni di Comunità 1964, 242 p
       French: Paris: Gallimard 1969
73129 La psicoanalisi e i fondamenti della psicoterapia. [Psychoanalysis and
       foundations of psychotherapy.] Sapere 1963. In author's *Nuovi Ori-
       entamenti nelle Psicoanalisi*
73130 La psychanalyse de la guerre. [The psychoanalysis of war.] RFPsa
       1966, 30(Suppl):135-260; 295-320
73131 Sentimenti di colpa e strutturazione del super-io. [Guilt feelings and
       the structure of the superego.] Riv Psa 1966, 12:277-282
       Sentiments de culpabilité et structuration du surmoi. RFPsa 1967,
       31:1081-1087
73132 Sociologia e psicoanalisi della società di massa. [Sociology and psy-
       choanalysis of mass-society.] Tempi Moderni 1966, 9:137-146
73133 Tecniche e problemi della psicoterapia delle psicosi. [Techniques and
       problems of psychotherapy of psychoses.] Ann Freniat 1961, 3:27-74.
       In author's *Nuovi Orientamenti nelle Psicoanalisi*
73134 La Vita Affettiva Originaria del Bambino. [Primal Affective Life of the
       Infant.] Milan: Feltrinelli 1963, 1966, 238 p
       Spanish: Madrid: Fax 1966
       German: Frankfurt: Fischer 1969

FORRER, GORDON RANDOLPH

73135 Hallucinated headache. Psychomatics 1962, 3:120-128
73136 The psychoanalytic theory of hallucination. Dis nerv Sys 1963, 24:
       721-727
73137 Psychoanalytic theory of placebo. Dis nerv Sys 1964, 25:655-661
73138 Psychosomatic compliance in an infant. Mich Med 1960, 59:1399-1402
73139 Weaning and Human Development. Roslyn Heights, NY: Libra Publ
       1969, 207 p

FORREST, ALISTAIR

73140 Critical notice. M 1965, 38:181-184

FORREST, DAVID V.

73141 New words and neologisms, with a thesaurus of coinages by a schizo-
       phrenic savant. Ps 1969, 32:44-73
73142 Poiesis and the language of schizophrenia. Ps 1965, 28:1-18. In Vetter,
       H. J. *Language Behavior in Schizophrenia*, Springfield, Ill: Thomas
       1968, 153-181

       See Glenn, Michael L.

FORREST, M. S.

See Kroth, J. A.

FORREST, TESS

73143 The combined use of marital and individual therapy in depression.
       Contempo Psa 1969, 6:76-83
73144 The family dynamics of the Oedipus drama. Ops 1967, 37:351-352.
       Contempo Psa 1968, 4(2):138-160
73145 Paternal roots of female character development. Contempo Psa 1966,
       3(1):21-38
73146 The paternal roots of male character development. R 1967, 54:51-68;
       277-295
73147 Treatment of the father in family therapy. Fam Proc 1969, 8:106-118

FORRESTER, ROLAND A. V.

73148 The patient, his doctor, and the psychiatrist. Canad Psychiat Assoc J
       1966, 11:508-511
73149 The untreatable patient. Canad Psychiat Ass J 1968, 13:288-290

FORSTER, EUGENE

See Cattell, James P.

FORSTER, W.

73150 The executive and neurosis. Canad Med Ass J 1963, 88:1244-1246

FORTES, MEYER

S-45788 Malinowski and Freud.
       Abs JLan An Surv Psa 1958, 9:15-16

FORTI, LIDIA

73151 Discussion of Fajrajzen, S. "Alcune considerazione sull' aggressività
       controtransferenziale nel trattamento di pazienti psicotici." Riv Psa
       1966, 12:107
73152 Discussion of Muratori, A. M. "Vicissitudini della relazione simbiotica
       e angosce d'identità." Riv Psa 1967, 13:323
73153 Discussion of Servadio, E. "Esperienze psicofarmacologiche ("psico-
       deliche") come fasi finali dell'analisi didattica." Riv Psa 1966, 12:83-84
73154 Utilizzazione della tecnica psicoanalitica in situazioni diverse durante

l'infanzia. [Use of psychoanalytic technique in various childhood situations.] Riv Psa 1966, 12:100-103. Inf Anorm 1966, 67:28-49

TRANSLATION OF:
Klein, M. [78959]

FORTIN, J.-N.

See Hillel, J.-M.

FORTIN, JOHN N.

S-45791 (& Abse, D. W.) Group psychotherapy with peptic ulcer.
Abs AaSt An Surv Psa 1956, 7:358-359

FORTMANN, HENRICUS MARTINUS MARIA

73155 Als Ziende de Onzienlijke; Een Cultuurpsychologische Studie over de Religieuze Waarneming en de Zogenaamde Religieuze Projectie. [On Seeing and Not Seeing. A Cultural-Psychological Study on Religious Observation, and So-called Religious Projects.] Hilversum: P. Brand 1964

FOSCHI, F.

See Cavazzuti, G. B.

FOSSI, G.

73156 [Psychoanalytic and psychotherapeutic trends in North American psychiatry.] (It) Rass Stud Psichiat 1962, 51:994-1000

FOSTER, RANDALL M.

73157 Intrapsychic and environmental factors in running away from home. Ops 1962, 32:486-491

FOSTER, SUSAN

See Alexander, Franz G.

FOUCAULT, MICHEL

73158 Folie et Déraison; Histoire de la Folie à l'Âge Classique. Paris: Plon 1961, xi + 673 p
Madness and Civilization. A History of Insanity in the Age of Reason. (Tr: Howard, R.) NY: Pantheon 1965; London: Tavistock 1967, xiii + 299 p
Rv J Am Psa Ass 1966, 14:237
73159 Maladie Mentale et Psychologie. [Psychologie and Mental Illness.]
Psychologie und Geisteskrankheit. (Tr: Botond, A.) Frankfurt a.M.: Suhrkamp 1968, 131 p

FOUDRAINE, J.

73160 Schizophrenia and the family. A survey of the literature 1956-1960 on the aetiology of schizophrenia. Acta psychother psychosom 1961, 9:82-110

73161 Symbiotic processes on and around a hospital ward. Psychother Psychosom 1966, 14:237-250

FOUGEROUSSE, C. E., JR.
See Melges, Frederick T.

FOUKS, LÉON
73162 (et al) Les limites de la psychiatrie morale. [The limits of moral psychiatry.] Ann méd-psychol 1967, 125(2):282-286

FOULARD, FRANÇOISE
See Corman, Louis

FOULDS, GRAHAM A.
73163 (& Mayo, P. R.) Neurotic symptoms, intropunitiveness and psychiatric referral. M 1967, 40:151-152
73164 Personality traits and neurotic symptoms and signs. M 1961, 34:263-270

FOULKES, A. P.
73165 Dream pictures in Kafka's writings. Germ Rev 1965, 40:17-30

FOULKES, DAVID
(See also FOULKES, WILLIAM DAVID)
73166 Dreams of the male child: Four case studies. J Child Psychol Psychiat 1967, 8:81-98
73166A Drug research and the meaning of dreams. Exp Med Surg 1969, 27: 39-52
73167 (& Pivik, T.; Ahrens, J. B.; Swanson, E. M.) Effects of "dream deprivation" on dream content: an attempted cross-night replication. JAbP 1968, 73:403-415
73168 (& Spear, P. S.; Symonds, J. D.) Individual differences in mental activity at sleep onset. JAbP 1966, 71:280-286
73169 (& Foulkes, S. H.) Self-concept, dogmatism, and tolerance of trait inconsistency. J Pers soc Psychol 1965, 2:104-110
73170 Theories of dream formation and recent studies of sleep consciousness. Psychol Bull 1964, 62:236-247. In Webb, W. B. *Sleep*, NY: Macmillan 1968, 115-130
73171 (& Larson, J. D.; Swanson, E. M.; Rardin, M.) Two studies of childhood dreaming. Ops 1969, 39:627-643

See Pivik, Terry; Swanson, Ethel M.; Vogel, Gerald W.

FOULKES, SIGMUND HEINZ
73172 The application of group concepts to the treatment of the individual in the group. Top Probl PT 1960, 2:1-56
73173 Discussion of Ivanov, N. V. "A Soviet view of group therapy." Int J Psychiat 1966, 2:214-217

73174 Einige Grundbegriffe der Gruppen-Psychotherapie. [Some basic concepts of group psychotherapy.] Z Psychother med Psychol 1965, 15: 125-130

S-9942 Group analysis in a military neurosis center. In Rosenbaum, M. & Berger, M. *Group Psychotherapy and Group Function,* NY/London: Basic Books 1963, 469-476

S-45797 Group-analytic dynamics with specific reference to psychoanalytic concepts.
    Abs AaSt An Surv Psa 1957, 8:277-278

73175 Group processes and the individual in the therapeutic group. M 1961, 34:23-31
    Abs RDT Q 1961, 30:610

73176 Group psychotherapy: the group-analytic view. A contribution to the discussion. Psychother Psychosom 1965, 13:150-154

S-45800 (& Anthony, E. J.) Group Psychotherapy: The Psychoanalytic Approach.
    Rv Semrad, E. V. & Day, M. J Am Psa Ass 1966, 14:591-618

73177 Illness as a social process. Psychother Psychosom 1966, 14:217-225

73178 On interpretation in group analysis. Int J grp PT 1968, 18:432-434

73179 A patient's view of psychotherapy. Lancet 1965, 1:433

73180 Psychotherapy 1961. M 1961, 34:91-102

73181 Theoretische und praktische Grundlagen der analytischen Gruppenpsychotherapie. [Theoretical and practical bases of psychoanalytic group psychotherapy.] Z Psychother med Psychol 1960, 10:229-237

73182 Therapeutic Group Analysis. NY: IUP; London: Allen & Unwin 1964, 320 p
    Rv Semrad, E. V. & Day, M. J Am Psa Ass 1966, 14:591-618

See Foulkes, David; Kadis, Asya L.

FOULKES, WILLIAM DAVID
(See also FOULKES, DAVID)

73183 Dream reports from different stages of sleep. ASP 1962, 65:14-25
    Abs Rosen, I. C. Q 1963, 32:295-296

73184 The Psychology of Sleep. NY: Scribner 1966, xii + 265 p

FOULKS, EDWARD FRANCIS

73185 Arctic hysteria—a research problem. Penn psychiat Q 1968, 7:50-55

73186 A historical review of the relations between anthropology and psychoanalysis. Penn psychiat Q 1968, 7:34-38

73187 Linguistic and its relation to personality, socialization and psychiatry. Penn psychiat Q 1968, 7:39-42

73188 A method of studying the psychology of the American. Penn psychiat Q 1968, 7:43-49

73189 On hearing profanity. Voices 1968, 4(4):55-60

73190 On teaching child development and psychoanalytic theory: views from nine cultures. Penn Psychiat Q 1969, 9(1):12-72

FOUNTAIN, GERARD

73191 Adolescent into adult: an inquiry. J Am Psa Ass 1961, 9:417-433
Abs FB Q 1962, 31:417-418. SAS RFPsa ℓ962, 26:618
73192 Discussion of Heilbrunn, G. "How "cool" is the beatnik?" Psa Forum
1967 2:44-45
73193 Obituary: Smiley Blanton, M.D. 1882-1966. Q 1967, 36:588

REVIEWS OF:
73194 Bennett, I. Delinquent and Neurotic Children. A Comparative Study.
Q 1961, 30:580-582
73195 The Boy Who Saw True. Q 1964, 33:445-446
73196 Child Study Assoc of Amer (Ed): A Reader for Parents. A Selection of
Creative Literature About Childhood. Q 1964, 33:444-445
73197 Coburn, K. (Ed): The Notebooks of Samuel Taylor Coleridge. Vol. II.
Q 1963, 32:271-273
73198 Symonds, P. M. & Jensen, A. R. From Adolescent to Adult. Q 1961,
30:582-583

FOWLER, GRACE R.

See Brown, Martha M.

FOWLER, RAYMOND D., JR.

73199 The current status of computer interpretation of psychological tests.
P 1969, 125(Suppl 7):21-27

FOWLER, WILLIAM

73200 Dimensions and directions in the development of affecto-cognitive systems. Hum Develpm 1966, 9:18-29

FOX, BEATRICE

73201 (& Di Scipio, W. J.) An exploratory study in the treatment of homosexuality by combining principles from psychoanalytical theory and conditioning: theoretical and methodological considerations. M 1968, 41:
273-282

FOX, EZRA G. BENEDICT

73202 Was General Lee a victim of group psychology? PPR 1961, 48(3):62-68

FOX, HENRY M.

73203 (& Daniels, E. M.; Wermer, H.) Applicants rejected for psychoanalytic
training. J Am Psa Ass 1964, 12:692-716
Abs JLSt Q 1967, 36:467
S-45822 Body image of a photographer.
Abs BEM An Surv Psa 1957, 8:114-115
73204 Discussant: "House Officers." Teach Dyn Psychiat 252-257
73205 Discussion of Sperling, M. "Migraine headaches, altered states of consciousness and accident proneness." Psa Forum 1969, 3:92-93

S-45824 Effects of psychophysiological research on the transference.
Abs HW An Surv Psa 1958, 9:396-398
S-45826 Narcissistic defenses during pregnancy.
Abs EMD An Surv Psa 1958, 9:144-145
73206 Obituary: Felix Deutsch. 1884-1964. J 1964, 45:615-616
73207 Psychiatric consultation in general medical clinics. An experiment in postgraduate education. JAMA 1963, 185:999-1003
73208 Psychiatric residency on a medical service. Arch gen Psychiat 1964, 11:19-23
73209 (& Gifford, S.; Valenstein, A. F.; Murawski, B. J.) Psychophysiology of monozygotic male twins. Arch gen Psychiat 1965, 12:490-500
73210 Some recent trends in psychophysiological research. Med Clin Amer 1960, 44:1341-1355

FOX, J. ROBIN

73211 Sibling incest. Brit J Sociol 1962, 13:128-250
73212 Witchcraft and clanship in Cochiti therapy. In Kiev, A. *Magic, Faith, and Healing,* Glencoe, Ill: Free Pr; London: Collier-Macmillan 1964, 174-200

FOX, M. W.

73213 A sociosexual behavioral abnormality in the dog resembling Oedipus complex in man. J Amer Vet Med Ass 1964, 144:868-869

FOX, PETRONELLA

73214 I'm Glad I Was Analysed. NY/Oxford: Pergamon Pr 1968, xi + 141 p

FOX, RENÉE C.

See Lief, Harold I.

FOX, RONALD E.

73215 (& Goldin, P. C.) The empathic process in psychotherapy: a survey of theory and research. JNMD 1964, 138:323-331
Abs Q 1965, 34:311-312
73216 (& Strupp, H. H.; Lessler, K.) The psychotherapy experience in retrospects: problems and potentials of an approach. In Lesse, S. *An Evaluation of the Results of the Psychotherapies,* Springfield, Ill: Thomas 1968, 38-48

See Ewing, John A.; Schopler, Eric

FOX, RUTH

73217 Alcoholism as a form of acting out. Acting Out 119-128
73218 (Ed) Alcoholism: Behavioral Research, Therapeutic Approaches. NY: Springer 1967, xii + 340 p
73219 The modification of group psychotherapy for alcoholics. J Psa in Groups 1966-67, 2(1):45-49
73220 A multidisciplinary approach to the treatment of alcoholism. Int J Psychiat 1968, 5:34-44; 65-71

73221 Psychiatric aspects of alcoholism. PT 1965, 19:408-416. Proc IV World Cong Psychiat 1966, 1383-1385
73222 Treatment of chronic alcoholism. Curr psychiat Ther 1965, 5:107-111

FOX, VERNON

73223 Psychopathy as viewed by a clinical psychologist. Arch crim Psychodyn 1961, 4:472-479

FOXE, ARTHUR N.

73224 The nature, quality and quiddity of psychopathic behavior. Arch crim Psychodyn 1961, 4:659-699
73225 Special remarks on a dynamic psychiatric view of psychopathy. Arch crim Psychodyn 1961, 4:811-814

FOX-KOLENDA, B. J.

See Freedman, David A.

FOY, JAMES L.

See Zimmer, Herbert

FRAENKEL, ERNEST

73226 L'originalité de René Laforgue. [The originality of Rene Laforgue.] Psyché, Paris 1963, 18 Sp Issue

FRAIBERG, LOUIS BENJAMIN

73227 Discussion of Miller, M. L. "Manic depressive cycles of the poet Shelley." Psa Forum 1966, 1:196-197
73228 Edmund Wilson and psychoanalysis in historical criticism. In author's *Psychoanalysis and American Literary Criticism*, 161-182
73229 Ernst Kris: ego psychology and art. In author's *Psychoanalysis and American Literary Criticism*, 90-119
S-45885 Freud's writings on art. In author's *Psychoanalysis and American Literary Criticism*, 1-46
        Abs JAL An Surv Psa 1956, 7:409-410
73230 Joseph Wood Krutch: Poe's art as an abnormal condition of the nerves. In author's *Psychoanalysis and American Literary Criticism*, 134-144
73231 Kenneth Burke's terminological medium of exchange. In author's *Psychoanalysis and American Literary Criticism*, 183-201
73232 Lionel Trilling's creative extension of Freudian concepts. In author's *Psychoanalysis and American Literary Criticism*, 202-224
73233 Ludwig Lewisohn and the Puritan inhibition of American literature. In author's *Psychoanalysis and American Literary Criticism*, 145-160
73234 New views on art and the creative process in psychoanalytic ego psychology. Lit & Psych 1961, 11:45-55. In Ruitenbeek, H. M. *The Creative Imagination*, Chicago: Quadrangle Books 1965, 223-243
73235 Summary. In author's *Psychoanalysis and American Literary Criticism*, 225-240
73236 Van Wyck Brooks versus Mark Twain versus Samuel Clemens. In author's *Psychoanalysis and American Literary Criticism*, 120-133

FRAIBERG, SELMA

73237 The American reading problem. Commentary 1965, 39(6):56-65

73238 The analysis of an eight-year-old girl with epilepsy. Ch Anal Wk 229-287

73239 An appraisal of group methods in case work agencies. In *Group Methods in the Practice of Casework*, Tulane Univ School of Social Work 1959

73240 A comparison of the analytic method in two stages of a child analysis. J Amer Acad Child Psychiat 1965, 4:387-400

73241 Contributions of psychoanalysis to medical practice with adolescents. Clin Proc Child Hosp DC 1963, 19:45-51

73242 Discussion of McDermott, J. F. "Residential treatment of children. The utilization of transference behavior." J Amer Acad Child Psychiat 1968, 7:169-192

73243 Further considerations of the role of transference in latency. (Read at Am Psa Ass, 4 Dec 1964) Psa St C 1966, 21:213-236

73244 Helping children develop controls. Child Study 1954-55, 32(1):12-19

73245 Homosexual conflicts. Adolescents 78-112

73246 How human bonds are formed. Learning to be human. Current 1968, (93):46-53

73247 Libidinal object constancy and mental representation. Psa St C 1969, 24:9-47

S-45892 The Magic Years. Understanding and Handling the Problems of Early Childhood. NY: Charles Scribners 1965, xiii + 305 p; London: Methuen 1968. Excerpts in Child Study 1959, 36(4):35-37

De Magiske Ar. Copenhagen: Reitzel 1962
Les Années Magique. Paris 1967
Hebrew: Folem 1965
De Magiske Arena. Norsk Forlog 1967
De Magiske Aren. Stockholm: Aldesbok 1965
Rv Harley, M. Q 1961, 30:127-129

73248 Management of disturbed children in foster care. Feelings 1965, Nov-Dec

73249 The mass media: new school house for children. Child Study 1960, 37:3-12. In Endleman, S. *Violence in the Streets*, Chicago: Quadrangle Books 1968, 119-134

73250 (& Freedman, D. A.) Observations on a congenitally blind child with severe ego deviations. (Read at Boston Psa Soc, 26 June, 1963) Abs Eger, W. H. Bull Phila Ass Psa 1963, 13:199-202

73251 On therapy. Child Welfare 1956, 35(6):11-12

73252 The origins of human bonds. Commentary 1967, 44(6):47-57

73253 The origins of identity. In Peters, M. *Self Identity in a World of Uncertainty*, Detroit: Wayne State Univ Pr 1968. Smith Coll Stud soc Wk 1968, 38:79-101

73254 Parallel and divergent patterns in blind and sighted infants. Psa St C 1968, 23:264-300

73255 Psychoanalysis and the education of caseworkers. Smith Coll Stud soc Wk 1961, 31:196-221. In Parad, H. J. & Miller, R. R. *Ego-Oriented Casework*, NY: Fam Serv Ass Amer 1963, 236-258

73256 Repression and repetition in child analysis. (Read at Boston Psa Soc, 22 June 1966)
       Abs Bullard, D. M., Jr. Bull Phila Ass Psa 1967, 17:99-106
73257 (& Siegel, B. L.; Gibson, R.) The role of sound in the search behavior of a blind infant. Psa St C 1966, 21:327-357
73258 The science of thought control. Commentary 1962, 33:420-429
S-45896 Some considerations in the introduction to therapy in puberty.
       Abs An Surv Psa 1955, 6:296-299
73259 (& Freedman, D. A.) Studies in the ego development of the congenitally blind child. Psa St C 1964, 19:113-169
73260 Technical aspects of the analysis of a child with a severe behavior disorder. J Am Psa Ass 1962, 10:338-367. In Haworth, M. R. *Child Psychotherapy,* NY/London: Basic Books 1964, 207-228
       Abs JBi Q 1963, 32:132-133
73261 A therapeutic approach to reactive ego disturbances in children in placement. Ops 1962, 32:18-31
73262 Two modern incest heroes. Partisan Rev 1961, 28:646-661
73263 A voyage to Brobdignag. In author's *The Magic Years.* In Rosenblith, J. F. & Allinsmith, W. *The Causes of Behavior,* Boston: Allyn & Bacon 1962, 226-227

       See McDermott, John F., Jr.

       REVIEWS OF:
73264 Alt, H. Residential Treatment of the Disturbed Child. Basic Principles in Planning and Design of Programs and Facilities. Q 1965, 34:121-123
73265 Blos, P. On Adolescence. A Psychoanalytic Interpretation. Q 1963, 32:432-436

FRAISSE, PAUL

73266 The Psychology of Time. (Tr: Leith, J.) NY/Evanston/London: Harper & Row 1963, vi + 343 p
       Abs J Am Psa Ass 1966, 14:620

       See Nuttin, Joseph; Piaget, Jean

FRAMO, JAMES L.

73267 Rationale and techniques of intensive family therapy. In Boszormenyi-Nagy, I. & Framo, J. L. *Intensive Therapy,* NY: Harper & Row 1965, 143-212
73268 (& Osterweil, J.; Boszormenyi-Nagy, I.) A relationship between threat in the manifest content of dreams and active-passive behavior in psychotics. ASP 1962, 65:41-47
73269 Symposium: Family treatment of schizophrenia. The theory of the technique of family treatment of schizophrenia. Fam Proc 1962, 1:119-131
73270 Systematic research on family dynamics. In Boszormenyi-Nagy, I. & Framo, J. L. *Intensive Therapy,* NY: Harper & Row 1965, 407-462

       See Boszormenyi-Nagy, Ivan

FRANCE, M. L.

See Bright, Florence

FRANCIS, JOHN J.

73271 (Reporter) Masturbation. (Panel: Am Psa Ass, 5 May 1967) J Am Psa Ass 1968, 16:95-112

73272 Passivity and homosexual predisposition in latency boys. Bull Phila Ass Psa 1965, 15:160-174
Abs EFA Q 1967, 36:628

FRANCK, ISAAC

73273 The concept of human nature: a philosophical analysis of the concept of human nature in the writings of G. W. Allport, S. E. Asch, Erich Fromm, A. H. Maslow, and C. R. Rogers. Diss Abstr 1966, 27:1079

FRANCO, DAISY

73274 The child's perception of "the teacher" as compared to his perception of "the mother." J genet Psych 1965, 107:133-141

73275 (& Levine, A.) Psychic reality and psychic structure as predicted from the manifest content of first dreams. Proc 77th Ann Convention Amer Psychological Assoc 1969, 4(2):493-494

FRANK, ALVIN

73276 (& Muslin, H.) The development of Freud's concept of primal repression. (Read at Am Psa Ass, May 1967) Psa St C 1967, 22:55-76

73277 The unrememberable and the unforgettable: passive primal repression. Psa St C 1969, 24:48-77

See Brugger, Thomas C.

FRANK, EDWARD C.

See Gottschalk, Louis A.

FRANK, GEORGE HUGH

73278 A review of research with measures of ego strength derived from the MMPI and the Rorschach. J gen Psychol 1967, 77:183-206

73279 The role of the family in the development of psychopathology. Psychol Bull 1965, 64:191-205

73280 (& Sweetland, A.) A study of the process of psychotherapy: the verbal interaction. J consult Psychol 1962, 26:135-138. In Goldstein, A. P. & Dean, S. J. The Investigation of Psychotherapy, NY: Wiley 1966, 283-287

73281 Why Oedipus. Psychol Rep 1960, 7:287-288

FRANK, GERDA

73282 The enigma of Michelangelo's Pietà Rondanini: a study of mother-loss in childhood. (Read at Chic Inst for Psa, 17 Nov 1965) Am Im 1966, 23:287-315
Abs JWS Q 1967, 36:630

FRANK, H.

See Johnson, R. C.

FRANK, IRVING

73283 (& Powell, M.) (Eds) Psychosomatic Ailments in Childhood and Adolescence. Springfield, Ill: Thomas 1967, xv + 578 p
Rv AL R 1968-69, 55:712-713

FRANK, JAN

73284 Communication and empathy. *Proc of the 3rd World Cong of Psychiat,* Univ Toronto Pr; McGill Univ Pr 1960, 360-366

73285 Indications and contraindications for the application of the "standard technique." J Am Psa Ass 1956, 4:266-284
Abs KOS An Surv Psa 1956, 7:312-313

73286 Nosological and differential diagnostic considerations in schizophrenias and regressophrenias: clinical examples. (Read at Psa Ass NY, 14 Nov 1966) J Hillside Hosp 1968, 17:116-135
Abs Fink, G. Q 1967, 36:638-639

FRANK, JEROME D.

73287 (& Nash, E. H.) Commitment to peace work. A preliminary study of determinants and sustainers of behavior change. Ops 1965, 35:106-119
Abs JMa RFPsa 1966, 30:523

73288 A conceptual framework of psychotherapy. In author's *Persuasion and Healing,* 18-34. With title: Modifications in the assumptive world. In Berenson, B. G. & Carkhuff, R. R. *Sources of Gain in Counseling and Psychotherapy,* NY/Chicago/San Francisco: Holt, Rinehart & Winston 1967, 99-113

73289 Discussion of Eysenck, H. J. "The effects of psychotherapy." Int J Psychiat 1965, 1:150-151

73290 Does psychotherapy work? Int J Psychiat 1967, 3:153-155

S-45908 The dynamics of the psychotherapeutic relationship. In Scheff, T. J. *Mental Illness and Social Processes,* NY: Harper & Row 1967, 168-206

73291 Emotions and the psychotherapeutic process. Curr psychiat Ther 1964, 4:25-34

73292 Evaluation of psychiatric treatment. Compreh Txbk Psychiat 1305-1309

* * * Foreword to Kiev, A. Magic, Faith, and Healing, Glencoe, Ill: Free Pr; London: Collier-Macmillan 1964, vii-xii

73293 Group psychotherapy. Ency Ment Hlth 707-715. *International Encyclopedia of the Social Sciences,* NY: Macmillan; The Free Pr 1968, 185-189

73294 Group psychotherapy with psychiatric outpatients. Group PT 1963, 16:132-140

73295 Group therapy in the mental hospital. Amer Psychiat Ass Mental Hospital Service Monogr Series No. 1, Dec 1955, 1-17. In Rosenbaum, M. & Berger, M. *Group Psychotherapy and Group Function,* NY/London: Basic Books 1963, 453-468

73296 (& Nash, E. H.; Stone, A. R.; Imber, S. D.) Immediate and long-term symptomatic course of psychiatric out-patients. P 1963, 120:429-439

73297 The influence of patients' and therapists' expectations on the outcome of psychotherapy. M 1968, 41:349-356

° ° ° Modifications in the assumptive world. See [73288]

73298 Neurosis. In Conn, H. F. Current Therapy, Phila: Saunders 1963, 535-539; 1964:549-553

73299 Persuasion and Healing: A Comparative Study of Psychotherapy. London: Oxford Univ Pr; Baltimore: Johns Hopkins 1961, xii + 282 p; NY: Schocken Books 1963, 282 p
      Rv Wallerstein, R. S. J Am Psa Ass 1966, 14:183-225

73300 Presidential address: contributions of behavioral scientists toward a world without war. Proc Amer Psychopath Ass 1966, 54:205-218

S-45912 Problems of controls in psychotherapy as exemplified by the psychotherapy research project of the Phipps Psychiatric Clinic. In Goldstein, A. P. & Dean, S. J. The Investigation of Psychotherapy, NY: Wiley 1966, 79-91

73301 The psychiatrist and international affairs. JNMD 1967, 144:479-484

73302 Psychotherapy. Ency Ment Hlth 1728-1736. In Encyclopedia Brittanica Vol. 18, Chicago: Encyclopedia Brittanica 1962, 721-723

73303 Psychotherapy and the assumptive world. In Recent Advances in the Study of Behavior Change, Proceedings of the Academic Assembly on Clinical Psychology, Montreal: McGill Univ Pr 1964, 50-75

73304 Psychotherapy and the sense of community. PT 1966, 20:228-234

73305 Recent American research in psychotherapy. M 1968, 41:5-13

73306 Relief of distress and attitudinal change. Sci Psa 1961, 4:107-121

73307 The role of cognitions in illness and healing. In Strupp, H. H. & Luborsky, L. Research in Psychotherapy, Vol. II, Wash DC: Am Psychiat Ass 1962, 1-12

73308 The role of hope in psychotherapy. Int J Psychiat 1968, 5:383-395

73309 The role of influence in psychotherapy. Ps 1959, 22:17-39. Comtempo PT 17-41

73310 (& Stone, A. R.; Imber, S. D.) The role of non-specific factors in short-term psychotherapy. Austral J Psychol 1966, 18:210-217

73311 Sanity and Survival: Psychological Aspects of War and Peace. NY: Random House 1967, 330 p

73312 Therapy in a group setting. Contempo PT 42-59

73313 Training and therapy. In Bradford, L. P. et al: T-Group Theory and Laboratory Method, NY: Wiley 1964, 442-451

73314 Treatment of the focal symptom: an adaptational approach. PT 1966, 20:564-575

See Hoehn-Saric, Rudolf; Imber, Stanley D.; Nash, Earl H.; Rosen, Harold; Scheidlinger, Saul; Stone, Anthony R.; Truax, Charles D.; Wheat, William D.

REVIEW OF:

73315 Bychowski, G. Evil in Man: The Anatomy of Hate and Violence. Am Im 1968, 25:384-386

FRANK, KLAUS

73316 Indikationen zur psychoanalytischen Gruppentherapie. [Indications for psychoanalytic group psychotherapy.] Psyche 1968, 22:778-785
　　　　Abs J 1969, 50:399

FRANK, LAWRENCE K.

73317 The Conduct of Sex. NY: Grove Pr 1963, 160 p
* * * Introduction to Hanfmann, E. et al: Psychological Counseling in a Small College. Cambridge, Mass: Schenkman 1963, xi + 131 p
73318 On the Importance of Infancy. NY: Random House 1966, 207 p
73319 Toward a projective psychology. J proj Tech 1960, 24:246-253

　　　　See Hartley, Ruth E.

FRANK, LEONARD

73320 Panel on the humanistic approach to sexuality: humanizing and dehumanizing aspects of human sexuality. Dis nerv Sys 1969, 30:781-783

FRANK, MARGARET G. (GRUNEBAUM)
(See also GRUNEBAUM, MARGARET GALDSTON)

73321 (& Zilbach, J.) Current trends in group therapy with children. Int J grp PT 1968, 18:447-460

FRANK, RICHARD L.

73322 Conversion and dissociation. NYSJM 1969, 69:1872-1877
73323 Obituary: Robert Thatcher Morse 1905-1964. J Am Psa Ass 1965, 13:468-470
73324 Some considerations in working with adolescents. Med Clin N Amer 1967, 51:1439-1451

FRANK, THOMAS

　　　　See Kaufman, Irving

FRANKE, JOACHIM

73325 Ausdruck und Konvention: Ein Beitrag zur Erfassung der sozial-kulturellen Bedingtheit des Ausdrucks. [Expression and Convention: a Contribution to the Understanding of Social-Cultural Restriction of Expressions.] Göttingen, W. Germany: C. J. Hogrefe 1967, 185 p

FRANKEL, EDWARD

73326 Theodor Reik and ego psychology. Am Im 1968, 25:32-51
　　　　Abs JWS Q 1969, 38:339

FRANKEL, MARVIN

73327 Morality in psychotherapy. Psychol Today 1967, 1:24-29

FRANKEL, NORMAN

See Rosenfeld, Eva

FRANKEN, R. E.

See Silverstein, Arthur B.

FRANKENSTEIN, CARL

73328 Impaired intelligence: an analysis of essential elements and types. Israel Ann Psychiat 1964, 2:209-227
73329 On transcending professional identity. Israel Ann Psychiat 1963, I: 23-30
73330 The Roots of the Ego: A Phenomenology of Dynamics and of Structure. Baltimore: Williams & Wilkins 1966, xi + 286 p

FRANKIE, G.

See Hetherington, Eileen M.

FRANKIGNOUL, M.

73330A (& Demoulin, C.) [A case of anorexia nervosa.] (Fr) Ann méd-psychol 1969, 2:655-666

FRANKIN, M.

See Abram, Harry S.

FRANKL, LISELOTTE

73331 Development of object constancy: stages in the recognition of the baby's feeding bottle. Discussion of a paper by O. Rubinow and L. Frankl. J humanist Psychol 1964, 4:60-71
73332 (& Hellman, I.) The effect of an early fixation on adolescent detachment from infantile ties. (Read at Phila Ass Psa, 17 April 1963)
    Abs Cowitz, B. Bull Phila Ass Psa 1963, 13:147-148
73333 (& Hellman, I.) The ego's participation in the therapeutic alliance. Symposium on child analysis. (Read at Int Psa Cong, July-Aug 1961) J 1962, 43:333-337. In Haworth, M. R. Child Psychotherapy, NY/London: Basic Books 1964, 229-236
    La participation du moi dans l'alliance thérapeutique. RFPsa 1964, 28:149-158
    Die Ich-Beteilingung am therapeutischen Bündnis. Hbh Kinderpsychother 294-301
    Abs RLG Q 1963, 32:605-606
73334 Die Hampstead Child-Therapy-Clinic, eine psychoanalytische Kinderklinik. [The Hampstead Child Therapy Clinic, a psychoanalytic child clinic.] In Federn, P. & Meng, H. Psychoanalyse und Alltag, 5, Bern/Stuttgart: Hans Huber 1964. Hbh Kinderpsychother 139-151
73335 Self-preservation and the development of accident proneness in children and adolescents. (Read at Cleveland Psa Soc; Phila Ass Psa; Chicago Psa Soc, 26 Mar 1963) Psa St C 1963, 18:464-483
    Abs Kavka, J. Bull Phila Ass Psa 1964, 14:162-166

73336 Some observations on the development and disturbances of integration in childhood. (Read at Los Angeles Inst Psa, May 1960) Psa St C 1961, 16:146-163
73337 (& Hellman, I.) A specific problem in adolescent boys; difficulties in loosening the infantile tie to the mother. (Read at Phila Ass Psa, 17 April 1963) Bull Phila Ass Psa 1963, 13:120-129
    Abs Cowitz, B. Bull Phila Ass Psa 1963, 13:147-148. EFA Q 1965, 34:133
73338 Susceptibility to accidents. A developmental study. M 1965, 38:289-297
    Unfallgefahrdung bei Kindern. Prax Kinderpsychol 1966, 15:161-167
    Abs JCS RFPsa 1967, 31:325

See Hellman, Ilse

FRANKL, VIKTOR EMIL

S-10193 Ärztliche Seelsorge.
    The Doctor and the Soul, From Psychology to Logotherapy. (Tr: Winston, R. & Winston, C.) NY: Knopf 1965, xxi + 289 p
    Rv Am Im 1965, 22:220
73339 Basic concepts of logotherapy. Confin psychiat 1961, 4:99-109. J existent Psychiat 1962, 2:111-118
73340 Beyond self-actualization and self-expression. J existent Psychiat 1960-61, 1:5-20
73341 The concept of man in logotherapy. J existent Psychiat 1965-66, 6:53-58
73342 Dynamics, existence and values. J existent Psychiat 1961-62, 2:5-16
73343 Existential dynamics and neurotic escapisms. J existent Psychiat 1963-64, 4:27-42
73344 Existenzanalyse und Logotherapie. Acta psychother psychosom 1960, 8:171-187
    Existential analysis and logotherapy. Surgo, Glasgow 1960, 26(2):65-71
    Abs SLe RFPsa 1961, 25:156
73345 Fragments from the logotherapeutic treatment of four cases. In Burton, A. *Modern Psychotherapeutic Practice*, Palo Alto, Calif: Sci & Behav Books 1965, 361-379
73346 Logotherapie und ihre klinische Anwendung. [Logotherapy and its clinical application.] WMW 1967, 117:1139-1143
* * * Man's Search for Meaning: An Introduction to Logotherapy.
    See [10199]
73347 "Nothing but ———" On reductionism & nihilism. Encounter 1969, 33(5):51-61
S-10199 Ein Psychologe erlebt das Konzentrationslager.
    From Death-Camp to Existentialism: A Psychiatrist's Path to a New Therapy. (Tr: Lasch, I.) (Pref: Allport, G. W.) Boston: Beacon Pr 1959, 111 p. With Title: Man's Search for Meaning: An Introduction to Logotherapy. (Tr: Lasch, I.) (Pref: Allport, G. W.) Boston: Beacon Pr 1962, 1963, 142 p
    Rv Coltrera, J. T. J Am Psa Ass 1962, 10:166-215

73348 Psychotherapy and Existentialism; Selected Papers on Logotherapy. NY: Washington Square Pr 1967, xii + 242 p

73349 The significance of meaning for health. In Belgum, D. *Religion and Medicine,* Ames, Iowa: Iowa State Univ Pr 1967, 177-185

73350 The Will to Meaning; Foundations and Applications of Logotherapy. NY: World Pub Co 1969, xi + 179 p

FRANKLIN, ALFRED WHITE

73351 Leontine Young and "Tess of the D'Urbervilles"—some thoughts on illegitimacy. Brit med J 1966(1):789-791

FRANKLIN, GIRARD

73352 (& Nottage, W.) Psychoanalytic treatment of severely disturbed juvenile delinquents in a therapy group. Int J grp PT 1969, 19:165-175

FRANKLIN, PAUL

73353 Family therapy of psychotics. Psa 1969, 29:50-58

See Ackerman, Nathan W.

FRANKLIN, R. T. D.

73354 School phobia. Brit med J 1960, 2:1238

FRANKS, CYRIL M.

73355 Alcohol, alcoholism and conditioning: a review of the literature and some theoretical considerations. In Eysenck, H. J. *Behaviour Therapy and the Neuroses,* Oxford, NY: Pergamon Pr 1960, 278-302

FRANSELLA, FAY

See Beech, Harold R.

FRANTZ, K. E.

73355A The analyst's own involvement with the process and the patient. J anal Psych 1969, 14:143-151

FRANZ, H.

See Prill, H. J.

FRANZ, MARIE-LUISE VON

73356 Conclusion: science and the unconscious. In Jung, C. G. et al; *Man and His Symbols,* NY: Doubleday 1964, 304-310

73357 The process of individuation. In Jung, C. G. et al: *Man and His Symbols,* NY: Doubleday 1964, 158-229

FRANZBLAU, ABRAHAM NORMAN

73358 Contribution of psychiatry to religious education. J relig Educ 1956, 51:335-338

73359 The contribution of psychiatry to the principal's task. Jewish Teacher 1955, May

73360 Conversion: psychologically speaking. In Eichhorn, D. M. *Conversion to Judaism: A History and Analysis*, NY: Ktav Publ 1965, 189-207

73361 Distinctive functions of psychotherapy and pastoral counseling. Arch gen Psychiat 1960, 3:583-589

73362 The dynamics of mixed marriages. J Central Conf Amer Rabbis 1954, Oct:21-25

* * *   Foreword to Spiro, J. D. A Time to Mourn, NY: Block Publ 1967, xi-xvi

73363 Functions of a chaplain in a mental hospital. Psychiat Q Suppl 1954, 28(2):181-191

73364 Highlights of the Franzblau-Bemporad papers. NATE News, UAHC 1967, Feb:4-5

73365 Judaism and psychoanalysis. Dimension 1967, 1(4):15-20; 30-31

73366 The ministry of counseling. J pastoral Care 1955, 60(3):137-144

73367 Physicians, clergymen, and the hospitalized patient. JAMA 1967, 200: 355-356

73368 A psychiatrist looks at "The Birthday Party" (Pinter). Letter. Sat Rev 1967, 50(Oct 28):46-47

73369 A psychiatrist looks at "The Homecoming" (Pinter). Sat Rev 1967, 50(April 8):58

73370 A psychiatrist looks at "Tiny Alice." Sat Rev 1965, 48(Jan 3):39

73371 Psychiatry in the classroom. Proceedings, Hebrew Union Coll Summer Inst 1947, June-July:1-11

73372 Psychotherapy and ministry. In *Psychiatry and Religion, International Symposia*, NY: MD Publ 1956, 47-51

73373 Rabbi or psychiatrist? J Central Conf Amer Rabbis 1953, Oct:46-50

S-45969 The Road to Sexual Maturity.
        Liebe und Reife. Heidenheim: Erich Hofman Verlag 1958

73374 (& Franzblau, R. N.) A Sane and Happy Life: A Family Guide. NY: Harcourt, Brace & World 1963

See Hulse, Wilfred C.; Kaufman, M. Ralph

REVIEW OF:

73375 Saul, L. J. Fidelity and Infidelity—And What Makes or Breaks a Marriage. Q 1969, 38:655-656

FRANZBLAU, ROSE N.

See Franzblau, Abraham N.

FRAS, I.

See Bernstein, N. R.

FRASER, ALAN W.

73376 A relationship between transitional objects and preconscious mental processes. In Solnit, A. J. & Provence, S. *Modern Perspectives in Child Development*, NY: IUP 1963, 144-161

ABSTRACT OF:

73377 Garma, A. Peptic Ulcer and Psychoanalysis. An Surv Psa 1958, 9:198-200

REVIEW OF:

73378 Muensterberger, W. & Axelrad, S. (Eds): The Psychoanalytic Study of Society. Vol. IV. Q 1968, 37:603-605

FRAZIER, SHERVERT H.

73379 (& Carr, A. C.) Introduction to Psychopathology. NY: Macmillan 1964, 168 p

73380 (& Carr, A. C.) Phobic reaction. Compreh Txbk Psychiat 899-911

73381 Principles of psychiatric emergency management. Curr psychiat Ther 1969, 9:106-115

73382 Problems in brief psychotherapy. Proc IV World Cong Psychiat 1966, 442-445

73383 Psychosomatic illness: a body language form of acting out. Acting Out 129-134

See Beckett, Peter G. S.; Woods, Joan B.

FREDE, M. C.

73383A (& Gautney, D. B.; Baxter, J. C.) Relationships between body image boundary and interaction patterns on the MAPS test. J consult Psychol 1968, 32:575-578

FREDENBURGH, F. A.

73383B An apologia for the hippie generation. MH 1968, 52:341-348

FREDERICK, CALVIN J.

73384 (Ed) The Future of Psychotherapy. (International Psychiatry Clinics 1969, Vol. 6, No. 3) Boston: Little, Brown 1969, xii + 415 p

73385 Future training in psychotherapy. Int Psychiat Clin 1969, 6(3):379-401

FREDMAN, SHIRLEY

See Goodrich, D. Wells

FREED, DONALD

73386 Freud and Stanislavsky. New Directions in the Performing Arts. (Foreword: Friedman, L. J.) (Introd: Stockwell, G.) NY/Washington/Hollywood: Vantage Pr 1964, viii + 128 p
        Rv HS Am Im 1965, 22:221. Seidenberg, R. 1966, 35:141-142

FREED, ELLEN S.

See Thomas, Caroline B.

FREED, HERBERT

73387 Combined use of psychotherapy and physical therapy. Int Psychiat Clin 1964, 1:483-491

73388   Comments on the present status of child analysis. Dis nerv Sys 1961, 22:404-407
73389   The current status of the tranquilizers and of child analysis in child psychiatry. Dis nerv Sys 1961, 22:434-437
73390   Psychoanalysis. Prog Neurol Psychiat 1960, 15:474-493; 1961, 16:486-503; 1962, 17:485-506; 1963, 18:579-603; 1964, 19:575-588; 1965, 20:682-703; 1966, 21:553-566; 1967, 22:476-491; 1968, 23:514-531; 1969, 24:463-477

FREEDMAN, ABRAHAM

73391   A biological correlation with Freud's theory of death instinct. Bull Phila Ass Psa 1967, 17:86-92
S-45973 Countertransference abuse of analytic rules.
           Abs AS An Surv Psa 1956, 7:350
S-45975 The feeling of nostalgia and its relationship to phobia.
           Abs AHM An Surv Psa 1956, 7:153-154
S-45976 (& Slap, J. W.) A functional classification of identification.
           Abs EFA Q 1961, 30:600
73392   Obituary. In memoriam: Robert Waelder. Bull Phila Ass Psa 1968, 18:10-11
73393   The role of the psychoanalyst in training psychiatric residents. Bull Phila Ass Psa 1966, 16:82-88
           Abs EFA Q 1968, 37:158

ABSTRACTS OF:
73394   Khan, M. M. R. Foreskin fetishism and its relation to ego pathology in a male homosexual. Bull Phila Ass Psa 1965, 15:50-53
73395   Saul, L. J. Technic and Practice of Psychoanalysis. An Surv Psa 1958, 9:368-380

REVIEWS OF:
73396   Boszormenyi-Nagi, I. & Framo, J. L. (Eds): Intensive Family Therapy. J 1968, 49:103-107; Q 1968, 37:140-141
73397   Levi, L. Stress Sources, Management, and Prevention. Bull Phila Ass Psa 1968, 18:204
73398   Lidz, T. The Person, His Development Through the Life Cycle. Bull Phila Ass Psa 1969, 19:223-225
73399   Socarides, C. W. The Overt Homosexual. Bull Phila Ass Psa 1969, 19:51-54

FREEDMAN, ALFRED M.

73400   Beyond "action for mental health." Ops 1963, 33:799-805
73401   (& Kaplan, H. I.) (Eds) Comprehensive Textbook of Psychiatry. Baltimore: Williams & Wilkins 1967, xxv + 1666 p
73402   (& Kaplan, H. I.) Conduct disorders and neurotic trait reactions. Compreh Txbk Psychiat 1384-1386
73403   The contribution of the school to mental illness. In Merin, J. H. & Nagler, S. H. The Etiology of the Neuroses, Palo Alto, Calif: Sci & Behav Books 1966, 95-109

73404 (& Sharoff, R. L.) Crucial factors in the treatment of narcotic addiction. PT 1965, 19:397-407
       Abs Auth Rev Psicoanál 1966, 23:72

73405 Discussion of Bender, L. et al: "Treatment of autistic schizophrenic children with LSD-25 and UML-491." Recent Adv biol Psychiat 1962, 4:177-179

73406 Discussion of Esman, A. H. "Drug use by adolescents: some valuative and technical implications." Psa Forum 1967, 2:345-346

73407 (& Deutsch, M.; Deutsch, C. P.) Effects of hydroxyzine hydrochloride on the reaction time performance of schizophrenic children. Arch gen Psychiat 1960, 3:153-159

73408 Mental health research and training. (Interviewed by Perkins, M. E.) In Ziskind, R. Viewpoint on Mental Health, NY: NYC Comm Ment Hlth Board 1967, 359-363

73409 (& Sager, C. J.; Rabiner, E. L.; Brotman, R. E.) Response of adult heroin addicts to a total therapeutic program. Ops 1963, 33:890-899

73410 (& Wilson, E. A.) Sociopathic personality disorders. III: Addiction and alcoholism. Compreh Txbk Psychiat 1429-1432

73411 Tertiary prevention. Compreh Txbk Psychiat 1548-1551

See Kaplan, Harold I.

FREEDMAN, DANIEL X.

73412 Commentary: psychopharmacology in relation to psychotherapy. In Shlien, J. M. et al: Research in Psychotherapy, Vol. III, Wash DC: Am Psychiat Ass 1968, 541-544

73413 On the use and abuse of LSD. Arch gen Psychiat 1968, 18:330-347

See Bowers, Malcolm B., Jr.; Redlich, Frederick C.; Schiff, Sheldon K.

FREEDMAN, DAVID A.

73414 (& Fox-Kolenda, B. J.; Margileth, D. A.; Miller, D. H.) The development of the use of sound as a guide to affective and cognitive behavior —a two-phase process. Child Developm 1969, 40:1099-1105

73415 The influence of congenital sensory deprivation on later development. Psychosomatics 1968, 9:272-277

73416 Observations on the early ego development in the absence of vision. Med Rec Ann 1966, 59:490-496

73417 (& Adatto, C. P.) On the precipitation of seizures in an adolescent boy. PSM 1968, 30:437-447

73418 (& Brown, S. L.) On the role of coenesthetic stimulation in the development of psychic structure. Q 1968, 37:418-438

73419 On women who hate their husbands. Ps 1961, 24:228-237

73420 Psychiatry and the law. Newsletter, Louisiana Psychiat Assoc 1965, 4(8)

73421 The role of early mother/child relations in the etiology of some cases of mental retardation. In Farrell, G. Advances in Mental Science I: Congenital Mental Retardation, Austin: Univ Texas Pr 1969, 245-261

See Adatto, Carl P.; Fraiberg, Selma

REVIEW OF:
73422 Harms, E. (Ed): Somatic and Psychiatric Aspects of Childhood Allergies. Q 1964, 33:593-594

FREEDMAN, JONATHAN LEWIS

73423 (& Wallington, S. A.; Bless, E.) Compliance without pressure: the effect of guilt. J Pers soc Psychol 1967, 7:117-124
73424 Involvement, discrepancy, and change. ASP 1964, 69:290-295

FREEDMAN, LAWRENCE ZELIC

73425 Childbirth while conscious: perspectives and communication. JNMD 1963, 137:372-379
73426 (& Lasswell, H. D.) Cooperation for research in psychiatry and law. P 1961, 117:692-694
73427 Forensic psychiatry. P 1964, 120:692-694; 1965, 121:708-710. Compreh Txbk Psychiat 1588-1604
73428 Psychiatry and the law. Prog Neurol Psychiat 1962, 17:421-424; 1963, 18:516-519; 1964, 19:513-516; 1965, 20:608-611; 1966, 21:487-491; 1967, 22:411-414; 1968, 23:445-447; 1969, 24:403-406
73429 Psychoanalysis, delinquency, and the law. Mod Psa 642-662
73430 Sexual, aggressive, and acquisitive deviates. JNMD 1961, 132:44-49
         Abs Powelson, H. Q 1961, 30:606
73431 (& Rosvold, H. E.) Sexual, aggressive and anxious behavior in the laboratory macaque. JNMD 1962, 134:18-27
73432 Social and legal considerations of psychiatric treatment in a general hospital. In Kaufman, M. R. *The Psychiatric Unit in a General Hospital,* NY: IUP 1965, 269-280; 281-304

See Berman, Leo H.; Kaswan, Jacques

FREEDMAN, NORBERT

See Hankoff, Leon D.

FREEDMAN, SANFORD J.

73433 (& Grunebaum, H. U.; Stare, F. A.; Greenblatt, M.) Imagery in sensory deprivation. In West, L. J. *Hallucinations,* NY: Grune & Stratton 1962, 108-117
73434 (& Grunebaum, H. U.; Greenblatt, M.) Perceptual and cognitive changes in sensory deprivation. In Solomon, P. et al: *Sensory Deprivation,* Cambridge, Mass: Harvard Univ Pr 1961, 58-71

See Grunebaum, Henry U.

FREEMAN, DANIEL M. A.

73435 Adolescent crisis of the Kiowa-Apache Indian male. In Brody, E. B. *Minority Group Adolescents in the United States,* Baltimore: Williams & Wilkins 1968, 157-204

FREEMAN, DAVID F.

See Boswell, John J., Jr.

FREEMAN, DEREK

73436 Shaman and incubus. Psa St Soc 1967, 4:315-343
73437 Thunder, blood, and the nicknaming of God's creatures. Q 1968, 37: 353-399
73438 Totem and taboo: a reappraisal. Psa St Soc 1967, 4:9-33

FREEMAN, EDITH H.

73439 (& Feingold, B. F.; Schlesinger, K.; Gorman, F. J.) Psychological variables in allergic disorders: a review. PSM 1964, 26:543-575

FREEMAN, HUGH

73440 The current status of human behavior. Comprehen Psychiat 1965, 6:355-368

FREEMAN, LUCY

73441 The Abortionist. NY: Doubleday 1962, 216 p
73442 The Available Woman. NY: Dell 1968, 175 p
73443 Chastise Me With Scorpions. NY: G. P. Putnams 1963, 283 p
73444 (& Hulse, W. C.) Children Who Kill. NY: Berkley Publ Corp 1962, 160 p
73445 The Cry for Love: Understanding and Overcoming Human Depression. NY: Macmillan 1969, x + 245 p
73446 (& Grennwald, H.) Emotional Maturity in Love and Marriage. NY: Harper & Bros 1961, xiv + 255 p
     Rv Lashinsky, B. K. PPR 1961, 48(4):141
73447 Exploring the Mind of Man: Sigmund Freud and the Age of Psychology. NY: Grosset & Dunlap 1968
73448 Farewell to Fear. NY: G. P. Putnams 1969, 379 p
73449 Fight against fears. In Nunokawa, W. D. *Readings in Abnormal Psychology: Human Values and Abnormal Behavior*, Chicago, Ill: Scott, Foresman 1965, 102-114
73450 (& Harris, S.) Lords of Hell. NY: Dell 1967, 225 p
73451 (Ed) The Mind: 12 Studies that Unlocked the Secrets of the Unconscious. NY: Crowell 1967, viii + 143 p
73452 Why People Act That Way. NY: Crowell 1965, 246 p
73453 (& Theodores, M.) (Eds) The Why Report: A Book of 45 Interviews with Psychiatrists, Psychoanalysts, and Psychologists. Purchase, NY: A. Bernhard 1964, xxxiv + 602 p

See Hartogs, Renatus; Rhodes, Laura; Spotnitz, Hyman

FREEMAN, PAUL K.

73454 An Introduction to Sigmund Freud, M.D. and Psychoanalysis. Englewood Cliffs, N.J.: Prentice-Hall 1965, 1 Vol.

FREEMAN, ROGER D.

73455 Child psychiatry. Prog Neurol Psychiat 1968, 23:454-468; 1969, 24: 414-423

73456 Controversy over "patterning" as a treatment for brain damage in children. JAMA 1967, 202:385-388
73457 Drug effects on learning in children. J spec Educ 1966, 1:17-44
73458 Emotional reactions of handicapped children. Rehabilitation Literature 1967, 28:274-282. Ann Prog child Psychiat 1968, 379-395
73459 The home visit in child psychiatry. J Amer Acad Child Psychiat 1967, 6:276-294. Ann Prog child Psychiat 1968, 419-436
73460 Psychopharmacology and the retarded child. In Menolascino, F. *Psychiatric Approaches to Mental Retardation in Childhood*, NY: Basic Books 1969
73461 Review of drug effects on learning in children. Proceedings of the 5th Annual Conference of the Association for Children with Learning Disabilities, Academic Therapy Publ 1968
73462 Special education and the electroencephalogram: marriage of convenience. J special Educ 1967, 2:61-73

FREEMAN, THOMAS A.

S-46006 Aspects of defence in neurosis and psychosis.
        Abs PCR RFPsa 1961, 25:287
S-46007 Aspects of perception in psychoanalysis and experimental psychology.
        Abs Frisch, A. An Surv Psa 1958, 9:89
73463 Clinical and theoretical notes on chronic schizophrenia. M 1960, 33:33-43
        Abs IH Q 1961, 30:152-153
S-46009 Clinical and theoretical observations on male homosexuality. PT Pervers 409-436
        Abs An Surv Psa 1955, 6:223-225
73464 A clinical approach to research in schizophrenia. M 1966, 39:275-280. New Zealand med J 1967, 66:722-725
73465 The clinical contribution to the study of the origins of schizophrenia. In Romano, J. *The Origins of Schizophrenia*, Amsterdam: Excerpta Medica Found 1967, 239-248
73466 The concept of narcissism in schizophrenic states. J 1963, 44:293-303
        Abs EVN Q 1965, 34:617-618
73467 Group psychotherapy in a mental hospital. New Zealand med J 1967, 66:726-730
73467A The learning component in the dynamic psychotherapeutic situation. Int Psychiat Clin 1969, 6:186-200
73468 Narcissism and defensive processes in schizophrenic states. J 1962, 43:415-425
        Abs EVN Q 1965, 34:307
73469 Obituary: David M. Kissen. M 1968, 41:93
73470 On the psychopathology of repetitive phenomena. Brit J Psychiat 1968, 114:1107-1014
73471 On the psychopathology of schizophrenia. JMS 1960, 106:925-937
73472 (& Gathercole, C. E.) Perseveration—the clinical symptoms—in chronic schizophrenia and organic dementia. Brit J Psychiat 1966, 112:27-32
73473 Postgraduate education in psychiatry. Lancet 1964, (2):304-305
73474 Problems of communication with psychotic patients. J Societal Issues 1965

73475 The psychiatrist and the training of nurses. New Zealand med J 1967, 66:758-762
73476 Psychoanalysis and the psychotherapy of psychoses. Anglo-German med Rev 1965, 2:780-786
73477 The psychoanalyst in the mental hospital. M 1960, 33:279-282
73478 A psycho-analytic approach to the diagnosis of schizophrenic reactions. JMS 1962, 108:286-299
73479 Psychoanalytic aspects of diffuse cerebral degenerations. Dyn Psychiat 1969, 2:83-93; Abs (Ger), 93-95
73480 A psychoanalytic critique of behaviour therapy. M 1968, 41:53-59
73481 The psycho-analytic observation of chronic schizophrenic reactions. In Richter, D. et al: *Aspects of Psychiatric Research,* London: Oxford Univ Pr 1962, 294-314
73482 Psycho-analytical psychotherapy in the National Health Service. Brit J Psychiat 1967, 113:321-327
73483 Psychopathology of the Psychoses. London: Tavistock Publ; NY: IUP 1969, vii + 215 p
73484 The role of learning in the dynamic therapeutic situation. In Ciba Symposium on "Research in Psychotherapy," London: Churchill 1968
73485 The role of psychoanalysis in the mental hospital. New Zealand med J 1966, 65:972-975
73486 Some aspects of pathological narcissism. J Am Psa Ass 1964, 12:540-561
     Abs JLSt Q 1967, 36:133. CG RFPsa 1968, 32:177
S-46012 (& McGhie, A.; Cameron, J. L.) The state of the ego in chronic schizophrenia.
     Abs CK An Surv Psa 1957, 8:146
73487 (& Cameron, J. L.; McGhie, A.) Studies on Psychosis. Descriptive, Psychoanalytic, and Psychological Aspects. London: Tavistock 1965; NY: IUP 1966, vii + 245 p
     Rv Richter, P. Q 1968, 37:612-615
73488 Symptomatology, diagnosis and clinical course. Schiz Rev Syn 1969, 311-342
73489 (& Kissen, D. M.) Teaching general practitioners psychosomatic medicine and psychotherapy by group discussions. Rev Méd psychosom 1964

See Cameron, John L.; Chapman, James; Davie, James M.

REVIEW OF:
73490 Jackson, D. D. (Ed): The Etiology of Schizophrenia. J 1962, 43:182-184

FREEMAN, WALTER

73491 The Psychiatrist; Personalities and Patterns. NY: Grune & Stratton 1968, x + 293 p
73492 Psychiatrists who kill themselves. P 1967, 124:846-847; 1270

FREEMANTLE, ANNE
REVIEW OF:
73493 Zilboorg, G. Psychoanalysis and Religion. Q 1962, 31:551-553

FREI, GEBHARD

73494   Obituary: C. G. Jung. (Ger) Arch Psicol Neurol Psichiat 1961, 22: 617-622

FREIJO BALSEBRE, ENRIQUE

73495   El Psicoanálisis de Freud y la Psicología de la Moral. [The Psycho-analysis of Freud and the Psychology of Morality.] Madrid: Editorial Razón y Fe 1966, 331 p

FREIMAN, GERALD

ABSTRACT OF:
73496   Muensterberger, W. Elements of creative imagination. Q 1961, 30: 476-479

FREISINGER, LEONA A.

TRANSLATION OF:
Freud, S. [10355, 10370]

FREIXA SANTFELIU, F.

73497   [Studies on the fundamentals of psychoanalysis. (Problems in Psy-choses.)] (Sp) An Med, Espec 1964, 50:175-181

FREMAN, EDITH MARIE HENRY

73498   Effects of aggressive expression after frustration of performance: a test of the catharsis hypothesis. Diss Abstr 1962, 23(3):1073

FRENCH, EDWARD L.

73499   (& Scott, J. C.) Child in the Shadows: A Manual for Parents of Re-tarded Children. Phila: Lippincott 1960, 156 p. With title: How You Can Help Your Retarded Child: A Manual for Parents. Phila: Lippin-cott 1967, 190 p

* * *   (& Scott, J. C.) How You Can Help Your Retarded Child: A Manual for Parents. See: [73499]

73500   Therapeutic education. Theory and practice in a residential treatment center for emotionally disturbed adolescents. In Hellmuth, J. *Educa-tion Therapy, Vol. I,* Seattle: Special Child Publ 1966, 425-437

FRENCH, JACQUELINE

73501   Dependency behavior and feeling of rejection in aggressive and non-aggressive boys. Diss Abstr 1964, 25:3108

FRENCH, THOMAS M.

73502   Analysis of the dream censorship. In Daniels, G. E. *New Perspectives in Psychoanalysis, Sandor Rado Lectures 1957-1963,* NY: Grune & Stratton 1965, 1-19

S-46182 Art and science in psychoanalysis. Psa Clin Inter 200-219
  Abs AL An Surv Psa 1958, 9:325-327
73503 Cognitive structure of a case of ulcerative colitis. (Read at Chicago Psa Soc, 23 Nov 1965)
  Abs Sadow, L. Bull Phila Ass Psa 1966, 16:222-226
73504 Discussion of Bion, W. R. "Notes on memory and desire." Psa Forum 1967, 2:274
73505 (& Fromm, E.) Dream Interpretation. A New Approach. NY/London: Basic Books 1964, vii + 224 p
  Abs J Am Psa Ass 1967, 15:218. Rv Radomisli, M. R 1964, 51:688-689. Joffe, W. G. J 1965, 46:532-533. Noble, D. Q 1965, 34:282-286
73506 A focal conflict view. In Kramer, M. *Dream Psychology and the New Biology of Dreaming*, Springfield, Ill: Thomas 1969
73507 (& Wheeler, D. R.) Hope and repudiation of hope in psycho-analytic therapy. (Read at Chicago Psa Soc, Nov 1958) J 1963, 44:304-316. In Daniels, G. E. *New Perspectives in Psychoanalysis, Sandor Rado Lectures 1957-1963*, NY: Grune & Stratton 1965, 20-44
  Abs EVN Q 1965, 34:618
S-46189 The Integration of Behavior, Vol. III: The Reintegrative Process in a Psychoanalytic Treatment.
  Abs Miller, M. L. An Surv Psa 1958, 9:382-385
° ° ° Introduction to Alexander, F. G. *The Scope of Psychoanalysis, 1921-1961*, NY: Basic Books 1961, v-xv
73508 Obituary: Franz Alexander (1891-1964). Beh Sci 1964, 9:98-100. PSM 1964, 26:203-206
S-686 Psychogenic Factors in Bronchial Asthma.
  Psicología y Asma Bronquial. Foreword: Grinberg, L.) Buenos Aires: Ed. Hormé 1966

See Alexander, Franz; Fromm, Erika

REVIEW OF:
73509 Storr, A. The Integrity of the Personality. Q 1963, 32:101-103

FRENKEL, HERBERT M.

73510 Fundamentals of the Frenkel Mirror Image Projective Technique. (Monograph) NY: Psychol Libr Publ 1969, 196 p
73511 (& Frenkel, R. E.) World Peace Via Satellite Communications: With a Psychoanalytic Examination of Its Aspects and Prospects. NY: Telecommunications Res Assoc 1965, xi + 166 p

FRENKEL, RICHARD E.

73512 Psychotherapeutic reconstruction of the traumatic amnesic period by the Mirror Image Projective Technique. J existent Psychiat 1964-65, 5:77-96

See Frenkel, Herbert M.

FRESTON, M.

See Gordon, Jesse E.

FREUD, ANNA

73513   Acting out. (Read at Int Psa Cong, July 1967) J 1968, 49:165-170
        Abs LHR Q 1969, 38:668

S-46236 Adolescence. In Weinreb, J. *Recent Developments in Psychoanalytic
        Child Therapy*, NY: IUP 1960, 1-24. In Rosenblith, J. F. & Allinsmith,
        W. *The Causes of Behavior*, Boston: Allyn & Bacon 1966, 328-334. In
        part in Goldstein, J. & Katz, J. *The Family and the Law*, NY: Fr Press
        1965, 907-908
            Probleme der Pubertät. Psyche 1960, 14:1-24
            Abs JA An Surv Psa 1958, 9:284-286

73514   Adolescence as a developmental disturbance. In Caplan, G. & Lebovici,
        S. *Adolescence*, NY/London: Basic Books 1969, 5-10

73515   Anna Freud doctoral award address. J Am Psa Ass 1967, 15:833-840

* * *   Answering teachers' question. See [10340]

73516   Assessment of childhood disturbances. Psa St C 1962, 17:149-158. In
        Miller, E. *Foundations of Child Psychiatry*, Oxford/NY: Pergamon Pr
        1968, 43-50. In part in author's *Normality and Pathology in Childhood*,
        140-147
            Abs SLe RFPsa 1964, 28:811

73517   Assessment of normality and pathology: clinical problems of young
        children. In *The Proceedings of the 18th Child Guidance Inter-Clinic
        Conference*, London: Nat'l Assoc Mental Hlth 1962, 22-29

S-10299 Über bestimmte Schwierigkeiten der Elternbeziehung in der Vor-
        pubertät.
            On certain difficulties in the preadolescent's relation to his parents.
        Writ AFr 4:95-106

S-10301 Certain types and stages of social maladjustment. Writ AFr 4:75-94
            Über bestimmte Phasen und Typen der Dissozialität und Verwahr-
        losung. In Bolterauer, L. *Aus der Werkstatt des erziehungsberaters*
        (Aichhorn-Festschrift), Vienna: Verlag für Jugend und Volk 1960,
        195-206

73518   Child and adult analysis; a summary of a seminar held in Chicago,
        December 19, 1966. Chicago, Ill: Chicago Institute for Psa

73519   The child guidance clinic as a center of prophylaxis and enlighten-
        ment. In Weinreb, J. *Recent Developments in Psychoanalytic Child
        Therapy*, NY: IUP 1960, 25-38

S-46238 Child observation and prediction of development: a memorial lecture
        in honor of Ernst Kris. In part in Goldstein, J. & Katz, J. *The Family
        and the Law*, NY: Fr Press 1965, 953-959; 1002; 1017. In part in
        Katz, J.; Goldstein, J. & Dershowitz, A. M. *Psychoanalysis, Psychiatry
        and the Law*, NY: Fr Press 1967, 399-402
            Abs Steinberg, S. An Surv Psa 1958, 9:230-233

S-46239 Clinical studies in psychoanalysis. Research project of the Hampstead
        Child-Therapy Clinic.
            Abs RTh J 1961, 42:469-470

S-46240 Comments on Joyce Robertson's "A mother's observations on the ton-
        sillectomy of her four-year-old daughter." Writ AFr 4:293-301

73520   Comments on trauma. In Furst, S. S. *Psychic Trauma*, NY: Basic Books
        1967, 235-245

73521   The concept of developmental lines. Psa St C 1963, 18:245-265. In author's *Normality and Pathology in Childhood*, 62-87

73522   The concept of the rejecting mother. Child Welfare 1955, 34(3):1-4. In Anthony, E. J. & Benedek, T. *Parenthood: Its Psychology and Psychopathology*, Boston: Little, Brown 1968. Writ AFr 4:586-602. Excerpts in Goldstein, J. & Katz, J. *The Family and the Law*, NY: Fr Press 1965, 1059, 1133. With title: Safeguarding the emotional health of our children. In *National Conference of Social Work, Casework Papers 1954*, NY: Family Service Association of America 1955, 5-17

S-10303 Concerning child-analysis.
      Erzieher und Neurose. [Educator and neurosis.] In Bittner, G. & Rehm, W. *Psychoanalyse und Erziehung*, Bern/Stuttgart; Hans Huber 1964

S-10305 The contribution of psychoanalysis to genetic psychology. Writ AFr 4:107-142

73523   Defense mechanisms. In *Encyclopaedia Britannica*, 1961 edition, Chicago/London/Toronto: Wm. Benton

73524   Diagnostic skills and their growth in psycho-analysis. J 1965, 46:31-38. In author's *Normality and Pathology of Childhood*, 10-24
      Abs EVN Q 1967, 36:312-313

73525   Difficulties in the Path of Psychoanalysis. (Read at NY Psa Soc, 16 Apr 1968) NY: IUP 1969, 83 p
      Abs Shapiro, S. H. Bull Phila Ass Psa 1968, 18:214-216. Barre, A. Q 1969, 38:676-679

73526   Discussion of Greenacre and Winnicott: "The theory of the parent-infant relationship. Further remarks." J 1962, 43:240-242

73527   Eine Diskussion mit Rene Spitz. [A discussion with Rene Spitz.] Psyche 1967, 21:1-3; 4-15

73528   Dr. Herman Nunberg: an appreciation. (Read at Herman Nunberg Lecture, celebrating his 80th birthday, April 1964) J 1969, 50:135-138

73529   The ego's defensive operations considered as an object of analysis. In Haworth, M. R. *Child Psychotherapy*, NY/London: Basic Books 1964, 193-200

S-10307 Einführung in die Psychanalyse für Pädagogen.
      Initiation à la Psychanalyse pour Éducateurs. (Tr: Delalande, C.) (Rev & Introd: Hahn, G.) Toulouse: E. Privat 1968, 118 p

S-10310 Emotional and instinctual development. Writ AFr 4:458-497

73530   The emotional and social development of young children. In Report of the 9th World Assembly, London, 16-21 July 1962 (World Organisation for Early Childhood Education, O. M. E. P.)

S-10312 The establishment of feeding habits. Writ AFr 4:442-457

S-10313 (& Dann, S.) An experiment in group upbringing. Writ AFr 4:163-229
      Gemeinschaftsleben im frühen Kindesalter. Jb Psa 2:201-248

73531   Expert knowledge for the average mother. Writ AFr 4:528-544

73532   Film review: *John, Seventeen Months: Nine Days in a Residential Nursery* by James and Joyce Robertson. Psa St C 1969, 24:138-143

* * *   Foreword. Dev Mind vii

* * *   Foreword and conclusion to Bergmann, T. & Freud, A. *Children in the Hospital*

* * * Foreword to Aichhorn, A. *Delinquency and Child Guidance: Selected Papers*, NY: IUP; London: Bailey Bros 1964

S-10313A Foreword to Buxhaum, E. *Your Child Makes Sense*. Writ AFr 4:610-613

* * * Foreword to Eddy, H. P. *Sex and the College Student*, NY: Atheneum 1966

* * * Foreword to Milner, M. *On Not Being Able to Paint*, (2nd ed) NY: IUP 1967, 184 p

* * * Foreword to Nagera, H. (Ed) *Basic Psychoanalytic Concepts on the Libido Theory*, London: George Allen & Unwin; NY: Basic Books 1969, 9-11

* * * Foreword to Nagera, H. (Ed) *Basic Psychoanalytic Concepts on the Theory of Dreams*, NY: Basic Books; London: George Allen & Unwin 1969, 6-8

* * * Foreword to Nagera (Perez), H. *Early Childhood Disturbances, the Infantile Neurosis, and the Adulthood Disturbances*, NY: IUP 1966, 9-10

* * * Foreword to Nagera, H. *Vincent Van Gogh: A Psychological Study*, NY: IUP; London: Allen & Unwin 1967

* * * Foreword to Ruben, M. et al: *Parent Guidance in the Nursery School*, NY: IUP 1960, 7-8

73533 Four contributions to the psychoanalytic study of the child. (Read at joint meeting of NY Psa Soc, Phila Ass Psa, Western New England Psa Soc and their Institutes, 15-18 Sept 1960)

   Abs Sachs, D. M. Bull Phila Ass Psa 1961, 11:80-87

S-10315 Freedom from want in early education. Writ AFr 4:425-441

* * * Geleitworte. [Preface.] Jb Psa 1960, 1:vii

73534 Hampstead child therapy clinic; a summary of a conference with Miss Anna Freud on September 26, 1957 held at Dr. Marianne Kris' apartment, 135 Central Park West, New York City. (multilithographed) Chicago, Ill: Chicago Institute for Psa, 7 p

73535 Heinz Hartmann: A tribute. J Am Psa Ass 1965, 13:195-196

73536 Hommage à Marie Bonaparte. [Tribute to Marie Bonaparte.] RFPsa 1965, 29:1-2

S-10318 Das Ich und die Abwehrmechanismen.

   The Ego and the Mechanisms of Defense. (Rev ed) *The Writings of Anna Freud*, Vol. 2, NY: IUP 1966

73537 The ideal psychoanalytic institute: a utopia. (Read at Chicago Inst for Psa, 21 Dec 1966) (multilithographed) Chicago, Ill: Chicago Institute for Psa, 11 p

73538 Die Identifizierung mit dem Angreifer. [Identification with the aggressor.] From author's *Das Ich und die Abwehrmechanism*. Hbh Kinderpsychother 287-294

73539 Indications and counterindications for child analysis. (Read at Amer Ass Child Psa, 21 Apr 1968) Psa St C 1968, 23:37-46

   Abs Shapiro, S. H. Bull Phila Ass Psa 1968, 18:217-220

S-10322 Indications for child analysis. Writ AFr 4:3-38

   Indikationsstellung in der Kinderanalyse. Psyche 1967, 21:233-253

S-46237 Instinctual drives and their bearing on human behavior. Writ AFr 4:498-527

73540 Interactions between nursery school and child guidance clinic. J child Psychotherapy 1966, 1:40-44

73541 Introduction to Balint, A. *The Psycho-Analysis of the Nursery Years,* London: Routledge & Kegan Paul 1953. Writ Afr 4:642-644

73542 James Robertson's *A Two-Year-Old Goes to Hospital.* Film Review. Writ AFr 4:280-292

73543 Links between Hartmann's ego psychology and the child analyst's thinking. Psa—Gen Psychol 16-27

73544 A list of the publications of Anna Freud. BMC 1963, 27:154-157

S-46247 About losing and being lost. Psa St C 1967, 22:9-19. Writ Afr 4:302-316

Über Verlieren und Verlorengehen. In van der Leeuw, P. J. et al: *Hoofdstukken uit de Hedendaagse Psychoanalyse,* Arnhem: Van Loghum Slaterus 1967, 91-100

73545 (& Nagera, H.; Freud, W. E.) Metapsychological assessment of the adult personality. The adult profile. Psa St C 1965, 20:10-41

73546 Ein metapsychologisches Entwicklungsbild des Kindes. [A metapsychological profile of the child's development.] In author's *Wege und Irrwege in der Kinderentwicklung* 130-138 Hbh Kinderpsychother 210-216

S-10327 The mutual influences in the development of the ego and id: introduction to the discussion. Writ AFr 4:230-244

73547 Normality and Pathology in Childhood. Assessments of Development. NY: IUP 1965, London: Hogarth 1966, xii + 272 p

Wege und Irrwege in der Kinderentwicklung. Bern: Huber 1968, 234 p

Abs J Am Psa Ass 1967, 15:213. Rv Hartmann, H. J 1967, 48:97-101. Kestenberg, J. Q 1967, 36:98-100. Mead, M. J 1967, 48:102-107. Wolman, B. B. Am Im 1966, 23:86-87

S-10328 Notes on aggression. In Flugel, J. C. *Proceedings of the International Conference on Child Psychiatry,* London: H. K. Lewis; NY: Columbia Univ Pr 1949, 16-23. Writ AFr 4:60-74. Excerpts in Goldstein, J. & Katz, J. *The Family and the Law,* NY: Free Pr 1965, 983-984

S-10329 Nursery school education: its uses and dangers. Writ AFr 4:545-559

S-10330 Obituary: August Aichhorn: July 27, 1878-October 17, 1949. Writ AFr 4:625-638

73548 Obituary: Willie Hoffer, M.D., Ph. D. Psa St C 1968, 23:7-9. J 1969, 50:265-266

73549 Obituary: James Strachey: 1887-1967. J 1969, 50:131-132

S-10331 Observations on child development. Writ AFr 4:143-162. Excerpts in Goldstein, J. & Katz, J. *The Family and the Law,* NY: Free Pr 1965, 1060

73550 Obsessional neurosis: a summary of psycho-analytic views as presented at the congress. (Read at Int Psa Cong, July 1965) J 1966, 47:116-122

Resumé presenté en conclusion du Congrès d'Amsterdam 1965. RFPsa 1967, 31:511-524

Neurosis obsesiva: resumen de los puntos de vista psicoanalíticos presentados ante el Congreso. (Tr: Díaz Portillo, I.) Cuad Psa 1967, 3:281-293

Abs EVN Q 1968, 37:308-309

73551   On the difficulties of communicating with children—the lesser children in chambers. Jean Drew. Cindy. In Goldstein, J. & Katz, J. *The Family and the Law*, NY: Fr Press 1965, 261-264, 960-962, 1051-1053. In part in Katz, J.; Goldstein, J. & Dershowitz, A. M. *Psychoanalysis, Psychiatry and the Law*, NY: Fr Press 1967, 417-419

73552   Pediatricians' questions and answers. In MacKeith, R. & Sandler, J. *Psychosomatic Aspects of Paediatrics*, London: Pergamon Pr 1961, 27-41

* * *   Preface to Bolland, J. et al: *The Hampstead Psychoanalytic Index: A Study of the Psychoanalytic Case Material of a Two-Year-Old Child*, NY: IUP 1965; London: Hogarth 1967

* * *   Preface to Freeman, T. et al: *Chronic Schizophrenia*, NY: IUP 1958, vii-viii

* * *   Preface to Freud, A. & Burlingham, D. *Infants Without Families* (new edition), London: Allen & Unwin 1964

* * *   Preface to Freud, S. *Gesammelte Werke*, Vol. 18. London: Int Psa Pr 1956

* * *   Preface to *Sigmund Freud: Psychoanalysis and Faith*, NY: Basic Books 1963

* * *   Preface to Spitz, R. A. & Cobliner, W. G. *The First Year of Life: A Psychoanalytic Study of Normal and Deviant Development of Object Relations*, NY: IUP 1965

       Preface to Spitz, R. A. *Die Entstehung der ersten Objektbeziehungen*, Stuttgart: Klett 1957

S-10332 Probleme der Lehranalyse.

       The problem of training analysis. Writ AFr 4:407-421

S-46252 Problems of infantile neurosis: contribution to the discussion. Writ AFr 4:327-355

S-46253 Problems of technique in adult analysis. Writ AFr 4:377-406

S-46254 Psychoanalysis and education. Writ AFr 4:317-326

S-10335 The psychoanalytic study of infantile feeding disturbances. Writ AFr 4:39-59

S-10336 The Psychoanalytical Treatment of Children; Lectures and Essays. (Tr: Proctor-Gregg, N.) NY: Schocken Books 1964, xiii + 114 p

       Rv Kramer, S. Q 1961, 30:271-275

73553   Die psychoanalytische Psychologie der kindheit und ihre Quellen. [The psychoanalytic psychology of childhood and its sources.] Psyche 1968, 22:405-409

73554   Regression as a principle in mental development. BMC 1963, 27:126-139. In author's *Normality and Pathology in Childhood* 93-107. In part in Goldstein, J. & Katz, J. *The Family and the Law*, NY: Fr Press 1965, 903-904. In part in Katz, J.; Goldstein, J. & Dershowitz, A. M. *Psychoanalysis, Psychiatry and the Law*, NY: Fr Press 1967, 351-353

       Abs HD Q 1964, 33:604-605

73555   Remarks on the fiftieth birthday of the International Journal of Psycho-Analysis. J 1969, 50:473-474

73555A Residential vs. foster care. In Witmer, H. L. *On Rearing Infants and Young Children in Institutions*. Wash DC: US Dept HEW, Children's Bureau Research Reports No. 1, 47-55

S-10339 The role of bodily illness in the mental life of children. Writ AFr 4:260-279
Die Rolle der körperlichen Krankheit im Seelenleben des Kindes. In Bittner, G. & Schmid-Cords, E. *Erziehung in früher Kindheit,* Munich: Piper 1968, 235-247. Hbh Kinderpsychother 827-837

73556 The role of regression in mental development. In Solnit, A. J. & Provence, S. A. *Modern Perspectives in Child Development,* NY: IUP 1963, 97-106

S-10340 The role of the teacher. With title: "Answering teachers' question." Writ AFr 4:560-568

* * * Safeguarding the emotional health of our children. See [73522]

73557 A 75th birthday tribute to Heinz Hartmann. J 1969, 50:721

73558 A short history of child analysis. (Read at Am Ass for Ch Psa, 9 Apr 1966) Psa St C 1966, 21:7-14

S-10321 The significance of the evolution of psychoanalytic child psychology. Writ AFr 4:614-624

73559 The sleeping difficulties of the young child: an outline. Writ AFr 4:605-609
Abs Bull Am Psa Ass 1952, 7:124-126

73560 Some aspects of the relation between neurotic pathology in childhood and in adult life. (Read at Chicago Psa Soc, 20 Dec 1966)
Abs Beigler, J. S. Bull Phila Ass Psa 1967, 17:111-114

73561 Some recent developments in child-analysis. Psychother Psychosom 1965, 13:36-46
Algunos adelantos recientes en psicoanalisis del niño. Cuad Psa 1965, 1:225-235

S-46256 Some remarks on infant observation. Writ AFr 4:569-585

73562 Some thoughts about the place of psychoanalytic theory in the training of psychiatrists. BMC 1966, 30:225-234

73563 Studies in passivity. Writ AFr 4:245-259
Abs (in part) J 1949, 30:145. Bull Am Psa Ass 1951, 7:117-118. Auth J 1952, 33:265

73564 Twentieth anniversary celebration of the Topeka Psychoanalytic Institute. Observations. BMC 1963, 27:148-149

73565 Visiting children—the child. Nursing Times 1952, 48(29 Mar):320. Writ AFr 4:639-641

73566 Why children go wrong. In *The Enrichment of Childhood,* Nursery School Association of Great Britain and Northern Ireland 1960, 23-24

S-46258 The widening scope of indications for psychoanalysis: discussion. Writ AFr 4:356-376

73567 The Writings of Anna Freud. Vol. IV. Indications for Child Analysis and Other Papers 1945-1956. NY: IUP 1968, xv + 690 p

S-10345 Zur Theorie der Kinderanalyse.
On the theory of analysis of children. Heirs Freud 129-143

See Arlow, Jacob A.; Bergmann, Thesi

FREUD, ERNST L.

* * * Editor of *Sigmund Freud—Arnold Zweig Briefwechsel.*
* * * (& Freud, L.) Editors of *Sigmund Freud Briefe 1873-1939.*

* * *   (& Meng, H.) Editors of *Sigmund Freud—Oskar Pfister: Briefe, 1909-1939.*

73568   (Ed) Jugendbriefe Sigmund Freuds. Neue Rundschau 1969, 80(4): 678-693
        Some early unpublished letters to Freud. J 1969, 50:419

* * *   Preface to *Sigmund Freud: Psychoanalysis and Faith,* NY: Basic Books 1963, 7

        See Abraham, Hilda C.; Meng, Heinrich

FREUD, LUCIE

See Freud, Ernst L.

FREUD, MARTIN

S-46261 Sigmund Freud: Man and Father
        Sigmund Freud: Mi Padre. Buenos Aires: Hormé 1966
        Abs Malev, M. An Surv Psa 1958, 9:3-5. Rv Carpinacci, J. A. Rev Psicoanál 1967, 24:210-213

FREUD, SIGMUND*

NON-PSYCHOLOGICAL WRITINGS

S-10350 Akute multiple Neuritis der spinalen und Hirnnerven.
[1886a]   Abs (Engl) Auth (Tr:JS) SE 3:236

S-10351 Über die Allgemeinwirkung des Cocaïns.
[1885b]   On the general effect of cocaine. (Tr: Edminster, S. A.) In author's *The Cocaine Papers,* 45-49

S-10352 Zur Auffassung der Aphasien. Eine kritische Studie.
[1891b]   Abs (Engl) Auth (Tr:JS) SE 3:240-241

73569   (Unsigned) The bacillus of syphilis. Medical News, Phila 1884, 45 (14 Dec):673-674. In Grinstein, A. "Freud's first publications in America," J Am Psa Ass 1971, 19:257-258

S-10353 Über den Bau der Nervenfasern und Nervenzellen beim Flusskrebs.
[1882a]   Abs (Eng) Auth (Tr:JS) SE 3:230

S-10354 Beitrag zur Kenntniss der Cocawirkung.
[1885a]   Contribution to the knowledge of the effect of cocaine. (Tr: Potash, R. S.) In author's *The Cocaine Papers* 35-41
           Abs (Eng) Auth (Tr:JS) SE 3:234

---

* As with the references for other authors, the citations given here include references published after the completion of this Index, Volumes 1, 5, and 6. Readers are urged to check these volumes for full bibliographic data for references with S-numbers. See also *Appendix* at the end of this volume which provides an alphabetical list of Freud's works according to their English titles together with their reference number in this Index and the *Standard Edition* reference.

S-10355 Bemerkungen über Cocaïnsucht und Cocaïnfurcht, mit Beziehung auf
[1887d] einen Vortrag W. W. Hammonds.
Craving for and fear of cocaine. (Tr: Freisinger, L. A.) In author's
The Cocaine Papers, 57-62
Abs (Eng) Auth (Tr:JS) SE 3:239

S-10356 Beobachtung einer hochgradien Hemianästhesie bei einem hysteri-
[1886d] schen Manne.
Observation of a severe case of hemi-anaesthesia in a hysterical
male. SE 1:25-31
Abs (Eng) Auth (Tr:JS) SE 3:239

S-10357 Beobachtungen über Gestaltung und feineren Bau der als Hoden
[1877b] beschriebenen Lappenorgane der Aals.
Abs (Eng) Auth (Tr:JS) SE 3:227

S-10358 Über die Bernhardt'sche Sensibilitätsstörungen am Oberschenkel.
[1895e] Abs (Eng) Auth (Tr:JS) SE 3:253

S-10359 (& Darkschewitsch, L.) Über die Beziehung des Strickkörpers zum
[1886b] Hinterstrang und Hinterstrangskern nebst Bemerkungen über zwei
Felder der Oblongata.
Abs (Eng) Auth (Tr:JS) SE 3:237

S-10360 Cerebrale Kinderlähmung.
[1898c]
[1899b] Infantile cerebral paralysis. (Tr: Russin, L. A.) Coral Gables,
[1900b] Fla: Univ Miami Pr 1968

S-10362 Über Coca.
[1884e] On coca. (Tr: Edminster, S. A.) In author's *The Cocaine Papers*,
1-28
Coca. (Abbrev, tr: Pollak, S.) In author's *The Cocaine Papers*, 29-31
Abs (Eng) Auth (Tr:JS) SE 3:233

73570 (Unsigned) Cocaine. Medical News, Phila 1884, 45(1 Nov):502. In
Grinstein, A. "Freud's first publications in America." J Am Psa Ass
1971, 19:255-256

73571 The Cocaine Papers. (Ed: Donoghue, A. K. & Hillman, J.) Vienna/
Zurich: Dunquin Pr 1963, 62 p. Includes [10351, 10354, 10355,
10362, 10370]
Rv Schusdek, A. Q 1967, 36:94-95

S-10365 Contributions to Villaret, A. *Handwörterbuch der gesamten Medizin.*
[1888c] Hysterie.
[1891c] Hysteria. SE 1:41-57
Hysteroepilepsie.
Hystero-epilepsy. SE 1:58-59

S-10366 Les diplégies cérébrales infantiles.
[1893e] Abs (Eng) Auth (Tr:JS) SE 3:247

S-10367 Ein Fall von Hirnblutung mit indirekten basalen Herdsymptomen
[1884a] bei Skorbut.
Abs (Eng) Auth (Tr:JS) SE 3:232

S-10368   Ein Fall von Muskelatrophie mit ausgebreiteten Sensibilitätsstörungen
[1885c]   (Syringomyelie).
          Abs (Eng) Auth (Tr:JS) SE 3:235

S-10369   Über familiäre Formen von cerebralen Diplegien.
[1893d]   Abs (Eng) Auth (Tr:JS) SE 3:247

S-10370   Gutachten über das Parke Cocaïn.
[1885e]   Opinion on Parke's cocaine. (Tr:Freisinger, L. A.) In author's *The
          Cocaine Papers*, 53

S-10371   Über Hemianopsie im frühesten Kindesalter.
[1885e]   Abs (Eng) Auth (Tr:JS) SE 3:240

S-10372   Die infantile Cerebrallähmung.
[1897a]   Abs (Eng) Auth (Tr:JS) SE 3:256

S-10374   Zur Kenntniss der cerebralen Diplegien des Kindesalters (im An-
[1893b]   schluss an die Little'sche Krankheit.
          Abs (Eng) Auth (Tr:JS) SE 3:245-247

S-10375   Zur Kenntnis der Olivenzwischenschicht.
[1885d]   Abs (Eng) Auth (Tr:JS) SE 3:234

S-10376   (& Rie, O.) Klinische Studie über die halbseitige Cerebrallähmung
[1891a]   der Kinder.
          Abs (Eng) Auth (Tr:JS) SE 3:241-242

S-10380   Eine neue Methode zum Studium des Faserverlauges im Central-
[1884b]   nervensystem.
          Abs (Eng) Auth (Tr:JS) SE 3:231

S-10382   Notiz über eine Methode zur anatomischen Präparation des Nerven-
[1879a]   systems.
          Abs (Eng) Auth (Tr:JS) SE 3:229

73572   (Unsigned) Spina's Studies on the Bacillus of Tuberculosis. Medical
          News, Phila 1883, 42(7 Apr):401-402. In Grinstein, A. "Freud's first
          publications in America," J Am Psa Ass 1971, 19:243-246

S-10383   Über Spinalganglien und Rückenmark des Petromyzon.
[1878a]   Abs (Eng) Auth (Tr:JS) SE 3:228-229

S-10384   Die Struktur der Elemente des Nervensystems.
[1884f]   Abs (Eng) Auth (Tr:JS) SE 3:230

S-10385   Über ein Symptom, das häufig die Enuresis nocturna der Kinder
[1893g]   begleitet.
          Abs(Eng) Auth (Tr:JS) SE 3:243

S-10386   Über den Ursprung der hinteren Nervenwurzeln im Rückenmarke
[1887a]   von Ammocoetes.
          Abs (Eng) Auth (Tr:JS) SE 3:228

S-10387   Über den Ursprung des Nervus acusticus.
[1886c]   Abs (Eng) Auth (Tr:JS) SE 3:238

PSYCHOLOGICAL WRITINGS AND LETTERS

S-10388   Abriss der Psychoanalyse.
[1940a]   An Outline of Psychoanalysis. SE 23:144-215
(1938)

S-10389   Die Abwehr-Neuropsychosen.
[1894a]   Abs (Eng) Auth (Tr:JS) SE 3:249

S-10391   Über die allgemeinste Erniedrigung des Liebeslebens.
[1912d]   Considérations sur le plus commun des ravalements de la vie
           amoureuse. (Tr: Laplanche, J.) In *La Vie Sexuelle*, Paris: PUF 1969,
           55-65

73573   (& Albrecht, A.) American interview (1909). R 1968, 55:333-341

S-10392   Analyse der Phobie eines funfjährigen Knaben.
[1909b]   Analyse d'une phobie d'un petit garcon de cinq ans (le petit
           Hans). (Tr: Bonaparte, M.) RFPsa 1928, 2:411-438. In *Cinq Psy-
           chanalyses*, Paris: Denoël & Steele 1936, 111-228. Paris: PUF 1954,
           1970, 93-198

S-10393   Aus den Anfängen der Psychoanalyse; Briefe an Wilhelm Fliess,
[1950a]   Abhandlungen und Notizen aus den Jahren 1887-1902.
(1887-   In part: Extracts from the Fliess letters (Drafts A-N; Letters 14,
1902)   18, 21, 22, 46, 50, 52, 55-57, 59-61, 64, 66, 67, 69-73, 75, 79, 84, 97,
           101, 102, 105) SE 1:177-280.
               In part: Cuatros cartas a Wilhelm Fliess. [Four letters to Wilhelm
           Fliess (Letters 69-72).] (Tr: Rosenthal, L.) Rev Psicoanál 1955,
           12:404-414

S-10394   Ansprache an die Mitglieder des Vereins B'nai B'rith.
[1941e]   Lettre aux membres de l'Association B'nai B'rith. (Tr: Berman, A.
(1926)   & Grossein, J. P.) In *Correspondances 1873-1939*, Paris: Gallimard
           1966, 397-399

73574   Anti-semitism in England. [To the editor of *Time and Tide.*] SE
           23:301
               Lettre à "Time and Tide." (Tr: Berman, A. & Grossein, J. P.) In
           Correspondances 1873-1939, Paris: Gallimard 1966, 497-498

S-10397   Zur Ätiologie der Hysterie.
[1896c]   Abs (Eng) Auth (Tr: JS) SE 3:254

S-10403   Beiträge zur Psychologie des Liebeslebens.
               Contributions à la psychologie de la vie amoureuse. In *La Vie Sex-
           uelle*, Paris: PUF 1969, 47-80

° ° °   Beobachtung einer hochgradigen Hemianästhesie bei einem hysteri-
           schen Manne. See [10356]

S-10407   Über die Berechtigung von Neurasthenie einen bestimmten Symptom-
[1895b]   enkomplex als "Angstneurose" abzutrenne.
(1894)   Abs (Eng) Auth (Tr:JS) SE 3:251

S-10408   Bericht über meine mit Universitäts-Jubiläums Reisestipendium un-
[1956a]   ternommene Studienreise nach Paris und Berlin. In Gicklhorn, J. &

(1886)   Gicklhorn, R. *Sigmund Freuds akademische Laufbahn im Lichte der Dokumente*, Vienna: Urban & Schwarzenberg 1960, 82.
           Report on my studies in Paris and Berlin: carried out with the assistance of a travelling bursary granted from the University Jubilee Fund (October, 1885–End of March 1886). SE 1:5-15
           Abs SLP An Surv Psa 1956, 7:29

S-10409   Über einen besonderen Typus der Objektwahl beim Manne.
[1910h]   D'un type particulier de choix objectal chez l'homme. (Tr: Laplanche, J.) In *La Vie Sexuelle*, Paris: PUF 1969, 47-55

S-10411   Brief an den Bürgermeister der Stadt Příbor, 25 Oct 1931.
[1931e]   Au maire de Příbor. (Tr: Berman, A. & Grossein, J. P.) In *Correspondances 1873-1939*, Paris: Gallimard 1966, 444-445

S-10413   Brief an Dr. Alfons Paquet, 3 Aug 1930.
[1930d]   Lettre au Dr. A. Paquet. (Tr: Berman, A. & Grossein, J. P.) In *Correspondances 1873-1939*, Paris: Gallimard 1966, 434

S-10415   Brief an Dr. Wittels
[1924g]   Extrait d'une lettre à Wittels. (Tr: Herbert) In Wittels, F. *Freud,*
(1923)   *L'Homme, La Doctrine, L'Ecole.* Paris: Alcan 1929. (Tr: Berman A. & Grossein, J. B.) In *Correspondances 1873-1939*, Paris: Gallimard 1966, 376-378

S-10417   Brief an Josef Breuer.
[1941d]
(1892)   Letter to Josef Breuer. SE 1:147-148

S-10419   Brief an Maxim Leroy über eines Traum des Cartesius.
[1929b]   Some dreams of Descartes. SE 21:203-204
           Lettre à Maxime Leroy sur "Quelques rêves de Descartes." In Leroy, M. *Descartes, L'Homme au masque*, Paris: Rieder 1930, 89-90.

S-10419A   Brief an Richard Sterba.
[1936b]   Preface to Richard Sterba's *Dictionary of Psycho-Analysis* SE 22:
(1932)   253

S-10420   Brief an Romain Rolland: Eine Erinnerungsstörungen auf der Akrop-
[1936a]   olis.
           A disturbance of memory on the Acropolis. An open letter to Romain Rolland on the occasion of his seventieth birthday. SE 22: 239-248.
           Un trouble de mémoire sur l'Acropole (Lettre à Romain Rolland). (Tr: Robert, M.) *L'Ephémère*, Paris: Editions de la Fondation Maeght 1967 (2:April): 3-13
           Un disturbo della memoria sull' Acropolis. Riv Psa 1966, 12:61-67

° ° °   Briefe an W. Fliess, Abhandlungen und Notizen. See [10393]

73575   Briefe 1873-1939. [Letters: 1873-1939.] (Ed: Freud, E. L.) Frankfurt: S. Fischer 1960, 511 p. 2nd edition (Ed: Freud, E. L. & Freud, L.) Frankfurt: S. Fischer 1968, 538 p. See [S-46284]
           Rv Illing, H. A. Q 1969, 38:126-127

73576   Briefwechsel. Von Sigmund Freud und Arnold Zweig. (Ed: Freud,
            E. L.) Frankfurt: S. Fischer 1968, 202 p
            Letters of Sigmund Freud and Arnold Zweig. (Ed: Freud, E. L.)
            (Tr: Robson-Scott, E. & Robson-Scott, W.) NY: Harcourt, Brace &
            World 1970, ix + 190 p
            Rv Illing, H. A. Q 1969, 38:643-644

S-10423   Charcot.
[1893f]   Abs (Eng) Auth (Tr:JS) SE 3:243

° ° °   The Complete Introductory Lectures on Psychoanalysis. (Tr, ed:
            JS) NY: Norton 1966, 690 p. Includes [10547, 10629]
                Abs J Am Psa Ass 1967, 15:729

° ° °   Contributions to the Neue Freie Presse. SE 9:253-256. Includes
            [10570, 10675, 10676]

S-10426   Über Deckerinnerung.
[1899a]   Les souvenirs écrans. (Tr: Anzieu, D. & Berman, A.) In Anzieu.
            D. L'auto-analyse, Paris: PUF 1959, 277-286

S-10427   Der Dichter und das Phantasieren.
[1908a]   The relation of the poet to daydreaming. In Dulany, D. E., Jr. et
            al: Contributions to Modern Psychology, NY: Oxford Univ Pr 1964,
            196-204.

73577   Dr. Reik und Kurpfuschereifrage. Neue Freie Presse 1926, (18 July):
[1926]   12
                Dr. Reik and the problem of quackery. A letter to the Neue Freie
            Presse. (Tr:JS) SE 21:247-248

S-10431   Dostojewski und die Vatertötung.
[1928b]   Dostoevsky and parricide. In Ruitenbeek, H. M. The Literary
            Imagination., NY: Quadrangle Books 1965, 329-348.
                Dostoiewski et le parricide. (Tr: Beucler, A.) In Dostoiewska,
            A. G. Dostoiewski, Paris: Gallimard 1930

° ° °   Drafts A-N (From the Fliess letters). See [S-10393]

S-46264   (& Oppenheim, D. E.) Dreams in Folklore.
                Abs JFr An Surv Psa 1958, 9:222-223

S-10432   Drei Abhandlungen zur Sexualtheorie.
[1905d]   Three Essays on the Theory of Sexuality. (Tr:JS) NY: Basic Books
            1962, 130 p
                Trois Essais sur la Theorie de la Sexualité. (Tr: Reverchon; rev.
            tr.: Laplanche & Pontalis) Paris: Gallimard 1968
                Rv Romagnoli, M. Q 1963, 32:444-445

S-10434   Zur Einführung des Narzissmus.
[1914c]   Pour introduire la narcissisme. (Tr: Laplanche, J.) In La Vie
            Sexuelle, Paris: PUF 1969, 81-105
                Introduzione al narcisismo. Riv Psa 1962, 8:155-175

S-10438   Einige psychische Folgen des anatomischen Geschlechtsunterschieds.
[1925j]   Quelques conséquences psychologiques de la différence anatom-
            ique entre les sexes. (Tr: Berger, D.) In La Vie Sexuelle, Paris: PUF
            1969, 123-132

S-10440 Die endliche und die unendliche Analyse.
[1937c]   Analysis terminable and interminable. SE 23:209-253

73578   Entwurf einer Psychologie. In author's *Aus den Anfängen der Psy-*
[1895]   *choanalyse.*
(1950)   Project for a scientific psychology. SE 1:281-397
         Esquisse d'une psychologie scientifique. (Tr: Berman, A.) In *La Naissance de la Psychanalyse,* Paris: PUF 1956, 307-386

S-10441 Entwurf zu einem Brief an Thomas Mann, Nov 29, 1936
[1941g]   Draft of a letter to Thomas Mann [on Napoleon]. In Jones 3:462-
(1936)   464. In *Letters of Sigmund Freud* [46284] 432-434.

S-10455 Ergebnisse, Ideen, Probleme.
[1941f]   Findings, ideas, problems. SE 23:299-300
(1938)   Résultats idées, problèms. (Tr: Briand, J. P. & Green, A.) L'Arc, Aix-en-Provence 1968, 34:67-70

* * *   Escritos de Sigmund Freud en primera version castellana. [First Spanish translation of some of Freud's writings.] Rev Psicoanál 1955, 12:115-182. See [10493, 10567, 10584]

* * *   Extracts from the Fliess papers. See [S-10393]

S-10448 Ein Fall von hypnotischer Heilung: nebst Bemerkungen über die
[1892–   Entstehung hysterischer Symptome durch den "Gegenwillen."
3b]   A case of successful treatment by hypnotism: with some remarks on the origin of hysterical symptoms through "counterwill." SE 1:117-128
         Abs (Eng) Auth (Tr:JS) SE 242-243

S-10451 Die Feinheit einer Fehlhandlung.
[1935b]   The subtleties of a faulty action. SE 22:233-235

S-10453 Fetischismus.
[1927e]   Fetishism. PT Pervers 204-219
         Le fétischisme. (Tr: Berger, D.) In *La Vie Sexuelle,* Paris: PUF 1969, 133-138

S-10458 Die Frage der Laienanalyse.
[1926e]   Psychanalyse et médicine. (Tr: Bonaparte, M.) In *Ma vie et la psychanalyse,* Paris: Gallimard 1928; 1949, 117-239; 1968, 93-184

73579   The Freud-Janet controversy: an unpublished letter [to E. A. Bennett.] Brit med J 1965, 5426 (Jan 2):52-53

S-10467 Geleitwort zu Hermann Nunberg *Allegemeine Neurosenlehre auf*
[1932b] *Psychoanalytischer Grundlage.*
(1931)   Préface à Nunberg, H. *Principes de psychanalyse. Leur application aux névroses.* (Tr: Rocheblave, A. M.) Paris: PUF 1957

S-10470 Zur Geschichte der psychoanalytischen Bewegung. Munich: Werner
[1914d] Fritsch 1966, 72 p
         On the History of the Psychoanalytic Movement. (Ed:JS; tr:JRiv) NY: Norton 1966, 79 p
         Contribution à l'histoire du mouvement psychanalytique. In *Cinq leçons sur la psychanalyse,* Paris: Payot 1968, 1969, 69-115

S-10472 Zur Gewinnung des Feuers.
[1932a] . The acquisition and control of fire. SE 22:187-193

S-10474 Gutachten über die elektrische Behandlung der Kriegsneuroti-
[1955c] ker.
(1920)   Abs JAL An Surv Psa 1956, 7:29, 296-297

S-10476 Hemmung, Symptom und Angst.
[1926d]   The Problem of Anxiety. NY: Norton 1964, 127 p
    Inhibition, Symptome et Angoisse. (Tr: Tort, M.) Paris: PUF 1968

S-10477 L'héredité et l'étiologie des névroses.
[1896a]   Abs (Eng) Auth (Tr:JS) SE 3:255

73580 Hypnose. In Bum, A. *Therapeutische Lexicon,* Vienna: Urban &
[1891] Schwarzenberg 1891, 724-734; 2nd edition 1893, 896-904; 3rd edition 1900, 1:1110-1119
    Hypnotism. (Tr:JS) SE 1:103-114

S-10479 Hypnotismus und Suggestion.
[1888–   Papers on hypnotism and suggestion. SE 1:63-128. Includes
89]   [10448, 10630, 10678, 73580]

S-10480 Hysterie. In Villaret, A. *Handwörterbuch der gesamten Medizin,*
[1888e] Stuttgart 1888, 1:886-892. Psyche 1953, 7:486-700
    Hysteria. (Tr:JS) SE 1:41-59

S-10482 Das Ich und das Es.
[1923c]   The Ego and the Id. (Tr, ed:JS) NY: Norton 1961, 88 p
    Le moi et le soi. (Tr: SJ) In *Essais de psychanalyse,* Paris: Payot
1927, 1951, 163-218. (Rev tr: Hesnard, A.) 1970, 177-234
    Rv Cuik, N. Rev Psicoanál 1966, 23:257

S-10483 Die Ichspaltung im Abwehrvorgang.
[1940e]   Splitting of the ego in the process of defence. SE 23:275-278
(1938)   Le clivage du moi dans le processus de défense. (Tr: Lewinter, R.
& Pontalis, J. B.) Nouvelle Revue de Psychanalyse 1970 (2):25-28

S-10484 Die infantile Genitalorganisation.
[1923e]   L'organisation génitale infantile. (Tr:Laplanche, J.) In *La Vie
Sexuelle,* Paris: PUF 1969, 113-116

S-10485 Über infantile Sexualtheorien.
[1908c]   Les théories sexuelles infantiles. (Tr: Pontalis.) In *La Vie Sexuelle,*
Paris: PUF 1969, 14-27

S-10486 Das Interesse an der Psychoanalyse.
[1913j]   L'interesse per la psicoanalisi. (Tr: Fachinelli, E.) In *Psicoanalisi:
Esposizione Divulgative,* Turin: Boringhieri 1963

S-10493 Ein Jungendbrief.
[1941i]
(1873)   Carta sobre el bachillerato. Rev Psicoanál 1955, 12:122-126

73581 Jugendbriefe Sigmund Freuds. Neue Rundschau 1969, 80(4):678-693
    Some early unpublished letters of Freud [to Emil Fluss]. (Intro:
Freud, E. L.) J 1969, 50:419-427

Lettres de Freud adolescent. (Tr: Pontalis, J. B.) Nouvelle Revue de Psychanalyse 1970 (1):167-184

S-10494A Kell-e az egyetemen a psychoanalysist tantitani? [On the teaching of
[1919j] psychoanalysis in universities.]
(1918)   Sobre la ensenanza del psicoanalisis en la universidad. Rev Psico-
            anál 1955, 12:111-114
            Abs SLP An Surv Psa 1956, 7:365

S-10495 "Ein Kind wird geschlagen." Beitrag zur Kenntnis der Entstehung
[1919e] sexueller Perversionen.
         "A child is being beaten." A contribution to the study of the origin
         of sexual perversions. PT Pervers 70-98
         "Un bambino viene picchiato." Contributo alla conoscenza dell' ori-
         gine delle perversioni sessuali. Riv Psa 1963, 9:3-21

S-10497 Eine Kindheitserinnerung des Leonardo da Vinci.
[1910c] Leonardo da Vinci and a Memory of His Childhood. NY: Norton
         1964, 101 p

S-10499 Konstruktionen in der Analyse.
[1937d] Constructions in analysis. Psa Clin Interpret 65-78. SE 23:255-259

S-10504 Zur Kritik der "Angstneurose."
[1895f] Abs (Eng) Auth (Tr:JS) SE 3:252

S-10505 Die "kulturelle" Sexualmoral und die moderne Nervosität.
[1908d] La morale sexuelle civilisée et la maladie nerveuse des temps
         modernes. (Tr: Berger, D.) In La Vie Sexuelle, Paris: PUF 1969,
         28-46

* * *   Letters to Karl Abraham. In Abraham, H. C. & Freud, E. L. A Psy-
         cho-Analytic Dialogue: The Letters of Sigmund Freud and Karl
         Abraham, 1907-1926, NY: Basic Books 1965

* * *   Letters to Lou Andreas-Salome. See [73591]

* * *   Letter to E. A. Bennett. See [73579]

73581A   Letter to Martha Bernays, 10 May 1883 (in part). In Grinstein, A.
         "Freud's first publications in America." J Am Psa Ass 1971, 19:241-
         242

S-10508A Letters to Ludwig Binswanger, 17 May 1909 to 19 July 1938.
         French: Binswanger, L. Discours, parcours et Freud. (Tr: Lewin-
         ter, R.) In Binswanger, L. Souvenirs sur Sigmund Freud, Paris: Gal-
         limard 1970, 278-366

73582   Letters to Eugen Bleuler. In Alexander, F. & Selesnick, S. T. "Freud-
         Bleuler correspondence." Arch gen Psychiat 1965, 12:1-9

73583   Letters to Leonard Blumgart and Philip Lehrman. 50 yrs Psa 89-91

S-10409A Letters to André Breton.
         French: In Breton, A. Les vases communicants, Paris: Gallimard
         1971, 173

73584   Letters to Wilhelm Fliess, (previously published). In Schur, M.
         "Some additional 'day residues' of 'The Specimen Dream of Psycho-
         analysis'." Psa—Gen Psych 45-85

° ° °   Letters to Emil Fluss. See [73581]

S-46275   Letter to Georg Fuchs.
English: SE 22:251-252

S-46276   Letter to G. Stanley Hall.
Abs Sapochnick, L. Rev Psicoanál 1962, 19:277

73585   Letter to Hermann Hesse. Postcard dated 23 August 1918. In Zeller,
B. "Ansprache bei der Eröffnung des Hermann-Hesse-Archivs im
Schiller-Nationalmuseum, Marbach A. N. am 23. Februar 1965."
Jahrbuch der Deutschen Schillergesellschaft, Stuttgart: Alfred Kröner
Verlag 1965, 9:637-642

73586   Letters to C. G. Jung. In Jung, C. G. *Memories, Dreams, Reflections*,
NY: Pantheon 1963

° ° °   Letters to Philip Lehrman. See [73583]

73586A   Letters to Jaacob J. Maitlis [30 Nov 1938; 20 Aug 1939]. In Maitlis,
J. J. "Späte Begegnungen mit Sigmund Freud." Neue Züricher Zeitung
1964, Dec 12

S-10520   Letter to Theodor Reik, 14 April 1929
[1930f]
(1929)   English: SE 21:195-196

73587   Letter to Herman M. Serota. (Tr: Eissler, R. S.) Bull Phila Ass Psa
1968, 18:12-13

73587A   Letters to Eduard Silberstein [1871-1910]. In Stanescu, H. "Unbe-
kannte Briefe des jungen Sigmund Freud an einen rumänischen
Freund." Neue Literatur, Zeitschrift des Schriftstellenverband der
RVR 1965, 16(3:June):123-129

73588   Letters to Ernst Simmel. J Am Psa Ass 1964, 12:93-109
Abs JLSt Q 1966, 35:154

73589   Letters to Edoardo Weiss. In Grotjahn, M. "Freud as a psychoanalytic consultant: from some unknown letters to Edoardo Weiss,"
Psa Forum 1966, 1:132-137. In Grotjahn, M. "Sigmund Freud as a
consultant and therapist: from Sigmund Freud's letters to Edoardo
Weiss," Psa Forum 1966, 1:223-231. In Weiss, E. *Sigmund Freud as
a Consultant*, NY: Intercontinental Med Book Corp 1970, 23-82

° ° °   Letters to Arnold Zweig. See [73575]

S-46284   Letters of Sigmund Freud. See also [73575]
Correspondance, 1893-1939. (Tr: Berman, A. & Grossein, J.-P.)
Paris: Gallimard 1966, 525 p
Rv MG Q 1961, 30:265-271. EG J 1962, 43:83-85. Payne, S. M.
J 1962, 43:85-86. Eissler, K. R. J Am Psa Ass 1964, 12:187-222. HS
Am Im 1966, 23:278-279

S-10525   Über libidinöse Typen.
[1931a]   Des types libidinaux. (Tr: Berger, D.) In *La Vie Sexuelle*, Paris:
PUF 1969, 156-159

S-10526   Lou Andreas-Salomé. (Obituary)
[1937a]   English: SE 23:297-298

S-10527   Der Mann Moses und die monotheistische Religion.
[1939a]
(1937-39)   Moses and Monotheism. SE 23:1-137

S-10533   Meine Berührung mit Josef Popper-Lynkeus.
[1932c]   My contact with Josef Popper-Lynkeus. SE 22:219-224

S-10534   Metapsychologische Ergänzung zur Traumlehre.
[1917d]   Complément metápsychologique à la science des rêves. (Tr: Bona-
             parte, M. & Berman, A.) In Métapsychologie, RFPsa 1936, 9:90-102;
             Paris: Gallimard 1940, 162-188. With title: Complément métapsy-
             chologique à la théorie des rêves. (Tr: Laplanche, J. & Pontalis, J. B.)
             In Métapsychologie, Paris: Gallimard 1968, 125-146

S-10535   Mitteilung des Herausgebers.
[1924h]   Editorial changes in the Zeitschrift. (Tr: JS) SE 19:293

S-10537   Moses ein Ägypter.
(1937b)   Moses an Egyptian. SE 23:7-16

S-10539   Das Motiv der Kästchenwahl.
[1913f]   The theme of the three caskets. In Manheim, L. F. & Manheim,
             E. B. Hidden Patterns, NY: Macmillan 1966, 79-92

S-10542   Nachschrift zur Analyse des kleinen Hans.
[1922c]   French: Epilogue 1922. In Cinq Psychanalyses, Paris: PUF 1954,
             198

S-10547   Neue Folge der Vorlesungen zur Einführung in die Psychoanalyse.
[1933a]   New Introductory Lectures on Psycho-Analysis. SE 22:5-182. NY:
(1932)   Norton 1965, 202 p. In The Complete Introductory Lectures on Psy-
             choanalysis, NY: Norton 1966, 690 p
             Abs J Am Psa Ass 1967, 15:729

S-10551   A note on the unconscious in psycho-analysis.
[1912g]   Quelques observations sur le concept d'inconscient en psychanal-
             yse. (Tr: Bonaparte, M. & Berman, A.) RFPsa 1936, 9:22-28. In
             Métapsychologie, Paris: Gallimard 1940, 9-25. With title: Note sur
             l'inconscient en psychanalyse. (Tr: Laplanche, J. & Pontalis, J. B.)
             In Métapsychologie, Paris: Gallimard 1968, 175-187

S-10552   Notiz "III".
[1941b]
(1892)   Memorandum "III." SE 1:49-150

S-10554   Obsessions et phobies. Leur méchanisme psychique et leur étiologie.
[1895c]
(1894)   Abs (Eng) Auth (Tr:JS) SE 3:250

* * *   Papers on hypnotism and suggestion. SE 1:75-114. Includes [10630,
             10678, 73580]

S-10561   Preface to Marie Bonaparte's Edgar Poe, étude psychanalytique.
[1933d]   Preface to Marie Bonaparte's The Life and Works of Edgar Allan
             Poe: A Psycho-Analytic Interpretation. SE 22:254

S-10561A Preface to Charcot, J. M. *Neue Vorlesungen über die Krankheiten*
[1886f] *des Nervensystems insbesondere über Hysterie.* Leipzig, Vienna:
Toeplitz & Deuticke 1886, iii-iv
Preface to the translation of Charcot's *Lectures on the Diseases of
the Nervous System.* (Tr:JS) SE 1:17-22

S-10562 Preface to Charcot, J. M. *Poliklinische Vorträge, I Band.*
[1892– Preface and footnotes to the translation of Charcot's Tuesday Lec-
93a] tures. SE 1:130-142

S-10565 Preface to J. J. Putnam's *Addresses on Psycho-Analysis.* SE 18:269-
[1921a] 270

* * * Preface to Richard Sterba's *Dictionary of Psycho-Analysis.* See
[S-10419A]

S-10567 Prefatory letter to Charles Berg's *War in the Mind.*
[1941h] Carta a Charles Berg sobre su libro *War in the Mind.* (Tr: Rosen-
(1939) thal, L.) Rev Psicoanál 1955, 12:126

S-10574 (& Breuer, J.) Über die psychischen Mechanismus hysterischer Phä-
[1893a] nomene.
(1892) Abs (Eng) Auth (Tr:JS) SE 3:244. JAL An Surv Psa 1956, 7:29

S-10575 Über Psychoanalyse.
[1910a]
(1909) Cinq Leçons sur la Psychanalyse. Paris: Payot 1969

* * * Psychoanalysis and Faith. See [73592]

S-10579 Psycho-Analysis: Freudian School.
[1926f] Psychanalyse: école freudienne. (Tr: Lauzun, G.) In Lauzun, G.
Sigmund Freud et la psychanalyse, Paris: Seghers 1966, 163-171

* * * A Psycho-Analytic Dialogue: The Letters of Sigmund Freud and
Karl Abraham. (Ed: Abraham, H. C. & Freud, E. L.) NY: Basic
Books 1965, xvii + 406 p. See [65093]

S-10584 Psychopathische Personen auf den Bühne.
[1924b] Personajes psicopáticos en el teatro. (Tr: Rosenthal, L.) Rev
(1905– Psicoanál 1955, 12:115-121
06?)

S-10585 Zur Psychopathologie des Alltagsleben.
[1901b] The Psychopathology of Everyday Life. (Tr: Tyson, A.) NY:
Norton 1965, 1966, xii + 310 p; London: Benn 1966, x + 310 p

S-10586 Über Psychotherapie.
[1905a] De la psychothérapie. (Tr: Berman, A.) In *La Technique Psy-*
(1904) *chanalytique,* Paris: PUF 1970, 9-22

S-10588 Quelques considérations pour une étude comparative des paralysies
[1893c] motrices organiques et hystériques.
Some points for a comparative study of organic and hysterical
motor paralyses. (Tr: JS) SE 1:160-172
Abs (Eng) Auth (Tr:JS) SE 3:248

73590 Record of Freud speaking. NY: The Psychoanalytic Review 1938

S-10591   Ein religiöses Erlebnis.
[1928a]   Religious experience. In Strunk, O. *Readings in the Psychology of Religion*. NY: Abingdon Pr 1959, 117-119
            Un évènement de la vie religieuse. (Tr: Bonaparte, M.) In *L'Avenir d'une Illusion*. Paris: Denoël & Steele 1932

S-10592   An Romain Rolland (zum 60. Geburtstag).
[1926a]   A Romain Rolland. (Tr: Berman, A. & Grossein, J. P.) In *Correspondances 1873-1939*. Paris: Gallimard 1966, 395

S-10594   Sándor Ferenczi (obituary).
[1933c]   Sándor Ferenczi. SE 22:227-229

S-10597   Zur Selbstmord-Diskussion.
[1919g]   Contributions to a discussion on suicide. In Friedman, P. (ed) *On Suicide*, NY: IUP 1967

S-10598   Die Sexualität in der Ätiologie der Neurosen. (Abs) Medical News,
[1898a]   NY 1899, 74(14 Jan):47-48

S-10599   Zur sexuellen Aufklärung der Kinder.
[1907c]   Les explications sexuelles données aux enfants. (Tr: Berger, D.) In *La Vie Sexuelle*, Paris: PUF 1969, 7-13

73591   Sigmund Freud. Lou Andreas Salome. Briefwechsel. (Ed: Pfeiffer, E.) Frankfurt: S. Fischer 1966, 291 p
            Andréas-Salomé, Lou: *Correspondance avec Sigmund Freud 1912-1936*. (Tr: Jumel, L.) Paris: Gallimard 1970:9-259
            Rv Simenauer, E. Am Im 1967, 24:374-377

* * *   Sigmund Freud in Übersetzungen. [Sigmund Freud Translated.] A Bibliography of Freud's Writings in Book Form and Anthology. (Compiled by Bentz, H. W.) Frankfurt: Hans W. Bentz 1961, 58 p
            Abs J Am Psa Ass 1966, 14:233-234. Rv Bendix, L. Q 1967, 36:129-130

73592   Sigmund Freud-Oskar Pfister; Briefe, 1909-1939. (Ed: Freud, E. L. & Meng, H.) Frankfurt A/M: S. Fischer 1963, 168 p
            Psychoanalysis and Faith. Dialogues with the Reverend Oskar Pfister. (Tr: Mosbacher, E.) London: Hogarth Pr; NY: Basic Books 1963, 152 p
            Correspondance avec le pasteur Pfister, 1909-1939. (Tr: Jumel, L.) Paris: Gallimard 1966, 216 p
            Abs J Am Psa Ass 1966, 14:621. Rv MG Q 1963, 32:574-578. Pruyser, P. W. Am Im 1964, 21:180-182

* * *   Sketches for the "Preliminary Communication" of 1893. SE 1:145-154. Includes [10417, 10532, 10606]

S-10600   Some elementary lessons in psycho-analysis. SE 23:279-286
[1940b]
(1938)

S-10601   Studien über Hysterie.
[1895d]   Abs (Eng) Auth (Tr:JS) SE 3:250-251. Rv Stein, G. Rev Psicoanál 1966, 23:247

S-10602   Das Tabu der Virginität.
[1918a]   Le tabou de la virginité. (Tr: Berger, D.) In *La Vie Sexuelle*,
(1917)   Paris: PUF 1969, 66-80

S-10606   (& Breuer, J.) Zur Theorie des hysterischen Anfalls.
[1940d]   On the theory of hysterical attacks. SE 1:151-154
(1892)

S-10607   Thomas Mann zum 60. Geburtstag.
[1935c]   Thomas Mann on his 60th birthday. SE 22:255

73593   (& Bullitt, W. C.) Thomas Woodrow Wilson: Twenty-Eighth Presi-
          dent of the United States. A Psychological Study. Boston: Houghton
          Mifflin 1967, 307 p; London: Weidenfeld & Nicolson 1967, 265 p
             Le Président Thomas Woodrow Wilson. Portrait Psychologique.
          (Tr: Tadié, M.) Paris: Ed. Albin Michel 1968
             Rv Erikson, E. H. J 1967, 48:462-468. Gorer, G. J 1967, 48:468-
          470. Lowenfeld, H. Q 1967, 36:271-279. HS Am Im 1967, 24:283.
          Gillibert, J. RFPsa 1968, 32:787-788. Gurvitz, M. S. R 1969, 56:
          346-349

S-10609   Trauer et Melancholie.
[1917e]   Deuil et melancholie. (Tr: Bonaparte, M. & Berman, A.) In *Méta-
          psychologie*, RFPsa 1936, 9:102-116; Paris: Gallimard 1940, 189-222.
          (Tr: Laplanche, J. & Pontalis, J. B.) In *Métapsychologie*, Gallimard
          1968, 147-174

S-10614   Die Traumdeutung.
[1900a]   L'Interprétation des Rêves. (Tr: Meyerson; rev. Berger, D.) Paris:
(1899)   PUF 1967
             L'Interpretazione dei Sogni. (Tr: Fachinelli, E.; Fachinelli, H. T.)
          Turin: Boringhieri 1966
             Rv Gillibert, J. RFPsa 1968, 32:788-790

* * *   Träume im Folklore. See [46264]

S-10616   Triebe und Triebschicksale.
[1915c]   Les pulsions et leur destin. (Tr: Bonaparte, M. & Berman, A.)
          In *Métapsychologie*, RFPsa 1936, 9:29-47; Paris: Gallimard 1940.
          With title: Pulsions et destins des pulsions. (Tr: Laplanche, J. & Pon-
          talis, J. B.) In *Métapsychologie*, Paris: Gallimard 1968, 11-44

S-10617   Über Triebumsetzungen insbesondere der Analerotik.
[1917c]   Sur la transformation des pulsions, particulièrement dans l'érotisme
          anal. (Tr: Berger, D.) In *La Vie Sexuelle*, Paris: PUF 1969, 106-112

S-10619   Das Unbehagen in der Kultur.
[1930a]   Civilization and Its Discontents. (Tr:JS) NY: Norton 1962, 112 p;
          1964, 109 p.

S-10620   Das Unbewusste.
[1915e]   L'inconscient. (Tr: Bonaparte, M. & Berman, A.) In *Métapsycholo-
          gie*, RFPsa 1936, 9:58-90; Paris: Gallimard 1940, 91-161. (Tr: La-
          planche, J. & Pontalis, J. B.] In *Métapsychologie*, Paris: Gallimard
          1968, 65-123

73594   An unknown review by Freud. [Review of Löwenfeld, L. *Die psychi-
           chen Zwangerscheinungen* (J Psychol Neurol 1904, 3:190-191).]
           (Tr:JS) J 1967, 48:319-320
           Abs EVN Q 1969, 38:191

S-10622   Der Untergang der Ödipuskomplexes.
[1924d]   La disparition du complexe d'Oedipe. (Tr: Berger, D.) In *La Vie
           Sexuelle,* Paris: PUF 1969, 117-122

S-10623   Die Verdrängung.
[1915d]   Le réfoulement. (Tr: Laplanche, J. & Pontalis, J. B.) In *Métapsy-
           chologie,* Paris: Gallimard 1968, 45-63

S-10629   Vorlesungen zur Einführung in die Psychoanalyse.
[1916–   Introductory Lectures on Psychoanalysis. In *The Complete Intro-
17]   ductory Lectures on Psychoanalysis.* NY: Norton 1966, 690 p

S-10630   Vorrede zur Übersetzung von Bernheim *Die Suggestion und ihre
[1888–   Heilwirkung.*
1889]   Preface to the translation of Bernheim's *Suggestion.* SE 1:75-85

S-10632   Vorrede zur hebräischen Ausgabe der *Vorlesungen zur Einführung*
[1932a]   *in die Psychoanalyse.*
(1930)   Preface to the Hebrew translation [of *Introductory Lectures in
           Psychoanalysis*]. SE 15:11-12

S-10634   Vortag über den psychischen Mechanismus hysterischer Phänomene.
[1893h]   On the psychical mechanism of hysterical phenomena [a lecture].
           SE 3:27-39

S-10635   Vorwort zu Max Eitingon *Bericht über die Berliner Psychoanalytische
[1923g]   Poliklinik.*
               Preface to Eitingon's *Report on the Berlin Psycho-Analytic Poli-
           clinic (March 1920 to June 1922).* SE 19:285

S-10640   Vorwort zu *Zehn Jahre Berliner Psychoanalytisches Institut.*
[1930b]   Preface to *Ten Years of the Berlin Psychoanalytic Institute.* (Tr:
           JS) SE 21:257

S-10642   Warum Krieg?
[1933b]   Why war? (Tr:JS) SE 22:203-215. In Ebenstein, W. *Great Po-
           litical Thinkers,* Rinehart 1960, 860-868. In Bramson, L. & Goethals,
           G. W. *War: Studies from Psychology, Sociology, Anthropology,* NY:
           Basic Books 1964, 71-80
               Pourquoi la guerre? RFPsa 1957, 21:757-768

S-10644   Über die weibliche Sexualität.
[1931b]   Sur la sexualité féminine. (Tr: Berger, D.) In *La Vie Sexuelle,*
           Paris: PUF 1969, 139-155

S-10645   Weitere Bemerkungen über die Abwehr-Neurosen.
[1896b]   Abs (Eng) Auth (Tr:JS) SE 3:253

S-10649   Wenn Moses ein Ägypter war. . . .
[1937e]   If Moses was an Egyptian. . . . SE 23:17-53

S-10653   Ein Wort zum Antisemitismus.
[1938a]   A comment on anti-semitism. SE 23:291-293

S-10655 Die Zukunft einer Illusion.
[1927c]　　The future of an illusion. (excerpts) In Kaufman, W. A. *Religion from Tolstoy to Camus*, NY: Harper 1961, 273-278

REVIEWS OF:
S-10673 Averbeck: Die akute Neurasthenie.
[1887a]　　English: (Tr:JS) SE 1:35

S-10675 Biedenkapp, Georg: Im Kampf gegen Hirnbacillen.
[1903a]　　English: (Tr:JS) SE 9:253-354

S-10676 Bigelow, John: The Mystery of Sleep
[1904b]　　English: (Tr: Richards, A.) SE 9:254-255

S-10678 Forel, A. Der Hypnotismus, seine Bedeutung und seine Handhabung.
[1889a]　　Review of August Forel's *Hypnotism*. (Tr:JS) SE 1:91-102

° ° °　　Lowenfeld, L. Die psychischen Zwangerscheinungen. See [73594]

S-10679 Mitchell, S. Weir: Die Behandlung gewisser Formen von Neurasthe-
[1887b] nie und Hysterie.
　　English: (Tr:JS) SE 1:36

° ° °　　(unsigned) Spina, A. Studien über Tuberculose. Medical News, Phila 1883, 42(7 Apr):401-402. In Grinstein, A. "Freud's first publications in America." J Am Psa Ass 1971, 19:243-246

COLLECTED WORKS—ENGLISH

S-10707A The Standard Edition of the Complete Psychological Works of Sigmund Freud.

Vol I (1886-1899) Pre-Psycho-Analytic Publications and Unpublished Drafts. London: HPI 1966, xxvi + 430 p
Rv MBr J 1947, 48:323-326

Vol III (1893-1899) Early Psycho-Analytic Publications.
Rv MBr J 1962, 43:468-471

Vol VI (1901) The Psychopathology of Everyday Life. London: HPI 1960, xiv + 310 p
Rv MBr J 1961, 42:288

Vol VIII (1905) Jokes and Their Relation to the Unconscious. London:HPI 1960, vi + 258 p
Rv MBr J 1961, 42:123

Vol XV (1915-1916) Introductory Lectures on Psycho-Analysis. Parts I and II. London: HPI 1963, vi + 239 p
Rv MBr J 1964, 45:584-586

Vol XVI (1916-1917) Introductory Lectures on Psycho-Analysis. Part III. London: HPI 1963, v + 256 p
Rv MBr J 1964, 45:584-586

Vol XIX (1923-1925) The Ego and the Id and Other Works. London: HPI 1961, vii + 320 p
Rv MBr J 1965, 46:251-254

Vol XXI (1927-1931) The Future of an Illusion, Civilization and Its Discontents and Other Works. London: HPI 1961, vi + 287 p
Rv MBr J 1965, 46:521-525

Vol XXII (1932-1936) New Introductory Lectures on Psycho-Analysis and Other Works. London:HPI 1964, vi + 282 p
Rv MBr J 1965, 46:251-254

Vol XXIII (1937-1939) Moses and Monotheism, an Outline of Psycho-Analysis, and Other Works.
Rv MBr J 1965, 46:521-525

COLLECTED WORKS—FRENCH

S-10710A Métapsychologie. (Tr: Laplanche, J. & Pontalis, J. B.) Paris: Gallimard 1968, 187 p

73595 La Vie Sexuelle. (Tr: Berger, D., Laplanche, J. et al) Paris: PUF 1969, 160 p. Includes [10391, 10403, 10409, 10434, 10438, 10453, 10484, 10485, 10505, 10525, 10599, 10602, 10617, 10622, 10644]

FREUD, WOLFGANG ERNEST

73596 Assessment of early infancy: problems and considerations. Psa St C 1967, 22:216-238
73597 Some general reflections on the metapsychological profile. (Read at Int Psa Cong, July 1967) J 1968, 49:498-501

FREUDENBERGER, HERBERT J.

73598 All the lonely people, where do they all come from? In Davis, E. *The Beatles Book*, NY: Cowles Publ 1968
73599 The case of the missing male authority. J Relig Hlth 1969, Fall
73600 (& Robbins, I.) Characteristics of acceptance and rejection of optical aids in a low-vision population. Amer J Ophthal 1959, 47:582-584
73601 A discussion of kleptomania. Journal of Offender Therapy 1962, 6(3)
73602 The drug scene in Haight-Ashbury, USA. Int J Offender Ther 1969, 13:13-17
73603 An investigation into certain personality characteristics as they relate to improvement in Parkinsonism: the influence of submissiveness, inactivity, pessimism and affective relatedness on the improvement of Parkinson patients with the pagitane drug. Diss Abstr 1956, 16: 1944-1945
73604 (& Overby, A.) Patients from an emotionally deprived environment. R 1969, 56:299-312
73605 Psychological planning, visual, occupational and travel survey of a visually handicapped population. (Monograph) NY: American Foundation for the Blind 1960, 110 p
73606 Some clinical observations for optometrists working with low vision patients. Amer J Optometry 1959, No. 248 (Monograph) 20 p
73607 Some psychological observations on work for the blind in Israel. The New Outlook for the Blind 1961, 55:21-24

73608 Treatment and dynamics of the "disrelated" teenager and his parents
       in the American society. Psychotherapy 1969, 6:249-255

       REVIEW OF:
73609 Jacobson, E. Psychotic Conflict and Reality. R 1969, 56:349

FREUND, KURT

73610 Die ätiologische Problematik der Homosexualität. [The etiologic prob-
       lem of homosexuality.] Stud Gen 1966, 19:290-302
73611 Aus der Krankengeschichten homosexueller Männer. [Case histories of
       male homosexuals.] Psychiat Neurol med Psychol 1960, 12:213-219
73612 Homosexualita u Muže. [Homosexuality in the Male.] Prague: State
       Publishing House 1962, 274 p
73613 (& Pinkava, V.) Homosexuality in man and its association with parental
       relationships. Rev Czech Med 1961, 7:32-40
73614 (& Pinkava, V.) K otázce "femininity" u homosexuálních muzù. [The
       question of "femininity in homosexual men.] Ceskoslov Psychiat 1960,
       56:386-394
73615 Laboratory differential diagnosis of homo- and heterosexuality—an ex-
       periment with faking. Rev zech Med 1961, 7:20-31
73616 (& Pinkava, V.) [On the relationship between homosexuality and pa-
       rental absence.] (Cz) Ceskoslov Psychiat 1959, 55:334-336
73617 Some problems in the treatment of homosexuality. In Eysenck, H. J.
       Behaviour Therapy and the Neuroses, Oxford, NY: Pergamon Pr 1960,
       312-326

FREUND, PHILIP

73618 The meaning of myth to modern man. J Otto Rank Ass 1967, 2(2):52-
       53
73619 Myths of Creation. NY: Wash Square Pr 1965, vi + 304 p. Excerpt in:
       J Otto Rank Ass 1967, 2(2):54-69

FREY, EGON C.

73620 Dreams of male homosexuals and the attitude of society. J ind Psych
       1962, 18:26-34

FREY, H.

See Eisenbud, Jule

FREYBERGER, HELLMUTH

73621 The concept of constitution in psychosomatic medicine. Adv Psm Med
       101-106
73622 Obesity. Abbottempo (Eng) 1963, 1:13-14

See Deutsch, Felix; Jores, Arthur; Reichsman, F.

FREYHAN, FRITZ A.

73623 The age of community psychiatry. Proc IV World Cong Psychiat 1966,
       351-353

73624 A comprehensive psychiatric center. Curr psychiat Ther 1964, 4:241-245

73625 (& Mayo, J. A.) A Comprehensive Psychiatric Center: Concept and Structure. Wash: US GPO 1963, 44 p

73626 (Ed) Family Therapy and Marriage Counseling: Why, When, How, and by Whom. (Sp Issue of Comprehen Psychiat) NY: Grune & Stratton

73627 Methodology of psychiatric investigation with special reference to collective investigation. Proc IV World Cong Psychiat 1966, 845-846

73628 The modern treatment of depressive disorders. P 1960, 116:1057-1064

73629 On the psychopathology of psychiatric education. Comprehen Psychiat 1965, 6:221-226

73630 Psychopathological issues in judging the outcome of psychiatric treatment. Proc Amer Psychopath Ass 1964, 52:106-121

73631 (& Zubin, J.) (Eds) Social Psychiatry. (The Proceedings of the 57th Meeting of the American Psychopathological Association, NYC, Feb 1967) NY: Grune & Stratton 1968, 382 p

73632 Symptomatology. Int Psychiat Clin 1965, 2:803-810

See Zubin, Joseph

FREY-ROHN, L.

73633 Von Freud zu Jung. [From Freud to Jung.] Stuttgart: Rascher 1969, 288 p

FREYTAG, FREDERICKA

73634 The hallucinated unconscious body image. Amer J clin Hypn 1965, 7:209-220

73635 Psychodynamisms with special reference to the alcoholic. In Fox, R. *Alcoholism*, NY: Springer 1967, 36-45

FRIBERG, RICHARD R.

73636 A study of homosexuality and related characteristics in paranoid schizophrenia. Diss Abstr 1965, 26:491

FRIED, EDRITA

73637 (et al) Artistic Productivity and Mental Health. Springfield, Ill: Thomas 1964, xiv + 177 p

73638 The Ego in Love and Sexuality. NY/London: Grune & Stratton 1960, 296 p
Rv Lowen, A. PPR 1961, 48(3):126-129. Nagelberg, L. PPR 1961, 48(3):124-125. WAS Q 1961, 30:119-120

73639 The ego in love and sexuality. JNMD 1961, 133:456-457

73640 The fear of loving. In Goldman, G. D. & Milman, D. S. *Modern Woman*, Springfield, Ill: Thomas 1969, 43-63

73641 Some aspects of group dynamics and the analysis of transference and defenses. Int J grp PT 1965, 15:44-56
Abs GPK Q 1967, 36:474

FRIED, J.

See Wittkower, Eric D.

FRIED, MARC

73642 Effects of social change on mental health. Ops 1964, 34:3-28. In Bergen, B. J. & Thomas, C. S. *Issues and Problems in Social Psychiatry,* Springfield, Ill: Thomas 1966, 358-399

* * * Functions of the working-class community in modern urban society. See [73650]

73643 Grieving for a lost home. In Duhl, L. J. *The Urban Condition,* NY: Basic Books 1963, 151-171. In Wilson J. Q. *Urban Renewal: The Record and the Controversy,* Cambridge: MIT Pr 1966, 359-379

73644 "Introduction" to Research Notes. J Amer Inst Planners 1963, 29:123; 1964, 30:234

* * * "Is work a career?" See [73645]

73645 The role of work in a mobile society. In Warner, S. B., Jr. *Planning for a Nation of Cities,* Cambridge: MIT Pr 1966, 81-104. With title: Is work a career?" Transactions 1966, 3:42-47

73646 Social problems and psychopathology. GAP Symp 1964, #10:403-446

73647 (& Lindemann, E.) Sociocultural factors in mental health and illness. Ops 1961, 31:87-101
    Abs JMa RFPsa 1962, 26:322

73648 (& Levin, J.) Some social functions of the urban slum. In Frieden, B. & Morris, R. *Urban Planning and Social Policy,* NY: Basic Books 1968, 60-83

73649 (& Gleicher, P.) Some sources of residential satisfaction in an urban slum. J Amer Inst Planners 1961, 27:305-315. In Bellush, J. & Hausknecht, M. *Urban Renewal: People, Politics, and Planning,* NY: Anchor Books 1967

73650 Transitional functions of working-class communities: implications for forced relocation. In Kantor, M. *Mobility and Mental Health,* Springfield, Ill: Thomas 1965. With title: Functions of the working-class community in modern urban society: implications for forced relocation. J Amer Inst Planners 1967, 33:90-103

See Robinson, Alice M.

FRIEDAN, BETTY

73651 The Feminine Mystique. NY: Norton 1963, 410 p

FRIEDEMANN, ADOLF

73652 Die Begegnung mit dem Kranken Menschen. [Meeting the Ill.] Bern: Verlag Hans Huber 1967, 163 p

73653 (Ed) Du und der Andere. [You and Others.] Biel: Inst f Psycho-Hygiene 1967, 112 p

73654 Hans Zulliger b. 1893. Psychoanalysis and education. (Tr: Grotjahn, M.) Psa Pioneers 342-347

73655 Heinrich Meng b. 1887. Psychoanalysis and mental hygiene. (Tr: Grotjahn, M.) Psa Pioneers 333-341

FRIEDEMANN, MAX WERNER

73656 Reflection on two cases of male transvestism. PT 1966, 20:270-283

FRIEDENBERG, EDGAR Z.

73657 Discussion of Erikson, E. "Eight ages of man." Int J Psychiat 1966, 2: 306-307
73658 New-Freudianism & Erich Fromm. Commentary 1962, 34:305-313
73659 The Vanishing Adolescent. Boston: Beacon Pr 1960, 144 p
Rv Strean, H. S. R 1964, 51:679-681

FRIEDENBERG, FRED S.

73660 Backward fixation, forward fixation and neurotic acting out. R 1963, 50:604-610
Abs SRS Q 1964, 33:608

FRIEDERICH, M. A.

73661 (& Romano, J.; Lund, C. J.) Psychologic aspects of obstetric-gynecologic practice. Amer J Obs Gyn 1965, 91:1029-1933

FRIEDHOFF, ARNOLD J.

See Frosch, William A.

FRIEDJUNG, JOSEPH K.

See Adler, Alfred

FRIEDLANDER, KATE

73662 On the "longing to die." In Ruitenbeek, H. M. *Death: Interpretations*, NY: Dell 1969, 39-49

FRIEDLANDER, WALTER A.

73663 (Ed) Concepts and Methods of Social Work. Englewood Cliffs, NJ: Prentice-Hall 1958, 308 p
Grundegriffe und Methoden der Sozialarbeit. Neuwied/Berlin: Hermann Luchterhand Verlag 1966
Principio e Metodo del Servizio Sociale. Bologna: Societa Editrice il Mulino 1963
Sosoyal Hizmentin Kazram ze Metodlari. Ankara, Turkey: Kardes Malbaasi 1965

FRIEDMAN, ALFRED S.

73664 (& Boszormenyi-Nagy, I.; Jungries, J. E.; Lincoln, G.; Mitchell, H. E.; Sonne, J. C.; Speck, R. V.; Spivak, G.) Psychotherapy for the Whole Family: Case Histories, Techniques, and Concepts of Family Therapy of Schizophrenia in the Home and Clinic. NY: Springer 1965, vii + 354 p

See Pollak, Otto

FRIEDMAN, ALICE R.

73665 Group psychotherapy in the treatment of the Medea complex. Acta psychother psychosom 1960, 8:457-461

FRIEDMAN, ARNOLD P.

73666 Headaches. Ency Ment Hlth 719-723

73667 (& Harms, E.) (Eds) Headaches in Children. Springfield, Ill: Thomas 1967, vii + 151 p

FRIEDMAN, C. JACK

See Wood, Alfred C., Jr.

FRIEDMAN, DAVID BELAIS

73668 (& Selesnick, S. T.) Clinical notes on the management of asthma and eczema. When to call the psychiatrist. Clin Ped 1965, 4:735-738

73669 Death anxiety and the primal scene. PPR 1961, 48(4):108-118
Abs LDr RFPsa 1962, 27:352

73670 (& Hansen, H.) Family therapy in pediatrics. Clin Ped 1968, 7:665-669

73671 Obsessive hypermnesia and free association as a transference resistance. PT 1967, 21:105-111

73672 On the phrase, "beautiful but dumb." PPR 1962, 49(4):100-102
Abs HL Q 1963, 32:611

73673 Toward a unitary theory on the passing of the Oedipal conflict. R 1966, 53:38-48
Abs Knobel, M. Rev Psicoanál 1967, 24:691. SRS Q 1967, 36:139. CG RFPsa 1968, 32:366

See Augenbraun, Bernice; Robertiello, Richard C.; Selesnick, Sheldon T.

FRIEDMAN, EMERICK

73674 (& Ackerman, N. W.) Newer methods in schizophrenia. Clin Med Surg 1938, 45:361-364

FRIEDMAN, ERWIN

73675 Individual therapy with a "defective delinquent." Clin Psych 1961, 17:229-232

FRIEDMAN, H.

See Pinderhughes, Charles A.

FRIEDMAN, HENRY J.

73676 Patient-expectancy and symptom reduction. Arch gen Psychiat 1963, 8:61-67. In Goldstein, A. P. & Dean, S. J. The Investigation of Psychotherapy, NY: Wiley 1966, 311-318

FRIEDMAN, IRA

See Rosen, Irving M.

FRIEDMAN, JACOB H.

73677 An organization of ex-patients for follow-up therapy. Current psychiat Ther 1963, 3:272-276

73678 (& Zaris, D.) Paradoxical response to death of spouse—three case reports. Dis nerv Sys 1964, 25:480-483

73679 (& Wechsler, H.) Psychogenic urinary retention? Case report. J Amer geriat Soc 1965, 13:447-448

73680 (& Kapp, F. I.) Refusal of surgical therapy as an immediate life saving procedure. Dis nerv Sys 1960, 22:54-56

73681 The vagarity of psychiatric indications for therapeutic abortion. PT 1962, 16:251-254

FRIEDMAN, JOSEPH

See Leopold, Robert L.; Wolfman, Cyrus

FRIEDMAN, LAWRENCE J.

73682 Ambivalence and the vicissitudes of the Oedipus complex. (Read at Los Angeles Psa Soc, 17 Oct 1963; at West Coast Psa Soc, 26 Sept 1964) Israel Ann Psychiat 1966, 4:16-29

73683 Discussion of Gaylin, W. M. "Psychiatry and the law." Columbia Univ Forum 1965, 8(2):45-46

73684 Drives and knowledge; a speculation. J Am Psa Ass 1968, 18:81-94

73685 An examination of Jay Haley's strategies of psychotherapy. Psychotherapy 1965, 2:181-188

73686 Fact and value: new resources for esthetics. R 1965, 52:117-129

73687 Foreword to Freed, D. *Freud and Stanislavsky,* NY/Wash/Hollywood: Vantage Pr 1964

73688 From Gradiva to the death instinct. Psa Forum 1966, 1:46-53; 62-63

73689 Japan and the psychopathology of history. Q 1968, 37:539-564

73690 Psychic determinism: an outmoded concept? P 1960, 116:1118-1122

73691 Psy'cho-a-nal'-y-sis: Uses and Abuses. NY: Paul S. Eriksson 1968, xvii + 172 p
   Us et Abus de la Psychanalyse. Paris: Editions Planete 1969
   Rv Anthony, R. A. Bull Phila Ass Psa 1969, 19:96. WAS Q 1969, 38:656-657

73692 The significance of determinism and free will. J 1965, 66:515-520
   Abs EVN Q 1967, 36:626

73693 The therapeutic alliance. J 1969, 50:139-153

S-46352 Toward an integration of psychoanalytic and philosophic esthetics. Abs EMD An Surv Psa 1958, 9:497-499

FRIEDMAN, LEONARD J.

73694 (& Zinberg, N. E.) Application of group methods in college teaching. Int J grp PT 1964, 14:344-359

73695 Virgin Wives: A Study of Unconsummated Marriages. (Foreword: Balint, M.) London: Tavistock; Springfield: Thomas 1962, xii + 161 p
  Virginität in der Ehe. Bern: Hans Huber; Stuttgart: Ernst Klett Verlag 1963, 155 p
73696 Virginität in der Ehe. Der Konflikt zwischen Liebe und Aggression. [Virginity in marriage. The conflict between love and aggression.] Psyche 1963, 17:185-196

See Zinberg, Norman E.

ABSTRACT OF:
73697 Zinberg, N. E. The mirage of mental health. Bull Phila Ass Psa 1969, 19:171-173

FRIEDMAN, MARIE R.
See Fries, Margaret E.

FRIEDMAN, MAURICE STANLEY

73698 The changing image of human nature. The philosophical aspect. Psa 1966, 26:138-147
73699 Dialogue and the "essential we": the bases of values in the philosophy of Martin Buber. Psa 1960, 20:26-34. In Rosenbaum, M. & Berger, M. *Group Psychotherapy and Group Function*, NY/London: Basic Books 1963, 604-613
73700 Existential psychotherapy and the image of man. J humanist Psychol 1964, 4:104-117
73701 Friedrich Nietzsche: father of atheist existentialism. J existent Psychiat 1966, 6:269-277
73702 Jung's image of psychological man. R 1966, 53:595-608
  Abs SRS Q 1968, 37:316
73703 To Deny Our Nothingness: Contemporary Images of Man. NY: Delacorte Books 1967, 383 p

FRIEDMAN, MERTON H.

73704 (& Andersson, J.) Body-image variability in peptic ulcer. A perceptual experiment with identical twins. Arch gen Psychiat 1967, 16:334-343
73705 On the nature of regression in aphasia. Arch gen Psychiat 1961, 5:252-256

FRIEDMAN, NEIL

73706 (& Jones, R. M.) On the mutuality of the Oedipus complex. Notes on the Hamlet case. Am Im 1963, 20:107-131

FRIEDMAN, PAUL

73707 Discussion of Hoppe, K. D. "The psychodynamics of concentration camp victims." Psa Forum 1966, 1:83-84
73708 An individual act. In Shneidman, E. S. *On the Nature of Suicide*, San Francisco: Jossey-Bass 1969, 48-52; 87-99
73710 Editor of Adler, A. et al: On Suicide, With Particular Reference to

Suicide Among Young Students. Discussions of the Vienna Psychoanalytic Society—1910

73711 Foreword to Adler, A. et al: On Suicide, With Particular Reference to Suicide among Young Students, NY: IUP 1967, 11-26

73712 (& Goldstein, J.) Some comments on the psychology of C. G. Jung. Q 1964, 33:194-225

73713 Some considerations on the treatment of suicidal depressive patients. PT 1962, 16:379-386

73714 Suicide. Ency Ment Hlth 1983-1991

73715 Suicide among police: a study of ninety-three suicides among New York City policemen, 1934-1940. In Shneidman, E. S. *Essays in Self-Destruction*, NY: Science House 1967, 414-449

REVIEWS OF:

73716 Anzieu, D. L'Auto-Analyse. Son Rôle dans la Découverte de la Psychanalyse par Freud. Sa Fonction en Psychanalyse. Q 1961, 30:431-433

73717 Loewenstein, R. M. et al (Eds): Psychoanalysis—A General Psychology. Essays in Honor of Heinz Hartmann. Q 1968, 37:596-597

73718 Margolis, J. Psychotherapy and Morality. A Study of Two Concepts. Q 1968, 37:620-622

73719 Meerloo, J. A. M. Suicide and Mass Suicide. Q 1963, 32:280-282

73720 La Psychanalyse. Recherche et Enseignement Freudiens de la Société Française de Psychanalyse. Q 1962, 31:554-556

73721 Winn, R. B. (Ed & Tr): Psychotherapy in the Soviet Union. Q 1963, 32:274-277

FRIEDMAN, S.

See Oltman, Jane E.

FRIEDMAN, S. THOMAS

See Sherrill, David

FRIEDMAN, SEYMOUR W.

73722 The diagnostic process as part of the treatment process. Reiss-Davis Clin Bull 1966, 3:62-67

73723 The diagnostic process during the evaluation of an adolescent girl. In Ekstein, R. *Children of Time and Space, of Action and Impulse*, NY: Appleton-Century-Crofts 1966, 15-62

73724 Discussion of Bender, L. "Childhood schizophrenia; a review." J Hillside Hosp 1967, 16:1. Int J Psychiat 1968, 5:211-236

See Ekstein, Rudolf; Motto, Rocco L.

FRIEDMAN, STANFORD B.

73725 (& Chodoff, P.; Mason, J. W.; Hamburg, D. A.) Behavioral observations on parents anticipating the death of a child. Pediatrics 1963, 32:610-625

See Chodoff, Paul

FRIEDMAN, STANLEY M.

S-46371 (& Fisher, C.) Further observations on primary modes of perception: the use of a masking technique for subliminal visual stimulation.
Abs JTM Q 1961, 30:595

73726 (& Fisher, C.) On the presence of a rhythmic, diurnal, oral instinctual drive cycle in man; a preliminary report. J Am Psa Ass 1967, 15:317-343

S-46372 One aspect of the structure of music. A study of regressive transformations of musical themes.
Abs JTM Q 1962, 31:126. SAS RFPsa 1962, 26:331

73727 Oral activity cycles in mild chronic schizophrenia. P 1968, 125:743-751

See Fisher, Charles; Kaufman, M. Ralph; Tarachow, Sidney

FRIEDMAN, T. I.

See Knight, James A.

FRIEDMANN, OSCAR

See Hellman, Ilse

FRIEDRICH, PETER

73728 Vergleichende Darstellung zweier Fälle von Wahnkrankheit. Ein Beitrag zur Differentialdiagnose der Wahnkrankheiten. [Comparative description of 2 cases of delusion. A contribution to the differential diagnosis of delusion.] Acta Soc Med Upsal 1963, 68:84-102

FRIEND, JEANNETTE

See Kaufman, Irving

FRIEND, MAURICE R.

73729 Discussion of Segal, H. "Melanie Klein's technique." Psa Forum 1967, 2:212-213

S-46383 (Reporter) Panel: On sleep disturbances in children.
Abs BEM An Surv Psa 1956, 7:271-273

73730 Psychoanalytic psychology of childhood schizophrenia. (Conference on childhood schizophrenia.) J Hillside Hosp 1967, 16:85-93

73731 Social service information in child psychiatry. Compreh Txbk Psychiat 1357

See Fries, Margaret E.

REVIEWS OF:
73732 Rosenberg, M. Society and the Adolescent Self-Image. Q 1967, 36:452-453

73733 Roucek, J. S. (Ed): The Difficult Child. Q 1967, 36:453-454

73734 Saul, L. J. Emotional Maturity: The Development and Dynamics of Personality. Q 1962, 31:261-262

73735 Simpson, G. People in Families. Sociology, Psychoanalysis, and the American Family. Q 1961, 30:589-590

73736   Spitz, R. A. & Cobliner, W. G. The First Year of Life. A Psychoanalytic
        Study of Normal and Deviant Development of Object Relations. Q
        1967, 36:281-283

FRIES, MARGARET E.

73737   (& Friedman, M. R.) A method of organizing clinical data: a teaching
        aid for training residents in psychoanalytic psychotherapy. A prelimi-
        nary report. J Hillside Hosp 1960, 9:23-47
73738   Problems of communication between therapist and patients with ar-
        chaic ego functions. J Hillside Hosp 1968, 17:136-160
73739   Some factors in the development and significance of early object rela-
        tionships. (Read at Am Psa Ass, Dec 1958) J Am Psa Ass 1961, 9:669-
        683
            Abs FB Q 1962, 31:424

REVIEWS OF:
73740   Alt, H. & Alt, E. The New Soviet Man. His Upbringing and Character
        Development. Q 1966, 35:304-305
73741   Kidd, A. H. & Rivoire, J. L. (Eds): Perceptual Development in Chil-
        dren. Q 1968, 37:139-140

FRIGHI, LUIGI

73742   (& Tolentino, I.) Réalisation de l'ideal du moi en tant que but de la
        psychotherapie. [Realization of the ideal-ego as an objective of psycho-
        therapy.] Acta neurol Psychiat Belg 1961, 61:879-892
73742A [Sociological foundations of psychotherapeutic action.] (It) Riv Sper
        Freniat 1969, 93:363-376

FRIJLING-SCHREUDER, BETS

73743   (& Lampl-de Groot, J.) Introduction to the scientific programme of the
        26th Congress of the International Psycho-Analytical Association, Rome
        (27 July 1969 to 1 August inclusive). J 1969, 50:3-4

FRIJLING-SCHREUDER, ELISABETH C. M.

73744   The adaptive use of regression. (Read at 24th Int Psa Cong, Amster-
        dam, July 1965) J 1966, 47:364-369
            Fonction adaptive de la régression. RFPsa 1968, 32:127-144
            Die Verwendung der Regression im Dienste der Anpassung. Psyche
        1967, 21:313-323
            Abs Cuad Psa 1967, 3:163-164. EVN Q 1968, 37:314
73745   (& Petri, M.) Algemene preventie. [General prevention.] Maandbl
        geest Volksgezondh 1962, 17(11)
73746   Anna Freud. In van der Velde, I. Grote Denkers over Opvoeding,
        Holland 1964
73747   Borderline states in children. (Read at San Francisco Psa Inst, 13 Oct
        1968) Psa St C 1969, 24:307-327
73748   Diagnostiek en indicatiestelling voor psychotherapie aan het M. O. B.
        [Diagnostics and indications for psychotherapy in the Child Guidance

Clinic.] In Hart de Ruyter: *Capita Selecta voor de Kinderpsychiatrie,* Zeist: E. de Haan 1963

73749 Discontinueit in de opvoeding. [Discontinuity in education.] Koepel 1967, 21(8)

73750 Enkele voorbeelden van psychische ontwikkelingsstoornissen in de kleuterfase. [Some examples of psychic disturbances of development during infancy.] N Tv G 1966, 110:749-753

73751 Honoré de Balzac—a disturbed boy who did not get treatment. (Read at Int Psa Cong, July-Aug 1963) J 1964, 45:426-430
     Honoré de Balzac, ein gestörter Junge, der nicht behandelt wurde. **Psyche 1965, 18:606-615**
     Abs EVN Q 1966, 35:466

73752 Huisarts en medisch opvoedkundig bureau. [Family doctor and child guidance clinic.] Huisarts en Wetenschap 1961, 4(11)

73753 Kleutermoeilijkleden. [Difficulties of toddlers.] In *Lectures on Child Psychiatry,* Holland: Stenfert Kroese 1961

73754 On individual supervision. Bull schweiz Gscht Psa 1968-69, No. 8:4-9

73755 De Ontwikkeling van het normale Kind in het onvolledige Gezin. [The development of the normal child in the incomplete family.] Koepel 1961, 15(9)

73756 De ontwikkeling van het protest bij het Kind. [The development of protest in childhood.] Wetenschap en Samenleving 1966, 20(11-12)

73757 Opmerkingen over de agressie. [Remarks about aggression.] In Hart de Ruyter: *Capita Selecta voor de Kinderpsychiatrie,* Zeist: E de Haan 1963

73758 Over sublimering. [About sublimation.] Maandbl geest Volksgezondh 1963, 18(11)

73759 De plaats van het M. O. B. gericht op het individu. [The place of the Child Guidance Clinic.] Maandbl geest Volksgezondh 1965, 20(9)

73760 Possibilities and limitations of child guidance treatment. Criança Port 1961-62

73761 Preventie van Neurotische Gezinrelaties. Prevention of Neurotic Family Relationships.] Assen, Holland: Van Gorcum 1965

73762 Problemen rondom de sexuele voorlichting in het Gezin. [Problems around the sexual instructions in the family.] Huisarts en Wetenschap 1963, 6

73763 (& Isaac-Edersheim, E.) Problems in determining indications for psychotherapy in children during the latency period. Psychiat Neurol Neurochir 1965, 68:34-49

73764 De psychiater en de dood. [The psychiatrist and death.] In Leeuw, P. J. van der et al: *Hoofstukken uit Hedenaagse Psychoanalyse.* Arnhem: van Loghumn Slaterus 1967

73765 Schoolziekte. [School phobia.] NTvG 1965, 109(5):225-230

73766 Sexuele ontwikkeling van het Kind. [Sexual development of the child.] Huisarts en Wetenschap 1963, 6

S-46394 Some remarks on transference and counter-transference in analytical child therapy.
     Abs An Surv Psa 1955, 6:285-287

73767 (& Velde, E. van der) De taak van het medisch opvoedkundig Bureau bij Rapportage. [The task of the Child Guidance Clinic in reporting to

the Children's Judge and to the Board for the Protection of Children.]
Maandbl geest Volksgezondh 1963, 18(5)

73768 Über Kinderanalyse. [About child analysis.] Jb Psa 1967, 4:157-180
73769 Übertragung und Gegenübertragung in der Psychoanalytischen Kindertherapie. [Transference and counter-transference in analytical child
therapy.] Psyche 1967, 21:16-30. In Hbh Kinderpsychother 302-313

See Leeuw, P. J. van der

FRISBIE, LOUISE V.

73770 (& Vanasek, F. J.; Dingman, H. F.) The self and the ideal self:
methodological study of pedophiles. Psychol Rep 1967, 20:699-706

FRISCH, ALAN

ABSTRACTS OF:
73771 Balint, M. The concepts of subject and object in psychoanalysis. An
Surv Psa 1958, 9:109-110
73772 Bellak, L. Psychoanalytic principles discernible in projective testing.
An Surv Psa 1958, 9:120
73773 Bellak, L. Studying the psychoanalytic process by the method of short-
range prediction and judgment. An Surv Psa 1958, 9:342-343
73774 Freeman, T. Aspects of perception in psychoanalysis and experimental
psychology. An Surv Psa 1958, 9:89
73775 Glover, E. The uses of Freudian theory in psychiatry. An Surv Psa
1958, 9:51-52
73776 Main, T. F. Perception and ego function. An Surv Psa 1958, 9:88-89
73777 Sperling, M. The analysis of a transvestite boy. A contribution to the
genesis and dynamics of transvestism. Q 1963, 32:471-472

FRISCH, GIORA R.

73778 (& Handler, L.) Differences in Negro and white drawings: a cultural
interpretation. Percept mot Skills 1967, 24:667-670

FRITZEN, EDWARD

73779 Review Notes and Study Guide to the Major Ideas and Writings of
Freud. NY: Monarch Pr 1964, 89 p

FROM, F.

73780 Beobachtungen aus dem Bereich des Traumes verglichen mit der Be-
griffsentwicklung beim Kind. [Observations from the realm of the
dream compared with conceptual development in children.] Z Psychol
1961, 165:240-252

FROM, FRANZ

73781 Drøm og neurose. Et forsøg pa et nyt synspunkt. [Dreams and Neuroses.] Copenhagen: Schultz 1968, 59 p

FROMM, ERICH

73782 Are we sane? In Nunokawa, W. D. *Readings in Abnormal Psychology: Human Values and Abnormal Behavior*, Chicago, Ill: Scott, Foresman 1965, 64-70

73783 The Art of Loving: An Enquiry Into the Nature of Love. NY: Harper & Row 1962, vii + 146 p

73784 [The bases and development of psychoanalysis.] (Sp) Rev Psicoanal Psiquiat Psicol 1965, 1:10-19
Abs de la Torre, A. Q 1968, 37:161

73785 Beyond the Chains of Illusion: My Encounter with Marx and Freud. NY: Simon & Schuster 1962, 182 p

73786 El carácter revolucionario. [The revolutionary personality.] Rev Psicoanal Psiquiat Psicol 1966, 3:25-35

73787 (& Narváez, F.) El complejo de Edipo: comentarios al "Análisis de la fobia de un niño de cinco años." [The Oedipus complex: commentaries on the "Analysis of a five year old child's phobia."] Rev Psicoanal Psiquiat Psicol 1966, 4:26-33
The Oedipus complex: comments on "the case of Little Hans." Contempo Psa 1968, 4(2):178-188

73788 La crisis actual en el psicoanálisis. [The present day crisis in psychoanalysis.] Rev Psicoanal Psiquiat Psicol 1967, 7:6-16

73789 The dogma of Christ. In author's *The Dogma of Christ, and Other Essays on Religion, Psychology and Culture*, 3-91

73790 The Dogma of Christ and Other Essays on Religion, Psychology and Culture. London: Routledge 1963, 151 p; NY/Chicago/San Francisco: Holt, Rinehart & Winston 1963, 1964, x + 212 p; NY: Doubleday 1966, ix + 218 p
Abs J Am Psa Ass 1966, 14:619

73791 (& Fuente, R. de la) [Editorial.] (Sp) Rev Psicoanal Psiquiat Psicol 1965, 1:3-4
Abs de la Torre, A. Q 1968, 37:161

S-11013 Escape from Freedom.
Die Furcht vor der Freiheit. Frankfurt a.M.: Europäische Verlags-Anstalt 1966, 292 p

° ° ° Foreword to Neill, A. S. *Summerhill: A Radical Approach to Child Rearing*, NY: Hart Publ Co 1960

° ° ° Foreword to Thompson, C. M. *Interpersonal Psychoanalysis*, NY: Basic Books 1964

73792 Die Grundpositionen der Psychoanalyse. [The basic positions of psychoanalysis.] Fortschr Psa 1966, 2:19-36

73793 The Heart of Man. Its Genius for Good and Evil. Religious Perspectives. (Ed: Anshen, R. N.) NY/Evanston/London: Harper & Row 1964; London: Routledge 1965, 156 p

73794 [Humanism and psychoanalysis.] (Sp) (Read at Inst Mexican Soc Psa, 8 March 1963) Prensa Méd Mex 1963, 28:120-126
Humanism and psychoanalysis. Contempo Psa 1964, 1(1):69-79

73795 Man for himself. In Koch, A. *Philosophy for a Time of Crisis*, NY: Dutton 1959, 159-173

73796   Man is not a thing. In Simonson, H. P. *Cross Currents*. NY: Harper 1959, 323-330
73797   (Ed) Marx's Concept of Man. NY: F Ungar 1961, xii + 260 p
73798   Marxův přínos k poznání člověka. [Marx' contribution to knowledge of man.] Ceskoslov Psychiat 1969, 65(3):174-180
73799   May Man Prevail?: An Inquiry into the Facts and Fictions of Foreign Policy. Garden City, NY: Doubleday & Co 1961, v + 252 p
73800   May man prevail; excerpt. In Ekirch, A. A., Jr. *Voices in Dissent*, NY: Citadel 1964, 377-381
73801   Medicine and the ethical problem of modern man. In author's *The Dogma of Christ, and Other Essays on Religion, Psychology and Culture* 169-187
73802   Memories of Dr. D. T. Suzuki. Psychologia 1967, 10(3-4)
73803   On the limitations and dangers of psychology. In author's *The Dogma of Christ, and Other Essays on Religion, Psychology and Culture* 191-200
73804   Problems of interpreting Marx. In Horowitz, I. L. *The New Sociology*, NY: Oxford 1964, 188-195
S-11028 Psychoanalysis and Religion.
            Psychanalyse et Religion. Paris: Éditions de l'Épi 1968, 160 p
73805   Psychoanalysis and Zen Buddhism. Psychologia 1959, 2:79-99
73806   Psychoanalysis—science or party line? In author's *The Dogma of Christ, and Other Essays on Religion, Psychology and Culture* 131-144
73807   Psychological problems of aging. J Rehab 1966, 32:10-12; 51-57
73808   The Revolution of Hope: Toward a Humanized Technology. (Ed: Anshen, R. N.) NY: Harper & Row 1968, xviii + 162 p
73809   Scientific research in psychoanalysis. An editorial. Contempo Psa 1966, 2(2):168-170
S-46411 Sex and character. In author's *The Dogma of Christ, and Other Essays on Religion, Psychology and Culture* 107-127
S-46412 Sigmund Freud's Mission: An Analysis of His Personality and Influence.
            Rv Waelder, R. J Am Psa Ass 1963, 11:628-651
73810   La situación psicológica del hombre en el mundo moderno. [The psychological situation of modern man.] Rev Psicoanal Psiquiat Psicol 1967, 5:6-16
73811   [Social factors and their influence in the development of the child.] (Sp) Prensa Méd Mex 1958, 23:227-228
73812   La teoría de la agresividad de Konrad Lorenz. [Konrad Lorenz' theory of aggressiveness.] Rev Psicoanal Psiquiat Psicol 1968, 6(9):5-16
73813   Teoría freudiana de la agresividad y la destructividad. [Freudian theory of aggressiveness and destructiveness.] Rev Psicoanal Psiquiat Psicol 1968, 8:19-48
73814   War Within Man. Phila: Amer Phila Service Committee 1963
73815   You Shall Be As Gods: A Radical Interpretation of the Old Testament and Its Tradition. NY: Holt, Rinehart & Winston 240 p
73816   (& Suzuki, D. T.; De Martino, R.) Zen Buddhism and Psychoanalysis. NY: Harper 1960, viii + 180 p

            See Kahn, Herman

FROMM, ERIKA

73818 Awareness versus consciousness. Psychol Rep 1965, 16:711-712
73819 Dissociative and integrative processes in hypnoanalysis. Amer J clin Hyp 1968, 10:174-177
73820 (& French, T. M.) Formation and evaluation of hypotheses in dream interpretation. J Psychol 1962, 54:271-283
73821 Hypnoanalysis: theory and two case excerpts. Psychotherapy 1965, 2:127-133
73822 (& Sawyer, J.; Rosenthal, V.) Hypnotic simulation of organic brain damage. ASP 1964, 69:482-492
° ° ° Introduction. In Sacerdote, P. *Induced Dreams,* NY: Vantage Pr 1967
73823 Let's keep our concepts straight. Percept mot Skills 1962, 15:217-218
73824 The manifest and the latent content of two paintings by Hieronymus Bosch: a contribution to the study of creativity. (Read at Chicago Inst Psa, 23 April 1968) Am Im 1969, 26:145-166
73825 Mental health, democracy and academic education. Sch R 1962, 70:405-409
73826 [Modern theories and practice of hypnotherapy.] (Jap) J Jap PSM 1967, 11:147-161
73827 Projective aspects of intelligence testing. In Rabin, A. I. & Haworth, M. R. *Projective Techniques with Children,* NY/London: Grune & Stratton 1960, 225-236
73828 Spontaneous autohypnotic age-regression in a nocturnal dream. Int J clin exp Hyp 1965, 13:119-131
73829 Transference and countertransference in hypnoanalysis. Int J clin exp Hyp 1968, 16:77-84

See French, Thomas M.

FROMME, ALLAN

73830 The Ability to Love. London: Allen & Unwin 1966, 366 p
73831 Our Troubled Selves: A New and Positive Approach. NY: Farrar, Straus & Giroux 1967, ix + 274 p
73832 Understanding the Sexual Response in Humans. NY: Pocket Books 1966, 79 p

FROMME, D. K.

See Heilbrun, Alfred B., Jr.

FROMM-REICHMANN, FRIEDA

S-46420 Basic problems in the psychotherapy of schizophrenia.
Abs WCW An Surv Psa 1958, 9:417-418
S-11048A Clinical significance of intuitive processes of the psychoanalyst.
Abs An Surv Psa 1955, 6:372-373
73833 Introduction. In author's *The Principles of Intensive Psychotherapy,* Chicago: Univ of Chicago Pr 1950. With title: The prerequisites of therapy from an analytic viewpoint. In Berenson, B. G. & Carkhuff, R. R. *Sources of Gain in Counseling and Psychotherapy,* NY: Holt, Rinehart & Winston 1967, 58-62

S-11058B Intuitive processes in the psychotherapy of schizophrenics.
Abs An Surv Psa 1955, 6:372

S-11068 Pädagogische Diskussionsbemerkungen zur psychoanalytischen Trieb-
lehre. In Bittner, G. & Rehm, W. *Psychoanalyse und Erziehung*, Bern/
Stuttgart: Hans Huber 1964

° ° °   The prerequisites of therapy from an analytic viewpoint.
See [73833]

S-46427 Psychiatric aspects of anxiety. In Stein, M. R. et al: *Identity and
Anxiety*, Glencoe, Ill: Free Pr 1960, 129-144

FRONTISI, F.

See Danon-Boileau, Henri

FROSCH, JOHN

73834   (& Ross, N.) (Eds) The Annual Survey of Psychoanalysis. A Compre-
hensive Survey of Current Psychoanalytic Theory and Practice. Vol.
VI, 1955. NY: IUP 1961, xi + 612 p
Rv MG Q 1962, 31:565

73835   (& Ross, N.) (Eds) The Annual Survey of Psychoanalysis: A Compre-
hensive Survey of Current Psychoanalytic Theory and Practice. Vol.
VII, 1956. NY: IUP 1964, 517 p
Rv MG J 1964, 45:607. Sloan, P. Q 1965, 34:119

73836   (& Ross, N.) (Eds) The Annual Survey of Psychoanalysis, Vol. VIII.
NY: IUP 1964; London: Hogarth 1966, 371 p
Rv Grinstein, A. Q 1967, 36:601-603

73837   (& Ross, N.) (Eds) The Annual Survey of Psychoanalysis. A Comprehensive Survey of Current Psychoanalytic Theory and Practice. Vol.
IX. NY: IUP 1968, viii + 527 p

73838   Clinical studies. An Surv Psa 1955, 6:143-231

73839   Delusional fixity, sense of conviction, and the psychotic conflict. (Read
at NY Psa Soc, 31 Mar 1964; at Phila Ass Psa, 15 Jan 1965) J 1967,
48:475-495
Abs Shorr, J. Q 1964, 33:617-618. Cowitz, B. Bull Phila Ass Psa
1965, 15:183-186. LHR Q 1969, 38:506

73840   Dream studies. An Surv Psa 1955, 6:232-246, 588-591; 1956, 7:222-
239; 1957, 8:171-180; 1958, 9:213-226

73841   A note on reality constancy. (Read at NY Psa Soc, 12 Oct 1965) Psa—
Gen Psychol 349-376

73842   Obituary: Sidney Tarachow, 1908-1965. (Read at NY Psa Soc, 25 Oct
1966) J 1967, 48:321-322

73843   Psychoanalytic education. An Surv Psa 1955, 6:380-396; 1956, 7:354-
375; 1957, 8:289-295; 1958, 9:431-438

73844   The psychotic character: clinical psychiatric considerations. (Read at
NY Psa Soc, 25 Oct 1960) Psychiat Q 1964, 38:91-96
Abs WAS Q 1961, 30:314-316. Gottreich, N. Q 1966, 35:312-313

73845   Reality constancy: a preliminary note. (Read at NY Psa Soc, 12 Oct
1965)
Abs EVN Q 1966, 35:477-479

73846 Severe regressive states during analysis. (Read at Am Psa Ass, Dec 1965) J Am Psa Ass 1967, 15:491-507, 606-625

S-46440 Transference derivatives of the family romance.
   Abs JTM Q 1961, 30:140

ABSTRACTS OF:

73847 Arlow, J. A. (Reporter) Panel: the psychoanalytic theory of thinking. An Surv Psa 1958, 9:90-100

73848 Buxbaum, E. (Reporter) Panel: the psychology of adolescence. An Surv Psa 1958, 9:274-284

73849 Calder, K. T. (Reporter) Panel: technical aspects of regression during psychoanalysis. An Surv Psa 1958, 9:350-357

73850 Freud, S. & Oppenheim, D. E. Dreams in Folklore. An Surv Psa 1958, 9:222-223

73851 Grinstein, A. The Index of Psychoanalytic Writings. Vol. I, Vol. II. An Surv Psa 1957, 8:294-295

73852 Grinstein, A. The Index of Psychoanalytic Writings. Vols. III, IV. An Surv Psa 1958, 9:437

73853 Kaufman, I. (Reporter) Panel: superego development and pathology in childhood. An Surv Psa 1958, 9:254-266

73854 Leach, D. (Reporter) Panel: technical aspects of transference. An Surv Psa 1958, 9:387-393

73855 Stanton, A. H. (Reporter) Panel: a comparison of individual and group psychology. An Surv Psa 1958, 9:42-50

73856 Valenstein, A. F. (Reporter) Panel: the psychoanalytic concept of character. An Surv Psa 1958, 9:149-152

FROSCH, WILLIAM A.

73857 Discussion of Flarsheim, A. "The psychological meaning of the use of marijuana and LSD in one case." Psa Forum 1969, 3:119-121

73858 (& Robbins, E. S.; Stern, M.) LSD casualties at Bellevue Hospital. The Bulletin, NY State District Branches, Amer Psychiat Assoc 1966, 9:5-8

73859 (& Robbins, E. S.; Robbins, L.; Stern, M.) Motivation for self-administration of LSD. Psychiat Q 1967, 41:56-61

73860 Physical and mental effects of LSD. NY Medicine 1968, 24:424-430

73861 (& Hekimian, L. J.; Warwick, K. W.; Friedhoff, A. J.) Statistical evaluation of the treatment response assessment method (TRAM) for psychiatric disorders. J clin Pharmacol 1969, 9:83-90

73862 (& Robbins, E. S.; Stern, M.) Untoward reactions to lysergic acid diethylamide (LSD) resulting in hospitalization. New Engl J Med 1965, 273:1235-1239

73863 Use and abuse of LSD. Acad Med New Jersey Bull 1967, 13:25-34

See Alpert, Murray; Robbins, Edwin S.

ABSTRACTS OF:

73864 Ajuriaguerra, J. de et al: Psychanalyse et neurobiologie. An Surv Psa 1956, 7:97-98

73865 Bouvet, M. La clinique psychanalytique: la relation d'objet. An Surv Psa 1956, 7:170-172

73866 Devereux, G. Normal and abnormal: the key problem of psychiatric anthropology. An Surv Psa 1956, 7:383-385
73867 Held, R. R. Psychanalyse et médecine. An Surv Psa 1956, 7:196-197
73868 Lebovici, S. et al: La psychanalyse des enfants. An Surv Psa 1956, 7:240-241
73869 Lesser, S. O. Fiction and the Unconscious. An Surv Psa 1957, 8:337-342
73870 Nacht, S. & Lebovici, S. Indications et contre-indications de la psychanalyse chez l'adulte. An Surv Psa 1956, 7:294-296
73871 Nacht, S. La thérapeutique psychanalytique. An Surv Psa 1956, 7:298-300
73872 Racamier, P. C. Psychothérapie psychanalytique des psychoses. An Surv Psa 1956, 7:328-330
73873 Reik, T. Adventures in psychoanalytic discovery. An Surv Psa 1956, 7:393-394
73874 Reik, T. Myth and Guilt. The Crime and Punishment of Mankind. An Surv Psa 1597, 8:296-298
73875 Siegman, A. J. Denial and screening of object-images. Q 1968, 37:478-479

REVIEW OF:
73876 Bellak, L. (Ed) Handbook of Community Psychiatry and Community Mental Health. Q 1966, 35:617

FRÜHMANN, EDMUND
See Caruso, Igor A.

FRUMKES, GEORGE
73877 Discussion of Miller, M. L. "Manic depressive cycles of the poet Shelley." Psa Forum 1966, 1:195-196

FRUMKIN, P.
See Sours, John A.

FRY, CAROL P.
See Kulka, Anna M.

FRY, P. S.
73878 Anxiety theory versus guilt theory of maladaptive behavior. Canadian Psychologist 1969, 10:398-408

FRY, WILLIAM F.
73879 The schizophrenogenic "who." PPR 1962, 49(4):68-73
       Abs Rev Psicoanál 1964, 21:86

FRY, WILLIAM FINLEY, JR.
See Heersema, Philip H.

FRYE, ROLAND LEE

73880 (& South, D. R.; Vegas, O. V.) The effect of parental orientation on the development of the child's orientation. J genet Psych 1965, 106: 315-318

73881 (& Spruill, J.) Type of orientation and task completion of elementary-grade students. J genet Psych 1965, 106:45-49

FRYER, DAVID GEORGE

73882 (& Rich, M. P.) Denial of illness in relation to intellectual function. JNMD 1960, 131:523-527

FUCHS, MARIANNE

73883 Atem-Entspannungstherapie bei psychosomatischen Störungen von Kindern und Jugendlichen. [Breathing-relaxation therapy for psychosomatic disturbances of children and adolescents.] Hbh Kinderpsychother 547-555

73884 Eigenrhythmus über Entspannung und Atmung ohne Selbsthypnose. [Proper rhythm for relaxation and breathing without self-hypnosis.] Z PSM 1964, 10:141-145

73885 "Der Weiherschlapp." Asthmabehandlung mit Atem-Entspannungstherapie. [The "Weiherschlapp." The course of a treatment for asthma.] Prax Kinderpsychol 1965, 14:209-213. Hbh Kinderpsychother 556-562

FUCHS-KAMP, ADELHEID

73886 Angst bei Psychotischen Patienten in Selbstzeugnissen. [Anxiety with psychotic patients in patient descriptions.] Fortschr Psa 1966, 2:211-221

73887 Hebephrenie, Grundsätzliches zu Struktur und Therapie. [Hebephrenia, fundamentals of its nature and treatment.] In Benedetti, G. & Müller, C. Psychotherapy of Schizophrenia (2nd Int Symp 1959), Basel/NY: Karger 1960, 156-178

S-46735 Zur Innenwelt einer paranoiden Psychose. Ausschnitte aus einer Behandlung. In Benedetti, G. & Müller, C. Psychotherapy of Schizophrenia (1st Int Symp 1956), Basel/NY: Karger 1957, 109-123

FUENTE, RAMÓN DE LA

73888 Fuentes y direcciones de la agresividad. [Origins and direction of aggressiveness.] Rev Psicoanal Psiquiat Psicol 1968, 8:3-18

73889 Guillermo Davila. In Memoriam. [Guillermo Davila. In memoriam.] Gac Med Mex 1968, 98:1478-1479

See Fromm, Erich

FUJII, H.

See Taketomo, Yasuhiko

FUJITA, CHIHIRO

73890 [Hitomishiri and anthropophobia: Symposium on "Hitomishiri."] (Jap) Jap J Psa 1969, 15(2):20-25

FULLER, J. L.

See Scott, John P.

FULLERTON, DONALD T.

73891 Infantile rumination, a case report. Arch gen Psychiat 1963, 9:593-600
       Abs KR Q 1964, 33:610
73892 (& Munsat, T. L.) Pseudo-myasthenia gravis: a conversion reaction.
       JNMD 1966, 142:78-86

FULTON, ROBERT

73893 (Ed) Death and Identity. NY/London/Sydney: John Wiley & Sons
       1965, xv + 415 p
       Abs J Am Psa Ass 1967, 15:218. Rv Brodsky, B. Q 1967, 36:106-108
73894 (& Geis, G.) Death and social values. Indian Journal of Social Research
       1962, 3:7-14. Death & Identity 67-75
73895 The sacred and the secular: attitudes of the American public toward
       death, funerals, and funeral directors. Death & Identity 89-105

FULTON, WALLACE C.

See Mudd, Emily H.

FURER, MANUEL

73896 The development of a preschool symbiotic psychotic boy. Psa St C
       1964, 19:448-469
73897 (Reporter) Panel on psychic development and the prevention of mental
       illness. (Read at Am Psa Ass, Dec 1961) J Am Psa Ass 1962, 10:606-
       616
73898 Some developmental aspects of the superego. (Read at Am Psa Ass,
       Mar 1964) J 1967, 48:277-280

See Mahler, Margaret S.; Pine, Fred

ABSTRACTS OF:
73899 Bychowski, G. The quest for beauty and the pitfalls of sublimation.
       Q 1963, 32:466-468
73900 Fisher, C. A cycle of penile erection synchronous with dreaming sleep.
       Q 1964, 33:614-617
73901 Hughes, J. E. Passivity: interpretative and theoretical aspects in psy-
       choanalytic treatment. Q 1962, 31:149-150

REVIEWS OF:
73902 Bolland, J. & Sandler, J. The Hampstead Psychoanalytic Index, A Study
       of the Psychoanalytic Case Materials of a Two-Year-Old Child. Q 1968,
       37:439-440
73903 Friedman, P. (Ed) Discussions of the Vienna Psychoanalytic Society,
       1910—On Suicide. With Particular Reference to Suicide Among Young
       Students. Q 1969, 38:130-132
73904 Harms, E. (Ed) Problems of Sleep and Dream in Children. Q 1965,
       34:120-121

73905   Koppitz, E. M. The Bender Gestalt Test for Young Children. Q 1965, 34:123
73906   Provence, S. & Lipton, R. Infants in Institutions. A Comparison of Their Development with Family-Reared Infants during the First Year. Q 1964, 33:289-291
73907   Solnit, A. J. & Provence, S. A. (Eds) Modern Perspectives in Child Development. In Honor of Milton J. E. Senn. Q 1965, 34:293-295

FURGER, RONALD

73908   Das analytisch orientierte Psychotherapiegespräch. [The psychoanalytically oriented psychotherapy interview.] Prax PT 1966, 11:258-267
73909   Kurzpsychotherapie. [Brief psychotherapy.] Proc IV World Cong Psychiat 1966, 485-460

FURHMAN, A.

See Rossi, Ascanio M.

FURLONG, E. J.

73910   Imagination. London: George Allen & Unwin; NY: Macmillan 1961, 125 p

FURMAN, ERNA

S-46781 An ego disturbance in a young child.
            Abs JA An Surv Psa 1956, 7:282-285
73911   The latency child as an active participant in the analytic work. Ch Anal Wk 142-184
73912   Observations on a toddler's near-fatal accident. Bull Phila Ass Psa 1964, 14:138-148
73913   Observations on entry to nursery school. Bull Phila Ass Psa 1969, 19: 133-152
73914   Some features of the dream function of a severely disturbed young child. (Read at Am Psa Ass, 4 Dec 1959) J Am Psa Ass 1962, 10:258-270
            Abs JBi Q 1963, 32:131. IBa RFPsa 1964, 28:455
73915   Some thoughts on the pleasure in working. (Read at Baltimore/DC-Cleveland-Phila Psa Cong, June 1968) Bull Phila Ass Psa 1969, 19: 197-212
S-46782 Treatment of under-fives by way of their parents. In Weinreb, J. *Recent Developments in Psychoanalytic Child Therapy*, NY: IUP, 123-134
            Behandlung von Kleinkindern durch Mütterberatung. Hbh Kinderpsychother 637-647
            Abs Skolnick, A. An Surv Psa 1957, 8:231-232
73916   Treatment via the mother. Ther Nurs Schl 64-132; 298-325

        See Furman, Robert A.

FURMAN, ROBERT A.

73917   Additional remarks on mourning and the young child. Bull Phila Ass Psa 1968, 18:51-64

73918 (& Schiff, E. J.; Benkendorf, J.; Furman, E.) Case reports. Ther Nurs Schl 124-203

73919 Comment on Dr. Stern's paper, "Fear of death and trauma. Remarks about an addendum to psychoanalytic theory and technique." (Read at Int Psa Cong, July 1967) J 1968, 49:461-463

73920 Death and the young child: some preliminary considerations. (Read at Cleveland Psa Soc, 21 Nov 1963) Psa St C 1964, 19:321-333
Der Tod und das Kind—Einige Vorlaufige Überlegungen. Psyche 1966, 20:766-777
Abs McDonald, M. Bull Phila Ass Psa 1964, 14:107-109

73921 Death of a six-year-old's mother during his analysis. (Read at Am Psa Ass 1963) Psa St C 1964, 19:377-397
Tod der Mutter wahrend der Analyse eines Sechsjahrigen. Psyche 1966, 20:778-796
Abs McDonald, M. Bull Phila Ass Psa 1964, 14:166-169

73922 Excerpts from the analysis of a child with a congenital defect. (Read at Int Psa Cong, July 1967) J 1968, 49:276-279
Abs LHR Q 1969, 38:669

73923 Experiences in nursery school consultations. (Separation anxiety.) Young Children 1966, 22:84-85

73924 Introduction. (Methodology of psychoanalytic investigation). Ther Nurs Schl 4-20

73925 Psychosomatic disorders. Ther Nurs Schl 231-273

73926 A technical problem: the child who has difficulty in controlling his behavior in analytic sessions. Ch Anal Wk 59-84

73927 (& Katan, A.) (Eds) The Therapeutic Nursery School: A Contribution to the Study and Treatment of Emotional Disturbances in Young Children. NY: IUP 1969, xi + 329 p

REVIEW OF:
73928 Wolfenstein, M. & Kilman, G. (Eds) Children and the Death of a President. Multidisciplinary Studies. Q 1967, 36:449-451

FURRER, W. L.

73929 Objektivierung des Unbewussten. [The Objectivization of the Unconscious.] Bern: Huber 1969, 76 p

FURST, HELEN B.

See Aronson, Marvin L.

FURST, SIDNEY S.

73930 (Ed) Psychic Trauma. NY: Basic Books 1967, 252 p
Abs J Am Psa Ass 1968, 16:181. Rv Beres, D. Q 1969, 38:132-135

73931 Psychic trauma: a survey. In author's *Psychic Trauma* 3-50

73932 (& Ostow, M.) The psychodynamics of suicide. Bull NY Acad Med 1965, 41:190-204

REVIEW OF:
73933 Stefan, G. In Search of Sanity. The Journal of a Schizophrenic. Q 1967, 36:457-458

FÜRSTENAU, PETER

73934 Erziehung als Schicksal vom psychoanalytischen Standpunkt aus gesehen. [Rearing as "fate" from an observed psychoanalytic standpoint.] Schweiz Z Psychol 1967, Suppl (51):145-149

73935 Ich-Psychologie und Anpassungsproblem; eine Auseinandersetzung mit Heinz Hartmann. [Ego-psychology and the problem of adaptation; a controversy with Heinz Hartmann.] Jb Psa 1964, 3:30-55

73936 Soziologie der Kindheit. [Sociology of Childhood.] Heidelberg: Guelle & Meyer 1967, 155 p

73937 "Sublimierung" in affirmativer und negativ-kritischer Anwendung. ["Sublimation," affirmatively and negative-critically applied.] Jb Psa 1967, 4:43-62

73938 Über Beratung, Therapie und Erforschung sozial definierter Neurotikergruppen. [On counseling, treatment and investigation of socially defined neurotic groups.] Z Psychother med Psychol 1968, 18:161-167

73939 (& Mahler, E.; Morgenstern, H.; Müller-Braunschweig, H.; Richter, H.-E.; Staewen, R.) Untersuchungen über Herzneurose. [Investigation of cardiac neuroses.] Psyche 1964, 18:177-190

73940 Wandlungen der Psychoanalyse als einer kritischen Gesellschafts-Theorie. [Changes in psychoanalysis as a critical association theory.] Psychother Psychosom 1967, 15:23

73941 Zur Psychoanalyse der Schule als Institution. [On psychoanalysis of the school as an institution.] Argument (Berlin) 1964, 29:65-78
    Contribution à la psychanalyse de l'ecole en tant qu'institution. Partisans 1967, 39:32-45

73942 Zur Psychologie der Nachwirkung des Nationalsozialismus. [On the psychology of the after-effect of national socialism.] In Huss, H. & Schröder, A. Antisemitismus, Frankfurt/Main: Europäische Verlagsanstalt 1965, 121-139
    Ripercussioni psicologiche del nationalsocialismo. In Pozzoli, C. Germania, Verso una Società Autoritaria, Bari: Laterza 1968, 233-257

FURTADO, D.

73943 [Psychoanalysis and its status among us.] (Por) J Med (Porto) 1959, 40:293-302

FUSCHILLO, JEAN

See Levine, Murray; Spivack, George

FUTTERMAN, SAMUEL

73944 The memory of the psychotherapist. PT 1966, 20:284-294

73945 Suicide: psychoanalytic point of view. In Farberow, N. L. & Schneidman, E. S. The Cry for Help, NY: McGraw-Hill 1961, 167-180
    Spanish: 1969

FYE, BONNIETA

See Varga, Laszlo

APPENDIX

ALPHABETICAL LISTING OF ENGLISH TITLES
OF THE WORKS OF SIGMUND FREUD

This appendix provides a ready reference to the works of Sigmund Freud as listed in the various volumes of THE INDEX OF PSYCHOANALYTIC WRITINGS.

Articles, books and monographs are listed alphabetically according to the principal words of their titles in English. Letters are alphabetized according to the name of the addressee. Prefaces, introductions, forewords and footnotes are alphabetized according to the author (or title, if no author is named) of the work for which these were written.

Although familiar translations are used for the most part, the translation by James Strachey is used where this is similar.

The Appendix contains three columns of numbers in addition to the titles. The first number is the reference number in THE INDEX OF PSYCHOANA-LYTIC WRITINGS. The second column gives the volumes of the INDEX in which material about this particular reference is given. The last column gives the volume and pages of the *Standard Edition* where the English translation of this work is to be found. The page numbers in this column refer to the pages on which Freud's work is to be found. They do not include the pages of editorial comments or appendices.

Abraham, Karl (obituary)	10494	1/6	20:277-278
Abstracts	10671	1	
Abstracts of the scientific writings of Dr. Sigmund Freud (1877-1897)	10373	1/6	3:227-257
The acquisition and control of fire	10472	1/10	22:187-193
Additions to the interpretation of dreams	10545	1	5:360-366; 408-409
Address delivered in the Goethe House at Frankfurt	10395	1/6	21:208-212
Address to the society of B'nai B'rith	10394	1/6/10	20:273-274
Advances in psychoanalytic therapy	10643	1/6	17:159-168

Goethe prize	10413	1/6/10	21:207
A "great achievement" in a dream	10424	1	5:412-413
"Great is Diana of the Ephesians"	10473	1/6	12:342-344
On the grounds for detaching a particular syndrone from neurasthenia under the description "anxiety neurosis"	10407	1/6/10	3:90-115 (Abs) 3:251
Group psychology and the analysis of the ego	10530	1/6	18:69-143
Halsmann case, expert opinion in	10447	1/6	21:251-253
Hammerschlag, Professor S. (obituary)	10570	1/10	9:255-256
The handling of dream-interpretation in psycho-analysis	10475	1/6	12:91-96
Hebrew University, opening of	10557	1/6	19:292
Hemi-anesthesia in a hysterical male	10356	1/10	1:25-31 (Abs) 3:238
Heredity and the aetiology of the neuroses	10477	1/6/10	3:143-156 (Abs) 3:255
On Hering, Ewald	10454A	1/6	14:205
From the history of an infantile neurosis	10471	1/6	17:7-122
The history of the psychoanalytic movement	10470	1/6/10	14:7-66
Hobman, J. B. *David Eder*, foreword to	10457	1	
Hoffman, E. T. A. on the function of consciousness	10446A	1/6	17:233n
Homosexuality in a woman	10582	1/6	18:147-172
"Human magnetism"	10550	1	
Humour	10478	1/6	21:161-166
Hypnotism	73580	10	1:105-114
Hypnotism, successful treatment by, with some remarks on origin of hysterical symptoms through "counterwill"	10448	1/6/10	1:117-128 (Abs) 3:242-243
Hypnotism and suggestion	10630	1/10	1:75-85
Hysteria [in A. Villaret]	10365	1/10	1:41-57
Hysteria, aetiology of	10397	1/6/10	3:191-221 (Abs) 3:254
Hysteria, fragment of an analysis of a case of	10421	1	7:7-122
On hysteria (lecture)	10480	5/6	
Hysteria in a male (hemianesthesia)	10365	1/10	1:5-31 (Abs) 3:238

Hysteria, studies on	10601	1/6/10	2:xxix-xxxi + 3-305
Hysterical attacks, some general remarks on	10390	1/6	9:229-234
Hysterical attacks, theory of	10606	1/10	1:151-154
Hysterical phantasies and their relation to bisexuality	10481	1/6	9:159-166
Hysterical phenomena, psychical mechanism of, lecture on	10634	1/5/10	3:27-39
Hystero-epilepsy [in A. Villaret]	10365	1/10	1:58-59
If Moses was an Egyptian . . .	10649	1/10	23:17-53
The infantile genital organization	10484	1/6/10	19:141-145
Infantile mental life: two lies told by children	10659	1/6	12:305-309
Infantile neurosis, history of an	10471	1/6	17:7-122
Infantile sexual theories	10485	1/6/10	9:209-226
Inhibitions, symptoms, and anxiety	10476	1/6/10	20:87-172
Instincts and their vicissitudes	10616	1/5/6/10	14:117-140
The interpretation of dreams	10614	1/5/6/10	4-5: 1-621
Introduction to* (*See also* Foreword; preface)			
Pfister's *The Psycho-Analytic Method*	10468	1/6	12:329-331
Psycho-Analysis and the War Neuroses	10439	1	17:207-210
Special psychopathology number of *The Medical Review of Reviews*	10563	1/6	21:254-255
Varendonck's *The Psychology of Day-Dreams*	10488	1	18:271-272
Edoardo Weiss's *Elements of Psycho-Analysis*	10469	1/6	21:256
Introductory lectures on psycho-analysis	10629	1/5/6/10	15:15-239 16:243-463
James J. Putnam (obituary)	10489	1	17:271-272
Janet-Freud controversy	73579	10	
Janet and psycho-analysis	10454	1	2:xiii
Jealousy, paranoia, and homosexuality, neurotic mechanisms in	10437	1	18:223-232
Jokes and their relation to the unconscious	10652	1/6	8:9-236

* Titles are listed as they appear in the *Standard Edition* but are alphabetized according to the last name of the authors of the books for which Freud wrote these prefaces. If no author is given, the title of the publication is used for purposes of alphabetization.

Leroy, Maxim: some dreams of Descartes	10419	1/6	21:203-204
Leyens, Mr. Erich	10515c	5	
Lopez-Ballesteros y de Torres, Señor Luis	10418	1/6	19:289
Low, Barbara	10516	1	
Magnes, J. L.	10516a	1	
Maitlis, Jaacob J.	73586a	10	
Mann, Thomas			
[on Napoleon]	10441	1/10	
on his 60th birthday	10607	1/10	22:255
Mordell, Albert	46278a	6	
Neue Freie Presse, on Dr. Reik and the problem of quackery	10518	1	21:247-248
	73577	10	21:247-248
Paquet, Dr. Alfons	10413	1/6	21:207
Pfister, O.	46279	6	
	46280	6	
	73592	10	
Psychoanalytische Volksbuch, [editors of]	10519	1	
Reik, Theodor	10520	1/10	21:195-196
	10521	1/6	
	10521a	1	
Roback, A. A.	10521b	6	
Rolland, Romain	46281	6	
on the occasion of his 70th birthday	10420	1/10	22:239-248
on the occasion of his 60th birthday	10592	1/6	20:279
Rubens, Mr. Victor [on smoking]	10521c	5	
Schnitzler, Arthur	10420a	6	
Serota, H. M.	73587	10	
Silberer	46282	6	
Silberstein, Eduard	73587a	10	
Simmel, E.	73588	10	
Sterba, Richard	10419a	1/10	22:253
Storfer, A. J.	10522	1	
Szondi, L.	46283	6	
Time & Tide, [editors of] (on anti-semitism in England)	73574	10	23:301
Tinty, Baron Karl Ferdinand	46283a	6	
Velikowsky, Immanuel [on telepathy]	10522aa	5	
Weiss, Edoardo	46283b	6	
	73589	10	
Weissman, Karl	46283c	6	
Wittels, Dr. Fritz	10415	1/6/10	19:286-288
Wortis, Joseph	10522a	1	

Popper-Lynkeus, Josef, my contact with	10533	1/10	22:219-224
Popper-Lynkeus, Josef, and the theory of dreams	10492	1/6	19:261-263
Position on awakening from a dream	10560	1/6	13:195
Postscript to the analysis of a phobia of a five-year-old boy	10542	1/10	10:148-149
Postscript (1935) to *An Autobiographical study*	10541	1/6	20:71-74
Postscript to the case of paranoia	10543	1/6	12:80-82
Postscript to paper on the Moses of Michelangelo	10544	1/6	13:237-238
Postscript (1927) to the question of lay analysis	10546	1/6	20:251-258
Predisposition to obsessional neurosis	10428	1/6	12:317-326
Preface to° (*See also* Foreword, Introduction)			
August Aichhorn's *Wayward Youth*	10465	1/6	19:273-275
translation of Bernheim's *Suggestion*	10630	1/10	1:75-85
Marie Bonaparte's *The Life and Works of Edgar Allan Poe: A Psycho-Analytic Interpretation*	10561	1/10	22:254
Bourke's *Scatological Rites of all Nations*	10466	1/6	12:335-337
translation of Charcot's *Lectures on the Diseases of the Nervous System*	10561A	1/10	1:21-22
and footnotes to translation of Charcot's *Tuesday Lectures*	10562	1/10	1:133-142
Max Eitingon's *Report on the Berlin Psycho-Analytical Policlinic (March 1920 to June 1922)*	10635	1/6/10	19:285
Sándor Ferenczi's *Psycho-Analysis: Essays in the Field of Psycho-Analysis*	10564	1/6	9:252
Sigmund Freud's *Sammlung kleiner Schriften zur*			

° Titles are listed as they appear in the *Standard Edition* but are alphabetized according to the last name of the authors of the books for which Freud wrote these prefaces.

Sketches for the "Preliminary	10417	1/10	1:147-148
Communication" of 1893	10553	1/10	1:149-150
	10606	1/10	1:151-154
On smoking (letter to Victor			
Rubens)	10521c	5	
Some additional notes on dream-			
interpretation as a whole	10436	1/6	19:127-138
Some character-types met with in			
psycho-analytic work	10435	1/6	14:311-333
Some dreams of Descartes: a letter			
to Maxime Leroy	10419	1/6	21:203-204
Some elementary lessons in psycho-			
analysis	10600	1/10	23:281-286
Some general remarks on hysterical			
states	10390	1/6	9:229-234
Some neurotic mechanisms in jeal-			
ousy, paranoia and homo-			
sexuality	10437	1	18:223-232
Some points for a comparative study			
of organic and hysterical			
motor paralyses	10588	1/10	1:160-172
			(Abs) 3:248
Some psychical consequences of the			
anatomical distribution be-			
tween the sexes	10438	1/6/10	19:248-258
Some reflections on schoolboy			
psychology	10583	1	13:241-244
Some remarks on the uncon-			
scious	10446в	1/6	19:3-4
A special type of choice of object			
made by men	10409	1/5/6/10	11:165-175
The specialist report in the Hals-			
mann case	10447	1/6	21:251-253
Splitting of the ego in the pro-			
cess of defense	10483	1/10	23:275-278
Steiner, M. *The Psychical Dis-*			
orders of Male Potency,			
preface to	10638	1/6	12:345-346
Stekel, W. *Nervous Anxiety States*			
and Their Treatment, pre-			
face to	10639	1/6	9:250-251
Stekel, W. *Zur Psychologie des*			
Exhibitionismus, footnote to	10455	1	18:274 note
Sterba, R. *Dictionary of Psycho-*			
Analysis, preface to	10419а	1/10	22:253
Studies on hysteria	10601	1/6/10	2:xxix-xxxi +
			3-305
The subtleties of a parapraxis			
(faulty action)	10451	1/10	22:233-235

Visual obsession, mythological parallel of	10540	1/6	14:337-338
War and death, thoughts for the times on	10654	1/6	14:275-300
War neuroses, electrical treatment of	10474	1/6/10	17:211-215
Weiss, E. *Elements of Psycho-Analysis*, introduction to	10469	1/6	21:256
Wilson, Thomas Woodrow, psychological study of	73593	10	
Why war?	10642	1/10	22:203-215
On "wild" psycho-analysis	10651	1/6	11:221-227
Wit and its relation to the unconscious	10652	1/6	8:9-236
"Wolf man"	10471	1/6	17:7-122
Worcester lectures on psycho-analysis	10575	1/6/10	11:9-55
Youthful letters	10493	1/10	
	73581	10	

NON-PSYCHOLOGICAL WRITINGS

Abstracts of the scientific writings of Dr. Sigmund Freud (1877-1897)	10373	1/6	3:227-257
Acoustical nerve, origin of	10387	1/10	(Abs) 3:238
Acute multiple neuritis of the spinal and cranial nerves	10350	1/10	(Abs) 3:236
Anatomical preparation of the nervous system	10382	1/10	(Abs) 3:229
Aphasia [in A. Villaret]	10365	1	
On aphasia, a critical study	10352	1/6/10	(Abs) 3:240-241
Bacillus of syphilis	73569	10	
On Bernhardt's disease (meralgia paraesthetica)	10358	1/10	(Abs) 3:253
Brain [in A. Villaret]	10365	1	
A case of cerebral hemorrhage with indirect basal focal symptoms in scurvy	10367	1/10	(Abs) 3:232
A case of muscular atrophy with extensive disturbances of sensitivity (syringomyelia)	10368	1/10	(Abs) 3:235
Cerebral diplegias in childhood	10364	1	
	10366	1/10	(Abs) 3:247
	10369	1/10	(Abs) 3:247
in connection with Little's disease	10374	1/10	(Abs) 3:245-247
Cerebral hemorrhage with indirect focal symptoms in scurvy, case of	10367	1/10	(Abs) 3:232

Infantile cerebral paralysis	10360	1/10	
	10363	1	
	10372	1/10	(Abs) 3:256
and infantile poliomyelitis	10361	1	
Infantile paralysis, spinal [in A. Villaret]	10365	1	
Intermediary layer of the olive	10375	1/10	(Abs) 3:234
Knowledge of cerebral diplegias in childhood in connection with Little's disease, contribution to	10374	1/10	(Abs) 3:245-247
Knowledge of the effects of coca	10354	1/10	(Abs) 3:234
Knowledge of the intermediary layer of the olive	10375	1/10	(Abs) 3:234
Medulla oblongata and restiform body	10359	1/10	(Abs) 3:237
Meralgia paraesthetica (Bernhardt's disease)	10358	1/10	(Abs) 3:253
Method for anatomical preparation of the nervous system	10382	1/10	(Abs) 3:229
Muscular atrophy with extensive disturbances of sensitivity (syringomyelia), case of	10368	1/10	(Abs) 3:235
Nerve fibers in the central nervous system, new method of the study of the course of	10379	1	
	10380	1/10	(Abs) 3:231
Nerve tracts in the brain and spinal cord, new histological method for the study of	10381	1	
The nervous system	10378	1	
method for anatomical preparation of	10382	1/10	(Abs) 3:229
structure of the elements of	10384	1/10	(Abs) 3:230
A new histological method for the study of the nerve-tracts in the brain and spinal cord	10381	1	(Abs) 3:231
A new method for the study of the course of nerve fibers in the central nervous system	10379	1	
	10380	1/10	(Abs) 2:231
Nocturnal enuresis in children, a symptom frequently accompanying	10385	1/10	(Abs) 3:243
Note on a method for anatomical preparation of the nervous system	10382	1/10	(Abs) 3:229
Note upon the inter-olivary tract	10375	1/10	(Abs) 3:234
Observations on the formation and more delicate structure of the lobe-shaped organs of the eel, described as testicles	10357	1/10	(Abs) 3:227